THE CAMBRIDGE HISTORY OF
TERRORISM

The Cambridge History of Terrorism provides a comprehensive reference work on terrorism from a distinctly historical perspective, offering systematic analyses of key themes, problems and case studies from terrorism's long past. Featuring expert scholars from across the globe, this volume examines the phenomenon of terrorism through regional case studies, largely written by local scholars, as well as through thematic essays exploring the relationship between terrorism and other historical forces. Each of the chapters – whether thematic or case-study focused – embodies new, research-based analysis which will help to inform and reshape our understanding of one of the world's most challenging problems.

RICHARD ENGLISH is Professor of Politics at Queen's University Belfast.

THE CAMBRIDGE HISTORY OF TERRORISM

*

Edited by
RICHARD ENGLISH
Queen's University Belfast

CAMBRIDGE
UNIVERSITY PRESS

University Printing House, Cambridge CB2 8BS, United Kingdom

One Liberty Plaza, 20th Floor, New York, NY 10006, USA

477 Williamstown Road, Port Melbourne, VIC 3207, Australia

314–321, 3rd Floor, Plot 3, Splendor Forum, Jasola District Centre,
New Delhi – 110025, India

79 Anson Road, #06-04/06, Singapore 079906

Cambridge University Press is part of the University of Cambridge.

It furthers the University's mission by disseminating knowledge in the pursuit of education, learning, and research at the highest international levels of excellence.

www.cambridge.org
Information on this title: www.cambridge.org/9781108470162
DOI: 10.1017/9781108556248

© Cambridge University Press 2021

This publication is in copyright. Subject to statutory exception and to the provisions of relevant collective licensing agreements, no reproduction of any part may take place without the written permission of Cambridge University Press.

First published 2021

Printed in the United Kingdom by TJ Books Limited, Padstow Cornwall

A catalogue record for this publication is available from the British Library.

Library of Congress Cataloging-in-Publication Data
NAMES: English, Richard, 1963– editor.
TITLE: The Cambridge history of terrorism / edited by Richard English, Queen's University Belfast.
DESCRIPTION: Cambridge, United Kingdom ; New York, NY : Cambridge University Press, 2021. | Includes bibliographical references and index.
IDENTIFIERS: LCCN 2021002029 (print) | LCCN 2021002030 (ebook) | ISBN 9781108470162 (hardback) | ISBN 9781108455329 (paperback) | ISBN 9781108556248 (ebook)
SUBJECTS: LCSH: Terrorism.
CLASSIFICATION: LCC HV6431 .C36 2021 (print) | LCC HV6431 (ebook) | DDC 362.88/931709–dc23
LC record available at https://lccn.loc.gov/2021002029
LC ebook record available at https://lccn.loc.gov/2021002030

ISBN 978-1-108-47016-2 Hardback

Cambridge University Press has no responsibility for the persistence or accuracy of URLs for external or third-party internet websites referred to in this publication and does not guarantee that any content on such websites is, or will remain, accurate or appropriate.

Contents

List of Figures *page* viii
List of Tables ix
Acknowledgements x
List of Contributors xi

PART I
INTRODUCTION

1 · History and the Study of Terrorism 3
RICHARD ENGLISH

PART II
FRAMEWORKS AND DEFINITIONS

2 · History and the Definition of Terrorism 31
MARTYN FRAMPTON

3 · Terrorism, History and Periodisation 58
WARREN C. BROWN

4 · Terrorism, History and Regionalisation 81
RORY MILLER

5 · A Processual Approach to Political Violence: How History Matters 106
LORENZO BOSI

6 · Terrorism, History and Neighbouring Disciplines in the Academy 124
BERNHARD BLUMENAU

PART III
HISTORICAL CASE STUDIES IN TERRORISM

7 · Terrorism in Israel/Palestine   *149*
JULIE M. NORMAN

8 · Terrorism in the Basque Country   *173*
LUDGER MEES

9 · Terrorism in African History   *199*
RICHARD REID

10 · The History of Terrorism in Pakistan   *223*
DAYYAB GILLANI

11 · Political Violence in Ireland   *254*
FEARGHAL MCGARRY

12 · Terrorism in the Russian Empire: The Late Nineteenth and Early Twentieth Centuries   *284*
EKATERINA STEPANOVA

13 · Terrorism in Post-Soviet Russia: 1990s to 2010s   *313*
EKATERINA STEPANOVA

14 · Terrorism in The Netherlands: A History   *333*
BEATRICE DE GRAAF

15 · Terrorism: An American Story   *361*
DENNIS DWORKIN

16 · Political Violence and Terrorism in Colombia   *387*
RODDY BRETT

17 · The Paths of Terrorism in Peru: Nineteenth to Twenty-First Centuries   *420*
CECILIA MÉNDEZ

18 · *Aiqtihams* (Whirlwind Attacks): The Rise, Fall and Phoenix-Like Resurgence of ISIS and Shiite Terrorist Groups in Iraq   *453*
BRIAN GLYN WILLIAMS

19 · Transnational Connections: Militant Irish Republicans and the World   *477*
KIERAN MCCONAGHY

PART IV
THEMATIC ESSAYS

20 · 'September 12 Thinking': The Missing Histories of Counterterrorism   *503*
STEVE HEWITT

21 · The History of Terrorism and Communication   *524*
BRIGITTE L. NACOS AND MELIH BARUT

22 · Terrorism, History and Religion   *551*
RICHARD ENGLISH

23 · History, Terrorism and the State   *571*
RORY COX

24 · Into the Labyrinth: Terrorism, History and Diplomacy   *594*
JOSEPH MORRISON SKELLY

25 · Gender Politics and Terrorist Histories   *623*
SYLVIA SCHRAUT

PART V
CONCLUSION

26 · Terrorism and History: Current Knowledge and Future Research   *647*
RICHARD ENGLISH

Index   *672*

Figures

8.1 Deaths caused by ETA and right-wing terrorism, 1968–75 (R. López Romo, *Informe Foronda: Los contextos históricos del terrorismo en el País Vasco y la consideración social de sus víctimas, 1968–2010* (Vitoria-Gasteiz, Instituto de Historia Social Valentín de Foronda, 2015)) *page* 185
8.2 Victims of political violence over various periods (R. López Romo, *Informe Foronda: Los contextos históricos del terrorismo en el País Vasco y la consideración social de sus víctimas, 1968–2010* (Vitoria-Gasteiz, Instituto de Historia Social Valentín de Foronda, 2015)) 187
11.1 Londoners view the aftermath of Fenian dynamiters' attempt to destroy Scotland Yard on 30 May 1884 (From *The Graphic*, 7 June 1884: photo by Hulton Archive/Stringer via Getty Images) 262
11.2 Following the assassination of the Chief Secretary for Ireland and his Undersecretary by militant Fenians in 1882, the Irish parliamentary party leader Charles Stewart Parnell was depicted as responsible for the violence, due to his support for the Irish Land League (From *Punch*, or the *London Charivari*, 20 May 1882: photo by The Cartoon Collector/Print Collector/Hulton Archive via Getty Images) 264
21.1 Terrorism and the triangle of political communication (Illustration by the authors) 527

Tables

14.1 Terrorist actions and fatalities in Germany and the Netherlands   *page* 349

Acknowledgements

Many people have helped with the creation of this book. Queen's University Belfast and Cambridge University Press between them funded a workshop to discuss earlier drafts of most of the chapters. The intense and productive conversations at that workshop, held at Queen's University, valuably enriched the arguments that are now published in this volume; colleagues at Queen's – especially Isabel Jennings, Nicola Skelly, Monica Salomeia and Catherine Pollitt – helped greatly with that event. At Cambridge University Press, Elizabeth Hanlon, Emily Sharp and Stephanie Taylor were superbly helpful throughout the process leading to the publication of the book. Jane Burkowski's copy-editing was meticulous and invaluable.

Contributors

MELIH BARUT is a communication science scholar at Hacettepe University. His fields of specialization are (1) strategic communications and engagement and public diplomacy; (2) civilian and military relations and military diplomacy; and (3) conflict studies, terrorism and counterterrorism. As a former air force officer and the Secretary General of Global Public Diplomacy Network, he has lectured and managed many programmes at military and civic institutions, including NATO and the United Nations. As a research scholar at Columbia University, he has explored the impact of digital media on collective behaviour. His latest co-edited book is *Public Diplomacy: Strategic Engagement in Conflicted Communities* (2nd ed., 2018).

BERNHARD BLUMENAU is a Lecturer at the Centre for the Study of Terrorism and Political Violence (CSTPV) at the University of St Andrews. He is interested in the history of terrorism, state terrorism and antiterrorism. More specifically, his research focuses on German antiterrorism policies, terrorism during the Cold War, multilateral antiterrorism efforts and the long history of state terrorism since the Middle Ages. Among others, he is the author of *The United Nations and Terrorism: Germany, Multilateralism, and Antiterrorism Efforts in the 1970s* (2014) and co-editor of *An International History of Terrorism: Western and Non-Western Experiences* (2013).

LORENZO BOSI is Associate Professor at the Scuola Normale Superiore (Florence). He is a political sociologist pursuing comparative analysis into the cross-disciplinary fields of social movements and political violence. In his research he is mainly interested in how and when contentious political actors shift their forms of action across time and space. He has published articles in *Historical Sociology, Mobilization, Qualitative Sociology, Social Forces, Social Science History* and numerous other academic journals. He is the author of *Vite di lotta armata: Storie di attivismo nella Provisional IRA* (2016) and co-editor of *The Consequences of Social Movements* (2016).

RODDY BRETT is Senior Lecturer in Politics and International Relations in the School of Sociology, Politics and International Studies (SPAIS) at the University of Bristol. Dr Brett was previously Senior Lecturer in International Relations at the University of St Andrews, Director of the Masters Programme in Peace and Conflict Studies and Director of the Centre for Peace and Conflict Studies. His fields of research include conflict, peace processes/peacebuilding, post-conflict reconstruction/reconciliation, genocide and transitional justice. His books include *The Politics of Victimhood in Post-Conflict Societies: Comparative and Analytical Perspectives* (2018); *The Origins and Dynamics of Genocide: Political Violence in Guatemala* (2016); *The Path Towards Reconciliation after Colombia's War: Understanding the Roles of Victims and Perpetrators* (2020).

WARREN C. BROWN is Professor for Medieval History at the California Institute of Technology. He studies the social and political history of medieval Europe, especially the history of conflict and power. His book *Violence in Medieval Europe* (2011) examines the social, cultural and legal norms that governed personal violence between 600 and 1500. He is currently exploring the instrumental use of terror in particular during this period.

RORY COX is Senior Lecturer in Medieval History at the University of St Andrews. He is a Fellow of the Royal Historical Society and an Associate Research Fellow of the Handa Centre for the Study of Terrorism and Political Violence (CSTPV). His interdisciplinary research examines violence, the ethics of war and comparative international history over a broad chronological range. He has published on a variety of topics, including ancient just war doctrine, medieval warfare, pacifism and the modern use of torture. He looks to engage different approaches pioneered in the disciplines of History, International Relations, Sociology and Anthropology.

BEATRICE DE GRAAF holds the Chair of History of International Relations and Global Governance at Utrecht University (since February 2014). In December 2019, she was awarded the title of Distinguished Professor. For her research into the history of security and terrorism she won the Stevin Prize (the highest academic distinction in the Netherlands) in 2018. Her book *Fighting Terror after Napoleon: How Europe Became Secure after 1815* was published by Cambridge University Press in 2020. She is currently leading an ERC Consolidator project, 'Securing Europe: The Emergence of a Security Culture in Europe and Beyond after 1815'.

DENNIS DWORKIN is Professor and Chair of the Department of History at the University of Nevada, Reno. He has a PhD in modern history from the

University of Chicago. He is a historian of Britain and Ireland with a specialty in cultural theory and intellectual history. His books include *Cultural Marxism in Postwar Britain: History, the New Left and the Origins of Cultural Studies* (1997), *Class Struggles* (2007) and *Ireland and Britain 1798–1922: An Anthology of Sources* (2012). He has been translated into Chinese, Portuguese and Turkish.

RICHARD ENGLISH is Professor of Politics at Queen's University Belfast. He is the author of eight books, including the award-winning studies *Armed Struggle: The History of the IRA* (2003) and *Irish Freedom: The History of Nationalism in Ireland* (2006). His most recent book, *Does Terrorism Work? A History*, was published in 2016. He is a Fellow of the British Academy, a Member of the Royal Irish Academy, a Fellow of the Royal Society of Edinburgh and a Fellow of the Royal Historical Society. In 2018 he was awarded a CBE for services to the understanding of modern-day terrorism and political history.

MARTYN FRAMPTON is Reader in Modern History at Queen Mary University of London. He is the author of three books on Irish Republicanism and 'the Troubles' in Northern Ireland, including *Legion of the Rearguard: Dissident Irish Republicanism* (2011). His most recent book marks a new departure in his research interests and is *The Muslim Brotherhood and the West: A History of Enmity and Engagement* (2018).

DAYYAB GILLANI has a Masters in Politics from the University of Warwick and a PhD in International Relations from the University of St Andrews. He is a fellow of HEC Pakistan and an Associate Fellow of HEA UK. Currently serving as Assistant Professor at the University of the Punjab, his research interests vary from political theory and moral philosophy to political violence and terrorism. Having returned to Pakistan, he has developed a keen interest in the region and has been working strenuously to study and understand the complex nature and history of terrorism and political violence in the country.

STEVE HEWITT is Senior Lecturer in the Department of History at the University of Birmingham in the United Kingdom. He has published extensively on security and intelligence, including counterterrorism, in the past and present and in a Canadian, American and British context. Currently, he is working on a history of terrorism and counterterrorism in Canada that will be published by McGill-Queen's University Press.

KIERAN MCCONAGHY is a Lecturer at the Centre for the Study of Terrorism and Political Violence (CSTPV) at the University of St Andrews, Scotland. He holds degrees in Law with Politics and Irish Politics (LLB, MA) from Queen's University Belfast, and in International Relations (PhD) from the University of St Andrews. He is the author of *Terrorism and the State* (2017) and has written on state terrorism, ethno-nationalist political violence and the impact and effectiveness of both terrorism and counterterrorism.

FEARGHAL MCGARRY is Professor of Modern Irish History at Queen's University Belfast. He has written widely on modern Ireland, particularly on political violence and radicalism in revolutionary and post-independence Ireland. He is the author of *The Abbey Rebels of 1916: A Lost Revolution* (2015) and *The Rising. Ireland: Easter 1916* (2010). With partners at the University of Edinburgh and Boston College, he is currently leading a major AHRC project, 'A Global History of Irish Revolution, 1916–23', which investigates how the Irish struggle for independence was shaped by international currents. His next book will explore anxieties about modernity in interwar Ireland.

LUDGER MEES completed his PhD in History at the University of Bielefeld (Germany) and was Assistant Professor at the same institution before taking up a Lectureship at the University of the Basque Country (Bilbao, Spain) in 1991. Since 2004 he has been Full Professor of Contemporary History at the University of the Basque Country and during 2004–9 he was also Vice-Chancellor. He is author, co-author or editor of twenty books and about 120 articles and book chapters in the fields of nationalism, social movements, historiography and agrarian history. One of his most recent books is *The Basque Contention: Ethnicity, Politics, Violence* (2020).

CECILIA MÉNDEZ is Associate Professor in the Department of History and Director of the Program in Latin American and Iberian Studies at the University of California Santa Barbara. She is a Peruvian historian specialising in the social and political history of the Andean region. She holds a PhD from the State University of New York, Stony Brook, and her publications include *The Plebeian Republic: The Huanta Rebellion and the Making of the Peruvian State, 1820–1850* (2005), which won the Howard F. Cline Award for the best book published on indigenous history in Latin America. Her work emphasises the importance of late eighteenth-century and nineteenth-century political developments in shaping modern conceptions of nationhood, citizenship and race.

RORY MILLER is a Professor of Government at Georgetown University in Qatar. Previously, he served in the War Studies Department and as head of the Middle East Program at King's College London. He is co-editor of the

Cambridge University Press book series on Intelligence and National Security in Africa and the Middle East. He is the author or editor of twelve books and has published extensively in academic journals and in policy and media outlets including *Foreign Affairs*, *The Economist*, *Foreign Policy*, *The New Republic*, *The National Interest* and *The Wall Street Journal*.

BRIGITTE L. NACOS is a political scientist and journalist who teaches at Columbia University, New York. Her fields of specialization are (1) mass media, public opinion and decision-making; and (2) terrorism and counter-terrorism. She has published a multitude of articles, book chapters and books. Among the books related to terrorism and counterterrorism are *Terrorism and Counterterrorism* (6th ed., 2019); *Mass-Mediated Terrorism,* (3rd ed., 2016); *Terrorism and the Media: From the Iran Hostage Crisis to the World Trade Center Bombing* (1994). She is co-author of *Selling Fear: Counter-Terrorism, the Media and Public Opinion* (2011).

JULIE M. NORMAN is a Lecturer in Politics and International Relations at the School of Public Policy (SPP) at University College London (UCL). Her research focuses on resistance, rights and security in protracted conflicts, and she is the author of four books on non-violent activism and multiple publications on Israel–Palestine. Prior to UCL, she was a Research Fellow at Queen's University Belfast, and a Lecturer in Politics at McGill University and Concordia University in Montreal, Canada. A native of Washington, DC, she has a PhD in International Relations from American University.

RICHARD REID is Professor of African History in the Faculty of History and a Fellow of St Cross College at the University of Oxford. His work has focused particularly on the history of political culture, historical consciousness, warfare and militarism in Africa, notably eastern and north-east Africa, including Eritrea, Ethiopia, Uganda and Tanzania. He is the author of a number of books, including *A History of Modern Uganda* (Cambridge University Press, 2017) and *Warfare in African History* (Cambridge University Press, 2012), while a revised third edition of his *History of Modern Africa: from 1800 to the Present* appeared in 2019. A former editor of the *Journal of African History*, most recently he has written a first-hand account of the social, political and cultural impact of conflict in the Horn, *Shallow Graves: A Memoir of the Ethiopia–Eritrea War* (2020).

SYLVIA SCHRAUT was Professor of German and European Modern History in the Department of History, Bundeswehr University Munich. Her main research topics are gender history and the history of political violence.

Publications about political violence include: S. Schraut and K. Weinhauer (eds.), 'Terrorism, Gender, and History', *Historical Social Research* 39 (2014); S. Schraut, *Terrorismus und politische Gewalt* (2018).

JOSEPH MORRISON SKELLY is Professor of History at the College of Mount Saint Vincent in New York City. He received a PhD in modern Irish history from University College Dublin. His books include *Irish Diplomacy at the United Nations, 1945–65: National Interests and the International Order* (1997), the volume *Irish Foreign Policy, 1919–1966: From Independence to Internationalism* (co-editor, 2000), and *Political Islam from Muhammad to Ahmadinejad: Defenders, Detractors, and Definitions* (editor, 2009). He is treasurer of the Association for the Study of the Middle East and Africa and an associate scholar at the Middle East Forum. An officer in the United States Army Reserve, he has served in Operation Iraqi Freedom, in West Africa and in Operation COVID-19 Support.

EKATERINA STEPANOVA heads the Peace and Conflict Studies Unit at the National Institute of World Economy and International Relations (IMEMO), Moscow, and teaches at MGIMO-University and European University in St Petersburg. Her books include *Terrorism in Asymmetrical Conflict* (2008), *Terrorism: Patterns of Internationalization* (2009), *Addressing Terrorism, Violent Extremism and Radicalisation* (2017) and *ISIS and the Phenomenon of Foreign Fighters in Syria and Iraq* (2020). She edits the journal *Pathways to Peace and Security*. In 2007–9, she led the Armed Conflicts Program at Stockholm International Peace Research Institute. She holds a PhD in History from Moscow State University and Dr.Habil. in Political Science from IMEMO. Website: estepanova.net.

BRIAN GLYN WILLIAMS is Professor of Islamic History at the University of Massachusetts Dartmouth and formerly taught at the University of London SOAS. He has worked in Afghanistan for the CIA's Counter-Terrorism Center and US Army's Information Operations. He is author of seven books based on his fieldwork in Islamic Eurasia. These include *Counter Jihad: The American Military Experience in Afghanistan, Iraq and Syria* (2018) and *The Last Warlord: The Life and Legend of Dostum, the Afghan Warrior Who Led Special Forces to Topple the Taliban Regime*, based on time spent living with pro-US Uzbek fighters and their commander. Website: brianglynwilliams.com.

PART I

★

INTRODUCTION

I

History and the Study of Terrorism

RICHARD ENGLISH

Terrorism[1] and responses to terrorism have repeatedly had a profound influence in shaping human experience. A terrorist incident was the detonator setting off the cataclysmic First World War explosion; terroristic violence was one of the important elements within the anticolonial reshaping of global politics during the twentieth century; responses to the September 2001 terrorist attack on the USA defined much subsequent international politics; terrorism has frequently been deployed by states against their own and other peoples; and the mutually shaping intimacy of non-state and state violence, together with the often agonising legacies emerging from that terrorising relationship, continue to determine the contours of many people's experience (in India, Pakistan, Afghanistan, Iraq, Spain, the UK, Colombia and across so much of the polarised world).[2]

Given this importance within the human past, what can we say about history and the study of terrorism?[3] In introducing the present volume, this chapter will ask five central questions. First, what has been the relative contribution of historians to the existing study of terrorism? Second, what

---

[1] The contributors to this volume have not been asked to subscribe to a single definition of terrorism. My own definition remains the capacious one that I published and defended in 2009: 'Terrorism involves heterogeneous violence used or threatened with a political aim; it can involve a variety of acts, of targets, and of actors; it possesses an important psychological dimension, producing terror or fear among a directly threatened group and also a wider implied audience in the hope of maximising political communication and achievement; it embodies the exerting and implementing of power, and the attempted redressing of power relations; it represents a subspecies of warfare, and as such it can form part of a wider campaign of violent and non-violent attempts at political leverage' (R. English, *Terrorism: How to Respond* (Oxford, Oxford University Press, 2009), p. 24).
[2] R. English (ed.), *Illusions of Terrorism and Counter-Terrorism* (Oxford, Oxford University Press, 2015).
[3] I refer to 'the past' as that which has happened before now; by 'history', I mean research and writing about the past; I use the term 'historiography' to refer to research and writing about history.

3

are the distinctive insights potentially brought by historians to our understanding of the subject? Third, what are the particular challenges for historians as they engage with the study of terrorism? Fourth, what are the opportunities for historians in studying this phenomenon? Fifth, given these aspects of the relationship between history and terrorism (the contribution to date, the distinctive insights, the challenges, the opportunities), what will this book decisively and originally offer?

Historians' Contribution to Date

First, what has been the relative contribution of historians to the existing study of terrorism?

Individual historians have, of course, made major contributions to our understanding of various aspects of terrorism, from wide-angled surveys of the phenomenon, to studies of particular non-state organisations, to works on state terrorism, to analyses of particular periods of terrorist activity, to consideration of the dynamics of counterterrorism, to specific national-level studies.[4] Some of that work will be alluded to in the concluding chapter of this book. But history, as a discipline, has been less conspicuous than some others (particularly some of the social sciences) within the study of terrorism to date.[5] In the prominent and influential academic journal *Terrorism and Political Violence* between 1998 and 2017, for example, there were 54 article authors who were historians and 957 who were not (so historians represented only 5.6 per cent of article authors during that twenty-year period). Perhaps this proportion will seem appropriate to some readers, since there are numerous disciplines with deep insights to offer regarding terrorism (including political science/international relations, psychology, sociology,

---

4 From many possible examples, see C. Townshend, *Terrorism: A Very Short Introduction* (Oxford, Oxford University Press, 2018); M. Burleigh, *Blood and Rage: A Cultural History of Terrorism* (London, HarperPress, 2008); R. Singh, *Hamas and Suicide Terrorism: Multi-Causal and Multi-Level Approaches* (London, Routledge, 2011); I. Kershaw, *The End: Hitler's Germany, 1944–45* (London, Allen Lane, 2011); R. B. Jensen, 'The International Campaign Against Anarchist Terrorism, 1880–1930s', *Terrorism and Political Violence* 21/1 (2009); R. B. Jensen, 'The Secret Agent, International Policing, and Anarchist Terrorism: 1900–1914', *Terrorism and Political Violence* 29/4 (2017); B. Blumenau, *The United Nations and Terrorism: Germany, Multilateralism and Anti-Terrorism Efforts in the 1970s* (Basingstoke, Palgrave, 2014); M. Fellman, *In the Name of God and Country: Reconsidering Terrorism in American History* (New Haven, Yale University Press, 2010).
5 Cf. Beverly Gage's comment that, 'on the subject of "terrorism", the form of violence that currently dominates American political discourse, historians have had comparatively little to say' (B. Gage, 'Terrorism and the American Experience: A State of the Field', *Journal of American History* 98/1 (2011), p. 73).

anthropology, law, philosophy, criminology, theology). But if we consider, for example, that during 2016 and 2017 alone *Terrorism and Political Violence* featured 59 article authors from political science/international relations (more than there were historians for 1998–2017 as a whole), then it might seem that historians have been rather under-represented in such scholarly debates.[6]

The situation regarding academic centres studying terrorism is somewhat similar. The Centre for the Study of Terrorism and Political Violence (CSTPV) at the University of St Andrews is housed in the School of International Relations; the Centre for Conflict, Security and Terrorism (CST) at the University of Nottingham is based in the School of Politics and International Relations; King's College London's International Centre for the Study of Radicalisation (ICSR) is housed in the Department of War Studies; the Centre for Research and Evidence on Security Threats (CREST) is coordinated by Lancaster University, where the director is a psychologist; the Terrorism and Political Violence Association (TAPVA) is an academic network based at the University of Leeds, its director working in the School of Politics and International Studies.

In the United States too the most prominent academic centres focusing on terrorism have tended not to be housed in History departments or led by historians. The Chicago Project on Security and Threats (CPOST, which has generated an influential Suicide Attack Database) was founded and is directed by a political scientist; START, the National Consortium for the Study of Terrorism and Responses to Terrorism, is headquartered at the University of Maryland, where its founding director was a criminologist and its current director another non-historian; CREATE (the Center for Risk and Economic Analysis of Terrorism Events) is an interdisciplinary centre based at the University of Southern California, drawing on the work of social scientists, engineers, economists and computer scientists; Georgetown University's Center for Security Studies (CSS) is housed in the Edmund A. Walsh School of Foreign Service, its director being a political scientist; Stanford University's Center for International Security and Cooperation (CISAC) is co-directed by a political scientist and a geologist, and is housed in an Institute for International Studies; the University of California's Institute on Global Conflict and Cooperation (IGCC) has an economist as its research director for work on conflict; the influential Empirical Studies of Conflict (ESOC) Project is co-directed by two political scientists; the director of the Terrorism

---

6 *Terrorism and Political Violence*, published by Taylor and Francis.

Research Center at the University of Arkansas is a criminologist; the Terrorism, Transnational Crime and Corruption Center (TraCCC) at George Mason University is based in its School of Policy and Government.

A similar pattern is evident elsewhere. In Israel, the founder and director of the International Institute for Counter-Terrorism (ICT) is a political scientist; in Australia, Macquarie University's programme on Policing, Intelligence and Counter-Terrorism (PICT) is housed in the Department of Security Studies and Criminology; in New Zealand, the University of Auckland's programme on Conflict and Terrorism Studies is explicitly multidisciplinary, but draws on politics/international relations, media and communications and criminology; the director of the Canadian Network for Research on Terrorism, Security and Society is a sociologist, and its associate director relating to terrorism is a political scientist.[7]

None of this undermines the excellent work pursued through these and other university initiatives. Nor does it mean that historians have not been at all involved in such ventures; CSTPV at St Andrews, for example, has had historians in its team in recent years. But what this short series of examples does suggest is that, institutionally and collectively, it has not tended to be historians who have been most prominent in the organised academic study of terrorism. Such a conclusion is reinforced by other kinds of evidence too. Lisa Stampnitzky's detailed analysis of the emergence of the terrorism expert reflects the greater influence of International Relations, Law, Maths and International Studies than of History;[8] another sustained study of the field identified forty-seven 'core members of the Terrorism Studies research community', of whom only four could be considered historians.[9] So, although some people have detected an increase in historical emphasis in very recent years,[10] this has to be considered in the context of the broadly non-historical centre of gravity which has so long prevailed in the field, and which continues still to dominate much debate.

---

7 These observations about university centres represent the situation at the time of writing and are open to later change, as universities potentially amend their organisational structures. Nonetheless, they represent a striking and telling situation at the time of their being observed, and I doubt that the situation will have greatly altered by the time of this book's publication.
8 L. Stampnitzky, *Disciplining Terror: How Experts Invented 'Terrorism'* (Cambridge, Cambridge University Press, 2013), pp. 88–90, 95–6, 124, 135, 139–40, 161.
9 S. Raphael, cited in A. P. Schmid (ed.), *The Routledge Handbook of Terrorism Research* (London, Routledge, 2011), p. 465.
10 G. M. Ceci, 'A "Historical Turn" in Terrorism Studies?', *Journal of Contemporary History* 51/4 (2016).

Historians' Distinctive Insights

Second, what are the distinctive insights potentially brought by historians to our understanding of the subject?

If historians have indeed been less prominent than some others within the debate on terrorism, might we be able to establish some of the disciplinary insights that have potentially been lost as a result? The study of terrorism has rightly and beneficially developed as a multidisciplinary endeavour.[11] Just as adherents to other disciplines rightly stress that history alone cannot provide full understanding of political violence,[12] so too it is reasonable to suggest that there might be elements of terrorism which cannot fully be apprehended without historians' contributions. This view is reinforced by the now widespread recognition, from scholars in various disciplines, of the decisive importance of history for our understanding of the present.[13] Even scholars studying how neurobiology and the genes relate to violence have stressed the decisive role that is played by particular, inherited, complex context;[14] that context is the very realm on which historians focus. So, while historians have not been especially salient in the terrorism debate so far, there is substantial agreement that their scholarly contribution might be important. Let me set out here five interwoven elements which, together, might be judged to represent a historian's distinctive approach,[15] as we collectively pursue a multidisciplinary route towards understanding terrorism.

---

11 See, for example, E. Chenoweth, R. English, A. Gofas and S. N. Kalyvas (eds.), *The Oxford Handbook of Terrorism* (Oxford, Oxford University Press, 2019).

12 F. Christia, *Alliance Formation in Civil Wars* (Cambridge, Cambridge University Press, 2012), p. 3.

13 D. Acemoglu and J. A. Robinson, *Why Nations Fail: The Origins of Power, Prosperity and Poverty* (London, Profile, 2012); A. Acharya, M. Blackwell and M. Sen, *Deep Roots: How Slavery Still Shapes Southern Politics* (Princeton, Princeton University Press, 2018); A. Roberts, 'Terrorism Research: Past, Present and Future', *Studies in Conflict and Terrorism* 38/1 (2015); J. Guldi and D. Armitage, *The History Manifesto* (Cambridge, Cambridge University Press, 2014).

14 R. M. Sapolsky, *Behave: The Biology of Humans at Our Best and Worst* (London, Bodley Head, 2017).

15 For earlier reflections on the particular approach brought by historians to the study of terrorism, see R. English, *Does Terrorism Work? A History* (Oxford, Oxford University Press, 2016), pp. 17–30. Clearly, historians have disagreed among themselves about the nature of historical work (e.g. M. Bentley, *The Life and Thought of Herbert Butterfield: History, Science and God* (Cambridge, Cambridge University Press, 2011); cf. D. W. Hayton, *Conservative Revolutionary: The Lives of Lewis Namier* (Manchester, Manchester University Press, 2019); see also J. D. Popkin, *From Herodotus to H-Net: The Story of Historiography* (Oxford, Oxford University Press, 2020), pp. xi–xii, 8, 230). But I think that a coherent case can still be made for a distinctive historical approach.

First, historians analyse the relationship between change and continuity with an eye to long pasts. Whether explaining the causes behind terrorism, the fluid dynamics characteristic of particular campaigns, questions of terrorist success or failure, the capacity of states to deal with non-state terrorism and even to end it – in all of this and much else we need to reflect not merely on the contemporary, but also on pasts that are long enough to enable us to produce strongly grounded assessments. And historians are crucial specialists here: good history 'looks at processes that take a long time to unfold'.[16] Whether or not the primary focus of a historian's particular piece of work is a long or short period, historians tend to be strongly conscious of the longer-term roots behind human behaviour. If one legitimate criticism of much current debate on terrorism is its short-term or even amnesiac quality, then historians might seem to have something particularly valuable to offer. In terms of terrorism's causation, its varied duration and its various endings, long-term frameworks are essential.

So, for example, the post-9/11 War on Terror seems to me imperfectly understood unless one recognises how deeply within America's past there runs the idea of the USA possessing a unique mission to bring freedom to the world.[17] Here, as in so many other ways, 9/11 did not so much represent an epoch-defining break, but rather a provocation into new versions of familiar behaviours and concepts. Continuity as well as change runs through early twenty-first-century counterterrorism, despite many people claiming that the world had changed utterly on that terrible Tuesday in 2001.[18] More broadly, one cannot understand even the recent politics of Hamas or ETA or the IRA without a deep sense of the long inheritances that are involved in each case.[19] Many terrorist groups themselves take a historically long view of their struggle; so too those analysing them need to do so.

If terrorism is a process intended to bring about change, then we can only assess its efficacy if we adopt this kind of long-term view. Such a historical approach does not necessitate a formally narrative-based analysis, but it will allow us to avoid the danger of anachronism[20] (terrorism necessarily being

---

16 Guldi and Armitage, *History Manifesto*, p. 12.
17 E. Foner, *Who Owns History? Rethinking the Past in a Changing World* (New York, Hill and Wang, 2003), pp. 58–65, 70.
18 R. English, 'Change and Continuity Across the 9/11 Fault Line: Rethinking Twenty-First-Century Responses to Terrorism', *Critical Studies on Terrorism* 12/1 (2019).
19 Singh, *Hamas and Suicide Terrorism*; C. J. Watson, *Basque Nationalism and Political Violence: The Ideological and Intellectual Origins of ETA* (Reno, Centre for Basque Studies, 2007); R. English, *Armed Struggle: The History of the IRA* (London, Pan Macmillan, 2012).
20 E. Hobsbawm, *On History* (London, Weidenfeld and Nicolson, 1997), p. 7.

different in some respects in 1820 as opposed to 1920 as opposed to 2020, because the technologies and also the imaginable worlds were so divergent between those various dates); it will also allow for more serious-minded evaluations of major phenomena. The outcomes of 1940s Jewish terrorism, or 1920s Irish republican terrorism, can only properly be considered if we are prepared to assess such activity and its outcomes over long periods of time. Again, the lengthy and complex historical roots of ISIS represent a necessary basis for understanding and responding to that organisation's violent politics,[21] and a historian's long-term framework will be a necessary part of any persuasive assessment of the group's full effect in due course.

In all this, we cannot properly understand the contemporary unless we 'plunge back into the lost world of yesterday',[22] and do so with respect for long time periods. Attention to long pasts allows us to avoid the dangerous solipsism of the present. Why dangerous? Partly because of the problems into which amnesia can lead us. So the frequent exaggeration of the threat that we supposedly now face from terrorism has led to some markedly unhelpful overreactions, and has been based on a forgetting of the extent of previous terrorisms and the threats that they posed. During 1971 and 1972, for example, the Federal Bureau of Investigation (FBI) noted more than 2,500 domestic terrorist bombings in the USA;[23] this far exceeds the number of jihadist attacks in the USA during the post-9/11 period, and yet alarmist fears about twenty-first-century threats have persisted.[24]

Indeed, when we consider in detail some of those previous experiences of terrorism, we see that much that has recently been presented as new should more accurately be read as a new version of historically familiar behaviour. On 4 February 1974 19-year-old Patricia Hearst was kidnapped by the

---

21 D. Byman, *Al-Qaida, The Islamic State and the Global Jihadist Movement: What Everyone Needs to Know* (Oxford, Oxford University Press, 2015); B. G. Williams, *Counter Jihad: America's Military Experience in Afghanistan, Iraq and Syria* (Philadelphia, University of Pennsylvania Press, 2017); B. H. Fishman, *The Master Plan: ISIS, Al-Qaida and the Jihadi Strategy for Final Victory* (New Haven, Yale University Press, 2016); J. Stern and J. M. Berger, *ISIS: The State of Terror* (London, William Collins, 2015); F. A. Gerges, *ISIS: A History* (Princeton, Princeton University Press, 2016); W. McCants, *The ISIS Apocalypse: The History, Strategy and Doomsday Vision of the Islamic State* (New York, St Martin's Press, 2015); M. Weiss and H. Hassan, *ISIS: Inside the Army of Terror* (New York, Regan Arts, 2015); G. Wood, *The Way of the Strangers: Encounters with the Islamic State* (London, Penguin, 2017).
22 E. Hobsbawm, *Fractured Times: Culture and Society in the Twentieth Century* (London, Little, Brown, 2013), p. x.
23 M. S. Hamm and R. Spaaij, *The Age of Lone Wolf Terrorism* (New York, Columbia University Press, 2017), p. 42.
24 M. Sageman, *Misunderstanding Terrorism* (Philadelphia, University of Pennsylvania Press, 2017).

Symbionese Liberation Army (SLA) from her apartment in Berkeley, California. The kidnappers included Donald DeFreeze, a low-level, rather pathetic criminal and high-school dropout who had suffered child abuse at the hands of his father, and who sought grandiose redemption and recognition through his political-liberation struggle. The SLA exhibited much that has recently been visible in jihadist violence in the West: a naïve grasp of an international belief system (in the SLA's case, a very crude, simplistic and vague Marxism); the importance of small group endeavour and of very small networks of association; the pursuit of redemption from former low-grade criminality; considerable ineptitude in tactics, but yet a lethal set of outcomes for the victims of the violence; the generation of revulsion on the part of many in the public, accompanied by some militant excitement and support; a blurring between self-serving criminal endeavour and a supposedly grand, revolutionary political ambition; dismal failure in terms of strategic outcomes; the publicity-grabbing potential of theatrically violent and transgressive acts; the campaign-sustaining impulse of a desire for revenge; and the violent death of numerous of the terrorists.[25] Even memory of this one historical case would therefore lead us to read twenty-first-century anti-Western jihadism as a more familiar, less automatically surprising or shocking or dangerous challenge than has sometimes been assumed. More broadly, a historically minded appreciation of the artificiality of periodisation, as well as of the long-term continuities that exist across putative fault lines in the past, suggests that what is often considered new in violent conflict is less novel than some have supposed. This can be true of supposedly epoch-inaugurating episodes of violence, as also of the experiences of particular groups of actors, as also of individually significant figures.[26] Relatedly, the popular idea of 'new' terrorisms sometimes depends on a lack of familiarity with terrorism's past; shrewd observers have repeatedly pointed out the continuities that have existed across different periods of terrorism year by year, decade by decade.[27]

---

25 J. Toobin, *American Heiress: The Kidnapping, Crimes and Trial of Patty Hearst* (London, Profile, 2017).
26 English, 'Change and Continuity'; S. Scheipers, *Unlawful Combatants: A Genealogy of the Irregular Fighter* (Oxford, Oxford University Press, 2015); P. R. Neumann, *Bluster: Donald Trump's War on Terror* (London, Hurst and Company, 2019).
27 M. Crenshaw, *Explaining Terrorism: Causes, Processes and Consequences* (London, Routledge, 2011), pp. 53–4; A. Gofas, '"Old" vs "New" Terrorism: What's in a Name?', *Uluslararası İlişkiler* 8/32 (2012); P. R. Neumann, *Radicalized: New Jihadists and the Threat to the West* (London, I. B. Tauris, 2016), pp. xv–xvi.

Second, historians tend to stress the complex particularity, and ultimately the uniqueness, of context.[28] So there remains something of an emphasis upon the unrepeatable specificity of what is being studied, and also a recognition of the decisive importance of local, small-scale and even individual action. In line with this, historians will tend to stress that it is terrorisms rather than terrorism that we have to explain. This approach points towards a careful distinction between cases, requiring sensitivity to geographical and temporal variation and to the specificities of setting;[29] it emphasises the jagged messiness of human experience as lived in complex relationships; and it leans towards many-layered multicausality. Such an approach, not least in relation to terrorism, represents the basis for valuable cross-case comparison rather than its enemy. So, with regard to context, how did those whom we analyse through the lens of terrorism see the world and interpret it themselves? Does the framework of terrorism make contextual sense of and for them? And what, in properly considered context,[30] was it feasible for those in that time and place to do, to think, to pursue? The avoidance of anachronism is one valuable advantage facilitated by this attitude of scholarly mind, and it has great significance as we reflect on terrorism's past.

Third, this complex particularity is analysed by historians through engagement with a vast range of mutually interrogatory sources, including first-hand sources drawn directly from those people under scrutiny. It remains unfortunate that so much research on terrorism is comparatively innocent of what terrorists themselves have actually said or left behind them.[31] It is not that such sources allow us to reach final or uncontested answers regarding major questions of terrorist definition, causation, consequences or best response. Nor is it the case that evidence from the past produces a straightforward reading of what has been remembered, since silences, reticence and the subtle retention of occluded pasts can also form a part of complex historical reality.[32] But the attempt to hear as many competing voices as possible and to evaluate their implications (an attempt so important

---

28 J. W. Scott, 'Gender: A Useful Category of Historical Analysis', in J. W. Scott (ed.), *Feminism and History* (Oxford, Oxford University Press, 1996), pp. 155, 157.
29 Bentley, *The Life and Thought of Herbert Butterfield*, pp. 9, 12.
30 Establishing the appropriate context to be considered is not, of course, straightforward (T. Shogimen, 'On the Elusiveness of Context', *History and Theory* 55/2 (2016)). But I believe that the point still stands, that historians attend to analysing people, their ideas and their behaviour with a particular eye to the complex and ultimately unique particularity of their setting in time and place.
31 E. Chenoweth and A. Gofas, 'The Study of Terrorism: Achievements and Challenges Ahead', in Chenoweth et al. (eds.), *Oxford Handbook of Terrorism*, p. 6.
32 D. MacCulloch, *Silence: A Christian History* (London, Penguin, 2013); G. Beiner, *Forgetful Remembrance: Social Forgetting and Vernacular Historiography of a Rebellion in Ulster* (Oxford, Oxford University Press, 2018).

in relation to something as contentious and painful as terrorism) is one to which historians' multi-evidence and primary-source inclinations can make a strong contribution. Naïvely conceived objectivity will be unattainable,[33] and it is important to recognise the power, distinctiveness and weight of rival voices of historical experience,[34] and the inappropriateness to some settings of analytical paradigms that have been generated within some others.[35] But that does not prevent us from distinguishing the more from the less plausible as we consider the past, nor even to separate truth from lies.[36] Pertinent here is reflection on a range of issues: what it is that rich first-hand sources compel us to say; what it is that they allow us legitimately to claim; what the constraints are upon what they tell us; and what it is that the crucial silences within them imply.[37] Deep-rooted professional scepticism about the origin and nature of sources is important, as is the combination of empathy and detachment.

This can be very valuable when political emotions become intense and polarised, and when restraint in contemporary judgement might make sense. US President Donald Trump's relationship with his former National Security Advisor H. R. McMaster was a potentially very important one for the history of terrorism and counterterrorism. It may indeed be that the views cited by Michael Wolff in his account of the Trump White House are accurate: that Trump considered McMaster 'boring', for instance, or that McMaster thought Trump a 'dope'. But since Wolff's book gives insufficient contextual specificity about these quotations (when exactly they were supposed to have been uttered, or where, or to whom, or how the author gained access to them or assessed their accuracy), they are less reliable as a source base than would be ideal.[38] All the more so when set against McMaster's own meticulous historical approach to sources,[39] and his rather impressive role in

---

33 L. Jordanova, *History in Practice* (London, Bloomsbury, 2006), pp. 3, 6; D. Lowenthal, *The Past is a Foreign Country – Revisited* (Cambridge, Cambridge University Press, 2015), pp. 336–40; P. Novick, *That Noble Dream: The 'Objectivity Question' and the American Historical Profession* (Cambridge, Cambridge University Press, 1988).
34 N. Mahuika, *Rethinking Oral History and Tradition* (Oxford, Oxford University Press, 2019).
35 M. H. Sommer, *Sex, Law and Society in Late Imperial China* (Stanford, Stanford University Press, 2000), pp. 3–4.
36 R. J. Evans, *Telling Lies about Hitler: The Holocaust, History and the David Irving Trial* (London, Verso, 2002); Popkin, *From Herodotus to H-Net*, pp. 174, 231–3.
37 MacCulloch, *Silence: A Christian History*.
38 M. Wolff, *Fire and Fury: Inside the Trump White House* (London, Little, Brown, 2018), pp. 189, 304.
39 H. R. McMaster, *Dereliction of Duty: Lyndon Johnson, Robert McNamara, the Joint Chiefs of Staff and the Lies that Led to Vietnam* (New York, HarperCollins, 1997).

countering non-state terroristic violence in military practice.[40] The only way of serious-mindedly engaging with such issues will be to gather a vast range of competing sources, many of them first-hand and all of them sceptically assessed.

A fourth instinct to which historians frequently tend is a scepticism about what might be considered an over-reliance on abstract theorising (on 'mechanistic theories'),[41] and about what might be thought a somewhat Procrustean attempt by some analysts to fit human experience into tidy theoretical models. It is not that empirical enquiry should (or even could) seriously exist without theoretical foundations.[42] But historians remain less prone to the establishment of a general theory about terrorism than are political and some other social scientists; thus, many historians tend more often towards a less neat and more jaggedly complex understanding of (for example) what success for a terrorist group might involve.[43]

This reflects a wider tendency, according to which historians' scepticism about an over-reliance on theory might complement more theoretically inclined approaches.[44] So, in relation to terrorism, many historians will want to complement a strictly instrumentalist explanation for political violence and its outcomes, with a recognition that – when explored in richly sourced and particular context – actors' motivations and concerns emerge possessing a complexity that involves sincere and significant attachment to particular beliefs, causes and identities.[45] And if Amartya Sen is correct to suggest that realisation-focused comparison is a better foundation on which to build than is transcendental institutionalism, and that we should attend to

---

40 Williams, *Counter Jihad*, pp. 209–10.
41 C. Townshend, *Political Violence in Ireland: Government and Resistance since 1848* (Oxford, Oxford University Press, 1983), p. ix.
42 Some of the most thoughtful of historiographical arguments reflect this, as is evident from journals such as *History and Theory*.
43 Compare, for example, the approaches respectively adopted towards this question in English, *Does Terrorism Work?*, and in studies such as M. Abrahms, *Rules for Rebels: The Science of Victory in Militant History* (Oxford, Oxford University Press, 2018); P. Krause, *Rebel Power: Why National Movements Compete, Fight, and Win* (Ithaca, NY, Cornell University Press, 2017); and E. Chenoweth and M. J. Stephan, *Why Civil Resistance Works: The Strategic Logic of Non-Violent Conflict* (New York, Columbia University Press, 2011).
44 R. J. Evans, *Altered Pasts: Counterfactuals in History* (London, Little, Brown, 2014), p. 62; P. Burke, *History and Social Theory* (Cambridge, Polity Press, 1992).
45 So the brilliant political scientists Daniel Posner and Fotini Christia, for example, might be judged by some historians to over-instrumentalise actors' motivations in settings of ethnic division: D. N. Posner, *Institutions and Ethnic Politics in Africa* (Cambridge, Cambridge University Press, 2005), pp. 11–13; Christia, *Alliance Formation in Civil Wars*, pp. 7, 32, 34, 170.

what we see as having actually happened in the world,[46] then historians seem well placed to provide very important thinking and evidence. The point here is not to dismiss more theoretically abstract approaches to terrorism. Rather, it is to use historians' scepticism as a complement to other methodological approaches, with historians as critical friends in the academic room when theories are being developed and adumbrated and defended. Indeed, the very best recent research on terrorism from non-historians seems to me to have benefited from this kind of multi-methodological approach, deploying sensitively qualitative analysis to complement its brilliant quantitative and model-generating scholarship.[47]

Fifth, despite some disagreement,[48] historians tend also to evince a scepticism about inevitability in human behaviour, preferring to stress the role of contingency within their analysis of complex pasts.[49] Indeed, historians have frequently found that luck can be decisive in determining important developments in the past.[50] Such an approach tends to clash with the teleological assumptions frequently evinced by non-state terrorists and their state opponents alike (as also by some of those who analyse them); it leans against seeing the past as a vindicating journey towards a known present; and it cautions also against overconfidence in the possibility of prediction. A careful reading of history might suggest that some things are more (or less) likely to occur in the future; it will probably not suggest human experience to be regular enough to allow for it to be confidently predicted: 'Time and again, history has proved a very bad predictor of future events'; 'history cannot create laws with predictive power'.[51]

Indeed, the possibility within the past for the emergence of various futures frequently appears in historical analysis. So the consideration of counterfactual possibility lies at the heart of much historical analysis[52] and, though it

46 A. Sen, *The Idea of Justice* (London, Allen Lane, 2009).
47 See, for example, the important study: E. Berman, J. H. Felter and J. N. Shapiro, *Small Wars, Big Data: The Information Revolution in Modern Conflict* (Princeton, Princeton University Press, 2018).
48 A. Tucker, *Our Knowledge of the Past: A Philosophy of Historiography* (Cambridge, Cambridge University Press, 2004), pp. 220–39.
49 J. W. Scott, 'Introduction', in Scott (ed.), *Feminism and History*, pp. 8, 13; Guldi and Armitage, *History Manifesto*, pp. 110–11; D. Cannadine, *Victorious Century: The United Kingdom, 1800–1906* (London, Penguin, 2017), pp. 3, 44, 92, 103, 528.
50 M. MacMillan, *History's People: Personalities and the Past* (London, Profile Books, 2016), pp. 12, 17, 73, 75.
51 R. J. Evans, *In Defence of History* (London, Granta, 1997), pp. 59, 61; cf. Foner, *Who Owns History?*, p. 4; J. Belich, J. Darwin, M. Frenz and C. Wickham (eds.), *The Prospect of Global History* (Oxford, Oxford University Press, 2016), p. 20.
52 MacMillan, *History's People*, pp. 55–8, 236.

does present complex challenges,[53] counterfactual reflection offers crucial insights when interrogating terrorism's past. Could the levels of Palestinian terrorism during the late twentieth century have been far lower? If not, what were the forces absolutely preventing that? If so, what could have been done to make this more eirenic past emerge? In either case, how far does such reflection inform our reading of other pasts and their possibilities during the same period (in western Europe, the United States, Latin America)?

I do not claim that only historians exhibit any of these approaches. But, taken together, these five elements – the detailed consideration of change and continuity over long pasts; a stress on the complex particularity and uniqueness of context; engagement with a vast array of sources (including many first-hand materials, drawn from those people under scrutiny); a scepticism about Procrustean and abstract theory; and a preference for contingency over inevitability – do constitute an interwoven and recognisably distinctive historical approach.

When we consider terrorism, such an approach potentially offers great rewards. Why has terrorist violence occurred, for example, when and where and at the levels that it has? What has terrorist violence achieved and caused? The problem of causation in human activities is recognised to be profound; 'In practice, the demonstration of cause in the social world is all but impossible.'[54] But one fruitful way of trying to address it is to examine human behaviour over long pasts in very particular contexts, read through first-hand sources and with an awareness both of multicausality and of the likelihood of unanticipated consequences; such an analysis will less frequently involve regularities, inevitabilities or theorisably predictable patterns of behaviour than it will contingent processes of contextual inheritance, intention, action and (often unexpected and unpredicted) outcome. But it might be no less valuable for that.

Challenges Facing Historians

Third, what are the particular challenges for historians as they engage with the study of terrorism?

It might be that some of these challenges or difficulties partly explain the comparative absence of history from the study of terrorism to date. My argument here is that the aspects of an interwoven historical approach that

---

53 Evans, *Altered Pasts*.
54 R. N. Lebow, *Constructing Cause in International Relations* (Cambridge, Cambridge University Press, 2014), p. 9.

have been identified above both demonstrate that historians have something distinctively valuable to offer, and also help to explain why historians have not been more visible in debates on terrorism thus far. For each of these qualities of methodological approach carries with it challenges when terrorism is the subject under scrutiny.

Discussion of terrorism is often driven by a public, popular, political and policy-focused obsession with a current crisis or threat. So historians' instinct towards long-termism can be seen by some people as a challenge or even a hindrance. If one wanted an immediate response to post-9/11 al-Qaida, for example, then those analysts focusing on the contemporary might have seemed more alluring in their answers than those whose focus is more on long-term continuities, sources and experiences than on the exigencies of day-to-day contemporary crisis. This is reinforced by the potential challenge that multicausal, long-rooted, contextually generated explanations of terrorism (ISIS in 2014, for example) can seem to many people less appealing than are simpler diagnoses or theories, based on less wide-ranging and deeply rooted interrogations of available evidence.

If historians also stress that the unrepeatable uniqueness of each human context makes predictions rather suspect, and that the contingency involved in human affairs suggests the need for caution about predicted policy outcomes, and about patterns or general laws, then again the historian might not be encouraged to be among the loudest voices in the room when terrorism is being discussed. Amid an understandable (though perhaps regrettable) urge towards generalisability when politicians and societies are faced with immediate political crisis, there might be challenges for a discipline which evinces doubts about general laws, about predictive rules and about inevitability in human behaviour. (In contrast, as Bernhard Blumenau points out in this volume, some other disciplines are more comfortable with generalisability and predictability.)

None of this undermines what historians have to offer this debate. It does, however, hint at some of the reasons why long-termist, particularising scholars, with a preference for wide-ranging, mutually interrogatory, first-hand sources from the past, and with a scepticism about rigid theory and also about predictions of future behaviour – it does suggest why some such scholars might not easily feel at home discussing terrorism amid contemporary crises, and why some other people will not have been as eager as perhaps they should have been to listen.

Central here is the issue of prediction. Many political scientists and other scholars within the social sciences, for example, explicitly seek to establish models which can allow for predictions relating to political violence.[55] Historians tend to be less comfortable with such patterns of prediction because, as one of them has put it, 'at no point have historians actually accepted that history is governed by laws operating in the sense of scientific laws; history is never rigidly predictable in the way that, say, chemical reactions are'.[56] Idiographic by instinct, historians tend to consider that history does not produce straightforward 'lessons'.[57] Indeed, some historians hold strongly to the view that their professional job is 'to understand the past' and not 'to change the future'.[58] Given that much of the public (and publicly funded) debate on terrorism is responsive to contemporary crises, and that amid such settings many people do seek that there should be some future-changing interventions by experts, the challenge for historians seems clear enough.

Historians' approach to source material presents further challenges when terrorism is the subject under interrogation. It is not that historians seek naïvely conceived objective judgements; but there does endure among them a strong sense of detachment rather than primarily partisan engagement. As Richard Evans has put it, 'the task the historian has to fulfil above all others is to enter into an understanding of the strange and often alien world of the past, not to condemn it on the one hand or identify with it on the other'.[59] This admirable approach can be difficult to sustain in relation to terrorism, as any scholar who has tried to write dispassionately on the subject is likely to have learned. 'When society feels under threat, attempts at rational analysis are often openly resisted as giving aid and comfort to, or even sympathising with, the enemy.'[60] If what society seems to demand is analysis which helps in the fight against terrorism as an enemy, then the challenges involved in producing source-driven historical interpretations of multicausal and non-Manichean conflicts can be painfully sharp.

There remains a popular expectation both that there is a truth (a set of facts to be known) about the past, and that the historian's job is disinterestedly to uncover this reality.[61] It is hard for anybody to be or to seem neutral about

---

55 Abrahms, *Rules for Rebels*; Christia, *Alliance Formation in Civil Wars*; Berman, Felter and Shapiro, *Small Wars, Big Data*; Krause, *Rebel Power*; A. M. Matanock, *Electing Peace: From Civil Conflict to Political Participation* (Cambridge, Cambridge University Press, 2017).
56 Evans, *Altered Pasts*, p. 62.   57 Jordanova, *History in Practice*, p. 5.
58 A. Marwick, *The New Nature of History: Knowledge, Evidence, Language* (Basingstoke, Palgrave, 2001), p. 8.
59 R. J. Evans, *Eric Hobsbawm: A Life in History* (London, Little, Brown, 2019), p. x.
60 Townshend, *Terrorism*, pp. 1–2.   61 Novick, *That Noble Dream*, pp. 1–2.

a subject that is as emotive and bloodstained as terrorism. And many readers and research funders might not even be keen that one should try.

Opportunities for Historians

Fourth, what are the opportunities for historians in studying this phenomenon?

Despite the challenges just discussed, the potential contribution of historians to debates on terrorism remains important, and there do seem to be profound opportunities for historical scholars in this field. There is the obvious point that historians are rightly drawn to compelling topics for which there exist rich, vivid and original sources, and on which there remains much to be said in scholarly ways; terrorisms offer multiple possibilities here. There is, to take one obvious example, a surprisingly small library of first-rate historical biographies of figures who have been involved in terrorism; yet the sources, significance and potential audience all exist to make further biographical studies alluring and appropriate projects for historians. More broadly, let me identify three arenas of opportunity for historians if they choose to make a larger contribution from their discipline to the study of terrorism: historical assessment of truly major phenomena in human affairs; the shaping of public debate in serious-minded rather than amnesiac fashion; and the influencing of public policy in a nuanced and constructive manner.

If history is to focus on the 'big questions',[62] then terrorism and responses to terrorism represent important fields of research in various ways. As indicated at the start of this chapter, there is no doubting that terrorism and reactions to it have done much to shape human experience. So, if history does represent 'a coherent intellectual project', one capable of making progress 'in understanding how the world came to be the way it is today',[63] then its contribution to explaining terrorism is surely vital. Put another way, to try to understand contemporary politics and society without a historical reading of the role that has been played by terrorism would seem ill judged.

But there are other dimensions to this 'big questions' point. Historians' informed scepticism about fault lines and periodisation will lead them to interrogate how far particular terrorist episodes (the 9/11 attack, for example) have in themselves transformed human experience. Eric Hobsbawm's claim (that historians' particular special interests should not prevent them from considering 'the major question of history', namely 'the transformations of

---

62 Guldi and Armitage, *History Manifesto*, p. 54. 63 Hobsbawm, *On History*, p. x.

human kind')[64] is important here. For historians will want to assess (and will be particularly well placed to assess, through closely focused, contextually specific, long-term, original-source-based analysis) exactly how much was continuous across terrorist attacks and across supposedly transformative campaigns of violence.

Historians might also have a contextually driven sense that what is most important about terrorist activity (about the PLO or ISIS or the IRA or ETA) is less those groups' actions than how these relate to far wider phenomena, such as the fluid relationship between nation and state, or the tensions between different religious movements or the wings within those movements, or the relationship between economic development and communal experience, or – more probably – the connections between elements of all of the above. That it is the nation or the state or religious community or economics that are the most important features of human experience does not minimise the importance of studying terrorism; this reality can indeed be made uniquely clear precisely because terrorism has been studied in its complex historical context over long pasts,[65] and as part of an integrated whole. Historians' instincts (towards understanding a phenomenon in its particular, complex context, as it has evolved through a lengthy past, and on the basis of first-hand sources) offer opportunities and rewards here for the scholar: there will be a distinctive understanding of terrorism (as something best understood as embedded within and reflecting larger relationships of nation, state, class, religious group); but there will also be sharp-edged readings of those major phenomena and of the extent to which they have or have not been transformed by terroristic violence. There is the opportunity here for two regrettable tendencies simultaneously to be averted by such historical work: the tendency towards amnesia about the role played by terrorism in broader histories;[66] and the tendency to examine terrorism as though it were a phenomenon existing beyond normal human activity or context or relationships.

---

64 Hobsbawm, *On History*, p. 67.
65 J. L. Gelvin, *The Modern Middle East: A History* (Oxford, Oxford University Press, 2016); J. L. Gelvin, 'Al-Qaida and Anarchism: A Historian's Reply to Terrorology', *Terrorism and Political Violence* 20/4 (2008); J. L. Gelvin, 'Al-Qaida and Anarchism: A Historian's Reply to Terrorology: Response to Commentaries', *Terrorism and Political Violence*, 20/4 (2008); L. Mees, *Nationalism, Violence and Democracy: The Basque Clash of Identities* (Basingstoke, Palgrave Macmillan, 2003); Watson, *Basque Nationalism*; English, *Armed Struggle*; R. English, *Irish Freedom: The History of Nationalism in Ireland* (London, Pan Macmillan, 2006).
66 See the excellent treatment in Fellman, *In the Name of God and Country*.

Since the division between political and other forms of history has now significantly dissolved (with our understanding of the politics of the past necessarily having all manner of social, cultural, geographical and economic elements),[67] there is an opportunity for historians to counteract decontextualised simplification, and to contribute to the understanding of major phenomena and human transformations through the lens of studying terrorism. A full understanding of terrorism will be impossible unless we integrate our reading of it into our explanations of the complex dynamics of the state, nationalism, major religions and the like.[68] It is also true that we cannot claim fully to have understood those more major phenomena unless we examine the role of terrorism within them.[69]

Such analyses might possess a doubly wide audience, therefore, presenting arguments of interest to those fascinated by terrorism, but also to those rightly intrigued by the historical evolution of nation, state, economy, religion and society. This leads to the second major opportunity, namely that there is the chance for historians studying terrorisms to generate and even perhaps to shape public debate. This might be judged important owing to the often ahistorical and amnesiac quality of so much existing public comment on terrorism.[70] Serious-minded understanding of this phenomenon must avoid short-termism.

There is, therefore, the opportunity here for an important public history, a history that engages audiences beyond other academics. Such an endeavour will not appeal to all. Public history is a complex phenomenon,[71] and historians who have become public scholars and public intellectuals have often enough been seen as controversial within the discipline. But they have seized attention for major insights about how the past illuminates various presents, and it is hard to sustain the view that public debate would have been richer without the discussion-generating arguments of figures as diverse as David Cannadine, Diarmaid MacCulloch, Linda Colley, Niall Ferguson, Richard Evans, A. J. P. Taylor, Lewis Namier or Herbert Butterfield.

---

67 P. Burke, 'Overture: The New History, Its Past and Its Future', in P. Burke (ed.), *New Perspectives on Historical Writing* (Cambridge, Polity Press, 1991), p. 19; Hobsbawm, *On History*, p. 66.
68 W. Pearlman and B. Atzili, *Triadic Coercion: Israel's Targeting of States That Host Non-State Actors* (New York, Columbia University Press, 2018).
69 K. McConaghy, *Terrorism and the State: Intra-State Dynamics and the Response to Non-State Political Violence* (Basingstoke, Palgrave, 2017), p. 9.
70 Williams, *Counter Jihad*, p. xi.
71 J. Tosh, 'Public History, Civic Engagement and the Historical Profession in Britain', *History* 99/335 (2014).

It is partly a question of diverse audiences. Some historians will, reasonably enough, prefer to remain with a specialist, technical readership. But public historians can sustain and have sustained the highest calibre of historical research and writing while reaching a wide public audience as well as being read by fellow scholars and specialists. Few subjects command public interest as dramatically as terrorism, and few things affect as many people as the contingent policy and societal responses to terrorist threats. There would seem, therefore, to be important opportunities here for positive public history,[72] and for arguing in relation to terrorism that, to borrow the words of Eric Hobsbawm, 'Historians should not write only for other historians.'[73]

Hobsbawm undoubtedly saw himself as a writer, and he reached a vast global audience, well beyond the world of the university library (and well beyond that which most historians will come close to reaching).[74] But the public audience for history remains vast, extending far beyond the academy, and political violence such as terrorism offers opportunities for historical insights to help to shape wide-ranging debate. This public-facing history involves not just the writing of books, but also the thinking and discussion behind memorials, museums, monuments and public acts of remembrance.

A third major opportunity for historians deciding to engage with the terrorism debate is a related one, and involves the possibility of influencing important public policy in a nuanced, complicating[75] and constructive manner.[76] This should not, I believe, be the primary goal of historical research, nor would such subtly benign policy influence be best achieved by those for whom it was. Nor do I suggest that historians (or any other scholars) are likely to have a mechanically decisive impact upon the decisions that are taken by governments or other wings of states. But it is clear that policymakers and practitioners do engage with expert analysis, not least in relation to counterterrorism, and that their thinking and decisions have

---

72 Guldi and Armitage, *History Manifesto*, pp. 112–13, 117–19, 123.
73 E. Hobsbawm, *Interesting Times: A Twentieth-Century Life* (London, Penguin, 2002), p. 282; cf. Foner, *Who Owns History?*, pp. 20–2, 35–6; E. Hobsbawm, *The Age of Empire 1875–1914* (London, Weidenfeld and Nicolson, 1995), p. ix.
74 Evans, *Eric Hobsbawm*.
75 'When the telling of our stories is left to policy makers and politicians, a simplistic summary can elide reality ... That's where historians matter most – where we carefully and judiciously complicate the story by confronting the evidence before us' (E. Lewis, 'History and the Common Good: Scholarship in the Public Eye', *Journal of American History* 106/3 (2019), p. 578).
76 J. D. Simon, 'The Forgotten Terrorists: Lessons from the History of Terrorism', *Terrorism and Political Violence* 20/2 (2008).

(among many other influences) on occasions been affected by these insights.[77]

Such influence from historians will not take the form of neat lessons from the past, nor of predictive laws offering certainty for the future. But it might involve deep and informed intuitions, based on the distinctive historical approach that was adumbrated earlier in this chapter: the interrogation of multiple (including first-hand) sources; a recognition of the importance of particular context; respect for the role of contingency; attention to the significance of long-term pasts and futures; and an acknowledgement of the unlikelihood that any Procrustean theory will adequately explain human behaviour.

Public history with a policy-facing dimension is not uncontroversial.[78] But it is hard to dismiss the suggestion that politicians and policymakers too often respond to terrorism on the basis of short-term thinking, or to dispute that there exists an opportunity for historians to help offset that problem. It may be that, as such, historians will sometimes take on the role of authoritative dissenters amid a more present-obsessed conversation; but that in itself might be a welcome contribution to a policy-serious responsibility of approach that should characterise all disciplines in relation to terrorism.[79]

Policy can, of course, be influenced by historians in other ways too. As teachers, historians can encourage an informed and reflective approach to the particular, long-term complexities of the human past, in relation to terrorism-generating settings as to others. As graduates, historians can and do affect the world of terrorism and counterterrorism. At the time of drafting an early version of this chapter, the US National Security Advisor was H. R. McMaster, a historian who (as noted) has written brilliantly on the violent past,[80] as well as someone whose military career has involved significant attempts to counter non-state terrorist violence.

The Contribution of This Volume

Fifth, given these aspects of the relationship between history and terrorism (the contribution to date, the distinctive insights, the challenges, the

---

77 For evidence both that counterterrorist practitioners listen to some academics, and also that there is more space for historians to occupy here, see J. Evans, 'Academic Research and the Intelligence Community: Some Reflections', in Chenoweth et al. (eds.), *Oxford Handbook of Terrorism*, and also 'CONTEST: The United Kingdom's Strategy for Countering Terrorism', June 2018.
78 AHR Exchange: On *The History Manifesto, American Historical Review* 120/2 (2015).
79 English (ed.), *Illusions of Terrorism and Counter-Terrorism*.
80 McMaster, *Dereliction of Duty*.

opportunities), what will this book decisively and originally offer? Despite the challenges adumbrated earlier in this chapter, the authors in this volume have produced analyses which demonstrate the particular insights that are available from historically minded work on terrorism.

Contributors to the book deal subtly with the challenges and opportunities involved in drawing on long pasts while discussing terrorism. Warren Brown points out that the modern idea of a state at which not-state actors direct their violence is somewhat anachronistic for much of the pre-modern past; he also identifies the difficulties that exist with distinguishing during such periods between civilian and military, or between combatant and non-combatant. Uncritically deploying the word terrorism for periods before the modern therefore carries its risks, and even looking for the origins of terrorism in a longer past can be challenging. But Brown's chapter nonetheless hints at some things that were inherited and later became significant for our understanding. He shows, for example, that while the distinction between military and civilian cannot be assumed in the pre-modern era, we can see in that earlier period (in the evolving relationships between nobles and the king) important foundations on which that later military/civilian distinction was built. Reinforcing this kind of insight, in his chapter on Africa, Richard Reid demonstrates the importance of appreciating African experience over lengthy periods if we are properly to understand contemporary terrorism. He shows that some patterns of recent terrorist violence in Africa (including the frequent and important eschewing of a distinction between combatant and non-combatant) have flowed from a deeper past. Joseph Morrison Skelly's analysis of diplomatic engagements with terrorism draws powerfully on the long-term effects of some of those endeavours. Cecilia Méndez's analysis of Peruvian violence demonstrates the long-term dynamics that are essential to understanding that country's more recent past, and long-term processes are central also to Lorenzo Bosi's chapter. My own arguments in this book about religion and terrorism are founded on the belief that only long-term frameworks will facilitate true understanding. Dennis Dworkin demonstrates in vivid detail why a proper understanding of US terrorism has to explore past centuries' experience, and the legacy of that experience for more contemporary crises.

Bernhard Blumenau points out that historians' distinctiveness of approach partly arises from their attention to long-term continuities, changes and patterns. Steve Hewitt points out that cultures of short-termism obstruct fuller understandings of terrorism (as of much else), with governmental instincts towards amnesia being a particular problem. His own chapter offsets this with a subtle and long-rooted consideration of the evolution of counter-terrorism and its relationship with terrorist violence. Ludger Mees's balanced account of Basque terrorism shows the vital significance of long pasts when understanding such complex political violence.

Echoing this, Julie Norman's very thoughtful discussion of terrorism in Israel/Palestine demonstrates how essential a long-term, historical approach is if we are properly to understand the interwoven, interlocking terrorisms of that region. Again, Brigitte Nacos and Melih Barut convincingly demonstrate how terrorist propaganda retains similarities even across very long time periods, an antidote to the exaggerated claims made by some about utterly new forms of terrorism. Kieran McConaghy shows that a full appreciation of what is new (or not new) about transnational terrorism in the twenty-first century depends on a profound historical reading of long-term behaviour; and Rory Cox's highly original examination of terrorism and the state shrewdly attends to the fact that the relationship between these two phenomena has been very lengthy. Likewise, Martyn Frampton's very subtle consideration of terrorist definition respects the long-term genealogy that must be involved in a properly historical understanding of this vital issue.

The significance of examining the complex particularity of historical context is repeatedly evident in these chapters on terrorism, whether in Roddy Brett's consideration of the Colombian case, Dennis Dworkin's reflections on the USA or Brian Glyn Williams's chapter on Iraq. Indeed, this book has benefited here from case-study analysis written by authors resident or long immersed in the setting itself. Again, Martyn Frampton's genealogical approach to the issue of definition reflects a deep respect for context, complexity and contingency, and alludes to historians' instinct towards recognising differences rather than similarities. Ekaterina Stepanova demonstrates the importance of complex historical context in her analyses of two very distinct periods of Russian terrorist activity: one in the late nineteenth and early twentieth centuries, and the other almost a century later in post-Soviet Russia.

What of mutually interrogatory and original sources? Fearghal McGarry shows what can be done with the rich, first-hand sources that are available to historians for the study of political violence. Likewise, Steve Hewitt's analysis of counterterrorism draws richly on newspapers, archives, memoirs and government sources. Beatrice de Graaf's fascinating account of terrorism in the Netherlands draws extensively on archives and newspapers, amid a wide source range; and first-hand sources are richly evident also in Lorenzo Bosi's analysis of the processes involved in political violence.

Contributors to this book offer explanations richer than would be generated through an over-reliance on rigidly abstract theory. So Joseph Morrison Skelly's historically contextualised analysis of terrorism and diplomacy approaches its subject in terms of its labyrinthine intricacy and its complex and varied dynamics, rather than according to more blunt analytical theories of explanation. Again, by adopting such a carefully historical approach to the relationship between terrorism and regionalisation, Rory Miller avoids the sweeping implausibility of some of the more mechanistic interpretations that have been offered to date.

Regarding inevitability, Ludger Mees demonstrates that the evolution of Basque terrorism owed more to contingency than it did to historical necessity; Warren Brown helpfully clarifies the degree to which terrorism is a culturally and historically contingent concept; and Brian Glyn Williams fascinatingly discusses the effect of COVID-19 on efforts to suppress what remains of ISIS.

So the authors featured in this book exemplify the distinctive aspects of a historically minded approach that were adumbrated earlier. They also show what can be done if one is prepared to avail of the opportunities available to those who engage with historical understandings of terrorism. In terms of analysing truly major phenomena in human affairs, for example, Dennis Dworkin's essay about American terrorism is also an interrogation of relationships that are central to defining the United States itself: domestic relationships between racial groups and between social classes; and important international relationships with external actors. Dayyab Gillani's assessment of terrorism in Pakistan locates and explains it within the wider sociopolitical realities of that important region. My own chapter on terrorism, history and religion recognises that terroristic violence has often emerged as a symptom of more significant phenomena (such as religiously fuelled nationalisms), and that understanding terrorism in these settings illuminates our reading of those more transformative forces. Rory Miller's interrogation of terrorism, history and regionalisation considers forces such as globalisation and economic interdependence in ways that engage with some of the most important features of world politics as they have evolved. Sylvia Schraut's analysis of terrorism engages powerfully with gender as an analytical category and, in so doing, interrogates one of the major themes for properly understanding any human past. Beatrice de Graaf considers terrorism in the Netherlands in relation to truly world-significant issues such as colonialism, decolonisation and the international effects of revolution.

In terms of shaping public debate on the basis of historical understanding, Julie Norman's impressively balanced account of Israel/Palestine and terrorism offers a corrective to much of the tendentious, self-serving commentary that still hampers serious-minded discussion of that vital context. Likewise, Brian Glyn Williams's historical reconstruction of the trajectory of terrorism in Iraq provides detailed evidence of complex developments, and thoughtful consideration of what we should be discussing when publicly reflecting on that turbulent setting. Few groups have elicited as widespread and emotive a public reaction as certain female terrorists have managed to do; in calmly analysing the relationship between terrorism and gender politics, Sylvia Schraut provides much-needed serious-mindedness to a subject far too often approached irresponsibly in public comment. My own arguments about religion and terrorism run contrary to much current debate and discussion, and are intended as contributions to a more nuanced public dialogue.

In terms of offering historically informed and nuanced arguments of relevance to public policy, there is much in this volume of high value. The long-term legacies of the early twenty-first-century US and allied engagement in Iraq will require honesty and some major rethinking if their most malign potential is to be mitigated. Brian Glyn Williams's close attention to particular context suggests the way forward here, just as Julie Norman's extraordinarily even-handed treatment of Israel/Palestine points towards the most fruitful means of addressing that seemingly perennial policy challenge. Joseph Morrison Skelly's arguments about the possible outcomes of diplomacy as a response to terrorism are of high value to practitioners in the field; so too Roddy Brett's thoughtful arguments about Colombia should inform the thinking of those dealing with contemporary politics and long-term legacies in that country. Likewise, Ekaterina Stepanova's identification of potential sociopolitical violence in the Russian future possesses clear policy significance, as does Rory Cox's sophisticated demonstration of the brutal effects than can emerge from the adoption of particular narratives of political interpretation.

Historiography may indeed be 'an unlovely word'.[81] But reflection on what it is that distinguishes historians from other scholars does possess real value as we think about what has, and what has not, been said about

---

81 K. L. Klein, *From History to Theory* (Berkeley, University of California Press, 2011), p. 20.

terrorism. Research in this field will continue to be collaborative, within and between disciplines, and that is just as things should be. The contributors to this book, however, do make clear that historically minded research and writing possess insights that are of profound value in relation to an enduringly significant and compelling phenomenon.

Further Reading

E. Chenoweth, R. English, A. Gofas and S. N. Kalyvas (eds.), *The Oxford Handbook of Terrorism* (Oxford, Oxford University Press, 2019)

R. English, *Does Terrorism Work? A History* (Oxford, Oxford University Press, 2016)

R. J. Evans, *Altered Pasts: Counterfactuals in History* (London, Little, Brown, 2014)

J. Guldi and D. Armitage, *The History Manifesto* (Cambridge, Cambridge University Press, 2014)

E. Hobsbawm, *On History* (London, Weidenfeld and Nicolson, 1997)

PART II
★
FRAMEWORKS AND DEFINITIONS

2

History and the Definition of Terrorism

MARTYN FRAMPTON

It is now a cliché to observe that, despite innumerable efforts to define terrorism, scholars are no nearer to arriving at a consensus.[1] Still, calls continue to be heard for a 'comprehensive, uniform – and above all functional – definition of just what we consider terrorism to be'.[2] In response, one approach has been to assemble the multitude of definitions produced by academics, commentators, governments and international organisations, in an attempt to identify common ground.[3] There is much to admire in this ethos of catholicity – though the final product can feel more like a catalogue of component parts than a cohesive and workable definition.

How, then, should historians approach the debate over defining terrorism? To explore this question, this chapter begins by reflecting on the 'genealogical turn' in historical method – a development closely associated with the 'Cambridge school' of intellectual history. It will then attempt to construct a genealogy for 'terrorism', as reflected in existing historical narratives of this subject. And finally, it will consider the key themes that emerge from such a genealogical examination.

The Question of Definition Amidst the 'Genealogical Turn'

'When we trace the genealogy of a concept, we uncover the different ways in which it may have been used in earlier times. We thereby equip

---

[1] See, for example, R. Jackson, 'An Argument for Terrorism', *Perspectives on Terrorism* 2/2 (2008).
[2] C. Carr, '"Terrorism": Why the Definition Must Be Broad', *World Policy Journal* 24/1 (2007).
[3] See, for instance, A. P. Schmid, 'The Definition of Terrorism', in A. P. Schmid (ed.), *The Routledge Handbook of Terrorism Research* (London, Routledge, 2011).

ourselves with a means of reflecting critically on how it is currently understood.'[4]

During the last two decades, the 'Cambridge school' of historians of political thought, foremost among them Quentin Skinner, have encouraged a healthy scepticism about the effort to produce categorical definitions. In making his case, Skinner has drawn especially from the reflections of Friedrich Nietzsche, whose writing on the genealogy of 'morality' recognized that this concept meant different things to different people, in different times and places. Nietzsche recognized too that any social phenomenon revealed a 'synthesis of "meanings"', and that anything which exists 'is continually interpreted anew'.[5] 'Only something which has no history', Nietzsche famously argued, 'can be defined'; conversely, 'all concepts in which an entire process is semiotically concentrated defy definition'.[6] These insights have become increasingly important for writing histories of political thought. They have meant a move away from a focus on 'classic texts', which were presumed to impart eternal ideas. Instead, historians now place a premium on setting any text within its immediate sociopolitical and cultural context, recognizing the malleable nature of any given concept.

The contemporary ascendancy of this methodological paradigm is not solely a product of the rediscovery of Nietzsche. Rather, it also owes much to the work of Michel Foucault and the wider 'postmodern' historiographical turn. Where Nietzsche had talked about 'the will to power' that underlay all interpretation, Foucault reflected more broadly, and more consistently, about the role of power relations in the construction of knowledge – and vice versa.[7] He too sought to unpick positivist assumptions about the origins of ideas, institutions and practices of the kind that informed attempts to establish stable, immutable conceptual definitions. Foucault understood that the 'attempt to capture the exact essence of things' assumed 'the existence of immobile forms', where in fact none could be found.[8] On this basis, he called

---

4 Q. Skinner, 'A Genealogy of the Modern State', *Proceedings of the British Academy* 62 (2009), p. 325.
5 F. Nietzsche, *On the Genealogy of Morality*, trans. C. Diethe (Cambridge, Cambridge University Press, 1994), p. 51. For Skinner on Nietzsche, see, for example, Skinner, 'Genealogy of the Modern State', p. 326.
6 Nietzsche, *Genealogy of Morality*, p. 53.
7 Ibid., p. 51; for Foucault, see, inter alia, M. Foucault, *Discipline and Punish: The Birth of the Prison*, trans. A. Sheridan (London, Penguin, 2019). Also, M. Foucault, 'Nietzsche, Genealogy, History', in D. F. Bouchard (ed.), *Language, Counter-Memory, Practice: Selected Essays and Interviews* (Ithaca, NY, Cornell University Press, 1977).
8 Foucault, 'Nietzsche, Genealogy, History', p. 142.

on scholars to practise intellectual 'archaeology', or the genealogical approach.[9]

Such an approach has informed the practice of an array of scholars more or less connected with the 'Cambridge school', including Skinner, John Pocock, John Dunn, Raymond Geuss and James Tully.[10] Of course, in its emphasis on critical analysis, context and the contingent nature of the past, this 'genealogical approach' corresponds to what many would already regard as the core elements of a sound historical method.[11] Certainly, in the hands of these scholars, it has not meant a collapse into a purely relativistic or deconstructionist posture.[12] Rather, it has entailed a recognition of the imperative of patient, empirical work – an ethos, as it happens, very much in keeping with the methodological injunctions of both Nietzsche and Foucault.

Nietzsche thus called for a 'real' history of morality and urged would-be researchers of genealogy to pursue the 'grey' – 'that which can be documented' – rather than to indulge in 'blue' skies thinking.[13] Similarly, Foucault argued that genealogy was 'gray, meticulous, and patiently documentary'; it required 'a knowledge of details' and the 'vast accumulation of source material'; it demanded 'relentless erudition'.[14] All of this, said Foucault, was to be put at the service of a systematic examination of 'descent' – the tracing of the complex ways in which a concept evolved, which occluded neither moments of continuity nor rupture.[15] This latter point is crucial. As Skinner has observed, it is important to avoid the trap of 'prolepsis', or the ironing out of discordant notes.[16]

Again, there is little here that would stir dissent among many academic historians. As scholars in other fields have noted, the elevation of the genealogical apparatus in some ways merely codifies much existing practice. In its emphasis on what Srdjan Vucetic termed 'the "three E" techniques of

9 For a useful dissection of Foucault on this issue, see U. Crowley, 'Genealogy, Method', in *International Encyclopaedia of Human Geography* (London, Elsevier Science, 2009).
10 See, for example, R. Geuss, *History and Illusion in Politics* (Cambridge, Cambridge University Press, 2001), pp. 6–13; M. Bevir, 'What is Genealogy?', *Journal of the Philosophy of History* 2 (2008).
11 Melissa Lane has described Skinner's 'genealogical turn' as only 'partially Nietzschean'. See M. Lane, 'Doing Our Own Thinking for Ourselves: On Quentin Skinner's Genealogical Turn', *Journal of the History of Ideas* 73/1 (2012).
12 For a further reflection on Skinner's methodology, see R. Lamb, 'Feature Book Review: Quentin Skinner's "Post-modern" History of Ideas', *History* 89/3 (2004).
13 Nietzsche, *Genealogy of Morality*, p. 8.
14 Foucault, 'Nietzsche, Genealogy, History', pp. 139–40.
15 Ibid., pp. 146–8. See also K. Ansell-Pearson, 'Introduction: On Nietzsche's Critique of Morality', in Nietzsche, *Genealogy of Morality*, p. xx.
16 Q. Skinner, 'Meaning and Understanding in the History of Ideas', *History and Theory* 8/1 (1969), esp. pp. 22–30.

inquiry – episodes, examples and effectiveness', genealogy is 'not radically different from more mainstream social science [or, we might add, historiographical] tools'.[17] For present purposes, though, the foregoing insights are valuable precisely because they underline the extent to which the search for a final and conclusive definition of a term like 'terrorism' is quixotic. Instead, the genealogical approach encourages us to make a virtue of its protean and disputatious character.

Moreover, we might also draw upon the interdisciplinary effort to understand other contested social phenomena, especially those that feature violence, such as revolution or civil war.[18] The former has been the subject of countless works that employ, inter alia, social scientific, historical, comparative or literary approaches.[19] There are as many definitions of 'revolution' as there are academics working on the subject. But this has hardly served to inhibit scholarly insight. The 'logic' and history of civil wars, meanwhile, has recently been explored in new and critical ways by scholars like Stathis N. Kalyvas and David Armitage.

Kalyvas, for instance, has shown through the use of comparative microhistory that we need to problematise 'master narratives' about the cause of war, exploring the dynamics of violence at the local level. His reflections on the ambiguous interplay between 'private' and 'political' motivations offer a new perspective on internecine conflict.[20] Armitage's history of civil wars is particularly interesting as a model for how historians can trace the evolution of a concept through time. In so doing, he seeks to render it explicable and show the contingency of the phenomenon.[21] Furthermore, Armitage shows that when tackling a subject like 'civil war' – or indeed, 'terrorism' – there is wisdom in recognising that these are 'fundamentally political concept[s]'.[22] The use of such

17 S. Vucetic, 'Genealogy as a Research Tool in International Relations', *Review of International Studies* 37 (2011).
18 On the role of historians in considering violence per se, and some of the controversies that can arise, see I. McBride, 'Historiographical Review. The Peter Hart Affair in Perspective: History, Ideology, and the Irish Revolution', *The Historical Journal* 61/1 (2018).
19 The literature on revolutions is voluminous, but for seminal contributions see T. Skocpol, *States and Social Revolutions: A Comparative Analysis of France, Russia and China* (Cambridge, Cambridge University Press, 1979); J. Dunn, *Modern Revolutions: An Introduction to the Analysis of a Political Phenomenon* (London, Cambridge University Press, 1972); C. Brinton, *The Anatomy of Revolution* (New York, Vintage Books, 1992).
20 S. N. Kalyvas, 'The Ontology of "Political Violence": Action and Identity in Civil Wars', *Perspectives on Politics* 1/3 (2003); S. N. Kalyvas, *The Logic of Violence in Civil War* (Cambridge, Cambridge University Press, 2006).
21 D. Armitage, *Civil Wars: A History in Ideas* (Totton, Yale University Press, 2017), esp. p. 11.
22 Ibid., pp. 13, 18.

terms has been, and will remain, a source of contention. Even so, this does not stop us from seeking to excavate their 'origins' – whilst remaining sceptical of ever discovering a singular point of origin – and being open to the different ways that an idea has been understood through history.[23]

If anything, all of this reinforces still further the importance of the kind of critical methods advocated by scholars like Marc Bloch, Richard Cobb or Clifford Geertz – an approach rooted in empirical investigation that allows for the 'layering' of individual episodes; that encourages the production of 'thick description' and draws on analysis from across the scholarly disciplines; and that sees the value of meaningful comparative approaches.[24]

Building upon these foundations, historians are able to offer an array of insights into, variously, the causes, character and context for terrorist violence. In particular, they are especially well placed to examine the *qualitative* dynamic of terrorist violence, drawing on more straightforwardly literary impulses, of the kind which have often allowed journalists and novelists to capture something of the essential nature of terrorism.[25] Naturally, this does not mean a rush to jettison painstaking, empirical research. But it is to acknowledge that there needs to be a place for reflecting on the role of mysticism and emotions. As Henry Patterson has recently argued, an overemphasis on the rationality of those who engage in terrorism can tend to obscure the delusionary/distorted world view to which they frequently adhere: 'Too much emphasis on the normality of terrorists also tends to screen out the Jihadi Johns, the Shankill Butchers and Freddie Scappaticcis.'[26] Historians are temperamentally inclined to seek out the unfamiliar and the outlandish – seeking to illuminate its provenance – whilst never losing sight of the bigger picture. As Mark Mazower has commented (when discussing an equally mutable term, 'genocide'), 'The lawyer may focus on the similarities ... the historian is struck by the differences.'[27] The historian's instinct is to grapple with the idiosyncrasies of an individual terrorist, whilst still trying to explain how particular

---

23 Bloch warned against the 'idol of origins'. See M. Bloch, *The Historian's Craft*, trans. P. Putnam (Manchester, Manchester University Press, 1992), pp. 24–9.
24 Ibid.; C. Geertz, *Interpretation of Cultures* (London, Hutchinson, 1975).
25 For particularly good examples, see F. Dostoyevsky, *The Devils*, trans. D. Magarshack (London, Penguin, 2004); D. Lessing, *The Good Terrorist* (London, Cape, 1985). On the place of terrorism within fiction, see W. Laqueur, 'Interpretations of Terrorism: Fact, Fiction and Political Science', *Journal of Contemporary History* 12/1 (1977), esp. pp. 15–32.
26 H. Patterson, 'The Limits of Empathy', *Dublin Review of Books*, 1 July 2019, www.drb.ie/essays/the-limits-of-empathy.
27 M. Mazower, 'Violence and the State in the Twentieth Century', *American Historical Review* 107/4 (2002), p. 1162.

terrorist campaigns/organisations have created environments permissive to the violation of social norms.

In undertaking this endeavor, then, it is vital never to lose sight of what might be termed the 'four Cs' that are central to any historical enquiry, not least one adopting the genealogical approach: Context, Complexity, Contingency and Contestation.[28] And in seeking to excavate a 'genealogy of terrorism' in this fashion, there is one final point on which the 'Cambridge school' has something important to say: namely, the link between belief and social action. We can learn a lot by examining the way in which a particular form of violence has been deployed and legitimated – assuming, as we surely must, that any political actor seeks to justify his/her actions, and uses language to make their case.[29] This means accepting what Herbert Butterfield called the 'operative force of ideas' and the reality that some – indeed, perhaps most – political actors are 'sincerely attached to the ideals' they invoke.[30] Or, as Raymond Geuss has argued, it means accepting that 'people do not simply wish to act, but they also wish to describe their actions in ways that they and others will find acceptable, to deflect possible criticism, to enlist (ideally) active support ... and so on.'[31]

This process of (self-)justification is absolutely critical, Skinner has noted, when people seek to rationalise 'questionable forms of social behavior' (and one could hardly think of a more questionable form of behaviour than terrorist violence). In those situations, their attempts at legitimation inevitably touch upon questions of 'moral identity'; and this involves the construction of broad conceptual schema and systems of belief.[32] At the same time, one has to situate those systems of belief within an immediate context that is simultaneously ideational, social and political.[33] Marc Bloch captured this sentiment with his observation that 'a historical phenomenon can never be understood apart from its moment

---

28 On the latter, see Bevir, 'What is Genealogy?'. For a neat encapsulation of the key analytical perspectives that historians might apply specifically to terrorism, see R. English, 'Review Article: The Future of Terrorism Studies', *Critical Studies on Terrorism* 2/2 (August 2009).
29 Q. Skinner, *Visions of Politics*, Vol. 1: *Regarding Method* (Cambridge, Cambridge University Press, 2002), p. xii.
30 Butterfield, cited in Q. Skinner, *Visions of Politics*, Vol. 2: *Renaissance Virtues* (Cambridge, Cambridge University Press), p. 351.
31 Geuss, *History and Illusion*, p. 2.
32 Skinner, *Visions of Politics*, Vol. 1, pp. 148–50, 160–5.
33 Ibid., pp. 3 and 27–56. See also J. Tully, 'The Pen is a Mighty Sword: Quentin Skinner's Analysis of Politics', in J. Tully (ed.), *Meaning and Context: Quentin Skinner and His Critics* (Princeton, Princeton University Press, 1988); Lamb, 'Quentin Skinner's "Post-modern" History of Ideas', esp. 428.

in time'.[34] Or, as Maurice Mandelbaum put it, 'if we are to understand the choices open to a specific person and the goals which he sought to attain, we must make reference to the social situations in which those choices took place'.[35]

For present purposes, this means understanding that the *meaning* of terrorism has evolved with the *practice* and *context* of the phenomenon; that the kinds of activity which the term has been able to sustain have been markedly different at different junctures.[36] A concept like terrorism, to paraphrase Raymond Geuss, carries its history with it.[37] It is for this reason that the question 'what is/was terrorism?' might better be replaced by those of '*when* was terrorism?' or '*how* was terrorism [manifested]?' To answer such enquiries we need next to turn our attention to a suitably caveated attempt to explore the origins and subsequent employment of the term.[38]

Towards a Genealogy of Terrorism

In trying to construct a genealogy for terrorism, it is striking that there are – across the relevant voluminous literature – the broad outlines of agreement in relation to both origins and the subsequent historical narrative.[39] With regards to the former, for example, most the scholars have identified the French Revolution as the critical context in which the idea of 'terror' first emerged. True, numerous popular histories of terrorism make passing references to the deeds of the Sicarii, the Assassins or the 'Thugs' – in order to suggest that terrorism is, to some extent, an indelible (and implicitly 'irrational') part of human nature. But, too often, this has been done without any clear explanation for why such groups should be considered relevant.[40]

---

34 Bloch, *Historian's Craft*, p. 29.
35 M. Mandelbaum, 'A Note on History as Narrative', *History and Theory* 6/3 (1997).
36 Skinner, 'Meaning and Understanding', pp. 37–8.   37 Geuss, *History and Illusion*, p. 10.
38 Skinner has stressed his interest in identifying the 'origin of a view of politics we still endorse'. See J. Lévy and E. Tricoire, 'Quentin Skinner: "Concepts Only Have Histories"' EspacesTemps.Net [online], Laboratory (2007), www.espacestemps.net/en/articles/quentin-skinner/.
39 For another illuminating application of the genealogical approach to this terrain, see M. Blain, 'On the Genealogy of Terrorism', paper delivered to Frontiers of Sociology: The 37th World Congress of the International Institute of Sociology, Stockholm, Sweden, 5–9 July 2005.
40 To give but a few examples, A. Sinclair, *An Anatomy of Terror: A History of Terrorism* (London, Macmillan, 2003); W. Laqueur, *Age of Terrorism* (London, Little, Brown, 1977); W. Laqueur, *A History of Terrorism* (London, Transaction Publishers, 2008); R. Law, *Terrorism: A History* (Cambridge, Polity Press, 2009); B. Hoffman, *Inside Terrorism* (New York, Columbia University Press, 2004); D. C. Rapoport, 'Fear and Trembling: Terrorism in Three Religious Traditions', *The American Political Science Review* 78/3 (1984).

And much writing in this vein has deployed loose, even ahistorical terminology (typified by references to 'holy terror').[41]

In contrast to this approach, the scholarly consensus would seem to be that 'terrorism' as a discrete phenomenon belongs to the post-French Revolutionary world. Its origins are usually traced to the period of the 'Great Terror' and, in particular, Maximilian Robespierre's rhetoric about the necessity of 'terror' for the inculcation of 'virtue'.[42] As John Gray has eloquently described, the Jacobins led the way in asserting that society could be transformed, for the better, through the application of systematic violence.[43] And Edmund Burke is credited with having first coined the English word 'terrorist', in reference to those Jacobins who presided over the first great wave of revolutionary violence.[44]

On the basis of these presumed foundations, there is something of a 'soft consensus' as to the subsequent *narrative* history of terrorism. The first half of the nineteenth century is usually deemed fallow territory, with precious few indications that 'terrorism' as a distinct form of violence had emerged. Certainly, there was nothing analogous to that which had taken place across France in the 1790s. The failure of the 1848–9 revolutions, however, seemed to be a seminal moment in reviving debates about the role and efficacy of violence for delivering radical sociopolitical change. Slowly thereafter, there emerged a more or less articulated doctrine of 'terrorism', increasingly understood to connote 'non-state' violence. Various individuals have been credited with making decisive intellectual contributions: Karl Heinzen, Johann Most, Mikhail Bakunin, Pyotr Kropotkin and Carlo Piscane, to name but a few. In their writings, violence 'from below' was held to be a liberating force, without which there could be no real 'revolution'. According to Susan Morrissey, the 'modern terrorism' thereby brought into being was defined by its transnational character; by its attachment to

---

41 Certainly this is the view of Rapoport, see Ibid. And for an incisive critique of Rapoport and the broader tendency to locate the phenomenon of 'Thugee' in a history of terrorism, see K. Wagner, '"Thugs and Assassins": "New Terrorism" and the Resurrection of Colonial Knowledge', in C. Dietze and C. Verhoeven, *The Oxford Handbook of the History of Terrorism* (Oxford, Oxford University Press, 2014).
42 See, for example, N. Hampson, 'From Regeneration to Terror: The Ideology of the French Revolution', in N. O'Sullivan (ed.), *Terrorism, Ideology, and Revolution* (Brighton, Wheatsheaf Books, 1986). And, in the same volume, P. Calvert, 'Terror in the Theory of Revolution'.
43 J. Gray, *Black Mass: Apocalyptic Religion and the Death of Utopia* (London, Penguin, 2007), pp. 25–39.
44 E. Burke, *Select Works of Edmund Burke*, Vol. 3: Letters on a Regicide Peace [1795], available at https://oll.libertyfund.org/titles/burke-select-works-of-edmund-burke-vol-3/simple.

different ideologies; by its urban locale; by its association with new forms of mass media and culture; and by the novel responses it engendered in terms of police/state practice.[45]

Terrorism was, from the beginning, clearly not the preserve of any single ideological predisposition. Historians have debated the question of which group properly deserves to be seen as the 'progenitor' of terrorism.[46] The global anarchist movement, Irish 'Fenians' and Russian Revolutionaries have each figured prominently in these discussions. In the early 1880s, for instance, it was those acting in the name of Irish self-determination who succeeded in conducting the first sustained campaign of terrorist violence, using explosive devices, aimed at symbolic targets. In Russia, attacks on the state perpetrated by radical members of the late nineteenth-century intelligentsia captured the imaginations of many, and came to embody the new age of 'terrorism'. Interestingly, such labels were in part a reflection of the extent to which several Russian Revolutionary leaders stressed the 'humane' character of terrorism, describing it as a preferable method for achieving their aims, as compared to mass insurrection.[47] Faced with the disproportionate power of the state, they saw violence as both a means for self-defence and a vehicle for striking back. They hoped too that violence could be used to awaken the slumbering masses – conceiving of themselves as an enlightened and just vanguard of 'the people'. Thinking of this kind inflected the pan-European emergence of ideas about the communicative effect of violence – imagined as 'propaganda of the deed'. There was, too, an identifiable 'cult of the revolutionary'.[48] All of this helped incite the era of the *attentats* that saw the assassination of several heads of state. As the 1901 murder of US President William McKinley confirmed, this phenomenon was not confined to Europe. And would-be revolutionaries around the world embraced the use of symbolic modes of assassination.

The global character of early twentieth-century terrorism has perhaps been underappreciated in much of the existing literature. But, in the first decade of the century, this mode of violence appeared in a range of settings. In British-occupied India, for example, there was a spate of attacks aimed at

---

45 S. K. Morrissey, 'Terrorism, Modernity, and the Question of Origins', *Kritika: Explorations in Russian and Eurasian History* 12/1 (2011).
46 L. Clutterbuck, 'The Progenitors of Terrorism: Russian Revolutionaries or Extreme Irish Republicans', *Terrorism and Political Violence* 16/1 (2004).
47 A. Hilbrenner and F. B. Schenk, 'Introduction: Modern Times? Terrorism in Late Tsarist Russia', *Jahrbücher für Geschichte Osteuropas* 58/2 (2010). For the best single-volume history of the revolutionary movement in Russia, see F. Venturi, *Roots of Revolution: A History of the Populist and Socialist Movements in Nineteenth Century Russia* (London, Phoenix, 2001).
48 N. O'Sullivan, 'Terrorism, Ideology and Democracy', in O'Sullivan (ed.), *Terrorism*.

governing officials and European settlers – many of them claimed by self-declared nationalist revolutionaries.[49] Bengal alone, in the decade prior to the First World War, experienced, by one estimate, 380 'terrorist outrages'.[50] Better known is the fact that Russia witnessed a second wave of revolutionary terror in the same period, one associated particularly with the Socialist Revolutionary Party and its 'Combat Organisation'. This group claimed responsibility for a series of high-profile political assassinations. Russian anarchists, too, launched intermittent attacks. Ultimately, though, these forces failed to dislodge the tsarist state.[51] When it did finally arrive, revolution in Russia came about only as a result of the strains caused by total, industrialised warfare.

Perhaps overly impressed by this, some scholars have tended to imagine a second hiatus in the materialisation of terrorist violence. Just as the first half of the nineteenth century has been judged quiet in relation to terrorism, the decades after 1914 are often represented in similar fashion. On this model, the chronology more or less jumps from *fin de siècle* to post-1945. Others, though, have noted that such elision requires an almost wilful neglect of the evidence pointing to the undiminished salience of terrorism. The immediate backdrop to the First World War itself, of course, was framed by the assassination of Archduke Franz Ferdinand by a member of a nationalist terrorist organisation. As one recent account of that conflict underlines, one cannot but be struck by the modern resonance of this self-conscious act of terrorism.[52] Furthermore, anarchist violence did not end in 1914, but rather continued during and after the world conflict. In the United States, for instance, the 'Galleani' movement was linked to a wave of small-scale bomb attacks; and anarchists of this stripe were blamed for the 1920 car bombing of Wall Street, which killed over thirty people.[53]

Elsewhere, a recognisably terrorist mode of violence continued to be deployed by those challenging imperial rule. In Egypt, terrorist 'outrages'

---

49 P. Heehs, *The Bomb in Bengal: The Rise of Revolutionary Terrorism in India, 1900–1910* (Oxford, Oxford University Press, 2004).
50 Sir Charles Tegart, 'Terrorism in India: A Speech Delivered Before the Royal Empire Society', 1 November 1932.
51 M. Perrie, 'Political and Economic Terror in the Tactics of the Russian Socialist-Revolutionary Party before 1914', in G. Herschfeld and W. J. Mommsen, *Social Protest, Violence and Terror in Nineteenth- and Twentieth-Century Europe* (London, Macmillan, 1982). And, in the same volume, M. Hildermeier, 'The Terrorist Strategies of the Socialist-Revolutionary Party in Russia, 1900–14'.
52 C. Clark, *The Sleepwalkers: How Europe Went to War in 1914* (New York, Harper, 2013).
53 B. Gage, 'Terrorism and the American Experience: A State of the Field', *Journal of American History* 98/1 (2011).

straddled the pre- and post-war period. In 1911, the Prime Minister Yousef Boutros Ghali was assassinated by a nationalist who deemed him overly sympathetic to the British occupation. The following decade, the 1924 murder of Sir Lee Stack, the British officer who commanded Egypt's army, came amidst an ongoing campaign of violence aimed at senior political/military figures.[54] Similarly, in India throughout this period, nationalist revolutionaries continued to deploy terrorist methods. Arguably the most famous of these was Bhagat Singh, who in 1928 murdered a policeman and, as a result, was executed by the British.[55] And across the interwar period, the British authorities and those loyal to the Raj lamented the 'terrorist outrages' that afflicted the country.[56]

Meanwhile, it was militant Irish nationalism that became virtually synonymous with the use of terrorism in the period immediately after the First World War. In January 1919, the self-declared Irish Republican Army (IRA) launched a 'war for independence', which combined rural guerrilla warfare with urban terrorism. The result was scarcely an unqualified success: the island of Ireland was partitioned, with a twenty-six-county 'Free State' effectively granted dominion status within the empire, while the six counties of Northern Ireland remained within the United Kingdom.[57] Even so, the campaign became an inspiration for other anti-imperialists, who saw in the IRA's use of violence a model worthy of emulation.[58] Consequently, similar campaigns appeared elsewhere, not least in Palestine, where, in the late 1930s, Zionist groups such as the Irgun initiated gun and bomb attacks on British forces.[59] In response, the imperial states tried to produce an international convention that might outlaw and suppress terrorism. Though unsuccessful, the effort was suggestive of the enduring salience of the issue.[60]

---

54 J. Gifford, 'Extracting the Best Deal for Britain: The Assassination of Sir Lee Stack in November 1924 and the Revision of Britain's Nile Valley Policy', *Canadian Journal of History* 48/1 (2016); S. Ball, 'The Assassination Culture of Imperial Britain, 1909–1979', *The Historical Journal* 56/1 (2013).
55 C. Moffat, *India's Revolutionary Inheritance: Politics and the Promise of Bhagat Singh* (Cambridge, Cambridge University Press, 2019).
56 *Tyranny and Terrorism* (Calcutta, The European Association (India), 1930); K. A. Khaleque, *Terrorism's Menace: How to Combat It* (Jalpaiguri, India, self-published, 1932); Tegart, 'Terrorism in India'.
57 P. Hart, *The I.R.A. at War, 1916–1923* (Oxford, Oxford University Press, 2003).
58 On this, see, in the current volume, K. McConaghy, 'Transnational Connections: Militant Irish Republicans and the World'.
59 J. Bowyer Bell, *Terror out of Zion: The Fight for Israeli Independence* (London, Routledge, 2007).
60 See, for example, League of Nations, 'International Repression of Terrorism: Draft Convention for the Prevention and Punishment of Terrorism: Draft Convention for the Creation of an International Criminal Court', Official No.: A.24.1936.V (Geneva, 7 September 1936).

As described above, the Second World War is, in many accounts, seen as marking another dividing line in the historical narrative of terrorism. On this view, the scale and character of that conflict eclipsed and rendered marginal more asymmetric forms of violence. There is obviously some truth in this. Again, though, it is possible to identify strands of continuity, with the chaos and instability arising from the war creating a context that made terrorist violence, in some settings, *more* rather than *less* appealing.

Moreover, what cannot be doubted is that the period *after* 1945 witnessed the proliferation of acts of terrorism, many of them again conducted by self-declared anti-imperialists. Palestine was an important crucible for such actions. The decision of Clement Attlee's government to abandon the British mandate for that territory – in the wake of renewed Zionist terrorism – fed the perception that campaigns of 'irregular' warfare could succeed. Other groups sought to apply that 'lesson' to their own struggles. The British thus soon confronted another nationalist insurgency prepared to utilise anti-state violence in nearby Cyprus, where the Ethniki Organosis Kyprion Agoniston (EOKA) hoped to expel imperial forces and achieve unity (*enosis*) with Greece.[61] The military leader of EOKA, Georgios Grivas, spoke openly of the need for 'terrorist attacks' to destabilise the British presence; and the British, in return, labelled EOKA a 'terrorist organization'.[62] Further afield, in Malaya, the struggle was with what the British labelled 'Communist terrorism', which was said to be pursuing its 'self-appointed mission by wholesale extortion and intimidation, by the destruction of property, and by the indiscriminate and brutal murder of civilians, men, women and children alike'.[63]

The French, meanwhile, faced arguably the most iconic campaign of modern terrorist violence in Algeria, where the Front de libération nationale (FLN) launched its own war. Though the governing authorities prevailed in purely military terms, the 'Battle of Algiers' proved another signature moment in the history of terrorism, indicative of the way in which non-state actors might use violence to exert a massive political toll on imperial governments. The polarising effects of that violence – coupled with the brutal *sale guerre*, or 'dirty war', waged by the French – sapped the health of 'French Algeria' and forced the government in Paris (eventually) to concede independence.[64]

---

61 W. Byford-Jones, *Grivas and the Story of EOKA* (London, R. Hale, 1959); R. F. Holland, *Britain and the Revolt in Cyprus, 1954–1959* (Oxford, Clarendon Press, 1988).
62 *Terrorism in Cyprus: The Captured Documents* (London, HMSO, 1956).
63 *The Fight Against Communist Terrorism in Malaya* (London, Colonial Office, November 1983).
64 A. Horne, *A Savage War of Peace: Algeria 1954–1962* (London, Macmillan, 1977).

In parallel with these events, and in part inspired by them, nationalist 'armed struggles' emerged around the world: in Spain (with the creation of Euskadi Ta Askatasuna, ETA); in Northern Ireland (with the formation of the Provisional Irish Republican Army, PIRA); again in Palestine (where Yasser Arafat created his Fatah movement and took over the Palestine Liberation Organisation, PLO); and in Sri Lanka (with the creation of the Liberation Tigers of Tamil Eelam, LTTE). In the same period, a new wave of radical, left-wing revolutionary movements also embraced terrorist methods: in Latin America, exemplified by groups like the Tupamaros or the Montoneros; and in Europe and the Global North, with groups such as the Red Army Faction, the Italian Red Brigades, the Symbionese Liberation Army and the Weathermen. This moment of revolutionary fervour was clearly connected with both the rise of the New Left and the geopolitical realities of the Cold War.[65] And it is striking that the end of that conflict between 1989 and 1991 coincided with the winding down of many campaigns of violence.

In the final decades of the twentieth century, terrorism of the kind practised by 'leftist revolutionaries' or 'traditional' nationalists was increasingly superseded by that which was framed through the language of religion and nationalism combined. Radical Islamists were the foremost expression of this new phenomenon, whether operating within a particular geographical territory – as do Hamas in Palestine, or Hezbollah in Lebanon – or seeking to transcend such divisions, as is the case with al-Qa'ida and, more recently, the Islamic State.[66]

The foregoing historical narrative, then, is one that many scholars would accept – at least in broad outline, even if they might contest some of the details. One of the virtues of such a narrative is that it cleaves closely to the path wrought by an explicit discourse of 'terrorism'. And, as Warren Brown helpfully observes elsewhere in this volume, there are serious problems with trying to impose some kind of 'objective, transtemporal' definition of terrorism on to terrain not already shaped by the term.[67]

One of the other benefits of taking a long-narrative view is that it allows us to reflect properly on evolution: of the term itself, and of the practice of

---

65 For a readable overview of terrorism across this era, see M. Burleigh, *Blood and Rage: A Cultural History of Terrorism* (London, HarperPress, 2008).
66 G. Kepel, *Jihad: The Trail of Political Islam* (Cambridge, MA, Havard University Press, 2002); W. McCants, *The ISIS Apocalypse: The History, Strategy, and Doomsday Vision of the Islamic State* (London, St. Martin's Press, 2015).
67 W. C. Brown, 'Terrorism, History and Periodisation', in the current volume.

violence with which it is associated. An influential attempt to do precisely that was David Rapoport's description of the four successive 'waves' of modern terrorism: anarchist, anticolonial, revolutionary leftist and religious.[68] Each of these waves, Rapoport suggested, had produced major technical developments that reflected an evolving 'science' of terror; and each, he reckoned, was 'driven by a common predominant energy' that shaped the 'characteristics and mutual relationships' of multiple groups.[69] The same idea was expressed by Walter Laqueur when he noted 'Terrorism always assumes the protective colouring of certain features of the *Zeitgeist*.'[70]

The notion of distinct terrorist 'waves' is therefore useful insofar as it allows us to discern moments of rupture. Yet, as has been pointed out by others, it is limited in that it offers only a partial picture. For one thing, it fails to engage with terrorism inspired by the 'right wing', despite the fact this has recurred throughout the last two centuries. Prior to 9/11, the most devastating terrorist attack to have occurred on American soil, for instance, was the bombing of the Federal Building in Oklahoma City by Timothy McVeigh. In Italy, a country beset by terrorist violence from the 1960s down to the 1990s, the deadliest episode was the 1980 bombing of the Bologna train station by neo-fascists. Yet all of this is lost in the construction of Rapoport's overarching narrative.[71] And this, in turn, arguably reflects the tendency of much 'terrorism studies literature' to adopt a Eurocentric, statist perspective, and to focus disproportionately on left-wing groups defined by their opposition to the dominant geopolitical order.[72]

Another problem with the 'wave' approach is that it requires the ironing out of intra-group complexity and the imposition of simplistic categories on to complex organisations. Where, for example, does the Provisional IRA sit on this spectrum? Or, indeed, Black September? These were movements committed primarily to the goal of national liberation (as they defined it), yet they also exhibited leftist/revolutionary pretensions. By the same token, a group like Hamas blends nationalist and Islamist imagery – and the same might even be said, up to a point, with regards to al-Qaeda, which prioritises the 'defence of Muslim lands', after the fashion of one of its intellectual forefathers.[73] The reality is that

68 For another version of this 'wave' theory, see W. F. Shughart II, 'An Analytical History of Terrorism, 1945–2000', *Public Choice* 128/1–2 (2006).
69 D. Rapoport (ed.), *Terrorism: Critical Concepts in Political Science* (London, Routledge, 2002), pp. 46–9.
70 Laqueur, 'Interpretations of Terrorism', p. 14.
71 Gage, 'Terrorism and the American Experience'.
72 Jackson, 'Argument for Terrorism'.
73 'Defence of Muslim Lands' was the title of a famous treatise written by Abdullah Azzam. See T. Hegghammer, *The Caravan: Abdallah Azzam and the Rise of Global Jihad* (Cambridge, Cambridge University Press, 2020).

it can often be hard to locate a given organisation solely within one specific 'wave'.

This highlights a further difficulty: the 'wave' thesis tends to imply a teleological evolution, marked by definable chronological boundaries. As suggested above, the construction of those boundaries seems to rely on presumed moments of hiatus – eras when terrorism is thought to have fallen back, or disappeared (as in the early nineteenth, or the interwar twentieth, centuries). Yet there is little attempt to explain why this should have happened. And it might be argued that these moments of hiatus are more imagined than real. In the post-First World War era, for example, it relies on both a neglect of what was happening within anti-imperial nationalisms, and on a degree of myopia about the multifarious forms of violence deployed by movements like the National Socialists in Germany. More broadly, this paradigm fails to account for underlying continuities, or more glacial processes of change.

At this point too, we might wish to re-examine the interpretation of 'origins' presented in the standard narrative. Until now, few scholars have been able to offer a compelling explanation for why it was that 'terrorism', if deriving ideational force from the French Revolution, should have then gone into several decades of hibernation. Why did it require an incubation period before emerging once again? And how do we explain the attendant transformation in the locus of terrorism – from a practice associated with those in control of the state, to one conducted by those wishing to challenge it? As mentioned, various scholars have identified the events of 1848–9 as a critical hinge in this evolution, after which terrorism became 'a kind of action directed against tyrannical rulers'.[74] Certainly there seems to be some truth in this. The biographies of early advocates of 'terrorism' reveal a common thread to be the experience of defeat in 1848 (one thinks of Heinzen, Most, Bakunin). But the precise dynamics of this shift remain to be explored; the links are more asserted than proven.

In addition, it is worth asking whether the focus on 1848 has perhaps led to the neglect of other important formative episodes – not least the 1871 creation and suppression of the Paris Commune.[75] The destruction of this body was accompanied by mass slaughter reaching, by some estimates, into the tens of thousands. To some later advocates of 'terrorist' violence, this episode – representing the brutal assertion of central state power – was at least as

---

74 J. Teichman, 'How to Define Terrorism', *Philosophy* 64/250 (1989); W. Laqueur, *Terrorism* (London, Weidenfeld and Nicolson, 1977), p. 26.
75 For one eloquent exception, see A. Butterworth, *The World That Never Was: A True Story of Dreamers, Schemers, Anarchists and Secret Agents* (London, Vintage Books, 2010).

important as the revolutionary upheavals of two decades earlier. For Leon Trotsky, for example (and indeed for Lenin), the lessons of 1871 underlined the importance of being organised and ruthless in the struggle to win and retain power.[76] To Trotsky this meant a readiness to engage in 'Red Terror' and 'the employment of all forms of violence'. 'The man who repudiates terrorism in principle', he wrote, 'must reject all idea of the political supremacy of the working-class and its revolutionary dictatorship.' The man who does that, according to Trotsky, 'digs the grave of Socialism'.[77]

The intensity with which Trotsky articulated this position was fired by his bitter public row with the social democrat Karl Kautsky, who had bemoaned the 'widely spread idea that Terrorism belongs to the very essence of revolution'. Kautsky argued that such views represented a fundamental misreading of both the French Revolution of 1789–94 and the Paris Commune, and the role of terror in each case. Kautsky also castigated the contemporary 'Regiment of Terror' established by the Bolsheviks, seeing this as the product of a 'militarist bureaucratic apparatus of power'.[78] 'Terrorism', he averred, 'which begins with the abolition of every form of freedom of the Press, and ends in a system of wholesale execution, is certainly the most striking and the most repellant of all.'[79]

The Kautsky–Trotsky dispute thus offers insight into two further issues, which are worth factoring in to any attempt to construct a historical narrative of terrorism. First, it illuminates the ongoing debate among revolutionaries about the place and character of violence defined explicitly as 'terrorism'. Second, it underlines the enduring relevance of ideas about 'terrorism from above'. Throughout the nineteenth century and into the first decades of the twentieth, individuals like Trotsky used the term 'terrorism' unashamedly to describe a mode of state-led violence, which they believed to be a necessary instrument in the struggle to conquer and hold political power.

From a different perspective too, those wishing to challenge imperial states in that period were clear that governments routinely deployed terrorism. During the First World War, Czech nationalists accused the Austro-Hungarian authorities of instituting a 'reign of terror' in Bohemia and Serbia, which left the people 'groaning under . . . terrorist oppression'.[80] In India, nationalists like Lala Lajpat

---

76 For Lenin, see Gray, *Black Mass*, p. 72.
77 L. Trotsky, *The Defence of Terrorism (Terrorism and Communism): A Reply to Karl Kautsky* (London, The Labour Publishing Company, 1921), pp. 22–4, 48–60.
78 K. Kautsky, *Terrorism and Communism: A Contribution to the Natural History of Revolution*, trans. W. H. Kerridge (London, George Allen & Unwin, 1920), pp. 1–2, 32–51, 113–40.
79 Ibid., p. 208.
80 Czech National Alliance in Great Britain, *Austrian Terrorism in Bohemia* (London, Jas. Truscott & Son, 1916), pp. i–iii, 15–18.

Rai denounced the 'military terrorism' of the British – charges later echoed by communist anti-imperialists.[81, 82] And wherever their focus, critics of empire continued to highlight what they judged to be its 'terrorist methods'.[83]

It was only gradually, as Laqueur has observed, that the word 'terrorism' became almost wholly identified with the 'systematic use' of violence by non-state actors.[84] By the early 1920s, the British authorities in India were referring to the 'terrorist mentality' exhibited by Bengali revolutionaries, and the threat posed by acts of 'terrorism'. Revealingly, this was frequently linked to concerns about the diffusion of 'Sinn Féin methods' – as well as comments about 'Russian ideas' – again, an indication of the important part played by events in Ireland and Russia, respectively, in creating a model for a particular kind of irregular violence directed against the state.[85]

It is thus evident that there are plenty of strands that require further exploration in order to establish a more thoroughgoing genealogy of terrorism. Yet one aspect that does seem incontrovertible is the fact that there were particularly decisive historic conjunctures. One such period was the three decades that followed the end of the Second World War, which saw something like a widespread 'cult of the insurgent' and the use of terrorist violence in a range of locales to try to secure political change.[86]

Unsurprisingly, this era proved productive in terms of scholarly reflections on the subject, with a rash of new courses and publications, including dedicated journals. Much of this came from a political science perspective and sought to identify the 'root causes' underpinning terrorism, tending to locate these in ongoing processes of socio-economic change, or in the existence of socio-economic grievances.[87] A key early contribution was made by T. P. Thornton, who sought to distinguish between what he called 'enforcement terror' and 'agitational terror'.[88] Others built on, or otherwise revised, this conceptual

---

81 L. L. Rai, 'Punjab's Sympathy with Bengal', in L. L. Rai, *Writings and Speeches*, Vol. 1, *1888–1919*, ed. by V. C. Joshi (New Delhi, University Publishers, 1966) (speech delivered at a protest meeting at Lahore, 9 December 1905, under the auspices of the Indian Association).
82 M. N. Roy, *Imperialist Terrorism in India: An Appeal to the Workers of Gt. Britain by the Communist Party of India* (India, unknown publisher, 1925).
83 See, for instance, F. E. Newton, 'Searchlight on Palestine: Fair-Play or Terrorist Methods?' (London, The Arab Centre, 1938).
84 Laqueur, 'Interpretations of Terrorism', p. 3.
85 *Sedition Committee, 1918: Report* (Calcutta: Superintendent Government Printing, India, 1918), pp. 93–101, 216–19; M. Silvestri, *Ireland and India: Nationalism, Empire and Memory* (Basingstoke, Palgrave Macmillan, 2009), pp. 46–75.
86 B. Hoffman, 'Terrorism in History', *Journal of Conflict Studies* 27/2 (2007), esp. pp. 15–25.
87 Laqueur, 'Interpretations of Terrorism', p. 4; Rapoport, 'Fear and Trembling', p. 658.
88 T. P. Thornton, 'Terror as a Weapon of Political Agitation', in H. Eckstein (ed.), *Internal War* (New York, Free Press, 1964).

framework.[89] H. Edward Price's study of the strategy and tactics of 'revolutionary terrorism' emphasised the 'conflict of legitimacies' involved in any situation where terrorist means had been deployed.[90] In the early 1970s, Martha Crenshaw put forward the concept of 'revolutionary terrorism', based on her analysis of events in Algeria. Such violence, she suggested, was 'part of insurgent strategy in the context of internal warfare or revolution: the attempt to seize political power from the established regime of a state, if successful causing fundamental political and social change'. Terrorism was, Crenshaw argued, usually symbolic in character, aimed at civilians, and sought to exert a psychological toll on opponents, so as to coerce political behaviour. Crenshaw's study was particularly interesting for its insights into the impact of this violence on the fabric of society, and its dialectical relationship with (repressive) state activity.[91]

Scholars like Crenshaw have done more than most to shape contemporary understandings of terrorism within the academy. Subsequent works explored variously the theory and tactics of terrorist actors, as well as different state responses; there have also been innumerable attempts to schematise different forms of terrorism.[92] From the 1970s onwards, too, there was an explosion of works aimed at a more general readership, which held it as axiomatic that terrorism was a form of 'revolutionary' violence from below.[93] As latter-day critics of such work have observed, this helped generate a shift in understanding at the popular level – one very much encouraged by governments that regularly sought to stigmatise their opponents as 'terrorists'.[94]

---

89 See, for example, C. Townshend, 'The Process of Terror in Irish Politics', in O'Sullivan (ed.), *Terrorism*.
90 H. Edward Price, 'The Strategy and Tactics of Revolutionary Terrorism', *Comparative Studies in Society and History* 19/1 (1977).
91 M. Crenshaw Hutchinson, 'The Concept of Revolutionary Terrorism', *The Journal of Conflict Resolution* 16/3 (1972).
92 See, for example, G. Wardlaw, *Political Terrorism: Theory, Tactics, and Counter-measures* (Cambridge, Cambridge University Press, 1982); P. Wilkinson, *Political Terrorism* (London, Macmillan, 1974); S. V. Marsden and A. P. Schmid, 'Typologies of Terrorism and Political Violence', in Schmid (ed.), *Routledge Handbook of Terrorism*.
93 See, for instance, L. A. Sobel (ed.), *Political Terrorism* (New York, Facts on File, 1975); A. Parry, *Terrorism: From Robespierre to Arafat* (New York, The Vanguard Press, 1976); Laqueur, *Terrorism*; G. Chaliand, *Terrorism: From Popular Struggle to Media Spectacle* (London, Saqi Books, 1987).
94 R. Jackson et al., *Critical Terrorism Studies: A New Research Agenda* (London, Routledge, 2009). In truth, 'Critical Terrorism Studies' seems not to object to an attempt to define terrorism, nor to disagree with much of what many would see as its key characteristics; in the end, it seems simply to be a plea for a more comprehensive application of the term – to include states (and primarily Western states) among those who are labelled 'terrorist'. See, for instance, Jackson, 'Argument for Terrorism'. Jackson agrees that

History and the Definition of Terrorism

The legitimacy or otherwise of this conversion of meaning is not our concern here. Instead, the focus is on the way in which the term 'terrorism' has come to be applied in more or less similar fashion, to describe a particular kind of violence. Amongst its characteristics are some or all of the following:

- It is planned by an individual/organisation acting beyond official state agencies;
- It is conducted as part of a wider conspiracy (whether real or imagined);
- It is always tied to some kind of political objective;[95]
- It serves a communicative purpose and is intended to have a psychological effect;
- It is therefore often of symbolic character;
- And it seeks fundamentally to coerce opponents to change their behaviour/policy.

Within these broad parameters, terrorist violence has shown an innate ideological promiscuity, and has been instrumentalised to achieve diverse objectives, whether conceived in terms of ideology, strategy or tactics.[96]

It is worth adding, too, that since at least the mid- to late twentieth century, most groups practising terrorism have not been solely 'terrorist' in character. Instead, they have often constituted broad sociopolitical movements engaged in a range of activity.[97] To such actors, terrorism was just one of several strategies that could be deployed within the context of 'wider political struggles'.[98] The point is an important one, because it shows the redundancy of many arguments about who is/is not a terrorist. If the metaphor can be excused, the mask of 'the terrorist' is usually just one of several worn interchangeably by its practitioners.

Such issues aside, though, the above descriptors can be said to constitute critical 'family resemblances' – to borrow from Wittgenstein – that have allowed for the identification of terrorist violence. Scholars today might

terrorism is rational, political activity, involving the use of violence that engenders fear, primarily (though not solely) against civilians, for communicative purpose. For a withering assessment of 'Critical Terrorism Studies', see D. M. Jones and M. L. R. Smith, 'We're All Terrorists Now: Critical – or Hypocritical – Studies on Terrorism?', *Studies in Conflict and Terrorism* 32/4 (2009).

95 Terrorists adhere to what O'Boyle calls a 'theory of justification'. See G. O'Boyle, 'Theories of Justification and Political Violence: Examples from Four Groups', *Terrorism and Political Violence* 14/2 (2002).
96 On the latter point, see W. L. Waugh, Jr., 'The Values in Violence: Organizational and Political Objectives of Terrorist Groups', *Conflict Quarterly* 3/4 (1983). See also A. Richards, 'Conceptualizing Terrorism', *Studies in Conflict and Terrorism* 37/3 (2014).
97 A. P. Schmid, 'Frameworks for Conceptualising Terrorism', *Terrorism and Political Violence* 16/2 (2004).
98 C. Tilly, 'Terror, Terrorism, Terrorists', *Sociological Theory* 22/1 (2004).

agree/disagree as to whether group 'X', or individual 'Y', truly deserves the epithet 'terrorist' – but they tend to have a similar idea of what is meant by the term.[99] As Gilbert Ramsay has adroitly observed, terrorism *has* effectively been defined – whatever one thinks of that process.[100] At a minimum, it might be said that we have arrived at a 'definition' that refuses to call itself by that name. To some extent, I see no reason to dispute this (and my own definition would be one framed by the parameters set out above). As Anthony Richards has argued, there are good reasons why any scholar working on terrorism should try to articulate their own intellectual (and definitional) first principles. He himself helpfully identifies it as a 'particular method of violence', which 'entails the intent to generate a wider psychological impact beyond the immediate victims.'[101] And yet, it is crucial to understand that such a definition can never be final, nor essential, in character. The labelling of any act of violence as 'terrorist' is always the product of a contested and contingent process. What is surely required, therefore, is to try and move beyond irresolvable and ultimately sterile debates about definition to consider what that process can tell us about the phenomenon.

Modernity, Violence and the State

At the core of the genealogical narrative laid out above is the fact that the concept of 'terrorism' has always been bound up with questions of the state. The 'fundamental truth' as identified by Paul Wilkinson is that 'one cannot adequately understand terrorist movements without paying some attention to the effects of the use of force and violence by states'. Such effects can be self-evident: the way in which misapplied state repression can often engender a reaction that sparks/exacerbates a terrorist challenge; or the way in which state violence might undermine or corrode the practice of liberal democracy. Alternatively, one might take a broader view and see the state–terrorism relationship as reaching to the heart of the matter.[102] For the state and terrorist violence are, in one important sense, mirror phenomena. One cannot understand the emergence of the latter without situating it in the

---

99 For the use of Wittgenstein here, I draw upon R. English, *Terrorism: How to Respond* (Oxford, Oxford University Press, 2009), p. 22. Skinner also has some invaluable insights on this issue; see Skinner, 'Meaning and Understanding', p. 6.
100 G. Ramsay, 'Why Terrorism Can, but Should Not Be Defined', *Critical Studies on Terrorism* 8/2 (2015).
101 Richards, 'Conceptualizing Terrorism'.
102 P. Wilkinson, 'Can a State be "Terrorist"?', *International Affairs* 57/3 (1981), p. 467.

context of state practice.[103] (Acknowledging this has the added benefit of going some way to obviating the criticism of those who believe that 'state terrorism' is perennially neglected within the field of 'terrorism studies'.[104])

All terrorist movements have been obsessed with the state: some seek its total destruction; others insist that it revise its political agenda. Either way, they are effectively parasitical upon state behaviour. Furthermore, they tend to view the state in a particular way. The Red Brigades thus sought to strike at 'the heart of the Italian State';[105] likewise, the Provisional IRA imagined 'the British State' to be a monolithic (colonial) oppressor. In both cases, they failed to understand that the idea of a single 'state' actor was itself an illusion.

What, then, do *we* mean by the state? One of the most influential characterisations has been that provided by Max Weber, who described the state as a community that successfully 'claims the *monopoly of the legitimate use of physical force* within a given territory' (emphasis in original).[106] A similar point has been made by Raymond Geuss, who has asserted that 'State-power' is 'in the last analysis coercive power'; and also, again in line with Weber, that the 'political' entails 'the use or threat of physical force' as an option of last resort (and conversely, 'Where the possible use of force is not an issue, there is no politics, strictly speaking').[107]

As can be seen, at issue here are interrelated ideas about coercion and violence, power and politics.[108] Hannah Arendt was another scholar who sought to disentangle concepts like power and violence, seeing the latter as a mere instrument of the former. Power, Arendt believed, rested ultimately on legitimacy, not on violence. Indeed, it was, to her mind, largely the opposite of violence:

> Nowhere is the self-defeating factor in the victory of violence over power more evident than in the use of terror to maintain domination ... Terror is not the same as violence; it is, rather, the form of government that comes

---

103 R. W. White, 'Issues in the Study of Political Violence: Understanding the Motives of Participants in Small Group Political Violence', *Terrorism and Political Violence* 12/1 (2000), esp. pp. 98, 100. On the need to situate terrorist violence alongside state responses and the broader question of a state's relationship to violence, see also, in the current volume, D. Dworkin, 'Terrorism: An American Story'.
104 For such a view, see Jackson, 'Argument for Terrorism'. On the effect of emphasising the role of the state, see also C. Wight, 'Theorising Terrorism: The State, Structure and History', *International Relations* 23/1 (2009).
105 Cited in Wilkinson, 'Can a State', p. 470.
106 M. Weber, 'Politics as a Vocation', in *From Max Weber: Essays in Sociology*, trans. H. H. Gerth and C. Wright Mills (Oxford, Oxford University Press, 1946), p. 78.
107 Geuss, *History and Illusion*, pp. 14–17, 28–42, 153.   108 Ibid., pp. 21–8.

into being when violence, having destroyed all power, does not abdicate but, on the contrary, remains in full control.[109]

This contrast between 'legitimate power' on the one hand, and 'illegitimate violence' or 'terror' on the other, takes us back to Weber's definition and his emphasis on the state's ability to exert a monopoly of *legitimate* physical force. Moreover, if one considers the question of 'legitimacy' from a narrowly legal perspective, then it is no surprise that 'terrorism' has come to be seen as an *illegitimate* form of violence; for by its very nature it seeks to challenge the state by transgression of the law. This, quite simply, is its *raison d'être*. There is therefore a logic to viewing terrorism through the lens of criminality (as many scholars and practitioners do). Terrorism is a particular kind of crime, which operates to undermine the state's sense of security at an ontological level – and, as Rory Cox points out, this is why states respond so fiercely to such activity.[110]

Further, it is this which also helps to explain why the *discourse* of 'terrorism' has become a device used by many states to pillory their opponents. Over the course of the twentieth century – an era in which the nation state became hegemonic both geopolitically and internally over society – states sought to set the terms of trade, and to define 'illegitimate' violence or 'terrorism' as that carried out by actors other than themselves. In the process, the term became imbued with pejorative meaning. As has been pointed out by others, this made the discourse of terrorism a 'calculated political act', used variously for mobilisation (of supporters), vilification (of enemies) and legitimation (of self).[111] The application of the word has thus come to reflect power relations – and equally, it has power in effect.[112] To label someone a terrorist is to place them beyond the bounds of acceptability and legality. Their actions are rendered 'criminal', which, setting aside for a moment any moral connotation of that term, *is* an accurate description. Terrorism is crime precisely because it deliberately contests the legitimacy of the state.

At this point, we might also note that there is no inherent contradiction either with those who insist on seeing terrorism as a distinct form of war.[113] As per the much cited observation of Carl von Clausewitz, war itself is

---

109 H. Arendt, *On Violence* (New York, Harcourt Books, 1970), pp. 35–55.
110 See, in the current volume, R. Cox, 'History, Terrorism and the State'.
111 Blain, 'Genealogy of Terrorism'.
112 On this point, see also, in the current volume, Brown, 'Terrorism, History and Periodisation'.
113 English, *Terrorism*; Schmid, 'Definition of Terrorism'; Schmid, 'Frameworks for Conceptualising Terrorism'.

nothing but politics continued through other means. And by virtue of its determination to challenge the power of the state through violence, terrorism is surely *both* warlike *and* fundamentally concerned with politics; the means by which it seeks to achieve its political aims is violence, which contravenes the laws of the state.

To return to the question of the relationship between the state and violence, few would dispute the assertion that all states are founded through, and rest upon, some kind of coercive force. Yet, historically, violence has been multivalent, used from below and across society to produce, impose and contest sociopolitical norms. Nietzsche was clear on the role of force and violence in shaping the human condition ('When man decided he had to make a memory for himself, it never happened without blood, torments and sacrifices'; 'the shaping of a population, which had up till now been unrestrained and shapeless, into a fixed form, as happened at the beginning with an act of violence, could only be concluded with acts of violence').[114] As Martin Miller has suggested, we cannot understand one kind of violence without situating it within that wider, interdependent context. He gives the example of Russia, where, throughout the nineteenth and twentieth centuries, the 'government and the insurgent sector of its society were in a continuous and conflicted relationship in which violence was an integral and frequently employed tactic'.[115] More broadly, the centrality of the state – and especially what Ian Kershaw calls the 'ideologically driven modern state' – to the practice of violence can scarcely be doubted when one considers the experiences of the twentieth century.[116]

Colin Wight is thus surely right to suggest that we need to reintegrate ideas about the state into research on terrorism.[117] When we say that terrorism is about the pursuit of political power, or political objectives – as we often do – we mean that it seeks to contest the state, understood in a Weberian light. As Wight observes, 'Terrorism cannot be defined in the absence of some or other account of the state. And the state can only be understood in terms of its history.'[118]

---

[114] Nietzsche, *Genealogy of Morality*, pp. 38, 58.
[115] M. A. Miller, 'Ordinary Terrorism in Historical Perspective', *Journal for the Study of Radicalism* 2/1 (2008), p. 142.
[116] I. Kershaw, 'War and Political Violence in Twentieth-Century Europe', *Contemporary European History* 14/1 (2005), p. 118; see also Mazower, 'Violence and the State'.
[117] Wight, 'Theorising Terrorism'.
[118] Ibid. On the importance of locating terrorism within the context of the state (or, as Laqueur puts it, the need to situate 'insurgent' in relation to 'incumbent'), see Laqueur, 'Interpretations of Terrorism', p. 14.

Significantly, as Skinner has shown, the concept of the 'state' is one with a distinct historical lineage of its own, arising in the early modern period – roughly the late sixteenth and early seventeenth centuries – and bound up with debates about the nature of the polity, sovereignty, the disposition of political authority, and the rights/obligations of government.[119] (The historical contingency of the idea of the state is also a theme for Warren Brown in his contribution to this collection; he suggests that it is only since the *eighteenth century* that the state has been understood in terms of purely secular politics.) On this view, different epochs and contexts have produced their own conceptions of the state. Modern political thought emerges at a distinct historical juncture; indeed, it is this that makes possible the very idea of 'the modern'. And this is significant precisely because it again takes us back to Weber's conception of 'the modern state' as distinct in form, possessing a complex, abstract structure, and resting on a particular kind of 'legal-rational' legitimacy.[120]

In similar vein, we can locate terrorism – not least by virtue of its relationship to the modern state – as a product of modernity. In fact, as Brown has underlined, it rests on a number of historically and culturally contingent concepts: about the legitimate use of violence; about the meaning of order and disorder; and about differences between 'civilians' and 'combatants'. Naturally, the phenomenon drew on earlier forms of violent practice, such as assassination, the destruction of property, or hostage-taking, which were then folded into a repertoire of recognisably 'terrorist' behaviour.[121] This is scarcely surprising. As Nietzsche observed with regard to changing conceptions of 'punishment', it was inevitable that any given 'procedure' was 'something older, pre-dating its use as punishment' – and only gradually did the two become conjoined.[122] The same point can surely be made in relation to the manifold manifestations of terrorist violence. But this does not abrogate the modern character of the phenomenon.

As Miller has pointed out, terrorism should be understood fundamentally as a product of modernity, an era which has seen the breaking down of old hierarchies and the emergence of new social collectives, subjectivities and imaginaries; a historical age tied to the transformation of the state and the metastasising of its relationship with society.[123] The modern bureaucratic state

---

119 Skinner, 'Genealogy of the Modern State'.
120 On all this, see too Geuss, *History and Illusion*, pp. 42–52.
121 Brown, 'Terrorism, History and Periodisation', in the current volume.
122 Nietzsche, *Genealogy of Morality*, p. 53.
123 Miller, 'Ordinary Terrorism'. See also Morrissey, 'Terrorism, Modernity', p. 225.

involves itself in the lives of its individual members in ways far more extensive than its antecedents. It seeks to regulate a much wider sphere of human activity than ever previously. And oftentimes it does so through coercion and violence.'[124] As Arendt noted, 'the greater the bureaucratization of public life, the greater will be the attraction of violence'.[125] The same dynamic has proven operative amongst those inclined to contest the state. The seemingly inexorable expansion of the modern bureaucratic state has inevitably generated resistance – and frequently this has taken the form of terrorist violence.

It is therefore unsurprising that the era of modern state formation, which began in the nineteenth century, and which has continued down to the present day – a process in which violence has been absolutely central – has witnessed repeated episodes of terrorist violence. After all, as Arendt observed, the introduction of violence into the body politic has predictable effects: 'The practice of violence, like all action, changes the world, but the most probable change is to a more violent world.'[126]

Furthermore, it seems clear that in particular the rise of popular sovereignty – another of the defining features of the modern age – has been a decisive generator of terrorism.[127] Almost all organisations that have engaged in this practice of violence have done so in the name of 'the people' – however defined. Though the terrorists have invariably comprised small minorities, they have nevertheless believed themselves to speak for a wider majority, and in addition, they have anticipated that history would bring retrospective legitimation. In this way, much modern terrorism has been possible only in contexts where popular sovereignty and democracy have been contested. It is jarring to note that terrorism and democracy have frequently gone hand in hand; and many terrorists have genuinely understood themselves to be the truest of democrats.[128]

* * *

To return, finally, to the question of definition, the suggestion here would be that an understanding of terrorism that foregrounds its relationship to

---

124 Geuss, *History and Illusion*, pp. 19–20.   125 Arendt, *On Violence*, p. 81.   126 Ibid., p. 80.
127 On this point, see O'Sullivan, 'Terrorism, Ideology and Democracy'.
128 This is the underlying argument of Richard Bourke's provocative book on the conflict in Northern Ireland. See R. Bourke, *Peace in Ireland: The War of Ideas* (London, Pimlico, 2003).

modernity and the state is valuable precisely because it allows us to historicise the phenomenon. The effect is thereby to liberate us from the hopeless pursuit of any singular definition. To invoke Nietzsche once more, the benefit of the genealogical approach is that it might provide 'an impression of how uncertain, belated and haphazard' are the meanings of a given concept.[129] Applied here, the genealogical approach reveals the contingency of 'terrorism' as both idea and practice.

None of this is to deny the salience of how the term is understood in our own time – but rather to encourage reflection on how it has been constituted in different eras, and with what consequence. As Mark Bevir has noted, 'On the one hand, genealogists continually question, exposing the particularity of perspectives that appear to be universal or timeless truths ... On the other hand, to question beliefs is not necessarily to reject them, and to expose the particularity of a perspective is not necessarily to deny its validity.'[130] Or, as Skinner has put it:

> An understanding of the past can help us to appreciate how far the values embodied in our present way of life, and our present ways of thinking about those values, reflect a series of choices made at different times between different possible worlds. This awareness can help to liberate us from the grip of any one hegemonal account of those values and how they should be interpreted and understood.[131]

In considering the question of how terrorism might be defined, then, the aim of the historian should not be to try to establish some new 'hegemonal account', which will inevitably falter under the weight of its own ambitions, but instead to glory in the multiplicity of voices and interpretations. To paraphrase the maxims that are drummed into first-year undergraduates, it is not the answers that really matter, but rather the questions that we ask, and the debates that these in turn stimulate. These are the lifeblood of the historiographical tradition – and it is that tradition, properly applied, which can do much to irrigate the otherwise arid ground of understanding, upon which singular definitions of terrorism wither and die.[132]

---

129 Nietzsche, *Genealogy of Morality*, p. 53.   130 Bevir, 'What is Genealogy?', p. 270.
131 Skinner, *Visions of Politics*, Vol. 1, p. 6.
132 Ramsay arrives at a similar conclusion with his assertion that 'Terrorism can never be defined ... because the meaning of terrorism lies in the debates which it itself produces regarding its own meaning and significance.' Ramsay, 'Why Terrorism Can', p. 226.

Further Reading

M. Crenshaw Hutchinson, 'The Concept of Revolutionary Terrorism', *The Journal of Conflict Resolution* 16/3 (1972)

G. Ramsay, 'Why Terrorism Can, but Should Not Be Defined', *Critical Studies on Terrorism* 8/2 (2015)

A. P. Schmid, 'Frameworks for Conceptualising Terrorism', *Terrorism and Political Violence* 16/2 (2004)

Q. Skinner, 'A Genealogy of the Modern State', *Proceedings of the British Academy* 62 (2009)

J. Teichman, 'How to Define Terrorism', *Philosophy* 64/250 (1989)

3
Terrorism, History and Periodisation

WARREN C. BROWN

Conventional historical periods, e.g. 'classical', 'medieval', 'early modern' etc., as Eurocentric as they are, help us as historians orient ourselves with respect to each other and to communicate what we do to a wider public. They give us a common language and set of temporal guideposts; when we try to interest colleagues who might work on different times and places in what we are doing, they let us quickly and easily anchor our specific subject in a wider and presumably recognisable meta-context. They allow us to generalise and to compare our work with that of others, secure in the knowledge that we share a common frame of reference. They also make it easier for us to bring non-specialists along with us, by anchoring what we are doing in historical narratives that many if not most people will at least recognise.

However, traditional periodisation is also dangerous. Giving a span of time a label such as 'Antiquity', 'the Middle Ages' or 'the Modern' tends to constrain our narratives within a set of assumptions about what the world was like then. If we try to use the past to inform our understanding of the present, we may bring those assumptions forward, to identify or contrast with contemporary events in a way that has little to do either with the past or with the present. We also risk triggering whatever associations about the period in question our readers or audiences happen to have, which can vary wildly. Unless all parties concerned are extremely careful, therefore, periodisation can powerfully shape both how we understand and present our evidence, and how our audience understands what they read or hear. Period labels can also be used not just to inform the present with the past, but to influence it. Calling something in the present 'medieval', for example, can be a shorthand for labelling it as barbaric, or conversely as an archetype of heroic, Christian European behaviour. 'Post-Enlightenment' or 'modern' can all too easily serve to cast something as rational and free of superstition, or as technologically superior.

Similar problems apply to the word 'terrorism' as an object of historical enquiry. We are interested in the history of terrorism because there is something going on in our own world that we have identified as a discrete pattern of behaviour (i.e. as an '-ism') and that we do not like. We want to understand it and stop it. We think we can get some help by looking at how this behaviour was carried out in the past and how past practice might have led to what is going on in the present. Bringing the label 'terrorism' with us as we look makes our task easier, because it tells us that we know what we are looking for. It helps us cut through some difficult complexities by letting us carry out a first-order triage: is what we are looking at 'terrorism' or not? If it is, well and good; if it is not, then we can safely move on and look for something that is.

The danger, of course, is that, as with conventional historical periods, going into the past armed with 'terrorism' inevitably shapes how we understand and make use of our sources. We risk misreading them, by filtering what they say through ideas about what terrorism 'is' that may be misleading. Terrorism is a historically and culturally contingent concept; it is modern, and it is Western. It depends in particular on modern and Western ideas about when and how violence should and should not be used, and for what, and about the very meaning of order and disorder. The word first shows up during the French Revolution, to describe the so-called 'Reign of Terror' imposed by the revolutionary government in 1793–4.[1] In this context, it labelled the behaviour of radical members of the French Revolutionary movement as they used fear to impose, from the top down, their views of right order on French society and to stifle dissent. As it is used and understood today, however, the word 'terrorism' generally means something different. Its meaning has been shaped in particular by a need to create a legal and moral category that delegitimises certain modern uses of violence and fear in order to justify action against them. Its semantic field is accordingly fluid and unstable; the contours of any given definition depend on who is formulating it, what their interests are, and whom they are talking about.[2] Nevertheless, most current definitions circle around a few core ideas.[3] Terrorism is violence carried out not by the strong against the weak but by

---

[1] C. Townshend, *Terrorism: A Very Short Introduction* (Oxford, Oxford University Press, 2011), p. 37.
[2] B. Saul, 'Defining Terrorism: A Conceptual Minefield', in E. Chenoweth, R. English, A. Gofas and S. N. Kalyvas (eds.), *The Oxford Handbook of Terrorism* (Oxford, Oxford University Press, 2019).
[3] Cf. the chapter by M. Frampton in this volume.

the weak against the strong, and especially violence carried out by non-state actors against the state; it is frequently, therefore, (though not always) distinguished from state terror. It is criminal; terrorism violates a public peace or public order. Most important, it is directed at civilians or non-combatants. Its aim is political change, though some definitions conceptually distinguish terrorism carried out with political goals from that carried out for religious reasons. It is said to show up first in the context of European revolutionary movements in the mid- to later nineteenth century, though important recent work has traced its appearance in part to the United States of the 1850s.[4]

This view of terrorism depends on analytical categories, norms of behaviour and ideas about order and the legitimate use of violence that for many times and places in the past, even the European past, simply do not apply. The state, for example: when we say that acts of terrorism are aimed at states by non-state actors, we have an idea in our heads of what a state is: a political entity, governing a fixed geographical area, that regulates the behaviour of citizens, and judges and punishes criminal offences, which it defines as actions against itself as the embodiment of the public weal. Most important, it claims a monopoly within its territory on the legitimate use of force. Although it is embedded in and tied to the economic, social, cultural and religious organisation of society, it is conceptually distinct.[5] For much of European history, however, it is very hard to talk about 'states', or to clearly distinguish 'public' from 'private' action or jurisdiction. It is hard sometimes even to separate out 'political' as a discrete category of action. Before the turn of the nineteenth century, it is virtually impossible in Europe to disassociate political order from religious order. Both theorists of power and wielders of power understood right order to be that which harmonised with the will of the Christian God. Similarly with social and economic order; in the centuries on either side of the first millennium, for example, order and the flow of power were based as much or more on personal and economic relationships than they were on defined relationships between governing and governed.

Past attitudes towards violence and who was entitled to use it were likewise very different from those that prevail in the modern West. The right of the individual to use violence on his (and sometimes her) own behalf, for example to take vengeance for a wrong or an insult, or to protect his or

---

4 C. Dietze, *Die Erfindung des Terrorismus in Europa, Russland und den USA 1858–1866* (Hamburg, Hamburger Edition, 2016).
5 See e.g. E. Cudworth, *The Modern State: Theories and Ideologies* (Edinburgh, Edinburgh University Press, 2007); cf. Frampton in this volume.

her property and interests, was taken for granted in Europe for centuries and even legally protected.[6] Accordingly, it is difficult if not impossible to draw a line between 'civilian' and 'military', and even the distinction between combatant and non-combatant is fluid. The idea of a government monopoly on the use of violent force, or of a professional soldiery, did not take root until the fourteenth century at the earliest, and even then continued to be contested. The term 'criminal' is similarly problematic. The word's root lies with the Latin word *crimen*, which simply meant an undifferentiated wrong. Its continued use in post-Roman Europe reflected the fact that, for much of Europe's early history, most wrongs were matters for individuals or kin-groups, as if society were entirely regulated by what we would call civil law. *Crimen* began to take on its modern meaning, as an offence against the state as the guarantor of public order that is qualitatively different from a civil wrong or tort, only gradually and at different rates in different parts of Europe from the twelfth century on, as kings and other rulers became sufficiently powerful to successfully assert an ideology of public order, ordained by God, that the ruler was duty-bound to uphold and which was injured by particular kinds of wrong.[7]

To study the history of terrorism, then, is not to go looking for an objective, transtemporal thing. In fact, if we push much earlier than the point at which the word 'terrorism' itself actually appears, the 'history of terrorism' as an object of enquiry quickly becomes unstable, even unsustainable. It cannot be divorced from the history of the ideas about order and disorder, and about the legitimate use of violence, on which the notion of 'terrorism' depends. This history involves the evolution of concepts such as criminal behaviour, state vs non-state actors, civilian vs military, and even of violence itself, through which people have come to view, understand and evaluate the instrumental use of terror. It does not map well on to conventional historical periods; the path of change for each conceptual thread cuts promiscuously across them.

There is another danger in studying the history of terrorism. Language shapes both our perceptions and actions. The word 'terrorism' has a particular power; it strongly affects how perpetrators, victims and observers behave and evaluate the behaviour of others. Calling something in the past 'terrorism', therefore, can affect how we respond to it, and provoke even unconscious judgements that can influence how we understand the people

---

[6] W. Brown, *Violence in Medieval Europe* (London, Longman, 2011).
[7] Brown, *Violence*; P. Hyams, *Rancor and Reconciliation in Medieval England* (Ithaca, NY, Cornell University Press, 2003).

we are studying. The word's power is only made stronger by the fact that it is used to delegitimise. Once it emerged at the end of the eighteenth century, it became a potent and malleable tool for a variety of people to use as they sought to condemn and punish a variety of actions.[8] This explains the stiff fights over its definition by people from different regimes and cultures who want to use it to combat everything from suicide bombings to public protests, or the concomitant debates over whether there is such a thing as 'state terrorism'.[9] When we put these problems with the word 'terrorism' together with those that attach to conventional historical periods, we get a witches' brew, out of which bubble terms such as 'medieval terrorism' as shorthand labels for behaviour in the present that is thought to be particularly heinous.

As we write a history of terrorism, we should forgo both the use of conventional periodisation and the use of the term 'terrorism', even in a lowest-common-denominator sense, as a transtemporal, objective object of enquiry. This does not mean that we should jettison the word 'terrorism' altogether. We should rather view the word itself as an actor on the stage – that is, as having a history that embraces an evolving and shifting set of ideas, and that fits into a much older story about humanity's views of order and disorder and its uses of violence and fear. Telling this story involves looking at how people in various pasts went about provoking extreme fear in order to achieve things, what sorts of things they were out to achieve, how they maximised the impact of the fear they created with the tools they had available, and how that fear was refracted through their own and their targets' beliefs about the right order of the world. Approaching the history of terror in this way gets us past the simple (and potentially simplistic) question of 'is this terrorism or not?' It allows us instead to make positive statements about what we see that can illuminate the different ways that people have understood and made use of violence and fear. This in turn will help us better understand a range of pasts that are messy and at times quite alien. More important, it will leave us better primed to understand the full range of ways that human beings can wield terror and understand what they are doing, or perceive terror and react to what they are experiencing, without the limits imposed by Western, state-based assumptions about violence and order. What we will find is a range of both similarities and differences in the connections between violence, terror, power and order between various pasts and various presents. Sometimes what we see will seem to fit easily

---

8 Cf. the chapter by C. Méndez in this volume.   9 Cf. Frampton in this volume.

with our ideas about terrorism, but often it will not. By the time we get to Europe in the later eighteenth and nineteenth centuries, some of the threads will come together in a way that observers have felt compelled to call 'terrorism'. If there is a useful periodisation in the history of terrorism, it is this: before the word appears, and the ongoing after, in which the word itself has influenced and continues to influence how people perceive others, or themselves.

For the purposes of illustration, I will work through a few examples over a range of time. For reasons of expertise, but also given that terrorism is a European concept born of European conditions and ways of viewing the world, I will focus on the history of Europe, including some periods when Europeans came into contact with or dominated cultures outside of Europe itself. To begin with the Romans: from their starting point on the banks of the Tiber River in Italy, this people erected in the Mediterranean basin over the last few centuries BC an extensive and clearly identifiable state, though they did not call it 'the state', but rather the *res publica*, which can be translated as the 'common matter', or the 'common weal', or even the 'community'. They also distinguished between public and private spheres of action, between civil and criminal wrong, and between civilians and soldiers. While much of this might sound familiar, the Roman view of terror, both outside and inside the *res publica*, was quite different from the one that prevails in the modern West. Successive Roman governments, both Republican and Imperial, regarded terror as a perfectly legitimate instrument of policy when dealing both with foreign enemies and with problematic citizens.[10] Non-combatants were far from off limits; Roman armies freely massacred entire city populations in their wars, especially those who had refused to surrender in time – as for example the population of New Carthage in Spain in the late third century BC, when the general in command let his troops loose to kill not just the entire human population but also the dogs and other animals. This policy was designed to make sure that conquered populations stayed conquered. It was captured perfectly in the late first century AD by Cornelius Tacitus, when, while writing about the Romans' conquest of Britain, he commented ironically through the voice of a British leader: 'they create a desolation and call it peace.'[11] Internal terror was aimed at deterring the potential rebel and/or criminal – perhaps the most well-known example being the crucifixion of the

---

10 J. Harries, 'Labelling the Terrorist in Ancient Rome', unpublished paper presented at the conference Terrorism: Interdisciplinary Perspectives, University of St Andrews CSTPV, 10 February 2010.
11 C. Tacitus, *The Agricola and The Germania*, trans. H. Mattingly and S. A. Handford (New York, Penguin, 1970), c. 30, p. 81.

rebel slave leader Spartacus and thousands of his followers along the Appian Way in AD 71. Criminal proceedings – i.e. criminal prosecutions, interrogations of subjects and witnesses etc. – took place in public. Those sentenced to death were executed by being made to fight in the arenas, providing members of the *res publica* with entertainment but also with a violent and bloody warning.

Non-Romans also sometimes resorted to terror against Romans, and citizens of the Empire used terror against each other. Among the former were the so-called Sicarii, or 'daggermen', who wielded violence and fear against the Roman occupation of Palestine in the first century AD.[12] The Sicarii look at first glance familiar, but some things about them are hard to pin down. They assassinated not only Romans but also pro-Roman or Roman-tolerant Jews, in an effort to frighten fellow Jews into fighting against the Roman regime. They killed by slitting their victims' throats with daggers. They often attacked in broad daylight, in crowded venues such as marketplaces; festivals were a favourite opportunity. Their attacks were generally aimed at high-profile leaders, for example in c.AD 58 a high priest named Jonathan. Sometimes, however, they killed indiscriminately. According to the Jewish historian Josephus, for example, they attacked the village at Ein Gedi, drove out the defenders, and killed over 700 women and children who could not flee. The Sicarii did not just kill, however; sometimes they captured prominent moderates in order to exchange them for prisoners from their own ranks held by the authorities. And, according to the Talmud, during the first Romano-Jewish War (AD 66–73), they destroyed Jerusalem's food supply, using starvation to force the population to resist a Roman siege rather than negotiate peace.

It is hard to tell how organised and self-aware the Sicarii as a group were. Their moniker may well have been a delegitimising label applied indiscriminately by Josephus and others to all violently radical revolutionaries, whether they belonged to the same group or not. Josephus also sometimes gives them another label: *latrones*, i.e. 'robbers' or 'bandits'. This was an all-purpose term used in Roman law that encompassed everything from the local outlaw who engaged in robbery, kidnapping, extortion or cattle-rustling, to someone who committed high treason.[13] Calling someone a *latro*, like calling someone a terrorist today, automatically placed them outside the law. But the term focuses conceptually on the physical disruption

---

12 M. A. Brighton, *The Sicarii in Josephus's Judean War* (Atlanta, Society of Biblical Literature, 2009).
13 Harries, 'Labelling the Terrorist'.

that they created, not the fear that they spread. Nevertheless, it does seem that many Sicarii sought to compel allegiance to an ideological agenda with fear. They acted, however, within a larger political culture in which indiscriminate terror was a legitimate tool of power and order. If today it is precisely the normally off-limits status of civilians that makes terrorist attacks on them so shocking, the Sicarii lived in a world that made no such distinction; from their perspective, everyone was a legitimate target.

Equally familiar-looking at first glance, but also somewhat strange on closer examination, are the so-called 'circumcellions' of late Roman North Africa. These stemmed from the separatist Christian movement of the fourth and fifth centuries AD called by their enemies the Donatists (from one of the movement's leaders, the priest Donatus).[14] The Donatists strongly resisted the cooperation, even intertwining, of the orthodox Catholic church with the Roman state that had developed after the emperor Constantine legalised Christianity in 312. They manifested their resistance in a separate church organisation that enjoyed broad popular support, particularly in the North African countryside. They faced an orthodox Catholic clergy, most famously represented by St Augustine (354–430), that favoured using the military power of the Roman state to enforce conformity. The circumcellions (those who hung around shrines, or *circum cellas*) represented the violent wing of the Donatist resistance. They attacked church buildings to reclaim them for a pure Christianity, destroying Catholic altars and holy objects and any trappings of Imperial authority. They were not averse to being caught and martyred, to the point sometimes of making sure that this would happen (though the stories that they acted to martyr themselves, by e.g. throwing themselves off of cliffs, appear to stem from a Catholic propaganda eager to label them as suicides). Faced with a severe government crackdown, they resorted to attacks on people. Their attacks were targeted; they went after their opponents' leadership, i.e. the Catholic clergy. They beat priests with clubs, blinded or otherwise mutilated them, and rarely but occasionally killed them. The point was apparently to terrorise the Catholics into leaving rural North Africa to the Donatists, and scare off those who might be tempted to collaborate or convert to the state-sanctioned church. The term used by hostile sources to describe the circumcellions is again *latrones* or 'bandits'; what they did was *latrocinium*, i.e. 'thuggery'. But the circumcellions were

---

14 B. D. Shaw, *Sacred Violence: African Christians and Sectarian Hatred in the Age of Augustine* (Cambridge, Cambridge University Press, 2011); M. Gaddis, *There Is No Crime for Those Who Have Christ: Religious Violence in the Christian Roman Empire* (Berkeley, University of California Press, 2005), pp. 103–30.

plainly using fear as a weapon; they were fighting a more powerful and institutionalised opponent by spreading terror, to keep both members of the laity and the clergy from cooperating with an institutional church that was acting like an arm of the state. The power of their tactics emerges in the story of a priest named Maximian, who was dragged away from his altar, beaten, stabbed in the groin and left for dead; Maximian lived to travel to Italy in person and shock the members of the Imperial court by displaying his scars. Nevertheless, not all of the categories associated with terrorism fit the circumcellions. Since, for example, the fight here was for the hearts and minds, or at least physical cooperation, of all Christian believers, and the leadership of the Donatists' opponents were clergy, the distinction between civilian and military, or even combatant and non-combatant, blurs. Was a priest serving mass at an altar a combatant? Were the Catholic clergy in general 'military' targets, because the fight was against a government-sanctioned church that was by this point very much the religious manifestation of the state?

As we move from the fifth into the sixth century, the Roman state in the West dissolved, though Roman legal traditions and patterns of political and social organisation persisted for quite some time. In Europe, power fell to kings of peoples that the sources (which were generally written from a Roman or Romanised perspective) identify as barbarian (i.e. Ostrogoths, Visigoths, Burgundians, Alemans, Franks), but whose political culture and power depended as much on their long histories in Roman military service as it did on outright conquest. How successful a given king was at controlling territory depended on how well he could mobilise the interests of his own followers and of the Roman population (including the powerful, aristocratic heads of what had been the orthodox state church, the bishops), and make use of the remaining Roman bureaucratic and military infrastructure. The most successful, it turned out, were the kings of the Franks, of north-western Gaul.[15]

Among the tools of power deployed by the Frankish kings, alongside military conquest and marriage, was terror. Early Frankish kings are reported as spectacularly and publicly killing other Frankish kings, or men who wanted to be kings, and even members of their own followings, in order to suppress dissent and coerce allegiance. These kings were Catholic Christian; the first Christian king of the Franks, Clovis, had converted himself and his

---

15 P. J. Geary, *Before France and Germany: The Creation and Transformation of the Merovingian World* (Oxford, Oxford University Press, 1988).

following to the orthodox faith in c.500. Whether the terror they provoked was judged good or bad by the Christian authors who tell us virtually all that we know about them depended on what they were using it for and against whom. Bishop Gregory of Tours, for example, at the end of the sixth century excused Clovis's murderous methods by casting him as God's instrument in supporting Catholicism in Gaul and suppressing heresy.[16] Authors such as Gregory wrote against the backdrop of a religious culture in which God and his saints used terror in much the same fashion. Lives of Christian saints from the fifth, sixth and seventh centuries describe God using violence, sometimes directly and sometimes through the saints, to persuade non-believers to convert, to punish men and society at large for their sins and to avenge injury and insult to himself and his followers both divine and human. The seventh-century *Life* of the Irish monk St Columbanus (d. 615), for example, which became one of the most popular and emulated saints' lives in Europe, has God wielding violence on Columbanus's behalf against those who had harmed the saint or his property, against disobedient monks, against disobedient kings, even against other saints who had fallen down on the job. The violence was carried out in spectacularly public fashion designed to deter repetition. In one vignette, Columbanus left some of his property in a boat on the River Loire at Tours while he went to pray at the tomb of Tours's patron saint, St Martin (d. 397). The property was stolen. Columbanus berated St Martin for not protecting his property; spurred into action, St Martin promptly tormented and tortured the thief. The miracle, says the life's author, struck such terror into everyone that no one dared further to touch anything belonging to Columbanus.[17]

The problems with interpreting past action uncritically through the lens of 'terrorism' are particularly pronounced under the greatest of the Frankish kings: Charlemagne (r. 768–814). Charlemagne took what had been a Frankish kingdom anchored primarily in the west and turned it into an empire that stretched from the English Channel to the Elbe and from the borders of Scandinavia to northern Italy and the marches of Spain. In the process, he built what many argue is a state, though his government and those of his immediate successors worked as much or more through personal relationships as they did through impersonal laws and

16 Gregory of Tours, *The History of the Franks*, trans. L. Thorpe (New York, Penguin, 1974), Book II, cc. 31, 37, 40, pp. 143–4, 151, 156.
17 Jonas of Bobbio, 'Life of St. Columbanus', in E. Peters (ed.) and W. E. McDermott (trans.), *Monks, Bishops and Pagans: Christian Culture in Gaul and Italy, 500–700* (Philadelphia, University of Pennsylvania Press, 1975), c. 22, p. 103.

offices.[18] Terror was one of Charlemagne's primary tools of power. His long and drawn-out conquest of the Saxons, for example, witnessed fire-and-sword devastation and destruction of religious sites, compulsory conversions to Christianity and the forcible implantation of a Frankish-style government and church organisation. In 782, a rebellion prompted him to round up and publicly execute a large number of Saxons (the source reports 4,500) all at once. Charlemagne cannot be accused here of slaughtering civilians; there was no concept 'civilian' in his world. All free men in his empire were subject to military service. In a war of conquest such as he was waging in Saxony, the entire population was fighting back. He was also heir to a learned, Christian just-war theory, rooted in the teachings of St Augustine, that saw killing non-combatants as justified if the war was a righteous one – which, from the Frankish perspective, a war waged to pacify and Christianise the Saxons certainly was.[19] Our principal source on this incident, the Royal Frankish Annals, reports the incident accordingly as a judicial execution, namely of those most responsible for prosecuting the rebellion, despite the huge numbers involved.[20]

While all this cost Charlemagne in terms of later reputation (the Nazis labelled him the *Sachsenschlächter* – 'the butcher of Saxons'), he does not seem to have faced undue criticism at the time. What criticism there was focused not on the king's use of terror per se but on its aims. A group of Spanish bishops complained that he was persuading people (i.e. to convert) by fear of his power rather than by justice. One of his principal advisors, the Anglo-Saxon intellectual Alcuin of York, wrote similarly in a letter to a friend at court that faith should not be coerced. Yet, in a letter to the king himself, Alcuin described Charlemagne (unsurprisingly) as a new King David who protected the Christian people and spread fear among the heathens.[21]

In the centuries that followed the disintegration of Charlemagne's empire in the later ninth century, as its component parts started down the paths that would lead to France and Germany, what emerged west of the Rhine river

---

18 J. L. Nelson, *King and Emperor: A New Life of Charlemagne* (Berkeley, University of California Press, 2019); Brown, *Violence*, pp. 69–96.
19 F. H. Russel, *The Just War in the Middle Ages* (Cambridge, Cambridge University Press, 1975); R. Cox, 'Asymmetric Warfare and Military Conduct in the Middle Ages', *Journal of Medieval History* 38/1 (2012).
20 'Royal Frankish Annals', in B. W. Scholz (ed. and trans.), *Carolingian Chronicles* (Ann Arbor, University of Michigan Press, 1972), pp. 35–125, here 61.
21 J. L. Nelson, 'Alcuin's Letter to Meginfrid', in A. Dierkens, N. Schroeder and A. Wilkins (eds.), *Penser la paysannerie médiévale, un défi impossible?* (Paris, Éditions de la Sorbonne, 2017); S. Weinfurter, *Karl der Grosse: Der Heilige Barbar* (Munich, Piper Verlag, 2013), p. 113.

has been characterised as 'stateless'.[22] The practical authority of the West Frankish king in Paris in the tenth and eleventh centuries was very limited; actual power was wielded by lords operating from castles with the support of their armed and mounted followings. These ranged from those who claimed the titles of count or duke, to mounted thugs who held a single castle with a few followers. The ability of anyone to control a territory of any size depended on his ability to build and maintain coalitions of lesser lords and to manage alliances with his peers. The more or less constant low-level conflict that resulted produced a great deal of terror.[23] In the pillaging and wasting of opponents' land that was a regular feature of local fighting, people lost their homes and property and/or their lives; they fled to seek sanctuary whenever they could. Nevertheless, it is hard to argue that the warriors responsible were in every case using terror instrumentally; in some cases terror seems, rather, to have been a by-product of the violence. The sources generally cast the pillaging not in terms of an intent to achieve some set of goals by deliberately spreading fear, but rather in terms of vengeance, or gathering supplies and plunder. Reading between the lines, we can also infer other motives: doing economic damage to an enemy; reducing his capacity to levy men and supplies; or provoking him into responding to an attack.

In many cases, however, combatants do seem to have intended to use fear instrumentally. Laying waste to an opponent's property and spreading terror among his people could serve to pressure him into a settlement – especially since doing so not only hurt him economically but also demonstrated his inability to carry out one of the fundamental tasks of lordship: controlling his holdings and protecting the people who lived on them. Moreover, it displayed publicly one's willingness to engage in violence, with the latent threat behind the display of a more direct use of force. Devastating an opponent's lands and terrorising his people, therefore, amounted to a non-verbal but nevertheless important tool of communication and negotiation among parties in conflict. Finally, in a world where political power depended on controlling land and its produce, terror was an effective way to persuade peasants to accept one's control, and to extort labour, supplies and other

---

22 P. J. Geary, 'Living with Conflicts in Stateless France: A Typology of Conflict Management Mechanisms', in *Living with the Dead in the Middle Ages* (Ithaca, NY, Cornell University Press, 1994).
23 See e.g. Brown, *Violence*, pp. 99–133; T. N. Bisson, *The Crisis of the Twelfth Century: Power, Lordship, and the Origins of European Government* (Princeton, Princeton University Press, 2008), pp. 22–83.

kinds of payments – a method of wielding power that Pierre Bonnassie has gone so far as to label *terrorisme seigneuriale*.[24]

Those responsible for the terror were not the only ones to exploit it. Records of property disputes kept by monasteries frequently accuse laymen of plundering and laying waste to monastery lands and driving out the inhabitants. Many of these accusations were probably accurate. But one cannot always assume that what the records said happened actually did; monks frequently demonised their opponents in lurid language that in some cases was demonstrably exaggerated. In these cases, the monks were creating or amplifying images of terror caused by others, in order to gain sympathy and support against their enemies, and to control the memory of events to their benefit.[25]

From the perspective of those with power, the lines separating legitimate from illegitimate violence did not follow distinctions between civilian and military, or combatant and non-combatant, but rather those of personal status. Rules that protected the women and children of aristocrats simply did not apply to ordinary people. Sometime around 1074, for example, according to a record preserved by the Abbey of St Mary at Noyers in the Touraine, one Acharius was entangled in a violent conflict with three other lords. He was losing badly, having already lost his own castle and lands. One night, he and his men rode out on a plundering raid. The band found a group of men gathered at a peasant's house and attacked. The people of the house fled to a cave below the house, so Acharius and his men burned the house down on top of the refugees, killing them all. This would not normally have been a problem, except that among the dead were some women and children belonging to a local aristocratic kindred. Acharius was promptly captured by his own nephew, and had to beg for the intercession of the monks of Noyers to make peace with the kin of the people he had killed.[26]

At the same time, however, commoners could wield terror themselves – or at least be used by their betters as instruments of terror. The *Miracles of St Benedict*, written by Andrew of Fleury c.1043, describes the activities of the so-called 'Peace League of Bourges' in 1038. According to Andrew, Archbishop Aimon of Bourges imposed a peace oath on all men above the age of fifteen throughout his diocese. To enforce the oath, Aimon created

---

24 P. Bonnassie, *La Catalogne du milieu du Xe à la fin du XIe siècle: Croissance et mutations d'une société*, 2 vols (Toulouse, Presses Universitaires Mirail, 1975–6), Vol. 2, p. 599.
25 See e.g. Brown, *Violence*, pp. 107, 124.
26 S. D. White, 'Feuding and Peace-Making in the Touraine Around the Year 1000', *Traditio* 42 (1986), Case 1, pp. 214–21.

a military force composed of clerics, some members of the local nobility, but also peasants. The army attacked violators of the peace and destroyed their castles:

> with the help of God they so terrified the rebels [i.e. the violators of the peace] that, as the coming of the faithful was proclaimed far and wide by rumor among the populace, the rebels scattered. Leaving the gates of their towns open, they sought safety in flight, harried by divinely inspired terror.

Archbishop Aimon was thus able to dominate the surrounding region until one magnate finally fought back and destroyed the archbishop's army.[27]

Among the most visible reactions to conditions in France in this period are the so-called Peace of God councils.[28] These were summoned by bishops and abbots, often with the cooperation of local lords, to reform a sinful, corrupt world and Church by imposing oaths on participants to reform their behaviour. Among the behaviour the councils sought to regulate was the predation and collateral damage caused by aristocratic brush wars. However, they did not focus on terror, or on the legitimacy of the violence that caused it. Whether violence and the terror it spread were legitimate depended on who was using them for what. The council acts acknowledged, respected and even incorporated the right of the aristocracy to wield violence on their own behalf, without royal sanction. They sought primarily to protect church spaces from unjustified invasion, church property from uncompensated seizure, and people such as peasants and merchants from uncompensated assault and plundering. They displayed a visible concern for those who were helpless, or not carrying weapons, but they still legitimated a great deal of aristocratic practice. Warriors were allowed to fight each other, to plunder land as long as it was their own, to devastate the property of legitimate enemies. Peasants, merchants, even women, who owed compensation for something or had committed some offence were fair targets – as were armed clerics, which reinforces evidence in other sources that plenty of clergy were wielding violence themselves.

That many Christian clergy and their audiences in this period sometimes saw terror as a good thing is revealed again by a persistent religious culture in which God and the saints used terror to achieve their ends. A telling example appears in a collection of miracle stories, the early eleventh-century *Miracles*

---

27 T. F. Head and R. Landes, *The Peace of God: Social Violence and Religious Response in France Around the Year 1000* (Ithaca, NY, Cornell University Press, 1992), pp. 339–42.
28 G. Koziol, *The Peace of God* (Leeds, Arc Humanities Press, 2018); Head and Landes, *Peace of God*; Brown, *Violence*, pp. 116–24.

of St Foy. Here we see a divine figure using terror as a tool in what can only be called extortion – extortion that was justified, however, because (according to the author concerned) it served a divinely mandated goal. According to one of the stories in the collection, the monks of St Foy's monastery at Conques decided that the high altar of the saint's church needed a new frontal. To make it, they needed gold. According to the story's author,

> this is the reason that few people are left in this whole region who have a precious ring or brooch or armbands or hairpins, or anything of this kind, because Sainte Foy, either with a simple entreaty or with bold threats, wrested away these same things for the work of the frontal.

One woman from the area, knowing that the saint was requisitioning gold, decided to hide a gold ring. St Foy promptly visited the woman with a painful fever for several nights in succession until she gave it up.[29]

A different relationship between violence, terror and the unarmed emerges from recent work by Hans-Jacob Orning on factional conflict in thirteenth-century Norway.[30] During this so-called 'Civil War Period' in Norwegian history, factions fought for control of the throne in a physical landscape in which significant towns and settlements were located almost entirely on the coast, and travel into the mountainous and forested interior was relatively difficult. Almost all communication, therefore – and certainly the projection of power – had to be by ship. Capturing a coastal town or strong point with a fleet was relatively easy; quick raids into territory that an opponent claimed to control could by spreading fear undermine that faction's local support. However, staying put and coercing the behaviour of widely scattered farmers over the long term was more difficult. This explains, says Orning, why all parties tended to use outright force only against the armed, and to avoid the sort of plundering and terrorising that characterised, say, France around the year 1000. Uncooperative or openly hostile peasants and townspeople could make it even harder than it already was for someone to conquer and hold territory over the long term. Contenders for power therefore needed their support, or at least their acquiescence. In other words, an ethic of not hurting the unarmed developed, not out of a sense that it was somehow unethical to harm the helpless,

---

29 *The Book of Sainte Foy*, trans. P. Sheingorn (Philadelphia, University of Pennsylvania Press, 1995), Book I, cc. 17–22, pp. 82–8.
30 H. J. Orning, 'Violence, Conflict and Order in Medieval Norway', *Global Intellectual History*, forthcoming.

but because they were not at all helpless and it was dangerous to alienate them.

During the Crusades into the Middle East of the late eleventh, twelfth and thirteenth centuries, Christian Europeans encountered the so-called 'Assassins'.[31] These were essentially hitmen from a small splinter group of Ismaili Islam, the Nizaris. They are best known for their targeted attacks on prominent Muslim and Crusader figures. It is hard to decide where the Assassins fit on the 'state'/'non-state' spectrum. They did represent an organised group that was busy building and maintaining its own political and religious structure based on strongholds in Persia and Syria.[32] But they acted within already extant (and hostile) states or proto-states: the principalities of the Seljuk Turks, the Crusader States, Fatimid Egypt, the Byzantine Empire. Their foremost victims were Muslim viziers (high-ranking ministers) and members of their families. But they also killed for hire; both Muslim and Christian power players in the region asked them to kill on their behalf. The Assassins were quite active; between 1092 and c.1147 they killed approximately forty-four major political figures in what are now Iraq and Iran, Syria–Palestine and Egypt. The unexpected and public nature of their attacks suggests that, in addition to killing prominent leaders, spreading to advance their religious and political aims was at least a secondary goal.[33] They usually killed with knives. They killed in public places, such as mosques, or they threatened death with such devices as leaving a knife on someone's bed. Their reputation certainly spread fear and forced potential victims to take precautions.

While the Assassins provide an example of terror used by the weak against the strong, in Europe proper the evidence remains firmly focused on terror wielded by the strong. This kind of terror is especially easy to see during the so-called Hundred Years War of the fourteenth and fifteenth centuries, which locked the burgeoning national kingdoms of England and France into an on-again/off-again series of conflicts that in fact went on for more than a century.[34] The fighting, which was touched off when the English King Edward III (r. 1327–77) laid claim to the French throne, took place almost exclusively in France, but the circumstances are quite different from those

---

[31] D. Cook, 'Ismaili Assassins as Early Terrorists', in C. Dietze and C. Verhoeven (eds.), *The Oxford Handbook of the History of Terrorism* (Oxford, Oxford University Press, online publication 2014).
[32] Cf. R. Cox in this volume, at p. 573.   [33] Cf. Cook, 'Ismaili Assassins', pp. 9–10.
[34] J. Sumption, *The Hundred Years War*, 4 vols (Philadelphia, University of Pennsylvania Press, 1990–2015).

that characterised France in previous centuries.[35] Both France and England had by this point become well-developed, bureaucratic kingdoms whose rulers were claiming ever tighter control over the right to wield violence and wage war. Their armies were not yet professional, but their heavy reliance on paid mercenaries was pointing in that direction. The increasing willingness of nobles to contribute money to the king rather than serve on campaigns themselves was laying the groundwork for an eventual distinction between nobles who fought and those who did not, i.e. between civilian and military.

A principal tactic in the wars of this period, especially beloved by but not exclusive to the English, was heir to the raiding and plundering of previous ages: the so-called *chevauchée*, or 'cavalcade'. Armies consisting of both foot and horse moved through the countryside burning, destroying and pillaging, sacking towns, raping women and killing or mutilating those who resisted them. The aim of these expeditions was to weaken the enemy by reducing an area's productivity and thus the opposing king's tax base. They were also designed to make the participants rich through plunder and ransoms; *chevauchées* were very much business ventures for both their leaders and the rank and file. A prime example is the raid into southern France led by Edward III's son, Edward the 'Black Prince' (1330–76), in 1355.[36] In October of that year, the younger Edward left English-held Gascony with between six and eight thousand men and plunged south-eastwards. Towns and cities throughout southern France panicked and bombarded the court of the French King John II (r. 1350–64) in Paris with pleas for help. John's commander in the field, the Count of Armagnac, decided to avoid the chances of direct battle, humiliating John and forcing him to redirect resources south from other theatres. Tax revenue from the region plummeted; what there was often had to be directed back to its sources to pay for rebuilding towns and villages and restoring fortifications for the case of another raid. A second *chevauchée* the following year provoked John into giving chase himself with a large army, and led to that army's devastating defeat, and John's capture, by the Black Prince's army at the Battle of Poitiers.

Although terror does not appear to have been the primary purpose behind these raids, it was clearly a secondary aim, and a successful one; they left psychological scars on the region that are still remembered today.[37] The Black Prince not only weakened the French materially; he discredited and undermined King John by spreading destruction and fear throughout one of the

---

35 Brown, *Violence*, pp. 255–61.   36 Sumption, *Hundred Years War*, Vol. 2, pp. 74–86.
37 P. Hoskins, *In the Steps of the Black Prince: The Road to Poitiers, 1355-56* (Woodbridge, Boydell Press, 2013).

richest areas of the French kingdom. John responded by coming out to fight, and lost (though whether in his second *chevauchée* Edward actually wanted to provoke John into fighting, or accepted battle at Poitiers because he could not avoid it, is a debated question).[38] Although the Black Prince's raids took place in a context where the lines between state and non-state actors are starting to get clearer, it is hard to say for certain that he was trying to spread terror by deliberately attacking civilians; as before, civilians or non-combatants are hard to pin down. Even though in 1355 the French royal army avoided battle, those defending their homes in the towns and cities did not; entire populations defended their town or city walls, forcing Edward to lay siege, sometimes for days, or to avoid the headache altogether and move on after plundering and torching the suburbs.

If the *chevauchées* of the Black Prince reveal terror wielded by what we might call states (or proto-states) in the context of warfare, it is only a few years later that we get a spectacular image of terror used by the weak against the strong in the context of revolt: the so-called Jacquerie of 1358. This rebellion among the peasantry and bourgeoisie of northern France (which earned its name from a common noble epithet for peasant, 'Jacques') was provoked by the political vacuum caused by the French defeat at Poitiers in 1356 and the English capture of King John II, by the fighting amongst several parties claiming to control the royal government in Paris during the truce with the English that followed, and by the infestation of the French countryside by companies of now unemployed mercenaries (as well as unpaid and unsupplied royal troops) seeking supplies and plunder. The most common picture of the Jacquerie is that projected by most of the surviving sources: it was a disorganised and savagely violent peasant rebellion against the power of a nobility that had completely failed to protect them. The reality turns out to be more complicated.[39] The Jacques's ranks included burgesses and a few members of the local nobility. They were in fact quite well organised and led. Their attacks focused on defending villages and towns against raids and

---

38 Hoskins, *Steps of the Black Prince*, pp. 153–64.
39 J. Firnhaber-Baker, 'The Eponymous Jacquerie: Making Revolt Mean Some Things', in J. Firnhaber-Baker and D. Schoenaers (eds.), *The Routledge History Handbook of Medieval Revolt* (London and New York, Routledge, 2017); J. Firnhaber-Baker, 'Soldiers, Villagers, and Politics: The Role of Mercenaries in the Jacquerie of 1358', in G. Pépin, F. Laine and F. Boutoulle (eds.), *Routiers et mercenaires pendant la guerre de Cent ans: Hommage à Jonathan Sumption* (Bordeaux, Ausonius, 2016); J. Firnhaber-Baker, 'À son de cloche: The Interpretation of Public Order and Legitimate Authority in Northern France 1355–1358', in H. R. Oliva Herrer, V. Challet, J. Dumolyn and M. A. Carmona Ruiz (eds.), *La comunidad medieval como esfera pública* (Seville, Universidad de Sevilla, 2014).

helping the rebellious citizens of Paris by destroying noble castles that threatened to strangle the city. Though many of the rank-and-file participants likely did want to punish and even get rid of a warrior class that was both failing and exploiting them, the atrocities attributed to them seem for the most part to be invented or exaggerated. It is precisely this invention and exaggeration, however, that is important. The narrative chronicles that record the Jacquerie mostly represent the perspective of the nobility. They surround the rebellion with a thick fog of terror. The chronicler Jean Froissart, for example, tells us that the Jacques deliberately created a reign of terror in the service of wiping out the aristocracy. Leaderless peasants who were little better than animals, moved solely by an irrational, disorganised rage, committed horrible atrocities against noble men, women and children (i.e. roasting noblemen on spits in front of their families, raping wives and daughters in front of their fathers before killing them all and burning their castle, etc.). Terrified women and their families sought refuge in walled towns, awaiting rescue by troops of armed nobles assembled to help them.[40] In other words, members of the nobility and the chroniclers who expressed their point of view perceived the Jacquerie as a deliberate use of terror to destabilise or overturn the noble regime. Whether or not this was actually the Jacques's aim, their victims and critics thought it was, and wanted posterity to think it was. This picture of the Jacquerie then justified the use of terror in response. Once the principal army of the Jacques was defeated in battle and its leader captured, bands of nobles went on the rampage, killing indiscriminately anyone they thought might have participated in the rebellion. They terrorised into submission those who had threatened their power and privileges, including their self-perceived status as the only social group entitled to wield violence.

When we move past the Protestant Reformation touched off by Martin Luther in 1517, we might expect that European ideas about violence and order would begin to overlap with the analytical categories on which 'terrorism' depends. The state as an institution and an idea was coming into focus; militaries were becoming professional, and thus the distinction between civilian and military begins to make sense (though, as the Wars of Religion of the seventeenth century amply demonstrate, the distinction between political and religious action was still a long way off). While previous ages had plenty of ways to communicate terror, after the middle of the fifteenth century the invention of the printing press enabled widespread, mass transmission of fear. It is in this context, for example,

---

40 J. Froissart, *Chronicles*, ed. and trans. G. Brereton (New York, Penguin, 1968), pp. 151–5.

that the so-called Gunpowder Plot of 1605 in England has been called an act of terrorism.[41] This was a conspiracy by a group of English Catholics who were frustrated by the continued persecution of their co-religionists in a now Protestant England. The conspirators planned to blow up the House of Lords while King James I was present, with an amount of gunpowder hidden in a room underneath that would have levelled the building and killed everyone in it. The explosion was to have been followed by an uprising in the English Midlands aimed at putting King James's 9-year-old daughter Elizabeth on the throne and installing a pro-Catholic government. Had the attack not been betrayed and stopped, it would have been sensational; it would have struck fear into the hearts of English Protestants and brought to worldwide (or at least Europe-wide) attention the plight of their Catholic countrymen. The terror that the attack inspired would have been amplified by the deaths of innocents, including the Queen and some of her other children, and pro-Catholic members of the House.

It is not entirely clear, however, that this is how the plotters were thinking (to the degree that it is possible to distil out what they were actually thinking and planning from the mostly hostile, pro-government accounts), that is, whether they consciously aimed to provoke and amplify terror by killing civilians, in order to coerce the government, frighten Protestants and inspire support from their fellow Catholics. When looked at purely for its immediate aims, the Gunpowder Plot looks more like a planned *coup d'état*.[42] The conspirators wanted to decapitate the government at a stroke, including the parliamentarians who had caused their co-religionists so much trouble. The Midlands rising and seizure of Princess Elizabeth was pre-planned; the plotters do not seem to have relied on inspiring a broader revolt by Catholics. If they hoped the attack would have any propaganda value, it would have been to inspire intervention in England by Catholic Spain. There is also evidence that the plotters agonised over the deaths of the innocent that they planned to cause, particularly the Queen, her children and the good Catholic members of Parliament. They were able to persuade themselves that what they were doing was justified with the help of a Catholic doctrine that justified doing something morally wrong if it was an unintentional and immediate consequence of doing a more important moral good.[43] In short, it is not

---

41 A. Fraser, *Faith and Treason: The Story of the Gunpowder Plot* (New York, Doubleday, 1996), p. 103.
42 M. Nicholls, 'Strategy and Motivation in the Gunpowder Plot', *The Historical Journal* 50/4 (2007).
43 The so-called 'double-effect' doctrine: A. McIntyre, 'Doctrine of Double Effect', in E. N. Zalta (ed.), *The Stanford Encyclopedia of Philosophy* (Spring 2019 edition), https://plato.stanford.edu/archives/spr2019/entries/double-effect/; Fraser, *Faith and Treason*, pp. 107–8.

obvious that 'terrorism' is the best way to understand what the plotters thought they were doing. After the plot was discovered, however, the English government and their Protestant allies magnified the terror of the plot with lurid accounts of what might have happened if the explosives had not been discovered and had gone off. If anyone can be said to have exploited the shock and horror of the Gunpowder Plot, it would be them.

In taking us through some of the ways that terror was deployed and understood in Europe's past, I have not been trying to push the origins of terrorism earlier. I have tried instead to suggest, first, that looking for the 'origins of terrorism', or even studying the deep history of 'terrorism' as a reified idea, is problematic, and, second, that studying how human beings used terror in the deep past is nevertheless important. The past provides us with examples of societies whose members thought very differently than do modern Westerners about order and disorder, legitimacy and illegitimacy, and the instrumental use of violence and fear. It thus gives us some tools and models for understanding the behaviour of violent actors in the present, many of whom likewise understand order and disorder, legitimacy and illegitimacy, and even violence itself differently than we do. At the same time, the past contains the threads out of which our current views of right order in the world were woven.

The 'invention of terrorism' (to lift the title of a recent book)[44] took place against a long backdrop in which human beings used terror instrumentally, in ways consonant with their own conceptual apparatus and world views. There are times and places where the necessary ingredients come into focus, that is, where people acted in ways that fit how we understand legitimacy and illegitimacy, order and disorder, and where we thus might be tempted to say 'this is plainly terrorism'. And then there are times and places where they do not, that is, where people's use of terror, and the norms through which they processed it, seem completely alien. The resulting patterns do not follow conventional historical periods; they have a rhythm of their own. To try to precisely define terrorism and then look for a point or points when it appears, as has been done for example with John Brown's raid on Harpers Ferry in 1859[45] – while usefully connecting some modern uses of terror to a particular set of precursors and contexts – masks the way that (to continue using the example) John Brown combined some very old traditions and attitudes in a new cause in a new set of circumstances with the particular tools he had available.[46]

---

44 Dietze, *Erfindung des Terrorismus*.   45 Dietze, *Erfindung des Terrorismus*.
46 P. Buc, *Holy War, Martyrdom, and Terror: Christianity, Violence, and the West* (Philadelphia, University of Pennsylvania Press, 2015), pp. 154–61.

There is a historical moment, however, with which we can usefully divide up time: it is the moment when the deliberate use of terror per se to achieve definable ends becomes enough of a concern that someone coins a word for it. We cannot, however, detach this word from its history and use it as an objective heuristic tool. It is part of the story; it takes on its own life, and has its own impact on the game of violence, fear and power. Organising our enquiry around this moment means exploring what imperatives produced the term 'terrorism', and how historical attitudes towards violence and fear, and towards order and disorder, came together in a way that prompted someone to come up with it. It also means exploring how the term has been deployed since, and how it has changed and continues to change, and what effects its existence as an idea has had on people.

If we understand this history of terrorism in this way, we are better positioned to understand and respond to terrorism in the present. The horror of planes being deliberately flown into the Twin Towers in New York on 9/11, for example, prompted politicians, commentators and scholars, especially in the United States, to claim that we faced a new period in the history of terrorism. This new threat justified unprecedented countermeasures that arguably violated long-standing Western norms of legitimate behaviour in conflicts and made the danger posed by the sorts of actors that staged the attacks worse.[47] Looked at historically, however, the attacks of 9/11 were not fundamentally new; they differed from earlier attacks in scale, not in kind. They were aimed at spreading terror by attacking civilians and at undermining the authority and control over its borders that define the modern state, by actors whom their enemies had defined as non-state. In other words, they worked within and took advantage of the very ideas about the primacy of state-based order that have shaped the term 'terrorism' itself. Calling them new and arguing for new kinds of countermeasures cut the government of the United States off from the long experience it and its allies had in dealing with attacks of this kind. The political response in the US was likewise nothing new, and could easily have been predicted. As we saw in the case of the noble response to the Jacquerie in the mid-fourteenth century, or the English government response to the Gunpowder Plot at the beginning of the seventeenth, a ruling elite or government inflaming and broadcasting terror, in order to justify and gain support for the actions it wants to take, has deep roots.

---

47 R. English, 'Change and Continuity Across the 9/11 Fault Line: Rethinking Twenty-First-Century Responses to Terrorism', *Critical Studies on Terrorism* 12/1 (2019).

Further Reading

W. Brown, *Violence in Medieval Europe* (London, Longman, 2011)

P. Buc, *Holy War, Martyrdom, and Terror: Christianity, Violence, and the West* (Philadelphia, University of Pennsylvania Press, 2015)

M. Gaddis, *There Is No Crime for Those Who Have Christ: Religious Violence in the Christian Roman Empire* (Berkeley, University of California Press, 2005)

P. Hyams, *Rancor and Reconciliation in Medieval England* (Ithaca, NY, Cornell University Press, 2003)

W. I. Miller, *Eye for an Eye* (Cambridge, Cambridge University Press, 2005)

4
Terrorism, History and Regionalisation

RORY MILLER

Introduction

There is a lack of empirical as well as theoretical literature examining the ways that terrorism spreads across different regions over different historical periods. This chapter looks to address one aspect of this deficit in the scholarship by locating the interrelationship between regionalisation and terror in its historical context. In doing so, it will examine the limitations of thinking about the regionalisation of terror in historical terms as well as the ways that the historical method enables us to understand more clearly some of the main aspects of the issue.

In particular, the chapter will assess the relationship between terrorism, history and regionalisation in terms of a number of distinct but overlapping factors: the connection between the nation state, non-state actors and the 'new' terrorism; and transnationalism and the contribution of region-specific factors in the formation, evolution and operational effectiveness of terror groups. Despite the absence of much relevant literature, these important issues will be placed in their historical context and will be examined in terms of their historical continuity as they relate to the regionalisation of terror.

There are hundreds of accepted definitions of terrorism. It is a widely contested term in the scholarly literature and among practitioners and policymakers. This article adopts its definition of terrorism from the United States Code of Federal Regulations, which describes it as 'the unlawful use of force and violence against persons or property to intimidate or coerce a government, the civilian population, or any segment thereof, in furtherance of political or social objectives'.[1] This definition has been chosen due to its

---

[1] US Code of Federal Regulations 28 Code of Federal Regulations Section 0.85, 'General Functions', Cornell Law School, Legal Information Institute, www.law.cornell.edu/cfr/text/28/0.85.

broad parameters and because of its equal application to state and non-state actors as perpetrators as well as victims.

There is also no agreed definition of regionalisation in the literature.[2] For the purposes of this study it describes an adaptive, even dynamic, 'bottom-up' process that can lead to the emergence of a new 'regional space'[3] occupied primarily but not solely by non-state actors. Regionalisation is widely viewed to be a recent development whose 'new patterns' are 'highly' relevant to our understanding of the contemporary world.[4] In particular, it is considered to be a reaction to two influential and interrelated processes. The first is the unprecedented rise in economic interdependence in the decades following the end of the Second World War. In South East Asia, for example, regionalisation is often traced back to the spread of ethnic Chinese business networks and the growth and expansion of, primarily, Japanese multinational corporations.[5] The second is globalisation, which can encompass rising economic interdependence and is defined here as the intensification of political, social and cultural, and economic relations across borders.[6]

It is undoubtedly the case that the rise of globalisation since the end of the Cold War has led to 'increased interconnectedness, interdependence and deterritorialization'.[7] This has shaped the move from a bipolar world to a 'world of regions',[8] as Katzenstein has termed it. In the process, this has disrupted traditional social, economic and political interactions between regional centres and peripheries. One consequence of this has been the rise of influential non-state actors and transnational networks, including terror groups, especially in environments characterised by economic neglect, poor

---

2 B. Hettne, 'Regional Actorship: A Comparative Approach to Inter-regionalism', in F. Baert, T. Scaramagli and F. Söderbaum (eds.), *Intersecting Interregionalism* (Dordrecht, Springer, 2014); T. J. Pempel (ed.), *Remapping East Asia: The Construction of a Region* (Ithaca, NY, Cornell University Press, 2005); V. R. Whiting, 'The Dynamics of Regionalization: Road Map to an Open Future?', in P. H. Smith (ed.), *The Challenge of Integration: Europe and the Americas* (Miami, North-South Center, 1993).
3 F. Söderbaum, *Rethinking Regionalism* (London, Palgrave Macmillan, 2016), p. 5.
4 B. Hettne, 'Globalization and the New Regionalism: The Second Great Transformation', in B. Hettne, A. Inotai and O. Sunkel (eds.), *Globalism and the New Regionalism* (London and New York, Palgrave Macmillan, 1999).
5 S. Breslin and R. Higgott, 'Studying Regions: Learning from the Old, Constructing the New', *New Political Economy* 5/3 (2000).
6 A. M. Kacowicz, 'Regionalization, Globalization, and Nationalism: Convergent, Divergent, or Overlapping?', *Alternatives* 24/4 (October 1999).
7 B. Lia, *Globalisation and the Future of Terrorism: Patterns and Predictions* (London and New York, Routledge, 2005), p. 20.
8 P. J. Katzenstein, *A World of Regions: Asia and Europe in the American Imperium* (Ithaca, NY, Cornell University Press, 2005).

governance and corruption, sectarianism, authoritarianism, excessive centralisation and cultural and political difference or alienation.[9]

Regionalisation, the Nation State and Terrorism

Historically, at least since the rise of the modern nation state in the sixteenth and seventeenth centuries until the end of the Cold War at the beginning of the 1990s, the overriding security preoccupation of sovereign states has been other states rather than violent non-state actors. When violent non-state actors holding grievances like those listed above rose to the top of a state's national security agenda, it was primarily due to the threat they posed to state authority and sovereignty from within. In recognition of this, as Rich has noted, research has extensively explored the roles of sub-state terror groups of all types – left-wing and right-wing, nationalist, separatist and irredentist, ethnic, nihilist and religious – in the making and unmaking of 'governments, societies and states'.[10]

The fact that most aspects of regionalisation apply primarily to the era of the modern nation state is evidenced by the fact that cross-border activity is of foundational relevance for regionalisation. This raises two questions: what role does history play in our understanding of regionalisation beyond extending the time frame and adding different methods compared to the social sciences? Is it anachronistic to even speak of regionalisation in terms of the historic, or certainly the pre-modern, experience? Interestingly, in these terms, leading scholars on regionalism including Fawcett and Söderbaum have argued that research on regions rarely adopts a sustained historical perspective and that one consequence of the focus on a shorter time frame is that it exaggerates the role of formal regional organisations at the expense of more fluid forms of regionalisation.[11]

In investigating these questions and issues, this chapter will specifically consider whether or not the most important relevant connection for this study is between regionalisation and terrorism, with history playing a distinctly secondary role. There are numerous cases throughout history

---

9 B. J. Lutz and J. M. Lutz, 'Economic, Social, and Political Globalization and Terrorism', *Journal of Political, Economic, and Social Studies* 39/2 (2014).
10 P. B. Rich, 'Terror and Its Limits: The Historical Understanding of Terrorist Movements, States and Tribes in an Age of Cultural Anxiety', *Studies in Conflict and Terrorism* 36/12 (2013).
11 See Söderbaum, *Rethinking Regionalism*, p. 3 and L. Fawcett, 'Regionalizing Security in the Middle East: Connecting the Regional and Global', in E. Monier (ed.), *Regional Insecurity after the Arab Uprisings* (London, Palgrave Macmillan, 2015).

when imperial ambitions or state repression (broadly conceived) served as a trigger for violent uprisings by local populations, which today might arguably be viewed as catalysts for the regionalisation of violent non-state action. One widely referenced historical case is the terror and insurgency tactics adopted by the Jewish population of Judaea during ancient times, notably during the Maccabean Revolt against Hellenic rule (167–160 BCE) and the subsequent uprising against Roman rule that spread across the region's eleven administrative districts (66 CE).[12]

Another example is the violent resistance across South and South East Asia in response to the arrival of Portuguese, Dutch, British and Spanish colonists from the start of the seventeenth century.[13] The excesses of the French imperial state in the late eighteenth century also fuelled guerrilla warfare across Napoleonic Europe from Tyrol in Austria, through Spain and Portugal and into Calabria in southern Italy.[14] A century later, on the eve the twentieth century, the Boxer Rebellion against foreign encroachment into China also employed classic terror tactics in its initial phase of resistance.[15]

The state-centric preoccupation of much of the research on terrorism goes beyond viewing state (and imperial) action as a cause of, as well as a response to, non-state violence on the regional level over the course of history. Inevitably, perhaps, it is particularly evident in the scholarship examining how non-state cross-border violent threats are addressed on the regional level,[16] with its focus on the 'top-down' policy coordination undertaken by geographically proximate, interdependent, nation states. Historically, such cooperation was informal. During the late nineteenth century, for example, the Okhrana, the tsarist secret police, operating out of the Russian embassy in Paris, established ad hoc frameworks for cooperation with government authorities across Europe to counter the threat posed by violent revolution-

---

12 B. J. Lutz and J. M. Lutz, 'The Role of Foreign Influences in Early Terrorism: Examples and Implications for Understanding Modern Terrorism', *Perspectives on Terrorism* 7/2 (2013). See also A. Pedahzur and A. Perliger, *Jewish Terrorism in Israel* (New York, Columbia University Press, 2011), p. 2.
13 Lutz and Lutz, 'The Role of Foreign Influences in Early Terrorism', p. 11.
14 See M. Rowe, *Collaboration and Resistance in Napoleonic Europe: State-formation in an Age of Upheaval, c.1800–1815* (London, Palgrave Macmillan, 2003).
15 Lutz and Lutz, 'The Role of Foreign Influences in Early Terrorism', p. 5.
16 S. Haggard, R. Cooper and C. Moon, 'Policy Reform in Korea', in R. Bates and A. Krueger (eds.), *Political and Economic Interactions in Economic Policy Reform* (Cambridge, Blackwell, 1993); J. Ravenhill, 'Understanding the "new East Asian Regionalism"', *Review of International Political Economy* 17/2 (2010); L. Fawcett, 'Exploring Regional Domains: A Comparative History of Regionalism', *International Affairs* 80/3 (2004).

ary groups, especially anarchists.[17] Subsequent Russian attempts to formalise such international cooperation culminated in their hosting of a conference in St Petersburg in 1904.[18]

In more recent times, nation states have dealt with the threats posed by violent non-state actors on the regional level by gradually transferring certain sovereign rights to more formal mechanisms. This can be seen in the proliferation of regional organisations (ROs) with a security function, including the European Union (EU), the African Union (AU), the Gulf Cooperation Council (GCC) and the Association of South East Asian Nations (ASEAN). As Robert Huggins has noted, 'prevailing critical discourse' tends to highlight differences in regional environments as limiting the utility of comparative study and 'one-size-fits-all' policymaking.[19] Different regions do have 'distinctive'[20] environments in terms of size and geographic spread, religion and ethnic composition, colonial history and culture, economic resources and political systems, historic levels of institutional cohesion, and the influence of external actors.

These and other variations can also result in state actors in the same region having divergent strategic and security cultures, operational capabilities and hierarchies of threat. This, in turn, can produce organisational structures, bureaucracies and institutional frameworks for cooperation in the realm of peace and security that differ greatly from one region to another in terms of sophistication and formality. As Kirchner and Dominguez argue, to take one example, the willingness of member states to increase the range of the RO's security provisions is influenced by the combination of high levels of economic and political development and low levels of dispersion among the members of a RO.[21]

Security governance can be understood as a system of rules conceived by individual and corporate actors aimed at coordinating, managing and regulating their collective existence in response to threats to their physical and

---

17 C. Verhoeven, *The Odd Man Karakozov, Imperial Russia, Modernity, and the Birth of Terrorism* (Ithaca, NY, Cornell University Press, 2009). See also B. B. Fischer, *Okhrana, The Paris Operations of the Russian Imperial Police* (College Park, MD, Central Intelligence Agency, 1997).
18 M. S. Barton, 'The Global War on Anarchism: The United States and International Anarchist Terrorism, 1898–1904', *Diplomatic History* 39/2 (April 2015). See also R. Jensen, 'Daggers, Rifles and Dynamite: Anarchist Terrorism in 19th Century Europe', *Terrorism and Political Violence* 16/1 (2004).
19 R. Huggins, 'Regional Competitive Intelligence: Benchmarking and Policy-Making', *Regional Studies* 44/5 (2009).
20 A. Pennisi di Floristella, 'Are Non-traditional Security Challenges Leading Regional Organizations Towards Greater Convergence?', *Asia Europe Journal* 11 (2013).
21 E. J. Kirchner and R. Dominguez, 'Security Governance in a Comparative Regional Perspective', *European Security* 23/2 (2014).

ontological security.[22] In some cases, structural and other differences that distinguish one region from another, like those noted above, will result in ROs that are either unwilling or unable to find the consensus among members required for the development of a coherent and agreed approach to major security threats like the regionalisation of terror. It also means that, even when ROs do enshrine governance policies relating to peace and security in their organisational treaties and other documents (including protocols, regulations, directives and resolutions),[23] members may still only pay rhetorical lip service to them. Even if they are willing to operationalise such statements of intent, they are still more often inclined to develop prevention and protection instruments rather than empowerment instruments in the area of peace management and peace enforcement.[24]

Reactive Consolidation on the Regional Level

On the other hand, one does see evidence over recent decades of ROs becoming increasingly willing to play a proactive role in conflict mediation and management and especially in providing legitimacy for the security action of member states in the face of threats posed by transnational non-state terror groups and proxy actors.[25] In doing so, the RO, or a subgroup of the RO's members, tends to develop a more institutionalised counterterror capability. I term this a process of reactive consolidation. On the most basic level, ROs provide a framework for member states to meet to discuss non-state threats through official channels. For example, members of the Organisation of African Unity, the forerunner to the African Union, first met formally to discuss the rising region-wide threat of Islamist terror in 1992. ASEAN members held their first official discussions on the same issue in 2002.[26]

---

22 E. Adler and P. Greve, 'When Security Community Meets Balance of Power: Overlapping Regional Mechanism of Security Governance', *Review of International Studies* 35 (2009).
23 For example, Article 1(1) of the ASEAN Charter (2007) and Article 3(1) of the Treaty on the Function of the European Union (TFEU) Lisbon Treaty (2007) declared the pursuit of peace and security as important goals of these major ROs.
24 Kirchner and Dominguez, 'Security Governance in a Comparative Regional Perspective', p. 166.
25 C. A. Crocker, F. Osler Hampson and P. Aall, 'A Global Security Vacuum Half-Filled: Regional Organizations, Hybrid Groups and Security Management', *International Peacekeeping* 21/1 (2014).
26 L. E. Cline, 'African Regional Intelligence Cooperation: Problems and Prospects', *International Journal of Intelligence and CounterIntelligence* 29/3 (2016); D. M. Jones and M. L. Smith, 'From Konfrontasi to Disintegrasi: ASEAN and the Rise of Islamism in Southeast Asia', *Studies in Conflict and Terrorism* 25/6 (2002).

Beyond providing a framework for such meetings, ROs are also used by members to develop and implement a wide range of formal prevention, protection, and occasionally enforcement, instruments to deal with region-wide threats.[27] Some ROs, for example, have changed their founding legislation to allow for security interventions in the case of breaches of 'regional norms and universally accepted standards'.[28] On a more informal level this can also result in the launch of ad hoc and 'improvised' collective conflict management arrangements to address specific problems, as Crocker, Osler Hampson and Aall have written about in their research on the Collective Conflict Management (CCM) model.[29] Such issue-specific security proactivism will only occur on the regional level among those local actors who have a shared understanding of the common threats that they face.[30]

One example is practical efforts of those state actors within the wider regional group most directly threatened by non-state violence to establish their own 'sub-sub-regional' mechanisms to deal with threats.[31] One case in point is the Multi-National Joint Task Force (MNJTF) launched by Nigeria, Chad, Niger, Cameroon and Senegal to counter the threat of Boko Haram, with the support of the African Union as well as France and the United States;[32] another is the Trans-Sahara Counterterrorism Partnership (TSCTP), a strategic counterterrorism mechanism sponsored by the United States that currently includes eleven countries from across north and north-west Africa.[33]

Compared to the large body of work dealing with contemporary state-level multilateral responses to terrorism in specific regions, there is much less research dealing with the types of informal, sub-level inter-state regional security cooperation outlined above. There is even less historical research that examines how informal and familial networks, population flows and

---

27 A. S. Bhalla and P. Bhalla, *Regional Blocs: Building Blocks or Stumbling Blocks?* (Houndsmills, Macmillan, 1997); F. K. Liu, 'East Asian Regionalism: Theoretical Perspectives', in F. K. Liu and P. Régnier (eds.), *Regionalism in East Asia: Paradigm Shifting?* (London, Routledge Curzon, 2003).
28 Crocker, Osler Hampson and Aall, 'A Global Security Vacuum Half-Filled', p. 7.
29 Ibid., p. 2.
30 S. Kingah and L. Van Langenhove, 'Determinants of a Regional Organisation's Role in Peace and Security: The African Union and the European Union Compared', *South African Journal of International Affairs* 19/2 (2012).
31 D. K. Kalinaki, 'Common Enemy Drawing Africa's Spy Chiefs Closer', *Daily Nation*, 30 August 2014.
32 D. M. Tull and A. Weber, 'Nigeria: Boko Haram and the Regionalization of Terrorism', *SWP Comments* (Berlin, Stiftung Wissenschaft und Politik, 21 April 2015), www.swp-berlin.org/fileadmin/contents/products/comments/2015C21_tll_web.pdf.
33 Kalinaki, 'Common Enemy Drawing Africa's Spy Chiefs Closer'.

other mobility-enhancing conditions impact informally on the spread of terror groups in distinct and defined geographic territories. Where such analysis exists, it once again tends to be state-centric in focus insomuch as it deals with how *sub-state* violent actors, often holding narrow separatist aspirations, have impeded the process of regionalisation or how *intra-state* conflicts have evolved into *inter-state* conflicts.[34]

This is understandable given that 'the boundaries' between regionalisation and regionalism[35] are often 'porous', as Mansfield and Solingen have put it.[36] It is especially difficult to distinguish where 'top-down' (state-driven) policies end and 'bottom-up' (non-state-initiated) processes begin. For Hurrell, this means that the regionalisation process can often be a form of 'soft regionalism'.[37] Best and Christiansen have even challenged the view that regionalisation is a process from 'below' at all, instead arguing that it can also be a state-led response to non-state actors that occurs when elite decision makers attempt to address regional imbalances through regional institutionalisation.[38]

Regionalisation, Non-state Actors and the 'New' Terrorism

It should not be forgotten that terrorism is not always, or even necessarily, foremost about non-state actors, or states for that matter, but rather can be more about employing violence as a communicative or symbolic tool to achieve political aims. That said, non-state actors are a crucial consideration in the recent history of terrorism, as well as the 'bottom-up' process of

---

34 B. McAllister and J. Khersonsky, 'Trade, Development, and Nonproliferation: Multilevel Counterterrorism in Central Asia', *Studies in Conflict and Terrorism* 30/5 (2007); A. Campana and J. F. Ratelle, 'A Political Sociology Approach to the Diffusion of Conflict from Chechnya to Dagestan and Ingushetia', *Studies in Conflict and Terrorism* 37/2 (2014).

35 Regionalism is widely viewed to be a political top-down process that describes cooperation in the economic, institutional, defence or security fields, occurring at a political decision-making level. See M. Legrenzi and M. Calculli, 'Regionalism and Regionalization in the Middle East: Options and Challenges', Research Report, International Peace Institute, 29 March 2013, www.ipinst.org/2013/03/regionalism-and-regionalization-in-the-middle-east-options-and-challenges.

36 E. D. Mansfield and E. Solingen, 'Regionalism', *Annual Review of Political Science* 13 (2010).

37 A. Hurrell, 'Regionalism in the Americas', in A. Hurrell and L. Fawcett (eds.), *Regionalism in World Politics* (New York, Oxford University Press, 1995).

38 E. Best and T. Christiansen, 'Regionalism in International Affairs', in J. Baylis, S. Smith and P. Owens (eds.), *The Globalisation of World Politics*, 6th ed. (Oxford, Oxford University Press, 2014).

regionalisation. More generally, they also play an important role in thinking about contemporary challenges to state authority and sovereignty.

The proliferation of 'Globalization's Bastards',[39] as Pollard has labelled today's violent non-state actors, has been heralded as something 'new' in the history of terror, unprecedented in terms of its transnationalism and internationalism, as well as its frequency, gravity and the lethality of its violence.[40] In 2004, British Prime Minister Tony Blair summed up this evolving attitude in an interview: 'The September 11 [Al Qaeda attacks on the United States] showed us a new type of terrorism, completely different.' In his widely debated book *Understanding Terror Networks*, published in the same year as Blair's interview, Marc Sageman echoed the then British premier's sentiments: 'A new type of terrorism threatens the world', he argued, 'driven by networks of fanatics determined to inflict maximum civilian and economic damages on distant targets in pursuit of their extremist goals.'[41]

It is important to frame any historical analysis of the interrelationship between terror and regionalisation in terms of the debate on 'new' versus 'old' terrorism, because the regionalisation of non-state violence is often explicitly linked to three phenomena that are widely considered, incorrectly, to be new and interchangeable: globalisation, transnationalism and ideologically driven extraterritorial violence. All three have undoubtedly deeply influenced and even exacerbated terrorism in the contemporary era. One interesting example of this interconnected process occurred in 2003 with the arrest on terror charges in Australia of a French citizen (Willie Brigitte) working for a Pakistani Islamist terror group (Lashkar-e-Taiba).[42]

39 N. A. Pollard, 'Globalization's Bastards: Illegitimate Non-State Actors in International Law', in R. J. Bunker (ed.), *Networks, Terrorism and Global Insurgency* (London and New York, Routledge, 2005).
40 P. Wilkinson, 'Why Modern Terrorism? Differentiating Types and Distinguishing Ideological Motivations', in C. W. Kegley, Jr. (ed.), *The New Global Terrorism: Characteristics, Causes, Controls* (Upper Saddle River, NJ, Prentice Hall, 2003); H. Ben-Yehuda and L. Levin-Banchik, 'Regime and Power in International Terror Crises: Strong Democracies Fight Back Hard', *Terrorism and Political Violence* 26/3 (2014); W. Enders and T. Sandler, 'After 9/11: Is It All Different Now?', *The Journal of Conflict Resolution* 49/2 (2005); B. Hoffman, 'Change and Continuity in Terrorism', *Studies in Conflict and Terrorism* 24/5 (2001); M. Morgan, 'The Origins of the New Terrorism', *Parameters* 34/1 (2004); A. Spencer, 'Questioning the Concept of "New Terrorism"', *Peace, Conflict and Development* 8/8 (2006); D. Tucker, 'What Is New about the New Terrorism and How Dangerous Is It?', *Terrorism and Political Violence* 13/3 (2001).
41 M. Sageman, *Understanding Terror Networks* (Philadelphia, University of Pennsylvania Press, 2004), p. vii.
42 R. Bonner and D. Van Natta, Jr., 'Regional Terrorist Groups Pose Growing Threat, Experts Warn', *New York Times*, 8 February 2004, www.nytimes.com/2004/02/08/world/regional-terrorist-groups-pose-growing-threat-experts-warn.html.

Identifying and exploring the historic conditions under which the regionalisation of terror has occurred can make a valuable contribution to thinking about the kind of 'new' terrorism exemplified by the Brigitte case – global, transnational and ideologically driven. It can also contribute a different perspective to the 'new' versus 'old' debate in terrorism studies. In particular, it can illuminate further whether the regionalisation of terror in the contemporary era is, to adopt and adapt Martha Crenshaw's words, one of the 'significant points of novelty in the historical development of campaigns of armed resistance', or 'one of those shifts that change the fundamental pattern of terrorist challenges to political authority'.[43]

Since its rise to international infamy in the late 1990s and early 2000s, Al Qaeda has been held up as the 'hallmark'[44] of the 'new' kind of terror group, one that no longer thinks in terms of specific grievances, conflicts or regions. Al Qaeda, as Lia summed up in his 2005 work *Globalisation and the Future of Terrorism: Patterns and Predictions*, was the 'first truly global terrorist organization'.[45] Neumann has described Al Qaeda as the apogee of 'new' terror, and has argued, more generally, that globalisation has been a facilitating factor in the transition from older to newer terrorism.[46] Al Qaeda's founder, Osama bin Laden, fostered this perception from the outset by calling his Islamist umbrella organisation, of which Al Qaeda was only one part, the International (World) Islamic Front for the Jihad Against Jews and Crusaders.

There exists an extensive literature that argues that contemporary Islamist terror groups differ greatly from non-state violent actors of earlier eras because they are pursuing an ideological victory over non-believers as part of an 'eternal global mission ... achieved in the distant future'.[47] This differentiates these actors, so the argument goes, from 'old' terror groups who viewed violence primarily as a means of pressuring opponents, and the international community at large, to make political concessions. This

---

43 M. Crenshaw, 'Innovation: Decision Points in the Trajectory of Terrorism', in M. M. Hafez and M. J. Rasmussen (eds.), *Terrorist Innovations in Weapons of Mass Effect: Preconditions, Causes and Predictive Indicators*, Workshop Report ASCO 2010-019, August 2010, www.hsdl.org/?view&did=9908.
44 V. Barber, 'The Evolution of Al Qaeda's Global Network and Al Qaeda Core's Position Within It: A Network Analysis', *Perspectives on Terrorism* 9/6 (2015), www.terrorismanalysts.com/pt/index.php/pot/article/view/469/html.
45 Lia, *Globalisation and the Future of Terrorism*, p. 37.
46 P. R. Neumann, *Old and New Terrorism: Late Modernity, Globalization and the Transformation of Political Violence* (Cambridge, Polity Press, 2009).
47 R. Paz, *The Brotherhood of Global Jihad*, South Asia Terrorism Portal, n.d., http://old.satp.org/satporgtp/publication/books/global/paz.htm.

necessitated, at some level, limited and achievable objectives, and an understanding that a balance must be struck between using violence to achieve publicity and political gains and avoidance of the mass killing of civilians for fear of discrediting the cause.

In these terms, it is no coincidence that the 199 commuters killed in the March 2004 Islamist attack on the Madrid rail system far exceeded the number of victims of any operation carried out by Spain's Basque separatist Euskadi Ta Askatasuna (ETA, also known as Basque Fatherland and Freedom) up to that point and claimed ninety more lives than ETA was responsible for killing in the whole of 1980, its bloodiest year of terror. It also explains why, over the entire course of the twentieth century, fewer than twenty individual terror attacks claimed more than one hundred lives.

Of course, this distinction is not clear-cut. Many of today's Islamist groups, regularly presented as leading examples of the 'new' kind of terror, have tangible and limited, often territorial, goals similar to those of 'old' groups. Despite its extraterritorial global endeavours (as highlighted by the Brigitte case), Pakistan's Lashkar-e-Taiba, for example, demands India's withdrawal from Kashmir. Nor do contemporary Islamist terror groups have a monopoly on killing in cold blood or on randomly targeting civilians. History is replete with examples of anticolonial insurgencies, social revolutions, independence struggles and secessionist movements that relied primarily on mass violence to attain their objectives. As Ekatarina Stepanova has pointed out, even with the rise of Islamist terror in the late 1990s and early 2000s, more international attacks were carried out by violent nationalist groups than by Islamist ones.[48]

Nor is suicide terrorism solely the preserve of twenty-first-century Islamist terror groups. Between 1980 and 2000, there were an estimated 271 suicide bombings worldwide. The Kurdish PKK, a Marxist separatist group fighting for national and cultural rights in south-east Turkey, carried out dozens of suicide attacks that killed scores and wounded dozens between 1996 and 1999.[49] The Liberation Tigers of Tamil Eelam (LTTE, or Tamil Tigers), a Sri Lankan separatist group fighting for the independence of the Tamil minority against the Sinhalese majority, carried out more suicide attacks between 1980 and 2003 than any other non-state actor.[50] The Tamil Tigers also consistently

---

48 E. Stepanova, 'Al-Qaeda Inspired Transnational Terrorism: Ideology and Organizational Forms', in J. Saikia and E. Stepanova (eds.), *Terrorism: Patterns of Internationalization* (Los Angeles, Sage, 2009).
49 S. Bolukbasi, 'Ankara, Damascus, Baghdad, and the Regionalization of Turkey's Kurdish Secessionism', *Journal of South Asian and Middle Eastern Studies* 14/4 (1991).
50 R. A. Pape, *Dying to Win: The Strategic Logic of Suicide Terrorism* (New York, Random House, 2005), p. 4.

demonstrated a willingness to carry out suicide attacks in densely populated civilian areas and was the first group in the modern era to use female suicide bombers.

The Home Region and the Making of Terror Groups

Though tempting, it is incorrect to think about the evolution of terror groups in binary terms: either as a sub-state problem with narrow and limited goals or as a process of 'excessive internationalism' during the Cold War that culminated in the post-Cold War era in the no-limits global phenomenon represented by Al Qaeda. Both of these framings fail to acknowledge that even in the contemporary era it is on the regional level, in geographically contiguous areas, that we see non-state violent actors linked by characteristics that are region-specific – historical, cultural, religious, familial or linguistic – operating most effectively.

This underscores the central importance of thinking about terror groups, even those perceived to be extraterritorial, in terms of regionalisation. As Bacon has pointed out, even groups that have extraregional relationships tend to have the home region as a focal point.[51] Drevon has noted, for example, that most of the radical Salafi groups that departed Afghanistan after the end of the war against the Soviets in the late 1980s subsequently focused their efforts on their home regions rather than on the international stage.[52]

This is also true, more recently, in regard to Islamic State (ISIS, also known by its Arab acronym Daesh). Launched in Iraq in 2011, following the official US military withdrawal from the country, the group focused on much more than its Islamist agenda. It was also a response to real economic, political and sectarian grievances that fostered a deep Sunni alienation from the Shia-dominated government in Baghdad and Alawi regime in Syria. Its regional focus is also apparent in its decision to break with Al Qaeda in order to focus its efforts on the establishment of a regional caliphate, as set out in its

---

[51] T. Bacon, 'Alliance Hubs: Focal Points in the International Terrorist Landscape', *Perspectives on Terrorism* 8/4 (2014), www.terrorismanalysts.com/pt/index.php/pot/issue/view/47.

[52] J. Drevon, 'The Jihadi Social Movement (JSM): Between Factional Hegemonic Drive, National Realities, and Transnational Ambitions', *Perspectives on Terrorism* 11/6 (2017), www.terrorismanalysts.com/pt/index.php/pot/article/view/656/html.

April 2013 proclamation of an 'Islamic State in Iraq and Levant', with its capital in the Syrian city of Raqqa.[53]

Even Al Qaeda, which launched an unprecedented franchising strategy from North Africa to Yemen following the US invasion of Afghanistan in 2001, has failed to establish a cohesive global movement. In recent years, it has become clear that despite Al Qaeda's attempts to dominate local affiliates, regional preferences have consistently been the 'strongest factor' in explaining relations between groups that ostensibly claim to be united under Al Qaeda's ideological banner.[54] Jemaah Islamiyah (JI or Islamic Group) is an illuminating contemporary example of a terror group that began as subnational actor with socio-economic grievances before gaining global attention as a champion of radical Islamist violence. Yet one can make a strong case that the main source of its significance, power and even legitimacy has stemmed from its engagement in the process of 'bottom-up' regionalisation.

Jemaah Islamiyah was established in 1993 in an area of Indonesia known for high levels of poverty, social and political marginalisation and poor governance. By the end of the 1990s, it had established a regional alliance called the Rabitatul Mujahidin (the International Mujahideen Association) that provided a framework for cooperation among like-minded groups, especially those in Malaysia and Southern Thailand. It also set up cells, operational bases and sanctuaries in Singapore, Thailand and the Southern Philippines. This regionally focused early history does not diminish the importance of extraregional drivers in Jemaah Islamiyah's regionalisation. The Afghan War of the 1980s was a 'watershed' moment for the group, as its members were among the thousands of volunteers from the Muslim world who fought together against the Soviet army over a prolonged period of time, in the process building up close ties with each other that were evident in subsequent decades. Even in Afghanistan, however, Jemaah Islamiyah tended to develop its closest ties with other groups engaged in the war against the Soviets that came from its home region, like the Moro Islamic Liberation Front (MILF).

Jemaah Islamiyah has also prioritised the development of cooperative links with pre-existing national separatist movements. In doing so, it has taken advantage of the region's porous land and maritime borders and long-standing informal trade and criminal networks to facilitate regional

---

53 E. Stepanova, 'Regionalization of Violent Jihadism and Beyond: The Case of Daesh', PONARS Eurasia, 5 July 2016, www.ponarseurasia.org/article/regionalization-violent-jihadism-and-beyond-case-daesh.
54 Barber, 'The Evolution of Al Qaeda's Global Network and Al Qaeda Core's Position Within It'.

expansion.[55] In this sense, the group provides an interesting, and quite representative, example of a regional actor that embraced Al Qaeda's globalist philosophy and benefited from the networks it built in Afghanistan in the 1980s without abandoning its own distinctive local character or its reliance on historic regional 'kin groups, marital alliances, cliques and religious schools'.[56]

The economist Alan Krueger and others have argued that there is no 'systematic empirical' evidence to back up the argument that economic deprivation and a lack of education are the main drivers of terror.[57] Even in cases where both are contributing factors to terrorist violence, they will still take a very local form. For example, the economic neglect, poor governance and excessive centralisation experienced by inhabitants of regions like Celebes (now known as Sulawesi) that have contributed to the rise of Jemaah Islamiyah in the late twentieth century can be traced back to the earliest days of the seventeenth century, with the arrival of the Dutch East India Company in the territories that now make up present-day Indonesia. The marginalisation and isolation of the country's interior from national power centres – a classic driver of regionalisation – was the norm over the entire course of the Dutch colonial era and continued even after independence in the mid-twentieth century.[58]

In the post-9/11 era, Jemaah Islamiyah did align itself with an 'Islamist discourse of forming a supranational Islamic state', and it even coordinated Al Qaeda meetings in South East Asia, as Mohamed Nawab Bin Mohamed Osman has recounted.[59] At the same time, the group's ideological adherence to a radical Islamic vision extending across South East Asia predates its involvement with the Al Qaeda phenomenon. Its origins can be found in the programme of groups like Darul Islam (DI) during the later anticolonial period and early era of independence in the 1940s. Jemaah Islamiyah's ideological, familial, clan and educational links to Darul Islam were so

55 L. C. Sebastián, *The ASEAN response to terrorism*, UNISCI Discussion Papers, 2, Universidad Complutense de Madrid (May 2003), pp. 1–8, https://www.ucm.es/data/cont/media/www/pag-72539/Leonard.pdf.
56 D. M. Jones, 'Informal Networks in Southeast Asia: The Case of Jemaah Islamiah and Its Affiliates', in D. M. Jones, A. Lane and P. Schulte, *Terrorism, Security and the Power of Informal Networks* (Cheltenham, Edward Elgar, 2002), p. 166.
57 A. B. Krueger, *What Makes a Terrorist: Economics and the Roots of Terrorism* (Princeton, Princeton University Press, 2018).
58 A. Rabasa, S. Boraz et al., *Ungoverned Territories: Understanding and Reducing Terrorism Risks* (Santa Monica, Rand Corporation, 2007), p. 111.
59 M. N. Bin Mohamed Osman, 'Regionalization of Terrorism: Jemaah Islamiyah in South East Asia', in J. Saikia and E. Stepanova (eds.), *Terrorism: Patterns of Internationalization* (New Delhi, Sage, 2009).

evident that on its launch it was widely assumed to be a faction of the earlier group.[60]

Regionalisation, Transnationalism and the Case for Historical Continuity

Regardless of the historic time period in which they exist, most terror groups can be described as transnational in some form or fashion. Apart from having implications for any discussion on the regionalisation of terror, this also complicates attempts to categorise specific terror groups as 'old' or 'new' solely, or even partly, on the basis of whether they have rejected a traditional hierarchical organisation and embraced a more horizontal or network-focused structure.

Duyvesteyn has specifically challenged the idea that transnationalism and cross-border networks in themselves are evidence of the existence of a 'new' kind of terrorism. Instead, she identifies many nominally national non-state violent actors from earlier times that operated transnationally and relied on networks to function during their most active years. The Japanese Red Army is one example. Founded in Lebanon in 1971, even after it called a halt to its international terror activity it established no formal base in Japan.[61] Similarly, Kassel's more focused research has illuminated how the anarchist movement of the late nineteenth and early twentieth centuries included several autonomous but interconnected groups across a wide region linked by a transnational network-based structure.[62]

One can find many other examples of what might be widely viewed as 'old' terror groups, including those well known for their explicitly narrow national ambitions, that did not limit their activities to one national territory. The Irish Republican Army (IRA), in both its earlier and more recent iterations, had two consistent objectives: to drive the British out of Northern Ireland and to unify the island of Ireland. Yet, from the 1970s onwards, it planned or carried out major operations across Europe, in Germany, the Netherlands and Gibraltar as well as in mainland Britain

60 Jones, 'Informal Networks in Southeast Asia'.
61 I. Duyvesteyn, 'How New Is the New Terrorism?', *Studies in Conflict and Terrorism* 27/5 (2004). See also M. Crenshaw, 'The Debate over "New" vs. "Old" Terrorism', in I. A. Karawan, W. McCormack and S. E. Reynolds (eds.), *Values and Violence: Intangible Aspects of Terrorism* (Dordrecht, Springer, 2008).
62 W. Kassel, 'Terrorism and the International Anarchist Movement of the Late Nineteenth and Early Twentieth Centuries', *Studies in Conflict and Terrorism* 32/3 (2009).

and built networks with other terror groups in the wider region, including ETA.[63]

Similarly, as Matthew Levitt has noted, even the most radical Palestinian groups that emerged during the era of decolonisation in the late 1960s and 1970s, such as George Habash's Popular Front for the Liberation of Palestine (PFLP), limited their objectives to the destruction of only one state – Israel.[64] Yet, in quantitative terms, the PFLP, alongside Yasser Arafat's Palestine Liberation Organization (PLO) and other Palestinian factions, were responsible for more attacks in the wider Middle East and Europe than on Israeli soil. Between July 1968 and the end of 1972, for example, Palestinian groups claimed responsibility for major attacks on airlines or aviation facilities in Jordan (twice), Lebanon (once), Italy (three times), Greece (three times), Switzerland (twice), Germany (twice), the Netherlands (once) and Belgium (once). Transnational terror on the regional or extraregional level should also be considered in qualitative as well as quantitative terms. The Tamil Tigers undertook hundreds of suicide operations in Sri Lanka, but the group's most significant attack occurred regionally, with the assassination of Rajiv Gandhi on the outskirts of the Indian city of Chennai in 1991. This represented the first ever killing of a prime-minister-in-waiting of another country by a foreign armed group.[65]

As noted above, almost all terror groups, including those claiming explicitly subnational goals and agendas, have acted transnationally. Not all transnational action is, however, necessarily evidence of the regionalisation of terror. One complex case that underscores this point is Hezbollah. The Shia group is a major player in the political, socio-economic and security life of Lebanon. The group has also looked to underscore its 'Lebanonisation' by framing its military role in terms of defending the country from Israeli aggression. Its spokesmen, especially in the post-9/11 era, publicly stressed that the group had no interests outside of Lebanon's borders. In reality, by the mid-1990s, Hezbollah had already claimed responsibility for attacks in Turkey and Belgium, as well against French economic targets in Iran and Jewish communal institutions in Argentina. More recently, Hezbollah has been accused of operating cells in Kuwait, Bahrain and Yemen and has openly

63 P. Jackson, 'The IRA's Foreign Connections', *BBC NewsOnline*, 14 August 2001, http://news.bbc.co.uk/2/hi/1490663.stm.
64 M. Levitt, *Hamas: Politics, Charity, and Terrorism in the Service of Jihad* (New Haven, Yale University Press, 2006), p. 33.
65 M. Sarvananthan, '"Terrorism" or "Liberation"? Towards a Distinction: A Case Study of the Armed Struggle of the Liberation Tigers of Tamil Eelam (LTTE)', *Perspectives on Terrorism* 12/2 (April 2018), https://papers.ssrn.com/sol3/papers.cfm?abstract_id=3172218.

acknowledged its involvement in Egypt and Iraq. It has also played a central and very public military role, alongside Iran, in support of the Assad regime over the course of the civil war in Syria.[66]

A far more clear-cut case of regionalisation is Al Qaeda in the Islamic Maghreb (AQIM), established in Algeria in 2003 as the Salafist Group for Preaching and Combat (GSPC). From its launch it was, as Marret described it, a 'Glocal'[67] organisation engaged both locally and further afield. However, its impact has primarily been a function of its regionalisation. In the mid-2000s, it expanded its operations into Mali and Niger, setting up training camps to support local affiliate groups.[68] It also gradually developed ties with a range of other radical groups across North Africa, including Morocco (the Moroccan Islamic Combatant Group), Libya (the Libyan Islamic Fighting Group) and Tunisia (the Tunisian Fighting Group).[69]

The AQIM case is a good example of how terror groups can embrace regionalisation in order to overcome the erosion of their influence at home. The group's cross-regional expansion peaked at those times when it faced the most intense domestic pressure from the counterterror campaign waged by the Algerian government. As the group acknowledged in one public statement: 'The destruction of war, the difficulty of the present situation, and the unified coalition of our enemies against us, make it necessary for us to confront this coalition with our own coalition.'[70] This culminated in the intensification of AQIM's engagement in Northern Mali, where state control was weaker than in Algeria and where much of the local Tuareg population supported the separatist aspirations of the National Movement for the Liberation of Azawad (MNLA). By 2012, AQIM had become a full participant in the Tuareg anti-government struggle, establishing itself in the process as a significant threat to the Mali state.[71]

Regionalisation has also provided other vulnerable terror groups with a way of distancing themselves from stronger state actors intent on undermining or neutralising them. In 2004–5, the Saudi government stepped up its

---

66 CNAS, 'The Regionalization of Hizbullah', Center for New American Century, Washington DC, 13 April 2009, www.cnas.org/publications/blog/the-regionalization-of-hizballah. See also R. Shanahan, 'Hizbullah as a Regional Brand: Not All Parties Are Equal', *Australian Journal of International Affairs* 71/2 (2017).
67 J. L. Marret, 'Al-Qaeda in Islamic Maghreb: A "Glocal" Organization', *Studies in Conflict and Terrorism* 31/6 (2008).
68 Bonner and Van Natta, Jr., 'Regional Terrorist Groups Pose Growing Threat, Experts Warn'.
69 Marret, 'Al-Qaeda in Islamic Maghreb', p. 543.   70 Bacon, 'Alliance Hubs', p. 11.
71 B. Didier, 'The Regionalization of Counter-Terrorism Strategies in the Sahel: The G5 as a Challenge for Transatlantic Relations', CEPOB #10.18, College of Europe Policy Brief, Bruges, June 2018, pp. 2–5, www.coleurope.eu/system/tdf/research-paper/didier_cepob_10-18.pdf?file=1&type=node&id=44989&force=.

counterterror campaign against Al Qaeda in the Arabian Peninsula (AQAP) following a series of attacks across the kingdom. The authorities rounded up suspected extremists, shut down money-laundering operations and drew up new plans to ready themselves for attacks on ports and airports, oil infrastructure and critical water and power facilities. This counterterror programme was highly effective. In 2004 alone, nineteen out of the twenty-six suspects on Saudi Arabia's most wanted terror list were either captured or killed.

This pushed AQAP, described at the time by Crown Prince Abdullah as a 'deviant' group and a 'scourge',[72] out of the kingdom and into neighbouring Yemen. Despite their displacement, those forced into Yemen took advantage of the lack of government control to find shelter, build new networks, attract more followers and gain access to training and weapons. By 2008–9, AQAP was able to relaunch operations against Saudi Arabia, including a daring assassination attempt on Saudi Arabia's deputy interior minister, Mohammed bin Nayef. The operation was carried out on Saudi soil by a twenty-three-year-old Saudi citizen, Abdullah Asiri, but the plot was conceived, and the perpetrator was trained, in Yemen.[73]

Ekaterina Stepanova has argued that, alongside shared beliefs, values, identities and practices, the capacity of terror groups to 'take advantage' of 'bottom-up' regionalisation is an important explanation as to why some violent non-state actors develop into resilient terror movements and others do not.[74] The AQAP case is another good example of how vulnerable terror groups can use regionalisation not only to gain new material resources and followers but also as a way to consolidate resilience through gaining geographic distance from stronger adversaries.

Throughout history, as Tore Refslund Hamming has noted, 'contestation and competition'[75] has often defined the interrelationship between various insurgent and terrorist groups. Regionalisation can provide groups with a way to overcome the challenges associated with operating in such

---

72 A. H. Cordesman and N. Obaid, *Al-Qaeda in Saudi Arabia: Asymmetric Threats and Islamist Extremists* (Washington, DC, Center for Strategic and International Studies, 2005), p. 11, www.csis.org/analysis/al-qaeda-saudi-arabia.
73 K. Coates Ulrichsen, 'The Geopolitics of Insecurity in the Horn of Africa and the Arabian Peninsula', *Middle East Policy* 18/2 (Summer 2011), www.mepc.org/geopolitics-insecurity-horn-africa-and-arabian-peninsula.
74 Stepanova, 'Regionalization of Violent Jihadism and Beyond'.
75 T. R. Hamming, 'Jihadi Competition and Political Preferences', *Perspectives on Terrorism* 11/6 (2017), www.terrorismanalysts.com/pt/index.php/pot/article/view/657/html. See also B. Phillips, 'Enemies with Benefits? Violent Rivalry and Terrorist Group Longevity', *Journal of Peace Research* 52/1 (2015).

a highly competitive environment. In 2017, for example, several North African groups loyal to Al Qaeda – including AQIM's Saharan branch, Ansar Din, Al-Murabitun and the Macina Liberation Front – joined together under the banner of the Group in Support of Islam and Muslims (GSIM). They did so in order to counter the threat they faced from increasingly influential and powerful ISIS-affiliated region actors who wanted to undermine their ambitions.[76]

This is not always an effective approach, and its success can be hampered if the group in question lacks dynamism or exists in a regional environment that prevents the process of regionalisation from taking place. During the 1980s, the West German Red Army Faction attempted to launch a region-wide network across Europe made up of like-minded terror groups – including France's Direct Action (AD), Belgium's Communist Combatant Cells (CCC) and Italy's Red Brigades.[77] Unable to overcome falling support for leftist ideologies and anticolonial causes in the final decade of the Cold War, this attempt at resilience-building through regionalisation failed, and the Red Army Faction dissolved in the 1990s.

Terrorism and Regionalisation: The Case for a Historical Perspective

Terror groups invariably reflect, represent and embrace the intellectual, political, socio-economic and technological developments of their time. For example, the rapid urbanisation and industrialisation of the nineteenth century led to the politicisation of insurgent groups across Europe.[78] Today's non-state violent actors are also a product of contemporary drivers and trends, including globalisation and technological advances that have transformed beyond recognition the contemporary security environment. This has necessitated a reimagining of the ways that we think about the role of geography, economics, the law and even state sovereignty on the regional level. At the same time, it is important to locate this current reality in its historical context.

A historical approach to the regionalisation of terror can allow for a more rounded analysis of the relevant interconnected issues by providing the opportunity to use a wide variety of primary and secondary sources that

---

76 Didier, 'The Regionalization of Counter-Terrorism Strategies in the Sahel', p. 2.
77 Bacon, 'Alliance Hubs', p. 18.
78 I. Sánchez-Cuenca, *The Historical Roots of Political Violence* (Cambridge, Cambridge University Press, 2019), p. 24.

are often not examined in social science research – court decisions, the minutes and records of group meetings, letters, diaries, declarations and proclamations. Removing specific start and end points for any analysis and adopting a longer time frame in thinking about the relationship between regionalisation and terror can also help us see variations in the 'synergistic interplay'[79] between 'top-down' and 'bottom-up' pressures and processes that drive regionalisation over different periods of history.

Past research has shown how the specific strategic objectives of a violent non-state actor on the intra-state level can determine the geographic location of its endeavour. Separatist groups attempting to gain independence in a particular part of a state's territory tend to focus their violence on that area; insurgents who are intent on overthrowing the state tend to fight nearer to the capital city or other places where the institutions of power are located.[80] Likewise, the physical location or relocation of terror groups to a particular territory can be an important consequence of regionalisation. Yet, in terms of causality and interdependence, this does not necessarily tell us anything about why they are established there in the first place. Nor does it explain internal dynamics within the group itself, including structures, memberships, resources and goals, but also historical memory and the traditions that drive location and relocation.[81] In these terms, a historical approach can help us to clarify better whether regionalisation is a centrifugal force pushing boundaries of terror from within or a centripetal factor that serves, at best, as a secondary driver of the process.

An historical perspective can also help us to understand better the regionalisation of terror in the current era by illuminating the different ways in which regions themselves have evolved gradually over the course of history. For example, a cultural geography approach, which assumes deep links between cultures and the physical geography of the environments in which they have evolved, can help us think about the regionalisation of terror outside of spatial terms and beyond existing legal and political boundaries.[82] Instead, we can

---

79 A. Moghadam, 'Top-Down and Bottom-Up Innovation in Terrorism: The Case of the 9/11 Attacks', International Institute for Counter-Terrorism (ICT), Working Paper 18, Herzliya, July 2013, p. 36, www.ict.org.il/UserFiles/ICTWPS%20-%20Assaf%20Moghadam%20-%2018.pdf.
80 W. H. Moore and S. M. Shellman, 'Conceptualizing a New School of Political Conflict and Terrorism Studies: From Attributes to Behavior and Why Policy Makers Will Care', Perspectives on Terrorism 2/12 (2008), www.terrorismanalysts.com/pt/index.php/pot/article/view/58/html.
81 J. N. Shapiro, The Terrorist's Dilemma: Managing Violent Covert Organizations (Princeton, Princeton University Press, 2013).
82 A. Philippopoulos-Mihalopoulos, 'Spatial Justice: Law and the Geography of Withdrawal', International Journal of Law in Context 6/3 (2010).

examine how cultures are formed in specific geographical spaces and, more importantly for the purposes of this chapter, how non-material factors including identity, ideology, power, meaning and values transform regions in ways that facilitate the regionalisation of terror.

To take one important example, it is widely held that the contemporary era has seen the rise of 'religious, internationalist [and] nomadic' networks,[83] and that these networks have facilitated, and even empowered, violent non-state actors. We also know that, throughout history, powerful ideologies, both religious and secular, transcended national boundaries with ease. A historical approach that takes into account the role of non-material factors in transforming regions over history can illuminate more clearly how shared ideologies over a longer time frame have contributed to contemporary processes of regionalisation. In particular, this can help us to assess the extent to which today's regionalisation is driven by the desire to promote and spread these long-held values and beliefs through physical expansion across different parts of the wider home region.

A historical approach can also help us to consider more deeply the importance of horizontal diffusion in the process of regionalisation, whereby relations evolve between actors located in the same region who share the same grievances, identities and goals but who have little or no history of formal contact with each other. One relevant example for this study is the evolving interactions between the Muslim communities of Indonesia and North Malaysia and the minority Muslim communities of southern Thailand and the Philippines over successive generations.[84] Beyond illuminating the significance of long-held ideologies, values and beliefs in driving the regionalisation of terror, a historical approach can also help us understand the contribution of other kinds of non-state identities and the role of cross-regional networks including clan and tribal loyalties to regionalisation in general and the regionalisation of terror in particular.

Today there are numerous online sources and databases that track terror attacks worldwide through the collection of detailed information on intra-regional and cross-regional patterns of terror under the categories of

---

[83] D. M. Jones and M. L. Smith, 'The Changing Security Agenda in Southeast Asia: Globalization, New Terror, and the Delusions of Regionalism', *Studies in Conflict and Terrorism* 24/4 (2001), p. 280.

[84] See W. Berenschot, H. Nordholt and L. Bakker (eds.), *Citizenship and Democratization in Southeast Asia* (Leiden and Boston, Brill, 2017).

frequency and deadliness.[85] There is wide-ranging agreement that these resources have 'transformed' the study of terrorism.[86] One of the major limitations of using the historical approach to understand the interrelationship between regionalisation and terror is the lack of accurate, especially real-time, data collection methods that allow for quantitative and qualitative analysis on the number, type and effectiveness of terror attacks during past periods of history. As Joshua Tschantret, one of the few scholars to attempt to build a terrorism database that predates the twentieth century, has acknowledged, 'the ability to generalize terrorism research across time is hindered by data limitations'.[87] This in turn has made research somewhat blind to historical trends.

Nevertheless, even the most cursory qualitative historical survey of non-state violence across different regions over different time periods underscores the extent to which terror is geographically concentrated and occurs disproportionately in different regions at different times, and that specific territories within particular regions have experienced far more terrorist violence than other parts of the same region. Building on this, the historical approach can illuminate the factors and conditions specific to particular regions with a history of terrorism, or other related forms of violence including insurgency and guerilla warfare. These can include the availability of reliable sources of informal income; the availability of adequate infrastructure and operational access; weak state governance; and favourable demographic and social conditions.[88]

In turn, this can shed light on the (uneven) distribution of terrorism across the world's regions and can help us to understand the reasons for such variations in cross-regional and intra-regional patterns of terror in the contemporary world. This has two potential practical benefits. The first is that it facilitates our efforts to understand more clearly why some specific territories in particular regions are being more easily exploited by violent non-state

---

[85] S. Pinero Kluch and A. Vaux, 'The Non-random Nature of Terrorism: An Exploration of Where and How Global Trends of Terrorism Have Developed over 40 Years', *Studies in Conflict and Terrorism* 39/12 (2016); C. C. Alcantara, '46 Years of Terrorist Attacks in Europe Visualized', *Washington Post*, 17 July 2017, www.washingtonpost.com/gdpr-consent/?destination=%2fgraphics%2fworld%2fa-history-of-terrorism-in-europe%2f%3f.

[86] See, for example, M. Crenshaw, 'Terrorism Research: The Record', *International Interactions* 40/4 (2014), p. 557.

[87] J. Tschantret, 'The Old Terrorism: A Dataset, 1860–1969', *International Interactions* 45/5 (2019). The dataset developed in this research contains 263 terrorist groups, which he defines as politically motivated, violent non-state actors, operating during the hundred-year period between 1860 and 1969.

[88] Rabasa, Boraz et al., *Ungoverned Territories*, p. 16.

actors than others in the present period. The second is that it can assist our efforts to identify those regions, and then pinpoint specific territories within those regions which are more likely to experience non-state violence at the hands of terrorist groups in the future.

It is often assumed that terror groups operating on the regional level prefer the non-territorial agility that comes with not being anchored to one particular territory or state. There are certainly advantages that come with being 'de-territorialised'. That said, many terror groups, especially those denied a permanent base elsewhere, often do look to regionalise across ungoverned or poorly governed territories that offer the potential to serve as safe havens or operational hubs. These 'grey zones'[89] are often 'historical regions in their truest sense': local areas that in the past had 'a cultural, ethnic, linguistic or political basis, regardless of present-day borders as well as an identity which is not understood, or considered by the contemporary world'.[90]

Russia and the former Soviet republics have experienced more terror-related fatalities than any other part of Europe since the end of the Cold War. One of the most violent regions in the former Soviet Union is the North Caucasus, which in recent years has served as a home base for a number of dedicated Islamist terror groups.[91] Examining this phenomenon in terms of the historic evolution of violent non-state activity in the region clarifies our understanding greatly. Notably, it highlights clearly that those areas that currently play host to the most active terror groups – Chechnya, Ingushetia and Kabardino-Balkaria – also had the most developed informal economies, the weakest state control and the most porous borders in the wider region in previous centuries. This made them highly natural bases for regional resistance to tsarist Russia's imperial ambitions, just as they now serve a similar function for Islamist opponents of the Russian post-Soviet state.

Since beginning its terror campaign in the early 2000s in north-eastern Nigeria, Boko Haram has not only been preoccupied with establishing a caliphate across Nigeria. It has also consistently addressed the socio-economic grievances experienced by local Muslim communities in one of

---

89 S. A. Kayani, R. Q. Ahmed and M. Shoaib, 'Regionalization of Political Violence: Arab Levant and Rise of Islamic State', *The Dialogue* 2/1 (October–December 2014), p. 4.
90 T. Gullberg, 'The Primacy of the Nation and Regional Identity: Carinthia, Burgenland and State-Formation after the Dissolution of the Dynastic System', in S. Tägil (ed.), *Regions in Central Europe: The Legacy of History* (London, Hurst & Co. Publishers, 1999), p. 151.
91 E. Pokalova, 'The North Caucasus: From Mass Mobilization to International Terrorism', *Small Wars and Insurgencies* 28/3 (2017); E. Pokalova, 'Islamic Radicalization in Russia's North Caucasus: Lessons from Russia's Handling of Religious Revival', *Journal of Balkan and Near Eastern Studies* 21/2 (2019).

the world's most economically deprived regions at the hands of indifferent, predominantly Christian, southern elites. The fact that the group openly pledged allegiance to ISIS at the same time as it regionalised, first into Northern Cameroon in early 2014 and then into Southern Niger and Western Chad in early 2015, has fuelled the impression that this was first and foremost an international, or at least extraregional, development.[92] It is true that Boko Haram embraced a process of regionalisation in part to attract new recruits from across its wider region and to draw on valuable training and support from other local groups.

Local factors are also important to consider. Interestingly, in terms of the points raised above, Boko Haram's regionalisation efforts took place within the boundaries of the nineteenth-century Bornu Empire, which covers some of the most ungoverned areas of what is today north-eastern Nigeria, the northern tip of Cameroon, south-western Chad and north-eastern Niger.[93] Likewise, another contemporary terror hotspot, the Sahal region, running south of the Sahara Desert and stretching east–west across the breadth of the African continent, also has a long history of weak governmental control and is home to centuries-old smuggling routes that run through Northern Mali and the Mauritania–Algeria borders.[94]

The famed philosopher Isaiah Berlin once noted that history 'details the differences among events'.[95] As the above demonstrates, the ways that terror groups and networks spread out across a region are not only a function of their contemporary goals and drivers. They are also a response to local, region-specific factors, including historical and cultural memories and experiences. One of the main advantages of adopting a historical approach to thinking about the regionalisation of terror is that it facilitates, or even requires, a long-term perspective on the causes and consequences of non-state violence that might not otherwise occur. Connected to this, by framing our investigation in historical terms we can also move beyond the natural tendency to think primarily, or even solely, about terror groups and the choices they make to regulate their own existence in terms of broad, generic

---

92 See, for example, H. Onapajo, U. Okeke Uzodike and A. Whetho, 'Boko Haram Terrorism in Nigeria: The International Dimension', *South African Journal of International Affairs* 19/3 (2012) and M. Goerg and S. Dembinski, 'Boko Haram Is Now a Global Threat', *Real Clear World*, 19 March 2015, www.realclearworld.com/articles/2015/03/19/boko_haram_is_now_a_global_threat_111059.html.
93 E. Karmon, 'Boko Haram's International Reach', *Perspectives on Terrorism* 8/1 (2014), www.terrorismanalysts.com/pt/index.php/pot/article/view/326/html.
94 Marret, 'Al-Qaeda in Islamic Maghreb', p. 547.
95 I. Berlin, 'History and Theory: The Concept of Scientific History', *History and Theory* 1/1 (1960).

economic, political, ideological and sociocultural drivers. Of course, some, or even all, of these factors will likely play a role in explaining the regionalisation of terror, but their significance will almost always be best understood if viewed from a local perspective.

Finally, a historical approach to the regionalisation of terror adds value to discussions on some of the most important, not to say controversial, debates addressed in the scholarly literature on terrorism, issues which have been discussed in detail in this chapter: the commonalities and differences between 'new' and 'old' terrorism; the interrelationship between terror tactics adopted by state and non-state actors; the distinctions, and lack thereof, between terror on the national and transnational levels; and even the appropriate state actor responses to terror, not only in terms of sovereignty, but also in terms of local interests and cultural, historical and political traditions and perspectives. In other words, thinking about the regionalisation of terror in historical terms ultimately serves to underscore one important reality, often ignored in terrorism studies: and that is, to paraphrase John Dewey, the American philosopher and social reformer, the local is the only universal upon which terror is built.

Further Reading

R. J. Bunker (ed.), *Networks, Terrorism and Global Insurgency* (London and New York, Routledge, 2005)

D. M. Jones, A. Lane and P. Schulte, *Terrorism, Security and the Power of Informal Networks* (Cheltenham, Edward Elgar, 2002)

E. D. Mansfield and E. Solingen, 'Regionalism', *Annual Review of Political Science* 13 (2010)

J. Saikia and E. Stepanova (eds.), *Terrorism: Patterns of Internationalization* (New Delhi, Sage, 2009)

F. Söderbaum, *Rethinking Regionalism* (London, Palgrave Macmillan, 2016)

5

A Processual Approach to Political Violence

How History Matters

LORENZO BOSI

> 'Men make their own history, but they do not make it just as they please; they do not make it under circumstances chosen by themselves, but under circumstances directly found, and given and transmitted from the past.'[1]

The long-term tendency in the scholarly literature has been to approach political violence as an outcome, as a discrete event in its own right, coming out of nowhere and relatively disconnected from history. Scholars have generally preferred to search for the most powerful predictor for a large number of cases (e.g. political, economic, organisational, cultural system), in an attempt to explain why collective actors adopt violent forms of action at a specific moment in time (i.e. root causes of political violence). They have thus shown an interest in the synchronic or 'snapshot' view of the studied phenomena, given that they are in search of a 'magic formula' for stopping political violence, rather than a means of explaining it. Moreover, strictly connected to this interest in a synchronic approach, these studies have mostly shown the uncritical use of existing terrorism data sets, media and official documents, as well as secondary sources.[2] Paul Pierson's critique of political science seems to apply very well also to political violence research:

> Both in what we seek to explain and in our search for explanations, we focus on the immediate – we look for causes and outcomes that are both temporally contiguous and rapidly unfolding. In the process, we miss a lot. There are important things that we do not see at all, and what we do see we often misunderstand.[3]

---

[1] K. Marx, 'The Eighteenth Brumaire of Louis Bonaparte', in T. Carver (ed.), *Marx: Later Political Writings* (Cambridge, Cambridge University Press, 1996), p. 32.
[2] L. Bosi, 'État des savirs et pistes de recherche sur la violence politique', *Critique internationale* 54 (2012).
[3] P. Pierson, *Politics in Time, History, Institutions, and Social Analysis* (Princeton, Princeton University Press, 2004), p. 79.

This chapter, rather than focusing on causal factors, explains political violence as a process, where the actions of differently situated actors are embedded in complex webs of sociopolitical relations, which are formed and transformed, in a constant state of flux. These relations do not start from scratch, but gradually shift through time, both shaped by history and shaping history. In other words, they affect and dynamically transform the process, thereby influencing the actual image and meaning of political violence at a given moment, in a given context. It is often forgotten that the concept of political violence is highly context-dependent, so that violent political behaviour at one time or in one space may not be recognised as such in another period or space. The concept of political violence itself is therefore a moving target. In this chapter, in referring to political violence I speak of 'a heterogeneous repertoire of actions aimed at inflicting physical, psychological and symbolic damage on individuals and/or property with the intention of influencing various audiences in order to effect or resist political, social, and/or cultural change'.[4]

A processual approach allows us to counter the ahistoricity and lack of context that characterises much of the work on political violence,[5] instead moving towards a dynamic, gradual and procedural perspective on how and when political violence develops. This means rejecting 'all attempts to explain human behaviour or social processes solely in terms of the categorical attributes of actors, whether individual or collective'.[6] In advancing such an approach, it is important to underline, as Stefan Malthaner has clearly pointed out,[7] that over the last two decades, processual approaches have become increasingly prominent in various subfields of research on political violence. Furthermore, several leading scholars in research on political violence have consistently insisted on analysing political violence within its historical, social and political context, developing contextual and process-oriented perspectives.[8]

---

4 L. Bosi, N. O'Dochartaigh and D. Pisoiu, 'Contextualising Political Violence', in L. Bosi, N. O'Dochartaigh and D. Pisoiu (eds.), *Political Violence in Context: Time, Space and Milieu* (Colchester, ECPR Press, 2015), p. 1.
5 R. Jackson, M. B. Smyth and J. Gunning, *Critical Terrorism Studies: A New Research Agenda* (New York, Taylor & Francis, 2009).
6 M. Emirbayer and J. Goodwin, 'Network Analysis, Culture, and the Problem of Agency', *American Journal of Sociology* 99 (1994), p. 1414.
7 S. Malthaner, 'Processes of Political Violence and the Dynamics of Situational Interaction', *International Journal of Conflict and Violence* 11 (2017).
8 M. Crenshaw, 'Thoughts on Relating Terrorism to Historical Contexts', in M. Crenshaw (ed.), *Terrorism in Context* (Pennsylvania, Pennsylvania State University Press, 1995); M. Crenshaw, *Explaining Terrorism: Causes, Processes and Consequences* (New York, Routledge, 2011); R. English, *Terrorism: How to Respond* (Oxford, Oxford University Press, 2009); R. English, *Armed Struggle* (London, MacMillan, 2003); J. Horgan, *The Psychology of Terrorism* (New York, Routledge, 2005); S. Malthaner,

The processual approach adopted in this chapter aims to reconstruct the historical understanding of how and when the Brigate Rosse (Red Brigades, henceforth BR) decided to adopt political violence as a form of action, leading to its first premeditated political assassination. The chapter will reconstruct the intermediate steps within this process of radicalisation from the late 1960s up to 1976. Notwithstanding the existence, from the outset, of an ideology that justified the use of political violence, of a radical sociopolitical agenda and of environmental stimuli for aggression, the BR's progression towards political assassinations as a strategic form of action was not inevitable. As Brubaker and Laitin have pointed out, 'even where violence is clearly rooted in pre-existing conflict, it should not be treated as a natural, self-explanatory outgrowth of such conflict, something that occurs automatically when the conflict reaches a certain intensity'.[9] The transition from structural causes to effects is not automatic, and we also need to take into account agency. A processual approach recognises structural conditions, while emphasising their less-than-determining character and the need to look at the relational processes put in motion by strategic choices. This attributes an important role to agency, and to the creativity with which armed groups can start new processes and make unexpected distinctions, with a capacity to transform social structures, while also recognising the limits of this creativity. Hence, the shift of the BR towards its first premeditated political assassination was contingent on a complex set of interactions between different actors, in the aftermath of the students' and workers' mobilisation of 1968–9.

The research conducted draws on a variety of qualitative sources: archival materials (biographical material, pamphlets, posters, leaflets, magazine reports, campaign officers' personal correspondence, political party records and programmes, parliamentary debates and official government reports), secondary sources, accounts taken from Italian newspapers, personal memoirs and autobiographies.

How History Matters in a Processual Approach to Political Violence

Time: Contingency and Conjuncture

Political violence is not a static occurrence that takes place in a fixed moment; rather, it is a process that unfolds over time. It develops in a non-linear fashion

---

Mobilizing the Faithful: The Relationship Between Militant Islamist Groups and Their Constituencies (Frankfurt and New York, Campus, 2011).

9 R. Brubaker and D. Laitin, 'Ethnic and Nationalist Violence', *Annual Review of Sociology* 24 (1998), p. 426.

along a continuum of patterns of violence, skipping steps or phases, remaining on a certain level or shifting back and forth, with different forms and levels temporarily coexisting in different spaces simultaneously. In contrast to static approaches, which consider actors independently of their interactions with others, a processual approach aims to reconstruct the interactive, unfolding, ongoing and open-ended nature of political violence within specific contexts. Those contexts must be understood as dynamic configurations of collective actors, rather than as static structures. Indeed, instead of conforming to a tendency to focus on immediate upheavals, or on presumably linear sequences of stages within the same form of political violence, it is crucial to analyse these processes if we are to understand the contingent, discontinuous, open-ended, unpredictable and fast-changing nature of violent conflicts. We must therefore acknowledge contingency and conjuncture in sequences of events that use violence,[10] and emphasise that a processual approach 'does not necessarily imply a simple deterministic account'.[11] As Ruud Koopmans has suggested,

> political processes consist of chains of many such sequences of innovation, selection (or not), and diffusion (or not), the end of one being at the same time the beginning of another. Time's arrow relentlessly pushes this process forward so that no sequence is ever repeated in the same way under the same circumstances.[12]

The processual approach allows us to imagine political violence as a long sequence of interactions involving many collective actors.

Sequences of Interactions

'When things happen within a sequence affects how they happen.'[13] A processual approach reconstructs when and how the choice of the form of action emerges gradually and diachronically, based on the interaction among actors when they are faced with strategic dilemmas, rather than on a mere behavioural response to the causal factors – such a response would limit the rich dynamic and open-ended

---

10 L. Bosi, C. Demetriou and S. Malthaner, *Dynamics of Political Violence: A Process-Oriented Perspective on Radicalization and the Escalation of Political Conflict* (Farnham, Ashgate, 2014), p. 4.
11 M. Taylor and J. Horgan, 'A Conceptual Framework for Addressing Psychological Process in the Development of the Terrorist', *Terrorism and Political Violence* 18 (2006), p. 590.
12 R. Koopmans, 'Protest in Time and Space: The Evolution of Waves of Contention', in D. Snow, S. Soule and H. Kriesi (eds.), *The Blackwell Companion to Social Movements* (Oxford, Blackwell, 2004), p. 41.
13 C. Tilly, *Big Structures, Large Processes, Huge Comparisons* (New York, The Russell Sage Foundation, 1984), p. 14.

nature of sociopolitical complexity. As illustrated by Doug McAdam in relation to the tactical innovations of the Civil Rights movement, tactical interaction between insurgents and opponents occurs 'in chess-like fashion in which one tries to offset the moves of the other'.[14] The goal of a processual approach is to reconstruct the temporal steps of a chronological sequence and how these steps connect to each other. Thus describing a path is to explain the process that enriches our understanding of complex political violent dynamics. 'When the adoption of a certain form of action is taken, whether this occurs before, during, or after a certain period, and how an actor arrives to that choice clearly affects the explanatory value of this choice.'[15] The order of steps produces an effect: if A precedes B and C, the outcome will be different than if A follows B and C. As Pierson puts it, 'it is not the past per se but the unfolding of processes over time that is theoretically central'.[16] From this perspective, we aim to understand when things happen in order to explain how they unfold into processes: 'to describe the unfolding of a process is to explain the process'.[17] Therefore, causality is 'conceived not as a relationship between dependent and independent variables, but as a property of the dynamics that they generate'.[18] This type of explanation is fundamentally a retrospective analysis, arranged in time sequences of 'what follows what' in the emergence, development, decline and impact of political violence.[19]

Historical Analysis

A processual approach aims to gain a temporal understanding of how complex social processes gradually unfold over time. This time-sensitive approach starts from the premises that context continuously changes and that collective action is the result of a dynamic interaction among relational actors rather than the outcome of pre-existing structures. It is also the result of earlier attempts to provoke social change. A processual approach can, then, hardly get anywhere without a meticulous historical analysis,[20] since

---

14 D. McAdam, 'Tactical Innovation and the Pace of Insurgency', *American Sociological Review* 48 (1983), p. 736.
15 L. Bosi and L. Zamponi, 'Paths Toward the Same Form of Collective Action: Direct Social Action in Times of Crisis in Italy', *Social Forces* (2020), p. 3.
16 P. Pierson, 'Increasing Returns, Path Dependence, and the Study of Politics', *American Political Science Review* 94 (2000), p. 264.
17 E. Alimi, C. Demetriou and L. Bosi, *The Dynamics of Radicalization* (Oxford, Oxford University Press, 2015), p. 34.
18 Bosi and Zamponi, 'Paths Toward the Same Form of Collective Action', p. 3.
19 D. McAdam, S. Tarrow and C. Tilly, *Dynamics of Contention* (Cambridge, Cambridge University Press, 2001), p. 3.
20 In this chapter I refer to the strong definition of history as Charles Tilly has described it: 'We can adopt either a weak or a strong definition of historical analysis. The weak

specific outcomes can be explained only by adopting an extensive temporal frame of reference. In a processual approach, history matters because time and temporality matter. As Charles Tilly has written, 'if political sociology is to escape from the cramped prison of the present, it must address directly the ways in which time and place affect the character of political processes'.[21] In fact, collective actors are 'historical', which means that they are embedded in concrete circumstances and relationships that do not start from scratch.[22] A processual approach considers the rise and fall of collective actors' actions across time, bringing history and interaction into close dialogue. It starts from the premise that collective action, including political violence, is a dynamic historical construction that continuously changes. Collective action, then, emerges, develops, advances and dissipates over time. Being intrinsically historical, such an approach embraces a depiction of social reality 'in dynamic, continuous and processual terms'.[23] It is an inductive–deductive approach, which – whilst drawing on the existing body of knowledge in the formulation of research questions and the clarification of concepts, based on a strong familiarity with relevant theories – is also data-driven in that it allows new insights and conceptual developments to emerge, when the history of the case under analysis is considered to be consistent with or challenging existing theories. As James Mahoney suggests, in reference to process-tracing, whose goal is theory development, 'these theories apply to the case at hand, but they remain general because they draw on more general theories and because they suggest more general propositions, including potentially ones not previously specified in the literature'.[24] A processual approach takes a middle ground between reductionism and idiographic ethnography, undertaking – as Tilly suggests – 'serious historical work without getting lost in historical particularism'.[25]

> version simply deals with events and processes that have taken place before the present. All study of the past, in the weak version, constitutes historical analysis. The strong version demands more. It identifies ways that a) when and where an event or process occurs affects b) how it occurs, c) why it occurs, and d) with what consequences it occurs' (C. Tilly, 'Historical Analysis of Political Processes', in J. Turner (ed.), *Handbook of Sociological Theory* (Berlin, Springer, 2001), p. 570).
> 21 Tilly, 'Historical Analysis of Political Processes', p. 567.
> 22 Marx, 'The Eighteenth Brumaire of Louis Bonaparte'; P. Staniland, *Networks of Rebellion: Explaining Insurgent Cohesion and Collapse* (Ithaca, NY, Cornell University Press, 2014).
> 23 M. Emirbayer, 'Manifesto for a Relational Sociology', *American Journal of Sociology* 103 (1997), p. 281.
> 24 J. Mahoney, 'Process Tracing and Historical Explanation', *Security Studies* 24 (2015), p. 217.
> 25 Tilly, 'Historical Analysis of Political Processes', p. 571.

Contextualising Political Violence

Challenging the 'de-contextual revolution' that generally characterises the social science literature,[26] the field of Social Movement Studies has suggested that we must situate political violence in the context of broader episodes of popular contention, and during long periods of time, if we want to explain its dynamic emergence, development and demise as well as its outcomes.[27] 'In order to reduce the structuralist bias, we should grasp the contextual dimension, not as a set of determining causes, addressed mechanically and from above, but as conducive elements, which refer to the characteristics of the environment, the collective actors and the individuals.'[28] We need to move away from an exclusive focus on the actions of armed groups and avoid positing them as separate from, and in opposition to, a given context. As Pierson observes, 'thinking about context means thinking about relationships'.[29] 'If we do not go relational', Tilly writes, 'we will not explain [political violence] ... All this amounts to saying that [political violence] is a strategy, that the strategy involves interactions among political actors, and that to explain the adoption of such a strategy we have no choice but to analyse it as part of a political process.'[30] This implies that we must investigate what Bosi, Demetriou and Malthaner term a relational field 'that includes state-agents, counter-movements, audiences, as well as groups and organisations which belong to the same movement – all of whom shape the evolution of the conflict as they are linked by asymmetrical power relations'.[31] Hence, we need to shift our focus to the study of interactions between collective actors across time, to an analysis of the way they make sense of and give meaning to the context in which they are embedded. Such collective actors, as McAdam and his colleagues suggest, 'are not neatly bounded, self-propelling entities with fixed attributes, but socially embedded and constituted beings who interact incessantly with other such beings and undergo modifications of their boundaries and attributes as they interact'.[32] Collective actors are profoundly interdependent on their efforts; choices are made in

---

26 Pierson, *Politics in Time*.
27 L. Bosi and S. Malthaner, 'Political Violence', in D. Della Porta and M. Diani (eds.), *Oxford Handbook of Social Movements* (Oxford, Oxford University Press, 2015).
28 M. Bennani-Chraibi, 'Beyond Structure and Contingency: Toward an Interactionist and Sequential Approach to the 2011 Uprisings', *Middle East Critique* 26 (2017), p. 376.
29 Pierson, *Politics in Time*, p. 171.
30 C. Tilly, 'Terror as Strategy and Relational Process', *International Journal of Comparative Sociology* 46 (2005), p. 21.
31 Bosi, Demetriou and Malthaner, *Dynamics of Political Violence*, p. 2.
32 McAdam, Tarrow and Tilly, *Dynamics of Contention*, p. 56.

anticipation of, and in reaction to, those of their counterparts. Aims are not long-lasting, but continuously adapted based on the interpretation of past experiences and future expectations. 'Rather than [a] comparison that generalizes across abstractly conceived variables, or schematic ideal types as in the Weberian tradition', as Joseph Ruane and Jennifer Todd suggest, 'this approach reconstructs complex contextualized unities out of simpler elements and identifies their specific dynamic.'[33] This perspective entails the contextualisation of political violence in three ways: first, it considers this form of action as a component of broader repertoires of action, without the willingness to equate violent forms of action with non-violent ones; second, political violence emerges, then, from interactive processes within heterogeneous arenas of actors, in which strategic choices become intertwined with self-reinforcing dynamics; third, political violence means locating it within larger political and social conflicts as well as shifting forms of control and political arenas that create opportunities for and constraints on political actors. Analysing political violence in context allows us to examine questions about how and when, rather than why, a group or an individual engages in violence, persists in using this repertoire of action, and eventually disengages from it. A similar approach thereby de-exceptionalises and de-essentialises political violence by considering it to be part of repertoires of action that include violent as well as non-violent forms of action.[34] Contextualising political violence implies a historically sensitive enquiry. Tracing the process through which political violence occurs implies for a processual approach recognising the interaction of multiple players.

The Red Brigades' Path to Political Assassination

Conflict Escalation: State Repression, Neo-fascist Violence and the Extra-Parliamentary Leftist Groups

In the aftermath of the Second World War, the Italian political system observed a stalemate whereby the Partito Comunista Italiano (Italian Communist Party, henceforth PCI) was forced into opposition from 1947 onwards, while the Democrazia Cristiana (Christian Democrats, henceforth DC) governed the country through patronage policies and periodic bouts of

---

33 J. Ruane and J. Todd, 'Social Movements, Long-term Processes, and Ethnic Division in Northern Ireland', in L. Bosi and G. DeFazio (eds.), *The Troubles in Northern Ireland and Theories of Social Movements* (Amsterdam, Amsterdam University Press, 2017), pp. 225–6.
34 Bosi, Demetriou and Malthaner, *Dynamics of Political Violence*.

severe repression, legitimated by the 'Red Threat'.[35] However, at the beginning of the 1960s, the Cold War 'thaw' process and the ongoing secularisation of Italian society shaped the conditions for transcending the left–right division at the level of elite politics. Such an early depolarisation was instrumental for the first centre-left governments, commencing from December 1963. The DC started to involve the Partito Socialista Italiano (Socialist Italian Party, henceforth PSI) in coalition governments, in order to open itself to the 'moderate' left.[36] These developments, as well as the promised 'season of reforms' (with regard to education, pensions and planning), raised great hopes for change and new demands in the country.

At this stage, collective actors saw new 'political opportunities' opening up, allowing them to push the government towards more progressive agendas;[37] part of their calculation was that the centre-left government would be more tolerant towards dissent, since the PSI 'could ill afford to be identified with repression'.[38] Inspired, to some degree, by the global revolt mounting in different Western societies in those years, people started taking to the streets with non-violent marches, sit-ins, mass assemblies, occupations of public buildings, unofficial strikes and so on.[39] As in other countries, the popular challenge was essentially an anti-authoritarian revolt, in which people demanded more democratic decision-making, rejected over-bureaucratisation and aimed for a more humanist understanding of politics. Initially led by students, who took to the streets in 1966, this wave of protests attracted different parts of Italian society, from 1969 onwards mostly workers. A consistent part of this mass mobilisation was made up of different militant groups and organisations, such as Il Manifesto, Lotta Continua, Potere Operaio and Avanguaria Operaia, as well as other minor ones. This was the Extra-Parliamentary Left.[40]

From 1969 onwards, non-violent protest was countered by, first of all, heavy state repression, where security forces charged crowds with jeeps and used tear gas on demonstrators, occasionally causing fatalities among

---

35 G. Crainz, *Il paese mancato: Dal miracolo economico agli anni ottanta* (Rome, Donzelli editore, 2005).
36 P. Ginsborg, *History of Contemporary Italy: Society and Politics, 1943–1988* (London, Penguin, 1990).
37 D. McAdam, *Political Process and the Development of Black Insurgency, 1930–70* (Chicago, University of Chicago Press, 1982); S. Tarrow, *Democracy and Disorder* (Oxford, Clarendon Press, 1989); Koopmans, 'Protest in Time and Space'.
38 S. Tarrow, *Power in Movement: Social Movements and Contentious Politics*, 3rd ed. (Cambridge, Cambridge University Press, 2011), p. 99.
39 Tarrow, *Democracy and Disorder*.
40 R. Lumley, *States of Emergency: Cultures of Revolt in Italy 1968–78* (London, Verso, 1990); Tarrow, *Democracy and Disorder*.

protestors and bystanders;[41] secondly, violence perpetrated by right-wing collective actors, who feared that the country could possibly become the target of worldwide communist forces or who deemed the centre-left government to be incapable of ensuring law and order in the face of mass mobilisation;[42] thirdly, indiscriminate killings,[43] orchestrated through a collaboration between different branches of the security forces, the Italian intelligence service (SID), the military, the upper echelons of the state administration, right-wing militants and the American CIA,[44] with the aim to push the Italian state to respond to the 'communist spectre' by suppressing the entire left.[45]

For the Extra-Parliamentary Left such responses were part of a conspiratorial, anti-leftist 'strategy of tension' which revealed the incapacity of the Italian state to break away from its authoritarian, fascist past. This prompted a general shift among these collective actors, towards vigilante and paramilitary operations as a means of defending street mobilisation, and Italian society generally, from the possibility of a fascist *coup d'état*. The security forces' 'policing of protest'[46] and the countermovement[47] violent strategies were fundamental for the onset of violence in the BR episode. The groups and organisations that belonged to the Extra-Parliamentary Left prided themselves on being the avant-garde, viewing themselves as workerist forces fighting for revolutionary change. They were also in a better position to resist the militarisation of the conflict imposed by security forces and by the neo-fascist countermovement. Sequences of interactions between the Extra-Parliamentary Left, the security forces and the countermovement gradually developed through reciprocal adaptation with innovative turns, so that each actor's choices were influenced by those of other actors. What kept these different collective actors united within the same movement was

---

41 D. Della Porta and H. Reiter, *Polizia e protesta: L'ordine pubblico dalla liberazione ai 'no global'* (Bologna, Il Mulino, 2003), p. 209.
42 F. Ferraresi, *Threats to Democracy: The Radical Right in Italy after the War* (Princeton, Princeton University Press, 1996).
43 On 12 December 1969, a bomb exploded in Milan, killing sixteen people and injuring ninety. This was not the first bomb to explode in the country in this period, nor would it be the last. After the bomb in Milan, other bombs exploded, including notable mass murders throughout the 1970s and early 1980s.
44 L. Pellegrino, *Luci sulle stragi per la comprensione dell'eversione* (Milan, Lupetti, 1996), p. 144.
45 Crainz, *Il paese mancato*, pp. 481–5.
46 D. Della Porta, *Political Violence and the State* (New York, Cambridge University Press, 1995).
47 D. Meyer and S. Staggenborg, 'Movements, Countermovements, and the Structure of Political Opportunity', *American Journal of Sociology* 101 (1996).

not only the sharp and unequivocal objection to the authoritarian features of the state, and the chronic ills and malfunctioning of the democratic system, but also, and in a related vein, their common criticism of the institutional left (i.e. PSI, PCI and the main trade unions), judged for being revisionist. They could no longer wait for a revolutionary situation to present itself. Yet, despite the existence of militant rhetoric and revolutionary ideologies, and despite such slogans as 'Smash the bourgeois state, don't change it', the rallies and marches organised by these collective actors were still predominantly non-violent, up until the early 1970s.

The Emergence of the BR: The Armed Propaganda

It was in this sociopolitical context that the BR was announced for the first time, on 20 October 1970, in the bulletin *Foglio di Sinistra Proletaria*. The BR's origins are to be found in the merging of several workers' and students' militant organisations. In an interview released for the weekly magazine *Espresso*, in 1974, the BR auto-defined its ideological background in these terms: 'Our ideological mould is communist. Our reference points are Marxism–Leninism, the Chinese Cultural Revolution, and the ongoing experiences of metropolitan guerrilla movements.'[48] As suggested by Donatella Della Porta, for the BR 'the working class [was] the revolutionary subject, the capitalist system [was] the enemy, the state [was] the guard dog of the bourgeoisie, and [the] Christian Democracy [was] its party'.[49] Like other left-wing militant groups of the time in Italy and internationally, the BR believed that it was no longer necessary to postpone the revolution until revolutionary conditions appeared. They thought it was possible to beat the oppressors of the working class by initiating a worldwide Marxist revolution to emancipate the oppressed.[50]

According to the BR, state repression and the 'strategy of tension' of the late 1960s and early 1970s embodied the authoritarian nature of the state; this, in turn, should be used to accelerate the working class's awareness of the need for armed organisations. References to the anti-fascist resistance and the spectre of a creeping civil war became central to a justification for violence. In a nutshell, the BR's strategy at this stage was to deafeat the system through

---

48 'A domanda rispondono', *Espresso*, 19 May 1974.
49 D. Della Porta, 'Terrorism in Context: Left-Wing Terrorism in Italy', in M. Crenshaw (ed.), *Terrorism in Context* (University Park: Pennsylvania State University Press, 1995), p. 125.
50 M. Albanese, *Tondini di ferro e bossoli di piombo: Una storia sociale delle Brigate Rosse* (Pisa, Pacini Editore, 2020).

exemplary actions, such as torching factory managers' motor vehicles and sabotaging industrial equipment, or breaking into factory offices and right-wing headquarters; through these actions, they sought to train the cadres of the group and propagate the only truly revolutionary political line – armed propaganda. These violent repertoires per se were not very different from those used by the more radical workers within the major factories; what set them apart was that they were designed as a continuous communication with the Extra-Parliamentary Left, aiming to demonstrate new possibilities of political action in a phase marked by a general decline of left-wing mobilisation.[51] During this phase the violence of the BR did not have human targets, but rather focused on symbolic property damage. The BR's violent actions were followed by the dissemination of explanatory texts, which defined such incidents as having two goals: to punish specific 'anti-worker' actions and to expose the secret management of capitalist power. The BR's violent actions did not target Italian society in general, but were, instead, designed to spark the workers' anger in their battle against the management and control of production and profits. 'The revolutionary struggle often takes place through secretly organised direct actions, but it is not our fault, but rather the fault of the repressive organisation of the bosses.'[52] Therefore, while the BR's initial violence was justified in defensive terms, it also had an offensive plan: to awaken awareness and activate commitment to the cause among the proletariat, without whom power could not be overturned. This is how the BR defined its strategy at this stage:

> The Red Brigades are the first sediments of the transformation process of what will become the armed political vanguard, the first armed steps in the direction of this construction ... Our point of view is that the armed struggle in Italy has to be conducted by a body that is a direct expression of the class movement and for that we are working on organising the factory workers in industrial centres and neighbourhood and metropolitan centres where a concentration of revolt and exploitation exists.[53]

In its first two years of operation, the BR was mainly active in large factories in Milan (Sit Siemens, Alfa Romeo, Magneti Marelli and Pirelli). Its leaders and rank and file participated openly in public activities, along with other organisations and with their supporters.

---

51 Della Porta, *Political Violence and the State*.
52 BR, 'Molti compagni o gruppi della sinistra rivoluzionaria', April 1971.
53 BR, 'Autointervista', September 1971.

From Armed Propaganda to Armed Struggle

In 1972, a first shift in the path of the BR occurred once it was pushed into clandestinity by the tightened repression of security forces, and in the aftermath of the national elections of May 1972, when the DC managed to form a centre-right government, constraining the opportunities of the Italian left. The PSI's exclusion from government, which at that time paralleled the traditional exclusion of the PCI, as well as the DC's turn towards the right and its readiness not only to block political changes but, more importantly, to overturn previously accomplished ones, were interpreted by the entire Italian left (i.e. political parties, trade unions and the Extra-Parliamentary Left) as unprecedentedly threatening. The shift of the governing coalition towards the right was viewed as a further sign of a state-backed project aimed at turning the young Italian Republic into an authoritarian regime. The PCI's fear of an imminent *coup d'état* similar to the one in Chile, which occurred in that same period, progressively precipitated the choice of the party's leadership to collaborate with other democratic forces – the 'historic compromise'. To promote this new strategy of compromise with moderate parliamentary forces, the PCI needed to appear as a reliable party and as a possible coalition partner, capable of taking governmental positions and maintaining stability in the country. Accordingly, the PCI withdrew its recognition from the Extra-Parliamentary Left and openly opposed its tactics, supporting many new laws meant to implement harsher repressive measures.

In this changed sociopolitical context, under the threat of what the BR considered as a neo-Gaullist restructuring of the state aimed at the 'centralisation of power, organisation of consent, institutionalised dispute and repressive law',[54] given also the threat induced by the strategic compromise between the DC and the PCI, and considering the timing of the security forces' crackdown on the BR, those militants who managed to stay out of prison reached the critical decision to renew and intensify the armed struggle. In January 1973 the BR wrote:

> The attack unleashed against us by the bourgeoisie in May sprang from their mistaken conviction that they could neutralise the political impact of the strategic proposal of armed struggle for communism by exploiting the organisational weakness which characterised us. This mistaken political evaluation is exactly what caused the police operation to fail, and we strengthened ourselves.[55]

---

54 Collettivo Politico Metropolitano, 'Lotta Sociale e organizzazione della metropoli', January 1970.
55 BR, 'Autointervista', January 1973.

The BR turned from a semi-clandestine organisation into a full-fledged clandestine organisation and concluded that it was necessary to start moving beyond the 'armed propaganda' in the factories and taking the struggle to the next level of intensity and lethality. As the BR later stated in one of its documents, 'the question of clandestinity was only posed in real terms after 2 May 1972. Up to then, enmeshed as we [BR] were in a situation of semi-legality, it was only seen in its tactical and defensive aspects rather than its strategic importance.'[56]

In only a few months the BR managed to expand its base of operation and support across Italy (Turin, Genoa, Venice/Mestre and Rome). These developments were accompanied by the compartmentalisation of the organisation's structure, now consisting of a Strategic Directorate (responsible for overall political and organisational guidance), an Executive Committee, urban and regional divisions, and brigade fronts which in turn were subdivided into cells. Caselli and Della Porta refer to this phase of the BR as its 'preparatory stage'.[57]

The BR's Shift Towards Political Assassinations: Strike the Heart of the State

The BR's shift towards a more violent repertoire came about gradually. The strategy behind the struggle moved from a focus on the national economic capital to an offensive against the state. Hence, its actions started to shift, strategically and progressively, from the local support of workers' struggles to more direct attacks on political targets, a shift meant to gain a wide social dimension. Rather than targeting only factories, the BR now started committing premeditated violent acts against the state and its 'fascist allies', such as politicians and state employees (i.e. judges, policemen and military officers). Its objectives were, on the one hand, to stop the neo-Gaullist, authoritarian attempt to transform the Italian democracy that had been 'born out of the Resistance'; on the other hand, to reveal the existence of secret links binding imperialist forces with political parties and the Italian state. This shift marked the evolution from low-level illegal actions, which remained mainly local and focused, towards a repertoire of action that involved proactive and deliberate violence against state representatives. Between 1974 and 1975, the BR's Strategic Directorate, via its 'Strategic Resolution', thus defined a 'new'

---

56 BR, 'Alcune questioni per la discussione sull'organizzazione', July 1974.
57 G. C. Caselli and D. Della Porta, 'The History of the Red Brigades: Organizational Structures and Strategies of Action (1970–1982)', in R. Catanzaro (ed.), *The Red Brigades and Left Wing Terrorism in Italy* (New York, St. Martin's Press, 1991), p. 78.

task: to attack and destroy capitalist power by 'striking the heart of the State', namely the imperialist state of the multinationals:

> the State becomes the direct expression of the will of the big multinational imperialistic groups, through a national focal point. In other words, the State becomes a specific function of the capitalistic development of the era of the multinational corporations' imperialism; it becomes the Imperialist Multinational State (SIM). Italian capitalism, therefore, is trying to exploit the present crisis in order to build the SIM.[58]

The counterterrorist efforts of the state apparatus, which involved 'widespread use of restrictive, preventive measures and of charges brought against activists and sympathizers',[59] and which extended to infiltrations into the organisation, resulted in the arrest and jailing – by September 1974 – of the BR's founding fathers.[60]

Increasingly isolated and struggling for its very survival, the BR was nonetheless able to muster resources and to channel them into a confrontation with the repressive apparatus of the state.[61] Being forced into the defensive and away from its initial 'armed propaganda' strategy inside the factories, BR militants who escaped captivity began to target political officials more directly; after all, from then on, its best form of defence was 'the attack on the heart of the State'. However, such a change in strategy was also possible due to a change in the composition of the armed organisation at the leadership level, first, and then at grassroots level. The BR's new leadership, which emerged after the arrest of its main leaders, saw violence as a means of sparking conflict within and between political parties, the state and its citizens. Consequently, it unleashed the latent 'civil war' from which a new communist order was expected to finally emerge.

> Parallel to the aggravation of regime crisis, with relentless frequency a process of counter-revolution is asserting itself, which unites the entire ruling class in the attempt to destroy the movement and the levels of autonomous and revolutionary organisation that the movement has produced. Well, if in the factories the Autonomia Operaia is strong enough to

---

58 BR, 'Risoluzione direzione strategica n. 1', April 1975.
59 H. Reiter and K. Weinhauer, 'Police and Political Violence in the 1960s and 1970s: Germany and Italy in a Comparative Perspective', *European Review of History* 14 (2007), p. 384.
60 D. Serafino, *La Lotta Armata a Genova: Dal Gruppo 22 Ottobre alle Brigate Rosse* (Pisa, Pacini Editore, 2016).
61 Della Porta, *Political Violence and the State*.

maintain a state of permanent insubordination and to conquer its own growing sphere of power, outside the factory it is still weak to the point of not being capable of opposing a resistance against the counter-revolution's attacks. For this reason, the forces of counter-revolution tend to shift the main contradiction outside the factories and to lead decisive battles in order to isolate the conflict within the factories, in order to better control and then destroy them.... The main contradiction is today that opposing the stack of counter-revolutionary forces. Because, if it is true that the regime crisis and the birth of a hardened and organised counter-revolution are the product of years of hard workers' and popular struggles, it is even truer that in order to win the mass movement, one must overcome today the spontaneous phase and organise oneself on the strategic terrain of the struggle for power. And the Working Class will conquer the power only through armed struggle.[62]

It was therefore not by coincidence that the target of the first premeditated lethal attack was the General Public Prosecutor of Genoa, Francesco Coco, who was killed along with two security guards in June 1976. As Caselli and Della Porta suggest, 'the triple assassination constituted a criminal bet to concentrate the forces of all regular militants who had avoided arrests (around ten) in the execution of an undertaking so sensational as to "relaunch" the BR, making it appear firmly in place and growing, regardless of the imprisonment of its "historic leaders"'.[63] With the violent attack on Coco, the BR wanted to assert, as David Moss has suggested in his in-depth analysis, 'that the "revolution" they represented could not be successfully halted by the use of ordinary judicial processes against participants'.[64]

Finally, it should also be stressed that the militarisation of the sociopolitical conflict the Italian state had provoked, and the detrimental influence of this situation on the mobilisation potential and readiness of the entire Extra-Parliamentary Left, became instrumental to the ramped-up radicalisation of the BR. In other words, the decline of mass movements produced a number of activists who had lost faith in legal and peaceful repertoires of action, and who therefore constituted a possible source of recruitment for clandestine organisations such as the BR. In the early 1970s the BR was one of several semi-clandestine organisations, but in the second half of the 1970s, it was recognised by both the security forces

---

[62] BR, 'Contro il neogollismo portare l'attacco al cuore dello stato', April 1974, quoted in G. DelVecchio, 'Political Violence as Shared Terrain of Militancy: Red Brigades, Social Movements and the Discourse on Arms in the Early Seventies', *Behavioral Sciences of Terrorism and Political Aggression* 8/3 (2016), p. 218.
[63] Caselli and Della Porta, 'The History of the Red Brigades', p. 83.
[64] D. Moss, *The Politics of Left-Wing Violence in Italy 1969–85* (London, Macmillan, 1989), pp. 69–70.

and other collective actors within the Extra-Parliamentary Left to be the most committed radical force within the left-wing milieu. Indeed, the changing of the guard within the organisation was meaningful in this regard, as the new recruits pushed forward meaningful organisational and ideological innovations, and tended to be less disciplined and loyal to the ideological orthodoxy of the armed organisation.[65] Not surprisingly, the following period (from 1977 to 1979) saw a dramatic rise in the lethality of violence; the injury and death toll as a result of BR-led violent operations almost tripled.

Conclusions

The proposed analytical framework aims to have resonance beyond the BR's path investigated in this chapter, and, for that matter, even beyond Western Europe during the 1970s, and may also be relevant to studies pitched at difference scales, whether international or subnational. Political violence, as the case of the BR has shown, needs to be explained within the complex web of contingent relationships and strategic interactions between different collective actors, 'as it happens' at specific points in history. The proposed approach situates our explanation of political violence in an ongoing, process-sensitive political and historical analysis, which is theoretically informed and capable of capturing the dynamic, relational interplay among multiple collective actors within the political system, therefore not only focusing on the armed group itself. Hence, any reading of the ways in which, and when, political violence is adopted needs to pay attention to the shifting and mutually influencing interactions between collective actors over an extended period of time. This means not only that we should not limit our analysis of the interrelation between collective actors to one moment in time, but that we must also capture their movements across time, in order to provide a fuller explanation of how and when these processes occur. Such an approach avoids falling into the trap of creating a rigid and deterministic vision of development sequences. It also offers more dynamic explanations of political violence processes by placing a stronger emphasis on time and history.

---

65 L. Bosi and D. Della Porta, 'Micro-Mobilization into Armed Groups: The Ideological, Instrumental and Solidaristic Paths', *Qualitative Sociology* 35 (2012).

Further Reading

E. Alimi, C. Demetriou and L. Bosi, *The Dynamics of Radicalization* (Oxford, Oxford University Press, 2015)

L. Bosi and D. Della Porta, 'Micro-Mobilization into Armed Groups: The Ideological, Instrumental and Solidaristic Paths', *Qualitative Sociology* 35 (2012)

L. Bosi, C. Demetriou and S. Malthaner, *Dynamics of Political Violence: A Process-Oriented Perspective on Radicalization and the Escalation of Political Conflict* (Farnham, Ashgate, 2014)

M. Crenshaw, *Explaining Terrorism: Causes, Processes and Consequences* (New York, Routledge, 2011)

C. Tilly, 'Terror as Strategy and Relational Process', *International Journal of Comparative Sociology* 46 (2005)

6

Terrorism, History and Neighbouring Disciplines in the Academy

BERNHARD BLUMENAU

Terrorism,[1] as this book demonstrates, is a complicated phenomenon with a long and complex history. Analytically it is a difficult issue to grasp, dissect and analyse, to evaluate and respond to. As a consequence of this complexity, different academic disciplines ask different questions on terrorism. Lawyers are eager to assess legal implications of terrorism, so they wonder how it is defined in law – both domestic and international. What legislations, if any, apply? What penalties does it incur? Meanwhile, for political scientists and International Relations (IR) scholars, generalisability and predictability might be of more interest: one needs to understand terrorism, model and theorise it appropriately to be able to make estimates about current and future trends, and thus to be able to develop possible (policy-relevant) solutions. Sociologists, then again, could be more interested in the individual or social circumstances that drive people to 'go terrorist' and to place themselves outside the social – and legal – order. Psychologists might want to dig even deeper and understand why some people become terrorists when others do not, while philosophers might go to the other extreme and look at the overshadowing moral and ethical questions related to this kind of political violence. Historians, finally, could be seen as the generalists in the field of Terrorism Studies. Motivated by many questions that are also asked in other disciplines, they are intrigued by the complexities that define terrorism, its long-term patterns, changes and continuities, but also by very detailed case studies of individual incidents, groups, responses and characters. Traditionally, historians would pick up where other, more topically interested disciplines had left a matter.

[1] This chapter will not enter into the debate about how best to define 'terrorism'. Other chapters in this book offer much more insightful discussions of the notion. To provide an understanding of what is meant here by 'terrorism', the following working definition will be applied: terrorism is a strategy of violence used by sub-state actors to gain power and achieve certain political goals. It is intended to have psychological effects beyond the immediate targets. If used by the state, terrorism is meant to secure power for a certain person (normally the leader) or elite by means of a deliberate campaign of orchestrated violent intimidation involving agents of the authority.

Against the backdrop of time passing, sources becoming available and the extra level of objectivity that temporal distance (should) provide, historians are best suited to reassess a topic. They try to make sense of it, in its complexity, but always with an eye to the particularities of every case. Traditionally, too, historians are not good at generalising, or theorising. This would be for others to do. But these classic division lines between the disciplines have become more blurred as of late. Social scientists turn towards historical case studies for their works. In that sense, historians provide the raw materials needed which others then process into theories. But historians nowadays also look at other disciplines to guide their research questions, seeking help from legal scholars, political scientists or sociologists in order to de- and re-fine a historical project. As a consequence, scholarship in the social sciences and humanities has become more intertwined, old walls have shown cracks and new projects are emerging that are marked by a diversity of research questions and approaches. It is difficult to imagine a topic where such collaboration is more desirable – and can indeed be more fruitful – than on an issue as diverse as terrorism and within a field as undefined – and unrestrained – as Terrorism Studies.

The latter is not (maybe yet) an academic discipline in its own right. To the author's knowledge, no university has a department of Terrorism Studies. Centres, projects, programmes and research clusters do exist, however, but they are normally situated within departments of political science, sociology, international relations, history or war studies. As Sageman lamented, there is still an absence of a large body of core scholars in Terrorism Studies.[2] Rather, practitioners but also historians, sociologists, lawyers et al. venture into (and out of) the field because of an, often only temporary, interest in the matter of terrorism and political violence. This results in a lack of clarity on the phenomenon and a diversity of approaches. However, this is not only a disadvantage. Indeed, the lack of a core corpus of people constantly committed to Terrorism Studies means a constant circulation of scholars, but that also allows for a perpetual stream of new ideas, questions, sources (or data) and approaches. The field is constantly in flux, but so is terrorism itself.

It will be the purpose of this chapter to look at what history can offer for the study of terrorism, how interdisciplinarity can be fruitful, what new themes and approaches can be developed by venturing beyond traditional division lines of established disciplines, and finally, to assess the limitations of multidisciplinarity in terrorism research. Thereby, hopefully, this text will

---

2 M. Sageman, 'The Stagnation in Terrorism Research', *Terrorism and Political Violence*, 26/4 (2014).

encourage further academic cross-fertilisation to advance all our understanding of the puzzle that is terrorism.

Historical Approaches to Terrorism; or Why the Past Matters

In the early 2000s, one of the deans of the field of Terrorism Studies, David Rapoport, observed that 'no good history of terrorism exists'.[3] Fortunately, some progress could be noticed since this rather devastating verdict was passed. Historians have (re-)discovered terrorism as a field deserving of more investigation. As such though, political violence, in general, is nothing new to scholars of the past. The term 'terror' found its way into scholarship through the works of Edmund Burke, a politician and amateur historian of his times. In 1795, he wrote about Maximilien de Robespierre's 'la terreur', which was unleashed after the French Revolution. Robespierre saw 'terror' as something positive and virtuous, as a process that would lead to the purification of the post-revolutionary society. But, through his writings, Burke started the process that would give 'terror' the negative connotation it now occupies in general debate:

> Every other ground of stability, but from military force and terrour (*sic!*), is clean out of the question. To secure them further, they have a strong corps of irregulars, ready armed. Thousands of those Hell-hounds called Terrorists, whom they had shut up in Prison on their last Revolution, as the Satellites of Tyranny, are let loose on the people. The whole of their Government, in its origination, in its continuance, in all its actions, and in all its resources, is force; and nothing but force ... They differ nothing from all the preceding usurpations, but that to the same odium a good deal more of contempt is added. In this situation, notwithstanding all their military force, strengthened with the undisciplined power of the Terrorists, and the nearly general disarming of Paris, there would almost certainly have been before this an insurrection against them, but for one cause. The people of France languished for Peace.[4]

---

3 D. C. Rapoport, 'The Four Waves of Modern Terrorism', in A. Kurth Cronin and J. M. Ludes (eds.), *Attacking Terrorism: Elements of a Grand Strategy* (Washington, DC, Georgetown University Press, 2004), p. 68, n. 3.

4 E. Burke, F. Canavan and E. J. Payne, *Select Works of Edmund Burke: A New Imprint of the Payne Edition* (Indianapolis, Liberty Fund, 1999), pp. 359–60. In fact, attempts to give 'terrorist' a positive connotation continued for a while with social revolutionaries and perpetrators of acts of violence in tsarist Russia referring to themselves as 'terrorists' in order to differentiate themselves from ordinary murderers. Since then, however, hardly anybody call themselves terrorist anymore, opting instead for terms such as 'freedom fighters' or 'social revolutionaries'. See for instance C. Tilly, 'Terror, Terrorism, Terrorists', *Sociological Theory* 22/1 (2004); L. Stampnitzky, *Disciplining Terror: How Experts Invented 'Terrorism'* (Cambridge, Cambridge University Press, 2014). See also Frampton's chapter in this volume.

In this tradition, political violence, committed by the state against its people, has attracted attention for a long time. It might just not have been framed as 'terrorism', and authors of such studies would have probably not considered themselves as scholars in a field of 'Terrorism Studies'. This academic identity issue notwithstanding, individual histories of the political violence committed by the Holy Inquisition, witch-hunters, or dictators such as Joseph Stalin, Adolf Hitler or Mao Zedong have been written aplenty; and not only in the past twenty years.[5] Likewise, state-instigated violence, or that benevolently ignored by authorities, which occurred within the context of (de-)colonisation or ethnic and racial discrimination has also received a great deal of attention.[6] Lastly, violence against civilians that occurred within the context of armed conflict is also often subjected to the scrutiny of historians.[7] So, while political violence by the state – whether it was explicitly called 'terrorism' or not – has been a rather usual field for historians to populate, historical cases of non-state terrorism, committed by groups or individual actors, have been less attractive a topic for academics for a long time. Granted, some important works were published long before 2001. One of the early masters of Terrorism Studies, Walter Laqueur, for instance, wrote *A History of Terrorism* in 1977. Others have followed suit: Rapoport (*Fear and Trembling: Terrorism in Three Religious Traditions*, in 1983), Bruce Hoffman (with a significant historical overview in his book *Inside Terrorism*, first published in 1996), and Michael Burleigh (*Blood and Rage: A Cultural History of Terrorism*, in 2010), to

---

5 A general history of state terrorism is still to be written. For accounts of individual episodes of state-organised terror, see for instance I. Kershaw, *Hitler*, reprint ed. (London, Penguin, 2009); J. R. Harris, *The Great Fear: Stalin's Terror of the 1930s* (Oxford, Oxford University Press, 2016); B. P. Levack, *The Witch-Hunt in Early Modern Europe*, 4th ed. (London and New York, Routledge, 2015); T. Green, *Inquisition: The Reign of Fear* (London, Macmillan, 2008); T. Snyder, *Bloodlands: Europe Between Hitler and Stalin* (New York, Basic Books, 2012).

6 See for instance K. Wagner, *Amritsar 1919: An Empire of Fear and the Making of a Massacre* (New Haven, Yale University Press, 2019); D. Walter, *Colonial Violence: European Empires and the Use of Force* (London, C Hurst & Co. Publishers, 2017); D. Anderson, *Histories of the Hanged: Britain's Dirty War in Kenya and the End of Empire: Testimonies from the Mau Mau Rebellion in Kenya* (London, Weidenfeld & Nicholson, 2006); M. Thomas, *The French Colonial Mind: Violence, Military Encounters, and Colonialism* (Lincoln, University of Nebraska Press, 2012); M. Thomas, *Violence and Colonial Order* (Cambridge, Cambridge University Press, 2015); P. Dwyer and A. Nettelbeck (eds.), *Violence, Colonialism and Empire in the Modern World* (New York, Palgrave Macmillan, 2017); C. Elkins, *Britain's Gulag: The Brutal End of Empire in Kenya* (London, Bodley Head, 2014). Studies of the Ku Klux Klan could also be listed here.

7 Many of the works cited above also fall into this category, but the literature on war crimes and civilians in war is too vast to cite here.

mention just a few.[8] However, it is noteworthy that some of these scholars are not historians by origin. They were political scientists that dealt with terrorism of the past as a prelude to extensive studies of contemporary terrorism. This points to two important, and insightful, observations on historical enquiries into terrorism: firstly, political scientists, by studying a contemporary phenomenon, opened the door to, and underscored the importance of, historicising terrorism. Even today, the fact that an overview of the history of terrorism is still often the first part of any book on contemporary terrorism shows just how important it is to understand the genesis of the phenomenon. Terrorism does not occur out of a vacuum, it is embedded in a complex social, political, legal and thereby, yes, – historical – context. Without an appreciation of the latter it is impossible to understand current instances of terrorism. Secondly, scholars from other disciplines, through their topical investigations, have pointed historians into the right direction to explore this topic themselves. This academic cross-fertilisation is one of the first, and important, benefits of interdisciplinary approaches towards terrorism, and bears witness to the advantages that other disciplines can offer to historians.

Over the past few decades some progress has been made, and important studies written by historians have emerged. Many address the rather general evolution of terrorism.[9] Others attend to more specific aspects, cases or methods.[10] Some scholars have also examined the flip side of the coin: the challenges of developing responses to terrorism, or the actors

---

8 There is now an updated version of Laqueur's 1977 book: W. Laqueur, *A History of Terrorism: Expanded Edition* (New Brunswick, NJ, Transaction Publishers, 2016); D. C. Rapoport, 'Fear and Trembling: Terrorism in Three Religious Traditions', *American Political Science Review* 78/3 (1983); Hoffman's book is now out in a revised edition as well: B. Hoffman, *Inside Terrorism*, 3rd ed. (New York, Columbia University Press, 2017); M. Burleigh, *Blood and Rage: A Cultural History of Terrorism* (New York, HarperPerennial, 2010).

9 Such as the authors listed above. See also R. D. Law, *Terrorism: A History* (Cambridge, Polity Press, 2009); G. Chaliand and A. Blin, *The History of Terrorism: From Antiquity to ISIS* (Oakland, University of California Press, 2016).

10 See for instance the chapters in this volume or in C. Dietze and C. Verhoeven (eds.), *The Oxford Handbook of the History of Terrorism* (Oxford, Oxford University Press, 2014); J. Hänhimaki and B. Blumenau (eds.), *An International History of Terrorism: Western and Non-Western Experiences* (Abingdon and New York, Routledge, 2013); E. Chenoweth et al. (eds.), *The Oxford Handbook of Terrorism* (Oxford, Oxford University Press, 2019). Sectarian violence, for instance in Northern Ireland, has also received more attention than other cases of terrorism; see e.g. R. English, *Armed Struggle: The History of the IRA* (Oxford and New York, Oxford University Press, 2004); T. K. Wilson, *Frontiers of Violence: Conflict and Identity in Ulster and Upper Silesia 1918–1922* (Oxford and New York, Oxford University Press, 2010); or the works by J. Bowyer Bell.

involved in formulating them.[11] And lastly, new and non-traditional questions for the history of terrorism have also been asked: for instance regarding the role of women in terrorism, non-Western cases of terrorism, or less well-studied motivations behind terrorist acts, such as those committed by environmentalist groups.[12]

The history of terrorism is hence a subfield in ascent, a fact which is due partly to the important works from non-historians that made the lack of historical studies embarrassingly obvious and hence gave important impetuses to the evolution of historical research on the topic. And historical studies are needed indeed. For one, and as explained above, historians can provide the context for more topical studies by showing evolutions, trends and differences. With more research on older cases of terrorism becoming available, it is hence possible to discover the long-term, larger patterns that would normally remain opaque if one only dealt with current cases. For instance, one could easily assume that nationalist terror started in early twentieth-century Ireland, Israel/Palestine from the 1930s onwards, or Algeria in the 1950s. Whether examples of nationalist terror committed in tsarist Russia's vast empire at the beginning of the 1900s – such as the assassination of Russian Governor-General Nikolai Ivanovich Bobrikov by Finnish nationalist Eugen Schaumann in 1904 – would be equally readily mentioned is questionable.[13] Granted, one of the more devastating nationalist terror attacks of the early 1900s, the assassination of Archduke Franz Ferdinand in Sarajevo by Gavrilo Princip, might appear in such chronologies, mostly because it triggered the World War that followed. But whether interested scholars – possibly even historians – would look back even farther, much farther in history, and identify the Jewish Sicarii of ancient times, in the first century AD, operating against the Roman occupation of their lands, as a documented starting point of the lineage of

---

[11] Again, see some of the chapters in the collections cited above and also, for instance, R. English, *Terrorism: How to Respond* (Oxford, Oxford University Press, 2010); K. McConaghy, *Terrorism and the State: Intra-State Dynamics and the Response to Non-State Political Violence* (London, Palgrave Macmillan, 2017); B. Blumenau, *The United Nations and Terrorism: Germany, Multilateralism, and Antiterrorism Efforts in the 1970s* (Houndmills and New York, Palgrave Macmillan, 2014); R. B. Jensen, *The Battle Against Anarchist Terrorism: An International History, 1878–1934* (Cambridge and New York, Cambridge University Press, 2014).

[12] For a good overview of non-conventional themes in the history of terrorism, see for instance Dietze and Verhoeven (eds.), *Oxford Handbook of the History of Terrorism*.

[13] R. B. Jensen, 'The 1904 Assassination of Governor General Bobrikov: Tyrannicide, Anarchism, and the Expanding Scope of "Terrorism"', *Terrorism and Political Violence* 30/5 (2018).

nationalist terror is doubtful.[14] Yet, this view of the history of terrorism as a phenomenon of *longue durée* has important implications: for one, it emphasises that terrorism is nothing new. It is a somewhat usual if horrific side effect of political relations: a group in dissent and without the means to conventionally assume power might ultimately choose violence in order to implement their goals. Thus, any aspirations as to the complete eradication of terrorism are probably illusionist.

Secondly, this awareness provides some encouragement for reason and moderation when dealing with terrorism. The knowledge that humanity has always survived terrorism, that it is nothing new, that terrorism has occurred before, and will probably strike again, might take some steam off the debates about how to respond to terrorism, and thereby replace heated activism with cool-headed rationality.[15]

Thirdly, historical, long-term studies might provide impetus for current enquiries, especially for those conducted in other disciplines. It might provide useful insights for answering questions such as: a) Why does terrorism occur? (History might provide insightful answers as to the context of previous acts of terrorism, and why people and groups resorted to it; or did, in fact, not. Looking beyond ISIL and Al Qaeda might point to the explanatory importance of long-hatched grievances, cultural and religious factors, perceptions of suppression, occupation, inequality and others in producing terrorism.)[16] b) Why do some people turn terrorist, and others do not? (Again, pre-9/11 history offers a wealth of sources, including biographical ones, that offer important insights, which could also be useful for the present.) c) Why do women become terrorists? (One of the questions that has recently experienced a revival around the role of women joining the Islamic State, the phenomenon as such greatly predates ISIL. Women played a prominent role in many of the social-revolutionary groups of the 1970s and 1980s, as demonstrated by Ulrike Meinhof and Gudrun Ensslin, Margherita Cagol and Bernadine Dohrn. Yet women also

---

14 For an overview of the history of nationalist terror, see for instance R. English, 'Nationalism and Terrorism', in Chenoweth et al. (eds.), *The Oxford Handbook of Terrorism*; B. Blumenau, 'Nationalism, Terrorism, and the State – Historical Perspectives', in C. Carmichael, M. D'Auria and A. Roshwald (eds.), *The Cambridge History of Nationhood and Nationalism* (Cambridge, Cambridge University Press, forthcoming).

15 For a much more eloquent and sound assessment of how to respond to terrorism, see for instance English, *Terrorism*.

16 Equally interesting is to investigate why in certain circumstances terrorism did not materialise; see for instance N. Brooke, *Terrorism and Nationalism in the United Kingdom: The Absence of Noise* (New York, Palgrave Macmillan, 2018).

had a part in violent nationalist movements, for instance when Leila Khaled attempted to hijack a plane in 1970, and were of great importance in nineteenth-century Russian groups such as the Narodnaya Volya.)[17] d) Does terrorism actually work? (Taking a historical approach can offer important insights on where, whether and why terrorism has historically worked – or has not worked.)[18]

And finally, lessons from the past can be drawn upon to ask how terrorism ends. History with its excess supply of case studies provides a great laboratory in which other disciplines can test theories on why terrorism does come to an end – and it always does eventually.[19] All of these questions can be more soundly and convincingly answered by taking history into account. Thus, it does not only provide worthwhile scholarship of its own but also (re)sources to other disciplines as well as important lessons for policymakers and practitioners outside of academia.

Moreover, methodologically, the historian's resort to detailed analyses of often thousands of documents – primary sources from national, international and non-state archives; interviews; newspapers; images; and personal collections – allows for a detailed, meticulous and comprehensive assessment of a specific case or question. Faced with a lack of information in one repository, historians often resort to triangulation amongst sources, examining discrepancies or a suspicious absence of documentation. More often than not, this approach provides the most important insights, which can enrich other scholars' analysis and theorising of specific questions. In that sense, historians not only provide context and the 'final product' of analysis but are often equally useful in supplying the 'raw material' that non-historians can use for their own research. The increasingly more available online archives or

---

17 Arguably, a good long-term historical study of the role of women in terrorism is still to be written. For studies coming from the social sciences, see for instance C. E. Gentry and L. Sjoberg, *Beyond Mothers, Monsters, Whores: Thinking about Women's Violence in Global Politics* (London, Zed Books, 2015); J. Davis, *Women in Modern Terrorism: From Liberation Wars to Global Jihad and the Islamic State* (Lanham, Rowman & Littlefield, 2017); L. Sjoberg and C. E. Gentry (eds.), *Women, Gender, and Terrorism* (Athens, University of Georgia Press, 2011).

18 See for instance the insightful history on this question written by R. English, *Does Terrorism Work? A History* (Oxford, Oxford University Press, 2016); Muro's edited volume could also offer some complementary insights: D. Muro (ed.), *When Does Terrorism Work?* (London and New York, Routledge, 2018).

19 Social scientist Audrey Kurth Cronin has produced a fine book on this question, one that can, however, only serve as a starting point for any such enquiry. A. Kurth Cronin, *How Terrorism Ends: Understanding the Decline and Demise of Terrorist Campaigns* (Princeton, Princeton University Press, 2011).

resources that nowadays often accompany historical projects provide additional and readily available resources.

Another advantage of historical studies is that historians normally know – at least roughly – what happened, and hence the level of speculation is limited. With social scientists challenged to predict the future, historians have the arguably more enviable, but perhaps equally complex, task of predicting the past.

Historians are also often less reliant on, or restricted by, specific theories than scholars of adjacent disciplines. While the latter frequently see that as a shortcoming, the historians' approach actually offers some advantages. It allows them to investigate topics with an open mind, without being confined to specific assumptions of just one school of thought. A topic can thus be examined in full, and in its complex nature. An analysis of terrorism, which is an extremely multilayered topic, certainly benefits from such an unrestricted approach. On a somewhat similar point, historians are often criticised for shying away from providing generalisations and predictions. This could be a major factor to explain why social and political scientists are more prominent in the public debates around terrorism. Yet historians have important contributions to make to those, too. In fact, being unable (or unwilling) to predict a regularised future is no great flaw, if what is on offer instead is a historically informed and deep intuition about likely outcomes. Those might prove much more valuable than precise predictions, which all too often never materialise.

Intellectual exchange is no one-way street. Knowledge, questions and approaches can travel both ways and provide better research on terrorism and political violence across the board. After having examined what benefits a historical approach provides for the study of terrorism, the next section will attend to the many advantages that other disciplines can offer to historians.

Challenges for Historical Research on Terrorism and the Benefits of Multidisciplinarity

Historical research aims to assess a question in its complexity. No simple answers exist to any research question, and any monocausal endeavour to make sense of historical instances of, and responses to, terrorism will hardly be successful. Because of this complexity, historical research on terrorism is often faced with challenges. On the one hand, those can derive from the availability and reliability of sources. Without sufficient documentation it is difficult, if not impossible, to examine the past properly. On a topic as controversial as terrorism, the accessibility of sources is a serious challenge. Governmental documentation on terrorist events, terror groups or counter-terrorism responses is often classified as top secret, and hence not normally released when standard embargo periods for archival material have passed. This is all the truer when one wants to draw on material from intelligence agencies, that often have their own, and even more restrictive, access regulations. Criminal records or personal files can also be subjected to special embargo periods. As data protection and privacy regulations are getting tighter, access to personal information related to victims, or potentially also perpetrators, will also become more difficult to obtain. This is not a challenge unique to terrorism research, as scholars looking into other subjects (contentious and high-profile international negotiations for instance, defence-related matters, or issues around war and peace) can confirm. One way around this is to triangulate. For instance, with different national archives or collections having different access rules, multi-archival research might fill some of the gaps. The evolution of ever growing levels of interconnectedness of states, societies and people over the course of, at least, the past 150 years has as a flip side that topics of relevance to, and within, one country were certainly also keenly observed by others. The acts of terrorism committed by Narodnaya Volya in Russia, for instance, were certainly the subject of conversations between Russian authorities and foreign diplomats. Assassination attempts on heads of state – whether it was on Otto von Bismarck (1866) or Kaiser Wilhelm I (1863, 1878, 1883), Tsar Alexander II (1881), US President William McKinley (1901), Archduke Franz Ferdinand (1914) or Yugoslavian King Alexander I and French Prime Minister Louis Barthou (1934) – were surely of enough significance to be reported back to foreign capitals, including assessments of the circumstances and responses. In more recent times, prominent terror attacks have reaped enough global public attention (for instance Dawson's Field 1970, the Munich Olympics 1972 or the Tehran Hostages Crisis 1979–1981, not to mention 9/11) to garner interest in capitals around the world, not least in order to assess what that country's own vulnerability to terrorism could be. Consequently, documentation is likely to exist in many different archives. At the same time, information classified as top secret in one country might not necessarily be regarded as so sensitive elsewhere and might hence be subjected to a laxer declassification procedure. Diversification and triangulation of archival documentations is, thus, one way around the lack of material. Another way to mine information is by diversifying the genres of sources. Newspaper articles might offer interesting and insightful glimpses into the historical context of terror crises, and point at the controversies around responses to them. While factually potentially not overly reliable due to the proximity to the events, they do provide a great survey of the topics that were of importance at the time, of theories developed about terror groups, and of how terrorism fitted within the broader societal environment. As one of the main mechanisms of terrorism is the spreading of fear and hysteria, newspaper articles provide an excellent snapshot at the societal reception of the attacks, and of attempts at explaining them. They might also be great indicators as to where to dig deeper and what other factors to consider when going back to the archives. Oral history can be another useful resource. With all the justified caveats – are interviewees available? How solid is their recollection of events? What is their own bias and agenda? Can they speak freely? – oral history not only provides an appreciation of the zeitgeist and of the issues debated at the time. Personal recollections can also point the scholar in the direction of other repositories, sources or avenues to explore. Lastly, artworks and images can also help to interpret events or their context – and Northern Irish murals come immediately to mind here. Many other potential sources exist, such as textiles.[20] The challenge for historical research into terrorism, more so than on other historical topics, is hence to think creatively with regards to what sources could be used and where further information might be available. Ideally, any information found in one source should be corroborated elsewhere. This might not always be possible, but great care has to be taken to avoid falling into the traps provided by rumours, conspiracy theories and fading memories.[21]

On the other hand, historical research into terrorism is challenged by the complexity of 'terrorism'. At the beginning of a project (or at any stage of it, really), historians can often be overwhelmed by the nebulous nature of events, the multitude of factors to consider, explanations to assess and consequences to evaluate. It is here that other disciplines can offer some help. Given the complicated nature of terrorism and the responses it provokes, a historian often also needs to be a psychologist, criminologist, political scientists, lawyer, cultural and religious scholar, philosopher and possibly even a nuclear scientist, chemist, biologist, medical doctor and, increasingly

---

20 See for instance the role that textiles can play in dealing with violence, C. Andrä et al., 'Knowing Through Needlework: Curating the Difficult Knowledge of Conflict Textiles', *Critical Military Studies* (2019), www.tandfonline.com/loi/rcms20.
21 On the role and impact of such theories, see for instance A. Hänni, 'Secret Bedfellows? The KGB, Carlos the Jackal and Cold War Psychological Warfare', *Studies in Conflict and Terrorism* 43/1 (2020).

more so, economist and computer expert. With the days of polymaths long gone, few people have the capacity, time and resources to acquire expertise in all these fields. And yet they matter. For instance, one can only really appreciate multilateral responses to terrorism when one has a notion of how international regimes operate and how international law works. Studying individual terrorists, or an evaluation of the implications of any counterterrorism policy on the broader public, is also hardly possible without some basic understanding of psychology. Discussing nuclear, biological or chemical terrorism remains vague without some understanding of how these potential weapons work and what effects they can have. Explaining religious terrorism will be difficult without an appreciation for underlying philosophical, cultural and religious references. In order to make sense of these things, other disciplines have to be drawn in to help the historian. They can provide the knowledge and context needed in order to write accurate and reliable histories – not to mention interesting ones.

Secondly, other disciplines' scholarship can serve a different purpose as well. Articles and books written by scholars in these fields at the time of terrorism occurring can pinpoint important issues at the time. Simply because the historian has to be a generalist of sorts but cannot possibly be an expert on everything, relying on this literature can help to identify the core issues around a specific case of terrorism, a group, individual or indeed counterterrorism responses. If such a topic received a lot of scholarly attention at the time, for instance by lawyers or political scientists, this indicates that it was deemed important and that this topic probably deserves further attention from historians.

Thirdly, history can benefit from other disciplines by gaining some help in setting out the design and direction of a project. As mentioned above, historians do not traditionally operate from specific theories, although they certainly have conceptual perceptions that shape their research. But theories used in other disciplines can offer some advantages for historians. Without our being limited by them overly restrictively, they can provide some initial guidance when approaching a topic, thereby helping to formulate and structure the research questions. In other words, they can be the spotlights that focus initial attention on specific aspects of a very chaotic past, and that help provide a better fundamental understanding of a topic. Once some focus has been achieved, the historian can move beyond the restrictions of the theories and examine the topic more comprehensively.

Aside from conceptual guidance, other disciplines can provide new directions and angles from which to examine the past as well. Historians are often rumoured to be conservative in principle – not necessarily politically, but in the way they define their projects. For a long time, for instance, diplomatic history was deemed the best form of historical enquiry, the purest kind of history and most worthy to be pursued. This was partly due to the fact that diplomacy in general was seen as a great art and held in the highest esteem. But it can also be attributed to the notion that history, for a long time, was thought to be made by great (white) men (occasionally, perhaps, some more progressive scholars would concede that a woman might have had some background influence on those as well). The fact that most sources available were often of a diplomatic nature aided this view on the supremacy of diplomatic history. Yet, due to the social and political upheavals of the twentieth century, other genres of history would slowly enter the mainstream as well: for instance, social history, cultural history and economic history. This was a reaction to developments elsewhere. With the education and democratisation of (Western) societies, the general interest in topics such as economics, politics, sociology, cultural studies and anthropology grew, and fields of studies dedicated to them expanded. Their proliferation then prompted historical enquiries to look into such topics as well. Historians began to ask what was known about the life of the 'common man or woman' in past centuries. How did economies work in the past? And how did societies? In that sense, other disciplines fertilised historical research and helped new topics to emerge and new subdisciplines to develop. But developing new fields of historical research aside, other disciplines also helped shaping existing ones. In the wake of emancipation, for instance, feminism became a legitimate school of thought in the social sciences. This development subsequently also prompted historians, even in the traditional field of 'state histories', to look at the role of women, and to realise that often they were more than just passive and obedient wives. This is certainly true when looking at the history of terrorism.

Transnationalism was another notion that spilled into history from the social sciences. As a consequence of globalisation and the erosion of national borders, social movements across states gained importance, and modern states and societies cannot be understood without looking at them as well. Terrorists are a prime example of this development. From the exchange of ideas between the anarchists of the nineteenth century via joint Palestinian–German terror operations in the 1970s, to fanatics joining ISIS from all corners of the world, transnational developments have had a major impact on the evolution of terrorism. Governments, in turn, then had to take this into account and develop coordinated responses amongst themselves. It will be difficult to comprehensively examine (even national) antiterrorism efforts since the second half of the twentieth century without also looking at international efforts at cooperation and coordination.[22] And the very notion of seeing international organisations as subjects worthy of study in their own rights is something that was first developed in politics and IR and then found its way into historical research.

This period of spillover effects from other disciplines into history is not over. With climate change becoming more prominent on the political agenda and in other disciplines, 'the environment' as a topic is entering history as well, and studies on the impact that environmental factors have had on the past are proliferating.[23] The effects of climate change and environmental factors on terrorism will also receive more attention in Terrorism Studies in general, and the history of terrorism in particular. Studying environmentalist groups and their use of terror (or, perhaps, why they did not use it) is another related subject worthy of more attention.[24]

Likewise, attempts to readjust the focus away from the 'West' and to look at global history, and developments that occurred outside the transatlantic arena, have also spilled over from other disciplines into history. The realisation gained traction that, historically, many regions of the world were at least as advanced as Europe, if not more so (and at a much earlier time). This appreciation that history is not confined to what the white men did is also affecting the history of terrorism, with the awareness taking hold that instances of terrorism in non-European regions need much more attention.[25] For good research to materialise here, the impetus of non-European scholars will be essential.

---

22 And, as Jensen has shown, even when examining late nineteenth- and early twentieth-century efforts, one cannot avoid looking at international efforts at coordination; see Jensen, *The Battle Against Anarchist Terrorism*.

23 See for instance W. K. Klingaman and N. P. Klingaman, *The Year Without Summer* (New York, St. Martin's Press, 2013); W. Behringer, *A Cultural History of Climate* (Cambridge and Malden, Polity Press, 2009); W. Behringer, *Tambora and the Year Without a Summer: How a Volcano Plunged the World into Crisis* (Medford, Polity Press, 2019); S. Winchester, *Krakatoa: The Day the World Exploded: August 27, 1883* (London, Penguin, 2004). Methods from other disciplines, for instance ice cores, are also used to reconstruct history and to examine what impact humans have had on the environment. See for instance J. R. McConnell and others, 'Lead Pollution Recorded in Greenland Ice Indicates European Emissions Tracked Plagues, Wars, and Imperial Expansion During Antiquity', *Proceedings of the National Academy of Sciences* 115/22 (2018); S. Preunkert et al., 'Lead and Antimony in Basal Ice From Col Du Dome (French Alps) Dated with Radiocarbon: A Record of Pollution During Antiquity', *Geophysical Research Letters* 46/9 (2019).

24 See for instance K. M. Woodhouse, 'In Defense of Mother Earth', in Dietze and Verhoeven (eds.), *Oxford Handbook of the History of Terrorism*.

25 See for instance R. Uz Zaman, 'Bengal Terrorism and the Ambiguity of the Bengali Muslims', in J. Hanhimäki and B. Blumenau (eds.), *An International History of Terrorism: Western and Non-Western Experiences* (London and New York, Routledge, 2013). See also for instance the various relevant chapters in Dietze and Verhoeven (eds.), *Oxford Handbook of the History of Terrorism*.

The rise of economics as an academic discipline has also led to economic history becoming a burgeoning subfield. This has impacted Terrorism Studies and histories of terrorism, too, and will continue to do so. Questions are asked as to how terrorists have financed themselves. What was their relationship with organised crime? How can terrorism financing be stopped? All of which are questions that are being examined now, but their study would also benefit from more contributions from historians.[26]

Finally, advances in technology and the ever-growing importance of the 'hard' sciences also affect historical work. For instance, the evolution of 'modern' terrorism can hardly be understood without looking at technological progress. In the nineteenth century, dynamite, faster and cheaper travelling by train or steamboat, and the telegraph made modern terrorism possible in the first place; live TV broadcasts and air travel helped make it more terrifying in the twentieth century; and the Internet and cryptocurrencies are important tools for terrorism today. Counterterrorism, likewise, used technology to fight terror: from the *portrait parlé* of the early 1900s, via espionage hardware, metal detectors at airports, grid net searches to spy software, CCTV and drones. The lingering sword of Damocles, the prospect of terrorists using ABC (atomic, biological, chemical) weapons, further amplifies this necessity to appreciate the impact of technology on terrorism, historically and in the present.[27]

This list of how developments in other disciplines have had an impact on historical research in general, and the history of terrorism in particular, is by no means exhaustive. But it was meant to provide an idea of the extent to which the social sciences and other disciplines have helped historians to overcome old assumptions, to develop new ideas and focuses, and to try out new methods. This has, no doubt, made History as such – and certainly the whole subfield of the history of terrorism – more complex but also more complete. Other

---

26 T. Makarenko, 'The Crime–Terror Continuum: Tracing the Interplay Between Transnational Organised Crime and Terrorism', *Global Crime* 6/1 (2004); A. P. Schmid, 'Revisiting the Relationship Between International Terrorism and Transnational Organised Crime 22 Years Later', *The International Centre for Counter-terrorism – The Hague* 9 (2018); M. Freeman, *Financing Terrorism: Case Studies* (Farnham, Ashgate, 2012); T. J. Biersteker and S. E. Eckert (eds.), *Countering the Financing of Terrorism* (London and New York, Routledge, 2006).

27 For the impact of technology on terrorism, see for instance A. Larabee, 'Propaganda of the Deed', in Dietze and Verhoeven (eds.), *Oxford Handbook of the History of Terrorism*; S. Werrett, 'The Science of Destruction', in Dietze and Verhoeven (eds.), *Oxford Handbook of the History of Terrorism*; Jensen, *The Battle Against Anarchist Terrorism*, shows how early attempts at using technology affected international antiterrorism efforts in the late nineteenth and early twentieth centuries; for an account of how counterterrorism uses technology, see for instance P. Lehr, *Counter-Terrorism Technologies: A Critical Assessment* (New York, Springer, 2018).

disciplines have helped historians shape projects, just as historical studies, too, can be an immensely useful resource for non-historical scholars. This dialogue and cross-fertilisation is a most welcome development in the study of the incredibly complex and multilayered topic of terrorism.

Avenues for Future Historical Research on Terrorism

The section above has already signposted possible avenues for future research: the relationship, for instance, between environmental factors and political violence, including terrorism, is one such path. It would be interesting to see if external pressures have pushed people into violence in the past, and what could be learnt from that. What if, for instance, ice cores were to reveal that peoples in the past experienced unusual weather phenomena – draughts or floods for instance – and that the pressures that those created would correlate with episodes of political violence? The role of women in terrorism is another subject where more research is still needed. Scholarship is becoming available on their role in social-revolutionary groups since the 1970s, and some awareness exists on the part women played in nineteenth-century Russian anarchist terrorism. But what about other cases? What roles did women play in ethnic and nationalist terror groups? How exactly were women involved in actual terror operations? Were they just passive bystanders when it comes to religious terror? These questions become even more intriguing when looking back farther into history: what role, for instance, did women play in *la terreur* in revolutionary France? Or during Stalin's great purges? To what extent did Madame Mao influence her husband's campaigns of violence? Taking this even further, could one argue that the witch-hunts of the Middle Ages and Renaissance were in fact political violence instigated by the male authority in order to keep women down? There are many interesting projects yet to be conducted on this.

The interconnectedness of today's world comes with implications for historical research, too. As IR scholars turn more attention to how international organisations are dealing with terrorism today – and most of them are in one way or another – not much is yet known on how those organisations have developed this focus on terrorism and what they have done in the past.[28] A focus on understudied organisations such as the International Civil Aviation

---

28 For some studies, some of them historical, on the international community and antiterrorism, see for instance R. B. Jensen, 'The International Campaign Against Anarchist Terrorism, 1880–1930s', *Terrorism and Political Violence* 21/1 (2009);

Organization or the Red Cross would be particularly interesting. Here, too, IR and legal scholars could help historians in designing research questions and approaches that are fit to answer these questions.

Victims of terrorism are another aspect of terrorism that would benefit from further research. Again a topic that has recently garnered more attention in social sciences and psychology, it would also be interesting for historians to ask how victims have dealt with terrorism.[29] It is a cruel side effect of terrorism research that the perpetrators have managed to steal the spotlight of enquiries from those that were targeted, adding thus insult to injury for those victims. As terrorism is so geared towards the (psychological) effects it creates within targets and the larger audience, studying those that were at the receiving end of political violence would be of enormous importance. It would, not least, help to inform our understanding of whether terrorism does actually work after all. At the same time, one still has to ask how the experience of having committed acts of political violence in the past influenced perpetrators. Some former terrorists have climbed to the highest echelons of power, especially in the context of successful national liberation struggles. But did this legacy of terrorism influence their actions later on? Some insightful research has been conducted for instance on the Polish national liberation struggle against the Russian occupation in the early 1900s and how it affected the leaders of the Polish state after the First World War.[30] But many other cases remain yet to be studied.

Blumenau, *United Nations*; B. Blumenau, 'The Group of 7 and International Terrorism: The Snowball Effect That Never Materialized', *Journal of Contemporary History* 51/2 (2016); B. Blumenau, 'Taming the Beast: West Germany, the Political Offence Exception, and the Council of Europe Convention on the Suppression of Terrorism', *Terrorism and Political Violence* 27/2 (2015); B. Blumenau, 'The European Communities' Pyrrhic Victory: European Integration, Terrorism, and the Dublin Agreement of 1979', *Studies in Conflict and Terrorism* 37/5 (2014); B. Saul, *Defining Terrorism in International Law* (Oxford and New York, Oxford University Press, 2006); J. Argomaniz, *The EU and Counter-Terrorism: Politics, Polity and Policies After 9/11* (London, Routledge, 2011); D. C. MacKenzie, *ICAO: A History of the International Civil Aviation Organization* (Toronto and Buffalo, University of Toronto Press, 2010), ch. 14; P. Romaniuk, *Multilateral Counter-Terrorism: The Global Politics of Cooperation and Contestation* (London, Routledge, 2010).

29 See for instance a collection of interesting articles in J. Argomaniz and O. Lynch (eds.), *Special Issue: The Complexity of Terrorism – Victims, Perpetrators and Radicalization*, *Studies in Conflict and Terrorism* 41/7 (2018). See also J. Argomaniz, 'A Battle of Narratives: Spanish Victims Organizations' International Action to Delegitimize Terrorism and Political Violence', *Studies in Conflict and Terrorism* 41/7 (2018).

30 F. Fischer von Weikersthal, 'From Terrorists to Statesmen: Terrorism and Polish Independence', *Studies in Conflict and Terrorism* 43/1 (2020).

The issue of state terrorism is another area deserving of more research: as traditional state power comes under distress and social sciences stipulate a more critical understanding of the state and its limits (of power), historians, too, could reflect upon state violence more critically. Dissecting the 'state' into different levels and clusters of power-yielding might open up a new understanding of the motives and methods of state-executed political violence. Interesting lessons could subsequently be learnt for understanding the return of the 'strong state' in many corners of the world today. These lessons might again cross-fertilise research in the social sciences, and possibly even trickle down into policy practice. Other disciplines have done a great job in paving the way for new enquiries to be developed by historians. Now it is up to us to continue down this path.

Historical research on terrorism and political violence could also benefit from borrowing research questions, knowledge and concepts from the 'hard sciences'. Much like questions on the effect of climatic fluctuations on terrorism, others could be asked: what impact did diseases have on political violence? Did they correlate with its inception, course or aftermaths? Linking, for instance, outbreaks of the plague with political violence (against minorities or women) in Europe makes sense. Other such historical connections certainly exist as well. One could also ask what new research in psychology reveals on why some people go terrorist and others do not, and apply this knowledge to historical cases.[31] Neurobiology and neuroscience are other fields where interesting insights can be sought on historical episodes of terrorism, and what factors pushed people towards violence.[32] Understanding what psychological, biological and social influences thrust people on a path towards terrorism might challenge the conventional understanding of previous acts (and actors) of terrorism. On the other end of the spectrum of the involvement in terrorism: how is the experience of being targeted processed by victims – not just psychologically but also biologically? And how does it influence people's recovery and well-being? One might also wonder what counterterrorism strategies actually work on the psychological and biological level, and which do not. This understanding could then be used to explain successes and failures of historical case studies of

---

31 See for instance S. Baron-Cohen, *Zero Degrees of Empathy* (London, Penguin, 2012).
32 For an insightful book that draws on many different disciplines to explain human behaviour, see R. M. Sapolsky, *Behave: The Biology of Humans at Our Best and Worst* (London, Vintage Books, 2018).

counterterrorism.[33] As terrorism and political violence affect many ways of life and draw from all possible fields and developments, hard sciences such as biology, chemistry and physics have a lot to offer to (historical) terrorism research.

Another way in which other disciplines can support historical research is by helping to get around the scarcity of sources. With only very few written or recorded documentations available, if any at all, other disciplines might provide data that helps to reconstruct the past: for instance, by samples from ice cores, statistical enquiries, genetical research or global climate patterns. As a historian, one has to be open-minded, and sometimes unconventional, when looking for sources, and other disciplines' methodologies and data might help us with this task.

Limitations

This chapter has shown that historians can benefit from an interdisciplinary approach. Observing which directions research in other disciplines takes, what sources they use and what methods they draw on can indeed give new impetus to historical enquiries; and historical research, in turn, can be of great use to scholars studying terrorism in adjacent disciplines. But despite the possible benefits of such endeavours, there are also significant limitations to such approaches. This section will address some of the pitfalls that might arise.

A general problem that could surface for anybody venturing into multidisciplinary projects is that one might not be taken seriously in one's home discipline (or institution). Old division lines between disciplines are still strong, and not everybody shares the enthusiasm for endorsing new approaches. This could have implications for funding, publishing, recognition and promotions. Hopefully, this will become less of a problem in the future, with many universities and granting agencies now encouraging innovative research that relies on different disciplines.

---

33 Research here is still in its infancy, but it could offer an interesting impetus to the understanding of historical cases of terrorism and their aftermath. See for instance J. Decety, R. Pape and C. I. Workman, 'A Multilevel Social Neuroscience Perspective on Radicalization and Terrorism', *Social Neuroscience* 13/5 (2018). On the flipside, when dealing with counterterrorism, scholarship from outside the social sciences/humanities offers insights as to what effects counterterrorism measures could, or could not, have. See e.g. S. M. O'Mara, *Why Torture Doesn't Work: The Neuroscience of Interrogation* (Cambridge, Harvard University Press, 2015).

As has been mentioned above, for historians, the availability of sources is a serious challenge, certainly when it comes to terrorism. State archives – police and judicial records – might provide some insights, but they are often heavily biased and might only offer very limited glimpses at individual motivations to join a terror organisation or commit acts of terrorism. And while interdisciplinary approaches and data might help to triangulate some of the existing lacunae, caution is of the essence when analysing these findings and drawing conclusions. A basic caveat for any serious research – correlation does not equal causation – certainly applies here. Just because two (or more) things occur at the same time does not necessarily mean that they have a causal (or any other form of) relationship to one another.

Moreover, while the bringing together of different approaches, sources and disciplines can be of value to historical research, there is also a risk that this can be done too well. As with most things, moderation is key, and great care has to be put into the design of interdisciplinary projects. Not every question lends itself to a multi-method or interdisciplinary approach, and rather than providing more clarity and a better understanding of the past, an ill-designed project can easily produce erratic findings and thereby add to the confusion. Another risk is that, whilst sources might be reliable, the interdisciplinary/multi-method project as such could be lacking focus, leaving the researcher (and the readers) rather lost as to what exactly is examined and in what fashion. This, again, might compromise the reliability of the results of such a project. This is certainly not a problem that is exclusive to multi-method research; any project can easily be overloaded and imprecise. But the risks are arguably even greater when a blurry topic such as 'terrorism' as well as other disciplines, their approaches and sources are involved. As with everything, sometimes less is actually more.

At the same time, there is another pitfall involved in multidisciplinary research. For scholars relatively new to a topic, when borrowing from other disciplines there is also the risk that a significant body of literature can be overlooked, outdated scholarship could be seen as state of the art, or a specific school of thought could be uncritically prioritised without a clear discussion and awareness of alternative, perhaps equally valid, approaches. Certainly, including knowledge from other disciplines offers great potentials. One has to be aware, though, that in all likelihood, as an outsider to a discipline, one will only get a somewhat superficial understanding of what can be very complex questions. For instance, a historian might have difficulties in fully understanding neuroscience and all the assumptions made and concepts used there. Another example is international law. For anybody who did not receive full legal training, the intricacy of international law – soft law, hard law, customary, codified, case law – can be challenging and confusing. This can, for instance, be a problem when examining international antiterrorism efforts, where, as a non-expert in law, one has to be careful when entering into a very legal debate on their meaning, relevance and applicability.

All this is not meant to discourage the use of interdisciplinary/multi-method research when studying terrorism. On the contrary, if proper consideration is given to the opportunities and limitations of such an approach, there can be great value in borrowing from other disciplines. However, this should not be done just for its own sake: interdisciplinarity for the sake of interdisciplinarity is not the *non plus ultra* of terrorism research. For many projects a mono-method approach might be completely adequate. Every design has to fit its research question. Where other disciplines are drawn in, however, good care has to be taken as to how that is done.

Conclusions

To state the obvious, certainly in an edited volume such as the present one: terrorism is a complex topic. It is highly politicised, vague, multifaceted, easily exploitable, headline-generating, intimidating and heavily dependent on context. It is also an issue that garners a lot of attention – mostly because that is exactly its point – and this tends to overemphasise its significance and danger. Extensive media and political spotlights do not make the academic study of this topic any easier.[34] Certainly, terrorism is a deplorable tactic; it relies on the deliberate use of violence, feeds off pain and fear and, more often than not, causes desolation, death and destruction. It has disastrous effects on victims, their relatives and friends as well as on communities, societies and sometimes even international relations. Because of all this, there is a considerable hype around terrorism. This, in turn, makes the threat appear uncontrollable, overwhelming and fatal. Yet, this is certainly not the case. Historical research in particular can help to counter this perception, and thereby play its part in robbing terrorism of its most pertinent weapon: fear. Non-colonial, non-state terrorism has never managed to achieve its goals – often because they were too utopian to persuade a critical mass of people of their achievability or desirability. And even in the context of successful

---

34 In fact, writing lots of emails with words such as 'bombs', 'attack', 'explosion' and 'assassination' can easily lead one to spend a lot of time in special interrogation rooms when crossing international borders.

colonial struggles, for the groups using it, terrorism was but one aspect of a multifaceted approach towards independence. It certainly was not the only factor that explains the successes or failures of national liberation campaigns. Terrorism, undoubtedly, is a threat, and there is the possibility that weapons could be used that would cause large-scale harm – virtual, nuclear, biological or chemical. Nevertheless, this risk is small and has no historical precedents. The average (Western) reader of this book is much more likely to die of cancer, a heart attack, a car accident, or even a lightning strike, than to become a victim of terrorism. Historians and their research can help to desensationalise terrorism, encourage a more rational understanding of its past and present, and show that it is not an exclusive feature of our current era. Terrorism has a recorded history that spans at least two millennia, and in all likelihood has been present ever since the first political relations were forged amongst humans. As is often stressed, 'terrorism is the weapon of the weak';[35] it is used by those that have, or see, no other means to gain or consolidate power. As such, it is a constant in human relations, and likely to remain that. Historical research can help to better appreciate and communicate this notion, but it can also contextualise and dissect the complexity of the phenomena of terrorism and political violence. Being extremely intertwined with many other developments, terrorism cannot be understood on its own – neither as a large-scale political occurrence nor as an individual's personal journey.

Context is of paramount importance for a proper comprehension of terrorism – or any form of political violence – and historians are supremely suited to provide it. They have the training as well as the chronological and emotional distance from the events that allows them to step back and look at the bigger picture; they have access to information unavailable to contemporaries, allowing them to conduct more informed assessments than what was possible at the time of things occurring; they have the toolbox and knowledge to provide multilayered, critical and balanced accounts of historical events of terrorism. Historians can reveal the context, but they can also examine long-term patterns, trends, parallels and ruptures. This perspective, and the data that comes with it, can be of great value to scholars working on more current aspects of terrorism. But historians are not just the sous-chefs for the social sciences. The latter can be useful for historians, too. They and other disciplines, including the 'hard sciences', can add their ingredients to

---

[35] L. Richardson, *What Terrorists Want: Understanding the Enemy, Containing the Threat* (New York, Random House, 2006), p. 20.

build a recipe for informative, sound and interesting terrorism research. Simply because terrorism is so complex, so difficult to fully grasp and apprehend, and information can be so sparse, interdisciplinary approaches – questions, designs and data – can be of immense help for historical research. There are limitations to this though. Just embarking on a multidisciplinary research project is not the automatic cure-all for the problems that research in terrorism entails. There are risks that poorly designed projects might add to the confusion around terrorism rather than reduce it.

The footnotes and literature used in this chapter make it evident that no discipline alone, certainly not history, can do justice to terrorism in its complexity. Therefore, drawing from multiple fields and sources of expertise might provide the most wholesome and suitable approach to the topic. Terrorism is an immensely sad topic of enquiry; it can be a frustrating one, too. But it puts the spotlights on the lows and the highs of human relationships, and thus it is also an extremely fascinating one to study. Most instances of contemporary terrorism have roots that reach far back into the past. And it is the past, in return, that can hence provide answers to the puzzles around terrorism today. Historical research can do that. And there is no harm in asking for a little help from our friends from across the disciplinary divide sometimes, too.

Further Reading

C. Dietze and C. Verhoeven, *The Oxford Handbook of the History of Terrorism* (Oxford, Oxford University Press, 2014)

C. Elman and M. Fendius Elman (eds.), *Bridges and Boundaries: Historians, Political Scientists, and the Study of International Relations*, BCSIA Studies in International Security (Cambridge, MA, MIT Press, 2001)

G. Lawson, 'The Eternal Divide? History and International Relations', *European Journal of International Relations* 18/2 (1 June 2012)

B. J. Lutz, 'Historical Approaches to Terrorism', in E. Chenoweth, R. English, A. Gofas and S. N. Kalyvas (eds.), *The Oxford Handbook of Terrorism*, pp. 193–206 (Oxford, Oxford University Press, 2019)

R. C. Williams, *The Historian's Toolbox: A Student's Guide to the Theory and Craft of History* (Armonk, NY, M. E. Sharpe, 2012)

PART III

★

HISTORICAL CASE STUDIES IN TERRORISM

7
Terrorism in Israel/Palestine

JULIE M. NORMAN

The history of terrorism in Israel/Palestine is a history of increasingly interwoven terrorism*s*. These terrorisms have been employed by both 'sides' in the conflict, Israeli and Palestinian, in different manifestations for over one hundred years, responding to internal and external pressures, and also reflecting and informing wider forces of change that have characterised the political histories of the twentieth and twenty-first centuries. A historical approach is thus not only helpful, but indeed crucial, for understanding the use of terrorism by various actors in Israel/Palestine, and also for recognising terrorism's short- and long-term influences on the trajectory of the conflict. Situating terrorism in Israel/Palestine in broader historical and political contexts can also help us answer broader questions, both academic and policy-oriented, regarding the causes, consequences and appropriate responses to political violence.

While terrorism is famously difficult to define, I will use an adaptation of Richard English's thoughtful definition, which seeks to overcome more narrow definitions that place primary emphasis on the actors, tactics or causes involved. Simply put, terrorism is the *use of violence against civilians for a political purpose with the aim of producing terror or fear among a directly threatened group and a wider implied audience.*[1] This definition is appropriate for the Israel/Palestine case study for two key reasons. First, this definition does not limit the potential use of terrorism to non-state actors, but rather recognises that states too use terrorism as a strategy, both within and beyond times of war. This definition is necessary for empirical accuracy in general, but it is essential in understanding terrorism in Israel/Palestine, where the actions of colonial powers, states, state-like actors and non-state actors have intersected in ways that have intensified cycles of terrorism throughout the conflict.

---

1 R. English, *Does Terrorism Work? A History* (Oxford, Oxford University Press, 2016), p. 10.

Second, the definition is dispassionate about the perceived justness of a political cause or seeming rationale of a security imperative. Rather, the focus is on the act(s) of political violence and the important inclusion of the psychological dimension of producing fear. This 'objective' approach again strikes me as most scholarly responsible regardless of the case study, but it is again crucial in the Israel/Palestine conflict, in which acts of terrorism have been simultaneously valorised, condemned and condoned by different actors across the conflict spectrum.

While one could attempt to divide the history of terrorism in the conflict into a Jewish/Israeli timeline and an Arab/Palestinian timeline, I choose to interweave them as much as possible, to indicate how intertwined and reactionary each has been to the other. In this chapter, I examine the history of terrorisms in Israel/Palestine in three periods of the conflict: first, 1920–48, from the mandate period through the establishment of the state of Israel and the Palestinian Nakba; second, 1949–93, including the start of the occupation in 1967 and the formation of the Palestinian Liberation Organisation (PLO), through the first intifada and the signing of the Oslo Accords; and third, 1994–2020, charting the rise of Hamas and Islamic Jihad, the second intifada and the series of Israeli operations in Gaza. I then reflect on this timeline as a whole, discussing the centrality of historical and political contexts both within and beyond Israel/Palestine that help us understand why and how terrorism has been employed in the conflict, and noting what we can learn from this context to give insights on larger questions regarding cycles of terrorism, particularly in protracted conflicts.

1920–1948: British Mandate to Independence and Nakba

Discussions of terrorism in Israel/Palestine often focus on more recent phenomena, such as suicide bombings during the second intifada or PLO hijackings and hostage-taking incidents in the mid-late twentieth century. But terrorism has been a significant factor in the conflict throughout its modern history, with increasing acts of violence between Jews[2] and Palestinians in the mandate years following the First World War, and the use of terrorist attacks against the British by violent Zionist organisations in the years preceding

---

2 I use the terms 'Jews' and 'Zionists' to refer to the Jewish population in Mandatory Palestine prior to the establishment of the state of Israel in 1948. Likewise, I use the term 'Palestine' when discussing pre-1948 events to refer to the region's historical name prior to Israel's founding.

Israeli independence. Indeed, as English noted as a perhaps unpopular point, 'the establishment of the state of Israel arguably embodies one of the most striking examples of terrorism actually managing to achieve major success'.[3] In this section, I first establish the historical-political context of the region in the post-First World War period. I then discuss the rising cycle of political violence between Jews, Palestinians and the British in the 1920s and 1930s (some of which fits within our definition of terrorism and some of which does not); the terrorist operations conducted by Zionist groups against the British in the 1930s and 1940s; and acts of terrorism committed during the War of 1948 and the Nakba.[4]

Historical Context

Jewish immigration to Palestine began in the 1880s as Jews fleeing increasing persecution in Russia and Eastern Europe emigrated to the Holy Land and started forming small agrarian settlements. Immigration increased further in the twentieth century with the growth of the Zionist movement, which, reflecting the nationalism movements of the time, sought to establish a national identity and ultimately homeland for the Jewish people, ideally in Palestine. It was thus to the president of the English Zionist Federation that the British Foreign Secretary, Arthur Balfour, issued a letter in 1917 that became known as the Balfour Declaration, expressing British support for the 'establishment in Palestine of a national home for the Jewish people'.[5]

British officials had already made similar promises to Arab leaders as well. Arab nationalism was also growing at this time, with the First Arab Congress of 1913 calling for independence from the Ottomans. It was in this context that Britain had committed to supporting Arab independence in support for military assistance against the Ottomans in a series of letters between Sir A. Henry McMahon, the High Commissioner of Egypt, and Sharif Hussein of Mecca between 1915 and 1916.[6] Thus, when the British were given the mandate from the League of Nations after the war to administer Palestine (and Transjordan) 'until such time as they are able to stand alone',[7] they found themselves with an impossible dual obligation to ensure the national

---

3 English, *Does Terrorism Work?*, p. 148.
4 Literally translated as 'disaster' or 'catastrophe', the term 'Nakba' refers to the forced displacement and subsequent refugee crisis of approximately 800,000 Palestinians during the War of 1948.
5 Balfour Declaration (1917), https://avalon.law.yale.edu/20th_century/balfour.asp.
6 McMahon–Hussein Correspondence (1915–16), www.jewishvirtuallibrary.org/the-hussein-mcmahon-correspondence.
7 Palestine Mandate (1920), https://avalon.law.yale.edu/20th_century/palmanda.asp.

aspirations of both Jews and Arabs in a region. This dual obligation was further complicated by the fact that the territory in question was highly religiously and historically significant (not to mention economically and geographically strategic) to both peoples. The next two decades saw the British unsuccessfully toggling between the Jewish and Palestinian communities, trying to manage the expectations and needs of both.

1920s–1930s: Riots and Revolts

As the national aspirations of both Jews and Arabs developed, the 1920s saw an increase in violence between the communities as each viewed the other as a threat to their security and potential statehood. Meanwhile, both felt increasing distrust of the British, who had reneged on their wartime promises. It would be too wide-sweeping to characterise all the violence and resistance of the 1920s as terrorism, but the incidents that occurred and the groups that formed during that time directly influenced the emergence of more 'clear-cut' terrorism in the following decade and are thus necessary to include here.

The roots of terrorism in the 1920s can best be described as a series of riots that devolved into violent confrontations between Jews, Palestinians and later the British. These included the Nebi Musa demonstrations in 1920 in Jerusalem that turned violent and left 5 Jews killed and 216 injured, and 4 Arabs killed and 23 wounded. This was followed the next year by a week of riots in the port city of Jaffa that left 47 Jews dead and 146 injured, and 48 Arabs killed and 73 wounded.[8] As many Zionists did not trust the ability or will of the British authorities to prevent or respond to the riots and more isolated attacks, a small group formed a clandestine paramilitary unit under Vladimir 'Ze'ev' Jabotinsky in 1920 called the Haganah (Defence), which began smuggling arms into Palestine. Elements of this group later evolved into the formally recognised Haganah and, after independence, the Israel Defence Force (IDF), while violent offshoots subsequently became the Irgun and Stern Gang.

For most of the 1920s, the Haganah units were mostly localised and lacked central coordination. Two events, however, would change the course of the Jewish armed resistance, first the 1929 riots, and second the 1936–9 Arab Revolt. The 1929 riots began when tensions rose around increasing Jewish demonstrations at the Western Wall, a Jewish holy site that abuts the Muslim holy site of the Haram al-Sharif (Dome of the Rock) in the Old City of

---

8 B. Hoffman, *Anonymous Soldiers* (New York, Knopf, 2015), pp. 11, 17.

Jerusalem. Riots spread outside Jerusalem, most notably in Hebron, where the Jewish community in the city was attacked by mobs in what can only be described as a massacre, with 64 Jews killed and 54 wounded, despite many Arab families attempting to hide and protect their Jewish neighbours.[9] The events of 1929 convinced the Jewish leadership that the Haganah lacked sufficient arms and training and needed further strengthening, consolidation and funding. Ideological issues caused the Haganah to see its first major split with the formation of the Haganah-Bet in 1931, which, unlike the Haganah, did not see itself only as a self-defence force, providing instruction in what Hoffman describes as 'the core tactics of terrorism', such as sabotage, bomb-making and hit-and-run attacks.[10]

The second event to transform both Arab and Jewish resistance was the Arab Revolt from 1936–9, a sort of precursor to the intifadas of the 1980s and 2000s. The revolt was influenced in part by Sheikh 'Izz al-Din Abd al-Qadir al-Qassam, whose secret Black Hand association aimed to 'spread terror' among Jewish communities in northern Palestine.[11] Though al-Qassam was killed in a gun battle in 1935, his followers continued targeting Jews, including robbing and killing three Jews on a bus near Nablus in April 1936, followed the next night by the Haganah-Bet killing two Arab labourers as revenge. Riots erupted in Jaffa two days later, and the Higher Arab Committee called for a general strike.

While much of the early months of the rebellion was characterised by non-violent actions such as strikes and demonstrations,[12] these were gradually overshadowed by the violence of the Qassamite-led gangs, which targeted not only Jews but also fellow Arabs and British security forces. Indeed, according to Kimmerling and Migdal, less than a quarter of the attacks targeted Jews, while over 40 per cent were on British military targets or involved sabotage on roads and other government infrastructure.[13] The Haganah-Bet continued carrying out reprisal attacks (which then in turn fuelled further Qassamite attacks) until Jewish leadership sought to consolidate it with the more defence-oriented Haganah in 1937. However, a number of Haganah-Bet officers refused the merger and formed the Irgun Zvai Le'umi (National Military Organisation), usually referred to as the Irgun, which would change the course of terrorism in the region.

---

9 Hoffman, *Anonymous Soldiers*, p. 32.   10 Hoffman, *Anonymous Soldiers*, p. 39.
11 Hoffman, *Anonymous Soldiers*, p. 39.
12 M. E. King, *A Quiet Revolution* (New York, Nation Books, 2009).
13 B. Kimmerling and J. Migdal, *The Palestinian People: A History* (Cambridge, MA, Harvard University Press, 2003), p. 119.

Irgun and Stern Gang/Lehi

Rejecting the Haganah's stated commitment to *havlagah* (restraint), the mobilisation of the Irgun shifted resistance beyond violence and revenge to full-fledged terrorism, first targeting Arab civilians and later the British. In 1938, the Irgun began a campaign of armed attacks in Tel Aviv and Jerusalem, using bombs, grenades and guns. A new form of terrorism emerged in Haifa in the form of 'market bombings', when an Irgunist disguised as an Arab would drop off a delivery of milk churns or pickle cans containing time bombs that would explode in succession nearly an hour after the 'porter' had disappeared. Like the suicide bombings of the 1990s and 2000s, in targeting civilians in crowded shopping areas, these bombings caused massive destruction and loss of life (60 Arabs were killed in one market bombing alone) and also encapsulated the psychological dimension of terrorism, creating a climate of fear in daily life. However, as Hoffman rightly notes, 'rather than paralysing the Arabs with fear or inaction and deterring them from further violence, the Irgun operations seemed only to incite greater bloodshed, locking both communities into a vicious upward spiral of intercommunal butchery that refused to abate'.[14]

The Irgun continued to carry out bombings and other operations through June 1939, with increasing attacks against British as well as Arab targets. The group decided to cease attacks against the British, however, with the start of the Second World War, causing a splinter with the formation in 1940 of the Stern Gang (later rebranded as Lehi), whose leader, Avraham Stern, had been inspired by the Easter Rising in Ireland to see the war as a time of vulnerability for Britain that could be exploited. Lehi thus continued attacks on British departments and in 1944 assassinated Lord Moyne, the British Minister Resident in the Middle East (and in 1948 assassinated United Nations Envoy Folke Bernadotte). The end of the war then saw the first joint operations between Lehi, the Irgun and the Haganah, operating as the united Jewish Resistance Movement.

The most noted act of terrorism in this period was carried out by the Irgun (led by Menachem Begin) against the British in 1946, with the bombing of the King David Hotel in Jerusalem. The attack took place when tensions between the British and the Yishuv (the Jewish community) were at an unprecedented high, with Britain's restrictive immigration policy preventing many Holocaust survivors in Europe from reaching Palestine. The site was chosen as it was the location of the British Military Command, but it was also

---

14 Hoffman, *Anonymous Soldiers*, p. 82.

a popular gathering point for diplomats, socialites, Jewish and Arab dignitaries and civilians. Despite warning calls being made before the explosion, the hotel was not evacuated, and 91 people were killed and 45 injured. The Irgun and Lehi continued operations against the British, increasing pressure for their withdrawal, which commenced in 1947.

War and Nakba

Britain's 1947 decision to withdraw from Palestine was not due solely to the terrorist attacks. In the post-war context, Britain was economically exhausted and unable to sustain its presence in much of the Commonwealth. But the attacks certainly had an impact and made it clear that the mandate, with its dual obligation, was not going to succeed. Britain thus worked with the newly formed United Nations on a partition plan for Palestine, which was issued in November 1947, with Britain's own withdrawal set for 15 May 1948. The rejection of the partition plan was followed by a 'civil war' between Jews and Palestinians, and then an inter-state war between the new state of Israel and the neighbouring Arab states (Egypt, Jordan, Syria, Lebanon and Iraq) after the British withdrawal.

It is important not to conflate acts of war with terrorism, but several incidents in the violence of early 1948 do fit within our definition of terrorism, particularly the massacre at Deir Yassin, a Palestinian village attacked by the Irgun and Lehi, with support from the Haganah, on 9 April in part of an offensive to clear the besieged road to Jerusalem. After the initial battle with Palestinian forces, Jewish fighters entered the village and killed an estimated 120 of the remaining civilians, raped and mutilated others, and paraded those taken captive through the streets of Jerusalem.[15] Four days later, a reprisal terrorist attack took place when Arab fighters surrounded a convoy en route to the Hadassah Hospital/Hebrew University campus on Mount Scopus, shooting the mostly civilian passengers and setting the buses on fire, resulting in more than 70 deaths.

Deir Yassin had further effects on how subsequent events that year played out. First, the media coverage of the massacre rallied Arabs around the region and may have contributed to decisions by Egypt and Jordan to become involved in the war against the new state of Israel in May.[16] Second, but perhaps even more significantly, the massacre at Deir Yassin understandably convinced most of the Palestinian population that they would be subject to

---

15 Kimmerling and Migdal, *The Palestinian People*, p. 161; B. Morris, *Righteous Victims* (New York, Knopf, 1999), p. 208.
16 Morris, *Righteous Victims*, p. 209.

the same types of attacks when the Jewish forces and later the Israeli army advanced on their villages, prompting many to flee and contributing to the displacement of over 800,000 Palestinians. Indeed, the IDF called Deir Yassin a 'decisive accelerating factor' in the Palestinian 'exodus',[17] and Menachem Begin later wrote that 'what was invented about Deir Yassin helped in fact carve the way of Jewish victories on the battlefield'.[18] It is thus clear that the quite literal terror created by the massacre at Deir Yassin contributed to the forced displacement that characterised the Nakba. The very real threat of violence, combined with the enforcement of Israeli policies to create Arab-free zones in strategic regions,[19] constituted a less 'spectacular' but ultimately 'successful' form of terrorism that set the course for the next phase of the conflict.

1949–1993: Occupation and PLO Resistance

The mid- to late twentieth century is the period when Israel/Palestine became closely associated with terrorism, primarily through the spectacular media-grabbing attacks orchestrated by groups within the Palestinian Liberation Organisation (PLO). However, it is important to unpack these events in the context of the conflict and regional and global events. Regarding the conflict itself, the establishment of the state of Israel reoriented the conflict from one that had been primarily Jewish–Palestinian to one that was Israeli–Arab, manifest most prominently in the wars between Israel and neighbouring Arab states in 1956 (Suez Crisis), 1967 (the Six Day War) and 1973 (the Yom Kippur War). However, a specifically Palestinian resistance was growing at this time as well, and the PLO emerged not just to counter Israel, but to take back the struggle for Palestine from the Arab states, especially after the losses in 1967 and the start of the occupation. All of this occurred over the backdrop of the Cold War and the emergence of guerrilla warfare and self-determination movements around the globe. With this context in mind, this chapter discusses the roots of resistance in the years between Israeli independence and the start of the occupation; the PLO's use of armed struggle and terrorism as primary means of resistance in the 1970s; and the shifts in tactics during the first intifada and early years of the peace process. I also discuss ongoing Israeli terrorism via groups like the Jewish

---

17 Morris, *Righteous Victims*, p. 209.
18 M. Begin, *The Revolt* (New York, Henry Schuman, 1951), p. 155.
19 Kimmerling and Migdal, *The Palestinian People*, p. 164.

Underground and policies such as targeted assassinations and collective punishment.

Roots of Resistance (1949–1967)

In the years following Israeli independence and the Nakba, most violence consisted of small but frequent cross-border attacks and reprisals. The extent to which these infiltrations constituted terrorism is not clear-cut. According to Morris, many were Palestinian refugees who, when prevented from legally returning to their homes in 1949, were forced to use illicit means to try to access their land, retrieve possessions, look for lost relatives or just see their homes, and the large majority were unarmed. Morris estimates that less than 10 per cent were engaged in guerrilla warfare or terrorism, though this minority caused significant Israeli casualties.[20] As a result, Israel saw all infiltrators as terrorists and responded with policies that fuelled violent reprisals and at times constituted terrorism themselves. From 1951–3 for example, Israel instituted a policy of 'indirect deterrence' (which was replicated in various forms in later years, notably in Lebanon) in which both army units and vigilante settlers crossed into Arab states attacking homes and sometimes killing civilians to try to force those states to curb infiltration.[21] The most notable of these operations was the 1953 raid on the Palestinian village of Qibya (then part of Jordan), in which 130 Israeli soldiers, led by Ariel Sharon, destroyed 45 houses and killed 70 civilians, mostly women and children.[22] As with prior and later 'indirect deterrence' attempts to prevent or punish terrorism, the raid on Qibya only furthered grievances, leading to an increase in *fedayeen* attacks until the Suez Crisis in 1956.

This period also saw the initial founding of Palestinian resistance groups that would make up the core of the PLO, including the founding of the Arab Nationalist Movement (a precursor to the leftist Popular Front for the Liberation of Palestine (PFLP) and Democratic Front for the Liberation of Palestine (DFLP)) by George Habash in 1951, and the founding of the Palestine National Liberation Movement (Fatah) by Yasser Arafat and Khalil al-Wazir in Kuwait in 1958. These groups later came under the umbrella of the PLO, established in 1964, and became dominant forces in Palestinian nationalism, resistance and ultimately terrorism after the War of

---

20 B. Morris, *Israel's Border Wars 1949–1956: Arab Infiltration, Israeli Retaliation, and the Countdown to the Suez War* (Oxford, Oxford University Press, 1993); I. Primoratz, 'Terrorism in the Israeli–Palestinian Conflict: A Case Study in Applied Ethics', *Iyyun: The Jerusalem Philosophical Quarterly* 55 (January 2006), p. 44.
21 Ibid.   22 Ibid., p. 45; Morris, *Israel's Border Wars*, pp. 245–55.

1967 and the subsequent Israeli occupation of the West Bank, Gaza Strip, Sinai Peninsula, Golan Heights and East Jerusalem.

Occupation and PLO Terrorism – Internal and External (1967–1980)

Assifa, the armed wing of Fatah, began operations in Israel prior to the Six Day War, undertaking nearly 100 acts of sabotage that killed 11 Israelis and wounded 62.[23] (Though favouring guerrilla warfare, Fatah denounced violence targeting civilians in this period;[24] however, by the 1970s, Arafat defended PLO operations that made no distinction between civilians and soldiers.[25]) However, it was after Israel's quick defeat of the Egyptian, Jordanian and Syrian forces in the 1967 War that Fatah was propelled to its dominant position in Palestinian resistance. As Kimmerling and Migdal explain, as humiliating as the 1967 War was for Arabs, it benefited Fatah, first by diminishing the prevalence of Nasserite pan-Arabism, and second by (re)uniting the Palestinians living under the Israeli occupation.[26] Essentially, Fatah took advantage of the failure of the Arab states, militarily and politically, to fight for the Palestinian cause, and represented 'taking back' the resistance from neighbouring government elites to the Palestinian people. Fatah's popularity burgeoned following the Battle of Karameh, where, though militarily defeated, they fought back against Israeli troops seeking to demolish the main Fatah camp in Jordan. After Karameh, recruitment for Fatah skyrocketed, and in 1969, Fatah took the majority of seats in the PLO and Arafat became the chairman, a position he held until his death in 2004.

Fatah was not without competition however; Habash's PFLP formed in 1967, with the DFLP splintering off into its own organisation shortly after. The violence and terrorism that would characterise Palestinian resistance for the next ten years was thus reflective in part of a conflict among Palestinian factions,[27] as each sought to outdo the others (similar to the rivalries in later years between Fatah and Hamas, and between Hamas and Islamic Jihad). In contrast to Fatah, which focused on guerrilla warfare and, at times, acts of

---

23 Kimmerling and Migdal, *The Palestinian People*, p. 252.
24 W. Pearlman, *Violence, Nonviolence, and the Palestinian National Movement* (Cambridge, Cambridge University Press, 2011), p. 68.
25 B. Rubin, *Revolution until Victory? The Politics and History of the PLO* (Cambridge, MA, Harvard University Press, 1994), p. 24.
26 Kimmerling and Migdal, *The Palestinian People*, p. 252.
27 Pearlman, *Violence, Nonviolence, and the Palestinian National Movement*, p. 82; Y. Sayigh, *Armed Struggle and the Search for Movement, 1949–1993* (Oxford, Oxford University Press, 1999), pp. 339–41.

terrorism within Israel–Palestine, the PFLP concentrated on creating international terrorism spectacles to force attention to the Palestinian cause. The PFLP carried out its first plane hijacking in 1968, seizing an Israeli El Al flight from Rome. Hijackings continued in 1969 with Leila Khaled's hijacking of a TWA flight from Los Angeles to Tel Aviv, and other hijackings and attacks carried out on Israeli aircraft and businesses. According to Byman, Palestinian groups hijacked sixteen airplanes and attacked thirty-three aviation targets (such as El Al offices) between 1968 and 1976,[28] and Ariel Merari and Shlomo Elad counted 435 acts of international terrorism between 1968 and 1984.[29] (It is notable that, of these 435, only one quarter were carried out by groups affiliated with the PLO, which declared a moratorium on external operations in 1974. But the PLO was unable to control groups and individuals who had split off or been expelled from its ranks, including the Abu Nidal Organisation, which broke off from Fatah, and Wadi Haddad, who continued to sponsor international attacks after being expelled from the PFLP. Together, Abu Nidal and Haddad were responsible for 38 per cent of the international attacks counted by Merari and Elad.[30])

Despite these splinters and internal disagreements on the strategy of such actions, some of the most notorious incidents of this period were orchestrated by groups under the PLO. These included the hijacking and blowing up of four planes at Dawson's Field in Jordan in 1970 by the PFLP, and the joint PFLP–Red Army attack on Lod Airport in Israel in 1972, which killed 26 people and wounded 80. Most famous, however, was the hostage crisis at the Munich Olympics in 1972, which played out to the world on live television, in which eleven Israeli athletes were taken hostage and killed by the Black September Organisation (BSO), a short-lived faction under the PLO. In response, Israel launched Operation Wrath of God, a campaign to assassinate the BSO/PLO militants involved in Munich, marking the first time that targeted assassinations became a full campaign rather than one-off strikes against individuals. As Byman notes, 'in theory the Mossad was using the killings to instill fear and deter future attacks – to terrorize the terrorists – but in reality revenge often drove the operations'.[31]

---

28 D. Byman, *A High Price: The Triumphs and Failures of Israeli Counterterrorism* (Oxford, Oxford University Press, 2011), p. 39.
29 A. Merari and S. Elad, *The International Dimension of Palestinian Terrorism 1968–1986* (Tel Aviv, Hakibbutz Hameuchad, Kav Adom, 1986).
30 Pearlman, *Violence, Nonviolence, and the Palestinian National Movement*, p. 79.
31 Byman, *A High Price*, p. 53.

Indeed, it is important to note that these terrorist acts like Munich, while abhorrent, did not occur in a vacuum, and reflected the clichéd but very real cycle of violence that has characterised the conflict from its early years to the present. For example, the Munich attack took place just after Israel had assassinated Ghassan Khanafani, a prominent Palestinian writer and editor of the PFLP's magazine, in retaliation for the Lod Airport attack. Like many of Israel's targeted assassination operations, the attack not only killed its target but civilians as well, this time killing Khanafani's young niece.[32] Meanwhile, Israel was regularly bombing Palestinian refugee camps in Lebanon in retaliation for cross-border raids, ostensibly targeting fighters, but resulting in civilian casualties as well. At the same time, the occupation was becoming more entrenched within the Palestinian Territories, with collective punishment policies that continue to the present, such as home demolitions and curfews in villages with suspected militant links, and arrest or deportation of leaders suspected of trying to organise any type of opposition.[33] Arrest and detention was (and continues to be) a common strategy for gathering intelligence, with approximately 500,000 (one in three) Palestinians detained or arrested in the first two decades of the occupation.[34] It is perhaps not surprising, then, that the majority of hijackings and hostage-taking actions carried out by the PLO involved demands for the release of Palestinian prisoners.

By the mid-1970s, resistance had shifted slightly. Organisations under the PLO, now based in Lebanon, began conducting more attacks by crossing the border into northern Israel. According to Rubin, Palestinian attacks in Israel between 1971 and 1982 killed 250 civilians and wounded over 1,600.[35] Among these was the 1974 Passover massacre at Kiryat Shimona, in which 18 Israelis (including 8 children) were killed in a shooting spree by the PFLP-General Command (PFLP-GC, a splinter group from the PFLP), followed a month later by the Ma'alot massacre, in which DFLP gunmen stormed a school, took more than 115 hostage, and ultimately killed 25 of the hostages, including 22 children.[36]

While brutally targeting Israeli civilians, these attacks, as Sayigh notes, were conducted largely to 'challenge the PLO leadership and demonstrate

32 L. Marlowe, 'Massacre in Munich', *Irish Times* (21 January 2006).
33 Byman, *A High Price*, p. 35.
34 R. Punamäki , 'Experiences of Torture, Means of Coping, and Level of Symptoms among Palestinian Political Prisoners', *Journal of Palestine Studies* 17/4 (Summer 1988).
35 Rubin, *Revolution until Victory?*, p. 48.   36 Byman, *A High Price*, p. 50.

opposition to the peace process'.[37] Encouraged by the United States, the first nascent peace process had begun following the 1973/Yom Kippur War, in which Israel, though suffering initial losses from Egypt's surprise attack, once again defeated the Arab armies, though not before the Arab oil embargo showed how the conflict could influence state interests well beyond the Middle East region. It was thus in 1974 that Arafat publicly renounced international attacks and gave his famous 'gun or the olive branch' speech at the United Nations, beginning the slow process of gradual Fatah openness to diplomacy alongside armed struggle. Though years away from any sort of peace agreement, these initial diplomatic steps activated a pushback response from other groups within the PLO. Indeed, while 'Fatah's direct involvement in terrorism against non-Israeli targets ceased at this point',[38] PLO groups continued to carry out attacks, including the 1976 hijacking of an Air France flight to Uganda, and a 1985 seizure of a passenger ship in the Mediterranean, as various spoiler groups sought to show their opposition to the peace process.

PLO factions were not the only ones using terrorism to disrupt the peace process. The 1978 signing of the Camp David Accords and the subsequent Egypt–Israel Peace Treaty, which returned the Israeli-occupied Sinai peninsula to Egypt in exchange for normalisation of relations, also spurred pushback in the form of terrorism from Jewish groups. Most notable was the Jewish Underground, or Makhteret, a radical organisation that emerged in 1979, formed by members of Gush Emunim, the right-wing organisation that had pushed for aggressive Israeli settlement in the West Bank (Judaea and Samaria) following the 1967 War.

The Jewish Underground had two main operational objectives, the first being a plot to blow up the Dome of the Rock, which was uncovered and pre-empted by Israeli intelligence officials. The second objective was to carry out punitive deterrence and revenge actions for Palestinian violence against settlers (which themselves were often justified by Palestinians as acts of reprisal to settler violence). The Makhteret carried out two major operations in this regard. First was the 1980 'bombing of the mayors', when a series of car bombs were deployed in one day against the Palestinian mayors of Ramallah, Nablus and El-Bireh (though the El-Bireh bomb was detected before explosion). Then, in 1983, Makhteret gunmen attacked students at the Islamic College in Hebron, killing 3 and wounding 33. Israel arrested 25 people

---

37 Sayigh, *Armed Struggle*, p. 339.   38 Byman, *A High Price*, p. 48.

affiliated with the Makhteret in 1984 and the organisation is considered a terrorist group by Israel.[39]

Meanwhile, the PLO in the late 1970s and early 1980s became increasingly consumed with their role in the civil war in Lebanon, especially during the Israeli invasions into southern Lebanon, until their eventual relocation to Tunis in 1982. The weakening of the PLO at this time gave space for a new form of resistance to emerge from within the Occupied Territories in the mid-1980s. Led by civil society and community-level 'popular committees', the first intifada involved Palestinians from all walks of life in directly confronting the occupation via mass protests, strikes, civil disobedience and forms of limited violence such as throwing stones and Molotov cocktails. Combined with global shifts with the end of the Cold War, and regional shifts with the defeat of Saddam Hussein, a PLO ally, in the Persian Gulf War, the first intifada provided a window for the first direct peace negotiations between Israelis and Palestinians, culminating in the signing of the Oslo Accords in 1993.

1994–2020: Hamas, the Second Intifada and the Gaza Wars

The peace process, and its failure, brought disillusionment and increased acts of terrorism from both sides of the conflict. However, terrorism looked different than it had in the past. In Palestine, the 'normalisation' of Fatah under Oslo from an armed movement to a political party, combined with the decline of the leftist parties with the end of the Cold War, created a vacuum for Palestinian armed resistance that was increasingly filled by Hamas, Islamic Jihad and, across the border in Lebanon, Hezbollah. Meanwhile, on the Israeli side, the 1990s saw expressions of extremist Israeli terrorism, while the twenty-first century saw an institutionalisation of terrorist policies by the state, rationalised in the post-9/11 world under the narrative of 'security'. These expressions have resulted in a bloody reality in the post-Oslo period, with unprecedented levels of violence in the second intifada and the Gaza Wars, manifesting what Thomas Schelling has called the 'capacity to hurt'.[40]

---

39 S. Sandler, 'Religious Zionism and the State: Political Accommodation and Religious Radicalism in Israel', in B. Maddy-Waitzman and E. Inbar (eds.), *Religious Radicalism in the Greater Middle East* (London, Routledge, 1997), p. 144; A. Pedahzur and A. Perliger, *Jewish Terrorism in Israel* (New York, Columbia University Press, 2009), pp. 39–40.

40 T. Schelling, 'The Diplomacy of Violence', in J. Garnett (ed.), *Theories of Peace and Security* (London, Palgrave Macmillan, 1970).

Post-Oslo (1990s)

Terrorism emerged from both sides of the conflict to challenge Oslo. In terms of Israeli terrorism, two incidents jeopardised the peace agreement almost from its start. First, on 25 February 1994, US-born Baruch Goldstein, a follower of the radical anti-Arab Rabbi Kahane, entered the Tomb of the Patriarchs in Hebron with a hand grenade and a machine gun and killed 29 Palestinians and injured 125 others. Dozens more died in clashes with the IDF when Palestinians protested the massacre. Then, on 4 November 1995, Yigal Amir, a young right-wing Israeli extremist, assassinated Israeli Prime Minister Yitzhak Rabin, whom he viewed as 'endangering innocent Jews by giving away Jewish land'[41] in the peace agreement. Both events, while tragic in their own right, were devastating to the already tenuous peace process. As Byman notes, 'Amir got what he wanted from killing Rabin', in that 'Jewish terrorism, along with Palestinian violence, "derailed the peace process"'.[42] Further, the Hebron massacre 'gave Hamas a pretext to launch attacks and proved a setback for ... negotiators on the peace process'.[43]

To be sure, Hamas's military wing, the Qassam Brigades, responded to the Hebron attack with their first suicide bombing, carried out in the Israeli town of Afula, which killed 8 Israelis and wounded 34, followed a week later by another suicide bombing at the central bus station in Hadera that killed 5. Suicide bombing would become the modus operandi of the Qassam Brigades, as well as that of their main rival, Islamic Jihad, with a combined fifteen suicide attacks between 1994 and 1999, and over one hundred attacks during the second intifada.[44] In terms of reflecting the psychological dimension of terrorism, the impact of suicide bomb attacks on Israel was, as Beverley Milton-Edwards and Stephen Farrell note, 'seismic. Hamas bombers now had the potential to be in every street, café, shopping mall, and bus', creating what a Hamas leader called a 'strategic balance of terror'.[45]

While the tactic of suicide bombing was new, Hamas and Islamic Jihad had been engaged in resistance since the 1980s. Islamic Jihad was formed in 1980–1 by a group of intellectuals in Gaza, and started pinprick attacks against Israelis in 1985–6. Meanwhile, in 1983–4, Sheikh Ahmed Ismail Hassan Yassin, an

---

41 Byman, *A High Price*, p. 283.
42 Byman, *A High Price*, p. 284, quoting former US peace negotiator Martin Indyk.
43 Byman, *A High Price*, p. 282.
44 Israel Ministry of Foreign Affairs, 'Suicide and Other Bombing Attacks in Israel Since the Declaration of Principles', https://mfa.gov.il/mfa/foreignpolicy/terrorism/palestinian/pages/suicide%20and%20other%20bombing%20attacks%20in%20israel%20since.aspx.
45 B. Milton-Edwards and S. Farrell, *Hamas* (London, Polity Press, 2010), p. 123.

imam and politician, started organising a military/terrorist wing inside the Muslim Brotherhood,[46] which had mostly refrained from participating in the Palestinian armed struggle. When the first intifada started, Yassin and his close associates decided to create an organisation affiliated with but distinct from the Brotherhood in order to take a more active role in the uprising, thus establishing Hamas.[47] (*Hamas* is an acronym of *Harakat al-Muqawama al-Islamiyya*, or Islamic Resistance Movement, and also an Arabic word meaning 'zeal'.) Hamas grew quickly, becoming the party most engaged in armed actions against Israeli targets by the latter years of the intifada, and becoming the second largest faction after Fatah by 1993. As Abu-Amr notes, Hamas's military activities were 'intended not only to strike at the occupation, but also to embarrass the negotiating factions and to bolster its own position as a major Palestinian force'.[48] In this way, from the outset, Hamas reflected other terrorist groups from earlier eras of the conflict in augmenting attacks to simultaneously disrupt peace processes, compete with other factions and fill a perceived void in the space of armed resistance.

Second Intifada (2000s)

Support for Hamas increased gradually in the 1990s as the hopes for statehood that many read in the Oslo Accords gave way to an increase of settlements and a further entrenchment of the occupation. Fatah and Arafat's role within the newly created Palestinian Authority constrained their ability to be a voice for resistance, obliged as they were by the peace process to cooperate with Israel and the United States. The space of resistance was steadily filled by Hamas, whose popularity and influence exploded in the second intifada, following the failed Camp David II Accords in 2000. As Mia Bloom summarises, 'Palestinians' disillusionment with Arafat, his Palestinian Authority, and the deadlocked peace process provided radical groups with an opportunity to increase their share of the political market by engaging in violence.'[49]

The second intifada, which lasted until 2007, was much bloodier than the first, defined almost from the start by armed attacks, harsh countermeasures and collective punishment. This is not to say that unarmed resistance and civil disobedience was absent amongst Palestinians; on the contrary, local

---

46 Morris, *Righteous Victims*, p. 570.
47 Z. Abu-Amr, 'Hamas: A Historical and Political Background', *Journal of Palestine Studies* 22/4 (Summer 1993), p. 11.
48 Ibid., p. 15.
49 M. Bloom, 'Palestinian Suicide Bombing: Public Support, Market Share, and Outbidding', *Political Science Quarterly* 119/1 (Spring 2004), p. 65.

campaigns, especially in villages affected by the erection of Israel's separation barrier,[50] organised weekly protests, demonstrations, strikes and boycott campaigns. However, these actions were widely overshadowed by suicide bombings and, later, rocket attacks.[51] Suicide bombing was by far the most significant form of Palestinian terrorism from 2001 to 2004, with 128 attacks causing over 500 deaths.[52] Some of the most infamous attacks included the bombing of the Dolphinarium discotheque in Tel Aviv in 2001, which killed 21 Israelis, 16 of them teenagers, and the 2002 Passover bombing of a hotel in Netanya, which killed 30, wounded 140, and was the deadliest attack against Israelis during the second intifada.

As Bloom notes, 'the waves of bombings demonstrated a competition between groups vying for power', reflecting a phenomenon she calls 'outbidding'.[53] To be sure, suicide bombing extended beyond Hamas and Islamic Jihad to include Fatah's Al-Aqsa Brigades and the PFLP in 2002. However, suicide bombings were also often direct responses to Israeli actions (with the timings of attacks initially correlated as responses),[54] representing again the escalating spiral of violence. Brym and Araj have likewise shown that 'strategic thinking is often overshadowed by the desire for revenge and retaliation',[55] with 82 per cent of suicide bombing attacks preceded by specific Israeli actions.[56] However, Brym convincingly argues that suicide bombing went beyond simple tit-for-tat violence to represent a response to harsh state repression more broadly, including the assassination of organisation leaders, the excessive use of force in the form of live ammunition against demonstrators, and collective punishment of civilians.

To be sure, harsh Israeli tactics, while ostensibly authorised to prevent or deter terrorism, only added to Palestinian grievances and increased support for armed resistance during the second intifada. First was the continuation of targeted assassinations, which, as mentioned previously, usually triggered reprisal operations. In January 1996, Shabak, the Israel Security Agency,

---

50 The separation barrier is a 723-km-long barrier, taking the form of a 6- to 8 m concrete wall in some areas and barbed wire and electric fence in others, built by Israel ostensibly to curb terrorism, but also viewed by critics as an attempt to create new borders encompassing West Bank settlements and sections of Palestinian land on the Israeli side of the barrier.
51 J. Norman, *The Second Palestinian Intifada: Civil Resistance* (London, Routledge, 2010).
52 Israel Ministry of Foreign Affairs, 'Suicide and Other Bombing Attacks'.
53 Bloom, 'Palestinian Suicide Bombing', p. 65.   54 Ibid.
55 B. Araj, 'Harsh State Repression as a Cause of Suicide Bombing: The Case of the Palestinian–Israeli Conflict', *Studies in Conflict and Terrorism* 31 (2008), p. 286.
56 Ibid., p. 293; R. Brym and B. Araj, 'Palestinian Suicide Bombing Revisited: A Critique of the Outbidding Thesis', *Political Science Quarterly* 123/3 (Fall 2008).

assassinated Yahya Ayyash, the leader of the West Bank's Qassam Brigades, and Hamas's chief bomb-maker, earning him the nickname 'the Engineer'. Just after the mourning period, Hamas launched four suicide bombings in Israel over ten days, resulting in 59 Israeli deaths.[57]

Targeted assassinations also frequently resulted in 'collateral damage', or death or injury of civilians in the premises. In 2002, for example, Salah Shehada, the head of Hamas's Qassam Brigades, was killed when the IDF dropped a one-ton bomb on the house where he was hiding in Gaza City, also killing 14 other Palestinians, 7 of them children, and wounding dozens of others. In 2004, Sheikh Yassin, the founder and leader of Hamas, was killed by Hellfire missiles as he was being wheeled in his wheelchair from morning prayers. Nine bystanders were also killed, and the incident brought international condemnation and mobilised 200,000 in his funeral procession.[58] This was followed less than a month later by the assassination of Abdel Aziz al-Rantisi, the co-founder of Hamas, in another Hellfire missile attack that wounded four bystanders, prompting then British Foreign Secretary Jack Straw to condemn the targeted assassinations as 'unlawful, unjustified, and counter-productive'.[59] Even Ami Ayalon, the former head of Shabak (Israel's internal security agency) from 1996 to 2000, acknowledged that 'all the punishment that we are using is in a way creating a wave of hatred that is not in our favour'.[60]

While Israel justified the assassinations as necessary for preventing further violence,[61] other harsh tactics were also used against unarmed protesters and civilians. Even in the first weeks of the intifada, when the uprising was characterised by large demonstrations, civil disobedience and stone-throwing, the protests were met with rubber-coated bullets, live ammunition and military incursions and mass arrests in Area A (the mostly urban areas of the West Bank administered by the Palestinian Authority). As human rights groups like Amnesty International documented, in just the first five days of the initafda, 47 Palestinians were killed and 1,885 wounded, 80 per cent of whom were not posing life-threatening danger to Israeli forces (the usual standard for deploying live ammunition), and in just the first month, 1,300,000

---

57 D. Ephron, 'How Israel's Most Fervent Peacemaker Squandered His Chance', *Washington Post* (16 October 2015).
58 I. R. Prusher and B. Lynfield, 'Killing of Yassin a Turning Point', *Christian Science Monitor* (23 March 2004).
59 'UK Condemns Hamas Leader Killing', *BBC News*, 18 April 2004.
60 A. Ayalon, interview with author, Jerusalem, 11 July 2013.
61 D. Byman, 'Do Targeted Killings Work?', *Foreign Affairs* 85/2 (March–April 2006).

bullets were fired by Israeli forces.[62] From 2000 to 2005, over 3,200 Palestinians were killed,[63] with thousands arrested and hundreds held detained without trial.[64] These tactics were compounded on the day-to-day level by means of collective punishment such as home demolitions, and 'security' measures that affected all forms of daily life, including curfews, checkpoints, movement restrictions and the erection of the separation barrier.

According to Byman, the separation barrier, combined with the targeted assassinations, increased arrests, intelligence and economic and military pressure, gradually quelled suicide bombing, though public support for the attacks also decreased as it became clear that the tactic was not working and was bringing further repression and international condemnation.[65] It is also important to note shifts among the Palestinian factions at this time, as the death of Arafat in 2004 decreased the strength of Fatah and the Al-Aqsa Brigades, and the surprise victory of Hamas in the 2006 Palestinian Legislative Council (PLC) elections further split the parties, with Hamas ultimately controlling Gaza and the Fatah-led Palestinian Authority (PA) controlling the West Bank.

At this point, rocket attacks replaced suicide bombing as the main terrorism tactic, first from Hezbollah in south Lebanon in the 2006 war with Israel, and later from Hamas and Islamic Jihad in Gaza, introducing another round of reprisal attacks with Israeli strikes on missile sites in the Strip. While gradually developing in sophistication, the rockets, known as Qassams, were crude and rarely fatal, but caused significant damage, injuries and, most importantly, fear in Israel, especially in towns near the Gaza border like Sderot and Ashkelon. They were also unpredictable, setting off sirens at all hours and 'terrifying Israeli residents'.[66] The sheer number was also notable, with more than 16,500 rockets launched between 2005 and 2014, causing 160 million dollars in damages and wounding over 2,600.[67]

Gaza Wars and Settler Terrorism (2010s)

Israel's responses to the rocket attacks from Gaza, though framed as defence and/or deterrence, have, according to our definition, constituted state

---

62 Just Vision, 'Second Intifada', www.justvision.org/glossary/second-intifada.
63 BBC, 'Intifada Toll 2000–2005', 8 February 2005.
64 B'Tselem, 'Statistics on Palestinians Held in the Custody of Israeli Security Forces' (26 September 2019).
65 Byman, 'Do Targeted Killings Work?'.
66 Milton-Edwards and Farrell, *Hamas*, p. 131.
67 M. J. Armstrong, 'The Effectiveness of Rocket Attacks and Defenses in Israel', *Journal of Global Security Studies* 3/2 (April 2018), p. 113.

terrorism, with three major and multiple 'minor' offences on Gaza. The first major assault, Operation Cast Lead, began on 27 December 2008 in response to Hamas-led rocket fire, but quickly became what Avi Shlaim describes as 'not a war, or even "asymmetric warfare", but a one-sided massacre', with over 1,400 Gazans killed, including 313 children, 5,500 wounded, and over 80 per cent estimated to be civilians.[68] The Goldstone Report, commissioned by the UN Human Rights Council and led by South African judge Richard Goldstone, concluded that the operation was 'a deliberately disproportionate attack designed to punish, humiliate and *terrorise* a civilian population, radically diminish its local economic capacity both to work and to provide for itself, and to force upon it an ever-increasing sense of dependency and vulnerability' (emphasis added).[69]

Operation Cast Lead was followed by Operation Pillar of Defence in 2012, a mostly aerial assault that killed 158 Palestinians, and Operation Protective Edge in 2014, in which over 2,200 Palestinians were killed, at least two-thirds of them civilians, and over 10,000 wounded. Over 90,000 homes were razed or damaged, and reconstruction was estimated at 6 billion dollars over twenty years, in a region already in humanitarian crisis.[70] The recurrent incursions into Gaza are known in Israel as 'mowing the lawn'. As Shlaim writes, 'this operative metaphor implies a task that has to be performed regularly and mechanically without end. It also alludes to the indiscriminate slaughter of civilians and the inflicting of damage on civilian infrastructure.'[71]

Meanwhile, in the West Bank, Palestinians have been subject to increasing settler terrorism from extremist groups. According to UN records, in 2011, extremist settlers launched over 400 attacks on Palestinians and 'nearly 300 attacks on Palestinian property, causing over 100 Palestinian casualties and destroying or damaging about 10,000 trees of Palestinian farmers'.[72] In 2018, figures were similar, with over 200 incidents characterised by arson, damaging trees and crops, vandalising homes, and physical assaults on farmers and herders. Referred to as 'price-tag' attacks, these actions are viewed as vigilantism by those who perpetrate them, with the UN's Office for the

---

68 A. Shlaim, 'Ten Years after the First War on Gaza, Israel Still Plans Endless Brute Force', *Guardian* (7 January 2019).
69 UN Human Rights Council, 'Report of the UN Fact-Finding Mission on the Gaza Conflict', A/HRC/12/48 (25 September 2009).
70 Associated Press, 'Housing Group: 20 Years to Rebuild Gaza after Fighting with Israel', *Ha'aretz* (30 August 2014).
71 Shlaim, 'Ten Years after'.
72 D. Byman and N. Sachs, 'The Rise of Settler Terrorism: The West Bank's Other Violent Extremists', *Foreign Affairs* 91/5 (2012), p. 75.

Coordination of Humanitarian Affairs (OCHA) recording 144 Palestinian attacks against Israeli settlers in the same period.[73] These two-way attacks, though much smaller-scale than the Gaza Wars, represent the everyday 'slow-burn' terrorism that affects both communities as reprisal attacks continue.

Discussion

The historical perspective on terrorism in Israel/Palestine helps us see how it is a history of interlocking terrorisms that cannot be fully understood in isolation. This is not to condone tit-for-tat or 'terrorism-for-terrorism' logic, nor to equate all actions as equal in severity or impact, but rather to show that terrorism in protracted conflicts is better understood as a process or a system, a double helix of sorts, rather than a series of isolated incidents. The form this double helix takes at any point is influenced by the conflict dynamics of the time, including pushback to peace initiatives, and also by the local and global contexts of each period.

Conflict Dynamics

In each of the three time periods discussed, the distinct conflict dynamics influenced the forms in which terrorism manifested. In the interwar period, the conflict was essentially a three-way battle between the British, the Jewish Zionists and the Palestinian Arabs. Direct Jew/Arab violence clearly existed, but most acts of terrorism, violence specifically for a political purpose, largely targeted the British, as the most powerful political actor in the region at the time. Both Jews and Arabs used violence to try to pressure the British to favour their group's national aspirations in the context of Britain's dual obligation, with terrorism peaking in the lead-up and aftermath of proposed partition plans and agreements.

In the late twentieth century, the conflict shifted to a double-stranded conflict, first between Israel and the Arab states (as manifest in the 1948 War, the Suez Crisis, the 1967 War and the 1973 War), and second between Israel and the PLO. In this context, the PLO was using terrorism alongside guerrilla warfare to force world attention to the Palestinian issue, and to take back the struggle from the Arab states. Israel's policies, however, often conflated the PLO with neighbouring Arab states, as evidenced by the incursions into

---

73 OCHA, 'High Level of Violence by Israeli Settlers, Rise in Israeli Fatalities', *The Monthly Humanitarian Bulletin* (October 2018), www.ochaopt.org/content/high-level-violence-israeli-settlers-rise-israeli-fatalities.

Jordan and most notably Lebanon, ultimately triggering grievances that arguably led to more terrorism over the years. Once again, terrorism was most evident at times when one or more parties began engaging in diplomacy alongside armed resistance.

Since the first intifada and the Oslo peace process, the conflict has come back to an Israeli–Palestinian conflict. While regional actors still play a role, and while the refugee issue cannot be overlooked, most acts of terrorism have been focused within Israel and the Palestinian Territories, shifting from more performative terrorism and militarily strategic counterterrorism to direct terrorism, aimed to inflict retributive pain and suffering on the opposing population. Despite the brief optimism around the Oslo Accords, their failure and the resulting disillusionment has only increased terrorism on both sides.

Internal Dynamics

At each phase of the conflict, internal dynamics also accelerated the use of terrorism. In the early years, competition between the Irgun and Stern Gang spurred the frequency and intensity of attacks carried out, and these were further exacerbated by the tensions between both the Haganah and the Jewish leadership. Then, in the mid-twentieth century, competition between Fatah, the PFLP and other organisations under the PLO accelerated the use of terrorism, and in the post-Oslo period, competition between Hamas and Islamic Jihad, and crucially Fatah and Hamas, have largely influenced the tactics used. Likewise, in Israel in the post-Oslo period, competition between political parties for appearing the toughest on terrorism and security has fuelled acceptance of policies like 'mowing the lawn'.

Global Context

The external backdrop of world events and historical trajectories is also crucial for understanding terrorism in Israel/Palestine and other protracted conflicts. In the interwar period, for example, the conflict can only be understood in the context of both national and anticolonialist movements that were sweeping the world at the time. Both Jews and Arabs felt a national birthright to the land with historical and religious roots, and each saw Britain as both a facilitator and an obstacle to that national realisation. For the Jewish population, the movement for statehood became crucial in the aftermath of the Second World War and the Holocaust; while the Zionist movement started long before that, it is not surprising that attacks against the British accelerated in the years following the war, as Britain continued to limit immigration to Palestine at the same time that most European states (including Britain) were resistant to accepting Jewish refugees.

In the latter half of the twentieth century, the conflict became increasingly influenced by Cold War dynamics, in terms of sources of arms, funding, alliances and political capital. Further, the number of proxy wars overlaid with non-Cold War self-determination movements introduced a new era of guerrilla warfare and political violence, with groups like the PLO looking to conflicts like Vietnam and Algeria as models. There was also increasing 'borrowing' of tactics and strategies, and vocalised solidarity, between the PLO and the Provisional Irish Republican Army (IRA) in the Northern Ireland conflict, and the African National Congress (ANC) in South Africa. At the same time, states were also sharing and learning from each other's counterterrorism strategies, with Israel adopting particular forms of torture and cruel, inhumane and degrading treatment, as well as the use of administrative detention, that had been used by the British in Northern Ireland and the apartheid government in South Africa.

Finally, in the post-Oslo period, the conflict has been transformed by the end of the Cold War, with the leftist parties severely weakened and the conflict increasingly influenced by the United States's role as sole global superpower. Further, after 11 September 2001, the use of religious 'jihadi' rhetoric increased in Hamas's and Islamic Jihad's recruitment, while the 'security' and 'war on terror' narratives allowed Israel to justify some of its 'deterrence' policies that can only be defined as state terrorism.

Conclusion

The history of terrorisms in Israel/Palestine is a long and complex one, and one that will no doubt continue to be written as the conflict eludes resolution, even one hundred years on. The historical approach, however, helps us understand the *longue durée* of terrorism in the conflict, and also provides insights into how terrorism manifests in protracted conflicts. Indeed, terrorism is not only a catalogue of tit-for-tat attacks, but rather a system of actors and events that is constantly influenced by conflict dynamics, intra-group competition and global trends and realities.

Further Reading

D. Byman, *A High Price: The Triumphs and Failures of Israeli Counterterrorism* (Oxford, Oxford University Press, 2011)

B. Hoffman, *Anonymous Soldiers* (New York, Knopf, 2015)

B. Kimmerling and J. Migdal, *The Palestinian People: A History* (Cambridge, Harvard University Press, 2003)

B. Milton-Edwards and S. Farrell, *Hamas* (London, Polity Press, 2010)

B. Morris, *Righteous Victims* (New York, Vintage Books, 2001)

W. Pearlman, *Violence, Nonviolence, and the Palestinian National Movement* (Cambridge, Cambridge University Press, 2011)

8
Terrorism in the Basque Country

LUDGER MEES

The Background: Terrorism and History

History matters, very much so. For years, it has been common practice to understand the phenomenon that journalists and academics coined as the 'Basque problem' in terms of a violent conflict provoked by the activity of an underground terrorist group that was carrying out 'armed struggle' in their fight for Basque sovereignty and independence from the Spanish and French states. This simplistic and reductionist interpretation failed to grasp the complex nature of the 'Basque problem' and its long historical roots. A more realistic and historically informed approach to the problem must substitute any unilateral understanding with a tridimensional perspective that focuses on the three elements inherent to the 'Basque problem'. Violence is only one of these three, the other two being, on the one hand, the century-old political conflict regarding the political and administrative relation between the Basque Country and the states; and on the other, the dispute between the various sectors of what is a pluralistic and heterogeneous society over the exact scope of Basque self-government. Thus, in the long history of what I have labelled the 'Basque contention', terrorism – although a key factor – emerged rather recently in the contention's 150-year history and only represented one minority sector of Basque society. No serious academic account of Basque terrorism can be written without this reference to history.[1]

Yet there is still a second indispensable preliminary observation that can be made in relation to the nexus between history and terrorism in the Basque Country. The master narrative disseminated by ETA (Euskadi 'ta Askatasuna, Basque Country and Freedom) activists and their like-minded

[1] To facilitate reading, I have reduced footnotes in this article to a minimum. Interested readers will find further references to scholarly literature and primary sources in my books *The Basque Contention: Ethnicity, Politics, Violence* (London, Routledge, 2020) and *Nationalism, Violence, and Democracy: The Basque Clash of Identities* (Houndmills, Palgrave Macmillan, 2003).

political followers uses history to legitimise their decision to take up arms. According to this narrative, ETA was but one link in a long chain of popular resistance against Spanish (and French) oppression and the fight for Basque independence. Within this discursive framework, Basque history was not sidelined but was reinterpreted from the Middle Ages as a succession of heroic struggles with one ulterior goal: the realisation of Basque freedom. Accordingly, the Carlist civil wars of the nineteenth century became national liberation wars. The significance of Franco's military uprising was manipulated and reduced to a new aggression against the Basque nation.[2] Under the dictatorship, and as a result of the futility of exiled Basque politicians, ETA was forced to take up arms as the only effective means of defending their people's interests. After Franco's death, nothing essentially changed. The new Spanish democracy continued to deny Basque sovereignty. ETA's task was to lift this pseudo-democratic veil, unmask the crude reality of continuing state repression and act as the armed vanguard in this new period of the Basque people's historical struggle.

This summary of ETA's master narrative suggests a second preliminary objection and premise for this analysis. Basque terrorism cannot be reduced to a mere direct and unavoidable consequence of the political contention over the claim to sovereignty. As I shall argue, the emergence of Basque terrorism and its evolution over half a century and within different political settings was not due to any historical necessity. It was a political decision taken by certain individuals and groups, one which reflected their views and convenient reactions to determined political situations. History is contingent, and even in 1959, when ETA was founded, there were other individuals, other groups, other views and other decisions. Of course, ETA's terrorism was related to and affected by the vicissitudes of the contention on sovereignty, but it was not a necessary and unavoidable result of it. The group's long endurance is owed to the confluence of different factors that developed their own dynamics beyond the evolution of the political contention itself. In other words: Basque political violence emerged within a context of contentious claim-making over identity and sovereignty issues, and throughout half a century it remained connected to these issues, but while this nexus is relevant for the explanation of political violence in the Basque Country, it is not sufficient to grasp the complexity of violent political activity from the late

---

2 For the nationalist interpretation of the Carlist and Civil War(s), see V. López de Maturana, 'Las Guerras Carlistas' and S. de Pablo, 'Guerra Civil', in S. de Pablo, J. L. de la Granja, L. Mees and J. Casquete (eds.), *Diccionario ilustrado de símbolos del nacionalismo vasco* (Madrid, Tecnos, 2012).

1960s to 2011. On the contrary, a brief glance at Basque history reveals that the Basque contention was shaped by a democratic and civic grassroots movement that reinterpreted the long tradition of Basque ethnic particularism in political terms.

Throughout the Middle Ages, the seven Basque territories on Spanish (Gipuzkoa, Biscay, Álava, Navarre) and French (Lapurdi, Zuberoa, Behe-Nafarroa) soil were parts of the Spanish and French kingdoms and enjoyed a high level of self-governance granted by specific pre-constitutional charters, known as the fueros. Although these territories had never formally established any kind of politico-administrative union within one single state, eighteenth- and nineteenth-century visitors from abroad coincided in their descriptions of the Basques as distinct from the Spanish or the French, governed by their own rules and institutions and bearers of an identity which the German intellectual and politician Wilhelm von Humboldt did not hesitate to describe as a sort of 'national pride'.[3] The core element of this particularist identity was the Basque language: Euskara. It was also the awareness of possessing a language different from any other that triggered the process of 'ethnogenesis'[4] among the sixteenth- and seventeenth-century Basque writers who invented a common name for the seven territories: 'Euskal Herria' ('land of Basque-speakers').[5] As long as self-governance was respected by the rulers, Basque citizens remained loyal subjects of the Spanish and French crowns.

From the end of the eighteenth and throughout the turbulent nineteenth century, this mutually accepted status quo came under pressure. The French revolutionaries abolished the Basque charters of self-government as obsolete vestiges of the *Ancien Régime* and initiated a coercive process of French nation-building. In Spain, the struggle between emerging liberal forces and the defenders of the *Ancien Régime* was decided across three civil wars and ended with the victory of a conservative form of liberalism that had managed to gain support from the Catholic Church for the establishment of the Bourbon 'Restoration Monarchy' in 1876. Akin to its French revolutionary neighbours before, Cánovas del Castillo's Spanish conservative government

---

3 W. von Humboldt, *Werke: Dritter Band 1799–1818* (Berlin, B. Behr Verlag, 1904), esp. pp. 119, 129 and 292.
4 See A. D. Smith, *Ethno-Symbolism and Nationalism: A Cultural Approach* (New York, Routledge, 2009), p. 46.
5 L. Mees, 'A Nation in Search of a Name: Cultural Realities, Political Projects, and Terminological Struggles in the Basque Country', in P. Salaburu and X. Alberdi (eds.), *The Challenge of a Bilingual Society in the Basque Country* (Reno, University of Nevada Press, 2012).

abolished the fueros, offering Basque elites a certain fiscal autonomy ('Concierto Económico') in order to placate and eventually silence opposition against the new regime in the Basque territories. Apart from minority liberal sectors in the Basque urban middle classes, the majority of the mostly agrarian country had aligned with the traditionalist defenders of the *Ancien Régime* who had utilised their commitment to the fueros as a powerful tool for mobilisation in the Basque region. Yet even significant sectors of Basque liberalism were opposed to the radical abolition of the fueros, demanding instead an *aggiornamento* of the charters and their incorporation into the constitutional framework of the Restoration monarchy. The unwillingness of liberal Spanish governments to attend to these claims gave rise to a powerful sociopolitical movement that soon gained political hegemony in the Basque territories. Fuerismo was a proto-nationalist movement that combined a resolute defence of Basque self-government with loyal recognition of Spanish sovereignty.

In the late nineteenth century, this particular 'double patriotism'[6] was put in jeopardy by two factors. First, the new liberal ruling elite's uncompromising rejection of any territorial project that was likely to undermine the unity of the Spanish nation turned the key element of the fuerist political message into wishful thinking, i.e. the idea of a negotiated settlement of the fuero question within the new constitutional framework. And second, the process of radical socio-economic industrial modernisation initiated in the two Basque coastal provinces of Biscay and Gipuzkoa since the late 1880s turned their social, economic and cultural structures upside down. Akin to other cases of rapid industrial growth in Europe, people's living environs were dramatically transformed within only a few years. One significant result was a massive influx of non-Basque migration to the mining, iron and steel areas, which in turn shaped a new working class and labour movement mostly under the control of socialist organisations. Frequently violent class conflicts with barricades on the streets of Bilbao and other cities provoked anxiety among the lower middle classes, who feared the consequences of this undesired turmoil they had sought to avoid.[7]

This middle-class anxiousness led to political radicalisation and the foundation of the Basque Nationalist Party (Partido Nacionalista Vasco – Euzko

---

6 The best account of nineteenth-century fuerismo and its inherent 'double patriotism' is C. Rubio, *La identidad vasca en el siglo XIX* (Madrid, Biblioteca Nueva, 2003).

7 J. P. Fusi, *Política obrera en el País Vasco (1880–1923)* (Madrid, Turner, 1975); M. González Portilla et al., *Los orígenes de una metrópoli industrial: la Ría de Bilbao*, 2 vols (Bilbao, Fundación BBVA, 2001).

Alderdi Jeltzalea, PNV/EAJ) in 1895 by Sabino Arana Goiri. The early PNV became the gathering point for the urban lower middle classes which had lost their political references as a result of the ongoing decline of the Carlist traditionalists and the fuerista movement, whose moderate and accommodative stance had become outdated in an increasingly polarised environment that required radical answers to radical challenges. Early Basque nationalism was a popular protest movement that combined reactionary discursive ingredients (anti-liberalism, anti-socialism, anti-migrant xenophobia, Ultramontane Catholicism) with democratic proposals for political modernisation (politics as the people's business and not a tiny elite's; women's participation in politics; severe criticism of the corrupt political system, vote-buying etc.). In order to escape juridical harassment and abandon its initial status as a semi-legal and anti-constitutional party, the PNV soon dropped its demands for independence and formulated the restoration of the fueros as its ulterior political goal, leaving the interpretation of this claim up to individual party members. This calculated ambiguity had a twofold positive effect. On the one hand, it led to the party's legalisation, permitting Sabino Arana's followers to involve themselves in politics without the coercive sword of Damocles hanging over them. And, on the other, it was the grounding for a steady broadening of the party's social base and its evolution towards a popular cross-class movement, since both pro-independence nationalists and those who favoured a regional form of home rule within the state could consider the party their political home. There was yet another effect linked to the party's political ambivalence. Translating the fuzzy formula of the restoration of the fueros into concrete political strategies was always likely to provoke internal disputes and perhaps a split. This happened in 1921, ending a period of moderate campaigning in favour of a limited regional autonomy that had been dismissed by the governing monarchic power elites in Madrid. Instead of initiating negotiations, the Spanish government and the monarchic parties had responded by categorically rejecting all of the PNV's demands while simultaneously launching a juridical offensive against the party and its office holders. With the PNV leadership's moderate position going unrewarded by any kind of concession from Madrid, the pro-independence sectors abandoned the party and founded a more radical one.[8]

---

8 On early Basque nationalism, see J. Corcuera, *La patria de los vascos* (Madrid, Taurus, 2001); A. Elorza, *Un pueblo escogido* (Barcelona, Crítica, 2001); S. de Pablo, L. Mees and J. A. Rodríguez Ranz, *El Péndulo Patriótico: Historia del Partido Nacionalista Vasco*, Vol. 1: *1895–1936* (Barcelona, Crítica, 1999), pp. 21–57; J. L. de la Granja, *Ángel o demonio: Sabino Arana. El patriarca del nacionalismo vasco* (Madrid, Tecnos, 2015), pp. 25–213.

Neither the moderate nor radical nationalists had much time to continue pursuing their political goals. In 1923, General Miguel Primo de Rivera's military coup inaugurated a new period of Spanish nationalist dictatorship, outlawing and persecuting Basque political nationalism for seven years. Only after the dictatorship's fall and the establishment of the Second Republic in 1931 could Basque nationalism, reunified into one party since 1930,[9] recover legal and institutional politics with the achievement of regional autonomy being the party's primary objective. However, having established an electoral alliance with the extreme right-wing Tradicionalistas, the PNV clashed with the new centre-left republican government, and Basque regional autonomy was not attained until October 1936,[10] after the PNV initiated a cautious strategic shift to the centre with the Civil War already under way. Standing before Gernika's historical freedom oak, the young PNV leader José Antonio Aguirre became the first Basque *lehendakari* ('president'), presiding over a multiparty government constituted by the PNV and the Popular Front's left-wing parties. Despite the enormous effort of the new Basque military forces under President Aguirre's command, just eight months after Aguirre's inauguration he and his ministers were pushed into exile as Franco, with German and Italian support,[11] conquered the Basque provinces, abolished regional autonomy and banned all 'separatist' parties. Again, as in 1923, violence and authoritarian Spanish nationalism silenced the Basque claim of self-governance. This time, however, the new dictatorial interregnum would last much longer. Neither geopolitical pressures nor domestic resistance was able to challenge Generalísimo Franco's rule. In the end, biology did the job: after a long disease, Franco died in 1975 at the age of eighty-two.[12]

---

9 A minority who rejected the PNV's ultra-Catholicism founded the liberal Acción Nacionalista Vasca (ANV).
10 The Statute of Autonomy included the three provinces of Biscay, Gipuzkoa and Álava, but Navarre, where Basque nationalism's presence was weaker, was excluded.
11 The most emblematic expression of this support was the April 1937 bombardment of Gernika by the German Condor Legion and several Italian fighter jets. This war crime became the motive for Picasso's famous masterpiece *Guernica*, presented at the Paris Universal Exhibition in September 1937. See L. Mees, 'Guernica/Gernika como símbolo', *Historia Contemporánea* 35 (2007).
12 J. L. de la Granja, *Nacionalismo y II República en el País Vasco: Estatutos de autonomía, partidos y elecciones. Historia de Acción Nacionalista Vasca, 1930–1936* (Madrid, Siglo XIX, 2008); S. de Pablo, L. Mees and J. A. Rodríguez Ranz, *El péndulo patriótico: Historia del Partido Nacionalista Vasco*, Vol. 2: *1936–1979* (Barcelona, Crítica, 2001), pp. 9–74. For the Spanish and international context of the Civil War, see P. Preston, *The Spanish Civil War: Reaction, Revolution, and Revenge* (New York, W. W. Norton, 2007).

From Politics to Violence: The Foundation of ETA

ETA's foundation in 1959 resulted from a split in the PNV youth organisation and their confluence with other nationalist youngsters in the interior. Recovering Durkheim's concept of anomie, the German sociologist Peter Waldmann described the context in which the new organisation emerged as a deep multilayered crisis.[13] In this situation, social bonds between individuals and the community break down, and the anxious search for orientation and guidance in a menacing context of radical social change surfaces among broad sectors of society. The process of social change, triggered by a second wave of Basque industrial revolution beginning at the end of the 1950s, provoked a double-barrelled reaction. On the one hand, economic growth, full employment, increasing wages and the new era of consumerism were strong incentives for the relaxation of political demands and a gradual accommodation of many Basques within the dictatorship. Yet, on the other hand, this very context of radical social change also opened up new windows of opportunity for contentious mobilisation against the regime: while full employment reduced the risk of mobilisation, a new law (1958) opened the door to collective bargaining agreements within the official vertical labour unions, giving rise to the founding of a new union (1963: Comisiones Obreras de Vizcaya) that was quickly outlawed; the Basque Catholic Church adopted an increasingly distant and critical stance towards the regime, while protecting and sponsoring cultural initiatives related to Basque culture and language; the new post-war generation was no longer attached to traditional political loyalties and behaviour patterns and was keen to respond to daily repression in the interior through deeds and not only words; Africa's and Asia's successful anticolonialist movements against powerful empires and their colonial rule inspired the Basques, who believed Franco and Spain's colonial occupation of the Basque Country might be similarly overthrown. Finally, the mixture of leftist thought and anticolonialist strategies offered a new and, in the eyes of many, meaningful discursive framework to criticise traditional Basque nationalism, which was suffering a deep crisis by the end of the 1950s, accentuated by President Aguirre's unexpected death in 1960.[14] With Aguirre's death, the PNV's traditional nationalism lost both its charismatic leader and the key proponent of its strategy since 1945, i.e. the hope that the Western democracies would remove Hitler's last ally Franco and reward the

---

13 P. Waldmann, *Militanter Nationalismus im Baskenland* (Frankfurt, Vervuert, 1990), p. 71.
14 L. Mees, J. L. de la Granja, S. de Pablo, J. A. Rodríguez Ranz, *La política como pasión: El lehendakari José Antonio Aguirre (1904–1960)* (Madrid, Tecnos, 2012).

Basques for their collaboration in the war against fascism. What happened was exactly the opposite: the Cold War served to assist Franco's transformation from an obsolete relic of the fascist past to a new indispensable ally in the fight against communist imperialism.

While ETA's foundational manifesto was rather moderate in demanding the 'salvation of the Basque essence through an exclusively patriotic and thus unpolitical and non-confessional channel',[15] without any reference to the use of violence, in 1963 a complete rupture with mainstream nationalism was initiated when the young Basque intellectual Federico Krutwig published his book 'Vasconia'. Krutwig's thesis would become a sort of bible for nationalists engaged in or attracted by the new project.[16] The book was crucial for several reasons. First, it was the first positive reception of Karl Marx and other leftist thinkers' ideas by a Basque nationalist. Second, it utilised that era's fashionable ethno-linguistic theories to present Euskadi, the Basque homeland, as a peripheral European nation that was being colonised by the Spanish (and French) centre. Third, drawing from various anticolonialist experiences, the book disseminated the encouraging message that efficient theories and strategies for the fight against the oppressor were already available: nothing had to be invented, the Basques need only learn from events occurring in Africa and Asia. And finally, unlike the foundational manifesto, Krutwig utilised the Third World liberation movement's example to present violence not as one of many tools Basques could employ, but rather as an indispensable necessity: 'If ... the only possibility of achieving national independence is through the means of victorious weapons, we also observe that the only people who have been able to have their rights recognised are those who have managed to defend them with arms in their hands.'[17]

According to Krutwig, there was no way back to institutional mainstream nationalism, which was blamed for defending the local bourgeoisie's interests, betraying the Basque nation and collaborating with the regime. The Basque government-in-exile, now presided over by Aguirre's successor Jesús María Leizaola, as well as the PNV leadership, had adopted a critical stance against ETA's first acts of sabotage: for instance, in 1961 some activists unsuccessfully tried to derail a train carrying Francoist Civil War veterans. The seven culprits' exorbitant sentences – ranging from five to twenty years of prison[18] – reflected badly on Leizaola's criticism, helped the new

---

15 See the manifesto in Pablo et al., *El péndulo patriótico*, Vol. 2, p. 236.
16 F. Sarrailh de Ihartza [pseud.: Federico Krutwig], *Vasconia: Estudio dialéctico de una nacionalidad*, 2nd ed. (Buenos Aires, Ediciones Norbait, 1973 [1st ed. 1963]).
17 Sarrailh de Ihartza, *Vasconia*, p. 328.
18 Pablo et al., *El péndulo patriótico*, Vol. 2, p. 267.

organisation shape its image as a group of selfless freedom fighters and added weight to Krutwig's argument that there should be a complete break with the PNV's nationalism. Consequently, it was not surprising that throughout the following years the PNV would effectively abandon any severe criticism of ETA. Instead, it developed an attitude of fatherly scolding, focused on what was considered a leftist 'deviation' from real nationalism and the dangerous weakening of the patriotic struggle that would emanate from any internal split of the movement and violation of basic rules of authority and hierarchy. This soft and cautious criticism went hand in hand with a sense of paternal empathy for the prodigal son who would return home after recognising his errors. ETA's first assassination in 1968 did nothing to change the PNV's attitude. When a Guardia Civil stopped two activists at a traffic control and the policeman realised the car was stolen, one of the *etarras* drew his gun and shot the officer dead. Although the drivers managed to escape, they were captured later that day at another control and one of them was killed: Txabi Etxebarrieta became ETA's first martyr. In response, ETA's Military Front implemented their first planned execution. The victim was Melitón Manzanas, a police officer infamous for his sadistic methods of torturing prisoners.[19]

Years before these first lethal attacks occurred, the underground group had already initiated a polemical discussion that remained unresolved until the mid-1980s. Resulting from the reappraisal of classic Basque pro-independence positions and the incorporation of leftist revolutionary ideas, including armed struggle as a necessary tool for any liberation movement, the unavoidable debate centred on the relationship between these elements within the new revolutionary nationalism. This debate can be reduced to several specific questions: should priority lie with social revolution or achievement of Basque independence? Who were the struggle's main allies, other (Spanish) revolutionary forces or traditional Basque nationalism? What was the armed struggle's function? Was the armed vanguard supposed to weaken the enemy, reveal its contradictions and trigger a popular war through spectacular strikes? Or was it a complementary tool under the strict control and at the

---

19 R. B. Clark, *The Basque Insurgents: ETA, 1952–1980* (Madison and London, University of Wisconsin Press, 1984); G. Jáuregui, *Ideología y estrategia política de ETA: Análisis de su evolución entre 1959 y 1968*, 2nd ed. (Madrid, Siglo XXI, 1985); A. Elorza (ed.), *La historia de ETA* (Madrid, Temas de Hoy, 2000); J. Zulaika, *Basque Violence: Metaphor and Sacrament* (Reno, University of Nevada Press, 2000); G. Fernández Soldevilla, *La voluntad del gudari: Génesis y metástasis de la violencia de ETA* (Madrid, Tecnos, 2016); L. Mees, 'Politics, Economy, or Culture? The Rise and Development of Basque Nationalism in the Light of Social Movement Theory', *Theory and Society* 33 (2004).

service of political leadership? From a historical perspective, it can be asserted that over the years those who controlled the arms and propagated radical nationalism rather than revolutionary socialism usually emerged as the winners in these internal clashes. Together with unanticipated factors, such as the police arresting an entire leadership, various arguments explain this outcome. First, the weakness of leftist thought in Euskadi's political culture and the strength, occasionally even hegemony, of the nationalist tradition gave an advantage to political projects that could be presented as a new contribution to the long history of struggle for sovereignty. Second, in the eyes of many Basques, the Francoist dictatorship's repression of Basque nationalism and culture gave greater rationale to the colonialist occupation thesis and the necessity of a *national* struggle for freedom. And third, the activists who controlled the arms and carried out assaults against the regime garnered all the attention. Indeed, for a wide audience, the armed militants' spectacular strikes were ETA's sole public image. By contrast, fellow comrades involved in mobilising Basque factory workers failed to make the headlines of the regime's media.

The first significant split occurred in 1966/7 when ETA militants gathered at the organisation's Fifth Assembly, carried out over two successive meetings. As a consequence of disagreements over goals and strategy, the more leftist sector abandoned the organisation and founded ETA-Berri ('New ETA') with the aim of creating a revolutionary party that would join with Spanish leftist worker organisations to foster socialist revolution in Spain as a first step to establishing a socialist and independent Basque Country. While this group quickly faded into political and social irrelevance, the 'old' ETA decided to restructure the organisation into four separate yet coordinated 'fronts' (political, military, economic/worker and cultural), without establishing any hierarchic relationship between the components.

It was therefore no surprise when the same polemics surfaced again a couple of years later. After ETA's entire leadership was arrested, José María Escubi, head of the organisation's more leftist (*obrerista*) wing, took advantage of the power vacuum to restore ETA-Berri's project to convert ETA into a revolutionary workers' party. In the summer of 1970 this new orientation was rejected by the more nationalist sectors, among which the Military Front were already playing a leading role. The nationalist sectors endorsed the Fifth Assembly's programme, while Escubi and his followers regrouped under the label ETA VI (their assembly was officially designated number six in the organisation's history), before abandoning ETA and merging with other insignificant Maoist, Trotskyist and communist groups.

The marginalisation of ETA VI came with a twist. When six ETA prisoners were sentenced to death during the famous Burgos trial of December 1970, all six declared their adherence to ETA VI. To recapture the spotlight, the Military Front kidnapped German consul Eugen Beihl, monopolised media coverage and won support from famous international intellectuals such as Jean-Paul Sartre. Wary of hampering popular mobilisations against the trial, the *milis* released the consul and celebrated the commutation of the death penalties to lifelong imprisonment as a triumph of the concerted pressure articulated by armed struggle and popular mobilisation. Once again, the Military Front had managed to emerge triumphant from an initially adverse situation by exploiting the prisoners' popularity for their own purposes. When in December 1973 the *milis* killed Admiral Luis Carrero Blanco, the Francoist government's new president and the main candidate to succeed the dictator in the event of his resignation or death, this image of ETA as fearless freedom fighters against a cruel dictatorship provoked, if not open admiration, at least silent consent even among many non-nationalist anti-Francoists in the Basque Country and Spain.[20]

Things changed almost a year later when, in September 1974, ETA bombed a Madrid cafe (Cafetería Rolando) near the regime's key police institution in charge of political repression (Dirección General de Seguridad). The bomb injured 80 and killed 13, all civilians bar one, a police officer. Since the group's foundation, ETA's public image had depended, to a great extent, on the selection of its targets, usually power-holders in the regime or members of the police and military forces. With the Rolando bomb, the paramilitaries had crossed that line and had killed 'innocent' people. Although from a scholarly vantage point the definition of terrorism as 'violence against noncombatants, usually common or ordinary people, in order to advance a political cause' seems problematic,[21] the Rolando bomb triggered a slow, gradual change in the public perception of ETA. Could a group willing to shed 'innocent' blood continue to be perceived as selfless fighters for democracy and freedom? Or should it be labelled a terrorist organisation, given that it performed 'heterogeneous violence used or

---

20 P. Eser and S. Peters (eds.), *El atentado contra Carrero Blanco como lugar de (no)memoria: Narraciones históricas y representaciones culturales* (Frankfurt, Vervuert, 2016).
21 If the targeting of non-combatants and 'innocent' civilians is the main criterion for the definition of terrorism, and given that in many terrorist acts civilians die alongside selected 'combatants' (politicians, police and army officers), does it make sense to distinguish between 'innocent' victims who must be labelled as victims of a terrorist act and others who would be victims of another kind of violence, whatever the label for this latter might be? The quotation is from J. Goodwin, 'The Causes of Terrorism', in E. Chenoweth, R. English, A. Gofas and S. N. Kalyas (eds.), *The Oxford Handbook of Terrorism* (Oxford, Oxford University Press, 2019), p. 253.

threatened with a political aim'? What surfaced for the first time in 1974 would achieve broad acceptance only years later, i.e. the typification of ETA's activity as terrorism, understood here according to Richard English as

> a variety of acts, of targets, and of actors; it possesses an important psychological dimension, producing terror or fear among a directly threatened group and also a wider implied audience in the hope of maximizing political communication and achievement; it embodies the exerting and implementing of power, and the attempted redressing of power relations; it represents a subspecies of warfare, and as such it can form part of a wider campaign of violent and non-violent attempts at political leverage.[22]

The fact that ETA did not claim official responsibility for the Rolando bomb and its lethal consequences indicates that the group was very much concerned about its public image. It was not until 2018, the year of ETA's dissolution, that the paramilitaries finally acknowledged authorship.[23]

The internal polemics that arose in the aftermath of the Rolando bombing, carried out by the Military Front without coordination with ETA's political leadership, resurfaced and intensified the aforementioned debate over the relationship between armed struggle and popular mobilisation. This eventually ended in ETA's last significant split. The Military Front opted to abandon the organisation in order to continue acting exclusively as the armed vanguard that would ideally trigger a social revolution, leaving the political work to other organisations. This new offshoot adopted the name 'ETA militar'. ETA's main wing, now denominated 'ETA político-militar', continued to embrace combining political and military activity within the same organisation, but with a clear hierarchy: the politicos would decide strategies and programmes, while the military branch carried out its activities at the direction of the former.[24] Following Franco's death in 1975, the *poli-milis*' story is one of continual, and ultimately futile, attempts to resolve the contradiction between mass mobilisation and armed struggle in the context of a democratic setting. ETA p.m.'s dissolution in 1982 was the only possible response to this inherent contradiction. In the meantime, however, three members of FRAP, an extreme left underground organisation, and two ETA p.m. members (Juan Paredes Manot ('Txiki') and Ángel Otaegi) were executed in 1975, just two months before the dictator's death. This act, in conjunction with the first extreme right-wing terrorist murders of two individuals for their alleged relations with ETA, was grist for

---

22 R. English, *Terrorism: How to Respond* (New York, Oxford University Press, 2009), p. 24.
23 *Gara*, 6 November 2018.
24 G. Fernández Soldevilla, *Héroes, heterodoxos y traidores: Historia de Euskadiko Ezkerra (1974–1994)* (Madrid, Tecnos, 2013), pp. 68–73.

the mill of those advocating for the continuity of armed struggle. Furthermore, the regime's violent reactions to massive mobilisations on Basque streets appeared to validate ETA's thesis regarding the likelihood of a popular uprising unleashed by the action–repression–action dynamic. In 1975, despite the Rolando bomb, ETA was more popular than ever, and most observers viewed it as the 'main protagonist of the opposition in the Basque Country'.[25] When Franco died in 1975, forty-five people had already lost their lives at the hands of ETA or right-wing killer commandos (Fig. 8.1).

The Violent Microcosm

The end of the Francoist dictatorship and the subsequent negotiated path towards democracy, a process that has been described as a 'transition through

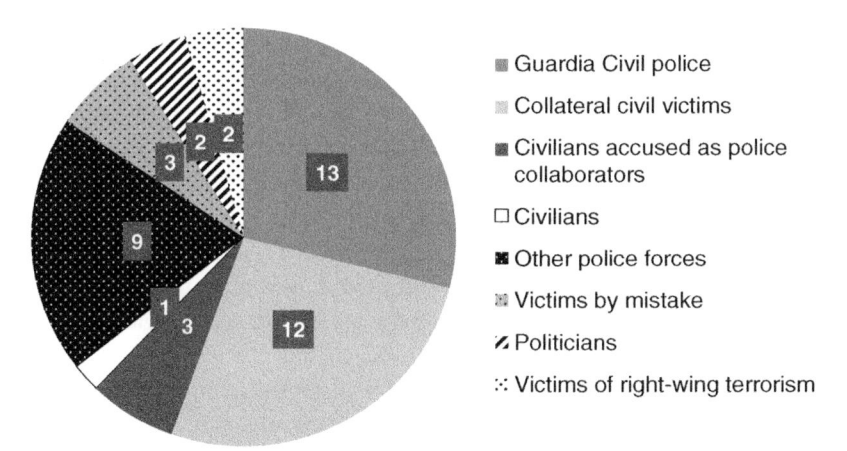

Figure 8.1 Deaths caused by ETA and right-wing terrorism, 1968–75 (R. López Romo, *Informe Foronda: Los contextos históricos del terrorismo en el País Vasco y la consideración social de sus víctimas, 1968–2010* (Vitoria-Gasteiz, Instituto de Historia Social Valentín de Foronda, 2015))[26]

---

25 S. de Pablo, 'La dictadura franquista y el exilio', in J. L. de la Granja and S. de Pablo (eds.), *Historia del País Vasco y Navarra en el siglo XX*, 2nd ed. (Madrid, Biblioteca Nueva, 2009), p. 108.
26 Unless otherwise indicated, Figures 8.1 and 8.2 and numerical information on victims are from R. López Romo, *Informe Foronda: Los contextos históricos del terrorismo en el País Vasco y la consideración social de sus víctimas, 1968–2010* (Vitoria-Gasteiz, Instituto de Historia Social Valentín de Foronda, 2015), pp. 125–8.

transaction' carried out by the democratic opposition and the regime's reformist sectors opened new opportunities for the settlement of the Basque contention.[27] After Franco's death, ETA's violence resulted in a new hierarchy between the contention's aforementioned three dimensions. Traditionally, an intra-Basque consensus regarding the desirable scale of self-governance gave way to negotiations with the state over the politico-administrative relationship between Spain and the Basque Country. Now a negotiated settlement on the demand for self-governance was no longer a goal per se, but rather a precondition for the end of terrorist violence. A broad consensus among the political actors, including moderate Basque nationalists and others, pivoted around the conviction that the concession of a certain degree of Basque self-government would undermine ETA's popularity and eventually end terrorism. During the transition years, the PNV presented itself as an indispensable broker in the process to cease violence while developing a strategy of critical participation that yielded two main achievements: first, the constitutionalisation of Basque 'historical rights', which were recognised in an amendment to the 1978 Constitution; and, second, regional autonomy for the provinces of Biscay, Gipuzkoa and Álava, endorsed by a Basque referendum in 1979.[28] This negotiation culminated in 1980 with the establishment of post-Francoist Basque autonomy under PNV leader Carlos Garaikoetxea, which the party presented as a first step on the gradual path towards sovereignty.

One basic problem soon emanated from the belief that limited Basque self-governance was a necessary precondition to end terrorism: those who were meant to be pressured by this strategy were not willing to play the game. On the contrary, ETA left no doubt they would not accept any political settlement short of Basque sovereignty. To them, the game was not between dictatorship and democracy in the form of Basque regional autonomy, but rather between

---

27 D. Share and S. Mainwaring, 'Transition Through Transaction: Democratization in Brazil and Spain', in W. Selcher (ed.), *Political Liberalization in Brazil* (Boulder, CO, Westview Press, 1986).

28 The PNV urged abstention from the Constitutional referendum, citing its non-recognition of the state's multinational character while asserting the 'indissoluble unity of the Spanish Nation', the one and only 'nation' that existed in Spain, together with other 'nationalities' and 'regions'. See S. Juliá, *Transición: Historia de una política española (1937–2017)* (Madrid, Galaxia Gutenberg, 2017); C. Molinero and P. Ysàs, *La Transición: Historia y relatos* (Madrid, Siglo XXI, 2018); D. Muro, 'Una larga Transición: Nacionalismo vasco y cambio político en Euskadi', in M. Ortiz Heras (ed.), *Culturas políticas del nacionalismo español: Del franquismo a la Transición* (Madrid, Los Libros de la Catarata, 2009); J. Ugarte (ed.), *La transición en el País Vasco y España: Historia y memoria* (Bilbao, Universidad del País Vasco, 1998); L. Mees, 'El nacionalismo vasco democrático durante la Transición (1974–1981)', in R. Quirosa-Cheyrouze y Muñoz (ed.), *Los partidos en la Transición: Las organizaciones políticas en la construcción de la democracia española* (Madrid, Biblioteca Nueva, 2013).

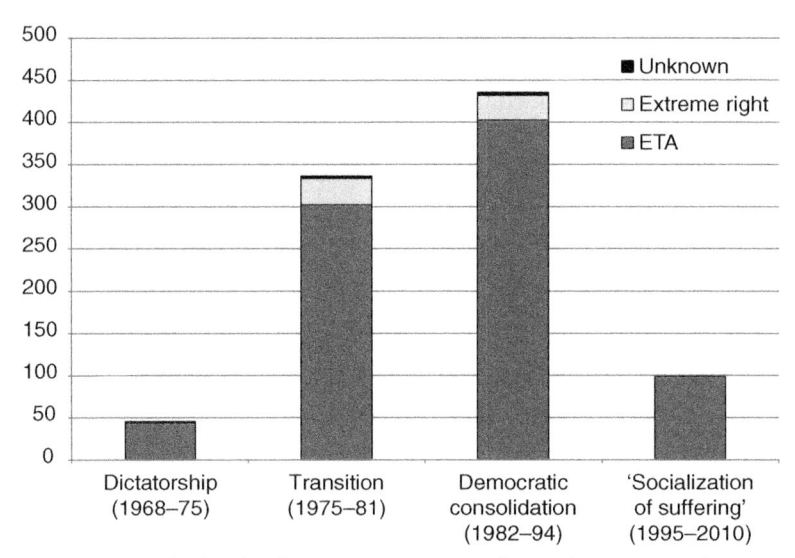

Figure 8.2 Victims of political violence over various periods (R. López Romo, *Informe Foronda: Los contextos históricos del terrorismo en el País Vasco y la consideración social de sus víctimas, 1968–2010* (Vitoria-Gasteiz, Instituto de Historia Social Valentín de Foronda, 2015))[29]

Spanish colonisation and Basque independence. If there were lingering doubts before 1975, afterwards it became increasingly evident that ETA's enemy was not Francoism, but Spain itself, irrespective of the country's constitutional form. The four years following Franco's death, when the new democracy's legal foundations were being set, represented the organisation's most lethal period in its history, with fatalities numbering 270. In 1980, ETA's bloodiest year on record, 96 people were killed, which amounted to one victim every 3.8 days. Some were assassinated because they refused to pay ransom after being kidnapped (48 people between 1976 and 1981). If we add to these the many, mostly entrepreneurs, who received death threats in an effort to extort ETA's so-called 'revolutionary tax', the impact of terrorist violence becomes evident (Fig. 8.2).

Until the cessation of ETA violence in 2011, about 42 per cent of all of those killed were police officers. The Guardia Civil (206) and the Policía Nacional or similar units (149) paid the highest death toll at the hands of ETA commandos. Both during and after Francoism, the police were allowed to respond with a high degree of impunity, partly because official state discourse asserted that the gravity of the terrorist challenge demanded firm

29 The meaning of the fourth period, 'Socialisation of suffering', will be explained below.

countermeasures. During the late 1970s and 1980s, the police took advantage of extremely fluid social and political mobilisation in the Basque provinces to stigmatise any kind of non-conformist behaviour as terrorist or pro-terrorist. In 1974–5, the police killed 22 people at public demonstrations and traffic controls, while at police barracks prisoners were frequently tortured during interrogations. After the dictator's death, arbitrary police violence continued. In March 1976, for example, police opened fire on striking workers leaving a church in Vitoria-Gasteiz, killing five and injuring about 150. And in July 1978, police forces occupied the centre of Renteria in Gipuzkoa, looting and destroying numerous shops. Police violence was exacerbated by right-wing paramilitary anti-ETA commandos, who killed 31 Basques from 1976 to 1981. Between 1983 and 1987, the Grupos Antiterroristas de Liberación (GAL) killed 25 Basques, mostly on French soil, with the objective of forcing the French government to reconsider its lax attitude towards ETA refugees and cooperate more directly with Spanish police forces. Many GAL victims were civilians without any link to ETA and were killed by mistake. This group was particularly relevant, because years later the courts found evidence that the Spanish Ministry of the Interior was implicated in its organisation and funding. High-ranking officials of the Ministry, including the former minister José Barrionuevo, were sentenced to prison terms.[30]

There is no doubt that these illegal practices in the fight against ETA terrorism provoked the opposite of their intended effect. For many, ETA's self-styled image as an armed vanguard in defence of a small nation that was being violently exploited and subdued by a powerful state rang true. Unlike other armed groups in Western Europe (the German Red Army Faction, the Italian Red Brigades), ETA could draw on a broad web of sympathetic organisations for the dissemination of their discourse. A milestone in the implementation of this organisational network came in 1978 when Herri Batasuna (HB, 'Popular Unity') was founded. HB was an electoral coalition encompassing different pro-ETA-m political parties (ANV, ESB, LAIA, HASI) and a number of formally independent personalities. In the following years and decades, HB – under changing names – would act as ETA-m's political and institutional wing, attracting 10 to 15 per cent of votes across various elections. A second key actor in the pro-ETA network was the labour union Langile Abertzaleen Batzordeak (LAB, 'Patriotic Workers' Committees'), which was created in 1974. Over the following years, a myriad of groups and initiatives from radical nationalist youth, feminists, ecologists and

---

30 P. Woodworth, *Dirty War, Clean Hands: ETA, the GAL and Spanish Democracy* (Cork, Cork University Press, 2001).

promoters of Basque culture also orbited the network. These groups frequently met in *Herriko Tabernak* (People's Bars), establishments that emerged throughout the Basque Country and served as gathering places for radical nationalists. As ETA prisoners continued to increase, new organisations dedicated to the defence of prisoners and to coordinating their families and friends also gained importance. The daily *Egin* – supported by a broadcasting station by the same name – was founded in 1977. The militant musical genre 'Basque Radical Rock' gave voice to radical nationalist claims and protests. Festivals and events displayed radical nationalist discursive symbols and stoked nationalist sentiment. ETA-m headed this self-declared Basque Movement for National Liberation, using KAS (Koordinadora Abertzale Sozialista, 'Patriotic Socialist Coordination', 1974) as a coordinating fulcrum to disseminate directives to the network's organisations and groups. KAS also established the conditions for the cessation of ETA violence in its political platform ('KAS Alternative', 1976). KAS sought Basque sovereignty and a socialist revolution that was to be implemented through several measures: amnesty for political prisoners; legalisation of all political parties; expulsion of the Spanish police forces from Euskadi; better living and working conditions for the popular classes; recognition of Basque national sovereignty and, as a first step towards this goal, implementation of a statute of autonomy that guaranteed substantial decision-making capacity.[31]

As mentioned, ETA's political control over this network and its robust organisational links to civil society made it unique among paramilitary groups in Western democracies. The Movement for National Liberation's expansive societal reach allowed a radical Basque nationalist to spend nearly the entire day in this particular milieu without any need to come into contact with people of different political affiliations. Control over this civil nationalist microcosm and its shielding against undesired external influences throughout the following decades was a key factor in ETA's long endurance even after Franco's death.[32]

---

31 S. de Pablo, J. L. de la Granja and L. Mees, *Documentos para la historia del nacionalismo vasco: De los fueros a nuestros días* (Barcelona, Ariel, 1998), pp. 153–5.
32 Among the numerous publications on ETA and the Liberation Movement, see J. M. Mata, *El nacionalismo vasco radical: Discurso, organización y expresiones* (Bilbao, Universidad del País Vasco, 1993); E. Majuelo, *LAB sindikatuaren historia: Langile Abertzaleen Batzordeak (1975–2000)* (Tafalla, Txalaparta, 2000); J. Casquete, *En el nombre de Euskal Herria: La religión política del nacionalismo vasco radical* (Madrid, Tecnos, 2009); I. Bullain, *Revolucionarismo patriótico: El Movimiento de Liberación Nacional Vasco (MLNV). Origen, Ideología y Organización* (Tecnos, Madrid, 2011); Clark, *The Basque Insurgents*; F. Domínguez, *ETA: estrategia organizativa y actuaciones* (Madrid, Taurus, 1998); Fernández Soldevilla, *La voluntad del gudari*; F. Letamendia, *Historia del*

The Decline: Towards Induced Suicide

If ETA's grip on their sociopolitical environment underpinned the organisation's apparent solidity, then it is unsurprising many would see cracks in the paramilitaries' legitimacy and strength were this grip to loosen. Precisely this occurred beginning in the late 1990s as an increasing alienation between the underground group and its followers began to emerge. Several factors account for this looming divorce. First, ETA's decision to broaden their spectrum of targets troubled many sympathisers. Almost anyone ETA considered an 'enemy' of the Basque nation became fair game: conservative and socialist town councillors, journalists, intellectuals, university professors, judges, businessmen unwilling to pay the 'revolutionary tax', Basque police officers and, in general, people who happened to be in the wrong place at the wrong time. Nobody was safe from ETA's violent strikes, although most targets continued to be citizens outside the nationalist community. In 1994, Herri Batasuna, ETA's political wing, issued a new programme ('Oldartzen') endorsing this radical stance. The party's leadership announced a more aggressive strategy to take violent conflict to the Basque Country's streets through a 'socialisation of the suffering'. In subsequent years, pro-ETA gangs initiated a campaign of sabotage and street violence that included defacing walls with bellicose slogans, burning buses and ATMs, or lobbing Molotov cocktails at non-nationalist party headquarters and private residences. In January 1995, ETA killed a Basque town councillor for the first time. Gregorio Ordóñez, a spokesman for the conservative Partido Popular (PP) in San Sebastián's municipal government, was assassinated while having lunch at a popular bar. But it was not until July 1997 that a point of inflection was reached in terms of ETA's popularity. On 1 July, Spanish police rescued José Antonio Ortega Lara, a prison worker who had been kidnapped and held by ETA in a small and wet dungeon for 532 days. The group's leadership had left him to die of starvation upon learning that the Spanish government was unwilling to transfer all Basque prisoners to Basque prisons in exchange for Ortega's release. When he was freed, TV images showed an emaciated, sick man who had lost 23 kg. In July, ETA kidnapped Miguel Ángel Blanco, a young PP town councillor from Ermua who was better known as the drummer for a local band than for his political activity. ETA's leadership again demanded the transfer of prisoners, but the Spanish government again

nacionalismo vasco y ETA (San Sebastián, R&B, 1994); R. López Romo, Años de claroscuros: Nuevos movimientos sociales y democratización en Euskadi (1975–1980) (Bilbao, Universidad del País Vasco, 2011).

refused to capitulate. Blanco's kidnapping ended in a televised killing. After two days of captivity, and despite massive popular mobilisations in Spain and the Basque Country, he was killed by a bullet to the back of the head. The wave of solidarity that had brought together hundreds of thousands of Basque and Spanish citizens in protest against ETA's cruelty and in favour of Blanco's release created a new atmosphere in the fight against terrorism that would later be called 'the spirit of Ermua'. This popular protest was channelled through various groups in a Basque peace movement that started to challenge the radical pro-ETA sectors' control of public space.[33]

A second factor that contributed to ETA's steady divorce from their political and social base was their growing isolation from mainstream PNV nationalism. The PNV, a centrist, moderate and pragmatic nationalist party, controlled the Basque government. In 1996, PNV leadership agreed to support Spain's new conservative government, led by José María Aznar, with its parliamentary votes in exchange for greater Basque autonomy. The pact was reached only a year after the newly elected Aznar had miraculously survived a car bomb planted by the Basque terrorists, and amidst the new political climate that the aforementioned 'spirit of Ermua' had generated, characterised by an increasingly fine line between Basque terrorism and democratic nationalism. This perceived approximation led many in Basque and Spanish society to criticise the PNV for an alleged reluctance to oppose ETA violence. Accordingly, PNV leadership concluded that ETA's existence was jeopardising the party's future and devised a new strategy to bring about its demise through a political rapprochement with its political wing. Their argument seemed unassailable: a new and resolute pro-sovereignty majority in the Basque parliament would obviate any need to continue armed struggle. In September 1998, under the impact of the peace process in Northern Ireland, this rationale led to the 'Lizarra Agreement', supported by twenty-three mostly nationalist organisations, including the PNV and Herri Batasuna.[34] Prior to this, the PNV and its minority partner EA had conducted secret negotiations with ETA in order to achieve an 'unlimited ceasefire'. As a precondition, ETA demanded several political concessions, including the foundation of a new institution that comprised representatives from all seven Basque territories in Spain and France, as well as an end to cooperation

---

33 M. A. Iglesias (ed.), *Ermua, 4 días de julio: 40 voces tras la muerte de Miguel Ángel Blanco* (Madrid, El País-Aguilar, 1997). For the peace movement, see Mees, *Nationalism*, pp. 91–100.
34 The English version of the accord is available at https://peacemaker.un.org/sites/peacemaker.un.org/files/ES_980912_LizarraGaraziAccord.pdf.

with forces intent on 'the destruction of Euskal Herria [the Basque Country] and the construction of Spain (PP and PSOE)'. Adding some qualifications to these demands, which ETA did not sign on, the PNV and EA accepted the deal. Both parties were well aware that what ETA would publicly call an 'indefinite' ceasefire would, in reality, be re-evaluated by them after four months to ascertain if the signatories had kept their word.[35]

In November 1999, the paramilitaries ended the ceasefire, blaming the PNV for failing to meet their commitments to progress towards Basque sovereignty. A secret meeting by President Aznar's emissaries in Zurich with ETA's leadership was also unable to prevent this outcome. In January of the following year, Pedro Antonio Blanco, a lieutenant colonel in the Spanish army, was killed by a car bomb and became the first victim in the aftermath of the Lizarra experiment. Another 22 people were killed in 2000 and 15 more the following year. As a consequence, political and media pressure against the PNV reached new heights. President Aznar, his party leadership and conservative media assailed the PNV for their alleged allegiance to ETA's political wing and unwillingness to fight terrorism. But, despite this unprecedented pressure, the PNV did not change course. Under Juan José Ibarretxe's leadership, who presided as *lehendakari* between 1999 and 2009, the PNV continued to seek – and gain – support from the pro-ETA party for Ibarretxe's investiture and for help in pushing polemical bills through parliament. These bills provoked strong criticism from the non-nationalist parties, who considered them first steps on the road towards Basque sovereignty and a rupture with the Spanish state.[36]

Despite these strategic rapprochements, ETA was unwilling to lay down arms. Nor was its political wing prepared to adopt a more critical stance, let alone reject the paramilitaries' lethal attacks. For the PNV, this experience resulted in political disaster: ETA continued to kill, Basque society was polarised into two opposing blocs, and the PNV lost the centrality that had historically allowed it to build majorities through alliances across the political

---

35 S. Morán, *PNV-ETA: Historia de una relación imposible* (Madrid, Tecnos, 2004), pp. 107–318; Mees, *Nationalism*, pp. 101–62; J. L. de la Granja and S. de Pablo, 'La encrucijada vasca: Entre Ermua y Estella', in J. Tusell et al., *El gobierno de Aznar: Balance de una gestión, 1996–2000* (Barcelona, Crítica, 2000); T. Whitfield, *Endgame for ETA: Elusive Peace in the Basque Country* (London, Hurst & Company, 2014), pp. 79–100.

36 L. Mees, 'Visión y gestión: El nacionalismo democrático 1998–2009', in W. L. Bernecker, D. Íñiguez Hernández and G. Maihold (eds.), *¿Crisis? ¿Qué crisis? España en busca de su camino* (Frankfurt, Vervuert, 2009); L. Mees, 'Nationalist Politics at the Crossroads: The Basque Nationalist Party and the Challenge of Sovereignty (1998–2014)', in R. Gillespie and C. Gray (eds.), *Contesting Spain? The Dynamics of Nationalist Movements in Catalonia and the Basque Country* (New York, Routledge, 2015).

spectrum. The party was dealt a loss in the 2009 elections as a result. For the first time since the establishment of regional autonomy in 1980, the Basque president was not a PNV member, but rather a socialist backed by the conservatives. Prior to its demotion to the opposition benches, the party had foreseen trouble ahead and set in motion a shift back towards its traditional position at the political centre. Under the leadership of its new president, Iñigo Urkullu, political rapprochement with ETA's political wing ceased and, in the wake of the 2008 economic crisis, the party's official discourse pivoted to issues concerning the economy, employment and welfare and away from identity politics.

The break with the PNV led ETA's political wing to lose more influence just as the police and courts were placing unprecedented pressure on the paramilitaries. This was a third factor in ETA's gradual decline. In March 2003 the Spanish Supreme Court, in accordance with a new Law of Political Parties, had illegalised Batasuna and its activities. The decision was upheld by the European Court of Human Rights in 2009 amid several successful attempts by the police to dismantle ETA leadership between 2008 and 2010. Complicating matters further, many former Batasuna leaders were detained and sentenced in 2009 to over six years in prison for attempting to reassemble the party. Within this context, the Basque Patriotic Left's normal political activities were stymied, although Batasuna maintained its representation in the Basque parliament and participated in several elections by resorting to legal subterfuges.

This political paralysis gave rise to a fourth crucial factor for the end of terrorism in the Basque Country: politicos' emancipation from the long-established tutelage of the Liberation Movement's military leadership. The first timid steps towards abandoning this traditionally passive submission were led by the charismatic spokesman for Herri Batasuna, Arnaldo Otegi, a former ETA activist and prisoner. By the time Batasuna was banned, Otegi was already involved in secret conversations with the Basque socialist leader Jesús Eguiguren. In 2002, both politicians had reached a provisional agreement on key issues they hoped would encourage a peaceful and democratic future for the Basques. These provisions included two-track negotiations between, on the one hand, ETA and the state over the 'consequences' of the violent conflict (prisoners, refugees, disarmament), and on the other, the Basque democratic political parties over constitutional issues. It was envisaged that these negotiations would be held without the interference of violence and that they would result in an inclusive transversal agreement likely to be accepted by all political and identity sectors in the Basque Country.

After the socialist leader José Luis Rodríguez Zapatero's surprising triumph in the 2004 elections to the Spanish parliament, this plan for a negotiated settlement to the Basque contention passed from the remote farmhouse where Otegi and Eguiguren had been meeting to the international realm. This was a decisive factor for the end of political violence in Euskadi. Supporting Otegi's strategy, ETA's leadership asked the new Spanish president for a formal meeting to discuss a democratic solution to the conflict. With majority support in parliament for initiating dialogue with ETA subject to an 'unequivocal willingness' to end violence, Zapatero sent Eguiguren to Geneva for a new round of secret talks. There, the Henry Dunant Centre for Humanitarian Dialogue hosted Eguiguren's meetings with high-ranking representatives of ETA's leadership. The Spanish president's decision was a risky personal gamble with an uncertain outcome. The conservative PP opposition had made it clear they were willing to exploit the situation and blame Zapatero for making political concessions to the terrorists.

Over the next few months, a series of encounters between ETA and Eguiguren, sometimes joined by other government emissaries, were held in Geneva, Oslo and Lausanne. Together, they became the most significant attempt to stop violence and address the political problem of Basque self-government in ETA's history. Meanwhile, the group's violence continued in the face of sustained police and juridical pressure. Although the meetings' minutes are still under seal at the Swiss Mediation Center, available scholarly publications, leaks and testimonies from key actors permit a relatively precise reconstruction of the talks. After the final meeting in February 2006, an agreement was reached on the guiding methodology for the process that would end ETA's violence and facilitate a settlement to the political conflict. ETA seemed to recognise its own lack of legitimacy as a negotiator on constitutional issues and the accord's key element was its acceptance of the aforementioned two-track negotiation. In order to set these negotiations in motion, ETA would declare a 'permanent cessation of their armed activities'. Concurrently, the Spanish government acceded to a series of concessions, such as respect for any political agreement reached among the Basques, a willingness to accommodate said agreement to the Spanish legislation, and a commitment to negotiate a 'state pact' with opposition parties so that the settlement would endure shifts in control of parliament. Furthermore, the government agreed to respect the political activity of all organisations in the Patriotic Left and to alleviate police pressure. In March 2006, ETA declared a ceasefire, and in June President Zapatero summoned the media for a declaration on the peace process. While his statement included the previously negotiated formula regarding respect for the decisions made by the Basques, he also announced that the government would not repeal the law that had banned Batasuna, which could be interpreted as contradicting what his emissaries had accepted in the final talks with ETA.[37]

A careful study of the ups and downs through which the ceasefire passed in its fourteen-month duration leads one to conclude that, notwithstanding a formal commitment, ETA's leadership was not ready to abandon its role as a political actor. Instead, the paramilitaries stuck to their understanding of the double-track negotiations. They demanded progress be made in negotiating the political strand as a precondition for opening talks on the second strand that would address the conflict's demilitarisation. Since the government, facing heavy criticism from the conservative PP and their media, was unwilling to make a further gesture of goodwill, ETA threatened to end the truce if political talks remained blocked. To avoid a return to violence, Otegi convinced the Basque socialists and the PNV leadership to initiate secret conversations at the Jesuit sanctuary of Loiola. From September to November 2006, the three parties outlined a preliminary agreement according to which any future alteration of the juridical status quo would be carried out within the existing legal framework, political projects would be accepted if they reflected the democratic will of Basque citizens, and the inclusion of neighbouring Navarre within a common institution would be promoted. After returning from a temporary break in conversations to consult with their respective parties, Otegi surprised the participants with new demands imposed by ETA and Batasuna zealots. Since neither the socialists nor the PNV were willing to accept these demands, which touched upon the sensitive question of Navarre, the conversations ended in failure. Despite some last-minute efforts, a return to violence was unstoppable. In December 2006, ETA detonated a car bomb at Madrid's airport, killing two people. Six months later the ceasefire officially ended, and in March 2008 the paramilitaries killed a former socialist town councillor.[38]

---

37 I. Murua, *Ending ETA's Armed Campaign: How and Why the Basque Armed Group Abandoned Violence* (New York, Routledge, 2017); J. M. Izquierdo and L. R. Aizpeolea, *El fin de ETA: Así derrotó la democracia al terror* (Barcelona, Espasa, 2017); Whitfield, *Endgame*.

38 I. Murua, *El triángulo de Loiola: Crónica de un proceso de negociación a tres bandas* (Donostia, Ttartalo, 2010); F. Munarriz, *El tiempo de las luces: Entrevista con Arnaldo Otegi* (Bilbao, Baigorri, 2012).

This return to violence shocked large segments of Basque society, including Otegi and the more pragmatic and reformist sectors of the Liberation Movement. In response to these dramatic events, which left them with few options to defend their political project, Otegi and his followers continued to distance politicos from the paramilitaries without formally breaking away. The Batasuna leader also mobilised grassroots support, a strategic move that proved decisive in ending terrorist violence. As noted above, Otegi was well aware that, unlike other European terrorist groups, ETA's strength was grounded on a large social and organisational network. Without this support, ETA's self-legitimation as a small nation's armed vanguard battling against a powerful colonialist state would be placed into further doubt. Thus, while new programmatic proposals (Summer 2009: 'Argitzen') were circulated among Batasuna members, the Batasuna leader organised a series of popular rallies, some from prison, where different manifestos were launched (2004: Manifesto of Anoeta; 2009: Declaration of Altsasu; 2010: Manifesto Zutik Euskal Herria). One basic notion emerged from this activity: a new political era demanded new democratic solutions. The era of armed struggle was over, and the Basque people were now ready to defend their rights through their own democratic means. The Northern Irish peace process and the Mitchell principles were prominent and frequently mentioned examples for what Otegi and his group had in mind. Otegi's strategy received significant international backing when several experienced mediators in other peace processes issued the 'Brussels Declaration' in March 2010, urging ETA to declare a permanent and verifiable ceasefire in order to facilitate a peaceful settlement of the Basque conflict.[39]

A core argument in this new strategy to push the paramilitaries towards their dissolution was the idea that powerful new political allegiances would emerge in a post-violence environment. In June 2010, cooperation between the Patriotic Left and the nationalist EA party demonstrated the possibilities of this new nationalist power. A year later, this coalition founded Bildu together with other minor nationalist and leftist parties, garnering significant support in the 2011 elections. For the first time since Batasuna was banned, judges allowed Bildu to participate due to the Patriotic Left's new commitment to democratic and peaceful principles, as well as to the 'permanent and general ceasefire' ETA declared earlier that year. Meanwhile, the presence of international mediators was helpful in combating the impression that the

---

39 Text available at https://icgbasquedotorg.wordpress.com/documents/brussels-declaration/.

Spanish state had forced ETA's retreat. This face-saving measure helped pave the path towards the group's dissolution. In November, an International Peace Conference held at San Sebastián's Aiete Palace reiterated the demand for a lasting ceasefire as a precondition for the peaceful settlement of the Basque contention. Three days later, ETA announced the definitive cessation of armed activity. The conservative PP's victory in elections to the Spanish parliament and the new administration's reluctance, under President Mariano Rajoy, to partake in any policy related to the end of ETA hampered, but did not abort the process of dissolution, which continued with renewed protagonism from international mediators and local peace movements. The final steps in this process came in April 2017, when spokesmen for the International Verification Commission certificated the decommission of ETA's weapons to the French police at a public gathering. In May 2018, ETA leader Josu Ternera, who had been Eguiguren's partner at the first Geneva talks, sent an audiotape to the BBC announcing that the organisation had fully dismantled, opening the beginning of a new political cycle in the struggle for Basque self-determination. ETA was no more. Its spokesman punctuated the text with one final grandiose and theatrical assertion: 'ETA was born from the people, and now it dissolves into the people.'[40]

Their 'commitment' to the people had resulted in nearly 850 deaths, thousands living under constant threat, and millions of euros spent in security and repairing material damage. And for many young Basques who fell (or not) into ETA's orbit, that same 'commitment' translated to long prison sentences that truncated their lives, torture in police barracks, or death at the hands of right-wing and state-sponsored commandos. Compared to this long list of human suffering and material damage, ETA's balance sheet of 'assets' is extremely poor. In fact, none of the group's major political goals were achieved: the seven Basque territories have not been unified and Euskal Herria is not an independent state, let alone a socialist society. Even with regard to minor 'secondary objectives' or 'tactical-operational successes', Richard English's balanced account does not permit a much more 'positive' view on ETA's efficacy.[41] Similarly to the fate shared by a large number of international terrorist groups, the Basque paramilitaries decided to dissolve without obtaining any feasible political

---

40 The English version of ETA's communiqué is available at www.naiz.eus/media/asset_publics/resources/000/494/627/original/20180503-eta-final-statement.pdf.
41 R. English, *Does Terrorism Work? A History* (Oxford, Oxford University Press, 2016), pp. 187–219.

dividend.[42] Why? While increasing political, juridical and police pressure on the group and its environment contributed unequivocally to the Liberation Movement's staggering weakness, the history of the group's dissolution is not exclusively a story of unconditional military defeat and surrender. I have suggested the notion of an externally induced suicide to better grasp the complex confluence of different factors that eventually led to the organisation's dissolution.[43] Like any suicide, the end of ETA's life cycle came about because it was the activists' will to finish it. This said, it must be added that this suicide was committed in a situation in which the suicide victim reached the conclusion that there was no alternative. As explained above, there seemed to be no escape from escalating police and juridical harassment, the unpopularity of terrorism in the aftermath of 9/11 and, above all, the Patriotic Left's enormous difficulties in fostering pro-independence politics within the traditional strategic politico-military framework. It was the politicos' decision to abandon their historical submission to the dictates of the armed activists and to articulate a new front of external pressure on the paramilitaries without formally breaking away that pushed the paramilitaries towards suicide. Instead of risking the loss of grassroots support, and pressured by the critical incomprehension of international agencies, ETA decided to embrace the rationale of the 'new cycle' in order to save, through its suicide, the self-adulating narrative of a legacy dedicated to the service of its people. One of the most urgent tasks of Basque society in the aftermath of terrorism will be to discuss and deconstruct this narrative.

Further Reading

J. E. Jacob, *Hills of Conflict: Basque Nationalism in France* (Reno, University of Nevada Press, 1994)
L. Mees, *The Basque Contention: Ethnicity, Politics, Violence* (New York, Routledge, 2020)
I. Murua, *Ending ETA's Armed Campaign: How and Why the Basque Armed Group Abandoned Violence* (New York, Routledge, 2017)
S. de Pablo and L. Mees, *El péndulo patriótico: Historia del Partido Nacionalista Vasco (1895–2005)* (Barcelona, Crítica, 2005)
T. Whitfield, *Endgame for ETA: Elusive Peace in the Basque Country* (London, Hurst & Company, 2014)

42 A. K. Cronin, *How Terrorism Ends: Understanding the Decline and Demise of Terrorist Campaigns* (Princeton, Princeton University Press, 2009); S. G. Jones and M. C. Libicki, *How Terrorist Groups End: Lessons for Countering Al Qa'ida* (Santa Monica, CA, Rand, 2008).
43 Mees, *Basque Contention*, pp. 242–4.

9

Terrorism in African History

RICHARD REID

Definitions and Historical Patterns

In 2008, in the final days of the Bush administration, it was discovered that Nelson Mandela – by that point arguably the most loved and revered person on the planet – was still on the US's 'terror watch-list', in addition to other senior figures in the African National Congress (ANC). This dated to 1986, when the Reagan administration concurred with P. W. Botha's apartheid government in South Africa that the ANC was indeed a 'terrorist group'. Just four years later, apartheid was collapsing, the ANC was unbanned, Mandela was the embodiment of a new optimism – and President Bush, Sr. invited the ANC leadership to Washington. Due to a bureaucratic error, however, their classification as 'terrorists' remained on the books until years later, when Secretary of State Condoleezza Rice embarrassedly noticed the 'glitch', which was swiftly corrected by means of a bill drafted by John Kerry.[1] This anecdote raises the hoary old issue of definition: *when is a terrorist not a terrorist?* Scholars have long wrestled with useable and comprehensive characterisations, in Africa and elsewhere.[2] To the ANC's detractors, there was little doubt that the movement was indeed a dangerous, violent, terrorist organisation. After all, it had dedicated itself to the overthrow of the existing, putatively legitimate political order. To many others, however, the ANC was in the vanguard of righteous struggle – as were a number of other similarly organised movements across Africa between the 1950s and the 1980s, waging war by any means possible against the last vestiges of imperialism and racial injustice. Yet, at the same time, the Mandela story reminds us how times change, and how dramatic the

---

1 'Why Nelson Mandela Was on a Terrorism Watch List in 2008', *Washington Post*, 7 December 2013.
2 For example, G. Chaliand and A. Blin, 'Introduction', in G. Chaliand and A. Blin (eds.), *The History of Terrorism: From Antiquity to ISIS* (Berkeley, University of California Press, 2016); R. D. Law, *Terrorism: A History* (Cambridge, Polity Press, 2016), pp. 2–10.

passage of time can be. The notion of Mandela being categorised as a terrorist is almost quaint, even otherworldly, in the age of al-Shabaab in Somalia and Boko Haram in Nigeria. The ANC was not inclined to shoot up shopping malls in urban areas, resulting in dozens of civilian deaths, as has happened in Nairobi (carried out by al-Shabaab); or seize schoolgirls and subject them to sexual assault and ideological indoctrination (as in the case of Boko Haram in north-east Nigeria).

There has been a marked increase in incidents of terrorism – and correspondingly a growth in the study of terrorism – in Africa over the last twenty years or so. Arguably, the bombings of the US embassies in Nairobi and Dar es Salaam in 1998 marked the beginning of a new era in terrorist activity on the continent. Christopher Clapham's prescient 2003 article, written in the wake of 9/11, provided a historical sketch and warned that it would be 'foolish to rule ... out' the prospect of Africa becoming a locus for radical Islam and the terrorism that often results.[3] Soon after, Lyman and Morrison likewise suggested that

> Africa may not rank with Iraq or Afghanistan as a top priority in the war on terrorism, nor with the Middle East or Southeast Asia as a primary focus of US antiterrorism programs. But if Washington continues to underplay the terrorist threat in Africa, its worldwide strategy against terrorism will falter – and the consequences may be dire indeed.[4]

Of course, while Africa may not have been a 'top priority' immediately after 9/11, the continent came to be defined in Washington, in many ways, in terms of security and antiterrorism.[5] No doubt, in the minds of the Bush-Cheney circle in particular, Africa conjured up the image of millions of disaffected Muslims ready to take up arms against an array of foreign enemies, the US foremost among them. However ill informed the image may have been, it was a trope which already had a fair degree of traction in foreign policy circles. After all, Robert Kaplan's gruesomely pessimistic assessment of a post-Cold War, 'Third World' dystopia had been circulated to US foreign missions across the globe just a few years earlier.[6] In many ways, each state collapse and the terrorist upsurge that was its corollary

---

3 C. Clapham, 'Terrorism in Africa: Problems of Definition, History and Development', *South African Journal of International Affairs* 10/2 (2003), p. 28.
4 P. N. Lyman and F. S. Morrison, 'The Terrorist Threat in Africa', *Foreign Affairs* 83/1 (2004), p. 86.
5 G. R. Olsen, 'The Ambiguity of US Foreign Policy Towards Africa', *Third World Quarterly* 38/9 (2017).
6 R. D. Kaplan, 'The Coming Anarchy', *Atlantic Monthly*, February 1994.

seemed to reinforce the 'Dark Continent' mythology in which Africa had been couched by outside observers since at least the late nineteenth century. One of the early post-9/11 foci was the Horn of Africa, long a place of fault lines and violent instability with the capacity for the export of terrorism globally.[7] Much of the analysis was understandably fixated with Al-Qaeda, and the global network of terror of which that organisation was deemed the conceptual centre. But since then, other, at least in part home-grown, movements have appeared: Boko Haram and al-Shabaab, most notably, and these have naturally attracted a great deal of attention.[8] Yet historians have generally been absent from the debate, which is dominated by political scientists, journalists, specialists in non-state military activity and policy-oriented analysts. Work on the *history* of terrorism in Africa is in its infancy, at least compared to other parts of the world.

The tendency to foreshorten the history of violence in Africa generally – the overwhelming analytical focus has been on the modern and contemporary era – has led to the identification of horrific novelty, rather than longer-term patterns, innovations and experiences. Terrorism itself is often understood as a distinctively modern phenomenon, associated with particular kinds of weaponry (most obviously, explosives, IEDs and the like) or tactics (such as the hijacking of aircraft). Terrorism is also, to a considerable extent, associated with the modern globalisation of violence, and more specifically the infiltration or influence of external dynamics. Yet a brief survey of the phenomenon in historical context reveals that terrorism in Africa has long been both complex and prevalent. Azar Gat observes that 'Terror – the targeting of civilians by small non-state groups for political purposes is probably as good a definition as any – is widely claimed to have been around throughout history.'[9] Two recent books likewise have chapters which trace the history of 'terror' and 'terrorism' into antiquity.[10] Nonetheless, Gat disagrees with this approach:

> More accurately . . . terror emerged only from the late nineteenth century on the back of the modern technological and social developments that had

---

[7] For example, see A. de Waal (ed.), *Islamism and Its Enemies in the Horn of Africa* (London, Hurst, 2004); R. I. Rotberg (ed.), *Battling Terrorism in the Horn of Africa* (Washington, DC, Brookings Institution Press, 2005).
[8] A sample would include: M. Smith, *Boko Haram: Inside Nigeria's Unholy War* (London, I. B. Tauris, 2015); A. Thurston, *Boko Haram: The History of an African Jihadist Movement* (Princeton, Princeton University Press, 2018); S. J. Hansen, *Al-Shabaab in Somalia: The History and Ideology of a Militant Islamist Group, 2005–2012* (London, Hurst, 2013).
[9] A. Gat, *War in Human Civilization* (Oxford, Oxford University Press, 2006), p. 637.
[10] Chaliand and Blin (eds.), *History of Terrorism*; Law, *Terrorism: A History*.

made it possible: high explosives and, later, automatic weapons gave individuals and small groups the ability that they previously lacked to cause damage disproportionate to their number.[11]

Thus, modern terrorist activity is framed as a universal response to alienation, oppression, marginalisation and persecution, made possible by technological innovation – and in that sense, Africa has much in common with other parts of the world. However, it might also be argued that terrorism is discernible in deeper historical patterns of violence in Africa – if not in terms of actual hardware, then in terms of modus operandi and tactics. In that sense I find myself diverging slightly from Clapham, who proposed that, in the broadest possible terms, precolonial Africa's abundance of land and its relative underpopulation meant that dissidents often simply moved away from unacceptable political systems, thus reducing 'the need for oppositional movements to adapt to the needs of operating in space they do not control' – one of the tenets of modern terrorism.[12] Clapham makes a powerful point. However, it *is* possible to identify modes of violence in African history which have 'terror' at their very core. Africans have used these tactics both against one another, and in response to the state terrorism inflicted by foreigners.

For much of Saharan and sub-Saharan Africa's history, these vast regions have been (and in some areas remain) relatively underpopulated, and it is important to note that a great deal of violence was aimed at the control of people rather than land per se. Often, there was no distinction between combatant and non-combatant, and violence was aimed at undermining the basic functions of society itself.[13] Episodic ambushes and raids on isolated, poorly defended communities in savannah country were designed to terrify and overawe non-combatants, took place suddenly and without warning, and were all over in a matter of minutes. This was a common form of violence in the savannah region in the deeper past and contains at least some of the hallmarks of 'terrorism' as broadly understood in our own era. The use of kidnapping and ambush were terrorising tactics directed at non-combatants in the forest zone, too, with some evidence pointing towards the evolution of such tactics in the early part of the second millennium.[14] In Africa's deeper past, the use of fear as a weapon against vulnerable communities was commonplace, and occurred outside what we might define as the normal

---

11 Gat, *War in Human Civilization*, pp. 637–8.   12 Clapham, 'Terrorism in Africa', p. 18.
13 R. J. Reid, *Warfare in African History* (New York, Cambridge University Press, 2012), p. 11.
14 See for example J. Vansina, *Paths in the Rainforests: Toward a History of Political Tradition in Equatorial Africa* (London, James Currey, 1990), pp. 80, 82, 106–7.

arena of contestation between armed groups. Indeed, fear and the need for some form of collective security and protection by armed benefactors drove state formation across sub-Saharan Africa, and legitimised ruling elites. The striking of fear into the heart of recalcitrant subjects was common.[15] The tactics of terror were adapted for the purposes of participation in the early modern Atlantic economy. Terror among communities subjected to the predations of slavers was certainly the outcome of such violence, though it was not necessarily the primary aim of the slavers themselves.[16] Nonetheless, terror was indeed intrinsic to the operation of the slave trade, witness the brutal kidnapping of people described so graphically, for example, by Olaudah Equiano.[17]

Similar arguments can be made for nineteenth-century eastern Africa, where the Indian Ocean-linked slave trade escalated across the region in the nineteenth century, with many of the same kinds of tactics deployed as in West Africa.[18] Terroristic tactics were developed by insurgent war leaders such as Mirambo and Nyungu-ya-Mawe to cow the wider population of north-central Tanzania, and to deliberately instil fear in communities in the hope that they would therefore offer no resistance. As the explorer Henry Morton Stanley had it, the very name of Mirambo struck terror into the hearts of the Nyamwezi people of the region, who believed he was everywhere, at all times, ready to strike. As Stanley wrote in the mid-1870s, as he marched through a Nyamwezi village: 'a messenger [arrived] to tell us that the phantom, the bugbear, the terror whose name silences the children of Unyamwezi and Usukuma, and makes women's hearts bound with fear; that Mirambo himself was coming ... '[19] Much of this was down to Mirambo's remarkable energy and a rare gift for *appearing* to be omnipresent – the great speed with which he moved armies from one neighbourhood to another, and his habit of attacking suddenly at night. He had, by general consensus, ripped

---

15 The concept of fear in a political context is explored in C. Robin, *Fear: The History of a Political Idea* (Oxford, Oxford University Press, 2004); see also D. L. Schoenbrun, *A Green Place, A Good Place: Agrarian Change, Gender, and Social Identity in the Great Lakes Region* (Portsmouth, NH, Heinemann, 1998).
16 The tactics deployed in the capture of slaves is examined in R. S. Smith, *Warfare and Diplomacy in Pre-colonial West Africa* (London, James Currey, 1989); and J. Thornton, *Warfare in Atlantic Africa, 1500–1800* (London, UCL Press, 1999).
17 O. Equiano, *The Interesting Narrative and Other Writings*, [1st ed. 1789], ed. V. Carretta (London, Penguin, 1995).
18 For a contemporary account, see V. Lovatt Cameron, *Across Africa*, 2 vols (New York, Harper & Brothers, 1877); and UK National Archives FO881/4189 Report on the slave trade in the East African interior, by Lt. V. L. Cameron.
19 H. M. Stanley, *Through the Dark Continent* [1st ed. 1878] (London, George Newnes, 1899), vol. 1, pp. 382–3.

up the rules of conventional local warfare. Mirambo's armies drew on young, unmarried, restless warriors known as *ruga ruga*, who terrorised communities across a wide area between the 1850s and the 1890s.[20]

Not coincidentally, eastern and central Africa in this period was defined by a new economics and, in particular, by heightened social aspiration and widening economic inequality. Mirambo was the entrepreneur of violence par excellence, but he was not unique. The use of these kinds of tactics was by no means uncommon in the late nineteenth century, an era of evolving political and economic transformation, of social upheaval and of military revolution. As particular groups competed violently for control of both people and resources, they resorted to deliberate terror against communities whose resistance was real or perceived. The trend is exemplified by Tewodros, embattled Emperor of Ethiopia in the 1850s and 1860s, whose acts of sudden violence against his own countrymen were notorious, as evidenced in both European and Ethiopian sources.[21] This was a distinctive and organic form of state terrorism in late precolonial Africa.

Considerable care is needed, of course, in identifying and contextualising this kind of violence, given the tendency of nineteenth-century Europeans to characterise African states as intrinsically barbaric and ferocious and rooted in the infliction of terror on the part of bloodthirsty monarchs upon cowering subjects. The popular treatment of the Zulu kingdom is illustrative.[22] Nonetheless, state-level terrorism rapidly evolved in new ways, with the incursion of European-led armies in the 1880s and 1890s. European imperial strategists saw no irony in the unleashing of terrible violence on Africans after a century or more of discourse on how violent Africans themselves were; such violence was constrained by neither moral code nor legal convention. In the late nineteenth and early twentieth centuries in Africa, violent terror was in effect racialised, and in the view of Colonial Secretary Joseph Chamberlain,

---

20 In addition to Cameron and Stanley, a vivid contemporary description is offered in LMS Central Africa, Southon's Journal, SOAS Special Collections. See also N. Bennett, *Mirambo of Tanzania, 1840–1884* (New York, Oxford University Press, 1971); and R. J. Reid, *War in Pre-Colonial Eastern Africa: The Patterns and Meanings of State-Level Conflict in the Nineteenth Century* (Oxford, James Currey, 2007).
21 S. Rubenson et al. (eds. and trans.), *Tewodros and His Contemporaries, 1855–1868* (Addis Ababa, Addis Ababa University Press, 1994); D. Crummey, 'The Violence of Tewodros', in B. A. Ogot (ed.), *War and Society in Africa* (London, Frank Cass, 1972).
22 P. Becker, *Rule of Fear: The Life and Times of Dingane, King of the Zulu* (London, Penguin, 1964); and by D. Wylie, see *Savage Delight: White Myths of Shaka* (Pietermaritzburg, University of KwaZulu-Natal Press, 2001) and *Myth of Iron: Shaka in History* (Scottsville, University of KwaZulu-Natal Press, 2006).

among many others, was indeed necessary to bring about the 'order' and civilisation which the continent so tragically lacked.[23]

Terror and Imperialism

The question of whether or not a state can be responsible for terrorism has been the subject of debate.[24] In the context of imperialism and the creation of the 'new' European empires in the late nineteenth and early twentieth centuries, the term terrorism seems apposite in considering the actions of European state-level actors (or their African agents). Indeed, tactics designed to instil terror in recalcitrant groups were more or less 'official policy', and resulted in some of the bloodiest atrocities in Africa's modern history.[25] In his minor classic *Small Wars*, a kind of handbook first published in 1896 for conquering colonial armies in far-flung places, Col. Charles Callwell openly proposed 'The destruction of the crops and stores of grain of the enemy' and, if necessary, 'the destruction of villages' in order to bring the intractable

---

23 J. Chamberlain, 'The True Conception of Empire' [1897], in E. Boehmer (ed.), *Empire Writing: An Anthology of Colonial Literature, 1870–1918* (Oxford, Oxford University Press, 1998).

24 For some, the term can only properly be applied to violent non-state actors, while the violence committed by states is generally described under different headings, including warfare and self-defence. But others have argued for the application of the term 'terrorism' to state actors, and I have followed that approach in this essay. This represents the resuscitation of the original conceptualisation of 'terror' – namely as something perpetuated by the state against its own citizens, beginning with the Terror in revolutionary France: D. M. F. Sutherland, *France 1789–1815: Revolution and Counterrevolution* (London, Fontana Press, 1985), pp. 192–247; H. Gough, *The Terror in the French Revolution* (Basingstoke, Palgrave, 2010). As Philippe Buc points out in his stimulating study, 'Terror' was official policy – not just an analytical category – between September 1793 and the overthrow of the Jacobin leadership in July 1794, whereupon the term took on the negative and derogatory connotations with which we have become familiar: P. Buc, *Holy War, Martyrdom, and Terror: Christianity, Violence, and the West* (Philadelphia, University of Pennsylvania Press, 2015), pp. 37–9. The term has also been applied to the period of Stalin's purges of suspected opponents and dissidents in Soviet Russia between 1936 and 1938, and – more pertinently for the present essay – to the state-led suppression of opposition in socialist Ethiopia in the late 1970s (the 'Red Terror'): R. Conquest, *The Great Terror: A Reassessment* (London, Pimlico, 2008); J. Harris (ed.), *The Anatomy of Terror: Political Violence under Stalin* (Oxford, Oxford University Press, 2013); A. Tiruneh, *The Ethiopian Revolution, 1974–1987: A Transformation from an Aristocratic to a Totalitarian Autocracy* (Cambridge, Cambridge University Press, 1993), pp. 208–14; J. Wiebel, '"Let the Red Terror Intensify": Political Violence, Governance, and Society in Urban Ethiopia, 1976–1978', *International Journal of African Historical Studies* 48/1 (2015).

25 For example, see D. Walter, *Colonial Violence: European Empires and the Use of Force* (London, Hurst, 2017), pp. 153–4 and *passim*; for a more global set of examples, M. Cocker, *Rivers of Blood, Rivers of Gold: Europe's Conflict with Tribal Peoples* (London, Pimlico, 1999).

savage to heel. Callwell conceded that this was 'unfortunate', but often unavoidable.[26] The deliberate and sudden targeting of non-combatants and their means of livelihood looks very much not like 'warfare' in the conventional sense, but state terrorism – though of course to European military strategists they were 'wars of pacification'. Instances abound of situations in which imperial violence morphed from combat between two armed groups – albeit often unequal in strength – into the targeting of non-combatants and their socio-economic bases, and the unleashing of horrific force against them. In the course of the 1890s, the kingdom of Bunyoro was laid waste by an Anglo-Ganda army, which involved the deliberate despoliation of food-producing areas and the systematic destruction of villages in order to depopulate and starve out potential resisters.[27] The brutal predations carried out by the notorious Force Publique in the Belgian Congo in the 1890s and 1900s were likewise designed to instil dread and compel submission among a traumatised populace, many of whom were consequently forced to supply rubber in the most dire conditions to foreign traders. The situation in the Congo was regarded as so terrible as to attract censure from other European powers – quite a feat in the age of violent imperialism.[28]

African responses to colonial invasion took numerous forms, but anti-colonial insurgencies, while usually short-lived, took on at least some of the attributes of 'terrorism' and were certainly seen as acts of illegitimate violence on the part of nascent colonial authorities. Uprisings in Southern Rhodesia on the part of the Ndebele and Shona (the 'Chimurenga') targeted 'civilians', at least initially, including scattered white settlers and their families, and mission stations.[29] Likewise, the rebels involved in the Maji Maji revolt in German East Africa undertook sudden attacks on soft targets,

26 Col. C. E. Callwell, *Small Wars: Their Principles and Practice*, 3rd ed. (London, HMSO, 1906), pp. 40–1.
27 J. Beattie, *The Nyoro State* (Oxford, Oxford University Press, 1971), pp. 73–5; E. I. Steinhart, *Conflict and Collaboration: The Kingdoms of Western Uganda, 1890–1907* (Princeton, Princeton University Press, 1977), pp. 58–97. Inevitably cleaned-up accounts are provided in A. B. Thruston, *African Incidents* (London, John Murray, 1900) and Sir Henry Colvile, *The Land of the Nile Springs; Being Chiefly an Account of How We Fought Kabarega* (London, Edward Arnold, 1895), ch. 7.
28 See for example A. Hochschild, *King Leopold's Ghost: A Story of Greed, Terror, and Heroism in Colonial Africa* (Boston, Houghton Mifflin, 1998). It forms the context, of course, of the classic novella of the era, Joseph Conrad's *Heart of Darkness and Two Other Stories* [1st ed. 1899] (London, The Folio Society, 1997).
29 D. N. Beach, 'Chimurenga: The Shona Risings of 1896–97', *Journal of African History* 20/3 (1979); T. O. Ranger, *Revolt in Southern Rhodesia, 1896–97* (London, Heinemann, 1967). For contemporary accounts, see D. Tyrie Laing, *The Matabele Rebellion, 1896* (London, Dean & Son, 1897) and F. C. Selous, *Sunshine and Storm in Rhodesia* (London, Rowland Ward, 1896).

although they also attacked local intermediaries in their attempts to clear the region of German rule.[30] Both the Chimurenga and Maji Maji rebellions were crushed, and many of the perpetrators (or suspected rebels) were summarily executed. But it was perhaps in German Southwest Africa – present-day Namibia – where the response to African recalcitrance was most horrific. Following the outbreak of rebellions by the Herero and the Nama in 1904–5, General Lothar von Trotha arrived in the territory at the head of 14,000 German troops. At a certain point, state terrorism becomes genocide, as it did in the case of the Nama, Herero and San: between 65,000 and 80,000 Africans were killed, and entire communities were simply wiped out.[31] But eruptions of terrorist violence did not always take the form of visible, widespread insurgency, as conventionally understood at least in subsequent nationalist historiography. Among the Tabwa in south-east Belgian Congo in the 1890s, dozens of killings were supposedly carried out by 'lions' – at least, that was the view of the missionaries stationed in the area – although local informants told the latter that the killings were in fact carried out by theriomorphic men who had taken the form of lions. It seems clear that the murders at least in part represented resistance to the growing influence of the mission station, especially in promoting a new group of Africans who owed their prominence to their association with the missionaries.[32]

The *pax colonia* – the idea that peace was imposed by the colonial order following an epoch of terrible violence – which followed the era of partition was only very rarely challenged by anything that might be described as 'terrorist insurgency'. Only in the late colonial period was the security of the imperial order seriously challenged. Here I draw attention to two particular cases – one well known, the other less so – but each in its way offering portents of things to come. In the highland border areas between Ethiopia and Eritrea in the 1940s, the term *shifta* – a catch-all term whose precise connotation has changed over time but which broadly means 'bandit'

---

30 G. C. K. Gwassa and J. Iliffe (eds.), *Records of the Maji Maji Uprising: Part One* (Nairobi, East African Publishing House, 1967). See also J. Giblin and J. Monson (eds.), *The Maji Maji War 1905–1907: Lifting the Fog of War* (Leiden, Brill, 2010); H. Schmidt, '(Re) Negotiating Marginality: The Maji Maji War and Its Aftermath in Southwestern Tanzania, ca. 1905–1916', *International Journal of African Historical Studies* 43 (2010).
31 See for example D. Olusoga and C. W. Erichsen, *The Kaiser's Holocaust: Germany's Forgotten Genocide and the Colonial Roots of Nazism* (London, Faber and Faber, 2010). See also J.-B. Gewald, *Herero Heroes: A Socio-political History of the Herero of Namibia, 1890–1923* (Oxford, James Currey, 1998).
32 A. F. Roberts, '"Like a Roaring Lion": Tabwa Terrorism in the Late Nineteenth Century', in D. Crummey (ed.), *Banditry, Rebellion and Social Protest in Africa* (London, James Currey/Heinemann, 1986).

in Amharic[33] – came to be applied to a disgruntled group of armed men with a tendency to attack soft rural targets without warning. They pointed their obsolete rifles and threw their Second World War hand grenades at tea shops, passing trucks, trading posts and lightly armed police patrols. They were the product of a peculiar set of circumstances: political instability in the region; a weak British administration; economic deprivation; uncertainty over the future of the former Italian colony of Eritrea (many of the *shifta* were 'unionist', actively seeking the unification of Eritrea with Ethiopia). Many of the men themselves were former *ascari*, Italian colonial soldiers summarily demobilised in the wake of the British victory in the Horn in 1941. The British were concerned enough to throw a sizeable chunk of the meagre resources at their disposal at the problem.[34] *Shifta* activities represented the first rumblings of a much larger storm to come in the Horn of Africa. The *shifta* of the 1940s were emblematic of the times, emerging in the cracks of the late colonial order, and motivated by an array of aims and grievances. They were squeezed between competing but incomplete power blocs which had enough strength to marginalise but not enough to either impose themselves fully on their territory or to offer lasting political or economic solutions to deep-rooted problems.

The *shifta* problem receded by the early 1950s – the outcome of a combination of British amnesties and the federation of Eritrea with Ethiopia. But, by then, a much more serious and substantial exemplification of the phenomenon had appeared in Kenya. The Mau Mau uprising was arguably the last of the major anti-colonial insurrections constrained by a relative lack of access to modern weaponry and by the inability to elaborate a wider ideology.[35] With around 12,000 insurgents, mostly Kikuyu, at its outset in 1952, the rebellion spread over the forested area of the central

---

33 D. Crummey, 'Banditry and Resistance: Noble and Peasant in Nineteenth-Century Ethiopia', in Crummey (ed.), *Banditry, Rebellion, and Social Protest*, p. 133. More broadly, see E. Hobsbawm, *Bandits* [1st ed. 1969] (London, Abacus, 2000).
34 G. K. N. Trevaskis, *Eritrea: A Colony in Transition, 1941–1952* (London, Oxford University Press, 1960), pp. 103ff.; and Trevaskis's report on the issue, 'A study of the development of the present shifta problem and the means whereby it can be remedied' (June 1950), Research and Documentation Centre, Asmara, Box/293 File SH/20 Vol II Acc 13406.
35 The body of scholarship on Mau Mau is vast. A brief sample would include J. Lonsdale, 'Mau Maus of the Mind: Making Mau Mau and Remaking Kenya', *Journal of African History* 31/3 (1990); D. M. Anderson, *Histories of the Hanged: Britain's Dirty War in Kenya and the End of Empire* (London, Weidenfeld & Nicolson, 2005); D. Branch, *Defeating Mau Mau, Creating Kenya: Counterinsurgency, Civil War, and Decolonisation* (Cambridge, Cambridge University Press, 2009). Official documentation on the British side is abundant, but fortunately there are also numerous Kenyan perspectives, albeit produced after the event: see for example W. Itote (General China), *'Mau Mau' General* (Nairobi, East African Publishing House, 1967).

highlands, and involved attacks on settlers and (more commonly) Kikuyu loyalists. The fighters were bound together by oathing ceremonies[36] and were broadly committed to Kenyan independence and the redistribution of land, the alienation of which to white settlers was the single biggest cause of social discontent in the highlands (hence their own term for themselves, the Land Freedom Army). The conflict swiftly became a remarkably bitter one, with terrorist tactics employed on both sides. Mau Mau attacks sometimes involved the massacre of non-combatants, including women and children, as well as the mutilation of victims. These tactics provoked a ferocious response on the British side: in addition to the reinforcement of conventional military forces, counterinsurgency gangs of Kikuyu loyalists were created which escalated a brutal war of attrition, while the British detained thousands of Mau Mau 'suspects' and subjected them to physical and psychological torture.[37] The revelation of British conduct in the late 1950s led to a political backlash at home, and in many ways pushed the Conservative government more rapidly towards decolonisation, despite the fact that, militarily at least, the insurgency had been largely crushed by 1956, although the state of emergency lasted until 1960.

In many ways, the Mau Mau revolt in Kenya resonated with long-standing white anxieties about Africa. White settlers in the Kenyan highlands, and indeed settlers everywhere, feared that in the night the native would sneak into their bedrooms with a vicious *panga* and hack them to death.[38] Meanwhile, Mau Mau 'terrorists' were regarded as certifiably insane, and one of the most common interpretations at the time was that the revolt was an outbreak of madness – a primordial, atavistic scream, as members of the Kikuyu struggled with modernity.[39] At the very least, as the psychiatrist Colin Carothers described it, they were 'in transition'.[40] The notion that there is

---

36 The subversion – and, for some, the bestial horrors – involved in these oaths captured the European imagination: see for example L. S. B. Leakey's contemporary assessment, *Mau Mau and the Kikuyu* (London, Methuen, 1952), as well as his *Defeating Mau Mau* (London, Methuen, 1954).
37 Anderson, *Histories*; Branch, *Defeating Mau Mau*; H. Bennett, *Fighting the Mau Mau: The British Army and Counter-Insurgency in the Kenya Emergency* (Cambridge, Cambridge University Press, 2013); C. Elkins, *Imperial Reckoning: The Untold Story of Britain's Gulag in Kenya* (New York, Henry Holt & Co., 2005). A series of legal cases brought by victims of counterinsurgency tactics have in recent years been brought to the UK High Court.
38 The psychological terror produced by Mau Mau has an echo in South African author Rian Malan's account of the Hammerman, a young Zulu who for a time breaks into whites' houses, smashing their heads in with a hammer while they sleep. He is eventually caught. R. Malan, *My Traitor's Heart* (London, Vintage Books, 1991).
39 Lonsdale, 'Mau Maus of the Mind'.
40 J. C. Carothers, *The Psychology of Mau Mau* (Nairobi, Government Printer, 1954).

something fundamentally psychopathic about the perpetrators of a particular kind of violence would prove an enduring one. At any rate, the government of independent Kenya, under Jomo Kenyatta – detained by the British during the emergency but with little direct involvement in Mau Mau itself – would remain ambivalent towards, and even suspicious of, Mau Mau veterans. They were a reminder of what could happen to his own state if the incipient violence of the unreconciled wasn't nipped in the bud.[41]

Mau Mau failed as an operational insurgency for various reasons, but chief among them were, as noted, Britain's brutal and effective counterinsurgency tactics, but also the fact that the British controlled the imagery around the insurgency itself. The insurgents themselves singularly failed to broadcast a wider message beyond the Kenyan highlands, one that might have spoken to anti-colonialism and mobilised support elsewhere in Africa and beyond it. It was not the last time an insurgent movement in Africa was unsuccessful in this way. But even as Mau Mau was unfolding, new forms of globally conscious violence were emerging, involving people willing and able to use terror to make political arguments and in so doing connect with increasingly transregional anti-colonial agendas. The failure of insurgents in Kenya contrasted starkly with the gruesome, hard-won success of their contemporaries in Algeria, and, in time, elsewhere in Africa.

Fanon's Wars

The relative monopoly on the use of armed force which undergirded colonial rule meant that the inherent autocracy and repression of the latter – evident in many territories by the 1930s and 1940s – could not be amended or confronted by conventional means.[42] Of course, on the African continent – as elsewhere in the imperial world – the notion of 'terrorism' is complicated. Struggles over its definition reflect a Manichaean dichotomy between righteous armed struggle (which came, and comes, in many guises) against oppressive colonialism on the one hand, and atavistic, needless and indiscriminate bloodshed versus the forces of progress and modernity on the other. Nonetheless, from the middle of the twentieth century, recourse to acts of terror was associated with the marginalised and dispossessed

---

41 In fact, newly independent Kenya was soon confronted with its own insurgency, in the predominantly Somali northern district, between 1963 and 1968: see for example H. Whittaker, *Insurgency and Counterinsurgency in Kenya: A Social History of the Shifta Conflict, c.1963–1968* (Leiden, Brill, 2014).
42 Law, *Terrorism*, chh. 11 and 12.

in situations where political access was closed and inclusive dialogue shut down. The 1950s, the late colonial moment, witnessed something of a shift in terms of the use of fear as both means and end in the exercise of killing.

In Algeria, the Front de libération nationale (FLN) launched its rebellion against French rule in October 1954, and the ensuing conflict swiftly became one of the bitterest in the age of decolonisation.[43] Although the French were initially caught off guard, they swiftly reinforced and, like the British in Kenya, launched a brutal counterinsurgency strategy which ultimately served to drive many politically neutral indigenous Algerians into the ranks of the insurgency. The FLN was in many ways no match for French military power, but it effectively used terrorist tactics in order to draw out (according to Leninist-Marxist thinking) the brutality of the colonial regime. The bloodshed of Philippeville in 1955, in which FLN fighters slaughtered dozens of *colons* (settlers) and Algerians, including women and children, demonstrated the lengths to which the FLN would go in order to take the war to the French authorities. But it also provoked a devastating backlash, on the part of both the French military and the *colons* themselves, who frequently took matters into their own hands. In 1956, the French military switched their focus from rural areas to the city of Algiers, and the ensuing Battle of Algiers (1956–7), captured in Gillo Pontecorvo's extraordinary 1966 film, involved FLN attacks followed by increasingly brutal French reprisals. French forces ultimately cleared Algiers, but the methods used marked the beginning of a political backlash.[44] By the beginning of the 1960s, the war had become a three-sided fight, with the Organisation armée secrète, set up by disgruntled French officers opposed to de Gaulle's decision to talk to the FLN, launching its own terrorist attacks on a regular basis.

Algeria, of course, ultimately became independent, in 1962: the FLN could never completely militarily destroy the French army, but it had created an uncontrollable level of violence in the territory and made it politically unsustainable for the French to retain it. Algeria set something of a benchmark for insurgents elsewhere willing to use terrorist tactics for political goals. Critically, the Algerian War had a chronicler, and one of the most articulate champions the FLN could have hoped for, in the psychiatrist and political activist Frantz Fanon. Fanon's *Wretched of the Earth*, first

---

43 The classic account in English is A. Horne, *A Savage War of Peace: Algeria 1954–1962* (London, Penguin, 1977), but there is also a useful summary in A. Clayton, *Frontiersmen: Warfare in Africa since 1950* (London, UCL Press, 1999), pp. 22–34.
44 *The Battle of Algiers* (1966), dir. Gillo Pontecorvo. The film was not screened in France until 1971.

published in 1961, was a powerful indictment of the impact of colonial rule on Algeria in particular, but also on conquered peoples everywhere – psychologically, socially, culturally – and became a handbook for liberation.[45] Young revolutionaries in Africa in the 1960s, confronted with various forms of state-level intransigence, read it eagerly and transferred the message, rooted in the Algerian experience, to their own situations. For them, and supposedly for Fanon, who did not live to see much of the violence carried out in his name, the colonial enemy must be confronted by whatever means necessary, and available. Such violence often took the form of guerrilla struggle, which might resemble conventional war in some respects – as it often did in the Horn of Africa, for example, and in parts of the Portuguese empire in Angola and Mozambique – with defined 'front lines', uniformed armies, and set battles, but which also (and sometimes at the same time) might look like what we would today define (and what was sometimes defined then) as 'terrorism'. This meant sudden attack on army and police outposts, using the 'bush' as rear base and cover, or on government or 'civilian' targets which were deemed to represent the enemy. Moral questions were generally set aside in pursuit of the larger goal, namely 'liberation', whatever that might mean in particular circumstances. For some, at least, Fanon exhorted the colonised to 'absolute violence' against the coloniser, up to and including terrorism.[46] This was the direct and logical outcome of colonial rule itself. Above all, perhaps, implicit in Fanon's argument is that violence begets violence; that the terror and brutality imposed on Africans during colonial rule – both physically and psychologically – justified, in Newtonian terms, an equal and opposite reaction.

Between the 1960s and the 1980s, an array of armed insurgencies appeared across the continent – though mostly in southern, central and north-east Africa – which, imbued with ideological fervour, sought the overthrow of minority or otherwise illegitimate regimes. Such asymmetrical warfare took various forms.[47] To their supporters, these insurgent groups were revolutionary guerrillas in the mould of Che Guevara, seeking the liberation of the oppressed masses; to others – including, of course, their military opponents – they were indeed 'terrorists', by which was meant illegitimate, dangerous

---

45 F. Fanon (trans. C. Farrington), *The Wretched of the Earth* (London, Penguin, 1990), was first published as *Les Damnés de la Terre* in 1961.
46 M. W. Sonnleitner, 'Of Logic and Liberation: Frantz Fanon on Terrorism', *Journal of Black Studies* 17/3 (1987).
47 The best single account is W. Reno, *Warfare in Independent Africa* (New York, Cambridge University Press, 2011).

radicals deploying violence indiscriminately. Foreign governments often followed the lead of local state-level actors. Politically motivated labelling aside, in general such movements did sometimes engage in activities which were 'terrorist' in a tactical sense: blowing up railway lines, or attacking airports, or hijacking civilian airliners. The Zimbabwean liberation forces and (rather less successfully, in military terms) the armed wing of the ANC in South Africa, Umkhonto we Sizwe (MK), often attacked 'civilian' as well as 'military' targets.[48] Acts of terror, involving the killing of non-combatants, occurred in the midst of larger, more complex guerrilla insurgencies – which we might categorise here as representing the more 'conventional' form of asymmetrical warfare during this period. After the fact, regret was often expressed at such casualties; but – as with the FLN in Algeria – an underlying objective was to provoke the oppressive state into revealing its true brutality, thus winning further recruits for the insurgencies themselves. Other movements, such as the Eritrean Liberation Front (ELF) and the Tigray People's Liberation Front (TPLF) in Eritrea and Ethiopia respectively, briefly dabbled in 'terrorist' tactics but generally eschewed them. The ELF, for example, was involved in abortive attempts at the hijacking of aircraft in the late 1960s and early 1970s,[49] before concentrating on a more urgent ground-level guerrilla war (and their own internal convulsions). The TPLF took some Westerners hostage in 1976, including a British journalist, but released them soon after, while their occasional partner and rival in the anti-Ethiopian struggle, the Eritrean People's Liberation Front (EPLF), distanced itself from such acts.[50]

In the violent age of late decolonisation, however, it was soon Fanon's wretched who were themselves being terrorised, and not just by recalcitrant and brutal colonial regimes. Armed insurgents deployed terror in a range of wars during the 1970s and 1980s. In Angola, for example, União Nacional para a Independência Total de Angola (UNITA) used terror to force the rural population into government-held urban areas in order to increase the burden on government resources.[51] Fanonesque 'revolutionary terrorism' was apparently morphing into something more brutal, less discriminate, than anything

---

48 D. Martin and P. Johnson, *The Struggle for Zimbabwe: The Chimurenga War* (London, Faber and Faber, 1981); K. Flower, *Serving Secretly: Rhodesia into Zimbabwe, 1964–1981* (London, John Murray, 1987); T. O. Ranger, *Peasant Consciousness and Guerrilla War in Zimbabwe* (London, James Currey, 1985). See also Nelson Mandela's own assessment of MK's objectives in *Long Walk to Freedom* (London, BCA, 1995), pp. 272–5.
49 See for example 'Terrorism: Brief and Bloody', *Time*, 18 December 1972.
50 D. Connell, *Against All Odds: A Chronicle of the Eritrean Revolution* (Lawrenceville, NJ, Red Sea Press, 1997), p. 30.
51 Reno, *Warfare*, pp. 75–7.

that had come before. Such violence was the result of new networks into which terrorist–guerrillas could tap; this was also what happened in the vortex created by collapsing states. In other ways, too, however, it seemed to be a reversion to older patterns of violence; it was certainly the outcome of weighty pasts, and not just the symptom of failed modernity. In particular, these forms of distinctively indiscriminate violence to some extent flowed out of the experience of imperial contact, and the roots of such violence were embedded in the very fabric of colonial rule.

The Dysfunctions of Modernity?

In some senses, contemporary Africa has witnessed the shift from the populist violence of revolutionary liberation to cells which are the vanguards of violence, which see the consensus and the hegemonic order as the enemy. This may partly explain why a distinctive image comes to the fore in the 1990s and 2000s, centred on the idea of a 'new', peculiar kind of brutality: a particularly 'modern' – or perhaps postmodern – form of seemingly nihilistic terror, characterised by the shocking brutality of the violence inflicted on civilians. These new terrorists are not necessarily 'global', although some do have global aspirations; but rather they are globally visible, as a result of the traumas and horrors they inflict at the local level. In recent years – and certainly since the end of the Cold War – there has been ever greater attention paid to terrorism and other forms of asymmetrical violence in Africa.[52] The rise of this scholarly strand is a reflection of the seeming proliferation of such violence in an era which has seen severe stresses placed on the African body politic. Since the 1980s and 1990s, a whole new genre (as some would have it) of terrorist violence has emerged – in northern Nigeria, across the West African Sahel and in the Maghreb; in Somalia, where religious insurgency has spawned attacks in the capitals of Kenya and Uganda; in Ethiopia; in northern Uganda and the eastern Democratic Republic of Congo (DRC). This was ostensibly the epoch in which crazed youth, recruited into roaming gangs of militia which were both the cause and

---

52 See for example the relevant sections in Paul D. Williams's excellent textbook survey, *War and Conflict in Africa* (Cambridge, Polity Press, 2016). A useful snapshot from 2009 is offered in P. Lyman, 'The War on Terrorism in Africa', in J. W. Harbeson and D. S. Rothchild (eds.), *Africa in World Politics* (Boulder, CO, Westview Press, 2009). It is perhaps interesting to note that this essay appeared in the fourth edition of this regularly updated text; but in the most recent (fifth and sixth) editions, it has disappeared – retired, it seems, to make way for other, more immediate concerns.

the effect of state collapse, inflicted extraordinary levels of both terror and physical suffering on vulnerable civilian populations.

In Sierra Leone and Liberia, from the late 1980s onward, rebels used horrifically violent ambush and widespread bodily mutilation to terrorise civilians into submission.[53] In the 1990s and 2000s, the Lord's Resistance Army (LRA), under the command of Joseph Kony, likewise terrorised a swathe of northern Uganda, mutilating victims, using rape as a weapon of war, and kidnapping children into its ranks.[54] Both perpetrators and victims were predominantly Acholi, an ethnic group long marginalised in economic and political terms. Despite much bluster on the part of Yoweri Museveni, Uganda's long-serving president, the Ugandan army never managed to fully defeat the LRA, or capture Kony, although the movement did eventually leave northern Uganda, relocating to the north-east corner of the Democratic Republic of Congo (DRC) and the Central African Republic. (Kony remains at large at the time of writing.) Indeed, for many observers, Museveni's own National Resistance Army, which swept to power in 1986, had fuelled the insurgency in the first instance by committing atrocities and human rights abuses on a large scale – state-level terrorism in action – as it subdued the north in the late 1980s and early 1990s.[55] In the wake of the Rwandan genocide of 1994, armed militias proliferated in the eastern DRC – some with links, at least initially, to the Ugandan and Rwandan governments – which acted with similar levels of shocking brutality towards the local population. 'Terror' was both tactic and way of life in a region consumed in a much larger war.[56]

---

53 P. Richards, *Fighting for the Rain Forest: War, Youth, and Resources in Sierra Leone* (Oxford, James Currey, 1996); S. Ellis, *The Mask of Anarchy: The Destruction of Liberia and the Religious Dimension of an African Civil War* (London, Hurst, 1999).

54 S. Finnstrom, *Living with Bad Surroundings: War, History, and Everyday Moments in Northern Uganda* (Durham, NC, Duke University Press, 2008); T. Allen and K. Vlassenroot (eds.), *The LRA: Myth and Reality* (London, Zed Books, 2010). See also contemporary reports by Human Rights Watch (HRW): *The Scars of Death: Children Abducted by the Lord's Resistance Army in Uganda* (New York, HRW, 1997); *Abducted and Abused: Renewed Conflict in Northern Uganda* (New York, HRW, 2003); *Uprooted and Forgotten: Impunity and Human Rights Abuses in Northern Uganda* (New York, HRW, 2005).

55 Amnesty International, *Uganda: The Failure to Safeguard Human Rights* (London, Amnesty International, 1992); S. Finnstrom, '"For God and My Life": War and Cosmology in Northern Uganda', in P. Richards (ed.), *No Peace, No War: An Anthropology of Contemporary Armed Conflicts* (Oxford, James Currey, 2005).

56 G. Prunier, *Africa's World War: Congo, the Rwandan Genocide, and the Making of a Continental Catastrophe* (Oxford, Oxford University Press, 2009); F. Reyntjens, *The Great African War: Congo and Regional Geopolitics, 1996–2006* (Cambridge, Cambridge University Press, 2009).

Some analysts debated whether greed rather than grievance wasn't a more powerful motivating factor in driving these insurgencies;[57] but, more broadly, they wondered whether such levels of killing and wanton brutality were the expression of ideology or of insanity. The use of terror and the horrific acts it involved came to define the rebels' very character and state of mind, and any larger agendas or aims were overlooked or at least relegated in importance. Some observers concluded – as an earlier generation did of Mau Mau – that the perpetrators of such violence could not possibly be 'sane'. Further, these were localised terrorisms which seemed, on one level, to be the product of modernity – or rather, for some, the failure of modernity. They emerged in periods of traumatic transition, as in Uganda, and occupied the spaces left by collapsing states, as in the case of DRC, Sierra Leone and Liberia. In that sense, in some places at least, they appeared to represent the failure of the postcolonial order. These movements represented the assertion of those unreconciled to, and marginalised from, the modern, mainstream, conventional political order as recognised as sovereign under international law. But they also represented profoundly *historical* grievances and practices. Historical roots and practices can be identified in various forms: in the reversion to the modus operandi, and an array of cultural and cosmological reference points, of the precolonial era – as in Sierra Leone and Liberia in the 1990s, or Darfur in the early 2000s.[58] They can be identified, too, in the use of disfigurement and mutilation as terrorising tactics, common, for example, in the precolonial Ugandan region; in the seizure of people as means of control and expansion; in the recruitment of the young to disruptive causes.

Meanwhile, the rise of militant Islam in recent years has involved violence enacted by historically marginalised and dispossessed people. But while religious violence is not in itself novel in African history, *religious terrorism* is, perhaps: in the precolonial era, conflict around faith generally involved conventional armed confrontation or, conversely, relatively peaceful adaptation. But modern religious terrorism in Africa is the result of a combination of autochthonous, endogenous dynamics and impulses, and a global network of clandestine, non-state activity. Al-Shabaab in Somalia partnered itself with Al-Qaeda early on in its development, while Al-Qaeda in the Islamic Maghreb (AQIM) has long operated across the West African savannah. Terrorist violence has been to some extent enabled, and in some cases strengthened,

---

57 P. Collier and A. Hoeffler, 'Greed and Grievance in Civil War', The World Bank: Development Research Group: Policy Research Working Paper No. 2355 (May 2000).
58 See for example M. W. Daly, *Darfur's Sorrow: A History of Destruction and Genocide* (Cambridge, Cambridge University Press, 2007).

by global connections and global causes through which to rally recruits – even when the primary targets of violence, and the grievances, are local, just as are the traditions of violence on which those transnational ideologies draw. The Horn of Africa, notably, has long been an arena of religious contest – no coincidence, given that Somalis and Amhara each possessed, as Gellner put it, the gun and their own version of 'the Book'[59] – but transnational, indeed global, connectivity has grown markedly in recent years.[60]

In Somalia, al-Shabaab (literally, 'the Youth') emerged following the controversial Ethiopian military intervention in 2006 aimed at the overthrow of the Union of Islamic Courts, which had, ironically, brought about some degree of order and stability in southern Somalia after years of civil war but which was regarded in Addis Ababa as a fundamental threat.[61] Al-Shabaab grew in strength – at least initially, in part, the result of the violent behaviour towards the populace by invading Ethiopian soldiers[62] – and its violence increased in reach and ferocity: it has been behind numerous attacks across southern Somalia, the most deadly being in Mogadishu, but also in Nairobi and Kampala. Only in recent years have its operations been pegged back somewhat, especially following a more robust African Union intervention, although it very much remains active. At its core, al-Shabaab represents the rejection of the international consensus on peacebuilding and national reconstruction in Somalia – dominated by the US and Ethiopia – and the creation of a pure Islamic state, hence its affiliation with al-Qaeda.[63] Al-Qaeda itself has remained alert to opportunities in Africa, having been behind the devastating US embassy bombings in Nairobi and Dar es Salaam in 1998, and has actively become involved in militant insurgency across the Sahel region. In north-east Nigeria, however, Boko Haram – the Hausa term broadly means 'Western education is forbidden' – has in many ways ploughed its own furrow. Founded in 2002 as a non-violent organisation, it soon embraced violence as a means of rejuvenating and purifying Islam in the region and has since

---

59 E. Gellner, *Nations and Nationalism* [1st ed. 1983] (Oxford, Blackwell, 2005), p. 84.
60 De Waal (ed.), *Islamism and Its Enemies*; Rotberg (ed.), *Battling Terrorism*.
61 Hansen, *Al Shabaab in Somalia*; K. Menkhaus, 'The Crisis in Somalia: Tragedy in Five Acts', *African Affairs* 106/424 (2007). For an earlier assessment, see also K. Menkhaus, 'Somalia and Somaliland: Terrorism, Political Islam, and State Collapse', in Rotberg (ed.), *Battling Terrorism*.
62 Human Rights Watch, 'Ethiopia's Dirty War', 5 August 2007; Human Rights Watch, 'Somalia: War Crimes Devastate Population', 8 December 2008; Amnesty International, *Routinely Targeted: Attacks on Civilians in Somalia* (London, Amnesty International, May 2008).
63 'Somalia's Al-Shabab Join Al-Qaeda', *BBC News*, 10 February 2012.

been responsible for the deaths of tens of thousands of people and the displacement of more than 2 million more. Located on an impoverished periphery, it has been broadly aligned with al-Qaeda and shares training and intelligence with other militant groups in the neighbourhood, while it was briefly affiliated with ISIL in 2015–16.[64] Despite repeated efforts by the Nigerian military, backed by the US and others, Boko Haram has proven difficult to overcome, to date.

Boko Haram and other movements in some ways emerge as the outcome of resistance to supposedly hegemonic political (and/or religious) orders, and as such belong to a tradition of resistance. Insurgents in Nigeria and Somalia, for example, can draw on histories of religious violence against various versions of infidel repression or apostasy.[65] Yet, at the same time, they demonstrate the fundamental *weakness* of the modern state, specifically its inability to secure and police borders, protect citizens, and to 'broadcast' power.[66] Historically, terrorism has a direct correlation with states – specifically, their perceived illegitimacy, their weakness and in many cases their disintegration and collapse. In the precolonial era, these were communities which might have 'moved on', or been left to their own devices, given the relative abundance of land vis-à-vis people. In the modern era, they have been incorporated into territories, and have responded by exercising violence in pursuit of resources and rights.

Terrorism and related insurgencies also serve a particular political purpose, enabling states to maintain a war footing, and to demonstrate martial muscle in their desire to achieve unity and peace. In turn, these agendas have tended to legitimise 'state terrorism' – as in the case of the National Resistance Movement (NRM) in northern Uganda, as noted earlier, a situation in which state action actually provokes the kind of violence which is subsequently labelled 'terrorist'. In the context of the securitisation of African politics and putatively 'new' forms of authoritarianism, 'terrorist'

---

64 Smith, *Boko Haram*; Thurston, *Boko Haram*.
65 Somalia has been the source, and the site, of religious violence against Christian Ethiopia for much of the last millennium, most famously the jihadist war of the mid-sixteenth century: S. A. A. Arabfaqih, *The Conquest of Abyssinia: Futuh Al Habasa* (Addis Ababa, Tsehai Publishers, 2005). Northern Nigeria was the site of one of the most successful theocracies in nineteenth-century Africa, the Sokoto Caliphate, with its origins in a widespread insurgency in between 1804 and 1810: see for example M. Last, 'Contradictions in Creating a Jihadi Capital: Sokoto in the Nineteenth Century and Its Legacy', *African Studies Review* 56/2 (2013), as well as Last's own classic study, *The Sokoto Caliphate* (London, Longmans, 1967).
66 J. Herbst, *States and Power in Africa: Comparative Lessons in Authority and Control* (Princeton, Princeton University Press, 2000).

became a particular form of political labelling. It always was, of course. But in the late twentieth and early twenty-first century, the use of the term for domestic purposes has only increased. Thus, 'terrorist' could be applied to any antagonist of the state, any opponent armed or otherwise. This was greatly facilitated by the security agendas of Western powers, especially the United States, which bolstered local partners and their capacity to combat terrorism (mostly seen as synonymous with Islamic extremism) on the front line. Those same partners then utilised the global antiterrorist agenda to target local opposition and consolidate extant regimes. What is most striking about the last few years is the use of terrorism to reinforce tight control of the domestic political space. The securitisation agenda has its echoes in other parts of the world, including in Europe and North America, but it is perhaps most stark in countries whose governments perceive any form of political opposition as an existential threat. It is not that terrorism did not exist in those places, but rather that – in addition – terrorism represented an opportunity and came to be considerably exaggerated in pursuit of heightened authoritarian control. Ethiopia offers a prime example, where antiterror legislation in 2009 was used to effectively suppress most forms of political dissent in the name of national security. Thus 'Ginbot 7', which emerged as a key opposition grouping in the years following the 2005 crackdown, was classified as a terrorist organisation – with all the legal implications for its members should they find themselves captured.[67] In so doing, the Ethiopian People's Revolutionary Democratic Front (EPRDF) regime was able to align itself with the US strategy in the region, whether under the Bush or Obama administration. Ethiopia cooperated in special renditions, moreover, and the trade-off was a closer security arrangement with the West.[68]

The Ethiopian government, of course, was indeed confronted with various internal 'terrorisms' which were very tangible. The Oromo Liberation Front (OLF) and the Ogaden National Liberation Front (ONLF) launched episodic attacks on economic and military targets, and represented groups adamantly hostile to the incumbent regime.[69] Even if they were low level and did not pose an existential threat to the state, these attacks further justified the

---

[67] There is a useful overview in International Crisis Group, 'Ethiopia: Ethnic Federalism and Its Discontents', Africa Report No. 153, 4 September 2009; also the author's own informal interviews and fieldwork notes, Addis Ababa, 2009–13.
[68] Human Rights Watch, '"Why Am I Still Here?"' The 2007 Horn of Africa Renditions and the Fate of Those Still Missing', 1 October 2008; A. Mitchell, 'US Agents Interrogating Terror Suspects Held in Ethiopian Prisons', *International Herald Tribune*, 4 April 2007.
[69] 'Chinese Energy Workers in Somalia Threatened', www.oilprice.com, 19 June 2011.

securitisation of the state and in particular a crackdown in the ethnically Somali province of Ogaden. The contrast between a seemingly omnipotent EPRDF and the ONLF seemed stark; and yet, part of the explanation for the EPRDF's brutal clampdown of all such insurgencies perhaps reflected an awareness of their own humble roots. The ONLF seemed far from challenging for power, and certainly lacked the capacity to achieve it; but then, as the story of the TPLF, the dominant force in the EPRDF coalition, demonstrates, no rebellious frontier, internal or external, rural or urban, seems threatening to the existing order until suddenly it is. Those terrorists, no longer the impoverished bandits on fly-blown peripheries, can become through organisation and the tipping point of 'popular support' the destroyers of regimes.

At the same time, it is important to note the emergence of state sponsors of terrorism in the same period – those regimes which used their security apparatus and other forms of material and ideological influence to reach into others' internal conflicts to support a range of armed groups. The most notable instance of this was Muammar Gaddafi's Libya, which in the 1970s and 1980s became the West's bête noire as Africa's chief sponsor of international terrorism.[70] Libya would later be joined by Sudan under Omar al-Bashir from 1989 onwards. In particular, Hassan al-Turabi, a leading figure of the Islamist movement in Sudan, expounded the promotion of Islamism by whatever means necessary. In the course of the 1990s, Sudan was widely associated – but particularly by the US – with Islamist terrorism across northeast Africa and the Middle East; Sudan was internationally isolated following the attempted assassination, in 1995, of Hosni Mubarak in Addis Ababa.[71] In their different ways, Libya and Sudan saw themselves as the champions of violent change as a means of challenging what they saw as occidental hegemony. The Horn of Africa illustrates the ways in which hostile neighbours use insurgencies as leverage. Eritrea's alleged interference in Somalia, and more specifically its supposed support for al-Shabaab, led to the imposition of international sanctions – the first case of such imposed isolation since Libya and Sudan. Eritrea denied the accusations.[72] But there was wide

70 B. L. Davis, *Qaddafi, Terrorism, and the Origins of the US Attack on Libya* (New York, Praeger, 1990).
71 P. M. Holt and M. W. Daly, *A History of the Sudan: From the Coming of Islam to the Present Day* (Harlow, Longman, 2000), pp. 187–94.
72 United Nations, meetings coverage and press releases: 'Security Council Imposes Sanctions on Eritrea over Its Role in Somalia, Refusal to Withdraw Troops Following Conflict with Djibouti', 23 December 2009, at www.un.org/press/en/2009/sc9833.doc.htm. See also R. Reid (ed.), *Eritrea's External Relations: Understanding Its Regional Role and Foreign Policy* (London, Chatham House, 2009), and International Crisis Group, 'Eritrea: The Siege State', Africa Report No. 163, 21 September 2010.

suspicion that the government in Asmara was only too willing to use terrorist organisations and other discontents to impose itself on a hostile neighbourhood, particularly in the wake of a disastrous war with Ethiopia between 1998 and 2000. Indeed, it was at least partly the result of that war that Eritrea refused to follow the Ethiopian-led conventional wisdom on Somalia, regardless of the extent of its actual support for al-Shabaab. In 2011, Eritrea was accused by a UN investigation of plotting to bomb an AU summit in Addis Ababa, using local proxies.[73] It was a shocking allegation, naturally rejected by Eritrea itself. But it was made all the more poignant considering that, in the 1990s, long before most people had heard of him, the Eritreans had been dealing with the threat posed by Osama bin Laden, then based in Sudan and supporting an organisation known as Eritrean Islamic Jihad.[74] It had been a remarkable and depressing journey for a country once, if briefly, held up as a symbol of progress in the region. But in the Horn no one had a monopoly on the use of terror as political weapon: everyone was caught up in a macabre dance of accusation and counter-accusation, and things were done to citizens and foreign antagonists alike in the name of security and particular interpretations of 'freedom'.

Concluding Reflections

The question of distinctive African perspectives and contours is to some extent a red herring, as much of what has been discussed in this chapter reflects a universal human experience. Nonetheless, some observations are perhaps in order. There is clearly novelty, in the course of the twentieth and early twenty-first century, in terms of external linkages, ideologies and technology at terrorists' disposal; this is true of both state and non-state actors. However, it is clear enough that some patterns of terrorist activity can be discerned as flowing from Africa's deeper past – notably in terms of the general (if not universal) eschewal of a distinction between combatants and non-combatants, given the nature of African war in general. Therefore, it is important to see terrorism, in its historical and its contemporary forms, as part of the totality of violence in Africa; in other words, as one branch of a range of violent options and cultures and practices. Connected to that, terrorism cannot be removed from the socio-economic and political conditions within which it takes place. There is something axiomatic in this

---

73 'UN Report Accuses Eritrea of Plotting to Bomb AU Summit', *BBC News*, 28 July 2011.
74 G. Kibreab, 'Eritrean–Sudanese Relations in Historical Perspective', in Reid (ed.), *Eritrea's External Relations*, pp. 87–8.

observation, but it is worth reiterating: that terrorism is an outcome of material circumstances, of perceptions of social convention and status, and of the state of political power in a given area at a given moment. Compelled by political and material dynamics (and shaped by political and material constraints), terrorism aims historically at the instilment of fear and the generation of shock, and it does so with particular aims in view; it is the expression of discontent. This is true even if violence becomes a way of life as much as a means to an end, for at the very least, in those cases, it is necessary to the acquisition of material goods, status and group cohesion, even if grander ideological visions are absent. Histories of terrorism in Africa are frequently histories of the marginalised, the oppressed, the persecuted.

Terrorism has long been a carefully calculated form of violence in which fear and unsettlement, not battlefield victories, have been the primary aims, and in which the capture and control of people has been the desired outcome. Africans have considerable experience of state terrorism – from the slave trade and the state-building exercises of the precolonial era, to imperial partition, to the brutal excesses of authoritarian systems in the recent past. Marginalised, subjugated or otherwise dispossessed communities have sought to curtail these projections of power and resist, using whatever tools available. Particular cultures of violence have long coalesced around both *killing* and *fear* in pursuit of effecting political and economic change. Terrorism cannot be segregated from wider contingencies – most obviously, economic and political aspiration and desperation, which fundamentally shape attitudes towards human life, or more precisely the taking of it, at particular moments in time.

Further Reading

C. Clapham, 'Terrorism in Africa: Problems of Definition, History and Development', *South African Journal of International Affairs* 10/2 (2003)

R. J. Reid, *Warfare in African History* (New York, Cambridge University Press, 2012)

W. Reno, *Warfare in Independent Africa* (New York, Cambridge University Press, 2011)

R. I. Rotberg (ed.), *Battling Terrorism in the Horn of Africa* (Washington, DC, Brookings Institution Press, 2005)

D. Walter, *Colonial Violence: European Empires and the Use of Force* (London, Hurst, 2017)

10

The History of Terrorism in Pakistan

DAYYAB GILLANI

Introduction

Analysis of terrorism in Pakistan has often suffered from simplifications, generalisations and stereotyping. Seen either as an extension of global Islamic extremism or worse a nursery that breeds this transnational threat, the country has regularly been ostracised and chastised by the international community. Since Islamic extremism has widely been regarded as a malevolent force that can only be perceived in apocalyptic terms, Pakistan therefore has attracted the attention of a number of alarmists and doomsday prophets. This negative attention has subsequently produced a discourse on one of the most dangerous countries in the world that narrowly focuses on the security threat posed by Pakistan.

Such superficial and shallow engagement with the problem is deeply unfair, as it selfishly presents terrorism in the country as a danger to the rest of the world and cruelly ignores its primary affectees – the people of Pakistan. Moreover, such a discourse is also largely unsustainable in the long run, as its parochial standpoint prevents it from appreciating the heterogeneity, complexity and interwovenness of terrorism in the country. In order to make sense of terrorism in Pakistan, it is necessary to both distance its understanding from the one-dimensional post-9/11 lenses and acknowledge it as an indigenous problem with a distinct pedigree that threatens first and foremost the citizens of the country. This can be accomplished by taking up a historically grounded context-specific approach, which traces the problem of terrorism back to the sociopolitical realities that produced it in the first place. This chapter will attempt precisely that.

It will start by first deconstructing the dominant discourse on the security threat posed by one of the most dangerous countries in the world, followed by a methodical dissection of the heterogeneity of terrorism in Pakistan. The analysis hopefully will not only expose the frivolity of stereotypical post-9/11 generalisations but will also allow us to appreciate the depth and density of terrorism in the country.

Primarily, however, this chapter will investigate in detail the sociopolitical factors that led to the emergence, diffusion and perpetuation of terrorism in the country. Most historical accounts of terrorism in Pakistan typically trace the phenomenon back to the Soviet–Afghan war and the subsequent rise of the jihadi/mujahideen culture in the region. Contrary to such postulations, it will be argued that the seeds for terrorism were as a matter of fact sown even before the country came into existence. This is because all variations of home-grown violence in Pakistan are in one way or another a product of its notoriously convoluted compound identity. It will be the central contention of this chapter that in order to cognise terrorism in Pakistan we must first understand and acknowledge the country's enduring identity crisis.

Terrorism is a complex phenomenon that can manifest itself in other forms of violence, like insurgency, militancy and state repression. It is important therefore to use a broad definition that can account for such trespassing. Accordingly I will utilise just such a definition, which was first proposed in my doctoral thesis. Terrorism generally, and for the purpose of this research specifically, is 'a fear generating political activity that psychologically influences an audience by means of targeting or threatening to target non-combatants with a credible threat of harm'.[1]

Discourse on the Security Threat Posed by the Most Dangerous Country – Pakistan

As an underdeveloped and underprivileged country, Pakistan always had an image problem. With a struggling democracy, chequered economy and rampant corruption, the country has always been presented poorly on the international stage. Nevertheless, the image Pakistan historically presented was not any different from a score of other countries that had secured independence from their European overlords in the twentieth century. All newly created countries in the postcolonial world order had their fair share of political, economic and social upheavals.

Rising from the abyss of centuries of colonial exploitation and manipulation, the newly created countries had to navigate through a treacherous path beset by their own inexperience and the onset of cold war. Caught up in the

---

[1] D. Gillani, 'The Definitional Dilemma of Terrorism: Seeking Clarity in Light of Terrorism Scholarship', unpublished PhD thesis, University of St Andrews (2017), p. 257.

middle of superpower rivalry and falling prey to their proxy wars and inescapable ideological preferences, the nascent countries had to start their recovery and development journey in egregious circumstances.

Given the geopolitical dynamics of the time, Pakistan and other newborn states would go on to acquire the support and sympathy of various Western scholars who cast their problems into moulds of neo-Marxist, dependency, postcolonial and other critical discourses.[2] Problems of nascent states were urged to be assessed in the light of broader frames of reference, historical facts and socio-economic realities. Arguably, while mainstream scholars were far less enthusiastic about the plight of the so-called Third World, they were nevertheless fairly conservative and guarded in their assessment. The developing world was at least not projected as a region of grave risk that posed an existential threat to the world at large.

As the Cold War ended and the focus shifted from bipolarity and ideological divides, much of the developing world suddenly emerged as a volatile and unstable region that threatened the very existence of not just the developed countries but the whole world itself. The threat posed was apparently being determined by means of a paradigm shift caused by the emergence of a phenomenon called terrorism.

Although the phenomenon itself had been around for centuries, terrorism's latter-day manifestation was deemed unique and novel. Articulated in the 'new terrorism thesis', one major feature of this supposedly unique threat emanating from the Third World was its radical Islamist character.[3] This threat was principally associated with the Middle East and South Asia, a region that was otherwise still recovering and convalescing from the legacy of colonialism and strategic exploits of the Cold War. Since the objective was to eliminate the threat of terrorism, little to no effort was spared to understand it. It was the single most dangerous threat faced by mankind, and the only way to deal with it was through ruthless military and strategic doctrines.[4]

It was only a matter of time until this logic would also be extended to the regions from where Islamist terrorism was evidently emanating. Consequently, countries like Pakistan and Afghanistan transformed into the

---

2 See e.g. I. Wallerstein, *The Capitalist World-Economy*, Vol. 2 (Cambridge, Cambridge University Press, 1979).
3 See e.g. M. Juergensmeyer, 'Understanding the New Terrorism', *Current History* 99 (2000).
4 In his 2001 presidential address, Bush stated that 'the only way to defeat terrorism as a threat to our way of life is to stop it, eliminate it, and destroy it where it grows', www.theguardian.com/world/2001/sep/21/september11.usa13.

most dangerous countries of the world. Since the prevailing policies and practices of the time only had a one-dimensional view of terrorism, the discourses that emerged as a result went only so far as to identify the regions of risk and the gravity of terrorist threat they posed.[5] All counterterrorism measures were subsequently directed at eradicating terrorism and neutralising the regions that allegedly produced it.

In the specific context of Pakistan – a predominantly Muslim country, home to one of the largest madrassa systems, professional and well-equipped armed forces with a nuclear arsenal at their disposal, and widespread anti-American sentiments – the country clearly possessed all the right ingredients to be characterised as a region of security risk. Against this backdrop, the prognosis that followed permitted and even facilitated the emergence of a discourse on the security threat posed by the most dangerous country in the world, Pakistan. Policy and even scholarly enterprises thereupon embarked on a quest to underscore the gravity of the threat posed and the methodology necessary to counter it.

This new security discourse effectively deprived Pakistan and its people of the empathy that had previously been extended to them. Gone were the critical postcolonial lenses and broader frames of reference that took into account historical contexts and socio-economic realities of the region. Questions over whether terrorism in Pakistan had a history and why and how it suddenly transformed into a threat of such gargantuan proportions were either ignored or taken for granted. Terrorism and terrorist organisations were simply treated as extensions of the Pakistani state or worse the Pakistani society. Even the colonial legacy and the resultant unfortunate state of economic and social affairs were used against the country. Given these dynamics, the notorious reputation Pakistan went on to acquire is hardly surprising.

This in no way is intended to suggest that Pakistan is not dangerous, nor does it in any way entail that there is no terrorism in the country. Pakistan, in effect, is a dangerous country confronting the very serious problem of terrorism. However, the danger posed by Pakistan is essentially to Pakistan itself, and the foremost affectees of terrorism have not been Westerners or foreigners but the citizens of the country. Therefore, instead of viewing it as a terrorist state or a region spewing terrorism, Pakistan must first be seen as a country that is effectively a victim of terrorism.

---

5 G. Bankoff, 'Regions of Risk: Western Discourses on Terrorism and the Significance of Islam', *Studies in Conflict and Terrorism* 26 (2003), p. 413.

What is required, therefore, is a significant discursive shift from the security threat posed by Pakistan to one that examines and investigates its internal dynamics and prioritises its most direct and greatest affectees. This will permit a deeper understanding of the underlying sociopolitical factors and a profound appreciation of the historical developments that produced them. Furthermore, it will allow us to replace the of late simplistic and narrow set of frames that typically explain terrorism only by dint of Islamic extremism with broader frames of reference that acknowledge both the heterogeneity and complexity of the problem.

The Heterogeneity of Terrorism in Pakistan

Undercutting terrorism's heterogeneity and highlighting Islamic radicalisation as its most imminent and pertinent manifestation, the post-9/11 events brought forth confining prisms that advanced the now familiar stereotypical understanding of the phenomenon. Predictably, therefore, terrorism in Pakistan was also perceived through similar confining lenses. On closer inspection, however, it becomes evident that Al Qaeda-style Islamic terrorism represents only a fraction of what actually happens in Pakistan.

To put it into perspective, Pakistan, to begin with, has been host to nationalist-inspired violence since its inception. The immense diversity of Pakistan often plays to its disadvantage, as nationalist aspirations run very deep and frequently pit disenfranchised and aggrieved communities against the state or each other. While the country has four distinct ethnicities (Punjabi, Pashtun, Sindhi and Balochi), it is also home to a large number of ethnic minorities (such as Siraiki, Hazara, Muhajir, Kashmiri and Brahvi). Usually overlooked or simply overshadowed by the dominant, stereotypical Islamist-centric view, the ethnic unrest and resultant terrorism pose a serious problem to the Pakistani state and, more importantly, the Pakistani people. With little to no signs of abating, ethnic and nationalist tensions have the potential to take centre stage in the years to come.

Admittedly, terrorism in Pakistan also has a pronounced religious dimension. However, the terrorist threat posed by religion is neither monolithic nor necessarily Al Qaeda- or ISIS-inspired (as the dominant discourse would have us believe). In fact, terrorism stemming from religion in Pakistan is hopelessly fragmented and mostly manifested along sectarian lines. Sectarian terrorism is arguably the most enduring form of terrorism in Pakistan and is statistically also the most dangerous, as it alone accounts for more fatalities than any other form of terrorism in the country.[6] Lumping it together or confusing it with ISIS/Al Qaeda-style terrorism is not only grossly misleading but also extremely unfair. This is because sectarianism fundamentally threatens the Pakistani citizens; associating it with the likes of Al Qaeda suggests that it principally poses a transnational threat.

Given the strategic location and geopolitical dynamics of the region, terrorism in Pakistan also has a very visible international footprint. From active state sponsorship to passive support, terrorism has frequently been utilised by competing powers to promote their respective political agendas in the country. Even though the main culprits are the regional actors (Saudi Arabia, Iran, Afghanistan and India), superpowers such as the US and USSR have also historically played a very crucial role in both encouraging and nurturing various terrorist movements for their respective strategic interests. While the complicity of the US, USSR and India is relatively better known,[7] the role of Iran and Saudi Arabia is somewhat underemphasised in comparison. Since 2015 the world has been witnessing the proxy war in Yemen being graphically played out between Saudi Arabia and Iran; however, their unremitting support of rival sectarian terrorist groups in Pakistan for decades is often conveniently overlooked.

It is not possible to discuss geopolitical dynamics and not talk about the complicity of the Pakistani state. In many such state-sponsored instances of terrorism, the Pakistani state was often a willing accomplice. Though it is true that the country has a history of political instability and dysfunctional economy that encourages trespassing, with a standing army of over half a million and a nuclear arsenal at its disposal, Pakistan can hardly be regarded as a sitting duck. From regional strategic preferences to individual and institutional political gains, the Pakistani state has been playing favourites to devastating effect.

With the USA's support, Pakistan infamously trained and equipped the Afghan mujahideen that later turned against their former patrons and posed one of the most notorious of all terrorist threats in recent times.[8] Moreover, following the sociopolitical collapse in Afghanistan after Soviet withdrawal, Pakistan created and nurtured the Taliban, who ideologically aligned with its

---

6 S. E. Hussain, 'Terrorism in Pakistan: Incident Patterns, Terrorists' Characteristics, and the Impact of Terrorist Arrests on Terrorism', unpublished PhD thesis, University of Pennsylvania (2010), p. 23.
7 See e.g. D. Byman, *Deadly Connections: States That Sponsor Terrorism* (Cambridge, Cambridge University Press, 2005).
8 P. Gasper, 'Afghanistan, the CIA, bin Laden, and the Taliban', *International Socialist Review* 20 (2001), p. 905.

own national interest and regional ambitions.[9] Even though the Taliban were forcefully removed from power by the US and coalition forces in 2001, they remain a serious political force and a key insurgency in both Pakistan and Afghanistan today. The Pakistani state also has an embarrassing record of assisting the Saudi Arabian-sponsored Wahabi extremist ideology that has over the years fuelled sectarian terrorism in the country and drawn in the Shia Iran to counter the Sunni Saudi influence.[10] Lastly, and perhaps most visibly, the Pakistani state has for a long time both mentored and discreetly supported the insurgency in Kashmir against its arch-enemy India. Terrorism stemming from Kashmir, both state and non-state, represents one of the most enduring and sustained violent campaigns in recent history.

The Pakistani state, much like its neighbours and the competing superpowers, has thus been supporting and sponsoring terroristic elements. What is ironic and perhaps also tragic is that this sponsorship is primarily directed inwards. Moreover, in addition to supporting and sponsoring, the state has on numerous occasions committed acts that some consider to be state terrorism.[11] The country has particularly shown little to no tolerance for any nationalist or ethnic unrest that was perceived by the state as a challenge to national cohesion. The state's active persecution of the Baloch nationalists is a case in point. It must of course be pointed out that, while it primarily engaged in such activities for political and strategic reasons (sometimes under the pretext of creating national unity and at other times to counter foreign threats), the Pakistani state at times was understandably incapacitated and intimidated by the likes of the USA. Forcing Pakistan to join the US-led war against terrorism after 9/11 is a case in point.

The multiple facets of terrorism identified thus far are in one way or another also heavily influenced by the prevailing socio-economic conditions of Pakistan. With one of the lowest Human Development Indexes and GDP per capita, the country, theoretically at least, maintains a healthy appetite for violence and radicalisation. Various statistical researches conducted in Pakistan typically suggest that most of the terrorist activities are carried out by young, impoverished individuals belonging to poor households.[12] For

---

9 A. Rashid, 'The Taliban: Exporting Extremism', *Foreign Affairs*, November/December 1999, p. 24.
10 M. Ahmar, 'Sectarian Conflicts in Pakistan', *Pakistan Vision* 9 (2007), p. 5.
11 See e.g. C. C. Fair, 'The Militant Challenge in Pakistan', *Asia Policy* 11 (2011), p. 107.
12 F. N. Peracha, R. R. Khan, A. Ahmad, S. J. Khan, S. Hussein and H. R. Choudry, 'Socio Demographic Variables in the Vulnerable Youth Predisposed Towards Militancy (Swat, Pakistan)', *Psychiatry, Psychology and Law* 19 (2012).

such desolate individuals, terrorism, sugar-coated in some religious or patriotic fervour, is an attractive alternative.

The socio-economic factor is thus an important variable that helps explain recruitment and the appeal of terrorism in Pakistan. However, economic factors mostly explain terrorism at the individual and not at the institutional level. Furthermore, while Pakistan is admittedly a poor country, there are a number of other countries that are far worse off, and yet their economic woes have not necessarily generated terrorism. Since economic woes on their own do not produce terrorism, and it is only when these conditions are exploited, it is vital instead to find out who exploits these woes and why. The focus here, therefore, will not be on individual choices or economic deprivation, but on ideological motivations and political aspirations of various state and non-state stakeholders that cash in on the country's socio-economic disadvantage.

With the advent of the new terrorism discourse in the late 1990s, there has been growing concern over the terrorist use of nuclear weapons, especially by Islamist terrorists. As it is a predominantly Muslim country in possession of a proven nuclear arsenal, it is not surprising that similar concerns were voiced about Pakistan as well. In fact, the discourse on the security threat posed by the dangerous Pakistan was in part due to the country's nuclear capability. Various commentators have used the socio-economic conditions, level of religiosity and political instability in Pakistan to highlight the dangers of nuclear terrorism.[13]

While the nuclear terrorist threat from Pakistan had an understandable appeal for millennial and doomsday conspiracy theorists, serious academics and policymakers should not have taken the threat at face value. Considering the serious backlash and consequences of such improbable and far-out scenarios, the scholarly community at least should observe more restraint and caution. Placing the existing security concerns in perspective, Leonard Weiss has shown how Pakistan has been running its nuclear weapons programme for over thirty years without any notable incident.[14] Michael Clarke similarly explains how terrorist seizure of Pakistani nuclear weapons is extremely unlikely and concludes that the nuclear terrorist threat from the country is generally overstated.[15]

13 C. D. Ferguson, *Preventing Catastrophic Nuclear Terrorism* (New York, Council on Foreign Relations, 2006), p. 4.
14 L. Weiss, 'On Fear and Nuclear Terrorism', *Bulletin of the Atomic Scientists* 71 (2015), p. 81.
15 M. Clarke, 'Pakistan and Nuclear Terrorism: How Real Is the Threat?', *Comparative Strategy* 32 (2013).

Pakistan's acquisition of nuclear weapons has certainly changed the country's outlook and the geo-strategic dynamics of the region generally. And while it may have raised the stakes for the two Himalayan rivals, India and Pakistan, it does not in any meaningful way pose a nuclear terrorist threat.

The heterogeneity of terrorism outlined so far thus demonstrates the density and diversity of terrorism in Pakistan. Judging this melange through the myopic lens of Islamic fundamentalism alone is therefore a gross oversimplification. Such generalisations not only prevent us from understanding the complexity of the problem but also deprive the real affectees of our well-deserved empathy and compassion. As the story of terrorism in Pakistan will demonstrate, its citizens have been the greatest victims, and yet the international community has regularly shunned and ostracised all Pakistanis as radical Islamists. From harassment at airports to visa restrictions, from public shaming to international seclusion, Pakistan has been treated as a pariah state for a good part of the last two decades.

Having rejected the dominant discourse on the grounds of being myopic and one-dimensional, it is important now to deduce the methodology most suitable for studying and understanding the diverse universe of terrorism in Pakistan. The different facets of terrorism when treated in isolation mostly fail to provide adequate explanation for terrorism in the country, which can only mean that, no matter how disparate, they must also be connected somehow. Understanding that connection, however hard it may be, could hold the key to unravelling the mystery of terrorism in Pakistan, as it would help resolve the paradox between the heterogeneity and complex interwovenness of terrorism's many faces.

It will be the contention of this chapter that this connection can and should be sought by means of untangling the compound Pakistani identity. In order to accomplish that we must undertake a brief journey down memory lane to find out how the Pakistani identity first came about and how it gradually evolved over the years.

Wherefore Art Thou Pakistan?

There is a widely held and largely undisputed collective belief in Pakistan that the country was created in the name of Islam. This feeling is perhaps best expressed by the popular national aphorism *Pakistan ka matlab kya? La Ilaha illalah*, which first raises a somewhat rhetorical question about the meaning of Pakistan and then styles the foremost pillar of Islam (*Shahada* – 'there is no god but God') as the obvious and straightforward answer. The slogan, used frequently during political rallies and protests across Pakistan, is given strong credence by the events that subsequently led to the creation of the country.

After the Great War, as Britain's grip over India began to fracture, apprehensions concerning an untimely British withdrawal led to renewed calls for independence. The calls for independence were directly inspired by the Westphalian nation-state system that had begun to attract a global audience in the twentieth century. This was in part due to the growing weakness of former colonial powers and the overall environment that 'had shifted against the proponents of colonialism'.[16] Credit must, however, be extended to indigenous leaders as well, who studied the Westphalian system and were able to mobilise their respective communities accordingly. One such standout leader was Muhammad Ali Jinnah.

Widely regarded as the father of the Pakistani nation, Jinnah is credited for outsmarting rival political heavyweights like Gandhi and Nehru and forcing the British to concede to his demands.[17] Initially, Jinnah and his All-India Muslim League party only demanded basic autonomy, separate electorate and reserved parliamentary seats for Indian Muslims. However, over time, as differences with the Congress party grew and British departure from the subcontinent seemed imminent, the Muslim League reassessed and greatly amended its political posture and ambitions.[18] Beginning in the 1930s, the party started floating the idea of either an independent Muslim country or a very loose federation with self-rule and significant devolution of power. Gradually, the demand for a loose federation was dropped in favour of complete independence.

This monumental transformation in the party's political aspirations was no plain sailing. The Muslim League first had the daunting task of convincing their own Muslim brethren of a shared sense of identity and nationhood. In addition to this, they also had to convince the British that the Muslims of India were indeed a distinct nation and their demands for a separate homeland complied with the *sine qua non* of the Westphalian state system. In due course, the party overcame its inhibitions as it went on to defend and propagate the idea of an independent Muslim country on the grounds of the *two-nation theory*.

---

16 H. Spruyt, 'The End of Empire and the Extension of the Westphalian System: The Normative Basis of the Modern State Order', *International Studies Review* 2 (2000), p. 84.
17 S. A. Wolpert, *Jinnah of Pakistan* (New York, Oxford University Press, 1984).
18 D. Gilmartin, 'Partition, Pakistan, and South Asian History: In Search of a Narrative', *The Journal of Asian Studies* 57 (1998), pp. 1078–9.

Officially adopted by the party in the late 1930s, the two-nation theory advanced the idea that there were two distinct nations in the Indian subcontinent, namely the Hindus and Muslims, with each having an equal legitimate claim to nationhood. Aware of the significance of the two-nation theory for mobilising the Indian Muslims on the one hand and satisfying the preconditions of Westphalian sensitivities on the other, Jinnah became one of its principal advocates.

As the two-nation theory steadily gained ground, the movement for an independent Muslim homeland acquired the name 'Pakistan',[19] coined in 1933 by a Cambridge-based scholar and activist, Choudary Rahmat Ali.[20] The Pakistan movement, at the behest of the two-nation theory, started making tremendous progress in the early 1940s. Under the dynamic and charismatic leadership of Jinnah, the movement was not only winning over the Muslim community to its cause but was also attracting the serious attention of the British overlords. Subsequently, the 1946 Indian general election, widely seen as a litmus test for the future of the Indian subcontinent, produced two clear victors – Congress and the Muslim League. The results finally granted Jinnah the authority to 'argue convincingly to others that he, and the Muslim League, represented the voice' of Indian Muslims.[21]

Thus, the Pakistan movement had ultimately been successful. Jinnah and his Muslim League had managed to pull off the unimaginable and unprecedented feat of creating a nation state in an astonishingly short period of time. On 14 August 1947, the Indian subcontinent was historically partitioned, paving way for India and Pakistan to emerge as independent states on the world stage. Impressive as this feat was, it was not without its fair share of contradictions and ironies.

While the Muslim League performed phenomenally in the 1946 elections, it is important to note that its overwhelming success was largely limited to Bengal, Punjab and to a lesser extent Sindh. The Muslim-majority North-West Frontier Province (now Khyber Pakhtunkhwa or simply KPK) and Balochistan were not part of this success story. Where KPK voted in favour of the Congress party, there on the other hand Balochistan never got the chance to vote.

---

19 An acronym for the five western Muslim-dominated provinces of the subcontinent and literally 'the land of the pure'.
20 Ali first presented his ideas in a 1933 paper titled *Now or Never, Are We to Live or Perish Forever?*
21 D. Gilmartin, 'A Magnificent Gift: Muslim Nationalism and the Election Process in Colonial Punjab', *Comparative Studies in Society and History* 40 (1998), p. 415.

In opposition to the Muslim League, the then Khan of Kalat (the principal representative of all Balochi princely states at the time), Ahmed Yar, had clearly expressed his desire to achieve an 'independent, united Balochistan after the departure of the British'.[22] Similar views were also expressed by Abdul Ghaffar Khan, who at the time was the most prominent leader in the KPK province. As an ardent Pashtun nationalist, Ghaffar bitterly opposed the Pakistan movement and launched an unsuccessful countermovement for independence in 1947 after feeling betrayed by the Congress party, which had agreed to the British partition plan.[23]

Although both Yar and Ghaffar eventually conceded, it is important to bear in mind that their initial quest for independence was completely ignored, as the British instructed all provinces and princely states of the subcontinent to decide in favour of either India or Pakistan. Both the KPK and Balochistan provinces were subsequently incorporated into Pakistan and now constitute more than 55 per cent of the country's total land mass.

Even though both provinces were predominantly Muslim, they were clearly not sold on the idea of an independent Muslim country. Nationalist sentiments ran very deep, and the Muslim identity, if not subordinate, was just as important as ethnic and tribal identities. The Baloch and the Pashtun attitude towards the Pakistan Movement visibly undermines the logic forwarded by the two-nation theory. It raises serious questions over Jinnah's advocacy of Indian Muslims being a distinct nation in the subcontinent. Clearly, for the Baloch and Pashtun, their regional ethnic identity had a stronger claim to nationhood than a united Muslim identity. Nevertheless, it was not them but the Muslim League that managed to convince the British, and it was not on ethnic but religious lines that the fate of the subcontinent was ultimately sealed.

Given that the Pakistan movement was essentially religion-centric, it is worth pointing out that the majority of the Muslim League leaders were not particularly religious. Jinnah and his associates had privileged backgrounds, were mostly Western-educated and held fairly liberal and secular world views. In addition to that, most of them belonged to the minority Shia sect, as opposed to the overwhelming Sunni majority of Pakistan.[24] On the other

---

22 A. Khan, 'Baloch Ethnic Nationalism in Pakistan: From Guerrilla War to Nowhere?', *Asian Ethnicity* 4 (2003), p. 285.
23 A. Saikal, 'Afghanistan and Pakistan: The Question of Pashtun Nationalism?', *Journal of Muslim Minority Affairs* 30 (2010).
24 E. Murphy, *The Making of Terrorism in Pakistan: Historical and Social Roots of Extremism* (London, Routledge, 2012), pp. 30–1.

hand, one of the strongest resistances to Pakistan's creation surprisingly came from some of the most conservative Muslim quarters in the subcontinent. Incidentally, these very critics would later claim to be the custodians and guardians of Pakistan once the subcontinent was formally partitioned.[25]

The fact that the cause for Pakistan, an independent Muslim country, was spearheaded by secular liberal Muslims and opposed by equally conservative orthodox Muslims is certainly ironic. Moreover, how the sceptical religious conservatives gradually sidelined the liberal ideals of the founding fathers and began claiming complete ownership of the country they once disavowed is perhaps even a touch comical. This comedy of ironies would soon transform into a tragedy of binaries as the newborn state of Pakistan wrestled with a profoundly confused sense of national identity.

Since the founding fathers had laid a claim to nationhood in the name of religion, the fact that it played to the advantage of religious conservatives even when they had initially rejected the idea outright is perhaps not all that surprising. Conversely, it can of course be argued that, while Islam was the driving force behind the Pakistan movement, the focus of Jinnah and his associates was on its adherents and not Islam per se.[26] However, separating religion from its adherents, especially when the former was being utilised to transcend ethnic and linguistic cleavages on the one hand and to propagate the divisive two-nation theory on the other, was far from straightforward. In hindsight, the pitfalls of this overambitious and portentous undertaking should not have been underestimated.

In order to forge a unified national identity at the behest of religion, the founding fathers inadvertently created one of Pakistan's most enduring and profoundest contradictions. The question over whether Pakistan was created for Islam or the Muslims of the subcontinent is one that has haunted the country since its inception. Not only does this question pose practical problems, but it is also a philosophical and intellectual quagmire. Eventually, it would become evident that the claim about Pakistan being a country for Muslims as opposed to Islam was unsustainable and somewhat self-contradictory.

As this inherent contradiction worked to the advantage of religious orthodoxy, the liberal and secular vision of the founding fathers increasingly became a distant reality. With religion now firmly in the driving seat,

25 Murphy, *The Making of Terrorism*, p. 46.
26 H. Alavi, 'Ethnicity, Muslim Society, and the Pakistan Ideology', in A. M. Weiss (ed.), *Islamic Reassertion in Pakistan: The Application of Islamic Laws in a Modern State* (Syracuse, NY, Syracuse University Press, 1986).

virtually all aspects of Pakistani society were subsequently questioned and scrutinised. Arguably, had Islam or at least its practice in Pakistan been homogeneous, this intrusion might have played a very constructive role in bringing together the country's immense diversity. However, far from being monolithic, Islam, especially in the subcontinent, is deeply fragmented and hopelessly fractured. Where disagreements over its preferred denomination cultivated an air of intolerance, there Islam's numerous manifestations produced a long-drawn sectarian strife. Despite this, the scope and reach of religious intrusion proliferated perennially, since every time it was checked or questioned, the Muslim state of Pakistan was harshly reminded of its alleged *raison d'être*.

Consequently, the history of Pakistan is replete with instances of religious concessions in both political and societal spheres, even when growing intolerance and divisions demanded moderation and containment. Admittedly, these religious compromises are also entangled profoundly with the power politics and geo-strategic dynamics of the region. Nevertheless, in the absence of any counter-rationale for Pakistan's inception and the source of its national identity, the ascendency wangled by religion stands on its own as well.

The cause of religion was clearly also helped by the country's rich ethno-linguistic diversity, since the people of Pakistan, in spite of all their differences, are predominantly Muslim. As discussed already, provinces like Balochistan and KPK from the outset had only reluctantly joined Pakistan owing to lack of preferred alternatives. To keep their separatist aspirations in check and to foster a sense of national unity, it was necessary to both stress and enforce the least common denominator of Islam.

Thus, the state of Pakistan from the start had a very visible and tangible stake in granting religion the space necessary for transgression. In comparison, the deep-rooted ethno-linguistic cleavages were blatantly shunned and brutally suppressed. The ruling elite neither addressed nor properly acknowledged the existence of any ethno-linguistic grievances in the country. Instead, the state of Pakistan constructed and propagated an inexact narrative of congruous local identities that were willingly subordinate to the overarching national identity.

Simultaneous appeasement of religious fundamentalists on the one hand and brutal oppression of ethno-linguistic dissent on the other would go on to spawn widespread sectarianism, factionalism, insurgency and terrorism in the country. Insecurity about the country's national identity and its unabating friction with local identities would ensure the continuation and perpetuation of this very grim and depressing state of affairs in the years to come. A brief chronological anatomy of political violence since independence will demonstrate how the problems inherent in compound Pakistani identity played out in the country.

Anatomy of Political Violence in Pakistan: A Perpetual Crisis of Identity

Drawing legitimacy from Pakistan's alleged *raison d'être*, the religious hardliners began to flex their muscle as soon as the country gained independence. They achieved their first major breakthrough with the passing of the 1949 Objectives Resolution, which was to serve as a guideline for future constitutional development in Pakistan. By attributing sovereignty to God and pledging to create a country where Muslims shall live their lives according to the teachings of Quran and Sunnah, the resolution made a somewhat ostensive 'allegiance of the state to Islam'.[27] Even though the rights of minorities were guaranteed, the use of Islamic terminologies in an intended framework for a future constitution was clearly divisive.

It is worth mentioning at the outset that the Objectives Resolution primarily made a commitment to ensuring the fundamental rights of Muslims of the subcontinent, as opposed to Islam per se. However, as discussed earlier, separating religion from its adherents was always an over-ambitious and precarious undertaking that would ultimately prove to be untenable. Moreover, the resolution's use of Islamic terminologies not only created a clear bias but also paved the way for future Islamisation of the constitution and the Pakistani society. Perhaps most damagingly, the resolution unwittingly provided religious hardliners with a state-sanctioned platform to increasingly demand persecution of any dissent and opposition.

Within months of the resolution's passing, the country witnessed its first sectarian strife, in the form of widespread anti-Ahmadiyya protests, which would serve as a prelude to decades of violence, intolerance and religious bigotry. Led by Majlis-e-Ahrar (or simply Ahrar), the countrywide protests demanded that the state declare the Ahmadiyya community non-Muslim.[28]

---

27 S. Saeed, 'Pakistani Nationalism and the State Marginalisation of the Ahmadiyya Community in Pakistan', *Studies in Ethnicity and Nationalism* 7 (2007), p. 137.
28 A. M. Khan, 'Persecution of the Ahmadiyya Community in Pakistan: An Analysis under International Law and International Relations', *Harvard Human Rights Journal* 16 (2003), p. 223.

Like most other mainstream fundamentalist Islamic parties, Ahrar drew its ideological inspiration primarily from the Deobandi school of thought.

In spite of its immense heterogeneity, the religion Islam has two standout sects – Sunni and Shia. Although the Muslim population of Pakistan is predominantly Sunni, the sect itself is far from homogeneous. The Sunni sect has two principal denominations in Pakistan, Deobandi and Barelvi. While both schools of thought have acquired their respective names from the towns of Deoband and Bareilly in the Northern Indian state of Uttar Pradesh, it is essentially the Barelvi School that is specific to the Indian subcontinent, with visible influence of local customs and traditions. Amid its strong reverence for saints and shrines and a firm belief in Sufi mysticism, the Barelvi School, in many ways, is a manifestation not only of how Islam was introduced in the subcontinent but also of how it has been influenced by indigenous values.

On the other hand, the Deobandi School can perhaps best be described as a product of Muslim agitation and dissatisfaction with the existing state of affairs in British India. Blaming Muslim decline and subservience on existing religious practices, Deobandis attempted to revive Islamic values associated with the time and life of Prophet Muhammad and his immediate successors. Deobandism was partly also inspired by Wahabism and Salafism, the ultra-conservative puritanical Islamic movements in Saudi Arabia and the broader Middle East.[29] With its total disregard and rejection of indigenous influences and a desire to emulate the time and life of Prophet Muhammad, the Deobandi sect from the outset had a very rigid and uncompromising standpoint.

In spite of their religious zeal and puritanical views, the Deobandis had vehemently opposed the creation of Pakistan – an independent Muslim state. They despised Jinnah and called him *Kafar-i-Azam* (the greatest infidel)[30] and his movement for Pakistan *Kafaristan* (land of the infidels).[31] In comparison, the Barelvis, who constitute the majority of the Sunni sect in the subcontinent, overwhelmingly supported Jinnah's cause for Pakistan. Perhaps it will not be an exaggeration to suggest that Pakistan was primarily created at the behest of liberal Shia leaders and their ardent Barelvi followers.

---

29 The foremost contemporary radical Islamist movements, from Al Qaeda to ISIS and from the Afghan Taliban to Tehrik-i-Taliban Pakistan, are generally adherents of Wahabi, Salafi and Deobandi denominations of Islam.
30 A crude and cynical parody of *Quaid-e-Azam* (the greatest leader), a title that had been bestowed upon Jinnah by his followers.
31 Hussain, 'Terrorism in Pakistan', p. 91.

Dismissing the general practice of Islam in the subcontinent owing to its allegedly being corrupted and contaminated by indigenous values and traditions, the Deobandis were profoundly critical of the majority Barelvi sect. They publicly condemned the mystical philosophy of Sufism and the practice of revering saints and shrines. Similarly, they were also extremely critical of the Shia strand of Islam, which they regarded as the first major defection that fractured Islam almost immediately after Prophet Muhammad's death. They openly denounced Shias as heretics, which in part also explains why they were so cynical about Jinnah and his associates. This utter disregard of Shias and Barelvis from the outset, coupled with constitutional and governmental concessions over the years, gradually paved the way for attacks on Shia mosques and Muharram processions, ruthless targeting of Sufi shrines and general widespread sectarian violence.

The Deobandi opposition of Shias and Barelvis, though rigid and uncompromising, appears somewhat piffling when compared with their loathing and contempt for the Ahmadiyya community. Moreover, whereas the antipathy towards Shias and Barelvis turned hostile gradually and over a period of several decades, the Ahmadis were the target of unbridled Deobandi aggression from the very beginning.

Following the Objectives Resolution, the Ahrar-led anti-Ahmadiyya protests turned violent as early as 1953. With widespread persecution, harassment and indiscriminate killing of Ahmadis, the year also marked the start of sectarian terrorism in Pakistan. In what would become a novelty in latter-day Pakistan, the government at the time responded strongly by banning Ahrar and vehemently rejecting all their demands.

The firm and unequivocal response of the then government is perhaps best encapsulated by the 1954 Munir Report (the official inquiry into the 1953 anti-Ahmadiyya riots). The extensive report not only offered an explanation for anti-Ahmadiyya riots but went above and beyond to raise philosophical and thought-provoking questions about the nature of religion and the basis of the Pakistani state. On the one hand, it highlighted the theological and doctrinal divisions among conservative religious leaders, their conflicting sociopolitical preferences and the controversy over reciprocal accusations of apostasy. On the other hand, it stressed the need for creating an inclusive and tolerant Pakistan by drawing attention to the secular and liberal vision of Jinnah and his associates.[32]

---

32 For details, see the 1954 Justice Munir Commission Report on the anti-Ahmadiyya riots of Punjab in 1953.

Given the contents of the report and the emphatic response of the government at the time, the menace of sectarian violence and intolerance should have been nipped in the bud. However, far from having settled the issue once and for all, both the Munir Report and the government response soon disappeared from public consciousness, just as the very religious hardliners they had cautioned and warned against steadily gained ground and pre-eminence. Arguably, this oversight was partly due to ongoing political instability and the imposition of the first martial law in 1958. Nevertheless, the role of national identity and the association of Pakistan first and foremost with Muslims and, by extension, Islam, should not be underestimated. The fact that the country adopted the phrase Islamic Republic in its first constitution of 1956 (just two years after the Munir Report) is a testament to this verity.

Thus, while the activities of Ahrar were largely shunned and disapproved of at the time, they would gain societal acceptance and government patronage in the decades to come. The Deobandi hardliners in particular would use Ahrar's 'propaganda as a basis to launch a unified campaign against Ahmadis', whom they would 'treat not only as non-Muslims but also as threats to Islam'.[33] It is important to note here that the Ahmadiyya persecution, though spearheaded by Deobandis, enjoyed the passive and at times even open support of Barelvis and Shias, who ironically would later themselves fall victim to Deobandi sectarian violence.

The major contention with Ahmadis is over the status they accord to their founder and spiritual leader, Mirza Ghulam Ahmed, with some revering him as a great reformer and others elevating him to the status of a Prophet.[34] In comparison, most, if not all, sects of Islam consider Muhammad to be the most pre-eminent and last of God's Prophets. As a cornerstone of all major sects of Islam, the hallmark of finality of prophethood not only served as a convenient rallying point but also exhibited a healthy appetite for ostracising dissent and opposition. Moreover, it had a distinctive appeal for religious hardliners across the fractured sectarian divides of Pakistan, who in due course began to treat it as the bedrock of Islam and associated any contrary claims with blasphemy and apostasy. Allegations of blasphemy and apostasy, with their inherent tendency to legitimise violence, inculcated a culture of harassment and persecution in the name of religion.

Denouncement of Ahmadis continued to grow relentlessly, and after the second wave of anti-Ahmadiyya violence, which began in the early

33 Khan, 'Persecution of the Ahmadiyya', p. 224.   34 Saeed, 'Pakistani Nationalism', p. 135.

1970s, the government, instead of reprimanding the religious hardliners as before, succumbed to their demands by constitutionally declaring the Ahmadis non-Muslim. The second amendment to the 1973 constitution (still in force today) categorically stated that anyone who denounces or questions the finality of Muhammad's prophethood 'is not a Muslim for the purpose of the constitution or law'.[35] The amendment thus categorically singled out the Ahmadis, formally reduced them to a religious minority and effectively also legalised their persecution.

The constitutional surrender to religious hardliners harshly exposed the Achilles heel of the Pakistani state, which hopelessly continued to appease and recede in spite of glaring ramifications. These religious concessions and the ensuing sectarian divide would receive prodigious impetus when the country was subjected to a decade-long dictatorial rule by the deeply religious General Zia ul Haq. Meanwhile, the resistance and defiance and subsequent appeals for inclusivity and tolerance that were witnessed in the wake of the 1953 riots, along with Jinnah's secular vision, simply became relics of a bygone age.

Zia came to power in 1977. Over the next eleven years, the country went through considerable transformation as a number of deeply controversial religious reforms were forcefully imposed. Where previous governments had only reluctantly and grudgingly conceded to fundamentalist demands, Zia would prove to be a willing and enthusiastic abettor. Although he is widely regarded as an opportunist and an astute political operator who used religion to legitimise his military rule, few would question 'Zia's devotion or resolute commitment to Islamic tenets'.[36]

Zia was a staunch Deobandi who frequented madrassas as a young man seeking guidance and counselling. Madrassas are Islamic seminaries that historically have been a vital part of the Indian subcontinent in general and Pakistan in particular. The role of madrassas traditionally was strictly restricted to teaching Quran, providing basic Islamic education and performing religious ceremonies at various social events. However, over time and especially after Pakistan's independence, the madrassas evolved into socially and politically active entities that often aggressively flaunted their respective brand of Islamic extremism. This transition was primarily due to the Islamic ideology that was the driving force behind the Pakistan movement and political opportunists that mobilised religion for their own relative gains.

---

35 Constitution of Pakistan, p. 155.
36 L. Ziring, 'Public Policy Dilemmas and Pakistan's Nationality Problem: The Legacy of Zia ul-Haq', *Asian Survey* 28 (1988), p. 796.

Incidentally, as fate would have it, Zia was both a religious ideologue and a political opportunist. Zia is now widely revered as a *mujahid* (holy fighter) and a patriot across Deobandi madrassas in Pakistan.[37]

With Zia's unequivocal support, there was a mushroom growth of Deobandi madrassas in Pakistan throughout the 1980s. Owing to immense theological similarities between Wahabism and Deobandism, the Zia regime also sent a large number of mullahs and muftis (the religious teachers that run mosques and madrassas) to Saudi Arabia for formal religious education. The Wahabi teachings did not just strengthen and corroborate the ultra-orthodox puritanical beliefs of the Deobandi scholars but also actively nurtured and fostered their antipathy towards other sects of Islam. Thus, upon their return, many of these mullahs and muftis condemned all other denominations of Islam with reaffirmed vigour and fervour.[38] This total rejection and denunciation of all other sects, coupled with active government patronage, formally ushered in the age of sectarian terrorism in Pakistan.

Although Deobandi hardliners had been critical of all other sects from the outset, their violence and aggression up until the 1980s had largely been limited to the Ahmadiyya community. Under Zia's patronage, however, sectarian violence and harassment increasingly became far less discerning. With an open pledge to convert Pakistan into a Sunni theocracy, the Deobandis turned their attention to the Shia community in particular.

Deemed to be the first formal sectarian defection, the Shias were projected as Islam's oldest enemy, who ideally needed to be eliminated or at least emphatically contained. Subsequently, a number of anti-Shia militant organisations like Sipah-e-Sahabah sprung into action that have since carried out violent acts of terrorism against the Shia community in Pakistan. The state-sponsored anti-Shia campaign consequently also led to the formation of Shia militant organisations like Tehrik-e-Jafaria that have carried out reciprocal acts of violence against Deobandi hardliners and Sunnis generally.[39] The madrassas meanwhile became the linchpin of sectarian feuds, providing fresh recruits for their respective allegiances.

Avowedly, the rise of madrassas, sectarian tensions and increasing religiosity can also be explained by the geopolitical and international developments of the time. The 1979 Islamic revolution in neighbouring Iran, for instance, had visible implications for Pakistan and the broader Middle East.

---

37 A sentiment that was shared by principal administrators at the Darul Uloom Islamia and Jamia Ashrafia, two prominent Deobandi madrassas in Lahore.
38 Conclusions drawn from my interviews conducted at madrassas in Lahore, 2019–20.
39 Hussain, 'Terrorism in Pakistan', pp. 111–14.

Establishment of the first Shia theocracy and calls by the Iranian supreme leader Ayatollah Khomeini for a worldwide Islamic revolution had spread alarm and panic throughout the Arab world. In order to balance or counter the perceived Iranian Shia threat, Saudi Arabia and other predominantly Sunni Arab countries therefore had a somewhat vested interest in financing and sponsoring Sunni madrassas and the Wahabi ideology in the neighbouring Pakistan.[40]

It is important to also bear in mind that these developments were taking place just when the climax of cold war was unfolding at Pakistan's doorstep. Fear of communism and Soviet domination had often provoked policy responses that lacked prudence and foresight. The role played by the US and other Western countries in nurturing and proselytising Islamic extremism at the time is now common knowledge. Owing to the overlap between its grand containment strategy and the short-term goals of Muslim extremists, the US, as we know, not only endorsed but also militarily and financially backed the radical Islamist ideology with little to no regard for its long-term implications for Pakistan and Afghanistan. This oversight in the long run proved to be detrimental, as these very events served as a precursor to global jihadist and Islamist terrorist movements.[41]

While the geopolitical developments of the 1980s help explain the rise of transnational Wahabi- and Salafi-inspired extremist movements in and outside Pakistan, they only partially explain the rise of home-grown sectarianism and religious intolerance. Admittedly, Zia benefited immensely from international sponsorship and patronage, which allowed him to roll out his overly ambitious and controversial policies. However, the nature of the policies implemented and the unconditional support he received from conservative religious quarters was highly reminiscent of a not very distant past. In fact, Zia's Islamisation process was in effect justified and legitimised by historical precedents and constitutional pledges.

Over the course of his numerous policy initiatives, Zia assertively stated that he wanted the constitution to be amended 'in such a way that the original Objectives Resolution of 1949 would take on a new substantive force'.[42] This was a direct reference to the first constitutional framework of Pakistan, which had expressly pledged to create a country where Muslims would live their lives according to Islamic injunctions. Additionally, Zia also

40 M. A. Zahab, 'The Regional Dimension of Sectarian Conflicts in Pakistan', in C. Jaffrelot (ed.), *Pakistan: Nationalism Without a Nation* (London, Zed Books, 2002).
41 E. Girardet, *Afghanistan: The Soviet War* (London, Routledge, 2012).
42 Khan, 'Persecution of the Ahmadiyya', p. 226.

believed that his Islamisation initiative was necessary 'to preserve the integrity of Pakistan, as a unified and independent state'.[43] This belief was clearly inspired by the doctrine of associating the creation and existence of Pakistan first and foremost with Islam.

Zia's first major religious reforms, known as the 'Hudood Ordinances', were introduced in 1979 'to bring Pakistan's legal system closer to the percepts of Islam'.[44] To ensure compliance, a federal Shariat Court was also established the following year. The Shariat Court, which still exists today, enjoys discretionary powers to challenge any law that is against the spirit of Islam. Over time, as the dictator grew in confidence, stricter and more rigid Islamic reforms were introduced and forcefully implemented. The most controversial and prominent of these reforms were related to blasphemy laws. Since the laws were originally designed by the British colonialists, they were far too vague for Zia's liking. Subsequently, the laws were thoroughly amended and modified to principally protect and preserve the honour of Islam (as envisaged by Zia and Deobandi hardliners). Violation and breach of the law could lead to lengthy imprisonment or even the death penalty.

While the blasphemy law has copious tangents, its most salient proviso concerns the sanctity of Prophet Muhammad and the finality of his prophethood. Given the theological disposition of the Ahmadiyya faith, the identity of the foremost affectees of these injunctions hardly requires any guessing. Hence, as the blasphemy law was honed and fine-tuned, the Ahmadis were brazenly singled out. Finally, in 1984, Zia passed an ordinance that categorically prohibited the Ahmadis from publicly confessing their faith, verbally or in writing. They were banned from building mosques, holding funeral prayers or even marking their graves with Islamic symbols. A blanket ban was also imposed on all Ahmadiyya publications, and the police were ordered to destroy their existing translations of Quran. 'In short, virtually any public act of worship or devotion by an Ahmadi could be treated as a criminal offence.'[45] By virtue of this ordinance, the state in effect denounced the Ahmadiyya faith as blasphemous and its adherents as living and breathing abominations.

Although the blasphemy laws were drafted under the watchful eye of Zia, a staunch Deobandi, they resonated strongly with other Sunni sects in Pakistan, especially the Barelvis. This resonance ultimately led to

43 Ziring, 'Public Policy Dilemmas', p. 798.
44 C. H. Kennedy, 'Islamization in Pakistan: Implementation of the Hudood Ordinances', *Asian Survey* 28 (1988), p. 307.
45 Khan, 'Persecution of the Ahmadiyya', p. 227.

a convergence of sorts between the Deobandis and Barelvis, who were united in their mutual contempt for blasphemy. Since the convergence was primarily on account of the proviso concerning Prophet Muhammad, it inexorably resulted in a united sectarian assault on the Ahmadis. With the state having formally criminalised the practice of Ahmadiyya faith, the attacks were carried out with great impunity.

As a shared hallmark of all major sects of Islam, the most serious charge of blasphemy has consistently related to disrespecting Prophet Muhammad and questioning the finality of his prophethood. The seriousness of this charge has rapidly intensified over the years, producing a new breed of far-right actors with a pledge to protect and preserve the sanctity of Prophet Muhammad at any cost. Organisations like Tehrik-e-Labbaik ('movement by dutiful followers [of the Prophet]') and Majlis-e-Tahafuz-e-Khatme Nabuwat ('assembly to protect the finality of prophethood') have increasingly become socially and politically relevant. These self-appointed 'blasphemy-watchers' have frequently carried out radical acts of vigilantism and terrorism in Pakistan, forcing the ordinary citizens to live in a constant state of fear.

In January 2011, Salman Taseer, the then Governor of Punjab, was assassinated by his own bodyguard Mumtaz Qadri for allegedly speaking against blasphemy laws.[46] Similarly, in 2017, a proposed parliamentary amendment to an election bill that omitted the clause on the finality of prophethood from the official oath-taking form caused furore and outrage in the conservative ranks. The ensuing violent protests and open death threats to members of parliament forced the government to retract and disregard the changes as mere clerical anomalies.[47] The recent acquittal of Asia Bibi (a Christian accused of insulting the Prophet and Islam) by the Supreme Court of Pakistan in 2019 generated the familiar uproar yet again.[48]

While blasphemy-related deaths in Pakistan, much like terrorism in general, are somewhat marginal, the extrajudicial killings, political assassinations, constant harassment of academics and persecution of minorities in the name of blasphemy has created an atmosphere of fear and intimidation. Admittedly, its most salient feature in Pakistan is related to the sanctity of

---

46 I. Khan, 'The Assertion of Barelvi Extremism', *Current Trends in Islamist Ideology* 12 (2011), p. 51.
47 'Anti-blasphemy Protesters Block Entrance to Islamabad', Al Jazeera, www.aljazeera.com/news/2017/11/anti-blasphemy-protesters-block-entrance-islamabad-17 1113102713450.html.
48 'Asia Bibi: Pakistani Christian Woman Breaks Silence in New Book', *BBC News*, 30 January 2020, www.bbc.com/news/world-us-canada-51317380.

Prophet Muhammad, and observing utmost caution in the matter can potentially spare charges of blasphemy. However, the notion of blasphemy is deeply contentious and divisive by nature. Blasphemy, especially in the context of Pakistan, has proven to be an elusive and obscure creed, varying from sect to sect and subject to degrees of religiosity. As a result, not just Ahmadis but religious minorities and even adherents of mainstream Islamic sects live in a constant state of fear, as accusations of blasphemy and apostasy could be affixed on anyone.

Terrorism in the name of blasphemy is essentially a product of excessive religious reforms that were introduced during the 1980s. Additionally, it can also be seen as a mutation of sectarianism that was carefully nurtured and proselytised by the Zia regime. The origins of other standout manifestations of religious extremism and terrorism in Pakistan are also typically traced back to the eighties. Given these dynamics, it is not surprising that the roots of modern-day terrorism in Pakistan are generally sought in the events that transpired during the Zia era.

Indeed, insofar as terrorism and its proliferation in Pakistan is concerned, Zia's decade-long dictatorial rule has no parallel. Moreover, his legacy has proven to be remarkably enduring, as Pakistan still continues to grapple with its fallout. Not only are his sweeping religious reforms and blasphemy laws just as sacrosanct as ever, but his transformation of madrassas into nurseries that bred hatred and intolerance has also consistently provided recruits for religious extremists.

While this may be so, it is critical not to get swayed by his towering legacy. For had it not been for earlier constitutional compromises and a history of political surrenders, Zia would never have enjoyed the freedom and legitimacy that he did. Commentators often credit Zia's religious predisposition for the initiation and success of his Islamisation process.[49] Indeed, Zia was a religious hardliner motivated by rigid Deobandi teachings that largely facilitated and prompted many of his policy initiatives. However, the Islamisation of Pakistan neither started nor ended with Zia. It is worth bearing in mind that the constitutional amendment of 1974 (still in force today) that granted the first major religious concessions was enforced during the reign of secular and socialist-leaning Zulfiqar Bhutto.

Zia's enduring legacy can alternatively also be attributed to his decade-long dictatorial rule and the geopolitical dynamics of the time – where the former gave him tremendous discretionary powers, the latter extended to

---

49 S. J. Burki, 'Pakistan under Zia, 1977–1988', *Asian Survey* 28 (1988).

him material and ideological support. Although the argument clearly has merit, it is important not to forget both the dictator and the events that followed Zia.

In 1999, just a decade after Zia, General Pervez Musharraf imposed yet another martial law in Pakistan. In comparison to Zia, Musharraf was fairly liberal and secular, as is evident from his famous 'plea for enlightened moderation'.[50] Musharraf's nine-year reign coincided with the US-led war against Islamic extremism and radicalisation. Siding with the US due to geopolitical pressures and his own personal preferences, Musharraf plunged Pakistan into a protracted war that led to the rise of Tehrik-i-Taliban Pakistan and other Islamist militant organisations that savagely punished Pakistan for its participation. Subsequently, suicide bombings and indiscriminate killings of ordinary citizens became mundane and a distinctive characteristic of the twenty-first-century Pakistan.

What is worth noting here is that, in spite of the dictator's own secular preferences, transmutation of the geopolitical sensitivities and the havoc unleashed over Pakistan in the name of Islamic extremism, no changes were made in the discriminatory religious policies and blasphemy laws of the country, even though Musharraf stayed in power for just as long as Zia. The same is also true for the succeeding democratic governments of Asif Zardari, Nawaz Sharif and Imran Khan, as none dared to revise the controversial blasphemy laws or question the constitutional compromises to religious fundamentalists.

Failure to engage with discriminatory religious policies, regardless of the consequences and circumstances, is evidence of the hold religion has over the national consciousness. This is certainly not surprising considering what is potentially at stake. As discussed already, in a country as ethnically and linguistically diverse as Pakistan, Islam as the least common denominator is believed to be the sole source of national identity that keeps vying and dissenting sentiments in check. However, since independence, Pakistan has confronted numerous irredentist and separatist movements that on the one hand demonstrate the resolve of ethno-linguistic struggles and on the other highlight the plight of national identity. Therefore, in a bid to strengthen national identity, the country inadvertently made an unconditional surrender to religion.

---

50 Available at www.washingtonpost.com/archive/opinions/2004/06/01/a-plea-for-enlightened-moderation/b01ff08e-f0c5-4ad5-8e96-b97a32ec084e/.

Analysis of major events since independence has demonstrated that the claim about Pakistan being a country for Muslims as opposed to Islam was indeed unsustainable, which ultimately and somewhat inevitably worked to the advantage of religious orthodoxy in the country. While this may be so, it is equally crucial to acknowledge the constant friction between the local ethno-linguistic and the national Islamic identities, which facilitated and accelerated the process of religious appeasement. As we know, the provinces of Balochistan and KPK from the outset had rejected the two-nation theory and the idea of an independent Muslim country. Having only joined Pakistan due to lack of preferred alternatives, both provinces had their fair share of grievances. These grievances, coupled with the state's incompetence, later inspired separatist movements and insurgencies, some of which are active even today.

Although nationalist sentiments run deep in both provinces, it is only Balochistan that has actively sustained an armed resistance against the Pakistani state. The province so far has witnessed several waves of insurgencies, with the first starting as early as 1948.[51] Each of these waves was brutally suppressed by the government, which neither acknowledged nor tolerated any form of nationalist dissent. Approving only its own brand of nationalism, the Pakistani state strongly denounces and actively represses all other forms of nationalist aspirations.

In the wake of the most recent wave of Baloch insurgency, which started in 2005 and continued for almost a decade, the state, under the pretext of counterterrorism, adopted ruthless methods like kidnapping, torture, assassination, extrajudicial killings and indefinite internments of suspected citizens. Provision for adopting such tactics and methods had been provided in abundance, courtesy of the global war against terrorism. Though the measures arguably proved to be effective, as the frequency of militant and terrorist attacks declined significantly, they were hugely unpopular among the local people, who felt both humiliated and intimidated. Amidst a strong presence of paramilitary forces and the overly vigilant intelligence agencies, one respondent observes that the ordinary people of Balochistan live in a constant state of fear.[52]

In spite of active state repression, the three most standout militant groups, the Balochistan Liberation Army (BLA), the Balochistan Liberation Front (BLF) and the Balochistan Republican Army (BRA), are still active today and

---

51 Z. L. Mirza, 'Balochistan – Past, Present and Future', *NDU Journal* 27 (2013).
52 Findings from my field research in Balochistan, September 2019.

in 2019 announced a merger by the name of Baloch Raaji Ajoi Sangar (loosely translated as 'Baloch nation independence front') or simply BRAS. Although these groups have carried out acts of sabotage, kidnappings, bombings and indiscriminate killings, the scale and potency of their actions is negligible when compared with the agency of sectarianism and religious extremism in Pakistan. Yet the state not only enforces a blanket ban on all Baloch militant groups but also subjects the entire province to harsh and oppressive restrictions, which fuels anti-state sentiments and breeds new defections.[53]

The state's uncompromising and one-dimensional response to Baloch nationalism bespeaks the deep-rooted insecurities that it inherited at the time of its birth. Not only did the newborn country have to deal with two estranged provinces that did not identify with the Pakistan movement but it also immediately confronted the paradox of the Pakistani national identity. Although supposedly enshrined in the two-nation theory, the requisites of national identity turned out to be inherently dubious, which continued to haunt and divide the country.

These inhibitions intensified exponentially when the country lost its other half, East Pakistan (Bangladesh) after the bloody war of 1971. Even though the loss was primarily due to the negligence and incompetence of West Pakistan, it triggered a serious existential crisis in the country. With the country dismembered and the basis for its existence seriously compromised, it grew ever more distrustful and apprehensive of ethno-linguistic cleavages and any remaining nationalist aspirations.

The East Pakistan debacle brutally exposed the facade of the Pakistani national identity and 'savagely destroyed the myth of two nation theory'.[54] The breakaway state of Bangladesh had at one point been the strongest supporter of Jinnah and his movement for Pakistan. Its rebellion and subsequent independence seriously undermined the credibility and workability of the Pakistan project. It was clear that if the country was to survive from here on then it had to first strengthen and revive its trampled national identity. In order to accomplish that, Pakistan had to resolve the long-running paradox of whether the country was created for Muslims or Islam, and also settle the issue of its subnational identities. Owing to the chronic misgivings over the task at hand, coupled with the enormity of the loss just incurred, the identity paradox was obliquely settled in favour of religion.

---

53 Conclusions drawn from my interviews in Balochistan in September 2019. Due to security concerns, all the subjects opted to remain anonymous.
54 Murphy, *The Making of Terrorism*, p. 75.

This haphazard and grudging settlement is clearly evident from the generous constitutional and political concessions to religious fundamentalists throughout the 1970s. It also puts Zia's Islamisation and enduring legacy in a broader context, which can be seen as a bid to strengthen the national identity. For, had Islam not been the primary source of Pakistani national identity, Zia's Islamisation agenda would not have had any merit or substance.

In addition to the developments outlined so far, the Kashmir problem has persistently been the most standout geopolitical issue in the country's history; however, its complexities are beyond the scope of this chapter. Suffice to say here, Pakistan claims Kashmir in the spirit of the same ideology that guided its movement for independence. As one of the largest Muslim-majority provinces, it is argued that Kashmir must have acceded to Pakistan not only to satisfy the demands of the two-nation theory but also to fulfil the presumed destiny of the Muslims of the subcontinent.

Thus, when the Hindu ruler of Kashmir acceded to India in October 1947, arguably against the wishes of the Kashmiri people, Pakistan felt it had no choice but to take Kashmir by force. Since then, India and Pakistan have been bitter enemies, with the state of Kashmir divided along a turbulent and heavily militarised line of control. The Kashmir conflict has not only led to all-out wars between the two countries, but has also sustained a healthy appetite for cross-border skirmishes, insurgency, militancy and terrorism. Due to Indian military superiority and geo-strategic dynamics, Pakistan has shown a preference for irregular warfare, covertly sponsoring the likes of Lashkar-e-Taiba and Hizbul Mujahideen.[55]

The Kashmir conflict in many ways is quintessential of the dilemma Pakistan has faced since its inception. Just as the claim about Pakistan being a country for Muslims as opposed to Islam proved to be unsustainable and inexorably played into the hands of religious fundamentalists, so did the Kashmir conflict. The cause of liberating fellow Muslims in Kashmir from Indian occupation has always resonated strongly with Pakistanis and the broader Muslim community. However, with the huge influx of Afghan mujahideen and madrassa-educated militants, the goal of liberating Kashmiri Muslims was subsequently conflated with extremist Islamist objectives. Consequently, the conflict in Kashmir has increasingly become a muddled affair, as it is not clear whether the insurgency is for Kashmiri Muslims or radical Islam.

55 C. C. Fair, 'The Militant Challenge in Pakistan', *Asia Policy* 11 (2011).

This is not to say that there is no legitimate struggle for emancipation in Kashmir. Having been at the epicentre of the bloody Indo-Pak conflict for a little over seventy years, the Kashmiri people have genuine grievances. However, owing to their being Muslim, the cause has been conflated with and in some cases even hijacked by Islamic extremists, which provides India with the pretext to simply denounce and disregard it as a mutation of terrorism. On the other hand, regardless of the conflation of objectives, Pakistan has consistently supported armed resistance in Kashmir. This somewhat unconditional support is not just due to military imparity with India or even the abundantly available aspiring mujahideen, but also because of what is potentially at stake.

Losing Kashmir will not only render the lives and resources sacrificed for the cause since independence somewhat meaningless but will also trigger a profound identity crisis in the country. Owing to the uncertain, confusing and at times contradictory nature of the Pakistani identity, Kashmir often serves as a stabilising force, as it unites the different sects and ethnicities of Pakistan in their mutual contempt of Indian aggression on Muslim Kashmiris. The Kashmir conflict can therefore be seen as a rallying point that brings the disparate local identities together under the banner of national identity. Thus, for the sake of national identity, cohesion and unity, sustaining the Kashmir conflict at any cost is often deemed necessary.

It needs to be pointed out here that the compound Pakistani identity is not just capable of explaining terrorism and its mutations inside the country, but can in fact also help explain Pakistan's foreign policy choices and initiatives in relation to violence abroad. In addition to its sponsorship of militancy in Kashmir, Pakistan has also been accused of covertly supporting certain strands of terrorism in Afghanistan.[56]

The country certainly has played favourites in Afghanistan, especially since the fateful Soviet–Afghan war ended. The actors it favoured were clearly determined by its ideological and geo-strategic preferences, since Pakistan shares not only a border with Afghanistan but also its rebellious and problematic subnational Pashtun identity. Owing to fears of irredentism, Pakistan has always been sceptical of Pashtun nationalist elements in Afghanistan. There is also apprehension that such elements could reignite the dormant nationalistic forces in the KPK province. This explains why during the 1990s Pakistan actively supported and guided the Taliban to the reins of power in

---

56 See e.g. L. Hanauer and P. Chalk, *India's and Pakistan's Strategies in Afghanistan: Implications for the United States and the Region* (Santa Monica, RAND Corporation, 2012).

Afghanistan. Although the Taliban were predominantly Pashtun, they were first and foremost strict adherents of orthodox Sunni Islam.[57] The fact that their ethnic Pashtun identity was subordinate to their ultra-religious identity aligned perfectly with Pakistan's own preferences and geo-strategic ambitions.

Throughout its history, Pakistan has distinctly favoured religious fundamentalists over nationalist forces, due to perennial insecurities over its national identity. However, it is worth pointing out in the end that religious fundamentalists enjoy this privilege only as long as they acknowledge the existence of the Pakistani state and pose no existential threat to Pakistan. The likes of Tehrik-i-Taliban and various other local affiliates or sympathisers of Al Qaeda and ISIS do not recognise the Pakistani state. With their ultimate goal of creating an Islamic caliphate and open declaration of jihad against the Pakistani state, they clearly pose an existential threat to the country.[58] Pakistan not only categorically denounces all such elements but has also launched a series of military campaigns to counter them.

To support one strand of religious fundamentalism in order to secure national unity and identity and denounce another for similar reasons, especially when the two strands are inspired by similar religious belief systems, is clearly a precarious and dubious undertaking. This duality often backfires, leaving the state stranded just as the ordinary people face the adverse effects of its fallout.

Analysis of major political and social upheavals in the country that have produced insurgency, sectarianism and terrorism thus clearly demonstrate a perpetual crisis of identity. The key to understanding terrorism or any of its mutations in Pakistan, therefore, is through untangling its compound identity.

Conclusion

Over the course of this historical investigation it has become evident that the roots of terrorism in Pakistan run very deep and can in fact be traced back to the movement and ideology that paved the way for the country to secure its independence.

A country that was claimed in the name of Islam felt helpless when confronted with its heterogeneity and reluctantly gave in to the demands

57 Saikal, 'Afghanistan and Pakistan', pp. 5–17.
58 J. Droogan, 'The Perennial Problem of Terrorism and Political Violence in Pakistan', *Journal of Policing, Intelligence and Counter Terrorism* 13 (2018).

of religious fundamentalists to prevent exposing its foundational weakness. Clearly, there is a real fear that challenging religion or its role in the society could trigger a serious identity crisis that could undermine Pakistan's unity and even its existence. These inhibitions have additionally been compounded by the ethno-linguistic cleavages that have threatened to undermine Pakistan's autonomy and national unity since independence. Faced with such existential odds, it became necessary to sustain and propagate a narrative about congruous local identities that were willingly subordinate to an overarching national identity rooted in Islam.

Hence, the prevailing conviction is that, if the country is to survive, the national identity must thrive no matter what the cost. This belief on the one hand strengthened religious fundamentalist forces and gradually paved the way for all forms of terrorism and violence in the name of religion. On the other hand, any form of dissent or challenge to national identity or unity has met the brute force of the state. Total disregard of ethno-linguistic grievances and nationalist sentiments has consistently produced active insurgencies and armed resistance against the Pakistani state.

The depth, density and diversity of terrorism in Pakistan can only be fully appreciated once we countervail the confining post-9/11 prisms that erroneously link it to transnational Islamic terrorism and focus solely on the threat posed by the country to the rest of the world. In order to do justice to the victims and in effect the study of terrorism in Pakistan, it is imperative to resist and repel existing practices and prevailing narratives that are effectively distorted and shortsighted. Instead, we must acknowledge the heterogeneity and complex interwovenness of terrorism and understand that it is essentially a product of its enduring identity crisis.

Further Reading

J. Droogan, 'The Perennial Problem of Terrorism and Political Violence in Pakistan', *Journal of Policing, Intelligence and Counter Terrorism* 13 (2018)

M. Gaborieau, 'From Al-Beruni to Jinnah: Idiom, Ritual and Ideology of the Hindu–Muslim Confrontation in South Asia', *Anthropology Today* 1 (1985)

E. Murphy, *The Making of Terrorism in Pakistan: Historical and Social Roots of Extremism* (London, Routledge, 2012)

S. Saeed, 'Pakistani Nationalism and the State Marginalisation of the Ahmadiyya Community in Pakistan', *Studies in Ethnicity and Nationalism* 7 (2007)

L. Ziring, 'Public Policy Dilemmas and Pakistan's Nationality Problem: The Legacy of Zia ul-Haq', *Asian Survey* 28 (1988)

11
Political Violence in Ireland

FEARGHAL MCGARRY

In Ireland, where the struggle for independence has transformed generations of former gunmen into established statesmen, 'political violence' offers a less contentious term than 'terrorism' for analysing how non-state actors used force to bring about political change. Conveying how violence was conceived 'as a form of politics, a bargaining tool in the negotiation process between state and opposition',[1] it offers a useful (if more diffuse) category to analyse the political impact of violence.[2] Given that 'terrorists don't just do terrorism',[3] there is a strong case for analysing terroristic forms of violence alongside other strands of political and armed struggle which it supplemented or displaced. This chapter will argue that the significance of political violence in Ireland stemmed primarily from its impact on non-violent nationalism and the state, and that the forms of violence adopted by republicans shaped that dynamic relationship in important ways.

What can an Irish case study add to our understanding of political violence? One means of addressing this question is to consider what was distinctive about its use in modern Ireland. The longevity and ubiquity (but not lethality) of the 'physical-force tradition' is striking. Republican insurrections against British rule occurred in 1798, 1848, 1867 and 1916. More sustained campaigns of violence, varying greatly in scale, were mounted in 1881–5 (Fenian dynamite campaign), 1919–21 (War of Independence), 1922–3 (Civil War), 1939–40 (English bombing campaign), 1956–62 (border campaign) and 1969–98 (Northern Irish Troubles). Other forms of collective violence – such

---

1 N. Whelehan, *The Dynamiters: Irish Nationalism and Political Violence in the Wider World, 1867–1900* (Cambridge, Cambridge University Press, 2012), p. 26.
2 For a typology of political violence incorporating terrorism, see S. N. Kalyvas, 'The Landscape of Political Violence', in E. Chenoweth, R. English, A. Gofas and S. N. Kalyvas (eds.), *The Oxford Handbook of Terrorism* (Oxford, Oxford University Press, 2019).
3 R. English, *Does Terrorism Work? A History* (Oxford, Oxford University Press, 2016), p. 16.

as agrarian, sectarian and class conflict, not always political in intent but with political implications – often overlapped with anti-state violence.[4]

Although this chapter focuses on republican organisations, the use of force was not confined to one political tradition. During the 1912–14 Home Rule crisis, the parliamentary leaders of nationalism and unionism mobilised over a quarter of a million armed 'Volunteers' to bolster their influence at Westminster. Supported by influential sympathisers within the British Conservative Party and British army, the Ulster unionist leader, Edward Carson, skilfully deployed the threat of violence against both the British state (which unionists sought to remain within) and Irish nationalists to impede Irish self-government before the First World War. Loyalist violence, threatened or (as in 1969) real, often provoked violent republican responses.

The British state, whose authority in Ireland rested on a greater degree of coercion (including a gendarmerie rather than constabulary) than in the rest of the UK, contributed to the process by which violence permeated Irish society during periods of conflict.[5] During the War of Independence, for example, the British government deployed a variety of unruly paramilitary organisations alongside the police and army, including 'Black-and-Tans' (temporary police constables), Auxiliaries (ex-army officers) and Ulster Special Constabulary (locally recruited Protestant loyalists) to suppress the IRA before finally conceding Irish self-government in 1921.

The outcome of that conflict – a nationalist Southern state that did not achieve full independence until 1949 and a Northern unionist regime which excluded its Catholic nationalist minority from power until its prorogation in 1972 – incentivised violent republican campaigns every decade from the 1920s until the 1960s, when the Troubles ushered in three decades of violent conflict. Despite the success of the 1998 Belfast/Good Friday Agreement in restoring devolution to Northern Ireland, low-level 'dissident' republican violence persists to the present day. Throughout all of these conflicts, each side accused their opponents of engaging in 'terrorism', although the term 'terrorist' was seldom used before the Troubles.[6]

A second distinctive feature of Irish political violence was its precociously transnational character. The emigration of 4 million Irish people to the United States between 1851 and 1921 enabled republicans to appeal to one of

---

[4] C. Townshend, *Political Violence in Ireland: Government and Resistance since 1848* (Oxford, Oxford University Press, 1983), pp. 407–8.

[5] C. Townshend, *The Republic: The Fight for Irish Independence* (London, Allen Lane, 2013), p. 452.

[6] D. Fitzpatrick (ed.), *Terror in Ireland 1916–1923* (Dublin, Lilliput Press, 2011), pp. 5–9.

the world's largest and most influential diasporas. The impact of 'long-distance nationalism' on politics and violence in Ireland was profound: as early as the 1880s, the British Home Secretary complained of 'an Irish nation in the United States ... absolutely beyond our reach'.[7] Better organised in America than Ireland, the Irish Republican Brotherhood (also known as the Fenians) was central to the planning of Irish insurrections, while financial and logistical support crossed the Atlantic throughout every republican campaign. Irish-American influence played a critical role in sustaining and ending the Troubles. Ireland consequently offers an 'illuminating historical example of the social causes, effects and patterns of political violence amongst a diverse immigrant community in a broad chronological framework' of relevance to contemporary violent movements.[8]

Third, a rich body of sources and literature exists for Irish political violence. While 'Ireland's may be the best-documented modern revolution in the world',[9] the Troubles is among the world's most extensively documented and analysed insurgencies. Almost every death in both conflicts has been the subject of biographical analysis.[10] State records and media coverage have generated abundant sources, while numerous inquiries have reconstructed seminal events such as the circumstances surrounding the outbreak of violence in Belfast in 1969 and the British army's killing of thirteen civilians in Derry on Bloody Sunday in 1972. Journalistic accounts and memoirs have exposed the inner workings of paramilitarism in intimate detail.[11] The longevity of the Irish insurrectionary tradition, Ireland's proximity to Britain, its relative safety and Anglophone environment further account for the disproportionate scale of scholarly research on Irish violence.

Given the sophisticated and extensive literature on republican and state violence,[12] Ireland provides a useful case study to address questions about the

7 D. Brundage, *Irish Nationalists in America: The Politics of Exile, 1798–1998* (Oxford, Oxford University Press, 2016), p. 6; quoted in R. Schmuhl, *Ireland's Exiled Children: America and the Easter Rising* (Oxford, Oxford University Press, 2016), p. 17.
8 C. Nic Dháibhéid, 'Political Violence and the Irish Diaspora', in E. F. Biagini and M. E. Daly (eds.), *The Cambridge Social History of Modern Ireland* (Cambridge, Cambridge University Press, 2017), p. 459.
9 P. Hart, *The I.R.A. at War 1916–1923* (Oxford, Oxford University Press, 2003), p. 5.
10 D. McKittrick, S. Kelters, B. Feeney, C. Thornton and D. McVea, *Lost Lives: The Stories of the Men, Women and Children Who Died as a Result of the Northern Irish Troubles* (Edinburgh, Mainstream, 2007 ed.); E. O'Halpin and D. Ó Corráin, *The Dead of the Irish Revolution* (New Haven, Yale University Press, 2020).
11 E. Moloney, *A Secret History of the IRA* (London, Penguin, 2002); P. R. Keefe, *Say Nothing: A True Story of Murder and Memory in Northern Ireland* (New York, Penguin Random House, 2019); E. Collins, *Killing Rage* (London, Granta, 1997).
12 See, for example, Townshend, *Political Violence*, and R. English, *Armed Struggle: The History of the IRA* (London, Pan, 2012).

relationship between terrorism and historical change at the heart of this book.[13] Described by the nineteenth-century French magistrate Gustave de Beaumont as 'a little country which raises all the great questions', Ireland was shaped by three developments central to modern Europe: territorial state formation; the sectarian divisions generated by the Reformation; and the challenge to empire posed by national self-determination.[14] Contrary to depictions of Irish violence as the product of insular, ancient enmities, conflict in Ireland usually coincided with wider European upheavals, demonstrating how external and modernising pressures shaped patterns of violence.

Rather than surveying the tradition of republican violence briefly introduced, this chapter analyses three discrete episodes: the Fenian 'dynamite war' (1881–5), Irish Revolution (1916–21) and Northern Irish Troubles (1969–98). Following a brief summary of each, the following questions will be analysed. How was violence rationalised by republicans? What impact did it have on Irish nationalism and the British state? What did violence achieve? One justification for comparing different republican campaigns over such a long period, notwithstanding important distinctions between late Victorian Fenians, Edwardian-era Volunteers and late twentieth-century paramilitaries, is that their activists perceived themselves as belonging to a coherent republican tradition. Just as the Easter 1916 rebels claimed a mandate from the 'dead generations' that preceded them, the Provisional IRA legitimised its violence by claiming the authority of the Irish Republic proclaimed in 1916. This snapshot methodology aims to identify continuities and changes over time: the long view allows both for comparison of similar scenarios in different periods, and analysis of the impact of shifts in political thought such as new understandings of civil rights and democracy.

The Fenian 'Dynamite War', 1881–1885

On 24 January 1885, Irish-American Fenians, posing as tourists, detonated bombs in the Tower of London, Westminster Hall and House of Commons. Condemned by *The Times*, whose offices had recently been bombed, as an attempt 'to strike terror into the souls of Englishmen; whether by the indiscriminate slaughter of holidaymakers and working people, or by the destruction of precious monuments', Dynamite Saturday marked the

---

13 G. de Beaumont, *L'Irlande sociale, politique et religieuse*, Vol. 1, p. ii, quoted in A. T. Q. Stewart, *The Shape of Irish History* (Belfast, Blackstaff Press, 2001), p. 139.

14 R. Bourke, 'Introduction', in R. Bourke and I. McBride, *The Princeton History of Modern Ireland* (Princeton, Princeton University, 2016).

culmination of the first urban bombing campaign in history.[15] Celebrated by one militant Irish-American newspaper as 'a victory that all patriotic Irishmen and justice loving Americans will appreciate', its audacity humiliated the Home Office and intelligence services, which placed the blame for this security failure on the London Metropolitan Police.[16] A transnational conspiracy; the destruction of symbolic targets; the sustained use of terror to maximise publicity and to provoke the state: there is much about this innovative campaign to explain why the Fenians have been described as the 'progenitors of terrorism'.[17]

The dynamite campaign was orchestrated by two militant Irish Republican Brotherhood (IRB) factions. Founded in 1858 in Ireland and the US, the IRB was a conspiratorial oath-bound movement committed to the use of violence to achieve an independent Irish republic. Beyond Ireland, Fenianism gained a large following throughout Britain, the Empire, and above all in the United States, where impoverished Catholic immigrants experienced discrimination and condescension. After an unsuccessful rebellion in 1867, the IRB softened its hostility to participation in politics, encouraging tenant agitation and supporting Charles Stewart Parnell's efforts to win Home Rule at Westminster. A movement whose appeal was social as well as ideological, the Fenians infiltrated cultural organisations, imported arms and, perhaps most influentially, sustained the romantic appeal of insurrectionary separatism through the commemoration of martyred patriots.

The campaign was hatched by a handful of conspirators. Since the mid-1870s Patrick Ford, a Famine emigrant, printer and American Civil War veteran, had called for attacks on Britain in his New York-based *Irish World* newspaper. He was supported by Jeremiah O'Donovan Rossa, a more recent emigrant whose reputation for belligerence and drunkenness never entirely dispelled the heroic status bequeathed by an arduous term of imprisonment for treason felony in English jails. By 1880, 90,000 dollars had been subscribed to the Skirmishing Fund.[18] Following disputes over control of these funds, O'Donovan Rossa broke with Clan na Gael, the largest American Fenian organisation, to establish the United Irishmen of America. Its campaign

---

15 Quoted in G. Beiner, 'Fenianism and the Martyrdom–Terrorism Nexus in Ireland Before Independence', in D. Janes and A. Houen (eds.), *Martyrdom and Terrorism: Premodern to Contemporary Perspectives* (Oxford, Oxford University Press, 2014), p. 214. The best account of the campaign, on which this essay relies, is Whelehan, *Dynamiters*.
16 Whelehan, *Dynamiters*, p. 110.
17 L. Clutterbuck, 'The Progenitors of Terrorism: Russian Revolutionaries or Extreme Irish Republicans?', *Terrorism and Political Violence* 16 (2004).
18 Beiner, 'Martyrdom–Terrorism Nexus', p. 211.

began in January 1881 with an attack on an army barracks in Salford, symbolically close to the location where three Fenians (the Manchester Martyrs) had been executed in 1867. In 1883 Clan na Gael began dispatching its own bombers across the Atlantic. Together, both organisations accounted for twenty-five explosions, targeting town halls, gasworks, bridges, newspaper offices and railway and underground stations in London, Liverpool, Manchester and Glasgow.

Why bomb Britain? According to O'Donovan Rossa, 'it was done to show England that she had better give Ireland her own parliament'.[19] The dynamiters rationalised their violence as a defensive response to English tyranny, in particular the renewal of coercion in Ireland to suppress agrarian agitation: 'England is at war with Ireland, and Ireland should be at war with England.'[20] By wreaking havoc in urban centres, the organisers sought to disrupt British economic life and revive Fenianism. They believed that dynamite, a recent invention, would facilitate the destruction of military targets with few casualties, and at little cost to Irish lives, thereby destabilising Britain, and encouraging a broader revolutionary challenge. The term 'skirmishing', associated with the irregular forces of the American Civil War whose deployment had eroded conventional distinctions between combatants and civilians, conveyed the idea of asymmetrical warfare as a pragmatic alternative to mass insurrection, which appeared to have been rendered obsolete by the power of the modern state.

Within Irish America, debate centred on the legitimacy of a strategy which was almost universally condemned beyond the US. Patrick Ford argued that the idea of 'civilised warfare' was based on a naïve 'sense of honour'.[21] Responding to press accusations of 'barbarism' after Dynamite Saturday, he accused Britain of hypocrisy: 'In the recent explosion in London not a single life was lost', whereas England 'has butchered some 1,300 Sudanese'.[22] Despite the lurid rhetoric of O'Donovan Rossa (who contemplated releasing poison gas in the House of Commons), most bombers understood the need for their violence to be seen as morally defensible, measured and competently executed: 'we must feel that we can justify the act'.[23] The campaign's fatalities were limited to one civilian (a seven-year-old boy killed in the first attack in Salford) and three dynamiters.

What accounted for the unprecedented strategy of a sustained urban bombing campaign? Depicted as part of an insurrectionary tradition, the

---

19 S. Kenna, *Jeremiah O'Donovan Rossa: Unrepentant Fenian* (Dublin, Merrion, 2015), p. 177.
20 Ibid.   21 Whelehan, *Dynamiters*, p. 111.   22 Ibid., p. 110.   23 Ibid., p. 95.

dynamiting campaign is better understood as the product of 'a peculiar juxtaposition of Irish inheritance and American environment'.[24] The skirmishers drew on the ideas of German émigré Johann Most, an advocate both of 'propaganda of the deed' and the power of 'scientific warfare'. Facilitated by innovations in transport, communications and science, and drawing on contemporary transnational influences, their strategy was a product of modernity. In what amounted to a very public conspiracy, the organisers sought to maximise publicity, announcing their plans to the world, and rhapsodising about the potential of modern technology to revolutionise conventional warfare. Public lectures and pamphlets explained how to manufacture 'infernal machines' from readily available materials, while 'Professor Mezzeroff' (a New York-born liquor salesman posing as a Russian nihilist) instructed international students from his Brooklyn 'dynamite school'.[25] The Fenians' innovative efforts to develop a submarine capable of sinking British commercial shipping reflected the same spirit. Rooted as it was in post-Civil War America's cultures of technology and violence, the 'host society, not ancestral animus, provides the critical framework' for understanding the emergence of the dynamite campaign.[26]

Who supported dynamiting? The skirmishing campaign's public subscribers were lower-class Irish-born immigrants rather than respectable Irish Americans. Only one of the thirty-six dynamiters arrested during the campaign was US-born.[27] Motivated by ethnic grievance, notably the horrors of the Great Famine, rather than a desire for social mobility, many Irish emigrants understood their presence in the US as a kind of involuntary political exile.[28] Supporting the campaign, Niall Whelehan suggests, allowed alienated immigrants 'to strike back without leaving their new home'.[29] Beyond the militants on the margins who funded and participated in the campaign, and were widely ridiculed in the press as fanatics or dupes, support for Fenian violence was occasionally voiced by prominent Irish Americans. Expressing his disappointment that an attempt to destroy the Home Office had not been more successful, Congressman John Finerty of Illinois declared that 'England brought this on herself.'[30] At a ceremony commemorating the

---

24 S. Kenna, *War in the Shadows: The Irish-American Fenians Who Bombed Victorian Britain* (Dublin, Merrion, 2014), p. 2.
25 Beiner, 'Martyrdom–Terrorism Nexus', p. 213.
26 Nic Dháibhéid, 'Irish Diaspora', p. 460; Whelehan, *Dynamiters*, pp. 138–75.
27 Ibid., pp. 178, 190.
28 K. Miller, *Emigrants and Exiles: Ireland and the Irish Exodus to North America* (New York, Oxford University Press, 1985).
29 Whelehan, *Dynamiters*, p. 216.   30 Kenna, *O'Donovan Rossa*, p. 178.

Manchester Martyrs in 1885, the Irish-born New York Congressman William Erigena Robinson praised 'God for the invention of dynamite'.[31]

Outside America, however, skirmishing was denounced by Irish revolutionaries as 'irrational, wasteful of revolutionary funds and highly immoral'.[32] Aside from some adherents in Scotland, Fenians in Britain offered little support for the campaign, with many denouncing the bombers for undermining Ireland's cause. O'Donovan Rossa was depicted as an embittered figure driven by vengeance rather than patriotism. Whether due to moral objections to the campaign's violence, or concerns about its impact on the Irish in Britain, police informers abounded. Whereas Fenian outrages in Britain during the 1860s had prompted attacks on the Irish community there, the British authorities attributed responsibility for the dynamite campaign 'to a handful of American specialists rather than to the immigrant population'.[33]

While the mainstream nationalist press in Ireland condemned the immoral dynamiter as 'a disgrace to his country, an enemy to her cause, a danger to the entire community', Fenian objections to the campaign were more nuanced.[34] Breaking with the insurrectionary tradition, skirmishing transgressed established notions of chivalrous combat. It also contravened the IRB's constitution, which had been modified after its disastrous 1867 insurrection to ensure that its next uprising commanded popular support. The strategy and morality of political violence were seen as interrelated. Whereas insurrection required drilled members imbued with a republican ethos, Fenians worried 'that an independent Ireland, born through assassination and outrage, not regular warfare, would be a place devoid of a moral centre or a sense of collective responsibility'. Skirmishing implied independence could be won by a revolutionary elite rather than 'an Irish population, politically conscious of itself as nation, arising to achieve fulfilment'.[35] Culturally determined ideas about the morality of violence were perhaps more important than its effectiveness. Despite killing the two most senior British officials in Ireland, the 1881 Phoenix Park murders carried out by a militant Fenian faction provoked widespread revulsion, including from most revolutionaries, due to the knife-wielding assassins' uncivilised methods.

---

31 Beiner, 'Martyrdom–Terrorism Nexus', p. 213.
32 O. McGee, *The IRB: The Irish Republican Brotherhood, from the Land League to Sinn Féin* (Dublin, Four Courts Press, 2005), p. 82.
33 D. Fitzpatrick, 'The Irish in Britain, 1871–1921', in W. E. Vaughan (ed.), *A New History of Ireland VI: Ireland under the Union 1870–1921*, p. 676.
34 *Freeman's Journal*, 10 August 1883, quoted in Whelehan, *Dynamiters*, p. 70.
35 Whelehan, *Dynamiters*, p. 90.

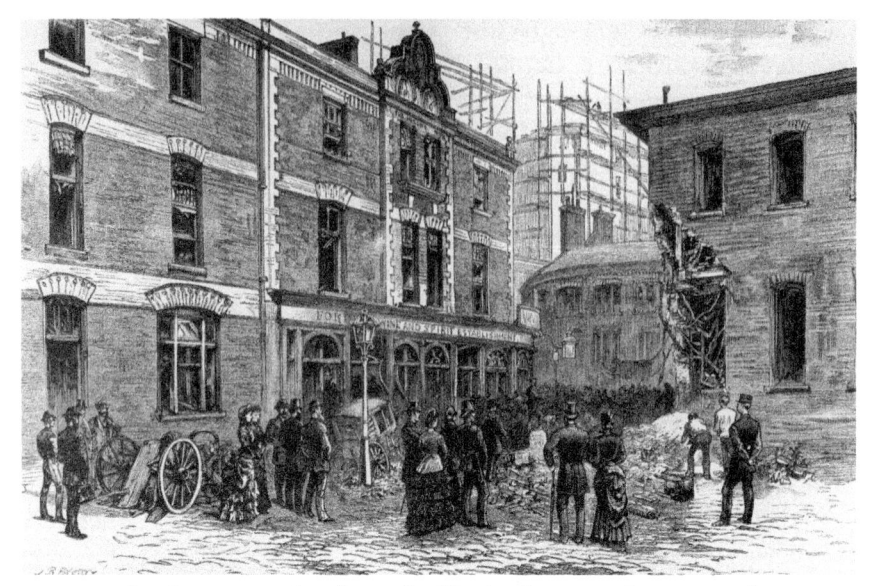

Figure 11.1 Londoners view the aftermath of Fenian dynamiters' attempt to destroy Scotland Yard on 30 May 1884 (From *The Graphic*, 7 June 1884: photo by Hulton Archive/ Stringer via Getty Images)

Arguably the most significant consequence of the bombing campaign was its impact on the British political and security establishment. The Fenians' targeting of the Criminal Investigation Department (established in the late 1870s to counter the IRB) at Scotland Yard on 30 May 1884 demonstrated an intent to provoke state repression (Fig. 11.1). A Crime Special Branch (initially known as the Special Irish Branch) was established by the London Metropolitan Police in 1883 following the bombing of the Home Office, while a 'Secret Service' section was also created to suppress the campaign. Although their use was disdained as a continental practice, greater reliance was placed on the role of plain-clothes policemen, informers and spies, with vast state expenditure (particularly in Ireland) devoted to the suppression of subversion. The creation of ill-defined roles for powerful figures such as the Assistant Undersecretary for Police and Crime in Ireland, Edward Jenkinson, and their willingness to use their influence to advance their own careers, ensured factional rivalries within the security services as marked as those within the Fenians.[36]

---

36 Ibid., pp. 118, 135.

British intelligence proved effective in recruiting agents provocateurs who undermined the IRB by encouraging reckless operations, fomenting crippling divisions within the fractious world of Fenianism and inveigling naïve militants in bogus plots. A network of informers and new legislative powers ensured that most dynamiters (such as a young Irish emigrant to the US named Tom Clarke) were arrested within weeks of their arrival in Britain. However, as had also proved the case in the 1860s, civil liberties were largely preserved in Britain, and there were no executions.[37] In the Irish part of the UK, where order was prioritised over law, the approach was different. Although condemning the dynamiters for 'injuring the Irish cause', nationalist politicians argued that Britain's reliance on coercion to suppress agrarian and Fenian violence represented 'the clearest possible demonstration of the incapacity of any English government satisfactorily to administer Irish affairs', an argument endorsed by some English liberals.[38] Fenian violence may have been easily suppressed, but the British state's reliance on force exposed its frail legitimacy in Ireland.

The most intriguing aspect of Britain's response to Fenian violence centred on this intersection between security and politics. Writing to both the prime minister and the leader of the opposition, the influential Dublin Castle spymaster, Edward Jenkinson, argued forcefully, if unsuccessfully, that the suppression of Fenian violence and long-term security of the Empire required a bipartisan political commitment to deliver Irish Home Rule. Although Gladstone, the Liberal leader, did proclaim his conversion to Home Rule in 1885, this reflected Parnell's success in winning the balance of power at Westminster rather than a belief in the need to address Fenian violence through political reform. Exploiting divisions among the Liberal Party, and Gladstone's failure to pass Home Rule in the Commons (which coincided with imperial reverses in Egypt and Africa), the manipulation of the Irish Question by the Conservative Party played a significant role in securing its return to power.[39] Conservatives misrepresented Parnell's indirect links to IRB figures to portray him as a Fenian ally (Fig. 11.2), while depicting Gladstone's support for Home Rule as appeasement.[40] The most remarkable example of the British state's exploitation of Fenian violence was the 1887 'Jubilee Plot', a conspiracy to assassinate Queen Victoria which was instigated by Irish-American agents

---

37 B. Jenkins, *The Fenian Problem: Insurgency and Terrorism in a Liberal State 1868–74* (Liverpool, Liverpool University Press, 2009).
38 E. Biagini, *British Democracy and Irish Nationalism 1876–1906* (Cambridge, Cambridge University Press, 2007), pp. 135–7.
39 D. M. Schreuder, *Gladstone and Kruger: Liberal Government and Colonial 'Home Rule' 1880–1885* (London, Routledge, 2018 ed.), p. 445.
40 McGee, *The IRB*, pp. 125–32.

PUNCH, OR THE LONDON CHARIVARI.—May 20, 1882.

THE IRISH FRANKENSTEIN.

"The baneful and blood-stained Monster * * * yet was it not my Master to the very extent that it was my Creature ? * * * Had I not breathed into it my own spirit ?" * * * (*Extract from the Works of* C. S. P-RN-LL, M.P.

Figure 11.2 Following the assassination of the Chief Secretary for Ireland and his Undersecretary by militant Fenians in 1882, the Irish parliamentary party leader Charles Stewart Parnell was depicted as responsible for the violence, due to his support for the Irish Land League (From *Punch*, or the *London Charivari*, 20 May 1882: photo by The Cartoon Collector/Print Collector/Hulton Archive via Getty Images)

provocateurs with the approval of the Conservative Prime Minister Lord Salisbury in order to discredit Parnell and suppress Fenianism.[41] A subsequent attempt by *The Times* to implicate the Irish Party leader through forgery led to

---

[41] C. Campbell, *Fenian Fire: The British Government Plot to Assassinate Queen Victoria* (London, HarperCollins, 2002).

a judicial inquiry that vindicated Parnell but drew unwelcome attention to the British state's use of espionage to undermine Irish nationalism.

British effectiveness in penetrating Fenianism, and Parnell's growing influence at Westminster, a development for which the dynamiters unconvincingly claimed some credit, led to the suspension of the dynamite campaign in 1885.[42] It was clear by then that the skirmishers' faith in technology was misplaced. Across America, Britain and Ireland, 'Fenian fever' was replaced by a growing press consensus 'that dynamite is not near so dangerous a thing as was generally supposed'. Dynamiters were often depicted as 'harmless idiots' rather than terrifying subversives.[43]

What did the campaign achieve? Although stimulating extensive public discourse and generating international publicity for Irish republicanism, the campaign served to identify their grievances with terror rather than liberty, undermining Irish-American efforts to portray Irish and American republicanism as analogous. The campaign also contributed to a growing consensus concerning the illegitimacy of Irish violence compared to 'acceptable Anglo-Saxon forms of resistance', which would shape official attitudes to international terrorism on both sides of the Atlantic.[44] In Britain, the revival of caricatures of Fenians as monstrous apes constructed the Irish as an irrational people incapable of self-government, a trope which served to justify Ireland's continued exclusion from Britain's liberal political culture.[45] Lacking political and public support, the dynamite war achieved little of substance. Coercion, penetration, infighting and paranoia devastated Fenianism in Britain and Ireland and divided the movement in the US.[46] The campaign indicated the ineffectiveness of forms of violence seen as lacking in moral and political legitimacy. Although some moderate nationalists sympathised with imprisoned bombers who served long sentences in harsh conditions, the campaign produced no martyrs. By the early twentieth century, political violence in Ireland was, if not discredited, widely viewed as an anachronism best consigned to history.

---

42 Whelehan, *Dynamiters*, pp. 295–303.   43 Ibid., p. 301.
44 J. Gantt, *Irish Terrorism in the Atlantic Community* (Basingstoke, Palgrave Macmillan, 2010), p. 16.
45 A. Martin, *Alter-Nations: Nationalisms, Terror and the State in Nineteenth-Century Britain and Ireland* (Columbus, Ohio State University Press, 2012).
46 McGee, *The IRB*, pp. 103–36.

The Irish Revolution, 1916–1921

The return of the gun to Irish politics resulted from developments beyond Ireland. The success of Parnell's heir, John Redmond, in winning the balance of power at Westminster in 1910 revived the Irish Question, resulting in the formation of rival paramilitary organisations in Ireland. In return for the Liberal government enacting Home Rule (albeit suspended for the duration of the First World War, when some form of partition would be implemented), the Irish Party committed itself to the British war effort. But, for the IRB, England's difficulty remained Ireland's opportunity. Its Easter 1916 rebellion collapsed within a week but led to popular support for republicanism, resulting in Sinn Féin's success in the 1918 UK general election. On 21 January 1919, the same day as Irish Volunteers in rural Ireland began killing policemen, an Irish parliament, Dáil Éireann, proclaimed Irish independence. Following two years of guerrilla struggle, resulting in 1,400 deaths, Britain conceded limited independence to southern Ireland. What was the rationale for the varying forms of violence adopted during these years, and why did they prove effective?

A military failure, the Easter rebellion was a remarkably successful act of political violence. Three key reasons can be identified: its mode of violence; the wider wartime context in which it occurred; and the manner of its suppression. An act of armed propaganda, its choreography was central to the Rising's impact. The strategy of occupying buildings in the centre of Dublin marked a conscious return to a seemingly archaic insurrectionary tradition. Although some Volunteers had advocated 'hedge-fighting' (guerrilla warfare), the Rising's 1848-style tactics, despite lacking much strategic rationale, accentuated its symbolic impact. The prominent role of Patrick Pearse, a cultural nationalist whose 'gospel of Irish nationalism' preached the necessity of a Christ-like act of redemption, ensured the leaders' actions were subsequently understood as an intentional 'blood sacrifice'. Although rather less mystically inclined, the rebellion's IRB organisers had also sought to revive militant nationalism among the apathetic masses, an aspiration which helps to explain their preoccupation with symbolism over strategy. Frustrated by popular nationalist support for Home Rule and the British war effort, they were motivated by their belief that the separatist tradition and spirit of nationality on which it rested was dying.

The Rising's effectiveness as 'propaganda of the deed' demonstrated the transformative impact of symbolic violence by a conspiratorial vanguard under the right circumstances. Little noticed at the time, the proclamation of the Irish Republic outside the General Post Office provided its seminal moment. Crucially, for posterity at least, this act of revolutionary violence underpinned a claim to national sovereignty, transforming marginal conspirators into a 'Provisional Government' responsible for 'the civil and military affairs of the Republic'. Their mandate rested not on popular support but on history and on the sacrifice of 'the dead generations' from which Ireland 'receives her old tradition of statehood', a justification which provided one point of continuity with the dynamite campaign (for which the Rising's most senior organiser, Tom Clarke, had served a life sentence). It was the funeral of O'Donovan Rossa, organised by Clarke in 1915, which offered a national stage for Pearse to articulate the powerful Fenian belief that violence was legitimised by martyrdom: 'Life springs from death, and from the graves of patriot men and women spring living nations ... while Ireland holds these graves, Ireland unfree shall never be at peace.'[47] The Proclamation depicted the Rising as a historical inevitability: 'In every generation the Irish people have asserted their right to national freedom and sovereignty: six times during the past three hundred years they have asserted it in arms.'

In reality, the rebellion was perceived by most contemporaries as shocking, anachronistic and futile. In explaining its causation and consequences, historians have increasingly emphasised the importance of external factors. The role of the US was central: 'No America, no New York, no Easter Rising.'[48] Despite its small scale in comparison to the violence of the Western Front, the American press was gripped by news of the rebellion (which made the front page of the *New York Times* for over two weeks).[49] Most obviously in terms of external pressures, the insurrection was a product of its wider wartime context: 'As surely as Verdun or the Somme, Dublin in 1916 was a First World War battlefield.'[50] Its leaders were united in their belief that, in time of war, action was preferable to inaction, and that the advantages of an unsuccessful insurrection – the reassertion of separatist credibility, the renewal of the physical-force tradition, the possibility of destroying popular support for Home Rule – outweighed the consequences of probable military defeat. The war provided a rationale that was as much emotional as strategic, with organisers speaking of their shame and humiliation should it end before an uprising. In this respect, their mentality reflected the pervasive

---

47 Beiner, 'Martyrdom–Terrorism Nexus', p. 219.
48 J. Lee, quoted in M. N. Grey, *Ireland's Allies: America and the 1916 Easter Rising* (Dublin, University College Dublin Press, 2016).
49 Schmuhl, *Ireland's Exiled Children*, p. 46.
50 K. Jeffery, *1916: A Global History* (London, Bloomsbury, 2015), p. 104.

militarism of the times. Pearse's sanguinary rhetoric resembled that of the 'generation of 1914', while James Connolly's embrace of violence demonstrated the war's radicalising impact on revolutionary socialists who had previously predicted an international workers' revolt against imperial militarism. The rebels' use of military titles, uniforms, fixed outposts, and their dignified formal surrender attested to their belief in the importance of conforming to idealised notions of military behaviour in order to win 'a glorious place among the nations'. Although there was little conventional about staging an insurrection in a densely populated city, which ensured that the largest proportion of the Rising's 500 fatalities were civilians, the idea that the rebels formed a legitimate army was central both to their self-perception and how their actions were perceived by nationalists.[51]

In striking contrast to the dynamite campaign, the rebels' claim to have exercised a legitimate form of violence on behalf of the Irish nation won (retrospective) popular support. Ensuring that the violence of the rebels was perceived as sacrificial rather than senseless, Britain's decision to execute fifteen leaders was important in shifting nationalist opinion. An emotional Westminster speech by Irish Party leader John Dillon conveyed the transformative impact of this heavy-handed response:

> You are letting loose a river of blood ... between two races who, after three hundred years of hatred and of strife, we had nearly succeeded in bringing together. It is the first rebellion that ever took place in Ireland where you had a majority on your side ... We are held up to odium as traitors by those men who made this rebellion, and our lives have been in danger a hundred times during the last thirty years because we have endeavoured to reconcile the two things, and now you are washing out our whole life work in a sea of blood.[52]

Yet Dillon's revealing admission that he was 'proud' of the rebels whose courageous 'conduct was beyond reproach as fighting men' indicates how the soldierly and sacrificial dimensions of their violence evoked approbation even from those who considered their strategy utterly misguided. Equally significant was the candid observation by the head of the Royal Irish Constabulary (when the government renewed efforts to implement Home Rule in the aftermath of the rebellion) that six days of violence had achieved more than twenty-five years of political agitation.[53] By 1918, public sympathy for the rebels had crystallised into a rejection of the Irish Party and its Home

---

51 F. McGarry, *The Rising: Ireland, Easter 1916* (Oxford, Oxford University Press, 2010).
52 *Hansard*, HC Deb. vol. 82, col. 940.   53 McGarry, *The Rising*, p. 285.

Rule project. Considering how the Irish Party's own political rhetoric was long suffused with an Anglophobic 'vocabulary of heroic struggle, suffering, grievance, injustice, and enemies', this popular shift from non-violent to revolutionary nationalism was less dramatic than may appear.[54]

Under the guidance of Michael Collins, who had complained about the rebellion's 'air of a Greek tragedy', theatrical violence was replaced by more brutally effective methods.[55] The targeting of political policemen in Dublin marked the beginning of a campaign of assassination which paralysed Dublin Castle's intelligence capabilities. The targeting of these 'G-men', seen as responsible for the 1916 executions, was symbolic and strategic. Although its propagandists insisted that civilians opposed to the Republic 'should be killed without mercy', the IRA's escalation from public defiance to guerrilla war occurred only gradually, partly due to widespread disquiet at the killing of Irish policemen, and its campaign was generally characterised by restraint. Notwithstanding an attempt to kill the Lord Lieutenant, politicians, judges and officials were rarely targeted. Violence in Britain was also discouraged by the IRA leadership, which did not implement its plan to assassinate the British cabinet. Evoking comparisons with the Phoenix Park murders, the opportunistic assassination of Field Marshal Sir Henry Wilson in London by IRA Volunteers in 1922 was seen by the British press as so shocking as to imperil Ireland's 'status as a civilised country'.[56]

It was not until the second half of 1920 that policemen were targeted in significant numbers. Denounced by the British government as murder, guerrilla methods provided a more formidable but less admired challenge than insurrection: 'we were a ghostly army of sharpshooters operating all over the country combining to deal with small bodies of the enemy and making Ireland too costly to hold; always choosing our own ground, and our own targets'.[57] Importantly, it was underpinned by extensive non-violent struggle. Transforming sites intended 'to "quell political dissent" into places where resistance, even revolution was nurtured', protests in prisons (where 6,000 republicans were incarcerated by 1921) exposed the limitations of British power.[58] Generating global headlines, the death of IRA hunger striker and

---

54 M. Wheatley, *Nationalism and the Irish Party: Provincial Ireland, 1910–1916* (Oxford, Oxford University Press, 2005), p. 94.
55 Quoted in T. P. Coogan, *Michael Collins* (London, Arrow, 1991), p. 54.
56 K. Jeffery, *Field Marshal Sir Henry Wilson: A Political Soldier* (Oxford, Oxford University Press, 2008), p. 287.
57 S. Robinson, quoted in Townshend, *The Republic*, p. 78.
58 W. Murphy, *Political Imprisonment and the Irish, 1919–1921* (Oxford, Oxford University Press, 2014), pp. 1, 10.

Lord Mayor of Cork Terence MacSwiney in Brixton jail in October 1920 provided a striking example of the power of martyrdom to evoke popular support.

Preoccupied with (more harshly suppressed) challenges in India and the Middle East, and unwilling for political reasons to designate the conflict a war, the British government struggled to formulate a coherent security response. Stiffening the police with paramilitary forces, the cabinet eventually resolved to fight terror with terror. As in 1916, heavy-handed measures proved militarily effective but politically counterproductive. Reprisals such as the sacking of Balbriggan and Cork undermined British legitimacy, as did night-time raids by police 'murder gangs'. Although placing the IRA under great pressure, these tactics polarised public opinion and, as *The Observer* noted, ensured 'the immense weakening of Britain's moral position throughout the world'. Republicans welcomed the exposure of the coercive essence of British rule. '[T]hings here are very thrilling', Collins cheerfully informed a colleague in Britain: 'Ireland is in for the greatest crucifixion she has ever yet been subjected to'.[59]

In contrast to the 1880s, Britain failed to penetrate the republican movement or generate significant intelligence from the public. Rivalry and poor coordination between its numerous intelligence organisations in Ireland was partly to blame, but the IRA's effective intelligence network and ruthless willingness to execute suspected spies and informers prolonged an increasingly dirty war. Around one-quarter of policemen killed by the IRA were unarmed, while a similar proportion of republicans were killed in circumstances that transgressed the 'rules of war'.[60] The death of thirty-five people on 'Bloody Sunday', 21 November 1920, when the IRA's execution of British agents provoked the retaliatory shooting of football spectators at Croke Park, appalled public opinion. In Britain, public revulsion at the IRA's willingness to shoot officers in their beds was accompanied by growing unease about the government's methods. In the wake of a war purportedly fought in defence of small nations and against 'German barbarism', substantial sections of British political opinion and civic society expressed deep disquiet at the news from Ireland.[61]

---

59 Quoted in F. McGarry, 'Revolution, 1916–23', in T. Bartlett (ed.), *The Cambridge History of Ireland*, Vol. 4: *1880 to the Present* (Cambridge, Cambridge University Press, 2018), p. 281.
60 O'Halpin and Ó Corráin, *Dead of the Irish Revolution*, p. 16.
61 E. Madigan, '"An Irish Louvain": Memories of 1914 and the Moral Climate in Britain During the War of Independence', *Irish Historical Studies* 44/165 (May 2020).

Functioning primarily as armed propaganda, republican violence framed the Irish conflict as a struggle for national self-determination against imperial oppression. Crucially, violence was only one element of a broader political strategy. Mass mobilisation, electoral politics, the establishment of a counter-state that could demonstrate popular allegiance, combined with sophisticated efforts to cultivate international support through propaganda and diplomacy, eroded British legitimacy in Ireland. It was less the effectiveness of republican violence than the belief that it was rooted in popular support that accounted for its impact, with even unsympathetic figures such as President Woodrow Wilson and dominion leaders impressing on Britain the need for a settlement. The post-war context was important also in the sphere of political thought, with popular enthusiasm for Wilsonian national self-determination strengthening the challenge to empire in Europe and beyond.[62]

What did republican violence achieve? While there was no question of forcing a British withdrawal, the IRA's ability to sustain an effective armed campaign, exemplified by the wiping out of an elite auxiliary unit at Kilmichael in November 1921, shook British public and political opinion. Army generals made clear that suppression of the IRA would require politically unacceptable methods: 'we shall have to do to Southern Ireland what we did to South Africa – barbed wire, blockhouses, drives, concentration camps, and the sweeping up of the population'.[63] Dublin Castle's pragmatic administrators also pressed for a political settlement. Although dismaying hardliners on both sides, the government's eventual shift from Home Rule to dominion self-government proved sufficient to secure a settlement. Republican violence played a significant role in winning Irish self-government, but British power ensured that Ireland ultimately left the union on British terms, which included the partition of the island and membership of the Empire. Beyond Ireland, this outcome was viewed as a remarkable achievement, particularly by anticolonial nationalists. Within Ireland, the failure to achieve a republic led to a vicious civil war followed by decades of rancour.

---

62 E. Manela, *The Wilsonian Moment: Self-Determination and the International Origins of Anticolonial Nationalism* (Oxford, Oxford University Press, 2007).
63 A. Dolan, 'Killing in "the Good Old Irish Fashion": Irish Revolutionary Violence in Context', *Irish Historical Studies* 44/165 (May 2020).

The Northern Irish Troubles, 1969–1998

Reconfiguring rather than resolving the Irish Question, the 1921 Anglo-Irish Treaty shifted the conflict over sovereignty to Northern Ireland, where unionists formed a substantial majority. Despite sporadic anti-Treaty IRA violence directed at the (Southern) Irish Free State after its defeat in the Civil War, the election of an anti-Treaty republican government in 1932 marginalised the IRA, as did the establishment of an Irish Republic in 1949. Subsequent republican violence, centring on partition, failed to mobilise significant southern support (as was demonstrated by the IRA's ineffective 1956–62 border campaign). But in Northern Ireland, where nationalists were excluded from power and subject to discrimination, political violence re-emerged after the failure of tentative unionist efforts to reform the state. External factors, including pressure from London and the inspiration of global civil rights movements in 1968, contributed to this crisis.[64] In 1969 loyalist attacks on civil rights protestors escalated into widespread disorder as Belfast Catholics were burned out of their homes. Communal violence was curbed only by the deployment of British soldiers, who were initially welcomed by Catholics.

Emerging from this chaos, the militant Provisional IRA (hereafter IRA) eclipsed the more left-wing 'Official' IRA from which it split. Inept British military responses, including the Falls Road curfew (July 1970), internment (August 1971) and Bloody Sunday (January 1972) inflamed nationalist opinion and boosted IRA recruitment. By 1972, when violence peaked at almost 500 deaths, riotous disorder had given way to a more concerted strategy of bombings and assassination, with the IRA heralding the car bomb as the weapon that would win the war.[65] 'Bloody Friday', on 21 July 1972, saw 20 bombs detonated across Belfast within 75 minutes, killing 9 and injuring 130. Violence returned to Britain when Westminster and the Tower of London were bombed in 1974. Displaying greater disregard for innocent life than their Fenian predecessors, the IRA's pub bombings in Guildford and Birmingham killed 25 people. Loyalist paramilitaries responded in kind: their targeting of Catholic civilians was intended not merely to pressure republicans but also the British government, whose 1972 truce with the IRA raised the spectre of British withdrawal. Following the collapse of a power-sharing initiative between moderate unionists and nationalists in 1974, and the failure of further talks with republicans in 1975, the IRA adopted a 'long war' strategy. Aiming

---

64 S. Prince, *Northern Ireland's '68: Civil Rights, Global Revolt and the Origins of the Troubles* (Dublin, Irish Academic Press, 2018 ed.).
65 B. Hanley, 'Terror in Twentieth-Century Ireland', in Fitzpatrick (ed.), *Terror*, p. 20.

to limit the conflict to what one British Home Secretary described as 'an acceptable level of violence', policies such as 'Ulsterisation' (police primacy) and 'normalisation' sought to contain the violence of the Troubles within Northern Ireland, where its political impact was limited. Enduring until 1998, the Troubles resulted in over 3,500 deaths.

What was the purpose of IRA violence, and how was it perceived by broader nationalist opinion? While the defence of besieged Catholics initially formed a key rationale, the IRA's ambitions soared, with each successive year during the early 1970s greeted as 'the year of victory'. The proroguing of the discredited Unionist regime in 1972 (blamed by London for the failure of security policy) and the British government's willingness to negotiate with the IRA made withdrawal (contemplated in the mid-1970s by the Labour Prime Minister Harold Wilson) appear feasible, further incentivising IRA violence. Heartened by the success of national liberation movements in Cyprus and Algeria, republicans saw the restoration of direct rule as placing 'the "Irish question" in its true perspective – an alien power seeking to lay claim to a country for which it has no legal right'.[66] These colonial interpretations were often shared by British army officers whose approach was informed by recent experiences in Kenya and Aden rather than historical Irish precedents.[67] The IRA also depicted its campaign as a defensive response to the structural injustices of partition, discrimination and state/loyalist violence. Conversely, its critics identified the IRA as primarily responsible for sustaining the conflict, depicting the British army as reluctant peacekeepers rather than colonial oppressors. While the notion of a defensive struggle was rendered less plausible by the escalation of IRA violence, the idea of republican agency as the key driver of conflict overlooks how the 'capacity of the British state and the shaping pressure of unionist resistance to British policy were much more significant sources of coercive power than was IRA violence'.[68] The security forces, for example, searched 300,000 houses in the early 1970s, interned 2,000 people and imprisoned over 20,000 paramilitaries. Over the course of the Troubles, 300,000 troops served in Northern Ireland, with Royal Ulster Constabulary (RUC) and Ulster Defence Regiment (UDR) membership reaching 20,000 by the mid-1980s.

---

66 P. Bew, *Ireland: The Politics of Enmity 1789–2006* (Oxford, Oxford University Press, 2008), pp. 508–9.
67 H. Strachan, *The Politics of the British Army* (Oxford, Oxford University Press, 1997), pp. 181–2.
68 N. Ó Dochartaigh, 'Northern Ireland since 1920', in Bourke and MacBride (eds.), *Modern Ireland*, pp. 152–3.

How much support existed for republican violence? Within working-class urban estates, such as Ballymurphy in west Belfast (where 1,000 men and women were imprisoned), and rural heartlands like South Armagh, deep communal support existed for the IRA: community defence, republican ideological goals and the impact of state repression were key motives.[69] Beyond such communities, support was more limited. Republicans formed a zealous minority within a larger nationalist community, which was itself a minority within the northern state, undermining the IRA's claim to a popular mandate. The shift from communal defence to more aggressive tactics further eroded support. With most northern nationalists sharing the 'revulsion, outrage and shame' expressed by the moderate nationalist Social Democratic and Labour Party (SDLP) after IRA atrocities, the 'condemnation, exclusion, and calculated isolation of the Provisionals helped give the movement something of the character of an angry militant sect, increasingly isolated and marginalized by the late 1970s'.[70]

Beyond Northern Ireland, the IRA's methods also hindered efforts to build support. As in the 1860s, a bombing campaign in Britain marginalised the Irish community there, which was subject to discrimination and miscarriages of justice. IRA violence saw mainstream British press coverage, which had been critical of the treatment of Northern Irish Catholics in the late 1960s, revert to a traditional pro-unionist line. Republican violence proved less alienating in America although, as in the 1880s, Irish-born immigrants provided the key activists within the IRA's support networks.[71] In political terms, however, the SDLP's John Hume proved more successful in mobilising Irish-American political support, with significant long-term consequences.

The counterproductive impact of IRA violence was most evident in the Irish Republic, where the Troubles initially generated much solidarity with northern Catholics. Bloody Sunday, for example, prompted extensive protests, culminating in the burning of the British Embassy. Atrocities like Bloody Friday, however, ensured that the IRA came to be viewed as the principal aggressors. Although elements within the Irish state had initially assisted the Provisionals (in preference to the more left-wing 'Officials'), the realisation that the Troubles threatened the Southern state, alongside genuine revulsion at republican violence, saw the near universal condemnation of the IRA by Southern politicians. It was widely asserted that the Provisionals

---

69 Ó Dochartaigh, 'Northern Ireland', p. 154.
70 R. English, *Irish Freedom: The History of Irish Nationalism* (London, Macmillan, 2006), p. 397; Ó Dochartaigh, 'Northern Ireland', p. 154.
71 English, *Armed Struggle*, p. 117.

shared little in common with their revolutionary predecessors who had enjoyed democratic support and eschewed terrorist methods. Arguing that the Troubles resulted from a poisonous virus rooted in veneration of 'the cult of 1916', influential intellectuals such as the government minister Conor Cruise O'Brien developed a more radical critique, attempting to forge a new nationalist consensus based on the rejection of republican violence, past and present, and an acknowledgement of unionists' right to self-determination. While hugely controversial, such 'revisionism' would dramatically reconfigure popular attitudes to political violence and partition over the longer term.[72]

Republican propagandists refuted any distinction between the Provisional IRA and its predecessors: 'the objective remains unchanged. The strategy remains unchanged. Only the tactics are different – but not all that different – and, of course, the weapons.'[73] The belief that Southern repudiation of the IRA rested on a denial of the Irish State's own violent origins led Sinn Féin to publish a remarkable pamphlet detailing the killing of informers, women and civilians during the War of Independence in order 'to confront those hypocritical revisionists who winsomely refer to the "Old IRA" whilst deriding their more effective and, arguably, less bloody successors'.[74] Even committed republicans occasionally struggled to maintain this line. Reflecting on the fate of three young Scottish soldiers, lured by women from a city-centre bar to their deaths in 1971, one IRA leader conceded 'it was not the type of job Patrick Pearse would have done'.[75]

Was the Provisional IRA, as many Southerners believed, more vicious or sectarian than its predecessors? Republican paramilitaries killed around 60 per cent of the Troubles' 3,500 fatalities, but the 'old IRA' accounted for a not insignificant 46 per cent of 2,141 fatalities between 1917 and 1921. Occurring in the most religiously divided region of Ireland, the Troubles was inevitably more sectarian than the War of Independence, but the earlier revolutionary conflict in Ulster – pitting the IRA against the Ulster Special Constabulary, and accompanied by extensive communal violence – had been shaped by similar dynamics. The most striking statistic calling into question clear moral distinctions between the two conflicts was the high proportion of civilian fatalities in each: non-combatants accounted for 48 per cent of

---

72 M. O'Callaghan, 'Conor Cruise O'Brien and the Northern Ireland Conflict: Formulating a Revisionist Position', *Irish Political Studies* 33/2 (2018).
73 B. Hanley, *The Impact of the Troubles on the Republic of Ireland, 1968–79: Boiling Volcano?* (Manchester, Manchester University Press, 2018), p. 166.
74 Hanley, 'Terror', p. 14.   75 Ibid., p. 19.

fatalities in 1917–21, compared to 52 per cent during the Troubles.⁷⁶ Perhaps the key factor driving Southern nationalist hostility to the IRA was revulsion at the bombing of civilian targets, the consequences of which were graphically brought home by television coverage. 'Can anyone now believe that anything worthwhile can be established by these methods?', asked the *Irish Times* after Bloody Friday.⁷⁷ Tom Barry, a legendary War of Independence leader who had initially supported the Provisional IRA, declared that he 'wouldn't have done the Birmingham job … if it was going to set Ireland free and flowing with milk and honey'.⁷⁸

How did the British state respond to IRA violence? Following the disastrous blunders of the early 1970s, British coercion was more effectively targeted against republicans rather than the wider nationalist community. As in earlier Irish conflicts, greater reliance on unconventional forces resulted in an essentially covert war. Adapting techniques inspired by recent colonial rather than Irish conflicts, shadowy counterinsurgency units (such as the Force Research Unit) operated with little oversight. Echoing 1920–1 controversies over reprisals, allegations of shoot-to-kill tactics saw efforts to formalise the use of lethal force with the introduction of the Special Air Service (SAS) in 1976. Britain's success in penetrating paramilitary organisations prompted similar dilemmas to the 1880s. A blind eye was turned to the murderous actions of informers such as Freddie Scappaticci, head of the IRA's internal security, if these were seen to marginalise militant republicans. Of 210 loyalist paramilitaries arrested during investigations into state collusion, a remarkable 207 were state agents or informants, calling into question the legality of the British state's actions.⁷⁹ British agents such as Brian Nelson, the modern-day equivalent of agents provocateurs, passed military intelligence to loyalists, facilitating the assassination of troublesome civilians such as the solicitor Pat Finucane. From the late 1980s, such collusion saw loyalists more effectively target non-combatant republicans in mid-Ulster, weakening the IRA's resolve.⁸⁰ Although the British Prime Minister David Cameron subsequently acknowledged 'frankly shocking levels of state collusion', the British security services' obstruction of investigations makes it difficult to evaluate its scale, and the level at which it was authorised.⁸¹ But, as in earlier

---

76 E. O'Halpin, 'Counting Terror: Bloody Sunday and the Dead of the Irish Revolution', in Fitzpatrick (ed.), *Terror*, p. 153; Sutton Index of Deaths, Conflict Archive on the Internet, https://cain.ulster.ac.uk/sutton/.
77 *Irish Times*, 22 July 1972.   78 Hanley, *Boiling Volcano*, p. 177.
79 *Panorama: Britain's Secret Terror* (BBC, 2015).
80 *Spotlight on the Troubles: A Secret History* (BBC, 2019).   81 Keefe, *Say Nothing*, p. 312.

conflicts, senior intelligence figures also used their contacts with republicans and Whitehall influence to press for the necessity of a political initiative. Like their predecessors, they were often favourably impressed by the calibre of IRA leaders such as Martin McGuinness: 'rather like talking to a middle-ranking British army officer from one of the tougher regiments like the Paras or SAS'.[82]

The emergence of prisons as sites of conflict capable of mobilising sufficient public support to effect far-reaching political developments represented another parallel with earlier conflicts. Comparable to the election of Easter rebels in Sinn Féin's 1917 by-election victories, the election to Westminster of IRA hunger striker Bobby Sands in 1981 reoriented a militaristic movement towards politics. Conscious of the precedent offered by the fate of Terence MacSwiney, republicans were more attuned than their opponents to the propaganda potential of the hunger strike, which centred on the prisoners' demand for the restoration of political status. Sands's funeral, one of the largest in republican history, demonstrated the enduring appeal of sacrificial violence. Rather than an endorsement of armed struggle, popular nationalist support for Sands represented a repudiation of Margaret Thatcher's intransigence and her characterisation of political violence as crime, sentiments rooted in the belief that Britain's presence in Ireland lacked legitimacy.

Although often directly linked to the peace process, by radicalising a younger generation and broadening the social basis of the republican movement, the hunger strikes helped to sustain seventeen further years of conflict. But the trajectory resulting from the gradual dominance of the republican movement's political wing led in only one direction. By the late 1980s some republicans acknowledged publicly the trouble with guns. Despite maintaining the need to 'sicken' Britain into withdrawal,[83] the subtle reframing of the campaign as one for 'equal citizenship' and 'parity of esteem' (in addition to national unity) signalled both greater realism and a growing acceptance that Irish unionism rather than British colonialism represented the principal obstacle to reunification. While particular forms of violence, such as the sniping of soldiers in South Armagh, the Downing Street mortar attack or the devastation wrought by enormous truck bombs in London's financial sector, continued to yield various dividends, the quotidian slaughter on Northern Irish streets was increasingly acknowledged as futile. Atrocities such as the Enniskillen bombing, which killed eleven civilians at

---

82 Quoted in P. Taylor, *Brits: The War Against the IRA* (London, Bloomsbury, 2001), p. 316.
83 Ó Dochartaigh, 'Northern Ireland', p. 159.

a Remembrance ceremony in 1987, led some republicans to question the morality and utility of further conflict. Such inevitable 'mistakes', an ever expanding range of 'legitimate targets', and ruthless innovations such as the use of 'human bombs' eroded grassroots support: '"Armed struggle" became a declining asset for republicanism as it came to be seen less as a form of "popular guerrilla warfare" and more as "terrorism".'[84]

As in 1921, Britain held out the lure of talks while turning the screw: penetration by spies and informers, mounting loyalist violence (surpassing that of the IRA by the early 1990s) and military successes in active areas such as east Tyrone indicated that the IRA was running out of road. Questioning whether they had been deafened by the 'deadly sound of their own gunfire', Sinn Féin leaders publicly contemplated an end to armed struggle, acknowledging that it would result in a potentially transformative political process rather than British withdrawal.[85] Reminiscent of de Valera's struggle to persuade his anti-Treaty supporters to participate in Irish Free State politics after the Civil War, a disciplined republican leadership embarked on a tortuous process to build support for concessions that would previously have been denounced as treachery. Originating in talks between Hume and Adams, and between officials and politicians in Dublin, London and Washington, imaginative initiatives sought to reconcile the need for unionist consent for reunification with republican commitment to the principle of national self-determination. A broad alignment with northern nationalism, the Irish state, and Irish America, reminiscent of late nineteenth-century 'new departures', was crucial in persuading republicans to end violence. A seemingly trivial matter, the granting of a visa to Adams to visit the US, demonstrated how Irish-American pressure and post-Cold War geopolitical shifts prompted the US government's willingness to internationalise what was previously regarded as an internal British matter.[86]

Other than lost lives and immeasurable misery, what did Irish republicans' longest and bloodiest campaign achieve? SDLP leader Seamus Mallon's withering description of the 1998 Good Friday Agreement as 'Sunningdale for slow learners' memorably conveyed how its central features – devolved power-sharing with an all-Ireland dimension – were achievable by 1974. The question of whether the ends justified the means had also preoccupied many after the War of Independence despite the more transformative nature of the

---

84 M. Mulholland, 'Irish Republican Politics and Violence Before the Peace Process, 1968–1994', *European Review of History* 14/3 (2007), p. 397.
85 R. Alonso, *The IRA and Armed Struggle* (Abingdon, Routledge, 2007), p. 189.
86 English, *Armed Struggle*, pp. 304–5.

1921 settlement. In both cases, militant republicans felt the outcome did not justify the violence endured and inflicted. Among the Good Friday Agreement's sharpest critics were disillusioned republicans such as Bernadette Sands McKevitt, who declared that her brother 'Bobby did not die for cross-border bodies with executive powers'.[87]

But there were important differences between Sunningdale, intended to marginalise the extremes, and the Good Friday Agreement, which constructed an international settlement around them. For all its weaknesses, its ingenuity lay in fashioning a structure capable of containing competing national aspirations. In shifting a zero-sum conflict over sovereignty from the sphere of violence to politics, it permitted the normalisation of Northern Irish society, albeit at the cost of hollowing out the political centre ground and entrenching sectarian divisions. From a republican perspective, the agreement delivered substantial reforms in areas such as policing, whose inequities dated back to partition, while allowing for future constitutional advances. Moreover, as de Valera had discovered in the 1920s, abandoning violence could reap electoral dividends: within three years of the agreement, Sinn Féin had replaced the SDLP as the largest party of northern nationalism. The confidence with which republicans asserted ownership of an agreement crafted by their moderate nationalist rival Hume contrasted with the defeatism demonstrated by northern unionists whose vision had rarely extended beyond maintaining an untenable status quo. As the British Prime Minister Tony Blair caustically observed, Northern Irish unionists 'are too stupid to realise they have won and SF too clever to admit they've lost'.[88]

Conclusion

Does the long sweep of republican history reveal a calculus of political violence? Although a near constant of the Irish political landscape, violence was rarely popular. Given its comparatively modest scale in Ireland, there is a need for greater understanding of the restraints on violence.[89] The forms violence took shaped public responses in ways that were difficult to predict or instrumentalise. Violence bereft of strategic purpose could yield political gains, while brutally effective tactics could lead to condemnation. The effectiveness of violence, more likely to delegitimise than validate the

---

87 *Irish Times*, 8 January 1998.
88 A. Campbell, *Diaries*, Vol. 3: *Power and Responsibility*, 25 June 1999 (London, Hutchinson, 2011), p. 66.
89 English, *Irish Freedom*, pp. 382–3.

cause, was generally overestimated. Shifting cultural attitudes were evident over time; by the end of the Troubles, few agreed with Pearse that 'bloodshed is a cleansing and a sanctifying thing'.[90] Mobilising a nationalist consensus around the desirability of independence rather than transformation of the state or society, political violence tended towards socially conservative outcomes even if radical ideals motivated many activists.

Although seldom appealing to more than a zealous minority, violence could win mass support when existing structures were perceived to illegitimately impede political progress. However, the gravitational pull of politics invariably lured and divided republican movements, much to the disappointment of purists. Wielded against a superior power, the utility of republican violence lay primarily in its impact as armed propaganda on popular nationalism and the British state. Most effective when provoking disproportionate responses, republican violence subverted the British state's liberal values,[91] exposing its lack of legitimacy in Ireland. Republicans could point to the 1921 and 1998 settlements as evidence that violence was effective – even necessary – in advancing self-determination and addressing communal grievances.

By generating international publicity, and focusing British attention on Ireland, violence could also prove effective by stimulating initiatives, effecting policy shifts and mobilising pressure for political settlements.[92] But violence led to change only when channelled into a realistic programme capable of mobilising broad nationalist and international support: only through democratic means could republicans liquidate 'the otherwise unrecoverable political capital amassed by the gunmen'.[93] Knowing when to abandon the diminishing returns of violence, and how to retain grassroots support during the transition to politics, was vital. An identification with violent means (as part of a broader rejection of British rule and an alternative claim to sovereignty) could also result in the eclipse of nationalist rivals, as demonstrated by the demise of the Irish Party (during a period of armed struggle) and decline of the SDLP (following the cessation of violence).

90 P. Pearse, 'The Coming Revolution', in *Political Writings and Speeches* (Dublin, Phoenix, 1924), p. 99.
91 English, *Does Terrorism Work?*
92 C. Townshend, *The British Campaign in Ireland, 1919–21* (Oxford, Oxford University Press, 1975), p. 206; R. Fanning, *Fatal Path: British Government and Irish Revolution 1910–1922* (London, Faber and Faber, 2013), p. 4.
93 A. Jackson, *Home Rule: An Irish History 1800–2000* (London, Weidenfeld & Nicholson, 2003), p. 287. On the process by which republican organisations have moderated their strategy without necessarily abandoning ideological goals, see M. Whiting, *Sinn Féin and the IRA: From Revolution to Moderation* (Edinburgh, Edinburgh University Press, 2018).

How do we explain the longevity of political violence in Ireland? A history of sectarian enmity is frequently identified as the principal culprit. Observing how 'the dreary steeples of Fermanagh and Tyrone' emerged with 'the integrity of their quarrel' intact after the deluge of the Great War had transformed the map of Europe, Winston Churchill lamented how atavistic hatreds enabled the Irish 'to hold, dominate, and convulse, year after year, generation after generation, the politics of this powerful country'.[94] For republican organisations, resistance to British rule formed part of a similarly timeless spirit. But British characterisations of Irish violence as the product of ancient hatreds usefully obscure the responsibility of the most powerful agent in shaping conflict in Ireland, just as the heroic continuities suggested by an unyielding struggle dating back to the misty origins of Irish nationhood conveniently legitimise the actions of movements whose violence rarely commanded popular support.[95] Scholars have also depicted the physical-force tradition as irrational. Fenian reasoning 'cannot be construed as a rational response to British domination, physical or cultural', Charles Townshend has argued, 'or even the emotional power of republican ideology, but only by an inheritance of communal assumptions validating its methods as much as its ends'. More persuasively, he observed, its persistence 'indicates the limitations of political talk'.[96]

Ultimately, any convincing explanation for political violence will remain untidy, incorporating a complex range of elements including the agency of revolutionaries and importance of ideology. As John Connelly notes in his compelling study of Eastern European nationalisms (with which the Irish variant shares much in common): 'as soon as patriots created national languages, nationalism itself became the language of politics'.[97] Central to the 'power of nationalist arguments to drive political imagination' is the importance of a deep level of popular historical memory which, although manipulated by patriots to imagine nations into being, was not simply invented.[98] This process was often a reaction to the pressures of modernisation, with resentment and humiliation of subjugation shaping the identities of

---

94 *Hansard*, HC Deb. vol. 150, col. 1270–1. In reality, post-war Wilsonian self-determination radically changed the terms of conflict between nationalists, unionists and the British state.
95 R. V. Comerford, 'Fenianism: The Scope and Limitations of a Concept', in F. McGarry and J. McConnel (eds.), *The Black Hand of Republicanism: Fenianism in Modern Ireland* (Dublin, Irish Academic Press, 2009).
96 Townshend, *Political Violence*, pp. viii–ix.
97 J. Connelly, *From Peoples into Nations: A History of Eastern Europe* (Princeton, Princeton University Press, 2020), pp. 19–20.
98 Ibid., pp. 21, 788.

national peoples on the edge of empire who strove for self-assertion against foreign domination.[99]

Rather than an atavistic tradition periodically erupting from the sectarian swamps of mid-Ulster, Irish political violence may be more convincingly understood as closely bound up with modernity. Niall Ó Dochartaigh has observed how the Provisional IRA's insistence on holding courts martial reflected a desire to legitimate itself through adherence to liberal democratic norms: 'While fanatical mind-sets and frozen ideologies were often identified as the defining features and driving forces behind the IRA, it is its bureaucratic structure, complexity, and the essential modernity of the organization that best explains its strength and persistence.'[100] A striking feature of many republican organisations was the importance placed on democratic and administrative structures: republican movements responded to changing ideas of popular sovereignty, mirroring the development of the modern state whose power it contested. The most successful not only aimed at achieving independence, they mimicked the British state, sought to control territory, established courts and claimed the authority of an established government. As Martyn Frampton notes elsewhere, 'terrorism and democracy have frequently gone hand in hand'.[101] Rather than an ancient island story, the long view suggests that the contours of Irish political violence were shaped by contemporary global developments as the age of empire gave way to the modern nation state. Transnational activism, cultural transfers and other international pressures including shifting norms of democracy and sovereignty frequently shaped political violence in Ireland.[102]

Partition, central to political violence in Ireland over the past century, offers one example of how political settlements were rendered unsustainable by evolving international norms. The depiction of the partition of Ireland in 1920 as a regrettable evil, reluctantly implemented by British administrators to effect 'an orderly transfer of power' to placate the irreconcilable demands of rival violent nationalisms obscures how it was the product of a particular historical moment 'that privileged ethnic nationalisms ... as the building blocks of a modern world order'.[103] Although partition exacerbated violence and division in Ireland, subsequent historians 'presented a paradigm which

---

99 Ibid., p. 798.   100 Ó Dochartaigh, 'Northern Ireland', pp. 154–5.
101 In this volume, p. 55.
102 R. Bourke, *Peace in Ireland: The War of Ideas* (London, Pimlico, 2003).
103 A. Dubnov and L. Robson, 'Introduction', in A. Dubnov and L. Robson (eds.), *Partitions: A Transnational History of Twentieth-Century Territorial Separatism* (Stanford, Stanford University Press, 2019), pp. 17, 27.

saw Ulster as a place of enduring and endemic sectarian strife, and partition less its cause than its result'.[104] In reality, the rationale shaping both Irish partition and the 1921 Anglo-Irish Treaty was the creation of new forms of informal British imperial authority rather than the fulfilment of democratic aspirations within Ireland.

Rather than irrational sectarian passions, it was the superseding of majoritarian understandings of democracy by internationally accepted principles of equality of citizenship that initially destabilised the Northern Irish state in the 1960s. Northern nationalist demands for 'British' civil rights created far more instability than the IRA's preceding border campaign, while the emergence of mass paramilitary organisations in the 1970s was a product rather than cause of Northern Ireland's 'descent into violent conflict'.[105] In contrast, political violence in Southern Ireland was marginalised from the 1930s, when it was demonstrated that the state's structures permitted the pursuit of full self-determination through political means. Not until 1998 did the Northern Irish state achieve something similar. If the Good Friday Agreement has a lesson to impart beyond Ireland, it concerns not merely the feasibility but the necessity of political solutions to the most intractable conflicts. The significance of political violence as 'an ineradicable theme of modern Irish history' rests primarily in the light it sheds on broader questions about Irish nationalism, the relationship between Ireland and Britain and the nature of the British state in Ireland, whose weak foundations rested more on coercion than consent.[106]

Further Reading

R. English, *Armed Struggle: The History of the IRA* (London, Pan, 2012)
R. English, *Irish Freedom: The History of Irish Nationalism* (London, Macmillan, 2006)
F. McGarry, *The Rising: Ireland, Easter 1916* (Oxford, Oxford University Press, 2010)
C. Townshend, *The Republic: The Fight for Irish Independence* (London, Allen Lane, 2013)
N. Whelehan, *The Dynamiters: Irish Nationalism and Political Violence in the Wider World, 1867–1900* (Cambridge, Cambridge University Press, 2012)

104 R. Lynch, *The Partition of Ireland* (Cambridge, Cambridge University Press, 2019), p. 8.
105 A. Guelke, 'Northern Ireland, Brexit, and the Interpretation of Self-Determination', *Nationalism and Ethnic Politics* 25/4 (2019), p. 388.
106 M. Mulholland, 'Political Violence', in Bourke and MacBride (eds.), *Modern Ireland*, p. 382.

12

Terrorism in the Russian Empire
The Late Nineteenth and Early Twentieth Centuries

EKATERINA STEPANOVA[1]

Russia was an integral part of the modern world's first historical wave of terrorism, which lasted from the final third of the nineteenth century to the first decades of the twentieth century. Some historians and terrorism experts even consider the Russian Empire to be the 'birthplace' of terrorism.[2] Indeed, in Russia, terrorism as a systematic tactic of revolutionary strategy, with its own ideological justification and organisational framework, took shape in 1869–81, is usually dated back to Sergei Nechayev's 'Catechism of a Revolutionary' and was developed and applied in practice by the Narodnaya Volya ('People's Will') organisation. By the start of the twentieth century, terrorist bombings in British India, the Balkans and elsewhere were often referred to as 'the Russian way', or 'the Russian method'.[3] Along with anarchist terrorism in Europe, which started to spread roughly at the same time, and the early resort to terrorist means by some national liberation and anti-colonial movements (in the Austro-Hungarian, Ottoman and British empires), Russian revolutionary terrorism of the late nineteenth century was certainly one of the first identifiable forms and clear manifestations of modern terrorism. That alone merits special attention to the phenomenon of pre-revolution terrorism in Russia.

This volume combines historical, theoretical and various national case-study perspectives. In addition to highlighting the specifics of a historical/

---

[1] Lead researcher and Head, Peace and Conflict Studies Unit, Primakov National Research Institute of World Economy and International Relations (IMEMO), Russian Academy of Sciences, stepanova@imemo.ru, www.estepanova.net.
[2] W. Laqueur, *Terrorism* (Boston, Little, Brown and Co., 1977), p. 11.
[3] Y. Varfolomeyev, '"Russkii sposob": fenomen revolutsionnogo terrorizma v Rossii nachala 20 v.' ['"The Russian Way": The Phenomenon of Revolutionary Terrorism in Early Twentieth-Century Russia'], *Rossiiskii istoricheskii zhurnal* [*Russian Journal of History*] 2 (2008); R. Jensen, 'Anarchist Terrorism and Counterterrorism in Europe and the World, 1878–1934', in R. D. Law (ed.), *The Routledge History of Terrorism* (London, Routledge, 2015).

national case, this also makes it possible to address the history of terrorism in Russia in two comparative dimensions. Placing the Russian case in a global historical context allows us to assess the extent to which its national experience forms, conforms to or deviates from global trends in terrorism. However, Russia's own case calls for historical comparison, as it displays two very distinct periods of intense terrorist activity, with almost a century between them: one in the Russian Empire in the late nineteenth to early twentieth century (addressed in this chapter) and another in post-Soviet Russia, in the late 1990s to early 2010s, which is the subject of the next chapter.

Definition and Concept of Terrorism

In this chapter and in the next one, terrorism is understood as 'premeditated use of violence by non-state actors against civilian and other non-combatant targets intended to create broader intimidation and destabilisation effects in order to achieve political goals by exercising pressure on the state and society'.[4] What distinguishes terrorism from criminal, profit-driven violence is its political goal. What makes terrorism different from rebel violence employed by non-state actors directly against government military and security forces in the context of ongoing armed conflict is its primary focus on political, civilian and other non-combatant targets. Finally, what distinguishes terrorism from such types of political violence as repressive state terror, genocide, ethnic, sectarian, class-based and other 'cleanses', and inter-communal violence is its asymmetrical, communicative, 'force multiplier' tactics. Terrorist methods are specifically designed to create political effect that goes far beyond the terrorists' immediate victims and is ultimately intended to affect and exercise pressure on a more potent actor – the state.

The extent to which this contemporary definition of terrorism applies, retrospectively, to the rise and fall of terrorism in the late imperial period of Russian history requires some clarification. Also, certain reservations have to be made about what this chapter (and the following one) are *not* about.

The fact that, in the nineteenth century, the first interpreters of the term 'terrorism' were terrorists and revolutionary ideologues themselves, and their main political opponents governments and state security structures, ensured a high degree of politicisation of the term and produced a lot of

---

4 E. Stepanova, *Terrorism in Asymmetrical Conflict: Ideological and Structural Aspects* (Oxford, Oxford University Press, 2008), pp. 13–20.

confusion about it, some of which persisted through the early twenty-first century. This included interchangeable use of the terms 'terrorism' and 'terror' or the use of either or both of them as a synonym of any intra-state political violence. This, however, should not prevent a modern researcher from defining the term 'terrorism' in a politically neutral, academic way and distinguishing it from other forms of political violence with which it was and is still confused.

The first clarification is particularly important in the Russian case. It is the distinction between revolutionary, anti-government terrorism and the use of terror methods by the state. Both in this chapter and in the following one, terrorism is understood as one of the violent tactics employed by *non-state actors only*. The notion of 'terror' is reserved for repressive, including violent, actions by the state against the society (individuals, social groups or the population at large). This includes terror by a 'revolutionary' state, i.e. by former revolutionaries *after* they came to power. This applies to the Jacobins in France in the late eighteenth century, the Bolsheviks in power in the former Russian Empire after 1917 and the Red Khmers in power in Cambodia in the mid-1970s alike. While, historically, Russia heavily suffered from, and became notorious for, prolonged periods of 'state terror', that is *not* the primary object of study in this chapter.

A popular assumption, also widespread in academic literature, is that state terror and anti-government terrorism by non-state actors are closely inter-linked. The two are often seen as mutually conditioned[5] and sometimes treated as interdependent variables in a closed system where more state repression always causes more terrorism, and vice versa. This claim, how-ever, appears to hold only partially and only for historical periods when some space for political activity exists, including periods of transition. For Russia, the link between non-state terrorism and state terror is quite relevant to the late tsarist period. It is even more relevant in the context of the armed conflict in the North Caucasus in the post-Soviet period covered in the next chapter. However, this link does not hold for much of twentieth-century Soviet Russia. In particular, the era of mass repressions under the rule of Joseph Stalin in the 1930s to early 50s was the worst period of domestic state terror in Russian history (at least since the later stage of Ivan the Terrible's rule in the sixteenth century), but did not see any major domestic terrorist activity.

---

5 D. Della Porta, 'On Violence and Repression: A Relational Approach', *Government and Opposition* 49/2 (2014); N. Naimark, 'Terrorism and the Fall of Imperial Russia', *Terrorism and Political Violence* 2/2 (1990).

The second reservation concerns a tendency, both in primary historical sources and in much of scholarly work on terrorism in the Russian Empire, to confuse terrorism either with revolutionary struggle as a whole or with any use of violence by political opponents of the government.[6] While it is important to follow the sources, there is no need for a modern analyst to join the nineteenth- and early twentieth-century revolutionaries and their antagonists in reducing all anti-government struggle or violence to 'terrorism'. The latter remained only one of the revolutionary movement's tactics and was employed by some groups but not others. For instance, direct combat between state and non-state actors – the exchange of armed violence between revolutionary groups and government security forces (police, gendarmerie, military units) in the context of ongoing armed conflict – should not qualify as terrorism, regardless of how it was labelled by its contemporaries. This also holds if, alongside combat, the same non-state combatants or their more radical factions *also* practised terrorist acts (high-profile, targeted political assassinations, bombings in public places etc.), if they employed a range of different violent tactics at once (combat/guerrilla warfare, terrorism, predator violence) or switched from one to another, depending on the context.

This reservation holds for the late nineteenth to early twentieth century as much as it does for the early twenty-first century. It also fully applies to domestic insurgencies, armed revolts and revolutions (i.e. to what modern International Humanitarian Law defines as 'non-international armed conflict').[7] While in Russia the main case in point has been the use of both combat and terrorism as tactics of the anti-government insurgency in the context and in the aftermath of two wars in Chechnya (in 1994–6 and 1999–2007/8),[8] an earlier historical case had been the first Russian revolution of 1905–7. The state of the sources on patterns of violence during the 1905–7 revolution often does not allow a historian to clearly distinguish between combat and terrorism (i.e. to establish whether a violent act's main intended targets were combatants or non-combatants); combat and terrorist tactics

---

6 A. Geifman, 'Aspects of Early Twentieth-Century Russian Terrorism: The Socialist-Revolutionary Combat Organisation', *Terrorism and Political Violence* 4/2 (1992); R. Hingley, *Nihilists: Russian Radicals and Revolutionaries in the Reign of Alexander II (1855–81)* (London, Weidenfeld and Nicolson, 1967).
7 Additional Protocol II to Geneva Conventions restricted the definition of non-international armed conflict to armed confrontation between state armed forces and organised armed opposition/dissident groups. Protocol Additional to the Geneva Conventions of 12 August 1949, and relating to the Protection of Victims of Non-International Armed Conflicts (Protocol II), 8 June 1977. Art. 1, Para. 1.
8 See next chapter.

were often employed simultaneously by the same groups. However, that does not change the fact that these are two different forms of violence.

The third, asymmetrical and communicative aspect of terrorism distinguishes terrorism as a modern form of political violence, in place since the late nineteenth century, from the individual political assassinations widespread in history and from mass killings and other atrocities committed by armed actors whose immediate victims remained their final targets. In contrast, terrorists' intent is to affect as many as possible by using violence against some or just a few, but in a demonstrative, event-setting and publicly impressive way. From the start, terrorists aimed to trigger political destabilisation and intimidation much broader than direct, physical harm from a terrorist attack and ultimately addressed to their main antagonist – the state. This helps explain why most studies of terrorism date its emergence to the last third of the nineteenth century. As disproportionally high, asymmetrical effect on politics through public, political and media hype from terrorist attacks on official or public figures or other citizens/subjects required real-time information flows, this only became possible at a certain stage of development of information and communication technology. In other words, terrorism, for the world at large and for Russia, is a product of modernity and modernisation.

Research Literature

Historical analysis of terrorism in the Russian Empire is dominated by chronological, factographic, ideographic and descriptive narratives. This is what this chapter seeks to avoid, offering a more critical and analytical perspective.

In Russia, the first quality research on the subject emerged in the post-Soviet period and the body of professional literature has remained limited. Most Soviet literature on the subject hardly met basic academic standards, for reasons ranging from ideological pressure, heavy censorship and absence of academic freedom to sheer lack of access to primary sources and archives.

Much historical evidence and many documents were lost in the flames of the revolution and the civil war or ended up abroad. Surviving direct actors or witnesses – socio-revolutionaries (the SRs), anarchists and radical nationalists who had had first-hand experience in the use and propaganda of terrorist tactics – ended up emigrating. Many of their critics within the revolutionary movement who had stayed in Soviet Russia perished in the civil war, the early Bolshevik terror or the later terror campaigns under Stalin. Security practitioners on the tsarist regime's side, some with solid experience in counterterrorism, were cleansed out and perished as part of their class.

The vast Soviet literature on the revolutionary/anti-tsarist movement notwithstanding, the prevalence of Marxist-Leninist approaches dictated an almost exclusive focus on mass-based upheavals, riots, strikes and propaganda among the working classes, and the connection between the revolutionary organisations, especially socio-democrats (and especially the Bolsheviks), with their 'broader' social base. While some of the early revolutionary terrorists (especially members of Narodnaya Volya) were often portrayed as 'heroes' or even 'iconised', they were not categorised as 'terrorists'. The later the period of terrorist activity in the Russian Empire, the more negative was the assessment of terrorism in the Soviet literature, especially when it came to terrorism by the SRs as the socio-democrats' boisterous rivals on the left, and the more terrorism was described as futile, counterproductive or a substitute for a lack of mass social base. In sum, in line with the Soviet ideological discourse, the tactic of 'individual terrorism' by 'underground conspiracy groups' was completely dismissed. As a result, terrorism as one of the *major* tactics of the Russian revolutionary movement was de-emphasised or neglected.

Hence, academic research work on the subject was primarily conducted in Europe and the United States, mainly by historians. That applies both to the Cold War period, when major studies were done by Hingley (UK), Laqueur (United States), Venturi (Italy) and others, and to more recent works, especially by Naimark and Geifman (United States), Hilbrenner (Germany) et al.

Due to availability of better sources and living witnesses, academic freedom and other standards, and relative lack of ideological bias, most Western literature on the Russian terrorism of the late nineteenth to early twentieth century avoided the defects that tainted the Soviet writings on the subject. However, Western historiography is not free from serious methodological and substantive flaws either, albeit of a different nature. Some of these flaws also surfaced in, or were replicated by, the emerging post-Soviet Russian works.

First, if heavily ideologically loaded Soviet studies de-emphasised the role of terrorism in the Russian revolutionary movement, most Western researchers overestimated, sometimes grossly, its role and place in, and impact on, the revolutionary movement and Russian history in general.

Second, terrorism in pre-revolutionary Russia was systematically confused or conflated with revolutionary struggle and revolutionary violence in general. A typical example is the common depiction of Russian ideologue and practitioner of revolutionary struggle, philosopher and publicist Mikhail Bakunin (1814–76) as a 'terrorist'. This runs against the fact that, while Bakunin called for the 'revolution' and 'revolutionary violence' more generally, none of his multiple practical roles in revolutionary struggle qualified as 'terrorism'.[9]

Third, while the Soviet discourse trumpeted the role of Marxists, especially socio-democrats, in the Russian revolutionary movement, much of the Western literature is heavily biased in favour of the more radical SRs and anarchists and overestimates their overall place and contribution, including through the use of terrorist means, to the fall of tsarism. This also reflects the primary exposure of Western authors to (the influence of) ex-revolutionary émigré sources, where these political segments were over-represented. Description of terrorism in the Russian Empire as largely anarchist and reduction of the Russian revolutionary movement mainly to anarchism[10] are particularly misleading: despite some manifestations of anarchist terrorism, it was never the main form of revolutionary terrorism in Russia. This distortion appears to stem from artificial projection of Europe's own, more typical and historically familiar nineteenth-century experience (which was, indeed, overwhelmed by anarchist terrorism) to the Russian realities.

Fourth, what often escaped Western researchers of Russian terrorism was the difference between a) revolutionary ideologies and ideologues, such as Pyotr Kropotkin (1842–1921), 'godfather' of Russian anarchism, who supported 'propaganda by the deed', which implied any form of active protest, but did not call for or prioritise terrorism, and b) terrorism as a certain violent tactic that may be inspired or employed in the name of various ideologies, but is not necessarily prescribed or predetermined by them. This is not to mention the frequent interchangeable use of the notions of 'terrorism' and 'terror', often in mere replication of the confused patterns of use of these terms in primary sources and by contemporaries during the period in question.

These problems permeate the field, but there are several positive exceptions. While a leading specialist on Russian terrorism at the turn of the nineteenth/twentieth centuries, Anna Geifman, also conflates terrorism with other revolutionary violence, especially in her analysis related to the period of the 1905–7 revolution, and overestimates the role of terrorism in the

---

9 See the subsection on 'Anarchist Terrorism'.
10 Hingley, *Nihilists*; F. Venturi, *Roots of Revolution: A History of the Populist and Socialist Movements in 19th Century Russia* (London, Phoenix Press, 2001).

fall of the empire, she accurately identifies the more systematic nature as a distinctive characteristic of Russian revolutionary terrorism and makes a genuine effort at deromanticising the phenomenon.[11] Richard Jensen points at the specifics of the revolutionary terrorism in Russia vis-à-vis European and North American anarchist terrorism and stresses the complex link between anarchism as an ideology and terrorism as a violent tactic.[12]

While Western scholarship still dominates the field, the balance between it and post-Soviet Russian research is getting better: e.g., historian Oleg Budnitskii not only became the most prominent Russian author on the subject, but also managed to avoid or overcome some of the methodological problems mentioned above.[13]

Causal Explanations

Methodological limitations and confusion have affected explanatory frameworks of terrorism. Systematic conflation of terrorism with revolutionary struggle in the more general sense projected itself into the analysis of causes and explanations of terrorism as just one, albeit the most extreme, of the tactics of revolutionary struggle. This fundamental problem tainted most explanations of Russian terrorism of the nineteenth to early twentieth century in the research literature and is reflected in the dominant 'root causes' approach.[14]

The problem is that most broad, underlying explanations, causes and preconditions (the so-called 'root causes') identified by researchers of Russian terrorism apply to the Russian revolutionary and protest movement *as a whole*. However, this approach hardly explains why some parts of that movement, in certain periods and contexts, systematically resorted to the use of terrorist means, out of the range of other tactics. *Tactics other than terrorism* were widely employed by

---

11 Geifman, 'Aspects of Early Twentieth-Century Russian Terrorism'; A. Geifman, *Thou Shalt Kill: Revolutionary Terrorism in Russia, 1894–1917* (Princeton, Princeton University Press, 1993).
12 Jensen, 'Anarchist Terrorism and Counterterrorism'.
13 O. Budnitskii (ed.), *Istoriia terrorizma v Rossii v dokumentakh, biografiyakh, issledovaniakh* [*History of Terrorism in Russia in Documents, Biographies, Studies*] (Rostov-na-Donu, Feniks, 1996); O. Budnitskii, *Terrorizm v rossiiskom osvoboditel'nom dvizhenii: ideologiya, etika, psikhologiya, vtoraya polovina XIX–nachalo XX v.* [*Terrorism in the Russian Liberation Movement: Ideology, Ethics, Psychology, the Second Half of the 19th–Early 20th Century*] (Moscow, ROSSPEN, 2000).
14 For critiques of this approach, see T. Bjorgo (ed.), *Root Causes of Terrorism: Myths, Reality and Ways Forward* (London, Routledge, 2005), pp. 2–40.

various revolutionary groups and currents (including terrorist actors themselves, such as the SRs who at a certain point switched to, or backed away from, terrorist methods, and combined them with other activities), as well as by social protest forces beyond the more organised revolutionary movement. These activities ranged from widespread non-violent forms (social work among the 'masses', propaganda, demonstrations, marches, strikes) to:

- Direct armed clashes *between* anti-government militants and government military and security forces during the revolution of 1905–7 (that better fall under the category of 'urban guerrilla' than under the notion of 'terrorism');
- Predatory criminal violence employed, to a varying extent, by most revolutionary actors, mainly as a fundraising tactic;
- Mass-based, grassroots riots and disturbances by peasants, workers, students etc., of varying degree of organisation, connection to the revolutionary movement and spontaneity.

At the most fundamental level, the roots of all of the above could be traced to *the same* underlying 'causes', structural problems and deficiencies of the Russian Empire, but none explains any of the variations. The more general and 'deeply rooted' a cause:

- The wider the range of various sociopolitical consequences and implications, of varying scale and gravity, it produces at different levels of social structure and the less directly it is connected with such specific, secondary phenomena as the revolutionaries' choice in favour of one tactic of struggle or another;
- The less dynamic such a 'cause' is, failing to explain ups and downs in resort to terrorism by segments of the Russian revolutionary movement and the interplay of terrorist action and counteraction;
- The more such 'static' causes fail to explain why some revolutionary actors chose to turn to terrorist means (individual political killings, bombing and other attacks in public places), while others did not support or prioritise terrorism, including those who generally accepted the use of violence and even, in the Bolsheviks' case, were more efficient in employing violence as one of the ways to reach their goals. 'Root causes' explanations are less actor-oriented: they underestimate the role of sociopolitical actors who are not just mechanical 'derivatives' of some underlying 'causes', but are conscious actors making wilful choices. There are also counter-actors on the government side whose actions may, in turn, affect the dynamics of

terrorist campaigns and organisations, but whose strategies and tactics/ behaviour may be shaped by factors that go beyond structural, 'root cause' explanations, such as bureaucratic politics, inter-agency tensions or corporate interests.

This does not mean that identifying underlying causes and facilitating conditions of terrorism in the Russian revolutionary movement is futile. While the main structural, or systemic, 'causes' are summarised below, it is useful to keep in mind that they, at best, explain the rise of the revolutionary movement in general – not a turn of its segments to one tactic or another at one stage or another.

All causal historical explanations are multifactorial. However, if the most critical structural cause of the emergence and persistence of the Russian revolutionary movement were to be identified, it would be a complex of factors and implications related to Russia's long overdue, highly uneven, painful and 'traumatic' modernisation. More specifically, the ultimate 'root cause' can be summed up as a fundamental contradiction and growing discrepancy between:

- Intensifying processes of capitalist modernisation since the last third of the nineteenth century that required new, reformed social-political structures, political system and representation of emerging social classes, and respective changes to, and adaptation by, the Russian state and
- The Caesarian, absolutist nature of the Russian monarchy, autarchic, obsolete character of the state, backwardness of Russia's political and administrative system and gross underdevelopment of its social structure, which largely remained that of an agrarian power.

Russia's long-term socio-economic transition to a capitalist system was never completed. It dates back to the liberation of peasants from slavery-type serfdom by Alexander II in 1861. Following the 1860s, that transition involved decades of industrialisation, urbanisation, emergence of new social classes and groups, modern financial, trade, transportation and educational systems, technological and other capitalist-age developments.

The modernisation processes, however, started much later than in Western or Central Europe, in more limited forms and in a less developed, agrarian, almost continent-size country, with a strong prevalence of traditionalist, including (semi-)feudal, social-political structures. This explains the persistent weakness of the emerging capitalist bourgeois class that, in contrast to Britain and France or even to Germany or Italy, had not become the main driver of political change. At the same time, some educational and public/ media space and a limited leeway for modern legal and technocractic/ bureaucratic practices emerged and periodically (re)opened on and off, but gradually expanded in the following decades. Modern liberal and radical ideas and ideologies, including from abroad, mainly Europe, spread more actively. A combination of these factors led to the emergence of a social stratum specific to Russia – the so-called *raznochintsy*, a relatively large number of educated urban intellectuals, professionals and technocrats, mostly with social roots other than the gentry. From the late nineteenth century to the first years of the First World War, the social (sub)class of *raznochintsy* became the main driver of sociopolitical change and revolutionary movement in Russia – not the bourgeoisie in the more classic sense, nor the peasant masses or the nascent working class.

For over half a century, capitalist modernisation in Russia was gaining momentum, in the absence of any political transition to speak of – all the way through to the February 1917 (Bourgeois) Revolution. Tsarism as an archaic type of governance that involved full personification of power and sacrality of the tsar increasingly collided with the evolving needs of the society and the economy. Any periodic attempts at reforming this system 'from the top' were too limited, inconsistent, belated, and did not address the mainstays of the tsarist rule. These facelifts could not produce any real change, but sufficed to (re)open minimal public space for the protest movement and political radicalisation, especially on the part of *raznochintsy*. They were increasingly frustrated with and nihilistic about the existing social order, acutely aware of the 'relative deprivation' of the peasant masses, emerging working class and urban underclass, and conscious about the lack of political representation for educated strata. At the same time, the failure of cosmetic reforms followed by periods of reaction and counter-reforms left few, if any, hopes for any possibility to change the system through incremental, reformist, non-revolutionary means.

While these fundamental controversies explain the rise of the Russian revolutionary movement, the non-linear dynamics, evolution and eventual success of that movement (which, along with other factors, ultimately brought down the Russian Empire) require more contextual explanations that should be the subject of another study.

The need to account for the *dynamics* of sociopolitical processes and changing political *context* and to take an actor-oriented approach is critical in explaining the resort of parts of the broader Russian revolutionary movement to terrorism as one of its main violent tactics. This need is also underscored by the wave-like, fluctuant dynamics of terrorism in the Russian Empire, with periods of surge followed by periods of decline and prevalence of other tactics of struggle. Terrorist campaigns by most radical segments of the revolutionary movement provoked the government's turn to more repressive behaviour, forming a cyclic interplay of terrorist action/government counteraction, with every next cycle deadlier than the previous one. While, in Russia, a degree of support or sympathy for revolutionary terrorism extended beyond the radical milieu to larger segments of the public, it was not just state repression that helped bring down waves of terrorism, but also terrorists' own excesses in the use of violence that often had counterproductive effects for their public support and made their own and other revolutionary groups de-emphasise or abandon this tactic, temporarily or for good.

The imperative to *contextualise* the turn to terrorist means was best summarised by Russia's lead theorist of anarchism, Pyotr Kropotkin, who noted that 'terrorism was generated by certain specific conditions of political struggle in a given historical moment. It was alive, but then died away. It can as well recur and die again.'[15] This imperative shapes the focus of the next section, devoted to the dynamics of the Russian terrorism of the late nineteenth to early twentieth century.

Different ideological-motivational types of terrorism may result from different combinations of drivers (or from similar sets of factors, but in different proportions). They differ in respective groups' main ideologies and final goals. As in other regions, countries and empires that started to face terrorist campaigns in the late nineteenth century, terrorism in the Russian Empire emerged in several types at once. However, in Russia, socio-revolutionary anti-government terrorism absolutely dominated over other types. It also formed a category of its own, compared to anarchist terrorism as the main form of left-wing political violence in Europe and North America, and was more radical, more explicitly revolutionary (anti-government), better organised, more systematic and deadlier. In contrast, while Russia produced several major ideologues of anarchism, anarchist terrorism remained a peripheral phenomenon. By spread and intensity, socio-revolutionary terrorism was followed by the use of terrorist means by the Polish, Armenian and other nationalist-separatist/liberation movements within the Russian Empire. Certain overlap between revolutionary

---

15 P. Kropotkin, *Zapiski revolutsionera* [*Notes of a Revolutionary*] (St Petersburg, 1902), section 'St. Petersburg', part XII, https://ru.theanarchistlibrary.org/library/petr-kropotkin-zapiski-revolyucionera.

(including anarchist) and nationalist-separatist terrorists and their shared opposition to the Russian Empire notwithstanding, they differed in their main political goals. Finally, in the early twentieth century, the first manifestations of right-wing (pro-imperial, loyalist) terrorism emerged in Russia, even though it never came close in scale and resonance to revolutionary and other anti-government terrorism.

Russian Revolutionary Terrorism

Russian revolutionary terrorism developed in waves and had two peaks. The first one fell in the late nineteenth century. It culminated in terrorist activities by the Narodnaya Volya group, including the assassination of Alexander II in March 1881. The second peak was primarily associated with terrorist activities by the Party of Russian Socialists-Revolutionaries in the early 1900s and by the SRs and other revolutionary groups during the first Russian revolution (1905–7).

Early Terrorism and Narodnaya Volya

The early stage of terrorism in Russia evolved from the early 1860s until the early 1870s. It came out in small, often tiny, conspiratorial cells. The more radical ones included Nikolay Ishutin's Moscow circle and Sergei Nechayev's Narodnaya Rasprava ('People's Reprisal'). They produced the first terrorist plots, such as Ishutin's plan to kill the tsar, and the first high-profile, albeit foiled, attack – an attempt by Ishutin's cousin Dmitri Karakozov to assassinate Alexander II in April 1866. However, the main input by these mini-cells into the history of Russian terrorism was less their practical activity and more their first ideological justifications of the systematic use of terrorist means in the name of and as an integral part of the revolutionary struggle.

Student Pyotr Zaichnevsky, following his arrest for spreading banned political materials, was the first to justify regicide, in his pamphlet 'Young Russia' (1861–2).[16] But the first explicit terrorist manifesto was 'Catechism of a Revolutionary' (1868),[17] authored by Sergei Nechayev (1847–82) as a charter for his group Narodnaya Rasprava. The manifesto declared terrorism, understood as political assassinations and other 'terrorising' actions against individuals, a mandatory tactic for any revolutionary group, while leaving regicide to the discretion of 'the people'. It offered the first known specification of

---

16 The full text in Russian is available at www.hist.msu.ru/ER/Etext/molrus.htm.
17 S. Nechayev, 'Katekhizis revolutsionera' ['Catechism of a Revolutionary'] (Geneva, 1868), www.hist.msu.ru/ER/Etext/nechaev.htm.

terrorist targets, singling out two main types: most zealous or economically affluent officials who most actively promote the interests of the state and the ruling classes, and key pro-government public figures. In addition to an 'the end justifies the means' principle, 'Catechism' promoted another main terrorists' thesis for centuries to come – 'the worse, the better': it called to avoid attacks against the most repressive and reactionary representatives of the ruling class, suggesting that the counterproductive effect of their brutal and misguided actions might be critical to provoke the people's uprising.

At this stage, the emerging Russian theory of terrorism was hardly matched with practice. Nechayev's terrorist activity did not go beyond composing the first 'blacklist' of potential targets, ranging from the chief of gendarmerie to well-known publicists and historians. The only assassination by Narodnaya Rasprava – the murder of a student who was its own member – produced public outrage and led to a high-profile trial and a twenty-year sentence for Nechayev.[18]

The counterproductive effect of the excesses of Nechayev's cell set a pattern for the next half a century. It manifested itself not only in the government's response to terrorism (after all, one of the terrorists' declared goals was to provoke disproportionately harsh counter-reaction by the state), but also in public outcry and in stimulating discussion within the revolutionary movement on 'ends vs means'. This usually led to reconsideration of the tactical arsenal in favour of alternative means of struggle, including non-violence and violent tactics other than terrorism – until the next 'wave' of resort on the part of the more radical factions to terrorist means. For almost a decade following Nechayev's case, terrorist methods gave way to the humanistic current in Russian revolutionary thought, embodied by the 'father' of Russian socialism, philosopher Alexander Herzen (1812–70), and writer Nikolay Chernyshevsky (1828–89). The dominant form of practical activity became propaganda among the working classes by the *chaikovtsy* movement[19] and Zemlya i Volya ('Land and Freedom') in the first half of the 1870s and their experiments in 'outreach to the people' – relocation of urban, educated *raznochintsy* to rural areas or small towns to engage in socialist advocacy among the peasants and other oppressed strata. These outreach campaigns would later expand into a broader *narodniki* movement (*narodnishestvo*).

---

18 The case inspired Fyodor Dostoyevsky's novel *The Devils* (1871–2).
19 Named after one of the movement's leaders, Nikolai Chaikovsky (1851–1926).

The first 'outreach to the people' experiments failed, due as much to financial/economic unsustainability and lack of response from the local population as to the government's aversion. This stimulated groups such as the originally non-violent Zemlya i Volya that had promoted peasant revolution and socialist federated communities to replace the state to reconsider the use of terrorism in the second half of the 1870s.

While at first terrorism was treated as a subsidiary, 'self-defence' tactic, political assassinations quickly became seen as a proactive way to provoke repressive response by the government, destabilise the tsarist regime and instigate anti-tsarist moods among the people. The year 1878 was marked by two high-profile terrorist attacks by members of Zemlya i Volya in St Petersburg. One was an assassination attempt on City Governor Trepov by Vera Zasulich, who undertook a spontaneous lone-actor attack in response to Trepov's illegal order to publicly beat *narodnik* Bogolyubov and was eventually acquitted by a jury. Another was an assassination of the chief of gendarmerie, Mezentsev, by Sergei Kravchinsky. While terrorist attacks were enthusiastically supported by radical segments of the revolutionary milieu and by many *raznochintsy*, the group's attempts to mount a broader rebellion failed as miserably as its earlier 'outreach to the people' experiments did.

These earlier, sporadic terrorist incidents set and sustained the lifeline of 'terrorist' current in the Russian revolutionary movement, with many of the same people, ideas and methods resurfacing in the next 'rounds' of terrorism campaigns. The next, most intense rise in terrorism in nineteenth-century Russia was linked to the Narodnaya Volya group. Its involvement in terrorism was marked by a paradox that would become typical for many terrorist organisations, in and beyond Russia, ever since.

On the one hand, terrorism never assumed a central place in the programme of Narodnaya Volya. Its members did not consider themselves to be primarily 'terrorists'. Even in their most radical writings, they presented political terrorism against certain individuals as a more selective mode of operation, aimed at punishing only the 'real' culprits (tyrants and other 'oppressors') and, hence, a more humanistic tactic than either mass revolts and uprisings or conspiratorial coups.[20]

On the other hand, Narodnaya Volya became one of the first historical illustrations of the creeping, self-perpetuating and addictive nature of

---

20 N. Morozov, *Terroristicheskaya bor'ba* [*Terrorist Struggle*] (London, Russkaya tipographiya, 1880), pp. 7–8.

terrorism that, once employed, quickly acquires its own logic and dynamics. Narodnaya Volya got sucked into terrorism that consumed more and more of the group's efforts and resources, marginalised its other activities and drew the bulk of public attention. In practice, the group followed the radical brochure 'Terrorist Struggle' (1880),[21] authored by Nikolai Morozov (1854–1946), who argued for a series of consecutive regicides that should lead to the 'total collapse' of tsarism. Notably, many of the group leaders and members, including Morozov and the masterminds of the regicide of Alexander II, Sofia Perovskaya and Andrei Zhelyabov, had previously been engaged in *narodnichestvo*, but got frustrated with the 'outreach to the people'.

Narodnaya Volya was drawn into a series of progressively more frequent and intense attacks killing up to a dozen people and became a symbol of political terrorism. They included the deadliest terrorist act in nineteenth-century Russia – a bombing inside the tsar's Zimnij (Winter) Palace on 5 February 1880 that killed 11 and wounded 56. A series of attempts on the life of one of Russia's most reform-oriented rulers, Alexander II, culminated in regicide on 1 March 1881. This attack had the largest effect on the Russian state and the society over the entire tsarist period. It was meant to destroy the perception of invulnerability and sacrality of the tsar (a purpose that it *did* achieve) and to undermine absolutism (a broader goal that it *did not* achieve and, perhaps, even delayed for decades).

The 1881 regicide not only led to the state's crackdown against Narodnaya Volya (destroyed by the mid-1880s) and the broader revolutionary movement, but also stimulated consolidation of absolutism and a backlash against reforms launched by Alexander II. For the rest of the century, this outcome had a no less discouraging effect for the use of terrorism by the Russian revolutionary movement than the tsarist regime's repressive policies. Terrorist plots were mostly confined to more radical splinter cells, such as the 'Young Party of Narodnaya Volya' led by Pyotr Shevyryov and Vladimir Lenin's older brother, Alexander Ulyanov. Remarkably, the cell argued for the decentralisation of terrorism towards more network-style activities and its relocation to the rural and industrial areas as a way to make up for the collapse and discreditation of 'central terror' and to force the government to make concessions through its 'systematic' disorganisation. Abroad, terrorist propaganda was confined to émigré publicists such as Vladimir Burtsev. More importantly, in the post-1881 period, the Russian socio-democratic movement, ideologically based upon Marxism, gained momentum and

21 Ibid.

became the mainstream current of the revolutionary struggle. Socio-democrats criticised the methods employed by Narodnaya Volya, stressed the imperative of a link to mass social movement(s), and reached out to guide and support the fledgling grassroots workers' protests.

Socialist-Revolutionary (SR) Terrorism

The growing influence of socio-democrats and the hard lessons of Narodnaya Volya led to the overall revision of the role of terrorism in the Russian revolutionary movement as a tactic that could supplement, but not substitute for, mass-based forms of struggle. This view was formally shared by the Socialist-Revolutionary Party, but did not prevent it from becoming the next symbol of revolutionary terrorism in Russia. This more radical group on the left formed in 1901–2 on the ideological basis of a mix of Marxism and *narodnichestvo*. Its terrorist activity can be divided into three periods: before, during and after the revolution of 1905–7.

At the first stage, like *narodovol'tsy*, the SRs pointed at the less deadly nature of terrorism, compared to 'revolution', and experimented with terrorist attacks as a means to instigate broader violence. However, the SRs tried to avoid being fully engulfed in terrorism. They structurally separated terrorist functions from the rest of the SR work (concentrating them in the party's 'combat organisation'). Political leadership was charged with coordinating terrorism with other forms of struggle and deciding upon the timing and high-profile targets for attacks, while execution was left to the combat organisation.

As the SR terrorism intensified in the first half of the 1900s, so did the socio-democratic criticism of it as an elitist tactic that diverted the revolutionaries from socialist work among the masses. Socio-democrats were hardly more moderate in terms of ideology, but insisted that class struggle did not allow for prioritising terrorist means. As noted by Russia's leading Marxist thinker, Georgi Plekhanov (1856–1918), 'a committed socio-democrat who firmly believes in his cause will never make a terrorist'.[22] Plekhanov saw terrorism as 'a natural product of the weakness of the revolutionary party' in Russia,[23] explained its recurrence by extreme resentment on the part of the

---

22 G. Plekhanov, 'Sotsial-demokratiya i terrorizm' ['Social Democracy and Terrorism'] (*Vorwärts* 187, 11 August 1904), in G. Plekhanov, *Sochineniya* [*Works*], Vol. 13 (Moscow, Gosuderstvennoye izdatel'stvo, 1926), http://az.lib.ru/p/plehanow_g_w/text_1904_sotzial-demokratia.shtml.
23 G. Plekhanov, 'O sotsial'noi demokratii v Rossii' ['On Social Democracy in Russia'], in Ibid., Vol. 9.

intelligentsia (raznochintsy) against police repression, and frustration about lack of conditions for mass armed uprising, and contrasted it with the working class's preference for grassroots street protests. Even Vladimir Lenin, one of the most persistent advocates of the admissibility of violent means among socio-democrats, dismissed SR terrorism as 'totally separated from the work with the masses, for the masses and along with the masses'.[24]

Socio-democratic critique of SR terrorism did not, however, offer protesters effective alternative means to resist state police and gendarmerie, and insisted, not without reason, that armed uprising was premature. Also, while workers' strikes, street protests and peasant disturbances often remained unreported to the wider public, terrorist attacks against high-profile officials had a large political-media effect across Russia. That did not discourage socio-democrats from prioritising propaganda, education and efforts to spur protest self-organisation among the working classes, but weakened socio-democratic appeal to *raznochintsy*, who were increasingly impressed by the terrorist successes of the SR combat organisation.

It took the first successful assassination, of Minister of the Interior Sipyagin on 2 April 1902, by the combat organisation, led by Grigori Gershuni, for the SRs to claim responsibility for it. At the pre-revolutionary stage, major terrorist acts by the SRs included the killing of the Ufa Governor Bogdanovich and their most popular attack – the assassination of a reactionary Minister of the Interior, von Pleve,[25] by Yegor Sazonov in St Petersburg in July 1904, under the pretext of the 1903 Jewish pogroms in Kishinev. In contrast to the post-1881 period marked by reaction and counter-reforms, von Pleve's assassination, committed amidst government crisis, Russia's defeats in the war with Japan, and rising popular resentment, opened space for short-lived liberalisation (associated with the next Minister of the Interior, Svyatopolk-Mirski). It was undercut by 'Bloody Sunday' – the regime's mass massacre of peaceful protesters led by a legal workers' organisation, on 9 January 1905, which marked the start of the first Russian revolution.

The revolution of 1905–7 was neither caused nor provoked by terrorism. It was the cumulative product of a deep internal crisis, military defeats abroad and failure of even limited attempts at social liberalisation that were still incompatible with absolutism. The state of the Russian monarchy

---

24 V. Lenin, *Polnoye sobraniye sochinenii* [*Collected Complete Works*], Vol. 6 (Moscow, Izdatel'stvo politicheskoi literatury, 1958), p. 380.
25 In the 1880s, von Pleve led the police crackdown against, and the investigation of the regicide by, Narodnaya Volya.

increasingly resembled a zugzwang in which *any* next move of the system only made its position worse. This zugzwang lasted through the last years of the Russian Empire until its ultimate collapse in 1917, sped up by Russia's engagement in the First World War.

The SRs were the only party that systematically employed terrorism both in peacetime, to instigate a broader uprising, and during 1905–7, when the level of violence between the state and the revolutionaries reached that of an internal armed conflict.

In 1905–7, terrorism reached its peak in terms of numbers of incidents and casualties, which increased manyfold. The SRs alone accounted for 59 terrorist incidents in 1905, 93 in 1906 and 81 in 1907 (compared to just 11 attacks committed by the combat organisation in all previous years).[26] On 12 August 1906, a more radical group of 'SR-maximalists' that split from the SRs to concentrate on 'pure terror' carried out a mass-casualty attack on Prime Minister Pyotr Stolypin's dacha, killing 27 (Russia's first attack with over 100 casualties). This excess by maximalists, coupled with their large fundraising 'expropriations', did much to discredit high-profile attacks in the eyes of the public and was even condemned by the mainstream SR party.

Terrorism, however, also transformed significantly through the revolution years. In the context of broader social upheavals and disturbances, it quickly spilled out of any central control and became fragmented, diffused and decentralised. The range of targets expanded beyond individual terrorism against senior officials towards indiscriminate, including mass-casualty, attacks in public places. While high-level government figures were systematically threatened and periodically targeted, the bulk of victims were already comprised of low-rank officials, local policemen and residents or passers-by. Most attacks were carried out by localised militant groups, some loosely affiliated with the SRs, but others linked to socio-democrats, anarchists or national separatists. These cells often acted without any higher sanction or guidance on choice of targets and other operational matters.

Another trend was the blurring of the notion of revolutionary terrorism (terror) in the context of a broader armed confrontation. Terrorism evolved from the main form of revolutionary violence in peacetime into just one

---

26 D. Pavlov, 'Iz istorii boyevoi deyatel'nosti partii eserov nakanune i v gody revolutsii 1905–1907 gg.' ['From the History of Eserys' Combat Activity on the Eve of, and During, the Revolution of 1905–1907'], in *Neproletarskiye partii Rossii v tryokh revolutsiyakh [Russia's Non-Proletariat Parties in Three Revolutions]* (Moscow, Nauka, 1989); M. Leonov, *Partiya sotsialistov-revolutsionerov v 1905–1907 gg. [The Party of Socialists-Revolutionaries in 1905–1907]* (Moscow, ROSSPEN, 1997), p. 128.

violent tactic, often combined with guerrilla-style activities – direct armed clashes and crossfire between revolutionary militants and state security forces. Both tactics were frequently employed by the same actors, who sometimes combined them with violent, predatory 'expropriations'. In most cases, revolutionary parties and militants did not distinguish between these tactics, using the notion of 'terror' as a synonym for any revolutionary violence. The more 'traditional' terrorism that centred on individual political assassinations got mired in the context of broader, more mass-based, organised and (semi-)spontaneous violence that increasingly became the means of direct elimination of the antagonist, losing much of terrorism's 'symbolic' and 'communicative' function.

This shift was well captured by Lenin, who saw 'the principal distinction between "insurgent activities" and "old terror" in the fact that they take place in the context of the uprising'.[27] On the ground, local combat groups of SRs and the main socio-democratic parties (the Bolsheviks and Men'sheviks) were almost indistinguishable in terms of their operational activities (clashes with security personnel, raids on prisons and police headquarters, attacks against officials etc.). This did not mean, however, that socio-democrats massively turned to the SR-style terrorism – instead, it was the SRs who had to shift from individual terrorism to more mass-based and combat-style forms of struggle. By some counts, in 1905–7, the death toll from all forms of revolutionary violence may have reached 9,000, out of the total of 17,000 people killed in such violence over the entire 1901–16 period.[28]

During the post-revolution stage, general violence subsided, but terrorism declined most radically. Major SR terrorist incidents fell to three in 1908, two in 1909, one in 1910 and two in 1911.[29] Notably, terrorism as such started to decline after, during the 1905–7 revolution, the theoretical thesis about terrorism as just one violent tactic to support other forms of revolutionary struggle was finally realised in practice.

The revolution led to certain shifts in the public mood and stimulated sociopolitical change, however limited and short-lived. Tsarism started to experiment with parliamentarianism and convened the First (April–June 1906) and Second (February–June 1907) State Dumas, which created the first opportunities for political engagement of the *raznochintsy*. Revolutionary parties boycotted elections to the First Duma, but not to the second one, where representatives of

---

27 Lenin, *Polnoye sobraniye sochinenii*, Vol. 14, p. 11.
28 A. Geifman, *Revolyutsionnyi terror v Rossii, 1894–1917* (Moscow, Kron Press, 1997), pp. 31–2; Budnitskii, *Terrorizm v rossiiskom svoboditel'nom dvizhenii*, p. 25.
29 Leonov, *Partiya sotsialistov-revolutsionerov*.

the Russian Socio-Democratic Workers' Party and the Party of Socialists-Revolutionaries got seats. In reaction to political developments, the SR leadership repeatedly decided to halt terrorist activity. Meanwhile, dissolution of the Second Duma made the SRs claim that the revolution was not over and legitimised for them the return to 'central terrorism'. However, the public got 'used to' violence, displayed a 'terrorism fatigue' and was overtaken by politics. Terrorism was losing much of its 'extraordinary', event-setting and, consequently, political effect. It was further discredited by blurring distinctions between 'terror' and banditry and degradation of some militant units to predatory gangs. Against this background, the SRs (and, to an extent, other revolutionary parties) became marginalised and their social base declined.

The worst blow to SR terrorism was the 'Azef case' of 1908. It revealed that Yevno Azef, head of the SR combat organisation in 1903–8, was a double agent for Russia's secret police.[30] Azef, inter alia, masterminded the 1904 assassination of minister von Pleve, designed the structure and logistics of the combat organisation that involved strict division of labour (between technicians, bombers, watchers and information-gatherers) and promoted the use of new technologies (dynamite, distance bombing). At the same time Azef gradually turned the combat organisation into a heavily centralised, autonomous enterprise linked to the SR central committee by his figure only, but co-funded from other SR activities. This made it easier to manipulate for a double agent at the top. As a result, in 1907–8, the combat organisation did not commit a single successful terrorist attack. Following Azef's exposure, the SR central committee sentenced him to death in 1909, but he fled to Germany. The combat organisation, led by Boris Savinkov, was revived to conduct 'central terrorism', but did not survive a range of failed plots and attacks and was dissolved in 1911.

The Azef scandal further discredited SR terrorism and had a damaging reputational and political effect for the broader revolutionary movement. It also compromised state counterterrorism practices. By the early twentieth century, Russia's counterterrorism had evolved from an overwhelmingly reactive and repressive response to a more preventive and pre-emptive approach, with more attention to human intelligence and undercover work.[31] Widespread use of double agents increased the efficiency of

---

30 A. Geifman, *Entangled in Terror: The Azef Affair and the Russian Revolution* (Lanham, MD, Rowman & Littlefield, 2000); B. Nikolajewsky, *Aseff the Spy: Russian Terrorist and Police Stool* (Garden City, Doubleday, Doran & Co., 1934).

31 See *Politicheskaya politsiya i politicheskii terrorizm v Rossii (vtoraya polovina XIX–nachalo XX vv.)* [*Political Police and Political Terrorism in Russia, Second Half of the 19th Century–Early 20th Century*] (Moscow, AIRO-XX, 2001), pp. 5–20.

counterterrorism in the short term, but also opened space for manipulation of terrorism by senior security officials and segments of the state apparatus for their own purposes, including those related to bureaucratic politics and inter-agency infighting. Provocation became one of the main counterterrorist tactics, eroding the boundary between undercover agents and terrorists. In another appalling incident, the 'Petrov case' (1909), a double agent killed the head of St Petersburg secret police, Karpov, at a safe address. On 1 September 1911, Russian Prime Minister Stolypin was fatally wounded by a terrorist – and police double agent – Dmitri Bogrov at the Kiev Opera Theatre. While this assassination did not provoke major outcry among the wider population, it was the final straw that discredited terrorist and antiterrorist methods at the time.

The start of the First World War (Russia went to war on 11 August 1914) was accompanied by a rise in patriotic feelings and the deceptive semblance of a new consolidation of the society and the state. Terrorism temporarily ceased to be a major issue. While some terrorist manifestations resurfaced in the age of 'Grand Turmoil' after 1917, they were marginalised by other forms of revolutionary (and counter-revolutionary) violence, and, later, by the rise of state terror by the Bolsheviks' Soviet regime. The age of 'historical terrorism' in Russia was over.

Other Types of Terrorism in the Russian Empire

Anarchist Terrorism

In contrast to Europe, where anarchist terrorism evolved since the 1870s and culminated in the 1890s, anarchist terrorism in Russia had not become a major current, even within the revolutionary/leftist milieu, and could only be discerned as it peaked in the early twentieth century, when its European analogues were already on the wane. It was heavily influenced by the theory and practice of European anarchist terrorism, and the first Russian cells of anarchist terrorists emerged among emigrants to Europe.

In Russia, anarchist terrorism was also peripheral in terms of geography and distribution by region. The first groups surfaced in émigré circles, especially in Switzerland (Khleb i Volya ('Bread and Freedom'), the Group of Russian Anarchists-Communists) and France (Beznachaliye ('Leaderless Resistance')) and later spread their activities to Russia. Inside Russia, anarchist terrorism was mainly confined to ethnically mixed areas at the southern and western edges of the empire. Among anarchists, ethnic minorities were heavily over-represented (especially Jews, who comprised almost 50 per cent of anarchist terrorists,[32] Poles and various ethnic groups from the Caucasus). In the Polish Kingdom and Transcaucasian governorates, anarchist groups, including terrorists, were often linked to or merged with the ethno-separatist (national-liberation) movements.

The largest anarchist movement in Russia was the 'Black Banner' confederation (*chernoznamentsy*), followed by Beznachaliye. The Black Banner movement, led by Judas Grossman, dominated in Belostok and was the leading violent anarchist current in Warsaw, Vilno, Ekaterinoslavl and Odessa. Anarchist terrorism peaked during the 1905–7 revolution, when it involved over 5,000 activists. Distinct from the mainstream Russian revolutionary movement in social composition, it was less elitist, involved younger people of lower educational level (less than 5 per cent were university graduates) and a larger proportion of workers and lumpenproletariat (over 60 per cent).[33] Anarchists quickly split into *bezmotivniki* (proponents of 'aimless', 'pure terror' who mounted or plotted attacks at cafes, restaurants and other public places from Odessa to Kishinev); anarcho-syndicalists (who insisted on more targeted violence against 'regime agents') and 'communars' (who gave up terrorism for a hope of raiding towns to build up the first communes).

Overall, Russia's main input into the anarchist movement came in the form of theory rather than practice, and mostly in ways other than propagating or justifying terrorism. This input dated back to the 1870s, embodied by Russian leading theorists of anarchism (Bakunin and Kropotkin), and predated the emergence of Russian anarchist terrorism. Bakunin was an ardent supporter and practitioner of 'armed propaganda'[34] and 'uncontrolled' revolutionary violence, but emphasised militant rather than terrorist tactics. Kropotkin saw terrorism more as a symptom and reflex of dramatic sociopolitical shifts than a conscious strategy to be 'directed' by the revolutionary movement 'from the top'. He argued that no political violence or regime change would make much difference as long as socio-economic mainstays of the existing system persisted and that revolutionary violence should

---

32 V. Ermakov, 'Portret rossiiskogo anarkhista nachala veka' ['Portrait of a Russian Anarchist of the Early Twentieth Century'], in *Sotsiologicheskiye issledovaniya* [*Sociological Studies*] 3 (1992), p. 98.
33 Ibid.
34 Bakunin took part in the 1848 French revolution, in clashes with Austrian security forces during the Prague uprising of 1848–9, in the Dresden uprising of 1849 and in the Polish uprising of 1862–3.

primarily target economic structures, and called for a mass peasant uprising in Russia.[35]

The main practical manifestation of anarchism in Russia came not so much in the form of peripheral (sub)urban anarchoterrorism of the 1900s as in the form of the anarchist orientation of the *makhnovtsy* – a grassroots peasant movement in south-eastern Ukraine led by Nestor Makhno starting in 1918. *Makhnovtsy* fought against both German–Austrian occupying forces and the 'Whites' in the civil war, but retained autonomy from the 'Reds' and were eventually suppressed by the Bolsheviks.

Nationalist/Separatist Terrorism

Terrorism by national-liberation movements took shape by the early twentieth century and mostly manifested itself at the 'national outskirts' of the Russian Empire, especially in the Polish Kingdom and Transcaucasia, but also, to an extent, in the Baltic region, Ukraine etc. This type of terrorism displayed three main characteristics.

First, minority nationalist terrorism in Russia was closely interrelated with revolutionary (and, in some cases, anarchist) terrorism. The official programmes of most nationalist parties proclaimed the unity of national goals – struggle against Russification, legal discrimination and Russian security presence, and for greater autonomy or separatism – and a left-wing sociopolitical agenda. The two currents developed in close contact and influenced one another. All Polish nationalist parties but one were also revolutionary left-wing organisations. The leading Polish national organisation was the Polish Socialist Party, founded in 1892. During the 1905–7 revolution, its fighting unit was responsible for 70 per cent of all anti-government violence in the Polish Kingdom governorates.[36]

Second, of all types of terrorism in the Russian Empire, nationalist-separatist terrorism suffers from the strongest bias towards undercounting – both in historical sources and in the research literature. In some regions (Poland, Armenia, the Baltic region) incidents of anti-government violence, including terrorism, occurred on a daily basis, especially in 1905–7.[37] However, they were mostly ignored in the Police Department centralised

---

35 Kropotkin, *Zapiski revolutsionera*, section 'Western Europe', part I.
36 N. Postnikov, 'Terror pol'skikh partii protiv predstavitelei russkoi administratsii v–1905–1907 gg.' ['Terror by Polish Parties Against Russian Administration Officials in 1905–1907'], in *Individual'nyi politicheskii terror v Rossii XIX–nachala XX v. [Individual Political Terror in Russia in the 19th–Early 20th Century]* (Moscow, Memorial, 1996).
37 See analysis of statistics by regional police departments in the Polish Kingdom in Geifman, *Revolyutsionnyi terror v Rossii, 1894–1917*, p. 38.

national-level data, which did not treat them as revolutionary 'terrorism', but used a separate category of ethnic strife and disturbances.[38] Nationalist-separatist violence also got much lower attention in the Russian media compared to high-profile terrorist attacks by the Russian revolutionaries. The same applied to data on terrorist tactics employed in the context of Armenian–Turkish, Armenian–Azeri and other inter-ethnic tensions and conflicts.

Third, a great deal of 'terror' by nationalists, especially in Poland and, to a lesser extent, Transcaucasia, was directed at the Russian government's military and security targets. In some cases, such violence hovered at the verge of a low-intensity conflict and, in 1905–7, fell more under the category of (counter)insurgency. If, prior to the first Russian revolution, only one out of four main Polish parties accepted 'terror' as a means of struggle, after 1905, all four did. The Russian government instigated violence in the Polish governorates by systematically disbanding protests and mass demonstrations by force. While violence by Polish nationalist parties' fighting units started as a more classic 'terrorism' against officials, it quickly shifted primarily to insurgent activity such as throwing bombs at government military targets and setting up ambushes against Russian security forces.

Apart from the Polish militants, Dashnaktsutyun,[39] the most radical party in the Armenian national movement,[40] founded in 1890 by Armenians in Tiflis (Georgia), actively employed violence, mainly in the form of terrorism. Historically, the *dashnaks* directed their violent activity mainly against the Ottoman, not Russian Empire (and were even backed by the Russian authorities in their struggle against Ottoman Turkey). However, in the early twentieth century, the *dashnaks* turned to terrorism against Russia and accounted for the majority of terrorist attacks in Transcaucasia through the 1900s. The most high-profile terrorist attacks by Armenian nationalists included an attempt to kill the Russian chief military commander in the Caucasus, Prince Golytsin, in October 1903 and the assassination of the Baku Governor Nakashidze for his role in backing the February 1905 pogroms against Armenians.

After the 1905–7 revolution, nationalist-separatist terrorism subsided. It was both harshly suppressed (over 60 per cent of the militants of the Polish

---

38 O. Kvasov, 'Kolichestvennyie parametry zhertv revolutsionnogo terrorizma nachala XX v.' ['Quantitative Parameters of Revolutionary Terrorism Casualties in the Early 20th Century'], *Vestnik VGU: Istoriya, Sotsiologiya, Politologiya* [*Voronezh State University Review: History, Sociology, Political Science*] 1 (2010), pp. 25, 31.
39 Armenian for the 'Armenian Revolutionary Federation' (ARF).
40 Another main Armenian party was the socio-democratic Gnchak.

Socialist Party's fighting units were arrested)[41] and degraded into infighting, splits and intra-party clashes. At some point, violence between militants of the Polish Socialist Party and the more radical nationalist-bourgeois Polish National-Democratic Party exceeded that between the Polish nationalists and the Russian authorities. During the post-revolutionary stage, nationalist militancy at the empire's peripheries, especially in Transcaucasia, also became heavily criminalised. However, signs of decline in nationalist terrorism were coupled with further radicalisation of some of the splinter groups, such as the revolutionary faction of the Polish Socialist Party, under the leadership of the head of the party's fighting unit, Józef Piłsudski (1867–1935). This radically nationalist faction inherited and integrated the party's fighting branch, seen by Piłsudski as a core of the future army of the independent Polish state that he eventually headed in 1918.

In contrast to Polish or Armenian nationalist groups, the Jewish national movement displayed a paradox. On the one hand, Jews dominated among anarchist terrorists and were over-represented in Russia's broader revolutionary movement. On the other, the largest Jewish political organisation – BUND (All-Jewish Workers' Union in Lithuania, Poland and Russia),[42] formed in Vilno in 1897 – was a distinctly socio-democratic/Marxist movement that later even joined the Russian Socio-Democratic Workers' Party as an autonomous branch. Its national goals were moderate and non-separatist, including cultural autonomy within Russia and opposition to Zionism. BUND never prioritised and hardly even practised terrorist means. While, during the 1905–7 revolution, BUND sided more with the Bolsheviks, it later shifted its affiliation to the more moderate Men'shevik current in the Russian socio-democratic movement.

Right-Wing Terrorism

Right-wing terrorism was a latecomer to the terrorist scene in Russia. It took shape during the 1905–7 revolution, peaked in 1905–14, and faded away afterwards. This type of terrorism was primarily associated with the 'Black Hundreds' – the radical part of the Russian far-right movement that pledged arch-loyalty to the ruling regime and especially to its most conservative linchpin – the monarchy. The Black Hundreds got representation in the Duma and were only banned after the Bourgeois Revolution of February 1917.

---

41 Postnikov, 'Terror pol'skikh partii', p. 117.
42 In Yiddish, Algemeiner Jiddischer Arbeter Bund in Lite, Poyln un Russland.

The movement involved a range of groups of varying degrees of radicalism and most had fighting squads to counter revolutionary actors. While the Russian far right was a cross-class movement, involving activists from the very top to the social bottom, its fighting squads were more grassroots and in social (not ethnic) terms resembled anarchist groups.[43] The Black Hundreds were composed of Russian nationalists, strongly anti-Semitic, and, like anarchists, most active in governorates with ethnically mixed populations. Terrorism was hardly their main violent tactic. Instead, the Black Hundreds were commonly associated with pogroms – a mix of inter-communal strife, repressive or punitive violence against civilians, and hate crimes against non-Russians, especially Jews. However, as revealed by the more recent research, the deadliest anti-Jewish pogroms in the Russian Empire, mostly in parts of Poland under Russian rule, predated the creation of the Black Hundreds and were closer to mass (semi-)spontaneous disturbances than to strictly organised operations.[44] While the Russian authorities, especially at levels from local to regional, were often inclined to close their eyes, or even sympathetic, to violence by the Black Hundreds and other far-right groups, the latter also had influential opponents, including at the top of the Russian government (with the notable exception of the tsar himself).

The Black Hundreds' main *raison d'être* was counter-revolution, and one of the main types of their fighting squads' violence was clashes with the revolutionary militants, especially in 1905–7. These armed exchanges were commonly labelled, including by the Police Department, as 'inter-party terror', alongside relatively few incidents of far-right terrorism. The latter were confined to political assassinations of liberal public and political figures considered to be 'enemies of the state', such as former Duma deputies and members of the Russian Cadet Party leadership Mikhail Herzenstein and Grigori Iollos, murdered by militants of one of the Black Hundreds movement's core groups, Soyuz Rysskogo Naroda ('Union of the Russian People'). At the same time, several far-right leaders and public figures were also targets of revolutionary terrorism from the left.

* * *

43 S. Stepanov, 'Chernosotennyi terror, 1905–1907 gg.' ['The Black Hundreds' Terror, 1905–1907'], in *Individual'nyi politicheskii terror v Rossii XIX – nachala XX v.*, p. 123.
44 See J. Klier and S. Lambrozo (eds.), *Pogroms: Anti-Jewish Violence in Modern Russian History* (Cambridge, Cambridge University Press, 2004).

Revolutionary terrorism in late nineteenth- to early twentieth-century Russia was one of the most active and sustained manifestations of historical forms of terrorism. National specifics notwithstanding, it was an integral part of the world's first historical wave of terrorism.

At that early stage, the Russian case already revealed the highly asymmetrical, symbolic, communicative and distinctively political nature of terrorism by radical oppositional non-state actors. The Russian state inadequately assessed the real potential of terrorists, overlooked their limited appeal among the masses, and generally exaggerated the scale of the problem. Despite gross disparity in power, terrorism as a 'weapon of the weak' allowed radical revolutionaries to exercise disproportionate political pressure on the state and played some, although hardly a decisive, role in destabilising politics and governance, and spurring further protests. While not always overly repressive or overreactive, the state's response was largely reactionary. Later, dangerous erosion of the border between state secret operations and subversive terrorist activities and growing possibilities for manipulation of terrorism by segments of the security apparatus further eroded public trust in state institutions. In fact, the very excesses of terrorists and routinisation of terrorism in the context of a broader armed uprising (the revolution of 1905–7) may have done more to reduce the political effect of terrorist incidents than antiterrorist efforts or propaganda.

On the one hand, terrorism in Russia became a customary, regular method of revolutionary struggle. Throughout the tsarist period, terrorism was dominated by individual attacks targeting state officials or public figures (including not only hardliners, but also progressive characters such as Stolypin), even as the early twentieth century was marked by the first mass-casualty attacks. Russian revolutionary terrorists were more radical than many of their foreign counterparts, in two ways. First, for most terrorist actors, terrorism was the sole method of choice and the only violent tactic they saw as feasible and effective. Second, compared to dominant anarchist forms of left-wing terrorism in the West, Russian revolutionary terrorism was more structured and systematic, with anarchist elements playing a marginal role.

On the other hand, terrorism in the Russian Empire did not become a cross-class or mass sociopolitical phenomenon. It mostly remained the realm of radical segments of the *raznochintsy* subclass. Most high-profile attacks were committed by students, and it is mainly among the *raznochintsy* that terrorism attracted some public support. Markedly, terrorism eventually tended to degrade into conspiratorial, socially marginalised or increasingly ferocious, senseless or predatory forms – regardless of its declared political goals, of whether it was prioritised as a tactic or seen as a way to instigate broader revolutionary violence, and of the organisational solution. Above all, terrorism (and counterterrorism) had no appeal or significant support among the masses.

Also, terrorism did not become a leading or winning tactic of the Russian revolutionary movement. For the Russian socio-democrats, including the Bolsheviks as a faction that accepted violence and ultimately won both the revolution and the civil war, terrorism was a marginal, heavily criticised tactic. Instead, the Bolsheviks prioritised the link to the mass movement, propaganda and agitation among the workers, soldiers and peasants, and armed uprising. However, the Russian case was also one of the first to question and confute the idea of the general incompatibility of terrorism with the grassroots, mass-based movement. During the 1905–7 revolution, terrorism in Russia became intertwined not only with insurgent-style violence, but also with more mass-based forms of revolutionary struggle. Still, the main lesson from Russia's historical case was the decisive role of the link to the mass movement for the success of a revolutionary (rebel) movement, regardless of whether or not it employed terrorist means.

Further Reading

O. Budnitskii, *Terrorizm v rossiiskom osvoboditel'nom dvizhenii: ideologiya, etika, psikhologiya, vtoraya polovina XIX–nachalo XX v.* [*Terrorism in the Russian Liberation Movement: Ideology, Ethics, Psychology, the Second Half of the 19th–Early 20th Century*] (Moscow, ROSSPEN, 2000)

A. Geifman, *Thou Shalt Kill: Revolutionary Terrorism in Russia, 1894–1917* (Princeton, Princeton University Press, 1993)

R. Hingley, *Nihilists: Russian Radicals and Revolutionaries in the Reign of Alexander II (1855–81)* (London, Weidenfeld and Nicolson, 1967)

N. M. Naimark, 'Terrorism and the Fall of Imperial Russia', *Terrorism and Political Violence* 2/2 (1990), DOI: 10.1080/09546559008427060

Politicheskaya politsiya i politicheskii terrorizm v Rossii (vtoraya polovina XIX–nachalo XX vv.) [*Political Police and Political Terrorism in Russia (Second Half of the 19th Century–Early 20th Century): Collection of Documents*] (Moscow, AIRO-XX, 2001)

13

Terrorism in Post-Soviet Russia

1990s to 2010s

EKATERINA STEPANOVA[1]

In Russia's case, historical study of terrorism implies analysis of at least two distinct periods of major terrorist activity. The first period, covered in the previous chapter, refers to terrorism in the late Russian Empire, from the last third of the nineteenth century through to the early twentieth century (technically, until 1917 and, substantively, until the formation and assertion of Soviet power in the early 1920s). This chapter looks at the second period, which started almost a century later, in post-Soviet Russia, and lasted from the mid-1990s to the 2010s. It was divided from the previous historical peak of terrorism by more than seven decades of Soviet rule, to the end of the 1980s. While the Soviet period was, at various stages, heavily associated with political violence, in the USSR, anti-government terrorism ceased to be one of the main or even noticeable forms of such violence. However, terrorism quickly gained momentum starting in the 1990s, albeit in ideological-motivational forms different from the dominant type(s) of terrorism in pre-Soviet Russia, and even reached some of the world's highest levels at the turn of the century.

While definitional aspects of terrorism, as applied to the Russian case, are addressed in the previous chapter, no historical comparisons between two different, unsuccessive periods of major terrorist activity in Russia can be made unless the more recent, post-Soviet peak in terrorist activity is also explored. Nor would the Russian case be complete, as placed in the global historical context, without its second peak of terrorism, which, from the early 2000s, became intertwined with the global wave of terrorism that lasted through the first two decades of the twenty-first century.

---

[1] Lead researcher and Head, Peace and Conflict Studies Unit, Primakov National Research Institute of World Economy and International Relations (IMEMO), Russian Academy of Sciences.

Remarkably, terrorism in post-Soviet Russia had no direct typological analogues or historical parallels to the peak of revolutionary terrorism in the Russian Empire. In modern Russia, levels of terrorism by ultra-left, anarchist and radical anti-fascist groups remained very low. The far-right extremism peaked a decade and a half after the fall of the Soviet Union. It sometimes involved terrorist acts, but was dominated by scuffle provocations, ethno-confessional vandalism, and attempts to seize upon spontaneous, grassroots, xenophobic, and increasingly anti-migrant, disturbances. Incidents of environmentalist and other 'single-issue' terrorism were even less frequent. None of these, however,[2] stood in any comparison to the two main forms of terrorism in post-Soviet Russia,[3] which unfolded in a certain sequence, but displayed some overlap.

The dominant type was explicitly conflict-related terrorism employed starting in the mid-1990s in the context of domestic insurgency in Chechnya and, starting in the late 2000s, as part of more fragmented, low-intensity conflict in the North Caucasus. While Chechnya's painful incorporation into the Russian Empire dated back to the mid-nineteenth century and was itself a result of prolonged Caucasian war,[4] the systematic use of terrorist means by ethnic separatists of an increasingly Islamist bent in post-Soviet Russia had no direct historical precedent or analogue. While the post-Soviet conflict in Chechnya was largely subnational and waged in one of Russia's peripheral regions, it remained the source of the most intense and protracted terrorism for decades. It is due to this type of terrorism that Russia became the only European and upper-middle-income country that, according to the Global Terrorism Index, made it into the world's Top Ten of terrorism-affected states in 2002–11.[5] As terrorism in Chechnya and the North Caucasus declined in the 2010s, Russia faced a new challenge posed by the broader

---

2 As of August 2020, Russia's list of terrorist organisations included two right-wing groups and two left-wing groups, in contrast to twenty-eight Islamist (Islamist/separatist) organisations: www.fsb.ru/fsb/npd/terror.htm. This proportion had held since the list was first compiled in 2003.
3 D. Pluchinsky, 'Terrorism in the Former Soviet Union: A Primer, a Puzzle, a Prognosis', *Studies in Conflict and Terrorism* 21/2 (1998); E. Stepanova, 'Russia's Approach to the Fight Against Terrorism', in J. Hedenskog et al. (eds.), *Russia as a Great Power: Dimensions of Security under Putin* (London, Routledge-Curzon, 2005); E. Stepanova, 'Russia's Response to Terrorism in the Twenty-First Century', in M. Boyle (ed.), *Non-Western Responses to Terrorism* (Manchester, Manchester University Press, 2019).
4 M. Gammer, *Muslim Resistance to the Tsar: Shamil and the Conquest of Chechnia and Daghestan* (London, Frank Cass, 1994).
5 'Global Terrorism Index: Capturing the Impact of Terrorism in 2002–2011', Institute for Economics and Peace, 2013, p. 4 (hereafter: Global Terrorism Index/year).

transnationalisation of terrorism and related radicalisation processes catalysed by the 'Islamic State' (ISIS)[6] factor.

Where does the Russian case or, rather, the two distinct periods of terrorism in Russia, stand vis-à-vis the world's historical waves of terrorism, from the late nineteenth century to the early twenty-first century? How does it play out in relation to general ideological-motivational types of terrorism (sociopolitical/ideological, nationalist and religious) and to their combinations? What are the key aspects specific to the main types of terrorism in post-Soviet Russia (i.e. terrorism by separatist-Islamist rebels in Chechnya and the broader North Caucasian region in the course of the first post-Soviet decades, and the more recent phenomenon of transnationalised, but home-grown, Islamist terrorism inspired by 'global jihad')? How specific are they, compared to typologically similar varieties of terrorism elsewhere (terrorism by modern Islamist-separatist insurgencies in a number of Asian and African states, or home-grown, but transnationalised, radical Islamist-jihadist terrorism in the West in the early twenty-first century, respectively)?

How does the rise and fall of terrorism in post-Soviet Russia relate to the factors of sociopolitical and socio-economic transition, regime type, functionality and legitimacy of state power, public perceptions and transnationalisation, in general and as compared to terrorism in the Russian Empire? How can very low levels of domestic terrorism during the Soviet period be explained?

Finally, does history teach us anything? How relevant is the historical case of revolutionary terrorism in the Russian Empire for the realities of contemporary terrorism? Can that distant past experience provide any useful lessons for policymakers, the security community, analysts and the broader public in a historically, culturally and geopolitically successive (albeit not directly so) twenty-first century Russia? Can they help prevent and address the main forms of terrorism in post-Soviet Russia, which are very different in ideological, motivational, organisational terms, degree of transnationalisation and other respects from political assassinations or bombings carried out by *narodniki* or socio-revolutionaries of the imperial times, and if so, how? Or should we think more in terms of certain, perhaps only limited, historical parallels than in terms of any direct lessons to be learnt? Do such parallels, if any, more closely apply to ideologically closer types and manifestations of modern terrorism elsewhere (e.g., to the rise of radical left terrorism in Europe in the 1970s and 1980s) than to Russia itself, which has never displayed

---

6 Acronym for 'Islamic State in Iraq and ash-Sham' (*ash-Sham* is Arabic for the Levant).

major manifestations of left-wing/revolutionary terrorism since the decline of its historical analogue in the early twentieth century?

Can any lessons be gleaned from almost three decades of the more recent, contemporary history of terrorism in post-Soviet Russia? Have they been? If so, do they apply to Russia alone or more generally? Which of these lessons matter in a more global sense and which are only relevant to similar or comparable types of state, and in which regions? These are just some of the questions that the angle taken in this volume raises in relation to Russia and that require both its main historical periods of terrorist activity to be addressed.

The Soviet Period

As, in the 1920s–50s, terrorism declined worldwide and remained at low levels, Soviet Russia was no exception. During this period, Soviet Russia lost tens of millions in battle-related deaths and one-sided violence during the Second World War and over 12 million in domestic state terror, but did not face any major, systematic anti-government violence in the form of terrorism. Minor exceptions were mostly confined to the aftermath of the October 1917 Bolshevik revolution, when, during and shortly after the civil war, some space for politics and political manipulation by non-state actors, including by use of political violence, was still open. At that time, terrorist manifestations, mostly by the remnants of the radical left and anarchist groups not yet incorporated or suppressed by the Bolsheviks, could be seen as fading aftershocks of the previous, anti-imperial wave of revolutionary terrorism.

Terrorism during the revolutionary year of 1917 and in the early Soviet period displayed a mix of residual aftershocks of the earlier terrorist wave with new post-revolutionary dynamics. They included some terrorist attacks directed against the new Bolshevik authorities, mainly by the more radical Left SRs and SRs, but also monarchists and anarchists, and terrorism as part of violent inter-party rivalries. On 6 July 1918, the Left SRs assassinated the German ambassador, Wilhelm von Mirbach. This was an attempt to derail the Brest peace deal with Germany (which was signed by the Bolsheviks in March 1918, causing a split with their radical partners in the coalition government) and a way to signal the uprising by the Left SRs (which was quickly suppressed). On 30 August 1918, the SRs carried out an attempt on Lenin's life and assassinated Moisei Uritskii, head of Petrograd's ChK, the Bolsheviks' nascent security service. These attacks had a dramatic, but counterproductive effect: they became the pretext for the launch of the 'Red Terror' campaign by the new revolutionary state. For some time, residual terrorism continued in émigré circles of Russia's large post-1917 diaspora, mainly in Europe.

The Russian civil war (1917/18–22) was dominated by combat activities, above all, direct fighting between the Red and White armies. Other widespread forms of violence included predatory local power-brokering and suppressive, punitive and other violence against civilians by all parties, gradually overtaken by terror by the Bolshevik state, especially at the stage of 'military communism' (1918–21). Following the early stage of the Bolshevik rule, anti-government terrorist acts carried out at home or terrorist attacks directed against Soviet citizens and other targets abroad became and remained rare exceptions for decades.

The Red Terror during the civil war paled in comparison to 'the Stalin repressions', which reached the scale of a domestic genocide.[7] At the time of Russia's worst state terror since medieval times, employed in the 1930s by the totalitarian system led by Joseph Stalin,[8] domestic terrorism came close to zero.

The post-Second World War USSR skipped the second historical wave of terrorism that manifested itself in Europe, the Americas and parts of Asia and the Middle East in the 1960s–80s. A few exceptions in the domestic use of terrorism included resort to terrorist means by localised anti-Soviet/pro-Nazi nationalist elements in the second half of the 1940s to early 50s (UNO/UPA in western Ukraine,[9] 'forest brothers' in the Baltic republics) and terrorist bombings by Armenian nationalists in Moscow on 8 January 1977.

This did not exclude support by the USSR and the Soviet bloc countries, such as the Warsaw Pact states and Cuba, for foreign communist and other left-wing insurgencies, anti-colonial movements and other militant groups, including those who, like the Palestinian Liberation Organisation, at some stage combined guerrilla warfare with terrorism.[10] To the extent that some of the Soviet (or Soviet allies') assistance to such groups was diverted to terrorist methods, it qualified as state support for terrorism by non-state actors. Following the logic of the bipolar world system, the same also applied to the Western bloc, including the US support for *contras* in Nicaragua and Western support for anti-Soviet jihad by the Afghan mujahideen.

However, anti-government terrorism inside the Soviet Union did not resume, in a systematic or statistically significant way, until the end of the Soviet period. It

---

7 According to the head of human rights group 'Memorial', Arseni Roginsky, direct victims of political repressions under Stalin's rule numbered approximately 12.5 million.
8 See D. Priestland, *Stalinism and the Politics of Mobilization: Ideas, Power, and Terror in Interwar Russia* (Oxford, Oxford University Press, 2007).
9 UNO and UPA (Ukrainian) stand for 'Organisation of Ukrainian Nationalists' and 'Ukrainian Insurgent Army', respectively.
10 R. Goren, *The Soviet Union and Terrorism* (London, George Allen & Unwin, 1984).

is only since the late 1980s, the last years of the Soviet era, when the state and its tight system of sociopolitical control started to disintegrate and political and media space reopened, that numbers of terrorist attacks, mostly by nationalists-separatists, started to grow, but they still remained low.

Terrorism and Insurgency in the North Caucasus

After Chechnya proclaimed its independence in 1991, as part of the general turmoil and disintegration at the time of collapse of the Soviet Union, it increasingly took up a separatist course, but was largely neglected by Moscow until late 1994. Russia's shift to armed intervention in Chechnya needs to be placed in the broader context of multiple, traumatic post-Soviet political, social and economic transitions that were going on simultaneously in the 1990s. More specifically, it needs to be placed in the context of the 1993 conflict between President Boris Yeltsin and the Parliament. That conflict ended in unconstitutional, violent suppression of the democratically elected parliament by a democratically elected president. Since the 1993 coup the authoritarian tendency gained ground in post-Soviet Russia and was later solidified during the 'Putin era'. The post-coup Yeltsin government lacked full legitimacy and had to show strength, reinforce its domestic position and direct public discontent against somebody else. In this spirit, Yeltsin launched the first military campaign in Chechnya, in December 1994 – officially, to 'restore constitutional order'. Thus, the war started more as a sign of regime weakness than of strength. What was meant to be a 'small victorious war' led to a sequence of two major armed conflicts of the type that can hardly be decisively won.

The first war involved fierce combat and several high-profile terrorist operations by Chechen separatists, including the June 1995 Budyonnovsk and the January 1996 Kizlyar attacks, with over 2,000 hostages taken in each case. Poorly managed by the federal centre, the war ended in the August 1996 Khasav-Yurt ceasefire, with the Russian troops to be withdrawn from Chechnya. That interim solution did not solve anything, nor did it address any of the underlying incompatibilities.

The conflict's underlying incompatibilities went well beyond the 'self-determination versus territorial integrity' dilemma to include painful and distorted modernisation of a North Caucasian society with significant traditionalist elements, as well as accompanying demodernisation processes,[11] and the

---

11 See V. Tishkov, *Chechnya: Life in a War-Torn Society* (Berkeley, University of California Press, 2004).

growing basic governance functionality gap between the federal state and the quasi-independent, secessionist Chechen Republic of Ichkeria. Whereas in Russia starting in the late 1990s a hybrid, anocratic regime started to consolidate and state functionality improved, Chechnya's self-governance experiment during its brief de facto independence period between the two wars (1996–9) did not work out, failed to provide basic order and public services and instead led to more militancy and instability.

The conflict in Chechnya became the main generator of terrorism in Russia for years. Certain conditions on both sides made this conflict particularly conducive to the use of terrorist means. Terrorism tends to be more effective when it is employed by a determined and capable opponent against a type of state that is neither a consolidated democracy, nor a full autocracy, neither too weak, nor too strong (which fully applied to Russia's transitional regime of the 1990s). The high level of determination and motivation on the part of the Chechen militants was catalysed by ideological extremism – a combination of ethnic separatism with growing Islamist radicalism, aggravated by such local norms and traditions as blood feud. In terms of organisation, the Chechen insurgency benefited from a dynamic, hybrid structure that combined network, clan and loose hierarchy elements. As the conflict became protracted, terrorist acts sharply increased in number and lethality (according to Russian official data, from 18 attacks in 1994 to 561 in 2003, amounting to a thirty-fold rise).

The federal response was brutal, but ineffective, poorly tailored to counterterrorist needs and often counterproductive. While Chechen terrorism became a serious challenge after, not before Russia launched its military campaign in December 1994, 'counterterrorism' was the main official rationale and post-hoc justification for the first war. Massive use of force in a poorly conducted counterinsurgency operation became the primary strategy to fight terrorism throughout the first war and into the second one. The short-term, reactive counterterrorist approach, based on poor (counter)intelligence, prioritised coercion, retaliation and post-hoc punishment and involved weak decision-making capacity. In a highly insecure environment, facing a capable armed opponent, unfriendly local population and difficulties in conducting patrolling or operating checkpoints, the federals often resorted to *zachistka* operations[12] that amounted to collective punishment and stimulated more violence than they were meant to quell. Outside Chechnya, especially in

---

12 A cordon and search operation.

Moscow, defensive measures were periodically upgraded, such as physical protection following every large-scale terrorist attack.

Russia's first antiterrorism law of 1998 legalised the use of armed forces in domestic counterterrorist operations, but still prioritised suppression, with minimal attention to terrorism prevention.[13] Unlike the first war in Chechnya, waged in an almost complete legal vacuum, the second one was squeezed into the category of a 'counterterrorist operation', applied to the entire territory of a federal republic. Russia's broad definition of terrorism did not explicitly acknowledge that terrorist actors pursue political goals, nor did it distinguish between terrorism against non-combatants and rebel attacks against military targets. The political, social and other underlying sources of Chechen terrorism and the Chechnya problem as a whole were also neglected at that stage.

The government of Vladimir Putin (Premier in 1999–2000 and 2008–12, President in 2000–8 and since 2012) made security and counterterrorism its top declared priorities. As Russia's main response to terrorism since the 1990s – the 'war' option – did not work, a relatively unorthodox approach had to be devised that went beyond military or counterterrorist measures. This revised approach did not materialise until a window of opportunity opened in Chechnya, in the context of the highly controversial impact of the rise of radical Salafism-jihadism *on the insurgency itself*. An originally ethno-separatist insurgency evolved to become an increasingly Islamist-jihadist movement with ambitions beyond Chechnya, across the North Caucasus. However, radicalisation of the insurgency along Salafist-jihadist lines in the late 1990s–2000s also set forth the dynamics that created conditions for the beginning of the end of a consolidated Chechen resistance.

Jihadisation became more salient as conflict became more intense and protracted,[14] and the rebels' state-building experiment during the quasi-independence period (1996–9) failed, leaving a vacuum of governance. This required additional mobilisation drivers and prompted further radicalisation of the insurgency, in terms of ideology and tactics. These key domestic drivers were exacerbated by external fundamentalist ideological influences and the inflow of foreign jihadists (mostly Arabs and diaspora Chechens from the Middle East).[15] Jihadisation of the insurgency first culminated in 1999

13 'Federal Law "On the Fight Against Terrorism"', *Rossiiskaya Gazeta*, 4 August 1998.
14 As noted by Gennadi Troshev, a native of Grozny and commander of federal troops in Chechnya in 1995–2002, 'we've bombed them into radical Islam'.
15 C. Moore and P. Tumelty, 'Foreign Fighters and the Case of Chechnya', *Studies in Conflict and Terrorism* 31/5 (2008).

when commanders Shamil Basayev and Khattab intervened in neighbouring Dagestan, with an explicitly Islamist goal of establishing an Islamic Republic of Ichkeria (Chechnya) and Dagestan.

On the one hand, resort to jihadist Islamism strengthened the resolve of the more radical elements of the insurgency and encouraged the use of more extreme tactics such as suicide terrorism and the new phenomenon of suicidal mass barricade hostage-taking (which culminated in the Nord-Ost and Beslan hostage crises, in 2002 and 2004, respectively). Also, jihadisation helped the insurgency both to cross multiple ethnic barriers, facilitating spillover of violence from Chechnya to other parts of the North Caucasus, and to bring in foreign funding from radical Islamist organisations, foundations and charities.

On the other hand, the rise of jihadism catalysed both the beginning of the end of major Chechen insurgency and one of the three main pillars of Russia's solution.[16]

To start with, the timing of jihadisation was extremely unfavourable for the insurgency, in view of the implications of the post-9/11 'war on terrorism'. Nothing facilitated the Kremlin's efforts to politically integrate the war in Chechnya into the global 'war on terrorism' more than jihadisation of the Chechen insurgency. A series of outrageous mass-casualty attacks against civilians, including children, such as the taking of hostages in a theatre centre in Moscow in October 2002 ('the Nord-Ost crisis') and at a school in Beslan, North Ossetia in September 2004,[17] passenger plane bombings etc. were undertaken explicitly under a jihadist banner, but were particularly counterproductive to the rebels' cause.

The growing role of jihadists also led to a series of major internal splits within the insurgency. Traditionalist ethno-confessional forces within the movement, led by the Chief Mufti of Chechnya and head of one of the two largest Sufi orders, the Qadiriyya, Akhmad Kadyrov, increasingly fell out with the Salafist-jihadists for reasons ranging from religious tensions to competition for turf and power. The followers of Kadyrov opted for leaving the insurgency, depriving it of significant manpower, clout and territory, and switched loyalty to the federal side. Once their main opponents left, the Salafist-jihadists won control over the insurgency from the remaining nationalists (such as independently elected President Aslan Maskhadov), but lost

---

16 'Solution' is used here as a euphemism for degrading the problem to a peripheral one.
17 A. Dolnik, *Negotiating the Impossible? The Beslan Hostage Crisis* (London, Royal United Services Institute, 2007).

Chechnya instead. Figuratively speaking, they won the battle, but lost the war.

The federal centre seized upon this split by shifting towards a new strategy of 'Chechenisation'. The strategy involved outsourcing stabilisation and most administrative tasks primarily to local Chechen forces who left the resistance and switched sides, and stepping up security and financial support to these forces. This produced the rise of formally pro-federal Chechen militias known as *kadyrovtsy*. In June 2000, the new Chechen administration headed by Akhmad Kadyrov was established. In 2001, the loyalist Chechen government moved to the republican capital of Grozny.

Russia's Chechenisation strategy was *literal*. The burden of keeping the order inside Chechnya was gradually, but fully shifted to the Kadyrov regime, which pursued a harsh security strategy and promoted traditional Sufi/Sunni Islam, while rigidly suppressing Salafism. Ramzan Kadyrov (who succeeded his father Akhmad, assassinated in a terrorist bombing on 9 May 2004) became the only republican head in Russia who controlled his security services and personally supervised counterterrorist operations. While heavily enforcement-centred, the *kadyrovtsy* response to terrorism and militancy was not confined to brutal suppression alone, and included reintegration of ex-combatants through amnesties and informal (clan, kin and other) ties and leverages.

Chechenisation was reinforced by the shift in federal security strategy from brutal to 'smart' suppression and prevention. This included a move away from controversial, *zachistka*-style, collective punishment operations in favour of more surgical special operations, focused on locating and systematically exterminating militant leaders (a tactic that proved to be a relatively effective way to counter violent networks). Following the Beslan tragedy, human and technical (counter)intelligence capacity was significantly improved, including creation of special Federal Security Service (FSB) units to collect intelligence on insurgent groups and the use of drones for reconnaissance purposes.

The third element of the solution was disbursement of massive reconstruction and development aid from the federal budget to Chechnya, without repayment requirements. In 2000–10, Russia allocated an enormous amount of federal funds to the North Caucasus; the Kadyrov regime received the bulk of 30 billion USD in exchange for loyalty and suppression of major violence. The funding increased from 0.6 billion USD in 2000 to 6 billion USD in 2010, or 600–700 USD per capita (four times Russia's average). By 2025, an additional 80 billion USD of federal funds were to be allocated.[18] Even as this massive economic support had a downside of 'privatisation' and siphoning off of state funds and reinforcing patronage–clientele resource distribution, it did result in visible, large-scale reconstruction of the basic infrastructure, economy and industrial production, educational system and public services in Chechnya.

A combination of Chechenisation, smarter suppression and large-scale financial assistance predetermined the outcome of the second Chechen war – disintegration of consolidated insurgency, decline in combat violence and terrorist activity by Chechens, general stabilisation of Chechnya, and the rise of a pro-Moscow Chechen government enjoying a very broad autonomy. In 2009, the ten-year 'counterterrorist operation' regime in Chechnya was lifted.

However imperfect, the three-pillar pacification strategy for Chechnya held through the 2010s. Even as occasional terrorist attacks in Chechnya continued, overall, the Kadyrov regime remained firmly in control. In fact, Chechnya became an island of relative stability amidst constantly emerging flashpoints of low-level violence across the broader North Caucasus. Chechenisation had worked for the time being, albeit at a high cost.

The main security costs were borne by the Chechen forces, who suffered heavy human losses in countering anti-government militants. While Kadyrov's strategy provided stabilisation in the short-to-mid term, it was hardly a substitute for long-term stability or applicable to contextual conditions in other North Caucasian republics. Financial costs were paid from Russia's federal budget and, as the economy slowed down in the 2010s, appeared to many to be excessively high. Political, civil and human rights repercussions were the most serious. If Putin's Russia was a hybrid regime that combined some formally democratic institutions with elements of autocracy and oligarchy, Kadyrov's Chechnya was a rigid autocracy. Chechenisation implied outsourcing not only counterterrorism, but also 'dirty work' (human rights abuse, forced disappearances, extrajudicial killings etc.). The ultimate political cost involved ceding an extensive amount of sovereignty to the Chechen republican authorities – almost everything short of formal sovereignty. As a result, Chechnya under Kadyrov pursued largely an autonomous state-building project even as Kadyrov himself played a major role in Russian politics. This heavy price for stabilisation may also be seen as Russia's specific, 'undeclared' way of addressing the main incompatibility over which the conflict was fought in the first place.

---

18 B. Judah, 'Putin's Medieval Peace Pact in Chechnya', *Bloomberg*, 26 April 2013.

Overall, Russia's solution to its main terrorist threat in the 1990s–2000s was partly made possible by a problem 'taking care of itself', through engagement of an indigenous Chechen element, but also resulted from a major shift in federal strategy towards Chechenisation, smarter suppression and massive reconstruction aid. No matter how dear the cost of that strategy was, it was much lower than the cost of war. While incomplete, Russia's solution helped to degrade the problem to a peripheral issue in national politics.

In the 2010s, peripheral, low-scale, increasingly segmented violence localised in the North Caucasus involved a mix of elements of communal, clan-based and ethnic strife, blood revenge, predatory and vigilante activities. Militant-terrorist actors with a more explicit Salafist-jihadist imperative became increasingly fragmented. A claim by the 'Islamic Emirate of the Caucasus' (Imarat Kavkaz), an umbrella network founded in 2007 by Doku Umarov, to control these cells was overstated – many operated on their own, with Imarat claiming responsibility for larger attacks only. Such violence was too elusive, non-linear and recurring to be decisively wiped out. Its underlying causes included deeply entrenched governance problems, prevalence of the patronage–clientele system, corruption and the region's lack of socio-economic development and of integration into the rest of Russia.[19] These problems may take decades to resolve. Against this background, Russia's approach to addressing such violence became containment (keeping it at the lowest possible level) as a more pragmatic and economical option.

Transnationalisation of Terrorism in the 2010s

Throughout the 2010s, Russia displayed a sustained decline in terrorism. Overall terrorist activity decreased 30-fold from 2010 to 2017,[20] including a 10-fold[21] to 7.5-fold[22] decline in terrorist attacks. Russia fell out of the Top Ten terrorism-affected states and, as of 2020, was down to no. 39 on the Global Terrorism Index scale, faring better than France, the UK and the United States.[23] While an upgrade of Russia's antiterrorism efforts at home

---

19 See 'North Caucasus: The Challenges of Integration (I–IV)', International Crisis Group (ICG) Europe reports nos. 220, 221, 226 and 237 (Brussels, ICG, 2012–15).
20 From 779 terrorism-related crimes in 2010 to 24 in 2017, according to the Head of Russia's National Security Council, Nikolai Patrushev: '[Security Council Marked a Ten-Fold Decline in Terrorist Crimes]', *RIA-Novosti*, 26 December 2017.
21 Ibid.
22 Global Terrorism Database, National Consortium for the Study of Terrorism and Responses to Terrorism (START), University of Maryland: www.start.umd.edu/gtd.
23 Global Terrorism Index/2020, p. 8.

contributed to a decline in terrorism,[24] the main substantive explanation remained de-escalation of the armed conflict in Chechnya. In 2008, it was downgraded by the Uppsala Conflict Data Program from a 'war' to a 'minor conflict' in the North Caucasus.[25]

Russia tried to ensure that this positive tendency was not reversed by any new destabilising factors, including transnational links. However, it is transnationalisation of terrorism and related radicalisation processes that became a growing challenge for Russia, actualised by the ISIS factor starting in the mid-2010s. These new challenges included transnationalisation of pre-existing domestic terrorism and violent extremism; emerging threats of the mixed, home-grown/transnationalised type; and growing transnational risks (from) abroad.

The first trend mainly involved transnationalisation of the pre-existing Islamist/separatist militancy in the North Caucasus. In the mid-2010s, segments of the fragmented violent underground pledged loyalty to ISIS. This led to their further radicalisation along the Salafist-jihadist line and to new splits, and weakened the indigenous Imarat Kavkaz. The outflow of local militants to Syria and Iraq starting in the early 2010s led to their transformation into transnational jihadists, actualising the issue of the subsequent return or relocation of survivors. The evolution of right-wing violent extremism, increasingly directed against labour migrants to Russia, predominantly Muslims from Central Asia, can also be seen as an extreme reaction to transnational processes.

A more recent trend involved radicalisation of small, self-generating cells and individuals into home-grown jihadist actors. These cells started to emerge in (sub)urban settings across Russia, with limited or no direct links to the North Caucasus. They were mainly comprised of Russian citizens, including native Muslims and converts to Islam, but also involved some migrants. While most radicalised at home, without having trained in or joined a terrorist group abroad, such cells demonstrated a better grasp of ISIS ideology and propaganda of 'global jihad', spread through modern means of information and communication. In many respects, these hybrid, home-grown/transnationalised cells more closely resembled jihadist cells in Europe than the North Caucasian militant underground.

24 There was a direct correlation with a nine-fold increase in terrorist convictions in 2013–17. Russia's Supreme Court statistics, quoted in '[One-Third of Convicted for Corruption Turned Out to Be Jobless]', *Rosbusinessconsulting*, 28 April 2018.
25 Uppsala Conflict Data Program and International Peace Research Institute in Oslo, Armed Conflict Dataset v.4–2009.

At least four risks for Russia were related to transnationalisation of terrorism in the broader sense and to transnational threats (from) abroad.

The first risk is Eurasia's physical proximity to both leading regions by intensity of terrorism and armed conflicts. One such region is the Near East, where Iraq and Syria were central areas of the ISIS violence, state-building experiment and other jihadist activity in the 2010s. Iraq was the world's most heavily terrorism-affected state through much of the early twenty-first century. Another region is South Asia, where Afghanistan accounted for more terrorism fatalities than any other country in 2017–19. This risk was compounded by relatively easy access and cross-border movement both from/to these regions and within much of Eurasia, due to Russia's visa-free policies with Central Asian states and Turkey and the porous nature of Afghanistan's borders.

Another risk was Russia's role as, in absolute numbers, perhaps the single largest country of origin of foreign terrorist fighters (FTFs) who headed for Syria and Iraq in the 2010s. Eurasia as a whole became a major region of FTF origin, second only to the Middle East. With the demise of the ISIS core in Syria and Iraq, the relocation and return of surviving FTFs threatened to become a major impulse to sustain the generational lifeline of jihadist terrorism in Europe, Eurasia, Asia and the Middle East.

The overall number of FTFs from Eurasia who fought as jihadists in Syria and Iraq was approximately 8,500–9,000 in 2017, including about 4,000 from Russia, of whom 619 were killed by May 2018.[26] The number of FTFs from Russia continued to increase longer than that from many other states and was officially estimated to have reached 5,500 by October 2019.[27] At the same time, due to fear of harsh prosecution and security control, FTF return rates to Russia (and to Central Asia) were considerably lower than return rates to the Middle East and Europe. Furthermore, the low rates of FTF returnees did not increase, and even declined somewhat over the second half of the 2010s, from 7.4 per cent in 2015 (compared, for instance, to almost 50 per cent FTF return to the UK at the time)[28] to 6 per cent in late 2019.[29]

---

26 '[Vladimir Putin: There Are up to 9,000 Militants from the Former USSR in Syria]', *Kommersant*, 23 February 2017; '[Over 600 Militants from Russia Killed Abroad]', *Rosbalt*, 16 May 2018.
27 '[FSB: 5.5 Thousand Russian Citizens Who Left to Fight in Terrorist Ranks Abroad Identified]', *RIA-Novosti*, 16 October 2019.
28 'CONTEST: The United Kingdom's Strategy for Countering Terrorism. Annual Report for 2015 Presented to Parliament by the Secretary of State for the Home Department. CM9310' (London, Controller of Her Majesty's Stationery Office, 2016), p. 7.
29 As estimated by the FSB, by the end of 2015, 214 out of 2,900 FTFs from Russia had returned; as of late 2019, only 337 out of 5,500 had. Quoted in: '[Russian Special Services Identified Hundreds of Fighters Who Returned from Syria and Iraq]', *Rosbusinessconsulting*,

Most FTF returns to Russia were from the first wave of the outflow of the early 2010s, which involved militants of the Imarat Kavkaz generation – mostly Russian-speaking Muslims from Eurasia and Europe who went to fight on the side of the Islamist opposition in Syria before the rise of ISIS. Not all of them joined ISIS once it became the lead jihadist force in Syria: some turned to other groups or left for Turkey. The second wave involved a younger, more urban generation of Russian-speakers who joined ISIS directly; in the late 2010s, the few returnees to Russia from this category were mostly FTF family members.

Through to the end of the 2010s, FTF returnees to Russia did not play a direct role in terrorist attacks, which remained of primarily home-grown character, sometimes with evidence of transnational connections (such as in the April 2017 bombing in the St Petersburg metro). Paradoxically, the closest connection to ISIS was displayed by several 'lone-wolf' attacks, such as the stabbing of passers-by by a young Dagestani on 19 August 2017 in Surgut (West Siberia), followed by a video of him pledging allegiance to 'Islamic State' published by the ISIS central media.

However, the risk of FTFs' engagement in violence and radicalisation at home cannot be discounted. While it was commonly expected that a natural place for them to come back would be the North Caucasus, federal containment strategy and security pressures inside the region imposed severe limits on such flow-back. In fact, there was a no lesser 'demand' for FTF returnees elsewhere in Russia, in view of proliferation of the new type of self-generating home-grown jihadist micro-cells across the country. Most of them, in contrast to the North Caucasian militants, but much like jihadist cells in Europe, displayed a mismatch between high ideological ambition and limited capacity to carry out deadly terrorist attacks. The undetected return of only a few seasoned FTFs, even if not all of them turned back to violent extremism, would suffice to bridge that gap by upgrading local cells' terrorist capacity through training, experience-sharing and ideological inspiration.

A no less, or more, disturbing challenge may be posed by Russian/Eurasian FTFs' relocation to third countries. Most surviving Russian-speakers and other FTFs from Eurasia, unlikely ever to return home, were located in or headed to third countries of the Middle East (such as Turkey, Egypt or Jordan), Europe and Asia. It was the third countries where FTFs from Eurasia caused the biggest trouble in the mid- to late 2010s: the two

---

25 December 2015; '[FSB: 5.5 Thousand Russian Citizens Who Left to Fight in Terrorist Ranks Abroad Identified]'.

deadliest of five attacks committed by terrorists of Eurasian origin outside their home region in 2016–17 involved FTFs or other ISIS-linked militants from the North Caucasus and Central Asia.[30]

FTFs of Eurasian origin in transit or stuck in third countries also threatened Russia, by their potential to attack Russian targets abroad and revive connections with, and exert ideological influence on, radicals at home. Another challenge to Russia was posed by the relocation and accumulation of some FTFs, especially Central Asians, in northern Afghanistan – a grey area populated by their ethnic kin and next to their home region. Relocation of FTFs from Syria and Iraq should not be confused with the regional ISIS branch Vilayat Khorasan, or Islamic State Khorasan Province (ISKP), in Pakistan and Afghanistan.[31] In 2018, Russia estimated the strength of all ISKP and self-identified ISIS militants at 4,000–10,000, with roughly half based in Afghanistan's north.[32] Even if FTFs relocating from Syria and Iraq to northern Afghanistan numbered in the low hundreds, they posed a serious concern to Central Asia, Russia as the main security ally of three Central Asian states and the Russia-led Collective Security Treaty Organisation.

Another challenge has been posed by the potential for returning Central Asian FTFs to use Russia's own territory for transit or as an alternative to returning home, by trying to 'get lost' amidst millions of formal and informal labour migrants from Central Asia in Russia. While some could head back to Central Asia via Russia, others would prefer to stay. If undetected, they could pose a security risk, along with the Russian FTF returnees.

The third risk involved growing terrorist threats to Russian citizens and targets abroad. This related to the overall transnationalisation of terrorism and to Russia's increased role and physical presence abroad, including in the Middle East, where Moscow launched its first military/antiterrorist campaign outside post-Soviet Eurasia (in Syria, beginning in 2015). The largest ISIS attack against Russian citizens – the bombing of a passenger aircraft over Sinai (Egypt) in October 2015, killing 224 – was committed abroad.

Finally, the radicalisation of segments of Russia's migrant labour population, dominated by Muslims of Central Asian origin, cannot be excluded in

---

30 The June 2016 Istanbul airport attack and the January 2017 attack on Istanbul's Reina nightclub.
31 A. Giustozzi, *The Islamic State in Khorasan: Afghanistan, Pakistan and the New Central Asian Jihad* (London, Hurst, 2018); E. Stepanova and J. Ahmad, 'Militant-Terrorist Groups in, and Connected to, Afghanistan', in *Terrorism in Afghanistan: A Joint Threat Assessment* (New York, East–West Institute, 2020).
32 According to Deputy Foreign Minister on antiterrorism Oleg Syromolotov, quoted in '[Afghanistan's North Becomes a Mainstay for Terrorism]', *RIA-Novosti*, 4 May 2018.

the longer run, at the second-generation stage. Even if only a small percentage were to become radicalised, it could be significant, as the total of Muslim migrants in Russia throughout the 2010s was approximately 7–8 million. In the late 2010s, radicalisation among first-generation migrants was not widespread yet, even as some jihadist cells, including perpetrators of the 3 April 2018 bombing in the St Petersburg metro, involved migrants from Central Asia. Notably, for the very few migrants who turned into violent extremists, radicalisation usually occurred not before, but *after* they arrived in Russia.[33]

Russia's capacity to address these new challenges depended on how well it could adjust to the changing nature of terrorism at home from predominantly internal to transnationalised home-grown threats, cope with transnational risks (from) abroad and engage in international antiterrorism cooperation.

* * *

In contrast to the post-Second World War part of the Soviet period, post-Soviet Russia displayed a growing overlap with global trends in terrorism, especially in the early twenty-first century. More generally, terrorism in Russia at both historical stages – in the late imperial and post-Soviet periods – largely conformed to global trends in terrorism at the time. The Russian case was an integral part of two out of three waves in the world history of terrorism – the first one (of the late nineteenth to early twentieth century) and the third and ongoing one (of the early twenty-first century).

Historically, terrorism in Russia was hardly unique in terms of its general causes, drivers and facilitating conditions. It largely conformed to several key broader explanatory frameworks. One such framework is centred on the role of traumatic, overdue and incomplete modernisation (especially if undertaken by or taking place in an eroding autocracy or in a weak/emerging democracy) as a structural cause of sociopolitical violence. Equally relevant to the Russian case is the role of social, political and economic transitions as major facilitating conditions for terrorism. Dynamic interaction and interdependence of anti-government terrorism and state terror also characterised both historical peaks of terrorism in Russia and applied to:

- The eroding tsarist autocracy in its final decades;
- The former totalitarian regime undergoing democratisation coupled with several other rapid, uneven transitional processes (post-Soviet Russia in the 1990s);

---

33 This also raised the issue of the return of radicalised migrants from Russia to Central Asia.

- The consolidating anocratic system that combined increasingly autocratic tendencies with some remaining political and media space and quasi-democratic institutions (the Putin regime in the early twenty-first century).

At both historical stages, terrorism in Russia was employed both as a method of political violence in peacetime (revolutionary and other terrorism in the Russian Empire and, over a century later, transnationalised/home-grown jihadist terrorism) and as a tactic in broader armed conflict – in the contexts of the 1905–7 revolution and of the conflict in Chechnya and the North Caucasus since the mid-1990s, respectively. All the differences between these two internal conflicts notwithstanding, conflict-related terrorism at any historical stage proved to be more intense and mass-based than in peacetime. However, its symbolic effect and ability to affect politics were the greatest either in peacetime, or during armed conflict, but in areas outside the conflict zone.

In the late nineteenth to early twentieth century, the specifics of Russian terrorism were relatively limited. The Russian case was not only integral to the world's first historical wave of terrorism – the Russian Empire was one of the leading candidates for the birthplace of modern terrorism and manifested all of its ideological types. While Russian terrorism developed under heavy influence by radical European ideologies, Russian ideologues of terrorism made a major contribution to the field. In terms of terrorist practices, the 'Russian way' had a model effect for terrorists in other regions. Russia's specifics were largely confined to the dominant variety of anti-government terrorism (socio-revolutionary, not anarchist) and better-organised, more persistent and systematic use of terrorist means. At the structural level, this could be explained by more acute and radical controversy between Russian absolutist monarchy's persistent unwillingness and failure to reform its political system, and the imperatives of belated, but rapid capitalist modernisation.

The Soviet Union bypassed the second historical wave of terrorism. While terrorism requires political space, the Stalin regime in particular exercised overwhelming control over the society and the state through means ranging from ideological mobilisation to mass repressive terror. This left no media, political or public space for terrorism. Whenever such control was weaker or eroded (at the earliest or the latest stage of the Soviet rule), political space for terrorism (re)opened.

Forestalled by the attacks of 11 September 2001 in the United States, the world's third historical wave of terrorism culminated in the mid-2010s.

Conflict-related, Islamist-separatist terrorism in post-Soviet Russia overlapped with, but also predated this global peak. In terms of type, scale and intensity of dominant terrorist threat, Russia's national specifics were more pronounced during the first two post-Soviet decades. The Islamist-separatist bent of Russia's main type of terrorism during that period, employed in the context of domestic (counter)insurgency, distinguished it from the dominant patterns of terrorism in Europe and in the West at large. However, by Asian standards, Russia's case was quite unexceptional: in the late twentieth to early twenty-first century, almost every Asian Muslim-minority state (India, China, the Philippines, Thailand) faced terrorism by a peripheral Islamist-separatist insurgency. If any lessons are to be gleaned from Russia's management of its main terrorism problem, which, following a series of failures, was degraded to a relatively marginal issue, they could apply to typologically similar Asian/Eurasian cases, if at all.

Finally, comparison between the two main periods of terrorism in Russia's own history reveals surprisingly few, if any, direct parallels or genetic links between them. If any parallels could be drawn, they mostly relate to the applicability of general explanatory frameworks to the Russian case. Ultimately, during both the pre-Soviet and post-Soviet historical stages, terrorism in Russia failed to achieve its perpetrators' declared goals. Almost everything else differs – historical context, typology, motivations and degree of transnationalisation of terrorism, type of state, political regime and terrorist actor(s), as well as state response to terrorism.

However, the domestic sociopolitical situation in twenty-first-century Russia displays some disturbing and growing parallels to the post-1881 public moods and climate. These parallels concern the widening gap between the unreformed, stagnant and increasingly obsolete character of the political order and rapid social modernisation, qualitatively enhanced in the contemporary stage by the imperatives of the information and globalisation age. While this gap has not led to any significant violent extremism, at some point it may spur sociopolitical violence, including in radical forms. If there is any lesson for Russia to learn from its more distant historical experience of terrorism, it is this one.

Further Reading

A. Dolnik, *Negotiating the Impossible? The Beslan Hostage Crisis* (London, Royal United Services Institute, 2007)

C. Moore and P. Tumelty, 'Foreign Fighters and the Case of Chechnya', *Studies in Conflict and Terrorism* 31/5 (2008)

North Caucasus: The Challenges of Integration (I–IV), International Crisis Group (ICG) Europe reports nos. 220, 221, 226, 237 (Brussels, ICG, 2012–15)

E. Stepanova, 'Russia's Response to Terrorism in the Twenty-First Century', in M. Boyle (ed.), *Non-Western Responses to Terrorism* (Manchester, Manchester University Press, 2019)

V. Tishkov, *Chechnya: Life in a War-Torn Society* (Berkeley, University of California Press, 2004)

14

Terrorism in the Netherlands
A History

BEATRICE DE GRAAF[*]

Introduction: 'Historicising Terrorism' as Part of a Security Culture

'Terrorism' as a history of and in a given country can only be written as global history. It is a phenomenon that cannot be studied in isolation, but only properly understood in its connectedness with the wider context of global trends in ideology, technology and political contestation.[1] In this chapter, terrorism is interpreted as a contested concept: as a discursive frame and a political attribution – oftentimes not even properly judicially delineated – with the power to transform conflicting political, ideological or religious positions into repertoires of action and governmental practices. Terrorism comprises various layers of analysis and description (is it an event, a historical trend, a policy, a framework?) and is a moving target, both discursively and legally. This makes it all the more challenging to write its history. Do we start with the emergence of terrorism as political discourse, with the definition of terrorism as a legal category, or with instances of disruptive terrorist events, and the media reporting and terrorist trials that often follow?

Elsewhere, I have introduced the notion of 'security cultures' to make it possible to historicise such notoriously contentious and open terms as 'security' or 'terrorism' throughout the last two centuries. A 'security culture' can be defined as 1) an open, and contested, process of threat-identification and interest-assessment, including the drawing of lines between friends and foes, insiders and outsiders; 2) enabled by institutional structures and agents involved in these processes of threat-assessment and neutralisation; 3) resulting in practices and action repertoires that are introduced and implemented to defend the allegedly

---

[*] The author wishes to thanks Carla Spiegel for her assistance.
[1] See S. Conrad, *What Is Global History?* (Princeton, Princeton University Press, 2017), p. 5.

endangered interests.[2] Studying 'terrorism' in these terms sheds new light on the nineteenth-century predecessors of the current 'War on Terror', and attention to the latter in turn helps nuance broader understandings of the categories and actors, ideas and practices. Current literatures on IR, security and terrorism already work with such concepts (security, security cooperation and counterterrorism), but apply them more often than not in a highly presentist or generalising fashion, giving little or no attention to manifestations of collective threat perceptions and counterterrorism cultures prior to 1945, let alone 1918. Here, 'historicising terrorism as a security threat',[3] that is, paying attention to the intersubjective and mediatised character of threat and interest constructions such as these developed within historical contexts, is explicitly widened to include the nineteenth century as well. Because, with the French Revolution and the emergence of a public space, the early nineteenth century was already seeing the outlines of a global marketplace of ideas, public scares, moral outrages and circulation of threat assessments and enemy images around the notion of 'terror' and 'terrorism'.

For this chapter, the methodological operationalisation of the notion of 'security culture' means that the chain of translating terrorism from incident via discursive frame and mediatised circulation to policymaking and concrete practices will be followed through time. Thus, we can historicise 'terrorism' as a semantic concept, a discourse, an occurrence of political violence and a reality of governmental interventions in public or social life. Terrorist events will be highlighted *inasmuch as they were reported on in the Netherlands*, or when threats posed by international terrorist organisations or foreign groups were mediatised within the Dutch context. We will also trace when indigenous Dutch radical groups and individuals triggered national debates – and estimate whether this was followed by national policy decisions and actions or not. As will transpire, the Netherlands were more often than not on the receiving end of international terrorism and global terrorist trends. Yet, there were some instances of terrorist groups and attacks originating in and from the Netherlands, inspired by injustice frames generated on the basis of misgivings about Dutch politics. By and large, the history of terrorism in the Netherlands did follow the trajectories of David

---

2 B. A. de Graaf, I. de Haan and B. Vick, 'Introduction', in B. A. de Graaf, I. de Haan and B. Vick (eds.), *Securing Europe after Napoleon* (Cambridge, Cambridge University Press, 2019), p. 18.
3 B. A. de Graaf and C. Zwierlein, 'Historicizing Security: Entering the Conspiracy Dispositive', *Historical Social Research* 38/1 (2013).

Rapoport's 'four waves' of terrorism, albeit with some national characteristics, and always situated within the specific confines of the Dutch national context.[4]

In 'historicising terrorism' in the Netherlands, the notion of 'path incrementalism' should be brought up as well. This chapter starts with the French Revolution as the major event that heralded the emergence of 'terror' and 'terrorism' as a salient political figure and discursive frame in the Netherlands. Interestingly enough, 'terrorism' was perceived by early nineteenth-century pundits as a modern phenomenon, carried out either by groups outside or within the state, and aiming to achieve revolutionary changes in government and society. The French Revolution and the 'Reign of Terror' thus very much set the stage and the tone regarding the introduction of 'terrorism' as a category of political change into the Dutch arena and as a 'bifurcated concept'. Terrorism would always have two faces: terror by non-state actors aimed at overthrowing the government and revolutionising society on the one hand, and terror by the government (the 'reign of terror') in order to quell opposition and dissent on the other. In the following, we will trace the introduction, trajectories and translations of terrorism as a concept, discourse and influence on concrete security practices in Dutch politics, society and law – and we will ask ourselves how this double-edged nature of terrorism played out in these interactions.

The French Revolution and the Birth of 'Terrorism' as a Two-Pronged Threat

The history of terrorism in the Netherlands as a discourse and a category of political change started with the French Revolution. Empirically, the first references to terrorism, terrorists and terror can be found in Dutch journal articles in the years after 1795. Before the French revolution, 'terror' (*terreur*) had been part of the political vocabulary as well, but back then (and this interpretation continued in public texts throughout the nineteenth and twentieth centuries[5]), it had denoted the righteous, salutary and majestic 'terror of God' – that capacity of gods and princes to instil fear in their enemies. Since Robespierre's Reign of Terror, however, the concept had morphed into a secularised version, the 'terror of the people', the 'tyranny of

---

4 D. C. Rapoport, 'The Four Waves of Modern Terrorism', in A. K. Cronin, J. M. Ludes and Georgetown University (eds.), *Attacking Terrorism: Elements of a Grand Strategy* (Washington, DC, Georgetown University Press, 2004).
5 *De Tijd*, 2 March 1864, which cites the 'terror of God's eternal predestination'.

the multitude': in short, into a 'term of abuse that could be used to discredit political adversaries'.[6] In Dutch discourse as well, references to terrorism pointed to the French Revolutionary or Bonapartist system of governance without law; it could indicate 'fanaticism', 'Jacobinism' or despotism – with the Dutch brand christened 'Batavian terror'. Moreover, through the revolutionary and Napoleonic wars, the semantic field of terror/terrorism became connected to chaos, disorder and anarchy as well. The securitising subject of this 'reign of terror' could, however, point in two directions: towards the government, engaging in 'terror' and abuses of power, or towards 'radicals' aiming at revolutionising society and overthrowing government.

After 1793, with the transnational spread of the scare of Robespierre's 'Reign of Terror' as a threat throughout Europe, with the continuation of the 'terror' inflicted by Napoleon's armies after 1803 and the reports on these instances of repression and violence by means of (military) bulletins, 'terror' became a unifying force for collective scares and moral outrages. Only a relatively small political faction favoured the use of 'terror' to revolutionise Dutch society and implement a modernised, centralised state system by force (for these Dutch radicals, 'terrorising' was not necessarily a negative concept). They remained marginal, by contrast with the French situation, never 'spilling one drop of blood'.[7] Subsequently, with the march of the Allied armies from 1813 onwards, a progressive institutionalisation of collective security policies to combat, neutralise and fend off terror, both in its revolutionary and its Napoleonic guise, was embraced. The peace treaties that marked the end of the Napoleonic wars – culminating in the Final Act of Vienna (June 1815), the Quadruple Alliance and the Paris Peace Treaty (November 1815) – created an international system that defined security as a collective obligation, referring both to the geopolitical challenge of restoring a balance of power and the domestic contexts of preventing revolutionary unrest from erupting ever again.[8]

The Netherlands featured here as well. The first concrete 'terrorist' event that was discursively linked to 'terrorism' both conceptually and in practice after 1815 took place in France, but had the Netherlands as its locus of origin. It started with an assault on the Paris palace where the supreme commander

---

6 See R. Schechter, *A Genealogy of Terror in Eighteenth-Century France* (Chicago, University of Chicago Press, 2018), pp. 204–5.

7 See N. van Sas, *Bataafse terreur: De betekenis van 1798* (Nijmegen, Van Tilt, 2011); N. van Sas, 'Scenario's voor een onvoltooide revolutie, 1795–1798', *BMGN/Low Countries Historical Review* 164/4 (1989).

8 B. A. de Graaf, *Fighting Terror: Securing Europe after Napoleon* (Cambridge, Cambridge University Press, 2020).

of the Allied forces and kingmaker of the post-Napoleonic peace, Arthur Wellesley, the Duke of Wellington, lived during the years of the Allied occupation of France. In the night of 10/11 February 1818 an aggrieved Jacobin from Brussels, named Catillon, awaited the Duke in front of the entrance and fired shots at him. The perpetrator missed – but sparked a massive public outrage. Via optic telegraph and couriers, the news of the attack was disseminated through France and Western Europe, alarm spreading everywhere. 'They did not aim at me, but at the allied army of occupation', Wellington correctly surmised.[9] Police officials in Paris and the Netherlands left no stone unturned in identifying the radicalist perpetrators and soon connected the attack to 'emigré Bonapartists' and former 'terroristes' from Brussels, where some of the exiled revolutionaries had indeed resettled and found a livelihood in printing and disseminating subversive pamphlets aimed at overthrowing the French and European order. Against this threat of 'armed Jacobinism',[10] the Allied ministers in Paris convened in the Allied Council and composed lists of allegedly 'dangerous radicals', including Bonapartists, members of Napoleon's family and a series of regicides and other 'terroristes dangereux'. These first European 'blacklists' were dispatched to all the foreign courts of Europe. Subsequently, after 1818, Metternich (with the support of Russia and Prussia) continued to try to transform the Allied coalition into a kind of 'European police', threatening minor countries with military action and enforcement if they would not comply and expel or imprison their radicals. The new King of the Netherlands, William I, was thus pressed into compliance and, reluctantly, introduced a number of new laws and deportation regulations (which they never seriously enforced). With censorship laws, the plotting and wrangling of French exiles and 'terroristes' in Brussels – 'this nest of traitors and libellers' – was curtailed somewhat.[11] Yet, in the Netherlands, the coming decades did not witness new, reported acts of 'terrorism'.

Over the course of the following decades, from the 1820s until the 1860s, terrorism did surface as a category in media and parliamentary debates, predominantly as a reference to the threat of revolution and anarchy by non-

---

9 R. Muir, *Wellington: Waterloo and the Fortunes of Peace, 1814–1852* (New Haven, Yale University Press, 2015), pp. 111–13.
10 Metternich, Memorandum to Hardenberg, 6 August 1815, GStA, PK III. HA I, nr. 1461, 75.
11 Wellington, Memorandum to ministers on the libels published in the Low Countries, 29 August 1816, attachment of Wellington to the protocol of the Allied Council of Ministers, 29 August 1816, The National Archives, Foreign Office, FO 146/14; see also De Graaf, *Fighting Terror*, chapters 5, 6.

state actors. As in 1818, 'terrorism' or 'terroristes' did first of all indicate the discrete category of 387 regicide representatives in the French Convention of 1793 and the direct followers of Robespierre, but was soon broadened to encompass newer generations of radicals. Sometimes the terminology was used to identify revolutionary uprisings in Belgium or Poland, as in 1830.[12] In the process of European radicalisation towards the uprisings of 1848, Dutch media indeed warned against the 'terrorism of the turbulent classes', pointing to the Swiss revolts in the canton of Vaud (1846), radicals in Italy, Belgium and Ireland, or Kossuth in Hungary. Terrorism was not just a political category, but also undermined social peace and order: 'La violence et le terrorisme sont les satellites du désordre social.'[13] Interestingly, at the same time, the threat of terrorism was also invoked to decry governmental despotism, in the form of Dutch governmental action against Belgian newspapers in 1830. 'Terrorism' was also attributed to a government, such as the Russian one, which did not refrain from infringing upon constitutional liberties and the freedom of the press in Poland.[14] The Italian and German governments were similarly chastised for their use of violence against oppositional factions. The culmination of this two-pronged threat was reached in 1851, according to the Dutch media, when Napoleon III used the fear for 'terrorism' and the memory of 'Red Terror' to install his own 'reign of terror'.[15]

In these first post-1815 decades, the security culture regarding 'terrorism' was still quite obfuscated and not sharply defined by law. It needs to be stressed that, in the decades before the 1880s, terrorism 'by the deed' and 'by the pencil' were not yet strictly separated. The epitaph 'radical' or 'Jacobin' could comprise both radical writers and those who committed violent or seditious acts; terrorism was a category of political unrest and social disorder, or an indication of governmental despotism.[16] Yet, this framing of any radical opposition to authoritarian monarchical rule as potentially terrorist and revolutionary abated somewhat after 1848, when the Dutch king accepted a constitution and made way for a parliamentary monarchy and democracy.

---

12 *L'éclaireur politique: Journal de la province du Limbourg*, 3 May 1829; *Journal de La Haye*, 17 June 1831.
13 *Journal de La Haye*, 18 April 1846; *Provinciale Overijsselsche en Zolsche Courant*, 21 April 1848; *Journal de La Haye*, 1 January 1849; *Rotterdamsche Courant*, 18 October 1849.
14 *L'éclaireur politique: Journal de la province du Limbourg*, 3 May 1829; *Journal de La Haye*, 17 June 1831.
15 *De Tijd*, 9 December 1851.
16 M. J. F. Robijns, *Radicalen in Nederland, 1840–1851* (PhD thesis, Leiden, Universitaire Pers, 1967).

The legal limbo regarding terrorism remained unchanged, however, and was only marginally adapted with the dawn of international anarchism.

A Failed Recipe: Anarchism in the Netherlands

With the emergence of the Fenians in Ireland, and the repression of the Paris Commune in 1870, the transnational spectre of 'terrorism' was both reawakened and depicted in sharper contours within the Dutch political and public arena.[17] Terrorism would now comprise concrete groupings of non-state actors who carried out political attacks or assassinations, such as the assassination attempts on Tsar Alexander II, and presented themselves as organisations – such as Narodnaya Volya, or 'the nihilists', as they were called in the Dutch media.[18] At the same time, such organisations were consciously and deliberately linked by confessional Catholic or Protestant journals to 'demonic liberalism', godless socialism and the 'terror of the masses', or 'the classes', that attempted to subvert the God-given order of society.[19] The national security culture became more polarised, divided into confessional, socialist and liberal factions – a situation mirrored in the fragmented media landscape.

Before any concrete incident of terrorism (such as a political murder or attack) took place, rumours and reports of foreign instances of violent attacks were feverishly collected and circulated by the Dutch authorities. Newspapers, telegraph, telephone and coffeehouse rumours contributed to this process of the public dissemination and securitisation of global anarchist threats. Due to the rise of financial markets and the diamond industry, cities like Amsterdam and Rotterdam experienced an economic high after 1871, followed by a corresponding upsurge in urban security and criminality problems. Public disturbances and riots increased, putting issues of public order and security high on the local and political agenda, advanced by political parties that were founded around that same period. Regarding

---

17 *Algemeen Handelsblad*, 22 December 1869; *De Locomotief*, 17 April 1871. On the concepts discussed in this section, see See B. A. de Graaf, 'The Black International as Security Dispositive in the Netherlands, 1880–1900', *Historical Social Research* 38/1 (2013); B. A. de Graaf and W. Klem, 'Joining the International War Against Anarchism: The Dutch Police and Its Push Towards Transnational Cooperation, 1880–1914', in R. van Dijk et al. (eds.), *Shaping the International Relations of the Netherlands, 1815–2000* (London, Routledge, 2018).
18 *Arnhemsche Courant*, 21 April 1879. The newspaper reported on failed attempts; the successful one occurred in 1881. *Tilburgsche Courant*, 5 May 1881; *Hoornsche Courant*, 9 July 1879.
19 *De Standaard*, 10 May 1883; 9, 14 September 1885.

these security concerns, it was not the marginal anarchists, but the increasingly organised socialists that represented the largest threat to the established order of confessional, conservative and liberal governments.[20] Police reports spoke of 'red flags' and subversive socialists roaming the streets.[21] Moreover, connections were drawn between socialists in the Netherlands and explosive events abroad. In 1887, a new article was added to the constitution, allowing the king to impose martial law and to declare a state of emergency 'in order to maintain external and international security'.[22]

Violent outbursts and attacks – such as those occurring in tsarist Russia, Spain or the United States – did not take place, but Parliament nevertheless felt the need to prohibit transporting and stockpiling explosives 'with malicious intent' per royal decree in 1885.[23] On 5 December 1888, on the occasion of the Dutch national celebration of Saint Nicholas, the mayor, police commander and public prosecutor of Amsterdam received 'hellish machines' – explosive devices, intended to blow up when they were unwrapped. The true content of the surprise packages was, however, detected before they exploded.[24] From the archives, it becomes clear that itinerant anarchists remained a threat in the years that followed. Police commissioners reported on 'strangers' within their area, purportedly preparing all kinds of subversive activities.[25] Newspapers reported on anarchist attacks abroad ('Read and tremble', the *Rotterdamsch nieuwsblad* commented on the Paris attack.[26]) *De Politiegids* pointed to a potential anarchist constituency in the Netherlands, where 'the violent school from which the Ravachols ... originated [knew] many students as well'. The police journal also expanded the threat definition, and turned it into a subversion of the overall public and moral order: 'And our country? ... Then a number of shocking attacks against public morality occurred. However different they

---

20 J. Charité, *De Sociaal-Democratische Bond als orde-en gezagsprobleem voor de overheid (1880–1888)* (PhD thesis, Utrecht, Zuid-Hollandsche Boeken Handelsdrukkerij, 1972); D. Bos, *Waarachtige volksvrienden: De vroege socialistische beweging in Amsterdam, 1848–1894* (Amsterdam, Bakker, 2001).
21 Telegrams of bureau section 5 to central bureau, 25 July 1886; see Gemeentearchief Amsterdam (GAA), 5225, 5.50 afternoon, no. 164 and idem, 7.56 afternoon, no. 148.
22 R. W. van Zuijlen, *Veiligheid als opdracht. Een onderzoek naar veiligheid als fundamenteel recht en als positieve verplichting van de staat in het licht van de politietaak tot strafrechtelijke rechtshandhaving* (PhD thesis, Nijmegen, Wolf Legal Publishers, 2000), p. 66.
23 'Royal Decree', *Staatsblad*, no. 187, 15 October 1885.
24 'Uit de Hoofdstad', *De Nederlandsche politiegids*, no. 37, January 1889.
25 Letter of the public prosecutor of Amsterdam to the Minister of Justice, 14 June 1894, National Archive, The Hague (NL-HaNA), 2.09.05. no. 8, 6486.
26 'Aanslagen', *Tilburgsche Courant*, 24 March 1892; 'Buitenland', *Rotterdamsch Nieuwsblad*, 29 March 1892.

might be, they seem to be connected by one single thread', the revolt against authority as such.[27]

Given the transnational spread of anarchism, the Dutch judicial authorities not only worried about any imminent danger of anarchist bombings in the Netherlands, but were even more concerned about their country becoming a safe haven for fugitive terrorists from abroad.[28] In May 1894, the prosecutor of The Hague wrote the Minister of Justice about the retrieval of a recipe for the making of a nitroglycerine bomb in May 1894, via a 'secret informer' within anarchist circles.[29] And after the assassination of French President Sadi Carnot in June, the Ministry of Justice warned all prosecutors of a heightened risk of incoming anarchist fugitives and dynamite attacks, and a manual was prepared to instruct the police services 'to deal with hellish machines'.[30]

Yet, these missives and some additional protective measures around Queen Wilhelmina aside, the Dutch Minister of Justice Van der Kaay remained reluctant to adopt new blanket antiterrorism laws similar to the French, Russian or Prussian ones. He kept to his liberal position and fended off those (represented by his prosecutors and the Prussian envoy), who demanded stricter laws on extradition or high treason. The minister did not see any merit in 'cultivating martyrs' or 'sowing the seed of resentment' amongst the social democrats, thereby 'nourishing that party'.[31] No war on anarchism was instigated, as far as the minister was concerned. What did change, however, was the level of connectedness and preparedness at police level. Dutch police commissioners participated in the Berlin Conference in 1897 and Rome Conference on International Anarchism in 1898, and undersigned the treaties on behalf of the Netherlands (thereby introducing the first international definition of terrorism to the Netherlands, albeit without legal implications in the form of antiterrorist paragraphs).[32] Moreover, after 1898,

---

27 'Aanranding van 't Gezag', *De Nederlandse politiegids*, no. 103, July 1894.
28 Letters of Serraris to the Minister of Justice, Den Bosch, 2 June 1894, NL-HaNA, 2.09.05, 6486, no. 2; 14 June 1894, NL-HaNA 2.09.05, 6486, no. 9.
29 Exchange between the regional police and Minister of Justice, 22 May–13 June 1894, NL-HaNA, 2.09.05, 6486, no. 10. Another reference to retrieved dynamite recipes can be found in *De Tijd*, 23 December 1892.
30 Letter of Serraris to the Minister of Justice (secret), 6 July 1894, NL-HaNA, 2.09.05, 6642, no. 12139; Minister of Justice to the Minister of War, 3 August 1894, NL-HaNA, 2.09.05, 6642, no. 36.
31 Exchange between the Minister of Justice, the Minister of Foreign Affairs and the German envoy, 18 December 1895 and 8 January 1896, NL-HaNA, 2.09.05, 6488, no. 6.
32 M. Deflem, *Policing World Society: Historical Foundations of International Police Cooperation* (Oxford, Oxford University Press, 2002). R. B. Jensen, *The Battle Against Anarchist Terrorism: An International History, 1878–1934* (Cambridge, Cambridge University Press, 2014).

structural surveillance and deportation of suspect foreigners, the creation of a central bureau for transnational information coordination and exchange within the Ministry of Justice, and the introduction of a new force of plain-clothes detectives ushered in a new mode of security governance: one that superseded the rather laidback and ad hoc measures applied by previous cabinets and that heralded a more internationally oriented, preventive and proactive governmentality.[33]

Terrorism Around the Wars

As a spillover of the late nineteenth-century anarchist threat, 'terrorism' as discourse and frame was carried into the twentieth century, but mostly to condemn socialist manifestations, strikes and picketing. With the installation of a staunch confessional, reformed government in 1901, chaired by the imposing Calvinist leader Abraham Kuyper, any social-democrat initiative or event, most notably the railroad strikes of 1903, was condemned as 'terrorist subversion' by the confessional and mainstream journals. At the same time, social and liberal outlets demanded the right to strike and form and join labour unions, and equally ostracised governmental prosecution and repression of strikers and union workers as 'police terror'.[34] Within the next few years, however, references to anarchist 'terrorism' and strikes were overshadowed by reports on 'terrorist' attacks in Spain, Russia and Serbia. 'The Black Hand' featured frequently, as did the rise of 'White and Red terrorism' in Russia after 1910, only to be paralleled by shocking reports on German terrorism in Belgium and France after the onset of the First World War, even amounting to the translated 'Yellow Book on German Terrorism in Northern France'.[35]

Obviously, the Russian Revolution and the murder of the tsar's family – reported in vivid pictures – gave the nineteenth-century moral scare of revolutionary terror a new boost, with 'Bolshevist terrorism' swiftly becoming the focus of most of the political and public outrage. With this new definition of violently overthrowing an existing order, the concept itself

---

33 See for a thorough analysis of transnational police cooperation in the battle against anarchism W. Klem, 'Founded on Fear: Transnational Police Cooperation Against the Anarchist "Conspiracy", 1880s–1914', unpublished PhD thesis, Utrecht University (2019).
34 *De Standaard*, 18 January 1898; *Nieuwe Tilburgsche Courant*, 19 February 1903; *Het Volk*, 8 March 1903; *Het Nieuws van den Dag*, 7 April 1903.
35 *De Telegraaf*, 2 August 1916; *Algemeen Handelsblad, Provinciale Geldersche en Nijmeegsche Courant*, 5 May 1915.

underwent an inflation. 'Red Terrorism' was considered far worse than the previous 'terrorism by the tsars', but other types of hyphenated terrorism were introduced in national discourse as well: 'automobile-terrorism', 'terrorism by guttersnipes and street kids', or 'barge-skipper terrorism' were headlined as the objects of public outcries, while the more serious race conflicts in the US attracted attention as 'terrorism by whites'.[36] A failed revolution attempt by Dutch socialist leader Pieter Jelles Troelstra in November 1918 sparked bouts of anti-revolutionary, 'antiterrorist' and pro-monarchist enthusiasm. Moreover, with the parliamentary ratification of general suffrage in 1918 (for men) and 1919 (for women), socialism and social democracy were no longer indiscriminately lumped together with 'terrorism' or 'bombings'. With Sinn Féin in Ireland on the rise, discussion on terrorism returned its focus to organised terrorism and political murders. The assassinations of German politicians Matthias Erzberger and Walther Rathenau were condemned as acts of terrorism, as was 'bomb-throwing' in Spain, the infamous bomb attack on Wall Street and the terrorism executed by the 'white extremists' of the Ku Klux Klan in the US.[37]

This new wave of post-1917 terrorist attacks manifested itself in the Netherlands as well, with a bomb attack carried out on 7 November 1921 by members of the International Antimilitarist Association. Four men, aged between twenty-four and thirty, conspired to bomb the house of a military judge who presided over a military tribunal against an indicted conscientious objector. Refusing service was still a punishable offence, and the perpetrators were trying to attract attention to their objections against the draft and in favour of the liberation of incarcerated draft dodgers. Interestingly enough, the media stated that the 'nature of the Dutch population was inherently democratic', that 'bomb attacks are fruits from foreign ground', and that the Dutch political climate was not prone to terrorist radicalisation.[38] Despite, or because of this climate, the prosecutors demanded stiff sentences (fifteen years). The four defendants (a student, an unemployed male, a mechanic and an electrician) were indicted based on criminal law paragraph 157, which penalised the wilful causation of explosions or inundations, and

---

36 See *Haagsche Courant*, 22 June 1918; *Algemeen Handelsblad*, 10 November 1918; *De Telegraaf*, 1 August 1919.
37 *De Telegraaf*, 12 December 1919; *De Tribune*, 20 December 1919; *De Tijd*, 28 July 1920; *Algemeen Handelsblad*, 30 September 1920; *Nieuwe Tilburgsche Courant*, 2 June 1921. See also *Nieuwe Rotterdamsche Courant*, 24 June 1922.
38 *Het Vaderland*, 8 November 1921.

were duly convicted (albeit with lesser sentences of eight and five years' imprisonment).[39]

For the Dutch government, the trigger to step up its antiterrorist measures and policies came with the assassination of Yugoslavian King Alexander I on 9 October 1934 by a member of the Bulgarian nationalist Internal Macedonian Revolutionary Organisation (IMRO or VMRO). The (aftermath of the) attack was captured on film and caused quite some indignation in Dutch media against countries (most notably Hungary and Italy) that let terrorists and regicides roam their lands without apprehending or expelling them.[40] The Dutch government actively participated in the drafting of a terrorism convention by the League of Nations, signed by the League Council on 10 December (the day after the attack), and dispatched to the member states for further comments in January 1935. Moreover, a Dutch delegation, including the Amsterdam police commissioner H. J. Versteeg, attended the International Conference for Unification of Criminal Law in Copenhagen, where a new general definition of terrorism was inaugurated.[41] Thus, the trend initiated by police commissioners around the turn of the century, in their efforts to establish transnational cooperation in the field of anti-anarchist police cooperation, was further institutionalised. Furthermore, the Netherlands were one of the founding members of Interpol in 1923 and actively supported the resolution to convince all European countries to report any sighting of fugitive terrorists to Interpol's central offices in Vienna.[42]

With the outbreak of the Second World War, discussions on international resolutions and definitions were shelved (the League's antiterrorism convention never came into existence) and *terreur* (interpreted as state terror) took over from 'terrorism' (still mostly a non-state activity). The Nazis had already taken over Interpol in 1938 and relocated its headquarters to Berlin, where it became a ploy in the persecution of political enemies and Jewish citizens ('terrorists', according to the Nazis). On 10 May 1940 the German forces invaded the Netherlands, the government and queen fled and the country

---

39 *Nieuwe Rotterdamsche Courant*, 5 January 1922; *De Maasbode*, 5 January 1922; *De Haagsche Courant*, 22 March 1922.
40 *Limburgsch Dagblad*, 10 December 1934; *De Tijd*, 11 December 1934; *Algemeen Handelsblad*, 30 December 1934.
41 *Algemeen Handelsblad*, 30 December 1934, 23 June 1935; *Het Vaderland*, 1 May 1935; *Algemeen Handelsblad*, 13 September 1935.
42 See also C. M. E. van Schelven, 'Het verdrag nopens bestrijding van terorisme', unpublished PhD thesis, Vrije Universiteit Amsterdam (1938). See *Friesch Dagblad*, 15 December 1938.

was placed under a civil occupation force. Active resistance, as carried out by a minority, was now considered 'terrorism', and punished by immediate death sentences.[43] Until 1942, newspapers printed in the Dutch East Indies (now Indonesia) were still able to vilify German acts of oppression as terrorism, but the printed press in the Netherlands had to obey the rules of the occupier (with the Japanese invasion of the Dutch Indies in 1942, freedom of the press was curtailed there as well).[44] After the liberation, a new framework was introduced in Dutch media: the antitotalitarian frame, branding both communist and fascist, national socialist rule as 'reigns of terror'. In 1945, a new security culture emerged, with the Netherlands abandoning pre-war neutrality and being a far more active partner in European and transatlantic partnerships. A domestic intelligence agency, the Binnenlandse Veiligheidsdienst (BVD), and a foreign one were created with the help of British and American partners, sharing information and threat assessments on communist targets. Left- and right-wing extremism were both considered a threat, but action repertoires were far more embedded and coordinated with partners in the international intelligence and military NATO community, which gave them a distinctly anti-communist emphasis.

Colonial and Decolonisation Terrorism

Parallel to the rise of political ideologies and extremisms from the left and the right in the 1920s and 1930s, another major global development affected the trajectory of terrorism and counterterrorism in the Netherlands: the onset of decolonisation movements in the non-Western world. For the Netherlands, this meant that their presence in the colonies of the East, most notably the Dutch East Indies, was forcibly contested by a rising class of nationalist activists and student protesters.[45] Others chose to follow the official line of anti-communist, colonial interpretation and saw the Komintern lurking behind the uprisings in the Indies, defaming the protesters as 'communist terrorists'.[46]

With the Japanese surrender in the Pacific in August 1945, the Japanese occupation of Indonesia ended. Two days later, on 17 August, Sukarno, the

---

43 *Nederlandsch Dagblad: orgaan van het Nationaal Front*, 20 January 1941.
44 See for example *Soerabaijasch Handelsblad, Bataviaasch Nieuwsblad*, 21 March 1941, reporting on 'terrorism by the Gestapo' versus the *Arnhemse Courant*, 25 October 1943, writing about a 'terror group' of resistance fighters being executed.
45 *Indische Courant*, 5 September 1923.
46 *Delftsche Courant, Nieuwe Rotterdamsche Courant*, 22 November 1926; *Sumatra Post*, 25 March 1927.

leader of the national movement, declared Indonesian independence, becoming the first Indonesian president himself. Yet, Indonesian forces would spend the next four years fighting the Dutch for independence, since the Netherlands did not acknowledge Sukarno's claim, and condemned the declaration of independence as an act of 'terrorism' by Sukarno's 'dictatorial republic'. 'It is hard to tell where nationalism stops and terrorism begins', the Catholic journal *De Tijd* lamented.[47] Indeed, tens of thousands of Indo-European civilians and internees were killed by radical republican youth groups, the *pemuda*, throughout the months of 1945 and 1946, a period called the Bersiap (which translates as 'get ready'). The son of the well-known historian Johan Huizinga, Leonhard Huizinga, ran an 'Indian diary' in the *Leeuwarder koerier*, in which he called for 'English and Dutch' presence 'to clear up the mess', and 'wipe out terrorism and banditism'.[48] Dutch Foreign Minister Van Kleffens presented similar arguments before the UN Security Council in blaming the UN for enabling the continuation of terrorism and violence by not assisting and supporting the Dutch forces in suppressing Indonesian independence. 'It is regrettable how the cliché of the poor Indonesian fighting for his freedom prevails', whereas these freedom fighters, according to Van Kleffens, were waging a campaign of terrorism and anarchy.[49] Consequently, the Dutch government launched two major military offensives in 1947 and 1948, euphemistically called 'police actions', to restore a Dutch civil government. Upon great international outrage and a resolution by the UN in January 1949, The Hague had to abandon its resistance against the Indonesian Republic. Under pressure at the prospect of losing its Marshall Plan funds, the Dutch government consented to the formal transfer of sovereignty in December 1949.

The end of the Dutch Empire in Indonesia ignited – with some delay – a new wave of anti-colonial terrorism. South Moluccans, from the Indonesian isle of Ambon, had fought on behalf of the Dutch colonial army until 1945 and, after the formal recognition of the Indonesian Republic, refused to be annexed, and proclaimed their own independent Republic of the South Moluccas (Republik Maluku Selaton) on 24 April 1950. The RMS government and its sympathisers fled to Ceram and continued their fight from the jungle; through New Guinea, which remained under Dutch control until 1962, weapons and commodities were

---

47 See *Amigoe di Curacao*, 4 October 1945; *Het Dagblad*, 17 November 1945; *De Tijd*, 10 November 1945.
48 *Leeuwarder Koerier*, 2 February 1946.
49 *Het Parool*, 15 February 1946; citations in *Friesch Dagblad*, 16 August 1947.

supplied.[50] Of the 8,000 Moluccan KNIL (Koninklijk – Royal Netherlands East Indies Army) soldiers, 4,000 did not want to demobilise in Indonesia, and in 1951, the soldiers and their families, over 12,500 people in all, arrived in the Netherlands as temporary refugees. The idea was that their stay would be temporary, and that after a 'cooling-down' period they would return. For the Moluccan KNIL soldiers and their wives, the damaged pride resulted in disappointment and depression. For the children who grew up in the new, cold country, their grudges against the Dutch government and the mirage of an independent RMS grew stronger by the year.[51]

When General Soeharto, the anti-communist Indonesian leader, executed the arrested RMS President Chris Soumokil, protests erupted in the Netherlands. The Indonesian embassy was set on fire, and raided by a group of young Moluccan radicals. As soldiers' children, they found a new Moluccan identity in guarding their respective leaders, practising with their weapons, and preparing for a future RMS army on their own terms. In the early seventies, criminality rates amongst South Moluccan male youths (up to twenty years of age) amounted to 8.4 per cent, against 4.7 per cent for the Dutch control group.[52] Militant young Moluccan men sought and found new role models in the Black Panthers, Che Guevara, the Palestinian Liberation Front and the Indian Movement in the United States.[53] 'The Ambonese are gambling away our sympathy with their terrorism', the *Nieuwsblad van het Noorden* protested.[54] RMS radicals occupied the residence of the Indonesian ambassador in Wassenaar and shot a police officer in 1970 – with the intent of forcing the hapless Dutch government to negotiate an independent Moluccan republic in Ambon on their behalf. In 1972, the Pemuda Masjarakat (Free South Moluccan Youth) carried out several violent actions, and in 1975 they tried to abduct Queen Juliana (the attempt failed, as they were arrested on their drive to the palace). Yet, another action drew worldwide attention to their cause. In December 1975, Free South Moluccan Youths hijacked a train and simultaneously occupied the Indonesian

50 H. Smeets and F. Steijlen, *In Nederland gebleven: De geschiedenis van Molukkers 1951–2006* (Amsterdam, Bert Bakker, 2006), pp. 36–72.
51 Smeets and Steijlen, *In Nederland gebleven*, pp. 73–207; P. Bootsma, *De Molukse acties: Treinkapingen en gijzelingen, 1970–1978* (Amsterdam, Boom, 2000), pp. 15–29.
52 Smeets and Steijlen, *In Nederland gebleven*, pp. 213–21; C. S. van Praag, 'Molukse jongeren in botsing met de Nederlandse maatschappij: De gevolgen van een beleid', *Beleid en Maatschappij* 2/12 (1975).
53 *De Tijd*, 2 September 1959, 27 September 1963; *De Volkskrant*, *Het Parool*, 7 June 1968; See also J. S. Wijne, *Terreur in de politiek: Politieke geheime genootschappen in deze tijd* (The Hague, Kruseman, 1967).
54 *Nieuwsblad van het Noorden*, 9 September 1970; *De Volkskrant*, 17 September 1970.

consulate in Amsterdam. Two passengers and the train machinist were executed before they surrendered. Two years later, out of frustration over the 'defeat' and imprisonment of their comrades in 1975, a group of fourteen Moluccans again staged an attack: a train was hijacked anew, but this time they also took 105 schoolchildren and five teachers hostage by occupying a primary school in Bovensmilde. After the train was raided by special forces and three out of nine hijackers were killed (including two passengers by accident), the school hijackers let the children go and surrendered. The last action took place in 1978, when a self-proclaimed Moluccan Suicide Squad raided the offices of the provincial authority in Assen, and killed two employees. This action ended the series of Moluccan atrocities. Although the three groups had claimed to be retaliating on behalf of the whole community, the Moluccans almost univocally condemned the action. Their leader Manusama called it out for what it was, despicable terrorism.[55] Moluccan spokesmen denounced the Free Moluccans' legitimacy and called out their youngsters to cease all violence and enter into negotiations with the Dutch government about socio-economic measures to facilitate their integration in the Netherlands.[56]

The Dutch Terror Letter of 1973

This wave of dramatically mediatised and televised anti-colonial, Moluccan terrorism was part of a global radical decade, that started around the end of the 1960s, lasted until the early 1980s and did spill over into the Netherlands as well.[57] Compared to West Germany with its 60 million inhabitants (see Table 14.1), the Netherlands with 14 million witnessed a relatively high number of terrorist actions. The mid-sixties had already seen a wave of student protests, but after 1966, radical 'Red Youth' groups took over, starting in 1967 in Amsterdam, and spreading out to other cities, such as Eindhoven, where the Philips industrial plant attracted violent anti-capitalist protests.[58] This Maoist urban guerrilla movement initiated several violent episodes, causing major material damage, but no deaths. Around that time, international

55 Het Parool, 16 June 1977.
56 A. P. Schmid, J. de Graaf and G. Teeling, Zuidmoluks terrorisme, de media en de publieke opinie: Twee studies van het Centrum voor Onderzoek van Maatschappelijke Tegenstellingen (Leiden, Rijksuniversiteit Leiden, 1982), p. 56.
57 See for a description of Dutch (counter)terrorism in comparison to revolutionary terrorism in the US, Italy and the Federal Republic of Germany in the 1970s B. A. de Graaf, Evaluating Counterterrorism Performance: A Comparative Approach (London and New York, Routledge, 2011).
58 See the first appeals for more measures in De Tijd, 12 September 1969; Trouw, 26 September 1969.

Table 14.1 Terrorist actions and fatalities in Germany and the Netherlands

	Germany (left-revolutionary) Terrorist actions	Fatalities	The Netherlands (left-revolutionary + Moluccan) Terrorist actions	Fatalities
1968	1	0	0	0
1969	0	0	2	0
1970	4	0	2	1
1971	12	2	2	0
1972	19	7	7	0
1973	7	0	0	0
1974	12	2	2	0
1975	23	10	4	4
1976	17	3	1	0
1977	33	10	4	9
1978	23	3	3	2
1979	13	2[a]	2	0
1980	10	0	2	0
1981	5	2	0	0
1982	3	0	0[b]	0
1983	2	0	0	0
Total	184	41	31	16

[a] These were the two RVF (Racial Volunteer Force) terrorist actions. In the same year, three terrorist incidents occurred for which the IRA and an Armenian terrorist group were responsible, as a result of which three people were killed. These actions were not included in these readings.

[b] This year featured ten terrorist actions organised by the newly formed Militant Autonomous Front, but they were part of a new protest cycle (squatters, environmental protests, anti-nuclear movement) and it is doubtful whether they can genuinely be labelled a terrorist organisation. Their actions are therefore not taken into account.

revolutionary, anti-colonial and anti-Zionist groups made themselves heard in the Netherlands as well. Palestinian commandos conducted operations in the Netherlands, as indeed they were doing in the rest of Western Europe.[59] Palestine el-Fatah commandos blew up a Gulf oil reservoir in Rotterdam, attacked gas piping in Ravenstein and Ommen in 1972 and attempted to hijack a train they presumed transported migrant Jews from Russia.

Initially, terrorism was not high on the political agenda. Within the intelligence service, for example, only five people were added to organise the new antiterrorism activities within the service. The hostage crisis during

---

59 'Arabische kinderen wierpen granaten', *De Telegraaf*, 9 September 1969.

the Munich Olympic Games on the night of 4–5 September 1972, broadcast nationwide, changed this abstinence from a counterterrorism approach.[60] The Minister of Justice promptly announced that 'at airports, security measures serving to prevent skyjacks and attacks on aeroplanes' would be implemented, and that 'the surveillance of objects such as embassies' would be coordinated as well.[61] Furthermore, the police force was expanded with three antiterrorism units, so-called Special Assistance Units (Bijzondere Bijstands Eenheden, BBEs).[62] In February 1973, Prime Minister Biesheuvel presented the first Dutch national strategy for 'combating terror' to parliament: 'The government would be forsaking its duty, if it were not to take into account the possibility that phenomena of a terrorist nature, such as those that have already occurred in this nation, were to repeat themselves. It finds that it is necessary to combat such phenomena vigorously.'[63] In this 'Terror Letter', as the note was referred to, the prime minister did reveal the creation of the antiterrorism units, but at the same time articulated a classical, liberal approach to public order and democracy: 'In accordance with the government's decision, counterterrorism will not be shaped in a way that will harm the open nature of our society.'[64] This implied that no additional laws would be adopted and no infringements of the existing security infrastructure would be made.

After 1973, this attitude of reserve persisted. Details on thwarted terrorist actions of Palestinian commandos in the 1970s were but sparsely disclosed to the press or the public. This reserve could only subsist on a public refraining from protest or demanding to have a say in the matter. Indeed, taciturn consent, indifference and the absence of public outrage concerning the new measures became the rule. Incidents were broadcasted, obviously, but discussions seldom ventured deep into the 'root causes' of the political violence; moreover, they were hardly defined as being terrorist at all. Criticisms were mainly vented at perceived intelligence failures.[65] When parliamentary

60 'Vragen van de leden Geurtsen, Berkhouwer en Portheine', 8 September 1972, Handelingen van de Tweede Kamer der Staten-Generaal (HTK), period 1972–3, Appendix, no. 705, p. 1415.
61 'Politie bewapend op Schiphol', Trouw, 12 September 1972.
62 'Conclusies van de bespreking over overheidsmaatregelen tegen terreuracties, gehouden in het ministerie van Algemene Zaken op dinsdag 26 september 1972 van 14.00 tot 16.00 uur', RA 1972/001, Archive Ministry of Justice, The Hague/National Archives.
63 HTK, Letter of the Prime Minister, Minister of General Affairs, 22 February 1973, 1973 National Budget, 12.000, No. 11.
64 Letter of the Minister-President to Parliament, 22 February 1973.
65 'Beveiliging van residentie onvoldoende geacht', De Volkskrant, 2 September 1970; 'BVD wist van exercities in kampen van Ambonnezen', De Telegraaf, 2 September 1970.

leaders asked to be informed of the reasons the BVD had repeatedly been surprised by South Moluccan hostage-taking actions, Head of the BVD Kuipers explained to them that this was due to the service being unable to set up a web of informants equal to that of the KGB in the Soviet Union and the Stasi in East Germany. Kuipers could not imagine that anyone in the Committee wished to transform the country into a comparable police state. Neither did the representatives – 'state terror' was a larger looming threat than non-state terrorism was.[66]

The lack of public debate on terrorism and its countermeasures changed temporarily with the occurrence of the two above-mentioned and eventful train hijackings, in December 1975 and May–June 1977. The ministerial antiterrorist committee called for 'increased vigilance for the country'.[67] Yet, after the surrender of the hijackers, the commotion subsided, and later that month, 41 per cent of the population was still sympathetic to the Moluccan cause.[68] Not terrorism, but the fear of governmental 'terror' prevailed: for Dutch leftist circles, counterterrorist policies in West Germany and the transition towards a police state there became the subject of their moral and activist outrage. During the Stammheim trial against the first-generation Red Army Faction (RAF) terrorists, Dutch radicals founded a solidarity network, Red Help (named after the Red Help organisation connected to the Communist International during the interwar period) and supported the fugitive German RAF members who had been apprehended and jailed in the Netherlands. Demonstrations were organised against the alleged rise of a police state 'next door'.[69] Only when shoot-outs in 1977 and 1978 with other fugitive German RAF terrorists resulted in the deaths of one police officer and two customs officers, with some more severely injured, did support for the RAF diminish.[70]

Substantial amendments to the liberal approach of the Terror Letter were, however, made during the second hijacking, in 1977. With special forces, military jets and help from the CIA the siege was ended, killing six out of nine hijackers and two hostages. Justice Minister Van Agt appeared on stage, arriving in a police Porsche and sporting a white police jacket, making

---

66 See for example D. Engelen, *Frontdienst* (Amsterdam, Boom, 2007), pp. 166–7, 181–2.
67 Which, in the end, was not passed. 'Kabinet bespreekt instelling "verhoogde waakzaamheid"', *NRC Handelsblad*, 5 December 1975.
68 NIPO Bericht, No. 1852; see Schmid et al., *Zuidmoluks terrorisme*, p. 61.
69 J. Pekelder, *Sympathie voor de RAF: De Rote Armee Fraktion in Nederland, 1970–1980* (Amsterdam, Mets & Schilt, 2007), pp. 81–101, 317–19.
70 And on 1 November 1978, on the Kerkrade border, two fugitive RAF members opened fire on customs officers Johannes Goemans and Dionysius de Jong. Both were killed.

national headlines.[71] These visible interventions notwithstanding, Van Agt still continued the line of pragmatic solutions and behind-the-scenes operations. To prevent prison radicalisation by second- or third-generation radicals, incarcerated and convicted perpetrators (German RAF fugitives, Palestinian plane-hijackers caught at Schiphol) were released or extradited as soon as possible. At the same time the departments of Culture and Welfare, Domestic Affairs and Foreign Affairs reached out to representatives of the unsettled Moluccan communities. Housing and schooling programmes were initiated to integrate Moluccan youngsters, while Red Youth and violent Palestine activist groups were monitored by means of secret intelligence measures. A last wave of left-wing, non-lethal, political violent activism resurfaced around 1985, but again, no new laws were deployed and the movement (named RaRa, Revolutionary Anti-Racist Action) was 'neutralised' by means of the intelligence services. In line with Kurth Cronin's thinking, patterns of very subtle, varied and nuanced repression went hand in glove with the transition of the groups themselves into legitimate patterns of political action and loss of support amongst the larger constituencies (Cronin's 'explaining factors' nos. 4, 5 and 6).[72]

To sum up the net result of the radical decade for the Dutch 'security culture': incidents of terrorist violence were not linked together into a homogeneously framed threat of global terrorism. Only in instances of major foreign attacks (Munich) or shocking domestic atrocities (the hijackings) were new policy measures adopted.[73] Not without some right, Member of Parliament Aad Kosto (PvdA – Labour Party) argued, rather indignantly, that the whole matter of the new antiterrorism units had been brought to light by accident.[74] With the German situation as the antithesis to the Dutch approach, this political culture drew from two ideological sources: on the one hand, conservative, liberal concepts of the democracy as an open marketplace of ideas, kept in rein by police and judicial forces, and on the other hand, new, progressive ideas about participatory democracy and civil action, resulting in an aversion to granting more power to the intelligence and police

---

71 See Bootsma, *De Molukse acties*, pp. 286–95.
72 See: B. A. de Graaf and L. Malkki, 'Killing It Softly? Explaining the Early Demise of Left-Wing Terrorism in the Netherlands', *Terrorism and Political Violence* 22/4 (2010); A. K. Cronin, *How Terrorism Ends: Understanding the Decline and Demise of Terrorist Campaigns* (Princeton, Princeton University Press, 2009), p. 8.
73 'Bijzondere commissie voor de brief van de Minister-President inzake bestrijding van terreuracties', 29 March 1973, HTK, period 1972–3, AA 18, 22.
74 'Bijzondere commissie voor de brief van de Minister-President inzake bestrijding van terreuracties', vergadering van 29 March 1973, HTK, period 1972–3, AA3.

services. Yet, internationally, this reluctant approach on the domestic political stage went hand in glove with close cooperation between Dutch and Western intelligence and police agencies behind the scenes. The Netherlands ratified all treaties and participated in all bodies on all levels. In the Club de Berne, the Dutch were particularly active. The Dutch head of the BVD participated as early as 1971 in exchanging information with other security officials on espionage and terrorism. The TREVI (the informal conference of European Community ministers in charge of police, justice and security) began in 1975 as a Dutch initiative to exchange information about terrorism.[75]

The Netherlands and the 'War on Terror'

Violent protests and demonstrations persisted throughout the 1980s, as elsewhere in affluent, post-industrialising societies. Squatters, radical anti-militarists, anti-apartheid and anti-nuclear activists joined forces, or quarrelled, with anti-racist, anti-fascist and radical feminist groupings. The 'movement', as it was called, consisted of several thousands of activists, and was closely monitored by Dutch security services, but was never identified as terrorist.[76] Not even the spectacular and successful actions of the anti-imperialist-inspired group RaRa were considered terrorist, although they included a series of (purposeful) non-lethal arson attacks against the multinationals Makro and Shell for their activities in South Africa, and (after the apartheid regime had collapsed) bomb attacks against governmental agencies and officials responsible for asylum policies and deportation of illegal aliens.[77] The frame of 'terrorism' was strictly separated from domestic political activism,[78] and remained reserved for well-known international terrorist organisations, such as the IRA, the Tamil Tigers, the Sandinistas (depending on the political leaning of the newspaper), the Indian Sikhs, Abu Nidal, the Red Brigades and the Red Army Factions. As a Dutch newspaper quite laconically stated, 'Terrorism' is a fruit of the 'wonders of modern life'; it is intrinsically tied to 'television and planes'.[79] Even with IRA attacks against

---

75 A. Daun, 'Intelligence – Strukturen für die multilaterale Kooperation europäischer Staaten', *Integration* 2 (April 2005).
76 Kwartaalbericht BVD 1987, 2e kwartaal 1987 Nr. 2056.843; Kwartaaloverzicht BVD 1980, 2e kwartaal 1980 – Nr. 1495.359.
77 E. R. Muller, *Terrorisme en Politieke verantwoordelijkheid: Gijzelingen, aanslagen en ontvoeringen in Nederland* (Arnhem, Gouda Quint, 1994), pp. 378–80.
78 See *Het Parool*, 23 August 1986, quoting Police Commissioner Martens on the Dutch 'reluctance' and 'soberness' in characterising something as terrorist.
79 *De Volkskrant*, 12 July 1985.

American GIs on Dutch soil, the IRA assassination of the British ambassador (1979) or the Armenian killing of the Turkish ambassador's son (1979), terrorism remained confined to the frame of 'foreign affairs', with 'Rambo Reagan' as an American anti-hero in whose footsteps Dutch authorities had best not follow.[80]

Indeed, as with the wave of anarchist and revolutionary terrorism, the Netherlands were a net receiver of international terrorism rather than being anywhere near the source. As the BVD already made clear in 1991, wars in Afghanistan and the Middle East (in Iraq for example) could trigger terrorist attacks in the West.[81] Undeniably, a new political religion was gaining footholds in the Netherlands from abroad. In 1986, the Saudi charity Al Haramain had founded the El Tawheed Foundation Amsterdam, thereby laying the groundwork for a Dutch Salafist intrastructure that would expand in the 1990s with three more Salafist mosques. These religious sites drew approximately 1,500 (As-Soennah) or 2,000 visitors (Al Fourqaan) a week from a Muslim population of around 850,000,[82] a relatively large support base in comparison to Germany, France or Belgium, where other movements, such as the radical Islamist Hizb al-Tahrir (Hizb ut-Tahrir) or Tablighi Jamaat enjoyed more popularity. Most visitors had a North African, Pakistani, Afghan, Turkish or Arab background, but Dutch citizens of Moroccan descent (or with a Moroccan passport) stood out. Only an obscure minority within these Salafist circles could be considered jihadi/*takfiri*, although their fundamentalist attitudes towards non-Muslims etc. overlap with mainstream or apolitical Salafis.[83] In 1998 the BVD issued a public warning against recruitment and financing attempts of Saudi, Libyan or Arab origin.[84] In April 2001, the intelligence service dedicated a whole report to the threat of radical Islam and identified the network around Osama bin Laden as the largest terrorist threat towards the West.[85]

---

80 *Het Vrije Volk*, 29 January 1986.
81 'BVD Alert on Terrorism', *Het Vrije Volk* and *Limburgs Dagblad*, 25 January 1991.
82 National Coordinator for Counterterrorism (NCTb), *Salafisme in Nederland* (The Hague, 2008), p. 65; M. de Koning, *Zoeken naar een 'zuivere' islam: Geloofsbeleving en identiteitsvorming van jonge Marokkaans-Nederlandse moslims* (Amsterdam, Bakker, 2008), pp. 373–7.
83 P. H. A. M. Abels and R. Willemse, 'Veiligheidsdienst in verandering: De BVD-AIVD sinds het einde van de Koude Oorlog', in *Justitiële Verkenningen* 30/3 (2004), p. 91; BVD, *Ontwikkelingen op het gebied van de binnenlandse veiligheid: Taakstelling en werkwijze van de BVD* (The Hague, 1992), p. 25.
84 BVD, *Jaarverslag 1999* (The Hague, 1999/2000), p. 15; BVD, *De politieke islam in Nederland* (The Hague, 1998).
85 BVD, *Terrorisme aan het begin van de 21e eeuw: Dreigingsbeeld en positionering BVD* (The Hague, 2001).

The events of '9/11' catapulted simmering fears regarding political Islam and terrorism high on the Dutch agenda and abruptly ended the previous 'reluctant' public and political approach. Tensions regarding immigration and national security had already heightened during the second social-liberal Kok administration (1998–2002).[86] A new populist movement, headed by professor in sociology Pim Fortuyn, declared Dutch multicultural society bankrupt.[87] With his provocative behaviour and sweeping statements against Islam and the 'leftist elites', Fortuyn's party was expected to achieve an unprecedented electoral victory in the coming general elections in May 2002. On 6 May 2002, Fortuyn (who had already been compared by political opponents and pundits to Hitler and Stalin) was murdered by Volkert van der Graaf, an environmental rights activist who justified his act in court by pointing to Fortuyn's attitude towards Muslims and 'vulnerable groups' in society.[88] This political assassination (the first high-profile political assassination since the seventeenth century) and Fortuyn's ensuing posthumous electoral success (17.5 per cent of the vote on 15 May 2002) further polarised the Dutch debate, turning 'Islam', immigrants and Turkish and Moroccan minorities into objects of public securitisation.

In 2001 and 2002 the first jihadist terrorist plots were uncovered in the Netherlands, with French and North African suspects apprehended for preparing attacks in France and Afghanistan (in the absence of terrorism laws, they could not be indicted for preparation of terrorist attacks or membership in a terrorist organisation). In 2002, two Dutch Moroccans were killed in Kashmir, both supposedly recruited in the Al Fourqaan Mosque in Eindhoven;[89] thirteen more individuals were arrested for terrorist activities, some of whom were regular visitors of the Al Fourqaan mosque as well.[90] In the summer of 2002, the service identified a group of Muslim youth, who met in and around the radical Salafist El Tawheed mosque in the north of Amsterdam and gathered around Redouan al-Issar (also named 'Abu Khaled' or 'the Shaykh'), an illegal immigrant from Syria, a former member

---

86 'Meer racistisch geweld in Nederland', *Trouw*, 6 September 2000.
87 P. Scheffer, 'Het multiculturele drama', *NRC Handelsblad*, 27 January 2000.
88 LJN: AF7291, District Court of Amsterdam, 13/123078–02.
89 This paragraph is partly based on B. A. de Graaf, 'The Van Gogh Murder and Beyond', in B. Hoffman and F. Reinares (eds.), *The Evolution of the Global Terrorist Threat: From 9/11 to Osama Bin Laden's Death* (New York, Columbia University Press, 2014); 'OM: moskee Eindhoven werft strijders', *NRC Handelsblad*, 3 May 2003.
90 S. Eikelenboom, *Jihad in de polder: De radicale islam in Nederland* (Amsterdam, Veen, 2004), p. 63; AIVD, *Annual Report 2002* (The Hague, 2003); AIVD, *Saoedische invloeden in Nederland: Verbanden tussen salafistische missie. Radicaliseringsprocessen en islamistisch terrorisme* (The Hague, June 2004).

of the Syrian Muslim Brotherhood and an al-Takfir wa al-Hijra adherent who came to the Netherlands in 1995, and who became a mentor for young radical Muslims.[91] He inspired some of them to try to join foreign jihadist groups in Chechnya and Pakistan. Other members of this group, later dubbed the 'Hofstad Group', travelled to Barcelona to meet with a jihadist Moroccan suspected of involvement in the Casablanca attacks of March 2003.[92]

Then, in the early morning of 2 November 2004, Mohammed Bouyeri, a 26-year-old Dutch Moroccan, born and raised in Amsterdam, awaited publicist and film-maker Theo van Gogh in an Amsterdam street, shot him off his bicycle and slaughtered him with a ritual knife in the street in front of many witnesses. This was the watershed event that converged the already existing fears and resentments on one focal point: the threat of jihadist terrorism. Moreover, it demonstrated a lack of preparedness on the part of the authorities. Bouyeri's action had taken the security services completely by surprise.[93] When Bouyeri's jihadist proclamation became public (in which he condemned the whole Dutch society, government and, amongst others, singled out Ayaan Hirsi Ali), the whole Salafist movement was put on trial in the eyes of the Dutch population.[94] In the perception of large parts of the Dutch population, the November attack showed that every orthodox Muslim could be a potential terrorist, and opinion polls showed that 80 per cent of the population wanted 'tougher policies against immigrants'.[95] In 2005, the Dutch population listed it as the most important issue facing the country.[96]

Yet, the Dutch Salafist movement immediately distanced itself from the attacks. Various Salafist leaders warned their followers against interpreting radical texts without consulting clerics.[97] No more attacks took place, and in its 2008 annual report, the Algemene Inlichtingen- en Veiligheidsdienst (AIVD – General Intelligence and Security Service) concluded that 'the

---

91 'Feitenrelaas', attachment to the Letter to Parliament (ministers of the Interior and Justice), 10 November 2004, Handelingen van de Tweede Kamer, no. 29854.
92 Court of Rotterdam (location, The Hague), verdict in the Hofstad Group case, 10 March 2006; see also E. Vermaat, *De Hofstadgroep: Portret van een radicaal-islamitisch netwerk* (Soesterberg, Aspekt, 2005), pp. 55–77.
93 National Prosecutor's Office, 'Requisitoir van de officier van Justitie', part I, 23 January 2006 and part II, 25 January 2006; District Court of Rotterdam, verdict in the Hofstad Group case, 10 March 2006.
94 BVD, *Terrorisme aan het begin van de 21e eeuw. Dreigingsbeeld en positionering BVD* (The Hague, 2001).
95 J. Sparks, 'Muslim Mole Panics Dutch Secret Service', *The Times*, 14 November 2004.
96 NCTb/RVD, Kwantitatief onderzoek risicobeleving *terrorisme 2008*, p. 5.
97 'Folderen in strijd tegen aanslagen', *Brabants Dagblad*, 10 June 2006; AIVD, *De radicale da'wa: De opkomst van het neo-radicalisme in Nederland* (The Hague, 2007); AIVD, *Annual Report 2006* (The Hague, 2007), p. 33 (in Dutch).

terrorist threat increasingly emanates from transnational and local networks with an international orientation, but less from local-autonomous networks'. Activities of 'home-grown' radicals and their networks had been effectively disrupted.[98] In December 2009, the level of security alertness regarding terrorism was therefore lowered from 'substantial' to 'restricted', since terrorist attacks against the Netherlands no longer seemed to be imminent.[99] The newfound balance of security provisions and societal resilience was, however, a fickle one.

Arriving in a Terrorist-Risk Society

After 2004, the security culture in the Netherlands changed fundamentally. Since 2001, the worldwide adoption of new laws and corresponding jurisprudence had ushered in a profound transformation in criminal law and risk assessment in formerly open, liberal societies. Substantial legal changes were initiated to enable the successful prosecution of terrorism suspects in the initial stages of planning and to reduce the risk of acquittals of terrorist suspects. In Europe, the cornerstone of the new legal edifice of precautionary criminal law was the 2002 EU Framework Decision on Combating Terrorism, which obliges member states to render punishable a broadly defined set of facilitating actions, including 'participating in the activities of a terrorist group by supplying information or material resources'.[100] Consequently – since a Framework Decision is binding EU law – the Dutch parliament was obliged (and willing) to adopt its first antiterrorism laws in 2004, criminalising various types and sorts of terrorist crimes and preparatory acts. Thus, under the new Dutch antiterrorism laws that passed on 10 August 2004, Bouyeri was arrested and tried for murder with 'terrorist intent'.[101] On 26 July 2005, he received a life sentence, without parole – unusually harsh in Dutch judicial history.

The AIVD tripled its staff, added a new directorate, 'Foreign Intelligence', and after the attacks in Madrid on 11 March 2004 a National Coordinator for Counterterrorism (now National Coordinator for Terrorism and Security) was established to oversee and streamline the still fragmented Dutch

---

98 AIVD, *Annual Report 2008* (The Hague, April 2009), pp. 20–2.
99 National Coordinator for Counterterrorism (NCTb), Letter to Parliament with the Eleventh Counterterrorism Progress Report, 15 December 2009.
100 The Council of the European Union, 'Council Framework Decision of 13 June 2002 on Combating Terrorism, (2002/475/JHA)', *Official Journal of the European Communities* (22 June 2002).
101 See the verdict against Bouyeri, Court of Amsterdam, 26 July 2005.

counterterrorism efforts.[102] The Interior Ministry introduced all kinds of programmes to neutralise the dangers of 'radicalisation and polarisation' and large-scale interventions on the local community level were initiated. Immigration and integration policies were also sucked into the vortex of counterterrorism efforts when conservative and populist parties demanded the constriction of dual nationality rights for immigrants (triggered by the fact that the Van Gogh murderer Bouyeri had two passports). Some Salafist imams were declared unwanted aliens and expelled from the country.[103]

Between 2009 and 2013 a spell of quiet and a decrease in terrorist incidents and reporting prevailed, while the new system of threat levels maintained a subdued 'restricted' stage. Yet, everything changed with the rise of IS and the proclamation of the 'Caliphate' in Syria and Iraq. The war in Syria and Iraq motivated thousands of young men and some women to join jihadi organisations in their struggle. Estimates suggest that around 30,000 foreign fighters joined terrorist organisations in Syria and Iraq, among them an estimated 4,000 fighters from Europe.

In the Netherlands, around three hundred Muslims left the country to join IS abroad, most of them radicalised via online forums, social media and virtual advertisement campaigns staged by IS. Consequently, new laws were adopted in the Netherlands to trace and prosecute such early, online trajectories of preparation, increasingly committed prior to or more detached from actual travel. Social media postings and other types of internet-based information were considered admissible evidence. Legal provisions were moreover introduced to enable the authorities to revoke the Dutch nationality of jihadists, or confiscate their passports. This transformation of criminal law in the wake of the fight against terrorism has shifted the burden of proof and evidence into the realm of virtual threats and possible violent futures that might be inaugurated by the defendants.[104] In this sense, the classical goals of criminal justice – retribution, deterrence, incapacitation and rehabilitation – have given way to the executive-oriented goal of security and risk management. This trend has, however, augmented the problem of having to deal with a growing number of young Muslim radicals (and some right-wing extremists) sentenced with relatively short prison times (for preparatory acts only) who will need to reintegrate into society again.[105]

102 AIVD, *Jaarverslag 2004* (The Hague, 2005), p. 15.
103 National Coordinator for Counterterrorism (NCTb), *Salafisme in Nederland*, p. 43; 'Ook tweede Eindhovense imam terecht uitgezet', *ANP*, 10 October 2007.
104 L. Amoore, 'Risk Before Justice: When the Law Contests Its Own Suspension', *Leiden Journal of International Law* 21/4 (2008), esp. p. 850.
105 S. Krasmann, 'Law's Knowledge: On the Susceptibility and Resistance of Legal Practices to Security Matters', *Theoretical Criminology* 16/4 (2012), esp. p. 381.

While jihadist suspects still figure most prominently in terrorism trials, after 2016, the security services also (or again) felt the need to monitor developments amongst right-wing extremists, animal rights activists and other left-wing militants. Yet, apart from jihadist terrorism convicts (over 300 since 2004), only five terrorism suspects have been condemned and sentenced for right-wing-inspired acts of terrorism, with no casualties involved.

Conclusions

Two centuries after the first involvement of the Netherlands in an act of international terrorism (if we may consider the 1818 attack on the Duke of Wellington in this way), vast transformations have affected the Dutch security landscape. It has transpired that, first of all, the semantic container of 'terrorism' was introduced into the Dutch language, political vocabulary and public debate after the French Revolution. From the onset, it has always been considered in close connection and association with that other part of the public scare, *terreur* ('terror'), in the sense of a state-led 'reign of terror'. Throughout the nineteenth century, the First and Second World War and into the anti-totalitarian 1950s and the decolonisation wave, 'terror' was always the twin risk of anti-state terrorism and state-led terror. Combating non-state terrorists, politically or religiously inspired, should never give way to strategies of blanket police surveillance or state repression – as various ministers of Justice from Van Maanen in the first half of the nineteenth century, via Van der Kaay at the end of the nineteenth century to Prime Minister Den Uyl compounded and defended. Keeping too tight a leash on political activism would merely promote it on to the stage of national attention (or, create a national public panic). Within the Dutch context of neutrality (until 1940), security served a depoliticised order, even throughout the radical decade and the many fatalities of the 1970s.

The largest landslide in the Dutch security landscape is still so recent that it is hazardous to historicise this transformation too unequivocally and emphatically. Yet, it does seem likely that the revolution in online communication in the 1990s may have fundamentally heightened Dutch vulnerability to trends and developments in terrorism from abroad. Throughout the nineteenth and largely the twentieth century as well, border controls, passports and special units were able to stem the tide of radicalism from abroad – arresting Russian agents provocateurs, fugitive RAF members, Palestinian plane-hijackers and rogue IRA killers in the Dutch border regions or at Schiphol. With access to the Internet and social media, the scale, speed and intensity of contacts and connections between Dutch citizens and radicals abroad underwent a shocking escalation. More foiled plots, arrested terrorist suspects, identified foreign fighters (and returnees) and vastly quicker patterns of radicalisation have been registered after 2004's fault line than ever before. *Terreur* as a political and discursive frame referring to 'state terror' has almost disappeared, whereas within the context of the twenty-first-century risk society the amorphous and morphing threat of non-state, transnational terrorism has captivated our digital imaginations and communications. While Dutch society is more secure than ever, in a physical sense that is (with decreasing homicide rates since the 1990s), it can be considered more vulnerable, in its immediate openness to international developments. It remains to be seen how the online power of nightmares, the lure of conspiracy theories and extremist ideas from left to right, from political to religious provenance, will further affect the historical traditions of the Dutch open and liberal approach to terrorism in the decades to come.

Further Reading

B. A. de Graaf, *Fighting Terror after 1815: Securing Europe after Napoleon* (Cambridge, Cambridge University Press, 2020)

B. A. de Graaf, *Evaluating Counterterrorism Performance: A Comparative Approach* (London, Routledge, 2011)

F. Demant and B. A. de Graaf, 'How to Counter Radical Narratives: Dutch Deradicalisation Policy in the Case of Moluccan and Islamic Radicals', *Studies in Conflict and Terrorism* 33/5 (2010)

N. Fadil, M. de Koning and F. Ragazzi (eds.), *Radicalization in Belgium and the Netherlands: Critical Perspectives on Violence and Security* (London, I. B. Tauris, 2019)

R. Schechter, *A Genealogy of Terror in Eighteenth-Century France* (Chicago, University of Chicago Press, 2018)

15
Terrorism: An American Story

DENNIS DWORKIN[*]

In June 2011, the *Journal of American History* published a forum in which historians and social scientists weighed in on the state of terrorism studies in the United States. The lead contribution, 'Terrorism and the American Experience: A State of the Field', was written by Beverly Gage, a prominent historian of terrorism in the United States.[1] Gage implored historians to intensify their efforts to explore terrorism in American history. Although she noted that 'we have a better understanding of terrorism's history than we did a decade ago', she believed that 'it would be hard to classify this surge of work as a flourishing subfield or even a coherent historiography'.[2] Reflecting on the state of the field, she wrote: 'Almost a decade out from 9/11, most US historians remain hard-pressed to explain what terrorism is, how and when it began, or what its impact has been. There is little consensus about how best to approach the subject or even whether to address it at all.'[3] Gage was aware that historians faced challenges when they took cues for their research and writing from current affairs: they risked lapsing into a stultifying presentism. Yet she regarded such work as an opportunity as well. It was a chance 'to ask new questions about the nature of American violence and national identity and to lend perspective to an often limited, polemical, and ahistorical contemporary debate'.[4]

---

[*] In writing this essay, I have benefited from conversations with numerous colleagues and friends, particularly James McSpadden. American historians Sarah Keyes and Elizabeth Raymond have read drafts of it and have made invaluable suggestions. This essay has benefited from discussions by the book's contributors at a workshop held at Queen's University Belfast in October 2019. I am greatly appreciative of the encouragement and suggestions given by the book's editor, Richard English. The multiple forms of love and support given by Suzanne Silverman defy words.
1 B. Gage, 'Terrorism and the American Experience: A State of the Field', *Journal of American History* 98 (2011).
2 Ibid., p. 74.   3 Ibid.   4 Ibid.

What follows is one historian's effort to synthesise the existing literature. If this essay is to have manageable proportions, it's necessary to spell out some parameters in advance.

Any analysis of terrorism must define what is meant by this illusive and contentious term. I adopt a definition in the spirit of this volume's editor, the historian Richard English. He defines terrorism as a heterogeneous form of political violence that is a subset of warfare; it is potentially a component of a political and military campaign; and it involves the expression of power and the redress of power relations. Critical to this definition is what classical anarchism called 'the propaganda of the deed', a psychological or symbolic dimension 'producing terror or fear among a directly threatened group and also a wider implied audience in the hope of maximizing political communication and achievement'.[5] In my deployment of this definition, terrorism can be carried out by individuals or groups, non-state or state actors.

In American history there have arguably been three types of terrorism – two domestic and one transnational. Domestic forms have emerged out of the most enduring social and political conflicts in the American past. The predominant expressions of domestic terrorism in the United States are rooted in ethnic and racial conflicts. Among the most important are aimed at the maintenance of racial hierarchies and specifically white supremacy. They have often been coupled with right-wing initiatives that view the government as inherently oppressive and tyrannical and the enemy of individual rights. Their most successful intervention in American history has been the remaking of the post-Civil War South following Reconstruction, but they have flourished intermittently subsequently.

A second domestic form is rooted in the class conflicts of a rapidly expanding industrial society at the end of the nineteenth century and the beginning of the twentieth. This 'revolutionary terrorism' is rooted in the anarchist tradition, which garnered substantial amounts of attention but had shallow roots in the labour movement. It was aimed at both people in positions of power and institutions that symbolised class oppression. Its actions were frequently matched or exceeded by the counterterrorism of the state.

'Transnational terrorism' is likewise important in the American context. While carried out on American soil or against American outposts abroad, it's often planned outside of it, or inspired by outside sources, and results from opposition to the United States' global role. While Americans often play little

---

5 R. English, *Terrorism: How to Respond* (Oxford, Oxford University Press, 2009), p. 24.

or no role in either the planning or execution of these transnational terrorist acts, it's inconceivable to imagine a history of terrorism in the United States without discussing them. This is in large part because the most prominent instance of transnational terrorism is 9/11, a watershed in American history, which placed its stamp on an entire era.

In thinking about the history of terrorism in the United States, we might well return to an argument made by the renowned American historian Richard Hofstadter more than fifty years ago (and referred to by Gage in her essay cited above). In the introduction to the path-breaking *American Violence: A Documentary History* (1970), Hofstadter viewed political violence in America in terms relevant to understanding terrorism.[6] He observed that while political violence had been ubiquitous in American history, much of it had been carried out by groups of citizens against other groups, and that it has rarely shaken the political order. He likewise suggested that the most successful forms have been socially and politically conservative.

Following this line of thought, terrorist acts in the United States have been numerous and varied. Hofstadter might have underestimated the extent of state terror, but with the notable exception of the racial terrorism that transformed the post-Civil War South, terrorist groups have neither produced (what Hofstadter describes as) 'chronic upheaval' nor 'political incapacity'.[7] This argument is explored in the three sections of my essay. The first two focus exclusively on domestic terrorism – racial/ethnic and revolutionary terrorism respectively. The third is more varied. Its emphasis is the transnational terrorism exemplified by September 11th, but it also explores domestic forms, notably the 1995 Oklahoma City bombing and recent terrorist attacks associated with the radical right. While this essay cannot hope to be comprehensive, my goal is to create a lucid story and put flesh on the bones of the principal themes that such a history might include.

Racial/Ethnic Terrorism

Ethnic and racial terrorism in the United States is part of a broader pattern of political violence in which dominant groups maintained their position through the actions of state agents, belligerent crowds and terrorist groups and their supporters. The focus of this section is the terrorist violence meted

---

6 R. Hofstadter, 'Reflections on Violence in the United States', in R. Hofstadter and M. Wallace (eds.), *American Violence: A Documentary History* (New York, Alfred A. Knopf, 1970).
7 Ibid., p. 11.

out against African Americans, especially those ex-slaves whose emancipation threatened the racial hierarchy of the American South. Yet they were not the only minority group to experience this form of violence. The American past is replete with instances of political terror used to eradicate the perceived threat posed by minorities and marginalised groups. These would include Loyalists during the American Revolution, Irish and German Catholics in the nineteenth century and Italians in the century that followed.[8] These would also include groups who are still vulnerable: Chinese immigrants and Asian Americans, Jews, Mexicans and Mexican Americans, and Native Americans among them.

Consider some examples. In the struggle between English colonists (later Americans) and Native Americans of various tribes over land and political control, both groups used political violence to terrorise their opponents. Ultimately, of course, it was Americans of European descent who prevailed, resorting to what we would describe today as ethnic cleansing. Following the Treaty of Guadalupe Hidalgo in 1848 (which ended the war between Mexico and the United States and brought California and other current western states into the American fold), regular forces and vigilante settlers were responsible for waves of violence against the Native Americans that lived in this region. As *The Yreka Settler* (a newspaper in California) stated in 1853: 'Extermination is no longer a question of time – the time has arrived, the work has commenced, and let the first man that says treaty or peace be regarded as a traitor.'[9] Historian Monica Muñoz Martinez has explored the violence experienced by ethnic Mexicans living on the Texas/Mexican border in the early twentieth century. She shows that, under the guise of policing the border, state agents in league with vigilantes executed residents, created 'a reign of social terror that denied residents their civil and social rights' and was responsible for the deaths of thousands of people.[10]

According to historian Beth Lew-Williams, 'while white citizens worried that Native Americans and African Americans would contaminate the nation, they feared the Chinese might conquer it'.[11] In 1885–6 at least 168 communities across the American West drove out Chinese residents. The violence was

---

8 See B. J. Lutz and J. M. Lutz, *Terrorism in America* (New York, Palgrave Macmillan, 2007), pp. 20–1, 38–41, 73.
9 M. Jennings, 'Terrorism in America from the Colonial Period to John Brown', in R. D. Law (ed.), *The Routledge History of Terrorism* (Abingdon, Routledge, 2015), p. 86.
10 M. M. Martinez, 'Recuperating Histories of Violence in the Americas: Vernacular History-Making on the US–Mexico Border', *American Quarterly* 66 (2014), p. 3.
11 B. Lew-Williams, *The Chinese Must Go: Violence, Exclusion, and the Making of the Alien in America* (Cambridge, MA, Harvard University Press, 2018), p. 6.

a consequence of the threat that whites felt from Chinese workers, but their hostility was expressed in racist terms, and they employed strategies that were fundamentally terrorist in nature: they planted 'bombs beneath businesses, shooting blindly through cloth tents, and setting homes ablaze'. Using physical violence as a threat, they 'drove them out using subtler forces of coercion, harassment, and intimidation'.[12]

American ethnic and racial violence against minorities developed in a uniquely American context, but it was certainly not unique to the United States. Rather than being exclusively an expression of American exceptionalism, violence perpetrated against African Americans, for instance, had similarities in form to the pogroms against Jews in late nineteenth- and early twentieth-century Russia. Indeed, the newspaper the New York Outlook described the violence against African Americans in the Atlanta, Georgia riots of 1906 as an 'American Kishinev', a reference to one of the most notorious pogroms against Jews in Russian history.[13] Furthermore, historian Hans Rogger suggests that terrorist actions perpetrated against northern blacks prior to the Civil War were animated by the same spirit as pogroms aimed at Jews. 'The similarities', in his view, 'extend to the flurry of feathers from pillows and comforters that became the hallmark of Russian pogroms, the hated or envied symbols of well-being that some Jews, like some blacks, had attained.'[14]

Thus far I have examined instances of group violence that have a symbolic or psychological dimension and thus fulfil an important part of the 'terrorism' definition. These groups tended to have weak organisations (if organisations at all), and may or may not have had the backing of the state. They had a kind of visceral racism yet very little in the way of a full-blown racist ideology. In other words, they might share the same underlying values as more archetypical terrorist organisations – notably the Ku Klux Klan – but they lacked either an articulate ideology or a discernible organisational form. For these modes of terrorism, we have to look first to the struggle over slavery prior to the Civil War and second to the southern white reaction to Reconstruction that followed in its aftermath.

The radical abolitionist John Brown is arguably the first notable American terrorist whose violence was based on ideological commitment. He preached

---

12 Ibid., p. 1.
13 H. Rogger, 'Conclusion and Overview', in J. Klier and S. Lambroza (eds.), *Pogroms: Anti-Jewish Violence in Modern Russian History* (Cambridge and New York, Cambridge University Press, 1992), p. 351.
14 Ibid., p. 353.

and practised violence aimed not only at punishing the slave-owners that he despised: he also envisioned it as lighting the fire of a slave revolt that would bring down the entire rotten system. While he failed miserably in the short term, he used his trial and execution as a soapbox to facilitate the ideological polarisation that led to the union being torn apart. Thus, as for many terrorists, violence was not an end in itself: it was one element in a broader strategy of political and social transformation.

Brown's radical abolitionism was a blend of fervent Calvinist Protestantism and passionate commitment to American ideals. 'I believe in the Golden Rule and the Declaration of Independence', he once said. 'I think they both mean the same thing: and it is better that a whole generation should pass off the face of the earth – men, women and children – by violent death, than that one jot of either should fail *in this country.*'[15] His transition from being a militant abolitionist to a terrorist took place in the context of the struggles over slavery in the Kansas territory of the 1850s. The Kansas–Nebraska Act of 1854 decreed that the future of slavery in those two territories would be decided by a vote of its inhabitants, thus producing a flurry of settlers and spurts of violence between supporters and opponents of slavery. After pro-slavery militias burned down most of the abolitionist town of Lawrence, Kansas, Brown and a group of loyal supporters struck back, murdering peaceful pro-slavery settlers near Pottawatomie Creek, a terrorist act that abolitionist opinion struggled to condone. None of the settlers had participated in the sacking of Lawrence, and none of them owned slaves, but Brown was determined to use terrorist violence to send a message to slave-owners and their supporters. In a letter dated 27 December 1859, less than a month after his execution, his son Salmon defended his father's deployment of violence: it 'was the first act in the history of the country that proved to the demon of slavery that there was as much room to give blows as to take them it was done to save life and to strike terror through there (*sic*) wicked ranks'.[16]

Brown's makeover from a religious and political terrorist to a self-styled Old Testament prophet took place following the event that will always be associated with him: the raid on the federal armoury at Harper's Ferry, West Virginia (then Virginia). Brown and a group of twenty-one men – mostly white but free blacks and a fugitive slave as well – seized the armoury. The

---

15 M. Fellman, *In the Name of God and Country: Reconsidering Terrorism in American History* (New Haven, Yale University Press, 2010), p. 27.
16 O. G. Villard, *John Brown 1800–1859: A Biography Fifty Years After* (New York, Alfred A. Knopf, 1943), p. 612.

scheme was meant to supply the weapons for a revolt. It was also meant to have a symbolic dimension: its ultimate goal was to inspire slaves to risk their lives for the cause of their freedom.

The armoury was easily seized, but things quickly fell apart. The slave revolt never materialised, and the US Marines stormed the engine house where Brown and his group were held up. In all, ten of Brown's men, including two of his sons, were killed, and Brown himself was wounded. In the trial that followed, the State of Virginia was determined to hang Brown for his challenge to the slave system. For many in the national audience, following the newspaper accounts of the trial, the state's determination to use Brown's trial and execution to send a broader message was itself an act of terror.

During the trial, Brown remained silent, as if indifferent to the world around him. When given the opportunity to make a statement, he assumed the cloak of martyrdom. 'I should forfeit my life for the furtherance of the ends of justice', he declared. 'And mingle my blood further with the blood of my children and with the blood of millions in this slave country whose rights are disregarded by wicked, cruel, and unjust enactments, I say let it be done.'[17]

Brown's trial and subsequent execution may not have directly led to the Civil War, but they played a critical role in exposing the fault lines in the fragile compromise between North and South. Indeed, it was his death more than his life that brought about the war against slavery for which he yearned. Among the attendees at Brown's execution was John Wilkes Booth, the future assassin of Abraham Lincoln. An accomplished actor from a well-known theatrical family, a devout white supremacist and an advocate of the Confederate cause, Booth had managed to infiltrate Brown's execution (which was not a public event) by putting on a uniform and posing as a guard. Booth hated what Brown stood for, describing him in a letter to his sister as a 'traitor and terrorist', but he could not help but feel respect and sympathy for Brown as he stood on the scaffold. Ironically, it was Brown that proved an inspiration for Booth's assassination of Lincoln. He contrasted Brown, 'a man inspired, the grandest man of this century', with Lincoln, a vulgar man of poor breeding. Booth likened Lincoln to the tyrannical Napoleon Bonaparte 'overturning the blind Republic and making himself a king'.[18] In assassinating Lincoln, which he viewed as a blow against the

---

17 Fellman, *In the Name of God and Country*, p. 42.   18 Ibid., pp. 95–6.

enslavement of the South, Booth emulated the terrorist strategy of Brown while seeking to restore the world that the latter had despised.

The historian Michael Fellman has memorably described Booth's assassination of Lincoln as both the last terrorist act of the Civil War and the first expression of terrorist resistance to Reconstruction. At a moment when the South was economically devastated and had lost hundreds of thousands of men in the war, the victorious North sought to revolutionise southern life, based on African Americans being accorded full rights as citizens, notably the right to vote and hold office. The response was a counter-revolutionary movement, known as the Redemption, which sought to restore white supremacy in economic and political life, widely thought by southern whites to be a restoration of the natural order. The centrepiece of this crusade was restoring the Democratic party to political dominance from the clutches of Republican intruders. Murder, beatings, property destruction, lynchings and physical and mental intimidation tilted elections in favour of Democrats by discouraging African Americans from voting and making it impossible for white and black reformers to hold political office.

In the twenty years following the Civil War, the Redeemers spawned terrorist organisations at the local level known by various names: the Knights of the White Camelia, the Red Shirts, the White Caps and the White Line, to name a few. The terrorist violence that these organisations spawned is exemplified by events that took place in Vicksburg in December 1874. When Peter Crosby, the beleaguered black sheriff, failed to enlist federal support to solidify his position in the summer of 1874, he established and trained a volunteer black militia to defend the community. It provided the justification for a corresponding effort among whites, which dwarfed that of blacks and caused Crosby to disband his units for fear of the slaughter that would take place. When the black volunteers began to leave the town, their white counterparts, riding on horseback, pursued them, killing about thirty. This group of whites subsequently swept the surrounding countryside, killing as many as 300 blacks whom they deemed as insurgents. This terrorism, borne of imagined fears of a black revolution, represented an assault on the entire black race.[19]

Undoubtedly, the best known of these white supremacist terrorist groups is the Ku Klux Klan. Founded in 1866 in Pulaski, Tennessee and soon spreading throughout the South, the Klan was founded as a 'post conflict fraternity of young returning Confederate officers' but quickly was

19 Ibid., p. 118.

transformed into 'a deadly serious reactionary movement'.[20] It's thought that the name comes from the Greek word *kuklos*, or 'circle', and 'clan', referring to the founders' Scottish–Irish heritage. Known for its elaborate initiation rituals and practices, the group was a terrorist organisation whose goal was the restoration of white supremacy in the transformed circumstances of southern defeat.

In his classical account of Reconstruction, Eric Foner suggested that the most massive Klan actions during this period took place in South Carolina in late 1870 and early 1871. A group of 500 masked Klansmen lynched eight blacks held in the Union County jail. In Spartanburg, they whipped hundreds of Republicans, black and white, and destroyed their property. In York County, the Klan, which comprised the majority of the white population, was behind at least eleven murders and hundreds of whippings. The victims included Elias Hill, a black teacher and minister, who was 'a dwarflike cripple'. In the company of sixty black families, he emigrated to Liberia.[21]

The extent to which Klan violence was successful in restoring white supremacy is stunning. Slavery itself was not reinstated, but the economic and political oppression of African Americans in the South by the early 1870s was virtually total. While this was partly made possible by the reluctance of the federal government to intervene, in fact federal action played an important role in driving the Klan underground. In 1871, Congress held hearings looking into Klan violence and was sufficiently horrified to pass the Ku Klux Klan Act, which allowed the federal (rather than state) government jurisdiction to prosecute perpetrators of Klan violence and to declare martial law in the affected localities. The federal government rarely used the powers that the Ku Klux Klan Act provided, but the national attention given to Klan violence contributed to prominent southerners distancing themselves from it. Most important, the Klan had been so effective in achieving its aims that there was little need for it to continue.

The Klan reinvented itself on multiple occasions. Perhaps the most prominent version was the one that briefly flourished in the 1920s. The founder of the second Klan was Atlanta physician William Joseph Simmons, a southern racist and Spanish–American War veteran who drifted from occupation to occupation and had a penchant for joining organisations. He was a member

---

20 C. L. Quarles, *The Ku Klux Klan and Related American Racialist and Antisemitic Organizations: A History and Analysis* (Jefferson, NC, McFarland & Company, 1999), p. 31.
21 E. Foner, *Reconstruction: America's Unfinished Revolution, 1863–1877* (New York, Harper & Row, 1988), p. 431.

of several churches and joined fifteen different fraternal orders. Simmons was inspired by two events in 1915: the film *The Birth of a Nation* and the lynching of the Jewish businessman Leo Frank. Frank was falsely accused of rape and murder, subsequently convicted and imprisoned, and eventually pardoned by the Governor of Georgia. He was 'liberated' from prison and subsequently lynched by white assailants who saw themselves as exercising popular justice.

The Birth of a Nation was among the first cinematic masterpieces of the silent era, the first Hollywood blockbuster, and a film that has elicited passionate defences and denunciations ever since. Based on Thomas Dixon's popular, blatantly racist novel *The Clansman*, the film embodied a white southern perspective on the Civil War and its aftermath. It portrays Reconstruction as corrupt and immoral, and the Klan as the saviour of the South and (white) Western civilisation. Blacks in the film are represented as sexual predators, uncivilised, driven by lust and avarice. In one scene set in the South Carolina legislature in the early 1870s, newly elected black legislators are portrayed slumping in their seats, going barefoot, gorging themselves on chicken and whiskey and eyeing white women in the visitors' gallery. In another, heroic Klansmen, wearing white sheets and riding horses, dump the dead body of the character Gus. He is an African American who is killed for driving Flora, an innocent white girl, to commit suicide rather than succumb to Gus's lechery.

The film was controversial from the moment that it was released. For Mary Childs Nerney, the secretary of the newly formed NAACP, which boycotted the film: 'The harm it is doing the colored people cannot be estimated. I hear echoes of it wherever I go and have no doubt that this was in the mind of the people who are producing it.'[22] The protests fell on deaf ears. The film was enthusiastically embraced by the highest levels of the political class, including a showing at the White House to rapturous applause. Indeed, it is an excerpt from President Woodrow Wilson's *A History of the American People* (1902) that introduces the Reconstruction phase of the film. As historian Melvyn Stokes wrote of the response to *The Birth of a Nation*: 'There can be little doubt that the attitudes expressed in the film were unexceptional to the vast majority of the white American population. Most critics who viewed the film could not understand why it generated such controversy, and it is probable that ordinary spectators reacted in much the same way.'[23]

---

22 M. C. Nerney to G. Packard, 17 April 1915, in 'The Birth of a Nation and Black Protest', Roy Rosenzweig Center for History and New Media, https://rrchnm.org/episodes/the-birth-of-a-nation-and-black-protest/.

23 M. Stokes, *D. W. Griffith's The Birth of a Nation: A History of 'The Most Controversial Motion Picture of All Time'* (Oxford, Oxford University Press, 2007), p. 285.

Simmons's initial efforts at reviving the Klan produced meagre results, but that changed after he hired Elizabeth Tyler and Edward Young of the Southern Publicity Association to market his organisation. They advised Simmons that the key to growth was to expand the targets of animosity. They argued that Jews and Catholics should be added to the mix. Immigrants and outsiders, they could be represented as un-American. The Klan's growth was founded on white supremacy redefined as being white, Protestant and anti-immigrant.

The second Klan took its name from its forebear, but it was different in a number of ways. It was more prominent in the North than in the South. It was not a secret organisation: it published recruiting ads in newspapers and held mass public events. It was much larger than its predecessor, having somewhere between 4 and 6 million members. Its values, if not its actions, possibly had the support of a majority of Americans. While terrorist violence or the threat of it was still a major part of its arsenal, it rarely entailed murder and physical assault.

An example of Klan violence during this period was the 1925 attack on the home of Baptist minister Earl Little in Omaha, Nebraska. Little was the father of the yet-to-be-born Malcolm Little, better known as Malcolm X. The elder Little was targeted for his subversive views of black empowerment, although, ironically, he was a recruiter for Marcus Garvey's 'back to Africa' movement, which supported expatriation. Little was speaking in Milwaukee when the attack happened, and his wife was at home pregnant with Malcolm. A group of Klan members, carrying torches and yelling at the top of their lungs, circled around the house on horseback several times and broke all the windows of the house before leaving. The threat of terror worked, as the family soon moved from the area. Just as important, it sent a message to the wider African-American community of Omaha of the consequences of challenging white supremacy. The threat was credible, given that there were 45,000 Klan members in Nebraska.[24]

The second Klan faded as quickly as it rose, but later incarnations and other organisations with similar agendas have surfaced on multiple occasions and in different localities. This was especially true during the Civil Rights era of the 1950s and 1960s, when racial terrorism proliferated, much of it by unaffiliated white supremacists.

---

24 L. Gordon, *The Second Coming of the KKK: The Ku Klux Klan of the 1920s and the American Political Tradition* (New York, Liveright Publishing Corporation, 2017), pp. 93–4.

The Klan has come into focus recently because of Spike Lee's film *BlacKkKlansman*, nominated for an Oscar for Best Picture in 2019. The film tells the remarkable story of Ron Stallworth, the first black police officer in Colorado Springs, Colorado, who in 1979 infiltrated the Klan through telephone conversations, while a white officer that worked with him attended meetings in his place. The film plays fast and loose with the truth, introducing a love interest and a bomb plot that do not appear in Stallworth's memoir on which the film is based. What the film and memoir vividly portray is that even though the Klan's ambition was to be a mainstream political organisation – in large part through the political ascension of David Duke – terrorism remained part of its arsenal. Stallworth never succeeded in bringing criminal charges against the Klan, but he was able to thwart a planned burning of crosses, a terrorist act in his view, as it implicitly carried with it the threat of further violence. As he states in his memoir: 'No child in the city limits of Colorado Springs ever had to experience firsthand the fear brought on by this act of terror. We prevented them from having such an incident burned into their consciousness, as many of their parents might have been imprinted as children.'[25] Noting that David Duke was in attendance at the Nazi march in Charlottesville in 2017 that resulted in the death of a protestor, killed by a white supremacist who drove into the crowd, Stallworth drew a line from the Klan that emerged in the aftermath of the Civil War to the recent surge in white supremacist violence.

Revolutionary Terrorism

The white supremacist premises on which racial terrorism was founded dug deep into American cultural and political soil. It's a different story when it comes to revolutionary terrorism. While some of the most spectacular terrorist events in American history fit this description, its roots in American culture are relatively shallow, and the reaction to it has often been repulsion, even by those who might have been supportive of its political goals.

Among the earlier instances of revolutionary terrorism was the Molly Maguires, a shadowy organisation that is shrouded as much in myth as in reality. It developed in the 1870s in the anthracite coal fields of Pennsylvania, where Irish immigrant coal miners were under the thumb of bosses of

---

25 R. Stallworth, *Black Klansman: Race, Hate, and the Undercover Investigation of a Lifetime* (New York, Flatiron Books, 2018), p. 164.

English and Welsh descent. Their confluence reproduced the ethnic and class oppression that the miners had thought they had left behind in Ireland and Britain. Part of efforts to form a union and more generally to challenge the power structure under which they lived, the Mollys were responsible for property destruction, assaults and occasionally murder. They were identified by the establishment as spreading terror and eventually smashed by the established order.

The event that exemplifies revolutionary terrorism in the United States is the Haymarket riot of 1886 that took place in Chicago on 4 May. Its context is the rapid industrialisation taking place in the United States in the late nineteenth and early twentieth centuries and the class conflicts that it engendered. An important component of this modernisation and urbanisation was the flood of European immigrants into American cities. They constituted a receptive audience to the revolutionary ideas that were circulating in newspapers, magazines and social gatherings. Of particular importance for American terrorism was the growth of anarchism, which advocated a series of violent acts aimed at triggering a revolutionary upheaval. Inspired by the example of the Paris Commune of 1871 and mesmerised by the potential of dynamite, invented by Alfred Nobel in the 1860s, anarchists preached the power of propaganda by deed. Their ideas were condemned by the mainstream labour movement and its supporters, but they frequently grabbed headlines and came to personify for industrial capitalists, government officials and the mainstream media the menace of organised labour. At the height of its influence in the 1880s, the anarchist movement probably attracted thousands of supporters.

A key event in this regard was the arrival in the United States of the German anarchist Johann Most, already prominent in European revolutionary circles. Most played a critical role in introducing anarchist ideas into American political culture. He composed the 1883 manifesto of the International Working People's Association. The group simultaneously embraced Marxist historical and social analysis and the revolutionary tradition of the Declaration of Independence. In his newspaper *Die Freiheit*, published throughout the 1880s (originally in London and subsequently in the United States), Most advocated liberating mankind by acts of terror that would trigger a revolutionary cataclysm. He romanticised dynamite's potential to create a level playing field between the working class and its bourgeois capitalist oppressors. However, arguably the most dramatic and explicit advocacy of the use of dynamite to advance the revolutionary cause came from Gerhard Lizius, secretary of the Indianapolis Group of the International. Fluent in German and English, he wrote in 1885:

> Stuff several pounds of this sublime stuff into an inch pipe, gas or water pipe, plug up both ends, insert a cap with fuse attached, place this in the immediate neighborhood of a lot of rich loafers, who live by the sweat of other people's brows, and light the fuse. A most cheerful and gratifying result will follow. In giving dynamite to the downtrodden millions of the globe, science has done its best work.[26]

The immediate trigger of the Haymarket events was a strike by workers at the McCormick Harvesting Machine Plant. When two unarmed picketers were murdered by the police, labour unions and anarchist groups called for a demonstration at Chicago's Haymarket Square the next day. The demonstration was peaceful, and, indeed, the anarchist labour leader August Spies softened his revolutionary rhetoric, imploring the protestors to refrain from violence. As the demonstration was petering out, the rhetoric heated up. It was at this point that the police tried to clear the square of a group a fraction of the original size. As the remaining demonstrators began to leave, someone in the crowd threw a bomb in the direction of the police. Immediately following the explosion, there was gunfire, which the police likely initiated. According to Paul Avrich, whose *The Haymarket Tragedy* is the definitive account of the events, one policeman died on the spot and six others were mortally wounded. Sixty other officers were wounded, one of them dying two years later. The extent of civilian death and injury has never been determined, although Avrich cites a police source suggesting that it was greater than that of the police.[27] In sum, the police were overwhelmingly responsible both for the wounding of the protesters and of their own colleagues.

The Haymarket massacre shocked mainstream American society, resulting in the wholesale arrests of revolutionary leaders and labour activists across the United States. Chicago became a police state in all but name. Constitutional rights were ignored; mail was seized and read; anarchist newspapers were closed down and their editors arrested; the meetings of trade unions were suspended; and the records of their organisations were seized. Richard T. Ely, an economist at Johns Hopkins University at the time, described Chicago after the Haymarket tragedy as a 'period of police terrorism'.[28] Ten anarchists were charged with murder, even though the

---

26 P. Avrich, *The Haymarket Tragedy* (Princeton, Princeton University Press, 1984), p. 170.
27 Ibid., p. 209.   28 Ibid., p. 222.

identity of the bomb-thrower was never established. In effect, they were prosecuted for their beliefs rather than their acts, and this stratagem found wide support in the mass media and among the American public. In the end, eight of the defendants were found guilty: four of them were hanged, one committed suicide in his cell and three received lengthy prison sentences.

The bomb thrown at the police in Haymarket Square was an act of terrorism that connected it to similar acts carried out in Europe. What distinguished revolutionary terrorism in the United States was perhaps the extent to which it was embedded in racial and ethnic discourses and anxieties about immigration. The fact that most of the Haymarket defendants were born outside of the United States made it possible to represent anarchism as fundamentally un-American. Or, as the chauvinistic *Chicago Tribune* stated it: 'Chicago has become the rendezvous for the worse elements of the Socialistic, atheistic, alcoholic European classes ... It is this alien and un-Americanized element ... which has been flaunting the red flag of blood and the black flag of murder in our midst.'[29]

The anarchists seized upon ethno-racial discourses as well. August Spies, one of the executed Haymarket defendants, portrayed working-class oppression as a form of slavery, comparable to that which had been abolished only a generation previous. African Americans during this period did not resort to terrorism in their struggle against racism. However, just as racial and ethnic discourses infused rhetoric around anarchism, the discourses around anarchist violence seeped into the African-American freedom struggle. T. Thomas Fortune, writing in *A. M. E. Church Review,* just prior to the Haymarket events, stated that 'the essential element in which the Afro-American character was most deficient [was] the *dynamite element*'. Six years later, Frederick Douglass echoed these sentiments, stating that 'if the Southern outrages on the Colored race continue the Negro will become a chemist'.[30]

The Haymarket tragedy set the terms for revolutionary terrorism and counterterrorist governmental response in the years to come: a bombing or assassination attempt would be greeted by massive state repression out of proportion to the original deed. It was aimed at suppressing not only the terrorists but also radicalism more generally and the labour movement writ large, which by and large abhorred terrorist violence. From this perspective, revolutionary terrorism ultimately worked against the interests of those that it claimed to champion.

29 J. A. Clymer, *America's Culture of Terrorism: Violence, Capitalism, and the Written Word* (Chapel Hill, University of North Carolina Press, 2003), pp. 54–5.
30 Ibid., p. 101.

The anarchist bombings of May 1919 adhere to this description. They took place at a time of rampant labour militancy and massive repression meted out against pacifists and Bolsheviks during the First World War and the immediate years following it. Much as Johann Most had been an inspiration for the anarchists of the 1880s, Luigi Galleani, an Italian immigrant, was the intellectual force behind the 1919 bombings: he advocated revolutionary acts of terror and published detailed descriptions of how to construct bombs. His followers were almost certainly behind the bold campaign of mail bombs sent to dozens of political and governmental figures, the great majority of which were defused before they reached their destination. These acts were followed by a spate of powerfully timed bombs aimed at government officials, resulting in three deaths, including one of the bombers. One of the bombs destroyed the home of the Attorney General of the United States, A. Mitchell Palmer. The government's response was swift. Palmer and his apprentice J. Edgar Hoover launched a massive campaign aimed at stamping out anarchism and eradicating radicalism more generally. The Palmer Raids resulted in thousands of arrests and hundreds of deportations. Their worst effects were thwarted by officials at the US Department of Labor, who had final authority for deportations and opposed Palmer's disregard for individual rights and due process.

The most spectacular anarchist attack during this period was undoubtedly the bombing of the J. P. Morgan bank in New York City on 16 September 1920, resulting in the deaths of thirty-eight people and injuries to more than 200 others. Until the 1995 Oklahoma City bombing, the Wall Street bombing was the most devastating terrorist attack in American history. Suspected to be the work of Galleanists (but never proven), it was part of the backdrop for the landmark Immigration Act of 1924, which limited immigration from Southern and Eastern Europe, where supporters of communism and anarchism were viewed as most likely to have originated. The historian Beverly Gage has suggested that these immigration policies 'were not so much a break with the past as the fruition of policies first proposed after Haymarket'.[31]

The terrorist act that arguably received the most attention in the 1920s was the murder of a paymaster and his guard at a shoe factory in South Braintree, Massachusetts in April 1920. It led to the arrests, trial and executions of Nicola Sacco and Bartolomeo Vanzetti. Italian immigrants and committed followers

---

31 B. Gage, *The Day Wall Street Exploded: A Story of America in Its First Age of Terror* (New York, Oxford University Press, 2009), p. 311.

of the anarchist Galleani, they were convicted on scanty and contradictory evidence in the courtroom of a judge who during the appeals process was reprimanded for his 'grave breach of official decorum'. Ultimately, their convictions and executions can be attributed to their foreign birth and radical beliefs. The trial attracted international attention. Protests demanding either pardons or a new trial took place in London, Paris and other cities throughout the world.

Anarchism as a form of revolutionary terrorism soon vanished from American life. It was revived in the 1960s and 1970s in the era of the Civil Rights movement and Black Power, protests against the Vietnam War, student activism and the explosion of youth countercultures. Like the anarchists before them, the groups advocating and/or practising terrorism – for instance, the Weathermen (subsequently renamed the Weather Underground) and the Symbionese National Army – found kindred spirits among revolutionaries outside the United States. American groups were a subset of the international New Left, an amorphous grouping that included a wide spectrum of radicals united as much by their opposition to mainstream left-wing parties as they were by their aspiration to overthrow bourgeois capitalist society. In the era of the American–Soviet confrontation, they frequently championed the anti-imperialist politics of the Third World. Lenin and Stalin were supplanted by Frantz Fanon and Che Guevara.

Ted Kaczynski, better known as the Unabomber, is best understood within this political and cultural milieu. A graduate of Harvard University (BA) and the University of Michigan (MA and PhD), he was a published mathematics professor at the University of California, Berkeley, a major hub of the counterculture and the student movement. He resigned his position and retreated to rural Montana, aspiring to live a solitary existence in harmony with nature. Frustrated by modernist interferences in his daily life, the continued destruction of the wilderness, and the catastrophic slide of American society, he advocated revolutionary eco-anarchism. 'To a large extent', he told an interviewer in 1999, 'I think the eco-anarchist movement is accomplishing a great deal, but I think that it could do better ... The real revolutionaries should separate themselves from the reformers ... And I think that it would be good if a conscious effort was being made to get as many people as possible introduced to the wilderness.'[32]

---

32 T. Kintz, 'Interview with Ted Kaczynski', The Anarchist Library, https://theanarchistlibrary.org/library/theresa-kintz-interview-with-ted-kaczynski.

Between 1978 and 1995, the year that he was apprehended, Kaczynski was responsible for multiple terrorist acts, resulting in the deaths of three people and the injuries of twenty-three others. He was the object of the most extensive manhunt in American history. Kaczynski regarded his bombings as extreme but necessary, the goal being to attract attention to the loss of human freedom and human dignity brought about by large-scale techno-capitalist organisations. This was the justification for the murder of Thomas J. Mosser, an executive at the international public relations firm Burson-Marsteller, who was killed by a mail bomb sent by Kaczynski to his home in North Caldwell, New Jersey. In a letter to *The New York Times* on 26 April 1995, Kaczynski argued that Moser was complicit in rehabilitating Exxon's public persona following the 1989 Exxon Valdez oil spill incident and, more generally, his company profited from manipulating people's attitudes. In the same letter, Kaczynski resisted the FBI's attempt to portray him as an 'isolated nut'. Whether he was a nut or not is an open question. His ideas were beyond doubt far from being isolated: they are part of a long-standing tradition of opposition to industrial capitalism founded on the advocacy of more 'natural' forms of existence.

In contrast to his reclusive years in Montana, Kaczynski's life in prison was far from 'isolated'. He carried on correspondences with scores of people, participated in interviews and reached out to the media on a regular basis. His 2016 book *Anti-Tech Revolution: Why and How* is a serious effort, based on wide reading, to reflect on the revolutionary politics that will be necessary when 'a failure of the system' creates the space for a sweeping transformation. He has likewise demonstrated a sardonic sense of humour. His response to the Harvard Alumni Association's directory enquiry at the time of the fiftieth-year reunion of his class was that his occupation was a prisoner and that his eight life sentences constituted awards. Ultimately, Kaczynski was no less an idealist than his anarchist predecessors. Like theirs, his terrorism did little to advance his political cause.

Transnational and Radical Right Terrorism

The first two sections of this essay, although chronologically organised, have been conceived thematically, the first focusing on ethnic and racial terrorism and the second on revolutionary terrorism. The subject matter for the final section casts a wider net. Its focus is on domestic and transnational terrorism since the 1980s.

In quantitative terms, the number of domestic terrorist acts in the United States since the 1970s has declined. Acts of terror between 2000 and 2011 comprise only 9 per cent of terrorist acts since 1970.[33] The data, however important, does not tell the entire story: the recent American experience of terrorism is far more powerful than the statistics capture. We live in a world where we fear terrorist-produced cataclysms. We are presented daily with a seemingly dizzying variety of causes advanced by those embracing terrorism: everything from ecoterrorists and anti-abortion activists to survivalists and separatists who see the American government as part of a worldwide authoritarian conspiracy. In a world in which the news cycle is 24/7 and mass communications are omnipresent (recently expanded through the explosion of social media), the organisational frameworks of terrorism have likewise been transformed. In contrast to classically organised groups such as the Irish Republican Army, recent atrocities have often been committed by lone-wolf terrorists, who seem to act of their own accord but frequently having found kindred spirits on political websites, Facebook and Twitter. According to the research of criminologist Mark Hamm and sociologist Ramon Spaaij, lone-wolf terrorists tend to blur the line between personal and political grievances. They are often unemployed, single white males with criminal records. They are older, less educated and more likely to have a history of mental illness than other violent criminals.[34]

Our fears and anxieties regarding terrorism are accentuated by a plethora of cable news channels, news websites and YouTube channels, which, like newspapers in the heyday of the anarchists (but more widespread and pervasive), have played an active role in representing terrorism, often accentuating and distorting its real effects. This mindset extends to the dominant political structures as well: the government, the major political parties, their affiliated groups and organisations, and various think tanks have an interest in intensifying public worries about terrorism. The anthropologist Joseba Zulaika views American counter-terrorist efforts as being founded on a self-fulfilling prophecy that has produced its own reality. He traces such a mindset to the 1980s, when, despite barely any terrorist fatalities in the United States, 'terrorism was still frequently hailed as the country's number-one threat – it was the

---

33 C. Gallaher, 'Contemporary Domestic Terrorism in the United States', in Law (ed.), *The Routledge History of Terrorism*, p. 326.
34 M. S. Hamm and R. F. J. Spaaij, 'Lone Wolf Terrorism in America: Using Knowledge of Radicalization Pathways to Forge Prevention Strategies', US Department of Justice, February 2015, pp. 6–7, www.ncjrs.gov/pdffiles1/nij/grants/248691.pdf.

fantasized enemy of the waiting for terror'.[35] In Zulaika's view, counter-terrorist ideology has its own self-confirming logic. When terrorist acts take place, they can be represented as confirming counterterrorist reason. When they do not materialise, they can be interpreted as justifying the counterterrorist actions that allegedly prevented them.

How are we to understand the recent history of terrorism in the United States? Arguably two events frame terrorism in contemporary America: one domestic and one transnational, the Oklahoma City bombing (1995) and 9/11 (2001).

On 19 April 1995, Timothy McVeigh – a white working-class Gulf War veteran – parked a rental truck filled with 4,800 pounds of homemade explosives outside the Murrah Federal Building. The bomb was set to go off at 9 a.m., which McVeigh knew to be the peak time when the building would be occupied. He left the car directly underneath the second-floor America's Kid Day Care Center. The blast killed 168 people and injured more than 680 others. It was responsible for destroying one-third of the building and destroying or damaging 324 others nearby. It remains the single most devastating act of domestic terrorism in American history.

McVeigh chose the federal building because it had a Secret Service office and housed the Bureau of Alcohol, Tobacco and Firearms (BATF). It was the BATF, following a fifty-one-day siege near Waco, Texas, that had raided the compound of the religious cult, the Branch Davidians, suspected of stockpiling illegal weapons. In the midst of the raid, a fire engulfed the group's compound, resulting in the deaths of seventy-six people. McVeigh held the federal government responsible for the tragedy, and he was determined to seek revenge and to send a message in the process. The Oklahoma City bombing was two years to the day after the Waco raid.

On the day of the bombing, McVeigh was wearing a windbreaker over a T-shirt, a black baseball cap, army boots and faded black jeans. His attire could have been worn by countless white men of his age and background. His T-shirt's content set him apart. On the front was a drawing of Abraham Lincoln and the phrase SIC SEMPER TYRANNIS – 'Thus ever to tyrants.' John Wilkes Booth had shouted this phrase immediately after shooting Lincoln. The back had an image of a tree with drops of blood dripping from the branches. There was a quote from Thomas Jefferson: 'The tree of liberty must be refreshed from time to time with the blood of patriots and

---

35 J. Zulaika, *Terrorism: The Self-Fulfilling Prophecy* (Chicago, University of Chicago Press, 2009), p. 5.

tyrants.' In short, McVeigh represented himself as a disciple of a hijacked American revolution and a descendant of a defeated white race.

McVeigh was a lone-wolf terrorist with tenuous ties to more organised reactionary movements. His claim to the American revolutionary tradition was framed in the language of the contemporary 'Minutemen' movement. Adherents regarded themselves as the descendants of the Minutemen of the 1770s, whom they saw as freedom fighters struggling against state tyranny. While consisting of various groups with different and often conflicting perspectives, in general the contemporary Minutemen advocated an armed response to the global tyranny of the New World Order personified by the United States government. The quotation from Booth suggests McVeigh's affinity to the Christian Identity movement, whose 'bible', the fictional *Turner Diaries*, was written by the neo-Nazi and white supremacist William Luther Pierce. Pierce envisions a deepening confrontation between the System – Jewish politicians and African-American enforcers who seek to disarm Americans – and a secretive organisation, the Order, which aspires to reclaim the country for oppressed white people. It contains the rudiments of McVeigh's attack: a bombing of the Washington headquarters of the FBI that kills 800 people. Pierce applauded the actions of his star pupil. 'I intended people to be inspired', he said. 'McVeigh was reacting to what he saw as tyrannical behaviour by the government in a society that alienates people and makes them feel they no longer have a role.'[36]

On the face of it, McVeigh and Theodore Kaczynski, the Unabomber, would seem to have little in common. There is a huge gap between the political formation of the white working-class veteran and the brilliant technophobic academic dropout. Yet they shared common ground. Both men not only detested the US government, they also saw it as part of a worldwide conspiracy threatening individual freedom. McVeigh himself seems to have believed in the convergence between the radical left and the radical right. According to Kaczynski, he said as much, when they had conversations while imprisoned in Colorado's Supermax Prison. Interestingly enough, Kaczynski regarded McVeigh's political views as 'rational and sensible' even as he was critical of the latter's use of violence. For Kaczynski, 'it could have been used far more humanely, and at the same time more effectively'. His belief that it would have been more effective for McVeigh to target a 'relatively small number of people who were personally

---

36 T. McVeigh, 'Dead Man Talking', *The Guardian*, 22 April 2001.

responsible for the policies or actions to which the protesters objected' reads like a defence of Kaczynski's own terrorism.[37]

A transnational rather than a domestic terrorist organisation, Al-Qaida was exclusively steeped in outrage against the United States' global role. In Al-Qaida's case, it was fierce opposition to American intervention in the Muslim world and the Middle East: its invasion of Iraq, its support for Israel and its propping up of a corrupt and authoritarian Saudi regime. For most Americans, the September 11th attacks were a bolt from the blue. They were the most devastating attack by a foreign power on American soil since Pearl Harbor. For many, the scale and symbolism were incomprehensible. Numerous pundits and academics focused on the enormity and daring of the attacks, describing them as a new stage in terrorism and a harbinger of a nightmarish epoch to follow. The anthrax attacks that killed five people and infected seventeen others which followed 9/11 only a week later seemed to confirm this perspective. But as the political scientist Martha Crenshaw has observed, the contention that there was a 'new' terrorism fundamentally different from an 'old' superseded one represented a rush to judgement. 'Analysis of what is new about terrorism', she wrote, 'needs to be based on systematic empirical research that compares a wide range of cases over extended time periods. Without knowing the contours of the old terrorism, the shape of the new cannot be identified. Comparisons must also take into account the historical context within which terrorism occurs.'[38]

If the jihadist terrorism on 9/11 appeared to many as a dramatic break with the past, for others its magnitude might have been shocking but its occurrence expected. It says a great deal of the cultural/political climate of the time that following the Oklahoma City bombing the immediate response of the mainstream media was to pin it on a jihadist. 'The betting here is on Middle East terrorists', asserted CBS News's Jim Stewart a few hours after the blast. For the syndicated columnist Georgie Ann Geyer, writing in *The Chicago Tribune*: 'It has every single earmark of the Islamic car-bombers of the Middle East.' According to the *New York Post*, 'in due course, we'll learn which particular faction the terrorists identified with – Hamas? Hezbollah? the

---

37 L. Michel and D. Herbeck, *American Terrorist: Timothy McVeigh and the Oklahoma City Bombing*, pp. 398–402, www.3-3-3.org/docs/Kaczynski%27s%20comments%20on%20McVeigh.htm.
38 M. Crenshaw, *Explaining Terrorism: Causes, Processes, and Consequences* (Milton Park and New York, Routledge, 2011), p. 65.

Islamic Jihad? – and whether or not the perpetrators leveled specific demands'.[39]

Such views, while the product of ideological blindness, were likewise founded on legitimate apprehensions. Al-Qaida and other jihadist groups had over the course of several years demonstrated their commitment to striking out at the United States. In 1993, a small group led by Ramzi Yousef targeted the World Trade Center, its goal to send a message regarding the consequences of American support of Israel and the corrupt regimes of the Middle East. The bomb that was planted created a seven-storey-deep crater, killing six people and injuring more than a thousand others when it exploded. Al-Qaida's terrorist attacks against American targets began in 1998 with bombings of American embassies in Nairobi, Kenya and Dar es Salaam, Tanzania. Together they killed 224 people and injured more than 4,000. This was followed by the bombing of the missile destroyer USS *Cole* in 2000, which at the time was refuelling in the Yemeni port of Aden. The blast killed seventeen American soldiers. The Clinton administration carried out unsuccessful reprisals against Al-Qaida in the Sudan and Afghanistan, inadvertently bolstering the group's claim to be a representative of Muslim interests.

The terrorism unleashed on 9/11, then, had clear continuities with previous events. Yet there can be no doubt that it represents the beginning of a new era in the American experience. A majority of Americans felt more insecure while at the same time more nationalistic and patriotic. The deeply entrenched idea that the United States had a mission to spread freedom to the rest of the world was given a boost. The ensuing global War on Terror, proclaimed by President George W. Bush, divided up the world with Manichean precision into those who opposed and those who supported terrorists and provided the justification for implementing regime change, notably in Iraq. Within the United States, it took the form of weeding out suspected home-grown and transplanted terrorists, given impetus by the passage of the 2001 Patriot Act. In its efforts to make America a safer place, it gave the government the power to wiretap, spy on suspected terrorists, open letters, read email and obtain records from institutions such as universities and libraries without the awareness of the person being investigated. The Patriot Act gave new life to the long-standing debate on the proper relationship between state authority and individual freedom in a democracy.

The post-9/11 period likewise produced an intensifying Islamophobia whose flames were fanned by government officials, news outlets, television news,

---

39 J. Naureckas, 'The Oklahoma City Bombing: The Jihad That Wasn't', *Fair*, 1 July 1995, https://fair.org/extra/the-oklahoma-city-bombing/.

internet websites, social media and politicians and pundits of various ideological stripes. This was in part because of deepening anxieties about global terrorist acts for which jihadists were responsible, exemplified by the terrorist bombings in London in 2005 known as 7/7. It was also because of terrorist actions in the name of radical Islam either directed at Americans or taking place in the United States. Richard Reid (better known as the shoe bomber) attempted but failed to ignite plastic explosives on a flight from Paris to Miami in 2001. Chechen Kyrgyzstani-American brothers Dzhokhar Tsarnaev and Tamerlan Tsarnaev detonated two bombs near the finish line of the Boston Marathon in 2013 that killed three people and injured hundreds of others. In 2017, fourteen people were killed and twenty-two others were seriously injured in a mass shooting and an attempted bombing of the Inland Regional Center in San Bernardino, California. The perpetrators were a married couple, Syed Rizwan Farook and Tashfeen Malik, the former a US-born citizen of Pakistani descent, the latter a permanent resident. In private messages to each other, they embraced jihadism and martyrdom.

Attitudes towards Muslims were reminiscent of the response of the media and the state to the anarchist scare of the late nineteenth and early twentieth centuries. Just as the assault on bomb-throwers became an assault on organised labour and immigrants, the war on terror tended to blur the lines between jihadists, Muslims and Arabs. In addition, the prevailing Islamophobia continued an American tradition which has both constructed and defended whiteness by attacking religious, ethnic and racial minorities. In the case of Islam, it was deemed dogmatic, resistant to reason, prone to violence and fundamentally anti-modern. For many Americans, those who came from Muslim backgrounds were assumed to be susceptible to its radical and militant political strains and hence prone to terrorism.

Without minimising the real terrorist threat of jihadism against American targets inside and outside the United States, the preoccupation with crushing radical Islam came at the expense of minimising the growing threat of domestic terrorism. According to a 2017 FBI and Department of Homeland Security Report, white supremacist groups carried out more terrorist acts than any other type of domestic terrorist group in the years since September 11th. Between 2008 and 2016, their plots and attacks surpassed comparable Islamist actions by almost 2 to 1. The report's prognosis that this 'likely will continue to pose a threat of lethal violence over the next year' continues to be true.[40]

---

40 J. Winter, 'FBI and DHS Warned of Growing Threat from White Supremacists Months Ago', *Foreign Policy*, 14 August 2017, https://foreignpolicy.com/2017/08/14/fbi-and-dhs-warned-of-growing-threat-from-white-supremacists-months-ago/.

The intensified Islamophobia produced in the aftermath of 9/11 contributed to a cultural and political atmosphere conducive to other types of discrimination and violence against minorities. In combination with the traumatic consequences of the Great Recession, an economic recovery widening income disparities, and the election of the first African-American president, the conditions were ripe for right-wing nationalist and populist ideas and groups to flourish. These ideologies were not defined by a commitment to terrorism per se, but terrorist acts on their behalf floated to the surface. They were typically committed by lone-wolf terrorists, connected to the broader pool of reactionary ideas via websites and social media. Their actions tended to blur the distinction between terrorism and hate crimes.

A brief inventory would include James Alex Fields, Jr., who ploughed his car into a crowd of protestors opposing the white supremacists rallying in Charlottesville, Virginia in 2017; Robert Gregory Bowers, who murdered eleven people at the Tree of Life Synagogue in Pittsburgh in 2018; John Earnest, who opened fire at a synagogue in Poway, California and killed one person; and the 2019 mass shooting of twenty-two people by Patrick Crusius at a Walmart in El Paso, Texas. He saw his actions as a statement protesting the Hispanic invasion of Texas. Each of these shooters had their own motives. However, their actions, as the historian Kathleen Belew has argued, were interconnected. In her words: 'We spend too much ink dividing them into anti-immigrant, racist, anti-Muslim or anti-Semitic attacks. True, they are these things. But they are also connected with one another through a broader white power ideology.'[41]

Such domestic terrorism does not exist in a vacuum. It's part of a global phenomenon, the most dramatic instance being the 2011 terrorist act by the Norwegian far-right nationalist Anders Behring Breivik. He killed eight people with a van bomb and then on the same day shot dead sixty-nine people of the Workers' Youth League sponsored by the Norwegian Labour Party. It's also part of a much longer domestic history that is as representative of the American experience as is the Bill of Rights and the Constitution. In the introduction to this essay, I argued that what is distinctive about American political violence, and by implication terrorism, is that it has (following Richard Hofstadter) neither led to 'chronic upheaval' nor 'political incapacity'. Like Hofstadter,

---

41 Quoted in L. Beckett and J. Wilson, '"White Power Ideology": Why El Paso Is Part of a Growing Global Threat', *The Guardian*, 5 August 2019, www.theguardian.com/us-news/2019/aug/04/el-paso-shooting-white-nationalist-supremacy-violence-christchurch.

I write at a time of heightened political turmoil. I still believe (although with less confidence than I once did) that this generalisation continues to hold true. Understanding contemporary terrorism within the broader sweep of American history is an important component in ensuring that it remains so.

Further Reading

J. Clymer, *America's Culture of Terrorism: Violence, Capitalism and the Written Word* (Chapel Hill, University of North Carolina Press, 2003)

M. Fellman, *In the Name of God and Country: Reconsidering Terrorism in American History* (New Haven, Yale University Press, 2010)

B. Gage, 'Terrorism and the American Experience: A State of the Field', *Journal of American History* 98 (2011)

B. J. Lutz and J. M. Lutz, *Terrorism in America* (New York, Palgrave Macmillan, 2007)

J. Zulaika, *Terrorism: The Self-Fulfilling Prophecy* (Chicago, University of Chicago Press, 2009)

16
Political Violence and Terrorism in Colombia

RODDY BRETT

Introduction

Since the nineteenth century, Colombia has experienced diverse, complex and mutually reinforcing forms of political and criminal violence. The ubiquity of such egregious violence in Colombia has led scholars to attest to its 'banal', ordinary quality.[1] Colombia has further been characterised as a country of 'permanent' and endemic 'warfare', typified by three stages of war and violence.[2] Firstly, a long and violent nineteenth century, shaped by civil wars between elites throughout the country. Secondly, *La Violencia* during the mid-twentieth century, a period of mass violence moulded by a combination of anarchy, peasant insurgency and official terror, the most evident motor of which was the viscerally hostile fracture between the Conservative and Liberal parties, which resulted in approximately 300,000 killings. Finally, a third cycle of violence imposed by Colombia's Cold War armed conflict. The armed conflict between the Colombian state, guerrilla insurgencies and paramilitary organisations, within which cartel violence played an increasingly decisive role, began in the 1960s and is ongoing at the time of writing, boasting a homicide rate akin to *La Violencia*.[3]

The aim of this chapter is to understand the role of terrorism and terrorist violence within the historical context of political violence in Colombia. English has defined terrorism as 'heterogeneous violence used or threatened with a political aim'. According to English, such violence may 'involve a variety of acts, of targets and of actors', and 'possesses an important

---

1 D. Pécaut, *Las FARC: Una guerilla sin fin o sin fines?* (Bogotá, Norma, 2008), p. 142.
2 G. Sánchez and P. Bakewell, 'La Violencia in Colombia: New Research, New Questions', *The Hispanic American Historical Review* 4 (1985).
3 The National Centre for Historical Memory identifies 95 terrorist attacks with 1,566 victims from between 1988 and 2012. See National Centre for Historical Memory, *Basta Ya!* (Bogotá, NCHM, 2012).

psychological dimension, producing terror or fear among a directly threatened group and also a wider implied audience in the hope of maximising political communication and achievement'. In this regard, for English, terrorism 'embodies the exerting and implementing of power, and the attempted redressing of power relations'.[4] Such a definition is relevant for the case of Colombia, given precisely that the use or threat of violence with a political objective that seeks to generate widespread fear and terror is not new to the country's social and political landscape. Nevertheless, over time, armed actors in Colombia have not limited their armed actions to a unique category of violence: armed groups, including both leftist insurgencies and paramilitary organisations, drug cartels and the state have employed terrorist methods and carried out acts of terrorism, whilst also resorting to irregular warfare, conventional warfare, widespread attacks on infrastructure, political activity and so on.[5] Consequently, there is some difficulty in identifying a 'single, concrete understanding' of terrorism in the case of Colombia.[6] A more precise and contextually driven approach would be to frame armed actors, whether state or non-state, as belonging to overlapping categories, according to the nature of their military strategies and the political context in which they have been levied. All groups mentioned above have, in fact, carried out both 'warlike actions' and 'terrorist actions'; nevertheless, over time said groups 'evolve and/or switch the targets and motivation of violence', from attacking non-combatants, to committing 'other terrorist acts' and targeting conventional armed forces.[7]

A further critical issue relating to the strategic employment of terrorism within the context of Colombia pertains to its communicative character, as identified by English. In a context such as Colombia, where multiple forms of violence have been executed against diverse targets by manifold armed groups – and where targets themselves have indeed often been victim to armed actions by multiple groups – this chapter is mindful of the capacity of an armed group to secure a coherent understanding of the message it originally aimed to communicate via atrocious violence. As Deas has noted, such messages have often been directed towards multiple publics; within such a context, there may, in fact, be a 'disarticulation between the

---

4 R. English, *Terrorism: How to Respond* (Oxford, Oxford University Press, 2010).
5 J. Holmes, 'Terrorism in Latin America', in E. Chenoweth, R. English, A. Gofas, and S. N. Kalyvas (eds.), *The Oxford Handbook of Terrorism* (Oxford, Oxford University Press, 2019); O. Palma, 'The Changing Meaning of Terrorism: A Matter of Discourse', in M. Boyle (ed.), *Non-Western Responses to Terrorism* (Manchester, Manchester University Press, 2019).
6 Palma, 'Changing Meaning', p. 266.   7 Holmes, 'Terrorism in Latin America'.

message that an actor seeks to transmit, the effect of the action and what is ultimately achieved by an episode of political violence'.[8]

Applying English's definition over a protracted historical period suggests that acts of terrorism have frequently been perpetrated by state and non-state actors alike – the latter including militia linked to political parties, guerrilla insurgencies, paramilitary organisations and, more recently, drug trafficking/producing organisations (DTOs), often themselves directly associated with state and non-state actors. However, categorising specific groups within the singular framework of 'terrorist' is conceptually problematic in Colombia; such an undertaking is not borne out by the empirical data. From this perspective, this chapter argues that acts of terrorism carried out by diverse state and non-state actors have been strategically employed within Colombia's broader historical experiences of civil war, internecine violence between political parties and internal armed conflict.[9] Acts of state and non-state terrorism have, in turn, represented core constitutive components of broader contested processes of state- and nation-building in Colombia, processes that remain, as yet, incomplete. As such, acts of terrorism have been strategically employed as 'a subspecies of warfare', often levied, as English has argued, as 'part of a wider campaign of violent and non-violent attempts at political leverage'.[10]

This standpoint differs from much of the recent and progressively influential scholarship addressing political violence in Colombia that has been concerned, above all, with violent actors and patterns of violence in the years since 9/11.[11] Reflecting the orientation of much of the wider scholarship that has emerged as part of the accelerated global growth in scholarly interest in terrorism since 2001, this scholarship crafts a narrative that frames contemporary Colombia as uniquely 'a boiling crucible of international efforts to combat global terror',[12] a narrative that is only, in part, accurate. Whilst said research contributes important insight to the study of political violence, it tends to restrict the study of terrorism principally to those violent phenomena perpetrated during the very late twentieth and early twenty-first centuries, and, in particular, to violent actions perpetrated principally by leftist insurgencies. By focusing upon the contemporary period, such research

---

8 M. Deas, *Dos ensayos especulativos sobre la violencia en Colombia* (Bogotá, FONADE, 1995), p. 60.
9 English, *How to Respond*.   10 Ibid.
11 See for example L. Nagle, 'Global Terrorism in Our Own Backyard: Colombia's Legal War Against Illegal Armed Groups', *Transnational Law and Contemporary Problems* 15 (2005).
12 Nagle, 'Global Terrorism', p. 5.

underplays the significance of the complex particularity of Colombia's widespread historically and locally driven patterns of political violence and the role that acts of terrorism have played therein. Such scholarship, in fact, constructs an amnesiac narrative, framing only the very last stage of the country's protracted internal armed conflict – specifically, the years since 2001 – as having been driven and shaped by terrorism. Such research appears, moreover, to buy into and further consolidate what has been characterised as a 'politically motivated' discourse propagated by both the Colombian and US governments aimed at 'delegitimising an agent'.[13] In the context of Colombia, replicating the discourse of the former Ambassador to Colombia, Lewis Tambs, and the country's former President Alvaro Uribe (2002–6; 2006–10), scholars and policymakers have tended to employ the term 'narco-terrorist'[14] to refer specifically to non-state actors, in particular to the leftist guerrilla insurgency, the Revolutionary Armed Forces of Colombia (FARC-EP) and, although to a far lesser degree, the paramilitary organisation the United Self-Defence Forces of Colombia (AUC). Such an enterprise is inaccurate and elides the role of the state in perpetrating acts of terrorism in the country.

This chapter offers a longer-term historical perspective with the aim of tempering the emergent scholarly narrative addressing Colombia's history of political violence – and of the operationalisation of acts of terrorism therein. The chapter argues that a historical perspective may assuage the narrowly focused and, arguably, ideological perspective of much literature, which in turn sidesteps a rigorous historically oriented, contextually driven analysis of acts of terrorism perpetrated by all violent actors, overshadows complex historical processes by linking them unhesitatingly to the international war on terrorism and marginalises the significance of state-sponsored terrorism. The chapter begins by discussing the patterns of violence that shaped Colombia's post-independence period and turbulent mid-twentieth century. The analysis then turns to the country's internal armed conflict, focusing upon the causes of the conflict, the principal state and non-state actors who have participated therein and the nature of the violence perpetrated by them. In this respect, the chapter discusses state terrorism, as well as those acts of terror that insurgent and paramilitary actors and DTOs have carried out.

---

13 Palma, 'Changing Meaning', p. 248.
14 See L. Nagle, 'Colombia', in K. Roach, *Comparative Counter-Terrorism Law* (Cambridge, Cambridge University Press, 2005).

A Violent Post-independence

Throughout much of the nineteenth century and well into the twentieth century, Colombia experienced ongoing war and political violence, punctuated by episodes of both bipartisan peace and incipient institution-building.[15] From the 1830s, wars were waged across every decade, as the Conservative and Liberal parties and their political, social and economic constituencies fought to establish hegemonic rule, control over the state and the ownership and management of key resources, such as land. From 1886, on the eve of the twentieth century, until 1930, the Conservative party asserted political and military hegemony,[16] with the Thousand Day War (1898–1902) leading to the third consecutive military defeat for the Liberals and the albeit temporary end to their 'military adventurousness'.[17] Significantly, the commencement of the period of Conservative Hegemony was inaugurated with the 1886 Constitution, which consecrated provisions to restrict the political activity of the Liberal party. The 1886 Constitution represented 'a definitive historical moment' which 'shaped modern terrorism', given that subsequent struggles to achieve liberal reforms have been 'at the centre of Colombia's violent history'.[18]

Following the political defeat of the Conservative party in 1930, for sixteen years, a series of Liberal party-run administrations, the so-called Liberal Republic, attempted to consolidate hegemony and craft a liberal government and society. With variegated levels of success, Liberal administrations sought to overturn Conservative domination, introducing, for example, land reform policies that limited ancestral privileges. During the Liberal Republic, Liberals carried out acts of vengeance against Conservatives throughout the country. Unsurprisingly, Liberal policies 'unleashed furious political opposition from the Conservatives'.[19] By the end of the Liberal Republic in 1946, a century of confrontation between Conservative and Liberal elites seeking to impose their own specific 'model of modernisation' through embedded 'local partisanship' throughout the country had exacerbated existing and acute societal cleavages framed across political party lines.[20] Such

15 R. Karl, *Forgotten Peace: Reform, Violence and the Making of Contemporary Colombia* (Los Angeles, University of California Press, 2017).
16 E. Posada-Carbo, 'Limits of Power: Elections under the Conservative Hegemony in Colombia, 1886–1930', *Hispanic American Historical Review* 77 (1997), p. 246.
17 Ibid.   18 Ibid.
19 A. Molano, 'The Evolution of the FARC: A Guerrilla Group's Long History', NACLA Report (2007), pp. 3–5.
20 F. Safford and M. Palacios, *Colombia: Fragmented Land, Divided Society* (Oxford, Oxford University Press, 2001).

conditions represented the tinderbox that would ignite the extreme and prolonged violence and terror, *La Violencia*, that would come in the wake of the assumption to the presidency on 7 August 1946 of Conservative leader Mariano Ospina Pérez.

La Violencia

The end of the Liberal Republic was precipitated by the early resignation of President López Pumarejo in 1944, which put the country on 'the brink of a catastrophic confrontation ... and augured a revolutionary explosion of unforeseen consequences'.[21] The abrupt end to the Liberal Republic in 1946 and, arguably, the collapse of the Liberal Party itself,[22] ushered in Colombia's modern period of political violence and partisan terror, 'a germinal period ... which sowed ... myths, representations, and modes of behaviour that would be harvested in later phases'.[23]

Conservative Mariano Ospina Pérez assumed the presidency in 1946, incorporating Liberals within what was to be a nominal transitional government. Despite a degree of goodwill on both sides, many Liberals throughout the country were unwilling to accept political defeat, whilst a wave of violent score-settling against Liberals accompanied the return of the Conservative party to government. Violence precipitously increased after 1946, as Liberal armed groups emerged to protect Liberals from armed opponents. In parallel, pro-government militias, the so-called *pajaros* (armed assassins) and *chulavitas* (Conservative police), grew in strength and number, and violence 'eventually engulfed most of the country'. Within this context, Liberals gradually coalesced around political leader Jorge Elécier Gaitán, who eventually withdrew Liberal support for the ruling coalition with the Conservative party.[24]

Gaitán was a polarising figure, who allegedly split the Liberal vote at the 1946 election, arguably leading to the Conservative victory. Whilst formally a Liberal, his populist policies diverged to some degree from the official party line;[25] in fact, his calls for land reform and for Colombians to unite against

---

21 See G. Sánchez and D. Merteens, *Bandits, Peasants, and Politics: The Case of 'La Violencia' in Colombia* (Austin, University of Texas Press, 2001), p. 11.
22 Safford and Palacios, *Fragmented Land.* 23 Ibid., p. 349.
24 D. Bushnell, *The Making of Modern Colombia: A Nation in Spite of Itself* (Berkeley and Los Angeles, University of California Press, 1993), pp. 201–7.
25 Sánchez and Bakewell, 'La Violencia in Colombia', p. 797; J. Mazzei, *Death Squads or Self-Defense Forces? How Paramilitary Groups Emerge and Challenge Democracy in Latin America* (Durham, NC, University of North Carolina Press, 2009), p. 75.

both Liberal and Conservative elites represented a significant threat to elite (partisan) hegemony.[26] Within this context, government repression of popular protest followed, leading the country to breaking point. On 9 April 1948, Gaitán was assassinated in Bogotá, under confusing circumstances, leading to accusations of his murder against both Liberal and Conservative party elites. An outbreak of spontaneous terror followed throughout the country, which would ultimately be sustained for a decade.

In the immediate aftermath of Gaitán's execution, Liberal-led popular insurrections and rioting, generalised and ritualistic violence – the so-called *Bogotazo* – broke out in the Colombian capital. Throughout the country, Revolutionary Boards (juntas), popular governments and peasant militias formed in response to the assassination.[27] Reaction to the *Bogotazo* and to the generalised revolutionary uprising was barbarous. Acts of state terror perpetrated by the police and military – who had been sent by the government to quell the uprising – sought to communicate a clear message to and to punish rebels. State forces cut off opponents' testicles, slashed open the bellies of pregnant women and executed babies, allegedly with the objective of preventing 'the seed of future rebellion'. The partisan terror represented the first phase in what would become 'a war of incredible cruelty'.[28] By the end of *La Violencia* in 1964, approximately 300,000 people had been killed and 2 million people displaced.[29]

Partisan violence displayed core characteristics of terrorism. Conservatives 'cut out the tongues and the eyes of ... Liberals, and disembowelled others', reflecting a 'sinister calculus of pain and cruelty. Pregnant women were disembowelled and foetuses destroyed, so new members of the opposition party would not be born.'[30] Ritualised violence was employed to communicate to party affiliates and allies; cadavers were mutilated and enemies were murdered using different 'cuts' – for example the 'necktie', 'florists' cut', 'monkey's cut' – as a means of signalling to party members that they should either flee or remain silent.[31]

In 1946 alone, 43,000 political killings took place, auguring 'the outgrowth of hostility' between the two formal political parties and local bloodletting by party members and sympathisers.[32] Much of the violence was 'state-sanctioned terror', of 'which the peasantry was the core

---

26 Sánchez and Merteens, *Bandits, Peasants*, pp. 11–17.   27 Ibid.
28 J. Pearce, *Colombia: Inside the Labyrinth* (London, Latin America Bureau, 1990), pp. 49–51.
29 F. Hylton, *Evil Hour in Colombia* (London, Verso, 2006), p. 40.
30 Hylton, *Evil Hour*, p. 43; Mazzei, *Death Squads*, p. 75; Pearce, *Inside the Labyrinth*, p. 65.
31 M. Palacios, *Between Legitimacy and Violence: Colombia 1875–2002* (Durham, NC, Duke University Press, 2007), pp. 49–51.
32 Palacios, *Legitimacy and Violence*.

victim',[33] as state terrorism increasingly became a 'salient characteristic' of patterns of violence[34] to crush the peasantry's democratic aspirations.[35] However, acts of terrorism were employed not only to prevent liberal reforms, but also in the struggle to achieve them. In the wake of Gaitán's murder, Liberals in Quindío and Tolima mobilised peasant clients, forming guerrilla militias to carry out grotesque violences. In Puerto Tejada in southern Colombia, for example, Liberals killed leading Conservative politicians, 'decapitated them and played football with their heads in the main plaza'.[36]

In the months following the *Bogotazo*, the government armed Conservative peasant groups, whilst Liberal peasants were armed with the support of the Communist Party and, at least initially, of the Liberal Party. In the years after 1948, the driving causes of *La Violencia* evolved, shifting away from their predominantly bipartisan roots. Whilst bipartisan animosity remained a crucial factor driving conflict onset and subsequently a core justification for the terror, patterns of rural social and economic development increasingly played a key role in its perpetuation,[37] edging the country towards 'more of a generalised civil war'.[38] In their crusade against communism and Liberalism,[39] Conservatives wielded terror 'to supress radical-popular politics',[40] spawning 'new modes of terror' in a war increasingly bereft of rules or limits.[41]

1948–1953: The Cold War and the Seeds of the Internal Armed Conflict

The initial 1948 uprising in Bogotá was crushed by the Conservative-controlled military within a relatively short period of time. Nevertheless, the *Bogotazo* and accompanying rural violence came to mark the commencement of a period of political violence and terror at national, subnational and local levels between 1946 and 1964 that would reach its 'most destructive force' between 1948 and 1953. The spark that had led to the immediate popular rage of 1948 would subsequently ignite a series of longer and more complex processes of violence and terror, a 'galaxy of social conflicts' that

---

33 Hylton, *Evil Hour*, p. 46. See also Palacios, *Legitimacy and Violence*.
34 Sánchez and Merteens, *Bandits, Peasants*, p. 15.   35 Ibid.
36 Bushnell, *Modern Colombia*, p. 202.   37 Ibid.
38 Safford and Palacios, *Fragmented Land*, p. 349.   39 Pearce, *Inside the Labyrinth*, p. 51.
40 Hylton, *Evil Hour*, pp. 39–48.   41 Ibid.

shared a 'national political history', yet acquired 'full significance in a history of local and provincial contexts'.[42]

Between 1949 and 1953, and emphatically during the presidency of Laureano Gómez Castro (1950–4), acts of terrorism such as massacres, decapitations, mutilations and sexual violence were meted out in similar measure by both Conservative and Liberal armed militias.[43] Initially, Liberal peasant guerrilla armies were organised by landowners in the coffee-producing regions of Valle and the minifundia regions of Boyacá, the Santanders and the Eastern Llanos, to confront the state's Conservative forces. Peasant farmers themselves carried out and bore the brunt of the killing. In 1950 alone, approximately 50,000 people were executed, principally in the name of partisan hostility and by peasant clients in bloody vendettas against neighbouring villages.[44]

In parallel, between 1950 and 1953, the 'foundations of the cold war national security state were established', whereby 'cold war objectives meshed with those of partisan sectarianism', leading to the perpetration of acts of terrorism as a central government policy linked to the wider ideological and political context.[45] From 1950, the Colombian state began to collaborate with paramilitary forces to levy terror against both armed Liberal factions and organised workers and peasants in its anti-Communist/anti-Liberal crusade.[46] In rural areas, Conservatives and Liberals executed acts of terrorism against their adversary, leading to a 'permanent state of siege'.[47] Entire families were frequently massacred, accompanied by rape, the burning of houses and the theft and destruction of harvests.[48] Such violence and plunder precipitated mass migration to those areas controlled by the party with which the victim identified, leading to 'politically homogeneous' neighbourhoods; rural terror thus reconfigured social classes and relations of power and leadership and shaped patterns of habitation.[49]

Within the political vacuum of the early 1950s and out of the structures of sectarian violence of the 1940s, armed Liberal groups, often referred to as Liberal 'guerrilla movements', emerged across the country, often with the support of Communist party activists.[50] Many who joined the groups had themselves survived the first years of brutal partisan violence, subsequently

---

42 Safford and Palacios, *Fragmented Land*, p. 345.
43 Pearce, *Inside the Labyrinth*, pp. 52–5.
44 Safford and Palacios, *Fragmented Land*, p. 340.   45 Hylton, *Evil Hour*, p. 47.
46 Sánchez and Merteens, *Bandits, Peasants*, pp. 17–20.
47 Palacios, *Legitimacy and Violence*, p. 135.   48 Ibid.
49 Sánchez and Merteens, *Bandits, Peasants*, pp. 17–20.   50 Ibid.

coming to form the first nuclei of the rural armed resistance. Accordingly, the seeds of Colombia's modern terrorism were sown in the country's rural areas during the 1940s.[51] Within the departments of Tolima, Huila, the Eastern Llanos, Boyacá, the Santanders, Antioquia and Caldas, these guerrilla groups were constituted by approximately 10,000 males. Liberal elites themselves gradually distanced themselves from the peasant guerrillas, refusing to accept requests for concrete alliances with or support to them.[52] By 1951, Liberal guerrillas began formally to break ranks with the Liberal landowning elite.[53] Significantly, it was those armed groups influenced by communism within the coffee-growing areas in Tolima that became increasingly radicalised, establishing the basis for the country's long-term guerrilla insurgencies that would form in the 1960s, in particular the Revolutionary Armed Forces of Colombia (FARC-EP). Within the wider context of the Cold War, the Conservative party imbued the war upon its Liberal enemy with a moral, religious and anti-Communist justification.[54] Party-led terrorism became increasingly organised, as the Conservative *chulavitas* and *pájaros*, on the one hand, and Liberal guerrillas and Communist self-defence groups on the other,[55] rampaged against each other.[56]

However, in 1953, Laureano Gómez was toppled in a *coup d'état* by General Gustavo Rojas Pinilla (1953–7), and a brief military dictatorship was installed. An anti-Communist military strongman, General Rojas Pinilla was backed by elements within both traditional parties and, significantly, by the US government. Assuming a mandate to pacify the country and bring an end to *La Violencia*, Rojas Pinilla offered amnesty to the Liberal guerrillas and peasant self-defence groups. With only limited success in its pacification programme, the regime became 'increasingly heavy-handed' against both the civilian opposition and armed groups,[57] launching in 1955 brutal military operations in rural zones representing the regional strongholds of the Liberal guerrillas and where Communist defence groups had crafted their political home. With the backing of Washington, and framed within the National Security Doctrine, Rojas Pinilla bombed guerrilla and opposition peasant positions,[58] operations which arguably radicalised peasant defence groups yet further

---

51 G. Paredes Zapata, 'Terrorism in Colombia', *Prehospital and Disaster Medicine* 18 (2003).
52 Mazzei, *Death Squads*, pp. 75–80.   53 Pearce, *Inside the Labyrinth*, p. 57.
54 D. Pécaut, *Violencia y política en Colombia: Elementos de reflexión* (Medellín, Hombre Nuevo/Universidad del Valle, 2003).
55 National Centre for Historical Memory, *Basta Ya!*, pp. 113–15.   56 Ibid.
57 Paredes Zapata, 'Terrorism in Colombia', pp. 53–7.   58 Bushnell, *Modern Colombia*.

and, in some cases, precipitated their subsequent transformation into revolutionary guerrillas.

During the mid-1950s, military campaigns in Tolima and the Eastern Llanos brought high numbers of homicides, whilst precipitating considerable displacement. Military operations against Communist and peasant defence groups and communities further radicalised armed peasants, many of whom reached a consensus not to disarm;[59] such groups came to form the 'early bastions of the Communist FARC-EP guerrillas of the 1960s'.[60]

The National Front and the Pillars of the Armed Conflict

After the failure of Rojas Pinilla to end *La Violencia*, in 1958, Conservative and Liberal elites reached a bipartisan power-sharing agreement, the so-called National Front (NF). The accord, which would endure formally for four presidential terms until 1974, obliged the Conservative and Liberal parties to alternate presidential power and governmental/public office every four years.[61] Partisan violence was reduced during the NF. However, the agreement simultaneously consolidated elite political control within the Conservative and Liberal parties,[62] therein marginalising other political parties – notably the Colombian Communist Party (CCP) – from participating in the political system. Consequently, the NF had a bearing upon the emergence of guerrilla insurgencies, cementing as it did oligarchic rule whilst excluding the CCP and other alternative political groups.[63] In fact, the latter remained subject to violent repression during the terms of the NF.[64]

In a context of accelerated rural discontent, growing poverty and displacement and formalised political exclusion, the CCP began to create militia units in those Communist enclaves that had been consolidated during the previous

---

59 National Centre for Historical Memory, *Basta Ya!*, p. 115.
60 Palacios, *Legitimacy and Violence*, pp. 160–8.
61 Bushnell posits that coalition rule lasted, in fact, until 1986, when Virgilio Barco (Liberal) took power (*Modern Colombia*, p. 225). See also D. Goldstein and E. Arias (eds.), *Violent Democracies in Latin America* (Durham, NC, Duke University Press, 2010) and F. Gutiérrez Sanín ¿*Lo que el viento se llevó? Los partidos políticos y la democracia en Colombia, 1958–2002* (Bogotá, Norma, 2007).
62 See Molano, 'Evolution of the FARC' and Pearce, *Inside the Labyrinth*, p. 64.
63 E. Posada Carbó, ¿*Guerra civil? El lenguaje del conflicto en Colombia* (Bogotá, Alfaomega y Fundación Ideas para la Paz, 2001).
64 See J. Brittain, *Revolutionary Social Change in Colombia: The Origin and Direction of the FARC-EP* (New York, Pluto Press, 2010) and C. LeGrand, 'The Colombian Crisis in Historical Perspective', *Canadian Journal of Latin American and Caribbean Studies* 28 (2003).

decade, whilst at the same time seeking to strengthen its links with active Liberal guerrillas.[65] The development of armed self-defence units within the so-called Communist enclaves, such as in southern Tolima, Huila and Cauca, posed a significant threat to the NF, to the Colombian state and to the rural elites.[66] The Liberal Party itself gradually aligned itself against CCP members, many of whom had sought refuge in communism during *La Violencia*, often collaborating with the Colombian military.

After the prolonged violent experiences of the late 1940s and 1950s, individual and collective barriers inhibiting the use of violence were arguably lowered.[67] The use of terror by both state and non-state actors thus became increasingly embedded as a permissible social and political strategy. In this context, the instrumentalisation of terror by peasants appeared logical: 'terror became not only an integral part but also, in most cases, the overarching element of their actions', incentivised by frustration, desperation and vengeance.[68] For those peasants that had survived the carnage and humiliation of *La Violencia*, and who were subsequently unable to organise collectively, 'disproportionate cruelty and massacres appeared as primitive but extreme expressions of power – as the only expressions available to them' through which they would be able *'to instil both awe and fear'*.[69]

Within this context, then, acts of terrorism during the first two governments of the National Front represented less the last remnants of *La Violencia* than the embers that would kindle the full-blown guerrilla insurgency and paramilitary brutality that commenced in the first half of the 1960s. Objective structural conditions, accompanied by a century of unbridled official and partisan terror, brought the country, once more, to a turning point at the beginning of the 1960s.

The Internal Armed Conflict (1964 Onwards)

Political violence in Colombia has been cogently characterised by Hylton as possessing a 'historical sense of tragic circularity and repetition'.[70] From Hylton's perspective, 'Patterns of counterinsurgent terror' employed against civilians during *La Violencia* were 'reinforced during the cold war, and repackaged under the anti-terrorist rubric after 11 September 2001'. Political

---

65 See Mazzei, *Death Squads*, p. 77 and National Centre for Historical Memory, *Basta Ya!*, p. 115.
66 Brittain, *Revolutionary Social Change*, pp. 9–12.
67 Sánchez and Merteens, *Bandits, Peasants*, p. 25.   68 Ibid.   69 Ibid.; emphasis added.
70 Hylton, *Evil Hour*, pp. 129–33.

violence and acts of terrorism therein have been reinterpreted and, oftentimes, replicated episodically over a period of 150 years: torture, homicide, massacre and dispossession have been consistently used against non-combatants by state and non-state actors, culminating in a 'limitless terror'.[71]

When *La Violencia* came to an end, rural grievances and political exclusion – the pillars of Colombia's internal armed conflict – had already been constructed. Within this context, Colombia's historical experience of armed conflict was shaped by a series of cross-cutting societal cleavages: ideological (left–right; social class) and demographic (urban–rural and, to a lesser extent, ethnic group identity), some of which possessed continuity with past drivers of violence. Said cleavages were reinforced by a series of systemic conflict drivers: *structural drivers* – rural exclusion/poverty/inequality (unequal land distribution/tenure) and the closure of the formal political system to effective political alternatives; and *proximate drivers* – drug trafficking and production and access to land for (il)legal resource extraction. Embedded within the ideological, military, political and economic logic of Latin America's Cold War, Colombia's revolutionary movements were a response to historically embedded structural drivers of conflict. In the aftermath of *La Violencia*, as the economic impact of the NF collided with the repercussions of the formal exclusion of the CCP from the political sphere, so armed groups consolidated their organisational forms – gradually developing into sophisticated armed organisations – and crafted military strategies aimed at confronting repression, political fraud, corruption, inequality and exclusion.[72]

The onset of the armed conflict came with the creation of the National Liberation Army (ELN) in 1962 and the FARC-EP in 1964, ushering in a wave of left-wing guerrilla violence that has persisted until the time of writing.[73] Shaped by a combination of Marxist-Leninism and, although albeit less so, Liberation Theology, the ELN emerged in the Middle Magdalena Valley of Santander. Formed by guerrillas trained in Cuba, the ELN initially became embedded in Santander and Norte de Santander.[74] The group lacked roots in a 'genuine peasants' movement', conforming instead to a more conventional model of Latin American insurgency, by drawing upon the disaffected middle class.[75] The political platform of the ELN focused upon land distribution,

---

71 Ibid. See also A. Steele, *Democracy and Displacement in Colombia's Civil War* (Ithaca, NY, Cornell University Press, 2017) for an excellent account of Colombia's conflict.
72 Brittain, *Revolutionary Social Change*, pp. 7–8; Pearce, *Inside the Labyrinth*, p. 165. See also Hylton, *Evil Hour* and J. Hristov, *Blood and Capital: The Paramilitarisation of Colombia* (Athens, Ohio University Press, 2009).
73 Safford and Palacios, *Fragmented Land*, p. 354.   74 See Deas, *Dos ensayos*.
75 Bushnell, *Modern Colombia*, p. 244.

poverty, corruption, access to resources and political participation. After military engagements with the Colombian armed forces in the early 1970s, the movement was in part weakened. Subsequently, the ELN became a less major military force, obtaining finance from kidnapping, extortion of petroleum companies, war taxes and, ultimately, from the illicit drug trade.

The FARC-EP grew out of grassroots peasant self-defence organisations formed across Tolima in Communist rural enclaves of the Upper Magdalena Valley. At least initially, the FARC-EP were less an offensive guerrilla than a defensive organisation, 'not given to sabotage or terrorism, nor to ambushes of the police or army', and focusing instead upon protecting peasant communities from 'clientilistic armed forces'.[76] However, in response to state military operations in the wake of the Yarborough survey, such as Plan Lazo in 1962,[77] and specifically to the bombing of the Communist enclave of Marquetalia in 1964, the organisation began to adopt more offensive guerrilla strategies. As Colombia's insurgencies became consolidated, so the 'unfinished business of La Violencia' merged with the country's incipient Cold War.[78]

Operation Marquetalia represented a turning point in Colombia's armed conflict. In the aftermath of the operation, Manuel Marulanda Vélez, alias Tirofijo, a Communist leader who had survived the bombing, garnered increasing support for his claim that armed struggle was the only feasible pathway towards transformation. The FARC-EP subsequently became a sophisticated military organisation under Marulanda's leadership,[79] over time becoming the largest and most capable armed group in Colombia.[80] During the 1960s and 1970s, the activities of the guerrillas were concentrated in rural areas. However, their territorial domination progressively expanded,[81] due, in part, to limited institutional presence across much of Colombia's vast territory. Consequently, the ELN and the FARC-EP – and other illegal armed groups – were gradually able to wield partial territorial control in diverse rural areas. Just as left-wing insurgencies grew, so the state's response to them escalated. Military operations aimed at defeating the

---

76 Ibid.
77 Between 1961 and 1967 the US provided Colombia with 100 million dollars for military equipment and 60 million dollars for economic development and military assistance. See J. Hristov, *Paramilitarism and Neoliberalism: Violent Systems of Capital Accumulation in Colombia and Beyond* (New York, Pluto Press, 2014), p. 80.
78 Hylton, *Evil Hour*, pp. 56–8.   79 Brittain, *Revolutionary Social Change*, pp. 12–16.
80 G. Leech, *The FARC: The Longest Insurgency* (London and New York, Zed Books, 2011), pp. 25–37.
81 Brittain, *Revolutionary Social Change*, pp. 155–6.

guerrilla groups increased in the 1960s, whilst death squads were legalised through Decree 3398 (1965) and subsequently Law 48 (1968), setting the precedent for the terrorist activities of the paramilitaries in the closing decades of the century.[82] At the same time, however, wealthy landowners also provided resources to the paramilitaries with the aim of preventing guerrilla hostilities, such as killings and kidnappings.[83]

Other guerrilla organisations emerged during the Cold War, as the FARC-EP's consolidation from the 1970s onwards was accompanied by the increasing capacity of diverse insurgencies to mobilise and craft effective social bases.[84] In the aftermath of allegedly fraudulent elections in April 1970, for example, the M-19 (19 April Movement) was formed. The M-19 espoused an ideology of nationalism, revolutionary socialism, equality/inclusion and populism, reflecting the experiences of insurgencies in the Southern Cone.[85] The M-19 had a 'gift for the spectacular', carrying out notorious high publicity operations, such as the theft of the sword of Simón Bolívar, the robbery of a mass weapons cache from a military base in Bogotá in 1978 and the occupation of the Embassy of the Dominican Republic in 1980. However, for Bushnell, the M-19 were instrumental in 'rural terrorism', as he accuses their ranks of having assassinated key figures, such as trade union leader José Raquel Mercado.[86]

The Evolution of Political Violence and Terror: the 1980s

The armed conflict had escalated during the 1970s, and, by the 1980s, the ranks of diverse insurgent groups had grown, whilst their geographic reach, military prowess and strategic capacity continued a process of consolidation. The response of the state was no less decisive, as military and paramilitary actors increased in number, preparing the ground for spiralling political violence between adversaries and what would be the enduring strategic employment of acts of terrorism.[87] With the assumption of Julio César Turbay Ayala (1978–82) to the presidency, the so-called Security Statute was

---

82 Hristov, *Blood and Capital*, p. 61.   83 See Mazzei, *Death Squads*, p. 80.
84 For example, the People's Liberation Army (EPL) in 1966 and the indigenous movement Quintín Lame, in 1972.
85 D. Villamizar, *Las guerrillas en Colombia: Una historia desde sus orígenes hasta los confines* (London, Penguin Random House, 2017).
86 Bushnell, *Modern Colombia*, p. 246.
87 See Brittain, *Revolutionary Social Change* and Leech, *The FARC*. The homicide rate tripled during the 1980s, as conflict and drug-related violence escalated.

passed, restricting fundamental freedoms and imposing an almost permanent state of emergency, whilst simultaneously framing counterinsurgency policy within the National Security Doctrine (NSD).[88] Counterinsurgency operations spread away from solely targeting revolutionary groups to target those legal groups perceived by the government to represent the guerrillas' political wing, such as trade unions, human rights organisations and other sectors of the legal political opposition,[89] resulting in ferocious levels of illicit state-sponsored violence against said groups. Within this context, state terrorism became a key characteristic of patterns of violence.[90]

By the end of the Turbay administration, despite the brutal counterinsurgency strategy, the FARC-EP had increased its size from a movement of approximately 500 combatants to a small army of 3,000, and, after having consolidated its forces in the Upper Magdalena Valley and Eastern Llanos, established new guerrilla fronts. By the following year, it would become an 'authentically offensive guerrilla movement',[91] boasting a centralised hierarchical structure, a general staff and military code, a training school and political programme. The ELN replicated this tendency, growing from 800 members eventually to reach 3,000 combatants.[92] Simultaneously, the M-19 grew steadily during the 1970s, and, by the 1980s, numbered over 2,000 combatants. Insurgent activity also expanded geographically, spreading from marginal rural areas to strategically more important zones and, eventually, to urban areas.

The 1980s brought, then, a considerable increase in guerrilla and death squad activity and combat hostilities between guerrilla groups, military forces and paramilitary organisations, whilst representing a key moment in which drug trafficking groups imposed their presence. The term 'terrorism' was first employed by the Colombian government in public discourse during the presidency of Virgilio Barco (1986–90), who referred to 'drug-dealing

---

88 See M. Iturralde, 'Guerra y derecho en Colombia: El decisionismo político y los estados de excepción como respuesta a la crisis de la democracia', *Revista de Estudios Sociales* 15 (2003).
89 See F. Gutiérrez Sanín and F. Barón, 'Estado, control territorial paramilitar y orden político en Colombia', in F. Gutiérrez Sanín, M. Wills and G. Sánchez (eds.), *Nuestra guerra sin nombre: Transformaciones del Conflicto en Colombia* (Bogotá, Norma, 2006).
90 See Bushnell, *Modern Colombia*, p. 256 and Comisión Colombiana de Juristas/Escuela Nacional Sindical, *Imperceptiblemente nos encerraron: Exclusión del sindicalismo y lógicas de la violencia antisindical en Colombia 1979–2010* (Bogotá, Comisión Colombiana de Juristas – Escuela Nacional Sindical, 2012).
91 See Safford and Palacios, *Fragmented Land*, p. 356 and T. Waisberg, 'Colombia's Use of Force in Ecuador Against a Terrorist Organisation: International Law and the Use of Force Against Non-state Actors', *ASIL Insights* 17 (2009).
92 Safford and Palacios, *Fragmented Land*, pp. 360–2.

terrorism', even before the term was used to refer to leftist insurgencies.[93] Whilst, in some cases, initial alliances existed between guerrillas and drug traffickers, an upsurge in violent hostilities between the revolutionary armed left and the latter took place during the 1980s, due, in part, to the fact that the latter were amassing land and the guerrilla itself was targeting wealthy landowners and cattle ranchers. As the insurgent threat grew, so alliances between ranchers, small farmers, police and narcos were forged with the aim of combating the guerrilla. Self-defence militias were formalised by wealthy landowners, cattle ranchers and drug lords throughout rural areas,[94] a direct antecedent to the paramilitaries of the 1990s, which would have their origins in the death squads of the Middle Magdalena Valley.[95] A key manifestation of this alliance was the formation of the organisation Death to Kidnappers (MAS), formed in Medellín between 1981 and 1982 by members of the Medellín Cartel, active and retired police and military, small industrialists, wealthy cattle ranchers and representatives of the US-based corporation Texas Petroleum. MAS confronted the guerrilla groups head-on, whilst subsequently perpetrating acts of terrorism against human rights defenders, members of left-wing political parties, journalists and lawyers through strategies reminiscent of the bipartisan terror employed during *La Violencia*.

By the mid-1980s, diverse rural and urban theatres of insurrectional and mafia war had appeared throughout the country, evidencing the emergence of an increasingly broad 'functional alliance' between the private sector, landowners, drug barons, sectors of the security forces and paramilitaries. The alliance waged a 'dirty war' against the guerrilla and the political left, whilst 'urban terrorism' grew sharply, linked to growing narco activity and the unchecked power of the drug lords, and exacerbated by the escalating grievances of the urban poor and the incapacity of successive governments to address urban discontent.[96]

In their bid to consolidate economic and political power, the drug cartels took on both the guerrilla and the government. Any attempts by the government to move against them were met with brutal and decisive force. In 1984, for example, during the government of President Belisario Betancur, Justice Minister Rodrigo Lara Bonilla was assassinated by Pablo Escobar's Medellín cartel due to the latter's attempts to persecute the cartels. The execution of Lara Bonilla pushed President Betancur to approve a law securing extradition to the US for cartel members, which the cartels took as a declaration of war.

---

93 Palma, 'Changing Meaning', p. 251.　94 Safford and Palacios, *Fragmented Land*, p. 265.
95 Hylton, *Evil Hour*, p. 68.　96 Bushnell, *Modern Colombia*, pp. 250–4.

Over the following years, the cartels employed acts of terrorism, supported by their 'virtually parallel security system', ravaging urban and rural Colombia. Magistrates connected with extradition cases were assassinated, as was Guillermo Cano, the editor of the Colombian newspaper *El Espectador*, after publishing an editorial on the mafia in 1986. In 1989, an airliner allegedly carrying police informants exploded in mid-air, killing all 107 people on board. The same year, a car-bomb attack on the country's intelligence agency in Bogotá killed more than 50 people and wounded over 1,000 others. In both cases, the Medellín cartel, and Pablo Escobar and Gonzalo Rodríguez Gacha, in particular, were purportedly responsible.[97]

Within this context, an emblematic episode took place on 6 November 1985, when the M-19 carried out a typical high-profile operation, occupying the Palace of Justice in downtown Bogotá.[98] The guerrilla's objective was allegedly to hold a symbolic trial of President Betancur, who, unsurprisingly, rejected the group's demands he go to the Palace to be tried by them. Once the M-19 had secured their position within the building, allegedly killing two security guards as they did, they took over 300 people hostage, including all Supreme Court Magistrates and over 20 other judges. The military operation to retake the Palace of Justice commenced the following day, coordinated by Colonel Alfonso Plazas. The armed forces stormed the building, utilising armoured cars and tanks to do so. During the military operation, over 100 people were killed, including 12 magistrates, civilians and 5 M-19 leaders, as both the guerrilla and the military unleashed their furies. In the aftermath of the operation, 11 individuals were forcibly disappeared by the military, a crime for which both Colonel Plazas and his commanding officer, General Armando Arias, were convicted in 2010 and 2014 respectively. Moreover, the Inter-American Court of Human Rights (IACHR) stated in 2012 that the Colombian authorities had carried out both torture and forced disappearances during the Palace siege.[99] By the mid-1980s, then, acts of terrorism by state and non-state terrorist actors had become uncontainable.

Terrorism Against the Left: The UP

In the same year as the sacking of the Palace of Justice, as part of the peace agreement between the FARC-EP and the Betancur government, former

---

97 Ibid.   98 Pearce, *Inside the Labyrinth*, p. 181.
99 The rationale for the M-19 operation has sparked deep controversy. During the operation, records for approximately 6,000 legal cases were destroyed, including files for the criminal case against Pablo Escobar, precipitating accusations that the M-19 were working with the backing of the drug lord.

FARC-EP combatants, dissidents from the CCP and social activists came together to establish the political party the Patriotic Union (UP).[100] In the context of the peace talks, and with a broad section of the country pushing for peace with the guerrilla, the UP rapidly became a political force. In the 1986 general elections, the party gained important inroads, winning 4.4 per cent of the presidential vote, 5 seats in the Senate and 9 in the Chamber of Representatives, alongside key wins at local level, including 14 deputies, 351 counsellors and 23 municipal mayors.

The UP's achievements precipitated a severely violent reaction from Colombia's political elites and right-wing illegal armed groups, culminating in the 'genocide of the UP'.[101] Acts of terrorism through formalised killing campaigns against the UP carried out by a 'perpetrator bloc' decimated the party,[102] leaving more than 3,000 of its politicians, including presidential candidates and parliamentarians, and UP supporters dead within less than a decade and a further 1,000 dead by 2002. Others were tortured, forced into exile or displaced. The 'bloc' itself was constituted by the armed forces, paramilitaries and self-defence groups, drug traffickers, political entrepreneurs and government officials, often in association or collaboration.[103] In a strategy reminiscent of Valentino's concept of 'collective punishment',[104] the killing campaign identified the entire political party, including leadership and social base, as a collective enemy to be physically eliminated. Massacres of UP members occurred throughout the country, including in regions such as Segovia, in the Middle Magdalena Valley, where the triumph of the UP precipitated alliances between traditional political parties and paramilitary groups. In the department of the Norte de Santander, perpetrators utilised crematoria, chainsaws and alligators to dispose of the bodies of assassinated UP officials. The extermination was ongoing throughout the 1990s, carried out through 'selective assassination of UP public figures, raids on UP offices and illegal detentions, assassinations and threats to

---

100 See Pearce, *Inside the Labyrinth*, S. Dudley, *Walking Ghosts: Murder and Guerrilla Politics in Colombia* (London, Routledge, 2004) and A. Gomez-Suarez, *Genocide, Geopolitics and Transnational Networks: Con-textualising the Destruction of the Unión Patriótica in Colombia* (London, Routledge, 2017).
101 Hylton, *Evil Hour* and Gomez-Suarez, *Genocide*.
102 A. Gomez-Suarez, 'Perpetrator Blocs, Genocidal Mentalities and Geographies: The Destruction of the Union Patriotica in Colombia and Its Lessons for Genocide Studies', *Journal of Genocide Research* 9 (2007), p. 468.
103 Ibid.; Leech, *The FARC*, p. 21.
104 B. Valentino, *Final Solutions: Mass Killing and Genocide in the 20th Century* (Ithaca, NY, Cornell University Press, 2004), p. 201.

relatives, families and local activists'.[105] The violence played a key role in radicalising those fighters that had previously demobilised, and once more pushing them back to the armed struggle, at the same time as the memory of the 'genocide' in turn prevented many combatants from disarming.

Barco and the Statute for the Defence of Democracy

The 'fight against terrorism on the judicial front' commenced in 1986, with the election of Virgilio Barco to the presidency. Midway through his term, Barco approved antiterrorist legislation, the so-called Statute for the Defence of Democracy, which sought to control and bring to justice both the drug cartels and armed insurgencies.[106] The Statute created ninety Specialised Judges of Public Order and Public Order Courts, at the same time as it authorised military forces to arrest individuals suspected of terrorist activities and, if required, detain them for up to ten days. The Statute restricted civilian freedoms, permitting the government to utilise the law to lay siege to leftist activists, trade unionists and human rights activists, at the same time as the military executed a 'policy of terror' against civilians, including bombings, intimidation, torture, killings and disappearances.[107] Rather than representing a legitimate instrument against terrorism, the Statute institutionalised state terror.

By the late 1980s, the paramilitaries had 'erased the broad Left from the electoral map, reinforced clientelist political controls, and began to acquire vast landholdings, chiefly through massacre and expropriation'.[108] Paramilitary 'social cleansing' in banana, logging and cattle-ranching regions – through massacres beginning in the 1980s – became a common feature of the paramilitary modus operandi. At the same time, urban terrorism by the paramilitaries and the cartels began to wield a significant effect: judges, activists and politicians were executed, and urban areas, such as Barrancabermeja, were cleansed of political oppositions, as well as 'petty thieves, prostitutes, homosexuals and other undesirables'.[109] Within this context, the state itself became 'part of an anachronistic political order', in which past and present violence propagated by political and economic elites became interconnected. Colombia's ruling class 'led its people into one of the

---

105 Gomez-Suarez, 'Perpetrator Blocs', p. 167.   106 Nagle, 'Global Terrorism', p. 97.
107 Pearce, *Inside the Labyrinth*, p. 234; Iturralde, 'Guerra y derecho'.
108 Hylton, *Evil Hour*, pp. 75–8.   109 Bushnell, *Modern Colombia*, p. 264.

bloodiest civil wars of the twentieth century, and three decades later, it unleashed a wave of right-wing terrorism against people that demanded their rights'.[110]

The 1990s: Terrorism in the Aftermath of the Cold War

Echoing processes across Latin America, the post-Cold War context brought a series of successful peace initiatives to Colombia, including the DDR (Disarmament, Demobilisation and Reintegration) process of the M-19 and Quintín Lame, amongst others. In the aftermath of the Cold War, however, the FARC-EP continued its war. The consolidation of its military and organisational capacity came at a cost, however:[111] the progressive loss of its political legitimacy, as it further turned to drug production and trafficking to finance its armed struggle.[112] As the FARC-EP sought to secure control and guarantee the sovereignty of its local territories, moreover, so the group perpetrated significantly higher levels of selective assassination and kidnappings. Violence once again spiked, as the paramilitary response to insurgent capacity escalated and, by the mid-1990s, terrorist actions – such as car bombings – by the cartels, in particular the Medellín cartel, became routinised. Consequently, the original structural causes of the conflict mutated and evolved.[113]

In this context, the FARC-EP began to execute increasingly arbitrary, diverse and widespread forms of violence and acts of terrorism, including against its own social base, subsequently alienating it from elements within its existing social constituency and broader Colombian society. Significantly, after 1990, the FARC-EP grew from under 8,000 to approximately 18,000 members in 2000. Between 1996 and 2003, the group averaged 1,000 offensive military actions, in contrast to 500 annually during the 1980s. By 1997, both the FARC-EP and the ELN would be placed on the US Department of State list of Foreign Terrorist Organisations, and in 2002 on the European Union Terrorist Organisation list.

The response to the FARC-EP's increasing military capacity was an expanded and progressively coordinated wave of paramilitary terror, sponsored, as before, by the state and the political and economic elites. Paramilitary expansion drew upon the historically enduring presence of

---

110 Pearce, *Inside the Labyrinth*, p. 234.
111 Safford and Palacios, *Fragmented Land*, pp. 86–8.
112 See Palma, 'Changing Meaning', p. 254.   113 Pécaut, *Las FARC*.

private armed groups and culminated in 1996 with the establishment of the United Self-Defence Forces of Colombia (AUC), an umbrella group that brought together diverse paramilitary fronts linked to the political and economic elites. During the late 1990s, as alliances were cemented with the military and between the paramilitary blocs themselves, so increasing acts of terrorism, including massacre campaigns, were executed against non-combatants throughout rural and semi-urban areas. Significantly, as was the case with the FARC-EP and ELN, both paramilitary and state security forces became intimately involved in drug production and trafficking during the 1990s, acutely transforming the nature of the armed conflict.

By the 1990s, then, the paramilitaries had crafted a degree of autonomy, collaborating variously with the state and military, landowners, cattle ranchers and cartels. They increasingly pursued an offensive strategy, cleansing areas of subversives and their supposed supporters through massacre and forced displacement, the latter often permitting cartels to move in or international companies to plant African palm. Paramilitaries often worked closely with the Colombian military 'to eliminate suspected guerrilla sympathizers, while at the same time they attacked Colombian authorities investigating drug trafficking and paramilitary activity'.[114] Paramilitaries were frequently employed as 'de facto shock troops', sent into rural areas suspected of supporting guerrilla activity prior to a formal military assault operation.[115] By the 1990s, beyond achieving relative autonomy, paramilitary groups were consolidated throughout the country, bolstered by income from illicit activities and, in some cases, legal decrees that formalised their mandates. For example, in 1994, Decree 356, promulgated by subsequent Colombian President Alvaro Uribe, created the so-called Convivir. Convivir security cooperatives were private organisations mandated with tasks of surveillance, information-gathering and rural security that articulated cooperation in security matters between the rural landowning elite and Colombia's armed forces. The group was established to combat the FARC-EP, and subsequently perpetrated egregious crimes against civilians, often in collaboration with military and police units.[116]

Paramilitary acts of terrorism spiralled between 1997 and 1999, organisations' ranks doubled; massacres represented a particular modus operandi of

---

[114] W. Tate, 'Paramilitaries in Colombia', *The Brown Journal of World Affairs* 8 (2001), p. 166 and Hristov, *Paramilitarism and Neoliberalism*, p. 53.
[115] Nagle, 'Global Terrorism', p. 19.
[116] The decree establishing the Convivir was struck down by the Constitutional Court in 1997; many of its ranks passed to the AUC.

the groups, increasing from 286 in 1997 to 403 in 1999. In 1996, across four municipalities of the so-called Banana Axis, the homicide rate was 500 per 100,000. Within this context, the military frequently allegedly removed troops tasked with the protection of civilians from the paramilitaries. For example, the massacre in the town of Mapiripán, perpetrated in July 1997, included five days of torture and murder, assisted by the military itself. Paramilitary terror wielded a significant effect on the capacity of the FARC-EP to control its territories. In 1996, for example, in the wake of a 'campaign of indiscriminate terror and cruelty', the Córdoba and Urabá Self-Defence Forces were able to displace the FARC-EP to neighbouring Chocó.[117]

Perhaps the key development with respect to paramilitary capacity to employ acts of terrorism as a strategy, however, was the establishment, in 1996, of the AUC by Carlos Castaño. Castaño sought to strengthen the anti-subversive campaign through a 'definitive and conclusive war against the guerrillas'.[118] Despite protestations that it would remain isolated from the narco sphere, the AUC took advantage of the illicit business both to finance its own struggle and to drive capital accumulation of its members, eventually appropriating 40 per cent of the drug economy.[119]

The AUC emerged with approximately 3,000 members, expanding rapidly; by 2005, they numbered between 8,000 and 11,000 armed combatants, with a logistical support base of approximately 18,000 members.[120] By 2003, it wielded a presence in over 25 of Colombia's departments and in a third of the country's municipalities. Castaño has claimed that the AUC ranks included 800 ex-guerrillas, 135 former military officers and over 1,000 former soldiers.[121] The organisation enjoyed broad operational, financial and technical support from the military high command, at the same time as it coordinated closely with landowning elites – often paid directly by them – and with local and national state and government officials.

The AUC was a significant terrorist actor in Colombia, linked, allegedly, to international terrorist organisations.[122] Collusion between the Colombian Armed Forces and the AUC was systematic from its creation up until the

---

117 Safford and Palacios, *Fragmented Land*, pp. 95–101.   118 Mazzei, *Death Squads*, p. 93.
119 V. Sanford, 'Learning to Kill by Proxy: Colombian Paramilitaries and the Legacy of Central American Death Squads, Contras, and Civil Patrols', *Social Justice* 30 (2003), p. 75.
120 Mazzei, *Death Squads*, pp. 93–4; N. Richani, 'Caudillos and the Crisis of the Colombian State: Fragmented Sovereignty, the War System and the Privatisation of Counterinsurgency in Colombia', *Third World Quarterly* 28 (2007), p. 409. There are estimates that the group numbered over 30,000 by the time of its DDR process in 2007.
121 Hristov, *Blood and Capital*, p. 71.   122 Nagle, 'Global Terrorism'.

DDR process with the group, which began in 2005. By 2000, the rapid spread of the AUC and its strategic use of acts of terrorism against non-combatants had polarised Colombian society yet further, transforming the social and political landscape. By the mid-2000s paramilitary terror played a key role in pushing both the FARC-EP and the ELN to withdraw from many areas in which they had historically asserted control and into peripheral zones of the country. The violence perpetrated by the group was both decisive and widespread in scale and grotesque in nature. In 2000, massacres increased by 22 per cent, whilst approximately 319,000 people were forcibly displaced.[123] Acts of terrorism – including the perpetration of massacres – were often facilitated or accompanied by state agents, either through direct collaboration in commissioning violence, or through acts of omission, or non-intervention, such as when state security forces would not respond to notifications of an imminent or probable paramilitary attack.

The paramilitaries' reach also extended to the political sphere. Between 2002 and 2006, 77 per cent of national Congressional representatives were linked to the paramilitaries, and, accordingly, to acts of terrorism; said links were replicated at the local level.[124] Significantly, the group also closely coordinated with transnational corporations, such as Chiquita Banana, on whose behalf it allegedly carried out terrorist actions against over 100 non-combatants, including organised Chiquita workers. For example, in 1998, the AUC forced Chiquita employees to watch as two co-workers were executed. In 1999, two AUC members beheaded a Chiquita employee with a machete on a Chiquita plantation, followed two years later by an action in which AUC members rounded up male civilians and smashed their skulls with 'stones and sledgehammers'.[125] In spite of such activity, however, the AUC would only be placed on the US Department of State list of Foreign Terrorist Organisations in September 2001, five years after its establishment.

The Uribe Years: 'Terrorism' in Colombia in the Aftermath of 9/11

Amidst the continued perpetration of acts of terrorism by state and non-state actors, the Caguán peace process (1999–2002) between the government of

---

123 Human Rights Watch, *World Report: Colombia* (New York, HRW, 2001), p. 5.
124 Hristov, *Paramilitarism and Neoliberalism*, pp. 103–4.
125 For discussion of the role of Chiquita in supporting terrorist actors, see Nagle, 'Global Terrorism' and V. Maurer, 'Corporate Social Responsibility and the Divided Corporate Self: The Case of Chiquita in Colombia', *Journal of Business Ethics* 88 (2009).

President Andrés Pastrana and the FARC-EP commenced. The guerrilla came to the talks from a militarily and politically robust position, bolstered by the impact of its politico-military strategy and illegal assets that had brought territorial expansion and, increasingly, key victories against the military. The government, whilst demonstrating political will, did not enjoy widespread political support, particularly from within the ranks of the military. Consequently, both parties were hesitant on major commitments, reluctant to compromise their political and ideological positions and, ultimately, to relinquish their perceived military superiority. Under these conditions, the peace talks languished ineffectively, and ultimately collapsed in July 2002, when the FARC-EP carried out an armed offensive, to which the government immediately responded by bombing guerrilla enclaves with the support of the US.[126]

The collapse of the talks paved the way for subsequent election of President Álvaro Uribe (2002–6; 2006–10), whose electoral platform had rejected a negotiated peace. What followed was an all-out war against the guerrilla and a dirty war against the FARC-EP's social base, executed with decisive support from Washington. The eight years of Uribe government would represent a significant moment in the extension of the perpetration of acts of state and non-state terrorism in Colombia.

President Uribe came to office in 2002, amidst a severe economic crisis and escalating drug trafficking violence. During 2002, approximately 19 terrorist attacks were executed, attributable to leftist and right-wing armed groups, all but one of which were bombings (car bombs; horse and bicycle bombs; collar bombs) against political, military and commercial targets. In May of that year, the FARC-EP perpetrated one of its most emblematic acts of terrorism. During hostilities between the guerrilla and the paramilitaries in the town of Bojayá, the FARC-EP fired a cylinder bomb at paramilitary positions located around the church and civilian residences. The gas cylinder fell upon the church where civilians were seeking refuge, killing more than a hundred civilians. The following year, a further egregious act of terrorism was perpetrated in February, when the El Nogal club in Bogotá was bombed, killing 36 people and injuring over 200. No group initially claimed responsibility, although the FARC-EP has since accepted responsibility for carrying out the attack. In response to the bombing, the United Nations Security Council issued Resolution 1465, in which it took the unprecedented step of

---

126 M. Chernick, 'The Dynamics of Colombia's Three-Dimensional War', *Conflict, Security and Development* 1 (2001).

terming the attack an act of terrorism and a 'threat to international security'.[127]

Within said context, Uribe adopted a dramatically different approach to the guerrilla than that of his predecessor, in particular with respect to the FARC-EP, who had executed his father some years before.[128] Finding an echo and seeking legitimation and justification in President Bush's 'War on Terror', Uribe appropriated the discourse of a global war on terror. In his inaugural address, Uribe stated that 'any violence against a [democratic state]' would now be defined as 'terrorist activity'.[129] In fact, presidents Uribe and Bush soon became staunch allies in their respective wars on terrorism: Colombia joined the 'Coalition of the Willing', and Bush channelled millions of dollars to Colombia's war on drugs (and later war on terror) through Plan Colombia, originally established in 1998.[130] The appropriation of the discourse of the global War on Terror by Uribe was key in securing both an effective militarised state response to the FARC-EP, and, significantly, garnering US support for his war. After reaching a peak during the early and mid-1990s, framed within the broader language of the War on Terror, the discourse of narco-terrorism re-emerged under Uribe, permitting him to frame 'the decades-old problem of violence in Colombia merely as a terrorist threat' and thus to intensify counterinsurgent strategy.[131]

US support was ultimately manifest through Plan Colombia, a multi-billion-dollar funding framework, which had initially engaged multiple donor governments, focused upon 'development' and conceived as a Marshall Plan for Colombia.[132] Under Clinton, the US government agreed to 1.3 billion dollars in support, oriented towards military assistance and crop eradication. During the Bush administration, funding was expanded and the original restriction upon wider support for counterinsurgency operations was vetoed. Plan Colombia was formulated as a national/international collaboration through which to restore rule of law, combat drug trafficking and address the insurgent problem, which morphed into a primarily counterinsurgency/antiterror intervention programme.[133]

Uribe's war against the FARC-EP and the ELN and political violence against their perceived bases of support quickly escalated. Uribe refuted

---

127 See United Nations Security Council Resolution 1465 (2003). See also Nagle, 'Global Terrorism'.
128 Ibid., p. 22; W. Monning, 'The Colombian Conflict: A War on Drugs? A War on Terrorism? A War on the Poor?', *Guild Practitioner* 59 (2002), pp. 161–4.
129 Ibid.   130 Nagle, 'Global Terrorism', p. 58.
131 Palma, 'Changing Meaning', pp. 259–64.
132 Monning, 'The Colombian Conflict', p. 164.   133 Nagle, 'Global Terrorism', p. 60.

that Colombia was experiencing an armed conflict, framing the state's strategy as counterterrorism. In August, Uribe declared a state of emergency, whilst building up a network of 'citizen spies' and 'peasant soldiers'.[134] Of significant importance was the Uribe government's ties with the paramilitaries, with whom the president had established a close relationship since the creation of the Convivir in 1994. Uribe, in part, abdicated the dirty war against the guerrilla's social base to the paramilitaries, who themselves subsequently became embedded in and captured state institutions, including through their legal arm, Colombia Viva. Shifting the narrative from both a counterinsurgency campaign and War on Drugs to his War on Terror, Uribe assumed a hard-line approach against the insurgencies through military campaigns and state reform bankrolled by an acutely receptive White House. In an effort to reassert state control across Colombia's vast territory, Uribe legislated a war tax to increase military revenue, whilst drawing upon Plan Colombia to improve military training and hardware.

In 2003, President Uribe formulated his government's security policy, the Policy of Democratic Defence and Security (Democratic Security Policy, DSP). Prioritising the elimination of the 'narco-terrorist' FARC-EP, the counterinsurgency/counter-'terror' strategy was undergirded by a series of interrelated goals, including strategic military pacification and stabilisation. The DSP sought to regain and consolidate state control and presence throughout the national territory, with the aim of denying sanctuary for illegal armed actors and perpetrators of violence ('terrorists'); to guarantee the protection of civilians through increasing state presence/control and reducing violence; to combat the illegal drug trade and eliminate resultant revenues financing illegal armed groups ('terrorism'); and to guarantee and efficiently manage resources with the aim of reforming and improving the performance of the government. The strategy ultimately sought, then, to restore control over transport infrastructure and demobilise and reintegrate armed groups.

The accompanying increase in military spending allowed the Colombian armed forces to acquire significant military hardware and, by 2010, the military had increased significantly. At the same time, elite counterinsurgent combat units were created, including Task Force Omega (in 2003), and, with US support, the Joint Commands were established to facilitate coordination between the army, air force and navy. Smaller, rapidly deployable units and specialised jungle and mountain units were also established,[135] improving mobility and logistics, enhancing reaction time to insurgent threats and

---

134 Hylton, *Evil Hour*, pp. 100–9.   135 Palma, 'Changing Meaning', p. 259.

operations, and improving capacity for night operations, all of which were central to bringing the fight to the guerrilla.[136] US financial assistance and training also permitted the reform of intelligence structures and networks, ultimately precipitating more streamlined and effective intelligence-gathering procedures.[137]

Under Uribe, the strategy of military pacification combined with the illegal paramilitary dirty war gradually reined in the guerrilla threat. Uribe's all-out war on the FARC-EP and its social base came at a significant cost, however. State institutions – such as the Constitutional Court – and politicians and activists that opposed or questioned the Uribe administration and international organisations were subject to illegal surveillance. Acts of terrorism against civilians carried out by the paramilitaries – often in coordination with the military – were as effective as they were brutal, as human rights and civil society organisations that opposed the DSP were identified as legitimate targets. Enjoying broad operational, financial and technical support from the military high command, AUC forces waged a war of terror against civilians, precipitating vast numbers of killings, massacres, torture, sexual violence and displacement across rural and urban areas.[138]

The US War on Terror, which had begun only a matter of months prior to the assumption of Uribe to the presidency, was then a critical enabling factor in the permissibility with which Uribe's discourse and actions were received. In the aftermath of 9/11, in a discursive conflation between war on terror, war on drugs and war on insurgents, the conceptualisation of the FARC-EP as 'narco-terrorists' was given robust support from Washington, a discourse that was, ultimately, operationalised through Plan Colombia. Significantly, 'the vast majority of abuses' in Uribe's 'war of terror' were perpetrated against the civilian population. In fact, the war precipitated the most dramatic humanitarian disaster in the western hemisphere: over 5 million people were displaced, thousands murdered, and entire zones destroyed.[139]

Uribe's strategy was resoundingly successful, weakening the guerrilla's command structure and strategic operational capacity, partially debilitating its communications capability and pushing it back from the country's central Andean departments towards increasingly peripheral areas.[140]

In numeric terms, the impact of the DSP was devastating for the guerrilla. Between 2003 and 2009, the security forces killed over 12,000 FARC-EP

---

136 Crisis Group, 'Colombia: Peace at Last?', *Report 45* (2012).   137 Ibid.
138 D. Stokes, 'Why the End of the Cold War Doesn't Matter: The US War on Terror in Colombia', *Review of International Studies* 29 (2003).
139 Ibid., p. 578.   140 Crisis Group, 'Peace at Last?'.

combatants and commanders and captured a further 12,000. In 2002, the FARC-EP had wielded operational presence in 377 municipalities; by the end of Uribe's second term, only 9,000 FARC-EP fighters remained active, with operational presence in only 142 municipalities. In parallel, the DSP achieved its objective of restoring state presence: by 2006, the state had operational presence in all the country's 1,100 municipalities.[141] As a consequence of their 'dirty war', the paramilitaries ultimately obtained enormous spoils (landed estates, illegal businesses, electoral networks, control of public services) and consolidated a foothold on local and national politics; in the latter case, in 2005, 35 per cent of Congress was controlled by paramilitaries.

As a result of its military success, direct paramilitary activity ended by 2007. The demobilisation of the AUC and other paramilitary groups took place between 2003 and 2006, within the framework of the so-called Justice and Peace Law (Law 975) passed in 2005 and its predecessor laws (Law 782 of 2002 and Decree 128 of 2003). However, and significantly, the DDR process pertaining to the paramilitaries has been a resounding failure. While approximately 32,000 paramilitaries formally demobilised, only 3,700 individuals applied as beneficiaries of Law 975. Furthermore, thousands of individuals have since integrated into post-AUC, so-called 'neo-paramilitary' organisations,[142] groups which continue to represent the principal challenge to peace and security in Colombia.

The Interminable Conflict? Some Concluding Thoughts on Terrorism in Colombia

This chapter has offered a longer-term historical perspective on terrorism in Colombia, providing a rigorous historically oriented and contextually driven analysis of acts of terrorism perpetrated since the nineteenth century by diverse violent actors, in this case understood as violence with a political aim that seeks to communicate and instil terror and maximise political gain. The research has depicted how complex interrelated political, economic, legal and social processes, themselves shaped by historical context and structural factors, have determined how, when and by whom acts of terrorism have been employed in Colombia. The research has argued that the employment of acts of terrorism predates Colombia's albeit brief articulation with the international war on terrorism since 2002 under former President

---

141 Ibid.
142 Office of the United Nations High Commissioner for Human Rights in Colombia, *Annual Report* (January 2015).

Uribe; in short, the use of terrorism as a military and political strategy has roots within the political, economic and social foundations of the Colombian state and society. Colombia has been defined less by the war on terrorism than by its own cyclical, home-grown wars of terrorism.

Since Colombia began its process to break free from Spanish rule in 1810, the country has suffered constant violent political confrontations. Independence ushered in a long period of violent instability throughout the nineteenth century, during which time civil war and poverty were significant factors determining the country's social and political dynamics. Broadly speaking, violent confrontation during the nineteenth and first half of the twentieth centuries was shaped by and further consolidated the cleavage between the Conservative and Liberal parties, and was manifest in complex patterns of conflict at national, subnational and local levels. Systematic, grotesque violence became the norm in Colombia's bipartisan conflict, as party elites and members and the armed militia groups through which their wraths were made manifest executed acts of terrorism against civilians. *La Violencia* represented the unfinished business of the post-indepedence period. However, the pillars of Colombia's internal armed conflict were, in turn, crafted during *La Violencia* and the National Front power-sharing agreement that sought to bring it to an end. Subsequently, with almost no meaningful or protracted hiatus, and in spite of important peacebuilding initiatives, the country embarked on what has been over five decades of egregious political violence, within which acts of terrorism against civilians have been employed systematically by multiple armed actors: the state, leftist guerrilla insurgencies, far-right paramilitaries and drug cartels.

Significantly, since the 1980s, violence in Colombia has become characterised by its sheer complexity, in particular in the aftermath of the Cold War, as the original structural causes of conflict that precipitated and decisively shaped the political violence of the second half of the twentieth century mutated and evolved. Guerrilla, paramilitary and state security forces became intimately involved in drug production and trafficking during the 1980s and, emphatically, the 1990s, acutely transforming the nature of the armed conflict and, in fact, exacerbating rural grievances as paramilitaries expropriated vast tracts of land. Since the early 1990s, drug trafficking organisations, criminal organisations and illegal armed groups – and not infrequently military and police forces – have generated complex alliances as they seek to maintain control of economic resources, including drug production and other illegal enterprises. In this regard, a mosaic of often connected subnationally and locally driven conflicts have emerged, converging around a set of objective conditions, common actors and patterns of violence, oftentimes melding political violence and criminal activity. The shifting motivations behind and targets of armed violence, including acts of terrorism, and the blurred line between political and criminal violence have since imbued the conflict with an unprecedented level of intricacy, in turn problematising the 'classification of violent acts'.[143] Armed actors have consistently resorted to acts of terrorism, often as a default strategy, whilst simultaneously waging regular and irregular warfare against conventional and unconventional forces, as well as engaging in the formal political sphere, as part of wider processes of war and state-building.[144] In this respect, the case echoes other Latin American cases, such as those in Central America.

The continuity of political violence within broader and more complex armed confrontations has been coherently evidenced within this chapter, as has the redundancy of categorising specific groups within the singular framework of 'terrorist'. The Colombia case, moreover, illustrates how the employment of terrorist violence has not been the sole preserve of leftist insurgencies. Party militias, right-wing paramilitaries, mafias, drug cartels and the state have, in turn, methodically commissioned widespread acts of terrorism, often collaborating together and, at other times, acting with the direct or indirect collusion of the private sector and transnational corporations. In this regard, the case would speak to other similar cases elsewhere. Significantly, mirroring other countries in Latin America such as Guatemala and Argentina, the state, then, has directly commissioned acts of terrorism, whilst also being responsible for such crimes through acts of omission. The acts of terrorism that have resulted from such complex interactions have, as has been illustrated, been intimately linked to the broader processes of state- and nation-building in Colombia, as politicians from distinct parties,

---

143 Holmes, 'Terrorism in Latin America'.
144 The violence exerted by the guerrillas included massacres, torture, homicide, disappearance. The guerrillas were responsible for the highest levels of kidnapping of civilians and members of the security forces in order to levy political pressure against the government or economic resources for the war (Leech, *The FARC*, pp. 109–10). According to the National Centre for Historical Memory, the paramilitary groups were the main perpetrators of massacres and selective assassinations, often in collaboration with the armed forces. They also systematically practised sexual violence. In addition, other types of violence are selective assassinations, forced disappearances, torture, threats, massive forced displacements and economic blockades against civilians. Consistently, the goal behind such activities was to increase civilian cooperation and force civilian support. Drug cartels have been responsible for massacres, homicides, torture, bombings and intimidation (National Centre for Historical Memory, *Basta Ya!*, pp. 44–84).

economic and political elites, armed actors and state agents have sought to sculpt a state and society wrought in their own image.

At the end of November 2016, after a four-year peace process, the Colombian Congress ratified a comprehensive package of five peace agreements negotiated between the government of President Juan Manuel Santos (2010–14; 2014–18) and the FARC-EP. After having been initially rejected by public referendum on 2 October 2016, and subsequently (and urgently) revised during the following weeks, the political settlement brought formal closure to the fifty-two-year armed conflict with the FARC-EP, although war with the country's other long-standing insurgency, the ELN, remains ongoing.

The end of the war with the FARC-EP has not, however, brought an end to the political violence and acts of terrorism that have blighted Colombia's social and political landscape since the nineteenth century. On the contrary, 'tragic circularity' persists. Whilst the homicide rate decreased in an unprecedented manner under President Santos, and conflict-related deaths reached their lowest levels for over five decades, acts of terrorism and levels of homicide have slowly increased once again since the end of the peace process and, in particular, the assumption of the presidency by Iván Duque. President Duque (2018–present) is the political heir of former President Uribe, who was the most vocal opponent of the Santos/FARC-EP peace process, along with his political party and elements of the private sector, including cattle ranchers. President Duque's government has done very little to implement the peace agreements signed with the FARC-EP. In fact, despite his commitments to the international community regarding governmental support to the peace process, he has, in practice, followed the political line aggressively imposed by his political chief and sponsor former President Uribe. Duque has sought to dismantle key institutions established through the negotiations, has reduced budget allocations and has decreased institutional capacity designated to respond to the state commitments to former combatants. Since 2015, neo-paramilitary organisations have augmented their killing campaigns, and been identified as the perpetrators of many of the murders of over 142 former FARC-EP combatants and over 500 social activists since the end of the peace process, in acts of despicable terror. Allegedly as a consequence of the extermination of former FARC-EP combatants and social activists and the lack of progress on the peace agreements, on 29 August 2019, Iván Márquez and Jesús Santrich, former FARC-EP commanders who were instrumental in the signing of peace with the government and in keeping the FARC-EP at the negotiating table, announced their return to the armed struggle. At the time of writing, Colombia is once again at a crossroads, as the country's fragile peace with the FARC-EP faces its most significant challenge yet, and as the weight of Colombia's violent past threatens to unleash further terror. At the beginning of this research, Colombia appeared to be treading a slow and precarious road to peace; it felt almost as if I were writing history. Today, however, it remains to be seen whether Colombia's recurrent wars of terror may indeed be assigned to the history books.

Further Reading

J. Brittain, *Revolutionary Social Change in Colombia: The Origin and Direction of the FARC-EP* (New York, Pluto Press, 2010)

B. Bushnell, *The Making of Modern Colombia: A Nation in Spite of Itself* (Berkeley and Los Angeles, University of California Press, 1993)

J. Hristov, *Paramilitarism and Neoliberalism: Violent Systems of Capital Accumulation in Colombia and Beyond* (New York, Pluto Press, 2014)

M. Palacios, *Between Legitimacy and Violence: Colombia 1875–2002* (Durham, NC, Duke University Press, 2007)

A. Steele, *Democracy and Displacement in Colombia's Civil War* (Ithaca, NY, Cornell University Press, 2017)

17

The Paths of Terrorism in Peru
Nineteenth to Twenty-First Centuries[*]

CECILIA MÉNDEZ

'The most important thing which can be done immediately towards stopping lynching is to gather all the facts of lynching and give them the widest publicity'

W. E. B. Dubois, 1916

The Paths of Terrorism: A Preliminary Framework

In Peru, the term 'terrorism' is unequivocally linked to the Communist Party of Peru-Sendero Luminoso (PCP-SL), best known in English as the Shining Path and in Spanish as Sendero Luminoso (SL), or simply 'Sendero'.[1] Formed in 1970 as a splinter of another Maoist communist party, the PCP-SL took up arms in 1980 to unleash the bloodiest and most lengthy insurgency recorded in Peru's modern history. The 'time of terrorism' refers to the years from 1980 to approximately 1998, in which Sendero launched their so-called 'people's war' (*guerra popular*) with the ultimate goal of taking over the state and establishing the 'dictatorship of the proletariat'. The insurgency took the form of attacks on infrastructure, such as electrical towers, bridges and emblematic buildings (from embassies to shopping malls), individual

---

[*] José Carlos Agüero, Elena Aronova, Ricardo Caro, Richard English and Juan Pablo Lupi provided insightful comments on earlier versions of this essay. Roberto Young, Ingrid Maza and Pilar Ramírez Restrepo provided crucial assistantship. Carlos Aguirre, Fernando Bryce, Guillermo Fernandez, José Miguel Munive and Ricardo Portocarrero generously shared their time and knowledge. I am grateful for the inspiring discussions at the *Cambridge History of Terrorism* 2019 Workshop at Queen's University Belfast. I also thank the University of California Humanities Research Institute for a Fall 2019 residential fellowship; in particular, I thank Can Aciksoz, David H, Anthony III, Javier Arbona, Shana Melnysyn, Diana Pardo Pedraza and Daphne Taylor-García for their valuable feedback.

[1] They most commonly signed simply as PCP, vindicating their Communist political allegiance, and did not like to be reduced to 'Sendero'. In this essay I use Sendero (or SL) at times, as a concession to the scholarship and common parlance, but I also adopt PCP-SL to emphasise their identity as a political party and the ideological roots they claimed.

assassinations, massacres and 'popular trials' that included summary executions and exemplary punishments. The latter were especially prevalent in peasant villages of the south-central Andean highlands of Peru, particularly the department of Ayacucho, the cradle of the movement. Sendero targeted a diverse array of people and social groups, from low-ranking policemen and military officers to elected civilian authorities such as city mayors and peasant community authorities, leaders of political parties, grassroots community leaders, merchants and, ultimately, anyone who dared to oppose their dictates. Though they were initially supported by groups of radicalised youth from public universities, and the impoverished peasantry of the south-central Peruvian Andes, peasants started turning against Sendero early on, and ended up becoming its foremost victims. Because of their systematic attack on all forms of organised society, some have described SL as the opposite of a social movement. Others have likened it to Cambodia's Khmer Rouge, in the light of their authoritarian ideology and methods, and their agrarian-based self-sufficient communist utopia.

Unlike Peru's previous twentieth-century armed insurgencies, the Shining Path war encompassed virtually the entire national territory, but was most devastating in the south-central Andean highlands, home to a majority of Quechua-speaking peasants, particularly in the department of Ayacucho, where it all started. According to the 2003 Truth and Reconciliation Commission (TRC – Comisión de la Verdad y Reconciliación) Report, nearly 70,000 people were killed or disappeared in the conflict, the majority of them (54 per cent) at the hands of the Shining Path, 1.5 per cent at the hands of another armed insurgent group, the Movimiento Revolucionario Túpac Amaru (MRTA), while the Armed Forces, paramilitaries and peasant patrols or *ronderos* were responsible for around 37 per cent of the remaining victims. Among them, nearly 29 per cent correspond to the Armed Forces. Approximately 75 per cent of the victims were rural, mostly illiterate, poor, and spoke Quechua or other indigenous languages as a mother tongue.[2] The population of Ayacucho was decimated. According to the late anthropologist and former TRC member Carlos Iván Degregori, 'If the ratio of victims to the population of Ayacucho were extended to the whole country, the violence would have resulted in 1,200,000 dead and disappeared.'[3]

---

2 Comisión de la Verdad y Reconciliación, *Informe Final, Perú: 1980–2000* (Lima, 2003), Vol. 1, p. 56 and Vol. 8, pp. 246–8.
3 C. I. Degregori, *How Difficult It Is to Be God: Shining Path's Politics of War in Peru, 1980–1999* (Madison, University of Wisconsin Press, 2012), p. 46. The figures of the TRC have been disputed by S. Rendón, 'Capturing Correctly: A Reanalysis of the Indirect Capture–

Today, the scars of the war are likely to be unnoticed by foreign visitors and a younger generation of Peruvians. Major cities, starting with Peru's capital, Lima, are bustling with shopping malls, gourmet restaurants, luxurious hotels and fast-food chain restaurants bearing typical US brand names. A celebratory mood that takes pride in the country's economic growth, tourist attractions and culinary riches has taken over since the first decade of the twentieth century, making references to the recent past of political violence an uncomfortable truth that many have preferred not to look at.[4]

But this national celebratory mood belies scars of violence that run deep. On the one hand, there is the staggering figure of the 'disappeared'. Calculated at around 20,000, it continues to grow. In 2003, the TRC identified 3,023 clandestine burial sites (by 2016, 2,244 have been exhumed), but the figure is now 4,000, and new sites continue to be reported, which suggests that the death toll estimated by the TRC may be conservative.[5] Considering both deaths and the 'disappeared', the figures greatly surpass those reported for the 1960s–80s dictatorships of Chile, Argentina and Brazil put together.[6]

On the other hand, there is the discursive legacy of the 'time of terrorism', which has powerfully affected language, politics and policies, determining the limits of what can be said – or not – in public. The defeat of Sendero's terrorism has not put terrorism to rest. On the contrary, at times it seems that 'terrorism' is invoked more often now than when the insurgency was in full swing. For, even though SL was disbanded as a political organisation shortly after the capture in 1992 of its main leader and founder, Abimael Guzmán (alias 'Presidente Gonzalo'), his wife Elena Iparraguirre, the second in

Recapture Methods in the Peruvian Truth and Reconciliation Commission', *Research and Politics* 6/1 (2019).

4 This celebratory mood is superbly analysed in G. Cánepa Koch and F. Lossio Chavez, *La Nación Celebrada: Marca País y Ciudadanías en Disputa* (Lima, Universidad del Pacífico/ Pontificia Universidad Católica del Perú, 2019).

5 Interview with Ricardo Caro, officer in charge of the Dirección General de Búsqueda de Personas Desaparecidas (DGBPD, General Directorate for the Search for Disappeared People of Peru's Ministry of Justice and Human Rights), Lima, 13 August 2019, and emails exchanged in August 2020. On the figures of the exhumed burial sites, see Equipo Forense Especializado (EFE), Ministerio Público, Fiscalía de la Nación website, www.mpfn.gob.pe/iml/efe/, accessed 15 August 2020.

6 Between 1973 and 1989, in Chile under the Pinochet dictatorship there were 3,065 dead or disappeared. In Argentina during the military junta from 1976 to 1983, the dead and disappeared amounted to nearly 30,000 people, and in Brazil's military dictatorship of 1964–85, the military was responsible for 421 assassinations and 'disappearances' of political adversaries of the regime. See A. Benites, 'La dictadura militar brasileña causó 421 muertos y desaparecidos', *El País*, 13 November 2014, https://elpais.com/internacional/2014/11/14/actualidad/1415926043_376239.html.

command in the party, and other high-ranking commanders – who are serving prison sentences – the 'threat of terrorism' is invoked by conservative politicians and media with such virulence and frequency that people unfamiliar with Peru could be led to believe that it is in fact a live threat.[7] The accusation of being a 'terrorist' is routinely brought up to crush political opponents, criminalise social protest, censor critical opinions and delegitimise any discourse calling for change, a scenario that replicates itself in other countries in the region, especially those that have passed through armed conflicts, such as Colombia. Even human rights activists can be dubbed 'terrorists', which is quite ironic, considering that Guzmán disparaged the discourse of human rights, which he deemed to be part of 'bourgeois ideology'. There is even a (racially tinged) neologism for the insult: *terruco*, which conflates the ideas of 'terrorist' and 'Indian', as historian Carlos Aguirre has insightfully analysed.[8] The term reflects the stigma attached to people who were actually, ironically enough, the majority of Sendero's victims. But because the cradle of the insurgency was also the department with one of the highest percentages of Quechua-speaking peasants – who are usually referred to in Peru as *indios* or *indígenas* (this is not necessarily a self-assumed category), they were often forced to put up with the stigma, even when most of the troops of the armed forces that repressed alleged and actual Senderistas shared with them the same linguistic and social characteristics and phenotypes. The PCP-SL's highest commanders themselves, though, including Guzmán, were rather mestizos or whites from the privileged provincial elites.[9] The noun *terruco*, in turn, brought with it a new verb: *terruquear*, or to call someone a *terruco*, and provides a good example of the way in which labels associated with terrorism are ethnicised. Yet, in contrast to cases in which the label of 'terrorist' is usually attached to those whom the mainstream deems foreigners – as happens in the US with Muslims and 'Arab-looking' people – in Peru the prime suspects were Peruvian themselves, especially if they were Quechua-speakers (or spoke a Spanish infused with Quechua or other indigenous languages' phonetics),

---

7 When in 1992 Abimael Guzmán was captured he called for a ceasefire. Although much of the party was disbanded, several of his former followers continued in arms until approximately 1999. Currently, some detachments are still active in the eastern rainforest mountains of south-central Peru, a region known as VRAEM, but their fight is no longer ideological; they are engaged in the lucrative business of cocaine production and trafficking.

8 C. Aguirre, 'Terruco de m... Insulto y estigma en la guerra sucia peruana', *Histórica* 35/1 (2011).

9 Aymara and Quechua are the most widely spoken but not the only languages of pre-Hispanic origin in Peru.

and poor.[10] In recent years, *terruqueo* has democratised its targets. Anyone who is critical of power, regardless of physiognomy or class, can be subject to *terruqueo*.[11]

* * *

The literature on the Shining Path insurgency – from its outbreak in 1980 to the beginning of its downfall in 1992, and into the 2000s 'post-conflict' period – is good and abundant. There are outstanding accounts of the early stages of the uprising and its roots, such as those by Carlos Iván Degregori and Gustavo Gorriti, studies on the peasant patrols (*rondas*) that fought them, SL's development in urban areas, and increasingly more works focusing on memory and the post-war aftermath. With notable exceptions, such as Jaymie Patricia Heilman's *Peru Before the Shining Path*, scholars generally do not venture into the *longue dureé* to understand the Shining Path and its particular commitment to violence.[12] Let me suggest two main reasons for this absence.

One is Sendero's own detachment from Peruvian historical referents. Unlike other well-studied terrorist and revolutionary organisations worldwide, Sendero does not make historical claims to the past or vindicate Peru's historical figures in search of legitimacy, even though their own name pays

10 See C. Méndez, 'Obama y Humala: ¿Nacionalismo o Democracia?', *Lamula.pe*, 15 December 2011, https://lamula.pe/2011/12/15/obama-y-humala-democracia-y-nacionalismo/lamula/.
11 For example, linguist Virginia Zavala was recently subject to *terruqueo* for stating that the 'groups of power' establish the hegemonic way of speaking Spanish, but that it was not the only correct way to do so. See V. Zavala, 'Sobre la discriminación lingüística, el "terruqueo" y los grupos de poder en el Perú', *Lamula.pe*, 13 May 2020, https://virginia zavala.lamula.pe/2020/05/13/castellanos-en-el-peru/virginiazavalac/.
12 For some important works on the Shining Path see C. I. Degregori, *Qué difícil es ser Dios: El partido comunista del Perú-Sendero Luminoso y el conflicto armado interno en el Perú, 1980–1999* (Lima, Instituto de Estudios Peruanos, 2013); G. Gorriti Ellenbogen, *Sendero: Historia de la guerra milenaria en el Perú* (Lima, Apoyo, 1990); C. I. Degregori, J. Coronel, P. del Pino and O. Starn, *Las rondas campesinas y la derrota de Sendero Luminoso* (Lima, IEP, 1996); J. P. Heilman, *Before the Shining Path: Politics in Rural Ayacucho, 1895–1980* (Stanford, Stanford University Press, 2010); P. del Pino, *En nombre del gobierno. El Perú y Uchuraccay: Un siglo de política campesina* (Lima/Juliaca, La Siniestra Ensayos/ Universidad Nacional de Juliaca, 2017); C. Tapia, *Las fuerzas armadas y Sendero Luminoso: Dos estrategias y un final* (Lima, IEP, 1997). For a comprehensive compilation in English see S. Stern (ed.), *The Shining and Other Paths: War and Society in Peru 1980–1995* (Durham, NC, Duke University Press, 1998). Regarding the *longue dureé* approach, J. L. Rénique in *La voluntad encarcelada* (Lima, IEP, 2013) sees the PCP-SL as part of a 'radical tradition' that he traces back to the progressive liberals of the second half of the nineteenth century, but his analysis is focused on intellectual and political history rather than ideology or political practice.

tribute to José Carlos Mariátegui, the celebrated Peruvian Marxist thinker of the early twentieth century. The 'Shining Path' alludes to their following of 'the shining path' of José Carlos Mariátegui.[13] Yet, unlike Sendero's rigid interpretation of Marxism, Mariátegui's vision of Peru's socialist future was shaped by his vison of Peru's pre-Columbian Andean society and its agrarian communal roots. Be that as it may, the references to Mariátegui that had marked Sendero's internal discussions in the 1970s, as they struggled to differentiate themselves from the rest of the left, faded to the background as they launched their long period of armed struggle in 1980. Henceforth, the word of Abimael Guzmán, their leader and founder, became the bible of the movement. Guzmán, a philosophy professor from the Universidad de Huamanga, in Ayacucho City in the south-central Andes of Peru, fashioned himself as the 'fourth sword' of the world revolution (after Marx, Lenin and Mao), and relished the personality cult the party lavished upon him as 'Presidente Gonzalo', his *nom de guerre*. His ideological script was referred to as *pensamiento guía* (the 'guiding thought').

More often than not, if the PCP-SL spoke of history, it was in the abstract terms of the laws of historical materialism and class struggle: the exploitation of men by men that had been going on for millennia, and history as a succession of 'modes of production' with communism as the final stage. In their view, Peru in the 1970s was a feudal society not unlike China of the 1930s, an overwhelmingly rural country with a large peasantry. Accordingly, if history mattered in their vision of communism, it was more that of China than Peru. They exhibited a particular admiration for Mao, borrowed heavily from his 'people's war' and guerrilla tactics and the idea of strangling the cities from the countryside, though, admittedly, they were not alone in this, as Maoism exerted a special allure among the Peruvian left. The absence of referents to Peruvian history in Sendero's conceptualisation of the revolution goes in tandem with their ideological rigidity and disregard for social organisations and movements, which other leftist parties sought to court. As Degregori put it: 'A fundamental characteristic of Sendero's activity is [its] disregard for grass-roots organizations: peasant communities, labor unions, neighborhood associations. These are all replaced by generated organisms – that is, by the party that decides everything.'[14]

---

13 Rénique, *La voluntad encarcelada* discusses Mariátegui's influence in Sendero at length. See also D. Asencios, *La ciudad acorralada* (Lima, Instituto de Estudios Peruanos, 2016).
14 C. I. Degregori, 'A Return to the Past', in D. S. Palmer (ed.), *The Shining Path of Peru*, 2nd ed. (New York, Palgrave Macmillan, 1994), p. 57.

Not surprisingly, their ideology was just as devoid of nationalist rhetoric and drives, a feature that sets Sendero apart from other Latin American leftist armed groups of the twentieth century (Marxist or not), which were highly nationalistic, as were most world revolutions of the twentieth century, if one follows Benedict Anderson (*pace* Marx) – from José Martí to Fidel Castro in Cuba, from Augusto César Sandino to Farabundo Martí in Central America, from the Tupamaros in Uruguay to the Montoneros in Argentina. All embraced nationalism. All denounced national elites (or 'comprador bourgeoisies') that colluded with foreign invading or interventionist powers. Unlike those movements (including Peru's own coeval of Sendero, the MRTA), Senderistas never wrapped themselves in the national flag. Theirs was, unmistakably, the red flag of the hammer and the sickle. To be clear, Sendero did embrace the 'anti-imperialist' rhetoric that was common to the left in the continent during the 1960s and 1970s, but this never translated into nationalism, references to the soil or the national past. Likewise, unlike other armed movements in the twentieth century worldwide, the PCP-SL did not claim to vindicate any racial or ethnic identity, nor did they raise racial or ethnic questions, though in this they were no different from the rest of the left in Peru and most of Latin America at the time.

Without national heroes to emulate, Senderistas saw themselves as 'the initiators', as Abimael Guzmán proclaimed in a speech announcing the start of their 'armed struggle'.[15] He envisioned Peru as the centre of the 'authentic' communist world revolution, one which Deng Xiao Ping's China had allegedly betrayed. This is no small detail. The year in which the PCP-SL launched its 'armed struggle', dead black dogs bearing a piece of paper that read 'Teng Siao Ping' appeared hanging from electrical light poles in Lima. If there was history, then, it was not Peruvian; it was the history of global communism. And it was in the future more than in the past.

The second reason why scholars have tended to keep their analyses of Sendero within rather constrained chronological boundaries, I will argue, may have to do with the nature of the violence that they elicited. Indeed, Sendero's violence was so openly reckless, and so seemingly gratuitous, that suggesting possible parallels with previous insurgencies or civil wars in Peru became taboo, and may even be subject to a 'soft' censorship (as I can witness in relation to my own work). Truth be told, Sendero was a fundamentalist organisation built around the cult of personality of Abimael Guzmán, which punished disloyalty with death. But the lack of empathy they elicited, in comparison to other armed insurgencies that took up arms in Latin America in the past century, may be attributable less to

---

15 The most detailed account of Sendero's origins is in Gorriti, *Sendero*.

the violence per se than to the fact that it was a deliberate strategy built into the party's ideology, not a last resort. The political context of their birth is important if we are to understand this. Sendero rose up in arms not to fight a repressive military dictatorship – like most Latin American revolutionary movements of the twentieth century – but to boycott an emerging democracy. They launched their war at the precise moment in which the country was transitioning to a democratic regime after twelve years of military dictatorship. Significantly, their first insurgent act was the bombing of the ballot boxes in the village of Chuschi, in the department of Ayacucho, on the eve of the presidential elections of May 1980. To consummate the irony, this was the first presidential election of the twentieth century in Peru in which illiterate people were allowed to vote; the detail is especially significant in a country where elections are mandatory. Their target, in other words, was not a particular regime, but democracy itself. This fact, in turn, explains why their violence had to be so reckless. Their attacks were meant to elicit a level of repression that would justify branding the state as 'fascist'. Such a situation, in turn, they hoped, would leave Peruvians no choice but to opt between them, Sendero, and the state. This is the way in which the PCP-SL hoped to create the 'conditions for the revolution'. Accordingly, it not only ordered its militants to kill but expected them to die – or give a 'quota' in blood – for the party.[16] Likewise, this is why Sendero broke with the rest of the left, which decided to take, instead, the electoral path.

* * *

Much has been written about the place of violence in the PCP-SL's ideology. Not unlike a fundamentalist religious organisation, they believed in the 'purifying' effects of bloodshed and cultivated a mystical relationship to violence, as Gustavo Gorriti early noted. Carlos Iván Degregori, for his part, suggested that the leadership's messianic zeal coexisted with an 'excess of reason', or an adherence to Marxist dogmas as 'scientific truth'. As he put it: 'They are the last children of the Enlightenment who, two hundred years later and isolated in the Andes, ended up converting science into religion.' Or, 'their vision, that sought to be absolutely scientific, became exceedingly emotional, offering its members a strong quasi-religious identity'.[17]

---

16 Ibid.
17 Degregori, 'Return to the Past', pp. 55–6. See also Gorriti, *Sendero*. Later on, sociologist Gonzalo Portocarrero used the concept 'reasons of blood' to describe the combination 'rational' and 'irrational' elements in Sendero's ideology, inspired by Remo Bodei's theories.

My goal in this essay is not further to examine this ideological distinctiveness, for which there exists an ample and superb literature. It is, rather, to understand where the violence that Sendero turned into such a rigid ideology came from. I start from the premise that the top-down violence that Sendero exerted was not precisely invented by them; it was already built into the pre-existing Peruvian social fabric. What Sendero did, I would suggest, was to turn this violence into ideology. I build in part on Carlos Iván Degregori's provocative thesis that, upon the breakdown of the latifundia regime in the southern-central Peruvian Andes following the 1969 agrarian reform, the Shining Path filled the void left by the oppressive landowners, or *mistis* (a Quechua term for mestizo, or white), also known as *gamonales*. They exploited peasant labour and exerted upon them forms of violence not unlike those that tend to be labelled 'terrorist', in complicity with or with the acquiescence of provincial and local authorities such as prefects, sub-prefects, governors, police and judges. Degregori likens the mixture of violence and paternalism that *mistis* displayed in their relationship with 'their' Indians – and the racism inherent in it – to the hierarchical structure of the Shining Path. Anthropologist Marisol de la Cadena, in turn, traced Sendero's disdain for the very indigenous peasants they sought to attract to an entrenched pattern of 'silent racism' among twentieth-century Peruvian intellectuals, or a sense of intellectual and cultural superiority that traverses the whole ideological spectrum.[18] With these considerations in mind, I proceed to take terrorism out of the Shining Path's exclusive compartment to trace its genealogy in Peru's republican history, starting with the story of its naming. The argument is presented in three parts.

In the first place – because terrorism is a term with its own history and terrorist actions are not the exclusive purview of non-state actors – I start by tracing the term 'terrorist' in the early nineteenth century, before it was used to designate the violence carried out by rebels in arms and when it was used to refer almost exclusively to the violence and abuse of power by states and statesmen, particularly in reference to monarchical or authoritarian regimes. The opposite of a terrorist was often a liberal. Nowhere is this clearer than in 1867, when a so-called 'law of terror' was debated in Congress. This case constitutes the second part of our analysis. The 'law of terror' was a draft law presented to the national Congress by three landowners (*hacendados*) of the southern department of Puno, which aimed at violently and militarily suppressing a wave of peasant uprisings in

---

See G. Portocarrero Maisch, *Razones de sangre: Aproximaciones a la violencia política*, 2nd ed. (Lima, Fondo Editorial de la Pontificia Universidad Católica del Perú, 2012 [1998]).

18 Degregori, *Qué difícil*; M. de la Cadena, 'Silent Racism and Intellectual Superiority in Perú', *Bulletin of Latin American Research* 17/2 (1998).

the region. Even though the 'law of terror' is a misnomer, as it never became law, due in great part to the fierce opposition of liberals and an emerging pro-Indian and pro-peasant-rights movement, the debate it elicited vividly illustrates the degree to which liberals effectively instrumentalised the term 'terrorism' to denounce the violence inherent in a system of exploitation of peasant labour and the dispossession of their resources. Lastly, I will discuss two key moments in the history of the Peruvian APRA Party (PAP), which at various points in its trajectory was deemed 'terrorist': the dictatorship of Luis M. Sánchez Cerro (1930-3), and the governments of José Luis Bustamante y Rivero and Manuel Odría (1945-56). APRA, an acronym for Alianza Popular Revolucionaria Americana (American Revolutionary Popular Alliance) was founded by Víctor Raúl Haya de la Torre in Paris, in 1926, while he was in exile. A centre-left political organisation of international scope, APRA fashioned itself as a revolutionary and 'anti-imperialist' alternative to communism. In an effort to repress APRA and other opposition forces, the government passed the 1932 Emergency Law. This law remained in force until 1945 but reverberated into the late 1940s, when, most likely for the first time, the state resorted to the term 'terrorist' in its search for a new legal framework to quell APRA and political dissent more broadly. In the final analysis – and without belittling the violence of the repression of the peasant uprisings of 1867 and 1868 – I will attempt to show that, as the state's repressive apparatus consolidated in the course of the twentieth century, it became more able not only to increase the level of violence it exerted over its citizens but to legitimise violence through law, thus nurturing a growing spiral of violence and disbelief in state institutions which may, in turn, help shed further light on the PCP-SL's formation, and its legitimacy in the eyes of a significant group of Peruvians.

A few cautionary words may be in order before we continue. Insofar as (as mentioned above) comparing the PCP-SL insurgency with prior political upheavals in Peru is a taboo of sorts for Peruvians, I am aware that my *longue durée* approach, and my attempt to understand terrorism from multiple angles, may be interpreted as a justification (or 'relativisation') of SL's cruelty and violence. It is not. To talk about state violence and terror is not to condone anti-state violence and terror. It is to put things in perspective. For, as historian David Andress has brilliantly analysed in his study of the Terror in the French Revolution: '... in the cold light of history, the Terror, is not, has not been, a unique aberration'.[19]

---

19 D. Andress, *The Terror: The Merciless War for Freedom in Revolutionary France* (New York, Farrar, Strauss and Giroux, 2005), p. 7.

Considering that I am only decades, and not centuries away from some of the themes to be studied, my task is even more daunting than Andress's. Sendero is still a threat in the minds of some generations of Peruvians in a way that the French Terror in France is not, and its destructive legacy runs deep: it is political, physical, emotional, ideological, juridical, cultural. But precisely because (unless you embrace the party's ideology) its ideological justification of violence is not self-evident, considering they had alternative political paths, a deeper exploration into the history of the violence that may, in turn, allow us to understand Sendero's violent path is necessary.

Liberals Versus Terrorists

Let us turn to the early nineteenth century, a time when 'terrorism' was used mainly to describe the violence of states or statesmen. By the 1820s most former colonies of the Spanish Empire in America had become national states following bloody independence wars that put an end to 300 years of European rule. Warfare did not recede quickly, though, as the former colonies continued to be embattled in internal and external wars for the control of the emerging national states and the shaping of national boundaries. Instability notwithstanding, newspapers proliferated with the new freedom of the press, and became a natural place for the expression of political ideas and debates. Newspapers followed world events very closely, particularly those of Europe, often reprinting and discussing political and historical documents. Our impressionistic look at Spanish American newspapers from the 1830s to the 1870s suggests that 'terrorist' had Robespierre's Reign of Terror as its main referent. Nevertheless, subsequent events in France, and Europe more broadly, imprinted new political meanings on the term.

At first glance, references to terrorism do not seem to be bound to a specific ideology so much as to a form of exercising violence through fear by powerful *caudillos* (political bosses) and 'tyrannical rulers'. But, at a time when political outcomes were decided in battle, it was hard to say who could be free of the charge of being a 'terrorist'. The enemies of Marshall Andrés de Santa Cruz, leader of the Peruvian–Bolivian Confederation (1836–9), claimed that his power derived from 'the terrorism and bayonets of his three numerous armies',[20] while others considered that 'the slogan of his administration

20 *El Comercio*, 18 October 1839. The words belong to Manuel Bulnes, a member of the Chilean military who allied with Santa Cruz's enemy, Mariscal Gamarra, to defeat the Confederation.

was terrorism'.[21] Nonetheless, the same charges could have been brought against his nemesis, Marshall Agustín Gamarra, a famed authoritarian president of Peru, who opposed Santa Cruz's free trade policies, and was backed by Lima's conservative elite and the government of Chile. Moving to the Río de la Plata region, we find slightly different examples. Members or sympathisers of the Unitarian Party, who tended to be (socially conservative) liberals, referred to Juan Manuel de Rosas, Governor of the province of Buenos Aires and leader of Federalist Party, as a 'tyrant' and a 'terrorist'.[22] Indeed, his reputation as such was well established in his time, as witnessed by the short story by Esteban Echeverría, eloquently titled 'The Slaughterhouse' ('El Matadero'), a direct reference to the Rosas regime.[23] Yet Rosas and Federalism were popular among gauchos and poor peasants. Earlier on, during the wars of independence, and also in the Río de la Plata, in the region corresponding to present-day Uruguay, José Artigas, *caudillo* and guerrilla leader whose political programme included agrarian reform, was also referred to as a 'terrorist' by his political enemies.[24] One might be tempted to deduce from these examples that 'terrorist' referred to politicians who favoured social causes, or 'Jacobins' of sorts, but this was not necessarily the case. Rosas, for instance, embraced Catholicism as a central tenet of his party's identity. What is significant here is that those deemed 'terrorists', far from being on the fringes of politics, were for the most part rulers, statesmen or aspirants to such roles.

In the 1850s and 1860s a clearer ideological pattern emerges. Even though one can find occasional associations between terrorists and liberals,[25] what becomes increasingly common is their opposition: 'terrorist' as the antithesis of 'liberal'. Liberals of different hues labelled their opponents as 'terrorist': from conservatives to partisans of the monarchy, to *godos* (a derogatory term for Spanish or conservative), 'enemies of freedom', and adherents to tyrannical rule. In 1851, an author who signed as 'El Indígena' in the Peruvian newspaper *El Comercio* referred to a columnist whom he charged with

---

21 *El Peruano*, 1 January 1840.
22 *El Mercurio de Valparaíso*, 30 December 1839 and 13 March 1841. See also J. Rivera Endarte, *Rosas y sus opositores* (Montevideo, Imprenta del Nacional, 1843), p. 210.
23 'El Matadero' was allegedly written in the late 1830s, but it was only published posthumously, in 1871. See E. Echeverría, 'El Matadero', *Revista del Río de la Plata* 1 (1871).
24 Letter from 'the government' to Belgrano, 26 April 1819, Ms. Archivo General, cited in 'Páginas históricas de la Independencia de Argentina por Bartolomé Mitre ... La guerra social, 1819 (continuación del capítulo XXVII)', reproduced in *La Nación* 7/1892, 21 September 1876.
25 See for example, the Mexican newspaper *El Siglo Diez y Nueve*, 10 June 1875, p. 2.

despising Indians as 'terrorist and *godo*'.[26] Into the 1860s, the association between terrorists and monarchists deepened, coinciding with European imperialist recolonising ventures in America, among them the French invasion of Mexico that resulted in the re-establishment of the monarchy (1862–7), and Spain's invasion of the Peruvian coasts in 1866. In this context, Mexican liberals, who tended to identify themselves as republican, fiercely opposed the monarchists as 'terrorists'. In April 1863, for instance, the liberal newspaper *Siglo Diez y Nueve* published reports decrying the violence and ransacking committed by the partisans of Napoleon III, who invaded the city of Aguascalientes under the cry 'Up with religion and France'. The writer claimed that the *chusmas* (vulgar people) were emboldened by their 'terrorist fame' and blamed the 'French tyrant' for the misery ravaging the city and especially the working poor.[27] A few years later, historian Mariano Felipe Paz Soldán denounced 'the forces and terrorism that the Spanish have availed themselves of to subjugate us' in Peru, in reference to the 1866 reconquest attempts.[28]

The 'Law of Terror'

But it is Peru of the 1860s that provides what may be the starkest example of liberals' use of the term 'terrorist' to attack reactionary politicians and the violence they promoted. On 8 May 1867, three congressmen, who were also *hacendados* in the southern department of Puno, drafted a law meant to suppress with brute force a wave of peasant unrest in that department and dissuade further rebellions. Five days later, on 14 May, the draft law was published in Peru's main newspaper, *El Comercio*, stirring a debate, mostly against the legislators' initiative. The following day, another newspaper, *El Nacional*, published one of three consecutive editorials against the proposed law, entitling all three columns 'The Law of Terror, the Indians'.[29] Henceforth, other commentators popularised the term, speaking of the terrorist attitude of *gamonales* and partisans of the project of law and the terrorist methods and practices aimed at exterminating Indians. Liberal public opinion criticised the proposed law so fiercely that one of the three congressmen who had drafted it withdrew his signature from the proposal,

---

26 *El Comercio*, 16 April 1851. Article signed by 'El Indígena'.
27 *El Siglo Diez y Nueve*, 30 April 1863, p. 3.
28 M. F. Paz Soldán, *Historia del Perú independiente: Primer periodo, 1819–1822* (Lima, 1868), p. 27.
29 Reprinted in E. Vásquez, *La rebelión de Juan Bustamante* (Lima, Juan Mejía Baca, 1980), pp. 341–51.

and it was ultimately rejected by both the Government Commission and the Legislation Commission in Congress. There is no record that the draft law ever passed, against what historiography has long assumed.[30]

What was at stake? In the course of 1866, as the demand for wool increased in the international market, peasants in the department of Puno, in the altiplano region bordering Bolivia, rich in pasture lands, felt an increasing pressure to sell their lands. Before the incursion of British traders in the region, peasants had owned most of the land in Puno and traded their wool at provincial fairs.[31] But as the demand for their lands soared, *hacendados* sought to enlarge their estates as well as get further control over the wool markets at the expense of the peasants. What made the situation untenable for the latter was a head tax (*contribución personal*) imposed by the government early in 1866, in part to compensate for the losses caused by the recent war against the Spanish invasion. In theory, the *contribución personal* applied to all adult men, but in practice it fell on indigenous peasants' shoulders, evoking the spectre of the colonial 'Indian tax' abolished in 1854.[32] Peasants felt the brunt heavily and protested by attacking and taking over offices of governors, prefects and sub-prefects – that is to say, the local authorities in charge of the collection of taxes – and in some cases demanding that they be returned to them.[33] Other grievances denounced included an alleged 'property tax' enforced illegally by the department's prefect, which forced all peasants who owned land to pay tax in exchange for a land title of no legal value.[34] This conjunction of factors became explosive in a society that had been enduring structural exploitation for centuries. Even though prohibitions against unpaid labour existed as early

---

30 For the ruling of the two congressional committees, see 'Dictamen relativo a la proposición sobre los indígenas de Puno', No. 24049, 9–21 May 1867, ff. 163–7, Archivo del Congreso de la República de Perú, Lima (ACRP). On the congressman who withdrew his signature from the proposal, Federico Luna, see 'Actas de las Sesiones del Congreso Constituyente, Cámara de Diputados', 20 May 1867, p. 432 (ACRP). On the historiography on the Puno rebellion, see Vásquez, *La rebelión*; M. Gonzales, 'Neo-colonialism and Indian Unrest in Southern Peru, 1867–1898', *Bulletin of Latin American Research* 6/1 (1987); N. Jacobsen, 'Civilization and Its Barbarism: The Inevitability of Juan Bustamante's Failure', in J. Ewell and W. Beezley (eds.), *The Human Condition in Latin America: The Nineteenth Century* (Wilmington, DE, Scholarly Resources, 1989); N. Jacobsen and N. Domínguez, *Juan Bustamante y los límites del liberalismo en el Altiplano: La rebelión de Huancané (1866–1868)* (Lima: Servicios Educativos Rurales/SER, 2011); C. McEvoy, 'Indio y nación: una lectura política de la rebelión de Huancané, 1866–1868', in C. McEvoy (ed.), *Forjando la nación: Ensayos de historia republicana* (Lima, Pontificia Universidad Católica del Perú/The University of the South, Sewanee, 1999).
31 Gonzales, 'Neo-colonialism'; Jacobsen and Domínguez, *Juan Bustamante*.
32 Jacobsen and Domínguez, *Juan Bustamante*, p. 54.   33 Gonzales, 'Neo-colonialism'.
34 Vásquez, *La rebelión*, pp. 388–93.

as the first colonial legislation, unpaid Indian labour was the norm in Andean society, the reason for the accumulation of wealth by many non-Indians and even essential for the state and public services to operate: community peasants were expected to work for free on tasks ranging from public works to serving as domestic servants in the houses and offices of authorities and as porters, jailers and servants of mayors, priests and the *hacendados* themselves. Peasants were even expected to give their children as servants to local authorities, who in turn gave them as 'presents' to people they wanted to be on good terms with.[35] In theory, peasants could vent their grievances in courts, and many chose to do so. In practice, though, they could hardly win any legal battle. Since many, if not most peasants were monolingual Quechua- or Aymara-speakers, language barriers added to class and racial discrimination, and the collusion of judges with *hacendados* and local and regional authorities prevented them from ever winning a case in court.[36]

The so-called 'law of terror' aimed to give legal legitimacy to this status quo, and it seemed particularly intent on denying peasants the right to property, for, in addition to punitive violence, it prescribed the dispossession of their lands. The lawmakers justified their stance by arguing that the peasant rebellions, rather than resulting from legitimate grievances, were the product of a 'caste war' (*guerra de castas*) 'poorly extinguished in 1814', and which had to be rooted out.[37] This is a remarkable statement. The reference alludes to the 1814–15 Cuzco Rebellion, which was part of Peru's wars of independence against Spain, thus showing the extent to which that fight was experienced by a privileged sector of the provincial elite of Puno as an affront to their privileged (white/mestizo) status (*casta* somehow blending race and status). Additionally, the draft law argued that the rebels destabilised 'public order' and threatened the 'life and property of the inhabitants of the Republic, which are under the government guarantee'. Yet, indigenous peasants clearly did not count as 'inhabitants of the republic', to judge from how the proposed law referred to their lives and property. Article 2 authorised the Executive to deport '*in perpetuity* ... to the inhabited points of the [rainforest] mountains of Carabaya the *communities* or *parcialidades* of Indians that have shown themselves to be the most sanguinary and

---

35 J. Bustamante, *Los indios del Perú* (Lima, J. M. Monterola, 1867), p. 9; Gonzales, 'Neo-colonialism'; A. Flores-Galindo, 'República sin ciudadanos', in *Obras Completas*, Vol. 3.1 (Lima, Casa de Estudios del Socialismo, 2005).
36 Gonzales, 'Neo-colonialism'; Jacobsen and Domínguez, *Juan Bustamante*.
37 'Dictamen', ACRP, ff. 165r and 166r.

defiant',[38] while establishing that their lands be sold at public auction, thus revealing the extent to which the rapaciousness for peasants' lands was a drive behind the lawmakers' intentions. Finally, and no less contentiously, the proposed law called for the deployment to the region of an army division 'made of the three branches' and the establishment of martial courts for the 'instigators and ringleaders of the insurrectionist Indians' (Articles 1 and 2). Lastly, it prescribed the same measures for similar cases that may eventually take place in other parts of the republic (Article 7).[39]

It was not hard for the two Congressional Commissions that discussed this draft law to debunk each one of its arguments, in a remarkable – legal and political – defeat for the *hacendados* of Puno. The Commissions' rulings alleged that the draft law infringed upon the division of powers, going beyond the functions of Congress, and questioned the legality of martial courts, deportations and the deprivation of anyone of their property as a form of punishment. Hence, they condemned the idea of perpetual deportations as much as the selling of the deported peasants' lands, because 'no one can be dispossessed of their property except for the juridically proven public good or owing to a condemnatory sentence in a criminal trial conducted according to law'.[40] Most importantly, the Government Commission decried the punitive sprit of the draft law, as it considered – in tune with most liberal commentators – that the peasants' rebelliousness was justified: 'The uprising of the *indígenas*', it asserted, 'has as a main cause the mistreatment that over long centuries, one could say, all their lives, they have been victim of.'[41] They considered that conciliatory methods would yield better results, and went on to draft an alternative law offering amnesty to the indigenous rebels who surrendered.

The forcefulness of the congressional commissions' rulings, added to the criticism of the liberal press, ultimately caused the proposed law to founder, yet the alternative conciliatory legislation seems not to have come to fruition either. In the meantime, peasant unrest continued in Puno, while the government of Mariano Ignacio Prado was besieged by conservative military uprisings, prompting a new civil war that eventually forced him to resign. At this point, Colonel Juan Bustamante decided to join the peasant uprisings. Bustamante was a Puno trader, former congressman, former prefect and subprefect, world traveller and a liberal-minded advocate of indigenous rights. Scholars contend that Bustamante joined the uprisings to defend the besieged

---

38 Ibid., f. 165v. Emphasis in the original. A *parcialidad* was a form of communal organisation in the Andes.
39 Ibid., ff. 165–6.   40 Ibid., f. 16rv.   41 Ibid., ff. 166v–167r.

reformist President Mariano Ignacio Prado in the ongoing civil war. But they also agree on his credentials as an honest and indefatigable intellectual and public servant. Amidst the turmoil of 1867, Bustamante founded the Friends of the Indians Society, an organisation that denounced the exploitation and abuses committed against Andean peasants, usually called *indios, or indígenas,* and advocated for their rights. It was the first institution of this kind in Peru. He ultimately met a tragic death as he and his rebel armies were captured by the Prefect's forces in the town of Pusi, in the province of Huancané, in Puno, where seventy-one peasants were crammed into one or two small rooms, which were eventually set on fire. Those who did not die asphyxiated were shot to death. Bustamante was forced to take the cadavers out, then he was hung upside down, naked, from a tree in the public square, where he was flogged and decapitated. It was 3 January 1868. A bloody percussion ensued in the rebel towns. Sixty-five rebels were taken prisoner and deported to the rainforest of Carabaya by orders of a military commander after receiving 200 lashes; among them were apparently national guards that had joined Bustamante. Several others died as a consequence of the floggings.[42]

The tragic end of Juan Bustamante and the Puno uprising shows that even though the 'law of terror' did not pass in Congress it was enacted in practice. The rebellion was put down by dint of terror and military force, including executions without trial and deportations. There are several important points to take from this story for our historical analysis of terrorism, and the first one has to do with the use of the term itself. 'Terrorism' was used as the most effective term to decry local state agents' violence and *hacendados'* violence against peasants. The three editorials published in *El Nacional* in mid-May 1867 under the title 'The Law of Terror – The Indians' described it as the 'terrorist project of the three congressmen of the Puno department'. The columns constituted, as did many other similar publications in the press at the time, a call to fight back against the systemic exploitation that indigenous peasants were subject to at the hands of prefects, sub-prefects, governors and priests. Nearly a year after the publication of those editorials, and with Bustamante already dead, a member of the Friends of the Indians Society, Antonio Riveros, a supporter of Bustamante, addressed a public letter to the Friends of the Indians Society shortly after having been released from prison, in which he resorted to the term 'terrorist' four times when describing those abuses at length. He argued that the repressive measures of the 'Pacification

---

42 Numbers and versions of the facts differ somewhat. I have tried to strike a balance between the following: Jacobsen and Domínguez, *Juan Bustamante,* p. 61, and Vásquez, *La rebelión,* pp. 205–9, 326–9 and 363.

Campaign' laid bare a wish to exterminate Indians – a theme that comes back again and again in liberal indictments. Said campaigns, he claimed, 'initiated terrorism against them [the Indians]'; he described, at times with proper names and places, crimes such as forcing them to work without pay, the stealing of their property, including cattle, and a host of other arbitrary aggressions. Like Bustamante and other liberals in the Friends of the Indians Society, Riveros asserted that peasants were being punished for the crime of defending their right as citizens. As he put it: 'Indigenous citizens are chastised . . . only for aspiring to equality before the law, for the right to keep their interests so that they are not ransacked and their persons not sacrificed to extermination.'[43] After the 'pacification', he asserted, 'terrorism has reached its height'.[44]

But what exactly did Riveros, and other pro-indigenous liberals, mean by terrorism? As one can glean from his letter and its larger context, terrorism did not just refer to the violence – physical or otherwise – that state authorities inflicted upon peasants; it referred to the authorities' capacity to coerce them to abide by their will by dint of threats. Terrorism alluded, in other words, to the systematic use of fear against a population that had little way of defending themselves, in order to take advantage of their resources and labour, a veritable labour regime. For example, if a peasant refused to comply with the forced, unpaid labour demanded by a prefect or other authority (say, building fences, ploughing the land or working as porters), or with the low price a mestizo offered to pay for their wool or other products, they could be threatened with floggings, with taking their children away from them and giving them to authorities or politicians, or with taking away their cattle, a practice known as *rebeque*.[45] And because, as already mentioned, peasants had no easy way of defending themselves in court, these threats were effective.

But terrorism was something more; it constituted 'a way of living', in Riveros's keen sociological observation, a habit (*costumbre*) that became entrenched in the absence of laws which corrupt authorities had no interest in enforcing, their preaching to the contrary notwithstanding. 'In these places', he lamented, 'there are no laws but habits acquired *velis nolis* [whether you want it or not], and fighting and pacification are carried out to re-establish them'. He added that in other towns 'the same abuses are starting by dint of terrorism, which has reached its height'.[46] He went on to note that some authorities lived off terrorism because they had lost their own means of

---

43 Letter from Antonio Riveros to the Secretariat of the Friends of the Indians Society, *El Comercio*, 18 March 1868, cited in Vásquez, *La rebelión*, p. 332.
44 Ibid.   45 Ibid., pp. 332–3.   46 Ibid., p. 332.

subsistence due to their own misdemeanours, in a statement that helps us further understand the pervasiveness of the practice, as well as its economic base.

Importantly, to the threats already described, it is necessary to add one more: the threat of being accused of being 'revolutionaries', 'insurgents', or *caudillos* or ringleaders of the rebellion.[47] Tragically, as Riveros witnessed, 'such a loathsome system' was so entrenched that peasants themselves began using it against other peasants, so that 'if one of them wants treacherously to seize the land from another, he accuses him of being a revolutionary, and the authority, upon hearing this slanderous accusation, humiliates the latter without a trial and without seeking the truth, and in this way the former succeeds'.[48] This means that the terrorist system put in place by authorities and local bosses to the detriment of peasants in the wake of the Puno rebellion had the capacity to contaminate the entire social fabric, a problem that resonates to this day, as the TRC noted of the Sendero Luminoso's terrorism: 'its "peasant war" against the state turned, in many cases, into confrontations between peasants'.[49]

Ultimately, the Puno case reinforces the association of 'terrorism' with state terror and conservative positions, in clear antagonism to liberalism, a pattern that we observed earlier in our analysis of the nineteenth-century press. It showcases a radical liberalism with a socially progressive agenda that antagonised local state agents and local bosses' terrorism. Significantly, the authorities who condemned or repressed the rebellion did not call the rebels 'terrorists', even when the so-called 'law of terror' accused them of instigating violence in the form of a 'war of castes'. They could be called 'savages' and 'uncivilised' (even by liberals), but not terrorists. Words such as 'insurgents', 'revolutionaries', 'rebels' or 'insurrectionists' were more common.

This lexical order was to be flipped in the course of the twentieth century, in tandem with strategies to repress APRA and the Communist Party and organised labour first, and Senderista violence later. Terrorism progressively ceased to be used to describe state terror in Peru (whether identified with monarchic absolutism, and tyrannical rulers, or exploitative provincial authorities colluding with *hacendados*). Rather, it now fell into the hands of the state to determine not only who was to be called terrorist but who was to be tried as terrorist. Terrorism became a question of law. And law's enactment required a more solid repressive apparatus than that which existed in the nineteenth century. Hence, although in 1867 a proposed law meant to put

---

47 Ibid., p. 333.   48 Ibid.
49 Comisión, *Informe*, Vol. 8, p. 247. For examples of such cases, see Del Pino, *En nombre*.

down peasant unrest in Puno by dint of blood and fire could not pass in Congress, in 1932 the 'Emergency Law' meant to put down APRA by similar means did pass, even if it was forced into Congress by the Executive power. The methods that the state used to repress the 1866–8 Puno rebellion were used again, but perfected to fight APRA, including martial courts, executions without trial, military force, suspension of constitutional rights. But this time around violence was legitimised by law. Yet, paradoxically, as state terror magnified, the idea of a terrorist state, or terrorist rulers, faded from the language. 'Terrorist' was applied increasingly to revolutionaries or insurgents that fought the state. In the grammar of politics, what started as an adjective became a noun. But the process was neither overnight nor uniform.

This resemanticisation of 'terrorism' from a term associated with the state to a term associated with insurgencies against the state was due to a complex set of factors that started to take shape around the mid-twentieth century. Some were international factors, such as the Cold War, McCarthyism, the birth of the Doctrine of National Security, the US training of Latin American militaries; all contributed to reinforcing the technologies to fight insurgencies along with their legitimating discourses. But the basis of it all was the strengthening of state institutions and the state's increasing capacity to claim the monopoly over 'legitimate violence', to use Max Weber's famous formula, that is to say, the state's control of the repressive apparatus. With more power at its disposal, the state was not only more able to dictate legislation instrumental to the repression of armed insurgents (and political opponents), but, along with that, and most importantly, to determine when terrorism was law, and when was it breaking the law. The professionalisation of the armed forces was central to this process. In Peru it started in 1895, in the aftermath of the last civil war of the nineteenth century, when a professional army and military schools were established with the help of a French military mission. This process cemented military institutions, delimiting the boundaries between civilians and militaries that had remained blurry for most of the – civil-war-plagued – nineteenth century. During that time, armed insurgencies (with the participation of both the military and civilians) were a routine path to state takeover.[50] But with the coming to power of a series of consecutively elected civilian presidents, a period Jorge Basadre called the 'Aristocratic Republic' (1895–1919), armed insurgencies aiming at state takeover had more difficulty in being accepted as routine. This does not mean

50 C. Méndez, 'Militares populistas: Ejército, etnicidad y ciudadanía en el Perú', in P. Sandoval (ed.), *Repensando la subalternidad: Miradas críticas desde/sobre América Latina* (Lima, Instituto de Estudios Peruanos, 2009).

they ceased to exist but that they would have a harder time achieving legitimacy.[51] In this new political context, different terms came to be used for armed insurgents, as their methods were progressively delegitimised; one of them was 'terrorist'.

In this way, 'terrorist', a term suggesting violence, was transferred lexically from state to non-state actors, paradoxically, when the state increased its capacity to exert violence. This point is crucial, for, as we shall see, legislation concerning terrorism as a crime was made from its inception with specific political groups in mind, tacitly excluding state actors. What I am trying to suggest, I think, is that the history of terrorism cannot be separated from the history of the power to name it.

The Peruvian APRA Party: Between Ballots and Bullets

Víctor Raúl Haya de la Torre founded APRA's first international cell in Paris, in 1926, while in exile. The Peruvian branch of the party, known as PAP (Peruvian APRA Party), was only formed in 1930, in the aftermath of the fall of the corrupt dictatorship of Augusto B. Leguía, the president who had sent a young Haya de la Torre into exile in 1923.[52] Haya was a prominent student activist and one of the leaders in the movements for workers' rights that Leguía repressed. The Peruvian APRA Party (henceforth referred to simply as APRA) had since its inception engaged simultaneously in armed actions and electoral politics but, as historian Iñigo García-Bryce rightly noted, historians tend to downplay the former.[53] It is not a glorious side of its history. APRA was responsible for the assassination of a standing Peruvian president, Luis Miguel Sánchez Cerro, in April 1933 (following an assassination attempt by an APRA militant the previous year), and the assassination

---

51 C. Méndez, 'La Guerra que no cesa: Guerras civiles, imaginario nacional y la formación del Estado en el Perú', in C. Thibaud et. al. (eds.), *L'Atlantique révolutionnaire* (Bécherel, Les Perséides, 2013), p. 385.
52 I. García-Bryce, *Haya de la Torre and the Pursuit of Power in Twentieth-Century Peru and Latin America* (Chapel Hill, University of North Carolina Press, 2018). See also M. Giesecke, *La insurrección de Trujillo, jueves 7 de julio de 1932* (Lima, Fondo Editorial del Congreso del Perú, 2010).
53 Except, perhaps, one may add, when it comes to the Trujillo insurrection of 1932, which has been thoroughly studied by Giesecke herself. See García-Bryce, *Haya,* and Giesecke, *Insurrección*. See also G. Thorndike, *El año de la barbarie, Perú 1932,* 2nd ed. (Lima, Mosca Azul Editores, 1972). For accounts written by former militants on Aprista insurrections, see V. Villanueva, *La sublevación aprista del 48: Tragedia de un pueblo y un partido* (Lima, Editorial Milla Batres, 1973); A. Villanueva and P. Macera, *Arrogante montonero* (Lima, Fondo Editorial del Congreso del Perú, 2011).

of the editor of Peru's main newspaper, *El Comercio*, and his wife in 1935. Later on, in 1947, two Aprista militants were convicted for the assassination of the editor of another important newspaper, *La Prensa*.[54] In 1948 APRA, in alliance with navy officers, launched a coup against the democratically elected government of Manuel Bustamante y Rivero, a former ally. Although the coup did not succeed, it helped to precipitate a military dictatorship shortly after.

APRA's terrorism has been recognised but not analysed by historians. One of the few to speak bluntly about it was Peru's major historian of the republic, Jorge Basadre. He defined APRA as a 'typical product of World War I'. After summarising its myriad of influences and the ideological evolution of APRA – ranging from Bolshevik communism to German national-socialism, to China's Kuo Ming Tang (from whom, Basadre claims, Haya adopted the anti-imperialist platform), to the Mexican revolution and its *indigenista* and agrarian agendas – he notes:

> At times it showed some terrorist and direct action aspects of rapturous groups of Eastern Europe or the Middle East, such as the Romanian 'Iron Guard' or the Iranian 'Islam Fadayam', a framework that can be explained and in part justified due to the persecutions it was subject to and which the passing of time has erased.[55]

Basadre was right. Whereas, on the one hand, the APRA of the early years did defend the principle of insurrectionary violence, its violent paths were enhanced by the persecution, censorship and brutal repression its militants endured from the party's inception up to the mid-1950s, when it abandoned its revolutionary stance to form a pact with conservative forces. To understand APRA's early commitment to revolutionary violence we must go to where it all began: APRA's fierce confrontation with the Unión Revolucionaria party (UR) and its founder, Army Colonel Luis Miguel Sánchez Cerro. Sánchez Cerro rose to the presidency through a coup that ousted then president Augusto B. Leguía, who by 1930 was ruling as a dictator, his government marred by corruption. Sánchez Cerro's coup proved to be very popular, and he subsequently sought to legitimise it in

---

54 A recent study by a journalist claims that the men convicted were not likely the authors, but does not discard the involvement of the APRA in the assassination of the editor. E. Rúa, *¿Quién mató a Graña? Crimen político y golpe de estado* (Lima, self-published, Industrial Gráfica San Remo, 2018).

55 J. Basadre, *Apertura: Textos sobre temas de historia, educación, cultura y política, escritos entre 1924 y 1977* (Lima, Ediciones Taller, 1978), p. 465, cited in Rénique, *La voluntad encarcelada*, p. 35.

a general election held on 11 October 1931. Sánchez Cerro won by a wide margin, 50.7 per cent over 35.4 per cent to his closest contender, APRA and Haya de la Torre. Significantly, it was the first national election in which direct popular vote was enforced.

But Apristas did not concede defeat. Alleging fraud, they contrived a variety of strategies to take power. Haya explicitly called for violence. The harangues he addressed to his militants from the city of Trujillo, on the northern coast of Peru – APRA's bastion – on the very day of Sánchez Cerro's inauguration, are hard to differentiate from those Abimael Guzmán would address to his own followers almost half a century later: 'More Aprista blood will run. The immortal list of our martyrdom will grow, the terror will begin again its hateful task.'[56] On that very day, Apristas set off bombs in Lima. Days before, APRA had staged a blackout in the same city, leaving it in darkness, not unlike Shining Path would recurrently do in the 1980s.[57] Concurrently, Apristas made plans for a more massive insurrection. On 5 December 1931, they launched a number of coordinated uprisings in various parts of the country, which drew considerable support. Participants included agricultural workers, the middle classes and disgruntled army and police personnel. They seized public offices such as telegraph stations, municipalities and police headquarters and staged strikes, all of which contributed to destabilising the government.[58] 'In the insurgent towns, half of the population was involved', states historian Margarita Giesecke.[59] But it was the Trujillo insurrection, which broke out on 7 July 1932, that sealed APRA's fate as a proscribed and persecuted party for years to come. That day, a group of a hundred APRA militants, among them agricultural workers, army licentiates, students, port workers and members of the 'special guard' of Haya de la Torre (who was then in jail), led by an APRA cadre known as 'Búfalo Barreto' and the schoolteacher Alfredo Tello, stormed the military headquarters of the city, causing over fifty deaths, most of them soldiers.[60] After their successful capture of the headquarters they proceeded to establish a revolutionary government in the city, while other armed columns took over the nearby sugar estates (a bastion of APRA militancy) and armed movements were sparked in neighbouring provinces and departments. Sánchez Cerro's response was swift and brutal. He deployed a war machinery comprising all three branches of the armed forces: the air force, the army and

---

56 V. R. Haya de la Torre, *Construyendo el Aprismo*, pp. 172–5, cited in García-Bryce, *Haya*, p. 60.
57 García-Bryce, *Haya*, p. 60.   58 Giesecke, *Insurrección*, pp. 195–235.   59 Ibid., p. 210.
60 Ibid., pp. 269–72.

the navy. This included 7,046 troops, one warship, two submarines and 'a squadron of seven airplanes and hydroplanes'.[61] The first airborne bombs were dropped in a packed main square of the city where people were celebrating the revolution. Bombs also targeted the headquarters where it all began, a hotel, a theatre, a hospital and the nearby port of Salaverry, while the army surrounded the city.[62] Never before had the republican state deployed such war machinery against its own civilian population. García-Bryce notes, 'Trujillo's residents witnessed one of the first civilian bombings in history, predating the more famous Guernica bombing in Spain.'[63] The bombing continued over the following days, showing the government's resolve to exterminate Apristas, or 'Aprocommunists' as they were often called. Those who could escape the city fled to the countryside in the Andean highlands, and continued resisting. Things soured further for Apristas when government forces found the lifeless bodies of a group of military and civil guard (police) officers and soldiers showing horrific signs of violence, including mutilations, in the city's prison.[64] Although APRA never acknowledged the crimes, they gave the government the perfect pretext for doubling down on the repression. Apristas were chased, sometimes taken from their homes, subjected to martial courts, or simply executed without trial, en masse. Approximately 400 men were executed in the pre-Columbian archaeological city of Chan Chan, on the outskirts of Trujillo, from 12 July to 16 July, according to Giesecke.[65] In less than a week, the government had recovered control of the city. But Sánchez Cerro did not live long enough to enjoy his bloody success. The following year, a young Aprista militant shot the president to death as he was leaving Lima's hippodrome. A new military dictatorship took power until 1939. After a brief amnesty, in 1933, APRA went underground again.

The bloody events in Trujillo marked decades of Aprista persecution and shaped the party's martyrdom identity in a considerable way. They also inaugurated a long-lasting rivalry between APRA and the army. The legal framework that Sánchez Cerro's government created in his war against APRA also had important repercussions. Of particular salience was the 'Emergency Law' tailor-made to 'exterminate' APRA, in the words of Giesecke. The Executive drafted the law and submitted it to Congress for

---

61 García-Bryce, *Haya*, p. 64.
62 Giesecke, *Insurrección*, pp. 286–7; García-Bryce, *Haya*, p. 64.   63 Ibid.
64 The exact number is disputed. Some say they were 34 or 35, but Margarita Giesecke in her thorough research came up with 52. See Giesecke, *Insurrección*, pp. 294–5.
65 Ibid., p. 311.

debate on 8 January 1932, but no debate took place, as the sessions were interrupted by armed law enforcement agents that had apparently broken into the building. Aprista congressmen protested, to no avail. The minutes of that day's session in Congress show some gaps, and a courageous dissenting legislator's minority opinion attests to the use of force. The Executive promulgated the law the following day.[66] The 'Emergency Law' was almost a verbatim copy of a law that the triumphant Republican government had recently passed in Spain, as Basadre noted. By virtue of this law a permanent 'state of exception' ensued, suspending many constitutional rights. The law was sweeping against all opposition. It decreed the suspension of their posts for state officials who questioned the government; it restricted the right of political and social gatherings, censored opinion, authorised suppression of publications, ordered the requisition of both legally and illegally owned arms; it imposed fines, confinement and even expatriations to opponents. Prior to that, Sánchez Cerro had passed other laws that went even further, such as a 'state of siege' establishing martial courts to try civilians, and dissolving workers' unions controlled by APRA.[67] In short, state repression did not just target violent insurgency and terrorist attacks but also unarmed opposition, and even organised labour, an attitude that the succeeding governments continued to embrace, if not perfect. Ultimately, APRA's fate was sealed in the Constitution of 1933 promulgated by Sánchez Cerro, which outlawed 'political parties of international organisation'.[68]

Yet neither in the legislation nor in other official documents issued under Sánchez Cerro does one find the term 'terrorist'. Apristas were most commonly referred to as 'Aprocommunists', or 'Communists' (even though at that time Peru had its own Communist Party, which competed with APRA but could never rival it in size or strength). One possible factor to explain this absence is the multiplicity of violent rebellions facing the government. APRA was the most visible, but hardly the only armed group conspiring against Sánchez Cerro; many more rebellions occurred, and the overwhelming majority of them came from within the army itself. Allegedly, as many as twenty-six military uprisings took place between 1930 and 1933 (including one in 1933 in which APRA colluded with a general to overthrow the president).[69] Indeed, whereas the state's repressive apparatus had grown

---

66 'Expediente Ley de Emergencia, Iniciado el 29 de diciembre de 1931, Terminado el 9 de enero de 1932, Ley No. 7479', Congreso Constituyente de 1931, 16 ff., ACRP, Lima.
67 *El Peruano*, 26 November 1930.   68 García-Bryce, *Haya*, p. 14.
69 Giesecke, *Insurrección*, interview with Víctor Villanueva, former Aprista militant, former army officer and historian.

considerably, the state was still weak, the ruthless deployment of military might in Trujillo notwithstanding. In fact, one may say that that spectacle of war was an expression of fear more than force, as the government was hardly in control of the country.

The discursive transformation of Apristas and Communists into terrorists would take a few more years and bloody events. The saddest part of the story may be APRA's own self-destructive path, which is no small thing to say, considering it was the largest, best-organised, and most important party in the history of Peru. In 1947, two alleged Apristas assassinated the editor of *La Prensa*, Francisco Graña. Subsequently, *La Prensa* and *El Comercio* published successive headlines denouncing terrorists' plots, and the discovery of bombs and explosives, all linked to Apristas. These were not mere inventions, or not all were. APRA did plan serious attacks with explosives and was getting armed.[70] On 3 October 1948, APRA, backed by sectors of the navy, took over the fortress of Peru's main port, Callao, in an attempt to overthrow President José Luis Bustamante y Rivero. But Bustamante was not a dictator, he was a former democratic ally. The insurrection – or coup – which took some two hundred lives, was quickly put down by the army but it left the already fragile government of Bustamante on the brink of collapse. Bustamante y Rivero, a centre-right moderate civilian, had run for president in a broad, momentous coalition that included APRA. Once in power he declared amnesty and repealed the Emergency Law, thus ending at least fifteen years of persecution of Apristas. But APRA was not content merely to play a secondary role. Having won the majority in Congress, it aspired to control or at least have a larger dose of power in the Executive (laws at that time had not allowed APRA to run with its own presidential candidate).[71] The short-lived democratic coalition led by Bustamante did not take long in falling apart. Besieged from within, by APRA, which activated both its legal and armed branches, and by members of his own cabinet, its days were numbered. On 27 October 1948, merely three weeks after APRA's failed coup, General Manuel Odría, Bustamante's own Minister of the Interior, backed by the army, deposed Bustamante in a new coup, putting an end to a significant, albeit short-lived, democratic experiment. Odría was a fiercely conservative,

---

70 *El Comercio* (Lima), October, various issues, 1948; *La Prensa* (Lima), October and November, various issues, 1948.
71 For this interpretation, see García-Bryce, *Haya*. For a different interpretation, see J. Lossio and E. Candela, *Prensa, conspiraciones y elecciones: El Perú en el ocaso del régimen oligárquico* (Lima, Pontificia Universidad Católica del Perú, Insituto Riva Agüero, 2015).

pro-US and anti-communist army general. His government inaugurated one of the most repressive dictatorships in twentieth-century Peru, enthusiastically backed by the oligarchy (1948–56). A new era of persecution of Apristas was unleashed, and it was to be the last one, as the party would soon abandon its revolutionary stance to co-govern with the most conservative political forces, obstructing the very reforms that it had once called for.[72] And it is under Odría that the discursive making of Apristas, *comunistas* and labour and peasant organisations as *terroristas* started to come into effect.

Odría outlawed APRA and the Communist Party, and on 1 July 1949 he promulgated the 'Law of Internal Security of the Republic', which sought to punish all forms of 'sociopolitical crime' including 'terrorist acts'. This was, in all likelihood, the first time that the term 'terrorist' was imprinted into law, though still as an adjective. Its reach was enormously wide, from 'propagating false news' to 'adhering to foreign doctrines' to attacking military and government personnel, public buildings and facilities, to fomenting illegal strikes and 'unrest in unions, workplaces or schools'. Sentences ranged from fines to expatriation and the death penalty.[73] According to this law, in stark resemblance to Sanchez Cerro's legislation, defendants would be tried in martial courts and summary trials, bypassing the judicial system and expanding the role of the police, which led to a host of arbitrary actions. Even though the law was abolished at the end of Odría's term, military jurisdiction did not cease to be expanded, even under constitutional regimes, in the apt analysis of jurist Diego García-Sayán.[74]

In a public speech given a few weeks after the passing of the 'Law of Internal Security of the Republic', Odría evoked again the legal figure of terrorism, this time as a noun. Appealing to the Geneva Convention, he defined terrorism as a 'crime against democracy', equivalent to genocide. His strange logic (don't forget he was a dictator) was intent on persuading the international community not to give political asylum to Haya and other Apristas.[75] Odría's targeting of Apristas and Communists as terrorists was

72 An exception was the first term of Alan García (1985–90), the first and only Aprista to make it to the presidency. He adopted a centre-left discourse, but his government, marred by corruption, brought the country to one of its worst social and economic crises.
73 'Decreto-Ley 11049', 1 July 1949, Archivo Digital de Legislación del Perú (ADLP), www.leyes.congreso.gob.pe/Documentos/Leyes/11049.pdf.
74 D. García-Sayán, 'Perú: Estados de excepción y régimen jurídico', paper presented at the seminar 'Regímenes de Excepión en los países de la region andina' (Lima, 1986), pp. 6–10.
75 'Mensaje a la nación del presidente del Perú, general Manuel A. Odría Amoretti', 27 July 1949, p. 5, ADLP, www.congreso.gob.pe/Docs/participacion/museo/congreso/files/mensajes/1941-1960/files/mensaje-1949.pdf.

significant because it was profoundly political. It was not just about – or not even principally about – fighting violent crimes so much as curbing the very possibility of social and political change, as the text of the Law of Internal Security suggests. Timing is important here. Odría's rule coincided with the Cold War and post-Second World War climate, when the US backed dictatorships that committed themselves to fighting (real or imagined) communists. Not coincidentally, with Odría the army achieved greater political clout. All this happened within the framework of the Doctrine of National Security, when fighting internal enemies and 'subversives' reached new levels of sophistication.

Later on, the military governments of 1968–80 created another new legal figure, 'the state of emergency', which was incorporated into the Constitution of 1979 (enforced in 1980) thus 'constitutionalising' the states of exception, which entailed suspending a great range of constitutional rights, to cite Garcia-Sayán again. At this point, on 17 May 1980, the PCP-SL unleashed its violent insurgency and the constitutional government of Belaúnde, who came to power shortly after, through the first presidential elections held after twelve years of military dictatorship, promulgated the first 'antiterrorist' law in 1981, explicitly to fight the PCP-SL. Shortly after, he expanded military jurisdiction over civilians even further by abdicating democratic authority and delegating all powers to 'politico-military commands' in the zones declared to be in a 'state of emergency', charging them with the responsibility of fighting the PCP-SL and the 'control of internal order' more broadly. Thus, ironically, whereas the 'politico-military commands' were established – unconstitutionally, according to García-Sayán – during the military dictatorship of 1968–80, it was Belaúnde's democratically elected government who gave them constitutional legality and a full range of powers. This situation further disempowered civilian authorities such as judges, state attorneys and prosecutors in the zone declared to be in emergency, as their jurisdiction was taken over by military personnel.[76] The 'dirty war' was unleashed, and with it tens of thousands of people were killed in the name of the nation, mostly poor, peasant and illiterate, without having been subject to any hearings, other than summary trials with either the armed forces or the PCP-SL, if at all.

The coup of Alberto Fujimori on 5 April 1992 introduced an even more expansive antiterrorist legislation that severely curtailed the rights of defendants in the processes of detention, interrogation and trial by establishing that

---

76 García-Sayán, 'Perú', 13.

the identity of the magistrates remain secret (the famous 'faceless judges', inspired by Italy and Colombia); by granting the National Police free rein to 'intervene without any restrictions' in the investigation process;[77] and by allowing the armed forces, yet again, to try civilians accused of terrorism according to military law.[78] As a consequence, thousands of innocent people were convicted.

With the return of democracy in the 2000s, some of the most controversial articles of Fujimori's 1992 law, such as the martial courts to try civilians and the faceless judges, have since been nullified, but his 'antiterrorism' legislation is otherwise in force and continues to be expanded, more recently to restrict the rights of citizens who have completed their sentences and have been released from prison.[79] Importantly, as jurist Carlos Rivera points out, if there is a constant in the antiterrorist legislation since 1981 it is 'the absence of a clear, precise and concrete definition of what act can be considered as terrorism', as a consequence of which, Rivera goes on, 'it is very easy to encompass any fact or act against people or property as terrorism'.[80] This point is crucial, with the caveat that this fuzziness does not start in 1981 but in 1949, when Odría first sought to sanction terrorist acts as a special type of crime 'against the organisation and internal peace of the republic'.[81] So, rather than an aleatory problem, this very fuzziness may be at the heart of what makes conceptualising terrorism as a distinctive crime such a powerful political weapon. The fuzzier the definition, the easier it is to use it publicly to disqualify a person or an act.

It should not come as a surprise that dictatorships such as those of Odría and Fujimori would indulge in such legislation. But the fact that the democratically elected, constitutional governments that have ruled Peru since 2000 have kept such an open definition of terrorism should be a matter of concern. As the TRC reflected, 'the antiterrorist legislation has generated a culture of emergency and a practice of the exception as the rule' that puts the 'reason of

---

77 Decreto-Ley No. 25475, 5 May 1992, Article 12, ADLP, www.leyes.congreso.gob.pe/Documentos/Leyes/25475.pdf.
78 Decreto-Ley No. 25659, 12 August 1992, ADLP, www.leyes.congreso.gob.pe/Documentos/Leyes/25659.pdf.
79 Ley No. 30794, 18 June 2018, ADLP. The title of this law is telling: 'Law that establishes as a requirement to provide services in the public sector not to have sentence for terrorism, apology of terrorism and other crimes'.
80 C. Rivera Paz, 'Ley penal, terrorismo y Estado de derecho', *Quehachacer* 167 (July–August 2007), p. 2.
81 After listing a wide range of acts that could qualify as such (some of which we described above), a clause adds that 'those who undertake any terrorist act in a way that has not been foreseen by the aforementioned dispositions' also commit such a crime. Decreto-Ley 11049, Chapter II, paragraph g.

state' above juridical security.[82] With this in mind, and considering the Peruvian state record in human rights violations (not by random chance is former president Alberto Fujimori serving a prison sentence for his responsibility in a number of such crimes), one wonders why the concept 'terrorism of state' never gained acceptance in Peru, as it did, for instance, in Argentina, Brazil or Chile after their 'dirty wars'. One possible explanation (in addition to the fact that the PCP-SL's distinctively cruel methods have drawn most of the attention to them) may have to do with the fact that, for most of the duration of the conflict, Peru was ruled by democratically elected, constitutional regimes (1980–92), not dictatorships like those countries, thus demanding more subtle explanations. Yet, it is precisely under those regimes that most human rights violations at the hands of the state were committed, as the TRC concluded.[83]

Final Thoughts

In his book *Persona*, poet and historian José Carlos Agüero, winner of Peru's National Literature Prize, questioned the widespread tendency in Peru to refer to the period of the PCP-SL insurgency as 'the time of terrorism'. Among other things, Agüero protested the singular. He did not mean to deny Sendero's terrorism as much as vindicate the right of, among others, his parents, who were both militants of the PCP-SL, to be remembered as something other than terrorists, perhaps as human beings. Most importantly, Agüero intimated that singularising terrorism in Sendero Luminoso led to the forgetting of the terror of the state that killed both his parents without a trial, among thousands of other Peruvians, most of them poor peasants, not Senderistas.

Agüero's reflections are in tune with the 'pluralistic' approach to terrorism that I have proposed in these pages. As we have seen, terrorism in Peru derived from multiple sources and existed in different times, almost as a constant in its national history. Why, then, reduce its analytical scope to the recent past and a single terrorist entity? Why use the term only according to the state prescription, especially knowing that the state's historical trajectory has been anything but democratic, even under elected democratic regimes? And knowing, moreover, that 'terrorist' has been deployed not only for juridical reasons but also political ones, to curb and crush social protest, organised labour and even discussion

---

82 Cited in Rivera Paz, 'Ley penal', p. 8.   83 Comisión, *Informe*, Vol. 1, p. 171.

about social change? Why, then, be surprised that after decades of 'ruling by abandonment' – to borrow Jaymie Patricia Heilman's expression – something other than a terrorist political organisation would come to fashion itself as the solution?

And yet, this is only part of the story. For, as responsible as the state may be for abandoning its citizens to the forces of terror – its own, and those of self-proclaimed twentieth-century revolutionaries – the state is made of people, who are in turn part of a society where it all converges or, rather, where it all springs from. So, a 'pluralistic' approach does not simply entail recognising the different sources of terrorism but also patterns. Along with authoritarian patterns that traverse the terroristic practices of state agents, political parties and *hacendados* that we have analysed in the preceding pages, there is also a pattern of racialised social hierarchies that have made some sectors of the society more likely to be on the receiving end of the various terrorist violences. This brings us back to De la Cadena's notion of 'silent racism', and Degregori's hypothesis that Sendero's 'racist conceptions and sense of superiority with regards to indigenous peoples'[84] reproduced those of the exploitative *mistis* they replaced in the rural highlands of Ayacucho. Nevertheless, as we have seen in our analysis of the terrorist labour regime that was at that basis of the wool export boom in Puno in the 1860s, these racialised patterns of violence have deeper roots and other geographies. But there is more.

We cannot conclude without bringing up the case of another, yet more ominous, terrorist labour regime that was put in place in Peru's northern Amazon region of Putumayo, bordering Colombia, half a century later, to extract rubber for export, which reached a genocidal scale. In the span of ten years, a population of 50,000 women, men and children was reduced to 7,000 or 10,000. They were killed by starvation, executions or floggings to death, among other forms of torture, for failing to fulfil their rubber quotas.[85] Even though this case became internationally well known and was denounced by the press in Peru, nothing stopped the terrorist genocide, and nobody was punished, because, according to Federica Barclay, everyone, from politicians in Lima to merchants and workers in Iquitos (the largest city in the Peruvian Amazon), drew some benefit, in one way

---

84 Ibid., Vol. 8, p. 248.
85 *Libro Azul Británico: Informes de Roger Casement y otras cartas sobre las atrocidades en el Putumayo*, translated from English by L. E. Belaunde (Lima, Centro Amazónico de Antropología y Aplicación Práctica, 2012 [1912]), p. 300.

or another, from the economic prosperity of the rubber boom. Everybody, except those who produced the wealth.[86] Closer to the century's end, the PCP-SL subjected other indigenous groups in the Amazon to a similar regime of terror. They forced Ashaninkas to join their armies or do the domestic chores for their armies in concentration camps of sorts. They executed many of their leaders and threatened to kill those who opposed them. The TRC estimates that out of a population of 50,000 Ashaninkas, 10,000 were forcibly displaced, about 6,000 died, and a total of thirty to forty communities 'disappeared'.[87] The TRC wrote bluntly about the PCP-SL's genocidal policies.[88] A common practice in the various terrorist regimes subjugating populations deemed *indígenas* was the practice of taking children away from their parents, whether to be servants, as in Puno in the 1860s, to force them to extract rubber, as in the Putumayo in the 1910s, or to indoctrinate them as Communist soldiers and teach them how to kill, as in the Andes and Amazon with the Shining Path.

These histories of terrorism are part of a whole and should be understood as a whole. The history of this whole is not taught in schools, but, as W. E. B. Dubois said about lynching in the US, the only way to stop violence is by making it known. We can take inspiration, perhaps, from those who already started that job: from Juan Bustamante, Antonio Riveros and other liberals in the 1860s; from those who put together the nine volumes of the TRC Report in the early 2000s, to mention only the ones I have cited most in this essay. But I know there are many more. In this learning process, let us not forget that terrorism has a history, which should not be detached from the history of terrorism, the term. It is the awareness of this history that will free us from reproducing the state's repressive gaze and to embrace our citizenship.

Further Reading

Comisión de la Verdad y Reconciliación, *Informe Final, Perú: 1980–2000*, 9 vols (Lima, 2003), http://www.cverdad.org.pe/ifinal/

C. I. Degregori, *How Difficult It Is to Be God: Shining Path's Politics of War in Peru, 1980–1999* (Madison, The University of Wisconsin Press, 2012)

---

86 F. Barclay Rey de Castro, 'La Asociación Pro Indígena y las atrocidades del Putumayo: Una misión autorestringida', *Boletín Americanista* 60.
87 Comisión, *Informe*, Vol. 5, p. 62.   88 Ibid., Vol. 8, p. 248.

M. Giesecke, *La Insurrección de Trujillo, jueves 7 de julio de 1932* (Lima, Fondo Editorial del Congreso del Perú, 2010)

M. Gonzales, 'Neo-colonialism and Indian Unrest in Southern Peru, 1867–1898', *Bulletin of Latin American Research* 6/1 (1987)

S. Stern (ed.), *The Shining and Other Paths: War and Society in Peru 1980–1995* (Durham, NC, Duke University Press, 1998)

18

Aiqtihams (Whirlwind Attacks)
The Rise, Fall and Phoenix-Like Resurgence of ISIS and Shiite Terrorist Groups in Iraq

BRIAN GLYN WILLIAMS

Iraq as a Global Terrorism *Platzdarm*

In the winter of 2016 I partook in a tour of the front lines facing the *Dawla al Islamia*, the Islamic State, in northern Iraq, when it still controlled an area the size of Britain, was home to as many as 12 million people, and stretched from near the Syrian Mediterranean coast near Aleppo, to the Israeli border south of Damascus, to the gates of Baghdad, to the Zagros Mountains of Kurdistan.[1] Two years earlier ISIS (the Islamic State in Iraq and Syria) had burst on to the world stage and conquered vast swathes of territory in a now borderless region known as 'Syraq'. ISIS's followers then promulgated new laws and constructed an, at times, remarkably efficient transnational state that may have been able to gather as much as 800 million USD a year in taxes and oil revenues, making it the wealthiest terror organisation in history.[2] ISIS also constructed a remarkably adaptive conventional army that may have had as many as 36,000 fighters in its ranks at its height, something Al Qaeda Central had only dreamed of creating.

From Iraq, which was the epicentre of the Islamic State hybrid terrorist group–war machine, ISIS leader Caliph al Baghdadi also forged a radical Sunni group that metastasised from a localised, anti-Shiite insurgency into a global terrorist movement.

On my winter 2016 tour of the front lines with the newly forged ISIS terror caliphate, I explored the murky Iraqi origins of the unprecedented Islamic State state-building, terror-exporting phenomena in an effort to understand the roots of a terrorist movement that dwarfed the original Al Qaeda in its ambitions, number of followers, control of territory and

---

[1] B. G. Williams, *Counter Jihad: The American Military Experience in Afghanistan, Iraq and Syria* (Philadelphia, University of Pennsylvania Press, 2018).
[2] R. M. Callimachi, 'The ISIS Files', *New York Times*, 4 April 2018.

devastating global impact. During my embeds with the legendary anti-ISIS Kurdish Peshmerga ('Those Who Confront Death') fighters, and my extensive interviews with the Yazidis' (an ancient ethnic group that worshipped pre-Islamic gods, who came to be defined as 'devil-worshippers' by ISIS) high priests, embattled Christians and Arab refugees living in sprawling camps who had fled the horrors of nearby caliphate territory, I came to know what it was like to live in the shadow of a militant theocracy that used terror as institutionalised foreign, military, economic, social and domestic policy.

The Kurds' top counterterrorism official, Masrour Barzani, the Chancellor of the Kurdistan Security Council, described to me ISIS's uniquely barbaric, but remarkably innovative, forms of terrorism. These included shooting mortars filled with chlorine gas into enemy villages, deploying waves of small 'off the shelf' IED-carrying ISIS quadrotor drones to drop jury-rigged explosives on civilians and troops, holding entire towns hostage as 'human shields', putting IEDs on cows, and burning oil fields to send poisonous gases drifting into neighbouring enemies' lands. There were also the executions, which ranged from crucifying Assyrian, Chaldean and Nestorian Christians, to blowing up Yazidi 'pagans' in their temples, to massacring thousands of Shiites with small arms. These atrocities formed a unique ISIS form of mass terrorism.

Peshmerga men and women fighters nervously manning the front lines facing the caliphate near Mosul also spoke to me of the ever present danger of ISIS's terrorist infiltrators who set off bombs in the towns of Kurdistan. Their greatest fear, however, came from a devastating battlefield terror tactic introduced by ISIS, 'up-armoured' Mad Max-style SVBIED (Suicide Vehicle-Borne Improvised Explosive Devices) war wagons that unexpectedly came barrelling into their positions, blowing up defenders and shattering the morale of demoralised survivors.

At the time of my journey, the ISIS *Jaish* (army) seemed to be a still unbroken war machine that used terror as a psychological tactic to break the spirit of its enemies through filmed beheadings of captured soldiers, slaughter of Arab tribes that dared to resist the caliphate, deployment of mass, almost suicidal assaults by shock troops known as *istimashiyoun* or *fedayeen* ('storm fighters' or 'those who sacrifice their lives'), and the weaponisation of suicide on the battlefield – via cars and unprecedentedly massive lorry or truck bombs – on a scale not seen since the Japanese Empire's deployment of kamikazes in the Second World War. As I learned in my journeys, for all the notoriety that the ISIS bloodbaths in places like Paris gained in the West, the majority of the terror group's attacks clearly took place in Iraq itself.

This was not surprising, as Iraq was the original crucible for the terror state/cult/war machine/ideological movement, and the people of the Iraqi 'Land of Two Rivers' suffered from this scourge more than any other. Since 2003, ISIS and its progenitors, Tawhid wal Jihad (Unity and Jihad), Al Qaeda in Iraq and the Islamic State in Iraq, have waged an unprecedented terror assault on those Iraqis whom its followers defined/define as 'apostates', 'disbelievers', 'American or Iranian stooges', *'rafida* (Shiite rejectionist) snakes' and 'infidels' that was to cost tens of thousands of Iraqis their lives and continues to take a heavy toll in post-caliphate Iraq.

This relatively untold story of terrorism in Iraq has not garnered as much attention in the West. The seemingly endless litany of mass-casualty chaos in Iraq is part of a wave of never-ending terror campaigns that blurs together and rarely makes headlines beyond the region. One need look no further than the attention the December 2015 killing of 130 in Paris by ISIS bombers and gunmen garnered in the Western media and compare it to the lack of Western reporting on the ISIS killing of more than twice as many Iraqis (340) in massive, neighbourhood-levelling ISIS suicide bomber truck attacks in the Karada district of Baghdad in July 2016 to see an example of this glaring discrepancy.

In the year I visited the peoples living in the shadow of the caliphate quasi-state, *The Atlantic* magazine published an article titled 'Iraq: The World Capital of Terrorism' that captured the widespread nature of the terrorist mayhem in the land that spawned ISIS.[3] In 2014, Iraq alone suffered a third of the world's terrorism fatalities and Baghdad became the world's deadliest city in terms of terrorism-related deaths. Baghdad was followed by the number two, three, four, five and six most 'terrorist incident cities', Mosul, Ramadi, Baqubah, Kirkuk and Al Hillah, all of which were also found in Iraq.[4] According to the Global Terrorism Index, Iraq suffered 17,500 terror attacks between 2006 and 2015, resulting in an astounding 52,000 deaths. In 2014, this source ranked Iraq as the country most impacted by terrorism and the location of the largest single terror attack globally that year, the killing of 671 Shiites by Sunni ISIS in a massacre in Mosul.[5] In that year, this source

---

3 U. Friedman, 'Iraq: The World Capital of Terrorism', *The Atlantic*, 5 July 2015.
4 '12 Capitals Face Extreme Terrorism Risk', *Verisk Maplecroft*, 19 May 2015.
5 'Global Terrorism Index 2014: Measuring and Understanding the Impact of Terrorism', Institute for Economics and Peace, 2014.

reported 9,929 terrorism-related fatalities in Iraq, the highest annual total ever recorded in a country.

But not all these deaths came at the hands of ISIS or its predecessor 'Al Qaeda in Iraq'. With Sunni ISIS garnering attention as the world's most deadly terrorist group, less attention has been paid to the terror campaign carried out by Shiite groups that was launched, in part, as a response to the terror campaign by Sunni AQI (Al Qaeda in Iraq) and ISIS. While the death toll from this campaign of Shiite terrorism has been lower, tens of thousands have nonetheless been killed by Shiite terrorists, paramilitaries and death squads, such as the Mahdi (Messiah) Army, Badr Brigades, Popular Mobilisation Fronts, the League of the Righteous and the Battalions of God.

Many observers who commented on this wave of terrorism described the spectacular rise of ISIS in 2012–14 and emergence of Iranian-backed Iraqi Shiite terrorist groups as coming 'out of the blue'. But there was a long and rarely studied prehistory to the rise of terrorism in this land that begins with the 2003 US–British invasion of this secular, Baathist-dominated country that had previously served as 'firewall' against both Shiite *and* Sunni sectarian radicalism. An understanding of this background history and the role of 2003's Operation Iraqi Freedom in opening the Pandora's box of sect-based terrorism in Iraq is crucial to explaining the origins, goals, tactics and local and global impact of the terrorists operating in this land. Locals I interviewed used the term *aiqtihams* ('whirlwinds' or 'lightning attacks') to describe the gale of jihad unleashed by 2003's Operation Iraqi Freedom, which created thousands of spin-off dust storms that buffeted the world with the winds of suicide bombings, beheadings, slavery, slaughter, ethnic cleansing, religious executions, terrorism, IEDs and fanaticism.

Kurdish Peshmerga general Shirwan Barzani, 'the Black Tiger', told me he put much of the blame for the spectacular rise of ISIS (and the concomitant rise of Shiite terrorist militias) squarely at the foot of one source: the George W. Bush administration. Pointing to a map of the sprawling ISIS *Dawla* on the wall of his command outpost, he reflected on the origins of the conflict: 'This nightmare state has its origins in mistakes made by the Americans in the aftermath of the overthrow of Hussein. That is when terrorism came to the lands of the Arabs . . . and to our lands as well. It all began in the chaos of 2003.'[6]

---

6 B. G. Williams, 'Journey to Iraqi Kurdistan – Realm of the Endangered Yazidi Pagans and Female Anti-ISIS Peshmerga Fighters', *Huffington Post*, 6 December 2017.

The history of how the ham-fisted US-led inversion of over a millennium of Sunni rule over Shiites in Iraq fulfilled the 'law of unintended consequences' and inadvertently created a terror threat that dwarfed the original Afghan–Pakistan-based Al Qaeda is the largely untold story of the unintentional spread of terroristic *aiqtihams* in a land previously dominated by Baathist Socialists who were the natural enemies of Islamic jihadism. It is also the story of the rise of the transnational ISIS Caliphate, an apocalyptic terrorist movement whose spectacular conquests most certainly did not 'come out of the blue'.

How to Create a Terrorist Insurgency: The Roots of 'Al Qaeda in Iraq' and ISIS

What can only be seen as an inadvertent recruitment drive for 'POIs' (Pissed-Off Iraqis in US military parlance) to join an anti-American terroristic jihad began on 11 May 2003 when Paul Bremer became de facto governor of post-US-invasion Iraq and enforced 'de-Baathification'. Among Bremer's first moves was firing all members of the ruling Baathist Party and Iraqi military. The vast majority of those purged/disenfranchised were Sunnis, who had held the levers of power in the country for centuries. The Iraqi military, which consisted of 385,000 soldiers in the army and 285,000 in the Ministry of Defence, was dominated by Sunnis, as was the Baathist government. Their sudden disbandment shocked Iraqi society, especially the 20 per cent of Iraqis who were members of the ruling Sunni sect that had long dominated the 60 per cent of the country who were members of the repressed Shiite sect.

Tens of thousands of Sunni soldiers who had taken their weapons home instead of fighting the American–British invaders felt deeply betrayed when they were fired. This purge of their ranks created an insurgent enlistment pool of trained, armed and disaffected soldiers who had access to command and control networks as well as stockpiles of weapons. The US military, CIA and State Department were all against these Republican neocon-inspired policies of broad de-Baathification, and one US general furiously said, 'You guys just blindsided Centcom [US Central Command]. We snatched defeat from the jaws of victory and created an insurgency.'[7] The straw that broke the camel's back was when Bremer's staff followed the firing of the Sunnis by creating a provisional government to rule Iraq that was dominated by Shiites,

---

7 T. E. Ricks, *Fiasco: The American Military Adventure in Iraq* (New York, Penguin, 2006), p. 163.

who had been under Sunni rule since the Middle Ages. One Sunni explained the impact this ill-conceived decision had on his disenfranchised community as follows:

> At first no one fought the Americans, not the Baath, not the army officers, and not the [Sunni] tribes. But when the Americans formed the Governing Council [in July 2003] with thirteen Shia [Shiites] and only a few Sunnis, people began to say 'The Americans mean to give the country to the Shia' and then they began to fight, and the tribes began to let Al Qaeda in.[8]

The blundering American administration had inadvertently become active participants in the post-1979 global struggle between the ayatollahs of Shiite Iran and the Wahhabi fundamentalists of Sunni Saudi Arabia by overturning over a millennium of Sunni rule in Iraq and putting Iranian-tied Shiites in power. It did not take long for this fast-spreading Sunni rage to morph into a terroristic Islamic insurgency under the leadership of a foreign terrorist mastermind who had not been classified as an HVT (High Value Target) by the CIA during the initial invasion. In failing to launch a 'decapitation strike' against a Jordanian *amir* (commander) named Abu Musab Zarqawi – who led a group of terrorists operating in a jihadist enclave known as Halabja in autonomous Iraqi Kurdistan prior to the invasion – the CIA lost the chance to kill a skilled leader who would 'jihadify' the budding Sunni insurgency and transform it into a full-blown holy terror campaign.

As the Sunni population was reacting with fury to the spring 2003 disenfranchisement of their community, Abu Musab Zarqawi, an itinerant jihadi paladin from Zarqa, Jordan, travelled to the Sunni heartlands of central and northern Iraq as the head of an independent, non-Al Qaeda Sunni Arab insurgent group known as Tawhid wal Jihad (Monotheism and Holy War). After the US–British spring 2003 invasion of Iraq, Zarqawi and his Sunni 'force multipliers' acted as missionaries/recruiters/terrorism 'enablers' for many previously secular Baathists and members of the Iraqi Army who quickly became radicalised under his followers' Islamist influence. Under the leadership of Zarqawi, newly disenfranchised, previously secular Sunni Socialist Baathists, Iraqi Army members and local and foreign jihadists united to create what ultimately became known as Al Qaeda in Iraq.

In many ways Zarqawi was the Pied Piper of Iraqi Sunni jihad, an emissary who called for a return to fundamentalist Salafite Islam and rejection of Baathist secularism as a means to defeat the Americans and the Shiite 'snakes'

---

8 J. D. Rayburn, *Iraq after America: Strongmen, Sectarians, Resistance* (Stanford, Hoover Institute, 2014), p. 105.

whom they had empowered. Many disenfranchised Baathists and Iraqi Army soldiers would go on to join the Zarqawi-led Sunni jihadi terrorist insurgency which began to take shape in the summer of 2003. The insurgents, including those from other Sunni terrorist groups, such as the Naqshbandi Army, the 1920s Brigade and the Islamic Army, offered unemployed ex-Iraqi Army soldiers salaries of up to 100 USD a month to shoot American 'Crucifixer occupiers' or plant IEDs. Bonuses were given if insurgents filmed the killing of a US solider, as Zarqawi's media-savvy followers launched an unprecedented, online jihad public relations campaign. Within a matter of weeks following the firing of the Sunni Party and Iraqi Army, the Sunni insurgents would commence a classic guerilla war via IED attacks on US patrols, mortar attacks on forward operating bases, sniper ambushes and, ultimately, faith-driven 'martyrdom operation' or suicide bombings.

Suicide bombing was to become the Sunni insurgents' most deadly and fear-inspiring terror tactic. Among Zarqawi's first strategic targets were the Jordanian embassy, which was suicide bombed on 7 August 2003, and the UN Mission in Iraq, which was suicide bombed on 19 August. Zarqawi's terrorists also blew up pipelines and oil production facilities that the Bush administration had hubristically claimed would be tapped into to pay for the war. As a result, oil production fell, as did electricity output, and the Americans were blamed for this and the general looting and chaos.

When the insurgency spread in the summer and fall of 2003, US troops responded by carrying out clumsy counterterrorism raids on Iraqi houses to arrest suspected insurgents, and this played into Zarqawi's hands. The Americans soon had thousands of prisoners and decided to reopen a notorious prison west of Baghdad known as Abu Ghraib. Abu Ghraib and other prison camps in essence became terrorist incubators where arrestees, many of whom were innocent, were radicalised by other inmates. The clumsy American counterterrorism sweeps and Abu Ghraib scandal involving photos of US National Guards torturing inmates also helped Zarqawi to recruit outraged Arabs from the neighbouring Sunni majority in Syria, Kuwait, Jordan, Libya, Tunisia and Saudi Arabia. Soon Iraq was filled with hundreds of fanatical foreign fighter–terrorists who were known to be willing to become suicide bombers as this new asymmetric tactic spread throughout the previously secular Sunni heartlands.

As part of a calculated master stroke to hurt the Americans and gain further publicity, in October 2004 Zarqawi then pledged *baya* (oath of allegiance) to bin Laden and announced that his independent jihad group, Unity and Jihad, was merging with Al Qaeda. Henceforth it would be known as

Tanzim Qaedat al-Jihad fi Bilad al-Rafidayn ('Al Qaeda in the Land of the Two Rivers') or simply Al Qaeda in Iraq (AQI). Thus the Bush administration's 2002 false claim that there was an Al Qaeda terrorist presence in secular Baathist Iraq became a self-fulfilling prophecy *two years later*. Bin Laden was thrilled by the overthrow of socialist Baathism in Iraq and the rise of an Al Qaeda affiliate in a land previously dominated by secular nationalist Baathist 'infidels'. He issued a statement from his place of hiding in Pakistan wherein he gloated 'Be glad of the good news: America is mired in the swamps of the Tigris and Euphrates. Here he [Bush] is now, thank God, in an embarrassing situation and here is America today being ruined before the eyes of the whole world.'[9]

By the spring of 2004, AQI had boldly set up its headquarters in the western Sunni town of Fallujah, a region that had seen most of its teachers and government employees fired as Baathists. At this time, Zarqawi, who became known as the 'Sheikh of Slaughterers' for his atavistic slaughter, was to declare after beheading an American civilian, 'the mujahideen [holy warriors] will give America a taste of the degradation you have inflicted on the Iraqi people'.[10] Zarqawi's Sunni terrorists brazenly used Fallujah as a launching pad for dispatching waves of suicide bombers into Baghdad to wreak havoc and deny Iraqis the security the new Shiite-dominated government and its American sponsors desperately sought to provide them.

As the situation deteriorated in Fallujah by the fall of 2004, it was decided that the notorious Al Qaeda in Iraq terror bastion would have to be taken. On 7 November, US and Iraqi security forces moved to encircle the roughly three to four thousand Islamist terrorists holed up in the city. The insurgents had dug into Fallujah and created everything from HBIEDs (house-borne improvised explosive devices, i.e. houses rigged to explode when entered by US troops) to interconnecting tunnels designed to turn the large city into an urban killing zone. The subsequent November 2004 Second Battle of Fallujah was the bloodiest battle of the entire Iraq War. When it was over, victorious US and Iraqi troops uncovered twenty-four bomb factories and 455 weapons caches in the terrorist haven. They also uncovered torture houses used by Zarqawi's followers, including one where the victims' legs had been sawed off, which demonstrated just how depraved and brutal the Sunni terrorists had become.[11]

---

9 J. R. Singal, C. Lim, and M. J. Stephey, 'Seven Years in Iraq: An Iraq War Timeline', *Time*, 19 March 2010.
10 'Qaeda Vows Iraq Defeat for Crusaders', *New York Times*, 4 April 2004.
11 M. R. Gordon and B. E. Trainor, *The Endgame: The Inside Story of the Struggle for Iraq, From George W. Bush and Barack Obama* (New York, Vintage Books, 2013), p. 118.

With the collapse of their capital in Fallujah, the Sunni AQI terrorists fled north to Mosul, Iraq's second largest city and a Sunni stronghold. Defeated in Mosul by US Stryker forces, the insurgents fled south to the city of Baqubah and declared it the capital. By 2005 it was obvious that the United States was essentially playing something similar to the funfair game of 'whack-a-mole' with elusive Sunni terrorist–insurgents. By 2006, American troops were dying in large numbers in the so-called Sunni Triangle, which stretched from Baghdad to Ramadi in the west to Mosul in the north. Tellingly, the US military was recording 1,000 attacks on their troops per week.[12] By this time, a classified American intelligence report would state that Iraq had become a 'cause célèbre for jihadists, breeding a deep resentment of US involvement in the Muslim world and cultivating supporters for the global jihadist movement'.[13] A 2006 National Intelligence Estimate (NIE) by America's various intelligence services stated that 'the Iraq war has made the overall terrorism problem worse'.[14]

I found evidence of the war making the global terrorism problem worse when I carried out fieldwork in Afghanistan in 2007 for the CIA's Counter Terrorism Center to try to find the origins of an alien, new terror tactic that had begun to be deployed by the Taliban: *istishahadayeen* (suicide bombing). During the course of my fieldwork in the insurgent-infested Pashtun belt, I found evidence of emissaries from AQI travelling from Iraq to Afghanistan to indoctrinate and train the Taliban rebels in the previously religiously forbidden tactic of suicide bombing.[15] This grafting of this previously unheard-of Arab ideology and terror tactic on to the Taliban insurgency was one of many unintentional, disastrous examples of the so-called 'Iraq effect' on the Islamic world.

Meanwhile, in Iraq itself, Zarqawi's Sunni terrorists increasingly attacked not only the American 'Crucifixer occupiers' but, in far greater numbers, Shiite 'apostates'. The Al Qaeda in Iraq *amir* referred to his sectarian foes, the Shiites, as 'the lurking snake', 'a sect of treachery and betrayal . . . the crafty and malicious scorpion, the true challenge', who had benefited from working with the occupation forces.[16] Zarqawi summed up the strategic logic for his terror jihad on Shiites as follows:

---

12 'The Road to the Surge', *Washington Post*, 2 November 2009.
13 M. Mazzetti, *The Way of the Knife: The CIA, a Secret Army, and a War at the Ends of the Earth* (New York, Penguin, 2013), p. 138.
14 M. Mazzetti, 'Spy Agencies Say Iraq War Worsens Terrorism Threat', *New York Times*, 24 September 2006.
15 B. G. Williams, 'Mullah Omar's Missiles: A Field Report on Suicide Bombers in Afghanistan', *Middle East Policy Council*, 15/4 (2008).
16 E. Friedland, 'Special Report: the Islamic State', *Clarion Project*, 15 May 2015, p. 7.

> Shi'ism is a religion that has nothing in common with Islam ... The Shiites have been a sect of treachery and betrayal throughout history and throughout the ages. It is a creed that aims to combat the Sunnis ... Targeting and hitting them in [their] religious, political, and military depth will provoke them to show the Sunnis their rabies and bare the teeth of the hidden rancor working in their breasts. If we succeed in dragging them into the arena of sectarian war, it will become possible to awaken the inattentive Sunnis.[17]

AQI suicide bombers targeted Shiite civilians going about their lives and killed hundreds doing mundane things like buying bread in the market or having tea in a Baghdad cafe. In a typical example of AQI terrorism against Shiites, Zarqawi's followers set off a car bomb in the Shiite holy city of Najaf in March 2003 that killed more than 85 people. The following March, his terrorist group set off coordinated explosives in Shiite shrines in the holy city of Karbala and in Baghdad, killing 181. Another AQI suicide car bomber struck a crowd of Shiite police and Iraqi National Guard recruits in the southern city of Hillah, killing 125, on 28 February 2005. One cannot overestimate the massive scale of the suicide bomber terrorism in this period, which far surpassed anything seen outside the region. One massive 2007 AQI SVBIED bombing using a fuel tanker against a Yazidi community, for example, levelled buildings, killed an astounding 800 people, and destroyed as much as 80 per cent of the targeted 'devil-worshipper' village.[18] In this case, and in many other cases of suicide bombing in Baghdad against Shiites, AQI deployed unprecedentedly massive truck bombs that killed hundreds and flattened whole neighbourhoods.

As Iraq's morgues filled with thousands of slain Shiites, it became obvious that Zarqawi was trying to inflame sectarian terrorism to shred the fabric of the democratic society the Americans were trying to construct in Iraq. He did so by using fear and hatred to turn Sunnis against Shiites. This sadistic killer, who personally introduced the AQI trademark terror tactic of beheading, was intent on starting not only a Sunni terrorist insurgency, but a civil war with the newly empowered Shiites. Sadly, history would show that Zarqawi's master plan of using terrorism to incite Shiites and Sunnis into waging a full-blown sectarian war that would both undermine US state-building objectives and make his Al Qaeda in Iraq terrorist force the primary defender of many Sunnis was resoundingly successful.

---

17 'Zarqawi Letter', *US Department of State Archive*, 20 January 2009.
18 'How Suicide Bombing Shattered Iraq', Al Jazeera, October 2010.

Warriors of the *Mahdi* (Messiah): The Rise of Shiite Terrorism in Post-invasion Iraq

It did not take long for Shiites to react to Zarqawi's terror war on their sect. For their part, many Shiites had also become more radicalised since the overthrow of the Baathist government and were increasingly led by extremist clerics who responded to Zarqawi's attacks on their community. The Shiite militias were guilty of having created kill lists of former Baathist Party members who were then tracked down and assassinated by terrorists. At this time, an Iranian-trained radical cleric named Moqtada al Sadr's Shiite militia created terrorist death squads which began to systematically hunt and kill Sunnis in Baghdad and elsewhere. Their most notorious modus operandi was to use power drills to drill holes in the heads of Sunnis who were kidnapped at random. Many of those who were killed by Shiite terrorists were Sunni teachers, doctors, artists, journalists, bureaucrats etc. who had been forced to join the Baathist party in order to get ahead in Iraqi society under Saddam Hussein.

But not all Shiites were engaged in Sadr's attacks on Sunnis, as the Shiites' main religious leader, Grand Ayatollah al Sistani, ordered his followers not to give in to the urge to fight back against the Sunnis. That changed on 22 February 2006, when Zarqawi's Sunni AQI terrorists blew up the gold-domed Al Askari mosque in Samarra (a medieval edifice that is the holiest shrine in Iraq for Shiites) in a terror act calculated to stir outrage. Devout Shiites across Iraq reacted in fury to this sacrilege and attacked Sunnis, killing over a thousand. In Baghdad, Shiites began to use terrorism to ethnically cleanse Sunnis from their neighbourhoods and vice versa, as this previously mixed city descended into a spiral of sectarian violence. Tens of thousands would die in the subsequent sect-driven terrorism, butchery, slaughter and mayhem.

Terrorism thus became a strategic tactic used by both Sunnis and Shiites as part of a full-blown sectarian civil war that would ultimately be won by the Shiites. By 2006, US troops were recording roughly 3,000 Iraqi deaths a month and more than 250 terrorist car bombings and suicide attacks a month.[19] A member of the US Army's EJK (Extra-Judicial Killing) Task Force captured the gruesome nature of the terroristic butchery, stating 'I remember those days when we'd have up to one hundred murders a day.'[20] Another US

---

19 K. E. Kagan, *The Surge: A Military History* (London, Encounter Books, 2009), p. 196.
20 Ibid., p. 228.

soldier would report, 'Every patrol, you're finding dead people. Their eyes are gouged out. Their arms are broken.'[21]

As the Americans tried to suppress the Shiite violence and related terrorism by moving against Moqtada al Sadr, they came under attack by his Mahdi Army followers and Shiites belonging to the Iranian-backed Badr Brigades. By 2006, the 'peaceful and self-governing nation' that President Bush had predicted would be established in Iraq after the invasion had devolved into a bloody Shiite and Sunni terrorism quagmire for the Americans and British.[22] Far from being welcomed as liberators, thousands of Americans were now dying at the hands of both the Shiites and the Sunnis whom they had ostensibly come to liberate. To compound matters, the US military had too few troops to crush the Sunni and Shiite terrorist insurgencies. But that was about to change.

Snatching Victory from Zarqawi: The 2007 Troop Surge and Sunni Anbar Awakening

By 2007 a group of American military officers had convinced President Bush to try to prevent a calamitous takeover of the country by Sunni and Shiite terrorist–militants by deploying reinforcements. Thus was born the famous 2007–8 eighteen-month Bush troop 'surge' of over 28,000 reinforcements that would bring the total number of US soldiers in Iraq to 168,000. The general chosen to lead the counteroffensive was General David Petraeus, who had a new plan for waging counterterrorism and COIN (Counter Insurgency). Petraeus's new counterinsurgency approach stressed the need to win over the population and rehabilitate Iraqi insurgents who might have joined the insurgency because of overly aggressive US tactics.

This latter point actually coincided with previous developments that were happening in the western Sunni province of Anbar at this time that ultimately helped Petraeus implement his ambitious COIN plans. As it transpired, many Sunnis in Anbar, Iraq's largest province, had by 2006 come to chafe under the rule of fanatical AQI Sunni insurgents. Several Sunni tribal leaders or sheikhs came to see the AQI militants who terrorised them on a daily basis, stole their daughters as 'wives' and enforced harsh Islamic law as a worse enemy than

---

21 D. P. Bolger, *Why We Lost: A General's Inside Account of the Iraq and Afghanistan Wars* (New York, Houghton and Mifflin, 2014), p. 229.
22 'President Says Saddam Hussein Must Leave Iraq Within 48 Hours', *George W. Bush White House Archives*, 17 March 2003.

the Americans. In this sense, Sunni AQI's terrorism backfired, and it lost local support among fellow Sunnis.

In response to these extraordinary developments among the Sunni tribes of the western province of Anbar, AQI (which, it must be stressed, was also Sunni) declared 'open war' on the so-called Anbar Awakening Sunni sheikhs who united with the US military to form anti-AQI militias. Ultimately, the AQI terrorists managed to kill Sheikh Abu Risha, the Anbar Awakening leader, in a bombing in September 2007. But by then the US surge reinforcement troops had bolstered the Sunni Anbar fighters and helped them spread to other Sunni provinces north of Baghdad. As the US surge reinforcements arrived in 2007 to work with the Anbar Awakening fighters, they pushed AQI out of most of the Sunni Triangle. The US reinforcements also denied AQI terrorists control of the so-called 'Baghdad belts', suburbs which had been used as bases for the manufacturing of SVBIEDs to attack Shiite neighbourhoods in the city.

US Centcom also achieved a victory in the killing of Al Qaeda in Iraq's almost demonic leader in a targeted air strike in June 2006. And Zarqawi was not the only terrorist leader to be killed by elite special operations terrorist hunters. By 2010 General Ray Odierno was able to announce that the United States had killed thirty-four of the top forty-two leaders of AQI.[23] The year 2008 was a low point in AQI's fortunes. The troop surge, special force raids, Anbar Awakening and loss of the Baghdad belts had pushed them out of their strongholds in Anbar Province and the Sunni provinces north of the capital. The Shiite-dominated Iraqi Army security forces had also taken control of such Sunni strongholds as Fallujah, Ramadi, Tikrit and Mosul. Then, in August 2007, the militant Shiite leader Moqtada al Sadr called a truce after his followers got into a bloody firefight with Iraqi government troops (mainly fellow Shiites) that cost scores of lives. Thus, the Sunni insurgency, the Shiite insurgency and the Sunni–Shiite civil war were, to a considerable extent, all tamped down by 2008. President Bush and Iraqi leader Prime Minister Nouri al Maliki were so confident of success that they signed an agreement in 2008 which called for US troops to withdraw from Iraq by 31 December 2011.

But despite the signing of a Status of Forces Agreement, the jihadi demons unleashed by Operation Iraqi Freedom were far from being exorcised and would return with a vengeance after the Americans departed.

---

23 T. Shanker, 'Al Qaeda in Iraq Leaders Neutralized, U.S. Says', *New York Times*, 4 June 2010.

Jihadi Phoenix: The Rise of ISIS out of the AQI and Reawakening of Shiite Militias

Despite the remarkable victories of 2007/8, there were still hundreds of diehard AQI terrorists operating in Iraq, and they continued to wage a low-level terror campaign. Zarqawi was quickly replaced as head of the down, but not out, AQI by an Iraqi cleric named Abu Omar al Baghdadi and his deputy, an Egyptian bomb expert named Abu Ayub al Masri. Abu Omar al Baghdadi and Abu Ayub al Masri subsequently dissolved AQI and renamed it the Islamic State in Iraq (ISI). While there have been retroactive efforts by Donald Trump to portray ISI or its subsequent iteration ISIS as somehow a creation resulting exclusively from President Barack Obama's decision to withdraw US troops from Iraq in 2011 (in fulfilment of the 2008 treaty signed by Bush), this terror group was simply Zarqawi's post-2003 US invasion Sunni insurgent organisation, only rebranded with a more ambitious title.

Meanwhile, despite ambitiously renaming itself, ISI's fortunes continued to deteriorate as its two leaders subsequently blew themselves up with suicide vests when they were tracked down and surrounded by Iraqi counterterrorism forces in April 2010. It was at this time that a relatively unknown Islamic scholar from Baghdad named Abu Bakr al Baghdadi, who had been arrested and radicalised at a US prison at Camp Bucca, took over as the leader of the weakened ISI. Defeated in the vast deserts of western Iraq's Anbar Province and Sunni lands to the north of Baghdad, al Baghdadi and the surviving ISI insurgents patiently bided their time in 2010 and 2011.

When President Obama completely withdrew all US troops from Iraq in December 2011, al Baghdadi awoke his remaining Sunni jihadi forces. Fortunately for al Baghdadi, the Shiite government of Prime Minister Nouri al Maliki cruelly repressed the Sunni minority once the US troops departed in December 2011. This gave the estimated 700–1,000 ISI insurgents the CIA felt were still active in 2011 the opportunity to once again spread their message of Sunni re-empowerment and jihadi terrorism among repressed and disenfranchised Sunnis.[24]

Al Baghdadi announced the revival of ISI by declaring a new terror campaign against the Maliki Shiite government known as 'Breaking the Walls'. Al Baghdadi also launched an attack on Abu Ghraib prison on 21 July 2013 that freed approximately 500 imprisoned Sunni insurgents. This prison break, which shocked the nation, was followed by seven more prison

---

24 D. Kenner, 'Panetta: 1,000 Al Qaeda Terrorists Still in Iraq', *Foreign Policy*, 9 June 2011.

breaks that freed more hard-core AQI terrorist veterans, many of them on death row. ISI also began waging an intensive IED and car-bombing terror campaign that brought 2013 casualty levels up to the point of the worst insurgent violence in the 2005–6 pre-surge period. This led to a staggering number of deaths, more than 1,000 (mainly Shiite) per month in 2013.[25]

The Shiite-dominated Iraqi government responded by launching a campaign of its own known as 'Revenge of the Martyrs', which saw mass arrests of Sunnis, thus further exacerbating the Sunni–Shiite divide and playing into ISI's hands. At this time, Iranian-backed Shiite militias were remobilised to fight against the Sunni insurgents, and this was akin to pouring gasoline on the flames of sectarianism. Many of these Iranian-backed Shiite paramilitary groups mobilised by Maliki's Shiite government had engaged in terrorism against Sunnis during the 2004–7 period, and Sunnis strongly resented their deployment in their lands to break up Sunni protest camps.

By 2013, ISI had also metastasised and spread like a cancer into neighbouring Syria following the outbreak of a Sunni vs Alawite Shiite civil war in that land in 2011, thus further fulfilling the 'law of unintended consequences' from the disastrous 2003 US-led invasion of Iraq.

As disputes broke out in 2014 between the newly declared ISIS Islamic State in Iraq *and* Syria and its breakaway Syrian faction Al Nusra, Al Qaeda leader Ayman al Zawahiri issued orders for ISI to remain in Iraq and for Al Nusra to lead the jihad in Syria.[26] But, far from heeding Zawahiri's orders, al Baghdadi made the momentous decision to break from Al Qaeda and declared that he would not take orders from anyone but Allah. In response, Al Qaeda cut its ties to the newly declared ISIS and stated '[Al Qaeda] has no connection with the group called the ISIS, as it was not informed or consulted about its establishment.'[27]

But despite this rejection from Al Qaeda, ISIS's power began to extend far and wide in Syria in 2014, from the eastern Syrian province of Deir es Zor, through the central Syrian deserts up the MERV (Middle Euphrates River Valley) to the desert town of Raqqa, which became the ISIS 'capital' in Syria in January of that year. At this time, ISIS was also able to make dramatic inroads in neighbouring Iraq. Maliki's Shiite government troops had been attacking Sunni protestors and militants in the Sunni Anbar Province cities of Ramadi and Fallujah, but the Iraqi prime minister abruptly withdrew his government forces on 30 December 2013. This unexpected move gave ISIS an opening and, on

---

25 J. D. Lewis, 'Al Qaeda in Iraq Resurgent', Institute for the Study of War, September 2013.
26 'Al Qaeda Iraqi Chief Rejects Zawahiri's Orders', Al Jazeera, 15 June 2013.
27 'Al Qaeda Disavows Militants in Syria', BBC, 3 February 2014.

3 January 2014, black-clad ISIS fighters swarmed in and seized control of most of Fallujah and much of Ramadi, the capital of Sunni-dominated Anbar province. The ISIS fighters then drove out or executed Iraqi government officials and policemen. The militants followed this up by boldly raising the *Rayah*, the notorious Eagle and black banner of ISIS, above the government buildings and police stations in these cities. ISIS fighters boldly declared Fallujah to be part of a newly proclaimed, transnational Islamic State.

While the winter 2014 conquest of most of Anbar by ISIS militants sent shock waves throughout Iraq, it did not cause much of a stir in America, where most people seemed to have put the unpopular, costly war behind them. At this stage, war fatigue still predominated, and what would later be described as 'ISISphobia' (following the shocking filmed beheading of captured US journalists by ISIS) had not yet begun to panic average Americans. The Obama administration was comforted by the fact that ISIS rebels were halted at Abu Ghraib to the west of Baghdad and did not have the strength to challenge the Maliki government for control of this Shiite-dominated capital city. Although Iraqis, who suffered immensely from ISIS's massive suicide bombing campaign, were aware that the Sunni terrorists posed a threat to their country, the group remained under the radar from January to June 2014 for most Americans.

But it later became clear that ISIS was plotting a bold 'Breaking the Walls'-style assault on Iraq's second-largest city, the northern Sunni-dominated town of Mosul. It was ISIS's subsequent surprise conquest of this metropolis of over 2 million and its looming threat to the oil-rich region of Kirkuk in neighbouring Kurdistan and the Yazidi 'pagans' that was to draw the reluctant warrior President Obama back to the killing sands of Iraq.

Khilafat (Caliphate): ISIS Carves out a Terrorist Theocracy in 'Syraq'

On 4 June 2014, hundreds of pickup trucks carrying ISIS fighters stormed out of the desert and began attacking government checkpoints in Mosul. The ISIS raiders' aim was to collude with local Sunnis in Baghdad, who were disgruntled with Shiite government repression, to set off powerful bombs downtown, overrun several districts, terrorise Shiites, and then retreat before the Shiite-dominated Iraqi Army could destroy them. The ISIS desert fighters' advance was spearheaded by unprecedentedly massive SVBIED attacks by captured army water trucks as Islamic State fighters became the first military force to systematically deploy suicide land vehicles in combat. As the attack unfolded, numerically superior government troops shocked the ISIS raiders by retreating after just four days of fighting. After less than a week of deploying massive suicide bombings and swarm attacks, a few hundred fanatically determined ISIS had done the seemingly impossible and had defeated a much larger, Shiite-dominated Iraqi army of five divisions and captured Mosul.

The triumphant ISIS conquerors lost no time in spreading terror and mayhem throughout the previously ethnically mixed, cosmopolitan city. Captured Iraqi government Shiite troops were crucified, beheaded and set on fire by victorious ISIS fighters. An unbearably gruesome cell phone video of triumphant ISIS fighters lining up and executing hundreds of captured Shiite government soldiers by shooting them point blank in the head on a blood-covered concrete deck overlooking the Tigris River subsequently went viral. Other blindfolded Shiite government defenders captured by ISIS's jubilant fighters were thrown in their thousands into a seemingly bottomless charnel pit east of Mosul known as the 'cursed Khasfa' sinkhole.

Having systematically butchered policemen, government officials and soldiers, and massacred hundreds of Shiites found in jail, the ISIS Sunni fighter–terrorists then fanned out from the charred and mutilated bodies of their enemies and attacked Mosul's ancient community of Assyrian, Chaldean and Nestorian Christians. Many of these had had *noons* (the letter *n* in Arabic, from the word Nazarene, a contemptuous term for Christians) painted on their houses by Sunni Arab neighbourhood informants. As they raped Christian women and girls or sold them in slave pens, defiled or dynamited churches and Christian shrines dating back to the sixth century, and killed 'Crucifixers' by nailing them to their doors, the ISIS fighters gave this peaceful community an ultimatum: 'We offer them three choices: Islam; the *dhimma* contract [of submission] – involving payment of *jizya* [a medieval Islamic tax on unbelievers]; if they refuse this they will have nothing but the sword.'[28]

A worse fate befell the 'devil-worshipping' Yazidi 'pagans' (whose main town of Sinjar was located to the west of Mosul near the Syrian border) when their unofficial capital was captured in an August 2014 ISIS blitz and almost every building systematically demolished with explosives. The mass ISIS terrorism against the Yazidis was genocidal and forced the majority of this ancient race of 500,000 to flee their ancestral lands. In what can best be described as sexual terrorism, thousands of Yazidi women and girls who could not escape in time were kidnapped from their burning villages as Koran-endorsed *sabbiya* (sex slaves) and raped and abused by ISIS fighters

---

28 D. J. Evans and I. A. Rubei'i, 'Convert, Pay Tax, or Die, Islamic State Warns Christians', Reuters, 18 July 2014; N. H. Shea, '"N" for Nazarene', Hudson Institute, 13 March 2018.

in what they considered an act of worship. Yazidis whom I interviewed spoke of seeing their priests' throats being ritualistically slit for not converting to Islam, of women over the age of forty (who were considered too old to be sex slaves) being massacred, and men being lined up and gunned down in ditches in their thousands. Since ISIS subsequently declared itself a caliphate or theocratic state on 4 July 2014, all of these atrocities could be designated 'state-sponsored acts of terrorism'.

But even as most of the world looked on in horror, ISIS adherents across the globe responded to the unbearable internet images of tormented Yazidi slave girls being sold online and other recruitment drives. They were thrilled by the bold ISIS conquest of Mosul and subsequent capture of northern Sunni towns including Tikrit, which was symbolic as Sunni leader Saddam Hussein's home town, and the cold-blooded execution of captured Shiite conscripts captured on film. Many global internet followers were drawn to join the cult of victorious holy slaughterers by its bold proclamation that its triumphant holy state was *baqiya* (remaining) and *tatamaddad* (expanding). Tens of thousands of Muslim extremists from Russia, the number one source of ISIS migration (mainly from the Caucasus republics of Chechnya and Dagestan), Tunisia (the second greatest source), Europe, Saudi Arabia, Uzbekistan, the USA and elsewhere began to partake in *hijra* (religious migration) via Turkey to Iraq and Syria to become martyrs in suicide terrorism, front-line combatants, or to live in and help build a 'pure' shariah Islamic law state.[29]

It was the unexpected June to July ISIS conquest of the northern Iraqi lands and declaration of a transnational militant state, which threatened the American-backed order in the Middle East, that finally awoke the somnolent Americans to the threat of al Baghdadi's expansionist jihadi theocracy/war machine. In a shockingly short time, ISIS had seemingly come out of nowhere and gained control of one-third of Iraq and one-third of Syria to create a terror state in the heart of the oil-rich Middle East. To 'degrade and destroy' this unexpected terror threat, whose adherents threatened to plant the flag of jihad on the Vatican and behead the US president, Obama ordered immediate air operations against ISIS. Operations commenced in August 2014 against ISIS fighters besieging thousands of trapped Yazidis atop their holy mountain, Mount Sinjar, and against ISIS troops surging towards Erbil, the capital of the pro-US autonomous Kurdistan region east of Mosul.

---

29 B. G. Williams, 'The Islamic State Threat to the 2018 FIFA World Cup', *West Point Counter Terrorism Center Sentinel* 11 (18 May 2018).

The US bombing halted ISIS's advance against Erbil, saved the besieged Yazidis and heralded the commencement of an air and local proxy counterterrorism campaign known as Operation Inherent Resolve. This proxy offensive would be the most successful surrogate war/counterterrorism campaign in modern history. Reluctant to redeploy conventional US troops to lead the fight against ISIS in what would essentially be Operation Iraqi *and* Syrian Freedom, Obama decided to work to enable local anti-ISIS forces to retake their lands. This UCW (Unconventional Warfare) approach translated to a 'light footprint' campaign of working 'by, with and through' the Iraqi Security Forces, Kurdish Peshmerga and Yazidi militias to halt ISIS's advances and roll it back.

Five thousand US 'enablers' were gradually deployed in waves to Iraq to act as 'accelerants', and train and assist 'partner units' like the famed Iraqi Golden Division special operations forces. This black-clad elite Iraqi Counter Terrorism Service unit was armed, trained and militarily supported by US Green Berets and other special forces to wage counterterrorism and ultimately to serve as shock troops in liberating the ISIS-held northern Sunni towns of Ramadi, Tikrit, Fallujah, Hit, Qaim, Rawa, Amerli, Baqubah, Hawija, Tel Afar and the diamond in Caliph al Baghdadi's turban, the massive metropolis of Mosul. While ISIS fighters fought back fanatically against US-backed local forces and died in the thousands to defend their dreamed-of state, they could not withstand the precision firepower of laser-/satellite-guided bombs or HIMARs (small satellite-guided rockets) directed by US 'combat controllers' or US-trained Iraqi or Kurdish ground spotters.

But progress was not immediate, and the ISIS repulse and Coalition counteroffensive did not gain traction until 2015. In the meantime, tens of thousands of foreigners flocked to the newly proclaimed theocracy/proto-state being brutally carved out of the deserts of Iraq and Syria. Most immigrants travelled through Turkey (whose Islamist president initially turned a blind eye to their transit) into Syria, where the foreign presence was more pronounced than in Iraq. It was from the Syrian town of Manbij, near the Turkish border in the so-called Al Bab 'terror corridor', that terror cells were dispatched to carry out attacks in Turkey, Russia, France and Belgium. But terror cells were also dispatched from ISIS's Iraq *wilayet* (province) to carry out a wave of devastating suicide bombing attacks against ISIS's primary target, Shiite neighbourhoods in the '*rafida* state of Baghdad', as well as against Shiite Iran, Saudi Arabia, Kurdistan and Kuwait.

Meanwhile, in the caliphate, tens of thousands of school-aged boys were indoctrinated to become terrorist 'Cubs of the Caliphate' (in classrooms that no longer taught secular school subjects) and many were dispatched to fight in the front lines or even used to execute prisoners of war and 'spies' on film. ISIS female 'Brides of Jihad' recruited foreign women online to travel to the caliphate, where many served in the hijab-wearing *Khansa*, a morality enforcement brigade that terrorised women and enforced strict shariah law. Many female ISIS adherents were far from passive actors and, most importantly, they helped raise a new generation of children who were fanatically dedicated to the cause of the caliphate and its terror war on those who lived in the 'camp of disbelief'.

But the terror state whose tens of thousands of devout adherents from abroad and from Iraq and Syria believed the caliphate would herald the end of times gradually fell to advancing US-backed Iraqi, Kurdish Peshmerga and Iran Revolutionary Guard-backed Shiite Popular Mobilisation Fronts (the last were accused of massacring Sunnis in Tikrit, Amerli and other cities as they advanced). But this cascading 2015–17 collapse did not dampen ISIS's belief in its divine terrorism. During the October 2016–June 2017 Battle of Mosul, the largest urban battle since Stalingrad, ISIS fighters, for example, terrorised the besieged city's population by keeping tens of thousands of terrified civilians trapped as human shields in apartments with fighters based in or on them (hundreds of civilians were killed in strikes on such enemy positions). ISIS fighters also massacred civilian 'traitors to the Caliph' who tried to flee the besieged city. In addition, ISIS 'martyrs' waged intensive suicide bombing attacks in Mosul against advancing Iraqi forces which, along with street fighting, killed as many as 10,000 Iraqi Security Forces.

While the rubbleised city of Mosul, filled with the bodies of thousands of ISIS fighters and many more civilians, finally fell in the summer of 2017 and Iraq was declared 'fully liberated' from ISIS on 8 December 2017, the terror continued. As it transpired, vengeful ISIS fighters had booby-trapped refrigerators, ovens, cars and houses with explosives to kill those refugee 'traitors' who had fled and now wanted to return to their homes. The terrorism continued from the Shiite side as well. Captured ISIS fighters were summarily executed by being thrown off of roofs or gunned down in the Tigris River by vengeful Shiite Popular Mobilisation militias.

Thousands more captured ISIS members, including foreign men and women from lands as far afield as France, Russia and Uzbekistan, were subsequently executed as terrorists by the new Iraqi government led by Prime Minister Abadi. Abadi had, despite condoning the swift and often summary executions, shown himself to be far more open to reconciling with the Sunnis than his disgraced predecessor the notorious Shiite Maliki. But the lack of development in the war-ravaged ruins of Sunni cities in northern Iraq continued to breed despair and provided a fertile recruiting ground for ISIS to recruit Sunnis who felt they no longer had a stake in a country that was dominated by victorious Popular Mobilisation Front Shiite militias.

Resilient Shadow Warriors: ISIS's Post-caliphate Insurgency

For all of its territorial losses from 2015 to 2017, and despite the triumphant, but unrealistic, boasts of President Donald Trump that he 'wiped out' and even 'absolutely obliterated' ISIS in the successful proxy campaign he inherited from Obama in January 2017, the terror group was far from being wiped out.[30] In a June 2019 report titled 'ISIS's Second Comeback', the Institute for the Study of War reported on ISIS's preservation of its forces since the beginning of its carefully planned retreat and regrouping, stating:

> ISIS responded with an intelligent strategy that prioritized setting conditions for reconstitution over retaining physical control. The U.S. underestimated how ISIS's hybrid style of warfare would enable it to adapt to military pressure and avoid defeat even if it lost terrain. ISIS began a staggered transition back to an insurgency from May 2017 to February 2018, dissolving large portions of its existing structure and dispersing its forces and committed supporters.[31]

This source also reported 'the U.S. intelligence community assesses that ISIS will attempt to resurge ... As of June 2019, ISIS likely has the capability to seize another major urban center in Iraq or Syria.' The Pentagon and UN estimated in 2019 that the surprisingly resilient terrorist group still had as many as 30,000 diehard followers in Iraq and Syria. ISIS had clearly reverted to its roots as a deadly guerilla, even as its final turf in eastern Syria was conquered by 21 March 2019 by US-backed Syrian Kurds and its leader al Baghdadi killed in an October 2019 Delta Force raid in north-western Syria.[32] Most worryingly, ISIS established fallback bases in the isolated Jazeera and Anbar deserts in the west and in the remote highlands to the

---

30 'A Presidential Epic Fail: Watch Trump Try to Explain His Syria Policy', *Haaretz*, 25 April 2018; 'Editorial: Wrong about ISIS', *Weekly Standard*, 26 September 2018.
31 J. Cafarella, B. Wallace and J. Zhou, 'ISIS's Second Comeback: Assessing the Next ISIS Insurgency', *Institute for the Study of War*, 23 July 2019.
32 'Overseas Contingency Operations: Operation Inherent Resolve, Operation Pacific Eagle-Philippines', *Media.Defense.gov*, 1 April 2018–30 June 2018.

south-east of Mosul in the Qara Chokh, Hamrin and Makhmoul Mountains. There, tensions between the Iraqi Security Forces and Kurdistan Peshmerga forces created a no man's land that the terrorists exploited to create a sanctuary.

From these redoubts, the US military reported ISIS 'resurgent cells' were (as of the time of this writing in June 2020) carrying out widespread terror attacks. These attacks included the systematic killing of pro-government Iraqi elders known as *mukhtars*, setting off massive car bombs, ambushing Shiite militias, dressing up as government troops at fake checkpoints and executing government employees, extorting money from locals as *zakat* (religious tax) and raiding the houses of government and police employees at night and executing them. In the summer of 2019, ISIS terrorists also took to burning thousands of acres of crops of their enemies in northern Iraq and gloated on their website, stating 'It seems that it will be a hot summer that will burn the pockets of the apostates as well as their hearts as they burned the Muslims and their homes in the past years.'[33]

Most worryingly, ISIS has an estimated 400 million USD in its war chest, which it laundered and used to fund what was essentially a Taliban-style war of guerilla terrorist attrition.[34] Such funds were used to pay for terror attacks by disgruntled Sunnis in a war-devastated, impoverished land where jobs and resources were few.

Before his death in the sort of targeted air strike that wiped out most of ISIS's leadership, ISIS's chief spokesman had warned this sort of resistance would come, stating:

> Do you think, O America, that victory is achieved by the killing of one commander or more? It is then a false victory ... victory is when the enemy is defeated. Do you think, O America, that defeat is the loss of a city or a land? Were we defeated when we lost cities in Iraq and were left in the desert without a city or a territory? No, defeat is the loss of willpower and desire to fight.[35]

A few months prior to his own death at the hands of US Delta Forces in the fall of 2019, Caliph al Baghdadi issued a 'proof of life' video and boldly proclaimed 'Our battle today is one of attrition and stretching the enemy.

---

33 'Deliberate Crop Burning by ISIS Remnants in Iraq and Syria Compounds Misery', *CBS News*, 30 May 2019.
34 P. B. Johnston, M. Alami, C. P. Clarke, H. J. Shatz, 'Return and Expand? The Finances and Prospects of the Islamic State after the Caliphate', Rand Corporation, 2019.
35 'ISIS Spokesman Abu Muhammad Al-Adnani Calls on Supporters to Carry Out Terror Attacks in Europe, U.S.', Middle East Media Research Institute, 20 May 2016.

They should know that jihad is ongoing until the day of judgment.'[36] Baghdadi's dedicated forever terrorists do not define their apocalyptic terror movement strictly by the towns or provinces they control. They have reverted to shadow jihadists who think in transgenerational, millennial terms and believe they are fighting an endless war for Allah against 'fickle' Americans and their local 'stooges'. Having learned from the mistake of making themselves targets for bombing by Coalition aircraft by trying to defend the turf of a physical state and waging costly frontal war against a vast array of powerful international forces backed by unprecedented precision firepower, ISIS's remaining post-caliphate fighter terrorists have returned to the shadows. Clearly al Baghdadi's resilient fighters define the 2015–19 defeat of their state, but not their ideology, as a test of the faith, not a permanent setback. The self-proclaimed 'Caliph's' terrorist–warriors have transitioned from planting black flags of conquest and ruling millions to waging a shadow war of terroristic attrition that they now define as *nikayah* – a grinding campaign designed to wear down their less determined enemies.

The Islamic State insurgents considered the outbreak of coronavirus in the spring of 2020 to be in many ways a gift from Allah. As the pandemic killed thousands of Coalition members' citizens, several members withdrew their troops from Iraq and halted their Iraqi Army training programmes in order to protect their soldiers from the spread of COVID-19. At this time, the US withdrew from its front-line operating bases at Mosul, Al-Qaim, Qayyarah, Kirkuk and Taqaddum. Most US forces were redistributed inside fewer, better-protected Iraqi bases, such as Al-Asad and Erbil Airport, to protect them from both rocket attacks by newly antagonistic Shiite militias (who were incensed by the Trump administration's drone killing of the anti-ISIS Shiite Iranian Revolutionary Guard general Qassem Soleimani in January 2020 at Baghdad Airport) and to limit their interaction with potentially infected locals. ISIS insurgents were also aided by the fact that the American overwatch and ISR (intelligence, surveillance, reconnaissance) by drones and aircraft was drastically diminished as a result and they were able to move with greater freedom in the newly permissive, comparatively unmonitored environment. The emboldened Islamic State called for stepped-up operations to take advantage of all these events the insurgents saw as fortuitous (ironically, General Soleimani had been an effective leader in the war on ISIS). In northern Iraq, increasingly bold Islamic State fighters

---

36 J. Gambrell and Z. Karam, 'ISIS Leader Outlines Path Forward for His Group Post-caliphate', *AP News*, 1 May 2019.

launched brazen attacks, killing Kurdish Peshmerga fighters, Shiite militiamen, policemen, Iraqi troops and two American Marines as the pandemic weakened their enemies in early 2020. Even before the coronavirus outbreak, Trump had telegraphed his lack of interest in continuing counterterrorism operations in Iraq and Syria, which he dismissed as 'endless wars' in 'bloodstained sand'. His strategic drawdown/retrenchment from the Middle East has been accelerated since the outbreak of the pandemic and, in addition to consolidating their soldiers on to fewer bases, US Defense Department officials indicate that they hope to reduce the US troop presence in Iraq by half. This is all good news for the scattered Islamic state cells as they work to move out of their remote mountain/desert hideouts, where ironically they had been unintentionally practising extreme 'social distancing', and move to recapture the towns and populations they used to control.

Further Reading

F. A. Gerges, *ISIS: A History* (Princeton and Oxford, Princeton University Press, 2017)

W. McCants, *The ISIS Apocalypse: The History, Strategy, and Doomsday Vision of the Islamic State* (New York, St. Martin's Press, 2016)

T. E. Ricks, *Fiasco: The American Military Adventure in Iraq* (New York, Penguin Press, 2007)

B. G. Williams, *Counter Jihad: The American Military Experience in Afghanistan, Iraq and Syria* (Philadelphia, University of Pennsylvania Press, 2018)

B. Woodward, *Obama's Wars: The Inside Story* (New York, Simon & Schuster, 2011)

19

Transnational Connections
Militant Irish Republicans and the World

KIERAN MCCONAGHY

Introduction

The narrative around contemporary terrorism and political violence has emphasised its transnational character.[1] There has been a tendency to see this dimension of terrorism as something novel, rendering contemporary terrorist threats as more dangerous than those experienced in the past.[2] The idea of globally networked violent actors is frightening, and understandably excites public anxiety. Yet the overwhelming majority of terrorism has tended to be not only domestic, but local, conducted by individuals in the country where they normally reside, usually striking at targets close to their home.[3] Transnational connections do exist, of course, but rather than being

---

1 Terrorism is a polarising concept, frequently doing more to frustrate and obfuscate than to clarify and allow for dispassionate analysis. It is also a term which has been applied unequally throughout history, being used far less often for state violence and system-affirming violence than revolutionary violence. As Fearghal McGarry highlights in his contribution to this volume, for all but the most recent phase of the conflict in Ireland, the term 'terrorism' has tended not to be applied to violent actors in Ireland. Of the multifarious definitions of terrorism that exist, the one I find most convincing is the one provided by Richard English in an earlier publication: 'Terrorism involves heterogeneous violence used or threatened with a political aim; it can involve a variety of acts, of targets, and of actors; it possesses an important psychological dimension, producing terror or fear among a directly threatened group and also a wider implied audience in the hope of maximising political communication and achievement; it embodies the exerting and implementing of power, and the attempted redressing of power relations; it represents a subspecies of warfare, and as such it can form part of a wider campaign of violent and non-violent attempts at political leverage', R. English, *Terrorism: How to Respond* (Oxford, Oxford University Press, 2009), p. 24.
2 See, for example, O. Lynch and C. Ryder, 'Deadliness, Organisational Change and Suicide Attacks: Understanding the Assumptions Inherent in the Use of the Term "New Terrorism"', *Critical Studies on Terrorism* 5/2 (2012).
3 There is solid evidence to suggest that, despite public perception of terrorism as a transnational phenomenon, something that visits 'us' in the West from other countries, the overwhelming majority of terrorist attacks occur in the perpetrator's country of origin, and indeed usually happen close to the place where they live. A. B. Krueger

the defining feature of some 'new' terrorism, they have been a feature of violent political movements, since long before 11 September 2001. Indeed, they arguably date back to the emergence of terrorism itself as some phenomenon discernable from other forms of violent contestation.

The hazard of accepting the flimsy argument that globally networked terrorism is somehow new is not purely an academic one. Rather, mischaracterising contemporary terrorism as an unprecedented threat because of its transnational character creates an even graver hazard. It renders the conventional wisdom on state responses to terrorism as anachronistic and promotes policy blind to the hard-learned lessons of history.[4] The cost here, though unquantifiable, is to human life, to societal norms and to dearly held political values. Rather than being redundant, when attempting to make sense of powerful political movements and ideologies, history is needed now more than ever.

Ireland may seem like a strange choice for a study on transnational connections between violent actors. It would be tempting to think that the history of political strife in Ireland, being mostly nationalistic in character, bears little relevance to current debates on 'international terrorism'. Yet, despite Ireland's diminutive proportions, it has been politically, economically and culturally networked for millennia. Analysis of its frequent episodic civil unrest and campaigns of political violence uncover important links across the globe. A small body of literature has aimed to understand and explain the nature of the transnational connections between contemporary non-state actors using terrorism.[5] This chapter has two aims. It will assess the importance of transnational links to radical and violent non-state actors for Irish Republicanism. Further, through an analysis of the Irish case study, it aims to contribute to our understanding of such transnational links more generally.

suggests in *What Makes a Terrorist: Economics and the Roots of Terrorism* (Princeton, Princeton University Press, 2018) that in almost 90 per cent of cases, perpetrators of terrorist attacks conduct them in their own country. L. Smith, J. Cothren, P. Roberts and K. R. Damphouse, 'Geospatial Analysis of Terrorist Activities: The Identification of Spatial and Temporal Patterns of Preparatory Behaviour of International and Environmental Terrorists', US Department of Justice, 2008, shows that over half of both 'international' and 'environmental' terrorists conducting attacks in the USA lived within 30 miles of the target, with only a quarter living over 800 miles from the target (see pp. 79–80).

4 M. Crenshaw, *Explaining Terrorism: Causes, Processes and Consequences* (London, Routledge, 2011), p. 51.

5 See for example, B. J. Philipps, 'Terrorist Group Cooperation and Longevity', *International Studies Quarterly* 58/2 (2014); T. Bacon, *Why Terrorist Groups Form International Alliances* (Philadelphia, University of Pennsylvania Press, 2018); A. Moghadam, *Nexus of Global Jihad: Understanding Cooperation among Terrorist Actors* (New York, Columbia University Press, 2017).

Irish Republicanism's Transnational Origins

There had been contact between the Society of United Irishmen, founded in 1791, and their contemporaries in Europe and North America prior to the 1798 revolution. Indeed, military assistance had been promised by revolutionary France, but bad weather and bad planning stymied those efforts.[6] However, in the nineteenth century, Irish nationalism took on a transnational dimension.

Economic uncertainty, political unrest and the Great Irish Famine of 1845–9 created a massive Irish diaspora across Britain, North America and further afield. In 1851 alone, 221,000 Irish immigrants arrived in the United States of America.[7] The Fenian movement, a secret Irish nationalist revolutionary organisation, was founded in 1858. It was a transatlantic movement, having parallel bases and organisational structures (Clan na Gael in North America and the Irish Republican Brotherhood at home in Ireland) among the Irish diaspora in North America and in Ireland, and support among the Irish communities in Scotland and England.[8] The Fenians remained in existence until 1924, and were responsible for a failed rebellion in Ireland in 1867, and were one of the organisations (alongside the Irish Volunteers and Irish Citizen Army) that launched the Easter Rising in 1916.

In addition to these open insurrectionary attempts, in the latter half of the nineteenth century, they conducted a campaign of sporadic dynamite bombing attacks and assassinations against targets across Ireland and Britain. These attacks had more in common with the kinds of political violence being seen elsewhere at the time than they had with the prior efforts of Irish Republicans. This new departure for the Fenian movement was contemporaneous with unrest surrounding labour agitation and anarchist violence in Europe and North America, as well as assassinations by Russian nihilists. Fenian dynamite attacks were unequivocally 'propaganda of the deed'. The same macro-processes that had made anarchism possible had given rise to this type of transnational threat from Fenianism.[9] Compared to their Continental counterparts, the Fenians were less fully engaged in Europe's

---

6 A. T. Q. Stewart, *The Summer Soldiers: The 1798 Rebellion in Antrim and Down* (Belfast, Blackstaff Press, 1995), pp. 9–10.
7 D. Brundage, *Irish Nationalists in America: The Politics of Exile, 1798–1998* (Oxford, Oxford University Press, 2016), p. 88.
8 P. Bew, *Ireland: The Politics of Enmity 1789–2006* (Oxford, Oxford University Press, 2007), p. 245.
9 N. Whelehan, *The Dynamiters: Irish Nationalism and Political Violence in the Wider World, 1867–1900* (Cambridge, Cambridge University Press, 2012), pp. 3, 13.

radical causes.[10] Despite their reluctance to become fully involved in conspiratorial secret societies in Europe, there was much contact between individual Fenians living in Paris and Continental revolutionaries like Louis Auguste Blanqui, and the Carbonari, from whom they borrowed ideas and strategy.[11] Indeed, the Fenian leadership went as far as recruiting European revolutionaries Gustave Cluseret and Octave Fariola to help plan the 1867 Fenian Rising.[12]

The Irish Revolution and Transnational Connections

The Easter Rising in 1916 was an insurrection against British rule that resulted in partial independence for four-fifths of Ireland and the partition of the island into Northern Ireland and the Irish Free State. While its purpose was manifestly national, and nationalist, the revolutionary generation that led the Rising and the subsequent Irish War of Independence owed much to a maelstrom of experiences overseas and transnational influences. Of the leadership of the 1916 Rising, roughly 40–50 per cent had spent considerable periods of time living outside of Ireland.[13] By the beginning of the twentieth century, both radical and moderate sections of Irish nationalists filled the ranks of the Irish pro-Boer movement, the largest such movement in Europe. This included many who would go on to play important roles in the Irish Revolution. John McBride, who would be executed in 1916 for his role in the Easter Rising in Ireland, had led one of two Irish Brigades to fight for the Boers; Arthur Griffith, who would found Sinn Féin in 1905, had been a journalist in South Africa before the war and edited the vociferously pro-Boer *United Irishman*. Irish rebels active during the Irish revolution such as Michael Collins, Dan Breen and Liam Mellows had grown up hearing the stories of the heroic feats of Boer generals in their fight against the British Empire.[14] The difficulty that Britain experienced in suppressing the Boers demonstrated to a generation of Irish nationalists that resistance to the Empire was not

---

10 P. Hart, 'Fenians and International Revolutionary Tradition', in F. McGarry and J. McConnell (eds.), *The Black Hand of Republicanism: Fenianism in Modern Ireland* (Dublin, Irish Academic Press, 2009), p. 196.
11 Whelehan, *Dynamiters*, p. 42.   12 Ibid., p. 53.
13 T. Garvin, *Nationalist Revolutionaries in Ireland 1858–1928* (Oxford, Clarendon Press, 1987), p. 54.
14 D. Lowry, '"A Fellowship of Disaffection": Irish–South African Relations from the Anglo-Boer War to the *Pretoriastroika* 1902–1991', *Études Irlandaises* 17/2 (1992), p. 106.

necessarily futile.[15] Turning attentions to South Africa and the plight of the Boers against the common enemies made up for the apparent lack of advancement of progressive causes in Ireland in the years leading up to the Easter Rising of 1916.

The Irish revolution, beginning with the Easter Rising in 1916 and the eventual Irish War of Independence from 1919 to 1921 sent reverberations throughout the world. While the 1916 Rising was quickly crushed and the War of Independence achieved only partial success against the stated objectives of establishing an independent Irish Republic, it demonstrated the frailty of British Empire. Thus, the Irish revolution became a precedent and an important study for other fledgling nationalist movements that wanted to break the connection with Britain through violence.

The 1916 Rising had inspired a raid on an armoury in 1930 in Chittagong, in British India (now Bangladesh), the opening salvo in the Chittagong Uprising, and the group that formed in its aftermath adopted the name Indian Revolutionary Army, influenced by their Irish counterparts who called themselves the Irish Republican Army (IRA).[16] Dan Breen's *My Fight for Irish Freedom* became thoroughly studied by revolutionaries.[17] Works like Breen's were deemed to be having such influence in India that the authorities prohibited their dissemination, according to *An Phoblacht* in 1929.[18] In Bengal, nationalism took a particularly militaristic tone, drawing more from the vitriolic anti-British sentiment of some Irish nationalists than the more socialist movements elsewhere in India.[19] Tactics were adopted from texts on the revolution in Ireland, and one Bengali nationalist, Jatin Das, embarked on a hunger strike in 1929, following the precedent of the Republican mayor of Cork, Terence MacSwiney, who died on hunger strike in

---

15 F. McGarry, *The Rising – Ireland: Easter 1916* (Oxford, Oxford University Press, 2010), p. 37.
16 F. McGarry, '"A Land Beyond the Waves": Transnational Perspectives on Easter 1916', in N. Whelehan (ed.), *Transnational Perspectives on Modern Irish History* (New York, Routledge, 2014), p. 174; K. O'Malley, *Ireland, India and Empire* (Manchester, Manchester University Press, 2008), p. 10; M. Chatterjee, *Do and Die: The Chittagong Uprising 1930–34* (New Delhi, Picador, 1999), pp. 55–61.
17 Kalpana Dutt (1945), quoted in E. Hobsbawm, *The Age of Extremes: The Short Twentieth Century 1914–1991* (London, Abacus, 1995), p. 199. See also M. Silvestri, '"The Sinn Féin of India": Irish Nationalism and the Policing of Revolutionary Terrorism in Bengal', *The Journal of British Studies* 39/4 (2000), p. 471.
18 O'Malley, *Ireland, India and Empire*, p. 38.
19 M. Silvestri, *Ireland and India: Nationalism, Empire and Memory* (Basingstoke, Palgrave Macmillan, 2009), p. 59.

Brixton Prison in 1920.[20] For Indian revolutionaries, the Irish precedent bore an almost mythical symbolism as the archetype of anticolonial resistance.[21]

The successes of Irish revolutionaries also became a model and inspiration for various elements of the Jewish Underground in British Mandate Palestine. The differences between the social and political situations in Ireland of the 1910s and 1920s and British Mandate Palestine in the 1930s and 1940s are clear. As are the differences in character between the nationalist movements themselves.[22] Nonetheless, that a small, determined group of revolutionaries representing a minority view within the wider population could achieve some success against the British Empire helped to convince Zionist radicals that they could be successful. Members of Jewish underground groups The Stern Gang (Lehi) and the Irgun studied Irish rebels' victory over the superior military might of Britain.[23] Ze'ev Jabotinsky, leader of the Irgun, had travelled to Ireland, meeting Irish Volunteer and IRA gunrunner Robert Briscoe, to discuss drilling, training and strategy in fighting the British[24] and to 'learn all he could in order to form a physical force movement in Palestine on the same lines as the IRA'.[25]

The Post-war Era

There was sometimes opportunistic contact between the IRA and other groups internationally. In the 1950s, there were a number of contacts made between members of the IRA and members of the Cypriot guerrilla organisation EOKA (Ethniki Organosis Kyprion Agoniston), ironically through the British prison system. IRA members Seán MacStiofáin and Manus Canning were introduced to members of EOKA in Wormwood Scrubs in 1956, where the two sets of prisoners developed strong affinities and supported each other's protest actions. MacStiofáin, who would later be IRA Chief of Staff, dedicated time in prison to the study of the Greek Cypriot campaign of

---

20 Ibid., p. 61.   21 McGarry, 'A Land Beyond the Waves', p. 175.
22 J. Spyer, 'The Birth of the Idea of Revolt: The Irish Example and the Irgun Tzvai Leumi', in R. Miller (ed.), *Ireland and the Middle East: Trade, Society and Peace* (Dublin, Irish Academic Press, 2007), p. 45.
23 See, for example, D. A. Charters, 'Eyes of the Underground: Jewish Insurgent Intelligence in Palestine, 1945–57', *Intelligence and National Security* 13/4 (1998), pp. 170, 177; J. B. Bell, *The Secret Army: The IRA* (New Brunswick, NJ, Transaction, 2003), p. 149; Spyer, 'The Birth of the Idea of Revolt', p. 46.
24 A. Selth, 'Ireland and Insurgency: The Lessons of History', *Small Wars and Insurgencies* 2/2 (1991), p. 301.
25 Robert Briscoe, cited in Spyer, 'The Birth of the Idea of Revolt', p. 47.

guerrilla warfare, leaving prison having learnt about EOKA's strategy against the British in Cyprus.[26] Indeed, the affinity between EOKA and the IRA grew so strong in Wakefield Prison that EOKA prisoners were included in plans for IRA jailbreaks.[27] Cathal Goulding took part in one such plan, which was aborted before the jailbreak could take place, with weapons being dumped and the assembled IRA team escaping to safety in England.[28] When the Wakefield jailbreak eventually went ahead in 1959, only one IRA prisoner, Seamus Murphy, escaped, while his IRA comrades and EOKA member Nicos Sampson were left behind.[29] Outside of the confines of prison, some contact was made in London between EOKA and the IRA with a view to cooperating on matters of mutual concern, but despite friendly relations, the connection did not result in any practical cooperation at that point in time, and the lines of communication soon fell dormant.[30] What is clear, though, is that EOKA left its mark on the IRA strategy. One IRA document seized in 1967 cited the need to 'learn from the Cypriots and engage in terror tactics only',[31] and the lines of communication would be reactivated a decade later.[32]

The IRA campaigns of 1945–52 and 1956–62 had been abject failures, with the IRA announcing the cessation of the latter, blaming the Irish people for their lack of support. It left many in the organisation demoralised and searching for new ways to gain relevance. The study of other revolutions and guerrilla campaigns became important both in the search for strategic direction and also in order to galvanise the idea that their course of action was right and could succeed. In the 1950s and 1960s, Pan-Celticism held some currency within the Republican movement. IRA leader Seán MacStiofáin recounts in his memoirs the sense of fraternity and solidarity that he felt and and which was reciprocated by members of Celtic nationalist underground organisations from Wales, Scotland and Brittany.[33] The exact nature of relationships between Irish Republicans and like-minded groups in other Celtic nations is hard to establish. There were many tenuous connections and efforts to establish more formalised working relationships, though they

---

26 Selth, 'Ireland and Insurgency', pp. 311–12. See also S. MacStiofáin, *Memoirs of a Revolutionary* (London, Gordon Cremonesi, 1975), pp. 74–9.
27 S. Murphy, *Having It Away: A Story of Freedom, Friendship and IRA Jailbreak* (Bray, Castledermot Press, 2017).
28 B. Hanley and S. Millar, *The Lost Revolution: The Story of the Official IRA and the Workers' Party* (Dublin, Penguin, 2009), pp. 10–11.
29 Bell, *The Secret Army*, p. 317. 30 Ibid., p. 320.
31 Hanley and Millar, *The Lost Revolution*, p. 59.
32 S. Boyne, *Gunrunners: The Covert Arms Trail to Ireland* (Dublin, O'Brien Press, 2006), p. 170.
33 MacStiofáin, *Memoirs of a Revolutionary*, p. 53.

seldom proved to be strategically important. It appears that prison offered other networking opportunities, as Goulding and MacStiofáin appear to have spent some time incarcerated alongside Welsh militant nationalist Pedr Lewis.[34] In 1962, militant Welsh nationalist Emyr Llywelyn Jones, who would found the group Mudiad Amddiffyn Cymru (Movement for the Defence of Wales) the following year, made contact with IRA veteran Máirtín Ó Cadhain, but the IRA, having only just called off their 'Border Campaign', were almost a spent force and were unable or unwilling to assist.[35] Some members of another group, the Free Wales Army (FWA) came to Ireland to train with the IRA in 1966, and an FWA contingency took part in that year's Easter Commemoration, paying their respects to Irish Republicans who died in the 1916 Rising.[36] Plans were hatched for some joint operations, including an arms raid that would furnish both movements with fresh weaponry. The IRA hoped to secure gelignite from FWA stocks. Collaboration on a level beyond training, parading and expressions of solidarity proved difficult. In one incident, gelignite being moved by the IRA from Glasgow to Salford at the request of the FWA had to be dumped in a canal over fears that it was becoming unstable, attracting the attention of the police.[37] Later, the shifting priorities of the IRA under Chief of Staff Cathal Goulding saw him sell off arms to the FWA in 1966, feeling that class agitation and direct action on social issues rather than armed action ought to become the mainstay of the IRA.[38] The arms (which were mostly obsolete, giving a sense of the state of the IRA in general) soon fell into the hands of the British police.

The IRA Split and the Conflict in Northern Ireland

The 1960s brought a change in the character of radical politics right across Europe and beyond. While there had been leftist strains to many nationalist movements since the early twentieth century, the increasing prominence of radical analyses of geopolitics from the interwar period was leading to a more visible chasm between traditionalists and Marxists in the Breton, Irish, Welsh and Basque nationalist

---

[34] W. Thomas, *Hands Off Wales: Nationhood and Militancy* (Llandysul, Gomer Press, 2013), p. 224.

[35] Thomas, *Hands Off Wales*, p. 32. [36] Ibid., p. 112.

[37] Hanley and Millar, *The Lost Revolution*, pp. 49–50.

[38] R. English, *Armed Struggle: The History of the IRA* (London, Pan Books, 2012), p. 86. See also Boyne, *Gunrunners*, p. 17.

movements.[39] Inspired by the burgeoning national liberation movements in the Third World and later the student radicalism of 1968, European nationalist movements adopted a more leftist ideological basis for their objectives. This tension between traditionalists and more radical leftist interpretations of nationalism led to the formation of Basque nationalist group ETA in 1959,[40] and later fomented splits within that organisation.[41] The 'softs' of the Breton Front de libération de la Bretagne (FLB-ALB), allegedly operating from a base in Ireland, saw terroristic violence as purely symbolic, and wanted nothing to do with Soviet-style communism or socialist interpretations of their struggle, whereas the 'hards' based in Paris were more Marxist, rejected what they saw as the fascistic tendencies of traditional Breton nationalists and were hopeful that violent action would ignite the revolution they hoped would bring Breton independence.[42] Forming late in the mid-1970s, Corsican militant nationalist group FLNC (Fronte di liberazione naziunale corsu) hoped to rise above the question of ideology, committing itself to straightforward nationalism,[43] aiming to keep older nationalists who had been collaborationist during the Second World War and younger Marxists within the same movement.[44] While tensions caused by debates over ideology in Europe's nationalist movements resulted in splits and fragmentation, ideological rebranding and the rhetoric of anti-imperialism drove energised and politicised youth into radical nationalist movements.[45] The same energy that filled the ranks of the IRA and Basque militant nationalist group ETA (Euskadi ta Askatasuna) filled the ranks of leftist organisations like the Red Army Faction (RAF) in Germany.[46]

The leftward turn in the IRA, mirroring the radicalisation of politics globally, meant that there was now a greater emphasis on the Republican violence in Ireland as an anti-imperialist struggle. Of course, there had long been an identification in the Republican movement with those independence movements that sought to achieve their freedom from the common enemy of the British Empire, but the shift towards Marxism meant an identification with

---

39 M. Treacy, *The IRA 1956–69: Rethinking the Republic* (Manchester, Manchester University Press, 2011), p. 32.
40 L. Mees, *Nationalism, Violence, and Democracy: the Basque Clash of Identities* (Basingstoke, Palgrave Macmillan, 2003), pp. 26–7.
41 R. P. Clark, *Negotiating with ETA: Obstacles to Peace in the Basque Country, 1975–1988* (Reno, University of Nevada Press, 1990), p. 15.
42 J. E. Reece, *The Bretons Against France: Ethnic Minority Nationalism in Twentieth-Century Brittany* (Chapel Hill, University of North Carolina Press, 1977), pp. 202–4.
43 R. Ramsay, *The Corsican Time-Bomb* (Manchester, Manchester University Press, 1983), p. 118.
44 D. Reid, 'Colonizer and Colonized in the Corsican Political Imagination', *Radical History Review* 90 (2004), p. 119.
45 Treacy, *The IRA 1956–69*, p. 132.   46 Ibid.

a whole new range of struggles. The *United Irishman* newspaper of the Republican movement began to carry in-depth articles about the conflict in Palestine and Zambia, while still not neglecting to mention the Free Wales Army and the two Welsh patriots the Abergele martyrs, who had been killed by their own bomb on 30 June 1969, which they were planting to protest the investiture of Prince Charles as 'Prince of Wales'.[47] By the end of 1970, tensions over strategic direction (military action versus politics), over rival cliques and centres of gravity (Belfast versus Dublin) and over ideology (traditional nationalism versus Marxism) had split the Republican movement, both Sinn Féin and IRA, into Provisional and Official Republican movements.[48]

While the orthodox Marxism of the Official IRA left them ideologically pure after the split, their reanalysis of the conflict and reluctance to act as the defenders of Northern Ireland's Catholic population in the early 1970s, as they were besieged by loyalist violence and police inaction, saw them haemorrhage support to the more militant and less verbose Provisional IRA. Ideologically, the Provisionals were populist, attempting to ride two horses at once, criticising communism sharply in the wake of the split with the Officials, while critiquing the inequalities of free-market capitalism.[49] This placed them on the left, where they could benefit from the perception of being fighters in a global revolution and receive materiel from Muammar Gaddafi, while maintaining enough distance from communism and thus not alienating traditionalists in the movement or the Irish diaspora in America – an important source of funding and weaponry for both the PIRA and Provisional Sinn Féin. By the end of 1972, the Official IRA were on ceasefire for all but defensive actions.

Despite the (sometimes vitriolic) anti-communism of PIRA leaders like MacStiofáin and Sinn Féin leader Ruairí Ó Brádaigh, who were suspicious of international progressive movements, many in the movement recognised the importance of radical politics.[50] Following a vote at the 1973 Ard Fheis (Party Conference), Provisional Sinn Féin established an International Bureau in Brusssels in 1974. Through this office, headed by Richard Behal,

---

47 See, for example, *United Irishman* 23/6 (June 1969), p. 3 on Palestine, *United Irishman* 23/7 (July 1969), pp. 4–5 on Palestine and Zambia, and pp. 10–11 on the Free Wales Army.

48 For more on the specifics of the 1969–70 split in Irish Republicanism, see English, *Armed Struggle*, pp. 81–119; J. Morrison, *The Origins and Rise of Dissident Irish Republicanism: The Role and Impact of Organizational Splits* (London, Bloomsbury, 2013), pp. 39–83; Hanley and Millar, *The Lost Revolution*, pp. 108–48.

49 M. McKinley, 'Of "Alien Influences": Accounting and Discounting for the International Contacts of the Provisional Irish Republican Army', *Conflict Quarterly* 11/3 (1991), p. 24.

50 M. Frampton, '"Squaring the Circle": The Foreign Policy of Sinn Féin, 1983–1989', *Irish Political Studies* 19/2 (2004), p. 48.

the Republican movement would seek out connections with sympathetic movements in Europe and beyond.[51] The Provisional movement's newspaper *An Phoblacht* began to carry many more stories and articles on international struggles, often penned by Behal himself. The pages of *An Phoblacht* in the 1970s and 1980s were replete with dispatches from conflicts overseas where the parallels between the armed struggle in Ireland and wars of national liberation (both historical and contemporary) were drawn. A near full-page article in *An Phoblacht* in July 1972 discussed the origins and activities of the OAS (Organisation armée secrète) and FLN (Front de libération nationale) in Algeria, drawing a comparison between the OAS and Northern Ireland's Loyalist Vanguard movement, implying the impending victory of the Republican cause in Ireland.[52] Other articles expressed the similarity of ideology and unity of struggle with independence movements in Scotland, Wales, Brittany,[53] reported on Basque national day celebrations,[54] reported screenings and reviews of documentaries about the Tupamaros in Uruguay,[55] reports on the death of Steve Biko in apartheid South Africa, dispatches from Rhodesia (Zimbabwe) sympathetic to the Zimbabwe African National Union (ZANU) and likening perceived treachery to examples from the Irish Civil War.[56] International themes became ubiquitous in murals in Republican areas across Northern Ireland during the conflict. Rolston lists a vast array of murals around Belfast from the 1980s, 1990s and early 2000s that variously proclaim their support for Basque nationalism, the Palestinian Liberation Organisation (PLO) and Palestinian political prisoners, a Turkish hunger striker, the South-West African People's Organisation (SWAPO), the Sandinistas and the African National Congress (ANC), as well as murals venerating figures like Frederick Douglass, Malcolm X, Leonard Peltier, Yasser Arafat, Che Guevara and Martin Luther King, Jr.[57]

Despite the expressions of support for the Latin American leftist movements and Third World guerrilla from Africa to East Asia, there was very little if any practical cooperation between such movements and the IRA in the 1970s and 1980s beyond statements of solidarity. That is not to say that

---

51 R. White, *Ruairí Ó Brádaigh: The Life and Politics of an Irish Revolutionary* (Bloomington, Indiana University Press, 2006), p. 211.
52 M. Quilligan, 'Vanguard: Ghost of the OAS', *An Phoblacht*, July 1972, p. 11.
53 'Nationalism and Socialism', *An Phoblacht*, 7 May 1974, p. 5.
54 'Basque Easter Demonstration', *An Phoblacht*, 4 April 1975, p. 4.
55 'Tupamaros in Dublin', *An Phoblacht*, 5 July 1975, p. 6.   56 *An Phoblacht*, 13 May 1978, p. 8.
57 B. Rolston, '"The Brothers on the Walls": International Solidarity and Irish Political Murals', *Journal of Black Studies* 39/3 (2009), pp. 457–8.

they played no role or should be discounted as irrelevant. While the PIRA never commanded the support of the majority of the nationalist population during its armed campaign, it nonetheless relied on the support of Republican communities and the acquiescence of a section of nationalist society to survive. The shift in the centre of gravity in the Provisional Republican movement from Dublin to Belfast, and the rise of more socialist figures like Gerry Adams, who was to lead Sinn Féin from 1983 to 2018, also facilitated a shift to the left, and while Adams and others were still coy about calling themselves Marxists, the Republican movement was increasingly framed as the vanguard of the anti-imperialist struggle in Ireland.[58] This framing created a powerful discourse that galvanised support from outside the organisation. Further, it steeled the motivation of PIRA volunteers, who could derive satisfaction and determination now that their fight was painted as a struggle of global importance. Indeed, the idea of playing a part in a transnational revolutionary struggle offered solace to those PIRA members in prison often serving long sentences. Many PIRA prisoners read and discussed wars of national liberation both past and present. Bobby Sands, who would die in 1981 on hunger strike, was among the PIRA members in prison who read copious amounts of literature on revolutionary struggle. His time in the Maze Prison before embarking on hunger strike was marked by the reading of Frantz Fanon, Camilo Torres, Amilcar Cabral and George Jackson, alongside the revolutionary writings of Irishmen like James Connolly, Patrick Pearse and Liam Mellows.[59] For many PIRA prisoners, reading and discussing wars of national liberation both past and present was a key pastime while in prison.[60]

Reading the prison diaries of senior Provisional Republicans such as Danny Morrison demonstrates the importance that some within the movement

---

58 Frampton, 'Squaring the Circle', p. 52.
59 D. Beresford, *Ten Men Dead: The Story of the 1981 Hunger Strike* (London, Grafton, 1994), p. 60; P. O'Malley, *Biting at the Grave: The Irish Hunger Strike and the Politics of Despair* (Boston, MA, Beacon Press, 1990), p. 47.
60 See, for example, R. English, 'Left on the Shelf', *Fortnight* 338 (2000). See also B. Campbell, L. McKeown and F. O'Hagan, *Nor Meekly Serve My Time: The H-Block Struggle 1976–1981* (Belfast, Beyond the Pale, 1994). Kevin Campbell recounts discussion of how movements in Cuba, China and Vietnam were successful (Ibid., p. 75), and Eoghan McCormaic (with less nostalgia) describes how INLA prisoner Patsy O'Hara, who would die on hunger strike in 1981, wrote out a summary of *Firepower in Angola* to be read out to all prisoners on the wing (p. 142). This author was unable to find a publication under that name, but irrespective of the book's title, the anecdote shows that some Republican prisoners found following the exploits of revolutionary movements in the Third World to be a great source of strength, while others were less enthused.

gave to international struggles. He writes a few times about developments in Palestine and he follows Nicaragua closely and the fortunes of the Sandinistas, writing to Gerry Adams to discuss the implications of their struggle for the Irish Republican movement and how it might affect their strategy in the early 1990s, when the Republican movement was seeking a way to bring an end to the conflict.[61] Morrison's journal is also peppered with references to the fortunes of the ANC as Mandela is released from prison and later calls upon the British government to talk to the IRA. The enthusiasm with which the Provisional Republicans declared their support for the ANC was not reciprocated from the South African side prior to the early 1990s. As Richard Davis has highlighted, there was less to be gained in propaganda value by the ANC in statements of support for Irish Republicanism, which had been more violent than the ANC's Umkhonto we Sizwe (MK).[62] As the peace negotiations in Northern Ireland began to emerge, however, ANC senior figures would become important supporters of the process.

When the PIRA made practical connections, it was more frequently in the form of other ethno-nationalist groups. The PIRA attended a conference in 1973 in Tripoli, Libya at the invitation of Muammar Gaddafi, who would go on to become a substantial supporter and donor to the IRA. At this conference there were militant organisations from Palestine, Germany, Uruguay, Turkey and Japan.[63] However, the old linkages to the Greek Cypriot organisation EOKA proved to be important in the 1970s for establishing contact with the Palestinians later in that decade.[64] It was via this channel that contact was made to the Palestinian Liberation Organisation for the importation of arms in 1977, though the substantial load was eventually intercepted by authorities at Antwerp.[65] On other occasions it seems that the PLO used its

61 D. Morrison, *Then the Walls Came Down: A Prison Journal* (Cork, Mercier, 1999). See particularly pp. 24, 79, 85 for Morrison's views on the ANC and Nelson Mandela, pp. 30–1 and pp. 288–92 on the Sandinistas, and pp. 77, 142 on Palestine. Danny Morrison's collected opinion editorial pieces in local newspapers can be found in D. Morrison, *Rebel Columns* (Belfast, Beyond the Pale, 2004). Here Morrison writes a number of articles focusing on the personal and political journeys of key people in national liberation movements around the world.
62 R. Davis, *Mirror Hate* (Aldershot, Dartmouth Publishing, 1994), p. 280.
63 J. Biggs-Davison, *The Strategic Implications for the West of the International Links of the IRA in Ireland*, Foreign Affairs Research Institute 17 (1976), p. 4.
64 EOKA remained apparently unaware that an article in the Provisional Republican movement's Belfast-based newspaper *Republican News* had described Georgios Grivas, EOKA's leader, in uncharitable terms, calling him a 'rather unpleasant and arrogant old Fascist', Davis, *Mirror Hate*, p. 217, citing *Republican News*, 2 June 1973.
65 According to Sean Boyne, the load included 29 AK-47s, 29 French-made sub-machine guns, 7 RPG-7 rocket launchers and 60 grenades, 2 Bren guns, over 100 grenades, 11,000

connections to Europe's radical leftist militants such as the Red Brigades and Action Directe to secure the transfer of arms to Ireland for use by the Provisionals.[66] It has also been suggested that the IRA, like many left-leaning militant organisations worldwide, benefited from visits to PLO training camps, including ones in Libya and South Yemen in 1979, where the training and materiel was acquired that allowed the PIRA to kill Lord Louis Mountbatten in August of that year.[67]

Links to Basque nationalist group Euskadi ta Askatasuna (ETA) proved to be the most long-standing and fruitful relationship that the PIRA had to other militant groups abroad. In 1971, a declaration of solidarity was signed between ETA, IRA and the FLB,[68] being followed in 1972 – the peak of the conflict in Northern Ireland – by a statement of support for the IRA signed by twelve armed groups around the world that included the PLO and ETA,[69] and a further declaration of support from ETA in 1973.[70] ETA had given revolvers to the IRA in exchange for training in the use of gelignite in the 1960s,[71] and over the course of the 1970s and 1980s more weaponry was traded between the two groups. Sinn Féin leader Gerry Adams and other prominent Irish Republicans made a number of trips over the years to the Basque country.[72]

It was through the connection to ETA that the IRA established their links to Colombian Marxist guerrilla organisation Fuerzas Armadas Revolucionarias de Colombia (FARC, Revolutionary Armed Forces of Colombia). In August 2001 three Irish Republicans were arrested in Colombia at a time when the IRA were on ceasefire, leaving Sinn Féin with some awkward questions to answer back in Ireland.[73] It is widely

rounds of SLR ammunition and 36 kg of 9 mm ammunition, as well as almost 200 kg of explosives. See Boyne, *Gunrunners*, p. 171.

66 I. Geldard and K. Craig, *IRA, INLA Foreign Support and International Connections* (London, Institute for the Study of Terrorism, 1998), pp. 32, 46.
67 Y. Alexander, 'The European–Middle East Terrorist Connection', *International Journal of Comparative and Applied Criminal Justice* 13/2 (1989), p. 2. See also Geldard and Craig, *IRA, INLA Foreign Support and International Connections*, p. 69.
68 R. Alonso, 'The International Dimension of ETA's Terrorism and the Internationalization of the Conflict in the Basque Country', *Democracy and Security* 7/2 (2011), p. 187.
69 E. Karmon, *Coalitions Between Terrorist Organizations: Revolutionaries, Nationalists and Islamists* (Leiden, Martinus Nijhoff, 2005), p. 222; McKinley, 'Of "Alien Influences"', p. 19.
70 Alonso, 'The International Dimension', p. 187.
71 M. McGuire, *To Take Arms: My Year with the IRA Provisionals* (New York, Viking Press, 1973) p. 66.
72 A. Oppenheimer, *IRA, The Bombs and Bullets: A History of Deadly Ingenuity* (Dublin, Irish Academic Press, 2008), p. 98.
73 English, *Armed Struggle*, pp. 331–2.

believed that the three were IRA members, there to train FARC members in the deployment of improvised explosive devices.[74] Some mortar attacks in Colombia in 2002 that resembled IRA tactics appeared to confirm these suspicions.[75] What the IRA were receiving in exchange for the technology was mooted in the press and by the public. The debacle soured relationships between the US government and Sinn Féin, a relationship that had been important in securing the peace agreement thus far, as the arrests came to light not long before the Al Qaeda attacks of 11 September 2001 and the emergence of a new era for the USA where 'terrorism' was treated very differently than it had been in the past.[76] In 2010, evidence of a long-suspected collaborative relationship between ETA and FARC was found when an ETA training camp in Venezuela was discovered, from which they were training FARC guerrilla fighters.[77]

As well as seeking refuge in Latin America, a small number of ETA members and supporters were discovered living in Belfast, with the Spanish authorities attempting to have them extradited to Spain to stand trial.[78] Whether this is evidence of cooperation between the IRA and ETA or simply individuals seeking refuge from the Spanish authorities in a community that is sympathetic to their plight is difficult to discern, but nonetheless demonstrates the degree of affinity between radical Basque and Irish Republican movements, as carefully fostered by ETA and the IRA over the years.

The Provisional IRA used its international connections, both rhetorical and practical, for the duration of its campaign in order to galvanise support for its actions at home and abroad, to supplement its arms and explosives supply, and to fine-tune its ability to deploy them successfully. Given the difficulty in sustaining practical linkages between covert organisations, however, these connections were of limited use. A rearmament from Palestinian sources was a bonus, but it could not be relied on as a principal source of weaponry. Likewise, connections with ETA were important rhetorically, given their similar interpretations of battling against powerfully repressive imperial states, yet the connection proved only to be of tactical importance for the PIRA in some instances, rather than being a crucial strategic alliance.

---

74 Oppenheimer, *IRA, The Bombs and Bullets*, pp. 283, 347.
75 'IRA Technology in Mortar Attack – Colombia', *Irish Times*, 12 August 2002, www.irishtimes.com/news/ira-technology-in-mortar-attack-colombia-1.432828.
76 Oppenheimer, *IRA, The Bombs and Bullets*, p. 347.
77 V. Eccarius-Kelly, 'Surreptitious Lifelines: A Structural Analysis of the FARC and the PKK', *Terrorism and Political Violence* 24/2 (2012), p. 249.
78 Alonso, 'The International Dimension', p. 187. See also 'Suspected Member of ETA Arrested in Belfast City Centre', *Irish Times*, 26 June 2010, p. 4.

The amount of assistance that was received from allied militant groups abroad pales in comparison to the assistance from other sources. Libya's Muammar Gaddafi became an important sponsor for the Provisional Republican movement, transferring tonnes of arms and explosives to the IRA throughout the 1970s and 1980s worth millions of dollars.[79] Similarly, connections to organised crime syndicates in America, and to the wealthy Irish America diaspora there, proved to be a much more important resource for the IRA, providing a stream of guns and money from the late 1960s until the 1990s.

Republicans, Republican Socialists and the European New Left

Formed in 1974 as the result of a split in the Official IRA, the Irish National Liberation Army (INLA) and its political wing, the Irish Republican Socialist Party (IRSP), were more eager to establish and exploit a range of relationships with armed groups abroad. The hard left INLA were more vociferously committed to socialism than the PIRA, and more militant than the OIRA. In the early days of the movement, the leadership was keen to play up both the indigenous ideological underpinnings and its internationalism. It portrayed itself as the inheritors of a tradition from the pantheon of Irish Republican heroes like James Fintan Lalor, Michael Davitt and Patrick Pearse, using a party name which harked back to a similarly named one founded by James Connolly in 1896, while at the same time using names like the 'National Liberation Army' and 'People's Liberation Army' as cover names, and welcoming the advances of the Vietnamese against the Americans at their first Ard Fheis (party conference) in 1975.[80]

The political orientation of the INLA meant that it found itself with more in common with Europe's New Left than the Provisionals, and some links that had existed between the Official IRA and European radicals were soon taken over by the IRSP and INLA. Such contacts were not only about expressions of solidarity. The INLA lacked the domestic support base that the PIRA could boast, and its overt Marxism meant that it had little appeal to the variety of conservative groups in the Irish diaspora in America who funded the Provisional Republican movement.[81] Thus, the INLA was more

---

79 English, *Armed Struggle*, p. 249; E. Moloney, *A Secret History of the IRA* (London, Penguin, 2002), p. 328.
80 J. Holland and H. McDonald, *INLA: Deadly Divisions* (Dublin, Torc, 1994), pp. 38, 72.
81 See, for example, Boyne, *Gunrunners*, p. 327.

dependent on Continental connections and, through these European socialists, links with Palestinians based in Eastern Europe and the Middle East for the weaponry and resources.

Connections to Europe proved crucial when the under-armed INLA were quickly able to procure semi-automatic rifles from contacts in France in 1975 for use in a feud with the OIRA.[82] Members of the INLA had carried over some connections to the European radical political milieu from their time in the Official IRA and used these connections to good effect to build gun-smuggling operations with materiel supplied by both European leftists and Palestinian nationalists. Through engaging with wider radical political movements, the INLA made contact with members of the German far-left group Revolutionary Cells (RZ) members Rudolf Raab and Joachim Stemler, through which contact was made to the PLO for arms procurement purposes. Between 1977 and 1981, the PLO furnished the INLA with six shipments of arms that included hundreds of Czechoslovak pistols, Browning pistols and Chinese SKS rifles.[83] The INLA even benefited from the use of PLO safe houses in Eastern Europe, and key INLA members based themselves on the Continent, secreted among radical milieus in France and making numerous trips over land, at times as far away as Beirut and Baghdad, to secure weaponry and explosives from PLO contacts.[84]

The Red Army Faction followed developments in Ireland closely and frequently expressed solidarity with the Irish Republican cause, though more often expressing their support for the IRA than INLA. PIRA had few connections with armed groups in Europe's far left. While Sinn Féin kept in touch with the radical political movements in countries right across Western Europe, their armed wing were keen to give armed groups such as the Red Brigades and the Red Army Faction a wide berth. There was obvious ideological divergence with the European ultra-leftists, and they were seen by the PIRA as 'indulgent middle-class nihilists'. There was also the idea that the reckless violence of the RAF alienated people, turning them against armed violence when otherwise they might have been inclined to support the actions of the PIRA.[85] In May 1976, Ulrike Meinhof, one of the leaders of the first generation of the Red Army Faction, died from suicide in Stammheim Prison. Despite the inclination of the Provisional Republican movement to distance themselves from the RAF's actions so as not to be

---

82 Geldard and Craig, *IRA, INLA Foreign Support and International Connections*, p. 28.
83 Holland and McDonald, *INLA*, p. 130.   84 Ibid., p. 146.
85 P. Bishop and E. Mallie, *The Provisional IRA* (London, Heinemann, 1987), pp. 244–5; Davis, *Mirror Hate*, p. 291.

associated with adventurist violence, *An Phoblacht* nevertheless published an article marking Meinhof's death, declaring her death to be murder at the hands of the West German state, and expressing its sympathy, and highlighting the parallels with poor treatment in prisons in Ireland.[86]

The Irish Republican use of hunger strikes had made an impression on the RAF in the 1970s and 1980s, and was almost certainly the inspiration for their adoption of the tactic. The RAF expressed solidarity with the IRA prisoners in English and Irish prisons in a communiqué announcing the RAF's fourth hunger strike in 1977.[87] The Irish Republican hunger strike of 1981 coincided with a hunger strike in West Germany by RAF prisoners. The INLA's Patsy O'Hara, who would die after sixty-one days on strike, wrote a message to RAF prisoners stating simply:

> To achieve our aim, our hope for socialism, we cannot, I believe limit ourselves to our national boundaries. Our perspective is internationalist, that is the nature of socialism ... Together with the other INLA-IRSP prisoners on the blanket I send you the warmest greetings and I hope that your struggle will succeed without loss of life.[88]

The relatives of those in prison in West Germany replied expressing their solidarity and hope for a successful conclusion to the hunger strikes in Ireland. There were to be other overtures towards the INLA from the RAF. A document entitled 'International Combat: A Revolutionary Task' was circulated to the INLA in 1984, promoting the idea of a joint front between the organisations, though such a connection never emerged.[89] The death of O'Hara had made an impact on the RAF, who, ever keen to demonstrate their internationalism, had named one of their commando units after him – a move which appears to have irked rather than flattered the INLA, who felt that the reckless violence of the RAF was an ill-fitting tribute for their fallen comrade and hero.[90] Thus, despite the internationalist rhetoric of the INLA, it retained a central focus on the conflict in Ireland, and the

---

86 'The Murder of Ulrike Meinhof', *An Phoblacht*, 21 May 1976, p. 4.
87 L. Passmore, 'The Art of Hunger: Self-Starvation in the Red Army Faction', *German History* 27/1 (2009), p. 44. See also J. Smith and A. Moncourt, *The Red Army Faction: A Documentary History*, Vol. 1: *Projectiles for the People* (Oakland, CA, PM Press, 2009), pp. 488–9.
88 J. Smith and A. Moncourt, *The Red Army Faction: A Documentary History*, Vol. 2: *Dancing with Imperialism* (Oakland, CA, PM Press, 2013), pp. 259–61.
89 'International Combat: A Revolutionary Task – Red Army Faction Document Circulated to INLA Promoting the Idea of a Joint Front Circa 1984', LHL NIPC P14208.
90 Smith and Moncourt, *The Red Army Faction*, Vol. 2, pp. 259–61.

forging of contacts with European socialists remained very much a secondary interest for the group, and usually for the procurement of equipment.

International Connections and the Peace Process

Perhaps ironically given the anxiety expressed by policymakers and commentators surrounding the likely effects of transnational connections between armed groups as some sort of multiplier of terror, the Provisional Republican movement's global outlook assisted it in making the switch from war to peace.

From the early 1980s, it was apparent to the leadership of the Provisional Republican movement that they would be unable to achieve their strategic end goals through the use of 'armed struggle' alone. Instead, the movement began a process of changing strategy. First, the shift was to a dual strategy of violence and electoral politics in the mid-1980s, and a later shift to a 'tactical use of armed struggle' in 1994 before declaring a ceasefire later that year.[91] A lasting ceasefire was declared again in 1997 that allowed for Sinn Féin's involvement in multiparty talks, culminating in the Good Friday Agreement in 1998. By 2005, the PIRA had announced a permanent cessation of violence. Given the tendency over the preceding decades for the Republican movement to fracture, this was a process that was necessarily slow and painstaking.

In the early 1990s, when the most decisive steps were taken to secure a lasting peace and political settlement in Northern Ireland, it was of great advantage to the leaders of the Provisional Republican movement that both the ANC and the PLO had both recently made political breakthroughs. In South Africa, the fall of apartheid, the release of Nelson Mandela and his subsequent election as president gave the Republican Movement a role model and a precedent that they could emulate in their own shift to purely peaceful pursuit of their political goals. Similarly, the breakthrough in the Israel–Palestine peace process in 1993 meant that Yasser Arafat and the PLO, whom the Republican movement had long admired and vocally supported in the pages of their newspaper and elsewhere, were elevated to hero status for delivering peace, rather than for delivering their strategic end goals.[92] Decades-long, intractable conflicts around the world appeared to be entering

---

91 The TUAS document is reproduced in M. Cox, A. Guelke and F. Stephen (eds.), *A Farewell to Arms? From 'Long War' to Long Peace in Northern Ireland* (Manchester, Manchester University Press, 2000), appendix 6.
92 B. O'Brien, *The Long War: The IRA and Sinn Féin 1985 to Today* (Dublin, O'Brien Press, 1993), p. 27.

a denouement. The continuation of a conflict in Ireland that looked unwinnable was increasingly seen as an embarrassment.[93]

During the peace negotiations in Northern Ireland, elements of a deal secured by the ANC in South Africa became the model for Sinn Féin,[94] despite the obvious divergence in their experiences, and Sinn Féin made some gestural steps, such as appealing to the UN and EC in a strategy document which appeared to emulate the ANC and PLO before them.[95] Later in the process, the engagement of ANC figures like Sathyandranath Maharaj and Cyril Ramaphosa at key junctures provided the Irish Republican movement with advice from movements they could trust as allies proved crucial to overcoming stalemate.[96] In May 1997, for example, a three-day conference was hosted by the South African government in Arniston, Western Cape. It assembled the chief negotiators of Northern Ireland's political parties, including David Trimble of the Ulster Unionist Party and Sinn Féin's deputy leader and former IRA commander Martin McGuinness. At the conference, Mandela warned Northern Ireland's political elite with an anecdote of the South African negotiations years earlier, and how their negotiations continued through deadlock because of the spectre of a return to bloodshed.[97] The conference was regarded positively by all Northern Ireland's political leaders, but for McGuinness in particular, seeing the reconciliation between former bitter enemies in South Africa first-hand convinced him that an agreement could be reached in Ireland.[98]

The eventual peace agreement was signed on Good Friday 1998 and ratified thereafter by referenda in Northern Ireland and the Republic of Ireland. As part of the peace deal, the PIRA and other paramilitary organisations were to decommission their weapons, not in surrender to the British government, but to a newly established Independent International Commission for Decommissioning. Cyril Ramaphosa of the ANC played a key role alongside Finnish Martti Ahtisaari, inspecting IRA arms dumps and writing a series of annual reports on their findings.[99]

Beyond Northern Ireland, the paramilitary ceasefires and the positivity generated by the peace process, along with attendant electoral boost for Sinn

---

[93] White, *Ruairí Ó Brádaigh*, p. 323.   [94] O'Brien, *The Long War*, p. 242.
[95] Ibid., p. 226.   [96] English, *Armed Struggle*, pp. 329–31.
[97] P. O'Malley, 'Northern Ireland and South Africa: "Hope and History at a Crossroads"', in J. McGarry (ed.), *Northern Ireland and the Divided World: Post-Agreement Northern Ireland in Comparative Perspective* (Oxford, Oxford University Press, 2001), p. 276.
[98] M. McGuinness, *Weekly Mail and Guardian*, 19 September 1997, quoted in P. O'Malley, 'Northern Ireland and South Africa', p. 300.
[99] Boyne, *Gunrunners*, p. 400.

Féin, made them serious electoral players. The peace process may not have delivered a united Ireland, but it nonetheless turned the Irish Republican movement into role models for war-weary guerrilla movements seeking to disarm and demobilise while retaining political relevance and credibility. While the IRA ceasefire in 1997 and the Good Friday Agreement of 1998 secured peace and the potential of Sinn Féin as a serious political player, it stopped well short of securing a united Ireland. Nevertheless, the positivity surrounding the Good Friday Agreement and the emergent political institutions provided a boost and precedent for other nationalist movements seeking ways out of violent conflict.[100] Basque nationalists interpreted the deal that Irish Republicans had secured as something for ETA and their political representatives in Batasuna to emulate. There were celebrations and slogans chanted in the Basque Country in 1998 when the Good Friday Agreement was signed, urging that the Basque country must be next.[101] From the late 1990s until 2012, Sinn Féin played an important role in the search for a peaceful conclusion to the Basque conflict. Though the differences between ETA and the IRA and, indeed, the conflicts in Ireland and the Basque Country were multifarious, Gerry Adams and other senior Irish Republicans facilitated dialogue and urged progress among the Basque nationalist left that included ETA, speaking with the legitimacy of their own conflict and peace process.[102]

Senior Sinn Féin personnel would play critical roles in facilitating and persuading other armed movements to search for peaceful conclusions to their campaigns. President of Sinn Féin Gerry Adams would also act as a go-between with Israel and Hamas while his second in command, former IRA commander Martin McGuinness, travelled to Sri Lanka, where he urged the Tamil Tigers to end their war.[103]

Conclusions

How might we characterise the connections of militant Irish Republicanism with other violent groups globally? The links that Irish Republican groups forged were first and foremost powerful in terms of the cross-pollination of ideas, and the galvanising effect brought on by a sense of belonging to

---

100 J. Loughlin and F. Letamendía, 'Lessons for Northern Ireland: Peace in the Basque Country and Corsica?', *Irish Studies in International Affairs* 11 (2000), p. 149.
101 Oppenheimer, *IRA, The Bombs and Bullets*, p. 98.
102 T. Whitfield, *Endgame for ETA: Elusive Peace in the Basque Country* (London, Hurst, 2013), p. 162.
103 Moloney, *A Secret History of the IRA*, p. 585.

a powerful global movement. The propaganda value of belonging to a transnational struggle against empire and oppression outweighed the impact of material connections or physical assistance in the Irish context. These effects were bidirectional, with Irish Republican exploits providing morale and encouraging radical political movements abroad, just as Irish Republicans were inspired by the revolutionaries they idolised and emulated.

Where concrete relationships existed with like-minded organisations abroad, these tended to be fruitful primarily for the acquisition of weapons and materiel, in exchange for money, training or goodwill. The PIRA had more productive channels from which it could acquire weaponry, namely through sympathetic Irish Americans, criminal gangs and the sponsorship of Libya's Muammar Gaddafi. Trading arms with other paramilitary groups overseas who were also fighting their own covert campaigns was more precarious and, in the long term, less productive. Such connections for the exchange of materiel did prove to be strategically important on some specific occasions. For example, the PIRA's acquisition of materiel from ETA that would allow them to engage in the highly symbolic process of decommissioning while retaining firepower and the likely provision of training to the FARC in exchange for either money, materiel or training opportunities that would have allowed the PIRA to retain its relevance would both have been tactically advantageous to the PIRA had they not been discovered. That they were discovered at a time when the PIRA and Sinn Féin were supposed to be committed to a permanent ceasefire demonstrates well the precarity of such arrangements and the associated risk.

Less prosperous than the PIRA, the INLA relied more heavily on connections to armed groups in Europe and the Middle East for weaponry. It is difficult to judge what percentage of INLA arms came from such sources, but there is little doubt that it afforded them the ability to continue an armed campaign that would have been difficult to effect otherwise, including providing the materiel for some of their most impactful attacks. Nonetheless, despite their global connections, the INLA remained smaller and less dangerous than the PIRA, save for a single year, when they were responsible for a greater number of casualties than the PIRA. While the INLA retained connections to Western Europe and the Middle East, they were semi-detached from the close kinds of cooperation that groups like Action Directe shared with the Red Army Faction, and there was no real effort by either the IRA or INLA to mount campaigns of collaborative attacks with their foreign allies.

Assessing the connections between Irish Republicans and armed groups abroad has necessitated a partial view of the ecosystem that sustained these movements. Armed actors have frequently had connections to trade union movements, political parties, diaspora associations, organised crime networks and of course states around the world. Only if taken together with the geographical community can we understand the transnational networks that precipitate, sustain and influence armed groups. Global connections, sponsors, allies and allegiances are the subject of much secrecy, speculation and deliberate misdirection on the part of paramilitary organisations and on the part of states that have sought to deter and disrupt them. Furthermore, Republican paramilitaries were not the sole protagonists in the conflicts on the island of Ireland that have spanned the twentieth century and lingered into the twenty-first. While loyalist paramilitaries in Northern Ireland have tended to be seen as more isolated and independent than Republicanism, their links to sympathetic movements globally demand further scrutiny.

What does the Irish case tell us about connections between armed groups more generally? Despite the assertions of some commentators during the Cold War that international terrorism was directed by the Soviet Union, it is clear from the Irish case that connections to allies overseas were organic, often serendipitous and frequently less productive than one could expect had there been an international terrorist conspiracy. Links can and do exist between organisations with apparently incompatible world views. Thus, such links should not be taken as evidence of ideological or strategic consensus. Our case study has also shown that groups have been keen to aggrandise the extent and importance of their transnational connections for propaganda purposes, and that we ought to be critical in evaluating the depth and importance of these connections rather than taking them at face value. Additionally, contrary to the contemporary perception that transnational connections make armed groups more dangerous, sometimes transnational connections were crucial for helping groups find pathways to peace. There was no domino effect leading organically from peace in South Africa, to the Middle East and then to Europe. Rather, where precipitous conditions existed, fraternal links to credible movements which could be emulated in peace as in war proved useful. The involvement of former violent actors in peace processes as official observers and arbitrators may have been difficult for governments and other stakeholders to stomach, but ultimately it imbued these processes with legitimacy and generated trust that would have been difficult to recreate otherwise. Most obviously, but most importantly, our Irish example demonstrates that global links between violent actors are not a recent development, but a long-standing one. As such, transnational connections between violent actors should provoke nuanced analysis rather than superficial sensationalism.

Further Reading

M. Frampton, '"Squaring the Circle": The Foreign Policy of Sinn Féin, 1983–1989', *Irish Political Studies* 19/2 (2004)

F. McGarry, '"A Land Beyond the Wave": Transnational Perspectives on Easter 1916', in N. Whelehan (ed.), *Transnational Perspectives on Modern Irish History* (London, Routledge, 2014)

M. McKinley, 'Of "Alien Influences": Accounting and Discounting for the International Contacts of the Provisional Irish Republican Army', *Conflict Quarterly* 11/3 (1991)

M. Silvestri, 'The Sinn Féin of India': Irish Nationalism and the Policing of Revolutionary Terrorism in Bengal', *The Journal of British Studies* 39/4 (2000)

N. Whelehan, *The Dynamiters: Irish Nationalism and Political Violence in the Wider World, 1867–1900* (Cambridge, Cambridge University Press, 2012)

PART IV

★

THEMATIC ESSAYS

20

'September 12 Thinking'
The Missing Histories of Counterterrorism

STEVE HEWITT

History and terrorism enjoy an intimately adverse relationship.[1] Terrorism has occurred for thousands of years, and in more modern forms since the nineteenth century. Despite this reality, the perception remains in some of the dominant scholarship that terrorism of the present or recent past, or aspects of it, represents something 'new'.[2] More generally, there is an anti-historical predisposition, not only among some academics but also within the ranks of counterterrorism professionals and even the wider public, to view terrorism as a problem uniquely of the twenty-first century.[3] Not surprisingly, many of these same attitudes coalesce around counterterrorism, the focus of this piece.

Undoubtedly, such attitudes reflect wider cultural trends in which 'short-termism' dominates, particularly in the political sphere.[4] A further

---

1 Terrorism in this chapter is taken to be violence or the threat of violence by non-state actors (as opposed to state terrorism) against non-combatants for ideological (including religious and racist motivations) and/or political purposes.
2 I. Duyvesteyn, 'How New Is the New Terrorism?', *Studies in Conflict and Terrorism* 27/4 (2004), p. 440; I. Duyvesteyn, 'The Role of History and Continuity', in M. Ranstorp (ed.), *Mapping Terrorism Research: State of the Art, Gaps and Future Direction* (London, Routledge, 2006), p. 52; I. O. Lesser, B. Hoffman, J. Arquilla, D. Ronfeldt and M. Zanini, *Countering the New Terrorism* (Santa Monica, RAND, 1999); W. Laqueur, *The New Terrorism: Fanaticism and the Arms of Mass Destruction* (Oxford, Oxford University Press, 1999). For a defence of 'new terrorism', see E. N. Kurtulus, 'The "New Terrorism" and Its Critics', *Studies in Conflict and Terrorism* 34/6 (2011). For more on the history of terrorism, see G. Chaliand and A. Blin, 'The Invention of Modern Terror', in A. Blin and G. Chaliand (eds.), *The History of Terrorism: From Antiquity to Al Qaeda* (Berkeley, University of California Press, 2007), p. 95; R. D. Law, *Terrorism: A History* (Cambridge, Polity Press, 2009 [Kindle edition]), locations 1932–40.
3 J. Evans, 'Academic Research and the Intelligence Community: Some Reflections', in E. Chenoweth, R. English, A. Gofas and S. N. Kalyvas (eds.), *The Oxford Handbook of Terrorism* (Oxford, Oxford University Press, 2019), p. 697; G. Aisch and A. Parlapiano, 'What Do You Think Is the Most Important Problem Facing This Country Today?', *New York Times*, 27 February 2017, www.nytimes.com/interactive/2017/02/27/us/politics/most-important-problem-gallup-polling-question.html.
4 J. Guldi and D. Armitage, *The History Manifesto* (Cambridge, Cambridge University Press, 2014), p. 2.

contributor is the prevalence of social media and twenty-four-hour news channels in the twenty-first century wherein terrorism exists as an ongoing menace, including in the minds of the public, even as it has declined, at least in Western Europe and the United States, from levels during the 1970s and 1980s.[5] Terrorism killed more people in Western Europe in the 1970s and 1980s, for example, than in Western Europe since the attacks of 11 September 2001 (hereafter 9/11).[6] That total included Italy, where, between 1969 and 1982, far-left and far-right terrorists carried out thousands of attacks that killed 351 and wounded 768.[7] In the United States, the single worst year in terms of the number of terrorist attacks between 1970 and 2019 was, in fact, 1970, although these attacks did not equate to the high loss of life experienced in Oklahoma City in 1995 or in Washington, DC, New York City and Pennsylvania in 2001.[8]

In the case of scholarship, there is an entwined problem. In recent decades, social scientists, mainly political scientists, have dominated writing about terrorism after a beginning in the 1970s that involved a cohort composed of scholars and non-scholars from diverse backgrounds.[9] A 2004 Andrew Silke survey documented the disparities. He catalogued that almost half of authors who published articles in major terrorism journals in the 1990s were political scientists. In contrast, historians popped up on Silke's list in sixth place, the equivalent of 4.2 per cent, or less than a tenth of the total number of political scientists.[10] Furthermore, he found that 13 articles out of a total of 490 that appeared in two significant terrorism journals related to 'non-contemporary

---

5 A. Nellis and J. Savage, 'Does Watching the News Affect Fear of Terrorism? The Importance of Media Exposure on Terrorism Fear', *Crime and Delinquency* 58 (2012); J. Mueller and M. G. Stewart, 'Public Opinion and Counterterrorism Policy', Cato Institute White Paper, 20 February 2018, www.cato.org/publications/whitepaper/public-opinion-counterterrorism-policy.
6 E. Luxton, 'Is Terrorism in Europe at a Historical High?', *World Economic Forum*, 24 March 2016, www.weforum.org/agenda/2016/03/terrorism-in-europe-at-historical-high/.
7 L. Weinberg, 'The Red Brigades', in R. J. Art and L. Richardson (eds.), *Democracy and Counterterrorism: Lessons from the Past* (Washington, DC, United States Institute of Peace, 2007), pp. 26–7.
8 B. Plumer, 'Nine Facts about Terrorism in the United States since 9/11', *Washington Post*, 11 September 2013, www.washingtonpost.com/news/wonk/wp/2013/09/11/nine-facts-about-terrorism-in-the-united-states-since-911/?utm_term=.c5091389aebe.
9 L. Stampnitzky, *Disciplining Terror: How Experts Invented 'Terrorism'* (Cambridge, Cambridge University Press, 2013), pp. 40–3.
10 A. Silke, 'The Road Less Travelled: Recent Trends in Terrorism Research', in A. Silke (ed.), *Research on Terrorism: Trends, Achievements, and Failures* (London, Frank Cass 2004), p. 193.

terrorism'.[11] These disparities have fuelled or reinforced critiques of terrorism studies, particularly from Critical Terrorism Studies (CTS) adherents, who warn, 'much terrorism research tends towards ahistoricity and acontextuality'.[12] However, it has not only been CTS scholars who have noted and critiqued the domination of certain disciplines when it comes to writing about terrorism. In *Terrorism: A History*, Randall D. Law warns that

> the domination of any field of interest by any one discipline produces certain distorting effects. The study of terrorism is an excellent case in point. 'Terrorism studies' within academia and the broader debates about terrorism and counter-terrorism raging in our society today have been dominated by social scientists, journalists, policy experts, and political pundits.[13]

He attributes this 'domination' to the post-Cold War period combined with 9/11 creating the overwhelming impression that terrorism is exclusively a contemporary issue. Hence, the focus of governments on the perceived threat of terrorism played into an emphasis on social scientists and an approach that Lee Jarvis labels as a 'problem-solving enterprise'.[14] Part of the momentum towards ignoring or downplaying the longer history of terrorism involved the assessment, which 9/11 seemed to endorse emphatically, that a 'new terrorism' associated with religion emerged in the 1980s and 1990s.[15] In that context, terrorism's lengthy past, much to the chagrin of long-time terrorism scholars such as Martha Crenshaw and others, was deemed insignificant.[16] More broad, and perhaps controversial, is the view that history as an academic discipline itself has yielded ground in terms of relevancy by an increasing preoccupation with researching shorter time frames, in the process abandoning expansive work, and a suspicion by

---

11 A. Silke, as quoted in M. Ranstorp, 'Introduction: Mapping Terrorism Research – Challenges and Priorities', in M. Ranstorp (ed.), *Mapping Terrorism Research: State of the Art, Gaps and Future Direction* (London, Routledge, 2006), p. 12.
12 R. Jackson, J. Gunning and M. Breen Smith, 'The Case for a Critical Terrorism Studies', paper presented to the American Political Science Association, 2007, p. 5, http://cadair.aber.ac.uk/dspace/bitstream/handle/2160/1945/APSA-2007-Paper-final2.pdf?sequence=1&isAllowed=y.
13 Law, *Terrorism*, locations 317–20.
14 Ibid., locations 317–24; L. Jarvis, 'The Spaces and Faces of Critical Terrorism Studies', *Security Dialogue* 40/1 (February 2009), p. 7; K. E. Brown, 'Blinded by the Explosion? Security and Resistance in Muslim Women's Suicide Terrorism', in L. Sjoberg and C. Gentry (eds.), *Women, Gender, and Terrorism* (Athens, University of Georgia Press, 2011), p. 197.
15 Laqueur, *The New Terrorism*; Lesser et al., *Countering the New Terrorism*.
16 Stampnitzky, *Disciplining Terror*, pp. 160–2.

some of working with state interests that mitigates against the exploration of solutions.[17]

Despite these pitfalls, scholarship about terrorism has evolved in the fifteen years since the emergence of Silke's study, which itself was documenting the landscape in the 1990s. Although it had already appeared when Silke was producing his survey, political scientist David Rapoport's 'four waves of modern terrorism' theory provides a historical context and approach (along with considerable fodder for classroom discussions) to some major terrorism trends since the final quarter of the nineteenth century. His interpretation has sparked challenges; these include a proposal of different historical periodisations and alternative theoretical frameworks through Nick Sitter and Tom Parker's 'strains' model that argues for greater continuity in the history of modern terrorism by putting forward a contagion approach connecting the development of terrorism in the past and present.[18] Historical scholarship, even if written by non-historians, also contests the notion that an era of 'new terrorism' began in the 1990s. The best examples here are Isabelle Duyvesteyn's article 'How New Is the New Terrorism?' and Lisa Stampnitzky's book *Disciplining Terror*. Marc Sageman has waded in to praise historical research because of its access to primary source material as an exception to what he perceives as a general malaise in Terrorism Studies in which 'academics understand everything but know nothing, while government analysts know everything but understand nothing'.[19]

Finally, several major historical surveys have appeared since 2009. Law's aforementioned book offers a wide-ranging academic examination of the history of terrorism. There is also popular historian Michael Burleigh's *Blood and Rage: A Cultural History of Terrorism*, which provides a more polemical take. Martin Miller's *The Foundations of Modern Terrorism* attempts to address core issues around definitions and accusations of politicisation by finding a model that incorporates both state and non-state violence by not privileging one over the other.[20]

---

17 Guldi and Armitage, *The History Manifesto*, pp. 8, 42, 45–8.
18 D. C. Rapoport, 'The Four Waves of Modern Terrorism', in A. Kurth Cronin and J. M. Ludes (eds.), *Attacking Terrorism: Elements of a Grand Strategy* (Washington, DC, Georgetown University Press, 2004), pp. 46–73; T. Parker and N. Sitter, 'The Four Horsemen of Terrorism: It's Not Waves, It's Strains', *Terrorism and Political Violence* 28/2 (2016); M. Sedgwick, 'Al-Qaeda and the Nature of Religious Terrorism', *Terrorism and Political Violence* 16/4 (2004). And see Rapoport's response to the 'strains' theory: D. C. Rapoport, 'It Is Waves, Not Strains', *Terrorism and Political Violence* 28/2 (2016).
19 M. Sageman, 'The Stagnation in Terrorism Research', *Terrorism and Political Violence* 26/4 (2014), p. 571; M. Sageman, *Misunderstanding Terrorism* (Philadelphia, University of Pennsylvania, 2016 [Kindle edition]), p. 20.
20 Law, *Terrorism*; M. Burleigh, *Blood and Rage: A Cultural History of Terrorism* (London, Harper Perennial, 2009); M. Miller, *The Foundations of Modern Terrorism* (Cambridge, Cambridge University Press, 2012).

The Missing Histories of Counterterrorism

In several respects, history is at the forefront of terrorism scholarship through challenging the domination of the social sciences and conventional wisdoms of the present that do not hold up to scrutiny once historicised. Moreover, historical research frequently accomplishes this by accessing a rich supply of primary source material that is more readily available than contemporary records because the passage of time has rendered it less sensitive.[21] Despite these factors, there remains a broader impression, especially among governments, that terrorism's past has little relevance to its present, hence the placing of resources into contemporary social science research instead of into the historicising of terrorism.[22]

Some of the problems identified with terrorism scholarship are even more relevant to the focus of this paper: the history of and historical scholarship on counterterrorism.[23] Here the issues identified in the paper's discussion of historical scholarship on terrorism appear especially pertinent. There are no grand historical studies of counterterrorism to parallel the monographs of Law, Miller and others. Nor are there similar broad explanatory models in relation to the historical evolution of counterterrorism comparable to Rapoport's 'four waves'. A 2006 reflection negatively contrasted counterterrorism scholarship in general in comparison to the work on terrorism.[24] The history of counterterrorism is the poorer cousin of the already impoverished cousin that is the history of terrorism. This chapter will focus on the reasons for that. A key explanation relates to an ongoing lack of access to primary sources. Another is the wider security environment in which other priorities, such as espionage and subversion during the Cold War, dominated relevant agencies, rendering counterterrorism a secondary pursuit, leading to scholarship that reflected similar emphases. Then there is the notion that counterterrorism is reactive, in that its historical evolution mirrors that of terrorism, so addressing the latter covers both topics simultaneously. Finally, there is the perception that the history of counterterrorism and terrorism is

---

21 Sageman, 'The Stagnation in Terrorism Research', p. 571.
22 D. K. Gupta, 'Terrorism, History and Historians: A View from a Social Scientist', *Journal of American History* 98 (June 2011), p. 96; Law, *Terrorism*, locations 320–4, 327–8. For a practical example, there is the Government of Canada's Kanishka initiative, named after the Air India airplane destroyed in a 1985 terrorist attack. Over the five rounds that the programme ran, only three of thirty-seven (8 per cent) grants awarded had any historical element, and one of those was for a project covering the post-2001 period. 'Kanishka Project', Public Safety Canada, www.publicsafety.gc.ca/cnt/n tnl-scrt/cntr-trrrsm/r-nd-flght-182/knshk/index-eng.aspx.
23 Ranstorp, drawing on Alex Schmid, provides a useful depiction of what constitutes the 'various elements of counterterrorism policies', Ranstorp, 'Introduction', p. 16.
24 Ibid., p. 15.

not worth examining because it offers no insights into responses to terrorism in the present. Jonathan Evans, the Director General of the British Security Service (MI5) from 2007 to 2013, in a reflection on the relationship between academia and counterterrorism, listed a 'range of disciplines that have been useful since 9/11' to battling terrorism, including international relations and epidemiology. Conversely, he added,

> there are wide areas of terrorism studies that are at best marginal so far as actual counterterrorism is concerned. I cannot remember much discussion of the definition of terrorism in the twenty-five years I spent working on counterterrorism, very little on history beyond the shortest of timescales, and virtually none at all on gender.[25]

In contrast to the notion of history lacking relevance to the current world of terrorism and counterterrorism, continuity might simultaneously account for the lack of attention paid to detailed histories of counterterrorism but equally why such histories are so important. My key argument is that counterterrorism issues and methods displayed in the present exist in the past as well – not as simplistic reproductions but with enduring similarities that are near enough to demonstrate parallels and continuity and yet variance, all of which are worthy of examination and reflection upon. These comprise the utilisation of human sources and difficulties associated with their deployment, including their reliability, the ethics around their usage, particularly in connection to agents provocateurs but similarly the targeting of certain communities for widespread infiltration, particularly through 'fishing expeditions'. These activities involve covert human sources, or 'mosque crawlers' as the New York Police Department called them, targeting specific communities in the hope of stumbling across relevant information.[26] There are other germane counterterrorism issues in the past and present around the 'politicisation' of terrorism and where the balance needs to be struck between civil liberties, human rights and security, including through the policing of diverse populations. This intersects with debates over counterterrorism tactics that go too far, particularly the use of violence by the state. Although the organisations involved in front-line counterterrorism in the present are clearly more expansive, complex and varied in the sense of the involvement of a range of agencies and thus a broader, sometimes even

---

25 Evans, 'Academic Research and the Intelligence Community', p. 697.
26 A. Goldman and M. Apuzzo, 'With Cameras, Informants, NYPD Eyed Mosques', *Associated Press*, 23 February 2012, www.ap.org/ap-in-the-news/2012/with-cameras-informants-nypd-eyed-mosques.

holistic, approach to the problem of terrorism, this does not obstruct the basics around methods and issues. This contribution will not be so crude as to suggest that there are 'lessons to be learned' from the history of counterterrorism. Rather, there are important parallels and similarities in responses to modern terrorism from the nineteenth to the twenty-first century that deserve more attention instead of being relegated to irrelevancy. Essentially, I argue that, if seeking to apply an analogous model to the 'waves' or 'strains' history of terrorism to counterterrorism, the latter approach would have the most relevance, because of its thematic and continuity-rich nature.

It is equally true that well-rounded histories of terrorism include state responses through counterterrorism as an important component of the wider story, since the two often have an intertwined trajectory, a point Magnus Ranstorp reiterates and which Martha Crenshaw has reflected on: '[f]ollowing the introduction of counterterrorism, subsequent generations are in part reacting to government approaches'.[27] Two excellent examples of this approach are Richard English's *Armed Struggle* and Richard Bach Jensen's *The Battle Against Anarchist Terrorism*.[28] Both deal with the interplay between the terrorists and the counterterrorists, and in the process shed light on both sides of the relationship. With English, there is repeated recognition of the impact of informers and intelligence more broadly for the British state on 'anti-state rebels' including the Irish Republican Army.[29] In turn, Jensen across his work on the history of state efforts against anarchist terrorists demonstrates indirectly the parallels around responses to transnational terrorism through attempts at broad cooperation, be it in the early twentieth century or 100 years later. The international conferences organised in the aftermath of the killing of several prominent public figures, most notably American President William McKinley in 1901, by anarchist terrorists were the most prominent example of this trend. Jensen's work usefully documents both the attempts and failures at intelligence cooperation, such as an unwillingness to share information that led intelligence agencies to recruit informants and spies even in allied countries, thus undermining efforts to counteract transnational terrorist threats.[30]

---

27 Ranstorp, 'Introduction', p. 15; M. Crenshaw, as quoted in S. Vertigans, *The Sociology of Terrorism: People, Places, and Processes* (London, Routledge, 2011), p. 74.
28 R. Bach Jensen, *The Battle Against Anarchist Terrorism: An International History, 1878–1934* (Cambridge, Cambridge University Press, 2013); R. English, *Armed Struggle: A History of the IRA* (London, Macmillan, 2003 [Kindle edition]).
29 English, *Armed Struggle*, locations 5535, 6146.
30 R. Bach Jensen, 'The Pre-1914 Anarchist "Lone Wolf" Terrorist and Governmental Responses', *Terrorism and Political Violence* 26/1 (2014); R. Bach Jensen, 'Anarchist Terrorism and Global Diasporas, 1878–1914', *Terrorism and Political Violence* 27/3 (2015).

Other scholarship does address counterterrorism in a historical context explicitly, but not always centrally. An example of this approach is Hillel Cohen's study of Israeli security forces and Palestinians before 1967.[31] Another is Bernard Porter's analysis of the Metropolitan Police's Special Branch before the First World War, which focuses heavily on its counterterrorism operations against both Fenians and anarchists.[32] Elsewhere, Laura K. Donohue provides a detailed examination of the evolution of counterterrorism law in the United Kingdom in relation to Ireland across much of the twentieth century.[33] In more contemporary fashion and in relation to the technology of counterterrorism, Christopher J. Fuller offers a history of the drone programme of the Central Intelligence Agency (CIA), a weapon that would be used to kill alleged terrorists after 9/11.[34]

Additionally, in a United Kingdom context, there are pieces that demonstrate the lack of centrality of counterterrorism within the burgeoning British Cold War security state. The first ever authorised history of the Secret Intelligence Service (MI6), by historian Keith Jeffery, offers little on the role of MI6 in counterterrorism, but that absence ably demonstrates the dominance of the Cold War and anti-communism in the realm of British security priorities.[35] Christopher Andrew's authorised history of MI5 contains considerably more material on counterterrorism than Jeffery, particularly because his work covers a broader and later time period, but, as with the study of MI6, it is not the essential focus. Nevertheless, Andrew's book, with its treasure trove of primary source material that he was able to draw upon in his role as a producer of an official history, is useful for what it reveals about the methods deployed in counterterrorism operations by MI5. These include the importance of informants, the domination of the Cold War after the Second World War in connection to security priorities, the emergence of non-Ireland-related counterterrorism in the 1970s, the prescient pessimism of senior Security Service members about the ability to stop terrorist attacks,

---

31 H. Cohen (trans. H. Watzman), *Good Arabs: The Israeli Security Agencies and the Israeli Arabs, 1948–1967* (Berkeley, University of California Press, 2010).
32 B. Porter, *The Origins of the Vigilant State: The London Metropolitan Police Special Branch Before the First World War* (London, Weidenfeld and Nicolson, 1987).
33 L. K. Donohue, *Counter-terrorist Law and Emergency Powers in the United Kingdom, 1922–2000* (Newbridge, Irish Academic Press, 2001). For a more contemporary take on counterterrorism law by the same author, see L. K. Donohue, *The Cost of Counterterrorism: Power, Politics, and Liberty* (Cambridge, Cambridge University Press, 2008).
34 C. J. Fuller, *See It/Shoot It: The Secret History of the CIA's Lethal Drone Program* (New Haven, Yale University Press, 2017).
35 K. Jeffery, *MI6: The History of the Secret Intelligence Service, 1909–1949* (London, Bloomsbury, 2010), pp. 109–10.

and the interaction of MI5 with other domestic counterterrorism agencies, specifically Special Branch. Although seemingly providing a new focus, the emergence of non-Ireland-related counterterrorism in the 1970s as a permanent feature was still heavily grounded within the Cold War environment: it was based within MI5's existing countersubversion branch until the 1980s.[36] This placement reflected wider attitudes evident in both the United Kingdom military and United States security agencies (and in comparable institutions in other nations) that lacked precise definitions of terrorism or which viewed terrorism as an element of subversion and/or insurgency.[37] Indeed, the head of one Western intelligence agency admitted in a public speech in 1974 that 'international terrorism like aggression or subversion, is not a precise concept which lends itself to definition . . . [there] is no internationally-accepted (*sic*) definitions of international terrorism'.[38] One of Andrew's research assistants for his book on MI5, Calder Walton, subsequently wrote his own history of MI5 efforts at home and abroad during the declining days of the British Empire. Among those duties were counterterrorism operations against the threat posed by Zionist terrorism, chiefly from Irgun and Lehi, and terrorism in Cyprus through EOKA.[39]

Smaller in number are those books that focus exclusively on the history of counterterrorism. Timothy Naftali's *Blind Spot: The Secret History of American Counterterrorism* began as an internal history for the 9/11 Commission of the early post-Second World War period of American counterterrorism. Overall, the book, although not an 'official history' in a British sense, features considerable cooperation from key American figures as it offers an extremely useful, if at times overly institutional and narrative-driven, history of the evolution of American counterterrorism. Somewhat problematically, Naftali begins the story after the Second World War and thus misses earlier American efforts to address the problem of 'international terrorism' in the

---

36 C. Andrew, *The Defence of the Realm: The Authorized History of MI5* (London, Penguin, 2009), pp. 350–64, 600–26.
37 F. Kitson, *Low Intensity Operations: Subversion, Insurgency and Peacekeeping* (London, Faber & Faber, 2013 [Kindle Edition] [1971]), locations 594, 1605; T. Naftali, *Blind Spot: The Secret History of American Counterterrorism* (New York, Basic Books, 2009 [Kindle edition]), location 26; L. Stampnitzky, *Disciplining Terror: How Experts Invented 'Terrorism'* (Cambridge, Cambridge University Press, 2013 [Kindle Edition]), locations 128–47; S. Hewitt, 'Cold War Counter-Terrorism: The Evolution of International Counter-Terrorism in the RCMP Security Service, 1972–1984', *Intelligence and National Security* 33/1 (2018), p. 76.
38 M. Dare, Director General of the RCMP Security Service, as quoted in Hewitt, 'Cold War Counter-Terrorism', p. 69.
39 C. Walton, *Empire of Secrets: British Intelligence, the Cold War and the Twilight of Empire* (New York, The Overlook Press, 2013 [Kindle edition]), locations 1790–2618, 6527.

early twentieth century.⁴⁰ In a similar vein to Naftali, although not in relation to the prominence of his narrative style, is Amy Zegart's *Spying Blind: The CIA, the FBI, and the Origins of 9/11*. In this comparative organisational examination of the Central Intelligence Agency (CIA) and the Federal Bureau of Investigation (FBI) in the context of their respective failures to stop the 9/11 attacks, Zegart connects some of the fiasco and institutional dysfunction to the individual and shared histories of the two American organisations.⁴¹

Transnational counterterrorism comparisons with varying degrees of historical content do exist. In *Democracy and Counterterrorism: Lessons from the Past*, editors Robert J. Art and Louise Richardson assembled a series of case studies by various scholars looking at post-1960s examples along national lines with an emphasis on a variety of responses to terrorism, including legislative and judicial.⁴² The book's style resembled a post-9/11 equivalent of Alex P. Schmid and Ronald D. Crelinsten's *Western Responses to Terrorism*, an edited collection that examined Western European experiences of and responses to terrorism in the 1968–93 period.⁴³

A similar comparative effort, albeit on a smaller and less historical scale, was produced by Peter Chalk and William Rosenau. Their work assesses counterterrorism in the UK, Canada, France and Australia, although the historical aspect of their study represents only brief overviews of the longer background in the four liberal-democratic states.⁴⁴ More ambitious is Frank Foley's comparative and detailed study of British and French counterterrorism, which includes important historical context, albeit in a contemporary sense, as his work delves back only to the 1990s.⁴⁵

A key text on counterterrorism more generally is Ronald Crelinsten's *Counterterrorism*. Although he does not engage in an explicit discussion of

---

40 Naftali, *Blind Spot*, location 162.
41 A. B. Zegart, *Spying Blind: The CIA, the FBI, and the Origins of 9/11* (Princeton, Princeton University Press, 2007). See also Zegart's earlier work on the CIA, A. B. Zegart, *Flawed by Design: The Evolution of the CIA, JCS and NSC* (Stanford, Stanford University Press, 1999).
42 R. J. Art and L. Richardson, 'Introduction', in R. J. Art and L. Richardson (eds.), *Democracy and Counterterrorism: Lessons from the Past* (Washington, DC, United States Institute of Peace Press, 2007), pp. 16–17.
43 A. P. Schmid and R. D. Crelinsten (eds.), *Western Responses to Terrorism* (London, Frank Cass, 1993).
44 P. Chalk and W. Rosenau, *Confronting the 'Enemy Within': Security Intelligence, the Police, and Counterterrorism in Four Democracies* (Washington, DC, Rand Corporation, 2004).
45 F. Foley, *Countering Terrorism in Britain and France: Institutions, Norms and the Shadow of the Past* (Cambridge, Cambridge University Press, 2013 [Kindle Edition]), locations 6998–7001.

the history of counterterrorism, implicit in his argument is the absence of history when discussing counterterrorism. Crelinsten contends that the two key models of counterterrorism are the 'law enforcement model' and the 'war model'. The former, as its name suggests, prioritises a traditional legal and law-enforcement approach that views terrorism as a type of criminal activity and responds to it accordingly. In contrast, the 'war model' emphasises military action, viewing terrorism as an act of war. Crelinsten remarks on the problematic discourse that emerged after the attacks of 11 September 2001, which argued that pre-9/11 counterterrorism treated terrorism as a law enforcement matter in contrast to the militaristic approach after 9/11. He notes that this interpretation parallels the 'old' versus 'new' terrorism dichotomy. This depiction of 'September 10 thinking', he adds, 'is an invention of "September 12 thinking" – a kind of projection which creates a straw man to argue with and criticize. They are two sides of the same coin, which represents narrow, conceptual models that distort the nature of the phenomenon to be dealt with and limit policy options.'[46]

Finally, there are occasional memoirs by professionals with some experience in counterterrorism. Stella Rimington, former Director General of MI5, provides considerable insight into the emergence of non-Ireland-related counterterrorism as a permanent function within the Security Service in the 1970s.[47] Former FBI counterterrorism agent Ali Soufan details the efforts against al-Qaeda, particularly in the lead-up to 9/11.[48] Robert Baer, Melissa Boyle Mahle, Jose A. Rodriguez and various other former CIA agents have all published books reflecting their different experiences of counterterrorism both before and after 9/11.[49]

Despite individual reflections by practitioners in post-retirement publications, there appears to be a lack of detailed engagement by security agencies and states, at least in public terms, with the history of terrorism and counterterrorism; one sign of this is the repeating or proposing of tactics, such as

---

46 R. Crelinsten, *Counterterrorism* (Cambridge, Polity Press, 2009), p. 9.
47 S. Rimington, *Open Secret: The Autobiography of the Former Director-General of MI5* (London, Arrow Books, 2002 [Kindle edition]), locations 1825–33.
48 A. Soufan, with D. Freedman, *The Black Banners: Inside the Hunt for Al-Qaeda* (New York, Allen Lane, 2011).
49 R. Baer, *See No Evil: The True Story of a Ground Soldier in the CIA's War on Terrorism* (New York, Arrow, 2002); D. R. Clarridge, *A Spy For All Seasons: My Life in the CIA* (New York, Scribner, 2002); M. Boyle Mahle, *Denial and Deception: An Insider's View of the CIA* (New York, Nation Books, 2004); G. C. Schroen, *First In: How Seven CIA Officers Opened the War on Terror in Afghanistan* (Novato, Presidio Press, 2005); P. Mudd, *Takedown: Inside the Hunt for Al Qaeda* (Philadelphia, University of Pennsylvania Press, 2013); J. A. Rodriguez, Jr., with B. Harlow, *Hard Measures: How Aggressive CIA Actions after 9/11 Saved American Lives* (New York, Threshold Editions, 2013).

torture and internment, either previously discredited or with complex and conflicting historical records.[50] In contrast, a number of terrorists have been keen students of certain aspects of history. Examples of terrorists examining past practices for inspiration and on other occasions for information, and sometimes for both, abound and frequently appear in the literature. A well-known example is Yitzhak Shamir, who took on the pseudonym 'Michael' while a member of the Zionist terrorist group Lehi as a tribute to Irish nationalist Michael Collins.[51] Another Zionist terrorist, Menachem Begin, looked to the Irish Republican Army and Russian extremist groups for a model for his own terrorist group, Irgun. In turn, al-Qaeda took interest in Begin's memoirs.[52] The leadership of the Provisional Irish Republican Army (PIRA) examined anticolonial struggles and the work of Frantz Fanon for relevant inspiration and ideas.[53] Sitter and Parker offer a myriad of other examples of groups and individuals seeking to learn from previous campaigns and organisations, such as Fatah learning from the Front de liberation nationale campaign in Algeria and Sayyid Qutb, inspirer of future faith-claimed terrorists, advising followers to look to Lehi and Irgun.[54]

Likewise, terrorists, as Martha Crenshaw suggests, learn from and react to counterterrorist tactics, such as the risk of having organisations infiltrated by agents of the state. This is evident in Johann Most's famous 'how to' guide, *The Science of Revolutionary Warfare*, which he published originally in German in 1883. The manual includes specific advice to those thinking of engaging in violence, such as how to protect information and what to do if arrested and interrogated.[55] It can be seen in more modern examples, as well, such as the

---

50 B. Myers, 'The Secret Origins of the CIA's Torture Program and the Forgotten Man Who Tried to Expose It', *The Nation*, 1 June 2015, www.thenation.com/article/secret-origins-cias-torture-program-and-forgotten-man-who-tried-expose-it/; J. Scott, 'Internment: Could It Help Fight Terrorism?', *BBC News*, 30 May 2017, www.bbc.co.uk/news/uk-40084280; English, *Armed Struggle*, locations 3040–55; S. Newbery, *Interrogation, Intelligence and Security: The Origins and Effects of Controversial British Techniques* (Manchester, Manchester University Press, 2015).
51 Burleigh, *Blood and Rage*, locations 1994–8; M. Sedgwick, 'Inspiration and the Origins of Global Waves of Terrorism', *Studies in Conflict and Terrorism* 30/2 (2007).
52 Law, *Terrorism*, locations 3666–9.   53 Ibid., locations 4783–5.
54 Parker and Sitter, 'The Four Horsemen of Terrorism: It's Not Waves, It's Strains', pp. 200–1.
55 J. Most, *Revolutionäre Kriegswissenschaft: Eine Handbüchlein zur Anleitung betreffend Gebrauches und Herstellung von Nitro-Glycerin, Dynamit, Schiessbaumwolle, Knallquecksilber, Bomben, Brandsätzen, Giften usw., usw.* (New York, Internationaler Zeitung-Verein, c.1883); J. Most, *Science of Revolutionary Warfare: A Little Handbook of Instruction in the Use and Preparation of Nitroglycerine, Dynamite, Gun-Cotton, Fulminating Mercury, Bombs, Fuses, Poisons, Etc.* (El Dorado, Desert Publications, 1978 [English translation]), pp. 58–61.

adaptability and innovation of the IRA in the late 1970s that even impressed British intelligence.[56]

Crelinsten's point about the interpretation of the history of responses to terrorism after 9/11 and the general absence of the historical context in his otherwise strong book illustrates the need for greater engagement with counterterrorism in the past. One explanation for the lack of historical writing about counterterrorism in its own right reinforces Sageman's critique of the wider field of Terrorism Studies, in that the primary source material can be lacking not because it does not exist but rather as it is restricted due to its perceived sensitivity. Writing about responses through police and intelligence agencies and the wider state, then, can be even more difficult than writing about terrorism itself. Whereas terrorism is regularly viewed as an aberration and outside of the pattern of normal conduct and, in the case of specific groups, potentially no longer an active threat as the result of them being destroyed or abandoning their campaigns, counterterrorism is different. Here considerable consistency exists, despite perceptions to the contrary, not only pertaining to agencies, including police forces and intelligence organisations that have participated in the counterterrorism milieu across human lifetimes, but, more explicitly, with the methods they use. Sensitivity around informants often does not wither with time, leading to records from decades or even more than a century earlier being kept completely closed or restricted. Other records can end up destroyed or kept out of archives completely because of their perceived sensitivity.[57]

There are several explanations for states and state agencies imposing restrictions on accessing primary source material despite the passage of considerable periods of time. There is, for instance, a reluctance on the part of security agencies to divulge a variety of counterterrorism methods and operations, even from much earlier time periods (and I have seen this firsthand in archives in Canada and the United Kingdom – it is less true in the United States). When it comes to human intelligence sources, part of the rationale for the lack of transparency is to ensure the safety of informants and their families, including those no longer active, out of concern that they might still face retribution years after their work. Such fears are not

---

56 L. Richardson, 'Britain and the IRA', in Art and Richardson (eds.), *Democracy and Counterterrorism*, p. 71.
57 I. Cobain and R. Norton-Taylor, 'Sins of Colonialists Lay Concealed for Decades in Secret Archive', *The Guardian*, 18 April 2012, www.theguardian.com/uk/2012/apr/18/sins-colonialists-concealed-secret-archive; I. Cobain, *The History Thieves: Secrets, Lies and the Shaping of a Modern Nation* (London, Portobello Books, 2017).

necessarily irrational, as exemplified by the case of Denis Donaldson, a senior member of the PIRA, who was revealed in 2005 to have been a British informant. In 2006, the Real IRA murdered him in retaliation.[58]

However, the reluctance to reveal records is not just about the safety of retired informants. It is also about future recruitment, as informants frequently wish, because of the unsavouriness often associated with the practice, to keep their work on behalf of the state perpetually secret. Additional openness might equate with increased difficulty in future recruitment.[59] Whatever the reason, restricted access to counterterrorism records for researchers will not disappear anytime soon.

The point about informants has dual applicability to the writing of the history of counterterrorism: while the previous reliance on informants by state agencies may hinder access to records, the use of human intelligence in counterterrorism connects the past to the present. This remains the situation despite the increased importance of technology as an intelligence gathering tool. Human intelligence, or Covert Human Intelligence Sources (CHIS), its official state label in the United Kingdom, encompasses not just informants whom agencies recruit within groups or who infiltrate them from the outside, but also applies to undercover police officers and intelligence agents who target terrorist groups.[60]

The deployment of CHIS abounds across the history of modern terrorism from the first rise of organised terrorist groups in the nineteenth century to the present. Their use was significant in Russia with Yevno Azev, an informant for the Okhrana, the Russian secret police, who by the early twentieth century was in charge of the terrorist wing of the Socialist Revolutionary Party.[61] He was the most prominent Russian example of what amounted to as many as 200 CHIS in 1899 and up to 500 by 1903 who were working on behalf of the Russian state within anarchist and socialist groups.[62] Even earlier than this, the British used CHIS to target Fenians from the 1860s onward on both sides of the Atlantic. In North America, the Fenians, many of

---

58 'D. Donaldson: Man to be Charged with MI5 Agent's Murder', *BBC News*, 3 July 2019, www.bbc.co.uk/news/uk-northern-ireland-48858481.
59 C. Sethna and S. Hewitt, *Just Watch Us: RCMP Surveillance of the Women's Liberation Movement in Cold War Canada* (Montreal, McGill-Queen's University Press, 2018), p. 173.
60 'Covert Surveillance and Covert Human Intelligence Sources Codes of Practice', Home Office, 10 December 2014, www.gov.uk/government/publications/covert-surveillance-and-covert-human-intelligence-sources-codes-of-practice.
61 S. Hewitt, *Snitch! A History of the Modern Intelligence Informer* (London, Continuum, 2010).
62 R. Bach Jensen, 'The Secret Agent, International Policing, and Anarchist Terrorism: 1900–1914', *Terrorism and Political Violence* 29/4 (2017), p. 738.

them US Civil War veterans, sought to capture British North America, after 1867 in the form of Canada, so as to barter for the freedom of Ireland. Here the British deployed Henri Le Caron and others as informants across several decades.[63] CHIS provided such detailed insight into Fenian plans that Le Caron advised that the issue for the authorities was whether to allow an attack to take place and crush it in the process or to do a pre-emptive strike and thus prevent future assaults.[64]

The use of CHIS continued across Rapoport's 'four waves'. In the initial anarchist wave, the work of Richard Bach Jensen provides insight into use of informants against anarchists in the late nineteenth and early twentieth centuries. He compares and contrasts the practices of the Special Irish Branch, which had as many as eighty-five informants targeting anarchists between 1888 and 1912 and achieved considerable success at generating actionable intelligence, with less successful operations of comparable agencies in Italy. This came down to handler practices, he argues, with meeting the needs of informants and their families translating into superior-quality intelligence. In contrast, the Italian unwillingness to pay decent salaries to informants led to the production of weak intelligence.[65] In the second terrorism wave, MI5 utilised informants to great success against Zionist groups. In turn, across the second and third waves, Israeli security forces have extensively used informants to undermine Palestinian organisations and to aid in targeted killings.[66] Informants and undercover police officers were deployed against the Weather Underground or wider New Left protest, two of whom wrote accounts of their experiences.[67] Canadian police used informants against the Front de libération du Québec (FLQ), with one prominent example producing a memoir about her undercover work.[68] Finally, security bodies in a number of countries have used informants and undercover police against Islamist terrorist organisations or cells in a number of countries,

---

63 H. Le Caron, *Twenty-Five Years in the Secret Service* (London, E. P. Publishing, 1893).
64 G. S. Kealey, *Spying on Canadians: The Royal Canadian Mounted Police Security Service and the Origins of the Long Cold War* (Toronto, University of Toronto Press, 2017), pp. 27–30.
65 Jensen, 'The Secret Agent, International Policing, and Anarchist Terrorism', pp. 736–7, 757.
66 Andrew, *The Defence of the Realm*, pp. 350–64; Cohen, *Good Arabs*; R. Bergman, *Rise and Kill First: The Secret History of Israel's Targeted Assassinations* (New York, John Murray, 2018).
67 L. Grathwohl and F. Reagan, *Bringing Down America: An FBI Informer with the Weathermen* (New Rochelle, Arlington House Publishers, 1976); W. Tulio Divale and J. Joseph, *I Lived Inside the Campus Revolution* (New York, NY Cowles Book Company, 1970).
68 C. de Vault, with W. Johnson, *The Informer: Confessions of an Ex-Terrorist* (Toronto, Fleet Books, 1982).

despite a perception that such organisations could not be infiltrated through such means;[69] several have written reminiscences about their infiltration activities.[70]

The relevance of the history of counterterrorism around CHIS extends beyond their simple use to a wider significance around the power of what they represent. This connects to their impact on targeted communities via the simple process of recruitment but also through disruption tactics carried out by agents provocateurs. Collectively, the wider significance connects to a broader pattern of the securitisation of specific communities often defined by specific characteristics such as ethnicity or religion.[71] This has emerged in the post-2001 world around the treatment of Muslim communities in a number of countries, including the United States and the United Kingdom. Their targeting by counterterrorism policies, including informants and collective profiling, has prompted criticism, allegations of Islamophobia and even lawsuits.[72] Yet, again, these matters emerged as part of counter-terrorism practices in earlier periods. In the twenty-first century, the label 'suspect community' has been applied to Muslim communities but, of course, the concept was created by Paddy Hillyard to describe the treatment of Irish communities in Great Britain during The Troubles.[73] Moreover, the targeting of entire populations emerged somewhat earlier in locales such as Algeria, where French counterterrorism affected the wider Muslim populace in response to terrorism by the Front de libération nationale (FLN).[74]

The danger of overreacting and stigmatising entire populations through counterterrorist methods has emerged as part of the discourse around the post-9/11 approach to terrorism. These and other issues associated with the

69 R. M. Gerecht, 'The Counterterrorist Myth', *The Atlantic*, July/August 2001, www.theatlantic.com/magazine/archive/2001/07/the-counterterrorist-myth/302263/.
70 See, for example, O. Nasiri, *Inside the Jihad: My Life with Al Qaeda, a Spy's Story* (New York, Basic Books, 2006); A. Speckhard and M. Shaikh, *Undercover Jihadi: Inside the Toronto 18 – Al Qaeda Inspired, Homegrown Terrorism in the West* (McLean, Advance Press, 2014); A. Dean and P. Cruikshank, *Nine Lives: My Time as MI6's Top Spy Inside Al-Qaeda* (Oxford, Oneworld Publications, 2018).
71 F. Vultee, 'Securitization: A New Approach to the Framing of the "War on Terror"', *Journalism Practice* 4/1 (2010).
72 A. Kundnani, *The Muslims Are Coming! Islamophobia, Extremism, and the Domestic War on Terror* (London, Verso Books, 2015).
73 P. Hillyard, *Suspect Community: People's Experience of the Prevention of Terrorism Acts in Britain* (London, Pluto Press, 1993). For a critique of the concept, including its application to Muslim communities, see S. Greer, 'Anti-Terrorist Laws and the United Kingdom's "Suspect Muslim Community": A Reply to Pantazis and Pemberton', *British Journal of Criminology* 50/6 (2010).
74 A. Horne, *A Savage War of Peace: Algeria, 1954–1962*, 3rd ed. (London, Pan Macmillan, 2012).

twenty-first century and the 'War on Terror' were evident to some involved in counterterrorism in previous eras as well. Witness this list of counterterrorism issues compiled by the Royal Canadian Mounted Police (RCMP) in a report prepared for and presented to the Canadian government of Prime Minister Pierre Trudeau in the early 1980s after Armenian nationalists murdered a Turkish military attaché in Ottawa:

(i) limited manpower resources, which necessitates the prioritization of targeting efforts;
(ii) the sensitivity of investigating ethnic and issue-orientated groups;
(iii) the difficulty in determining the line that distinguishes legitimate dissent from terrorist sympathy and support;
(iv) the problem of balancing the rights of the individual with the security requirements of the State;
(v) the lack of coordinated analytical resources within the Security and Intelligence community;
(vi) the different interpretation and definitions that various States apply to the field of terrorism which makes it difficult for the Security Service to verify information and threat assessments;
(vii) problems of a legal nature in the conduct of some types of Counter-Terrorism investigations, these have been identified by the McDonald Commission [a commission that looked into unethical and illegal counterterrorist activities by the RCMP in the 1970s].[75]

Other potential problematic parallels available from the history of counterterrorism exist that provide occasional coherent but often cautionary and complex messages that at least call out for greater consideration of tactics before introducing them. There is the repeated danger of overreacting to terrorism by responding militarily to a criminal justice matter or by deploying methods that blur boundaries around ethics and civil liberties, such as torturing and murdering terrorism suspects. The French famously used torture and killings against the FLN in Algeria.[76] In Canada, the RCMP Security Service, in its desire to crush the faltering FLQ in the aftermath of the 1970 October Crisis and years of bombings stretching back to 1963, engaged in a campaign of 'dirty tricks' that involved disinformation campaigns but also illegal activities including burglary and arson. The ensuing outcry that emerged when the details of the 'dirty tricks' became public led to an official inquiry and the replacement of the RCMP Security Service by the

75 Hewitt, 'Cold War Counter-Terrorism', p. 76.   76 Horne, *A Savage War of Peace*.

Canadian Security Intelligence Service in 1984.[77] Similarly, the FBI found itself enmeshed in scandal in the 1970s that at least in part emanated from an exaggerated response to the Weather Underground through the illegal acquiring of evidence, which meant that, in the end, many Weather Underground members could not be prosecuted because the material acquired against them by the Bureau was inadmissible.[78] Of course, the best example of a damaging counterterrorism overreaction was the American militarisation of counterterrorism after the attacks of 11 September 2001. The reliance on a war model of counterterrorism, including the invasions of Afghanistan and Iraq, led to more American deaths than did the terrorist attacks of 9/11, while being responsible for hundreds of thousands of Iraqi and Afghani deaths, the displacement of millions more, and widespread and ongoing regional instability.[79]

Finally, there is relevancy in the past to the central element of terrorism and counterterrorism: how do you define what it is you are attempting to counter?[80] Although this might appear as a problem of the recent past, agreeing on a definition of terrorism has long been a contentious matter. A relevant historical example is the little-remembered 1937 League of Nations' 'Convention for the Prevention and Punishment of Terrorism'. It represented the first transnational effort at a coordinated counterterrorism campaign since the 1904 St Petersburg Protocol attempted to respond to anarchist violence against high-profile individuals. The effort in the 1930s emerged after the 1934 public killing in Marseilles, captured live on film, of King Alexander I of Yugoslavia by a Bulgarian nationalist, an attack that also resulted in the death of French Foreign Minister Louis Barthou.[81] The subsequent League of Nations' efforts at tackling terrorism through a concerted international endeavour failed decisively. Ultimately, thirty member countries of the League did agree to the draft Convention that a panel of experts first assembled, but, finally, only one ratified it. Randall

---

77 J. Sallot, *Nobody Said No: The Real Story About How the Mounties Always Get Their Man* (Toronto, Lorimer, 1979).
78 A. M. Eckstein, *Bad Moon Rising: How the Weather Underground Beat the FBI and Lost the Revolution* (New Haven, Yale University Press, 2016).
79 J. Mueller and M. G. Stewart, 'The Terrorism Delusion: America's Overwrought Response to September 11', *International Security* 37/1 (Summer 2012).
80 A. P. Schmid, 'Terrorism: The Definitional Problem', *Case Western Reserve Journal of International Law* 36/2 (2004); J. Blackbourn, F. F. Davis and N. C. Taylor, 'Academic Consensus and Legislative Definitions of Terrorism: Applying Schmid and Jongman', *Statute Law Review* 34/3 (2012).
81 'Live Footage of King Alexander's Assassination (1934)', *The Public Domain Review*, https://publicdomainreview.org/collections/live-footage-of-king-alexanders-assassination-1934/.

D. Law attributes this to the commitment of some 'to the use of state-sponsored terrorism' and a broader fear about the impact on national sovereignty.[82] However, that is only part of the story. A major country involved in the talks, the United Kingdom, which did not endorse the final Convention, pushed to have the definition 'considerably narrowed, if possible to cases of death of [a] statesman' and sought to avoid any requirement that it introduce legislation, arguing in part that it had relevant laws in place already.[83] The original drafts designed by the panel of experts sought to 'enumerate acts which constitute "acts of terrorism", and are henceforth to be the subject of provisions in the criminal law of the contracting parties and to form grounds for extradition'. The League effort identified a number of counterterrorism issues, including the movements of weapons across national boundaries, the creation of false passports and the need for transnational cooperation by state security agencies, which still resonate in the twenty-first century as they did in the 1930s and earlier. Nevertheless, a perpetual obstacle bedevilled the League's task:

> Much of the discussion turned upon the definition of the word terrorism. It was pointed out by several delegates that the meaning of this word should be strictly delimited and that as a starting point they should take the tragic event which has led to the constitution of the Committee: the murder of King Alexander of Yugoslavia. The extension of the notion of terrorism to acts which were not recognized as crimes by national laws could hardly be expected in liberal countries.[84]

It was not as if the complexity of the undertaking came as a surprise to those tasked with assembling the draft convention. In the report of their first session, held in 1935, they acknowledged the difficulties:

> The first question to be settled is what is the actual subject of the convention. In other words, in what does terrorism consist, and what are the arguments in favour of international co-operation for its prevention and punishment?

---

82 R. Law writes that twenty-five countries supported the agreement, but the Canadian delegation that took part in the actual talks said in 1937 that the figure was thirty. Law, *Terrorism*, locations 2914–16; Library and Archives Canada (LAC), Record Group (RG) 25, Records of the Department of External Affairs, vol. 1723, file R219-100-6-E, Convention for the Prevention and Punishment of Terrorism, Telegram from Canadian Advisory Office, 17 November 1937; LAC, RG 25, vol. 1723, file R219-100-6-E, League of Nations to Secretary of State for External Affairs, 24 July 1937.
83 LAC, RG 25, vol. 1723, file R219-100-6-E, Telegram from Canadian Advisory Officer to Secretary of State, 8 October 1937; LAC, RG 25, vol. 1723, file R219-100-6-E, Instructions for United Kingdom Delegation at Diplomatic Conference, 25 October 1937.
84 LAC, RG 25, vol. 1723, file R219-100-6-E, Canadian Advisory Office to Secretary of State, 4 May 1937.

Unlike the subjects of the conventions already in force for the suppression of certain offences such as counterfeiting currency, the traffic in women and children, the drug traffic, slavery, the circulation of obscene publication, etc., *terrorism is not an offence* sui generis. It is not 'a distinct and uniform type of criminal activity' ... Terrorism is the name applied to a number of crimes and offences the great majority of which are punishable under national laws. In certain circumstances, however, these crimes and offences assume an international character, whether because their preparation is a process that takes place in the territory of several States, or because they involve damage to highly valuable lawful property, the protection of which is an essential condition of the maintenance of friendly relations between States, and hence of international peace.[85]

Later efforts by the United Nations, particularly in the 1970s, to find a common international characterisation of terrorism would similarly flounder, and even the United States in the twenty-first century, despite being engaged in a 'War on Terror' since 2001, still lacks a single definition among its agencies tasked with counterterrorism responsibilities.[86]

The example of the definitional issue inhibiting efforts at transnational cooperation in the 1930s reiterates in a broad sense that counterterrorism is a complex and difficult task. As the PIRA observed famously after the Brighton hotel bombing failed to decapitate the British government, despite killing five and wounding dozens more, '[t]oday we were unlucky, but remember we only have to be lucky once. You will have to be lucky always.'[87] Luck is certainly an element of counterterrorism since, as in the past, it remains anything but a scientific practice, because of the complicated and diverse nature of terrorism. Nonetheless, as with terrorism, counterterrorism is not solely a phenomenon of the present day. It has a history as long as that of terrorism. Whether it is in the form of counterterrorism methods, such as the reliance on human intelligence, the difficulty in striking a balance between civil liberties, human rights and security or how to define the threat needing to be countered, the issues of the twenty-first century are,

---

85 LAC, RG 25, vol. 1723, file R219-100-6-E, Committee for the International Repression of Terrorism, Report to the Council on the First Session of the Committee, 8 May 1935.
86 N. Rostow, 'Before and After: The Changed UN Response to Terrorism since September 11th', *Cornell International Law Journal* 35/3 (Winter 2002), p. 480; C. A. Baker, 'We May Be Better Off Without a Clear Definition of Terrorism', *Fair Observer*, 23 July 2019, www.fairobserver.com/region/north_america/terrorism-definitions-legislation-extremism-turkey-us-security-news-14231/.
87 J. Bingham, 'Margaret Thatcher: Seconds from Death at the Hands of an IRA Bomber', *Daily Telegraph*, 8 April 2013, www.telegraph.co.uk/news/politics/margaret-thatcher/9979915/Margaret-Thatcher-Seconds-from-death-at-the-hands-of-an-IRA-bomber.html.

to varying extents, re-emergent, not nascent. As scholars make increasing inroads into excavating the difficult and convoluted history of terrorism, the need to exhume another inherent element of the complex equation, counter-terrorism responses in both the micro and macro, grows ever greater.

Further Reading

R. Bach Jensen, *The Battle Against Anarchist Terrorism: An International History, 1878–1934* (Cambridge, Cambridge University Press, 2013)

L. K. Donohue, *The Cost of Counterterrorism: Power, Politics, and Liberty* (Cambridge, Cambridge University Press, 2008)

F. Foley, *Countering Terrorism in Britain and France: Institutions, Norms and the Shadow of the Past* (Cambridge, Cambridge University Press, 2013)

S. Hewitt, 'Cold War Counter-Terrorism: The Evolution of International Counter-terrorism in the RCMP Security Service, 1972–1984', *Intelligence and National Security* 33/1 (2018)

L. Stampnitzky, *Disciplining Terror: How Experts Invented 'Terrorism'* (Cambridge, Cambridge University Press, 2013)

21

The History of Terrorism and Communication

BRIGITTE L. NACOS AND MELIH BARUT

In December 2018, as thousands of revellers enjoyed the festive atmosphere and offerings at Strasbourg's century-old Christmas Market in front of the Alsatian city's majestic Catholic cathedral, a young man screamed 'Allahu akbar' (Allah is Great) and aimed his handgun indiscriminately into the crowd, killing five persons and injuring eleven more. As it turned out, a 29-year-old extremist Muslim was shooting 'infidels' in the name of the Islamic State, or ISIS. Hundreds of eyewitnesses fled the scene, telling strangers, friends, neighbours, family members and reporters about their shocking experience. Most of all, they took to social media platforms to describe their haunting experiences to global audiences. One month after the incident a Google search for the '2018 Strasbourg attack' produced more than 6 million results.

Almost two millennia earlier, in the middle of the first century AD, members of the Sicarii sect attacked fellow Jews who collaborated with or tolerated Roman rule in Palestine. They stabbed their targets with short daggers in crowded places. As David Rapoport noted, Sicarii 'atrocities occurred on the most holy days to exploit the potential for publicity therein, and, more importantly, to demonstrate that not even the most sacred occasions could provide immunity'. The Zealots, contemporaries of the Sicarii, targeted Roman occupiers.[1] While both sects sought publicity to enlist broad support for their fight against the political and religious status quo, they had different objectives. According to one historian, Zealots and Sicarii were distinctly different groups. The Zealots 'sought democratic rule, were opposed to the priestly aristocracy and did not maintain any "philosophic" approach, as did the Sicarii'. On the other hand, the Sicarii rejected 'human leadership', because their credo was that 'God

---

[1] D. C. Rapoport, 'Fear and Trembling: Terrorism in Three Religious Traditions', *American Political Science Report* 78/3 (September 1984), p. 670.

is the only ruler'.[2] The Sicarii sect's Jewish utopia sought in the first century AD was very similar to ISIS's Islamic version of an ideal religious community ruled by the word of God in the twenty-first century.[3]

The Assassins (eleventh to thirteenth century), members of the militant arm of an extremist Shia sect active in Persia, attacked and killed Sunni leaders and sometimes Christian crusaders with daggers in bright daylight and in front of many witnesses. Unlike Sicarii and Zealots, who disappeared in the crowd after their attacks, the Assassins made no effort to flee the sites of their violence and were typically killed on the spot. They may well have been precursors of modern-day suicide bombers, seeking shocking publicity and martyrdom like their modern-day successors.

These groups operated before the advent of the press. Yet, the Sicarii, Zealots and Assassins were highly successful in maximising their quest for publicity in the form of word-of-mouth communication by the people who had seen their deadly attacks to those who had not been eyewitnesses.[4]

Publicity: The Lifeblood of Terrorism

Whether in biblical times, during the Middle Ages, or in the twenty-first century, terrorist strikes were then and are now first of all communicative acts intended to get attention in particular communities, countries, regions or even around the globe. In the words of one terrorism scholar, 'Terrorism is aimed at the people watching, not the actual victims. Terrorism is theater.'[5] Others have claimed that publicity is the lifeblood or oxygen of terrorism. The more people witness terrorist violence or learn of horrific attacks from news reports, the more successful are the perpetrators of political violence in furthering the universal goal of terrorists throughout history: achieving the greatest amount of publicity.

Communication scholars distinguish between three types of communication: interpersonal, mass communication and mass self-communication. Interpersonal communication can be in the form of actual conversations

---

2 S. B. Honig, 'The Sicarii in Masada: Glory or Infamy?', *Tradition: A Journal of Orthodox Jewish Thought* 11/1 (Spring 1972), pp. 6, 7.
3 This chapter is exclusively devoted to communication and political violence or terrorism committed by *non-state actors*, groups or individuals. Moreover, the emphasis is on self-communication.
4 See Warren C. Brown's chapter in this volume for a history of early practitioners of political violence, including Sicarii, Zealots, Assassins and other groups.
5 B. Jenkins, 'International Terrorism: A New Kind of Warfare', *The Rand Paper Series* (1974), p. 6.

between two or more persons who are together in one space or connected via some media they control: print, radio, television, phone, email or social media messages and images. Mass communication refers to traditional media and the dissemination of news and other content by the few in charge of media organisations to the many consumers of news and entertainment. Finally, in the age of digital media there is mass self-communication, meaning that individuals or groups have the potential of reaching worldwide audiences by posting their written, spoken and visual messages on platforms such as Facebook, Twitter and YouTube. Importantly, these three modes of communication 'coexist, interact, and complement each other rather than substituting for one another'.[6]

As Figure 21.1 shows, terrorist publicity or propaganda, depicted on top of the communication triangle, is directed at targets shown in the other two corners of the figure: (1) governments, elites and all those directly involved in governmental decision-making and (2) domestic and international publics. All terrorists have had in the past and continue to have today distinct publicity objectives; most of all, they want and need

(1) **ATTENTION**, most of all in their target societies, as a precondition for intimidating and spreading fear and anxiety among their foes. They aim for public pressure on governments. Beyond that, they want attention beyond their immediate target countries or regions. Once a target society is intimidated, the mere threat of further attacks will heighten fear and anxiety.
(2) **RECOGNITION**, most of all of their grievances, causes, justifications – and their demands. Terrorists want their targets to know why they are hated, why they are attacked and what they must do to avoid further violence.
(3) **RESPECT**, most of all of those in whose name they claim to act, with the aim of winning supporters, even recruits.[7]

Research has shown that terrorists at all times understood and were quite successful in achieving their propaganda goals by exploiting the communication means available at their time. In this chapter, we focus particularly on communication modes and media controlled by non-state perpetrators of political violence against civilians or non-combatants – in other words, terrorism.

6 M. Castells, *Communication Power* (New York, Oxford University Press, 2011), p. 55.
7 B. Nacos, *Mass-Mediated Terrorism: Mainstream and Digital Media in Terrorism and Counterterrorism* (Lanham, Rowman & Littlefield, 2016), chapter 2.

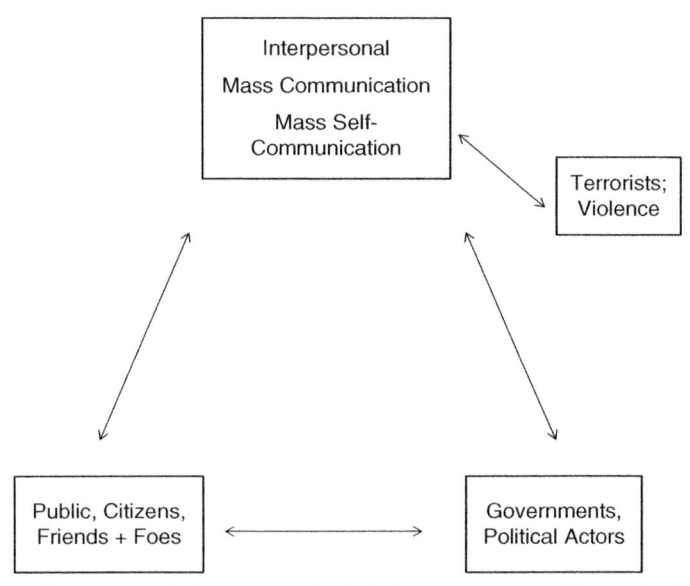

Figure 21.1 Terrorism and the triangle of political communication (Illustration by the authors)

The Muenster Anabaptists: Propagating the 'New Jerusalem'

More than 250 years after the Assassins' demise, when another religious sect carried out political violence, a new communication technology was available, thanks to Gutenberg's invention of the printing press. Besides interpersonal communication, with its limited reach, there was now the beginning of the press or media in form of books, pamphlets and leaflets with the potential of reaching many thousands of people. The Anabaptists of Muenster, Germany utilised both.

When Martin Luther nailed his Ninety-Five Theses criticising the Roman Catholic Church to the door of Wittenberg's Castle Church in 1517, he fired the opening salvo in the Protestant Reformation. During the following years of religious and secular upheaval a quickly growing movement arose that insisted on adult baptism; hence the name Anabaptists. One extremist sect formed within and then split from the mainstream, non-violent Anabaptists: the Muenster Anabaptists, who in the mid-1530s established what they called the 'New Jerusalem', where they were to prepare for the Second Coming of Christ and their salvation.

To gain complete control of the Westphalian city of Muenster the sect drove mainstream Protestants and Catholics who did not convert to Anabaptism violently out of town. Even mild disagreements with the strict church rules resulted in severe punishment. The sect's spiritual leader, Bernhard Rothmann, published increasingly militant tracts and gave fiery sermons using the Scriptures to justify violence – what would be called terrorism today. In 'A Consoling Message of Vengeance', addressed to Baptists outside of Muenster, Rothmann wrote,

> Now, probably, many are of the opinion, indeed expect confidently, that God himself and his angels will come from heaven to punish the godless. No, my dear brothers, he will come, that is true. But the punishment must first be executed by God's servants, and injustice justly punished as God has ordered.[8]

In the first half of the sixteenth century, Germany and neighbouring countries had plenty of printers willing to publish Lutheran and Anabaptist books and pamphlets – even in Catholic cities – but not of the extreme variety that the Muenster Anabaptists preached. Thus, once in control of Muenster, they immediately 'established their own press in the cellar of the former mayor's house ... after plundering the materials of Dietrich Tzwyvel's press, the most important printing shop in Muenster'.[9] They had emissaries distribute Rothmann's tracts and other propaganda material in surrounding German and Dutch regions to win followers. According to one historian, 'some 700–800 men, and twice the number of women, came to Muenster annually'.[10] In a letter to the Anabaptists of Muenster, Martin Luther, himself a gifted propagandist, condemned the sect's propaganda for 'paint[ing] in brightness and color your devilish doings'.[11]

Yet, the Anabaptists' best-laid propaganda did not match the military might of secular and religious authorities that besieged the city and eventually conquered it. Rothmann was killed; Jan van Leyden, who had proclaimed himself king of the New Jerusalem, and two other leaders were captured and

---

8 M. Driedger, 'Norman Cohn, Anabaptist Muenster, and Polemically Inspired Assumptions about Apocalyptic Violence', *Nova Religio: The Journal of Alternative Religions* 21/4 (2018).
9 K. Hill, 'Anabaptism and the World of Printing in Sixteenth Century Germany', *Past and Present* 226 (February 2015), p. 92.
10 H. J. Hillerbrand, 'The Propaganda of the Muenster Anabaptists', *The Mennonite Quarterly Review* 62/4 (1988), p. 508.
11 P. E. Lewis, 'The Anabaptist Kingdom of Muenster', April 2017, https://cccrh.files.wordpress.com/2017/04/anabaptist-kingdom.pdf.

executed; their corpses were hung in metal cases from the top of the city's St Lambert's Church as a warning to other potential rebels. To this day, these metal cases can be seen at St Lambert's as relicts of violent terrorism – and brutal counterterrorism – in the sixteenth century.

The Sons of Liberty: Shaping Public Opinion

Historical accounts of the period leading up to the American War of Independence tend to describe the frequent attacks by colonialists on British administrators, British soldiers and home-grown Loyalists to the crown as mob violence. But while many of these attacks seemed spontaneous actions, many others were well planned and carefully staged for the best possible propaganda effects. At the forefront of the organised political violence designed to intimidate the British and radicalise people in the Thirteen Colonies were Boston's Sons of Liberty (1765–76) and their leader Samuel ('Sam') Adams. The self-described patriots formed a secret group of well-regarded and influential citizens of Boston in reaction to the Stamp Act of 1765 that laid taxes on all printed material. Similar groups, often with other names, were organised in towns and counties in all colonies. It is telling that, two centuries after the Sons of Liberty functioned as a covert cell system, the white supremacist Louis Beam praised this early organisational mode as proof that 'leaderless resistance' was and is superior to a hierarchical form.

The autonomous cells were held together by their quest for independence and, most importantly, by so-called Committees of Correspondence that spoke, wrote, printed and circulated subversive propaganda to enflame colonial sentiments against the British and influence public opinion to support the coming War of Independence. Because newspapers were particularly hard hit by the stamp tax, many of the up to then non-political presses joined the opposition against the Crown. Indeed, some printers and editors became Sons of Liberty, including 'Benjamin Edes of the *Boston Gazette* [who] not only mingled on intimate terms with the local leaders of the Sons of Liberty, but belonged to the inner circle – the "Loyal Nine" – which directed the movements of rank and file from behind the scenes'.[12]

Those 'movements of rank and file' staged events to showcase colonists' fearless resistance to the British, with the Boston Tea Party of 1773 the most iconic of all. In response to the Tea Act that laid taxes on imported tea, a well-organised group of men boarded vessels of the East India Company in Boston

---

12 A. M. Schlesinger, 'The Colonial Newspapers and the Stamp Act', *The New England Quarterly* 8/1 (March 1935), p. 73.

Harbor, casting 342 chests of tea into the water. Ashore, a huge crowd witnessed the spectacle. Two hundred years later, Samuel Adams, who orchestrated this event and others, was remembered as 'progenitor' of modern-day public relations.[13]

But, aside from staging publicity stunts and spreading propaganda, the Sons of Liberty and the mobs they inspired carried out violence against civilians and non-combatants for political objectives.[14]

Contrary to the Sicarii, Zealots and Muenster Anabaptists, the Sons of Liberty's propaganda, their staged events and the violence of political mobs they inspired were successful in furthering their ultimate objective: intensifying public sentiments in favour of support for the War of Independence.

The Age of Modern Terrorism

Modern terrorism emerged during the nineteenth century at a time of political and social upheaval. According to David Rapoport's wave theory, there were four major waves during which particular types of terrorism were carried out: (1) the Anarchist Wave, from about 1870 through the first two decades of the twentieth century; (2) the Anti-colonial Wave, in the post-Second World War decades through to the 1960s; (3) the New Left Wave, from the late 1960s through to the 1980s; and (4) the Religious Wave, starting with the Iranian Revolution and the Soviet Invasion of Afghanistan in 1979 and reaching well into the twenty-first century.[15] While Rapoport's model captured major terrorist movements and groups during pinpointed time periods, it failed to accommodate groups that preceded waves or lasted through or even emerged during subsequent waves. For this reason, Tom Parker and Nick Sitter reject the wave theory and distinguish between strains of terrorism, starting in the nineteenth century: nationalist, socialist, religious and social exclusion terrorism, the last category including groups such as the Ku Klux Klan and lone wolves that respond violently to alleged threats against their racial, ethnic and/or religious supremacy.[16]

---

13 S. M. Cutlip, 'Public Relations and the American Revolution', *Public Relations Review* 2/4 (Winter 1976), p. 11.
14 At the time, though, the terms 'terrorist' and 'terrorism' were not used yet, because they were coined later in the eighteenth century during the French Revolution.
15 D. C. Rapoport, 'The Fourth Wave: September 11 in the History of Terrorism', *Current Events* 100 (2001).
16 T. Parker and N. Sitter, 'The Four Horsemen of Terrorism: It's Not Waves, It's Strains', *Terrorism and Political Violence* 28/2 (2016).

Utilising both wave and strain theories, and aware that some groups fit more than one category, we discuss in the following sections the propaganda schemes of terrorist movements and groups that were particularly innovative in utilising the available communication technologies of their times.

Anarchist Wave/Early Socialist Strain

As Walter Laqueur observed, 'It has been possible since time immemorial to make love and to cook without the help of textbooks; the same applied to terrorism. In some cases the decision to adopt a terrorist strategy was taken on the basis of a detailed political analysis. But usually the mood came first, and ideological rationalization only after.'[17] In case of the anarchist movement in the West and the revolutionary movement in Russia, philosophies of terrorism and 'textbooks' in the form of pamphlets and articles called for and described violent tactics against monarchs or elected officials before groups and individuals plotted and carried out assassinations and other terrorist attacks.

In 1849, a radical journal in Switzerland published a tract under the headline 'Der Mord' ('Murder'), in which Karl Heinzen laid out the rationale for terrorist action against reactionaries, accusing people in power of 'mass murder, organized murder, or war, as it is called'. He advocated murder for political ends and anticipated the development of weapons that would make this sort of violence far more lethal and effective – what were later called weapons of mass destruction. 'The greatest benefactor of mankind will be he who makes it possible for a few men to wipe out thousands', he wrote.[18] Heinzen's essay contained all terrorist publicity aims; it called for attention-getting, horrific attacks that would drive fear into targeted societies, detailed the grievances of anarchists and justified their violence, and assumed the recruitment of revolutionaries devoted to the cause. According to one expert account, 'The quantum leap into the modern age of terrorist theory made by Heinzen in his essay "Murder" was matched in deed by the daring attempt on the life of Napoleon III by Felice Orsini nine years later. Although there had been earlier assassination attempts on European rulers, Orsini's was the first to be carried out for explicitly political reasons.'[19]

---

17 W. Laqueur, *A History of Terrorism* (New Brunswick, NJ, Transaction Publisher, 2002), p. 77.
18 K. Heinzen, 'Murder', in W. Laqueur and Y. Alexander (eds.), *The Terrorism Reader: The Essential Source Book on Political Violence Both Past and Present* (New York, Penguin, 1987).
19 M. A. Miller, 'The Intellectual Origins of Modern Terrorism in Europe', in M. Crenshaw (ed.), *Terrorism in Context* (University Park, Pennsylvania State University Press, 1995), pp. 36–7.

In Russia, Sergei Nechayev, Nikolai Morozov and Pyotr Kropotkin were among the radical leaders who justified terrorist means in their writings and prescribed rules of conduct for the true revolutionary. The terms 'revolutionary' and 'terrorist' were used interchangeably. Although living for most of his political life in Switzerland, Mikhail Bakunin, who advocated his own brand of anarchism, had devoted followers in Russia who eventually translated his radical philosophy into violent actions.

In 1879, Johann Most, a German immigrant, established the anarchist newspaper *Freiheit* ('Freedom') in New York to propagate the idea that political violence was needed to rid the world of capitalists and governments that served them. For him, terrorism was a communicative act or 'propaganda of the deed'.[20] Most argued that only anarchists' own spoken and written words could inform friend and foe correctly about the anarchist cause and the need for political violence. By 1885 Johann Most was 'the world's leading anarchist'.[21] His newspaper and pamphlets were not only read by radicals in the United States but in Europe as well. 'For the police [in Europe] it was as though Most and [other] anarchists were directing an invisible army of warriors who were following their instructions with frightening precision', Martin Miller noted. 'In Germany, anarchist cells across the country were uncovered. Searches revealed that members had copies of *Freiheit*.'[22]

Most inspired followers to establish their own anarchist newspapers. In the mid-1880s, for example, Chicago 'had five major anarchist newspapers (three in German, one in Czech, and *The Alarm* in English) with a combined circulation of thirty thousand'.[23] The editors of these and other anarchist newspapers published incendiary material urging their comrades to get dynamite sticks to attack the enemy.

Besides publishing books, articles and pamphlets, leading anarchists cultivated interpersonal communications. When Most made his first trip to Chicago in 1882, '6000 people came to hear him speak. The crowd spilled into the aisles and massed outside ... Speaking English with a heavy German accent and performing like a seasoned actor, Most elicited thunderous applause from the huge immigrant audience.'[24] The Russian anarchist Emma Goldman, who moved to the United States in 1885, was also

---

20 Scholars are not clear about the origin of the term 'propaganda of the deed' (or 'propaganda by deed'). Some credit Most, others the International Anarchist Conference of 1881, and still others the Italian anarchist Luigi Galleani, who in the early twentieth century led the most violent anarchist group in the US.
21 J. Green, *Death in the Haymarket* (New York, Pantheon Books, 2006), p. 129.
22 Miller, 'The Intellectual Origins of Modern Terrorism in Europe', p. 45.   23 Ibid., p. 49.
24 Green, *Death in the Haymarket*, pp. 95–6.

a prolific writer and gifted orator. While newspapers referred to her as 'high priestess of anarchy', Goldman attracted thousands of enthusiastic admirers. She 'took her message to the people wherever they might be, crossing class, ethnic, and language barriers to reach them. She delivered her lectures in large community halls and university lecture rooms as well as from open cars in crowded squares, and even in the backs of barrooms.'[25] Leon Czolgosz, who assassinated US President William McKinley in 1901, was a Goldman fan who had met her after one of her speeches in Cleveland before he killed McKinley. After his arrest he mentioned Goldman among anarchists who had inspired his deed. Immediately after the assassination Johann Most reprinted Heinzen's article 'Der Mord' and published an editorial in his newspaper justifying the killing of a ruler. He was convicted for endangering the public peace and served a short prison sentence.

Besides receiving ample news coverage in the wake of their violent deeds, anarchists utilised interpersonal communication and their own, alternative presses to disseminate their propaganda.

Comparing Terrorist Propaganda Tactics in the Late Nineteenth and Early Twenty-First Centuries

Anarchist propaganda designed to radicalise, recruit and instruct was very similar to the propaganda of terrorist organisations in the twenty-first century – although communication technology changed in dramatic ways. One instructive example is a comparison of the following bomb-making instructions, publicised by Johann Most in 1885 and by the Islamic State in 2017:

> Here is another way to make bombs: take a piece of iron pipe, as commonly used for water or gas mains, and cut it into short lengths. For home-made 'hand-grenades', six inch lengths of pipe of one and a half to two inches diameter are suitable ... We carried out tests with these bombs, also, and the results were always satisfactory. It should be clear to everyone that such devices are easy to make, and not expensive at all (which is very important to us), and that they can achieve spectacular results when used against large assemblies of people (riff-raff of the upper-class variety) ... These weapons are to the proletariat an effective substitute for artillery, and inflict surprise, confusion and panic on the enemy.
>
> (From Johann Most's pamphlet 'Science of Revolutionary War', 1885)

---

25 C. Falk, 'Emma Goldman: Passion, Politics, and the Theatrics of Free Expression', *Women's History Review* 11/1 (2002).

> (cont.)
>
> All that is required are pieces of polystyrene (Styrofoam), which is commonly found in boxed packaging of children's toys and household appliances or in the form of foam cups used for hot coffee at donut shops. One only has to pack the pieces of crushed foam inside the bottle (two thirds of which is filled with gasoline), gently shaking it, until the polystyrene dissolves, turning the mixture into a thick solution. He should continue adding polystyrene until the desired sticky glue-type consistency is reached. This stickiness will assist in allowing the area of the Molotov cocktail's impact to burn for a longer period. Alternatively, instead of Styrofoam, one can add liquid laundry detergent or dishwashing liquid in the same manner, to thicken the gasoline and slow its burning. The piece of cloth is then inserted into the bottle, the protruding end should be soaked in gasoline, and the bottle's mouth must then be sealed as explained before. Also, the exterior of the bottle should be cleansed of any napalm. Additionally, if needed for the arson attack, the mixture can be prepared and stored in a larger container and poured directly on the intended target before lighting the fire.
>
> (From ISIS's *Rumiyah* online magazine, issue 5, 2017)
>
> Similarly, anarchists in the late nineteenth and early twentieth centuries claimed responsibility for violent attacks just as later terrorists did and contemporary groups still do. Thus, the Galleanists, the most active American anarchists in the second decade of the twentieth century, included printed messages in each letter and package bomb shipment they sent in 1919 to prominent public officials, signing with 'The Anarchist Fighters'. After a dynamite-packed horse-drawn wagon exploded in the Wall Street area in 1920, killing thirty-three persons and injuring many more, a printed leaflet was found nearby signed by 'American Anarchist Fighters' that warned of more violence unless political prisoners were released.
>
> Following generations of terrorists have typically phoned news organisations to claim responsibility for their attacks or, more recently, made such claims in social media posts.
>
> Same tactics, different communication technologies!

Anti-colonial Wave/Nationalist Strain

Following the First World War and the crumbling of the empires of defeated states, the push for national self-determination began to take hold in various parts of the world, and intensified after the Second World War. The Zionist Lehi and Irgun, the Algerian Front de liberation nationale (FLN), the Palestinian Fatah/Palestinian Liberation Organistion (PLO) and the Popular Front for the Liberation of Palestine (PFLP), the Basque ETA, the Provisional Irish Republican Army (PIRA), the Kurdistan Workers' Party

(PKK), the Tamil Tigers and many more nationalist and separatist groups utilised propaganda means to further their causes. Some of these organisations fit more than one strain. For example, ETA, secular Palestinian groups and PKK were nationalists and socialists, but their desire for national independence seemed always stronger than their socialist ideology. Organisations like Hezbollah and Hamas fit the nationalist but also the religious wave or strain. The following case studies demonstrate how some of these groups utilised propaganda by deed and word to further their causes.

The Algerian FLN: First radio and eventually television were the new communication technologies which were directly or indirectly available to guerillas and terrorists. The Algerian FLN became a striking example for the power of propaganda not only by violence but also by word. Domestically, FLN propaganda was to a large extent a word-of-mouth effort. Pro-independence and anti-French posters and leaflets could not be disseminated openly but changed hands underground. Occasionally, messages and images were sprayed on streets and sidewalks. But the FLN's secret weapon was the 'Voice of Algeria' or 'Voice of Fighting Algeria', which began airing in 1956. For a time, the French managed to jam FLN broadcasts so that liberation broadcasts were often interrupted and rarely received clearly. Nevertheless, many Algerians listened to whatever they were able to hear. As Frantz Fanon wrote,

> Listening to the Voice of Fighting Algeria was motivated not just by eagerness to hear the news, but more particularly by the inner need to be at one with the nation in its struggle, to recapture and to assume the new national formulation, to listen to and to repeat the grandeur of the epic being accomplished up there among the rocks and on the djebels [mountains]. Every morning the Algerian would communicate the result of his hours of listening in. Every morning he would complete for the benefit of his neighbor or his comrade the things not said by the Voice and reply to the insidious questions asked by the enemy press. He would counter the official affirmations of the occupier, the resounding bulletins of the adversary, with official statements issued by the Revolutionary Command.[26]

When the French were no longer able to jam the 'Voice of Algeria', many more Algerians were able to listen to broadcasts originating in Tunis, Rabat, Cairo and Damascus.

---

26 F. Fanon, *A Dying Colonialism* (New York, Monthly Review Press, 1965), p. 86.

Equally important were FLN efforts to get international media attention. The FLN leadership went out of its way to accommodate foreign reporters who wanted to accompany FLN fighters; they also provided the international press with pictures of civilian victims of French attacks taken by FLN mujahideen. In the United States in particular leading TV networks and their star anchors interviewed FLN leaders, covering them prominently and sympathetically as they made their pleas to the American government and public as well as to the United Nations.

This sort of international news took its toll on the French elite and public. Whereas the French military won the war in Algiers, the FLN, not the French government, won the international propaganda war and Algeria's independence.

The Palestinian Liberation Movement: Some national liberation movements inspired others to take up the struggle for self-determination. Thus, 'Yasser Arafat's intelligence chief Salah Khalaf, better known to posterity by his nom de guerre Abu Iyad, noted in his memoirs: "The guerrilla war in Algeria, launched five years before the creation of Fatah, had a profound influence on us . . . [It] symbolized the success we dreamed of."'[27]

Like the FLN, Fatah and similar Palestinian groups were well aware of violence as a means to draw public and elite attention to their cause. PFLP leader Dr George Habash made no secret of what he and other Palestinians aimed for when they hijacked commercial airliners with predominantly Western passengers. 'We force people to ask what is going on', he explained.[28]

In 1970, PFLP commandos hijacked four New York-bound planes nearly simultaneously. While security guards aboard an El Al airliner overwhelmed the hijackers, the three other planes, with hundreds of passengers aboard, were forced to land in a remote area of Jordan that was not quickly accessible for the press. The incident did receive international news coverage but not to the extent the hijackers had hoped for.

This changed drastically two years later, when Black September, a breakaway group from the PLO, kidnapped and killed members of Israel's national team during the 1972 Olympic Games in Munich. Reporters from around the world, who were in Munich to report on the

---

27 Parker and Sitter, 'The Four Horsemen of Terrorism', p. 201.
28 M. Crenshaw, 'The Logic of Terrorism: Terrorist Behavior as a Product of Rational Choice', in W. Reich (ed.), *Origins of Terrorism* (New York, Cambridge University Press, 1990), p. 18.

sports events, turned all their attention to the tragic attack on Israel's young athletes. An estimated global audience of more than 500 million people witnessed the drama and its deadly end non-stop on live television. In the process, the cause of Palestinian nationalists was put on the map of global public attention. When asked about their violent means to get attention, one Palestinian extremist answered, 'We would throw roses if it would work.'[29]

Hezbollah: While accounts about the formation of the organisation differ, there seems to be agreement that various militant Shia groups grew in the early 1980s with the assistance of the Iranian Revolutionary Guards into a well-organised, well-trained and well-financed group with political, social service and military wings. Eventually, Hezbollah's political arm participated in Lebanon's elections, won seats in parliament and became part of the government. Whereas some Western countries such as the United States and the United Kingdom considered and treated Hezbollah as a terrorist organisation, other countries did not.

During the 1980s, Hezbollah operatives were responsible for a wave of terrorist hijackings, facility attacks and kidnappings predominantly of Westerners that brought global attention to its political causes: rejection of Western presence and influence in Lebanon and the Middle East and the destruction of Israel.

To publicise threats, grievances and demands and to win supporters and recruits, the group established its own, formidable media that came to include print, radio, television and eventually online sites. In 1984, the organisation founded the weekly newspaper *Al-Ahed* ('The Pledge'), followed by several other weekly and monthly periodicals. In 1988, Al Nour 9 ('The Light') radio began to operate; in 1991 Hezbollah's television station Al-Manar ('The Beacon') beamed its first programmes into parts of Beirut. By 2000 Al-Manar beamed its programmes throughout the Arab world and soon thereafter went global, airing its programmes in several languages twenty-four hours a day. The satellite network was particular influential in the Arab and Muslim diaspora. In short, well before the advent of the Internet as a popular means of communication Hezbollah did not rely only or mostly on traditional media reporting but was in control of its own formidable media empire to spread propaganda, win supporters and recruit members.

Like other secular and religiopolitical groups, Hezbollah established its own website early on and eventually utilised social media platforms, such as

---

29 D. M. Schlagheck, *International Terrorism* (Lexington, Lexington Books, 1988), p. 69.

Facebook, Twitter, YouTube and Telegram. Unlike ISIS and like-minded jihadist groups that we discuss below within the religious wave or strain, Hezbollah's own social media posts avoided outright terrorist propaganda, leaving the groups' many supporters to glorify martyrs and political violence.

Long before Hezbollah came to participate as a political party in Lebanon's legitimate political process, the group established and operated a multi-pronged and far-reaching media empire as no other group had done before.

The Kurdistan Workers' Party (PKK): On 20 June 1987 the PKK carried out its first major terrorist attack by assaulting the tiny Turkish village of Pınarcık, killing sixteen children, six women and eight men. In its monthly newspaper *Serxwebun* the group celebrated the massacre as a 'noble deed' in the fight against 'Turkish colonialism'.[30] More importantly, this massacre and quickly following similar actions were widely reported by the Turkish press and international media. At the time, Western correspondents described the attackers as 'insurgents', 'rebels' and 'separatists' – not terrorists.

While many terrorist organisations have appealed to their brethren abroad for support, including in the form of propaganda, the Kurdistan Workers' Party was unique in establishing or exploiting Kurdish satellite TV channels headquartered in Europe that beamed nationalist programmes to the sizeable Kurdish diaspora in Western European countries and Kurdish minorities in the Middle East and North Africa.

The first of these channels, Med-TV, began in 1995 to beam its programmes in six languages (Kurdish, Turkish, Arabic, English, Assyrian and Zaza) from London to several dozen countries. But, because of its pro-separatist/pro-PKK content and its popularity among Kurds, the channel was forced off the air by 1999 as a result of the Turkish government's pressure on the British licence provider and the Polish satellite server. Whether established in France, Denmark, Belgium or elsewhere in Europe, subsequent channels, too, lost out when Ankara, supported by Washington, pressed for a united front against media allegedly supporting terrorists and terrorism. This became an easier task when the European Union and a number of its members declared the PKK a terrorist organisation – although, in some cases, European courts ruled in favour of Kurdish TV channels in the name of freedom of the press.

Whenever PKK-friendly TV channels were banned, they seemed to re-emerge with different names and different satellite providers. Others

---

30 *Serxwebun*, June 1987.

streamed their programmes online. There were also a multitude of radio stations beaming their programmes from studios inside and outside of Kurdish areas. When print presses were banned, they became available online – just like the PKK's original monthly print organ *Serxwebun*, which became more widely accessible as an online publication. Eventually, there was also a strong social media presence of the PKK and the group's supporters. Taken together, these media enlisted support and sympathy for the PKK and in certain cases radicalised and recruited young Kurds to fight for the nationalist cause. As one PKK fighter testified after his arrest,

> After the second year of high school, I started surfing the websites about the organisation under the influence of my friends. I was also watching Roy TV and listening to Mesopotamia FM. I was very influenced by the guerillas I saw and the news I heard. I was especially inspired by the female guerillas' fight for the people. I talked about these things with my cousin (my maternal uncle's daughter) and, finally, we decided to join the organisation.[31]

The New Left Wave (1960s–1980s)

Clandestine groups cannot openly communicate with friends and foes. Thus, the Western anti-capitalist/anti-imperialist groups that formed in the late 1960s relied mostly on the mainstream media to cover their revolutionary violence, receive public attention and cause widespread fear and anxiety. The Weather Underground in the US, the Red Army Faction (RAF) in Germany and the Red Brigades in Italy did not publish their own newspapers like the early anarchists; they did not have their own radio transmitters like the FARC in Colombia. But they all understood the power of 'propaganda by deed', or what the Latin American revolutionary Carlos Marighella called 'armed propaganda'.

The Red Army Faction (also called Baader–Meinhof Gang in reference to its founders Andreas Baader and Ulrike Meinhof): Although frequently mentioning Lenin and Mao in their programmatic declarations, the group portrayed itself as a European version of Latin American urban guerrillas. In 'Das Konzept der Stadtguerrilla' ('The Concept of the Urban Guerrilla') the group mentioned advice Marighella provided in his *Minimanual of the Urban Guerrilla*. According to Marighella,

---

31 'Uluslararası Terörizm ve Sınıraşan Suçlar Araştırma Merkezi-UTSAM (2012). Terör Örgütlerinde Militan Kimlik İnşası ve Eleman Profili: PKK/KCK Örneği', UTSAM Raporlar Serisi: 20. Ankara, Turkey. Polis Akademisi Başkanlığı. TBMM Kütüphanesi, 2011, p. 534.

> The coordination of urban guerrilla activities, including each armed action, is the primary way of making armed propaganda. These actions, carried out with specific objectives and aims in mind, inevitably become propaganda material for the mass communication system. Bank robberies, ambushes, desertions and the diverting of weapons, the rescue of prisoners, executions, kidnappings, sabotage, terrorism and the war of nerves are all cases in point. Airplanes diverted in flight by guerrilla action, ships and trains assaulted and seized by armed guerrillas, can also be carried out solely for propaganda effect.[32]

RAF leaders were obsessed with the news media. They kept meticulous records of everything publicised about the group in print and broadcast media. They frequently contacted newsrooms by phone and letters to the editor to complain about allegedly biased or erroneous reporting. The leadership distinguished between the 'hostile' press, most of the mainstream media, and 'friendly' media, mostly leftist, alternative presses with very small circulations. Rank and file members distributed pamphlets and flyers among sympathetic groups and spray-painted threatening slogans on walls. But Ulrike Meinhof, a well-known leftist journalist before going underground, knew that news coverage in the mainstream media could be manipulated to the RAF's advantage. She was aware, for example, that the volume of coverage could be maximised by the timing of attacks. Because heavy advertising towards the end of the week increased the news hole in the print media, the RAF preferred to strike on days when their violence was most likely to be reported most extensively.

Most of all, RAF leaders heeded Marighella's credo that the most shocking terrorist actions guarantee the most prominent and most extensive news coverage. This was never more obvious than during the most horrendous of all RAF operations, which began in early September 1977 with the kidnapping of Hanns-Martin Schleyer, a leading industrialist and chair of the German employers' association, and ended forty-three days later with his violent death. The hostage-holders' demand was categorical: either release Andreas Baader and three other RAF leaders from prison or Schleyer will die. The government was less clear in its responses, because officials were stalling for time, hoping to find and rescue the prominent hostage. During the hostage situation the news media became the transmitter of messages dispatched by the RAF and the German government. While the two sides communicated with each other through the media, both tried to influence the German

---

32 C. Marighella, *Minimanual of the Urban Guerrilla* (Montreal, Abraham Guillen Press, 2002), p. 30.

people. The government wanted the public to support its refusal to give in to the terrorists' demands; the Red Army Faction hoped that public pressure would force the government to save Mr Schleyer's life by releasing their imprisoned comrades.

News organisations, regardless of their political leanings, cooperated with the government by refusing to publicise certain RAF messages while printing and airing even those government declarations designed to mislead the captors. The RAF became the first terrorist organisation to produce and make available to news organisations a video in which its hostage was seen and heard. The sensational material was aired by television networks after a few days of collective delays. But the impact was disappointing for the RAF, because the German public became outright hostile towards the group after watching Schleyer in distress and even more so after learning that the kidnappers had killed their victim.[33]

Like the Weather Underground in the United States and the Red Brigades in Italy, the Red Army Faction was a rather small gang weakened by constant internal disagreements and rivalries. Yet, these groups' 'armed propaganda' was instrumental in convincing their respective governments, security agencies and publics that they posed existential threats to the democracies they wanted to destroy.

Social Exclusion Terrorism: From the KKK to Lone Wolves

The Ku Klux Klan

Parker and Sitter categorise KKK violence fittingly as 'social exclusion' terrorism carried out by white supremacists. After the Civil War, the first wave of Klan violence targeted freed African-American slaves in the South to deny them the civil rights and civil liberties that white Americans enjoyed. Since the history of the Ku Klux Klan spans 150 years from its inception in 1865 through the first decades of the twenty-first century, the movement has utilised the whole range of communication technologies progressively coming available from the second half of the nineteenth through the first decades of the twenty-first century – print, broadcast and online-based media – after originally relying exclusively on interpersonal communication. However, in the early twentieth century the fate of the KKK and of many of its victims was

---

33 For an excellent account of the RAF's propaganda, including the news coverage of the Schleyer case, see A. Elter, *Propaganda der Tat: Die RAF und die Medien* (Frankfurt, Suhrkamp Verlag, 2008).

uniquely affected for years to come by the controversial content of one motion picture, a product of the emerging new entertainment media.

In what was and remained for more than a century unprecedented in the history of communicative terrorism, a Hollywood silent film released in 1915, D. W. Griffith's *The Birth of a Nation*, was instrumental in reviving the then dormant KKK. What came to be known as the Second Klan grew into a potent organisation in the South and won many recruits, supporters and admirers in the North. The three-hour blockbuster portrayed the Klan as a heroic force saving whites from the onslaught of inferior and violent blacks. African-American males were stereotyped as rapists of white women. Eighty years after the premiere, film critic Molly Haskell wrote in the *New York Times*, 'The major source of the movie's racial bigotry was "The Clansman", Thomas Dixon's overwrought novel of hate and intolerance, from which the film was adapted ... The film's most inflammatory scenes involve the sexual pursuit of two white women by liberated black slave men, and the heroic rescue of the women by members of a glorified Ku Klux Klan.'[34] According to one media expert, 'The film is one of the most racist films ever made. Maybe the most racist film ever. The politics of the film was essentially to say certain black people are worthy of being lynched. In that sense it's extremely racist.'[35]

Fascist Movements

During their ascents to power, the post-First World War fascist movements in Italy and Germany resembled modern-day terrorist organisations in that they had political and paramilitary wings, with the latter physically attacking political opponents, all the while claiming that these squads were merely protecting fellow partisans and their nations' values. Fascist violence was more extreme in Germany. As two terrorism scholars concluded, 'In the 1920s Germany saw the emergence of the Nazi party's Sturmabteilung (the SA, or Stormtroopers), a paramilitary organization that used terrorism in support of the political party (which included its own internal body responsible for terror in the shape of the Schutzstaffel – the SS).'[36]

---

34 M. Haskell, 'How the Earlier Media Achieved Critical Mass: Motion Pictures; In "The Birth of a Nation", Birth of Serious Film', *New York Times*, 20 November 1995, www.nytimes.com/1995/11/20/business/how-the-earlier-media-achieved-critical-mass-motion-picturesin-the.html?searchResultPosition=2.
35 Ellen Scott, author of the book *Cinema Civil Rights*, cited by Tom Brook, 'The Birth of a Nation: The Most Racist Film Ever Made?', BBC, 8 February 2015, www.bbc.com/culture/story/20150206-the-most-racist-movie-ever-made.
36 Parker and Sitter, 'The Four Horsemen of Terrorism', p. 210.

The fascist movements in both Italy and Germany utilised their own alternative media to disseminate their propaganda. Mussolini established the newspaper *Il Popolo d'Italia* ('The People of Italy') as his propaganda outlet. For Hitler, *Völkischer Beobachter* ('People's Observer') was the 'fighting newspaper' of his party. Both Mussolini and Hitler spoke regularly at mass rallies to persuade the masses to join their movements in their fights to take over their respective governments.

However, when it came to propaganda, the Nazis were in a league by themselves. Hitler was a natural propagandist. In his two-volume autobiographical manifesto *Mein Kampf* he devoted two chapters to propaganda, focusing on the effects of various forms of persuasion. In one section, Hitler compared textual and visual propaganda and concluded that still photographs and motion pictures were more effective than the written word. As he noted, 'It is sufficient if one be careful to have quite short texts, because many people are more ready to accept a pictorial presentation than to read a long written description. In a much shorter time, at one stroke I might say, people will understand a pictorial presentation of something which it would take them a long and laborious effort of reading to understand.'[37]

While Hitler was well versed in propaganda, the Nazi party's propagandist-in-chief Joseph Goebbels understood the power of persuasion in theory and practice. He had studied American public relations literature and was an admirer of Edward L. Bernays, a pioneer of modern public relations who argued that the consent of the public could be manufactured.

In the first issue of the Nazi magazine *Wille und Weg* ('Will and Path') Goebbels wrote,

> No other political movement has understood the art of propaganda as well as the National Socialists. From its beginnings, it has put heart and soul into propaganda. What distinguishes it from all other political parties is the ability to see into the soul of the people and to speak the language of the man in the street. It uses all the means of modern technology. Leaflets, handbills, posters, mass demonstrations, the press, stage, film and radio – these are all tools of our propaganda ... In the long run, propaganda will reach the broad masses of the people only if at every stage it is uniform. Nothing confuses the people more than lack of clarity or aimlessness.[38]

---

37 A. Hitler, *Mein Kampf*, Vol. 2, chapter 6 (London, Pimlico, 1992). The first volume of *Mein Kampf* was first published in 1925, the second volume in 1926.
38 J. Goebbels, *Wille und Weg* 1 (1931), pp. 2–5. English translation available at http://research.calvin.edu/german-propaganda-archive/wille.htm.

Most of all, the Nazis understood the communicative power of public displays. In their propaganda manuals for local and regional party functionaries, they listed public rallies and marches as effective propaganda means. In one instruction pamphlet there was even a reference to the effectiveness of choral propaganda during particular meetings – but only if the singers had rehearsed and, ideally, were 'supported by a trumpet'.[39]

In sum, while the violence carried out by Hitler's Brown Shirts or Storm Troopers intimidated and struck fear into their political opponents, the Nazis' multi-pronged propaganda scheme was equally, if not more important on their road to power.

White Supremacist Lone Wolves

Violent online extremism made its debut in 1995, when the one-time KKK leader Don Black established the white supremacist/neo-Nazi website 'Stormfront'. In short order, similar groups followed his example. But towards the end of the twentieth century and even more so in the twenty-first century the most lethal terrorist attacks by white supremacists were plotted and carried out not by terrorist organisations but by lone wolves. These individuals were every bit as interested in and capable of attracting massive coverage in traditional news media and utilising mass self-communication via social media.

Timothy McVeigh, whose truck bomb attack on a government building in Oklahoma City in 1995 killed 168 people, had personally scouted venues housing federal offices in several states because he wanted a building 'with plenty of open space around it, to allow for the best possible news photos and television footage'.[40] Google Maps were not yet available at that time, nor were social media platforms. McVeigh was happy with the massive news coverage his attack received. While on death row he referred to the phrase 'the shot heard around the world' when he told reporters contently that 'the Oklahoma City blast was heard around the world'.[41]

Anders Breivik, whose 2011 attacks in Oslo and on a nearby island killed a total of 77 persons, emailed a 1,515-page manifesto to acquaintances before he began his killing spree in the name of protecting a white and Christian Europe from Muslim invaders. Soon, his tract was available on the Internet.

---

39 From a pamphlet on 'modern political propaganda', available at http://research.calvin.edu/german-propaganda-archive/stark.htm.
40 L. Michel and D. Herbeck, *American Terrorist: Timothy McVeigh and the Oklahoma City Bombing* (New York, Regan Books, 2001), p. 169.
41 Ibid., p. 382.

According to Breivik's testimony in court, he had originally planned to behead Gro Harlem Brundtland, former prime minister of Norway, and 'film the killing using an iPhone and upload the footage to YouTube'.[42] But this plan failed.

Eight years later, in 2019, an Australian white Supremacist succeeded with a much more ambitious publicity coup, when he livestreamed his 36-minute shooting attacks on two mosques in Christchurch, New Zealand that killed 51 men, women and children. According to one account,

> Somewhere between 10 and 20 minutes before the first mosque was attacked, Tarrant logged on to the /pol/ section of 8chan, an image board popular with the extreme right. As an anonymous user, Tarrant announced himself with a post entitled '*ahem*'. It read: 'Well lads, it's time to stop shitposting and time to make a real life effort post. I will carry out and (sic) attack against the invaders, and will even live stream the attack via facebook.'[43]

He also posted a link to his manifesto titled 'The Great Replacement', which praised Breivik and other notorious white nationalists, asking 8chan comrades to spread his message.

If major terrorist attacks were like shots heard around the world before the advent of online communication, as McVeigh recognised, as the second decade of the twenty-first century neared its end lone-wolf online propaganda was eventually seen and heard during or soon after deadly terrorist attacks – and often imitated by like-minded extremists.

The Modern Religious Wave or Strain

According to Rapoport, modern terrorism's religious wave began in 1979 with upheavals in the Muslim world, most importantly, the Islamic (Shia) revolution in Iran and the invasion of Afghanistan by the Soviet Union that was successfully fought by a multinational group of Sunni mujahideens – among them the later Al-Qaeda founder and leader Osama bin Laden. Although other religious groups (i.e. Christian, Jewish, Buddhist and Hindu) carried out terrorist attacks during this period, Islam was predominant in terms of the number of terrorists and the number of attacks.

The young Islamists that stormed the US embassy in Tehran in 1979, holding fifty Americans hostage for 444 days, disseminated their

---

42 G. Macklin, 'The Christchurch Attacks: Livestream Terror in Viral Video Age', *CTC Sentinel*, July 2019, p. 19.
43 Ibid., p. 18.

propaganda via mainstream media; bin Laden's Al-Qaeda Central and some of its affiliates operated before and after the advent of social media; but the young media specialists of the self-proclaimed Islamic State, or ISIS in Iraq and Syria, belonged to the first generation growing up in the age of social media.

The Iranian Hostage-Holders

Based on incident data collected by the RAND Corporation, Brian Jenkins found that forty-three successful embassy takeovers and five unsuccessful attempts occurred between 1971 and 1980 in twenty-seven countries.[44] It is plausible that terrorists and would-be terrorists learned about these incidents from media reports, since the takeovers took place in a host of different countries on different continents. By late 1979, when a group of young Islamists, so-called 'students', seized the US embassy in Tehran, they knew about the prominent news coverage such incidents received. While followers of the Ayatollah Khomeini, a foe of modernity, the captors proved very resourceful in their efforts to use modern Western media to get attention and explain their demands to America and the rest of the world.

In the United States, the incident was the most reported news story for the full duration of the crisis – fourteen months.[45] The captors staged massive protests around the embassy ground on a daily basis, directing a seemingly angry crowd to shout anti-American slogans, burn effigies of President Jimmy Carter and set American flags on fire. Those scenes dominated TV screens in America and elsewhere. Unknown to TV audiences was that the spectacle in the streets of Tehran was not non-stop but staged daily for a limited time in order to create media events. Before Western TV cameras began filming the crowds, some Iranians were often helpful in setting up tripods and other equipment. And when cameras and microphones were packed away, the crowds disappeared.

While the hostage holders did not have their own alternative media, they tried hard to control news content in the mainstream media. As one American TV correspondent explained, 'The students have even attempted to buy off television networks by offering an unpublished American embassy

---

44 B. M. Jenkins, 'Embassies Under Siege: A Review of 48 Embassy Takeovers, 1971–1980', Rand Corporation, January 1981, www.rand.org/content/dam/rand/pubs/reports/2005/R2651.pdf.
45 B. L. Nacos, *Terrorism and the Media* (New York, Columbia University Press, 1994), chapter 3.

secret document in return for five minutes *unedited* [emphasis added] airtime.'[46]

The Al-Qaeda Network

Before social media became the vehicle for mass self-communication, the close-knit group of Arab jihadists led by Osama bin Laden was the most feared terrorist group. Originally, Al-Qaeda Central relied on the traditional mass media to get global attention. In the 1990s, when bin Laden issued his fatwa, or religious edicts, that declared war on the West, he invited TV reporters to his residence in Afghanistan to explain his grievances and plans. To cultivate Western media, he had a press liaison in London. Bin Laden and his close associates had the mainstream media in mind when they selected the targets of their 9/11 attacks; they wanted to set a new publicity record, held by the Black September since the Munich Olympics. After 9/11, one leading Al-Qaeda operative boasted, 'September 11 was an even greater propaganda coup. It may be said that it broke a record in propaganda dissemination.'[47]

When US-led military actions in Afghanistan forced the group's leadership to flee and go underground, bin Laden and his directorate had limited communications. In order not to be located by foreign intelligence agencies they used messengers to communicate with associates or deliver material to friendly media. Ayman al-Zawahiri, Al-Qaeda Central's second in command, and others, especially a Californian convert to Islam, Adam Gadahn, managed to produce propaganda videos that they placed into the hands of the Arab television network Al Jazeera or posted on the Internet. CDs with fake images of American soldiers mistreating Muslim women and the elderly during the invasion and occupation of Iraq were Al-Qaeda Central's most powerful recruitment tools.

Anwar al-Awlaki, a Yemeni-American leader of Al-Qaeda on the Arabian Peninsula, became the organisation's most prominent online propagandist. His powerful written and spoken online sermons that urged Muslims around the world to attack Western infidels radicalised and recruited a multitude of young Muslims, particularly in the West. He inspired terrorist attacks in the US and elsewhere during his lifetime and even after being killed in a US drone

---

46 Tom Fenton reported this on the CBS Evening News on 6 December 1979. Similar experiences were reported by other reporters.
47 B. Rubin and J. C. Rubin, *Anti-American Terrorism in the Middle East* (New York, Oxford University Press, 2002), p. 274.

attack in 2011. Indeed, a survey of individuals accused of ISIS-related offences in the US during a twenty-nine-month period from 2014 to 2016 revealed that the Al-Qaeda propagandist was very well regarded by ISIS supporters. Of those who saw ISIS videos, '37% [also] reported watching video versions of lectures by American-born imam Anwar Al-Awlaki'. One woman planning to join ISIS in Syria 'left behind a pile of Awlaki DVDs' and one male recruit reported that he watched 'almost all of [al-Awlaki's] lectures'.[48]

The Islamic State

Internet and especially social media have been utilised by terrorists for a multitude of reasons, among them searching for valuable information, planning and coordinating terrorist operations, radicalising and recruiting susceptible individuals, raising funds and providing instructions for lone wolves. Most importantly, social media platforms have allowed terrorists to report their own violence in words, pictures, videos and live-stream transmissions. The mainstream media were left to report on what terrorists self-reported.

No other terrorist organisation established so potent an online propaganda machine as the Islamic State, or ISIS. Take the carefully staged and marketed executions of hostages. On a Tuesday in August 2014, the media centre of the Islamic State uploaded its video '#NewMessagefromISIStoUS' to YouTube, which depicted the desperate pleas of the American journalist James Foley and his gruesome beheading. While the video was soon removed from YouTube, the horrific content dominated the news in the United States and elsewhere. The same scenarios unfolded after ISIS posted videos of subsequent decapitations and the burning of a Jordanian pilot. These and similarly atrocities were staged and filmed to get global attention and spread fear and anxiety, particularly among Westerners. From ISIS's perspective, they scored major propaganda coups.

While President Barack Obama, other leaders and most of the general public condemned the executions, some individuals were empowered by the videos' cruelty. Thus, Sayfullo Saipov, a naturalised US citizen, who drove his pick-up truck on to a busy bike lane in a Manhattan park on Halloween Day 2017, killing eight persons, told FBI investigators that his attack was inspired by ISIS videos. Among his possessions the police found some ninety videos with thousands of images of ISIS fighters killing infidels.

---

48 R. A. Page et al, 'The American Face of ISIS', report released by the Australian Strategic Policy Institute, February 2017.

At its height, the organisation had a well-equipped media centre in Raqqa that produced many short videos, a 50-minute Hollywood-like film, 'Flames of War', that glorified the Islamic State, a glitzy online magazine, *Dabiq* (later renamed *Rumiyah*), and propaganda products for people living in ISIS-controlled territories.

Just as important as the in-house media staff were the thousands of online jihadis who spread ISIS propaganda. As one of the more prominent of them, Nasser Balochi, explained, 'This is a war of ideologies as much as it is a physical war, and just as the physical war must be fought on the battlefield, so must the ideological war be fought in the media.'[49] Both ISIS and Al-Qaeda considered online jihadists as valuable as those on the battlefield.

The military defeat of ISIS – first in Iraq and then in Syria – the loss of the media centre in Raqqa and the deaths of dozens of media staffers responsible for global and local propaganda reduced the daily output significantly. But there were still daily online releases. Whether issued directly by Media Diwan, ISIS's department of propaganda, or by affiliated and independent online jihadists around the globe, whether on social media platforms or on the dark web, the group's propaganda machine continued to function; it was weakened but not defeated; it claimed to be ready for the physical revival of the caliphate.

Conclusion

The one trait that all non-state terrorist groups and lone wolves have shared throughout the history of terrorism has been their quest for attention and spreading fear among their enemies, the recognition of their grievances and demands, and the sympathies of those in whose name they claimed to act. In that respect nothing changed in the maxim that terrorism is 'propaganda by deed'. Once communication technology was invented, from the printing press, radio, television to the Internet and particular social media platforms, all terrorists have striven for and many have found alternative media to disseminate their own propaganda in written and spoken words, visuals and even motion pictures. Yet, even in the age of mass self-communication, made possible by social media, the traditional media have remained central in the propaganda calculus of all terrorists, in that old and new communication modes have complemented each other.

---

49 Quoted in H. Solomon, 'The Evolution of Islamic State's Strategy', *Scientia Militaria: South African Journal of Military Strategy* 45/1 (2017), p. 26.

Further Reading

C. Archetti, *Understanding Terrorism in the Age of Global Media: A Communication Approach* (Houndsmills, Palgrave Macmillan, 2013)

A. Hoskins and B. O'Loughlin, *Television and Terror: Conflicting Times and the Crisis of News Discourse* (Houndsmills, Palgrave Macmillan, 2007)

D. Paletz and A. P. Schmid (eds.), *Terrorism and the Media: How Researchers, Terrorists, Government, Press, Public, Victims View and Use the Media* (Newbury Park, Sage, 1992)

T. Shaw, *Cinematic Terror: A Global History of Terrorism on Film* (New York, Bloomsbury, 2015)

G. Weimann, *Terror on the Internet: The New Arena, the New Challenges* (Washington, DC, United States Institute of Peace Press, 2006)

22

Terrorism, History and Religion

RICHARD ENGLISH

It seems unarguable that religious belief and practice have contributed on occasions in the past to the generation and sustenance of terrorism.[1] Moreover, the contemporary persistence of religious commitment suggests that such long-rooted processes may have life in them yet. As the mischievous Terry Eagleton has put it, 'The Almighty has proved remarkably difficult to dispose of';[2] vast numbers of people in the USA, for example, retain a Christian belief (though even scholars working in relevant fields of study sometimes tend to ignore this important fact);[3] in relation to terrorism as to much else, those who espouse a religious faith probably deserve more serious-minded, respectful attention than scholars sometimes afford them.[4] Certainly, in settings where religious values and beliefs have undeniably contributed in complex ways to the dynamics of terroristic violence (such as Afghanistan and Israel/Palestine), the assumption of an evaporative quality to religion and its effects would seem profoundly ill judged.[5] And if

---

1 As suggested earlier in this book, my approach to defining the word 'terrorism' allows for such violence to be practised by states as well as by non-state actors. The space allowed in a book chapter such as the current one, however, precludes full treatment of both state and non-state terrorism, so this chapter will focus on non-state activity, albeit with due attention to the mutually shaping relationship that exists between state and non-state actions.
2 T. Eagleton, *Culture and the Death of God* (New Haven, Yale University Press, 2014), p. ix; cf. C. McCrudden, *Litigating Religions: An Essay on Human Rights, Courts and Beliefs* (Oxford, Oxford University Press, 2018), p. 3.
3 As pointed out by K. L. Klein, *From History to Theory* (Berkeley, University of California Press, 2011), pp. 140–1, 145–6; cf. the valuable account in F. FitzGerald, *The Evangelicals: The Struggle to Shape America* (New York, Simon and Schuster, 2017).
4 T. Eagleton, *Reason, Faith and Revolution: Reflections on the God Debate* (New Haven, Yale University Press, 2009), p. 33; A. R. Holmes, *The Irish Presbyterian Mind: Conservative Theology, Evangelical Experience and Modern Criticism, 1830–1930* (Oxford, Oxford University Press, 2018).
5 T. H. Johnson, *Taliban Narratives: The Use and Power of Stories in the Afghanistan Conflict* (London, Hurst and Co., 2017); R. English, *Does Terrorism Work? A History* (Oxford, Oxford University Press, 2016), pp. 148–85.

terrorism is potentially most revealing in regard to the world-historical forces with which it intersects, then examination of the multilayered relationships between terrorism, history and religion represents a major challenge.

Accordingly, this chapter suggests that the precise nature of the important and complex relationships between terrorism and religion might helpfully be examined through addressing the following four historically minded questions.[6] First, should religious belief and practice be seen more as causes of terroristic violence, or as restraining influences upon it? Second, has religious terrorism represented an existential threat, or more of a horrific nuisance? Third, is religious terrorism a novel phenomenon, or a recognisably familiar one? Fourth, is religion a detachable part, or an organically inextricable feature, of the beliefs which can lead to terrorist activity?

Causes or Restraining Influences?

First, should religious belief and practice be seen more as causes of terroristic violence, or as restraining influences upon it?

One eminent scholar of religious terrorism has pointed out that 'The rhetoric of warfare is evoked in virtually every religious tradition';[7] elsewhere, he has also suggested that 'Religion seems to be connected with violence virtually everywhere', and that religious terrorism involves 'public acts of violence ... for which religion has provided the motivation, the justification, the organisation and the world view'.[8] Equally, however, one distinguished neurobiologist with great expertise on violence has argued that 'religion fosters the best and worst of our behaviours'.[9] So it might reasonably be proposed both that religious commitment in the past has on occasions

---

[6] Two further definitional points might usefully be made here, one about the word 'history' and one about the word 'religion'. I refer to 'the past' as that which has happened before now; by 'history', I mean research and writing about the past; I use the term 'historiography' to refer to research and writing about history. By 'religion', I mean 'belief in, recognition of, or an awakened sense of, a higher unseen controlling power or powers, with the emotion and morality connected therewith; rites or worship; any system of such belief or worship' (*Chambers 20th Century Dictionary* (Edinburgh, W. and R. Chambers, 1983), p. 1093).

[7] M. Juergensmeyer, *Global Rebellion: Religious Challenges to the Secular State, from Christian Militias to al-Qaida* (Berkeley, University of California Press, 2008), p. 212.

[8] M. Juergensmeyer, *Terror in the Mind of God: The Global Rise of Religious Violence* (Berkeley, University of California Press, 2001), pp. xi, 7.

[9] R. M. Sapolsky, *Behave: The Biology of Humans at Our Best and Worst* (London, Bodley Head, 2017), p. 305.

stimulated terrorist violence, and also that it has on others restrained its occurrence.

Close examination of first-hand evidence gathered from various long pasts makes clear that religiously based grievances and religiously fuelled commitments have frequently contributed to the emergence of terrorist violence. Twenty-first-century jihadist terrorism, for example, seems to have had at least some foundation in people's long-standing perception of wrongs done by Western countries against Muslims;[10] there have also been attempts (however unpersuasive) to justify jihadist violence according to explicitly religious thinking and teaching.[11] Again, unless we dismiss what vast numbers of those involved have actually said,[12] it is clear that the grievances central to numerous other major forms of terrorism have, from Israel/Palestine to Ireland and beyond, possessed some religious dimensions in terms of the communities, organisations and perceptions that have generated the violence. Each of these cases is unique, each of them has complex causation behind it, and each has evolved over time; but the sincerity of religiously informed thinking and emotion is one important element within all of their histories.[13]

It is true that the processes involved here are far from straightforward when examined within the complex particularity of their context. So, Jewish

---

10 In addition to violence in places such as Afghanistan or Iraq, there is also the issue of anti-Muslim discrimination within Western countries (C. L. Adida, D. D. Laitin and M. Valfort, *Why Muslim Integration Fails in Christian Heritage Societies* (Cambridge, Harvard University Press, 2016)). It is clear that perceived wrongs against Muslims partly motivate (and are certainly used in attempts to justify) jihadist terrorism (English, *Does Terrorism Work?*, pp. 42–91).

11 See the excellent treatment in A. Brahimi, *Jihad and Just War in the War on Terror* (Oxford, Oxford University Press, 2010).

12 *Republican News*, 9 February 1974; Millar to Pope John Paul II, 30 November 1980, Linen Hall Library Political Collection Archive, Belfast; M. Begin, *The Revolt: Story of the Irgun* (Jerusalem, Steimatzky's, 1977).

13 As is clear from detailed studies that draw on first-hand, contextually based evidence: R. Singh, *Hamas and Suicide Terrorism: Multi-Causal and Multi-Level Approaches* (London, Routledge, 2011); S. Mishal and A. Sela, *The Palestinian Hamas: Vision, Violence and Coexistence* (New York, Columbia University Press, 2006); M. Ruthven, *A Fury for God: The Islamist Attack on America* (London, Granta, 2002); D. Byman, *Al-Qaida, the Islamic State and the Global Jihadist Movement: What Everyone Needs to Know* (Oxford, Oxford University Press, 2015); P. L. Bergen, *The Osama bin Laden I Know* (New York, Free Press, 2006); G. Wood, *The Way of the Strangers: Encounters with the Islamic State* (London, Penguin, 2017); W. McCants, *The ISIS Apocalypse: The History, Strategy and Doomsday Vision of the Islamic State* (New York, St Martin's Press, 2015); G. Aran and R. E. Hassner, 'Religious Violence in Judaism: Past and Present', *Terrorism and Political Violence* 25/3 (2013); R. English, *Armed Struggle: The History of the IRA* (London, Pan Macmillan, 2012); English, *Does Terrorism Work?* Other modes of impressive scholarly research have reinforced the point: N. Saiya, 'Religion, State and Terrorism: A Global Analysis', *Terrorism and Political Violence* 31/2 (2019).

terrorism has possessed profoundly religious dynamics; but it is also a phenomenon which can be powerfully explained in relation to the politics of nationalism as such, involving the desire of a particular national community to struggle for the establishment and then the defence of political power within a designated territory in Israel; a similar point could be made about Israel's opponents in Hamas, or indeed about religiously infused nationalist terrorisms in Ireland: all are cases which embody important religious themes but which also require explanation in regard to nationalism itself.[14] In each of these cases, there have existed religiously fuelled nationalisms within which religion is one of a set of important motivating forces.[15] As so often, terrorism here has been an emergent symptom of far more significant and globally transformative phenomena.

So, in the generation of terrorist violence there can be varying kinds of religious contribution. Al-Qaida's politics and terrorism have involved both primarily religious and also politically Muslim elements; the same is true of Hamas, but the violence of the latter owes far more than does that of al-Qaida to nationalism and to its profound impulses; the IRA has drawn on a nationalism that has been heavily influenced historically by Catholic experience, community and grievance, but the degree to which this has involved religious commitment has varied over periods and between different IRA activists at any given moment; some religiously related terrorist violence involves intra-religious rivalries and tensions, while some relates more to hostility towards enemies who exist beyond one's own religion or religious grouping.[16] Every terrorism (and, ultimately, every terrorist) is unique. But the central points to consider here are these. First, historically, religious

14 B. Hoffman, *Anonymous Soldiers: The Struggle for Israel, 1917–1947* (New York, Alfred A. Knopf, 2015); Singh, *Hamas and Suicide Terrorism*; R. English, *Irish Freedom: The History of Nationalism in Ireland* (London, Pan Macmillan, 2006); R. English, 'Nationalism and Terrorism', in E. Chenoweth, R. English, A. Gofas and S. N. Kalyvas (eds.), *The Oxford Handbook of Terrorism* (Oxford, Oxford University Press, 2019).

15 As is vividly clear from archival sources, such as IRA man Ernie O'Malley's 1923 statement: 'one feels that one is always fighting for God and Ireland, for the spread of our spirituality such as it is, to counteract the agnosticism and materialism of our own and other countries' (O'Malley to Childers, 5–7 December 1923, Trinity College Dublin Library (Manuscripts), TCL 7850 909); cf. Mary MacSwiney's view that, for the Irish republican movement of which she was a member, a 'social programme in accordance with Catholic principles is quite good enough for anyone' (MacSwiney to Brugha, 23 January 1935, Brugha Papers, University College Dublin Archives Department P15/8).

16 Byman, *Al-Qaida, the Islamic State and the Global Jihadist Movement*; Singh, *Hamas and Suicide Terrorism*; English, *Armed Struggle*; R. English, *Ernie O'Malley: IRA Intellectual* (Oxford, Oxford University Press, 1998).

motivation has frequently been one among the many factors contributing towards generating terrorist violence. Second, such motivation tends overwhelmingly to be interwoven with other elements in a multicausal process.

If religiously inflected grievances and religiously united communities can represent one part of the causal foundation for terrorist activity, then it is also true that the levels and precise types of violence that people actually carry out can be affected by distinctively religious dynamics. Eli Berman's powerful study of major terrorist groups that carry out high levels of violence, for example, suggests that one reason for their lethality lies in their religiously specific organisation. More particularly, Berman argues that groups like Hamas, Hezbollah and the Taliban have proved able to avoid defection and infiltration (and therefore to remain resiliently more violent) partly because they are religious movements which require high-cost sacrifice as a commitment-demonstrating part of the process of joining, and that they are organisations which also possess strong ties of loyalty-sustaining mutual aid once one has become part of the group. As a result of this, shirkers and potential defectors are more likely to have been separated out from the movement.[17]

Again, in terms of religion's relevance to the actual types of violence that are practised, Ariel Merari has argued that the contingent religious valorising within Muslim cultures of a certain form of self-sacrifice can make suicide terrorism a more frequent occurrence than it would have been without such religious thinking.[18] In other ways too, the specifically religious dynamics of terrorist causation can prove complex rather than straightforward. Richard Nielsen's ingenious argument about the motivation of some militant jihadist clerics offers an example. Nielsen suggests that some such clerics seem to have been jihadists who then turned to clerical careers, while others appear to have been people whose frustrated clerical careers have nudged them towards militant jihadism; the respective roles played here by religious belief, behaviour and practice clearly vary, but religious dynamics are causally and integrally involved in each instance.[19]

---

17 E. Berman, *Radical, Religious and Violent: The New Economics of Terrorism* (Cambridge, MIT Press, 2009).
18 A. Merari, *Driven to Death: Psychological and Social Aspects of Suicide Terrorism* (Oxford, Oxford University Press, 2010).
19 R. A. Nielsen, *Deadly Clerics: Blocked Ambition and the Paths to Jihad* (Cambridge, Cambridge University Press, 2017). I am grateful to Jasmine English for kindly alerting me to this book, as also to some other valuable publications of relevance to this chapter.

Yet again, the work of Diego Gambetta and Steffen Hertog suggests that religious beliefs can reflect and reinforce instincts which increase someone's propensity to carry out terrorist violence. Addressing the puzzle that 'engineers are overrepresented among violent Islamist extremists', they explore the mechanisms behind such jihadist violence, and argue that the personality traits on which engineers tend to score highly ('proneness to disgust', 'need for closure', 'in-group bias', politically naïve 'simplism') are also ones which resonate with Islamist ideology ('a desire to keep society clean or purify it, a preference for social order, and rigid in-group/out-group distinctions'). Gambetta and Hertog are clear that they do not view their findings as proof that religiosity as such is a cause of violence.[20] But their work does suggest the significance of religion, in that its attractions are here seen as reflecting and reinforcing people's deep (and violence-generating) instincts. The kind of violent politics that a significant group of jihadists engages in is, according to their argument, at least partly related to what a particular religious ideology distinctively offers them and reinforces.

All of this demonstrates that, within a multicausal, complex and contingent set of processes, religious beliefs, behaviours, instincts, cultures, grievances, organisations and practices have historically played a role in generating some terrorism and in partly defining the types and levels of violence that have emerged. This is not to mark religious terrorism out as a neatly or entirely separate form of violence. Some distinguished scholars have indeed suggested that religious terrorism is different from other kinds; but, even here, much of the evidence adduced can be read as involving group dynamics and motivations which also exist in non-religious movements (instrumental warfare, defence, retaliation, social provision, theatrically symbolic violence, deliberate terrorising of opponents, the seizing of public attention, intra-communal competition).[21] In any case, we do not require a separate category of religious terrorism in order to recognise the central point that is being established here: that theological but also social, communal, institutional, organisational, behavioural and attitudinal aspects of various religions have historically contributed towards the generation of terrorist violence in significant ways.

Less frequently discussed and less famous is the capacity of religious belief and practice to limit the incidence of terrorism. Not only has religious motivation been non-essential to the generation of fanatical terrorist zealotry

20 D. Gambetta and S. Hertog, *Engineers of Jihad: The Curious Connection Between Violent Extremism and Education* (Princeton, Princeton University Press, 2016), pp. viii, 154, 156, 158.
21 Juergensmeyer, *Terror in the Mind of God*, pp. 10, 73–8, 124, 139–40, 167, 216–17, 220.

in the past;[22] religion might also be proposed as having been one of the most important means, on occasions, of counteracting it. Scriptural injunctions to behave with empathy and compassion might seem to point in this direction (within the Christian tradition, for example, Matthew 7:12 or Luke 6:36); so too does much other historical evidence. Most British Muslims have had no role at all in generating terrorism, and many Muslims have very openly condemned it;[23] some of the most authoritative voices that have limited the appeal and momentum of groups like al-Qaida and ISIS have been explicitly Muslim voices;[24] intensified Muslim fervour and devotion can on occasions generate a more tolerant, rather than a more aggressively antagonistic, approach on the part of those involved;[25] amid the terrorism of the post-1968 Northern Irish conflict, there were powerful instances of religious belief and commitment leading towards restraint, forgiveness and peace rather than towards violence and retaliation;[26] likewise, powerful voices from within the Jewish faith have argued that religion should be seen as a major venue for countering terroristic and other violence: 'Religiously motivated violence must be fought religiously as well as militarily'; 'To invoke God to justify violence against the innocent is not an act of sanctity but of sacrilege.'[27] It is not, of course, essential that one should possess a religious faith in order to espouse the constructive potential of a quality such as compassion;[28] but that does not diminish the reality that, for very many people, religious belief and practice have led powerfully and decisively in that eirenic direction.

Indeed, subtle and contextual historical thinking shows how mistaken it is to assume that the religious past has been dominated by enmity and hostility between major faiths. As David Cannadine has put it,

22 T. J. Kaczynski, *Anti-Tech Revolution: Why and How* (Scottsdale, Fitch and Madison, 2016); S. Aust, *Baader–Meinhof: The Inside Story of the RAF* (Oxford, Oxford University Press, 2009).
23 S. Warsi, *The Enemy Within: A Tale of Muslim Britain* (London, Allen Lane, 2017), pp. 5, 62, 80, 143–5, 161.
24 M. Sageman, *Misunderstanding Terrorism* (Philadelphia, University of Pennsylvania Press, 2017), pp. 122–3.
25 M. A. Alexseev and S. N. Zhemukhov, *Mass Religious Ritual and Intergroup Tolerance: The Muslim Pilgrims' Paradox* (Cambridge, Cambridge University Press, 2017).
26 M. O'Doherty, *Fifty Years On: The Troubles and the Struggle for Change in Northern Ireland* (London, Atlantic Books, 2019), pp. 292, 296; English, *Armed Struggle*, pp. 255–6; M. M. Scull, *The Catholic Church and the Northern Ireland Troubles, 1968–1998* (Oxford, Oxford University Press, 2019), pp. 24, 34, 43, 45, 51, 55, 61, 135, 142, 160, 164, 166–7, 170–81, 197–8; J. D. Parker, *On the Waterfront* (Durham, Pentland Press, 2000).
27 J. Sacks, *Not in God's Name: Confronting Religious Violence* (London, Hodder and Stoughton, 2015), pp. ix, 5.
28 J. R. Doty, *Into the Magic Shop: A Neurosurgeon's True Story of the Life-Changing Magic of Compassion and Mindfulness* (London, Yellow Kite, 2016).

the evidence is clear that Christians and Muslims have often lived together constructively and amicably, that they have taught one another much about how to live, and that they have learned a great deal from each other. When looked at as a whole, the 'Islamo-Christian world' has much more in common and binding it together than it has forcing it apart.[29]

And the eirenic possibilities and resources evident here might yet become more powerful in the future; 'The revival of tolerant forms of religion may therefore be a part of the cure for the excesses of its rebellious and intolerant extremes.'[30] Certainly, there have been religious roots to some powerfully moderating arguments about politics in the past.[31] None of this requires a diminution in religious belief or even in religion's capacity for major historical transformation; religious faith can indeed be revolutionary (indeed, some would see that as one of its central strengths), but that need not have any violent aspect to it at all.[32] Quite the contrary.

With an eye to policy, it is therefore intriguing to detect the religious silences that are evident in many current efforts to counteract religious terrorism. The 2018 *National Strategy for Counter-Terrorism of the United States of America* (an important strategic document setting out 'a new approach to combatting and preventing terrorism', and one emphasising 'the use of all elements of national power to combat terrorism and terrorist ideologies'), stated that the USA's 'principal terrorist enemies are radical Islamist terrorist groups'. But, apart from a passing reference to working with 'religious leaders' (among others), there is no engagement in the document with the extraordinary resources embodied in religious faith, commitment and practice in terms of opposing terrorist violence.[33]

An Existential Threat?

Second, has religious terrorism represented an existential threat, or more of a horrific nuisance?

---

29 D. Cannadine, *The Undivided Past: History Beyond Our Differences* (London, Penguin, 2013), pp. 36–7.
30 Juergensmeyer, *Global Rebellion*, p. 263.
31 See, for example, A. Jackson, 'J. C. Beckett: Politics, Faith, Scholarship', *Irish Historical Studies* 33/130 (2002).
32 D. English, 'Faith in the New Testament', in J. Stacey (ed.), *About Faith* (Letchworth, Garden City Press, 1972), p. 45; H. Kung, *On Being a Christian* (London, Collins, 1977), p. 191.
33 *National Strategy for Counter-Terrorism of the United States of America* (October 2018), quotations at pp. i, 1, 21.

There are distinguished figures who have argued for the former interpretation. Alan Dershowitz, for example, has suggested: 'The greatest danger facing the world today comes from religiously inspired terrorist groups ... that are seeking to develop weapons of mass destruction for use against civilian targets.'[34]

However, in terms of the detailed historical record, such claims seem ill founded. Compared with genocidal killing, or with large-scale wars (whether civil or international),[35] non-state terrorism (whether religious or not) remains a low-level threat to most societies and to most individuals most of the time. Indeed, contrary to what many people assume, the historical evidence in fact suggests that terrorism has been a comparatively trivial threat to most people in most parts of the world.[36] Terrorist groups using violence can on occasions be an existential threat to some governments; and the threat to individual existence for those who are victims of terrorist violence is appalling and extreme. But the threat presented by terrorism at societal level (and the threat to most individuals' existence most of the time) has been and continues to be minimal when compared with other contextual dangers that are faced. In relation to specifically religious-terrorist danger, for example, there has undoubtedly been 'a great inflation of the terrorist threat to the United States'; 'a misunderstanding of terrorism in the West has dramatically inflated fear of the actual danger posed by neojihadis'.[37]

None of this means that we should dismiss the terrible suffering that religious and other terrorism causes for its victims, nor that we should be casual about trying to prevent it or defend people against it. But it does imply that there is a need for a clear-eyed sense of proportion when responding to the threat. Given some of the exaggerated responses to Islamic terrorism over recent decades, and given the historically repeated problem that overreaction has actually contributed to generating *more* terrorism, this is a vitally

---

34 A. M. Dershowitz, *Why Terrorism Works: Understanding the Threat, Responding to the Challenge* (New Haven, Yale University Press, 2002), p. 2; cf. Sacks, *Not in God's Name*, p. 14; 'Terror Chief: Threat Is Worst for a Generation', *Sunday Telegraph*, 26 February 2017.

35 J. Waller, *Becoming Evil: How Ordinary People Commit Genocide and Mass Killing* (Oxford, Oxford University Press, 2007); S. N. Kalyvas, *The Logic of Violence in Civil War* (Cambridge, Cambridge University Press, 2006); D. Armitage, *Civil Wars: A History in Ideas* (New Haven, Yale University Press, 2017); R. English, *Modern War: A Very Short Introduction* (Oxford, Oxford University Press, 2013).

36 J. Mueller and M. Stewart, *Chasing Ghosts: The Policing of Terrorism* (Oxford, Oxford University Press, 2016); Berman, *Radical, Religious and Violent*, p. 239; Sageman, *Misunderstanding Terrorism*, pp. 30–5, 45, 58; E. Hobsbawm, *Globalisation, Democracy and Terrorism* (London, Little, Brown, 2007), p. 135.

37 Sageman, *Misunderstanding Terrorism*, pp. 21–2.

important, practical point. Moreover, there exist historically based and proportionate ways of diminishing and containing the threat that is actually posed by terrorism, approaches which are as relevant to religious actors as they are to other terrorists.[38]

A Novel Phenomenon?

Third, is religious terrorism a novel phenomenon, or a recognisably familiar one?

There are certainly those who have suggested a novelty to recent terrorism of a religious kind;[39] and it is axiomatic that every terrorist organisation is, in its uniqueness, to some extent new. But the broader historical reality is that, as Bruce Hoffman has pointed out, 'The connection between religion and terrorism is not new.'[40] There are impressive scholars who are sceptical about the value of applying the term terrorism to very early periods within the human past,[41] and I have profound respect for that view. But there are also distinguished scholars who do apply the word to periods of ancient history,[42] and the use of deliberately terrorising violence with a politico-religious dimension is traceable as far back as the Christian Old Testament (the books of Isaiah and Jeremiah, for example); and there are many varieties of religiously informed terrorisms from the more modern but still very far from contemporary past.[43] Moreover, some of these examples (including those in Palestine and Ireland) have clearly pre-echoed and influenced more recent forms of terrorism which possess a strong religious flavour.

Given all this, it is important to stress the longer-term continuities as well as the genuine novelties that exist within contemporary religious terrorism. So, for all that distinguishes them,[44] what are the consequences of seeing

---

38 R. English, *Terrorism: How to Respond* (Oxford, Oxford University Press, 2009), pp. 118–43.
39 D. C. Rapoport, 'The Four Waves of Rebel Terror and September 11', *Anthropoetics* 8/1 (2002); E. N. Kurtulus, 'Is There a "New Terrorism" in Existence Today?', in R. Jackson and D. Pisoiu (eds.), *Contemporary Debates on Terrorism* (London, Routledge, 2018).
40 B. Hoffman, *Inside Terrorism* (New York, Columbia University Press, 2017), p. 85; Begin, *The Revolt*; F. Gallagher, *Days of Fear* (London, John Murray, 1928), pp. 13, 35–6, 57, 60–1, 75, 110; M. Brennan, *The War in Clare 1911–1921: Personal Memoirs of the Irish War of Independence* (Dublin, Four Courts Press, 1980), p. 81.
41 W. C. Brown, 'The Pre-History of Terrorism', in Chenoweth et al. (eds.), *Oxford Handbook of Terrorism*.
42 See, for example, M. Beard, *SPQR: A History of Ancient Rome* (London, Profile Books, 2015), p. 21.
43 Hoffman, *Anonymous Soldiers*; English, *Irish Freedom*.
44 Hoffman, *Inside Terrorism*, pp. 91–100.

a group such as al-Qaida or ISIS as a new version of a historically recognisable reality? I think there are three central benefits. Less exaggeration of the novelty of such groups helps us avoid the amnesiac laziness which so often and so damagingly greeted the movements just mentioned above; many of the egregious errors that were made in responding to al-Qaida and to ISIS were facilitated by the unhistorical suggestion that these groups were so utterly new and completely different from what had preceded them that we could ignore hard-learned wisdom in counterterrorist approach;[45] many lives were lost as a consequence. It is also true that recognition of historical continuities and inheritances offsets the unnecessary panic that some have evinced regarding religious terrorism supposedly representing a more cataclysmic threat because it is religious. In fact, with the exception of the 9/11 atrocity, the scale of terrorist violence as practised by recent religious terrorists has not been utterly different in scale from that which was characteristic of previous periods or actors. Finally, a historically informed recognition of what is shared between contemporary and previous terrorists who had a religious commitment clarifies the profound multicausality behind terrorism as carried out by (say) al-Qaida and ISIS; deep understanding of the Irgun, of the 1920s IRA, of the PLO and of other pre-contemporary groups makes clear the likelihood that more recent actors too have had motivations and causal contexts which separate them less neatly from non-religious terrorists than is sometimes assumed, and which represent essential elements in our understanding of their violence and its complex, contextual emergence.

Detachable or Inextricable?

This hints at our fourth question: is religion a detachable part, or an organically inextricable feature, of the beliefs which can lead to terrorist activity?

My argument here is that, when we consider the complex particularity of terrorist context, as seen through the lens of multiple sources, it is hard to argue that religion is mechanically or easily detachable from the other beliefs and behaviours of those whom we are studying. This is implied strongly in the work alluded to earlier by scholars such as Berman, Nielsen, Merari, Gambetta and Hertog, whose findings suggest a deep entanglement between religion and social dynamics within terrorist groups. That religious terrorism is not merely about theology but also about social organisation is one aspect of this; but the

---

45 L. Richardson, *What Terrorists Want: Understanding the Terrorist Threat* (London, John Murray, 2006); English, *Terrorism: How to Respond*.

interwovenness (in the eyes and actions of the actors themselves) between the specifically religious and the socially broader aspects of their activity is the weightier point. If your religious belief and level of religious commitment affect the membership and efficacy of your terrorist group, for example,[46] then it is impossible either to remove the religion from the group and still understand it, or to deny that organisational dynamics which are explicable in social terms are also, interwovenly, at play. In this sense religion cannot be read as a somewhat lesser element in the mixture, as a mere surface badge which can be removed in order to reveal the deeper explanation behind human activity; rather, it is inseparably integrated into what has historically occurred, and is an essential part of the explanation of activities which are both religious and also about social behaviour and relationships. For serious religion is of course numinous (and therefore different from secular approaches to politics and society, and distinct from non-religious ideologies);[47] but such religion necessarily concerns the ways in which such sincere spiritual beliefs affect society, economy, daily behaviour, morality, interactions with neighbours, political power.[48] Indeed, to pretend otherwise is to misrepresent what vast numbers of people have historically thought and felt.

There might seem to be a tension here between this historical approach and arguments that have been offered within the instrumentalist literature generated by some political scientists. In terms of ethnicity, for example, Daniel Posner has argued that ethnic identities are 'instrumental', viewing the relationship between someone's environment and their identity 'as the product of a deliberate decision designed to maximise payoffs'. This is, as Posner himself describes it, a 'strict instrumentalist approach', featuring the central argument 'that ethnic groups are mobilised or joined not because of the depth of attachment that people feel toward them but because of the usefulness of the political coalitions that they define – a usefulness determined exclusively by their sizes relative to those of other coalitions'.[49] Strongly influenced by Posner, Fotini Christia's analysis of alliances and identities in civil war settings 'is essentially an instrumentalist one'; alliances and their associated identity narratives are not 'intrinsic' but rather 'invented'.[50] Where ethnicity and religion interact (as they frequently do) this

---

46 Berman, *Radical, Religious and Violent.*
47 See, for example, K. Barth, *The Faith of the Church: A Commentary on the Apostles' Creed According to Calvin's Catechism* (London, Fontana, 1960), pp. 27, 63–4.
48 K. Armstrong, *Fields of Blood: Religion and the History of Violence* (London, Bodley Head, 2014).
49 D. N. Posner, *Institutions and Ethnic Politics in Africa* (Cambridge, Cambridge University Press, 2005), pp. 11–12.
50 F. Christia, *Alliance Formation in Civil Wars* (Cambridge, Cambridge University Press, 2012), pp. xiii, 7.

kind of approach has implications for the argument of this chapter. To see someone's attachments as instrumental towards maximum payoffs involves a very different reading than one which accepts that the beliefs themselves (whether about religion, ethnicity or a combination of the two) are sincere and integral to people's attachments.

Political scientists Brendan O'Leary and John McGarry have argued that 'The vital feature of ethnic markers is not their particular religious, linguistic or cultural signs, but rather that they provide evidence of common origin and shared experiences, a basis for recognising members and non-members, and therefore potential friends and potential "strangers".' In their view, 'as long as groups have *any* way of telling each other apart – names or clothes can be substituted for religion or language – ethno-national divisions can be maintained'. With regard to Northern Ireland, they assert that 'Protestants and Catholics are divided by religion, by definition, but they are also divided by differences in economic and political power, by historical experience, and, most intensely, by national political identity.'[51]

But in understanding the role of religion within the violent national conflict in Northern Ireland, it is important not to underestimate its interwovenness with other historical factors, its inherent significance or its possibly crucial effects. McGarry and O'Leary here present ethno-nationalism as the truly important phenomenon, with religion being a mere 'ethnic marker', something far less significant and somewhat detachable or replaceable. But the ethno-national identities and communities involved here (rival Irish and British nationalisms) emerged from and were defined by episodes and relationships within which religion was an integral, inseparable element. To suggest that ethnicity rather than religion was the crucial issue in the period of the seventeenth-century Plantation, or that nationalism was the issue and religious conviction merely a replaceable badge during the Home Rule or Irish Revolutionary eras, would be anachronistic. To very many of the people involved in those crucial phases of the Irish past, politics and religion were inextricably intermingled. The religious outlook, background and identity of many early twentieth-century Irish republicans, for example, profoundly shaped their nationalism and the goals for which they were violently fighting. To present the religious aspects of that violent nationalism as comparatively insignificant, or as something which could be detached or replaced while

---

51 J. McGarry and B. O'Leary, *Explaining Northern Ireland: Broken Images* (Oxford, Blackwell, 1995), pp. 212, 357. A subtler version of this argument is offered in B. O'Leary, *A Treatise on Northern Ireland*, Vol. 1: *Colonialism* (Oxford, Oxford University Press, 2019).

leaving the main motivations still intact, would have made little sense to many of the historical actors themselves.[52]

Religion's interwoven prominence within nationalism was more marked before the Northern Ireland Troubles than it was during them, and religion grew less crucial for many people during the Troubles themselves. But it remains important to acknowledge that, even in modern Northern Ireland, the reason for many people having cared so much about their group origins and their shared experiences has often related to the very particularity and profundity of their religious beliefs, practices and identities. Indeed, the important Northern Irish differences to which McGarry and O'Leary point (in economic and political power, historical experience and rival national political identities) are incomprehensible without respecting the vital, integral role of particular religious beliefs, practices and adherences in forging but also in long maintaining those differences. The suggestion that religion could be removed and replaced with an alternative and equally effective ethno-national 'marker' is one that disrespects what many have historically considered to be profound and special and what, even now, some of those involved in Northern Ireland politics would consider inherently and uniquely important.[53]

This is not to present religion as the main or primary cause of the Northern Ireland conflict, or to reduce ethno-national politics there to religious conviction or affiliation. It is rather to stress (first) that religious commitment and belonging have, for many people, been much more than mere markers within the long-term political conflict between national communities in the Irish and Northern Irish contexts, and (second) that trying to disentangle the national from the religious in such cases makes less sense than respecting the interwovenness of religion with the other important elements of national identity and attachment. In playing down the significance of religion in the

---

52 R. F. Foster, *Vivid Faces: The Revolutionary Generation in Ireland 1890–1923* (London, Penguin, 2014), pp. 36, 229, 232, 248–9; English, *Ernie O'Malley*, pp. 89–94.
53 Holmes, *Irish Presbyterian Mind*; A. Jackson, *Ireland 1798–1998* (Oxford, Blackwell, 1999); D. Keogh, *The Vatican, the Bishops and Irish Politics 1919–39* (Cambridge, Cambridge University Press, 1986); D. Ferriter, *The Transformation of Ireland 1900–2000* (London, Profile, 2004); M. Elliott, *When God Took Sides: Religion and Identity in Ireland – Unfinished History* (Oxford, Oxford University Press, 2009); English, *Irish Freedom*; English, *Armed Struggle*; S. Millar, *On the Brinks* (No place or publisher given, 2003), pp. 35, 153; L. Clarke and K. Johnston, *Martin McGuinness: From Guns to Government* (Edinburgh, Mainstream Publishing, 2001), p. 15; E. Collins, *Killing Rage* (London, Granta, 1997), pp. 36–7; A. Edwards, *UVF: Behind the Mask* (Newbridge, Merrion Press, 2017), pp. 10–12, 36–9; J. Tonge, M. Braniff, T. Hennessey, J. W. McAuley and S. A. Whiting, *The Democratic Unionist Party: From Protest to Power* (Oxford, Oxford University Press, 2014), pp. 133–60.

Northern Ireland conflict, McGarry and O'Leary point to the fact that the clashing communities in the north of Ireland are not only 'religiously differentiated', but also 'divided by broader cultural differences, national allegiances, histories of antagonistic encounters, and marked differences in economic and political power'.[54] But each of these other elements of division has been informed and affected and significantly shaped by the role of religion.

My broader argument here is that it is mechanically ahistorical to present the religious elements of ethnic or national division as somewhat superficial, as surface badges rather than anything more substantial or integrally significant, and as elements easily detachable from the essence of the conflict. For a historian, one key issue is to try to identify and recover the world as those living in the past saw it; in the case of much religious politics, this demands that we respect the profundity of people's religious beliefs (and the interwovenness of the latter with questions of power, identity, economics and belonging), rather than that we try to present these beliefs as markers of something mechanically separable and more important.

It is also true that the particularity of ethno-national divisions can have an important effect on the actual nature of violent conflict as it is practised. Tim Wilson's research strongly reinforces this point. Wilson shows that the nature of ethno-national division between violently opposed groups (the issue of whether the dividing line is primarily religious, for example, or linguistic) can play a powerful role in determining the levels and kinds of non-state terrorising violence that actually occur in ethno-nationalist conflicts. The idea that one could see religion as merely a superficial element, or an analytically detachable badge of some deeper ethnic reality, seems implausible when set against Wilson's close historical reading of grassroots evidence and experience.[55] In other geographical settings and periods of high relevance to terrorism, a similar point can be established by research that is closely and contextually focused on first-hand sources.[56]

The hermeneutical and practical implications of this argument are significant. For such an approach precludes two common errors of response regarding religious terrorism: first, the error of presenting religious belief and motivation as somehow more trivial and detachable than other, more foundational elements; second, the error of assuming that religion operates in

---

54 McGarry and O'Leary, *Explaining Northern Ireland*, p. 172.
55 T. K. Wilson, *Frontiers of Violence: Conflict and Identity in Ulster and Upper Silesia, 1918–1922* (Oxford, Oxford University Press, 2010).
56 Johnson, *Taliban Narratives*.

a separate world from other factors (social, economic), that it should be treated as if utterly different in kind from other world views, and that its extirpation would therefore bring the relevant terrorism to an end.[57]

So it is not appropriate to suggest that, for example, what is *really* going on in Israel/Palestine is about nationalism, and that the religious cultures and beliefs involved are badges and can be seen as more trivial elements; but nor is it accurate to assert that, if only one could rid people of religious belief, then their terrorism would simply not occur. In the latter case, there would have been different pasts, and different possibilities of violence; but religion is neither an incidental, detachable badge nor an isolated and independent cause of terrorism.

The argument offered in this chapter resonates with the work of those scholars who have questioned the drawing of a stark distinction between 'religious' and 'secular' terrorisms;[58] and it reflects a historian's scepticism about binary definitions and approaches. For serious historical study of the evolution of major religions shows repeatedly the complex interweaving of faith, economics, identity, personal and family histories and opportunities, nationalist context, gender relations, social inheritances and issues of state and secular power.[59] The idea that one could mechanically remove religion while leaving those other elements essentially unchanged, or that one can explain religious behaviour without simultaneous attention to these other, interwoven dynamics, therefore seems unhistorical.[60] Similarly, terroristic religious violence involves interwoven, but non-religious, dynamics: these might be social, psychological, nationalistic, state-related; and they can relate to power, identity, cultural processes and personal relationships.[61] Careful analysts of religious fundamentalism reinforce this argument, by stressing the interwovenness of such belief with social and political concerns and goals.[62]

---

57 R. Dawkins, *The God Delusion* (London, Transworld Publishers, 2006).
58 J. Gunning and R. Jackson, 'What's So "Religious" about "Religious Terrorism"?', *Critical Studies on Terrorism* 4/3 (2011).
59 D. MacCulloch, *A History of Christianity: The First Three Thousand Years* (London, Allen Lane, 2009); Holmes, *Irish Presbyterian Mind*; D. H. Akenson, *Discovering the End of Time: Irish Evangelicals in the Age of Daniel O'Connell* (Montreal, McGill-Queen's University Press, 2016); D. H. Akenson, *Exporting the Rapture: John Nelson Darby and the Victorian Conquest of North-American Evangelicalism* (Oxford, Oxford University Press, 2018); D. English, *Christianity and Politics* (Belfast, Queen's University Belfast, 1993); FitzGerald, *The Evangelicals*; S. Ozment, *Protestants: The Birth of a Revolution* (London, Fontana, 1993).
60 Kung, *On Being a Christian*, p. 31.
61 Waller, *Becoming Evil*; English, *Does Terrorism Work?*
62 M. Ruthven, *Fundamentalism: The Search for Meaning* (Oxford, Oxford University Press, 2004).

As suggested, this has practical as well as analytical implications, requiring a more serious understanding of religion than is sometimes evident in state or policy-oriented responses to non-state terrorism. As an example of what needs to be challenged, in the wake of 9/11 at one US National Laboratory a leading scientist asked whether, 'from reading the Koran', it would be possible to derive al-Qaida's tactics and strategy and thereby allow him and his team to predict the organisation's next attacks.[63] Whatever one's religious beliefs (or lack of them) we need to be more serious-minded in our policy response than that.

Even with famously religious lone-wolf terrorism, the motivation behind the attacks turns out very often to be complex, involving religious but also personal-biographical, regional-political and other motivations and considerations.[64] It is in the complex, contextual interweaving of these elements that explanation really lies, rather than in the clumsy labelling of it as a religious phenomenon which operates in a mechanical fashion. Someone from a Muslim background in the West, whose life has involved personal and cultural marginalisation, who has had a history of low-level crime and drug use and mental illness, who has become outraged by the experiences of fellow Muslims during the early twenty-first century and who seeks revenge, who is mentored by a somewhat charismatic figure, and who seeks redemption as well as fame through an act of violence in ostensible support of a famous terrorist organisation – such a person is clearly pursuing something which is, in part, religious terrorism; but there is also much else involved, of a potentially non-religious character. All of these aspects must be considered.

Indeed, the importance of not ascribing complex phenomena to single causes spreads far beyond lone-actor terrorism. Even in contexts of group violence, close examination of terrorist killings frequently demonstrates that, even in settings where the causal processes cannot be reduced to (or even primarily based on) religion, there can be important religious dynamics involved in terms of communal grievance, attachment, identity and enmity, and in terms of the generation of particular, local-level hostility and brutality.[65] Religion cannot be mechanically detached from religious

---

63 Sageman, *Misunderstanding Terrorism*, pp. 8–9.
64 M. S. Hamm and R. Spaaij, *The Age of Lone Wolf Terrorism* (New York, Columbia University Press, 2017).
65 P. R. Keefe, *Say Nothing: A True Story of Murder and Memory in Northern Ireland* (London, William Collins, 2018).

terrorism if we are properly to understand it; its inextricability from other elements of human activity are far too profound for that.

ISIS commitment, for example, frequently involved an explicitly religious dimension, but one which was entangled with daily realities of a social and economic nature, and with questions of identity, politics and power; moreover, the roots of these questions were historically very long indeed. Theology, politics, economics, identity and emotion are inextricable here if the group is properly to be explained.[66] ISIS violence represents a certain form of religious vision. But it has also been about, for some, adventure and an escape from quotidian dullness and – especially for some foreign fighters – an exhilarating apotheosis; for some it has been about psychopathology and gangsterism; for some it has been about being part of something grand and historically significant; it has been about revenge for things done to neighbours and families and co-religionists; it has been about seeking legitimate and stable authority in Syria and Iraq for a disaffected Sunni community – so yes, a religious community, but one whose problems of order and of legitimate, acceptable government are explicable in terms very recognisable to a secular audience; ISIS appealed to so many people for a time partly because, for many Sunnis in Iraq and Syria, the existing governments in Baghdad and Damascus respectively were seen as hostile to their interests and community.

To think that one could mechanically read off ISIS's activities from religion, or that if one removed theological thinking then the basis for violent conflict in that region would simply be removed, are both mistaken. The absence of particular theological interpretation and religious argument would, of course, change the existing nature of the conflict and tension; it would not remove all of its elements.

Significantly, ISIS violence partly also emerged from the consequences of Western states' foreign policies after 9/11: 'ISIS can be seen as an extension of AQI [al-Qaida in Iraq], which was itself a creature of the 2003 US-led invasion of Iraq and its aftermath';[67] 'By destroying state institutions and establishing a sectarian-based political system, the 2003 US-led invasion polarised the country along Sunni–Shia lines and set the stage for a fierce, prolonged

---

66 Byman, *Al-Qaida, the Islamic State and the Global Jihadist Movement*; Wood, *The Way of the Strangers*; F. A. Gerges, *ISIS: A History* (Princeton, Princeton University Press, 2016); J. Stern and J. M. Berger, *ISIS: The State of Terror* (London, William Collins, 2015); McCants, *The ISIS Apocalypse*; B. H. Fishman, *The Master Plan: ISIS, Al-Qaida and the Jihadi Strategy for Final Victory* (New Haven, Yale University Press, 2016).
67 Gerges, *ISIS: A History*, p. 8.

struggle driven by identity politics';[68] 'Many diverse factors contributed to the rise of ISIS, but its roots lie with Zarqawi and the 2003 invasion of Iraq that gave him purpose ... ISIS was born from the crucible of America's "War on Terrorism"';[69] and some of the anti-US violence in Iraq from 2003 onwards drew on motivations that were not specifically religious.[70]

The first American to conduct a prolonged interrogation of the captured Saddam Hussein in 2003–4 (the then CIA analyst, John Nixon) has put this very crisply: 'The rise of Islamic extremism in Iraq, chiefly under the rubric of ISIS (or Islamic State in Iraq and al-Sham), is a catastrophe that the United States needn't have faced had it been willing to live with an aging and disengaged Saddam Hussein.' That there emerged a religiously inflected violence in Iraq is indisputable; that this had some of its roots in actions contingently taken by Western states is equally so: 'Saddam's removal created a power vacuum that turned religious differences in Iraq into a sectarian bloodbath.'[71]

Echoing this, ISIS's own tactics have drawn inspiration from some decidedly non-Muslim authorities, and their politics have combined explicit and stringent adherence to a particular reading of Islam with a preparedness to deviate from it frequently enough.[72]

So yes, religion is crucial here (including intra-Islamic tensions); yes, if you removed the explicitly religious dimensions then the political conflict would be changed significantly; but no, ISIS is not a movement which can be crudely explained purely as an outgrowth of religious belief or fanaticism. ISIS 'is both a symptom of the breakdown of state institutions in the heart of the Arab world and a clash of identities between Sunni and Shia Muslims'.[73]

So, just as al-Qaida's politics was and is religious, but simultaneously and inextricably focused on matters which relate to secular realms (US foreign policy, political power within particular states such as Saudi Arabia, personal motivations for revenge),[74] so too with ISIS. So too, in different historical contexts, with other groups designated as exponents of religious terrorism.

---

68 Ibid., p. 68; cf. Fishman, *Master Plan*, p. 23.
69 Stern and Berger, *ISIS*, pp. 13, 177; cf. pp. 58, 62–3; B. G. Williams, *Counter Jihad: America's Military Experience in Afghanistan, Iraq and Syria* (Philadelphia, University of Pennsylvania Press, 2017).
70 Gerges, *ISIS: A History*, pp. 67, 70.
71 J. Nixon, *Debriefing the President: The Interrogation of Saddam Hussein* (London, Bantam Press, 2016), pp. 1, 4.
72 McCants, *The ISIS Apocalypse*, pp. 81–2.   73 Gerges, *ISIS: A History*, p. 260.
74 Byman, *Al-Qaida, the Islamic State and the Global Jihadist Movement*.

Further Reading

E. Berman, *Radical, Religious and Violent: The New Economics of Terrorism* (Cambridge, MIT Press, 2009)

R. English, *Irish Freedom: The History of Nationalism in Ireland* (London, Pan Macmillan, 2006)

F. A. Gerges, *ISIS: A History* (Princeton, Princeton University Press, 2016)

M. Juergensmeyer, *Terror in the Mind of God: The Global Rise of Religious Violence* (Berkeley, University of California Press, 2001)

R. Singh, *Hamas and Suicide Terrorism: Multi-Causal and Multi-Level Approaches* (London, Routledge, 2011)

23

History, Terrorism and the State

RORY COX

Introduction

The relationship between terror and the state is a long and intimate one.[1] While the origin of our modern term 'terrorism' can be found in the language describing the state-led violence of the French Jacobin government – the so-called 'Reign of Terror' (1793–4) – it is clear that ruling powers have a long history of using terror to enforce their authority and subjugate populations. Indeed, some argue that 'state terrorism has been central to the development of the modern state in general'.[2]

Terrorism, of course, is a contested term: there are literally hundreds of definitions at work in the academic literature alone.[3] Terrorism can be examined as a social product or as a set of actions committed by those labelled as 'terrorists'; it can be approached as a method of action or a logic of action.[4] Part of the difficulty in defining terrorism, as Walter Laqueur

---

1 The history of terrorism and the state is a subject that has produced a broad literature, and the following list is purely indicative: W. Laqueur, *A History of Terrorism*, expanded ed. (New Brunswick, NJ, Transaction, 2016); R. D. Law (ed.), *The Routledge History of Terrorism* (Abingdon, Routledge, 2015); C. Dietze and C. Verhoeven (eds.), *The Oxford Handbook of the History of Terrorism* (Oxford, Oxford University Press, 2014); T. Wilson, 'State Terrorism: An Historical Overview', in G. Duncan, O. Lynch, G. Ramsay and A. Watson (eds.), *State Terrorism and Human Rights: International Responses since the End of the Cold War* (London, Routledge, 2013); M. Thorup, *An Intellectual History of Terror: War, Violence and the State* (London, Routledge, 2010); R. D. Law, *Terrorism: A History* (Cambridge, Polity Press, 2009); M. Burleigh, *Blood and Rage: A Cultural History of Terrorism* (London, Harper, 2009); M. Carr, *The Infernal Machine: A History of Terrorism* (New York, New Press, 2007).
2 Wilson, 'State Terrorism: An Historical Overview', p. 15. Wilson also draws on the language of barbarism in his discussion of state terrorism: Ibid., pp. 21–4, 27; T. Wilson, 'State Terrorism', in E. Chenoweth, R. English, A. Gofas and S. N. Kalyvas (eds.), *The Oxford Handbook of Terrorism* (Oxford, Oxford University Press, 2019), p. 334.
3 Richard Jackson has recorded over 200 definitions: see R. Jackson, 'An Argument for Terrorism', *Perspectives on Terrorism* 2/2 (2008), p. 25.
4 M. Wieviorka, 'Terrorism in the Context of Academic Research', in M. Crenshaw (ed.), *Terrorism in Context* (University Park, Pennsylvania State University Press, 1995), pp. 598, 601.

points out, is its 'multifaceted and often-changing character', so that 'it is usually easier to define what terrorism is not, rather than what it is'.[5] Martha Crenshaw notes that: 'Both the phenomenon of terrorism and our conceptions of it depend on historical context – political, social, and economic – and on how the groups and individuals who participate in or respond to the actions we call terrorism relate to the world in which they act.'[6] The overriding importance of historical context has led historians such as Warren Brown (see chapter in present volume) to question whether our modern understanding of the term 'terrorism' can ever be accurately or usefully applied to describe pre-modern uses of terror. Brown argues that conceptions of violence (including whether actions are even understood to be 'violent') and the terminology of terrorism are too culturally contingent to be universally applied across such large chronological periods and across such socially and linguistically distinct societies.[7]

I am sympathetic to these concerns. Yet, ultimately, I subscribe to a broad understanding of terrorism as 'violent intimidation for political effect'.[8] In other words, fear, violence and coercion are at the heart of terrorism.[9] This can describe sub-state/non-state[10] actors seeking radical political change. Nevertheless, as Paul Wilkinson remarks, 'The tendency of modern governments to apply the terms terror and terrorism exclusively to sub-state groups is blatantly dishonest and self-serving.'[11] Consequently, I believe a definition of terrorism which focuses on political *effect* is better able to describe state

---

5 Laqueur, *History of Terrorism*, p. xvi; see also B. Hoffman, *Inside Terrorism*, revised ed. (New York, Columbia University Press, 2006), pp. 3, 21–36.
6 M. Crenshaw, 'Thoughts on Relating Terrorism to Historical Contexts', in Crenshaw (ed.), *Terrorism in Context*, p. 3.
7 W. C. Brown, 'The Pre-History of Terrorism', in Chenoweth et al. (eds.), *Oxford Handbook of Terrorism*; W. C. Brown, 'Instrumental Terror in Medieval Europe', in Dietze and Verhoeven (eds.), *Oxford History of Terrorism*, Oxford Handbooks Online: DOI: 10.1093/oxfordhb/9780199858569.013.003.
8 Wilson, 'State Terrorism', p. 331.
9 Following Freudian psychoanalysis, anxiety is distinguished from fear as lacking a referent object; or, as Giddens puts it, anxiety is 'an unconsciously organised state of fear', A. Giddens, *Modernity and Self-Identity: Self and Society in the Late Modern Age* (Stanford, Stanford University Press, 1991), p. 44. See also S. Starkstein, *A Conceptual and Therapeutic Analysis of Fear* (Cha, Switzerland, Springer/Palgrave, 2018), pp. 231–57; K. De Castella and C. McGarty, 'Two Leaders, Two Wars: A Psychological Analysis of Fear and Anger Content in Political Rhetoric about Terrorism', *Analyses of Social Issues and Public Policy* 11/1 (2011).
10 While these two terms are conceptually and politically distinct, for the sake of economy I will henceforth refer solely to 'sub-state' actors and terrorism – readers should take this to embrace both terms.
11 P. Wilkinson, *Terrorism Versus Democracy: The Liberal State Response*, 3rd ed. (Abingdon, Routledge, 2011), p. 10; Wilson, 'State Terrorism', p. 1.

terrorism than the more common focus on terrorism as seeking political *change*.[12] This is because the intended effect of state terrorism may not be political change, but rather maintenance of a dominant political status quo.

Conceived in these broad terms, both state and sub-state actors have been, and continue to be, willing and able to engage in terrorism.[13] Some will object that this expansive understanding of terrorism reduces the analytical utility of the term. Tim Wilson cautions against a conflation of state terrorism and anti-state terrorism, claiming that such a conflation is naïvely ahistorical.[14] I would argue, however, that by focusing on the coercive power of fear and violence (i.e. 'terror') as political tools, we return to the most important and historically salient aspect of terrorism. And, as far as I can see, both states and sub-state actors are capable of wielding fear and violence in a bid to achieve their intended political effects.

Historically, the vast majority of coercion through terror has been performed by states or their proxies. Evidence can be found from ancient Egypt to medieval Europe, from the Chinese Warring States to Soviet Russia, and on into the present day. Even the medieval Shiite sect of the Assassins, often cited as one of the earliest sub-state terrorist organisations,[15] operated (and conceived of itself) as a state-like entity, holding considerable territory around their capital of Alamut in the Alborz Mountains (modern northern Iran).[16]

I will not attempt to chart a comprehensive history of how states have experienced or practised terrorism. A single chapter would hardly be capable of offering such a survey, and there are many good resources already available. Instead, this chapter will focus on some of the ways in which states and their citizens have sought to describe and identify terrorists and terrorism, and why they have adopted certain historical tropes and language in the

12 For example, Bruce Hoffman's influential definition of terrorism as 'the deliberate creation and exploitation of fear through violence or the threat of violence in the pursuit of political *change*', Hoffman, *Inside Terrorism*, p. 44, emphasis added.
13 In contrast, Hoffman asserts that one of the defining features of terrorism is an act or threat of violence 'perpetrated by a *subnational group or non-state entity*', Ibid., emphasis added.
14 Wilson, 'State Terrorism', pp. 332, 343–4.
15 For example, B. Lewis, *The Assassins: A Radical Sect in Islam* (New York, Oxford University Press, 1967), pp. 129–30; R. H. T. O'Kane, *Terrorism*, 2nd ed. (Harlow, Pearson, 2012), pp. 7–8; D. Cook, 'Ismaili Assassins as Early Terrorists?', in Dietze and Verhoeven (eds.), *Oxford History of Terrorism*, Oxford Handbooks Online: DOI: 10.1093/oxfordhb/9780199858569.013.004; D. Taylor and Y. Gautron, 'Pre-Modern Terrorism: The Cases of the Sicarii and the Assassins', in Law (ed.), *Routledge History of Terrorism*.
16 F. Daftary, *A Short History of the Ismailis: Traditions of a Muslim Community* (Edinburgh, Edinburgh University Press, 1998), pp. 120–53.

process. All states use 'History' in some way or another, but the present discussion will focus on the United States and United Kingdom. This focus is partly dictated by my own expertise, but also because these states have been at the forefront of the so-called 'War on Terror' since 2001, and because anglophone media and popular culture enjoys global consumption.

Over the last three decades a growing body of scholars has sought to apply critical theory in order to reflect upon how states and societies respond to, and construct, 'terrorism'. Such works are loosely grouped under the label Critical Terrorism Studies (CTS). This approach has its theoretical roots in the Frankfurt School and the French deconstructivist and post-structuralist movements, and its most prominent proponents include Joseba Zulaika, Richard Jackson, John Mueller and Ruth Blakeley.[17] While this chapter does not strictly adhere to the formal theories espoused by CTS scholars, it explores the ways in which 'History' – that is, the attempt to understand, write and construct the past[18] – has been used and abused by states as a means to frame the experience of terrorism and to justify a variety of counterterrorism policies. It could thus be said to sit broadly within the Critical Terrorism Studies project; for the fact remains that although the dominant focus of modern Terrorism Studies, the popular media and the public imagination has been on sub-state terrorism and its threat to the security of established states and their citizens, state-engineered terror has harmed, and continues to harm, vastly more people than sub-state terror – by several orders of magnitude.[19]

---

[17] Major works include J. Zulaika and W. Douglass, *Terror and Taboo: The Follies, Fables and Faces of Terrorism* (Abingdon, Routledge, 1996); R. Jackson, *Writing the War on Terrorism: Language, Politics and Counter-Terrorism* (Manchester, Manchester University Press, 2005); J. Mueller, *Overblown: How Politicians and the Terrorism Industry Inflate National Security Threats, and Why We Believe Them* (New York, Free Press, 2006); R. Blakeley, *State Terrorism and Neoliberalism: The North in the South* (London, Routledge, 2009); J. Zulaika, *Terrorism: The Self-Fulfilling Prophecy* (Chicago, University of Chicago Press, 2009); R. Jackson, L. Jarvis, J. Gunning and M. Breen-Smyth, *Terrorism: A Critical Introduction* (London, Red Globe Press, 2011); R. Jackson (ed.), *Routledge Handbook of Critical Terrorism Studies* (Abingdon, Routledge, 2016).

[18] On how to define and describe 'History', the four classic studies remain: R. G. Collingwood, *The Idea of History* (Oxford, Oxford University Press, 1973 [1946]); E. H. Carr, *What is History?*, 2nd ed. (London, Penguin, 1987 [1961]); G. R. Elton, *The Practice of History* (Sydney, Sydney University Press, 1967); R. J. Evans, *In Defence of History* (London, Granta, 2000).

[19] As Tim Wilson puts it (paraphrasing Bruce Hoffman): 'Although popular usage has since shifted, in its earliest usages terrorism thus belonged to the state before it belonged to the anti-state', Wilson, 'State Terrorism', p. 1; Hoffman, *Inside Terrorism*, pp. 2–3. See also E. Murphy, S. Poynting and R. Jackson (eds.), *Contemporary State Terrorism: Theory and Cases* (London, Routledge, 2009); Blakeley, *State Terrorism and*

Modern states have utilised a number of long-standing historical tropes as lenses through which to view the nature and threat of modern sub-state terrorism, in turn adopting corresponding historical narratives to condemn and counter terrorism. 'History' has therefore proved a useful tool in helping states legitimate counterterrorism policies. As a historian, I would argue that knowledge about the past can help us to reflect upon the nature of contemporary challenges: a process which may, in turn, help to elucidate certain contemporary issues. But historical lenses do not guarantee an accurate picture of contemporary reality; indeed, they can distort it. A distorting effect is all the more likely (and potentially harmful) if the historical lenses in question are constructed from tropes which are themselves fundamentally inaccurate, as historical tropes tend to be. Claims to direct analogues or parallels must therefore be treated sceptically. The risk of obfuscation is higher when certain institutions or governments are highly motivated to frame terrorism in a way that can garner public support for various counter-terrorism and security policies, especially if such policies would be controversial under normal circumstances.

'History' has also played a role in the scholarship of Terrorism Studies, with commentators looking to the past in order to differentiate between 'old' and 'new' terrorism. Unfortunately, looking to the past often involves a glance over the shoulder rather than a sustained examination, and it is telling that more historically nuanced accounts of terrorism argue that the so-called distinctions between 'old' and 'new' terrorisms are not so great after all.[20] Nonetheless, this old/new binary has fed into a narrative that presents modern terrorism as posing an original and unique existential threat to modern states and Western civilisation: a degree of threat absent from the 'old' sub-state terrorism experienced prior to the late twentieth century.[21]

Neoliberalism; R. Rummel, *Death by Government* (New Brunswick, NJ, Transaction, 2011); L. Jarvis and M. Lister, 'State Terrorism Research and Critical Terrorism Studies: An Assessment', *Critical Studies on Terrorism* 7/1 (2014); R. Blakeley and S. Raphael, 'Understanding Western State Terrorism', in Jackson (ed.), *Routledge Handbook of Critical Terrorism Studies*.

20 Notable defences of the 'new terrorism' interpretation include W. Laqueur, *The New Terrorism: Fanaticism and the Arms of Mass Destruction* (London, Oxford University Press, 1999); P. R. Neumann, *Old and New Terrorism* (Cambridge, Polity Press, 2009); E. N. Kurtulus, 'The "New Terrorism" and Its Critics', *Studies in Conflict and Terrorism* 34/6 (2011). Bruce Hoffman, among others, has argued against such a distinction: B. Hoffman, 'Change and Continuity in Terrorism', *Studies in Conflict and Terrorism* 24/5 (2001). For a useful overview of the debate, see A. Spencer, 'New Versus Old Terrorism', in Jackson (ed.), *Routledge Handbook of Critical Terrorism Studies*.

21 See J. Wolfendale, 'The Narrative of Terrorism as an Existential Threat', in Jackson (ed.), *Routledge Handbook of Critical Terrorism Studies*.

The historical evidence for the old/new terrorism thesis may be fragile, but the presentation of 'new terrorism' – characterised by religious fanaticism (notably Islamic extremism), irrationality and unlimited violence – has drawn heavily upon the historical trope of civilisation struggling against barbarism.[22] This trope is frequently orientalist and intrinsically morally partisan in nature, playing on long-standing dichotomies between East and West, civilised and uncivilised, secular and religious, good and evil. In other words, 'History' has played a key role in how states and popular media have constructed an understanding of modern, sub-state terrorism, as reprehensible and thus intrinsically barbaric.

Terrorists have become the paradigmatic *new barbarians* of our current political era. The wider cultural resonances of this linguistic association between barbarism and terrorism is important because, as Crenshaw rightly argues, language is not neutral and 'what one calls things matters . . . political language affects the perceptions of protagonists and audiences, and such effect acquires a greater urgency in the drama of terrorism'.[23] By using the language of barbarism in reference to terrorism, states are able to situate terrorists immediately within a deep cultural understanding of threat and the Other.

The importance of the civilisation/barbarism narrative has been noted in International Relations scholarship.[24] In the epilogue of a book published shortly after the 2001 World Trade Center attacks, Mark Salter wrote:

> In rhetorically distancing these terrorists as 'barbarians', the administration hopes that all manner of extra-legal international violence will be tolerated by the society of nations and that other Muslim countries may be appeased and co-opted to the American alliance. The US is shoring up this image of itself as the 'crusader' of civilization, at war not with the general barbarian of Islam, but the specific barbarian of the terrorist.[25]

---

22 'From the moment that Powell and Bush categorized the perpetrators of the [9/11] attack as "barbarians", the enemies of "America's new war" were directly linked with the legends of other enemies whose existence predates the United States itself . . . the men who attacked the World Trade Center towers and the Pentagon are the postmodern Attila or Genghis Khan', M. A. Llorente, 'Civilization Versus Barbarism', in J. Collins and R. Glover (eds.), *Collateral Language: A User's Guide to America's New War* (New York, New York University Press, 2002), p. 41.
23 Crenshaw, 'Relating Terrorism to Historical Contexts', p. 7. See also Jackson, *Writing the War on Terrorism*, pp. 21–2.
24 M. Wight, '*De systematibus civitatum*', in M. Wight, *Systems of States*, ed. H. Bull (Leicester, Leicester University Press, 1977), p. 34; 'Hellas and Persia', Ibid., p. 105.
25 M. B. Salter, *Barbarians and Civilization in International Relations* (London and Sterling, VA, Pluto Press, 2002), pp. 163–4. See also S. P. Huntington, 'The Clash of Civilizations?', *Foreign Affairs* 72/3 (1993).

It is likely that Salter has been surprised by how accurate his prediction has proven to be: the 2003 invasion of Iraq, the CIA torture and rendition programme and the revelations of abuse at Abu Ghraib were still in the future. Yet all of the aforementioned were types of extra-legal or illegal violence partly enabled by the identification of terrorists as new barbarians.

The trope of barbarism has also been noted by Richard Jackson, in his analysis of the discourse of the 'War on Terror'. Indeed, the civilisation/ barbarism metanarrative has played a key role in the creation of this discourse, being so engrained in the collective Western consciousness that it can even lurk beneath the surface of political language, present without being overtly referenced.[26] Jackson notes that in 'both popular culture and the counter-terrorism discourse, terrorists are seen as "the new barbarians", the epitome of savagery for the Western psyche'.[27] Such sentiments are evident in the remarks of John Ashcroft, US Attorney General at the time of the 9/11 attacks: 'the attacks of September 11 drew a bright line of demarcation between the civil and the savage ... On one side of this line are freedom's enemies, murderers of innocents in the name of a barbarous cause. On the other side are friends of freedom.'[28] Of course, such a stark delineation places the West on a moral pedestal – a shining beacon of freedom and civilisation – with no recognition that Western states have indulged in their fair share of savagery.

I would suggest that the reason why states have utilised this association between terrorism and barbarism in their approach to sub-state terrorism might be understood in terms of ontological security, which concentrates on the 'security of being' as opposed to the more traditional 'security of survival'.[29] This subfield of Critical Security Studies has blossomed over the last decade.[30] Thinking about states as ontological security-seeking agents, and the potential influence this may have on motivating state behaviour, is

---

26 Jackson, *Writing the War on Terrorism*, pp. 21, 31–58.   27 Ibid., pp. 47–8.
28 J. Ashcroft, 'Testimony Before the House Committee on the Judiciary Committee, 24 September 2001', https://fas.org/irp/congress/2001_hr/h092401_ashcroft.html. Cited in Jackson, *Writing the War on Terrorism*, p. 49.
29 C. Kinnvall and J. Mitzen, 'Introduction: Ontological Securities in World Politics', *Cooperation and Conflict* 52/1 (2017), p. 4.
30 At least three special issues on ontological security have appeared: *Cooperation and Conflict* 52/1 (2017); *Journal of International Relations and Development* 21/4 (2018); *European Security* 27/3 (2018). See also J. Huysmans, 'Security! What Do You Mean? From Concept to Thick Signifier', *European Journal of International Relations* 4/2 (1998); J. Mitzen, 'Ontological Security in World Politics: State Identity and the Security Dilemma', *European Journal of International Relations* 12/3 (2006); B. J. Steele, *Ontological Security in International Relations: Self-Identity and the IR State* (Abingdon and New York, Routledge, 2008).

increasingly recognised as important in regards to both building and disrupting inter-state and intra-state relations. An emphasis on the importance of identity in shaping how international actors behave is pertinent to an approach which stresses the importance of 'History' in determining how states interpret and present terrorism. This will be discussed further below.

A Summary of Barbarism

The etymology and idea of the barbarian, as conceived in the contemporary West, has its roots in classical Greece. However, comparable concepts of dangerous and irrational foreigners, posing an existential threat to society, date back as far as the ancient Akkadians and Egyptians (third to second millennium BCE). Such tropes are also identifiable in China from the first millennium BCE, with the Great Wall of China standing as a physical manifestation of the binary separation of sedentary 'civilisation' from nomadic 'barbarism'.[31] Ancient Greeks designated all non-Hellenic-speakers as *barbaroi*/βάρβαροι (the word is onomatopoeic, imitating the babbling sounds of foreign languages), and with this came an implication that they did not think 'properly', especially in terms of political organisation.[32] As a result of the trauma of the Greco-Persian wars of the fifth century BCE, Hellenic writers such as Herodotus discovered a fervent streak of xenophobia (itself a Greek term) aimed squarely at the 'barbarian' Persians. The Persians were not viewed as savages, but were deeply feared as an existential threat to Hellenic culture, autonomy and *politics* – literally the life of the polis. Ironically, it was the eventual – rather unexpected – Greek victory against Persia that 'not only gave them self-confidence; it made them overweening, and produced attitudes of racial superiority'.[33] From this time, *barbaros*/βάρβαρος became an increasingly pejorative and derogatory term, yet it also continued to embody a genuine fear of a destructive force against which victory was not guaranteed.

---

31 W. R. Jones, 'The Image of the Barbarian in Medieval Europe', *Comparative Studies in Society and History* 13/4 (1971), pp. 376, 378; G. Beckman, 'Foreigners in the Ancient Near East', *Journal of the American Oriental Society* 133/2 (2013); T. Schneider, 'Foreigners in Egypt: Archaeological Evidence and Cultural Context', in W. Wendrich (ed.), *Egyptian Archaeology* (Chichester, Wiley-Blackwell, 2010); Y. Huang, 'Perceptions of the Barbarian in Early Greece and China', *Centre for Hellenic Studies Research Bulletin* 2/1 (2013).
32 M. Boletski, *Barbarism and Its Discontents* (Stanford, Stanford University Press, 2013), pp. 4–6.
33 Wight, *Systems of States*, p. 85.

This concept of the barbarian contained, almost from the outset, an understanding that barbarism was utterly opposed to the culture and language of civilised society – those vital elements that contribute to its ontological sense of self. Moreover, barbarians posed an existential physical threat to civilised society, threatening to destroy it entirely, just as the Persians had burned and desecrated Athens and its temples.[34]

The 'ancient antithesis of civilization and barbarism' was steadily developed in the West through the Roman, medieval and early modern periods.[35] Particularly from the time of Rome, the antagonism between civilisation and barbarism was portrayed in moral terms, with the barbarian coming to embody an evil force opposed to civic virtue.[36] This moral judgement was also projected into the past. According to the Greco-Roman writer Plutarch (47–127 CE), Alexander the Great believed that 'the distinction between Greek and barbarian should not be a matter of clothes and weapons, but the mark of the Greek should be seen in virtue, and the mark of the barbarian in an evil character'.[37] Christianity adopted this trope of barbarism and made its danger more severe by endowing civilised (i.e. Christian) society with a soteriological role. Unbelievers threatened the salvific function of society and government, and the language and imagery of barbarism was deployed to represent non-Christians who threatened the terrestrial and spiritual security of Christendom.

The hallmarks of the historical barbarian were ferocity, brutality, treachery and irrationality. Nevertheless, a single, concise definition of barbarism is difficult because its characteristics are inherently cultural and therefore relative, with different societies producing slightly differing concepts of barbarism. Indeed, in the nineteenth-century roots of modern sub-state terrorism, it was the terrorists who claimed that state governments were barbarians. An article by Karl Heintzen, entitled 'Der Mord' (1849), declared:

> Even if we have to blow up half a continent or spill a sea of blood, in order to finish off the barbarian party, we should have no scruples about doing it. The

---

34 According to Arrian (92–175 CE), Alexander the Great burned the Persian capital of Persepolis two centuries later in order 'to punish the Persians for sacking Athens and burning the temples when they invaded Greece', Arrian, *Anabasis Alexandri*, trans. P. A. Brunt, 2 vols (Cambridge, Harvard University Press/Heinemann, 1976), Vol. 1: 3.18.12, pp. 288/9.
35 Jones, 'Image of the Barbarian', p. 405.
36 Ibid., p. 379; G. Woolf, *Tales of the Barbarians: Ethnography and Empire in the Roman West* (Chichester, Wiley-Blackwell, 2011), pp. 32–58, 90–4.
37 Eratosthenes, in Plutarch, *De Alexandri fortuna*, 329 C–D, cited in Wight, *Systems of States*, pp. 87–8.

man who would not joyfully give up his own life for the satisfaction of putting a million barbarians into their coffins carries no Republican heart within his breast.[38]

A separate strand of post-Enlightenment Western thought steered towards an association between barbarism and the irrationality of religion. In his *Decline and Fall of the Roman Empire* (published 1776–88), Edward Gibbon remarked that he had 'described the triumph of barbarism and religion'.[39] The legacy of this association is arguably evident in the ease with which modern Western observers have equated religious fanaticism – a defining feature of so-called 'new terrorism' – with a new strain of barbarism.

A few nineteenth- and twentieth-century writers bucked this trend of condemning the barbarian, most notably Friedrich Nietzsche, who argued that the 'blond beast' of the barbarian remained 'at the centre of every noble race'. Nietzsche claimed that the identification of the power and violence of the barbarian as 'evil' was a product of the Judaeo-Christian 'slave morality' that he so despised.[40] Other defenders included Matthew Arnold, Jacob Burckhardt and Oswald Spengler, who saw a raw creative force of *Kultur* in the post-Roman barbarian peoples of Europe, acting as a necessary replacement of the declining rationalism of Late Antique Western civilisation.[41] Such positive appraisals of the 'barbarian spirit' were subsequently adopted by the myth-makers of the Nazi Third Reich.

One common denominator we can observe is that all concepts of barbarism are founded upon the identification of an Other, whose actions and/or ideals are opposed, or are widely believed to be opposed, to the dominant cultural values and norms of the 'civilised' group. Accordingly, all images of the barbarian, regardless of historical context, have been 'the invention of civilized man who thereby expressed his own strong sense of cultural and moral superiority'.[42]

A fundamental assumption of the antagonistic civilisation/barbarism trope is that it creates a threat of violence and a challenge to the virtuous civilised culture. Here, therefore, we must note a distinction between the concept of

---

38 Cited in B. L. Nacos, *Terrorism and Counterterrorism: Understanding Threats and Responses in the Post-9/11 World* (New York, Pearson Longman, 2008), p. 37.
39 E. Gibbon, *The History of the Decline and Fall of the Roman Empire*, ed. D. Womersley, 3 vols (London, Allen Lane, 1994), Vol. 3, p. 1068; J. G. A. Pocock, *Barbarism and Religion*, 6 vols (Cambridge, Cambridge University Press, 1999–2010), Vol. 1, p. 2.
40 F. Nietzsche, *On the Genealogy of Morality*, ed. K. Ansell-Pearson, trans. C. Diethe (Cambridge, Cambridge University Press, 1997), pp. 22–4.
41 See Boletski, *Barbarism and Its Discontents*, pp. 76–7, 108ff.
42 Jones, 'Image of the Barbarian', p. 405.

the barbarian and that of the savage. One could sum up the distinction by saying that the savage has been thought to live in isolation from civilisation, while the barbarian lives in opposition to civilisation. Images of the noble savage are identifiable diachronically from Roman depictions of Germano-Gauls to modern European depictions of Native Americans or indigenous peoples of Africa and the Far East.[43] The language of barbarism and savagery can bleed into one another, but images of the noble savage (often products of Western Orientalism) tend towards romanticism and sentimentalism, as well as being deeply patronising.[44] Such 'savages' are noble in as far as they are uncorrupted by the moral and physical laxness of certain 'civilised' societies (thus providing a vehicle for self-reflective critique), but pose no serious threat to such societies, whose burden it is to civilise them.

This stands in stark contrast to dominant ideas of the barbarian, who is defined by his antipathy to civilisation and is thus fundamentally uncivilisable. This is nowhere better expressed than in a lecture given by Foucault in 1976, condensing Western historiographical attitudes:

> The barbarian ... is someone who can be understood, characterized, and defined only in relation to a civilization, and by the fact that he exists outside it. There can be no barbarian unless an island of civilization exists somewhere, unless he lives outside it, and unless he fights it. And the barbarian's relationship with that speck of civilization – which he despises, and which he wants – is one of hostility and permanent warfare. The barbarian cannot exist without the civilization he is trying to destroy and appropriate ... He does not make his entrance into history by founding a society, but by penetrating a civilization, setting it ablaze and destroying it.[45]

The barbarian is thus understood to be intrinsically and inescapably dangerous. From this conceptual starting point, it is just a short hop, skip and a jump to dehumanisation followed by the necessity of eradication.[46]

---

43 Tacitus, *Germania* [*De origine et situ Germanorum*], ed. J. G. C. Anderson (London, Bristol Classical Press, 1997); R. F. Berkhofer, Jr., *The White Man's Indian: Images of the American Indian from Columbus to the Present* (New York, Vintage Books, 1979), esp. Part 3; D. P. S. Goh, 'Imperialism and "Medieval" Natives: The Malay Image in Anglo-American Travelogues and Colonialism in Malaya and the Philippines', *International Journal of Cultural Studies* 10/3 (2007).
44 See E. W. Said, *Orientalism* (London, Routledge, 1978); D. Gutmeyr, *Borderlands Orientalism, or How the Savage Lost His Nobility: The Russian Perception of the Caucasus between 1817 and 1878* (Vienna, Lit, 2017), p. 191; Salter, *Barbarians and Civilization*, p. 26.
45 M. Foucault, *'Society Must Be Defended': Lectures at the Collège de France, 1975–76*, ed. M. Bertani and A. Fontana, trans. D. Macey (London, Penguin, 2004), p. 195.
46 '[T]he "barbarian" is never afforded the same rights as "insiders" ... The barbarian always marks the foreign, dangerous and threatening', Salter, *Barbarians and Civilization*, pp. 25–6.

Terrorism and the New Barbarians

Modern associations between barbarism and terrorism as the antithesis of civilisation, particularly as reported in the popular media, are commonplace and broadly accepted. The strongest association is with radical Islamist groups, who are routinely described as posing an existential threat to modern civilised society. While this has gained considerable pace since 2001, the association predates the World Trade Center attacks. President Reagan equated terrorism with both cancer and barbarism, stating that 'this barbarism is abhorrent, and all those who support it, encourage it, and profit from it, are abhorrent. They are barbarians.'[47]

The reality of the existential threat posed by modern terrorism has been called into question by sceptical commentators – most notably John Mueller and Mark Stewart[48] – but the threat narrative goes hand in hand with the civilisation/barbarism narrative. In the wake of 9/11, the US ambassador to Japan cautioned that the World Trade Center attacks were 'an attack not just on the United States but on enlightened, civilized societies everywhere'; President George W. Bush stated that 'terrorists have chosen to live on the hunted margins of mankind … they have divorced themselves from the values that define civilization itself.'[49] Bush repeatedly stated that Al Qaeda sought 'to harm civilization as we know it' and therefore individual nations are 'either with us or against us in the fight against terror'.[50] Bush warned that 'no civilized nation can be secure in a world threatened by terror'.[51] This was reinforced by the evocation of a civilisational

---

47 Cited in D. Campbell, *Writing Security: United States Foreign Policy and the Politics of Identity*, revised ed. (Minneapolis, University of Minnesota Press, 1998), p. 88.

48 Mueller and Stewart calculate that the risk of an American dying from a terrorist attack in any given year is 1 in 3.5 million, J. Mueller and M. Stewart, 'The Terrorism Delusion: America's Overwrought Response to September 11', *International Security* 37/1 (2012), pp. 95–6. See also Mueller, *Overblown*; J. Mueller and M. Stewart, *Chasing Ghosts: The Policing of Terrorism* (New York, Oxford University Press, 2016); J. Mueller and M. Stewart, 'Terrorism and Bathtubs: Comparing and Assessing the Risks', *Terrorism and Political Violence* (2018), DOI: 10.1080/09546553.2018.1530662; Wolfendale, 'Narrative of Terrorism', pp. 114–23.

49 Cited J. Matusitz, *Terrorism and Communication: A Critical Introduction* (Thousand Oaks, Sage, 2013), p. 194.

50 G. W. Bush, CNN, 6 November 2018, http://edition.cnn.com/2001/US/11/06/gen.attack.on.terror/. This repeated an earlier statement made by President Bush in his State of the Union address: 'Every nation, in every region, now has a decision to make. Either you are with us, or you are with the terrorists. From this day forward, any nation that continues to harbor or support terrorism will be regarded by the United States as a hostile regime', G. W. Bush, 'Address to a Joint Session of Congress and the American People', 20 September 2001, https://georgewbush-whitehouse.archives.gov/news/releases/2001/09/20010920-8.html.

51 G. W. Bush, 6 November 2001, cited in De Castella and McGarty, 'Two Leaders', p. 185; Wolfendale, 'Narrative of Terrorism', p. 114.

struggle painted not only in stark moral, but also historical and theological, terms: 'Freedom and fear, justice and cruelty, have always been at war, and we know that God is not neutral between them.'[52] In justifying the war in Afghanistan, President Bush claimed that 'we destroyed one of the [most] barbaric regimes in the history of mankind. A regime so barbaric, they would not allow young girls to go to school. A regime so barbaric, they were willing to house al Qaeda'.[53]

The collapse of distinct friend/enemy mediations in the post-Cold War era has arguably added to a more general 'impression of chaos' at the geopolitical level, exacerbated by the media transformation of threat into 'spectacle'.[54] From this perspective, one might read George W. Bush's 'with us or against us' stance as an attempt to forge and create a new 'fixed enemy', thereby helping to consolidate Western self-identity. It is possibly more than mere coincidence that so-called 'new terrorism' is said to have emerged in the 1990s, exactly the same time at which the Cold War was drawing to an end. Thus, one 'existential threat' was immediately replaced by another.

Other politicians soon adopted the barbarian narrative. In 2002, Prime Minister Tony Blair stated: 'If we do not deal with the threat from this international outlaw [Osama bin Laden] and his barbaric regimes, it may not erupt and engulf us this month or next; perhaps not even this year or next. But it will at some point.'[55] In 2015, Prime Minister David Cameron condemned the Paris *Charlie Hebdo* attack as a 'barbaric' act, while Jean-Claude Juncker, President of the European Commission, was 'shocked by the brutal and inhumane attack ... a barbaric act that concerns us all, as humans, as Europeans'[56] After the Manchester Arena attack in 2017, the French press reported Queen Elizabeth II's condemnation of 'un acte "barbare"'.[57] The killing of 13 people in Barcelona in 2017 was described by Didier Reynders, the Belgian Foreign Minister, as a 'barbaric act'.[58]

---

52 G. W. Bush, 'Address to a Joint Session of Congress and the American People', https:// georgewbush-whitehouse.archives.gov/news/releases/2001/09/20010920-8.html.
53 G. W. Bush, 2 May 2003, cited in Jackson, *Writing the War on Terrorism*, p. 50.
54 Huysmans, 'Security!', pp. 243–4; Campbell, *Writing Security*, pp. 136–47, 169–89; T. Delpech, *Savage Century: Back to Barbarism*, trans. G. Holoch (Washington, DC, Carnegie Endowment for International Peace, 2007), p. xiii.
55 De Castella and McGarty, 'Two Leaders', p. 186.
56 N. Morris, 'Charlie Hebdo Attack: World Leaders Unite in Condemning "Barbaric" Paris Killings', *The Independent*, 7 January 2015, www.independent.co.uk/news/world/ europe/charlie-hebdo-attack-world-leaders-condemn-barbaric-killings-9963622.html.
57 F. Collomp and A. L. Frémont, 'Manchester: le terrorisme islamiste poursuit sa guerre contre l'Europe', *Le Figaro*, 23 May 2017, www.lefigaro.fr/international/2017/05/23/0 1003-20170523ARTFIG00366-manchester-daech-poursuit-sa-guerre-barbare-contre-l-eur ope.php.
58 '"Barbaric Act": World Reacts to Barcelona Attack', *Al Jazeera News*, 18 August 2017, www.aljazeera.com/news/2017/08/act-world-reacts-barcelona-attack-170818060019 13 1.html.

Even mainstream Muslim commentators and politicians buy into the language of jihadist barbarism. In the wake of attempted car bombings in London and Glasgow in 2007, Dr Muhammad Abdul Bari, Secretary General of the Muslim Council of Britain, condemned the actions because 'There is no cause whatsoever that could possibly justify such barbarity.'[59] Sadiq Khan, the Mayor of London and a practising Muslim, described the Barcelona 2017 killings as 'this barbaric terrorist attack'.[60]

Nor are such descriptions restricted to Western politicians. The United Nations Security Council jointly condemned 'the barbaric and cowardly terrorist attack' that killed 25 people on a bus in Mali in January 2018.[61] Likewise, when an ISIS suicide bomber killed 29 people at a Shiite shrine in Kabul, Afghanistan (March 2018), the Indian government released a statement decrying the 'inhumane and barbaric' attack.[62]

The sensationalist elements of barbarism as a cultural trope have led to an enthusiastic adoption of the language of barbarism by the print and visual media when reporting on terrorist activities. A 2013 article in *The Spectator* (UK) argued that referring to the murder of British soldier Lee Rigby in Woolwich (May 2013) as an 'act of terrorism somehow dignifies the barbarism'.[63] The link between terrorism and barbaric violence is made explicit here, with the two attackers also labelled as 'savages'. Writing for CNN in the wake of the 2013 London Bridge attacks, one journalist lauded the stoic response of British citizens and police, proudly declaring that 'we don't give in to terrorists. A barbarian cannot change a country as old and civilized as ours.'[64] A year later, Forbes magazine compiled a list of the world's ten

---

59 C. Davies, 'Muslims Must Fight Terrorist Barbarians', *The Telegraph*, July 2007, www.telegraph.co.uk/news/uknews/1556458/Muslims-must-fight-terrorist-barbarians.html.
60 '"Barbaric Act"', *Al Jazeera News*; see above, n. 58.
61 'Security Council Condemns "Barbaric" Terrorist Attack in Central Mali That Killed Dozens on Civilian Bus', *UN News*, 27 January 2018, https://news.un.org/en/story/2018/01/1001391.
62 'India Condemns "Barbaric" Terrorist Attack in Kabul', *The Times of India*, 21 March 2018, https://timesofindia.indiatimes.com/india/india-condemns-barbaric-terrorist-attack-in-kabul/articleshow/63402627.cms.
63 R. Liddle, 'The Words "Terrorist Attack" Only Dignify the Barbarism', *The Spectator*, 23 May 2013, https://blogs.spectator.co.uk/2013/05/terrorist-attack-or-not/.
64 T. Stanley, 'A Barbarian Cannot Change Britain', CNN, 24 March 2017, www.cnn.com/2017/03/22/opinions/london-terror-attack-stanley/index.html. Online readers' comments to the article include: 'Barbarians indeed. Even that description is too kind'; 'No more saracen barbarians! Take a page out of our noble Arthurian tradition. Let them convert like Sir Palomides or let them go back to their barbarian lands which they themselves destroyed.'

richest terrorist organisations, which included a description of Boko Haram's 'barbaric actions of cruelty'.[65]

Further examples of commentators and politicians describing terrorists as barbarians and their acts as barbaric could be provided ad nauseam. Yet there are some examples of pushback: those who argue that the barbarian analogy is overly simplistic and fails to address the root causes of terrorism, thus hampering effective responses;[66] or those who draw attention to the fact that so-called 'barbaric' violence should not imply strategic mindlessness. For example, Abraham H. Miller insists that terrorist attacks on civilians are 'brutal, violent, and barbaric – but hardly senseless'; such acts are perpetrated with a cool logic, being both empowering for the terrorists and aimed at encouraging reprisals against a sympathetic population that the terrorist hopes to attract to their cause.[67]

One can find more radical positions in pseudo-academic works produced by and for the American Christian right, embracing a theologically infused Huntingtonian vision of a 'clash of civilisations'. A book entitled *The Barbarians Are Here: Preventing the Collapse of Western Civilization in Times of Terrorism* describes an existential battle between the Christian 'West' and the forces of radical 'Islamist barbarians'. The author sees 'historical parallels between the collapse of Rome and the current decline of America', and warns that the 'barbarian invasion of Western civilization has begun', yet again.[68] While such sentiments will strike many readers as outlandish, the considerable influence of the Christian right among American voters and the political establishment – especially at the states level – should not be underestimated.[69]

More measured analyses by public intellectuals are still inclined to persevere with the barbarian descriptor. The French philosopher Roger-Pol Droit

---

65 I. Zehorai, 'The World's 10 Richest Terrorist Organizations', *Forbes International*, 12 Dec 2014, www.forbes.com/sites/forbesinternational/2014/12/12/the-worlds-10-richest-terrorist-organizations/#139bafb84f8a.

66 G. Benhessa, 'Le terrorisme n'est pas le fait de quelques "barbares", il est durablement ancré au cœur de nos territoires', *Le Huffington Post, édition Français*, 23 August 2017 www.huffingtonpost.fr/ghislain-benhessa/terrorisme-pas-le-fait-de-quelques%20-barbares-il-est-durablement-ancré-au-cœur-de-nos-territoires_a_23156643/.

67 A. H. Miller, 'Terrorism Is Not Senseless: It Is Calculated Barbarism', *The American Spectator*, 20 October 2015 https://spectator.org/64401_terrorism-not-senseless-it-calculated-barbarism/.

68 M. Youssef, *The Barbarians Are Here: Preventing the Collapse of Western Civilization in Times of Terrorism* (Franklin, Worthy, 2017), see ch. 3, 'The Barbarian Invasion', ch. 9, 'Clash of Cultures'.

69 K. H. Conger, 'A Matter of Context: Christian Right Influence in U.S. State Republican Politics', *State Politics and Policy Quarterly* 10/3 (2010).

rejects Lévi-Strauss's call to abandon the condemnatory language of barbarism (see below, n. 93) by arguing that 'barbarian' remains a valid identifier to describe those who seek to justify murder through appealing to absolute truths, cutting themselves off from the basic 'human bond' of empathy.[70] The English political philosopher, John Gray, interprets contemporary conflict between centralised states and terrorist groups as merely a novel expression of a repeating cycle of antagonism between civilisation and barbarism: 'Civilization is not the endpoint of modern history, but a succession of interludes in recurring spasms of barbarism.'[71] Gray posits that the ideology and actions of ISIS, and groups like them, challenge the dominant Western liberal metanarrative of steady and irreversible 'progress'. In reality, ISIS's 'acts of barbarism have modern precedents', including the cultural revolutions of Leninist Russia and Mao Zedong's China, postcolonial civil wars in African states, and the Balkans conflict of the 1990s. Indeed, Gray argues that technological innovation 'has repeatedly interacted with human conflicts and passions to produce new kinds of barbarism ... some of the most modern movements are the most barbaric'. ISIS has expertly utilised modern technologies – especially communications – for its own benefit, and is thus 'a peculiarly modern form of barbarism'.[72] Seen in this light, terrorism is a barbaric force, but its current prominence is not historically atypical.

Formal academic literature also contributes to the conflation of terrorism and barbarism. In her analysis of the re-emergence of violence in the early twenty-first century, Thérèse Delpech believes that 'Barbarous deeds are preceded by barbarity of spirit.'[73] Significantly, in a book with the subtitle *Back to Barbarism*, Delpech offers no definition of barbarism itself, assuming (presumably) that the term is self-evident. In *Return of the Barbarians: Confronting Non-State Actors from Ancient Rome to the Present*, Jakub Grygiel sees clear analogues between modern terrorists and pre-modern 'barbarian' actors.[74] The Huns and Goths, the Mongols, the early Ottomans and the

---

70 R.-P. Droit, 'Lévi-Strauss und die Barbarei', *Philosophie Magazin*, 1 June 2017, https://philomag.de/artikel/levi-strauss-und-die-barbarei/.
71 J. Gray, 'The Anomaly of Barbarism: The Brutality of Islamist Terrorism Has Many Precedents', *Lapham's Quarterly*, www.laphamsquarterly.org/disaster/anomaly-barbarism.
72 Gray is willing to see barbarism on both 'sides', condemning the post-9/11 Bush administration for its 'rehabilitation ... of the barbarous practice of torture', Ibid.
73 Delpech, *Savage Century*, p. xix.
74 J. J. Grygiel, *Return of the Barbarians: Confronting Non-State Actors from Ancient Rome to the Present* (Cambridge, Cambridge University Press, 2018), p. 5. The following discussion is adapted from my review of the book in *Ethics and International Affairs* 32/4 (2018).

Plains Indians of North America are frequently cited as examples of barbarians. Accordingly, while providing the caveat that 'I do not want to suggest that … modern Islamist terrorists are exactly like the Huns or the Comanches', Grygiel believes that there are sufficient similarities that 'using the old word of "barbarians" is appropriate'.[75] Grygiel presents premodern and modern barbarians as peoples who were, and are, predominantly a violent negative force: 'They destroyed more than they built … They were more interested in blood than law', as he says.[76] To put it bluntly: 'Barbarians were barbaric.'[77]

Despite the insinuation of cultural inferiority and moral reprehensibility connected with the term 'barbarian', Grygiel insists that he uses the term descriptively rather than normatively, returning to 'its simplest usage' to describe opposing cultures dominated by a lack of understanding and possessing conflicting ideologies and objectives.[78] Such a claim is all well and good; unfortunately, the reality is that the term 'barbarian' is not simple or neutral. As Martha Crenshaw observed, no language is neutral.[79] Jef Huysmans demonstrated that terms such as 'security' are thick signifiers, informed by their own history and usage: equally, the term 'barbarian' carries a great deal of negative cultural baggage.[80] We are increasingly aware that emotions play an influential role in international politics and security; therefore, any claim to deploy the terminology of barbarism in a purely neutral sense – especially when discussing policy – is deeply unconvincing.[81]

The essential problem that all of the aforementioned commentators fail to confront is, what happens when you apply the term 'barbarian' to actors who are already widely feared and vilified? By equating terrorism with barbarism, politicians, journalists and academics contribute to the 'spillage' of metanarratives between the analysis and practice of security and International Relations.[82] Identifying terrorists as barbarians encourages further dehumanisation of such individuals as brutes who are, at best, undeserving of restraints

---

75 Grygiel, *Return of the Barbarians*, p. 9. Marina Llorente had critiqued exactly these kinds of comparisons as early as 2002: Llorente, 'Civilization Versus Barbarism', pp. 41, 45; cf. Jackson, *Writing the War on Terrorism*, p. 48.
76 Grygiel, *Return of the Barbarians*, pp. 9, 10.   77 Ibid., p. 10.   78 Ibid., pp. 8, 49–50.
79 Above, n. 23.   80 Huysmans, 'Security!', p. 228.
81 See, for example, Neta C. Crawford's work on emotions: 'The Passion of World Politics: Propositions on Emotion and Emotional Relationships', *International Security* 24/4 (2000); 'Emotions and International Security: Cave! Hic Libido', *Critical Studies on Security* 1/1 (2013); 'Institutionalizing Passion in World Politics: Fear and Empathy', *International Theory* 6/3 (2014).
82 On the idea of 'spillage', see S. Smith, 'Singing Our World into Existence: International Relations Theory and September 11', *International Studies Quarterly* 48/3 (2004); C. Lynch, *Beyond Appeasement: Interpreting Interwar Peace Movements in World Politics*

granted to 'civilised' enemies or, at worst, deserving of the harshest treatment and complete eradication. History is full of examples of how enemies understood as barbarian have been the targets of extreme cruelty and violence, from ancient Egypt through the medieval Crusades to the Second World War. Even the identification of terrorists as barbarians is not an entirely novel phenomenon. From the late 1940s, in both Malaysia and Indonesia, colonial and postcolonial authorities justified anti-communist violence by depicting communists as 'terrorists, barbaric, immoral and hence uncivilized'.[83] Such depictions played a central role in the construction of postcolonial nationalist narratives and state memories, emphasising 'the idea of a menacing communist threat, of communist terrorism and communist barbarism and the need for constant vigilance against this threat'.[84] The similarities to contemporary Western narratives concerning Islamist terrorism hardly need stating. Over the last two decades, the new barbarians have been subjected to treatment otherwise considered morally unacceptable or illegal, most notably the erosion of the anti-torture norm.[85] While enemies can be dehumanised in any number of ways, the trope of the barbarian remains particularly effective – evident from political speeches to newspaper cartoons – precisely because of its long historical pedigree.[86]

Terrorism, Ontological Insecurity, and the Comforting Familiarity of Barbarism

The identification and condemnation of sub-state terrorists as barbarians is arguably a reaction to the ontological *insecurity* created by terrorism: it is an attempt to restore a secure sense of being and identity to the state and its citizens. Such identity is based principally on a sense of superiority. Opposing

(Ithaca, NY, Cornell University Press, 1999), p. 217; Steele, *Ontological Security*, pp. 160, 163.

83 K. MacGregor, 'Cold War Scripts: Comparing Remembrance of the Malayan Emergency and the 1965 Violence in Indonesia', *South East Asia Research* 24/2 (2016), p. 247, and pp. 244, 246, 249, 255.

84 Ibid., p. 255.

85 J. Wolfendale, 'The Myth of "Torture Lite"', *Ethics and International Affairs* 23/1 (2009); R. Cox, 'Historicizing Waterboarding as a Severe Torture Norm', *International Relations* 32/4 (2018).

86 See Matusitz, *Terrorism and Communication*, pp. 193–7; W. B. Hart, II and F. Hassencahl, 'Dehumanizing the Enemy in Editorial Cartoons', in B. S. Greenberg (ed.), *Communication and Terrorism: Public and Media Responses to 9/11* (Cresskill, Hampton Press, 2002), esp. pp. 142–9. The authors note that representations of Islamic terrorists in the type 'enemy-as-barbarian' was the 'fourth most frequent metaphor' used by the cartoons: Ibid., p. 146.

'barbaric' ideologies (e.g. radical jihadism) by killing or detaining individual 'barbarians' (i.e. terrorists) contributes to and reinforces the ontological security of states and their citizens who self-identify as civilised and thus ipso facto *not* barbaric. After all, the concept of barbarism is rooted in the perception of a fundamental dichotomy of culture and values: the barbarian standing in stark contrast (and posing an existential threat) to civilised society. From a sociological perspective, civilisation arguably depends upon the barbarian Other in order to fully define itself.[87] These convictions are deeply rooted in historical narratives stretching back through the Middle Ages and into the classical world, but that does not prevent them from being fantastical. As Aristotle recommended, certain dangers are useful in maintaining the unity of the state, and sometimes they must be invented.[88]

The end of the Cold War and the challenges of globalisation are forcing Western states and their citizens to face new physical and ontological insecurities.[89] After the removal of the Soviet/communist Other, Western states have had to find new ways to differentiate themselves from their global competitors. Amidst this landscape of evolving identity, terrorism has introduced a physical, as well as a vivid ontological, security threat. The fact of modern 24/7 media coverage is that any terrorist attack against Western interests is given such massive exposure that, regardless of the physical proximity of individual citizens to the events, they nonetheless feel immediate to them. This unique feature of late modernity has contributed to what Giddens describes as a 'climate of risk'.[90] This fear of terrorism far outstrips the real threat posed by terrorists to individual citizens, leading to a perpetual 'terrorism delusion', in the words of Mueller and Stewart.[91]

Western states are compelled to respond to the long-term challenge that sub-state terrorism poses to their identity and role as security providers. Under these circumstances, the trope of barbarism is highly attractive and legitimises extreme forms of counter-violence. In 1915, Freud despaired that the bitter divisions separating 'the civilized nations' of the West had provoked a similar conceptual move against Germany, which had become branded as a barbaric enemy in order that the Allied nations could more

---

87 A. Linklater, 'Torture and Civilisation', *International Relations* 21/1 (2007), p. 114.
88 Aristotle, *The Politics*, ed. S. Everson, trans. J. Barnes (Cambridge, Cambridge University Press, 1988), Book 5, 1308a24–30.
89 Giddens, *Modernity and Self-Identity*, pp. 183–4; S. J. Flanagan, E. L. Frost and R. L. Kugler, *Challenges of the Global Century* (Washington, DC, Institute for National Strategic Studies, 2001), pp. 13–18; Campbell, *Writing Security*, pp. 136–47, 169–89.
90 Giddens, *Modernity and Self-Identity*, pp. 123–4.
91 Mueller and Stewart, 'Terrorism Delusion', p. 107.

easily comprehend and continue the bloodbath on the Western Front.[92] By conflating terrorism with barbarism, Western states can establish a familiar and easily understood dichotomy, refashioned for the twenty-first century, through which they can reassert a traditional understanding of their cultural and moral superiority – a narrative of the civilised and the uncivilised. This is what could be described as the comforting affect of barbarism.

Here we can see the substantial work being done by 'History' in providing comforting narratives that help to anchor state responses to terrorism. Historical narratives can unify disparate contemporary threats (multiple organisations and individuals, with varying agendas) into a single threat identity (the barbarian). In a highly dynamic modern world, widely accepted historical dichotomies can help to sustain a secure sense of self. Appealing to historical tropes of barbarism is one way in which Western states have turned *anxiety* about ill-defined and poorly understood terrorist agendas into a focused *fear* of barbarians, who are culturally familiar and identifiable.

It must be realised that the invention of new – albeit historically informed – narratives of terrorism is as much about what we wish to tell ourselves about *ourselves* as it is about the reality of terrorism and why it occurs. Such a realisation is crucial when considering how we react to terrorism and whether our reactions are effective (i.e. likely to reduce the threat), ineffective or actually make the threat worse. Equally important for the long-term ontological and physical security of liberal democratic societies is the realisation that narratives of barbarism have been harnessed to justify actions otherwise considered at odds with liberal democratic values. Indulging in cultural relativism and simplistic vilification of our enemies is dangerous in itself. Writing for the newly established UNESCO in the early 1950s, Claude Lévi-Strauss warned that

> the paradox inherent in cultural relativism . . . [is that] the more we claim to discriminate between cultures and customs as good and bad, the more completely do we identify ourselves with those we would condemn. By refusing to consider as human those who seem to us to be [the] most 'savage' or 'barbarous' of their representatives, we merely adopt one of their own

---

92 '[T]he civilized nations know and understand one another so little that one can turn against the other with hate and loathing. Indeed, one of the great civilized nations is so universally unpopular that the attempt can actually be made to exclude it from the civilized community as "barbaric", although it has long proved its fitness by the magnificent contributions to that community which it has made', S. Freud, *Thoughts for the Times on War and Death* [1915], in *The Standard Edition of the Complete Psychological Works of Sigmund Freud*, Vol. 14: *1914–1916*, trans. and ed. J. Strachey (London, Hogarth Press and the Institute of Psycho-Analysis, 1957), p. 279.

characteristic attitudes. The barbarian is, first and foremost, the man who believes in barbarism.[93]

Such relativism and vilification produces dichotomies of good/bad and civilised/barbaric that, although easily grasped and providing some degree of comfort, are, in the longer term, potentially harmful to cultural diversity and non-violent international relations.

To an extent, the War on Terror and the threat of barbarism is a crisis constructed by the state. Such 'crisis production' is not novel. Analysing the 1962 Cuban Missile Crisis as a paradigmatic example, Jutta Weldes posits that all 'crises are social constructions that are forged by state officials in the course of producing and reproducing state identity'.[94] Therefore, it is plausible that, over the last two decades, Western states (notably the US, the UK and France) could have reacted to terrorism – even the 9/11 attacks – very differently. After 2001, the US and its allies chose to escalate the threat of terrorism into a global struggle for civilisation, tapping into rich historical veins in the process. But it should not be forgotten that there are numerous historical narratives that might have de-escalated and played down the threat. Richard Jackson argues that the 'use of alternative narrative frameworks would have helped to create a different set of meanings and interpretations'.[95] It seems possible that the US administration and others acted in such a way because it fulfilled their ontological security needs, in spite of the potential damage it has done to their physical security and international prestige.

Language possesses illocutionary force, it both reflects and constructs reality, shaping ideas and actions. Once the state has committed itself to the linguistic move of synonymising 'terrorist' and 'barbarian', it thereby commits itself to a certain set of possible material responses to terrorists *as* barbarians. Such counterterrorism responses are unlikely to be lenient or even level-headed; they are more likely to be uncompromising and potentially deleterious to national physical security interests. An ill-conceived war in Iraq and the use of torture by US agencies are examples of actions committed more for the sake of securing self-identity than enhancing physical security.[96]

---

93 C. Lévi-Strauss, *Race and History* (Paris, UNESCO, 1952), p. 12.
94 J. Weldes, 'The Cultural Production of Crises: U.S. Identity and Missiles in Cuba', in J. Weldes, M. Laffet, H. Gusterson and R. Duvall (eds.), *Cultures of Insecurity: States, Communities, and the Production of Danger* (Minneapolis, University of Minnesota Press, 1999), p. 37; cf. Steele, *Ontological Security*, p. 70.
95 Jackson, *Writing the War on Terrorism*, p. 51.   96 Steele, *Ontological Security*, p. 162.

Conclusion

Undoubtedly, tropes and concepts other than barbarism feed into current Western reactions to terrorism. But I have tried to show why adopting and adapting historical narratives of barbarism is particularly attractive to Western states and their citizens as they attempt to maintain their identity in the face of emerging security threats and an evolving global order. On the one hand, imagining themselves as actors in the historical grand narrative of civilisation's struggle against barbarism – a narrative in which all 'great states' have been embedded – is a coping mechanism, easing the disappointment of failure by contextualising it within a trans-historical process that is presented as somehow inevitable. On the other hand, identifying terrorists as barbarians is a strategy of reductionism in the face of a complex threat. Attempting to understand why terrorists act in the manner they do, or to reflect self-critically on how one's own actions may be implicated in exacerbating a conflict, is a difficult and jarring process. Identifying terrorists as new barbarians removes the need for such self-reflection or self-critique. It answers the complex question, 'Why do they hate us?'[97] with the simple answer, 'Because we are good and they are evil.'

The removal of the need to think about the enemy on any kind of complex level also removes the need to feel shame about the enemy's suffering or destruction. When the expanding dumdum bullet was prohibited by the Hague Conventions of 1899, the British delegate (supported by the US delegate) argued for an exception to be made when fighting against 'the savage' and the 'fanatical barbarian', because 'there is a difference in war between civilised nations and that against savages'.[98] Identified as enemies of civilisation, barbarians have rarely been considered deserving of the protections offered by 'civilised' society.[99] The range of highly controversial military tactics, incarceration methods and interrogation techniques used against terrorists and suspects of terrorism have starkly illustrated this.

---

97 G. W. Bush, 'Address to a Joint Session of Congress and the American People', https://georgewbush-whitehouse.archives.gov/news/releases/2001/09/20010920-8.html.
98 R. Coupland and D. Loye, 'The 1899 Hague Declaration Concerning Expanding Bullets: A Treaty Effective for More Than 100 Years Faces Complex Contemporary Issues', *International Review of the Red Cross* 85 (2003), p. 137.
99 Linklater, 'Torture and Civilisation', p. 114; R. Cox, 'Asymmetric Warfare and Military Conduct in the Middle Ages', *Journal of Medieval History* 38/1 (2012); B. J. Steele, 'Organizational Processes and Ontological (In)Security: Torture, the CIA and the United States', *Cooperation and Conflict* 52/1 (2017), pp. 71–2; Thorup, *Intellectual History of Terror*, pp. 28, 36, 61, 67–8.

A final point that should give us pause for thought is Jennifer Mitzen's argument that routines of conflict actually create ontological security for states. As a result, the longer these routines persist, the more difficult it is for states to disassociate themselves from such routines or to form new behaviours.[100] If this assessment is accurate, then the longer the association between terrorism and barbarism persists, the more difficult it will be for states to detach themselves from the conflict routines produced by this particular historical narrative. The 'civilised us' versus the 'barbaric them' narrative may create ontological security, but left unchallenged it will be ever harder to break out of, reducing the likelihood of finding long-term solutions that can generate better physical security outcomes. Put bluntly, our historical imagination will forge a cage for our future actions.

Further Reading

D. Campbell, *Writing Security: United States Foreign Policy and the Politics of Identity*, revised ed. (Minneapolis, University of Minnesota Press, 1998)

R. Jackson, *Writing the War on Terrorism: Language, Politics and Counter-Terrorism* (Manchester, Manchester University Press, 2005)

M. B. Salter, *Barbarians and Civilization in International Relations* (London, Pluto Press, 2002)

B. J. Steele, *Ontological Security in International Relations: Self-Identity and the IR State* (Abingdon, Routledge, 2008)

M. Thorup, *An Intellectual History of Terror: War, Violence and the State* (London, Routledge, 2010)

---

100 Mitzen, 'Ontological Security', pp. 360–2.

24

Into the Labyrinth
Terrorism, History and Diplomacy

JOSEPH MORRISON SKELLY

'We do not negotiate with terrorists.' For decades world leaders have asserted this principle. In July 1985, President Ronald Reagan insisted, following Hezbollah's murder of Navy diver Robert Stethem during a plane hijacking in Beirut, that 'America will never make concessions to terrorists – to do so would only invite more terrorism – nor will we ask nor pressure any other government to do so.'[1] When Nelson Mandela suggested, soon after his release from prison, that British officials should talk with Irish paramilitaries, a spokesman for Prime Minister Margaret Thatcher avowed, 'We do not negotiate with terrorists and have no intention of negotiating with the IRA or their political wing.'[2] In response to the Madrid bombings in 2004, Prime Minister José María Aznar of Spain declared, 'There can be no negotiation with these murderers. We will only stop these attacks by taking a hard line.'[3] The historical record demonstrates otherwise, however. Contrary to their public pronouncements, statesmen have repeatedly engaged in diplomacy with terrorist organisations. As one of the contributors to this volume, Martyn Frampton, and his colleagues have written, 'Governments talk to terrorists. This is a statement of fact rather than a critique; it is an acknowledgement of reality rather than a value judgement.'[4] President William Clinton epitomises this divergence between theory and practice. The United States 'will continue to take the fight to terrorists', he said after al Qaeda's attack on the American embassies in Nairobi and Dar es Salaam in

---

1 'The President's News Conference: Trans World Airlines Hijacking Incident', 18 June 1985, Ronald Reagan Presidential Library and Museum, www.reaganlibrary.gov/research/speeches/61885c.
2 R. C. Longworth, 'Britain Scolds Mandela over IRA Comment', *Chicago Tribune*, 4 July 1990, www.chicagotribune.com/news/ct-xpm-1990-07-04-9002230746-stoary.html.
3 'Aznar: We Will Not Back Down', Al Jazeera, 13 March 2004, www.aljazeera.com/arc hive/2004/03/200849135635749864.html.
4 J. Bew, M. Frampton and Í. Gurrachaga, *Talking to Terrorists: Making Peace in Northern Ireland and the Basque Country* (New York, Colombia University Press, 2009), p. 1.

1998.[5] Yet burnished in our collective memory is the famous image of Yitzhak Rabin, the Israeli prime minister, Yasser Arafat, erstwhile international terrorist and the chairman of the Palestinian Liberation Organisation (PLO), and William Clinton clasping hands on the South Lawn of the White House after signing the Oslo Accords in September 1993. So much for the claim 'We do not negotiate with terrorists.' Some practitioners argue that we are better off for the judicious violation of this ironclad rule. Jonathan Powell, who served as Prime Minister Tony Blair's chief negotiator during the peace process in Northern Ireland, admits that initially he was hesitant to meet with paramilitaries, but is now certain that 'talking is the right thing to do'.[6] His role there has convinced him that 'no conflict – however bloody, ancient or difficult – is insoluble'.[7] According to this logic, conferring with militants has sometimes led to progress, if not to peace. Or has it? The record of government officials engaging with terrorist organisations is ambiguous. Yes, inclusive dialogue has coincided with reductions in political violence in places like Colombia, Aceh, the Basque region of Spain, and Northern Ireland. But is that the only cause of these declines? What about other locations? In Israel and Palestine, the path to peace since President Clinton's historic meeting with Yitzhak Rabin and Yasser Arafat has been rocky, pockmarked by acts of terror and reprisal, with no permanent settlement in sight. In Turkey, intermittent consultations between the government and insurgent groups like the Kurdistan Workers' Party (PKK) have failed to quell decades of hostility. Against this unsettled background, the question arises: what does a comprehensive historical analysis of the intersection of armed extremism and statecraft reveal? This chapter's central argument asserts that historically the interrelationship of terrorism and diplomacy has often been, for the array of actors who have experienced it, like entering into a labyrinth. But which type? We are not referring to the mazes inside medieval cathedrals or modern churches designed for rituals, meditation and prayer. We mean the labyrinth of classical mythology at Knossos, that warren of cul-de-sacs and trapdoors designed by Daedalus. Today it is defined as 'a place constructed of, or full of, intricate passageways and blind alleys; something extremely complex or tortuous'.[8] This metaphor is apposite. It reflects the direction the negotiating

---

5 White House Communications Agency and William Jefferson Clinton, 'The President's Radio Address on August 8, 1998', Clinton Digital Library, https://clinton.presidentiallibraries.us/items/show/13140.
6 J. Powell, *Talking to Terrorists: How to End Armed Conflicts* (London, The Bodley Head, 2014), p. 3.
7 Ibid., p. 4.
8 *Merriam-Webster Online Dictionary*, www.merriam-webster.com/dictionary/labyrinth.

path has taken when terrorists have been travelling companions. On rare occasions it has been straightforward, but more often winding, circuitous, labyrinthine, in fact. The central motif of a labyrinth unifies the strands of this chapter's historical assessment. Its conceptual apparatus consists of three supporting arguments. Some participants have accrued benefits; others have incurred costs; and they have occasionally encountered limits to the efficacy of diplomacy as a vehicle for achieving their objectives. Certain actors have managed to follow the thread to the light at the end of the tunnel. Others have crashed like Icarus, the architect's son. A few have become disoriented once inside the maze. The concepts of benefits, costs and limitations provide a useful analytical framework for assessing the experiences of protagonists at the crossroads of militancy and mediation. Several qualifications should be noted. These are not clear-cut, zero-sum outcomes. They are subtle, often calculated by weighing one against another. Participants have faced several simultaneously. Some in the same location have had contrasting experiences: one may have gained while another lost. The historical record, like a labyrinth itself, is complex, with competing perspectives and unexpected combinations, depending on the circumstances.

Parameters

This chapter's analysis of history, terrorism and diplomacy utilises several critical terms, or parameters. First, it focuses on specific agents instead of only assessing broad cases studies like the Basque peace process or the Colombian peace process. This methodology generates a multifaceted perspective. It reveals the historical complexity of the interaction of radicalism and statecraft. The participants relevant to studies of this nature encompass several characteristics: they are state and non-state, democratic and undemocratic, violent and non-violent, domestic and global in scope. They include government officials, the voting public, their elected representatives, security forces, terrorist groups, their political fronts, victims of state and non-state violence, international organisations and others. Groups that have resorted to terrorism are central to this study. First, we must define this elusive term. Terrorism, Daniel Pipes reminds us, 'is a tactic'.[9] Boaz Ganor elaborates further: 'Terrorism is the deliberate use of, or the threat to use, violence against civilians in order to attain political, ideological and religious

---

9 D. Pipes, 'What Bush Got Right – and Wrong?', *Jerusalem Post*, 26 September 2001, posted at Daniel Pipes/The Middle East Forum, www.danielpipes.org/70/what-bush-got-right-and-wrong-in-his-speech.

aims.'[10] The US Department of State notes that terrorism is 'premeditated, politically motivated violence perpetrated against noncombatant targets by subnational groups or clandestine agents',[11] and the US Department of Defense adds that it is 'often motivated by religious, political, or other ideological beliefs'.[12] Large-scale insurgencies often rely on it. So do governments, through state sponsorship of terrorism, acts of state terrorism, or by being terrorist states. Militants, some insurgents, and selected states thus employ a tactic – violence – against civilians or non-combatant targets for political, religious or ideological motivations. These entities occupy points along a spectrum of increasing size, from discrete cells to small-to-medium-sized organisations to large-scale domestic and transnational insurgencies to proto-states to actual states. The boundaries between these categories are fluid. Some units expand or contract in size over their lifetimes, so cross-over occurs. They can jump from being a terrorist group to an insurgency to a quasi-state and then, after coming under pressure from conventional security forces, shrink considerably in size or even face extinction. This chapter concentrates on small-to-medium subnational organisations along the terrorist continuum that have engaged in asymmetric warfare in many parts of the world from the 1960s to today. Examples from Europe are Euskadi Ta Askatasuna (ETA), the Red Army Faction, the Red Brigades, the Provisional IRA and Revolutionary Organisation 17 November. Case studies from the Middle East include the Palestinian Liberation Organisation, Palestinian Islamic Jihad and al Qaeda. Several organisations originate in the United States or its territories: the Weather Underground, the Black Liberation Army and Fuerzas Armadas de Liberación Nacional (FALN), which sought independence for Puerto Rico. Insurgent groups and terrorist-linked states located at the upper end of the spectrum cast light on this chapter's central themes. The former include Fuerzas Armadas Revolucionarias de Colombia (FARC), Sendero Luminoso (the Shining Path), the Moro Islamic Liberation Front, the Abu Sayyaf Group (ASG), the Taliban, the Islamic State of Iraq and Syria (ISIS), Hamas and Hezbollah. Some of these movements have links to illegal narcotics trafficking. Several have risen to the level of nascent or actual states, controlling territory and administering government functions, albeit for some only temporarily. They

---

10 B. Ganor, 'Defining Terrorism: Is One Man's Terrorist Another Man's Freedom Fighter?', *Police Practice and Research* 3/4 (2002), p. 288.
11 The Department of State utilises the definition of terrorism found in the United States Federal Criminal Code, Title 22, Chapter 38, US Code §2656f, available at the Legal Information Institute, Cornell Law School, www.law.cornell.edu/uscode/text/22/2656f.
12 United States Department of Defense, 'Terrorism', *Department of Defense Dictionary of Military and Associated Terms* (June 2020), p. 215.

have features in common with state sponsors of terrorism and perpetrators of state terrorism like Iran and North Korea, which offer insights into our discussion. This wide variety of militants draws attention to an important insight in the Introduction to this volume by its editor, Richard English, about the constructive propensity of some scholars of the past to focus on specific cases of extremism rather than treat it only as a monolithic phenomenon. As Professor English writes, 'historians will tend to stress that it is terrorisms rather than terrorism that we have to explain'.[13] They often consider 'the complex particularity, and ultimately the uniqueness, of context. So there remains something of an emphasis upon the unrepeatable specificity of what is being studied, and also a recognition of the decisive importance of local, small-scale and even individual action.' History reminds us that a good deal of terrorism, like all of politics, is local. This study utilises an expansive conception of diplomacy. It includes secret contacts, indirect communications, direct talks, more formal peace processes, bilateral relations, the diplomatic components of military alliances, multilateral frameworks and international organisations. It explores how interlocutors have operated in these critical settings. It also considers instances where adversaries have rejected statesmanship. States have now and then lived up to their declared policy not to negotiate with terrorists, while the latter have occasionally rebuffed overtures from the former.[14]

Accruing Benefits

The first pillar of this chapter's conceptual framework argues that some actors navigating through the labyrinth of terrorism and diplomacy have accrued benefits. Governments have frequently utilised statesmanship vis-à-vis extremism to bolster their security interests. One compelling example is the international response to al Qaeda and its host in Afghanistan, the Taliban, in the months following 11 September 2001, when diplomacy served as the catalyst for common action. It activated existing regional alliances and created ad hoc ones in Europe, the Middle East, the Indo-Pacific and Latin America. It galvanised multilateral organisations, energised international law and mobilised public opinion (at least temporarily). Like-minded nations, many of whom were targets of domestic and global terrorists, synchronised overlapping strategies and interlocking tactics in order to respond to the new threat environment.

13 See above, p. 11.
14 This chapter's definition of diplomacy does not encompass tactical diplomacy or public diplomacy relative to terrorism, but extensive scholarly literatures assess these important themes.

The first steps took place in Brussels and New York on 12 September 2001. At its headquarters in Belgium, the North Atlantic Treaty Organization (NATO) took resolute diplomatic action. Its nineteen ambassadors, meeting in the North Atlantic Council, unanimously invoked for the first time Article Five of its founding treaty, which assures all members of collective defence.[15] 'If it is determined that this attack was directed from abroad against the United States, it shall be regarded as an action covered by Article Five of the Washington Treaty', promised Lord George Robertson, the NATO Secretary General.[16] He issued a joint statement that same day with the European Union High Representative for Common Foreign and Security Policy, Javier Solana, and other envoys in the Euro-Atlantic Partnership Council, denouncing the assaults and pledging 'to undertake all efforts to combat the scourge of terrorism. We stand united in our belief that the ideals of partnership and co-operation will prevail.'[17]

The United Nations reinforced NATO's assertive statesmanship. The Security Council unanimously approved a resolution that condemned 'in the strongest terms the horrifying terrorist attacks which took place on 11 September 2001'.[18] It called on member states 'to work together urgently to bring to justice the perpetrators, organizers and sponsors of these terrorist attacks', exhorted 'the international community to redouble their efforts to prevent and suppress' terrorism, and expressed 'its readiness to take all necessary steps to respond to the terrorist attacks of 11 September 2001'. The General Assembly followed suit the same day. It condemned 'the heinous acts of terrorism, which have caused enormous loss of human life, destruction and damage', expressed its 'solidarity with the people and Government of the United States of America' and requested worldwide assistance 'to prevent and eradicate acts of terrorism'.[19] True, United Nations action has been constrained in several respects since 9/11 (it has failed to define terrorism, for instance), but diplomacy there in the autumn of 2001 did help to consolidate a global response to

---

15 S. Daley, 'After the Attacks: The Alliance; for First Time, NATO Invokes Joint Defense Pact with U.S.', *New York Times*, 13 September 2001.
16 'NATO Reaffirms Treaty Commitments in Dealing with Terrorist Attacks Against the U.S.', NATO Update, North Atlantic Treaty Organization, 12 September 2001, www.nato.int/docu/update/2001/0910/e0912a.htm.
17 'Statement by the Euro-Atlantic Partnership Council', North Atlantic Treaty Organization, 12 September 2001, www.nato.int/docu/pr/2001/p01-123e.htm.
18 United Nations Security Council Resolution 1368, 12 September 2001, https://undocs.org/S/RES/1368(2001).
19 United Nations General Assembly Resolution 56/1, 12 September 2001, https://undocs.org/en/A/RES/56/1.

al Qaeda.[20] Bolstered by this diplomatic support, the United States took major action on 18 September 2001 in Washington, DC. Congress ratified the Authorization for the Use of Force, which approved the use of military action 'against those nations, organizations, or persons [the President] determines planned, authorized, committed, or aided the terrorist attacks that occurred on 11 September 2001, or harbored such organizations or persons, in order to prevent any future acts of international terrorism against the United States by such nations, organizations or persons'.[21] It was, in essence, a declaration of war.

Statecraft thus helped to solidify a multinational coalition against al Qaeda and the Taliban. The stage was set for a coordinated military response, and on 7 October 2001 the United States, supported by NATO and other allies like Australia, launched Operation Enduring Freedom against these foes.[22] Within months this campaign degraded the former's capability and blunted its momentum; al Qaeda was not defeated, but disrupted, at least temporarily.[23] NATO partnered with the Northern Alliance to oust the Taliban from power in November 2001. Its despotic rule ended in parts of Afghanistan and its support for foreign terrorist organisations like al Qaeda diminished.[24] The new government in Kabul, with international assistance, slowly consolidated its authority and augmented security in some parts of the country.[25] Conditions for the people of Afghanistan improved slightly: some experienced basic political reform, expanded access to education, and modest – but still fragile – rights for women.[26] This is not to suggest that diplomacy and its attendant military action resolved every dilemma. Remnants of al Qaeda escaped. The Taliban transitioned into a resilient

20 See, for example, J. Dhanapala, 'The United Nations' Response to 9/11', *Terrorism and Political Violence* 17/1–2 (2005); for a more critical view, see V. D. Comras, *Flawed Diplomacy: The United Nations and the War on Terrorism* (Washington, DC, Potomac Books, 2010).
21 Authorization for the Use of Military Force/Public Law 107-40, United States Congress, 18 September 2001, www.congress.gov/107/plaws/publ40/PLAW-107publ40.pdf.
22 D. L. Hanagan, *NATO in the Crucible: Coalition Warfare in Afghanistan* (Stanford, Hoover Institution Press, 2019), pp. 33–41.
23 Ibid., pp. 38–9; P. Bergen, *The Longest War: The Enduring Conflict Between America and Al-Qaeda* (Free Press, New York, 2011), pp. 68–9, 93–4.
24 A. Giustozzi, *The Taliban at War, 2001–2018* (Oxford, Oxford University Press, 2019), pp. 17–19.
25 Hanagan, *NATO in the Crucible*, pp. 39–47.
26 R. D. Lamb and B. Shawn, 'Political Governance and Strategy in Afghanistan: A Report of the CSIS Program on Crisis, Conflict and Cooperation', Center for Strategic and International Studies, April 2012, x–xiii, https://csis-website-prod.s3.amazonaws.com/s3fs-public/legacy_files/files/publication/120426_Lamb_PolGovernanceAfgha_Web.pdf.

transnational insurgency that remains deadly.[27] NATO's mission evolved into a protracted counterinsurgency. A substantive scholarly literature assesses its effectiveness,[28] and its impact on the alliance.[29] Stalled negotiations in 2020 aimed at resolving this conflict underscore how actors sometimes encounter limits to diplomacy with respect to terrorism.[30] Still, it is reasonable to conclude that NATO's early achievements, facilitated by international cooperation, were noteworthy. Statesmanship in the aftermath of 11 September 2001 produced some short-term benefits in Afghanistan – and elsewhere.

Diplomacy, Security, Peace

In the years after 9/11, some governments used the anti-al Qaeda and anti-Taliban diplomatic framework – multilateral relations, bilateral contacts, consultations with military allies – to forge international partnerships that countered local or regional opponents situated across the terrorist continuum. They occasionally achieved moderate progress when an improved defence calculus bolstered government confidence, diminished terrorist certitude about the inevitability of victory, and thereby established the conditions for brief dialogue or even extended peace processes. Foreign policy experts have reflected on how diplomacy, and then security, have sometimes been precursors to peace.[31]

Colombia is a case in point. In 2002, President George W. Bush and President Álvaro Uribe signed an agreement that galvanised Colombia's counterinsurgency campaign against FARC with greater backing from the United States, and eventually created the right circumstances for a resumption of multiparty talks that had recently stalled. They built upon

---

27 See 'Global Terrorism Overview: Terrorism in 2019', National Consortium for the Study of Terrorism and Responses to Terrorism, University of Maryland, July 2020, pp. 1–4, www.start.umd.edu/pubs/START_GTD_GlobalTerrorismOverview2019_July2020.pdf.
28 See, for example, R. English, *Terrorism: How to Respond* (Oxford, Oxford University Press, 2009), pp. 99–104, 107–9; S. G. Jones, *In the Graveyard of Empires: America's War in Afghanistan* (New York, W. W. Norton and Company, 2009).
29 See E. Hallams, *The United States and NATO since 9/11: The Transatlantic Alliance Renewed* (Abingdon, Routledge, 2010); S. M. Saidman, *NATO in Afghanistan: Fighting Together, Fighting Alone* (Princeton, Princeton University Press, 2014).
30 See S. G. Jones, 'A Failed Afghan Peace Deal', Council on Foreign Relations, Contingency Planning Memorandum 37, 1 July 2020, www.cfr.org/report/failed-afghan-peace-deal.
31 'The Role of Diplomacy in Combating Terrorism: Selected U.S. Perspectives', The Inter-University Center for Terrorism Studies, Potomac Institute for Policy Studies, November 2017, www.potomacinstitute.org/images/ICTS/RoleofDiplomacyNov2017.pdf.

the work of their predecessors, William Clinton and Andrés Pastrana, who had drafted 'Plan Colombia' a year earlier. This new approach, part of a wider project called the Andean Regional Initiative, provided Colombia with hundreds of millions of dollars in military assistance, intelligence support and counter-drug resources.[32] President Uribe's goal was to deal from a position of strength. With an infusion of men and material, the government gradually tilted the playing field in its favour. The number of insurgents under FARC's command declined, its grip on the narcotics trade was mildly disrupted, and the territory it controlled decreased, while internal reforms gradually enhanced the government's legitimacy.[33] Uribe was able to rein in some right-wing paramilitary groups, although scholars have denounced some of his tactics, widespread violations of human rights, and the modalities of American support.[34] Having improved security overall, President Uribe made covert contacts with FARC in the late 2000s. Due to continued pressure, it agreed to enter formal talks with his successor, Juan Manuel Santos, in 2012. The Colombian peace process, which continued for four excruciating years, resulted in a comprehensive agreement that was signed in late 2016.[35] Its implementation has faced several serious tests, human rights abuses persist in some parts of the country, and murders on both sides have continued.[36] It demonstrates, nonetheless, how statecraft can advance security and thereby promote a moderate degree of stability. In Asia, the Philippines and the United States used diplomacy to coordinate their counterterrorism policies. The Filipino government has been battling secessionists

---

32 For an assessment of the early stages of Plan Colombia, see D. Stokes, 'Better Lead Than Bread? A Critical Analysis of the US's Plan Colombia', *Civil Wars* 4/2 (June 2001); for a more sympathetic review of its later phases, see H. F. Kline, *Fighting Monsters in the Abyss: The Second Administration of Colombian President Álvaro Uribe Vélez, 2006–2010* (Tuscaloosa, University of Alabama Press, 2015), pp. 50–9.

33 L. Beehner and L. Collins, 'Welcome to the Jungle: Counterinsurgency Lessons from Colombia', Modern War Institute at West Point, 23 May 2019, pp. 36–40, https://mwi.usma.edu/wp-content/uploads/2019/05/Welcome-to-the-Jungle.pdf; L. E. Taylor II, 'Case Analysis: The FARC in Colombia', *Small Wars Journal* (5 March 2020), https://smallwarsjournal.com/jrnl/art/case-analysis-farc-colombia.

34 For critiques of these and other aspects of the Colombian–American partnership, see J. D. Rosen, *The Losing War: Plan Colombia and Beyond* (Albany, SUNY Press, 2014); W. Tate, *Drugs, Thugs, and Diplomats: U.S. Policymaking in Colombia* (Stanford, Stanford University Press, 2015).

35 For a first-hand account of the peace process by the former president of Colombia, see J. M. Santos, *La batalla por La Paz* (Bogotá, Planeta Colombia, 2019).

36 For a review of the implementation of the Colombian peace agreement, see J. Meernik, J. H. R. DeMeritt and M. Uribe-López (eds.), *As War Ends: What Colombia Can Tell Us about Sustainability of Peace and Transitional Justice* (Cambridge, Cambridge University Press, 2019). For an analysis of recent violence, see Human Rights Watch, 'Colombia: Events of 2019', www.hrw.org/world-report/2020/country-chapters/Colombia.

in the southern Philippines for decades. According to the United States Institute for Peace, in 1996 it reached a deal with one group, the Moro National Liberation Front, which has generally persisted, albeit with serious difficulties.[37] In 2001 its main antagonists were two indigenous Islamist movements, the Moro Islamic Liberation Front and the Abu Sayyaf Group. The former sought 'independence for the 'Bangsamoro' (literally, 'Moro nation') across the southern part of the country and held sway over parts of Mindanao.[38] The ASG launched its operations primarily out of nearby Basilan and Sulu, notes one scholar of the organisation.[39] Both had established ties to al Qaeda and Jemaah Islamiyah, the South East Asian terrorists responsible for the Bali bombings.[40]

President George W. Bush and President Gloria Macapagal Arroyo pledged mutual cooperation after 9/11 and instructed their representatives to draft a series of agreements. The combined effort was called Operation Enduring Freedom – Philippines. The United States committed to providing military aid, logistics support, intelligence analysis and Special Operations advisors (although they were not authorised to engage in direct combat), while the Philippines allowed American forces to use some of its bases as staging grounds for Afghanistan. From 2002 to 2015, several thousand US soldiers supported Filipino counter-insurgency operations, especially on Mindanao, Basilan, Sulu and Jolo.[41] This joint campaign gained some traction. The Moro Islamic Liberation Front tentatively agreed to sporadic talks, which were interspersed with fighting, and by 2007 'had abandoned its goal of an independent homeland and accepted in principle an autonomy agreement'.[42] An early version of a settlement failed in 2008, while conflict flared on and off. Because they could not stand up to increasingly effective government forces, the insurgents resumed political

---

37 Z. Abuza and L. Lischin, 'The Challenges Facing the Philippines' Bangsamoro Autonomous Region at One Year', United States Institute for Peace, Special Report 468, June 2020, pp. 4–5, 14–16, www.usip.org/sites/default/files/2020-06/20200610-sr_468-the_challenges_facing_the_philippines_bangsamoro_autonomous_region_at_one_year-sr.pdf.
38 Ibid., pp. 3, 4.
39 R. C. Banlaoi, 'The Abu Sayyaf Group: From Mere Banditry to Genuine Terrorism', *Southeast Asian Affairs* (2006), pp. 248, 252–3.
40 Banlaoi, 'The Abu Sayyaf Group', pp. 249, 254–5; Z. Abuza, *Forging Peace in Southeast Asia: Insurgencies, Peace Process, and Reconciliation* (Lanham, Rowman and Littlefield, 2016), p. 77.
41 See, for example, L. Robinson, P. B. Johnston and G. S. Oak, *U.S. Special Operations Forces in the Philippines, 2001–2014* (Santa Monica, Rand Corporation, 2016); B. M. Stentiford, *Success in the Shadows: Operation Enduring Freedom – Philippines and the Global War on Terror, 2002–2015* (Fort Leavenworth, Combat Studies Institute Press, 2019).
42 Abuza and Lischin, 'The Challenges Facing the Philippines' Bangsamoro Region', p. 4.

dialogue, 'leading to the Framework Agreement of 2012 and its four annexes in February 2013, and then to the Comprehensive Agreement on the Bangsamoro in March 2014'.[43] Further challenges delayed the plan, but by 'mid-2018, the Philippine Congress passed the implementing legislation for the peace process, and in January 2019 the Bangsamoro Autonomous Region of Muslim Mindanao (BARMM) was formally established by plebiscite'.[44] The Filipino military, by the same token, was able to reduce the ASG's capabilities in the early 2000s,[45] but because it has periodically staged attacks while resisting mediation, it is discussed in the section below on limitations. Yet the relevant argument about these Filipino groups applies to al Qaeda, the Taliban, FARC and similar organisations: namely, statesmanship in relation to terrorism procured advantages for governments and societies following 11 September 2001.

Peace Processes Before and After 11 September 2001

States – and by extension the general publics they govern – have accrued benefits not only when they used diplomacy to counter terrorists in the wake of 11 September, but also to engage with them in comprehensive peace processes before and after this historic date. These gains include a decline in violence, the dissolution of some militant groups, a degree of political stability, economic growth, international investment and post-conflict reconciliation. A substantial literature highlights these and some of the other rewards that inclusive dialogue has sometimes generated.[46]

Northern Ireland

Various commentators maintain that the peace process in Northern Ireland has secured advantages for the governments of the United Kingdom and Ireland, for the new administration in the province, for the people living there and beyond. Several have knowledge born of experience in the crucible of the Ulster labyrinth. George Mitchell, the former United States Senator and President Clinton's envoy to Northern Ireland who was deeply involved in hammering out the Belfast Agreement, says that the peace process convinced the people of Northern Ireland 'that peace and political stability will

---

43 Ibid.
44 Ibid., p. 3. For a review of the Filipino peace process in its regional context, see Abuza, *Forging Peace in Southeast Asia*, pp. 65–120.
45 Banlaoi, 'The Abu Sayyaf Group', pp. 253–5.
46 For general studies, see, for example, J. Tonge, *Comparative Peace Processes* (Cambridge, Polity Press, 2014); A. Özerdem and R. MacGinty (eds.), *Comparing Peace Processes* (Abingdon, Routledge, 2019).

enable them to enjoy unprecedented growth and prosperity'.[47] Jonathan Powell asserts, in his memoir of the talks, that the day in 2007 when Ian Paisley of the Democratic Unionist Party (DUP) and Martin McGuinness of Sinn Féin were sworn in as leaders of the Northern Ireland executive was 'a great moment for the people of Ireland and the people of Britain', one that gave him a profound sense of satisfaction.[48] The major milestones of the peace process are well known. In 1993 the British and Irish governments issued the Downing Street Declaration, which created a framework for dialogue based on the principles of Irish self-determination and the consent of the majority in Northern Ireland. Five years later, four parties – the Ulster Unionist Party (UUP), the Social Democratic and Labour Party (SDLP), Sinn Féin and the Alliance Party – joined them in signing the Belfast Agreement. This pact established a regional government with mandatory cross-community power-sharing (or consociation), an assembly with some powers devolved from London and an executive with seats apportioned to Unionists and nationalists according to representation in the assembly.[49]

These and other landmarks were achieved through gruelling deliberations. George Mitchell describes his role as 'the most difficult task I have ever undertaken, far more demanding than the six years I served as majority leader of the United States Senate'.[50] Daunting disputes slowed the passage through this diplomatic thicket. Inter-party tensions periodically immobilised government institutions. The number of Catholics in the Police Service of Northern Ireland (PSNI) in 2020 continues to lag, at 31.81 per cent.[51] Some victims of terrorist violence and state security forces have not received justice. The destabilising complexities of Brexit loom large.[52] Still, statistics highlight how participants in the peace process have accrued some benefits. Political violence has dropped steadily. The University of Ulster's fifth 'Northern Ireland Peace Monitoring Report', published in 2018, notes that data from 2016–17 'confirms the downward trend of conflict-related crimes reported in previous

---

47 G. J. Mitchell, *Making Peace* (New York, Alfred A. Knopf, 1999), pp. 186–7.
48 J. Powell, *Great Hatred, Little Room: Making Peace in Northern Ireland* (London, The Bodley Head, 2008), p. 1.
49 For a review of the major stages of the peace process, see, for example, T. Hennessey, *The Northern Ireland Peace Process: Ending the Troubles?* (New York, Palgrave, 2001); A. Edwards and S. Bloomer (eds.), *Transforming the Peace Process in Northern Ireland: From Terrorism to Democratic Politics* (Dublin, Irish Academic Press, 2008).
50 Mitchell, *Making Peace*, p. 1.
51 'Workforce Composition Statistics', Police Service of Northern Ireland, 1 May 2020, www.psni.police.uk/inside-psni/Statistics/workforce-composition-statistics/.
52 M. Russell, 'Northern Ireland after Brexit', European Parliamentary Research Service, 6 May 2020, www.europarl.europa.eu/RegData/etudes/BRIE/2020/649416/EPRS_BRI(2020)649416_EN.pdf.

Peace Monitoring Reports. The figures are the lowest recorded' since the signing of the Belfast Agreement in 1998.[53] Deaths linked to terrorism have dropped from 55 in 1998 to 2 in 2017.[54] Annual bombings have decreased from 127 to 29 during the same period.[55] The decline in civil unrest has contributed to modest economic development. According to the 'Northern Ireland Peace Monitoring Report', the economy 'grew rapidly from 1998 up to the recession [of 2008–9], ahead of the UK rate'.[56] It rebounded in the following decade, so by 2018 employment was 'at its highest level on record and unemployment at a historic low' in the province.[57] Foreign direct investment 'has improved markedly since the signing of the [Belfast] Agreement as job creation levels have more than doubled over the past two decades'.[58] Twenty years after the conclusion of the Belfast Agreement, 'there are clear signs of economic progress', and 'Peace is an important element' of this recovery.[59] These numbers add up. They support the conclusion that some communities in Ulster have mapped a course through the twisting maze of the peace process in Northern Ireland to find rays of light at the end of a long, dark tunnel.

The Basque Peace Process

The Basque region of Spain is also a place where states and societies have consolidated advantages by interacting with terrorists in a lengthy peace process. There were several primary interlocutors, including the Spanish government, the moderate Basque Nationalist Party, which has ruled the Basque autonomous region for most of the past forty years, elements of the more uncompromising umbrella group Basque National Liberation Movement, the violent separatist organisation Basque Homeland and Freedom, or Euskadi Ta Askatasuna (which experienced several splits during its lifetime), and its political arm Batasuna (previously Herri Batasuna).[60] The more extremist Basque parties were, according to a scholar of the peace process, Teresa Whitfield, committed to 'the independence of a Basque

---

53 'Northern Ireland Crime Survey (NICS), 2018', quoted in A. M. Gray, J. Hamilton, G. Kelly, B. Lynn, M. Melaugh and G. Robinson, 'Northern Ireland Peace Monitoring Report', Ulster University, 5 October 2018, p. 89, https://cain.ulster.ac.uk/events/peace/docs/nipmr_2018-10.pdf.
54 'Security Situation Statistics, 2018', Police Service of Northern Ireland, quoted in Gray et al., 'Northern Ireland Peace Monitoring Report', p. 107.
55 'Police Recorded Security Situation Statistics', Police Service of Northern Ireland, quoted in Gray et al., 'Northern Ireland Peace Monitoring Report', p. 109.
56 Ibid., p. 19.   57 Ibid., p. 23.   58 Ibid., p. 27.   59 Ibid., p. 28.
60 For a detailed discussion of these parties, and the Basque peace process, see Bew et al., *Talking to Terrorists*, pp. 169–238; R. Leonisio, F. Molina and D. Muro (eds.), *ETA's Terrorist Campaign: From Violence to Politics, 1968–2015* (Abingdon, Routledge, 2016).

homeland, Euskal Herria, that extends across seven administrative units in Spain and France'.[61] All of these antagonists entered into a labyrinth haunted by historical grievance, contemporary contempt and seemingly irreconcilable political objectives. ETA launched its violent campaign in 1968. In 1989, following years of discreet consultations, the Spanish government and ETA held low-level direct talks for the first time in Algiers, but they collapsed over unbridgeable differences, and the latter predictably returned to violence.[62] In 1996 the new prime minister, José María Aznar, the leader of the Popular Party whom ETA had tried to assassinate the previous year, intensified police pressure on the group. Meanwhile, according to Whitfield in her study *Endgame for ETA*, 'Social opposition to ETA increased dramatically after July 1997 when ETA kidnapped Miguel Angel Blanco, a young [Popular Party] counselor from the Vizcayan town of Ermua, and two days later killed him.'[63] Aznar's prioritisation of security over politics accelerated after 11 September 2001, when the government passed laws making it easier to prosecute radical Basque groups, enhanced its cooperation with France and the EU, and banned Batasuna.[64] Critics compare these harsher tactics to some of the unlawful ones applied during the dirty war of the 1980s by the secret paramilitary force, Grupos Antiterroristas de Liberación (GAL), but they were not the same – and Aznar's successor continued some of them.[65] In 2005 the new Socialist prime minister of Spain, José Luis Rodríguez Zapatero, renewed contacts that resulted in another ETA cessation in March of 2006. When a third round of negotiations stalled, ETA detonated a bomb at the Madrid airport in December that killed two but sparked a major public backlash.[66] After a pause, the government tried again in 2007; the two parties met without success; and ETA returned to the armed struggle. Two factors then focused the collective mind of ETA. On the security front, by 'the end of 2009, with substantial cooperation from France, some 277 alleged members of ETA had been detained', including many of its leaders.[67] Elements of the international community also weighed in. The Centre for Humanitarian

---

61 T. Whitfield, 'The Basque Conflict and ETA: The Difficulties of an Ending', United States Institute for Peace, Special Report 384, December 2015, p. 1, www.usip.org/sites/default/files/SR384-The-Basque-Conflict-and-ETA-The-Difficulties-of-An-Ending.pdf.
62 Ibid., pp. 5–6.
63 T. Whitfield, *Endgame for ETA: Elusive Peace in the Basque Country* (Oxford, Oxford University Press, 2014), p. 80.
64 Whitfield, 'The Basque Conflict and ETA', p. 6.
65 For a discussion of GAL's campaign, see P. Woodworth, *ETA, the GAL and Spanish Democracy*, 2nd ed. (New Haven, Yale University Press, 2003).
66 Whitfield, *Endgame for ETA*, pp. 179–82.
67 Whitfield, 'The Basque Conflict and ETA', p. 8.

Dialogue in Geneva had already been acting as an intermediary in the peace process for several years, and in late 2010 six winners of the Nobel Peace Prize issued the Brussels Declaration, which implored ETA to issue another ceasefire.[68] It responded affirmatively in January 2011. Next, at a conference in San Sebastián in October, a group of international dignitaries 'issued a declaration calling on ETA to announce the end of its violence. Three days later, as previously agreed, ETA responded by declaring the definitive end of its armed activities.'[69]

The following month the Popular Party returned to power, headed by Mariano Rajoy. It continued making arrests and made no major diplomatic overtures. ETA refrained from violence, while low-level international contacts continued. In 2017 it surrendered its arsenal, which French authorities verified.[70] In May of 2018 the Centre for Humanitarian Dialogue announced that ETA had in fact dissolved.[71] ETA confirmed this step in a final statement.[72] Unlike the way other conflicts have ended, there was no final agreement nor a signing ceremony in Madrid, Bilbao or Vitoria-Gasteiz. Still, actors in the Basque peace process accrued some benefits. There was a marked decrease in violence over time. More than 800 were killed and 2,000 wounded from 1968 to 2011, but the 'count remained low during much of the 1990s', while ETA murdered 'zero between 2003 and late 2006, and only twelve between 2006 and the cessation of violence in 2011'.[73] There was a gradual reduction in popular support for ETA, the decommissioning of weapons, and the dissolution of one of the most radical organisations in Europe. A transition to democratic politics ensued: in 2011, for example, some elements of Batasuna joined 'a new political party, Sortu (Create), which clearly rejected violence and ETA's violence explicitly' and which gravitated to a new, legal coalition of the national left, Euskal Herria Bildu.[74] The Basque peace process found itself on life support several times, but those

---

68 Whitfield, *Endgame for ETA*, pp. 131–2, 150–4, 223–5.
69 Whitfield, 'The Basque Conflict and ETA', p. 10.
70 C. Canellas and S. Dowsett, 'Basque Militants ETA Surrender Arms in End to Decades of Conflict', Reuters, 7 April 2017, www.reuters.com/article/us-spain-eta/basque-militants-eta-surrender-arms-in-end-to-decades-of-conflict-idUSKBN1790YK.
71 'HD Announces ETA's Official Final Declaration That It Has Disbanded Forever', Center for Humanitarian Dialogue, 3 May 2018, www.hdcentre.org/updates/hd-announces-etas-official-final-declaration-that-it-has-disbanded-forever/.
72 'Final Statement from ETA to the Basque Country', Center for Humanitarian Dialogue, 3 May 2018, www.hdcentre.org/wp-content/uploads/2018/05/ETA-declaration-English.pdf.
73 Whitfield, 'The Basque Conflict and ETA', p. 4.   74 Ibid., p. 9.

who travelled along this arduous pathway managed to emerge with modest but tangible gains.

A Multi-component Strategy

In retrospect, it is worth noting that peace processes have usually yielded the best results for states, societies and individual citizens when they have been one part of a multi-component counterterrorist strategy. A comprehensive approach has sometimes created the conditions for negotiations, which, in turn, have generated progress. In other words, the counterterrorist strategy is the overarching policy (which in some contexts can be defined as conflict resolution), and the peace process (or diplomacy) is one spoke in that wheel. Several of the features of this unified plan may be described in soft power terms, including a focus on the root causes of terrorism, political change and economic development. Others fall under the umbrella of criminal justice reform. Important components are linked to law, order and security, such as robust policing, the prosecution of extremists, decisive intelligence and in certain cases the tactical use of force; their accumulated effect occasionally induces militants to reconsider the use of terror. The resolution of terrorist conflicts in the Basque country and Ulster demonstrates the efficacy of a multidimensional strategy in which statecraft is one of several important elements. In the former location, according to Teresa Whitfield:

> When an end to ETA's violence eventually appeared possible, it could be attributed to many factors. Foremost among them were the decimation of the organization by successful police action against it in Spain and France, the intensity of the legal campaign against Batasuna and others associated with the nationalist left, and the widespread rejection of ETA's violence among elements of Basque society ... [and] it would not have been achieved without Zapatero's initiative of the peace process in 2005, the changes set in motion by Batasuna after this process's collapse in 2007 and limited but essential assistance from international actors.[75]

Several components thus contributed to ETA's renunciation of terror and subsequent progress: state security, law enforcement, civic engagement, intra-Basque dialogue, the peace process and international statesmanship.

Bew, Frampton and Gurrachaga sum up well the value of reconceptualising diplomacy within an integrated counterterrorist strategy. 'Conventional wisdom is fast coalescing around the idea that talking to terrorists is *the*

---

75 Whitfield, *Endgame for ETA*, p. 7.

pre-requisite for a solution to violent conflicts in which a terrorist organization is a key protagonist', they observed in 2009, but this and related ideas 'are removed from the many other ingredients which feed into violent conflict, as well as those which are required to bring it to an end'.[76] Instead,

> a variety of other factors can be decisive in determining when and how governments talk to terrorists – and with what result. Inclusive dialogue with terrorists has been a feature of government policy in the Basque Country and Northern Ireland on several occasions over the last thirty years. But it has not, in itself, provided a magic solution to either conflict, particularly in the Basque Country where ETA is yet to renounce violence [as of 2009]. Ultimately, if talking to terrorists can be said to have had some success in Northern Ireland, this was only when the terrorists had come to accept the rules of the game and agreed to abide by them in the search for a settlement.

Terrorist Organisations

Like states, terrorist organisations and their political fronts have from time to time accumulated advantages at the nexus of political violence and statecraft. Some of their gains include greater political legitimacy, rising popularity and international acceptance. The consolidation of these benefits has set the stage for subsequent ones, such as the achievement of political objectives, enhanced electoral performance and, in several cases, a grip on the levers of state power. It is not surprising that militants have profited from diplomacy, for many have demonstrated prowess at combining strategic theorising with tactical dexterity extending back to the 1950s. Anti-imperialist movements in places like Algeria and Vietnam grasped that the fluid nature of political deliberations presents opportunities to seize the initiative at the expense of their negotiating partners, and they did just that, often by integrating dialogue with force. Many of the contemporary terrorists and insurgents they have inspired, from FARC to the Taliban to the PLO, have adopted the same strategy.[77]

The Provisional IRA and Sinn Féin

Throughout the course of the peace process in Northern Ireland, the Provisional IRA and its political arm, Sinn Féin, have accrued benefits.

---

76 Bew et al., *Talking to Terrorists*, p. 259.
77 See, for example, J. J. Byrne, *Mecca of Revolution: Algeria, Decolonization and the Third World Order* (Oxford, Oxford University Press, 2016); S. G. Jones, *Waging Insurgent Warfare: Lessons from the Vietcong to the Islamic State* (Oxford, Oxford University Press, 2017).

Their participation in multiparty talks conferred political legitimacy on them. After President Clinton invited Gerry Adams, the leader of Sinn Féin, to a reception at the White House on Saint Patrick's Day in 1995, the *Washington Post* recognised that 'A personal meeting with the president bestows a legitimacy on Adams and Sinn Fein considered unthinkable a few years ago.'[78] Jonathan Powell admits this transpired, but defends the result: 'Bestowing temporary legitimacy on armed groups is not necessarily too high a price to pay for a peace process', since it can evaporate quickly if mediation ends, and so long as governments do not recognise them as the only representatives of their side.[79] As the party gained admission into the inner sanctums of decision-making in Washington and London, it earned plaudits at home for securing republican objectives like police reform and prisoner releases. As a result of these achievements, Sinn Féin steadily expanded its share of the Catholic-nationalist vote at the expense of its rival, the SDLP. In the elections to the new Northern Ireland Assembly in 1998 it won 17.6 per cent of first preference ballots and 18 out of 108 seats.[80] In 2003 it supplanted the SDLP as the largest nationalist party.[81] Four years later its totals jumped to 26.2 per cent and 28 seats, and Martin McGuinness became Deputy First Minister.[82] It surged in 2017, as its first preference vote increased by 3.9 per cent (the largest gain of any of the parties) to 27.9 per cent and it secured 27 seats out of a reduced total of 90 in the Assembly.[83] The executive, which had been suspended just before the elections, was fully restored in January 2020, with Sinn Féin's Michelle O'Neill appointed Deputy First Minister (following the death of Martin McGuinness in 2017) and the DUP's Arlene Foster named First Minister. Several factors have fuelled the ascent of Sinn Féin. Diplomacy has been one of them. The peace process has legitimised it, polished its domestic image and burnished its international reputation. It has translated these concrete gains into stepping stones on its long march to power. Sinn Féin and the Provisional IRA, relying

---

78 F. Barbash and A. Devroy, 'Sinn Fein Leader Can Raise Funds Here', *Washington Post*, 10 March 1995, www.washingtonpost.com/archive/politics/1995/03/10/sinn-fein-leader-can-raise-funds-here/4ac7519b-5123-43b4-a891-c38e887ff7e6/.
79 Powell, *Talking to Terrorists*, p. 27. For a scholarly defence of legitimising terrorists during negotiations, see H. Toros, '"We Don't Negotiate with Terrorists!": Legitimacy and Complexity in Terrorist Conflicts', *Security Dialogue* 39/4 (August 2008).
80 'Northern Ireland Assembly Elections 1998', ARK, www.ark.ac.uk/elections/fa98.htm.
81 'Northern Ireland Assembly Elections 2003', ARK, www.ark.ac.uk/elections/fa03.htm.
82 'Northern Ireland Assembly Elections 2007', ARK, www.ark.ac.uk/elections/fa07.htm.
83 'Northern Ireland Assembly Elections 2017', ARK, www.ark.ac.uk/elections/fa17.htm.

on shrewdness and cunning, have plotted a deft course through the maze of the Northern Ireland peace process.

Incurring Costs

This chapter's second supporting argument contends that historically some actors who have banked on diplomacy as a profitable means of responding to terrorism or as a potential vehicle for disengaging from it have incurred costs instead. They are one of the potential hazards of charting a path through this Byzantine web of alleyways. The analytical ability of participants to assess costs has been critical to their journey. Some have demonstrated impressive navigational skills: their gains have outweighed their losses. Others have failed to discern pitfalls, so their scales have balanced out at best or tilted towards deficits at worst. Officials, politicians and scholars have affirmed this chapter's recognition of costs in first-hand accounts and academic research.[84] Historians should consider them, too, in order to reach a fuller appraisal of how radicalism and statecraft have interacted in the past.

Political Leaders

Some of the non-terrorist protagonists in this study have experienced losses by bargaining with militants. One political figure who suffered was Yitzhak Rabin, the prime minister of Israel. His decision to cooperate with the Palestinian Liberation Organisation and sign the Oslo Accords in 1993 earned him widespread gratitude abroad. He received the Nobel Peace Prize the following year, along with Shimon Peres, the Israeli Foreign Minister, and Yasser Arafat. When presenting the awards in Oslo, Francis Sejersted, Chairman of the Nobel Committee, alluded to the *longue durée* of the diplomatic quest: 'Peace has to be perpetually won. That means that every award must contain an element of entering into a process, a process with a promise of peace. The Nobel Peace Prize is awarded both in recognition of efforts which have been made, and to encourage still further

---

[84] See, for example, in the context of Asia, Abuza, *Forging Peace in Southeast Asia*, pp. 2–5; in the Middle East, E. W. Said, *Peace and Its Discontents: Essays on Palestine in the Middle East Peace Process* (New York, Vintage Books, 1996); M. Ma'oz, K. Shikaki, and R. L. Rothstein (eds.), *The Israeli–Palestinian Peace Process: Oslo and the Lessons of Failure: Perspectives, Predicaments, Prospects* (Eastbourne, Sussex Academic Press, 2004); O. Seliktar, *Doomed to Failure? The Politics and Intelligence of the Oslo Peace Process* (Santa Barbara, Praeger Security International, 2009); in Northern Ireland, R. McCartney, *Reflections on Liberty, Democracy and the Union* (Dublin, Maunsel and Company, 2001); G. K. Peatling, *The Failure of the Northern Ireland Peace Process* (Dublin, Irish Academic Press, 2004).

efforts.'[85] In his acceptance speech, Rabin recognised he was inside something like a labyrinth or, as he put it, 'We are in the midst of building the peace. The architects and engineers of this enterprise are engaged in their work even as we gather here tonight, building the peace layer by layer, brick by brick, beam by beam. The job is difficult, complex, trying.'[86] Rabin's consultations with the PLO, however, divided opinion at home. Many Israelis supported his outreach, as they did his signing of the Israel–Jordan peace treaty in 1994. Other elements of the population were sceptical. Some were overtly hostile, including settlers in the West Bank and Gaza, religious conservatives and opposition political parties. The latter constellation shared their fury with numerous Palestinians. 'Rabin's diplomacy', according to Dan Ephron, 'triggered a violent backlash by Israelis and Palestinians opposed to the conciliation process'.[87] He was acutely aware of this criticism. So was Francis Sejersted: in Oslo he had said, with a hint of presentiment, 'The three prize-winners are all in positions in which they have power to intervene in the course of events. But their positions are also exposed.'[88] Rabin persisted, for which he would pay the ultimate price. On 4 November 1995, Yigal Amir, an Israeli extremist opposed to his overtures to the Palestinians, assassinated him at the end of a political rally in Jerusalem.[89] His death provoked a national and international outpouring of grief. During his eulogy two days later, President Clinton affirmed that 'His spirit lives on in the growing peace between Israel and her neighbors.'[90] Dan Ephron believes his murder had a profound effect on the peace process: it 'set off a chain reaction that would shift the power in Israel from the pragmatists to the ideologues. Two decades later, the coveted peace remains elusive.'[91] In Rabin's death are echoes of the fate of Anwar Sadat, the president of Egypt who brokered a treaty with Israel in 1978, only to incur a tremendous cost at the hands of his own countrymen when a group of hardcore Egyptian Islamists determined to asphyxiate the budding peace between Egypt and Israel assassinated him in Cairo in 1981.

---

85 F. Sejersted, 'Award Ceremony Speech', The Nobel Prize, 10 December 1994, www.nobelprize.org/prizes/peace/1994/ceremony-speech/.
86 Y. Rabin, 'Nobel Lecture', The Nobel Prize, 10 December 1994, www.nobelprize.org/prizes/peace/1994/rabin/lecture/.
87 D. Ephron, *Killing a King: The Assassination of Yitzhak Rabin and the Remaking of Israel* (New York, W. W. Norton, 2015), p. xii.
88 Sejersted, 'Award Ceremony Speech'.   89 Ephron, *Killing a King*, pp. 175–9.
90 W. Clinton, 'Eulogy for Yitzhak Rabin', The Yitzhak Rabin Center, 6 November 1995, www.rabincenter.org.il/Items/01104/clinton.pdf.
91 Ephron, *Killing a King*, p. xii.

Political Parties

Some democratic political parties that have negotiated with armed radicals have subsequently waned at the ballot box. Two of them in Northern Ireland are the Social Democratic and Labour Party and the Ulster Unionist Party. The SDLP, an enthusiastic participant in the Irish peace process, was in a strong position at its start. At the 1998 Assembly elections it won 21.9 per cent of first preference votes (the highest of any party), 24 seats, was the largest Catholic party, and its deputy leader, Seamus Mallon, became Deputy First Minister.[92] These achievements were fleeting. By 2007 its share of the vote fell to 15.2 per cent, its seats to 16, and Mallon surrendered his post to Martin McGuinness.[93] This disappointing trend continued through 2017, with only 11.9 per cent of the vote total and 12 seats.[94] The SDLP also faded in the United States in comparison to Sinn Féin, despite the popularity of John Hume, its leader throughout the peace process and the recipient of the Nobel Peace Prize in 1998. Several factors precipitated the SDLP's decline. One of them may have been its decision to enter into dialogue with the political representatives of the Provisional IRA, which, along with the Hume–Adams initiative,[95] bestowed a measure of respectability on Sinn Féin. Seamus Mallon admits in his memoir that, when his colleagues joined talks with Sinn Féin, 'we also legitimized them'.[96] He understood that his party, which 'had struggled for so long to keep the flame of decency and democracy alive, paid a high price for conceding that republican ground to the Provos'. It still strains to find its footing. As one analyst wrote in 2019, 'in the years since the culmination of their flagship achievement, the Good Friday Agreement, the SDLP has lost its "message"', just as 'they have struggled to find a role in a post-civil rights, post-peace process era' in Ulster.[97]

Another organisation whose ranking tumbled after engaging in diplomacy with terrorists was the Ulster Unionist Party. The largest unionist party at the

---

92 'Northern Ireland Assembly Elections 1998', ARK, www.ark.ac.uk/elections/fa98.htm.
93 'Northern Ireland Assembly Elections 2007', ARK, www.ark.ac.uk/elections/fa07.htm.
94 'Northern Ireland Assembly Elections 2017', ARK, www.ark.ac.uk/elections/fa17.htm.
95 See J. Hume, *A New Ireland: Politics, Peace and Reconciliation* (Boulder, Roberts Rinehart Publishers, 1996), pp. 113–18.
96 S. Mallon, with A. Pollak, *A Shared Home Place* (Dublin, The Lilliput Press, 2019), p. 94.
97 C. Kelly, 'The Decline of the SDLP and Their European Election Brexit Headache', *E-International Relations* (22 April 2019), p. 1, www.e-ir.info/pdf/78526.

start of the peace process, it reluctantly joined inclusive dialogue with Sinn Féin in 1997.[98] It received some kudos at home. In the 1998 elections to the Assembly it remained the leading unionist party, with 21.25 per cent of first preference votes, 28 seats, and its leader, David Trimble, appointed First Minister.[99] That same year he shared the Nobel Peace Prize with John Hume. The UUP's electoral performance faltered in 2007, however, when its numbers collapsed to 14.9 per cent of the vote and 18 seats, and Trimble relinquished the position of First Minister to Ian Paisley of the DUP.[100] In 2017 its totals slid again to 12.9 per cent and 10.[101]

The deterioration of the UUP's position had several causes. One of them was its decision to confer with republican and loyalist militants, which sowed internal discord. The signing of the Belfast Agreement, Jonathan Powell recalls, eventually 'cost Trimble his job as leader, and broke up the party. He made the brave and right decision on Good Friday, but he paid a terrible price for it'.[102] The UUP's policy also alienated vocal segments of the Unionist electorate opposed to collaborating with terrorists, who gravitated towards other parties, especially the DUP, which steered a more effective electoral route through the peace process maze.[103] Some observers in Northern Ireland and the Republic of Ireland have decried another shortcoming of the peace process: it has enabled Sinn Féin and loyalist parties to camouflage their continuing links to terrorists. In 2015 the Police Service of Northern Ireland and MI5 concluded that 'All the main paramilitary groups operating during the period of the Troubles remain in existence', which includes the Provisional IRA.[104] They have not been quiescent, but continue to mete

---

98 For a discussion of this and other UUP decisions during the peace process, see T. Hennessey, M. Braniff, J. W. McAuley, J. Tonge and S. Whiting, *The Ulster Unionist Party: Country Before Party?* (Oxford, Oxford University Press, 2014), pp. 41–61.
99 'Northern Ireland Assembly Elections 1998', ARK, www.ark.ac.uk/elections/.
100 'Northern Ireland Assembly Elections 2007', ARK, www.ark.ac.uk/elections/fa07.htm.
101 'Northern Ireland Assembly Elections 2017', ARK, www.ark.ac.uk/elections/fa17.htm.
102 Powell, *Great Hatred, Little Room*, p. 106. For assessments of David Trimble's policies, see F. Millar, *David Trimble: The Price of Peace* (Dublin, The Liffey Press, 2005); D. Godson, *Himself Alone: David Trimble and the Ordeal of Unionism* (New York, HarperCollins, 2005).
103 For an analysis of the DUP's evolution during the peace process, see J. Tonge, M. Braniff, T. Hennessey, J. W. McAuley and S. Whiting, *The Democratic Unionist Party: From Protest to Power* (Oxford, Oxford University Press, 2014).
104 'Paramilitary Groups in Northern Ireland', Police Service of Northern Ireland and MI5 Security Service, Northern Ireland Office, 19 October 2015, https://assets.publishing.service.gov.uk/government/uploads/system/uploads/attachment_data/file/469548/Paramilitary_Groups_in_Northern_Ireland_-_20_Oct_2015.pdf.

out rough justice in the form of punishment attacks.[105] The Irish Taoiseach, Leo Varadkar, asserted in early 2020 that 'It is our view that Sinn Féin is not a normal party.'[106] He and other Irish officials have reason to be concerned. In the 2020 elections for the Irish Dail, Sinn Féin, sanitised by the peace process, achieved a major breakthrough, winning 24.5 per cent of first preference votes (the highest of any party) and 37 seats (second only to Fianna Fáil).[107] A three-party coalition has denied it a place in government, at least for now.[108] Can civil society coexist with paramilitary organisations? Adherents of the peace process assured its sceptics that they would wither away.[109] History has confirmed that they still exist. This revelation reminds us of one of the imperatives of the historian's craft, which Richard English highlights in his Introduction: they 'analyse the relationship between change and continuity with an eye to long pasts.'[110]

Limits to Diplomacy

This chapter's third supporting argument asserts that actors deliberating at the crossroads of terrorism and diplomacy have now and again encountered limits. They may have participated in peace processes, but have failed to resolve the contentious issues dividing them; they advanced into Daedalus' maze, but are still wandering inside. Some potential participants have decided not to do business at all; they have refused to cross the threshold into the labyrinth's knot of alleyways. Others have briefly joined multiparty talks only to abandon them; they have rapidly backed out before falling through a trapdoor.

The Israeli–Palestinian Peace Process

The historical record reveals several examples of how terrorists and non-terrorists have tried to settle their differences, without success. The Israeli–Palestinian peace process is one of them. Modest improvements followed the Oslo Accords of 1993, as the two parties signed several interim

---

105 Gray et al., 'Northern Ireland Peace Monitoring Report', p. 95.
106 B. Roche, 'Taoiseach Claims Sinn Féin Not "a Normal Political Party"', *Irish Times*, 21 January 2020, www.irishtimes.com/news/ireland/irish-news/taoiseach-claims-sinn-f%C3%A9in-not-a-normal-political-party-1.4146758.
107 'Election 2020', *Irish Times*, www.irishtimes.com/election2020/results-hub.
108 'Irish Government: Parties Agree to Form a Coalition Government', *BBC News*, 26 June 2020, www.bbc.com/news/world-europe-53181237.
109 For critiques of paramilitary involvement in the peace process, see, for example, McCartney, *Reflections on Liberty, Democracy and the Union*, pp. 151–75.
110 See above, p. 8.

agreements.[111] Israel gradually transferred control over some domestic affairs to the newly created Palestinian Authority. Backsliding, alas, overshadowed this early progress. We have discussed the assassination of Yitzhak Rabin. In July of 2000, President Clinton hosted a summit at Camp David with Yasser Arafat and another Israeli prime minister, Ehud Barak, where all three were scheduled to sign an agreement settling several outstanding issues, but it unravelled at the last minute.[112] Tensions soon escalated. Palestinians unleashed the second intifada (or the al-Aqsa Intifada) in late September 2000,[113] while Israel responded with punishing air and ground attacks. This downward spiral persisted for more than four years, with thousands of casualties.[114] Consultations continued amid the bloodshed, without resolution. In 2002 the Arab League held a summit in Beirut; in 2003 the Quartet outlined the Road Map to Peace; in 2005 the Israeli prime minister, Ariel Sharon, met the new Palestinian prime minister, Mahmoud Abbas, at Sharm el-Sheikh.[115] Later, the Obama administration sponsored direct talks between Israel and Palestine that lasted on and off for several years. None of these initiatives succeeded, as attitudes between Israelis and Palestinians hardened. Radical Islamist groups like Hamas in Gaza and Hezbollah in Lebanon increased the pressure. Israel withdrew completely from the Gaza Strip in 2005, only to launch two major wars against Hamas there: Operation Cast Lead in 2008–9 and Operation Protective Edge in 2014.[116] In January 2020, new American and Israeli leaders, Donald Trump and Benjamin Netanyahu, met at the White House to announce another blueprint for peace. Missing from this summit was Mahmoud Abbas, who boycotted this round of consultations.[117] On the eve of the publication of this volume, no resolution to this intractable conflict appears in sight. The peace process in the vexed lands of Palestine and Israel has reached its limits, at least for now. From the perspective of the Palestinians, there has been little movement

---

111 D. Ross, *The Missing Peace: The Inside Story of the Fight for Middle East Peace* (New York, Farrar, Straus and Giroux, 2004), pp. 122–6, 133–6, 302–13, 415–59.
112 Ibid., pp. 710–11.
113 A. Qurei, *Peace Negotiations in Palestine: From the Second Intifada to the Roadmap* (London, I. B. Tauris, 2015), pp. 11–30.
114 Ross, *The Missing Peace*, pp. 781–2.
115 Qurei, *Peace Negotiations in Palestine*, pp. 76–9, 221–4, 260–3, 315–21.
116 For contrasting views of these issues, see S. Zuhur, 'Gaza, Israel, Hamas and the Lost Calm of Operation Cast Lead', *Middle East Policy* 16/1 (Spring 2009); J. L. Gleis and B. Berti, *Hezbollah and Hamas: A Comparative Study* (Baltimore, Johns Hopkins University Press, 2012).
117 'Trump Releases Long-Awaited Peace Plan', *BBC News*, 28 January 2020, www.bbc.com/news/world-middle-east-51288218.

on the issues most critical to them: the right of return for refugees, the final status of Jerusalem, settlements in the West Bank. Ahmed Qurei, who served as one of the Palestinian negotiators at the Camp David summit in 2000, places blame for its collapse (and subsequent diplomatic failures) on the Israelis: 'The truth was that Israel had more to gain from violence than we did, and less from negotiation. In due course, this became the basis of Israeli policy.'[118] From Israel's point of view, repeated fiascos like Camp David, and endless rounds of futile negotiations, have fortified the Palestinians' refusal to accept Israel as a Jewish state and reinforced its reliance on terrorism. Scholars disagree about the efficacy of dialogue in the region, including the role America should play. Steven L. Spiegel and his colleagues in the Study Group on Arab–Israeli Peacemaking argue that the 'challenge for the United States is to craft a policy and a strategy – not simply a succession of tactics – that speak to the core issues in dispute, are sensitive to the domestic politics and constraints of the parties, and stay within the narrowing confines of American views about the Middle East'.[119] Achieving these outcomes requires a proactive mindset: 'We are firmly of the view that opportunities do not "knock", but rather that political leaders and diplomats must create them, often from the smallest of leads and threads.' The Middle Eastern scholar Seth Frantzman has a different view. He asks, 'Why is the U.S. so addicted to the notion that so many of the world's problems can be solved with "deals" – especially given the track record of previous failed efforts?'[120] He believes this 'approach to international affairs has its limits', especially in unsettled locations like the Middle East. 'The nature of modern open-ended conflicts that take place in ungoverned spaces, or through proxies and non-state actors, makes the ability to get a deal more complex', he avers. 'An entity like Hezbollah doesn't have to adhere to a "deal", and the Palestinian Authority can sign on to a "deal" while Hamas doesn't, allowing a kind of "good cop/bad cop" strategy.' Frantzman may be right; perhaps the Israeli–Palestinian conflict is not amenable to a solution, at least for the moment. Yes, contacts continue on the ground level, as Palestinians go to work in Israel and the two

118 Qurei, *Peace Negotiations in Palestine*, p. 3.
119 D. C. Kurtzer, S. B. Lasensky, W. B. Quandt, S. L. Spiegel and S. Z. Telhami, *The Peace Puzzle: America's Quest for Arab–Israeli Peace, 1989–2011* (Ithaca, NY, Cornell University Press, 2012), p. 269.
120 S. Frantzman, 'From Taliban to "Deal of Century", Why Is America Addicted to "Deals?"', *Jerusalem Post*, 9 September 2019, www.jpost.com/Middle-East/From-Taliban-to-Deal-of-Century-why-is-America-addicted-to-deals-601005.

governments cooperate on economic issues. Yet whatever momentum the peace process accumulated in its early stages has run into the sand. These actors have been wandering in a labyrinth. The resolution of this dispute may require its fundamentals to evolve, which takes time. As Israel, Saudi Arabia and the other Arab Gulf states consider a rapprochement to counter Iran, for example, the former may become more flexible in its demands, while the latter two might be able to exert leverage on the Palestinian Authority (but not Hamas) to halt its terror attacks. The recent announcement of a peace agreement between Israel and the United Arab Emirates, whereby Israel has agreed to suspend the annexation of some settlements in the West Bank, may be an indication that tectonic plates are shifting ever so slightly in the right direction.[121] Meanwhile, the historical evidence here is a reminder of the limitations that sometimes clog the intersection of terrorism and diplomacy, despite the best of intentions.

The Rejection of Negotiations

Several protagonists have demonstrated a second limit to diplomacy in relation to terrorism: they have rejected the feasibility of prolonged deliberations from the start or, in some cases, have abandoned them after briefly testing the waters. The United States government, the American people and their allies have refused to bargain with some international terrorist organisations. Two decades after the attacks of 11 September, there is not a great deal of eagerness within official circles or the public at large to open talks with al Qaeda. There is virtually no enthusiasm for embarking on a peace process with ISIS. These groups are beyond the pale. Speaking in June 2020, Ambassador Nathan Sales, the American Coordinator for Counterterrorism, said, when releasing the State Department's '2019 Country Reports on Terrorism', that the US and its allies 'took major strides last year to defeat and degrade international terrorist organizations. In Iraq and Syria, we destroyed ISIS's so-called caliphate and eliminated its leader. Now we're taking the fight to ISIS and al-Qaida affiliates' throughout the world.[122] Missing from his remarks were any references to opening discussions with them.

---

121 A. Kalman, 'The Abraham Accords Prove That Israel and the UAE Are True Peace Seekers', *The National Interest*, 15 August 2020, https://nationalinterest.org/blog/middle-east-watch/abraham-accords-prove-israel-and-uae-are-true-peace-seekers-167023.
122 Quoted in 'U.S. Report: ISIS and Al Qaeda Threats in 2019', Wilson Center, 30 June 2020, www.wilsoncenter.org/article/us-report-isis-and-al-qaeda-threats-2019.

Likewise, there is no real backing in the United States Congress for rescinding the Authorization for the Use of Military Force (although there have been calls to revise it to take account of new contingencies and to rein in possible action by the Trump administration against Iran).[123] Numerous international experts have strongly argued the case for negotiations with both al Qaeda and ISIS, however.[124] This is not to say that talks will never transpire, but they are very unlikely in the near future. Various governments have recognised the limitations of inclusive dialogue with domestic radicals. The United States rejected compromise with the Weather Underground, the Symbionese Liberation Army, the Black Liberation Army and FALN, opting to prosecute them instead (although this strategy was not always successful).[125] In Europe, Germany showed little interest in discussions with the Red Army Faction.[126] The Italian state did not pursue lengthy mediation with the Red Brigades, only periodic tactical negotiations.[127] Greece declined to compromise with Revolutionary Organisation 17 November.[128] The Irish and British governments have not started a peace process with dissident republican groups like the Real IRA or the Continuity IRA. Israel has not spoken regularly with Hamas or Palestinian Islamic Jihad, unlike the Palestinian Authority, other than low-level discussions regarding prisoner exchanges.[129]

Some of these and other terrorists have reached a similar conclusion: diplomacy has its limits as a vehicle for achieving their objectives. In the

123 J. Gould and L. Shane III, 'House Votes to Curb Trump's Military Action on Iran', *Defense News*, www.defensenews.com/congress/2020/01/30/house-votes-to-curb-trumps-military-action-on-iran/.
124 For a discussion of some early calls to confer with al Qaeda, see Bew et al., *Talking to Terrorists*, pp. 4–5. For more recent arguments, see S. Cantey, 'Beyond the Pale? Exploring Prospects for Negotiations with Al Qaeda and the Islamic State', *Studies in Conflict and Terrorism* 41/10 (June 2017).
125 See, for example, B. Burrough, *Days of Rage: America's Radical Underground, the FBI, and the Forgotten Age of Revolutionary Violence* (New York, Penguin Press, 2015).
126 S. Aust, *Baader–Meinhof: The Inside Story of the R.A.F.*, revised ed., trans. A. Bell (Oxford, Oxford University Press, 2009), pp. 231–301.
127 See A. Orsini, *Anatomy of the Red Brigades: The Religious Mind-Set of Modern Terrorists*, trans. S. J. Nodes (Ithaca, NY, Cornell University Press, 2011); S. Clark, *Terror Vanquished: The Italian Approach to Defeating Terrorism* (Fairfax, Center for Security Policy Studies, George Mason University, 2018).
128 See G. Kassimeris, 'Fighting for Revolution? The Life and Death of Greece's Revolutionary Organization 17 November, 1975–2002', *Journal of Southern Europe and the Balkans* 6/3 (December 2004).
129 'Negotiating with the Enemy: Hamas and Israeli Prisoner Exchange Talks', *Middle East Monitor*, 7 May 2020, www.middleeastmonitor.com/20200507-negotiating-with-the-enemy-hamas-and-israeli-prisoner-exchange-talks/.

Philippines, the Abu Sayyaf Group and allied Moro extremists have rejected consultations with the government, unlike the Moro Islamic Liberation Front. While state security forces have gained traction against them, with American support, they remain resilient opponents, especially the ASG.[130] According to the United States Institute for Peace, 'Enormous security challenges are posed by militant Moro groups that have eschewed the peace process.'[131] These diehard Islamists 'have pledged allegiance to the Islamic State, continue to attract foreign fighters, and are determined' to wreck multiparty talks.[132] The past reminds us how statesmanship has run up against some barriers when dealing with terrorism. Dialogue has not resolved all quarrels, some antagonists have refused to parley with their opponents and others, once inside the maze of mediation, have quickly exited. In the face of these hurdles, some actors have periodically resorted to alternatives to diplomacy. States have prioritised other options – political reform, law and order, security – or several at the same time. Political parties have boycotted talks. Paramilitaries have maintained their reliance on violence. Several of these protagonists have sought victory over their adversaries rather than peace with them, consigning emissaries to the sidelines while more imposing forces take centre stage.

Terrorism, History, Diplomacy

This chapter has aspired to answer the question: what does a comprehensive historical analysis of the intersection of terrorism and diplomacy reveal? Its central thesis contends that historically the interrelationship of terrorism and diplomacy has often been, for protagonists who have attempted it, like crossing into a labyrinth. Its conceptual framework has relied on three supporting arguments. Some actors have accrued benefits; they have exited relatively unscathed, with something to show for their efforts. Others have incurred costs; they have struggled before escaping or have been mauled by the Minotaur. Some have occasionally encountered limitations, expending effort without result or avoiding the challenge altogether. Participants in the same country or conflict have often had different experiences and divergent

---

130 'Mapping Militant Organizations: Abu Sayyaf Group', Center for International Security and Cooperation, Stanford University, p. 4, https://stanford.app.box.com/s/dtmf26g5t0q0nh77w8sndon01c8rlsu5.
131 Abuza and Lischin, 'The Challenges Facing the Philippines' Bangsamoro Region', p. 17.
132 Ibid., p. 18.

perspectives. A peace process may have succeeded for those who accumulated benefits, failed for those who paid a high price, or demoralised those who experienced its constraints. Which brings us to terrorism, history and diplomacy. Terrorism is explosive; history is subtle; diplomacy is inventive. Whereas the militant is zealous, the historian is patient, the envoy is deliberate. One destroys; one reveals; the other resolves. This chapter resonates with the historian's mission to explain the interaction of the former and the latter. Its aim has been to uncover some of the labyrinthine layers of meaning that have concealed, to one degree or another, the complex interplay of these three subjects. In the process, it has sought to reveal some of the enduring ripple effects of the vital intersection of terrorism, history and diplomacy.

Further Reading

J. Bew, M. Frampton and I. Gurrachaga, *Talking to Terrorists: Making Peace in Northern Ireland and the Basque Country* (New York, Colombia University Press, 2009)

E. Hallams, *The United States and NATO since 9/11: The Transatlantic Alliance Renewed* (Abingdon, Routledge, 2010)

D. L. Hanagan, *NATO in the Crucible: Coalition Warfare in Afghanistan* (Stanford, Hoover Institution Press, 2019)

T. Hennessey, *The Northern Ireland Peace Process: Ending the Troubles?* (New York, Palgrave, 2001)

D. Ross, *The Missing Peace: The Inside Story of the Fight for Middle East Peace* (New York, Farrar, Straus and Giroux, 2004)

25

Gender Politics and Terrorist Histories

SYLVIA SCHRAUT

For a long time, studies on terrorism as a historical phenomenon have neglected gender as analytical category.[1] In political science, and especially gender studies or gendered security studies, however, gender has become an issue since 9/11 and the growing participation of Muslim women in terrorist attacks, as an overview of the published research results in these fields shows.[2] A remarkable number of recent publications deal with the question of how to explain that *oppressed* Muslim women became suicide bombers.[3]

---

1 This paper is based on a definition of terrorism which was developed in 1988. According to Alex P. Schmid and Albert Jongman, terrorism is 'an anxiety-inspiring method of repeated violent action, employed by (semi-)clandestine individual, group or state actors, for idiosyncratic, criminal or political reasons, whereby – in contrast to assassination – the direct targets of violence are not the main targets. The immediate human victims of violence ... serve as message generators. Threat- and violence-based communication processes between terrorist (organization), (imperiled) victims, and main targets are used to manipulate the main target (audience(s)), turning it into a target of terror, a target of demands, or a target of attention, depending on whether intimidation, coercion, or propaganda is primarily sought', A. P. Schmid and A. Jongman, *Political Terrorism: A New Guide to Actors, Authors, Concepts, Data Bases, Theories and Literature* (New York, Routledge, 2017), p. 28. In contrast to Schmid and Jongman I will only focus on terrorism by non-state actors. Following the definition of Schmid/Jongman in historical perspective, terrorism as a political strategy is in several respects interwoven with the European bourgeois society and the political systems which have developed since the Age of Enlightenment and the French Revolution: terrorism needs a type of government which is legitimised by majorities, irrespective of the way these majorities are gained. Terrorism needs the existence of a central space in which, for the purpose of winning sympathisers, negotiations about the state's legitimacy, the legitimacy of attacks on the system, and the right of the actors to commit such acts are possible.
2 A. Nachtigall, *Gendering 9/11: Medien, Macht und Geschlecht im Kontext des 'War on Terror'* (Bielefeld, transcript Verlag, 2012), pp. 389–405.
3 For example: F. S. Hasso, 'Discursive and Political Deployments by/of the 2002 Palestinian Women Suicide Bombers/Martyrs', *Feminist Review* 81 (2005); C. Brunner, *Wissensobjekt Selbstmordattentat: epistemische Gewalt und okzidentalistische Selbstvergewisserung in der Terrorismusforschung* (Wiesbaden, VS Verlag, 2011); V. G. J. Rajan, *Women Suicide Bombers: Narratives of Violence* (Hoboken, Taylor & Francis, 2011); A.-M. McManus, 'Sentimental Terror Narratives: Gendering Violence, Dividing Sympathy', *Journal of Middle East Women's Studies* 9/2 (2013).

Others analyse the female careers into terrorism and the changing structures of terrorist organisations when women come on board.[4] They deal with gender and agency or the discursive representation of gender and terrorism.[5] Counterterrorism and security studies have added gender to their analytical categories. Research projects on peacebuilding and peacekeeping in international political affairs or on human security discuss questions of gender.[6] Last but not least, the gender-concept of the male Islamist terrorist has come into view.[7]

All authors, more or less, stress the strong gender-bias which characterises the representation of the terrorist, be it in self-representations, in the media or in analyses of the social background of terrorism. Often they assume that men and women have a different historical or anthropological relation to political violence, or, at least, that terrorists are gender-specifically treated by their organisations. Especially the first political or sociological studies in the aftermath of 9/11 stress the point that terrorism seems to be a male phenomenon, and they emphasise that male and female violence cannot be the same.[8] Therefore, there are more problems associated with legitimising political violence committed by women than political violence committed by men.[9] Some recent studies describe female political violence as growing female agency. Candice Ortbals and Lori Poloni-Staudinger (both political scientists) state in their 2018 book: 'This distinction of men as aggressors and

---

4 C. O. N. Moser and F. C. Clark (eds.), *Victims, Perpetrators or Actors? Gender, Armed Conflict and Political Violence*, 2nd ed. (London, Zed Books, 2005); C. D. Ness (ed.), *Female Terrorism and Militancy: Agency, Utility and Organization* (London, Routledge, 2008); M. H. Alison, *Women and Political Violence* (London, Routledge, 2009); L. Sjoberg and C. E. Gentry (eds.), *Women, Gender, and Terrorism* (Athens, University of Georgia Press, 2011); M. Bloom, *Bombshell: The Many Faces of Women Terrorists* (London, Hurst & Company, 2011).

5 L. Åhäll and L. J. Shepherd (eds.), *Gender, Agency and Political Violence* (Basingstoke, Palgrave Macmillan, 2012); L. Poloni-Staudinger and C. D. Ortbals, *Terrorism and Violent Conflict: Women's Agency, Leadership, and Responses* (New York, Springer, 2013); C. D. Ortbals and L. Poloni-Staudinger, *Gender and Political Violence: Women Changing the Politics of Terrorism* (Cham, Springer, 2018).

6 N. Detraz, *International Security and Gender* (Cambridge, Polity Press, 2012); M. L. Satterthwaite and J. C. Huckerby (eds.), *Gender, National Security and Counter-terrorism: Human Rights Perspectives* (London, Routledge, 2013); C. E. Gentry, L. J. Shepherd and L. Sjoberg (eds.), *The Routledge Handbook of Gender and Security* (London, Routledge, Taylor & Francis Group, 2018).

7 M. Aslam, *Gender-Based Explosions: The Nexus Between Muslim Masculinities, Jihadist Islamism and Terrorism* (New York, United Nations University Press, 2012); M. Aslam, 'Islamism and Masculinity: Case Study Pakistan', *Historical Social Research* 39/3 (2014).

8 For example, C. D. Ness, 'In the Name of the Cause: Women's Work in Secular and Religious Terrorism', *Studies in Conflict and Terrorism* 28/5 (2005).

9 C. E. Gentry and L. Sjoberg, *Beyond Mothers, Monsters, Whores: Thinking about Women's Violence in Global Politics* (London, Zed Books, 2015).

women as passive victims denies women their voice and agency.'[10] Their book is an investigation of 'how women cope with and influence violent politics, and is both a descriptive and analytical attempt to describe in what ways women are present or absent in political contexts involving political violence, and how they deal with gender assumptions, express gender identities, and frame their actions regarding political violence encountered in their lives'.[11]

The studies mentioned here mostly interpret terrorism as a phenomenon which emerged first in the twentieth century and, if they work historically, they compare case studies dealing with post-Second World War phenomena with recent examples of political non-state violence. The important varieties of nineteenth-century terrorism are frequently neglected. Moreover, these authors use terms with a centuries-old gendered tradition, for example 'hero' or 'martyr', without reflecting the historically rooted gendered implications of these terms and without taking account of the gendered traditions of the representation of male or female political violence which go back more than two hundred years. This paper wants to address this lack of historical contextualisation.

In a gendered historical perspective we ask: what role has gender played in the development of modern terrorism during the nineteenth century? What are the gendered stereotypes concerning political violence which have been constructed and transmitted since the early nineteenth century? And in what way do these stereotypes influence recent interpretations of terrorism and historical research on terrorism? To use gender as a historical category firstly requires defining its explanatory force for the analysis of terrorism. It is the merit of women's history, which developed in Europe and the USA in the 1970s, to add *her*story to history and to make women and their agency visible. Since the 1980s gender history has interpreted gender as social construction. The meaning of masculinity and femininity differs through time and historical context. In an often quoted paper, Joan W. Scott understands gender as a 'constitutive element of social relationships based on perceived differences between the sexes, and ... a primary way of signifying relationships of power'.[12] Both elements – gendered social relationships and gendered relationships of power – are relevant for the analysis of the history of terrorism.

---

10 Ortbals and Poloni-Staudinger, *Gender and Political Violence*, cover/introduction of the book.
11 Ibid.
12 J. W. Scott, 'Gender: A Useful Category of Historical Analysis', *American Historical Review* 91/5 (1986), p. 1067.

Does the view on terrorism change, if gender is used as a category? Not at first glance. In general, definitions of terrorism seem to be sex- and gender-neutral. But gender studies taught us that even apparently neutral terms have a gender bias. Some examples may verify the gender bias of so-called *gender-neutral* terrorism studies: a survey on the connection of terrorism and media which does not use the category gender will neglect the fact that in specific historical situations men and women had different access to the media. For a long time women had no chance to write articles under their own name. Even today most of the chief editors of political magazines are male, and in television it is mostly male experts who discuss aspects of terrorism and security. Furthermore, the answer to the question whether there were legal ways to enter politics in specific historical situations will fundamentally differ for men and women in the nineteenth century. Therefore, it makes no sense to define female terrorists during the nineteenth century as a group with particularly weak influence on politics – as definitions of terrorism commonly do – when women in general did not have voting rights. In historical analyses it is misleading to define regulatory agencies or courts in a gender-neutral perspective, because until the second half of the twentieth century violent women were confronted with male policemen and male judges who in general had exact ideas about what constitutes a male or a female character and about male or female scopes of action. Therefore, as a rule, historical analyses of terrorism should take into account that, in the nineteenth century, women's agency was more restricted than today. But historically minded gender studies do not only show the gender bias of seemingly neutral definitions of terrorism. If the category gender actually helps to analyse the perceived differences between sexes and their relationships of power we can assume that the historical discussions in the media and the courts about the gender of the terrorist reflect the general social relations of men and women in a specific historical society.

If we examine historical publications on political violence in general, gender plays a minor role.[13] When historical publications deal with political violence against the state in the nineteenth and twentieth centuries we often find the same gender-blindness which characterises studies on recent

---

13 Overviews of historical terrorism and gender, especially in Europe, are given in C. Hikel and S. Schraut (eds.), *Terrorismus und Geschlecht: politische Gewalt in Europa seit dem 19. Jahrhundert* (Frankfurt, Campus, 2012); S. Schraut and K. Weinhauer, 'Terrorism, Gender, and History: Introduction', *Historical Social Research* 39/3 (2014); S. Schraut, *Terrorismus und politische Gewalt* (Göttingen, Vandenhoeck & Ruprecht, 2018), pp. 193–208.

terrorism. I would like to mention only one example: Joachim Wagner, who pioneered the research on the biographies of German anarchists of the late nineteenth century, had only men in his sample and saw no necessity to explain why he ignored supporting women.[14] Since the nineteenth century, when the media or scholars have set out to study the participation of women in political violence in history, they have mostly claimed that men and women have a different relation to political violence just as political and sociological researchers do today. Consequently, the motivation of women to commit acts of political violence is explained by the existence of particular or extraordinary circumstances in the specific historical situation which is examined.[15] It can be assumed that the traditionally linked terms male = active = fighting versus female = passive = peaceful persist although there is no historical evidence substantiating these associative chains. What is important, however, is not only the fact that political opponents, academic researchers and even brothers in arms seem to consider it necessary to find particular explanations for female participation in violent political acts in the nineteenth or twentieth century. This participation also provokes specific interpretations which are closely linked with the debate on the legitimacy or reprehensibility of politically motivated violence in history. Before discussing this phenomenon more closely it is necessary to define a starting point for studying terrorism under a gender perspective and to analyse our knowledge about male and female participation in terrorism.

Historically, female participation in terrorism starts with the French Revolution. During this period we can see the shaping of modern gender models and the development of gendered representations of male and female terrorists. When in France the Third Estate declared 'we are the nation' it appeared that this newly defined political sphere would be open for women too. But in 1793 women's political clubs were prohibited. The French male revolutionaries justified this decision with what they considered to be the bizarre and unnatural behaviour of women in politics and women's low knowledge, attention span, devotion and capacity. From then on, *he* has

---

14 J. Wagner, *Politischer Terrorismus und Strafrecht im Deutschen Kaiserreich von 1871* (Heidelberg, Decker, 1981).
15 An overview can be found in C. Harders, 'Geschlechterverhältnisse in Krieg und Frieden: eine Einführung', in C. Harders and B. Roß (eds.), *Geschlechterverhältnisse in Krieg und Frieden: Perspektiven der feministischen Analyse internationaler Beziehungen* (Opladen, Leske und Budrich, 2002) or in K. Hagemann, 'Krieg, Frieden und Gewalt: Friedens- und Konfliktforschung als Geschlechterforschung – Eine Einführung', in J. A. Davy et al. (eds.), *Frieden – Gewalt – Geschlecht: Friedens- und Konfliktforschung als Geschlechterforschung* (Essen, Klartext Verlag, 2005).

represented rationality, activity and authority in the political sphere, whereas *she* has represented emotionality, passivity and privacy. *He* is linked with armed violence, *she* is linked with peacefulness. The decision to ban female political clubs and its gender-based justification had its effects throughout the whole nineteenth and even throughout the twentieth century. Not only the bourgeois gender-model is rooted in the French Revolution, but also the female terrorist. We can start with the early forms of terrorism, namely with Charlotte Corday, who assassinated Jean-Paul Marat at the outset of the *terreur* in 1793 in Paris.[16] She herself interpreted her deed as a symbolic assassination to raise the awareness of the public, as an appeal to make peace between the revolutionary parties. This legitimisation already contains fundamental elements of modern definitions of terrorism. Marat's assassination by a woman became famous and was vigorously discussed by the European audience in the following decades. Soon afterwards imitators tried to copy Charlotte Corday. One of them was the German student Karl Ludwig Sand, one of the most prominent European assassins of the early nineteenth century. His use of a violent political strategy was comparable with those of modern terrorists; he wanted to provoke the media and an audience by political violence. When he killed the well-known author August von Kotzebue in 1819 he saw himself in the tradition of Charlotte Corday. In the following decades of the nineteenth century a large number of terrorists saw themselves as followers of Charlotte Corday and Karl Ludwig Sand, and their contemporaries interpreted these perpetrators as founding mother and father of modern terrorism.[17] Even Alexander Pushkin built a memorial for Corday and Sand in his poem 'Kinzhal' of 1821, where he wrote about the 'virgin goddess of vengeance' (Eumenide) Corday and the 'noble young man Sand'; both are depicted as 'avengers', 'threatening to the tyrant's power'.[18]

What do we know about the participation of women and men in terrorism during the nineteenth and twentieth centuries? There is a still a lack of knowledge. But it seems that, from a historical point of view, the participation of women has not intensified recently. As shown before, women using political violence can already be found in the French Revolution. Moreover,

---

16 S. Schraut, 'Charlotte Corday und Karl Ludwig Sand: populäre Repräsentation von Geschlecht und politischer Gewalt im 19. Jahrhundert', in E. Cheauré et al. (eds.), *Geschlecht und Geschichte in populären Medien* (Bielefeld, transcript Verlag, 2013).

17 For example: L. Patyk, *Written in Blood: Revolutionary Terrorism and Russian Literary Culture, 1861–1881* (Madison, University of Wisconsin Press, 2017).

18 See the translation of the poem in German in A. S. Pushkin, *Gedichte, Poeme, Eugen Onegin* (Berlin, SWA-Verlag, 1947). In English: *The Complete Works of Alexander Pushkin*, Vol. 2: *Lyric Poems, 1820–1826* (Norfolk, Milner and Company, 1999).

the anarchist movement in the second half of the nineteenth century was supported by men and women.[19] Especially the Russian nihilists were discussed by their contemporaries as a movement with strong women at the front line. It is assumed that about 25 per cent of the Russian anarchists were female. The statement of Sergei Nechayev in his 'Catechism of a Revolutionary' (1869) is well known. He described three types of women important for the revolution. As the first type he mentioned prominent women who could support the revolutionary movement by their social reputation and with their property. As the second type he defined enthusiastic, devoted and talented women, who should be recruited. The third type: the women belonging to the anarchist movement were characterised by Nechayev as 'most valuable, or our treasures'.[20] Three years before, the Russian anarchist Bakunin had developed the utopia of a future anarchist society in which women and men had the same political rights. Both should work, and caring for the children was defined as a task of the society.[21] The anarchist programmes were mostly much more feminist than the concepts of the contemporary (non-violent) socialists.[22] These circumstances may perhaps explain the remarkable number of female Russian terrorists in the anarchist era of the late nineteenth century. Female anarchists participated in international meetings and gave speeches. As the Prussian police reported from the International Anarchist Conference in London in 1881, which decided to support violent activities, there had been three famous speakers: the Italian Errico Malatesta, Louise Michel from France and the American female delegate Lecompte.[23] The American Lecompte was probably Marie Le Compte, who was born in France and had immigrated to the USA. She translated texts of Bakunin, but we know nothing about her further life. By

19 An overview without aspects of gender is provided by O. Hubac-Occhipinti, 'Anarchist Terrorists of the Nineteenth Century' and Y. Ternon, 'Russian Terrorism, 1878–1908', in G. Chaliand and A. Blin (eds.), *The History of Terrorism* (Berkeley and Los Angeles, University of California Press, 2007).
20 S. Naechev, 'Katechismus eines Revolutionärs', published in W. Laqueur (ed.), *Zeugnisse politischer Gewalt: Dokumente zur Geschichte des Terrorismus* (Kronberg/Ts., Athenäum, 1978), p. 59. An English translation is available at www.marxists.org/subject/anarchism/nechayev/catechism.htm.
21 M. Bakunin, 'Revolutionary Catechism', in *Bakunin on Anarchy: Selected Works by the Activist-Founder of World Anarchism*, ed. by S. Dolgoff (London, George Allen & Unwin, 1973), pp. 76–97.
22 On the ambivalences of feminism and patriarchy in the anarchist programmes, compare S. Gemie, 'Anarchism and Feminism: A Historical Survey', *Women's History Review* 5/3 (1996).
23 *Dokumente aus geheimen Archiven: Übersichten der Berliner politischen Polizei über die allgemeine Lage der sozialdemokratischen und anarchistischen Bewegung 1878–1913*, Vol. 1: *1878–1889*, ed. by D. Fricke and R. Knaack (Berlin, BWV, 1983), pp. 121ff.

contrast, German anarchism of the late nineteenth century is known as a male movement. But there are descriptions by some anarchist contemporaries about their (sometimes) bad experiences with the wives of their supporters.[24] Have research studies neglected these women because they were *only* wives?[25] Ulrich Linse, who, until now, has published the only detailed analysis of anarchism in the German Empire, gender-neutrally describes workers and craftspeople as the heart of the movement, not intellectuals.[26] Might the common negative attitude towards female industrial work in late nineteenth-century Germany, with its affinity to the bourgeois gender model, perhaps explain the absence of German female anarchist terrorists? The historical comparison of Russian and German anarchism demonstrates the surplus which gender analysis will bring in historical research on the social and cultural conditions of terrorism.

But women were not only ordinary members of the anarchist movement in the late nineteenth century. As Charles Townshend wrote, there was a 'remarkable prominence of women in terrorist operations. From Vera Zasulich, who carried out the first Narodnik armed attack when she shot the governor of St. Petersburg in 1878, to Waffa al-Endress, the first female Arab "suicide bomber" in Israel in January 2002, women have been front-line actors and, consequently, pioneer recasters of gender roles.'[27] We know of female terrorists in the national movements, as, for example, the Ukrainian one after 1929.[28] We also know that the nationally orientated terrorist groups in Spain (ETA) or in Ireland (IRA) had female members.[29] It was only in 1968 that the IRA decided to accept female members. But much earlier, in 1914, Cumann na mBan was founded, an Irish republican women's organisation which actively and violently operated between the 1960s and 1986.[30] S. V. Raghavan and V. Balasubramaniyan (wrongly) believe that female

24 J. Most, *August Reinsdorf und die Propaganda der That* (New York, J. Mueller, 1890), pp. 48–50.
25 F. Lemmes, 'Der anarchistische Terrorismus des 19. Jahrhunderts und sein soziales Umfeld', in S. Malthaner and P. Waldmann (eds.), *Radikale Milieus: das soziale Umfeld terroristischer Gruppen* (Frankfurt, Campus, 2012), p. 91.
26 U. Linse, *Organisierter Anarchismus im deutschen Kaiserreich von 1871* (Berlin, Duncker & Humblot, 1969).
27 C. Townshend, *Terrorism: A Very Short Introduction* (Oxford, Oxford University Press, 2002), p. 16.
28 O. Petrenko, 'Makellose HeldInnen des Terrors: die Organisation der Ukrainischen Nationalisten im Spannungsfeld zwischen Heroisierung und Diffamierung', in Hikel and Schraut (eds.), *Terrorismus und Geschlecht*.
29 T. Riegler, *Terrorismus: Akteure, Strukturen, Entwicklungslinien* (Innsbruck, Studienverlag, 2009), p. 188.
30 D. Reinisch, 'Cumann na mBan and Women in Irish Republican Paramilitary Organisations, 1969–1986', *Estudios Irlandeses* 11 (2016).

terrorism started in the late 1950s, and they compiled information about leading female terrorists in thirteen terrorist groups over the whole world from this date on. For the 1960s they mention the Palestinian groups Harakat al-Tahrir al-Watani al-Filastini (Fatah) and the Popular Front for the Liberation of Palestine (PFLP), the Euskadi Ta Askatasuna (ETA) in Spain, the Fuerzas Armadas Revolucionarias de Colombia (FARC) in Colombia and the Maoists in India.[31] The New Left terrorism which developed in Germany, France, Italy, the USA or even Japan in the 1970s was an array of movements in which men and women participated as equal partners.[32] Charles Russell and Bowman Miller counted about 10 per cent women in a sample of 350 well-known terrorists from eighteen terrorist organisations which were active in urban areas in the 1970s.[33] It is supposed that a third of the members of the German RAF and half of the members of the US Weathermen were female.[34] Some terrorist groups, for example in Japan, had female leaders.[35] According to Charles Townshend, 33 per cent of the Comunisti Organizzati per la Liberazione Proletaria (COLP) and 31 per cent of the Brigate Rosse (Red Brigades), both Italian groups, were women.[36] Eighteen per cent of the people who were arrested as terrorists in Italy between 1970 and 1984 were female.[37] Some terrorist groups, such as the German Rote Zora, had only female members and a feminist programme. From the 1970s onwards female terrorists have also become more important in the left-wing liberation groups in South America.[38] In general, we can assume that terrorist groups of the

31 S. V. Raghavan and V. Balasubramaniyan, 'Evolving Role of Women in Terror Groups: Progression or Regression?', *Journal of International Women's Studies* 15/2 (2014), pp. 198ff.
32 C. E. Gentry, 'The Relationship Between New Social Movement Theory and Terrorism Studies: The Role of Leadership, Membership, Ideology, and Gender', *Terrorism and Political Violence* 16/2 (2004); L. Churchill, 'Exploring Feminism's Complex Relationship with Political Violence: An Analysis of the Weathermen, Radical Feminism and the New Left', *A Feminist History Journal* 16 (2007).
33 C. A. Russell and B. H. Miller, 'Profile of a Terrorist', *Terrorism* 1/1 (1977).
34 I. Bandhauer-Schöffmann and D. von Laak (eds.), *Der Linksterrorismus der 1970er-Jahre und die Ordnung der Geschlechter* (Trier, WVT, 2013); J. Varon, *Bringing the War Home: The Weather Underground, The Red Army Faction, and Revolutionary Violence in the Sixties and Seventies* (Berkeley and Los Angeles, University of California Press, 2004), p. 172.
35 P. Steinhoff, 'Hijackers, Bombers, and Bank Robbers: Managerial Style in the Japanese Red Army', *The Journal of Asian Studies* 48/4 (1989); S. Shigematsu, 'The Japanese Women's Liberation Movement and the United Red Army', *Feminist Media Studies* 12/2 (2012).
36 Townshend, *Terrorism*, p. 18.
37 W. L. Eubank and L. Weinberg, 'Italian Women Terrorists', *Terrorism* 9/3 (1987).
38 See for example L. Churchill, *Becoming the Tupamaros: Solidarity and Transnational Revolutionaries in Uruguay and the United States* (Nashville, Vanderbilt University Press, 2014), pp. 119–54.

political left welcomed female sisters in arms relatively early, a fact which correlates with their gender model, which was and is based on gender equality. In contrast – due to their traditional gender model – terrorist groups with a nationalist background, of the political right wing or Islamist groups at first welcomed women only as assisting, non-violent supporters. It is only mostly since the 1980s that they seem to have accepted women who decide on their own to take part in violent attacks as equal partners. Leonard Weinberg and William Eubank pointed out that 'women have played strong leadership roles in left-wing, revolutionary bands, while these roles have been far fewer with right-wing and racist aggregations. Women have tended to be late-comers to contemporary, religiously-inspired terrorism: Muslim religious authorities first had to endorse their participation.'[39] But in general we can observe: terrorist women were and are 'ideologues; they plan violent activities; they lead; and they commit suicide attacks. Thus women's involvement is more than just nurturing the men – their participation is active.'[40]

How can we explain the fact that the participation of women in terrorism is often neglected by researchers or is often over-scandalised by state authorities or contemporary media? Despite the above-mentioned known or estimated gender quotas in terrorist groups, their contemporaries and historical researchers mostly seem to be convinced of the peaceful nature of *normal* women, and they interpret the female use of violence as unnatural. In this perspective they agree with most of the recent researchers on present terrorism. Therefore, female terrorism calls for explanation, even in history. Clare Bielby, among others, has emphasised that the connection of manliness with armaments, politics and the propensity for violence and the reverse characterisation of women have a long history which goes back (as mentioned before) to the nineteenth century.[41] And we may ask whether the distance from violence which is assumed for the female gender has delivered an argument for the exclusion of women from politics even to this day.[42] Nineteenth-century observers who were convinced that women act more emotionally than men described female terrorists – who transgress their

---

39 L. Weinberg and W. L. Eubank, 'Women's Involvement in Terrorism', *Gender Issues* 28 (2011), p. 22.
40 C. E. Gentry, 'Women and Terrorism', in E. Chenoweth, R. English, A. Gofas and S. N. Kalyvas (eds.), *The Oxford Handbook of Terrorism* (Oxford, Oxford University Press, 2019), p. 418.
41 C. Bielby, *Violent Women in Print: Representations in the West German Print Media of the 1960s and 1970s* (Rochester, Camden House, 2012).
42 S. Schraut, 'Terrorismus, Heldentum, Martyrertum: die historische Entwicklung von Terrorismusbildern, Deutungsversuchen und Geschlechterstereotypen', in Bandhauer-Schöffmann and Van Laak (eds.), *Der Linksterrorismus der 1970er-Jahre*, p. 23.

traditional gender boundaries – as persons who are particularly cruel and irrational when using violence. Already Friedrich Schiller described the female republicans of the French Revolution in his poem *The Song of the Bell* as inhuman hyenas and panthers. And in the middle of the nineteenth century Jules Michelet, the author of a book about the women of the French Revolution, explained: 'During the whole course of the Revolution, I see them violent and intrigant, and often more guilty than men.' He concluded:

> It is not our fault if nature has made them, not only weak, as it is said, but infirm daughters of a starry world, as by their unequal temperaments, they are unable to perform all the stern duties of a political world ... [T]his has plainly been shown in our Revolutions. It was principally women who have caused them to fail. Their intrigues have undermined, and their deaths (often merited, but always impolitic) have powerfully served the contre-revolution.[43]

Statements on politically violent women until the 1970s often combine the postulated emotional female character with the fortitude and perseverance produced by that emotionality. At the end of a long series of similar statements, Christian Lochte, head of the Office for the Protection of the Constitution of Hamburg, Germany, who was in the 1970s confronted with the RAF, explained that female terrorists were more dangerous than male ones because they were emotionally more bound to their aims than men. He is quoted as having made the proposition: 'Who loves his life, should shoot at the female terrorists at first.'[44] The finding that violent women have since the early nineteenth century often been seen as *abnormal* or *unnatural* women leads to an aspect of the gender analysis of terrorism which similarly involves male and female terrorists: the gender-transgressing qualities of terrorism.[45]

The analysis of historical statements and of historically minded biographical studies shows: both women and men seem to transgress their gender roles, if they carry out acts of violence against their own governments or

---

43 J. Michelet, *The Women of the French Revolution* (Philadelphia, Henry Carey Baird, 1855), pp. 23ff.
44 E. MacDonald, *Shoot the Women First* (London, Fourth Estate, 1991), pp. xiv and 222; G. Diewald-Kerkmann, 'Frauen in der RAF: Erklärungsmuster von Strafverfolgungsbehörden und Gerichten für den Weg in die Illegalität', in V. F. Drecktrah (ed.), *Die RAF und die Justiz: Nachwirkungen des 'Deutschen Herbstes'* (Munich, Meidenbauer, 2010).
45 See S. Schraut, 'Wie der Hass gegen den Staatsrath von Kotzebue, und der Gedanke, ihn zu ermorden, in Sand entstand: ein politischer Mord und seine Nachwirkungen', in Hikel and Schraut (eds.), *Terrorismus und Geschlecht*; Schraut, 'Charlotte Corday und Karl Ludwig Sand'; S. Malvern and G. Koureas (eds.), *Terrorist Transgression: Gender and the Visual Culture of the Terrorist* (London, I. B. Tauris, 2014).

against foreign ones, against political systems or, very simply, against randomly selected people. How can we describe the representation of the gender-transgressing nature of male terrorists, which has developed since the French Revolution? We may start with the image of the German Karl Ludwig Sand, who in 1819 murdered the conservative politician and playwright August von Kotzebue. Even the representations of the murder in the (mostly liberal) media which defend Sand describe him as a man who transgressed masculine gender roles.[46] They draw the image of a sensitive (feminine) man who was emotionally unable to bear the restorative conditions after the Congress of Vienna (1814/15) in which freedom of speech was oppressed. Even the conservative critics portrayed Sand as a feminine man, a man whose (feminine) emotions were too strong and who had been primarily educated by his mother, a man who was not able to rationally participate in politics. To quote one example of 1831: according to the German lawyer and conservative author Carl Jarcke, Sand was a young man, underdeveloped in mind and body. His writings show (female) 'depression', 'melancholy' and 'disappointment' as well as 'a true impression of the chaos in which Sand's mind was destroyed in those times'.[47]

This depiction of Sand – by supporters and opponents – as an effeminate man influenced the image of the male terrorist throughout the nineteenth and twentieth centuries, up to the present.[48] To give one example: the French anarchist bomber of the 1890s Ravachol was described by the American journalist Alvan F. Sanborn in 1905 as 'an unusually kind-hearted man ... In his young manhood he supported his mother and younger brother, and treated them with the greatest consideration. He was fond of children, and remonstrated fiercely against cruelty to animals.'[49] In the same manner Emma Goldman, the famous anarchist and contemporary witness of the Russian revolution, tried to explain the use of political violence (by men) with attributes which were commonly ascribed to women. She wrote in 1917:

> The ignorant mass looks upon the man who makes a violent protest against our social and economic iniquities as upon a wild beast ... Yet nothing is

---

46 Schraut, 'Wie der Hass gegen den Staatsrath von Kotzebue'.
47 C. Jarcke, *Carl Ludwig Sand und sein an dem kaiserlich-russischen Staatsrath v. Kotzebue veruebter Mord, e. psychol.-criminalist. Eroerterung aus d. Geschichte unserer Zeit* (Berlin, Dümmler, 1831), p. 75.
48 Rainer Emig argues along these lines in his paper about terrorist masculinities. See R. Emig, 'Terrorist Masculinities: Political Masculinity Between Fiction, Facts and Their Mediation', *Men and Masculinities* 22/3 (2019).
49 A. F. Sanborn, *Paris and the Social Revolution: A Study of the Revolutionary Elements in the Various Classes of Parisian Society* (London, Hutchinson, 1905), p. 157.

further from the truth. As a matter of fact, those who have studied the character and personality of these men, or who have come in close contact with them, are agreed that it is their supersensitiveness to the wrong and injustice surrounding them which compels them to pay the toll of our social crimes.[50]

She mentions the 'tenderness and kindness' of violent anarchists,[51] and quotes the characterisation of anarchists by Sanborn, who detected in them 'a rare love of animals, surpassing sweetness in all the ordinary relations of life, exceptional sobriety of demeanor, frugality and regularity, austerity, even, of living, and courage beyond compare'.[52]

But, if we are to achieve an understanding of such assumptions about the feminine character of male terrorists, they have to be embedded into a larger frame, namely the two competing interpretations of political (violent) masculinity which emerged in the nineteenth century; they were deeply connected with the writers' attitudes towards democracy and political violence against the state. On one side we have the man who acts rationally in interior political affairs. He is on the way to democracy, or is already a democrat, who denies the necessity of political violence and distances himself from the weak (feminine) man who uses violence against the state and its representatives. On the other side we find the strong man who uses violence to defend his country against exterior enemies in wartime. This image, developed since the French Revolution, was and perhaps is commonly accepted to this day as an attribute of the manliness of the citizen in the Western world.[53] As a democrat he has to defend the nation. From the perspective of right-wing ideologies, he has to defend not the democratic nation but his fatherland – and this of course even against interior (mostly left-wing) enemies and against 'wrongful' state authorities. Finally, the positive or negative stance towards the state's monopoly on force decides about the gendered representation of the male terrorist. But even writers of the political right wing in the first half of the twentieth century who sympathised with the male terrorist who acted against the state's authorities could not describe him as a *normal* man. In general, their hero was not given female attributes; he was, however, a man without a sex life and a hero without a family. 'You know that I do not trail women's skirts', Sand explains, for example, in a novel by the German

---

50 E. Goldman, *The Psychology of Political Violence* (New York, Gordon Press, 1974), p. 2.
51 Ibid., p. 3.   52 Ibid., p. 4.
53 See for example R. A. Nye, 'Western Masculinities in War and Peace', *American Historical Review* 112/2 (2007); L. Braudy, *From Chivalry to Terrorism: War and the Changing Nature of Masculinity* (New York, Vintage Books, 2005).

nationalist Hans Schönfeld, a dismissed captain and writer during the 1920s and 30s.[54] A good example for the fluctuating representation of manliness in connection with political violence and disagreement with or acceptance of the political system even today is provided by Graham Dawson's research about masculinities and the terrorist in the process of conflict transformation in post-conflict Northern Ireland. Throughout the Troubles the critical discourse represented republican and loyalist combatants as irrational (meaning feminine) and evil men, while their supporters talked of strong manliness and sketched the image of the terrorist as a soldier-hero. Today, people have problems integrating the terrorist hero into the memory of the now largely non-violent Northern Irish society.[55]

Fluctuating representations of the male hero defending his nation and the feminine-connoted terrorist and enemy can also be observed after 9/11. In the debates following the attack on and the destruction of the Twin Towers the well-fortified Western man had to defend Western values (and Western women) with violence against Islamist attacks. As the American President George W. Bush pointed out in his speeches after 9/11, the Western world needs (male-connoted) courage in fighting against the terrorist enemy. 'We're facing coldblooded killers who have an ideology that is the opposite of ours. These people believe that there should be no dissent, no freedom, no rights for women ... They want to shake our will and to weaken our determination.'[56] And in 2003 Condoleezza Rice, the later Secretary of State, stressed the huge importance of the (masculine) combat-readiness of the soldier for American society:

> Every one of America's soldiers, like every one of you, took an oath to defend this nation. There is no higher calling, and America and the world are a better place thanks to your labors. All of you are also part of a rich military tradition that reaches back more than two centuries and which is being carried forward today by our men and women in uniform.

---

54 H. Schönfeld, *Karl Ludwig Sand* (Berlin, Martin Wasservogel Verlag, 1927), p. 12.
55 G. Dawson, 'Masculinities and the "Terrorist" in Conflict Transformation: Representation, Identity and Reconciliation in Post-conflict Northern Ireland', in S. Malvern and G. Koureas (eds.), *Terrorist Transgression: Gender and the Visual Culture of the Terrorist* (London, I. B. Tauris, 2014), pp. 157–80.
56 G. W. Bush, 'Remarks on the Patriot Act in Baltimore, Maryland, July 20, 2005', in *Public Papers of the Presidents of the United States: George W. Bush*, 2005, Book 2 (Washington, DC, United States Government Printing Office, 2009), pp. 1250ff.

Referring to Western values shared over generations, she added: 'There is a common bond of duty and honor among those who have served, and a respect for those who have marched down the same path.'[57] What can be seen here is a phenomenon already analysed by historical gender studies for the epoch of the Napoleonic Wars in the early nineteenth century: violent times influence the concepts of manliness and bring together manliness and combat readiness.[58]

By contrast, soon after 9/11 and before the rise of IS the Islamist terrorist was often described as an enemy of women and/or as a sexually oppressed man. The media intensively discussed the fact that Mohammed Atta, one of the assassins of 9/11, had forbidden pregnant women to participate in his funeral and that he had ordered in his testament: 'The person who will wash my body near my genitals must wear gloves on his hands so he won't touch my genitals.'[59] Some media described Muslim terrorists as weak men humiliated by Western mothers or wives. This was, for example, the attitude of an article in *Der Spiegel* about Nizar Trabelsi, a Tunisian terrorist who was arrested in Brussels before he could blow up the French Embassy in 2011. Nizar Trabelsi had started a career as a football player in Germany, but this failed. According to *Der Spiegel*, he was an inconspicuous man, who grew up without a father and who was too weak to succeed in German football. This was because 'Nizar was soft. The boxers would say, he has a chin of glass.' His marriage to a German wife failed, and even as a father he was no good, 'because he had enough to do with himself, like a big kid. He jumped back and forth between the options of life, joyfully, later with drugs, increasingly aggressively, irascibly, compulsively.'[60] It was only when IS became a massive danger that the media presentation of Islamist terrorists with female characteristics vanished. It was impossible to describe a dangerous militant enemy as a female-connoted inferior adversary.

In order to demonstrate the gender-transgressing quality of the political violence of female terrorists we may go back once more to Charlotte Corday. Only some weeks after the assassination in 1793, at the memorial service for

---

57 'National Security Advisor Condoleezza Rice Remarks to Veterans of Foreign Wars at the 104th National Convention of the Veterans of Foreign Wars', 25 August 2003, https://georgewbush-whitehouse.archives.gov/news/releases/2003/08/20030825-1.html.
58 K. Hagemann, 'The Military and Masculinity: Gendering the History of the Revolutionary and Napoleonic Wars, 1792–1815', in R. Chickering and S. Förster (eds.), *War in an Age of Revolution, 1775–1815* (Cambridge, Cambridge University Press, 2010).
59 The testament has been published by the Public Broadcasting Service (PBS), www.pbs.org/wgbh/pages/frontline/shows/network/personal/attawill.html.
60 'Allahs Reservist', *Der Spiegel*, 22 October 2001.

Marat, the Marquis de Sade called Corday a hermaphrodite, or at least 'an androgynous creature without sex, which descended from hell to the despair of men and women'.[61] This interpretation established a long-lasting and influential narrative about the transgressive gender-code of female assassins. In 1891, for example, the Italian criminologist Lombroso lectured on the Russian female anarchists following Charlotte Corday:

> Petersburg counts 168,000 unmarried or separated women and 98,000 married women ... The consequences are evident ... The women cannot live their natural lives, and they turn to politics ... Here we can find these female students or, as they call themselves, 'tomboys' (Weib-Männer), who are fond of severe conspiracies, hunt after rich inheritors, in order to fill the treasury of their group, who kidnap prisoners, bribe prison guards, find everywhere entrance as maids and nurses and make propaganda, at which they are extraordinary.[62]

In 1905, Karl von Levetzow wrote of the French anarchist Louise Michel: 'There is a certain beauty in the face; but then it is a hard, severe, pure masculine beauty, all female softness and gentleness is totally lacking ... Is it a man, is it a woman?'[63] Fantasising about the gender of female terrorists and referring to Charlotte Corday, the Austrian writer and psychoanalyst Fritz Wittels came to the conclusion in 1908: 'The female assassins are the burning mountains of the imprisoned female libido ... The loneliness of the female political assassins may be voluntary or involuntary; the result is the same, and means rejection of sexuality: they do not want to kiss.'[64]

Even female writers of the first half of the nineteenth century who admired Corday could not describe their female hero as a *normal* woman. Many of them wrote of the sweet temper of Charlotte Corday, which seemed to heal the assassination. Sometimes they emphasised her strong male character or they described a political (sexless and bodiless) angel. These explanations vanished in the second half of the nineteenth century when the bourgeois gender model became predominant in Western societies. Now the (female) admirers of Corday looked for familiar explanations of the assassination, for example, revenge for the death of her boyfriend. Or they transformed the

---

61 D. A. F. de Sade, *Ausgewählte Werke*, ed. by M. Luckow (Frankfurt, Zweitausendeins, 1978), Vol. 3, p. 81.
62 C. Lombroso and R. Laschi, *Der Politische Verbrecher und die Revolutionen in anthropologischer, juristischer und staatswissenschaftlicher Beziehung* (Hamburg, Verl.-Anst. und Druckerei, 1891), Vol. 1, p. 230.
63 K. von Levetzow, 'Louise Michel (La vierge rouge)', *Jahrbuch für sexuelle Zwischenstufen unter besonderer Berücksichtigung der Homosexualität* 7/1 (1905), p. 311.
64 F. Wittels, 'Weibliche Attentäter', *Die Fackel* 9/246–7 (1908), p. 32.

character of the angel into a more secular figure of entrancement. Emma Adler, for example, a well-known Austrian socialist writer of the early twentieth century, is the author of a book about the women of the French Revolution. She characterises Corday as follows:

> The only picture we have of her is painted shortly before her death. It shows an enormous softness. Nothing is less in accord with her appearance than the bloody remembrance which her name evokes ... If we look thoroughly into her sad and soft eyes, we feel something which might explain her whole destiny: she was always lonesome! Yes ... in this charming, good being was this harmful power, the demon of loneliness.[65]

A similar writing tradition existed until the 1980s. 'Charlotte Corday, the gentle woman with the dagger' the feminist writer Salomé Kestenholz wrote, 'moved by the destiny of Ulrike Meinhof, other women, and by the denunciation of emancipated women which was to follow'.[66]

Against the background of this tradition the male members or sympathisers of terrorist groups have seldom had arguments to legitimise female political violence. Often, they refer to the family relationships of female terrorists to explain their actions. In this view, female terrorists resort to political violence because their father/husband/brother was killed or imprisoned. One example is a text in the anarchist journal *Freiheit* about Helene Marković, who in 1883 attempted to assassinate the Serbian king, but failed:

> Soon a number of fighters were dead, amongst them Zephrem Marković, the worthy brother of Svetozar and the worthy husband of the steadfast and heroic Helene Marković. The latter had aroused the suspicion of Milan[67] and was thrown into prison and executed without any judgement by a court – just like a dog. This was the reason why Helene Marković armed herself to take revenge on the villain Milan, but unluckily without success. Hats off to this martyr![68]

It is only a short way from there to today's Palestinian brides and the Chechen Black Widows. Similarly, male members or sympathisers of terrorist groups have encountered some problems in describing their female comrades as heroes, in contrast to their male members. Terms such as hero or martyr are deeply gendered. A hero in the ancient Greek tradition

---

65 E. Adler, *Die berühmten Frauen der französischen Revolution 1789–1795* (Vienna, Stern, 1906), pp. 26ff.
66 S. Kestenholz, *Die Gleichheit vor dem Schafott: Portraits französischer Revolutionärinnen* (Darmstadt, Luchterhand, 1988), pp. 7 and 16.
67 King Milan Obrenović IV (1882–9).   68 'Helene Marković', *Freiheit*, 16 June 1883.

was always a supernatural man, the son of a god or a goddess. How should it then be possible to describe a female hero? The sympathisers of terrorism had to mix the male attributes of a hero with the female attributes of a female martyr if they wanted to create the image of a female hero. Martyrs are traditionally more often described as male than female. However, the passive suffering of a martyr seems to be closer to female-connoted suffering and compassion. Rudolf Rocker, a German anarchist, who in the 1890s met the famous French anarchist Louise Michel, a supporter of political violence, had nothing more to write about this woman than to describe her as a human being of 'indescribable goodness of heart'.[69] What was important for him was the following anecdote:

> Once a friendly comrade donated a beautiful coat to her, which he had especially designed for her ... For some weeks we had the pleasure of admiring Louise in her new coat, until she suddenly wore her old dress again. As it turned out, late one evening on her way home, a ragged female beggar had been asking for charity. So she gave her her beautiful, warm coat.[70]

This is the story of St Martin sharing his coat, and not the description of a female anarchist and terrorist. It is into this tradition that the image of female terrorist idols, as for example Leila Khaled, the Palestinian skyjacker of 1969, can be integrated. In many ways her pictures published in the 1970s evoke associations with the Virgin Mary. If the supporters could not or cannot use the positively connoted representations of suffering (holy) women, they have difficulty in gaining acceptance from the sympathising public. According to Elena Bergia's analysis, the struggle of imprisoned male members of the IRA for better conditions of imprisonment in the 1970s was very famous and qualified to win the sympathy of the audience, as well as 'seductive capital':

> The male republican prisoners who engaged in radical forms of protest for political status often came out glorified by their experiences ... The ex-prisoners' deeds, difficult to comprehend as they may have been, echoed with the glory of Irish anti-colonial history; their suffering and endurance read as signs of strength. The women who engaged in similar battles were less fortunate. Their blood smeared on the walls of their cells clashed with widespread views of femininity as synonymous with propriety, cleanliness, and modesty; and their solitary battles, with notions of gender as a shared enterprise.[71]

---

69 R. Rocker, *Aus den Memoiren eines deutschen Anarchisten* (Frankfurt, Suhrkamp, 1974), p. 139.
70 Ibid., p. 140.
71 E. Bergia, 'Unexpected Rewards of Political Violence: Republican Ex-Prisoners, Seductive Capital, and the Gendered Nature of Heroism', *Terrorism and Political Violence* (2019), p. 17, DOI: 10.1080/09546553.2019.1629423.

All in all, we can interpret the difficulties of the sympathisers in legitimating the participation of women in violent activities as a counterpart to the mainstream perspective of violent women as gender-transgressing women.

Especially in the 1970s, the mainstream or dominating topos of female terrorists as genderless or gender-transgressing women occupied the media. It seems possible to interpret this hype as a reflection of the contemporaneous rising women's movement.[72] If female terrorism was not explained as caused by the unwillingness of women to behave like *real* women, their search for gender equality and emancipation served as an explanation. As a result, there were three typical gendered patterns to explain, for example, German female terrorism in the 1970s: 1) Women are not able to do politics rationally; 2) Women become terrorists because they want to achieve emancipation, and this demonstrates that they are not proper women; 3) Women are handicapped twice, by patriarchy and capitalism, and therefore act as terrorists.[73] These explanatory approaches can even be found in research studies about recent terrorism across the world.[74]

Are there really arguments for connecting female terrorism with female emancipation in specific historical circumstances? Many contemporary authors who have published on recent female terrorism would agree. Let us first examine the nineteenth century. If we interpret the call for female political rights in these times as a call for emancipation then it is logical to interpret female terrorists as emancipated women, because they not only called for political rights, but defined political participation as the possibility of participating in violent political affairs.

Do we have statements from female terrorists themselves about their gender role? In the nineteenth century there are demands for equal rights by female terrorists, but statements by them which deal with their gendered self-conception seem to be rare. We know of only one early reflection on the female gender character and participation in violent political actions: when Amalie Struve, the wife of Gustav Struve, a radical democrat and German

---

72 D. Grisard, *Gendering Terror: eine Geschlechtergeschichte des Linksterrorismus in der Schweiz* (Frankfurt, Campus-Verlag, 2011); D. Grisard, 'Das feminisierte Geheime: der Terrorismusbegriff der 1970er- und frühen 1980er-Jahre' and I. Bandhauer-Schöffmann, 'Österreichische Terrorbuben? Zeitgenössische und retrospektive Deutungen des Linksterrorismus in Österreich während der 1970er-Jahre', in Hikel and Schraut (eds.), *Terrorismus und Geschlecht*.
73 S. Schraut, 'Terrorismus und Geschlecht', in C. Künzel and G. Temme (eds.), *Täterinnen und/oder Opfer? Frauen in Gewaltstrukturen* (Hamburg, Lit, 2007).
74 Poloni-Staudinger and Ortbals, *Terrorism*, pp. 33–50; Raghavan and Balasubramaniyan, 'Evolving Role of Women', p. 206.

Eighteen Forty-Eighter, was not allowed to accompany her husband during the revolutionary struggle, she wrote:

> I never felt so deeply the degrading position to which, compared to that of the male sex, the female sex is bound until today. Why should a woman who is capable of working not work at the moment of decision? Why should the wife who shared her husband's danger not partake in his actions? In truth, as long as even in the storm of revolution one shows so much consideration for traditional prejudice the yoke of tyranny will not be broken.[75]

Also known is the critical attitude towards patriarchy which characterises Louise Michel: 'The proletarian is a slave, the wife of the proletarian is the slave of all slaves ... Will you [the men] dare to share rights, when men and women shall have won human rights?', she wrote in her autobiography, first published in 1886.[76] After the First World War, left-wing female politicians and authors began to discuss gender roles fundamentally; for them emancipation meant more than gender equality. An article in the journal *Social Revolution* states:

> The revolutionary man who fights for his freedom today only fights against the outside world ... Conversely, the revolutionary woman has to fight in two arenas. At first for her external liberty – in this fight she finds her comrade in the man, she fights together with him for the same aims, for the same topic. But she has also to fight for an internal liberty, a liberty which the man has owned for a long time; and in this fight she stands alone.[77]

Similar statements, reformulated, were discussed, for example, in Germany when the second women's movement separated itself from the student movement in the 1970s. But none of the (German) female terrorists of these times defined herself as a feminist or a woman primarily fighting for female emancipation. Gilda Zwerman, who interviewed women of the left-wing liberation movements in the United States in the 1970s, made similar observations. She reported that all the women interviewed had some contact with feminism during the late 1960s or 1970s. They 'note that their contact gave cause for reflection and pause before casting or recasting their lot with armed insurgents', but feminism as a political strategy was not going far enough for them.[78]

---

75 A. Struve, *Erinnerungen aus den badischen Freiheitskämpfen: den deutschen Frauen gewidmet* (Hamburg, Hoffmann & Campe, 1850), pp. 68ff.
76 L. Michel, *Buch vom Bagno: Erinnerungen einer Kommunardin* (Berlin, Rütten & Loening, 1962), pp. 117 and 119.
77 *Social Revolution* 12 (1 May 1937), quoted in *Frauen in der Revolution*, Vol. 1: *Louise Michel – Ihr Leben – Ihr Kampf – Ihre Ideen* (Berlin, Karin Kramer Verlag, 1976), p. 14.
78 G. Zwerman, 'Mothering on the Lam: Politics, Gender Fantasies and Maternal Thinking in Women Associated with Armed, Clandestine Organizations in the United States', *Feminist Review* 47 (1994), p. 43.

They said that they were socialist feminists. They said they were trying to figure out how to reactivate a mass [left] movement that was rapidly disintegrating. And they said they were committed to maintaining their identity as radicals. I thought we had more similarities than differences. But I was wrong. They were ambitious, would-be professionals, who ultimately relied more on European radical traditions as a basis for their politics. And what did they do? Talk. Talk. Talk. Read. Read. Read. In the face of the National Liberation Front's struggle in Vietnam and the rise-up at Attica [Prison] and Black Nationalism, feminism seemed completely self-serving, limited . . . and boring.[79]

We probably have to turn the emancipation argument upside down. There is no direct way from the demand for emancipation – interpreted by its opponents as unnatural – to political violence. But women (and this applies to the past and the present) who define themselves as emancipated and who therefore demand political participation use political violence if they are part of a violent political movement. And it is another question whether politically active women, peacefully or not, developed or develop feminist attitudes. To quote Zwerman once more: 'The female guerrilla symbolizes the stereotypical extremes of gender identity. It permits the traditional character and dichotomy between masculinity and femininity to remain intact, while giving the women access – albeit temporary and highly supervised – to the male realm of power and aggression.'[80]

All in all, we can conclude: in the present and in history, terrorism, with all its symbolic aspects of violent communication, challenges and confuses political systems, especially democratic ones, which have to legitimate themselves and their security policy. These systems are theoretically open to general political and social participation. How is it possible, then, that some people come to the conclusion that they can only violently participate in such systems? This confusion also extends to the gender concept which has been dominant since the nineteenth century. Therefore, in gender perspective, the representation of the terrorist reflects the confusion of the society which is confronted with terrorism. Sympathising as well as critical descriptions of female and male terrorists in the nineteenth and twentieth centuries share the assumption that these persons transgress their gender roles. This is only one result which demonstrates the benefit of the analytical category gender in historical studies when examining terrorism and its representations.

---

79 Women using political violence, quoted in Zwerman, 'Mothering on the Lam', p. 43.
80 Zwerman, 'Mothering on the Lam', p. 44.

Further Reading

M. Aslam, *Gender-Based Explosions: The Nexus Between Muslim Masculinities, Jihadist Islamism and Terrorism* (New York, United Nations University Press, 2012)

C. E. Gentry, L. J. Shepherd and L. Sjoberg (eds.), *The Routledge Handbook of Gender and Security* (London, Routledge, Taylor & Francis Group, 2018)

C. D. Ortbals and L. Poloni-Staudinger, *Gender and Political Violence: Women Changing the Politics of Terrorism* (Cham, Springer, 2018)

S. Schraut and K. Weinhauer, 'Terrorism, Gender, and History: Introduction', *Historical Social Research* 39 (2014)

J. Scott, 'Gender: A Useful Category of Historical Analysis', *American Historical Review* 91/5 (1986)

PART V

★

CONCLUSION

26

Terrorism and History
Current Knowledge and Future Research

RICHARD ENGLISH

This book has involved scholars thinking historically about terrorism. In relation to the four main areas of understanding in the field – definition, causation, consequences and appropriate response – what can we therefore say that we know, and what should we prioritise next in our research? This chapter will identify some of what the contributors themselves have valuably argued, and it will consequently have a historical dimension. But it will also relate such ideas to wider understandings, findings and agendas, recognising that the study of terrorism is and should be collaborative between disciplines.[1]

Definition

The precise definition of terrorism has practical (legal and political) consequences, and it continues to possess enduring academic appeal as a subject of research.[2] But the lack of definitional consensus among scholars might be less problematic than is often assumed.[3] Indeed, as Martyn Frampton points out in this volume, we know that we know a considerable amount about what people mean (and agree on meaning) when they use the term terrorism. Where there have been and remain

---

1 R. English, 'The Enduring Illusions of Terrorism and Counter-Terrorism', in R. English (ed.), *Illusions of Terrorism and Counter-Terrorism* (Oxford, Oxford University Press, 2015).
2 See, for significant examples, A. Richards, *Conceptualising Terrorism* (Oxford, Oxford University Press, 2015); A. P. Schmid (ed.), *The Routledge Handbook of Terrorism Research* (London, Routledge, 2011).
3 B. Saul, 'Defining Terrorism: A Conceptual Minefield', in E. Chenoweth, R. English, A. Gofas and S. N. Kalyvas (eds.), *The Oxford Handbook of Terrorism* (Oxford, Oxford University Press, 2019). As examples of the richly illuminating work that is possible, definitional disagreements notwithstanding, see C. Townshend, *Political Violence in Ireland: Government and Resistance since 1848* (Oxford, Oxford University Press, 1983); C. Townshend, *Terrorism: A Very Short Introduction* (Oxford, Oxford University Press, 2018).

differences of interpretation, Frampton's Skinneresque approach might make us less anxious than scholars sometimes seem to be about the absence of a consensual definition. Indeed, historians might instinctively feel comfortable concentrating on what it is that meanings in varied contexts have told us about those who perceived them within those particular cultural and sociopolitical settings. This, rather than a Procrustean attempt to force varied human experience into one definitional shape, seems to me an important historical contribution and approach.

It is not that there exist no conceptual challenges within the enduringly contested definitional arena. Some scholars define terrorism more narrowly, whether specifying that it must involve attacks on civilian targets[4] or that it must be practised by non-state actors.[5] Others suggest that the victims of terrorism can be drawn from various categories (including non-civilians) and that states as well as non-state organisations or individuals can practise terrorist violence.[6] In addition to these disputes about definition in terms of target and in terms of practitioner, there are also issues regarding the potential overlap between terrorism and other categories of political violence (such as civil war, insurgency, guerrilla warfare), and concerning the validity of using an analytical term which undeniably carries such pejorative weight.[7] As Warren Brown valuably points out in this volume, there is also the question of how applicable the term terrorism is to some historical periods of human experience, when the latter are examined with due respect for detailed context.

It is important, however, not to exaggerate the definitional problems that we currently face. The authors contributing to this book have demonstrated both that those working with different definitions can engage meaningfully in collective dialogue on the subject, and also that there exists considerable overlap between the rival definitions that tend to be employed. Moreover, constructive dialogue amid definitional non-consensus is common in fields that focus on major social phenomena, including some whose labels also

---

4 L. Richardson, *What Terrorists Want: Understanding the Terrorist Threat* (London, John Murray, 2006), p. 22; M. Abrahms, *Rules for Rebels: The Science of Victory in Militant History* (Oxford, Oxford University Press, 2018), pp. 8–9.

5 Richardson, *What Terrorists Want*, pp. 21–2; C. Wight, 'State Terrorism: Who Needs It?', in R. Jackson and D. Pisoiu (eds.), *Contemporary Debates on Terrorism* (London, Routledge, 2018).

6 A. Richards, 'Is Terrorism Still a Useful Analytical Term, or Should It Be Abandoned?', in Jackson and Pisoiu (eds.), *Contemporary Debates on Terrorism*, p. 19; R. English, *Terrorism: How to Respond* (Oxford, Oxford University Press, 2009), p. 24.

7 English, *Terrorism: How to Respond*, pp. 1–26.

carry considerable pejorative power (nationalism, empire, revolution, colonialism, fascism, Marxism, class, security).[8] Indeed, instead of lamenting our lack of agreement concerning the word terrorism, it might be more honest and helpful to recognise that definitional divergence is actually a sign that healthy, critical perspectives exist within the field. Put another way, what kind of scholarly debate could be judged to exist on a subject as Protean and painful as terrorism, if scholars *could* comfortably agree on a definitional consensus?

More fruitful than any sense of immobilisation through definitional dispute would be future investigation of three definitionally relevant areas of enquiry. First, historical analyses show that terrorism is a phenomenon defined by relationships. These are rarely straightforward to categorise. Historians have rightly been wary of binary thinking,[9] and close analysis of the relationships involved in terrorism will certainly require such caution. It is important, for example, in analysing the often decisive relationship between non-state terrorists and state actors, to acknowledge the heterogeneity of each of these players. Similarly, I doubt that contextual analysis in particular settings of the relationship between terrorism and insurgency, or terrorism and civil war, will yield satisfactorily binary conclusions. Far more likely is a continuum between different modes of violence, with much overlap along it as many acts turn out to be simultaneously terroristic and insurgent, or to embody terrorism and civil war violence at the same time. My suggestion here is that historians will be well placed (owing to their analysis of first-hand and multiple sources in unique context over long periods, and their instinctive scepticism about rigid frameworks of theoretical analysis), to explain the complexity and multiple identities involved in terrorist violence, and to assess the analytical work being done (or obstructed) by the use of the T-word in the context of relevant human relationships. As Warren Brown's chapter in this volume suggests, one of the best ways to respond to the issue of terminology and terrorism is to use our consideration of the T word, as used in its various settings, to illuminate our reading of how people have understood important behaviour in context.

A second research opportunity would be to explore systematically the actual policy effects of definitional dispute and variation. As Brian Glyn Williams's chapter on Iraq suggests, some groups that have dominated discussion of terrorism have also been capable (as with ISIS) of operating in

---

8 R. English, *Does Terrorism Work? A History* (Oxford, Oxford University Press, 2016), p. 9.
9 D. Cannadine, *The Undivided Past: History Beyond Our Differences* (London, Penguin, 2013).

ways that go beyond usual definitions of the subject (running a quasi-state, for example, or operating a sizeable army). The issue, therefore, is how far analytical and practical responses will be shaped by whether or not one characterises such a group as a terrorist organisation. Steve Hewitt's chapter in this volume rightly stresses that there is a long past to definitional dispute about terrorism. And it is clear that there can be practical implications arising from definitional choices (regarding which laws can be used, for example, to respond to particular actions within a given state). It is sometimes suggested that use of the word terrorism gets in the way of fruitful state engagement with the causes behind terrorist violence, and that such use makes it difficult for states to pursue negotiation or conflict resolution. Examining first-hand sources in contextual detail could help to demonstrate how far this assumption is accurate. My own intuition would be that this suggestion might turn out to be an exaggerated one, as reflection on the UK's involvement in the Northern Ireland peace process would suggest. The UK's Chief Negotiator in that process, Tony Blair's Chief of Staff Jonathan Powell, clearly considered the IRA to be a terrorist organisation; but, despite this, he engaged in extensive, fruitful and successful dialogue with them to produce a significant shift towards peace in Northern Ireland.[10]

So I think that more could be researched regarding the contextual ways in which definitional problems have, or have not, hindered beneficial responses to terrorism. The USA has multiple wings of the state, and they sometimes diverge in their definitions of terrorism. But to what extent has that had a damaging effect on US counterterrorism in practice?

A third related area of future enquiry would be to extend the definitional debate beyond the anglophone world in which it overwhelmingly occurs. Have the supposed problems generated by the pejorative meanings of the word terrorism been equally important in the multilingual setting of Pakistan? How useful and how important have disputes about defining terrorism been in Turkey? Put another way, are the connotations of the word that distress some and divide many in English as significant in, for example, Pashto or Punjabi or Turkish? My initial suspicion here is that the unfortunate geographical bias of research base for most terrorism scholars[11] has been reflected in an untested and possibly erroneous assumption that the

---

10 J. Powell, *Great Hatred, Little Room: Making Peace in Northern Ireland* (London, Bodley Head, 2008); J. Powell, *Talking to Terrorists: How to End Armed Conflicts* (London, Bodley Head, 2014).
11 R. English, 'The Future Study of Terrorism', *European Journal of International Security* 1/2 (2016).

anglophone debate over definition is equally significant elsewhere (including countries which have experienced far more terrorism than most English-speaking ones).

Causation

Turning from definition to causation, the chapters of this book have repeatedly demonstrated the complex multicausality behind terrorism. This is strikingly the case with Roddy Brett's analysis of Colombia, where long-term, fluid dynamics have involved economic, ideological, legal and social elements of causation, and a mutually shaping relationship between those with state power and those various groups without it. But it is also the case with Ludger Mees's chapter on the heterogeneous causality behind Basque terrorism, with Julie Norman's account of the interwoven terrorisms of Israel/Palestine, with Ekaterina Stepanova's stress upon the multifactorial quality of all historical causal explanations and with Dayyab Gillani's account of the ways in which terrorism in Pakistan has emerged out of economic, colonial, internationalist interventionist, religious, nationalistic and ethnic elements, together with the instability and complicity of the state itself. In line, therefore, with the arguments about history set out in the Introduction to this book, contributors have demonstrated that we must indeed recognise the complex particularity and the many-layered multi-causality involved in satisfactory explanations of terrorism.

So, contrary to some suggestions,[12] we actually know a significant amount about why people turn to terrorism. Its practitioners evince complex, tangled motivation at group but also at individual level.[13] Ideology or belief system, suffering and grievance, individual and group desire for revenge or retaliation,[14] the influence of mentors or of influential friends and family,[15] support or encouragement from external sponsors or actors,[16] tactical

---

12 M. Sageman, 'The Stagnation in Terrorism Research', *Terrorism and Political Violence* 26/4 (2014).
13 Richardson, *What Terrorists Want*, p. 2; P. R. Neumann, *Radicalized: New Jihadists and the Threat to the West* (London, I. B. Tauris, 2016), pp. 42, 89–97, 153; J. Goodwin, 'The Causes of Terrorism', in Chenoweth et al. (eds.), *Oxford Handbook of Terrorism*.
14 M. Crenshaw and G. LaFree, *Countering Terrorism* (Washington, DC, Brookings Institution Press, 2017), p. 98; Richardson, *What Terrorists Want*, pp. 62–3, 100–1, 113–20; A. Edwards, *UVF: Behind the Mask* (Newbridge, Merrion Press, 2017), pp. 56–7; A. Pedahzur and A. Perliger, *Jewish Terrorism in Israel* (New York, Columbia University Press, 2009), pp. 51, 63, 143, 155.
15 M. O'Doherty, *Gerry Adams: An Unauthorised Life* (London, Faber and Faber, 2017).
16 D. Byman, *Deadly Connections: States That Sponsor Terrorism* (Cambridge, Cambridge University Press, 2005); G. Ó Faoleán, *A Broad Church: The Provisional IRA in the Republic of Ireland 1969–1980* (Newbridge, Merrion Press, 2019).

imitation and inspiration,[17] organisational and other inherent rewards – again and again in the past these elements have variously combined to make terrorist violence seem justified and necessary for the tactical pursuit of various strategic objectives.

Even lone-actor terrorism tends to be emphatically multicausal (and this is true at the individual level as well as across different lone-actor cases).[18] In analysing Anders Breivik's 22 July 2011 Norway attacks, for example, Hemmingby and Bjorgo have shown what a dynamic, contingent, complex and improvised process small-scale terrorist-attack planning and execution can be.[19] It seems likely that mental illness plays a larger role in generating lone-actor than group-based terrorism.[20] But, in considering causation, it is worth stressing also that, across the universe of terrorist cases past and present, it is the psychological normality of its practitioners and supporters that is striking.[21] This does not mean that psychology plays no role. Rather, it means that explanations founded on psychopathology are unlikely to be helpful when dealing with the major terrorist formations that demand analysis. The contextual evidence available in the chapters of this book reinforces such a conclusion.

How important is ideology within these causal dynamics? Some observers have stressed its role starkly. In relation to jihadist terrorism, the former UK Prime Minister David Cameron argued that 'The problem was, predominantly, the ideology of Islamist extremism. Hate preachers had twisted and perverted the religion of Islam and turned it into a dogma of hatred, division and ultimately violence.'[22] Scholarly opinion has varied here,[23] but the

---

17 C. Hemmingby and T. Bjorgo, *The Dynamics of a Terrorist Targeting Process: Anders B. Breivik and the 22 July Attacks in Norway* (Basingstoke, Palgrave Macmillan, 2016), p. 54; M. S. Hamm and R. Spaaij, *The Age of Lone Wolf Terrorism* (New York, Columbia University Press, 2017), pp. 45–8, 185; J. Toobin, *American Heiress: The Kidnapping, Crimes and Trial of Patty Hearst* (London, Profile Books, 2017), pp. 42, 56.
18 Hamm and Spaaij, *The Age of Lone Wolf Terrorism*; P. Gill, *Lone-Actor Terrorists: A Behavioural Analysis* (London, Routledge, 2015).
19 Hemmingby and Bjorgo, *Dynamics of a Terrorist Targeting Process*.
20 Gill, *Lone-Actor Terrorists*.
21 J. Horgan, *The Psychology of Terrorism* (London, Routledge, 2005); Richardson, *What Terrorists Want*, pp. 32–4; Jackson and Pisoiu (eds.), *Contemporary Debates on Terrorism*, p. 150; English, *Does Terrorism Work?*, pp. 1–2.
22 D. Cameron, *For the Record* (London, William Collins, 2019), p. 421.
23 A. Brahimi, 'Ideology and Terrorism', in Chenoweth et al. (eds.), *Oxford Handbook of Terrorism*; A. Moghadam, *Nexus of Global Jihad: Understanding Cooperation among Terrorist Actors* (New York, Columbia University Press, 2017), pp. 69–75, 262; T. Bacon, *Why Terrorist Groups Form International Alliances* (Philadelphia, University of Pennsylvania Press, 2018), pp. 4, 32–3; J. Mulqueen, *'An Alien Ideology': Cold War Perceptions of the Irish Republican Left* (Liverpool, Liverpool University Press, 2019).

predominant weight of analysis in this book's chapters has been towards seeing ideology as one part of a wider set of causal elements, and as always needing to be interpreted in terms of the contingency and complexity of particular circumstance rather than with a mechanical view that ideology X will produce terrorism. Indeed, the mutually shaping intimacy of political relationships in adversarial contact emerges often as more decisive than the direct role of ideological principle. Dennis Dworkin's chapter on the USA, for example, shows how long into the past the mutually shaping relationship between non-state terrorism and state response has been rooted, and this has been true across different ideological realms in that country. This state/non-state enmity and friction emerges in the different contexts of Africa, Ireland/UK, the Basque Country/Spain, Israel/Palestine, Peru, as is richly evident from the respective chapters in this volume.

In order to explain the emergence and sustenance of terrorism, attention has been paid in this book to the particularity and uniqueness of context. That has reinforced the fact that it is terrorisms, rather than terrorism, that we are analysing. Dayyab Gillani's chapter, for example, clarifies the heterogeneity of terrorisms in Pakistan, and in studying terrorist violence we are simultaneously looking at the dynamics of the very local and also of the global. Moreover, in line with the argument set out regarding historical method in the opening chapter of this book, Kieran McConaghy's chapter shows that an understanding of particular, long-rooted context is the basis for international understandings, not its opponent.

So these chapters have sought less to establish general laws about terrorist causation than to explain in detailed context the reasons why people decided that violence was the best or the only way of achieving precious and necessary political change. This is not to present terrorist activity as purely a rational calculation. That emotions play a causal role in generating and sustaining various forms of political violence has been recognised by scholars across different disciplines; as noted, the fact that revenge is crucial among these emotions has also been well established, not least in relation to terrorism.[24] But it is vital to recognise (from Israel/Palestine to Ireland to Spain/the Basque Country to Iraq to numerous African countries and beyond) how repeatedly central to the generation of terrorism has been the issue of the legitimacy of existing political and/or social and/or religious arrangements in each setting.

24 R. D. Peterson, *Understanding Ethnic Violence: Fear, Hatred and Resentment in Twentieth-Century Eastern Europe* (Cambridge, Cambridge University Press, 2002); Richardson, *What Terrorists Want*.

Repeatedly crucial also in the generation of terrorist violence has been the large effect of small numbers of enthusiasts, zealots, initiators and entrepreneurs.[25] John Brown and his small group of colleagues in Dennis Dworkin's chapter on the USA, Mohammed Bouyeri (the killer of Theo van Gogh) in Beatrice de Graaf's essay on the Netherlands, the small group of rebels who produced the 1916 Easter rebellion in Fearghal McGarry's Irish chapter – these and other activists featured in these historical essays exemplify the decisive role that small numbers of individuals (and their motivations) can play in the causation of terrorism and its effects.[26] This also allows for close analysis of the causation behind particular kinds of terrorist act: why attack *this* target rather than *that* one? Such issues, on close scrutiny, seem often to be determined by practical considerations and locally determining factors in particular context.[27]

Despite understandable twenty-first-century attention to religiously inflected terrorism, it is clear from this book how vital nationalism has been and remains to the generation of terrorist violence. It is not that there is anything inevitable here, or that nationalism only creates violence in relation to terrorism; indeed, it could be argued that nationalism often helps to create and sustain the consensual and stable state legitimacy which renders terrorism less likely.[28] But, as is clear from the chapters here by Julie Norman, Ludger Mees, Richard Reid, Dayyab Gillani, Fearghal McGarry and Kieran McConaghy (and as is evident from other impressive research produced recently),[29] nationalist politics has represented and continues to represent a world-significant part of terrorist causation. This again demonstrates the extent to which terrorism can only be understood if it is explained in the context of more significant historical forces.

Future research will be able to establish how far greater understanding of these complicated, contextual, causal processes might or might not have informed and altered political decision-making at crucial moments in the

---

25 R. F. Foster, *Vivid Faces: The Revolutionary Generation in Ireland 1890–1923* (London, Penguin, 2014); R. English, '"The Inborn Hate of Things English": Ernie O'Malley and the Irish Revolution 1916–1923', *Past and Present* 151 (1996), p. 199.
26 English, *Does Terrorism Work?*, p. 42; R. English, *Ernie O'Malley: IRA Intellectual* (Oxford, Oxford University Press, 1998), pp. 77–9; E. Burke, *An Army of Tribes: British Army Cohesion, Deviancy and Murder in Northern Ireland* (Liverpool, Liverpool University Press, 2018).
27 C. Hemmingby, 'Exploring the Continuum of Lethality: Militant Islamists' Targeting Preferences in Europe', *Perspectives on Terrorism* 11/5 (2017).
28 R. English, 'Nationalism and Terrorism', in Chenoweth et al. (eds.), *Oxford Handbook of Terrorism*.
29 K. Rekawek, 'Career Break or a New Career? Extremist Foreign Fighters in Ukraine', report published by the Counter Extremism Project, April 2020.

past. Given that state responses to non-state terrorism change the world more decisively than non-state terrorist violence itself, this is a major point. In relation to jihadist terrorism, for example, it is clear that key political and policy-significant figures in the US and UK saw al-Qaida as representing an utterly new form of terrorism, requiring an utterly different kind of response.[30] It is equally clear that much influential counterterrorist thinking in such circles involved little reflection on history, even among very intelligent, educated practitioners.[31] Yet it is plausible also to suggest that, while al-Qaida was (like all terrorist organisations) unique, there existed family resemblances between its motivations and the motivations of familiar groups from the terrorist past, and also that there existed strong continuities between what would be effective in countering this terrorism and what had worked previously.[32] The chapters in this book have shown the value of establishing source-based, contextual explanations for even the most brutal and appalling terrorist violence. It will be important that future historical scholarship assesses how far a more contextually historical understanding of the supposedly epoch-changing violence of 9/11 might have averted some of the clumsier, counterproductive responses that emerged to that atrocity.

Another important area of future historical research regarding terrorist causation is to consider cases in which the sustaining causes do not endure, and where terrorism from particular sources subsides. Pioneering work has been done by scholars (mostly from other disciplines) into the ending of terrorism.[33] But historians could contribute more substantially to this debate than they have done to date, both through case-study analysis in contextual detail, and in terms of integrating the endings of particular groups or campaigns with the wider-angled arguments of more nomothetically oriented scholars from other disciplines. Issues of long-termism, multicausality in specific context, contingency and the significance of first-hand source material will be profoundly important again here.

30 R. English, 'Change and Continuity Across the 9/11 Fault Line: Rethinking Twenty-First-Century Responses to Terrorism', *Critical Studies on Terrorism* 12/1 (2019), pp. 78–9.
31 J. Evans, 'Academic Research and the Intelligence Community: Some Reflections', in Chenoweth et al. (eds.), *Oxford Handbook of Terrorism*, p. 697.
32 Richardson, *What Terrorists Want*; English, *Terrorism: How to Respond*.
33 A. K. Cronin, *Ending Terrorism: Lessons for Defeating Al-Qaida* (London, Routledge, 2008); A. K. Cronin, *How Terrorism Ends: Understanding the Decline and Demise of Terrorist Campaigns* (Princeton, Princeton University Press, 2009); J. Horgan, *Walking Away from Terrorism: Accounts of Disengagement from Radical and Extremist Movements* (London, Routledge, 2009); I. Murua, 'No More Bullets for ETA: The Loss of Internal Support as a Key Factor in the End of the Basque Group's Campaign', *Critical Studies on Terrorism* 10/1 (2017).

Consequences

As with causation, so also with consequences, historical analysis will stress complexity and a far from neat pattern of outcomes and legacies, when carefully scrutinised over long pasts. Julie Norman's chapter in this book demonstrates that the pressure applied by Jewish terrorism did have an impact in relation to the establishment of the state of Israel, but that the latter's emergence was also caused by other significant factors. Beatrice de Graaf shows that late nineteenth-century anarchism represented a threat in the Netherlands, but that it remained a violent politics which failed to achieve significant success. Fearghal McGarry's cross-period analysis involves episodes of Irish republican violence (1881–5, 1916–21, 1969–98) which resulted in markedly varied outcomes in relation to political strategy and goals.

These and other historically informed insights from the volume's contributors show how complex a question it is to ask how far terrorism works. Though some scholars have argued more strongly than others that terrorist violence is effective,[34] it is fair to suggest that historians are likely to be among those who are dissatisfied with answers along the lines of a binary 'yes' or 'no'. Close reading of the chapters in this book reinforces the scholarly judgement of those who have opted for complex, layered answers to the question of whether terrorism works,[35] and who have emphasised that long pasts and long futures need to be considered when addressing this question. It is striking how many of this book's judgements about terrorism's effects are framed in relation to very lengthy and tangled political and social relationships; this is true of Julie Norman's chapter on Israel/Palestine, as also of Richard Reid's on African terrorism, Fearghal McGarry's on Ireland, Roddy Brett's on Colombia, Dayyab Gillani's on Pakistan and Cecilia Méndez's on Peru.

---

34 Those suggesting a greater degree of terrorist efficacy include A. M. Dershowitz, *Why Terrorism Works: Understanding the Threat, Responding to the Challenge* (New Haven, Yale University Press, 2002); A. H. Kydd and B. F. Walter, 'The Strategies of Terrorism', *International Security* 31/1 (2006); R. A. Pape, 'The Strategic Logic of Suicide Terrorism', *American Political Science Review* 97/3 (2003). Those much more sceptical about how far terrorism works include C. Gearty, *Terror* (London, Faber and Faber, 1991); M. Abrahms, 'Why Terrorism Does Not Work', *International Security* 31/2 (2006); D. C. Rapoport, 'The International World as Some Terrorists Have Seen It: A Look at a Century of Memoirs', in D. C. Rapoport (ed.), *Inside Terrorist Organisations* (London, Frank Cass, 2001).

35 P. Wilkinson, *Terrorism Versus Democracy: The Liberal State Response* (London, Routledge, 2006), pp. 6, 22, 26, 195; Richardson, *What Terrorists Want*, pp. 105–6; D. Muro (ed.), *When Does Terrorism Work?* (London, Routledge, 2018); English, *Does Terrorism Work?*; R. W. White, *Out of the Ashes: An Oral History of the Provisional Irish Republican Movement* (Newbridge, Merrion Press, 2017), pp. 341–56.

Repeatedly, it has been the case that strategic victory has eluded terrorists but that they have gained other goods through their violence. This has been historically reflected in the experience of the PLO, the IRA, Hamas, ETA, FARC, al-Qaida, ISIS and numerous other important groups; it has been a contingent process, difficult to capture through rigid theoretical explanations or without contextual precision and particular detail; and it has been repeatedly argued in the scholarly literature on terrorist violence.[36] The extent of terrorist strategic failure is vividly implied in the remarkable nature of the Basque separatist group ETA's profound apology to its victims: 'We know that we caused a lot of pain during that long period of armed struggle'; 'We wish to show our respect for those who were killed or wounded by ETA and those who were affected by the conflict. We are truly sorry.'[37] But it is also well established that, whatever its limitations in relation to central, strategic goals, terrorism has had greater efficacy at a tactical level: terrorist violence can be part of how groups ensure organisational sustenance and survival;[38] indeed, terrorism can help to create and sustain groups' organisational power and momentum.[39]

In terms of terrorism's consequences, we also know how frequently such violence has produced or reinforced polarisation; that it has often provoked states into acting aggressively or repressively against the population in whose name terrorists have been claiming to act; relatedly, that terrorism has frequently prompted states into acting in ways that profoundly limit civil liberties;[40] and that, as terrorism is produced, small numbers of people (and even key individuals) can have a disproportionately large effect, albeit not usually in terms of securing the strategic goals that they most desire.[41] This last point reinforces the importance of contingency, given the degree to which individual and small-group action can be decisively affected by chance; it also strengthens the case for attending to the particularity and complexity

---

36 English, *Does Terrorism Work?*; Cronin, *How Terrorism Ends*; E. Chenoweth and M. J. Stephan, *Why Civil Resistance Works: The Strategic Logic of Nonviolent Conflict* (New York, Columbia University Press, 2011); Abrahms, *Rules for Rebels*; Muro (ed.), *When Does Terrorism Work?*
37 Quoted in *Irish Times*, 21 April 2018.   38 Moghadam, *Nexus of Global Jihad*, pp. 20–3.
39 A. Moghadam and M. Wyss, 'The Political Power of Proxies: Why Nonstate Actors Use Local Surrogates', *International Security* 44/4 (2020).
40 C. Gearty, 'No Golden Age: The Deep Origins and Current Utility of Western Counter-Terrorism Policy', in English (ed.), *Illusions of Terrorism and Counter-Terrorism*; L. K. Donohue, *The Cost of Counter-Terrorism: Power, Politics and Liberty* (Cambridge, Cambridge University Press, 2008).
41 D. Byman, *Al-Qaida, the Islamic State and the Global Jihadist Movement: What Everyone Needs to Know* (Oxford, Oxford University Press, 2015), p. 160; Pedahzur and Perliger, *Jewish Terrorism in Israel*, p. 161; English, *Does Terrorism Work?*

of local context. In terms of this volume, the point about context and locality has been shown to be vital. Dayyab Gillani, for example, makes the important point that, whatever Western anxieties and priorities of focus, most victims of Pakistani terrorism are people in Pakistan itself.

We also know that terrorism has had and continues to have a marked capacity for generating conspicuous publicity. As Brigitte Nacos and Melih Barut show in this volume, across very long time periods and across very different kinds of terrorist actor, the pursuit and achievement of publicity has been an enduring consequence of terrorist violence. This has been stressed also by practitioners themselves. As Popular Front for the Liberation of Palestine leader George Habash once put it, 'For decades world opinion has been neither for nor against the Palestinians. It simply ignored us. At least the world is talking about us now.'[42]

But we also know that there is a paradox of publicity, also relevant to Palestinian activists: terrorism gains publicity, but it does so through acts which most observers find repellent. This contradiction has represented a frequent problem for groups such as ETA, the IRA, al-Qaida and Hamas.

Where next in terms of studying terrorism's effects? There are some important areas where complex consequences still require much more treatment by historically minded scholars. Despite some pioneering work,[43] for example, there is still much more to be explored concerning the participation of women in terrorism (as Sylvia Schraut rightly suggests in this volume). This involves consideration of the long-term effects of that participation on activists, victims and wider society; it also involves broader questions of gender and power, as some scholars have begun to demonstrate.[44] Again, historians have much to offer in terms of the longer-term, contextual legacies of terrorist violence. In analysing complex societal effects, this work could complement, for example, the brilliant economic analysis that has been offered regarding the effects that cessations of terrorist violence have on aspects of local economies;[45] it could also extend the excellent work that has been pursued on post-violent disillusionment.[46]

---

42 Quoted in Bacon, *Why Terrorist Groups Form International Alliances*, p. 63.
43 D. Reinisch, 'Women's Agency and Political Violence: Irish Republican Women and the Formation of the Provisional IRA, 1967–70', *Irish Political Studies* 34/3 (2019).
44 E. Bergia, 'Unexpected Rewards of Political Violence: Republican Ex-Prisoners, Seductive Capital and the Gendered Nature of Heroism', *Terrorism and Political Violence* (published online 28 June 2019), DOI: 10.1080/09546553.2019.1629423.
45 T. Besley and H. Muller, 'Estimating the Peace Dividend: The Impact of Violence on House Prices in Northern Ireland', *American Economic Review* 102/2 (2012).
46 Foster, *Vivid Faces*; F. Flanagan, *Remembering the Revolution: Dissent, Culture and Nationalism in the Irish Free State* (Oxford, Oxford University Press, 2015).

Current Knowledge and Future Research

More broadly still, in assessing the extent to which terrorism has brought into being the new worlds that its practitioners actually sought, two obvious candidates for historically informed research suggest themselves. One is to apply a wide-angled framework of analysis about efficacy (of which there are now numerous examples)[47] to a wider and wider set of long-term, contextual case studies, to assess the extent to which these cases reinforce or contradict or necessitate a modification of the frameworks in question. Given the points often made in the literature about there being a lack of engagement with firsthand data relating to terrorist violence,[48] the richness of historical evidence and analysis could be of high importance here, as we collectively harmonise the insights of the idiographic and the nomothetic within our research community.

The other important area in terms of efficacy would be systematically to pursue the implications of the historian's instinctive scepticism about supposed inevitabilities. Sharp-eyed scholars have noted elsewhere how often people fail to get the futures they wanted and for which they have striven.[49] As a cross-case basis for exploration, it would be valuable to examine how often this was indeed the case with terrorist actors, what it was that made it so and how the various participants in the terrorist drama adapted and responded to this outcome.

One final area of proposed research regarding consequences would be this: to devote more collective expertise than has hitherto been the case to studying the experiences of the victims of terrorism. There has been some pioneering work done in recent years in this field.[50] But, as with the targets of other forms of political mobilisation,[51] so too there is room for much more historical research into the many contexts and contours of terrorist victimhood, and the long-lasting, heterogeneous nature of that phenomenon.[52]

---

47 English, *Does Terrorism Work?*; Muro (ed.), *When Does Terrorism Work?*; Abrahms, *Rules for Rebels*.
48 See, for example, R. Jackson, M. Breen Smyth and J. Gunning (eds.), *Critical Terrorism Studies: A New Research Agenda* (London, Routledge, 2009), pp. 17, 219.
49 R. F. Foster, *The Irish Story: Telling Tales and Making It Up in Ireland* (London, Penguin, 2001).
50 J. Argomaniz and O. Lynch (eds.), *Victims of Terrorism: A Comparative and Interdisciplinary Study* (London, Routledge, 2015); J. Argomaniz and O. Lynch (eds.), *Victims and Perpetrators of Terrorism: Exploring Identities, Roles and Narratives* (London, Routledge, 2018); R. Alonso, 'Victims of ETA's Terrorism as an Interest Group: Evolution, Influence and Impact on the Political Agenda of Spain', *Terrorism and Political Violence* 29/6 (2017).
51 L. Bosi, M. Giugni and K. Uba (eds.), *The Consequences of Social Movements* (Cambridge, Cambridge University Press, 2016), p. 9.
52 T. Knatchbull, *From a Clear Blue Sky: Surviving the Mountbatten Bomb* (London, Hutchinson, 2009); R. O'Rawe, *In the Name of the Son: The Gerry Conlon Story* (Newbridge, Merrion Press, 2017).

When terrorist violence has harmed civilians, this has tended to damage the cause of those behind the violence;[53] it has often also produced intensified polarisation and complex responses which have damaged those in whose name the violence was supposedly justified.[54] But there has been less historical analysis of this and other aspects of victim experience than would be ideal. One key aspect of this would be to analyse historically the long-term effects of terrorist violence and its consequences on already vulnerable groups and individuals.

Brian Glyn Williams's chapter in this volume reflects on the appalling cruelty of violence practised by various jihadist groups in Iraq upon civilian victims there. This represents surely a central aspect of such terrorists' effect; it should define much of what we think about groups like ISIS (in contrast to so much Western focus, which has been on the much lower-level threat to people beyond the Middle East). And the long-term, evolving nature of this brutal legacy is something to which historical enquiry could continue powerfully to contribute.

Appropriate Response

A vast amount has been written in the literature about what we supposedly know about appropriate responses to non-state terrorism. This is a vital theme since, as noted, responses to terrorism tend to change the world far more than do acts of non-state terrorism themselves.[55] There can, of course, be far more than the countering of terrorism going on in counterterrorist activities: economic, political, sectional and individual agendas can also find their home in that complex realm of action. This book's chapters do imply, however, that serious-minded attention to long and complex pasts provides an important foundation for thinking about best response, when the latter is considered to focus on countering and diminishing terrorist violence.

Effective responses to terrorism will concentrate on containing and limiting it rather than extirpating it entirely.[56] Reflection on the contextual cases

---

53 E. Berman, J. H. Felter and J. N. Shapiro, *Small Wars, Big Data: The Information Revolution in Modern Conflict* (Princeton, Princeton University Press, 2018); Byman, *Al-Qaida, the Islamic State and the Global Jihadist Movement*, pp. 135–6; Abrahms, *Rules for Rebels*.
54 T. Abbas, 'Muslim Minorities in Britain: Integration, Multiculturalism and Radicalism in the Post-7/7 Period', *Journal of Intercultural Studies* 28/3 (2007).
55 G. Chaliand and A. Blin (eds.), *The History of Terrorism: From Antiquity to ISIS* (Oakland, University of California Press, 2016), p. xv.
56 Crenshaw and LaFree, *Countering Terrorism*, p. 175; Richardson, *What Terrorists Want*, pp. 10–11; 246–9.

carefully studied in this book – Israel/Palestine, Ireland, Pakistan, Colombia, Russia, Peru, the Netherlands, Spain, Iraq, the USA, Africa – make that point very forcibly in their drawing attention to the persistence of various kinds of terrorism in those contexts. Individual terrorist campaigns and most terrorist organisations will come to a conclusion; but terrorism as such does not do so,[57] traditions of resistance can endure longer than particular organisational adherents to it, and even when terrorism largely seems to conclude, it very often continues in changed form.[58]

In tune with this book's historical centre of gravity, it is important that responses to terrorism are realistic in their recognition of the long duration of the enmities and the polarisation that can be involved in serious terrorist conflicts and their legacies. After the Northern Ireland conflict had effectively ended, Irish republican ex-prisoner Sam Millar wrote fascinating novels which repeatedly and gruesomely depicted Ulster unionist enemies as vile villains. So, for example, in *The Darkness of Bones* (2006) a child-abuser bears the name of a former Northern Ireland prison officer from the jail in which Millar himself had been incarcerated. This was an officer whom the IRA had killed in 1978, and a man whose fictional namesake in Millar's novel is vengefully killed by having his genitals and head cut off, and a metal rod forced into his anus.[59] So the brutal hatreds that ignite violence are reinforced by it and can long endure. The terrorist groups in which states have most interest are in fact long-term in two senses: they exist for a lengthily violent time (as with the PLO, Hamas, the FARC, the IRA, the UVF (Ulster

---

57 B. Hoffman, 'Rethinking Terrorism and Counter-Terrorism since 9/11', *Studies in Conflict and Terrorism* 25/5 (2002), p. 314.
58 Major terrorist campaigns or traditions are less likely to end completely than they are to fade into comparative triviality (with residual lethality). For one well-studied case, see 'New IRA: Our War Goes On', *Sunday World*, 11 February 2018; M. Frampton, *Legion of the Rearguard: Dissident Irish Republicanism* (Dublin, Irish Academic Press, 2011); S. A. Whiting, *Spoiling the Peace? The Threat of Dissident Republicans to Peace in Northern Ireland* (Manchester, Manchester University Press, 2015); J. Horgan, *Divided We Stand: The Strategy and Psychology of Ireland's Dissident Terrorists* (Oxford, Oxford University Press, 2013); J. F. Morrison, *The Origins and Rise of Dissident Irish Republicanism: The Role and Impact of Organisational Splits* (New York, Bloomsbury, 2013); P. M. Currie and M. Taylor (eds.), *Dissident Irish Republicanism* (London, Continuum, 2011); M. McGlinchey, *Unfinished Business: The Politics of 'Dissident' Irish Republicanism* (Manchester, Manchester University Press, 2019).
59 S. Millar, *The Darkness of Bones* (Dingle, Brandon, 2006); D. McKittrick, S. Kelters, B. Feeney, C. Thornton, *Lost Lives: The Stories of the Men, Women and Children Who Died as a Result of the Northern Ireland Troubles* (Edinburgh, Mainstream, 2001), p. 771. See also S. Millar, *Bloodstorm* (Dingle, Brandon, 2008); S. Millar, *The Dark Place* (Dingle, Brandon, 2009).

Volunteer Force), al-Qaida and other major actors), and the political struggles to which they relate have very long roots in the past.

Major terrorist organisations themselves recognise the need to prepare for and engage in long-term struggle.[60] It may be less appealing for people to hear that living with and containing terrorism are more appropriate responses than striving to eradicate it completely. But terrorism's long past suggests that the more modest goal here is the more effective, life-saving one. Frequently, there have been disastrous consequences when states have exaggerated the threat faced from non-state terrorism and when they have consequently overreacted. This can take the form of counterproductive military endeavours which help to stimulate the terrorism that they are intended to uproot;[61] but there are also major questions about the economic costs involved in vast counterterrorism, and the societal consequences of these.[62]

The UK's 2018 iteration of its counterterrorism strategy sensibly reflected an emphasis on risk-reducing containment, and on the continuation of normality: 'CONTEST's overarching aim remains to reduce the risk to the UK and its citizens and interests overseas from terrorism, so that our people can go about their lives freely and with confidence.'[63] What is required is a proportionate, commensurate response to the actual danger generated by terrorism: 'sensible and moderate policy decisions based on a realistic appraisal of the threat'.[64]

Does terrorism's long past suggest that countering terrorism involves a need to address root causes behind the violence? The evidence from this book suggests that any other approach would be myopic. It is not that easy answers regarding responses to terrorism will automatically emerge from deep knowledge of why African, Dutch, Pakistani, American, Russian or other violence has occurred. But to respond without such understanding

---

60 S. McChrystal and E. Chapin, 'The Business of Terrorism', *PRISM* 8/2 (2019); English, *Does Terrorism Work?*
61 B. G. Williams, *Counter Jihad: America's Military Experience in Afghanistan, Iraq and Syria* (Philadelphia, University of Pennsylvania Press, 2017); K. McConaghy, *Terrorism and the State: Intra-State Dynamics and the Response to Non-State Political Violence* (Basingstoke, Palgrave, 2017); English (ed.), *Illusions of Terrorism and Counter-Terrorism*.
62 J. Mueller and M. G. Stewart, *Terror, Security and Money: Balancing the Benefits, Risks and Costs of Homeland Security* (Oxford, Oxford University Press, 2011); J. Mueller and M. G. Stewart, *Chasing Ghosts: The Policing of Terrorism* (Oxford, Oxford University Press, 2016).
63 'CONTEST: The United Kingdom's Strategy for Countering Terrorism', June 2018, p. 7; cf. D. Omand, *Securing the State* (London, Hurst and Company, 2010).
64 Crenshaw and LaFree, *Countering Terrorism*, p. viii; cf. M. Sageman, *Misunderstanding Terrorism* (Philadelphia, University of Pennsylvania Press, 2017), pp. 21–2.

makes that response far more difficult to craft appropriately. Again and again in this book, brutal terrorist violence has been shown to emerge from a complex set of causes, within which problems of state or societal legitimacy and power have been prominent. Likewise, the actions of states (whether Israel, Spain, the USA, the UK or others) have repeatedly been part of a mutually shaping, escalatory relationship of violence. Responding effectively to non-state terrorism requires a framework of explanation which looks at state as well as non-state action in the turbulent past.

Historians are well placed here to offer ever-richer analyses of relevance to such effective responses to terrorism, since their approach is likely to focus on long-term, contextually nuanced, very specific relational dynamics and inheritances, involving world-historical forces of nation, state, religion, economy and culture.[65] Complex power relationships in the past do not necessarily legitimise merciless violence in response, especially given the strategic inefficacy so evident in terrorist experience;[66] but amnesiac condemnation of contemporary violence is both ill-informed and likely to be counterproductive, as it prevents full appreciation of why the violence seems legitimate to its supporters. Greater historical awareness in public and political and journalistic discussion would offer an important contribution here, and historians' public voice could be of value. For one thing, the often-assumed binaries in settings of terrorist violence (Basque versus Spanish, Irish versus British, Sunni versus Shia) imply both a neater division than historians know to have existed, and also a greater sense of inevitability than is justified.[67] In terms of religion and terrorism, it is very often intra-religious as well as inter-religious tension that is significant; and it is frequently (as chapters in this book have made clear) simultaneously about religion and also nationalism and also social and personal networks.[68]

As just suggested, the counterproductive aspects of exaggerated and clumsy military state response to terrorism are well documented from a wide variety of sources.[69] This has been reflected in the chapters in this

---

65 For an excellent statement of this point in relation to a region that frequently features in analyses of terrorism, see J. L. Gelvin, *The Modern Middle East: A History* (Oxford, Oxford University Press, 2016).
66 English, *Does Terrorism Work?*
67 Gelvin, *Modern Middle East*; Cannadine, *Undivided Past*; English, *Irish Freedom*; English, *Does Terrorism Work?*
68 Cf. Pedahzur and Perliger, *Jewish Terrorism in Israel*.
69 R. A. Clarke, *Against All Enemies: Inside America's War on Terror* (London, Free Press, 2004); J. Nixon, *Debriefing the President: The Interrogation of Saddam Hussein* (London, Bantam Press, 2016); M. Stohl, R. Burchill and S. Englund (eds.), *Constructions of Terrorism: An Interdisciplinary Approach to Research and Policy* (Oakland, University of California Press, 2017), p. 228; Berman, Felter and Shapiro, *Small Wars, Big Data*, pp. 7, 198–200; N. Brooke, *Terrorism and Nationalism in the United Kingdom: The Absence of*

book, including Julie Norman's analysis of Israel/Palestine, Fearghal McGarry's treatment of Ireland and Rory Cox's essay on history, terrorism and the state. It is also important to note that terrorists have repeatedly sought to provoke states into just such counterproductive overreaction,[70] that aggressively far-reaching responses to perceived threats have long been offered by states (including liberal-democratic ones)[71] and that the effects of non-violent engagement with terrorists can be complex and multifaceted also (a theme explored carefully by Joseph Morrison Skelly in this volume). More broadly, again and again, state action and non-state action have existed in a mutually shaping antagonism and intimacy, and (as Steve Hewitt suggests in this volume) there remains a need for more historical research on counterterrorism and its complex effects. Significantly, the fact that military means have severe limits in terms of what they can achieve against terrorism has been widely recognised in the existing scholarly literature.[72]

It is important to stress the contingency of much of this state action. Brian Glyn Williams's chapter in this book reflects that in his explanation of the rise of ISIS, and of the role within that process of the contingent decisions made and actions taken by Western states in their responses to 9/11 and other terrorism. Crucial to understanding such subjects is another area in which contextually focused historians might make an ever-greater contribution: the recognition of just how divergent different geographical points of vision and experience can be in terms of terrorism and responses to it. Primary-source-attentive historians can do something, at least, to offset the profound imbalance that exists in the scholarly centre of gravity within the study of terrorism (with the vast preponderance of academic work being generated in Western countries, and far less in settings most likely to undergo large-scale and enduring terrorism and counter-terrorism). Richard Reid's chapter on Africa, Dayyab Gillani's on Pakistan and Cecilia Méndez's on Peru all point the way impressively here.

Historians will increasingly be able to offer long-term analysis of some crucial aspects of contemporary responses to terrorism. It seems plausible to hypothesise, for example, that the use of drones in Western states'

Noise (Basingstoke, Palgrave Macmillan, 2018), p. 170; Byman, *Al-Qaida, the Islamic State and the Global Jihadist Movement*, pp. 115–16, 203.

70 T. Parker, *Avoiding the Terrorist Trap: Why Respect for Human Rights Is the Key to Defeating Terrorism* (London, World Scientific Publishing, 2019), pp. 117–39.

71 A. Thomson, *Outsourced Empire: How Militias, Mercenaries and Contractors Support US Statecraft* (London, Pluto Press, 2018).

72 A. Roberts, 'Terrorism Research: Past, Present and Future', *Studies in Conflict and Terrorism* 38/1 (2015); Cronin, *Ending Terrorism*, p. 8; J. Stern and J. M. Berger, *ISIS: The State of Terror* (London, Williams Collins, 2015), p. 235.

counterterrorism will prompt various forms of counterproductive outcome, including the stimulation of violent reaction, to accompany the kinetic, tactical value that some have also identified. As so often in previous periods, the history of twenty-first-century drone counterterrorism is likely to demonstrate some tactical efficacy, complemented by considerable blowback in terms of popular and political opinion in areas that are targeted (and in which civilian casualties have sometimes been high).[73] There has already emerged a very useful literature on drones,[74] but long-term analysis will require further historical approaches, since full assessment of the efficacy or effect of drone use will have to move beyond the short term. Contextually sensitive analysis, based on a wide range of first-hand and other data, will also be essential, and this could represent a policy-serious and intellectually significant contribution by historians to the understanding of terrorism and counterterrorism.

There is widespread agreement on the significance of intelligence in countering non-state terrorism,[75] and this has been reinforced by the observations of many different kinds of practical actor.[76] Put another way, when insufficiently accurate and up-to-date intelligence is the basis for counterterrorist operations, the consequences can be lastingly counterproductive.[77] But, while the vital importance of gaining, accurately interpreting and effectively responding to intelligence about terrorist opponents is a crucial aspect of successful state response, there remains sharp dispute about precisely how decisive it has been in particular historical contexts, and about some of the darker aspects of legacy

---

73 J. Zulaika, *Hellfire from Paradise Ranch: On the Front Lines of Drone Warfare* (Oakland, University of California Press, 2020).

74 Birmingham Policy Commission, 'The Security Impact of Drones: Challenges and Opportunities for the UK', 2014; Zulaika, *Hellfire from Paradise Ranch*; M. J. Boyle, 'The Costs and Consequences of Drone Warfare', *International Affairs* 89/1 (2013); B. G. Williams, 'The CIA's Covert Predator Drone War in Pakistan, 2004–2010: The History of an Assassination Campaign', *Studies in Conflict and Terrorism* 33/10 (2010).

75 A. Roberts, 'The "War on Terror" in Historical Perspective', *Survival* 47/2 (2005), p. 109; M. Howard, 'What's in a Name? How to Fight Terrorism', *Foreign Affairs* 81/1 (2002), p. 9; Berman, Felter and Shapiro, *Small Wars, Big Data*; Townshend, *Political Violence in Ireland*, p. 403; S. Hewitt, *Snitch! A History of the Modern Intelligence Informer* (London, Continuum, 2010).

76 W. Matchett, *Secret Victory: The Intelligence War That Beat the IRA* (Lisburn, Hiskey, 2016); W. Matchett, 'Security: Missing from the Northern Ireland Model', *Democracy and Security* 11/1 (2015); G. Bradley and B. Feeney, *Insider: Gerry Bradley's Life in the IRA* (Dublin, O'Brien Press, 2009); E. McGuire, *Enemy of the Empire: Life as an International Undercover IRA Activist* (Dublin, O'Brien Press, 2006); E. Collins, *Killing Rage* (London, Granta, 1997); D. Omand, 'What Should Be the Limits of Western Counter-Terrorism Policy?', in English (ed.), *Illusions of Terrorism and Counter-Terrorism*; English, *Does Terrorism Work?*, pp. 124–6.

77 M. J. McCleery, *Operation Demetrius and Its Aftermath: A New History of the Use of Internment Without Trial in Northern Ireland, 1971–75* (Manchester, Manchester University Press, 2015).

that are involved.[78] These long legacies require that, among others, historians are involved in the debate; the policy and political effects of such discussions make them a site for potentially valuable societal contribution from such scholars. In democracies, the issue of obtaining secret intelligence remains a complex and problematic one. Who should oversee those who pursue and hold such intelligence? What should be the limits placed upon those who are engaged in intelligence work? How should societies deal with the issue of clashing freedoms: the freedom from surveillance, for example, but also the freedom to live safely and to be protected from violent harm? There have been valuable contributions regarding the morality and proportionality to which democracies should adhere.[79] But our understanding of long-term historical outcomes and their implications remains an area for further historical investigation. Moreover, in assessing the counterterrorist efficacy of various different approaches here, historical approaches can complement those which rely more heavily upon metrics.

This relates to another aspect of appropriate response, certainly from democratic states as they deal with terrorist threats. Lawyers have contributed brilliantly to our reflections on what is necessary, and on what should be avoided, when states react to terrorism. Restraint, proportionality, accountability, an adherence to democratic legal process and a respect for human rights have all emerged here as important themes.[80] Other scholars have contributed very helpfully too: 'The more western society reacts to terrorist assault with an answerable illegality, the more it depletes the very spiritual and political resources which it takes itself to be protecting.'[81] But prescriptions from non-historians could be very valuably complemented by further historical analysis of context and contingency on the basis of a wide range of first-hand sources. It is important to understand, for example, the historical context and dynamics of a particular state response at a particular time (Spain in the 1970s, Israel in the 1980s, the UK in Northern Ireland in the 1990s, the USA after 2001). Historical dynamics of those states and their evolution and practice; historical contextualisation of what was practically possible within the choice-range available at particular moments of

---

78 T. Leahy, *The Intelligence War Against the IRA* (Cambridge, Cambridge University Press, 2020); M. Cochrane and R. Monaghan, 'Countering Terrorism Through the Use of Informants: The Northern Ireland Experience', *Behavioral Sciences of Terrorism and Political Aggression* 4/1 (2012).
79 D. Omand and M. Phythian, *Principled Spying: The Ethics of Secret Intelligence* (Oxford, Oxford University Press, 2018).
80 C. Gearty, *Liberty and Security* (Cambridge, Polity Press, 2013); Donohue, *The Cost of Counter-Terrorism*.
81 T. Eagleton, *Holy Terror* (Oxford, Oxford University Press, 2005), p. 50; cf. Parker, *Avoiding the Terrorist Trap*.

crisis; the longer-term legacies of particular state responses, when viewed through the lenses of multiple first-hand sources – all of these provide areas in which historians could offer vital work to complement that of other disciplines.

One striking possibility relates to the use of torture during the post-9/11 period. It has been well established that interrogational torture is less effective than other methods in terms of gaining reliable and valuable counter-terrorist information.[82] It is also true that torture can frequently damage the state which practises it, in terms of undermining state legitimacy and morality, and through giving propaganda gifts to contemporary terrorist opponents.[83] But, given that states repeatedly engage in the same kinds of activity across different eras, it would be valuable to have systematic historical explanation for this pattern's occurrence, and long-term analyses of how much lasting damage is actually done, and in what ways. There is also the issue of what occurs beyond democracies. The historical study of authoritarian responses to terrorism remains at an early stage of development. Its importance is, however, undeniable, and it would be a very significant development were this comparative historical silence to be addressed. It might also be illuminating, as so often, to consider what this historical silence tells us about the wider societal and political contexts that produced it.[84] And terrorist silences also offer significant, wider opportunities for historians of the subject. There might be great benefit, for example, in examining historically those cases where significant terrorism did not emerge, despite there having existed some of the foundational elements which have elsewhere generated such violence. Some good work has already begun to emerge here, pointing to the long-term complexity of causation behind violence and also its absence,[85] and further opportunities for fruitful analysis exist elsewhere.

Existing research suggests that it is probably unhelpful to consider best responses to terrorism as involving the binary choice between either a war-based or a law-enforcement-based approach;[86] in cases of sustained terrorism, the

---

82 J. W. Schiemann, *Does Torture Work?* (Oxford, Oxford University Press, 2016); Matchett, *Secret Victory*, pp. 149–50; S. O'Mara, *Why Torture Doesn't Work: The Neuroscience of Interrogation* (Cambridge, Harvard University Press, 2015); E. G. Arsenault, *How the Gloves Came Off: Lawyers, Policy Makers and Norms in the Debate on Torture* (New York, Columbia University Press, 2017).
83 J. Comey, *A Higher Loyalty: Truth, Lies and Leadership* (London, Macmillan, 2018), pp. 100–10; Stern and Berger, *ISIS*, p. 253; Arsenault, *How the Gloves Came Off*, pp. 168–79; S. Raphael, C. Black and R. Blakeley, *CIA Torture Unredacted: An Investigation into the CIA Torture Programme* (The Rendition Project, 2019).
84 D. MacCulloch, *Silence: A Christian History* (London, Penguin, 2013).
85 Brooke, *Terrorism and Nationalism*. 86 Donohue, *The Cost of Counter-Terrorism*, p. 9.

most appropriate responses will probably draw on aspects of both. The central point seems to be that, in their reactions to terrorism, democratic states should adhere to established, proportionate and accountable frameworks of legal behaviour.[87] This is as relevant to the decision to go to war and to the behaviour of the military as it is to intelligence-led policing or the work of the courts. It does not preclude the introduction of special powers in times of perceivedly heightened threat, nor the possibility that those provisions might help save lives.[88] But the drafting and passing and monitoring of such provisions should all take place within appropriate, democratically supervised structures, and with a sense of what is proportionate to the actual threat being faced, and of what is appropriate within the rule of law. These suggestions are reinforced by the research embodied in this book, including the chapters by Joseph Morrison Skelly and Fearghal McGarry.

Similarly, this volume's historically minded chapters reinforce other aspects of what seems best in terms of response to non-state terrorism: the coordination of effort within and between states, and the maintenance of strong credibility in counterterrorist argument and analysis. As Beatrice de Graaf points out in her chapter on the Netherlands, terrorism in any given setting can only be understood if there is due attention to its connectedness with wider trends; Kieran McConaghy's and Rory Miller's chapters strongly echo that insight. These concentric circles of activity imply a need for connected responses. The effectiveness of terrorists is strengthened when they engage in successful alliances,[89] and – as so often – there are echoes here with counterterrorism. Successful reactions to terrorism tend to involve integrated, coordinated efforts within and also between states,[90] and much is known about the difficulties that can emerge when such coordination is absent.[91] After 9/11 there emerged far greater levels of counterterrorist intelligence-sharing and cooperation (intra-state as well as

---

87 English, *Terrorism: How to Respond*, pp. 133–6.
88 Donohue, *The Cost of Counter-Terrorism*, p. 333.
89 Moghadam, *Nexus of Global Jihad*; Bacon, *Why Terrorist Groups Form International Alliances*.
90 Crenshaw and LaFree, *Countering Terrorism*, pp. 55, 87–8; A. Pedahzur, *The Israeli Secret Services and the Struggle Against Terrorism* (New York, Columbia University Press, 2009), p. 9; R. Cormac, *Confronting the Colonies: British Intelligence and Counter-Insurgency* (London, Hurst and Company, 2013); English, *Terrorism: How to Respond*, pp. 136–40; B. Blumenau, *The United Nations and Terrorism: Germany, Multilateralism and Anti-Terrorism Efforts in the 1970s* (Basingstoke, Palgrave, 2014).
91 Byman, *Al-Qaida, the Islamic State and the Global Jihadist Movement*, pp. 33, 36–7; A. B. Zegart, *Flawed by Design: The Evolution of the CIA, JCS and NSC* (Stanford, Stanford University Press, 1999); A. B. Zegart, *Spying Blind: The CIA, the FBI and the Origins of 9/11* (Princeton, Princeton University Press, 2007); Neumann, *Radicalized*, p. xiv; McConaghy, *Terrorism and the State*, p. 129.

inter-state);[92] international and intra-state trust and coordination were interwoven when this worked well.

How can historians contribute most powerfully to the next stage of analysis here? Some recent developments yet await systematic historical enquiry, and these include the important question of how far Brexit will in practice affect inter-state coordination in counterterrorism. There is also scope for far more work to be done, on the basis of first-hand sources, to analyse the historical development and effects of the Five Eyes community (the USA, UK, Australia, Canada, New Zealand) and its counterterrorist work.

In terms of credibility, the United States was profoundly, lastingly damaged in its counterterrorist efforts by the flawed justifications that were offered for the early twenty-first-century Iraq War, and by the bloodstained imbroglio which ensued in the years after the 2003 invasion of that country. Attention to first-hand sources, and to long-term historical analyses, makes this unavoidably clear,[93] and it is underlined by Brian Glyn Williams in his contribution to this current volume. Credibility in counterterrorist argument clearly possesses various dimensions. These include the amount of information that is publicly provided about those counterterrorist measures which have had some success;[94] there is also the issue of whether claims by the state are sustainedly trusted, as well as the degree to which terrorist organisations themselves are sophisticated in their communication.[95] Not only is the validity of the message important, therefore, but the reliable credibility of the messenger is crucial too.[96] This is rarely straightforward, of course. President Donald Trump said many implausible and incredible things about terrorism; yet some of the policies of his regime in regard to terrorist violence were nonetheless marked by successes (the military campaign against ISIS being an example). There can be, as here, a dichotomy between public pronouncements and day-to-day policy implementation,[97] though

---

92 Comey, *A Higher Loyalty*, p. 81; J. Argomaniz, *The EU and Counter-Terrorism: Politics, Polity and Policies After 9/11* (London, Routledge, 2011); Omand and Phythian, *Principled Spying*, p. 32.
93 Clarke, *Against All Enemies*, pp. xvi–xix, 267–8; Williams, *Counter Jihad*; Nixon, *Debriefing the President*.
94 A. M. Hoffman and W. Shelby, 'When the "Laws of Fear" Do Not Apply: Effective Counter-Terrorism and the Sense of Security from Terrorism', *Political Research Quarterly* 70/3 (2017).
95 M. Feyyaz, 'Communication (Un)savviness and the Failure of Terrorism: A Case of Pakistani Terrorist Organisations', *Dynamics of Asymmetric Conflict* 13/1 (2020).
96 Byman, *Al-Qaida, the Islamic State and the Global Jihadist Movement*, p. 219.
97 P. R. Neumann, *Bluster: Donald Trump's War on Terror* (London, Hurst and Company, 2019).

there seems little doubt that the effective work done here by the president's regime has gained less widespread recognition precisely because of the credibility challenges that he possesses for many observers.

State credibility can often gain momentum through shrewd focus on the lack of credibility in the claims of one's terrorist adversaries. The inconsistencies and weakness in terrorists' own arguments can often be used effectively against them;[98] indeed, this is partly why communication (so valuably analysed in this volume by Brigitte Nacos and Melih Barut) remains so important an issue. There is also the issue of how far a state appears genuinely to want to improve the lives of the relevant populations. Service provision can be an important aspect of this, if well targeted to address local needs and if complemented by the creation of sufficient security through state capacity and control; so too the avoidance of harming civilians can clarify credible commitment to popular well-being.[99]

In all of this, historians' contribution to understanding the efficacy of counterterrorism in practice could yet make a much more powerful contribution. Martha Crenshaw has rightly and recently observed that 'A satisfactory understanding of what constitutes effective counter-terrorism also escapes us.'[100] That understanding will benefit greatly from historically minded work, including a contextual, primary-source-based appreciation of the ways in which different political and cultural contexts have shaped various states' responses to terrorism.[101]

As Bernhard Blumenau notes in this volume, different academic disciplines will tend to approach terrorism by asking different kinds of question, and interaction between disciplines therefore allows for understanding that would otherwise be unobtainable. The implications of genuinely interdisciplinary dialogue will be profound for our understanding of terrorism and of our responses to it. Neurobiological research has begun to question how much room remains for traditional understandings of individual free will,[102] and the consequences of this for research on (and public as well as legal responses to) terrorism might be very significant. Each scholarly discipline offers its own range of methodologies and distinctive insights; the only

---

98 D. Holbrook, 'Al-Qaida and the Rise of ISIS', *Survival* 57/2 (2015).
99 Berman, Felter and Shapiro, *Small Wars, Big Data*.
100 M. Crenshaw, 'Constructing the Field of Terrorism', in Chenoweth et al. (eds.), *The Oxford Handbook of Terrorism*, p. 719.
101 F. Foley, *Countering Terrorism in Britain and France: Institutions, Norms and the Shadow of the Past* (Cambridge, Cambridge University Press, 2013).
102 R. M. Sapolsky, *Behave: The Biology of Humans at Our Best and Worst* (London, Bodley Head, 2017), pp. 580–613.

effective way of generating cumulatively reliable understanding of a subject as vast and Protean and complex as terrorism is for scholars from different disciplines to listen to each other and, where feasible, to generate and test ideas in conversation and collaboration with one another. Amid this set of conversations, historians' questions allow us to see both the things that we think we know, and also areas of exciting future research on one of the most illuminating and compelling subjects open to historical interrogation.

Historians have made valuable contributions in the uncovering of previously silent pasts, respecting the unique particularity of each setting (as the basis for cross-case comparison), and being attentive to the need to avoid comfortable narratives in the aftermath of terrorising violence.[103] Exploring long-term legacies, on the basis of a wide range of mutually interrogatory (often first-hand) sources, with an eye to contingency and to the uniqueness of context, and with a scepticism regarding suspiciously neat models – such work allows historians to make a distinctive contribution to a fuller and more honest appreciation of the true legacies of terrorist violence. It is hoped that the historically minded essays in this current volume further enrich that process of understanding and debate.

Further Reading

E. Chenoweth, R. English, A. Gofas and S. N. Kalyvas (eds.), *The Oxford Handbook of Terrorism* (Oxford, Oxford University Press, 2019)

M. Crenshaw, *Explaining Terrorism: Causes, Processes and Consequences* (London, Routledge, 2011)

R. English, 'The Future Study of Terrorism', *European Journal of International Security* 1/2 (2016)

B. Hoffman, *Inside Terrorism* (New York, Columbia University Press, 2017)

L. Richardson, *What Terrorists Want: Understanding the Terrorist Threat* (London, John Murray, 2006)

---

103 D. M. Anderson and D. Branch (eds.), *Allies at the End of Empire: Loyalists, Nationalists and the Cold War, 1945–76* (London, Routledge, 2018).

Index

1920s Brigade, 459
7/7 London bombings 2005, 384
8chan (image board), 545
9/11 attacks, 79, 382–3

A History of Terrorism, 127
Abbas, Mahmoud, 617
Abdul Bari, Dr Muhammad, 584
Abergele bombing 1969, 486
Abu Ghraib prison, 459
   ISI attack 2013, 466
Abu Iyad (Salah Khalaf), 536
Abu Nidal Organisation, 159
Abu Sayyaf Group (ASG), 597, 603, 621
Action Directe, 490
Adams, Gerry, 488, 497, 611
Adams, Sam, 529
Adler, Emma, 639
African terrorism, 199
  American embassy bombings 1998, 200
  Angola, 213
  asymmetrical warfare, 212
    Angola, 213
    Eritrea, 213
    South Africa, 213
    Zimbabwe, 213
  complex and prevalent, 201
  control of people rather than land, 202
  Dark Continent mythology, and, 200
  Eritrea, 213
  Ethiopia, 219
  imperialism, and, 205
    anti-colonial insurgencies against, 206, 207
    official policy, 205
    targeting of non-combatants, 206
  Mau Mau uprising 1952–60, 208
    bitter fighting, 209
    British response, 209
    failure of, 210
    reinforcing white anxieties, 209
  modernity of, 214
    expression of ideology or insanity, 216
    historical grievances and practices, 216
    Rwandan genocide, 215
    Uganda, 215
  modes of violence, 202
  nineteenth century
    control of people and resources, 204
    European colonialism, and, 204
    slave trade, 203
  religious-based, 216
  shifta campaign, 207–8
  South Africa, 213
  state-sponsored, 220
    Libya, 220
  use of fear as weapon, 202
  vanguard of righteous struggle, 199
  Zimbabwe, 213
African Union (AU), 85
  al-Shabaab, curtailing, 217
Afula suicide bombing 1995, 163
agents provocateurs
  Irish Republican Brotherhood (IRB), undermining of, 263
  Provisional IRA (PIRA), undermining of, 276
agitational terror, 47
Aguirre, José Antonio, 178, 179
al-Abadi, Haider, 472
Al-Ahed ('The Pledge') (newspaper), 537
Al Askari mosque bombing, 463
al-Awlaki, Anwar
  assassination, 547
al Baghdadi, Abu Bakr, 466
al Baghdadi, Abu Omar, 466
  assassination, 473
al-Bashir, Omar, 220

Index

al-Endress, Waffa, 630
al-Issar, Redouan (Abu Khaled/the Shaykh), 355
Al Jazeera, 547
al Maliki, Nouri, 465, 466
Al-Manar ('The Beacon') (television station), 537
al Masri, Abu Ayub, 466
Al-Murabitun, 99
Al Nour 9 ('The Light') radio station, 537
Al Nusra, 467
Al Qaeda
  global movement, failure to establish, 93
  mass communication, use of, 547
Al Qaeda in Iraq (AQI). *See also* Islamic State in Iraq and Syria (ISIS)
  2008 reversals, 465
  Al Askari mosque bombing, 463
  al Baghdadi, Abu Omar, named as new leader of, 466
  Anbar Awakening, opposition to, 465
  establishment in Fallujah 2004, 460
  fleeing to Mosul and Baqubah 2006, 461
  loss of Sunni support, 464
  renamed as Islamic State in Iraq (ISI), 466
  Second Battle of Fallujah 2004, 460
  sectarian war, creating, 462
  Shiite response to, 463
    Al Askari mosque bombing, reaction to, 463
    American attempts to suppress, 464
    death squads, 463
  Shiites
    opinion of, 461
    suicide bombings against, 462
  Taliban, training for suicide bombing, 461
Al Qaeda in the Arabian Peninsula (AQAP)
  relocation to Yemen, 98
  Saudi Arabia
    counterterror campaign against, 98
    relaunching operations against, 98
Al Qaeda in the Islamic Maghreb (AQIM)
  transnationalist activities, 97
al Rantisi, Abdel Aziz
  assassination, 166
al Sadr, Moqtada, 463, 464, 465
al-Shabaab ('The Youth')
  core idealogy, 217
  emergence, 217
al-Takfir wa al-Hijra, 356
al-Turabi, Hassan, 220
Al-Wazir, Khalil, 157

al Zarqawi, Abu Musab, 458
  assassination, 465
al Zawahiri, Ayman, 467, 547
Alexander I, Tsar
  assassination, 344
Alexander II, Tsar
  assassination, 296, 299
Alexander the Great, 579
Algerian War, 1954–62, 211–12
Alianza Popular Revolucionaria Americana (APRA – American Revolutionary Popular Alliance), 429
Alliance Party
  Belfast Agreement, signing, 605
All-India Muslim League
  initial demands, 232
  two-nation theory, 233
American embassy bombings 1998, 200, 383, 594
American terrorism
  9/11 attacks, 382–3
  class conflicts, rooted in, 362
  domestic attacks
    declining since 1970s, 379
    failure to minimise white supremacist threats, 384
    increasing fears of, media representation, 379
    increasing fears of, underlying causes, 379
    Oklahoma City bombing 1995, 380–2
    overseas examples, 385
    right-wing ideologies, flourishing, 385
    self-fulfilling prophecy, 379
  ethnic and racial terrorism. *See* ethnic and racial terrorism
  political violence, and, 363
  post-9/11 attacks, 383
  revolutionary terrorism
    anarchist bombings 1919, 376
    Haymarket riot 1886, 373, 374
    immigrants, blamed on, 375
    Molly Maguires, 372
    revival of, 1960s and 1970s, 377
    South Braintree robbery and murders 1920, 376
    state repression, 375
    Unabomber, 377–8, 381
    Wall Street bombing 1920, 376
  transnationalist, 362
American Violence: A Documentary History, 363
Amir, Yigal, 163, 613

673

Index

An Phoblacht (Provisional Sinn Féin newspaper), 487
anarchist bombings 1919, 534
anarchist terrorism
  bombings 1919, 376
  Netherlands
    attempted Saint Nicholas bombing 1888, 340
    constitutional changes, 340
    foreign attacks, reports circulated, 339
    government reluctance to adopt antiterrorism laws, 341
    police preparedness, 341
    safe haven for fugitive terrorists from abroad, 341
  Russian Empire, and, 305–7
anarchist wave of terrorism, 531–4
anarchists
  newspapers, 1880s, 532
  pamphlets and leaflets, 534
anarcho-syndicalists, 306
Anbar Awakening, 465
Ancien Régime, 175, 176
Andean Regional Initiative, 602
Andrew, Christopher, 510
Angola, 213
Ansar Din, 99
anthrax attacks 2001, 382
anti-Ahmadiyya protests, 237
  Munir Report 1954, 239
  second wave, 240
  violence of, 239
anti-colonial insurgencies, 206
anti-colonial wave of terrorism, 534–9
Anti-Tech Revolution: Why and How, 378
Antonio Blanco, Pedro
  assassination, 192
Arab Nationalist Movement, 157
Arab Revolt 1936-9, 153
Arafat, Yasser, 487
Arana Goiri, Sabino, 177
Arendt, Hannah, 51, 55
Argitzen programme, 196
Arias, General Armando, 404
Aristocratic Republic 1895–1919, 439
Armed Struggle, 509
Armitage, David, 34
Arnold, Matthew, 580
Arroyo, Gloria Macapagal, 603
Art, Robert J., 512
Artigas, José, 431
ascari, 208
Ashaninkas, 451

Ashcroft, John, 577
Asiri, Abdullah, 98
Assassins, 525
Assifa
  initial attacks, 158
Association of South East Asian Nations (ASEAN), 85
  Islamist terror discussions 2002, 86
asymmetrical warfare
  Africa, 212
    Angola, 213
    Eritrea, 213
    South Africa, 213
    Zimbabwe, 213
  alternative to mass insurrection, 259
Atta, Mohammad, 637
Attlee, Clement, 42
Authorization for the Use of Force, 600, 620
Ayalon, Ami, 166
Ayatollah Khomeini, 243
Ayyash, Yahya
  assassination, 166
Azef, Yevno, 304

Baader–Meinhof group. *See* Red Army Faction (RAF)
Back to Barbarism, 586
Badr Brigades, 456, 464
Baer, Robert, 513
Bakunin, Mikhail, 290, 306, 532, 629
Balfour Declaration, 151
Baloch Raaji Ajoi Sangar ('Baloch nation independence front') (BRAS), 249
Balochi, Nasser, 549
Balochistan Liberation Army (BLA), 248
Balochistan Liberation Front (BLF), 248
Balochistan Republican Army (BRA), 248
Bangsamoro Autonomous Region of Muslim Mindanao (BARMM), 604
Barak, Ehud, 617
barbarians, 66–8
barbarism, 576–8
  existential threat
    adoption by Western politicians, 582, 583
    Christian radical/fundamentalist viewpoint, 585
    dehumanisation, and, 587
    formal academic literature, and, 586
    intellectual analyses, 585
    language use, media, 584
    Muslim condemnation, 584
    pushback against, 585

term not neutral or devoid of
meaning, 587
UN condemnation, 584
fundamentally uncivilisable, 581
hallmarks of, 579
identification of an Other, 580
modern associations broadly accepted, 582
ontological security/insecurity, and, 588
  challenge to security provider role, 589
  Cold War, end of, 589
  comforting narratives, 590
  crisis production, 591
  justification for non-liberal democratic actions, 590
opposition to civilised society, 579
religion and, association between, 580
replacing Cold War as existential threat, 583
roots of
  ancient era, 578
  Roman era, 579
savages, distinguished from, 581
support for, 580
threat of violence to civilised cultures, 580
Barcelona killings 2017, 583
Barco, Virgilio, 402, 406
Barelvi School of Islam, 238
Barrionuevo, José, 188
Barry, Tom, 276
Barzani, Masrour, 454
Barzani, Shirwan, 456
Basque Movement for National Liberation, 189
Basque Nationalist Party (Partido Nacionalista Vasco – Euzko Alderdi Jeltzalea, PNV/EAJ)
  2009 election loss, 193
  break with ETA, 193
  clashes with centre-left government, 178
  critical of ETA sabotage, 180
  dealings with ETA ceased, 193
  foundation, 177
  negotiations with ETA, 191
  post-Lizarra conservative criticism, 192
  pro-independence split, 177
  restoration of fueros policy, 177
  support for Aznar conservative government, 191
  two main achievements, 186
Basque Patriotic Left, 193, 196
Basque terrorism. *See also* Spain
  contentious claim-making, and, 174
  historical background

Basque Nationalist Party. *See* Basque Nationalist Party (Partido Nacionalista Vasco – Euzko Alderdi Jeltzalea, PNV/EAJ)
  double patriotism, and, 176
  industrial modernisation, and, 176
  Middle Ages, 175
  nineteenth-century conservative rule, 175
  master narrative, 173
  political decision by individuals, 174
Battalions of God, 456
Battle Against Anarchist Terrorism, 509
Battle of Algiers 1956–7, 42, 211
Battle of Karameh 1968, 158
Battle of Mosul 2016–17, 472
  atrocities during, 472
  execution of ISIS members, 472
Beam, Louis, 529
Begin, Menachem, 154, 156
Behal, Richard, 486
Beihl, Eugen, 183
Belaúnde Terry, Fernando, 447
Belew, Kathleen, 385
Belfast Agreement, 605, 615
Bengali nationalism, 481
Bergia, Elena, 640
Berlin, Isaiah, 104
Bernadotte, Folke
  assassination, 154
Bernays, Edward L., 543
Beslan hostage crisis 2004, 321
Betancur, Belisario, 403, 404
bezmotivniki (proponents of 'pure terror'), 306
Beznachaliye (Leaderless Resistance), 305
Bhutto, Zulfiqar, 246
Bibi, Asia, 245
Bielby, Clare, 632
Bildu
  formation, 196
bin Laden, Osama, 460, 547
Bin Mohamed Osman, Mohamed Nawab, 94
bin Nayef, Mohammed, 98
binary evolution of terrorism, 92
Birth of a Nation, 370, 542
Black Hand, 153
Black Hundreds, 309
Black Liberation Army, 597, 620
Black September Organisation (BSO), 159
  Munich Olympic Games attack 1972, 536
Black, Don, 544
Black-and-Tans, 255
Blair, Tony, 89, 583

675

Index

Blanco, Miguel Ángel
   execution, 190
Blanqui, Louis Auguste, 480
blasphemy-watchers, 245
Blind Spot: The Secret History of American Counterterrorism, 511
Blood and Rage: A Cultural History of Terrorism, 127, 506
Bloody Friday bombings 1972, 272
Bloody Sunday shootings
   1905, 301
   1920, 270
   1972, 272, 274
Blumenau, Bernhard, 670
Bobrikov, Nikolai Ivanovich
   assassination, 129
Bogotá car bombing 1989, 404
Bogotazo riot, 393
Boko Haram
   founding, 217
   transnationalist activities, 103, 104
Bologna train bombing 1980, 44
bombing of the mayors 1980, 161
booby traps, 472
Booth, John Wilkes, 367
Boston Marathon bombing 2013, 384
Boston Tea Party 1773, 529
bottom-up regionalisation, 88
Boutros Ghali, Yousef
   assassination, 41
Bouyeri, Mohammed, 356
Bovensmilde hostage crisis 1975, 348
Bowers, Robert Gregory, 385
Boxer Rebellion 1899–1901, 84
Boyle Mahle, Melissa, 513
Branch Davidians, 380
Breaking the Walls terror campaign, 466
Breen, Dan, 480, 481
Breivik, Anders Behring, 385, 544
Bremer, Paul, 457
Brexit
   counterterrorism, impact on, 669
Brides of Jihad, 472
Brigate Rosse. *See* Red Brigades (BR)
Brigitte, Willie, 89
Briscoe, Robert, 482
British Mandate Palestine, 482
Brown, John, 365–7
Brown, Warren, 572
Brundtland, Gro Harlem, 545
Brussels Declaration 2010, 196, 608
Búfalo Barreto, 442

BUND (All-Jewish Workers' Union in Lithuania, Poland and Russia), 309
Burckhardt, Jacob, 580
Burleigh, Michael, 127, 506
Burtsev, Vladimir, 299
Bush, George W., 583
Bustamante, Colonel Juan, 435
Bustamante y Rivero, José Luis, 445
   deposed by coup, 445
Bustamante y Rivero, Manuel, 441
Byzantine Empire, 73

Cagol, Margherita, 130
Callwell, Colonel Charles, 205
Cameron, David, 276
Camp David Accords
   1978, 161
   2000, 164
Canadian Network for Research on Terrorism, Security and Society, 6
Canadian Security Intelligence Service, 520
Canning, Manus, 482
Cano, Guillermo
   assassination, 404
Cánovas del Castillo, Antonio, 175
Carbonari, 480
Carrero Blanco, Luis
   assassination, 183
Carson, Edward, 255
Castaño, Carlos, 409
'Catechism of a Revolutionary', 284
caudillos, 430
Center for International Security and Cooperation (CISAC), 5
Center for Risk and Economic Analysis of Terrorism Events (CREATE), 5
Center for Security Studies (CSS), 5
Centre for Conflict, Security and Terrorism (CST), 5
Centre for Research and Evidence on Security Threats (CREST), 5
Centre for the Study of Terrorism and Political Violence (CSTPV), 5
chaikovtsy movement, 297
Chalk, Peter, 512
Chamberlain, Joseph, 204
Charlie Hebdo shooting, Paris 2015, 583
Charlottesville rally 2017, 385
Chechenisation strategy, 322
chernoznamentsy (Black Banner), 306
Chernyshevsky, Nikolay, 297
chevauchée (cavalcade), 74

Index

Chicago Project on Security and Threats (CPOST), 5
Chimurenga, 206
Chiquita Banana murders, 1990s–2000s, 410
Chittagong armoury raid 1930, 481
ChK (Bolshevik security service), 316
Christchurch mosque shootings 2019, 545
chulavitas (Conservative police), 392
circumcellions, 65–6
civil disobedience
　First Intifada, 162
　Second Intifada, 164, 166
Clan na Gael, 258, 479
Clansman, The, 370
Clapham, Christopher, 200, 202
Clarke, Tom, 263
climate of risk, 589
Cluseret, Gustave, 480
Coco, Francesco
　assassination, 121
Cohen, Hillel, 510
collateral damage, 166
collective conflict management arrangements, 87
collective punishment
　Chechnya, 319, 322
　Colombia, 405
　Palestinian Territories, 160
　Second Intifada, 167
Collins, Michael, 269, 480
Colombia Viva, 413
Colombian Communist Party (CCP), 397
　militias, 397
Colombian terrorism
　1980s
　　drug cartels, 403
　　FARC, alliances against, 402, 403
　　FARC, growth of, 402
　　M-19 occupation of Palace of Justice, 404
　　right-wing violence against UP, 404
　　Security Statute passed, 402
　　Statute for the Defence of Democracy, 406
　1990s
　　Convivir security cooperatives, 408
　　Córdoba and Urabá Self-Defence Forces, 409
　　FARC, ongoing struggle, 407
　　paramilitary operations, 408, 409, 410
　　United Self-Defence Forces of Colombia (AUC), 409, 410
　9/11 attacks, and
　　United Self-Defence Forces of Colombia (AUC), demobilisation, 415
　barriers to violence lowered, 398
　Cold War 1948–53, 394
　　armed militia attacks, 395
　　Liberal guerrilla movements, 395
　　paramilitary terror, 395
　communicative character, 388
　historical background, 387
　　Conservative Hegemony, 1886–1930, 391
　　La Violencia, 392–4
　　Liberal Republic 1930–46, 391
　　Thousand Day War 1898–1902, 391
　internal armed conflict 1964–present, 398
　　FARC, change into military organisation, 400
　　FARC, creation of, 400
　　M-19 (19 April Movement), 401
　　National Liberation Army (ELN), creation of, 399
　　National Liberation Army (ELN), territorial control, 400
　　Operation Marquetalia, 400
　　systemic conflict drivers, and, 399
　narco-terrorism, 390
　National Front, 397
　　CCP militias, creation of, 397
　　communist parties marginalised, 397
　　precursor to full-blown insurgency, 398
　post-9/11 attacks
　　Bogotá bombing 2003, 411
　　Bojayá cylinder bomb attack 2002, 411
　　Caguán peace process 1999–2002, 410
　　FARC, Uribe campaign against, 412–15
　　paramilitary operations, 413
　　United Self-Defence Forces of Colombia (AUC), operations, 414
　post-9/11 narrative, 389
　Rojas Pinilla coup 1953, 396
　strategically employed within historical experience, 389
comforting narratives
　ontological security, and, 590
Comisiones Obreras de Vizcaya, 179
communars, 306
communication. *See also* publicity
　interpersonal, 525
　　American anarchists, 1880s, 532
　mass, 526
　　Al Qaeda, 547
　　fascist movements, 542
　　Hezbollah, 537, 538
　　Iran hostage crisis 1979, 546

677

Index

communication (cont.)
  ISIS (Islamic State in Iraq and Syria), 548, 549
  Ku Klux Klan, 541
  Kurdistan Workers' Party (PKK), 538
  lone-wolf terrorism, 544
  Front de libération nationale (FLN), 535, 536
  Popular Front for the Liberation of Palestine (PFLP), 536
  Red Army Faction (RAF), 539, 540
  mass self-communication, 526
Communist Combatant Cells (CCC), 99
Communist Party of Peru-Sendero Luminoso (PCP-SL). *See* Shining Path
comparative micro-history
  exploring dynamics of violence, 34
Comunisti Organizzati per la Liberazione Proletaria (COLP), 631
Concierto Económico, 176
Conflict and Terrorism Studies (NZ), 6
conflict of legitimacies, 48
Connolly, James, 268
Conservative Hegemony 1886–1930, 391
consociation, 605
conspicuous publicity, 658
Convivir security cooperatives, 408
Corday, Charlotte, 628, 637, 638
Córdoba and Urabá Self-Defence Forces, 409
counterinsurgency campaigns
  Afghanistan, 600
  Algeria, 211
  Chechnya, 319, 320, 322, 323
  Colombia, 402, 601
  Dutch East Indies, 346
  Iraq, 459, 464
  Ireland, 276
  Kenya, 209
  Pakistan, 249
  Peru, 442, 447
  Philippines, 603
  Uganda, 215
counterterrorism
  histories
    state responses, 509
  human sources, utilisation of, 508
  law enforcement model, 513
  overreactions, 519
  relevant issues, 518
  scholarship
    Covert Human Intelligence Sources (CHIS), 516–18
    disciplines of, 504
    exclusive focus on history, 511
    grand historical studies, lack of, 507
    historical context, 510
    history challenging social sciences, 507
    human intelligence, use of, 516
    lack of centrality, British security state, 510, 511
    lack of engagement by security agencies and states, 513
    primary sources, lack of access to, 507, 515, 516
    professional memoirs, 513
    terrorists examining past practices for inspiration, 514
    terrorists learning from and reacting to, 514
    transnational comparisons, 512
Counterterrorism, 512
Covert Human Intelligence Sources (CHIS), 516
  continuation across four waves, 517
  historical background, 516
covert human sources, 508
Crelinsten, Ronald D., 512, 515
Crenshaw, Martha, 48, 514, 572, 587
crisis production, 591
Critical Terrorism Studies (CTS), 505
critical theory, 574
Crosby, Peter, 368
cross-border activity, 83
Crusius, Patrick, 385
Cuban Missile Crisis 1962, 591
Cubs of the Caliphate, 471
cult of personality, 425, 426
cult of the insurgent, 47
cult of the revolutionary, 39
cultural geography
  regionalisation of terror, understanding, 100
cultural relativism, 590
Cumann na mBan, 630
Cuzco Rebellion 1814–15, 434
Czolgosz, Leon, 533

Dabiq/Rumiyah (online magazine), 549
Daesh. *See* Islamic State in Iraq and Syria (ISIS)
Darul Islam (DI), 94
Das, Jatin, 481
'Das Konzept der Stadtguerrilla' ('The Concept of the Urban Guerrilla'), 539
Dashnaktsutyun, 308

Dawson, Graham, 636
Dawson's Field hijacking 1970, 159
death squads
    Colombia, 401, 403
    Shiite, Iraq, 456, 463
Death to Kidnappers (MAS), 403
de-Baathification, 457, 458
Declaration of Altsasu 2009, 196
Decline and Fall of the Roman Empire, 580
decolonisation terrorism
    Republic of the South Moluccas, 346–8
definitions of terrorism
    accepting multiple interpretations, 56
    'Cambridge school' scepticism, 32, 33
    characteristics, 49
    civil war studies, application of, 34
    constituted in different eras, 56
    critical method approach, 35
    effectively defined, 50
    evolved with practice of context, 37
    historiographical turn, and, 32
    Nietzsche, morality and, 32, 33
    operative force of ideas, 36
    US Code of Federal Regulations, 81
DeFreeze, Donald, 10
Degregori, Carlos Iván, 421, 425, 427, 428
Deir Yassin massacre 1948, 155, 156
    impact of, 155
Delpech, Thérèse, 586
Democratic Front for the Liberation of Palestine (DFLP), 158
Democratic Unionist Party (DUP), 605, 611, 615
Democrazia Cristiana (Christian Democrats), 113
Deng Xiao Ping, 426
Deobandi School of Islam, 238
    critical of Barelvi School, 239
    General Zia ul Haq, support from, 241
    hatred of Ahmadiyya community, 239, 240, 244
    opposition to creation of Pakistan, 238
    Shia sect, attacks on, 242
Dillon, John, 268
diplomacy
    accrued benefits, 596
        9/11 attacks, and, 598–601
        Basque peace process, 606–9
        international partnerships, 601–4
        IRA and Sinn Féin, 610–12
        multi-component strategy, 609–10
        Northern Ireland peace process, 604–6
    ambiguous results, 595
    incurred costs, 596, 612
        political leaders, 612–13
        political parties, 614–16
    limits to efficacy, 596, 616
        Israeli–Palestinian peace process, 616–19
        negotiations, rejection of, 619–21
    private negotiations, 594
    public non-negotiation principle, 594
    specific agents, focus on, 596, 597
    winding and circuitous process, 596
diplomatic history, 136
Direct Action (AD), 99
Disciplining Terror, 506
Dohrn, Bernadine, 130
Dolphinarium discotheque bombing 2001, 165
Donaldson, Denis
    assassination, 516
Donatists, 65
Donohue, Laura K., 510
double patriotism, 176
Douglass, Frederick, 487
Downing Street Declaration 1993, 605
Droit, Roger-Pol, 585
drones
    counterterrorism operations, and, 664
    ISIS use, 454
Duque, Iván, 418
Dutch East India Company, 94
Dutch East Indies, 345
    independence movements, 345
        declaration of Indonesian independence, 345
        Dutch government counterinsurgency operations, 346
        Republic of the South Moluccas, 346–8
Dutch terrorism
    1960s, 348
    1970s
        anti-terrorism units, creation of, 350
        information exchange with other officials, 353
        Munich Olympic Games attack 1972, impact of, 349
        Red Help network, 351
        superficial coverage and analysis of foreign attacks, 350
        sympathy with Moluccan separatists, 351
        Terror Letter, 350
    1980s, 353
        domestic activism, separation from, 353
        Salafist movement, 354
    9/11 attacks, impact of, 355

Dutch terrorism (cont.)
   El Tawheed mosque, radicalisation and, 355
   jihadist terror plots uncovered, 355
   populist movement against multiculturalism, 355
   Salafist distancing from, 356
   Theo van Gogh assassination, 356, 357
  anarchist
   attempted Saint Nicholas bombing 1888, 340
   constitutional changes, 340
   fears of becoming safe haven for foreigners, 341
   foreign attacks, reports circulated, 339
   government reluctance to adopt antiterrorism laws, 341
   police preparedness, 341
  Dutch East Indies, 1940s, 345
   Dutch government counterinsurgency operations, 346
   Indonesian independence, 345
   Republic of the South Moluccas, 346–8
  French Revolution, and, 335
   reign of terror, 336
  General Intelligence and Security Service (AIVD), restructuring, 357
  Jacobinism, and, 336–7
  mid-nineteenth century, 337, 338
  Second World War, and, 344
  security culture, 352
   fundamental changes, early twentieth century, 357
   post-Second World War, 345
  twentieth century, 342
   Alexander I assassination, impact of, 344
   Bolshevist terrorism, focus on, 342
   condemnation of foreign attacks, 343
   International Antimilitarist Association bombing 1921, 343
   Interpol, Netherlands as founding member, 344
  twenty-first century
   antiterrorism laws, 357
   decrease in reporting, 358
   monitoring of non-jihadists, 359
   Muslims joining IS abroad, 358
Duyvesteyn, Isabelle, 506

early socialist strain of terrorism, 531–4
Earnest, John, 385
Easter Rising 1916
  perceived as failure, 267
  popular support, 268
  propaganda of the deed, 266
  successful act of political violence, 266
  transnational elements of, 480
economic deprivation
  terror, driver of, 94
education
  terror, driver of, 94
Edward III, King of England, 73
Edward the Black Prince, 74–5
Eguiguren, Jesús, 193
Egypt–Israel Peace Treaty 1979, 161
El Paso shootings 2019, 385
El Tawheed Foundation, 354, 355
Emergency Law 1932, 429, 439, 443, 445
Empirical Studies of Conflict (ESOC) Project, 5
Endgame for ETA, 607
enforcement terror, 47
English bombing campaign 1939–40, 254
English, Richard, 509
Enniskillen bombing 1987, 277
Ensslin, Gudrun, 130
EOKA (Ethniki Organosis Kyprion Agoniston)
  IRA, contacts with, 482, 483
Ephron, Dan, 613
Eritrean Islamic Jihad, 221
Eritrean Liberation Front (ELF), 213
Eritrean People's Liberation Front (EPLF), 213
Erzberger, Matthias
  assassination, 343
Escobar, Pablo, 403
Escubi, José María, 182
ETA-Berri (New ETA), 182
ETA político-militar
  assassination of members by right-wing groups, 184
ETA VI, 182
Ethiopian People's Revolutionary Democratic Front (EPRDF), 219
ethnic and racial terrorism
  abolitionism, 365–7
  Abraham Lincoln, assassination, 367
  Harpers Ferry raid 1859, 366
  Ku Klux Klan
   early activities, 369
   foundation, 368
   recent focus on, 372
   reinvention, 1920s, 369, 371
   reinvention, post-Second World War, 371
   white supremacy, restoring, 369

minorities, against, 363, 365
  Native Americans, 364
  nineteenth century, 364
  similarities to foreign violence, 365
  symbolic or psychological dimension, 365
  Redemption movement/Redeemers, 368
Etxebarrieta, Txabi, 181
Euro-Atlantic Partnership Council, 599
European Union (EU), 85
  9/11 attacks, response to, 599
  Framework Decision on Combating Terrorism 2002, 357
  PKK declared as terrorist organisation by, 538
  Terrorist Organisations list, 407
Euskadi ta Askatasuna (ETA)
  anti-colonialist movements, inspiration from, 179
  Basque Nationalist Party, break from, 193
  Basque Nationalist Party, negotiations with, 191
  Brussels Declaration, 196
  costs of armed struggle, 197
  declaration of end of armed struggle, 194
  decommissioning of weapons, 197
  definitive cessation of armed struggle, 197
  ETA-Berri split, 182
  ETA VI split, 182
  foundation, 179
  Geneva discussions, 194
  gradual loss of support, 190
  isolation from PNV nationalism, 191
  kidnappings 1997, 190
  late 1970s attacks, 187
  Liberation Movement, moving away from, 196
  links to civil society, 189
  Madrid airport bombing 2006, 195
  Madrid cafe bombing 1974, 183, 184
  manifesto, 180
  Military Front
    Eugen Beihl kidnapping, 183
    first execution, 181
    self-governance as precondition for ending of violence, 186
    split from, 184
  PNV criticism of early sabotage, 180
  police response to, 187, 188
  restructuring, 182
  sabotage and street violence, 190
  'spirit of Ermua' protests against, 191
  sympathetic organisations, 188, 189
Euskadi ta Askatasuna (ETA) militar, 184
Euskadi ta Askatasuna (ETA) político-militar, 184
Euskal Herria, 175
Evans, Jonathan, 508
exemplary actions, 117
Extra-Parliamentary Left, 114, 115

family relationships
  female terrorists, explaining actions of, 639
Fanon, Frantz, 211, 514, 535
FARC, 396
  Bogotá bombing 2003, 411
  Bojayá cylinder bomb attack 2002, 411
  Caguán peace process 1999–2002, participation in, 411
  change into military organisation, 400
  creation, 400
  paramilitary response to, 407
  political legitimacy, loss of, 407
  political settlement of insurgency 2016, 418
  return to armed struggle 2019, 418
  size
    1980s, 402
    1990s–2000s, 407
  territorial domination, 400
  Uribe campaign against, 412–15
Fariola, Octave, 480
Farook, Syed Rizwan, 384
fascist movements
  mass communication, use of, 542
  social exclusion terrorism, 542
Fatah
  rise after Six Day War, 157–8
Fatimid Egypt, 73
Fear and Trembling: Terrorism in Three Religious Traditions, 127
fedayeen (storm fighters), 454
female agency
  political violence as, 624
Fenian Rising 1867, 480
Fenians
  formation, 479
  nineteenth-century dynamite attacks, 479
Fields, Jr., James Alex, 385
Final Act of Vienna 1815, 336
Finerty, John, 260
Finucane, Pat, 276
First Arab Congress 1913
  independence calls, 151
First Intifada, 162
fishing expeditions, 508

Five Eyes community, 669
'Flames of War' (ISIS film), 549
Foley, Frank, 512
Foley, James, 548
Force Publique, 206
Force Research Unit, 276
Ford, Patrick, 258, 259
foreign terrorist fighters (FTFs)
   Russia, a main source of, 326
      home radicalisation and violence, 327
      overall numbers, 326
      relocation to third countries, 327, 328
      returning to, 327
Fortuyn, Pim
   assassination, 355
Foucault, Michel
   barbarianism, and, 581
   descent, examination of, 33
   power relations, and, 32
Foundations of Modern Terrorism, 506
'four Cs' of historical enquiries (context, complexity, contingency and contestation), 36
four waves of terrorism, 44, 530
   anarchist wave, 531–4
   anti-colonial, 534–9
   New Left Wave, 539–41
   religious, 545–9
   right-wing terrorism, ignored, 44
   simplistic categories, 44
   teleological evolution, implying, 45
Franco, Francisco, 174, 178, 179
Frank, Leo
   lynching, 370
Frankfurt School, 574
Frantzman, Seth, 618
Franz Ferdinand, Archduke
   assassination, 40, 129
Free Wales Army (FWA)
   IRA, contact with, 484
Freiheit ('Freedom') (anarchist newspaper), 373, 532, 639
French Revolution, 335
   female participation in terrorism, 627–8
   Reign of Terror, 336
Friends of the Indians Society, 436
Front de libération de la Bretagne (FLB-ALB), 485
Front de libération du Québec (FLQ), 517, 519
Front de liberation nationale (FLN)
   French counterinsurgency against, 211
   mass communication, use of, 535, 536
   Philippeville massacre 1955, 211

Fronte di liberazione naziunale corsu (FNLC), 485
Fuerzas Armadas de Liberación Nacional (FALN), 597
Fuerzas Armadas Revolucionarias de Colombia. *See* FARC
Fujimori, Alberto, 447, 448, 449
Fuller, Christopher J., 510
future research
   causation, 651
      context, particularity and uniqueness, 653
      emotion, role of, 653
      ideology, importance of, 652
      lone-wolf terrorism, 652
      nationalism, vital part, 654
      political decision-making, impact on, 654
      significant knowledge of factors, 651
      sustaining causes subsiding, 655
      zealots, enthusiasts and initiators, large effects of, 654
   consequences, 656
      conspicuous publicity, 658
      how far terrorism works, 656
      non-strategic victories, 657
      paradox of publicity, 658
      polarisation and contingency, 657
   cruelty of violence, 660
   efficacy
      analysis for case studies, 659
      implications of scepticism about inevitabilities, 659
   extension of definitional debate beyond Western/English-speaking countries, 650
   female participation, 658
   policy effects of definitional dispute, 649, 650
   relationships, 649
   responses to terrorism, 660
      analyses of relevance, 663
      binary war-based or law-enforcement-based approach, 667
      Brexit, impact of, 669
      containing and limiting, 660, 662
      credibility in counterterrorist argument and analysis, 668, 669, 670
      intelligence, importance of, 665, 666
      long-term analysis, 664
      overreactions, 662, 663, 664
      polarisation, and, 661
      root causes, addressing, 662

state adherence to democratic
processes, 666
state coordination, 668
torture, use of, 667
victims of terrorism, 140, 659

Gadahn, Adam, 547
Gage, Beverly, 376
Gaitán, Jorge Elécier, 392
  assassination, 393
Galleani, Luigi, 376
Gamarra, Marshall Agustín, 431
gamonales, 428
Gandhi, Rajiv
  assassination, 96
Ganor, Boaz, 596
Garaikoetxea, Carlos, 186
gender politics
  female agency, 624
  female heroes, difficulty describing, 639, 640
  female violence seen as unnatural, 632
  French Revolution, 627–8
  gender, defining explanatory force, 625
  gender-transgressing qualities of terrorism, 633–8
  nineteenth century
    anarchist movements, 628–30
    emancipation, and, 641–3
    family relationships as factors explaining actions, 639
    female emancipation, and, 641
    heroes not normal women, 638
    women described as cruel and irrational, 632
  nineteenth-century terrorism, 625
    gender playing minor role, 626
  string gender-bias, 624
  twentieth-century terrorism
    female members, 630
    female participation, 630–2
  women's movement, and, 641
  women's participation, 130
  women's role, 139
gender-neutral terrorism studies, 626
genealogy of terrorism
  Algerian War, 42
  early twentieth century, global character, 39
  evolution of term and practice of violence, 43
  hiatus between 1914 and 1945, imagining of, 40

hibernation and re-emergence, 45
imperialism, challenging, 40, 42, 46, 84
narrative history, consensus on, 38
nationalist armed struggles, 43
non-state actors, identification with, 47
not preserve of any single ideology, 39
origins and historical narrative, 37
Paris Commune, neglecting of, 45
perspectives, post-Second World War, 47, 48
post-First World War, 41
post-French Revolutionary world, 38
religious nationalism, 43
Second World War as dividing line in narrative, 42
state-led violence, nineteenth and twentieth century, 46
wider political struggles, part of, 49
General Intelligence and Security Service (AIVD)
  restructuring, 357
  terrorism threat, identifying 2008, 356
Gershuni, Grigori, 301
Geuss, Raymond, 37
Ghulam Ahmed, Mirza, 240
Gibbon, Edward, 580
Ginbot 7, 219
Gladstone, William, 263
Global Terrorism Index
  Iraqi terror attacks, 2006–2015, 455
  Russian inclusion, 2002–2011, 314
global War on Terror
  Colombian appropriation, 412
  justification for regime change, 383
globalisation
  regionalisation, and, 82
Goebbels, Joseph, 543
Goldman, Emma, 532, 634
Goldstein, Baruch, 163
Goldstone Report, 168
Gómez Castro, Laureano, 395, 396
Good Friday Agreement 1998, 278, 279, 283, 496, 497
Gorriti, Gustavo, 424, 427
Goulding, Cathal, 483, 484
Graña, Francisco
  assassination, 445
Grand Ayatollah al Sistani, 463
Gray, John, 586
Great Irish Famine 1845–9, 479
grey zones, 103
Griffith, Arthur, 480
Grivas, Georgios, 42

Grossman, Judas, 306
Group in Support of Islam and Muslims (GSIM), 99
Grupos Antiterroristas de Liberación (GAL), 188, 607
Grygiel, Jakub, 586, 587
Guevara, Che, 487
Gulf Cooperation Council (GCC), 85
Gunpowder Plot 1605, 76–8
Gush Emunim, 161
Guzmán, Abimael (Presidente Gonzalo), 422, 425, 426

Habash, George, 96, 157, 158, 536, 658
hacendados (landowners), 428, 432, 433, 435
Hadera suicide bombing 1995, 163
Haganah (Defence)
  first major ideological split, 153
  formation, 152
Haganah-Bet
  formation, 153
Hamas
  military activities, 164
Harakat al Tahrir al-Watani al Filastini, 631. *See* Fatah
Harakat al-Muqawama al-Islamiyya (Islamic Resistance Movement). *See* Hamas
hard sciences
  historical research, borrowing from, 141
Harpers Ferry raid 1859, 78, 366
Haya de la Torre, Víctor Raúl, 429, 440
  call for violence against Cerro government, 442
Haymarket riot 1886, 373, 374
head tax (*contribución personal*), 433
Hearst, Patty, 9
Heilman
  Jaymie Patricia, 424
Heinzen, Karl, 531
Henry Dunant Centre for Humanitarian Dialogue, 194
Herero/Nama rebellion 1904–5, 207
heroes
  gendered meaning, 639
Herri Batasuna ('Popular Unity'), 188
  Argitzen programme, 196
  made illegal, 193
  Oldartzen programme, 190
Herzen, Alexander, 297
Herzenstein, Mikhail
  assassination, 310
Hezbollah
  mass communication, use of, 537, 538

transnationalist activities, 96
Higher Arab Committee, 153
Hillyard, Paddy, 518
Hitler, Adolf, 543
Hizb al-Tahrir, 354
Hizbul Mujahideen
  Pakistani sponsorship, 250
Hoffman, Bruce, 127
Hofstad Group, 356
Hofstadter, Richard, 363
Holland terrorism. *See* Dutch terrorism
Home Rule crisis 1912–14, 255
Hoover, J. Edgar, 376
horizontal diffusion
  regionalisation of terrorism, importance of, 101
house-borne improvised explosive devices (HBIEDs), 460
Hudood Ordinances 1979, 244
human intelligence. *See* Covert Human Intelligence Sources (CHIS)
human shields, 472
Hume, John, 274, 279, 615
Hundred Years War (1337–1453), 73
hunger strikes
  India, 481
  IRA political strategy, 277, 481, 488
  Red Army Faction (RAF), 494
Hussein, Saddam, 162, 569
Huysmans, Jef, 587

Ibarretxe, Juan José, 192
Il Popolo d'Italia ('The People of Italy'), 543
illegitimate violence, 51
  African resistance to colonisation, 206
  defining, 52
  Middle Ages, 70
Imarat Kavkaz (Islamic Emirate of the Caucasus), 324, 325, 327
Independent International Commission for Decommissioning, 496
Indian Revolutionary Army
  Chittagong armoury raid 1930, 481
Indianapolis Group of the International, 374
indirect deterrence, 157
informants
  historical use of, 517
  Irish Republican Brotherhood (IRB)
    execution of, 270
    undermining of, 261
  loyalist paramilitaries, number of, 276
  protection and safety of, 515
  records of, and access to, 515

Index

Inland Regional Center shooting 2017, 384
Inside Terrorism, 127
Institute on Global Conflict and Cooperation (IGCC), 5
Inter-American Court of Human Rights (IACHR), 404
Internal Macedonian Revolutionary Organisation (IMRO/VMRO), 344
International (World) Islamic Front for the Jihad Against Jews and Crusaders, 90
International Antimilitarist Association, 343
International Centre for the Study of Radicalisation (ICSR), 5
International Conference for Unification of Criminal Law 1935, 344
International Institute for Counter-Terrorism (ICT), 6
International Peace Conference 2011, 197
International Working People's Association, 373
interpersonal communication, 525
  American anarchists, 1880s, 532
Interpol
  creation of, 344
  German control, 344
Iollos, Grigori
  assassination, 310
Iparraguirre, Elena, 422
Iran hostage crisis 1979
  mass communication, use of, 546
Iraqi Counter Terrorism Service, 471
Iraqi terrorism
  Abu Ghraib prison scandal, 459
  American fatigue 2014, 468
  American troop surge 2007–8, 464, 465
  American troop withdrawal 2011, 466
  de-Baathification process, and, 457, 458
  Global Terrorism Index
    terror attacks, 2006–2015, 455
  ISIS (Islamic State in Iraq and Syria), 453
    Baghdad suicide bombings 2016, 455
    barbaric methods, 454
    Suicide Vehicle-Borne Improvised Explosive Devices (SVBIED), 454
  Operation Iraqi Freedom 2003, and, 456, 457
  Shiite terror campaign, 456
  Status of Forces Agreement 2008, 465
Irgun Zvai Le'umi (National Military Organisation)
  IRA collaboration, 482
  King David Hotel bombing 1946, 154
  market bombings, 154
  Second World War, cessation of attacks, 154

Irish Auxiliaries, 255
Irish border campaign 1919–21, 1956–62, 254
Irish Civil War 1922–3, 254
Irish Home Rule, 263, 266
  rejection of, 268
Irish National Liberation Army (INLA), 492
  Palestine Liberation Organisation (PLO), contact with, 493
  political orientation, 492
  procurement of weapons, 493
  Red Army Faction, overtures from, 494
  Revolutionary Cells (RZ), contact with, 493
Irish Republican Army (IRA). *See also* Official IRA; Provisional IRA (PIRA)
  transnationalist activities, 95
Irish Republican Brotherhood (IRB), 258, 479
Irish Republican Socialist Party (IRSP), 492
Irish terrorism, 254, *see also* Provisional IRA (PIRA)
  Anglo-Irish Treaty 1921, impact of, 272
  British paramilitary organisations, 255
  Fenian dynamite campaign 1881–5, 254, 257
    achievements, 265
    British agents provocateurs, 263
    British political exploitation, 263
    criticism of, 261
    defence of, 259
    Fenian objections, 261
    impact on British political and security establishment, 262
    Irish Republican Brotherhood, orchestrating, 258
    main conspirators, 258
    public support, 260
    rationale for, 259
    suspension, 265
  historical examples, 254
  IRA marginalisation in Irish Republic, 272
  Ireland, shaping and development, 257
  Irish Revolution 1916–21, 266
    achievements, 271
    British failure to penetrate republican movement, 270
    Easter Rising 1916, 266, 267, 268
    incoherent and counterproductive British response, 270
    struggle for self-determination against imperialism, 271
    targeting of police officers, 269
  loyalist violence, 255
  Northern Irish Troubles 1969–98
    British military responses, 272
    IRA car bombing campaign, 272

Irish terrorism (cont.)
　IRA long war strategy, 272
　Sunningdale and Good Friday
　　Agreements, differences between, 279
　partition, and, 282
　rich body of literature and sources, 256
　transnational character, 255
Irish War of Independence 1919–21, 254
Ishutin, Nikolay, 296
ISIS. *See* Islamic State in Iraq and Syria
Islamic Army, 459
Islamic College attack 1983, 161
Islamic Jihad, 163
Islamic State. *See* Islamic State in Iraq and
　Syria (ISIS)
Islamic State in Iraq and Levant, 93
Islamic State in Iraq and Syria (ISIS), 453, *see
　also* Al Qaeda in Iraq (AQI)
　Abu Ghraib prison break 2013, 466
　al Baghdadi, Abu Bakr, new leader, 466
　American air strikes against 2014, 470
　barbaric methods, 454
　　Baghdad suicide bombings 2016, 455
　　Suicide Vehicle-Borne Improvised
　　　Explosive Devices (SVBIED), 454
　Battle of Mosul 2016–17, 472
　　atrocities during, 472
　　execution of ISIS members, 472
　breaking from al Qaeda, 467
　Breaking the Walls terror campaign, 466
　Fallujah, recapture of 2014, 468
　mass communication, use of, 548, 549
　Media Diwan propaganda department, 549
　Mosul, capture of 2014
　　atrocities during, 469
　　strategy, 468
　　support and radicalisation for, 470
　movement into Syria, 467
　non-religious dimensions, 568
　Operation Inherent Resolve, against, 471
　post-caliphate insurgency, 473
　　American withdrawal, 476
　　nikayah (war of attrition), 474
　　resurgence cell attacks, 474
　　sanctuary in Western Iraq, 474
　Shiite Revenge of the Martyrs campaign
　　against, 467
　Sinai aircraft bombing 2015, 328
　Syrian civil war, involvement with, 471
　war chest, 474
　Western states' foreign policies,
　　influencing, 568, 569
Islamophobia, United States, 383, 384, 385

Ismaili Islam, 73
Israel–Jordan Peace Treaty 1994, 613
Israel–Palestine terrorism, 149
　1920s–30s riots and revolts, 152–3
　1949–67
　　founding of Palestinian resistance
　　　groups, 157
　　Israeli indirect deterrence policy, 157
　1967–80
　　Assifa attacks, 158
　　attacks on Israeli soil, 160
　　cyclic nature of violence, 160
　　Fatah, rise after Six Day War, 158
　　First Intifada, 162, 163
　　Jewish disruption of peace process, 161
　　Munich Olympic Games attack 1972, 159
　　non-Fatah factions, 158
　　Palestine splinter factions, 159
　　Palestinian aircraft hijackings, 159
　　Palestinian disruption of peace
　　　process, 160
　British obligations to Arabs and Jews,
　　151, 152
　Cold War dynamics, influence of, 171
　conflict dynamics, influence of, 169
　Gaza, Israeli responses
　　Operation Cast Lead, 168
　　Operation Pillar of Defence, 168
　　Operation Protective Edge, 168
　internal dynamics, influence of, 170
　Irgun campaigns. *See* Irgun Zvai Le'umi
　　(National Military Organisation)
　late nineteenth century and early twentieth
　　century, 151
　Lehi campaigns. *See* Lehi
　peace process, 616–19
　post-Cold War dynamics, influence of, 171
　post-Oslo Accords (1990s), 163–4
　Second Intifada, 164–7
　UN partition plan, 155
　West Bank settler attacks, 168
istimashiyoun (storm fighters), 454
istishahadayeen (suicide bombers), 461
Italy. *See also* Red Brigades (BR)
　post-Second World War political system
　　challenges to, 114
　　left vs right division, 113
　　PSI exclusion after 1972 election, 118
　　state repression of protests, 114, 115

Jabotinsky, Vladimir 'Ze'ev', 152, 482
Jackson, Richard, 577, 591
Jacobinism, 336–7, 571

Index

Jacquerie, 75–6
Jaffa riots 1921, 152
Japanese Red Army
   transnationalist activities, 95
Jarcke, Carl, 634
Jeffery, Keith, 510
Jemaah Islamiyah (JI or Islamic Group), 603
   establishment, 93
      links with Darul Islam (DI), 94
      links with existing nationalist movements, 93
Jensen, Richard Bach, 509, 517
Jerusalem riots 1929, 152
Jewish Resistance Movement, 154
Jewish Revolt (66 CE), 84
Jewish Underground. *See* Makhteret
John II, King of France, 74
Jubilee Plot 1887, 263
Juncker, Jean-Claude, 583

Kabul Shiite suicide bombing 2018, 584
Kaczynski, Ted, 377–8, 381
Kadyrov, Akhmad (Chief Mufti of Chechnya), 321
   assassination, 322
Kadyrov, Ramzan, 322
kadyrovtsy militias, 322
Kalyvas, Stathis N., 34
Karakozov, Dmitri, 296
Kautsky, Karl
   Bolshevism, criticism of, 46
Kenyatta, Jomo, 210
Kestenholz, Salomé, 639
Khaled, Leila, 131, 159, 640
Khan of Kalat (Ahmed Yar), 234
Khan, Abdul Ghaffar, 234
Khan, Imran, 247
Khan, Sadiq, 584
Khanafani, Ghassan
   assassination, 160
Khansa brigade, 472
Khasav-Yurt ceasefire 1996, 318
Khleb i Volya ('Bread and Freedom'), 305
King David Hotel bombing 1946, 154
King, Jr., Martin Luther, 487
Knights of the White Camelia, 368
Kony, Joseph, 215
Koopmans, Ruud, 109
Koordinadora Abertzale Sozialista (Patriotic Socialist Coordination), 189
Kravchinsky, Sergei, 298
Kropotkin, Pyotr, 290, 295, 306, 532
Krutwig, Federico, 180

Ku Klux Klan
   early activities, 369
   foundation, 368
   mass communication, use of, 541
   recent focus on, 372
   reinvention
      1920s, 369, 371
      post-Second World War, 371
   white supremacy, restoring, 369
Kurdistan Security Council, 454
Kurdistan Workers' Party (PKK)
   mass communication, use of, 538
Kuyper, Abraham, 342

La Violencia, 392–4
Lajpat Rai, Lala, 46
Langile Abertzaleen Batzordeak ('Patriotic Workers' Committees'), 188
Laqueur, Walter, 44, 127
Lara Bonilla, Rodrigo
   assassination, 403
Lashkar-e-Taiba, 89, 91
   Pakistani sponsorship, 250
Latin American terrorism
   nationalism, key elements of, 426
   nineteenth century
      terrorism as antithesis of liberalism, 431
      violence through fear by ruling interests, 430, 431
latrones, 64, 65
Law, Randall D., 505, 521
Le Caron, Henri, 517
Le Compte, Marie, 629
Leaderless Resistance, 529
League of Nations
   Convention for the Prevention and Punishment of Terrorism
      1937, 520–2
League of the Righteous, 456
legitimate power, 51
Leguía, Augusto B., 440, 441
Lehi
   attacks on British targets, 154
   Deir Yassin massacre 1948, 155, 156
Leizaola, Jesús María, 180
Lenin, Vladimir
   assassination attempt on, 316
   insurgent activities and old terror, distinguishing, 303
   SR terrorism, criticism of, 301
Lévi-Strauss, Claude, 590
Lew-Williams, Beth, 364
Lewis, Pedr, 484

Index

Liberal Republic 1930–46
  actions, 391
  attacks against Conservatives, 391
  end of, 392
Libyan Islamic Fighting Group, 97
Lincoln, Abraham
  assassination, 367
Linse, Ulrich, 630
Little, Earl
  attack on home, 371
Lizarra Agreement, 191
Llywelyn Jones, Emyr, 484
Lochte, Christian, 633
Lod Airport hijacking 1972, 159
London bombings 1974, 272
lone-wolf terrorism
  future research, 652
  mass communication, use of, 544
  mental illness, and, 379
  social exclusion terrorism, 544
  Surgut stabbings 2017, 327
López Pumarejo, Alfonso, 392
Lord Moyne
  assassination, 154
Lord Salisbury, 264
Lord's Resistance Army (LRA), 215
Loyal Nine, 529
Loyalist Vanguard movement, 487
Luther, Martin, 76, 527

M-19 (19 April Movement), 401
  growth, 402
  high publicity operations, 401, 404
Ma'alot massacre 1974, 160
Maccabean Revolt (167–160 BCE), 84
Macina Liberation Front, 99
MacStíofáin, Seán, 482, 483, 486
MacSwiney, Terence, 270, 481
madrassas, 241
  1980s growth, 242
Madrid airport bombing 2006, 607
Madrid cafe bombing 1974, 183, 184
Madrid railway bombing 2004, 91, 594
Mahdi (Messiah) Army, 456, 464
Maji Maji revolt 1905–7, 206
Majlis-e-Ahrar, 237
Majlis-e-Tahafuz-e-Khatme Nabuwat
  ('assembly to protect the finality of prophethood'), 245
Makhno, Nestor, 307
makhnovtsy peasant movement, 307
Makhteret
  formation, 161
  modelled on IRA, 482
  operational objectives, 161
Malatesta, Errico, 629
Malcolm X, 487
Mali bus bombing 2018, 584
Malik, Tashfeen, 384
Mallon, Seamus, 278, 614
Manchester Arena attack 2017, 583
Manifesto of Anoeta 2004, 196
Manifesto Zutik Euskal Herria 2010, 196
Manzanas, Melitón, 181
Marat, Jean-Paul
  assassination, 628
Mariátegui, José Carlos, 425
Marighella, Carlos, 539
market bombings, 154
Marković, Helene, 639
Marković, Zephrem, 639
Marquetalia bombing 1964, 400
Márquez, Iván, 418
Maskhadov, Aslan, 321
mass communication, 526
  Al Qaeda, 547
  fascist movements, 542
  Front de libération nationale (FLN), 535, 536
  Hezbollah, 537, 538
  Iran hostage crisis 1979, 546
  ISIS (Islamic State in Iraq and Syria), 548, 549
  Ku Klux Klan, 541
  Kurdistan Workers' Party (PKK), 538
  lone-wolf terrorism, 544
  Popular Front for the Liberation of Palestine (PFLP), 536
  Red Army Faction (RAF), 539, 540
Mau Mau uprising 1952–60, 208
  bitter fighting, 209
  British response, 209
  failure of, 210
  reinforcing white anxieties, 209
Mazower, Mark, 35
McAdam, Doug, 110
McBride, John, 480
McKinley, William
  assassination, 39, 509, 533
McMahon, Sir A. Henry, 151
McMaster, H. R., 12
McVeigh, Timothy, 44, 380–2, 544
Media Diwan, 549
Med-TV (television station), 538
Mein Kampf, 543
Meinhof, Ulrike, 493, 540
Mellows, Liam, 480, 488

688

Index

mental illness
  lone-wolf terrorism, and, 379
Mezentsev, Nikolai
  assassination, 298
MI5, 510, 511, 517
MI6, 510
Michel, Louise, 629, 638, 640, 642
Michelet, Jules, 633
Middle Ages
  Assassins, 73
Millar, Sam, 661
Miller, Abraham H., 585
Miller, Martin, 53, 506
Minimanual of the Urban Guerrilla, 539
Mirambo, 203, 204
mistis, 428
Mitchell, George, 604, 605
Mitzen, Jennifer, 593
modern state
  fundamental weakness of, 218
modernity
  terrorism, product of, 54
Molly Maguires, 372
Moluccan Suicide Squad, 348
Montoneros, 43
Moro Islamic Liberation Front (MILF), 93, 603, 621
Moro National Liberation Front, 603
Moroccan Islamic Combatant Group, 97
Morozov, Nikolai, 299, 532
Morrison, Danny, 488
mosque crawlers, 508
Mosser, Thomas J.
  murder, 378
Most, Johann, 260, 373, 532, 533
Mountbatten, Lord Louis
  assassination, 490
Movimiento Revolucionario Túpac Amaru (MRTA), 421
'mowing the lawn', 168
Mubarak, Hosni
  attempted assassination, 220
Mudiad Amddiffyn Cymru (Movement for the Defence of Wales)
  IRA, contact with, 484
Muenster Anabaptists, 527
  attacks against Protestants and Catholics, 528
  defeat of, 528
  printing pamphlets, 528
Multi-National Joint Task Force (MNJTF), 87
Munich Olympic Games attack 1972, 536
Munir Report 1954, 239

Muñoz Martinez, Monica, 364
Muralanda Vélez, Manuel (Tirofijo), 400
Murphy, Seamus, 483
Museveni, Yoweri, 215
Musharraf, General Pervez, 247
Muslim Brotherhood, 164

Naftali, Timothy, 511
Nakashidze, Mikhail
  assassination, 308
Naqshbandi Army, 459
narco-terrorism, 390, 412
Narodnaya Rasprava ('People's Reprisal'), 296, 297
Narodnaya Volya ('People's Will'), 284, 296–300
  addiction to terrorism, 299
  categorisation of, 289
  frequent and intense attacks, 299
  terrorism never central, 298
  terrorist activities, 296
  transnationalist activities, 133
narodniki movement, 297
National Consortium for the Study of Terrorism and Responses to Terrorism (START), 5
National Coordinator for Terrorism and Security (Netherlands), 357
National Front (NF), 397
National Intelligence Estimate (NIE)
  Iraq war 2006, 461
National Liberation Army (ELN), 399
  growth, 402
  insurgency ongoing, 418
  middle-class support, 399
  political platform, 399
  territorial control, 400
National Liberation Front. *See* Front de libération nationale
National Movement for the Liberation of Azawad (MNLA), 97
National Resistance Army, 215
National Security Doctrine (NSD)
  Colombia, 402
nationalist strain of terrorism, 534–9
nationalist/separatist terrorism
  Russian Empire, 307–9
Nebi Musa demonstrations 1920, 152
Nechayev, Sergei, 284, 296, 532
Nelson, Brian, 276
Netanyahu, Benjamin, 617
Netherlands terrorism. *See* Dutch terrorism
New Left Wave of terrorism, 539–41

newspapers. *See* mass communication
Nietzsche, Friedrich
  barbarianism, and, 580
  force and violence, shaping human condition, 53
  morality
    genealogy of, 32
    real, 33
  will to power, 32
Nizaris, 73
non-violent protest
  repression, Italy 1969, 114
  Russian Empire, 292
Nord-Ost hostage crisis 2002, 321
North Atlantic Treaty Organization (NATO)
  9/11 attacks, response to, 599
North Caucasus, 103
Northern Alliance, 600
Northern Ireland Peace Monitoring Report 2018, 605
Northern Ireland Troubles 1969–98, 254
Norwegian bombings and shootings 2011, 385, 544
Norwegian civil war 1130–1240, 72
Nyungu-ya-Mawe, 203

Ó Brádaigh, Ruairí, 486
O'Brien, Conor Cruise, 275
Ó Cadhain, Máirtín, 484
O'Donovan Rossa, Jeremiah, 258
O'Hara, Patsy, 494
O'Neill, Michelle, 611
Objectives Resolution 1949, 237
Odierno, General Ray, 465
Odría, General Manuel, 445
  fighting terrorism as political control, 446
  PAP
    outlawing, 446
Official IRA, 272
  creation of Irish National Liberation Army (INLA) and Irish Republican Socialist Party (IRSP), 492
  reluctance to defend Northern Ireland Catholics, 486
Ogaden National Liberation Front (ONLF), 219, 220
Okhrana
  ad hoc cooperation with European governments, 84
Oklahoma City bombing 1995, 44, 380–2, 544
Oldartzen programme, 190
ontological security, 577, 589
Operation Cast Lead, 168, 617

Operation Enduring Freedom, 600
Operation Enduring Freedom – Philippines, 603
Operation Inherent Resolve, 471
Operation Iraqi Freedom 2003, 456, 457
Operation Marquetalia, 400
Operation Pillar of Defence, 168
Operation Protective Edge, 168, 617
Operation Wrath of God, 159
Ordóñez, Gregorio
  assassination, 190
Organisation armée secrète (OAS), 211, 487
Organisation of African Unity (OAU)
  Islamic terror discussions 1992, 86
Oromo Liberation Front (OLF), 219
Ortbals, Candice, 624
Ortega Lara, José Antonio
  kidnapping, 190
Oslo Accords 1993, 162, 595, 612, 616
  limits of, 164
  post-Oslo terrorism, 163–4
Ospina Pérez, Mariano, 392
  assassination, 392
Otaegi, Ángel, 184
Otegi, Arnaldo, 193
outbidding, 165

Pacification Campaign, Peru, 437
Paisley, Ian, 605, 615
pajaros (armed assassins), 392
Pakistani independence, 232
  All-India Muslim League
    1946 election success, 233
    initial demands, 232
    opposition to, 234
    two-nation theory, 233
  Cold War tensions, effect of, 243
  created for Muslims or as an Islamic state, 235
  ethno-linguistic grievances suppressed, 236
  Islamic revolution in Iran 1979, effect of, 242
  partitioning, 233
  religious compromises and concessions, 236
  religious rule
    Ahmadiyya persecution, 244
    anti-Ahmadiyya protests, 237, 239, 240
    blasphemy against Prophet Muhammad, 244–6, 247
    constitutional changes, 1974, 241
    enforcement of 1974 constitution, 246

General Zia ul Haq, enabling, 241–2, 243, 244
martial law, imposition in 1958, 240
Objectives Resolution 1949, 237
post-Bhutto leaders, 247
secular and conservative Muslims, role of, 235
secular vision diminished, 235
Pakistani terrorism, 223
Afghanistan, and
Taliban, support for, 251
analysis of nascent state, 225
Balochistan province
insurgencies, 248
militant groups, 248
state counter-insurgency against, 249
Bangladeshi independence, and, 249
characterisation of country as security risk, 226
danger to Pakistani citizens, 226
deemed unique and novel, 225
fundamentalist appeasement and ethno-linguistic dissent, and, 236
Kashmir dispute, and, 250
extremist Islamist objectives, and, 250
state-sponsored covert warfare, 250
myopic understanding of, 231
nationalist violence, history of, 227
nuclear weapons, use of, 230, 231
religion favoured over nationalism, 252
religious dimension, 227
socio-economic conditions, and, 229
state-based terrorism, 229
state complicity, 228
stereotypical understanding of, post-9/11, 227
superficial and shallow engagement with, 223
visible international footprint, 228
Palestine Liberation Organisation (PLO)
move to diplomacy alongside armed struggle, 160
transnationalist activities, 96
Palestine National Liberation Movement. *See* Fatah
Palmer, A. Mitchell, 376
pan-Arabism, 158
pan-Celticism, 483
paradox of publicity, 658
Paredes Manot, Juan (Txiki), 184
Paris Commune
creation and suppression, 45, 46, 339
Paris Peace Treaty 1815, 336

Paris shootings 2015, 455
Parker, Tom, 514
strains of terrorism model, 506
wave theory, rejection of, 530
Parnell, Charles Stewart, 258, 263
partisan violence
Colombia, 393, 397
Partito Comunista Italiano (Italian Communist Party), 113
Extra-Parliamentary Left, withdrawal of recognition, 118
Partito Socialista Italiano (Socialist Italian Party), 114
Party of Russian Socialists-Revolutionaries, 296
Pashtun nationalism, 251
Passover bombing 2002, 165
Passover massacre 1974, 160
Pastrana, Andrés, 411
path incrementalisation, 335
Patriotic Union (UP), 405
right-wing response to, 405
Patterson, Henry, 35
pax colonia, 207
Peace League of Bourges, 70
Peace of God councils, 71
Pearse, Patrick, 266
Peltier, Leonard, 487
Pemuda Masjarakat (Free South Moluccan Youth), 347
Peres, Shimon, 612
periodisation of terrorism
9/11 attacks, 79
advantages, 58
barbarians, 66–8
dangers of, 58
filtering of sources, 59
language shaping perceptions and actions, 61
state violence, 60
evolving and shifting set of ideas, 62
finding similarities and differences across past and present, 62
hard to fit into conventional periods, 61
imperatives producing, 79
Middle Ages
Assassins, 73
chevauchée (cavalcade), 74
commoners, violence used by, 70
fear used instrumentally, 69
Gunpowder Plot 1605, 76–8
Hundred Years War (1337–1453), 73
Jacquerie, 75–6

periodisation of terrorism (cont.)
  lack of royal authority, 68
  legitimate and illegitimate violence, 70
  Peace of God councils, 71
  pillaging, 69
 Norwegian civil war 1130–1240, 72
 past attitudes of violence, 60
 Roman Empire, 63–6
Perovskaya, Sofia, 299
perpetrator bloc
 Colombia, 405
Peru Before the Shining Path, 424
Peruvian agrarian reform 1969, 428
Peruvian Apra Party (PAP), 440
 1931 election, response to, 442, 443
 assassinations carried out, 440
 Bustamante y Rivero, 1948 coup against, 445
 early commitment to revolutionary violence, 441
 ideological evolution, 441
 Law of Internal Security of the Republic, use of against, 446
 outlawing of, 444
Peruvian terrorism
 accusation of terrorism used politically, 423
 Alianza Popular Revolucionaria Americana (American Revolutionary Popular Alliance), 429
 Aristocratic Republic 1895–1919, 439
 disappeared persons, 422
 eighteenth century
  Friends of the Indians Society, 436
 law of terror 1867, 428
 Movimiento Revolucionario Túpac Amaru (MRTA), 421
 mystical relationship to violence, 427
 nineteenth century
  law of terror, 434, 435, 436
  state terror and conservatism, link with, 438
  state use of fear against population, 437
  terrorism as antithesis of liberalism, 432, 433
  threat of accusations, 438
  way of living/habit, 437
 Peruvian Apra Party (PAP)
  1931 election, response to, 442, 443
  1931 election, Sánchez Cerro counterinsurgency against, 442
  assassinations carried out, 440
  Bustamante y Rivero, 1948 coup against, 445

  early commitment to revolutionary violence, 441
  foundation, 440
  ideological evolution, 441
  Law of Internal Security of the Republic, use against, 446
  outlawing of, 444
 Puno rebellion 1866–8, 439
 Shining Path
  Abimael Guzmán, influence of, 425
  Ashaninkas, terror against, 451
  Belaúnde counterinsurgency against, 447
  disbandment, 422
  disregard for social organisations and movements, 425
  establishment, 420
  Fujimori anti-terrorism legislation, 447, 448
  initiators of revolution, 426
  nationalist rhetoric, lack of, 426
  no reference to historical past, 424
  operations, 420
  Quechua peasants, attacks on, 421
  violence as deliberate strategy, 427
  violence turned into ideology, 428
 twentieth century
  Emergency Law 1932, 429, 439, 443, 445
  factors shaping, 439
  multiple rebellions against Sánchez Cerro government, 444
  Odría dictatorship 1948–56, 445, 446
  Putumayo rubber industry, 450
  question of law, as, 438
  transfer from state to non-state actors, 440
 twenty-first century, anti-terrorism legislation, 448
Peruvian–Bolivian Confederation 1836–9, 430
Peshmerga ('Those Who Confront Death'), 454, 472, 476
Petraeus, General David, 464
PFLP-General Command (PFLP-GC), 160
Philippeville massacre 1955, 211
Philippines
 Operation Enduring Freedom, 603
Phoenix Park murders 1881, 261
Pierce, William Luther, 381
pillaging
 motives for, 69
Piłsudski, Józef, 309
Pipes, Daniel, 596
PIRA (Provisional IRA)

692

change of strategy
  acceptance of failure of stand-alone armed struggle, 495
  ANC and PLO political developments, and, 495, 496
  Good Friday Agreement 1998, positive dimensions of, 497
  Good Friday Agreement 1998, signing of, 496
  participation in other conflicts, 497
connections with ethno-nationalist groups
  Euskadi ta Askatasuna (ETA), 490
  Fuerzas Armadas Revolucionarias de Colombia (FARC), 490, 491
  Libya, 489
  limited use, 491
  Palestine Liberation Organisation (PLO), 489
Pittsburgh synagogue shootings 2018, 385
Plan Colombia, 412
Plan Lazo 1962, 400
Plazas, Colonel Alfonso, 404
Plekhanov, Georgi, 300
Plutarch, 579
pogroms
  anti-Armenian, 308
  anti-Jewish, 310
Police Service of Northern Ireland (PSNI)
  Catholic officers, 605
Policing, Intelligence and Counter-Terrorism (PICT), 6
Policy of Democratic Defence and Security (Democratic Security Policy, DSP)
  impact on guerrillas, 414
  role, 413
Polish National-Democratic Party, 309
Polish Socialist Party, 307
political (violent) masculinity
  interpretations of, 635
political violence
  outcome disconnected from history, 106
  processual approach, 107
    contextualising, 112–13
    contingency and conjuncture, acknowledging, 109
    countering ahistoricity and lack of context, 107
    historical analysis, 110–11
    non-linear fashion, 108
    recognising structural conditions, 108
    Red Brigades. See Red Brigades (BR)
    sequences of interactions, 109
Poloni-Staudinger, Lori, 624

Popular Front for the Liberation of Palestine (PFLP), 158, 631
  aircraft hijackings, 159
  mass communication, use of, 536
  transnationalist activities, 96
Popular Mobilisation Fronts, 456, 472
popular sovereignty
  terrorism, generator of, 55
Popular Unity. See Herri Batasuna ('Popular Unity')
Porter, Bernard, 510
Post-Soviet Russian terrorism, 1990s–2010s, 313
  Chechnyan insurgency, 318
    ending of federal counterinsurgency operations, 323
    federal Chechenisation strategy, 322, 323
    federal reconstruction and development aid, 322
    federal response, 319, 320
    federal smart suppression, 322
    first war, 318
    internal splits within, 321
    main generator of terrorism, 319
    Salafism-jihadism, 320, 321
  conflict-related, 314
  contributing factors, 315
  Global Terrorism Index ranking, 314
  no direct parallels to Russian Empire terrorism, 314
  North Caucasus, 324
  Russian Empire terrorism, relevance of, 315
Post-Soviet Russian terrorism, 2010s–present
  foreign terrorist fighters (FTFs)
    home radicalisation and violence, 327
    overall numbers, 326
    relocation to third countries, 327, 328
    returning to Russia, 327
    source of, 326
  North Caucasus, 325
    radicalisation into jihadists, 325
    physical proximity to regions of conflict, 326
    possible radicalisation of labour migrant population, 328
    sustained decline, 324
    threats to Russian citizens abroad, 328
Poway synagogue shootings 2018, 385
Powell, Jonathan, 595, 605, 611, 615, 650
Prado, Mariano Ignacio, 435
Price, H. Edward, 48
price-tag attacks, 168
Primo de Rivera, General Miguel, 178

Princip, Gavrilo, 129
process-tracing, 111
prolepsis, 33
propaganda of the deed, 39
  definition, 362
  Easter Rising 1916, 266
  Fenian dynamite attacks, 479
  Johann Most, and, 260, 532
  New Left Wave 1960s–80s, 539
Protestant Reformation, 527
Provisional IRA (PIRA), 272. *see also* Irish terrorism
  building political support for concessions, 278
  Irish Republic hostility to, 275
  legitimising of violence, 257
  long war strategy, 272
  marginalisation in Irish Republic, 272
  prisons, use for mobilising public support, 277
  Red Army Faction (RAF), adoption of hunger strikes, 494
  shift towards Marxism, 485
  similarity between Provisional IRA and Official IRA, 275
  violence
    achievements, 278
    British response, 276
    counterproductive impact, 274
    gradual loss of public support, 277
    longevity, explaining, 281
    mobilising pressure for political agreements, 280
    modernity, and, 282
    purpose of, 273
    rarely popular, 279
    support for, 274
    support for, outside Northern Ireland, 274
    winning mass support, 280
Provisional Sinn Féin
  International Bureau, establishment, 486
proxies
  coercion through terror, 573
pub bombings 1972, 272
publicity. *See also* communication
  conspicuous, 658
  distinct objectives, 526
  oxygen or lifeblood of terrorism, 525
  paradox of, 658
Puno rebellion 1866–8, 439
Pushkin, Alexander, 628
Putin, Vladimir, 320

Qadri, Mumtaz, 245
Qassam Brigades, 163
Qibya raid 1953, 157
Quadruple Alliance 1815, 336
qualitative dynamic of terrorist violence, 35
Queen Juliana of the Netherlands
  abduction attempt 1975, 347
Qurei, Ahmed, 618
Qutb, Sayyid, 514

Raab, Rudolf, 493
Rabbi Kahane, 163
Rabin, Yitzhak
  assassination, 163, 613
  Nobel Peace Prize, awarding of, 612
Rabitatul Mujahidin (International Mujahideen Association), 93
radical abolitionism, 365–7
radio. *See* mass communication
Rahmat Ali, Choudary, 233
Rajoy, Mariano, 197, 608
Rapoport, David, 44, 127, 506, 524, 530
RaRa (Revolutionary Anti-Racist Action), 353
Rathenau, Walther
  assassination, 343
Ravachol, 634
raznochintsy (intelligentsia)
  political engagement of, 303
  public support for terrorism, 311
  resentment against police repression, 301
Reagan, Ronald, 582, 594
rebeque, 437
Red Army Faction (RAF), 43
  European network, failure to establish, 99
  hunger strikes, adoption of, 494
  mass communication, use of, 539, 540
  propaganda by deed, understanding, 539
Red Brigades (BR), 15 *See also* Italy
  armed struggle, 118
  arrest of leaders, impact of, 120
  compartmentalisation of structure, 119
  Francesco Coco, assassination, 121
  proactive and deliberate, 119
  recognition as committed force, 121
  shift from local struggles to direct attacks, 119
  sociopolitical conflict, impact of, 121
  early activities, 117
  exemplary actions strategy, 116
  ideological background, 116
  origins and announcement of, 116
  propaganda by deed, understanding, 539
  symbolic property damage, focus on, 117

Index

Red Help network, 351
Red Shirts, 368
Redeemers/Redemption movement, 368
Redmond, John, 266
regional organisations (ROs)
  proliferation of, 85
  reactive consolidation, 86–8
  security governance, 85
regionalisation
  definition, 82
  economic interdependence, and, 82
  globalisation, and, 82
  modern nation-state, application to, 83
regionalisation of terrorism, 81
  distinct and overlapping factors, 81
  factors limiting or stopping, 99
  historical perspective, 99
    geographical concentration, 102
    grey zones, 103
    horizontal diffusion, and, 101
    major limitation, 102
    non-territorial agility, and, 103
    objectives determining geographical location, 100
    regions, illustrating change and development, 100, 101
    Russia and former Soviet republics, 103
    scholarly debates, adding value to, 105
  home region as focal point, 92
  non-state actors
    crucial role, 88
  Okhrana, nineteenth century, 84
  online sources and databases, tracking, 101
  reactive consolidation, 86–8
  regional organisations (ROs), 85
  replacing waning local influence, 97
  self-preservation, as, 98
  state actors, distancing from, 97
  transnationalism, 136
    historical examples, 95, 96
    not necessarily evidence of regionalisation, 96
  uneven distribution across world, 102
Reid, Richard (shoe bomber), 384
religion, 551
  complex interweaving of factors, 566
  contribution to terrorism, 552
    context, and, 553
    dynamics, and, 555
    grievances and commitments, and, 553
    reflecting and reinforcing instincts, 556
    varying kinds of contributions, 554

  limiting terrorism, 556
  lack of references in combating religious terrorism, 558
  mistaken enmity between faiths, 557
  part of beliefs leading to terrorism
    ethno-nationalism, and, 563–6
    instrumentalism, and, 562, 563
    not detachable, 561
  state lack of understanding, 567
religious strain of terrorism, 545–9
religious terrorism
  complex interweaving of factors, 567
  existential threat, 558
  ISIS
    other dimensions, and, 568
    Western states' foreign policies, influencing, 568, 569
  novel or familiar phenomenon, 560
  single causes, complex phenomena, and, 567
  suffering not to be dismissed, 559
religious wave of terrorism, 545–9
Republic of the South Moluccas (Republik Maluku Selaton), 346
res publica, 63
Return of the Barbarians: Confronting Non-State Actors from Ancient Rome to the Present, 586
Revenge of the Martyrs campaign, 467
Revolutionary Antifascist Patriotic Front (FRAP), 184
Revolutionary Armed Forces of Colombia (FARC-EP). *See* FARC
Revolutionary Boards (juntas), 393
Revolutionary Cells (RZ), 493
Revolutionary Organization 17, 620
revolutionary terrorism, 48, 213, *see also* Russian Empire terrorism
  anarchism, rooted in, 362
  Johann Most, and, 373
  Russia, 291, 295
    active and sustained, 311
    blurring of, 302
    customary, regular method of struggle, 311
    not cross-class or mass sociopolitical phenomenon, 311
    not lead or winning tactic, 312
  United States
    anarchist bombings 1919, 376
    Haymarket riot 1886, 373, 374
    immigrants, blamed on, 375
    Molly Maguires, 372

Index

revolutionary terrorism (cont.)
  Oklahoma City bombing 1995, 380–2
  revival, 1960s and 1970s, 377
  South Braintree robbery and murders 1920, 376
  state repression, 375
  Unabomber, 377–8, 381
  Wall Street bombing 1920, 376
Reynders, Didier, 583
Rice, Condoleezza, 199
Richardson, Louise, 512
Rigby, Lee, 584
right-wing terrorism, 44
  Colombia, 404, 405
  four waves model, ignored by, 44
  Russian Empire, 309–10
  Spain, 184
  Yitzhak Rabin assassination, 163
Rimington, Stella, 513
ritualised violence
  Colombia, 393
Riveros, Antonio, 436
Road Map to Peace 2003, 617
Robertson, Lord George, 599
Robespierre, Maximilien de, 126
Robinson, William Erigena, 261
Rocker, Rudolf, 640
rocket attacks, 167
  Israeli response, 167
Rodríguez, Jose A., 513
Rodríguez Gacha, Gonzalo, 404
Rojas Pinilla, General Gustavo, 396
Roman Empire, 63–6
Romano-Jewish War, AD 66–73, 64
Rosas, Juan Manuel de, 431
Rosenau, William, 512
Rote Zora, 631
Rothmann, Bernhard, 528
routines of conflict
  ontological security, and, 593
Royal Canadian Mounted Police (RCMP)
  counterterrorism issues list 1980s, 519
  Front de libération du Québec (FLQ), campaign against, 519
ruga ruga, 204
Russian civil war 1918–22, 317
Russian Empire terrorism. *See also* revolutionary terrorism
  anarchist terrorism, 305–7
  causal explanations, 291
    contextualising the turn, 295
    dominant root causes approach, 291, 293
    dynamic sociopolitical processes, 294
    failed transition to capitalist system, 293, 294
    first peak, 296
    non-terrorism tactics, 292
    second peak, 296
    socio-revolutionary anti-government, domination of, 295
  definition, 285
    asymmetrical nature, 288
    direct combat between non-state and state actors excluded, 287
    non-state actors, 286
    non-state actors and state actors, intertwined, 286
    political violence, distinguishing, 285
    state actors, 286
  integral part of first historical wave, 284
  Narodnaya Volya, 296–300
  nationalist/separatist terrorism, 307–9
  research literature
    limited, 288
    prevalence of Marxist-Leninist approaches, 289
    Western sources, 289
    work conducted in Europe and United States, 289
  revolutionary ideologies and violent tactics, difference between, 290
  right-wing terrorism, 309–10
  socialist-revolutionary (SR), 300–5
Russian Revolution 1905–7
  Polish Socialist Party violence, 307
  terrorist attacks, statistics, 302
  underlying reasons, 301
Russian Socio-Democratic Workers' Party, 309

Sacco, Nicola, 376
Sadat, Anwar
  assassination, 613
Sadi Carnot, Marie François
  assassination, 341
St Petersburg Protocol 1904, 520
Saipov, Sayfullo, 548
Salafism, 238
  Chechnya, 320
  Netherlands, 354
Salafist Group for Preaching and Combat (GSPC). *See* Al Qaeda in the Islamic Maghreb (AQIM)
Sales, Nathan, 619
Salter, Mark, 576, 577
Sampson, Nicos, 483

696

Sanborn, Alvan F. 634, 635
Sánchez Cerro, Luis Miguel, 440
  assassination, 443
  response to PAP attacks, 442
  rise to presidency, 441
Sand, Karl Ludwig, 628, 634
Sands, Bobby, 277, 488
Sands McKevitt, Bernadette, 279
Santa Cruz, Marshall Andrés de, 430
Santos, Juan Manuel, 418
Santrich, Jesús, 418
Saudi Arabia
  Al Qaeda in the Arabian Peninsula (AQAP), counterterror campaign against, 97
savages
  barbarians, distinguishing from, 581
Savinkov, Boris, 304
Sazonov, Yegor, 301
Scappaticci, Freddie, 276
Schiller, Friedrich, 633
Schleyer, Hanns-Martin, 540
Schmid, Alex P., 512
Schönfeld, Hans, 636
Schutzstaffel (SS), 542
Science of Revolutionary Warfare, 514, 533
Scott, Joan, 625
Second Battle of Fallujah 2004, 460
Second Intifada, 164–7
  civil disobedience, 166
  civilian deaths and injuries, 166
  collective punishment, 167
  Israeli response, 165, 166
  Palestinian power struggles, 165, 167
  rocket attacks, 167
  violence of, 164
security culture
  definition, 333
  Netherlands, 352, 357
    post-Second World War, 345
  nineteenth century, 338
security governance, 85
Security Statute, 401
Sejersted, Francis, 612, 613
self-determination
  twentieth century, 534
Seljuk Turks, 73
Senderista violence, 438
Senderistas. *See* Shining Path
Sendero Luminoso (SL). *See* Shining Path
September 12 thinking, 513
Serxwebun (newspaper), 538
sexual terrorism
  Iraq, 2014, 469

Shabak, 165
Shamir, Yitzhak, 514
Shariat Court, 244
Sharif Hussein of Mecca, 151
Sharif, Nawaz, 247
Sharon, Ariel, 157, 617
Shehada, Salah
  assassination, 166
Sheikh Abu Risha
  assassination, 465
Sheikh Ahmed Ismail Hassan Yassin, 163
Sheikh 'Izz al-Din Abd al-Qadir al-Qassam, 153
Sheikh Yassin
  assassination, 166
Shevyryov, Pyotr, 299
shifta, 207–8
Shia theocracy, 243
Shiite terror campaign, 456
Shining Path
  Abimael Guzmán, influence of, 425
  Ashaninkas, terror against, 451
  Belaúnde counterinsurgency against, 447
  disbandment, 422
  disregard for social organisations and movements, 425
  establishment, 420
  Fujimori anti-terrorism legislation, 447, 448
  initiators of revolution, 426
  mystical relationship to violence, 427
  nationalist rhetoric, lack of, 426
  no reference to historical past, 424
  operations, 420
  Quechua peasants, attacks on, 421
  violence as deliberate strategy, 427
  violence turned into ideology, 428
shoe bomber, 384
short-termism, 503
Sicarii ('daggermen'), 64–5, 524
silent racism, 450
Silke, Andrew, 504, 506
Simmons, William Joseph, 369, 371
Singh, Bhagat, 41
Sinn Féin
  2020 electoral success, 616
  accrued benefits, 610–12
  Belfast Agreement, signing, 605
  role in Basque peace process, 497
Sipah-e-Sahabah, 242
Sipyagin, Dmitri
  assassination, 301
Sitter, Nick, 514
  strains of terrorism model, 506
  wave theory, rejection of, 530

Index

Six Day War 1967, 156
skirmishing. *See* Irish terrorism, Fenian dynamite campaign 1881–5
slave trade, 203
Small Wars, 205
smart suppression and prevention
   Chechnya, 322
Social Democratic and Labour Party (SDLP)
   Belfast Agreement, signing, 605
   electoral downturn, 614
social exclusion terrorism
   fascist movements, 542
   Ku Klux Klan, 541
   lone-wolf terrorism, 544
social media. *See* mass self-communication
Social Movement Studies
   political violence, positioning, 112
Socialist-Revolutionary (SR) terrorism, 300–5
societal cleavages
   Colombia, 399
Society of United Irishmen, 479
soft power, diplomacy, 609
soft regionalism, 88
Solana, Javier, 599
Soleimani, Qassem
   assassination, 475
Song of the Bell, 633
Sons of Liberty
   Boston Tea Party 1773, 529
   Committees of Correspondence, 529
   establishment, 529
   violence used for political objectives, 530
Sortu (Create), 608
Soufan, Ali, 513
Soumokil, Chris
   execution, 347
South Braintree robbery and murders 1920, 376
South West African People's Organisation (SWAPO), 487
Soviet Union terrorism, 1920s–80s, 316–18
Soyuz Rysskogo Naroda (Union of the Russian People), 310
Spain. *See also* Basque nationalism; Basque Nationalist Party (Partido Nacionalista Vasco – Euzko Alderdi Jeltzalea, PNV/EAJ); Euskadi ta Askatasuna (ETA)
   Basque double-track negotiations, 195
   double patriotism, 176
   Franco dictatorship, end of, 185
   fueros, conservative abolition of, 175
   Primo dictatorship, 178

Second Republic, 178
Special Assistance Units (Bijzondere Bijstands Eenheden, BBEs), 350
Special Irish Branch, 262, 517
Spengler, Oswald, 580
Spiegel, Steven L., 618
Spies, August, 374, 375
spirit of Ermua, 191
Spying Blind: The CIA, the FBI, and the Origins of 9/11, 512
SR-maximalists, 302
Stack, Sir Lee
   assassination, 41
Stalin, Joseph
   repressions, 1930s, 317, 330
Stampnitzky, Lisa, 6, 506
state, the, 55
   bureaucratisation of, 55
State Department (US)
   2019 Country Reports on Terrorism, 619
states
   definition, 51
   historical lineage, 54
   legitimate and illegitimate force, 51, 52
   terrorism used to attack enemies, 52
   terrorism, bound up with, 50
   terrorist movements, obsession with, 51
   violence, founded through, 53
states and terrorism, 571
   coercion of through terror, 573
   critical theory, 574
   future research into, 141
   historical tropes, 575
      civilisation/barbarian narrative. *See* barbarism
      modern terrorism posing original/unique threat, 575
   use of language, and, 573
Status of Forces Agreement
   withdrawal of US troops from Iraq, 2011, 465
Statute for the Defence of Democracy, 406
Stemler, Joachim, 493
Stepanova, Ekaterina, 98
Stern Gang. *See* Lehi
Stern, Avraham, 154
Stethem, Robert, 594
Stokes, Melvyn, 370
Stolypin, Pyotr, 302
Stormfront (website), 544
strains of terrorism, 530
   early socialist, 531–4
   nationalist, 534–9

religious, 545–9
Strasbourg shooting 2018, 524
strategy of tension, 115
Straw, Jack, 166
Struve, Amalie, 641
Struve, Gustav, 641
Study Group on Arab–Israeli Peacemaking, 618
Sturmabteilung (SA), 542
sub-state terror groups, 83
Suez Crisis 1956, 156
suicidal mass barricade hostage-taking Chechnya, 321
Suicide Attack Database, 5
suicide bombings
    Qassam Brigades, mid-1990s, 163
Suicide Vehicle-Borne Improvised Explosive Devices (SVBIED), 454
Sunni sect, 238
    Barelvi School of Islam, 238
    Deobandi School of Islam, 238
        critical of Barelvi school, 239
        General Zia ul Haq, support from, 241
        hatred of Ahmadiyya community, 239, 240, 244
        opposition to creation of Pakistan, 238
        Shia sect, attacks on, 242
Sunni Triangle, 461, 465
Sunningdale Agreement 1973, 279
Surgut stabbings 2017, 327
suspect community, 518
Symbionese Liberation Army (SLA), 43
    Patty Hearst kidnapping, 10
Syrian civil war, 467
    foreign fighters, and, 471
systemic conflict drivers
    Colombia, 399

Tablighi Jamaat, 354
Taliban
    suicide bombing, and, 461
Tamil Tigers
    transnationalist activities, 96
Tanzim Qaedat al-Jihad fi Bilad al-Rafidayn ('Al Qaeda in the Land of the Two Rivers'). *See* Al Qaeda in Iraq (AQI)
Tarrant, Brenton, 545
Taseer, Salman
    assassination, 245
Task Force Omega, 413
Tawhid wal Jihad (Monotheism and Holy War/Unity and Jihad), 455, 459
    Al Qaeda, merging with, 459

America, counterinsurgency against, 459
    recruitment of Sunnis, 458
    rejection of Baathist secularism, 458
    suicide bombings, 459
technological innovation
    barbarism, and, 586
Tehrik-e-Jafaria, 242
Tehrik-e-Labbaik ('movement by dutiful followers [of the Prophet]'), 245
Tehrik-i-Taliban Pakistan, 247
television. *See* mass communication
Tello, Alfredo, 442
temporary legitimacy
    peace process, and, 611
Ternera, Josu, 197
terrorism
    contemporary issue, perceived as, 505
    definition
        Dayyab Gillani, 224
        focus on political effect, 572
        Joseph Morrison Skelly, 596
        League of Nations Convention for the Prevention and Punishment of Terrorism 1937, 520–2
        non-consensus on, 647
        problems exaggerated, 648
        Richard English, 149, 362, 387
        sex- and gender-neutral, 626
    different disciplines asking different questions, 124
    distinct form of war, as, 52
    historical context deemed insignificant, 505
    path incrementalism, 335
    scholarship
        contesting new terrorism paradigm, 506
        evolving, 506
        historical surveys, post-2009, 506
    security culture. *See* security culture
    two faces, 335
    women. *See* gender politics
Terrorism: A History, 505
Terrorism and Political Violence Association (TAPVA), 5
Terrorism Studies
    historical approaches
        avenue for future research, 139–42
        complexity challenge, 134
        current enquiries, providing impetus, 130
        designing and directing projects, 135
        determining ending of terrorist activities, 131
        documentation, 131, 132–4

Terrorism Studies (cont.)
  economics, and, 138
  humanity surviving, 130
  interdisciplinary limitations, 142–4
  issues identified by other scholars, 135
  new areas and topics from other disciplines, 137
  new directions from other disciplines, 135
  non-state terrorism, ignored by scholars, 127
  non-Western global approach, 137
  past scholarship, 126
  political scientists, role in, 128
  recent studies, 128
  scholars aiding historians, 128
  sources from other disciplines, 142
  speculation limited, 132
  state-instigated violence, 127
  subfield in ascent, 129
  technology, and, 138
  no formal structure, 125
Terrorism, Transnational Crime and Corruption Center (TraCCC), 6
terroristic religious violence, 566
terruco, 423
Tewodros, 204
theatrical violence, 269
Thornton, T.P., 47
Thousand Day War 1898–1902, 391
'three E' techniques of enquiry (episodes, examples and effectiveness), 34
Tigray People's Liberation Front (TPLF), 213
Tilly, Charles, 111
Tomb of the Patriarchs bombing 1994, 163
top-down regionalisation, 88
torture
  Al Qaeda in Iraq (AQI), 460
  counterterrorism operations, and, 667
Trabelsi, Nizar, 637
tragic circularity of events, 418
transnationalism, 478
  historical examples, 95, 96
  Indian Revolutionary Army, modelled on IRA, 481
  Ireland
    Easter Rising 1916, 480
    Fenian dynamite attacks, 479
    importance of international struggles to some members, 488
    little practical support for other movements, 487
    origins, 479
    pan-Celticism, and, 483
    post-Second World War links to other groups, 482–4
    War of Independence 1919–21, 481
  Irgun Zvai Le'umi (National Military Organisation)
    IRA collaboration, 482
  Makhteret, modelled on IRA, 482
Trans-Sahara Counterterrorism Partnership (TSCTP), 87
Treaty of Guadalupe Hidalgo 1848, 364
Trepov, Fyodor, 298
TREVI (Terrorisme, Radicalisme, Extrémisme et Violence Internationale), 353
triangle of political communication, 525, 527
Trimble, David, 496, 615
Troelstra, Pieter Jelles, 343
Trotsky, Leon, 46
Trudeau, Pierre, 519
Trujillo insurrection 1932, 442
Trump, Donald
  Barack Obama, blaming for ISIS creation, 466
  counterterrorism, lack of interest in, 476
  credibility of, 669
  H.R. McMaster, relationship with, 12
  ISIS, claims wiped out, 473
  Middle East peace process, and, 617
Truth and Reconciliation Commission (TRC) Report 2003, 421
Tsarnaev, Dzhokhar, 384
Tsarnaev, Tamerlan, 384
Tunisian Fighting Group, 97
Tupamaros, 43
Turbay Ayala, Julio César, 401
Turner Diaries, 381
two-nation theory, 233

Ulster Special Constabulary, 255
Ulster Unionist Party (UUP)
  Belfast Agreement, signing, 605
  electoral downturn, 614, 615
Ulyanov, Alexander, 299
Umarov, Doku, 324
Umkhonto we Sizwe (MK), 213, 489
UN (United Nations)
  9/11 attacks, response to, 599
UN Human Rights Council
  Goldstone Report, 168
UN Office for the Coordination of Humanitarian Affairs (OCHA), 169
Unabomber, 377–8, 381

unarmed resistance
  Second Intifada, 164
Unconventional Warfare (UCW)
  Iraq, 2014–15, 471
União Nacional para a Independência Total de Angola (UNITA), 213
Union of Islamic Courts, 217
Unión Revolucionaria (UR), 441
United Irishmen of America, 258
United Self-Defence Forces of Colombia (AUC), 390, 408
  Chiquita Banana murders, 1990s–2000s, 410
  demobilisation, 415
  establishment, 409
  military support for, 414
  significant actor, 409
United States. *See* American terrorism
Uritskii, Moisei
  assassination, 316
Urkullu, Iñigo, 193
US State Department
  Foreign Terrorist Organisations list, 407, 410
USS Cole attack 2000, 383

Van der Graaf, Volkert, 355
Van Gogh, Theo
  assassination, 356, 357
Van Leyden, Jan, 528
Vanzetti, Bartolomeo, 376
Varadkar, Leo, 616
'Vasconia' (book), 180
Vicksburg shootings 1874, 368
victims of terrorism
  future research, 140, 659
Vilayat Khorasan (Islamic State Khorasan Province – ISKP), 328
Völkischer Beobachter ('People's Observer'), 543
'Voice of Algeria', 535
von Clausewitz, Carl, 52
von Kotzebue, August
  assassination, 634
von Levetzow, Karl, 638
von Mirbach, Wilhelm
  assassination, 316
von Pleve, Vyacheslav
  assassination, 301
von Trotha, General Lothar, 207

Waco siege 1993, 380
Wadi Haddad, 159

Wagner, Joachim, 627
Wahabism, 238
Wakefield jailbreak 1959, 483
Wall Street bombing 1920, 40, 376, 534
Walton, Calder, 511
War of Independence 1919–21, Ireland
  transnational elements of, 481
wars of pacification, 206
Weathermen, 43
  FBI, illegal acquisition of evidence, 520
  female membership, 631
  propaganda by deed, understanding, 539
Weldes, Jutta, 591
Wellesley, Arthur (Duke of Wellington), 337
Western Responses to Terrorism, 512
White Caps, 368
White Line, 368
Whitfield, Teresa, 606, 607, 609
Wilkinson, Paul, 50, 572
Wille und Weg ('Will and Path'), 543
Wilson, Harold, 273
Wilson, Marshal Sir Henry
  assassination, 269
Wilson, Tim, 565, 573
Wilson, Woodrow, 271, 370
Winter Palace bombing 1880, 299
Wittels, Fritz, 638
women and terrorism. *See* gender politics
World Trade Center bombing
  1993, 383
Wretched of the Earth, 211

Yazidis, 454, 470
  ISIS atrocities against, 469
Yom Kippur War 1973, 156
Young Party of Narodnaya Volya, 299
'Young Russia' (pamphlet), 296
Yousef, Ramzi, 383

zachistka operations, 319, 322
Zaichnevsky, Pyotr, 296
Zapatero, José Luis Rodríguez, 194, 195, 607
Zardari, Asif, 247
Zasulich, Vera, 298, 630
Zealots, 524
Zegart, Amy, 512
Zemlya i Volya ('Land and Freedom'), 297
Zhelyabov, Andrei, 299
Zia ul Haq, General Muhammad, 241
  Ahmadis oppression, 244
  fallout from rule, 246

Zia ul Haq, General Muhammad (cont.)
    fundamentalist supporter, 241
    Hudood Ordinances 1979, 244
    Islamisation initiative, 243
    legacy, 246
    supporting Deobandi madrassas, 242

Zimbabwe African National Union (ZANU), 487

Zwerman, Gilda, 642